Introductory Econometrics
with Applications

Fifth Edition

Upper Percentage Points of the Chi-Square Distribution
(ν is the Degrees of Freedom and Q is the Area in the Right Tail)

ν \ Q	0.250	0.100	0.050	0.025	0.010	0.005	0.001
1	1.32330	2.70554	3.84146	5.02389	6.63490	7.87944	10.828
2	2.77259	4.60517	5.99146	7.37776	9.21034	10.5966	13.816
3	4.10834	6.25139	7.81473	9.34840	11.3449	12.8382	16.266
4	5.38527	7.77944	9.48773	11.1433	13.2767	14.8603	18.467
5	6.62568	9.23636	11.0705	12.8325	15.0863	16.7496	20.515
6	7.84080	10.6446	12.5916	14.4494	16.8119	18.5476	22.458
7	9.03715	12.0170	14.0671	16.0128	18.4753	20.2777	24.322
8	10.2189	13.3616	15.5073	17.5345	20.0902	21.9550	26.125
9	11.3888	14.6837	16.9190	19.0228	21.6660	23.5894	27.877
10	12.5489	15.9872	18.3070	20.4832	23.2093	25.1882	29.588
11	13.7007	17.2750	19.6751	21.9200	24.7250	26.7568	31.264
12	14.8454	18.5493	21.0261	23.3367	26.2170	28.2995	32.909
13	15.9839	19.8119	22.3620	24.7356	27.6882	29.8195	34.528
14	17.1169	21.0641	23.6848	26.1189	29.1412	31.3194	36.123
15	18.2451	22.3071	24.9958	27.4884	30.5779	32.8013	37.697
16	19.3689	23.5418	26.2962	28.8454	31.9999	34.2672	39.252
17	20.4887	24.7690	28.5871	30.1910	33.4087	35.7185	40.790
18	21.6049	25.9894	28.8693	31.5264	34.8053	37.1565	42.312
19	22.7178	27.2036	30.1435	32.8523	36.1909	38.5823	43.820
20	23.8277	28.4120	31.4104	34.1696	37.5662	39.9968	45.315
21	24.9348	29.6151	32.6706	35.4789	38.9322	41.4011	46.797
22	26.0393	30.8133	33.9244	36.7807	40.2894	42.7957	48.268
23	27.1413	32.0069	35.1725	38.0756	41.6384	44.1813	49.728
24	28.2412	33.1962	36.4150	39.3641	42.9798	45.5585	51.179
25	29.3389	34.3816	37.6525	40.6465	44.3141	46.9279	52.618
26	30.4346	35.5632	38.8851	41.9232	45.6417	48.2899	54.052
27	31.5284	36.7412	40.1133	43.1945	46.9629	49.6449	55.476
28	32.6205	37.9159	41.3371	44.4608	48.2782	50.9934	56.892
29	33.7109	39.0875	42.5570	45.7223	49.5879	52.3356	58.301
30	34.7997	40.2560	43.7730	46.9792	50.8922	53.6720	59.703
40	45.6160	51.8051	55.7585	59.3417	63.6907	66.7660	73.402
50	56.3336	63.1671	67.5048	71.4202	76.1539	79.4900	86.661
60	66.9815	74.3970	79.0819	83.2977	88.3794	91.9517	99.607
70	77.5767	85.5270	90.5312	95.0232	100.425	104.215	112.317
80	88.1303	96.5782	101.879	106.629	112.329	116.321	124.839
90	98.6499	107.565	113.145	118.136	124.116	128.299	137.208
100	109.141	118.498	124.342	129.561	135.807	140.169	149.449
X	+0.6745	+1.2816	+1.6449	+1.9600	+2.3263	+2.5758	+3.0902

Note: For 25 d.f., $P(\chi^2 > 37.6525) = 0.05$.
 For $\nu > 100$ take

$$\chi^2 = \nu\left\{1 - \frac{2}{9\nu} + X\sqrt{\frac{2}{9\nu}}\right\}^3 \quad \text{or} \quad \chi^2 = \tfrac{1}{2}\{X + \sqrt{(2\nu - 1)}\}^2,$$

according to the degree of accuracy required. X is the standardized normal deviate corresponding to $P = 1 - Q$ and is shown in the bottom line of the table.

Source: Biometrika Tables for Statisticians, Vol. I. Edited by E. S. Pearson and H. O. Hartley, 3rd edition, 1966. Reprinted with the permission of the Biometrika Trustees.

Introductory Econometrics
with Applications

Fifth Edition

Ramu Ramanathan
University of California–San Diego

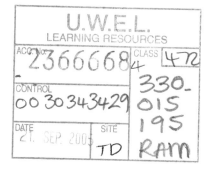

SOUTH-WESTERN

THOMSON LEARNING

Australia · Canada · Mexico · Singapore · Spain · United Kingdom · United States

Publisher	Michael P. Roche
Acquisitions Editor	Tom Gay
Developmental Editor	Amy Porubsky
Marketing Strategist	Janet Hennies
Project Manager	Angela Williams Urquhart

Cover image provided by PhotoDisc © 2002.

ISBN: 0-03-034186-8 (book), 0-03-034193-0 (CD), 0-03-034342-9 (pkg)

Library of Congress Control Number: 2001092277

For more information
contact South-Western,
5191 Natorp Boulevard,
Mason, Ohio 45040.
Or you can visit our Internet site at
http://www.swcollege.com

For permission to use materal from this
text or product, contact us by
Tel (800) 730-2214
Fax (800) 730-2215
http://www.thomsonrights.com

Printed in the United States of America

3 4 5 6 7 8 9 0   039   9 8 7 6 5 4 3

To my family: Vimala, Sadhana,
Pradeep, and Sridhar

Preface

It is indeed quite flattering that this book is in its fifth edition, and for that I am grateful to the numerous professors, both within and outside the United States, who have found the balance between the theoretical foundations of econometrics and practical applications presented in this book appropriate for their courses. This edition continues the tradition established in the previous editions, namely (1) a clear specification of the theoretical assumptions, with proofs of properties mostly in appendices, (2) detailed steps for the estimation of models and for diagnostic testing to improve model specification and/or the estimation procedures, (3) walk-through practical applications that show exactly how econometric methodology is applied to real-world data, and (4) intuitive interpretation of the results. Other salient features of the book are described on the back cover and need not be repeated here.

Chapter 1 now includes a discussion of different types of data: experimental, observational, and sample survey. Because most of econometrics deals with modeling one or more variables for given values of other variables that influence the former, the theory parts of Chapters 2 and 3 have undergone the most changes. In Chapter 2, the section on joint probabilities has an extensive discussion of conditional probability, conditional expectation, and conditional variance. Properties involving multivariate distributions have been moved from the appendix to the chapter, but these sections are marked with an asterisk so that they can be skipped, if desired, without loss of continuity. In the theoretical part of Chapter 3, all the assumptions on the error terms have been stated as conditional on given X. Proofs of unbiasedness and the Gauss–Markov theorem are initially done with X given and then extended to the case where it is a random variable. Chapter 4 has a new section on generating the forecast and confidence interval for the dependent variable in a multiple regression model. Also added here is a section on interpreting regression coefficients, especially those for variables measured as percents or proportions. This emphasis on the proper interpretation of the results has been reinforced and extended in Chapter 6 with a discussion and a table summarizing the interpretation of regression coefficients in models involving logarithms of variables. Chapter 7 presents modified interpretation of dummy coefficients in the case of log-linear models. Chapter 10 has also undergone substantial changes with new sections on vector autoregressive (VAR) models and the treatment of panel data. Chapter 11 extends the forecast combination section to include serial correlation, ARCH effects, and time-varying weights. In Chapter 14, on the steps for carrying out empirical projects, there is now an extensive discussion of how index numbers are computed and the importance of dealing appropriately with changes in the base periods.

Several new data sets, end-of-chapter exercises, and references have been added. All the data are now available in a variety of formats: ASCII (that is, text format), B34S, EViews, Excel, GRETL, PcGive, and SHAZAM. Appendix D has a list of the data with the names of the variables, units of measurement, and the data sources. The Web site set up for the book, *http://econ.ucsd.edu/~rramanat/ embook5.htm,* has also undergone substantial changes, with suggested test questions, links to data sets in the book as well as outside databases, and econometric software packages. Details about these links are provided in Appendix C. The instructor's manual has also been revised to include answers for the new exercises.

People familiar with the fourth edition of the book are aware of the econometrics programs ESL/ESLWIN included with the book. Professor Allin Cottrell has spent numerous months developing GRETL (Gnu Regression, Econometric, and Time-series Library), the successor to his ESLWIN, which is now a completely Windows-based and more user-friendly program with numerous additional econometric methods, and has graciously consented to including it with this book. There are not enough thanks to express my deepest appreciation for his effort and generosity in giving GRETL free to the world. All the Computer Practice Sessions set up for ESL/ESLWIN have been redone to be accessible by GRETL. The program, its manual, the book's data sets in different formats, ready-made commands for practice sessions, and GRETL databases are all included in the CD accompanying this book. A brief introduction to the program is provided in Appendix C.

Many professors expressed annoyance at the interruption of the flow of the text material by computer outputs with commands tailored to the ESL program in the previous edition of the book. To accommodate this complaint, I have now deleted all references to commands and kept only essential outputs, which are basically independent of the software that readers use, so that the comments in these outputs will be beneficial to all. This, combined with the new feature of having data sets readily readable by a variety of econometric packages, should make the task of empirical analysis considerably easier. The text references to Practice Computer Session files such as PS2-1.INP can be ignored by non-GRETL users or, better yet, the commands may be used as a guide to reproducing the examples using their own regression package.

I would like to acknowledge with gratitude the kindness of Professor Ken White and his colleagues for access to SHAZAM and for preparing a supplementary disk with the program's commands for reproducing all the book's examples, Professors David Hendry and Jurge Doornik for setting up the book's data files in a form accessible by the PcGive program, and Professor Houston Stokes for doing the same for the B34S program.

I am deeply indebted to all the instructors who have used the previous editions of the book and to the numerous students who compiled many of the data sets included here (their contribution is acknowledged in Appendix D). I am also greatly thankful to a number of professors who made extensive comments on the manuscript. They are David Brasington (Tulane University), Randy Campbell (Trinity University), Anthony M. Carilli (Hampden-Sydney College), Allin Cottrell (Wake Forest University), Graham Elliot (University of California, San Diego), Lily Huang (University of California, San Diego), Oscar Jorda (University of California, Davis), Jan Kiviet (University of Amsterdam), Judy Mann (University of California, San Diego), Brad Tuck (University of Alaska), Ayse Pinar Tutus (University of Minnesota), H. van Ophem (University of Amsterdam), and Phanindra V. Wunnava

(Middlebury College). Most of their page-by-page comments have been incorporated, but some of the suggestions for drastic changes could not be accommodated because of time pressures. I hope to address these changes through supplementary pages on the Web site set up for this book. Many thanks are also due to Gail Gavin at Clarinda Publication Services, as well as Angela Urquhart, Project Manager, and Janet Hennies, Marketing Strategist, for making the production and marketing processes smooth. Also deserving thanks are Lynn Reichel, Randy Campbell, and Ayse Pinar Tutus, who painstakingly proofread the technical aspects of the book. Finally, I would like to acknowledge the help of Amy Porubsky for the years of dedication to helping me in a variety of ways, particularly with reviews of the fourth edition, requests from professors for the instructor's manual, and so on.

I welcome comments from readers on any aspect of the book (e-mail address: *rramanathan@ucsd.edu*). I would be particularly grateful to users who point out the typographical errors that invariably crop up even after scrupulous proofreading. The errors discovered will be posted at *http://econ.ucsd.edu/~rramanat/errata5.htm*.

Ramu Ramanathan
San Diego, California
August 2001

About the Author

Ramu Ramanathan has an M.A. in Mathematics from the University of Madras, India, an M.Stat. in Statistics from the Indian Statistical Institute, and a Ph.D. in Economics from the University of Minnesota.

His areas of interest are applied econometrics, energy economics, economic growth, and international trade. His articles in these areas have appeared in leading journals in the United States, United Kingdom, Australia, and India. He is the author of *Statistical Methods in Econometrics* and *Introduction to the Theory of Economic Growth,* and co-author of the books *San Diego: An Economic Analysis, Measuring External Effects in Solid Waste Management,* and *Regional Load Curve Models.* He is a professor emeritus at the University of California, San Diego, where he has been a faculty member since 1967. He has been an associate editor of *ENERGY: The International Journal,* a member of the University of California Energy Research Group Advisory Committee, and the President of the Quantitative Economic Research Institute (QUERI), a consulting firm. Dr. Ramanathan also served as a member of the Energy Finance Committee for the San Diego Association of Government and played a leading role in its functions.

Contents

Part 1: Background   1

Chapter 1: Introduction   1

1.1 What Is Econometrics?   2
1.2 Basic Ingredients of an Empirical Study   4
1.3 Empirical Project   13
Summary   14
Key Terms   15
Exercises   15

Chapter 2: Review of Probability and Statistics   16

2.1 Random Variables and Probability Distributions   16
2.2 Mathematical Expectation, Mean, and Variance   20
2.3 Joint Probabilities, Covariance, and Correlation   26
2.4 Random Sampling and Sampling Distributions   35
2.5 Procedures for the Estimation of Parameters   38
2.6 Properties of Estimators   42
2.7 The Chi-square, t- and F-distributions   47
2.8 Testing Hypotheses   50
2.9 Interval Estimation   56
Key Terms   58
References   59
Exercises   60
Appendix 2.A: Miscellaneous Derivations   63
2.A.1 Certain Useful Results on Summations   63
2.A.2 Maximization and Minimization   64
2.A.3 More on Estimation   71

Part 2: Basics   75

√*Chapter 3: The Simple Linear Regression Model   76*

3.1 The Basic Model   76
3.2 Estimation of the Basic Model by the Method of Ordinary Least Squares (OLS)   80
3.3 Properties of Estimators   85
3.4 The Precision of the Estimators and the Goodness of Fit   91
3.5 Tests of Hypotheses   95
3.6 Scaling and Units of Measurement   105
3.7 Application: Estimating an Engel Curve Relation between Expenditure on Health Care and Income   106
3.8 Confidence Intervals   110

3.9   Forecasting   110

3.10 Causality in a Regression Model   113

3.11 Application: Relation between Patents and the Expenditures on Research and Development (R&D)   116

Summary   119

Key Terms   121

References   122

Exercises   122

Appendix 3.A: Miscellaneous Derivations   133

3.A.1   Three-Dimensional Representation of the Simple Linear Model   133

3.A.2   More Results on Summations   133

3.A.3   Derivation of the Normal Equations by Least Squares   135

3.A.4   Best Linear Unbiased Estimator (BLUE) and the Gauss–Markov Theorem   135

3.A.5   Maximum Likelihood Estimation   137

3.A.6   Derivation of the Variances of the Estimators   138

3.A.7   Unbiased Estimator of the Variance of the Error Term   139

3.A.8   Derivation of Equation 3.26   140

3.A.9   Derivation of Equation 3.27a   140

3.A.10 Proof That $r^2_{xy} = R^2$ for a Simple Regression Model   141

3.A.11 Derivation of Equation 3.29   142

3.A.12 Derivation of Equation 3.30   143

Chapter 4: Multiple Regression Models   144

4.1   Normal Equations   145

4.2   Goodness of Fit   148

4.3   General Criteria for Model Selection   151

4.4   Testing Hypotheses   153

4.5   Specification Errors   165

4.6   Application: The Determinants of the Number of Bus Travelers   171

4.7   Application: Women's Labor Force Participation   177

4.8   Empirical Example: Net Migration Rates and the Quality of Life   183

4.9   Empirical Project   185

Summary   185

Key Terms   187

References   187

Exercises   188

Appendix 4.A: Miscellaneous Derivations   205

4.A.1 The Three-Variable Regression Model   205

4.A.2 Bias Due to the Omission of a Relevant Variable   206

4.A.3 Proof of Property 4.4   208

Chapter 5: Multicollinearity   210

5.1   Examples of Multicollinearity   210

5.2   Exact Multicollinearity   213

5.3   Near Multicollinearity   214

5.4   Applications   220

Summary   225
Key Terms   226
References   226
Exercises   227
Appendix 5.A: Derivation of Equations (5.4) through (5.6)   229

Part 3: Extensions   231

Chapter 6: Choosing Functional Forms and Testing for Model Specification   232
    6.1   Review of Exponential and Logarithmic Functions   232
    6.2   Linear-Log Relationship   235
    6.3   Reciprocal Transformation   238
    6.4   Polynomial Curve-Fitting   238
    6.5   Interaction Terms   241
    6.6   Lags in Behavior (Dynamic Models)   243
    6.7   Application: Relation between Patents and R&D Expenses Revisited   244
    6.8   Log-Linear Relationship (or Semilog Model)   250
    6.9   Comparison of R^2 Values between Models   254
    6.10 The Double-Log (or Log-Log) Model   255
    6.11 Application: Estimating Elasticities of Bus Travel   257
    6.12 Miscellaneous Other Models   258
    6.13 The Hendry/LSE Approach of Modeling from "General to Simple"   261
    6.14 "Simple to General" Modeling Using the Lagrange Multiplier Test   262
    6.15 Ramsey's RESET Procedure for Regression Specification Error   270
    Summary   271
    Key Terms   272
    References   272
    Exercises   274
    Appendix 6.A: More Details on LR, Wald, and LM Tests   284
    6.A.1 Likelihood Ratio Test   284
    6.A.2 The Wald Test   286
    6.A.3 The Lagrange Multiplier Test   287

Chapter 7: Qualitative (or Dummy) Independent Variables   290
    7.1   Qualitative Variables with Two Categories Only   290
    7.2   Qualitative Variable with Many Categories   298
    7.3   The Effect of Qualitative Variables on the Slope Term (Analysis of Covariance)   302
    7.4   Application: Covariance Analysis of the Wage Model   305
    7.5   Estimating Seasonal Effects   312
    7.6   Testing for Structural Change   314
    7.7   Empirical Example: Motor Carrier Deregulation   320
    7.8   Application: The Demand for a Sealant Used in Construction   320
    7.9   Empirical Project   324

Summary 325
Key Terms 325
References 325
Exercises 326

Part 4: Some Special Issues with Cross-Section and Time Series Data 343

Chapter 8: Heteroscedasticity 344
8.1 Consequences of Ignoring Heteroscedasticity 346
8.2 Testing for Heteroscedasticity 347
8.3 Estimation Procedures 355
8.4 Application: A Model of the Expenditure on Health Care in the United States 363
8.5 Empirical Project 365
Summary 366
Key Terms 367
References 367
Exercises 368
Appendix 8.A: Properties of OLS Estimators in the Presence of Heteroscedasticity 378

Chapter 9: Serial Correlation 380
9.1 Serial Correlation of the First Order 382
9.2 Consequences of Ignoring Serial Correlation 383
9.3 Testing for First-Order Serial Correlation 386
9.4 Treatment of Serial Correlation 389
9.5 Higher-Order Serial Correlation 398
9.6 Engle's ARCH Test 401
9.7 Application: Demand for Electricity 406
Summary 416
Key Terms 417
References 417
Exercises 419
Appendix 9.A: Miscellaneous Derivations 431
9.A.1 Proof That the DW d is Approximately $2(1-\hat{\rho})$ 431
9.A.2 Properties of u_t When It Is AR(1) 431
9.A.3 Treatment of the First Observation under AR(1) 432

Chapter 10: Distributed Lag Models 434
10.1 Lagged Independent Variables 434
10.2 Lagged Dependent Variables 442
10.3 Lagged Dependent Variables and Serial Correlation 446
10.4 Estimation of Models with Lagged Dependent Variables 449
10.5 Application: A Dynamic Model of Consumption Expenditures in the United Kingdom 453
10.6 Application: Hourly Electricity Load Model Revisited 454

10.7 Unit Roots and the Dickey–Fuller Tests   455
10.8 Error Correction Models (ECM)   461
10.9 Application: An Error Correction Model of U.S. Defense
      Expenditures   464
10.10 Cointegration   472
10.11 Causality   475
10.12 Pooling Cross-Sectional and Time Series Data (or Panel Data)   478
10.13 Empirical Project   481
Summary   482
Key Terms   484
References   484
Exercises   487

Part 5: Special Topics   493

Chapter 11: Forecasting   494
11.1 Fitted Values Ex-post, and Ex-ante Forecasts   495
11.2 Evaluation of Models   496
11.3 Conditional and Unconditional Forecasts   497
11.4 Forecasting from Time Trends   498
11.5 Combining Forecasts   504
11.6 Forecasting from Econometric Models   510
11.7 Forecasting from Time Series Models   514
Summary   524
Key Terms   525
References   526
Exercises   527

Chapter 12: Qualitative and Limited Dependent Variables   528
12.1 Linear Probability (or Binary Choice) Models   529
12.2 The Probit Model   530
12.3 The Logit Model   532
12.4 Limited Dependent Variables   534
Summary   538
Key Terms   539
References   539
Exercises   539

Chapter 13: Simultaneous Equation Models   542
13.1 Structure and Reduced Forms of Simultaneous Equation
     Models   542
13.2 Consequences of Ignoring Simultaneity   544
13.3 The Identification Problem   546
13.4 Estimation Procedures   551
13.5 Empirical Example: Regulation in the Contact Lens Industry   556
13.6 Application: A Simple Keynesian Model   558
Summary   561

Key Terms   561
References   562
Exercises   562
Appendix 13.A: Derivation of the Limits for OLS Estimates   565

Part 6: Practice   567

Chapter 14: Carrying Out an Empirical Project   568
14.1 Selecting a Topic   568
14.2 Review of Literature   573
14.3 Formulating a General Model   574
14.4 Collecting the Data   574
14.5 Empirical Analysis   579
Key Terms   582
References   583

Appendix A: Statistical Tables   585
Appendix B: Answers to Selected Problems   607
Appendix C: Practice Computer Sessions   635
Appendix D: Descriptions of the Data and Practice Computer Sessions   639
Copyrights and Acknowledgments   675
Name Index   677
Subject Index   679

Background

Part 1 consists of two chapters that are intended to provide a background for those that follow. The introductory chapter describes what econometrics is all about and gives examples of real-world applications. It goes on to provide a brief description of each of the steps an econometrician takes in carrying out an empirical study. Chapter 2 summarizes the concepts of probability and statistics as used in econometrics. This chapter is written so that those of you who have had a basic statistics course but have no calculus background can still obtain enough knowledge to understand the later material.

CHAPTER 1

Introduction

1.1 What Is Econometrics?

*In simple terms, **econometrics** deals with the application of statistical methods to economics. Unlike economic statistics, which is mainly statistical data, econometrics is distinguished by the unification of economic theory, mathematical tools, and statistical methodology. More broadly, it is concerned with (1) estimating economic relationships, (2) confronting economic theory with facts and testing hypotheses involving economic behavior, and (3) forecasting the behavior of economic variables. In the following sections we illustrate each of these activities with a number of short, real-world examples.*

Estimating Economic Relationships

Empirical economics provides numerous examples of attempts to estimate economic relationships from data. A brief list of examples might include the following:

1. Analysts from both the government and the private sector are interested in estimating the demand/supply of various products and services.
2. A private firm might be interested in estimating the effect of various levels of advertising on sales and profits.
3. Stock market analysts seek to relate the price of a stock to the characteristics of the company issuing the stock, as well as to the overall state of the economy.
4. Federal and state governments might want to evaluate the impact of monetary and fiscal policies on such important variables as employment or unemployment, income, imports and exports, interest rates, inflation rates, and budget deficits.
5. Local governments are concerned with the relationship between revenues and the various factors, such as tax rate and population, that determine those revenues.
6. Municipalities might be interested in the impact of a company locating in their area. Of particular interest would be the effects on housing demand, employment levels, sales and property revenues, such public service requirements as schools, sewage treatment facilities, electricity, and so on.

Testing Hypotheses

As in any science, a good deal of economics is concerned with **testing hypotheses** about economic behavior. This point can be illustrated by these examples:

1. A fast-food chain might want to determine whether its new advertising campaign has been effective in increasing sales.
2. Both government and private analysts should be interested in whether demand for a given commodity or service is elastic or inelastic with respect to price and income.
3. Virtually any company might want to know whether returns to the scale of operation are increasing or decreasing.
4. Government policy makers, tobacco companies, and medical researchers would be interested in whether the surgeon general's reports on smoking and lung cancer (and other respiratory illnesses) have resulted in a significant reduction in cigarette consumption.
5. Macro economists might want to measure the effectiveness of various government policies.
6. A public utilities commission should be interested in whether regulations requiring better insulation of homes and buildings have significantly reduced energy consumption.
7. Law enforcement agencies and state legislatures might want to measure the effectiveness of tightening laws against drinking and driving in reducing deaths and injuries attributable to them.

Forecasting

Once variables have been identified and we have measured their apparent effect on the subject of study, we might want to use the estimated relationships to project future values. A few examples of such **forecasting** are as follows:

1. Firms forecast sales, profits, cost of production, and inventory requirements.
2. Utilities project demand for energy so that adequate generating facilities can be built and/or arrangements can be made to buy power from outside.
3. Numerous firms forecast stock market indices and the price of specific stocks.
4. The federal government projects such things as revenues, expenditures, inflation, unemployment, and budget and trade deficits.
5. Municipalities routinely forecast local growth in such areas as population; employment; numbers of residential, commercial, and industrial establishments; needs for schools, roads, police and fire stations, and utilities; and so on.

Because the three general steps identified at the opening of the chapter are usually based on sample data rather than on a complete census, there will be uncertainty in these standard investigations; in particular, (1) estimated relationships are not precise, (2) conclusions from hypothesis testing are subject to either the error of not rejecting a false hypothesis or that of rejecting a true hypothesis, and (3) forecasts based on estimated relationships are almost never exactly on target. To reduce the level of uncertainty, an econometrician will usually estimate several different relationships among the variables under study. He or she will then conduct a series of tests to determine which relationships most closely describe or predict the actual behavior of variables of interest.

This uncertainty makes statistical methodology very important in econometrics. The next chapter presents a summary of the basic statistical concepts needed in this book and should be referred to, as needed, in later chapters. Let us now take a look at the basic steps for developing an empirical study.

1.2   Basic Ingredients of an Empirical Study

An investigator conducting an empirical study follows a number of basic steps: (1) formulating a model, (2) gathering the data, (3) estimating the model, (4) subjecting the model to hypothesis testing, and (5) interpreting the results. Figure 1.1 presents these steps in flowchart form. In this section we give a brief description of each of these activities. Chapter 14 goes into each of these topics in more detail. If an instructor plans to require an empirical project as part of a course on econometrics, Chapter 14 should be assigned early.

Formulating a Model

Every analysis of an economic, social, political, or physical system is based on some underlying logical structure (known as a **model**) that describes the behavior of the agents in the system and is the basic framework of analysis. In economics, as in the physical sciences, this model is set up in the form of equations, which, in this case, describe the behavior of economic and related variables. The model that an investigator formulates might consist of a single equation or a system involving several equations.

SINGLE-EQUATION MODELS   In a single-equation specification, the analyst selects a single variable (denoted by Y) whose behavior the researcher is interested in explaining. Y is referred to by a number of names; **dependent variable** is the most common term, but it is also called *regressand* and *left-hand side variable*. The investigator then identifies a number of variables (denoted by Xs) that influence the dependent variable. These variables are also referred to in a number of ways; **independent variable** is the usual term, but they are also called the *exogenous variable, explanatory variable, regressor,* and *right-hand side variable*. The choice of independent variables might come from economic theory, past experience, other studies, or from intuitive judgment. As an example, consider a firm that is interested in determining its labor requirements. The company's economic analyst might use the basic microeconomic theory of profit maximization to determine how many persons to hire. The profit of the firm would depend on the price and quantity of the product it sells, the number of persons it employs, the wage rate, interest rate, costs of capital and raw materials, and so on. The principle of profit maximization would lead to a theoretical relationship between the number of persons (or worker-hours) and the

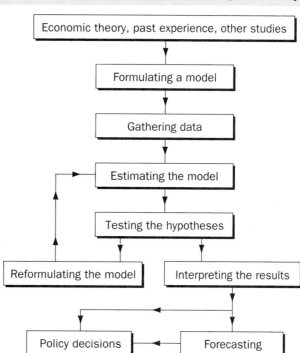

Figure 1.1 Flowchart for the Steps of an Empirical Study

other variables just listed. In this example, Y would be the number of persons (or worker-hours) to be employed, and the Xs would be the price of the good, wage and interest rates, the cost of raw materials, and so on. The goal would be to estimate the theoretical relation and use it to make policy decisions.

SIMULTANEOUS-EQUATION MODELS In some econometric studies, the investigator may be interested in more than one dependent variable and hence formulate several equations at the same time. These are known as **simultaneous-equation models.** Estimating demand and supply equations is an example of this type of formulation. Macroeconomic models are another example of simultaneous-equation specification. One of the equations might be a consumption function that relates aggregate consumption to disposable income and the interest rate. Another might be the investment function, relating investment to disposable income and the interest rate. There would also be a money demand function, relating money demand to income and the interest rate. Other equations could be equilibrium conditions that relate aggregate demand to aggregate supply and money demand to money supply.

EXAMPLE 1.1

The basic structure of an econometric model will be better understood with a simple example in which the dependent variable (Y) is related to a single independent variable (X). Consider a real estate agent who is interested in relating the sale price of a house to its characteristics, such as the lot size, the living area, the number of bedrooms and bathrooms, the types of built-in appliances, whether it has a swimming pool, whether it has a view, and so on. In particular, the agent would want to know what the contribution of a specific attribute is toward determining the value of the property. This example is a special case of a **hedonic price index model,** in which the price of a commodity depends on its characteristics (another example is the relationship between the price of a car and its characteristics).

Although all the characteristics listed are important in explaining the differences in prices across houses, for purposes of illustration let us consider a single characteristic, say the living area. Suppose PRICE is the sale price of a house and SQFT is the living area in square feet. Assuming for simplicity that the relationship between these two variables is linear, we obtain the equation PRICE = α + βSQFT, where α is the intercept and β is the slope of the straight line. Suppose we identify two houses with the same living area. In spite of this, their sale prices need not be the same. This might be due to pure random chance or, more likely, to differences between the two houses in characteristics that were not taken into account by the model (such as the yard size). Thus, the relationship is not likely to be precise but rather subject to errors. To allow for these errors, an **econometric model** would be formulated as follows:

$$\text{PRICE} = \alpha + \beta\text{SQFT} + u \qquad (1.1)$$

where u is an unobserved random variable called the **error term** (also known as the *disturbance term* or *stochastic term*) with certain statistical properties described later. The error term will vary from observation to observation. Equation (1.1) is known as the **linear regression model** or the **simple linear regression model.** The straight line α + βSQFT is called the *deterministic* part of the model, and the error term u is called the *stochastic* part.

Continuing with the real estate example, suppose we fix SQFT at the five levels 1,500, 1,750, 2,000, 2,250, and 2,500, enumerate *all the houses in a given locality* that have SQFT at (or very close to) one of these levels, and obtain their sale prices.[1] As pointed out earlier, even if two houses had the same living area, their sale prices might be different. What we are interested in here is measuring how much of the variation in price is statistically due to the factor "SQFT." If the pairs of values PRICE and SQFT are plotted on coordinate axes, they form a graph like the one in Figure 1.2 in which the circles denote the plotted points. Because larger homes command higher prices, we expect the points in the diagram to exhibit an upward shift as we move to the right on the horizontal axis.

Next we calculate the average price at each of the five levels of SQFT. In Figure 1.2 these points are denoted by ✕. The assumption behind Equation (1.1), which is of course subject to critical examination, is that these average points lie on the straight line α + βSQFT. The deterministic part can be thought of as a "statistical av-

---

[1]In practice, such a complete census of the population of houses would not be done because of the high cost. Instead, a sample would be drawn and observations made on it.

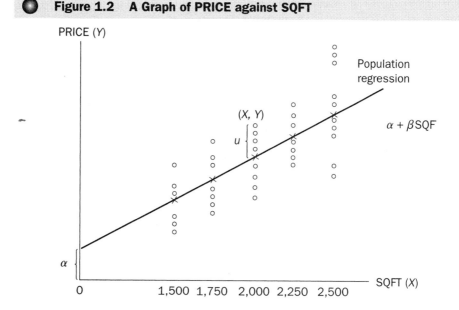

Figure 1.2 A Graph of PRICE against SQFT

erage" relation between the dependent variable and the independent variable(s) *for the entire population* of houses in the locality under study. For this reason, α and β are known as the **population parameters** (or sometimes as the **true parameters**). The "true" average relationship $\alpha + \beta$SQFT (referred to as the **population regression**) is never known but, as will be described in detail in Chapter 3, an "estimated" relationship (known as the **sample regression**) is obtainable from a sample. The unobservable error term u represents the effects of the omitted variables (yard size, age of house, and all the other characteristics that influence the sale price), as well as those of any inherently unpredictable effects.

Since it would be prohibitively expensive to survey all the houses in an area to determine the values of α and β, an investigator would instead obtain a sample of houses and use the information obtained for this sample to draw inferences not only about the population values of α and β but also about the adequacy of the linear regression assumption behind Equation (1.1). Because the conclusions are based on a sample of houses, they too are subject to errors. It is important to study these errors to find out whether the formulations can be improved and the conclusions strengthened.

As pointed out earlier, variables other than the living area would also affect the sale price of a house. An extension of the model above is thus the **multiple regression model,** an example of which follows. (Since several parameters are used, the standard convention is to use the Greek symbol β with subscripts.)

$$\text{PRICE} = \beta_1 + \beta_2\text{SQFT} + \beta_3\text{YARD} + \beta_4\text{BATHS} + \beta_5\text{BEDRMS} + u \quad (1.2)$$

where YARD is the yard size, BATHS is the number of bathrooms, and BEDRMS is the number of bedrooms. The estimation and interpretation of this model is discussed in detail in Chapter 4. Extensions of this model that include nonlinearities are discussed in Chapter 6.

EXAMPLE 1.2

Suppose that we survey all the households in a city and measure their monthly incomes (Y) and total consumption expenditures on all goods and services (C). If we plot C against Y, we would obtain a diagram such as Figure 1.2, but with income on the X-axis and consumption on the Y-axis. Next let us take all the households with an income of $500 (or more realistically, in a small interval around 500) and then average the corresponding consumption expenditures. We repeat the process for households with the approximate monthly incomes of $1,000, $1,500, $2,000, and so on, and we compute the corresponding average consumption levels. Then we plot these averages against 500, 1,000, 1,500, and so forth. Again assume that these average points lie on a straight line ($\alpha + \beta Y$). Because households with the same income will differ in consumption levels (perhaps because of differences in other characteristics such as the number of members in the household), a typical observation (C, Y) is not likely to lie exactly on the straight line. Thus, the simple linear regression model corresponding to this example will be of the form

$$C = \alpha + \beta Y + u \tag{1.3}$$

In practice, we would not survey all households but draw a sample from them and use the observations to estimate the unknown parameters α and β, as well as conduct tests and examine the validity of the assumption that the average relationship between consumption and income is linear.

EXAMPLE 1.3

In the study of finance, the **capital asset pricing model (CAPM)** provides a general framework for analyzing risk–return relationships for all types of assets. Suppose r is the return on a particular security (such as the stock in a company), r_m is the return on the market portfolio (such as the Standard and Poor's Composite Index), and r_f is the return of a risk-free return (such as a 30-day U.S. Treasury bill). Let $Y = r - r_f$ be the excess returns of the given security and $X = r_m - r_f$ be the excess returns of the market average portfolio. Then the following is the standard CAPM formulation:

$$Y = \beta X + u$$

Note that the model does not have an intercept term. This is because the returns are expressed as deviations from the risk-free return. If we have historical data on security returns, we can estimate the model. Financial magazines often report the "betas" of securities. What they refer to are estimates of β in the model above. A security for which the estimated β is greater than 1 is considered more "aggressive" or volatile than the market, and one for which the value is less than 1 is considered "conservative" or less volatile.

● EXAMPLE 1.4

In consumer demand theory, an analyst usually formulates a "utility function" and maximizes it subject to the budget constraint. This leads to derived demand functions for commodities. In particular, one can show that, under certain assumptions, the expenditure on a commodity (E) is proportional to income (Y). Such a relationship is known as the **Engel curve.** This leads us to the following econometric model, in which α is theoretically expected to be zero:

$$E = \alpha + \beta Y + u$$

The coefficient β is interpreted as the **marginal propensity** to spend on the commodity, with respect to income. Thus, a one-dollar increase in income is expected to increase the average spending on the commodity by β dollars. With data on individual households, we can estimate the preceding expenditure function and test the hypothesis that the intercept term α is zero.

OTHER EXAMPLES   Although this book is primarily concerned with economic relationships and tests of hypotheses on them, the techniques are equally applicable in other disciplines. Here we present a few examples from other fields.

● EXAMPLE 1.5

It is well documented by now that smoking is a leading cause of death due to lung cancer. A simple linear regression model formulation for this is

$$\text{DEATHS} = \alpha + \beta \text{SMOKING} + u$$

where DEATHS is the number of deaths due to lung cancer per 1 million population in a region over a specified period such as a year and SMOKING is the per capita consumption of tobacco in pounds. Because increased smoking is likely to cause more deaths, we would expect β to be positive. As in the real estate example, a researcher would include other variables that would also account for affecting the number of deaths due to lung cancer (for instance, the amount of air pollution).

● EXAMPLE 1.6

Many sociologists and criminologists have argued that capital punishment is a significant deterrent to violent crimes. To test this, we may formulate a model such as the following (again ignoring other causes of changes in violent crimes):

$$\text{CRIMES} = \alpha + \beta \text{PUNISHMENT} + u$$

Here CRIMES stands for the number of violent crimes per 1,000 population and PUNISHMENT might be the percent of convictions that resulted in the death sentence. The expected sign for β is negative because increased punishment is likely to deter crime.

● EXAMPLE 1.7

When a law that imposes restrictions on smoking is defeated, one often cites the reason to be the heavy lobbying against the law by the tobacco industry. A way to estimate this impact is by means of a model such as the following:

$$VOTE = \alpha + \beta EXPENSE + u$$

where VOTE is the percent of voters against the law and EXPENSE is the expenses per voter by the tobacco industry. We would expect a positive sign for β because an increase in EXPENSE is likely to increase the number of voters against the law.

Two of the approaches to model formulation differ considerably in philosophy. One method starts with a basic model (such as Equation 1.1), which usually comes from economic theory, intuition, other studies, and previous experience, and then performs diagnostic tests to see if a more complex model (such as Equation 1.2) is appropriate. This approach, known as **simple to general modeling,** is in predominant use in North America. In contrast, **general to simple modeling** starts with a general formulation and carries out a data-based reduction to a simpler model. This methodology, also referred to as the **Hendry/LSE approach,** is more prevalent in the United Kingdom and other European countries. Both approaches have their merits and weaknesses, which are discussed at length in Chapter 6, Sections 6.13 and 6.14. My advice is that one should not be dogmatic about either approach but use them both to arrive at the most robust conclusions.

Gathering Data

In order to estimate the econometric model that a researcher specifies, sample data on the dependent and independent variables are needed. In broad terms, there are three types of data an investigator can gather: **experimental, sample survey,** and **observational.** Experimental data are obtained by an investigator performing a controlled experiment. For example, a chemical company manufacturing fertilizers would want to measure the effectiveness of various doses of a fertilizer. The investigator would choose several plots of land with similar characteristics in terms of soil fertility, amount of irrigation done, pesticide applied, and so on and apply different levels of the fertilizer. As another example, a pharmaceutical company that wants to study the effectiveness of a particular new medicine would choose two groups of patients with similar characteristics and apply the medicine to one group and a placebo to the second group, which would be treated as control. Electric utilities often have time-of-day pricing in which prices vary depending on the time of day when electricity is used. They identify homes or companies with matching characteristics and then measure the response to the different prices faced by the consumer. In all of these examples, the experimenter chooses specific inputs and then observes the responses.

As the name indicates, obtaining sample survey data involves a researcher devising a questionnaire that addresses the issues for which he or she wants answers and then surveying a segment of the population. Some surveys are conducted on a regular basis: Survey of Current Business, Current Population Surveys, Panel Studies of Income Dynamics, monthly surveys by the Bureau of Labor Statistics and the Federal Reserve are some examples of sample surveys that are conducted periodically. An investigator may also devise special surveys to meet specific needs.

Observational data (sometimes also referred to as **nonexperimental data**) are data on variables that are not observations obtained from sample surveys or from controlled experiments. Variables such as the gross domestic product, inflation, unemployment, stock market indices, volume of shares sold on the New York Stock Exchange, and so on are examples of data that are nonexperimental in nature.

If an analyst is interested in explaining the variation of the dependent variables over time, he or she must obtain measurements at different points in time (referred to as **time series data**). For instance, a municipality might want to forecast the demand for housing for five or ten years into the future. This requires identifying the variables that influenced past demand for housing in that municipality, obtaining time series data over several years in the past, and using them in an appropriate model to generate forecasts of future demand. The interval or **periodicity** of the time series will be annual, quarterly, or monthly, depending on whether the municipality wishes to account for changes in annual, quarterly, or monthly demand for housing. The type of data available often dictates the periodicity of the data gathered.

While time series data represent observations for different time periods, **cross-section data** represent measurements *at a given point in time.* For example, a state's department of housing might wish to explain why housing demand varies across municipalities. This objective calls for obtaining observations on the characteristics of various municipalities at a certain period.

Most data are obtained from readily available public or private sources (Chapter 14 has more details on this). Frequently, however, these sources are not adequate for the problem in hand, or such data might simply not be available. In such a case, a special survey is conducted to gather the relevant information. For instance, some years ago several public utility commissions were interested in studying how consumers would respond to time-of-day pricing of electricity. Time-of-day pricing means that the price of electricity varies over different hours of the day, with higher prices during peak periods and lower prices during off-peak hours. In order to obtain the relevant data, utilities selected a number of residential customers and equipped their homes with meters that recorded the usage during every hour of the day. The usage was then monitored for at least a full year so that the utilities could record the response over different seasons. Because this type of data collection results in time series data for a cross section of households, it is known as **pooled cross-section and time series data** or more commonly as **panel data.** Special econometric techniques are needed to handle these types of data.

Another type of data a researcher often encounters involves **aggregation.** For example, consider the relation between the expenditure on food and income. The data for this could be one of several types: (1) for a selected family over time (that is, time series), (2) for a group of families at a given point in time (that is, cross-section), (3) for a group of families for several periods (that is, panel data), (4) total expenditures and total income of all the residents in a number of cities, counties, or states (that is, aggregated cross-section data for the residents of several geographical areas), and (5) total expenditures and total income over time of all residents in a given geographical area (that is, aggregated time series data for the residents of the area). The nature of the questions the investigator is interested in answering will dictate the type of data he or she would be gathering and the level of aggregation, if any.

In the process of obtaining the data, an empirical investigator must consider the fact that the available data may not exactly match the analyst's requirements. As an example, a great deal of economic theory is concerned with the interest rate. Yet there is no such thing as a single interest rate. If the analyst is interested in studying the demand for housing, he or she would use the mortgage rate. If, however, the focus is on capital expenditures for new plants and equipment, the "prime rate" or some other borrowing rate tied to it would be the proper interest rate measure.

A great deal of caution must be exercised in using data in the form of **index numbers** because the government periodically changes the **base period,** which is the basic reference period. For example, the **consumer price index (CPI)** is an average measure of the value of a fixed bundle of goods at a given point in time (say December 2000) relative to its value in a fixed year (for instance, the base period January 1995). If the base is changed to January 2000, then all data measured with January 1995 as the base period must be converted to the new base. Chapter 14 has more details about how index numbers are computed and how base period conversions can be made.

Thus, a good deal of judgment as well as care is needed in the data processing stage of an empirical study. An investigator should not only select data appropriate for the problem studied but should also be aware of the limitations of the data used, because the validity of the conclusion will also depend on the accuracy of the data.

Estimating the Model

After the model has been formulated and the relevant data gathered, a basic task of an investigator is to estimate the unknown parameters of the model. In the preceding examples, we would obtain estimates of the intercept term α, the slope term β, and the parameters (such as the mean and variance) of the probability distribution of u. The estimated equation may then be used for testing hypotheses or forecasting the values of the dependent variable, given the values of the independent variables. A variety of estimation procedures are available for model estimation. As will be studied later, the nature of the problem under investigation and that of the model specified usually dictate the procedures used.

Testing the Hypotheses

The preliminary estimation of an econometric model does not always give satisfactory results. The formulation of the basic econometric model is typically guided by economic theory, the analyst's understanding of the underlying behavior, and past experience or studies. These ingredients of a model provide only a general framework for the econometric specification. Consequently, the first results might surprise the investigator because variables that were thought to be important a priori appear after the fact to be empirically unimportant or they may have effects going in unexpected directions. The economic analyst would therefore subject the model to a variety of diagnostic tests in order to make sure that the underlying assumptions and estimation methods are appropriate for the data. The goal is to find robust conclusions—that is, conclusions that are not sensitive to model specification. To achieve this objective, one usually has to reformulate the models, and perhaps reestimate them with different techniques. Testing hypotheses is not done just to improve model specification, but also to test the validity of a body of theory.

Interpreting the Results

The final stage of the empirical investigation is to interpret the results. The conclusions might support an economic theory or contradict it, thus requiring a reexamination of the theory. If the results are relevant for making policy decisions, then such decisions will also be made at this stage. Alternatively, the empirical analyst might use the final set of models to forecast one or more dependent variables under different scenarios of the future and use these results for policy purposes.

Summary of Important Considerations

In carrying out an empirical project, an investigator must have satisfactory answers to the following questions:

1. Does the model make economic sense? In particular, does it capture all relevant relationships that are behind the **data generating process (DGP)?**
2. Are the data reliable?
3. Is the method of estimation used appropriate? Could there be any bias in the estimates obtained?
4. How do the results of the models compare with those obtained from other competing models?
5. What do the results show? Are they what economic theory or intuition would lead one to expect?

● 1.3   Empirical Project

If an empirical project is contemplated as part of a course on econometrics, it is useful to digress temporarily and proceed to the task of selecting a topic and then gathering the data. This is because the process of selecting a topic, formulating models, and collecting data is time-consuming, and one need not wait to learn all of the theory before starting the process.

Here we distinguish between two levels at which a project can be carried out: the *advanced* and the *intermediate*. Which level is chosen depends on the length of the course and the time the instructor and the student want to spend on the empirical project. If the advanced track is chosen, then read Section 14.1, which describes how to go about choosing a topic for study, then review the literature on the topic (see Section 14.2), identify variables that will be in the models (Section 14.3), decide whether cross-section or time series data are appropriate, and start collecting the data (Section 14.4).

The intermediate approach could make the task easier. To use this level, choose one of the data files listed in Appendix D, update it or find similar data for a different region or country, and carry out an analysis similar to the one discussed in the book. As an example, the data file DATA9-7 in Appendix D relates the sale of new cars to a new car price index, income, interest rate, and so on. The data sources are also listed there. Either those series can be updated for the United States, or similar data may be obtained for other countries. For a number of data sets, however, data sources are not cited but can be obtained from sources listed in Section 14.4.

If you updated any of these data files or gathered your own data and would like to include them in future editions of this book (with proper acknowledgement), please send the data file to me. My e-mail address is rramanathan@ucsd.edu, and my U.S. mail address is Department of Economics, University of California, San Diego, La Jolla, CA 92093-0508, USA.

Practice Computer Sessions

You are strongly encouraged to use your own program and try to reproduce the results of various examples and applications discussed in this book. All the data files are stored on the accompanying disk in several formats, including the ASCII (that is, text) form, and may be readily imported into any regression program (see Appendix C). The data files are labeled DATAX-Y, where X stands for the chapter number and Y stands for the file number within the chapter (e.g., DATA3-1). Associated with each data file is a header file labeled DATAX-Y.HDR (see DATA3-1.HDR) that contains the variable names, data sources, units of measurement, and so on. Appendix D has a complete listing of all the header files. Table D.1 identifies the data file associated with each practice session.

If you plan to use the GRETL program included on the disk, you should read Appendix C, which has both the directions for installing the program as well as how to obtain the documentation. The appendix also has information on how to obtain and use the data with a number of well-known regression packages.

Summary

The field of econometrics is concerned with estimating economic relationships, subjecting economic theory to hypothesis testing, and forecasting economic or other variables. An econometrician generally starts with a body of theory, then combines this with intuitive judgment (or past experience or studies) to formulate an econometric model. This process involves deciding upon one or more dependent variables and identifying the independent variables that influence them. The economic analyst should also decide whether time series or cross-section data are appropriate. The next step is to gather the relevant data. At this stage, an investigator often finds that compromises will have to be made because the measured data might not match what the theory requires. Once the data have been obtained, the practitioner estimates the parameters of one or more preliminary models. These models are then subjected to a variety of tests to identify possible misspecification and erroneous methodology. Based on these tests, the model or models are reformulated and reestimated until the investigator is satisfied that any conclusions drawn from them are robust. The final stage is interpreting the results and deciding whether they support or refute the body of theory that the econometrician is testing empirically. The final models may also be used for deriving policy implications or for forecasting the values of the dependent variables under alternative scenarios.

Key Terms

Aggregation
Base period
Capital asset pricing model (CAPM)
Consumer price index (CPI)
Cross-section data
Data generating process (DGP)
Dependent variable
Econometric model
Econometrics
Engel curve
Error term
Experimental data
Forecasting
General to simple modeling
Hedonic price index model
Hendry/LSE approach
Independent variable
Index numbers
Linear regression model

Marginal propensity
Model
Multiple regression model
Nonexperimental data
Observational data
Panel data
Periodicity
Pooled cross-section and time series data
Population parameter
Population regression
Sample regression
Sample survey data
Simple linear regression model
Simple to general modeling
Simultaneous-equation models
Testing hypotheses
Time series data
True parameter

Exercises[2]

1.1   Write down a multiple regression model relating the average amount of ice cream consumed in a given week by the residents of a city to a number of independent variables that affect consumption. For each independent variable, describe whether you would expect consumption to go up or down when the value of the variable goes up (that is, whether the effect is positive or negative). For this problem, is cross-section data or a time series more appropriate? Explain.

[†]1.2   Let OUTPUT be the total number of bushels of corn produced in a given state. Write down a model that relates output to various input variables. Carefully justify your choice of variables. Note that it is not enough to list a variable, but you should explain how the input variable is likely to affect the output.

1.3   Let SALARY be the salaries of the employees in a firm. Provide a list of variables that will influence SALARY. For each variable describe whether the effects are likely to be positive or negative.

1.4   In a regression model such as Equation (1.2), what is the distinction between a "parameter" and a "variable"? Also explain the difference between a "population parameter" and an "estimated parameter."

[†]1.5   When asked to write a regression model (as, for example, in Exercises 1.1, 1.2, and 1.3), a few past students have written the model as follows:

$$Y = \beta_1 + X_2 + X_3 + X_4 + \cdots$$

Explain what is wrong with this formulation.

---

[2]Here and throughout the book, exercises indicated by (†) are answered in Appendix B. Those marked by (*) are more difficult and may be skipped at the discretion of the instructor.

CHAPTER *2*

Review of Probability and Statistics

*I*n this chapter, we summarize the concepts of probability and statistics that are used in econometrics. Because a prior knowledge of basic probability and statistics is assumed in this book, this review is designed to serve only as a refresher course on topics that are of use in later chapters. It is not meant to be a rigorous and complete treatment of the subject. For this reason, we present very few proofs. Instead, we define important concepts under the heading "Definition" and summarize useful results under the heading "Properties." For a detailed discussion of the topics, you should refer to the excellent books listed in the bibliography at the end of the chapter. Sections indicated with an asterisk (*) are more advanced and may be skipped without losing the gist of the subject matter.

   This chapter reviews all of the relevant topics in probability and statistics. If it has been some time since you studied the subject, you should quickly go over this chapter to refresh your memory. However, if you have just completed a course on these materials, we recommend that you read Sections 2.1 through 2.5 (with particular emphasis on covariance and correlation discussed in Section 2.3) and then proceed directly to Chapter 3 rather than read the rest of this chapter. You can return to review relevant sections of this chapter as needed. Sections in Chapter 2 parallel those in Chapter 3, and this cross-reference is indicated so that a smooth switchover can be accomplished. This will enable you to understand the underlying econometric theory better and to appreciate the usefulness of probability and statistics more readily.

2.1 Random Variables and Probability Distributions

An investigator typically conducts an experiment that might be as simple as tossing a coin or rolling a pair of dice or as complicated as making a survey of economic agents or conducting an experimental medical treatment program. Based on the outcomes of the experiment, an analyst would measure the values of variables of interest that characterize the outcomes. Such variables are known as **random variables** (or *stochastic variables*) and are usually denoted as X. Examples include the temperature at a certain time, the number of calls coming through a switchboard in a five-minute interval, the income of a family, the inventories of a firm, and the sale price of a house as well as its characteristics, such as the living area or the size of the lot. A random variable is *discrete* if it can take only selected values. The number of defective TV tubes in a lot of 20 and the number of heads in ten tosses of a coin are examples of discrete random variables. A random variable is *continuous* if it can take any value in a real interval. When measured accurately, the height of a person, the temperature at a particular instant, and the amount of energy consumed in an hour are examples of continuous random variables. The convention used in this book is to denote a random variable by an uppercase letter (such as X or Y) and its specific outcomes by a lowercase letter (such as x or y).

To keep the presentation simple, we illustrate the various concepts using mostly discrete random variables. The propositions extend easily to the case of a continuous random variable.

Associated with each random variable is a **probability distribution** [denoted by the function $f(x)$] that determines the probability that the random variable will take values in specified intervals. The formal definition of a random variable is not presented here but may be found in all the books listed in the bibliography.

In this book we discuss only those distributions that are of direct use in econometrics. Ramanathan (1993) has numerous examples of both continuous and discrete distributions not presented here.

⬤ EXAMPLE 2.1

As an illustration, the U.S. Internal Revenue Service has the information about the adjusted gross incomes from all individual (including jointly filed) income tax returns for the entire United States. Suppose we form the income intervals 1–10,000, 10,000–20,000, 20,000–30,000, and so on and calculate the fraction of the tax returns that falls in each income group. This gives rise to a **frequency distribution.** The fraction of the returns that falls in the income group 40,000–50,000 can be taken to be the probability that a tax return drawn at random will have income falling in that interval.

In Figure 2.1 the proportion of returns is plotted against the midpoints of the intervals in the form of a bar diagram (known as a **histogram**) in which the areas of the rectangles equal the corresponding proportions. If the size of the population is sufficiently large and the intervals are small enough, we can approximate the frequencies with a smooth curve (as shown in the diagram), which is the probability distribution of incomes.

⬤ EXAMPLE 2.2

The grade point average (GPA) of a student varies from 0 to 4. Table 2.1 has an example of the probability distribution of GPAs. Figure 2.2 is a graphic representation of the probability distribution. The probability that a student selected at random will have a GPA between 2 and 2.5 is given by 0.244. The interpretation of the other numbers is similar.

⬤ Table 2.1   Probability Distribution of Grade Point Averages

Range	0–0.5	0.5–1.0	1.0–1.5	1.5–2.0	2.0–2.5	2.5–3.0	3.0–3.5	3.5–4.0
x	0.25	0.75	1.25	1.75	2.25	2.75	3.25	3.75
$f(x)$	0	0.002	0.010	0.049	0.244	0.342	0.255	0.098

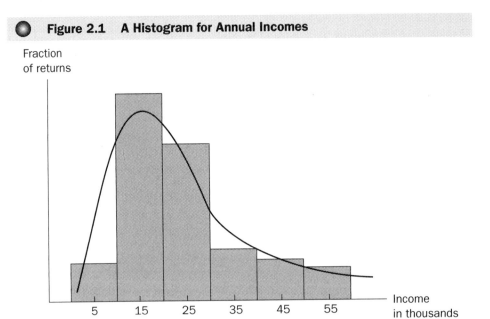

Figure 2.1   A Histogram for Annual Incomes

Fraction
of returns

Income
in thousands
of dollars

5   15   25   35   45   55

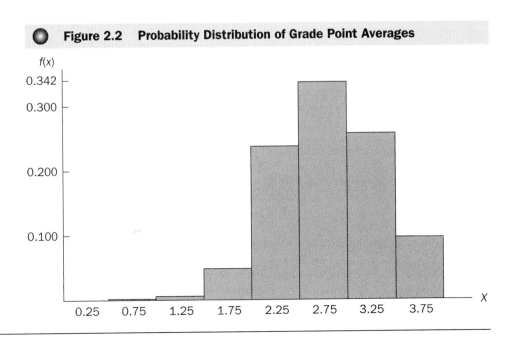

Figure 2.2   Probability Distribution of Grade Point Averages

f(x)

0.342

0.300

0.200

0.100

0.25   0.75   1.25   1.75   2.25   2.75   3.25   3.75   X

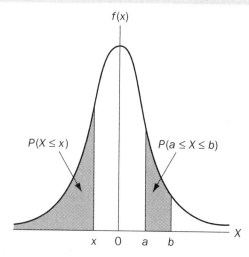

● **Figure 2.3   Graph of the Standard Normal Density**

Users of the GRETL program should try the Practice Computer Session described in Appendix C. Others are encouraged to use their own regression program to obtain the frequency distributions for DATA2-1 and DATA2-2 (see Appendix D).

The Normal Distribution

The most widely used continuous distribution is the **normal distribution** (also known as the *Gaussian distribution*). In its simplest form, known as the **standard normal distribution** (or **standardized normal**), its **probability density function (PDF)** is

$$f(x) = \frac{1}{\sqrt{2\pi}} \exp(-x^2/2) \qquad -\infty < x < \infty$$

where *exp* is the exponential function. The normal density $f(x)$ is symmetric around the origin and is bell-shaped (see Figure 2.3). $P(a \leq X \leq b)$ is given by the shaded area between a and b.

● **EXAMPLE 2.3**

Appendix Table A.1 has the area under the standard normal curve between 0 and any point z. Thus, for example, the area from 0 to 1.72 is 0.4573. Because the normal curve is symmetric around the origin, the area from 0 to -1.72 is also 0.4573. The area from 0.65 to 1.44 is obtained as the difference in the areas from 0 and is hence $0.4251 - 0.2422 = 0.1829$. Using this technique and the symmetry property, it is easily verified that $P(-0.65 < X < 1.44) = 0.2422 + 0.4251 = 0.6673$ and that $P(-1.44 < X < -0.65) = 0.1829$. To get $P(X > 1.12)$, we use the relation $P(X > 1.12) = P(X > 0) - P(0 < X < 1.12) = 0.5 - 0.3686 = 0.1314$.

Table 2.2   **Probability Distribution for the Number of Heads in Three Tosses of a Coin**

x	0	1	2	3
$f(x)$	$\frac{1}{8}$	$\frac{3}{8}$	$\frac{3}{8}$	$\frac{1}{8}$

The Binomial Distribution

As an example of a discrete probability function, let X be the number of heads in three tosses of a coin. X can take the values 0, 1, 2, or 3. The eight mutually exclusive outcomes, each of which is equally likely with probability $\frac{1}{8}$, are given by (HHH), (HHT), (HTH), (THH), (HTT), (THT), (TTH), and (TTT). It follows from this that $P(X = 2) = P(\text{HHT}) + P(\text{HTH}) + P(\text{THH}) = \frac{3}{8}$. By proceeding in the same way, we can obtain the probabilities for each possible value of X. Table 2.2 gives the probability function $f(x)$ for the four possible values of X.

The distribution is a member of a family of distributions known as the **binomial distribution.** It arises when there are only two possible outcomes to an experiment, one designated as a "success" and the other as a "failure." Let p be the probability of a success in a given trial. The probability of a failure is $1 - p$. Also assume that the probability of a success is the same for each trial and that the trials are independent. Let X be the number of successes in n independent trials. Then $f(x)$ can be shown to be [see Freund (1992), pp. 184–185]

$$f(x) = \binom{n}{x} p^x q^{n-x} = \frac{n!}{x!\,(n-x)!} p^x q^{n-x} \qquad x = 0, 1, \ldots, n$$

where $1 - p = q$ and $n! = n(n-1) \cdots 1$ (0! is defined as 1).

EXAMPLE 2.4

A particular leukemia treatment has a 25 percent probability of a complete cure. If 40 patients chosen at random are given the treatment, what is the probability that at least 15 patients will be cured?

Let X = the number of successes in 40 trials. Then we need $P(X > 15)$ for $p = 0.25$. Appendix Table A.6 has the desired upper cumulative probability as 0.0544.

Try Exercises 2.1 through 2.5 and study the answers to Exercise 2.4 in Appendix B.

2.2   Mathematical Expectation, Mean, and Variance

Consider the binomial experiment described earlier in which a coin is tossed three times. Suppose we were paid $3 if the outcome were three heads, $2 if there were two heads, $1 if there was only one head, and none if all three tosses resulted in tails. On average, what would we expect to win *per trial* of three tosses? We note from Table 2.2 that in eight trials we can expect, *on average*, one event in which all three tosses are heads (resulting in a payoff of $3), three events with two heads (with a total payoff of $6, calculated as $2 for each of the three events), and three events with one head (with a total payoff of $3). We can thus expect a grand total payoff of $12 (3 + 6 + 3) in eight trials, giving an average payoff of $1.50 per trial.

The Mean of a Distribution

The average value computed in the previous section is called the **mean of the distribution** (also known as the *mathematical expectation of X* and the **expected value of X**). It is also known as the *first moment around the origin*, or **first central moment**, and is a measure of location. It is denoted by $E(X)$ or by μ. $E(X)$ is a weighted average of X, with the weights being the corresponding probabilities. In the general case, suppose a discrete random variable can take the values $x_1, x_2, \ldots, x_n$. $P(X = x_i) = f(x_i)$ is its probability function. If the payoff for the outcome $X = x_i$ were x_i dollars, the average payoff would be $x_1 f(x_1) + x_2 f(x_2) + \cdots + x_n f(x_n) = \Sigma[x_i f(x_i)]$, where Σ denotes the summation over each of the terms, for $i = 1$ to n. (See Appendix 2.A.1 on summation.) We thus have the following definition.

DEFINITION 2.1   (Mean of a Distribution)

For a discrete random variable, the mean of the distribution (μ) is defined as

$$\mu = E(X) = \sum_{i=1}^{i=n} [x_i f(x_i)] \tag{2.1}$$

Because $E(X)$ is weighted by probabilities, it might differ from the arithmetic mean, $\bar{x} = (\Sigma x_i)/n$.

There is no reason why the payoff described earlier should be limited to x. It can be any function of x. Suppose the payoff were x^2. The average payoff would then be $\Sigma[x_i^2 f(x_i)]$. This is called the *second moment of the distribution of X around the origin*. The concept of mathematical expectation can be extended to any function of x. Thus, we have the following expression for the expected value of a general function $g(X)$:

$$E[g(X)] = \sum [g(x_i) f(x_i)] \tag{2.2}$$

● **EXAMPLE 2.5**

The Verbal Scholastic Aptitude Test (VSAT) score for a student applying for college ranges from 0 to 700. Table 2.3 has an example of the probability distribution of VSAT scores for a large population of college students. The mean of this distribution is calculated as $100 \times 0 + 225 \times 0.003 + \cdots + 675 \times 0.063 = 506.25$.

● **Table 2.3   Probability Distribution of VSAT Scores**

Range	x	$f(x)$
0–200	100	0
200–250	225	0.003
250–300	275	0.021
300–350	325	0.033
350–400	375	0.061
400–450	425	0.131
450–500	475	0.201
500–550	525	0.234
550–600	575	0.169
600–650	625	0.084
650–700	675	0.063

● **PRACTICE PROBLEM 2.1**

Suppose 10,000 $1 lottery tickets are sold and three prizes are being offered: first prize $5,000, second prize $2,000, and third prize $500. What is the expected win?

● **PRACTICE PROBLEM 2.2**

A baker has the following probability function for the demand for loaves of bread (in dozens per day). What should the average stock be?

x	0	1	2	3	4	5	6 or more
$f(x)$	0.05	0.10	0.25	0.30	0.20	0.10	0

We write without proof a number of results involving expectations. It is recommended that these be studied carefully because they will be used frequently in later chapters. (Try to prove them.)

Property 2.1

a. $E(X - \mu) = E(X) - \mu = 0$.

b.   If c is a constant or a nonrandom variable, $E(c) = c$.

c.   If c is a constant or is nonrandom, $E[cg(X)] = cE[g(X)]$.

d. $E[u(X) + v(X)] = E[u(X)] + E[v(X)]$.

In words, the expected value of the deviation from the mean is zero. The expected value of a constant or a nonrandom variable is itself. The expected value of a constant times a random variable is the constant times the expected value. The expected value of a sum of functions of X is the sum of the expectations. Answers to Exercise 2.6 in Appendix B have the proof of Property 2.1 for the discrete case.

The Variance and Standard Deviation of a Random Variable

Let $\mu = E(X)$ be the mean of the distribution of X. A special case of the function $g(X)$, whose expectation was defined in Equation (2.2), is of considerable interest. Let $g(X) = (X - \mu)^2$. $X - \mu$ is a measure of how far X deviates from the mean μ. Squaring this magnifies large deviations and treats positive and negative deviations alike. The probability-weighted average of these squared deviations (or, more specifically, their expected value) is a measure of the dispersion of the values of X around the mean value μ. It is called the **variance of the distribution** (or the **second central moment**) and is denoted by σ^2 or Var(X). It is a measure of the spread of X around μ. Formally, we have the following definition.

DEFINITION 2.2   (Variance and Standard Deviation)

The variance of X is defined as

$$\sigma^2 = \text{Var}(X) = E[(X - \mu)^2] = \sum (x_i - \mu)^2 f(x_i) \tag{2.3}$$

The positive square root (σ) of this is called the **standard deviation (s.d.).**

Property 2.2 lists several properties of the variance that hold for both discrete and continuous distributions.

Property 2.2

a. $\sigma^2 = E[(X - \mu)^2] = E[X^2 - 2\mu X + \mu^2] = E(X^2) - 2\mu E(X) + \mu^2$
    $= E(X^2) - \mu^2.$

b. It follows from this that if c is a constant or is nonrandom, Var$(c) = 0$.

c. If a and b are constants or nonrandom, Var$(a + bX) = b^2\sigma^2$.

● **EXAMPLE 2.6**

The probability function of a discrete random variable is given as follows:

x	0	1	2	3
$f(x)$	0.1	0.3	0.4	0.2

Compute the mean, variance, and standard deviation.

$$\mu = E(X) = \sum x_i f(x_i)$$
$$= (0 \times 0.1) + (1 \times 0.3) + (2 \times 0.4) + (3 \times 0.2)$$
$$= 0 + 0.3 + 0.8 + 0.6 = 1.7$$
$$E(X^2) = \sum x_i^2 f(x_i) = (0 \times 0.1) + (1 \times 0.3) + (4 \times 0.4) + (9 \times 0.2)$$
$$= 0 + 0.3 + 1.6 + 1.8 = 3.7$$
$$\mathrm{Var}(X) = E(X^2) - \mu^2 = 3.7 - (1.7)^2 = 0.81$$
$$\sigma = \sqrt{\mathrm{Var}(X)} = 0.9$$

● PRACTICE PROBLEM 2.3

Compute the mean, variance, and standard deviation for the distributions in Tables 2.1 and 2.3.

● PRACTICE PROBLEM 2.4

Show that if the random variable X has mean μ and standard deviation σ, the transformed random variable $Z = (X - \mu)/\sigma$ (often referred to as the **z-score**) has mean zero and variance 1.

The General Normal Distribution

The normal distribution presented in Section 2.1 has mean zero and variance unity. A general normal distribution, with mean μ and variance σ^2, conventionally written as $N(\mu, \sigma^2)$, has the following density function:

$$f(x) = \frac{1}{(\sigma\sqrt{2\pi})} \exp\left[-\frac{(x - \mu)^2}{2\sigma^2} \right] \qquad -\infty < x < \infty \qquad \textbf{(2.4)}$$

where exp stands for the exponential function. If X is distributed normally, it is written as $X \sim N(\mu, \sigma^2)$. Three normal probability distributions are presented in Figure 2.4. Several properties of the normal distribution are listed in Property 2.3.

Property 2.3	The normal distribution, with mean μ and variance σ^2 [written as $N(\mu, \sigma^2)$], has the following properties:

a.   It is symmetric around the mean value μ and has a bell shape.

b.   The area under a normal curve between $\mu - \sigma$ and $\mu + \sigma$—that is, within 1 standard deviation from the mean—is slightly over $\frac{2}{3}$ (0.6826). 95.44 percent of the area lies between 2 standard deviations from the mean—that is, between $\mu - 2\sigma$ and $\mu + 2\sigma$. 99.73 percent of the area lies within 3 standard deviations from the mean. Thus, virtually the entire distribution lies between $\mu - 3\sigma$ and $\mu + 3\sigma$.

Figure 2.4 Three Normal Distributions

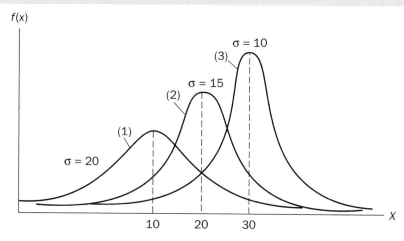

c. If X has the normal distribution, with mean μ and standard deviation σ, then the "standardized" random variable $Z = (X - \mu)/\sigma$ has the standard normal distribution $N(0, 1)$. Because of this property, the area between the points a and b in $N(\mu, \sigma^2)$ is the same as the area between the *standardized endpoints* $(a - \mu)/\sigma$ and $(b - \mu)/\sigma$ in $N(0, 1)$. Table A.1 has the areas under the standard normal between the mean zero and various values of Z.

d. If X is distributed as $N(\mu, \sigma^2)$, then $Y = a + bX$, where a and b are fixed constants, is distributed as $N(a + b\mu, b^2\sigma^2)$.

EXAMPLE 2.7

A manufacturer of tires has found that the lifetime of a certain kind of tire is a normal random variable with a mean of 30,000 miles and standard deviation 2,000 miles. The company wishes to guarantee it for N miles with a full refund if the tire does not last that long. Suppose it wants to make sure that the probability that a tire will be returned is no more than 0.10 (that is, no more than 10 percent of the tires sold will be returned). What value of N should the company choose?

Let X be the life of the tire. Then X is distributed as $N(30,000, 2,000^2)$. We want

$$P(X \le N) \le 0.10. \quad P(X \le N) = P\left(\frac{X - \mu}{\sigma} \le \frac{N - \mu}{\sigma}\right) \le 0.10. \quad \text{Let } Z = \frac{X - \mu}{\sigma}$$

be the standard normal. Then $P\left(Z \le z = \frac{N - \mu}{\sigma}\right) \le 0.10$. We see from Figure 2.5 that to get an area of 0.10 to the left of z, we need to find the point $d(= -z)$ such that the area between 0 and d is 0.40 (because of the symmetry property). From Table A.1 of the appendix, we note that $P(0 \le Z \le d = 1.282) = 0.40$, which

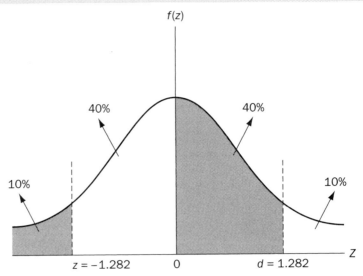

Figure 2.5   Graph of the Standard Normal Density

means that if $\dfrac{N - \mu}{\sigma} \le -1.282$ then the above inequality will hold. Thus, $N \le \mu - 1.282\sigma = 30{,}000 - (1.282)2{,}000$; that is, $N \le 27{,}436$ miles.

Coefficient of Variation

The **coefficient of variation** is defined as the ratio σ/μ, where the numerator is the standard deviation and the denominator is the mean. It is a measure of the dispersion of a distribution *relative to its mean*. We will encounter this concept again in Chapter 14 on carrying out an empirical project.

For a discussion of other measures characterizing a distribution, see Ramanathan (1993, Section 3.5). Practice Computer Session 2.2 (see Appendix Table D.1) illustrates these concepts for GRETL users, using sample data on the grade point averages of 427 students.

2.3   Joint Probabilities, Covariance, and Correlation

Probability functions defined over a pair of random variables (such as, for example, PRICE and SQFT or consumption and income) are known as *joint probability distributions* or as *bivariate distributions*. To keep the presentation simple, our discussion focuses only on discrete random variables. The generalization to the continuous case is quite straightforward. Let X and Y be discrete random variables, and x and y be possible values they can respectively attain. The probability that $X = x$ and $Y = y$ is called the *joint probability function* for X and Y and is denoted by $f_{XY}(x, y)$. Thus,

$f_{XY}(x, y) = P(X = x, Y = y)$, which stands for $P(X = x$ and $Y = y)$. Because a probability function is generally represented by $f(\ )$, we use the subscript XY to identify the fact that the random variables in question are X and Y jointly.

EXAMPLE 2.8

Consider the experiment of rolling a pair of dice. There are 36 possible outcomes that can be denoted by $(1, 1)$, $(1, 2)$, . . . , $(6, 6)$, where the first number is the outcome of the first die and the second number is the outcome of the second die. Each outcome is equally likely, and hence the probability of a typical outcome is $\frac{1}{36}$. Now construct the random variable $X =$ the number of 3s in a typical outcome. Thus, if the outcome is $(1, 5)$, then $X = 0$; if it is $(3, 6)$, then $X = 1$; and $X = 2$ if and only if the outcome is $(3, 3)$. X can take only the values 0, 1, and 2. Next define the random variable $Y =$ the number of 5s in a typical outcome, which also can take only the values 0, 1, and 2. The outcome $(1, 3)$ corresponds to $X = 1$ and $Y = 0$. It is easy to verify that the joint probabilities are as given in Table 2.4. For instance, the joint event $\{X = 1, Y = 1\}$ can occur only when the outcome is either $(3, 5)$ or $(5, 3)$, each with a probability of $\frac{1}{36}$. Therefore, $f(1, 1) = P(X = 1, Y = 1) = \frac{2}{36}$. Other probabilities are calculated similarly (verify these as a practice problem).

Statistical Independence

The discrete random variables X and Y are said to be **statistically independent** if $P(X = x$ and $Y = y) = P(X = x)P(Y = y)$. Thus, in this case, the joint probability is the product of individual probabilities. For the continuous case, we have $f_{XY}(x, y) = f_X(x) \cdot f_Y(y)$.

Conditional Probability*

In addition to knowing the probability of the joint occurrence of two random variables X and Y, we might also be interested in knowing the probability of a particular random variable (Y) *given* that another random variable (X) has already occurred. For instance, we might want to know the probability that the price of a house is $200,000, given that its living area is 1,500 square feet. This comment leads us to the

Table 2.4   Joint Probability Distribution for the Number of 3s (X) and the Number of 5s (Y) when a Pair of Dice Is Rolled

Y \ X	0	1	2
0	$\frac{16}{36}$	$\frac{8}{36}$	$\frac{1}{36}$
1	$\frac{8}{36}$	$\frac{2}{36}$	0
2	$\frac{1}{36}$	0	0

notion of **conditional probability,** which is defined, for discrete random variables, as follows:

$$P(Y = y \mid X = x) = \frac{P(X = x, Y = y)}{P(X = x)} \qquad \text{provided } P(X = x) \neq 0$$

The symbol "|" stands for *given*. The **conditional probability density function** is defined (both for discrete and continuous random variables) as

$$f_{Y|X}(x, y) = \frac{f_{XY}(x, y)}{f_X(x)} \qquad \text{for all values of } x \text{ such that } f_X(x) > 0$$

where $f_{XY}(x, y)$ is the joint probability density of X and Y and $f_X(x)$ is the separate density function of X by itself, commonly referred to as the **marginal density of X.** Note that the conditional probability depends on both x and y. When two random variables are statistically independent, the conditional probability distributions become the corresponding marginal distributions. To see this, note that statistical independence implies that $f_{XY}(x, y) = f_X(x) f_Y(y)$. It follows from this that $f_{Y|X}(y|x) = f_{XY}(x, y)/f_X(x) = f_Y(y)$ and that $f_{X|Y}(x|y) = f_{XY}(x, y)/f_Y(y) = f_X(x)$.

● **EXAMPLE 2.9**
_____

Table 2.4 has the joint probabilities of the number of 3s (X) and the number of 5s (Y) when a pair of dice is rolled. Let us first derive the marginal densities of X and Y. Because $X = 0$ can occur when $Y = 0$ or 1 or 2, $P(X = 0)$ can be calculated as $P(X = 0, Y = 0) + P(X = 0, Y = 1) + P(X = 0, Y = 2) = \frac{16}{36} + \frac{8}{36} + \frac{1}{36} = \frac{25}{36}$. By proceeding similarly, we get $P(X = 1) = \frac{10}{36}$ and $P(X = 2) = \frac{1}{36}$. Note that the three probabilities add up to 1, which is as it should be. The marginal distribution of Y is obtained in a similar manner. Table 2.5 shows the marginal densities of X and Y as the last row and the last column, respectively. Note that they happen to be the same.

● **Table 2.5   Marginal Distributions for the Number of 3s (X) and the Number of 5s (Y) When a Pair of Dice Is Rolled**

X \ Y	0	1	2	$f_Y(y)$
0	$\frac{16}{36}$	$\frac{8}{36}$	$\frac{1}{36}$	$\frac{25}{36}$
1	$\frac{8}{36}$	$\frac{2}{36}$	0	$\frac{10}{36}$
2	$\frac{1}{36}$	0	0	$\frac{1}{36}$
$f_X(x)$	$\frac{25}{36}$	$\frac{10}{36}$	$\frac{1}{36}$	1

● **Table 2.6   Conditional Distribution for the Number of 5s (Y) Given the Number of 3s (X) When a Pair of Dice Is Rolled**

Given X \ Y	0	1	2
0	0.64	0.32	0.04
1	0.80	0.20	0
2	1.00	0	0

The conditional probability that $Y = 0$, given that $X = 0$ is obtained as

$$P(Y = 0 \mid X = 0) = P(X = 0, Y = 0)/ P(X = 0) = \frac{16}{36} \div \frac{25}{36} = 0.64$$

By proceeding similarly, we get the conditional distribution of Y given X presented in Table 2.6.

Mathematical Expectation in a Two-Variable Case

The concept of mathematical expectation is easily extended to bivariate random variables. Given the function $g(X, Y)$ and the joint probability function $f(x, y)$, the expected value of $g(X, Y)$ is obtained (again for the discrete case) by multiplying $g(x, y)$ by $f(x, y)$ and summing it over all the possible values of x and y. We thus have the following definition.

DEFINITION 2.3   (Expected Value)

The expected value of $g(X, Y)$ is defined as

$$E[g(X, Y)] = \sum_{x} \sum_{y} g(x, y)f(x, y)$$

where the double summation indicates summation over all the possible values of x and y. (The expectation is thus a weighted sum with the joint probability as the weight.)

Let μ_x be the expected value (that is, mean) of the random variable X, and let μ_y be the expected value of the random variable Y. Their variances are defined as in the univariate case:

$$\sigma_x^2 = E[(X - \mu_x)^2] \quad \text{and} \quad \sigma_y^2 = E[(Y - \mu_y)^2] \tag{2.5}$$

● **PRACTICE PROBLEM 2.5**

For the joint probabilities given in Table 2.4, compute the means $\mu_x = E(X), \mu_y = E(Y)$, and the variances σ_x^2, σ_y^2. Also verify that X and Y are not statistically independent.

Conditional Expectation and Conditional Variance*

The expected value of Y given X is known as the **conditional expectation of Y given X.** More formally, for a discrete pair of random variables, $E(Y \mid X = x) = \sum_{Y=y} y f_{Y\mid X}(x, y)$. In other words, it is the mean of Y using the conditional density $f_{Y\mid X}(x, y)$ as weights. The expectation of Y given X is also referred to as the **regression of Y on X.** We can see from Table 2.6 that $E(Y \mid X = 0) = (0.64 \times 0) + (0.32 \times 1) + (0.04 \times 2) = 0.32 + 0.08 = 0.4, E(Y \mid X = 1) = 0.2$, and $E(Y \mid X = 2) = 0$. In the simple regression model illustrated in Example 1.1, PRICE $= \alpha + \beta$ SQFT $+ u$. If $E(u \mid \text{SQFT}) = 0$, then $E(\text{PRICE} \mid \text{SQFT}) = \alpha + \beta$ SQFT. Thus, the deterministic part of the model is the conditional expectation of PRICE given SQFT, when $E(u \mid \text{SQFT}) = 0$.

The concept of conditional expectation is easily extended to variances to obtain the **conditional variance,** defined as follows. Let $\mu^*(X)$ be the conditional expectation of Y given X, namely, $E(Y \mid X)$. Then the conditional variance of Y given X is defined as $\text{Var}(Y \mid X) = E_{Y\mid X}[(Y - \mu^*)^2 \mid X]$. In other words, fix the value of X, obtain the conditional mean of Y given X, and then obtain the variance around this mean, using the conditional density $f_{Y\mid X}(x, y)$ as the weight.

A number of properties of conditional expectations that are used in econometrics are summarized next. For proofs, see Ramanathan(1993, Section 5.2).

Property 2.4

For any function $u(X)$, $E[u(X) \mid X] = u(X)$. This implies that, when it comes to conditional expectation given X, the function $u(X)$ behaves like a constant. As a special case of this, if c is a constant, $E(c \mid X) = c$.

Property 2.5

$E([a(X) + b(X)Y] \mid X) = a(X) + b(X) E(Y \mid X)$.

Property 2.6

$E_{XY}(Y) = E_X[E_{Y\mid X}(Y \mid X)]$. This means that the unconditional expectation of Y, using the joint density between X and Y, can be obtained by first getting the conditional expectation of Y given X (which is the expression in the square brackets), and then taking the expectation of that over X. This property is known as the **law of iterated expectations.**

Property 2.7

$\text{Var}(Y) = E_X[\text{Var}(Y \mid X)] + \text{Var}_X[E(Y \mid X)]$. In other words, the variance of Y obtained using the joint density function $f_{XY}(x, y)$ is equal to the expected value of the conditional variance of Y given X plus the variance of the conditional expectation of Y given X.

Covariance and Correlation

When we are dealing with two random variables, one of the main items of interest is how closely they are related. The concepts of **covariance** and **correlation** are two ways to measure the "closeness" of two random variables.

Consider the function $g(X, Y) = (X - \mu_x)(Y - \mu_y)$. The expected value of this function is called the *covariance between X and Y* and is denoted by σ_{xy} or by $\mathrm{Cov}(X, Y)$.

DEFINITION 2.4   (Covariance)

The covariance between X and Y is defined as

$$\sigma_{xy} = \mathrm{Cov}(X, Y) = E[(X - \mu_x)(Y - \mu_y)] = E[XY - X\mu_y - \mu_x Y + \mu_x \mu_y] \quad (2.6)$$

$$= E(XY) - \mu_y E(X) - \mu_x E(Y) + \mu_x \mu_y = E(XY) - \mu_x \mu_y$$

It readily follows from this that $\mathrm{Cov}(X, X) = \mathrm{Var}\,(X)$.

The definitions of variance and covariance are the same for both discrete and continuous distributions. Just as variance is a measure of the dispersion of a random variable around its mean, the covariance between two random variables is a measure of the joint association between them. Suppose the discrete random variables X and Y are positively related so that Y increases when X increases, as illustrated in Figure 2.6. The circles represent pairs of values of X and Y that are the

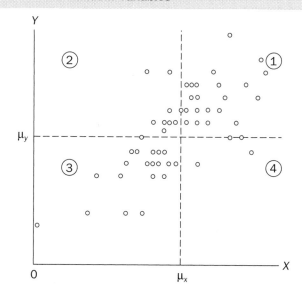

● **Figure 2.6   An Illustration of the Covariance between Two Random Variables**

finite possible outcomes. The dashed lines indicate the means, μ_x and μ_y. By translating the axes to the dashed lines with origin at (μ_x, μ_y), we can see that $X_i - \mu_x$ and $Y_i - \mu_y$ are the distances from the new origin, for a typical outcome denoted by the suffix i. It is evident from the figure that the points in the first and third quadrants will make the product $(X - \mu_x)(Y - \mu_y)$ positive, because the individual terms are either both positive or both negative. In contrast, the points in the second and fourth quadrants will make the product negative, because one of the terms is positive and the other is negative. When we compute the covariance measure, which is a weighted sum of these products, the net result is likely to be positive because there are more positive terms than the opposite. Therefore, the covariance is likely to be positive. In the case when X and Y move in opposite directions, $\text{Cov}(X, Y)$ will be negative.

Although the covariance measure is useful in identifying the nature of the association between X and Y, it has a serious problem—namely, the numerical value is very sensitive to the units in which X and Y are measured. If X were a financial variable measured in dollars rather than in thousands of dollars, the covariance measure would go up by a factor of 1,000. To avoid this problem, a "normalized" covariance measure is used. This measure is called the **correlation coefficient** between X and Y and is denoted as ρ_{xy}.

DEFINITION 2.5   (Coefficient of Correlation)

The coefficient of correlation between X and Y is defined as

$$\rho_{xy} = \frac{\sigma_{xy}}{\sigma_x \sigma_y} = \frac{\text{Cov}(X, Y)}{[\text{Var}(X)\text{Var}(Y)]^{1/2}} \tag{2.7}$$

If X and Y are positively related, the correlation coefficient will be positive. If X and Y are negatively related, they will move in opposite directions. In this case, the covariance and correlation coefficient will both be negative. It is possible for the correlation coefficient to be zero. In this case, we say that x and y are **uncorrelated.** It can be shown that $\rho_{xy}^2 \leq 1$ or equivalently that $|\rho_{xy}| \leq 1$. $|\rho_{xy}|$ will be equal to 1 if and only if there is an exact *linear relation* between X and Y of the form $Y - \mu_y = \beta(X - \mu_x)$. If $|\rho_{xy}| = 1$, then X and Y are said to be **perfectly correlated.** It should be noted that perfect correlation occurs only when X and Y are *exactly linearly related.* Thus, for instance, Y may be of the form $Y = X^2$, which is an exact relation, but the correlation coefficient between X and Y will not be 1. The coefficient of correlation thus measures the extent of linear association between two variables.

If X and Y are independent, $f_{XY}(x, y) = f_X(x)f_Y(y)$; that is, the joint probability is the product of individual probabilities. Note from the definition of σ_{xy} that in this case,

$$\sigma_{xy} = \sum_x \sum_y (x - \mu_x)(y - \mu_y)f_X(x)f_Y(y)$$

Because x and y are now separable, we have

$$\sigma_{xy} = \left[\sum_x (x - \mu_x) f_X(x) \right]\left[\sum_y (y - \mu_y) f_Y(y) \right]$$
$$= E(X - \mu_x) E(Y - \mu_y)$$

But $E(X - \mu_x) = E(X) - \mu_x = 0$ (see Property 2.1a). Hence, $\sigma_{xy} = 0$ and $\rho_{xy} = 0$ if two random variables are independent. In other words, *if X and Y are independent random variables, then they are uncorrelated.*

The converse need not be true (that is, zero correlation need not imply independence), as may be seen from the following counterexample. Let $f_{XY}(x, y)$ be as in Table 2.7.

$$\text{Cov}(X, Y) = E(XY) - E(X)E(Y)$$
$$E(X) = (1 \times 0.4) + (2 \times 0.2) + (3 \times 0.4) = 2$$
$$E(Y) = (6 \times 0.4) + (8 \times 0.2) + (10 \times 0.4) = 8$$
$$E(XY) = (6 \times 1 \times 0.2) + (6 \times 3 \times 0.2) + (8 \times 2 \times 0.2) + (10 \times 1 \times 0.2)$$
$$+ (10 \times 3 \times 0.2) = 16$$

Hence, $\text{Cov}(X, Y) = 0$. But X and Y are not independent because $P(X = 2, Y = 6) = 0$, $P(X = 2) = 0.2$, and $P(Y = 6) = 0.4$. Hence the joint probability is not the product of individual probabilities.

● PRACTICE PROBLEM 2.6

For the random variables X and Y with joint probabilities given in Table 2.4, compute $\text{Cov}(X, Y)$ and ρ_{xy}. (Note that you have already computed the means and variances in Problem 2.5.)

● PRACTICE PROBLEM 2.7[†]

Suppose the random variable X can assume only the values 1, 2, 3, 4, and 5, each with the equal probability 0.2. Let $Y = X^2$. Compute the coefficient of correlation

● **Table 2.7   An Example Showing That Zero Covariance Need Not Imply Independence**

X ╲ Y	6	8	10	$f_X(x)$
1	0.2	0	0.2	0.4
2	0	0.2	0	0.2
3	0.2	0	0.2	0.4
$f_Y(y)$	0.4	0.2	0.4	1

between X and Y and show that it is not equal to 1, even though X and Y have an exact relationship.

Property 2.8 lists a number of properties involving two random variables.

Property 2.8

a. If a and b are constants, then $\text{Var}(aX + bY) = a^2\text{Var}(X) + b^2\text{Var}(Y) + 2ab\,\text{Cov}(X, Y)$. As a special case of this, $\text{Var}(X + Y) = \text{Var}(X) + \text{Var}(Y) + 2\text{Cov}(X, Y)$. Also, $\text{Var}(X - Y) = \text{Var}(X) + \text{Var}(Y) - 2\text{Cov}(X, Y)$.

b. The correlation coefficient ρ_{xy} lies between -1 and $+1$.

c. If X and Y are independent, then $\sigma_{xy} = \text{Cov}(X, Y) = 0 = \rho_{xy}$; that is, X and Y are uncorrelated. It follows from this and (a) that, in this case, $\text{Var}(X + Y) = \text{Var}(X) + \text{Var}(Y)$ and $\text{Var}(X - Y) = \text{Var}(X) + \text{Var}(Y)$.

d. $|\rho_{xy}|$ will be equal to 1 if and only if there is an exact linear relation between X and Y of the form $Y - \mu_y = \beta(X - \mu_x)$.

e. The correlation between X and itself is 1.

f. If $U = a_0 + a_1 X$, $V = b_0 + b_1 Y$, and $a_1 b_1 > 0$, then $\rho_{uv} = \rho_{xy}$; that is, the correlation coefficient is invariant under a rescaling of units. If $a_1 b_1 < 0$, then $\rho_{uv} = -\rho_{xy}$. However, if $U = a_0 + a_1 X + a_2 Y$ and $V = b_0 + b_1 X + b_2 Y$, then $\rho_{uv} \neq \rho_{xy}$. This means that correlation is not invariant under a general linear transformation (a_i and b_i are assumed to be nonzero).

g. If a_1, a_2, b_1, and b_2 are fixed, then $\text{Cov}(a_1 X + a_2 Y, b_1 X + b_2 Y) = a_1 b_1 \text{Var}(X) + (a_1 b_2 + a_2 b_1)\,\text{Cov}(X, Y) + a_2 b_2 \text{Var}(Y)$.

Multivariate Distributions*

In this section the concepts just discussed are extended to more than two random variables. Let $x_1, x_2, \ldots, x_n$ be n random variables. Then their joint probability density function is $f_X(x_1, x_2, \ldots, x_n)$. As before, they are independent if the joint PDF is the product of the individual PDF. Thus, we have

$$f_X(x_1, x_2, \ldots, x_n) = f_{X_1}(x_1) \cdot f_{X_2}(x_2) \cdot \cdots \cdot f_{X_n}(x_n)$$

In the special case when each of the x's is independently and identically distributed (denoted as iid), we have

$$f_X(x_1, x_2, \ldots, x_n) = f_X(x_1) \cdot f_X(x_2) \cdot \cdots \cdot f_X(x_n)$$

where $f_X(x)$ is the common distribution of each of the x's. A number of useful results on multivariate distributions are listed in Property 2.9.

Property 2.9

a. If $a_1, a_2, \ldots, a_n$ are constants or nonrandom, then $E[a_1 x_1 + a_2 x_2 + \cdots + a_n x_n] = a_1 E(x_1) + a_2 E(x_2) + \cdots + a_n E(x_n)$. Thus, the expectation of a linear combination of terms is the linear combination of the expectations. In summation notation, $E[\Sigma(a_i x_i)] = \Sigma E(a_i x_i) = \Sigma a_i E(x_i)$.

b.   If each x_i has the same mean so that $E(x_i) = \mu$, we have $E(\Sigma a_i x_i) = \mu \Sigma a_i$. In particular, if the a_i's are all equal to $1/n$, we have $E(\Sigma x_i / n) = E(\bar{x}) = \mu$. Thus, the expected value of the mean of several identically distributed random variables is equal to their common mean.

c. $\text{Var} [\Sigma (a_i x_i)] = \Sigma_i a_i^2 \text{Var}(x_i) + \underset{i \neq j}{\sum \sum} a_i a_j \text{Cov}(x_i, x_j)$, where the a_i's are assumed to be constant or nonrandom.

d.   If $x_1, x_2, \ldots, x_n$ are all independent, then every pair of correlations (ρ_{ij}) and covariances will be zero so that $\text{Cov}(x_i, x_j) = 0 = \rho_{ij}$ for all $i \neq j$.

e.   It follows from (c) and (d) that when the x's are independent, $\text{Var}[\Sigma(a_i x_i)] = \Sigma a_i^2 \text{Var}(x_i)$, because the covariance terms will disappear. Thus, the variance of the sum of independent random variables is the sum of the variances. In particular, if the variances are the same, so that $\text{Var}(x_i) = \sigma^2$ for each i, then $\text{Var} [\Sigma(a_i x_i)] = \sigma^2 \Sigma a_i^2$.

f.   If $x_1, x_2, \ldots, x_n$ are independent random variables such that x_i is normally distributed with mean μ_i and variance σ_i^2—that is, $x_i \sim N(\mu_i, \sigma_i^2)$—then the linear combination of the x's given by $a_1 x_1 + a_2 x_2 + \cdots + a_n x_n$ also has the normal distribution with mean $a_1 \mu_1 + a_2 \mu_2 + \cdots + a_n \mu_n$ and variance $a_1^2 \sigma_1^2 + a_2^2 \sigma_2^2 + \cdots + a_n^2 \sigma_n^2$. In summation notation, $U = \Sigma(a_i x_i) \sim N[\Sigma(a_i \mu_i), \Sigma(a_i^2 \sigma_i^2)]$.

g.   If $x_1, x_2, \ldots, x_n$ are independently and identically distributed (iid) as $N(\mu, \sigma^2)$, their mean $\bar{x} = (1/n)\Sigma x_i$ has the normal distribution with mean μ and variance σ^2/n; that is, $\bar{x} \sim N(\mu, \sigma^2/n)$. Also, $z = \sqrt{n}(\bar{x} - \mu)/\sigma \sim N(0, 1)$.

2.4   Random Sampling and Sampling Distributions

A statistical investigation arises out of the need to solve a particular problem. It might be an attempt to rationalize past behavior of agents or to forecast their future behavior. In formulating the problem, it is important to identify the relevant *statistical universe*, or the *population*, which is the totality of elements about which some information is desired. The term *population* is used in a general sense and is not restricted to living things. All the seeds in a storage bin, all the firms in a city, and all the containers of milk produced by a dairy are examples of populations. Sometimes a population is also referred to as the **parent population.**

An analyst is interested in drawing inferences about several attributes of a population. It would clearly be prohibitively expensive to study every element of a population in order to derive the inferences. The investigator would therefore draw a sample of the elements, make observations on them, and use these observations to draw conclusions about the characteristics of the parent population that the sample represents. This process is known as *sampling*. Several types of sampling are possible: random sampling, judgment sampling, selective sampling, sampling with and without replacement, stratified sampling, and so on. In this book we focus our attention only on **random sampling,** the most common type of sampling.

DEFINITION 2.6   (Random Sampling)

A simple random sample of n elements is a sample that has the property that every combination of n elements has an equal chance of being the selected sample. A random sample of observations on a random variable X is a set of **independent, identically distributed (iid)** random variables $X_1, X_2, \ldots, X_n$, each of which has the same probability distribution as that of X.

Sampling Distributions

A function of the observed values of random variables that does not contain any unknown parameters is called a **sample statistic.** The two most frequently used sample statistics are the **sample mean** (denoted by $\bar{x}$) and the **sample variance** (denoted by s^2):

$$\text{Sample mean: } \bar{x} = (x_1 + x_2 + \cdots + x_n)/n = \frac{1}{n} \sum x_i \tag{2.8}$$

$$\text{Sample variance: } s^2 = \frac{1}{n-1}(x_1 - \bar{x})^2 + \frac{1}{n-1}(x_2 - \bar{x})^2 \tag{2.9}$$

$$+ \cdots + \frac{1}{n-1}(x_n - \bar{x})^2$$

$$= \frac{1}{n-1} \sum (x_i - \bar{x})^2$$

The reason for dividing by $n - 1$ rather than by n is given in Section 2.7. The square root of the sample variance (s) is called the **sample standard deviation** or **standard error.** The distinction between a *sample statistic* and a **population parameter** must be clearly understood. Suppose the random variable X has expected value μ and variance σ^2. These are the population parameters that are fixed and not random. In contrast, however, the sample mean $\bar{x}$ and the sample variance s^2 are random variables. This is because different trials of an experiment result in different values for the sample mean and variance. Because these sample statistics are random variables, it makes sense to talk about their distributions. If we draw a random sample of size n and compute the sample mean $\bar{x}$, we get a certain value. Repeat this experiment a large number of times, each time drawing a random sample of the same size n. We will obtain a large number of values for the sample mean. We can then compute the fraction of times these mean values fall in a specified interval. This gives the *probability that the sample mean will lie in that interval* (refer to the frequency concept of probability presented in Section 2.1 and in Example 2.1). By varying this interval, we can obtain the whole range of probabilities, thus generating a probability distribution. This distribution is called the **distribution of the sample mean.** In a similar manner, we can compute the sample variance for each replication of the trial and use the various values generated this way to obtain the **distribution of the sample variance.** Because the sample mean and variance were for a sample of the specified size n, we would expect their sampling distributions to depend on n as well as on the parameters of the parent distribution from which the sample was drawn.

Sampling from a Normal Population

The sampling distributions of the mean and the sample variance are of considerable interest in econometrics and statistics, especially when the parent population from which the observations are drawn has the normal distribution. Let X be a random variable that has the normal distribution with mean μ and variance σ^2. Thus, $X \sim N(\mu, \sigma^2)$. Let us draw a random sample of size n from the population, measure the random variable, and obtain the observations $x_1, x_2, \ldots, x_n$. What are the sampling distributions of $\bar{x}$ and s^2? We note that the sample mean is a linear combination of n random variates. From Property 2.9g, we see that this linear combination also has a normal distribution. In particular, $\bar{x}$ also has mean μ and $\mathrm{Var}(\bar{x}) = \sigma^2/n$. We thus have the following property.

Property 2.10

a. If a random sample $x_1, x_2, \ldots, x_n$ is drawn from a normal population with mean μ and variance σ^2, the sample mean $\bar{x}$ is distributed normally with mean μ and variance σ^2/n. Thus, $\bar{x} \sim N(\mu, \sigma^2/n)$. We note from this that the distribution of the sample mean has a smaller dispersion around the mean, and the larger the sample size the smaller the variance.

b. The distribution of $Z = (\bar{x} - \mu)/(\sigma/\sqrt{n}) = \sqrt{n}(\bar{x} - \mu)/\sigma$ is $N(0, 1)$.

The derivation of the distribution of the sample variance defined in Equation (2.9) is postponed to Section 2.7.

Large-Sample Distributions

When the sample size is large, we can derive a number of properties that are quite useful in practice. Two of these are the **law of large numbers** and the **central limit theorem** stated in Property 2.11.

Property 2.11

a. **The law of large numbers:** Let $\bar{Z}$ be the mean of a random sample of values $Z_1, Z_2, \ldots, Z_n$, which are independently and identically distributed. Then $\bar{Z}$ converges to $E(Z)$. In simple terms, this means that as n increases, the sample mean of a set of random variables approaches its expected value. A special case of this arises when $\bar{Z} = \bar{x}$, the sample mean. Because $E(\bar{x}) = \mu$, the population mean, $\bar{x}$ converges to μ. Similarly, $s^2 = [\Sigma (x_i - \bar{x})^2]/(n - 1)$ converges to σ^2 as n approaches infinity.

b. **The central limit theorem:** Let $x_1, x_2, \ldots, x_n$ be a random sample of observations from the same distribution and let $E(x_i) = \mu$ and $\mathrm{Var}(x_i) = \sigma^2$. Then the sampling distribution of the random variable $Z_n = \sqrt{n}(\bar{x} - \mu)/\sigma$ converges to the standard normal $N(0, 1)$ as n converges to infinity.

The central limit theorem is very powerful because *it holds even when the distribution from which the observations are drawn is not normal.* This means that if we make sure that the sample size is large, then we can use the random variable Z_n defined above to answer questions about the population from which the observations are drawn, and we need not know the precise distribution from which the observations are drawn.

2.5   Procedures for the Estimation of Parameters

We have discussed the particular topics in probability and statistics given so far in order to prepare ourselves for the two basic objectives of any empirical study: the estimation of unknown parameters and the testing of hypotheses. In this section we discuss the problem of estimation. Hypothesis testing is covered in Section 2.8.

In an empirical investigation, the analyst very often knows, or can approximate, the general form of the probability distributions of the random variables of interest. The specific values of the population parameters of the distributions are, however, unknown. As mentioned earlier, a complete census of the population is out of the question because of the enormous cost that would involve. The investigator therefore obtains a sample of observations on the variables of interest and uses them to draw inferences about the underlying probability distribution.

As an illustration, suppose we know that the height of a person is approximately normally distributed but we don't know the mean, μ, of the distribution or its variance, σ^2. The problem of estimation is simply one of selecting a sample of people, measuring each person's height, and then using the measurements to obtain estimates of μ and σ^2. The term **estimator** is used to refer to the formula that gives us a numerical value of the parameter of interest. The numerical value itself is referred to as an **estimate.**

In this section we present two alternative procedures for estimating the unknown parameters of the probability distribution from which the observations $x_1, x_2, \ldots, x_n$ are obtained. In the appendix, Section 2.A.3, we describe an additional advanced method. In the following discussion it is assumed that the investigator knows the nature of the probability distribution but not the values of the parameters.

The Method of Moments

The oldest method of estimating parameters is the **method of moments.** If a distribution has k unknown parameters, the procedure is to calculate the first k **sample moments** of the distribution and use them as estimators of the corresponding **population moments.** In Section 2.2, we noted that the **population mean** of the distribution (μ) is also referred to as the *first moment* of the distribution around the origin. It is the weighted average of all possible x's, the weights being the corresponding probabilities. The sample mean ($\bar{x}$) is the arithmetic average of the sample observations $x_1, x_2, \ldots, x_n$. By the method of moments, $\bar{x}$ is taken as an estimator of μ. The variance of a random variable is $\sigma^2 = E[(X - \mu)^2]$ and is known as the *second moment around the mean.* The sample variance (s^2), defined in Equation (2.9), is used as an estimator of the **population variance** of the distribution. In many cases (for example, the normal distribution), the mean and variance completely characterize a distribution, and hence there is no need to use higher-order moments such as the expected value of $(X - \mu)^3$. We will see later that the sample mean possesses several desirable properties, described in Section 2.6.

The same principle can be applied in estimating the coefficient of correlation between two random variables X and Y (see Definition 2.5). Let $x_1, x_2, \ldots, x_n$ and $y_1, y_2, \ldots, y_n$ be independent random samples of observations (of the same size n) on X and Y, respectively. The population covariance between them is given in Definition 2.4 as $E[(X - \mu_x)(Y - \mu_y)]$, where μ_x and μ_y are the population means of X and Y, respectively. An estimate of this is given by the **sample covariance**

$$s_{xy} = \widehat{\mathrm{Cov}(X, Y)} = \frac{1}{n-1} \sum (x_i - \bar{x})(y_i - \bar{y}) \qquad (2.10)$$

If the pairs of values x_i and y_i are plotted, we obtain a graph such as Figure 2.7, in which X and Y are positively related (that is, X and Y generally move in the same direction). We have already mentioned that such a plot is known as a *scatter diagram*. Figure 2.6 is similar to this except that in that figure the points referred to the *population*, whereas here they refer to the *sample*. By translating the axes to the dashed lines with origin at $(\bar{x}, \bar{y})$, we can see that $x_i - \bar{x}$ and $y_i - \bar{y}$ are the distances from the mean point $(\bar{x}, \bar{y})$. If the relationship is positive, we would expect most of the points to lie in the first and third quadrants in which the product $(x_i - \bar{x})(y_i - \bar{y})$ will be positive. Because the negative products from the points in the second and fourth quadrants are likely to be dominated by the positive products, we would expect the covariance to be positive. By a similar argument, we can see that if the relationship is negative, most of the points will lie in the second and

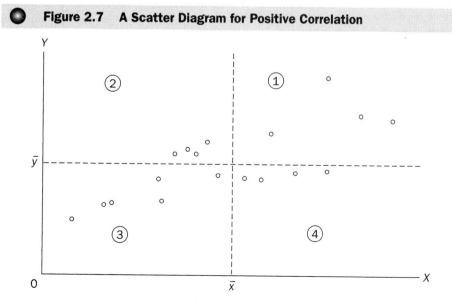

Figure 2.7   A Scatter Diagram for Positive Correlation

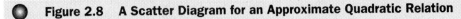

Figure 2.8   A Scatter Diagram for an Approximate Quadratic Relation

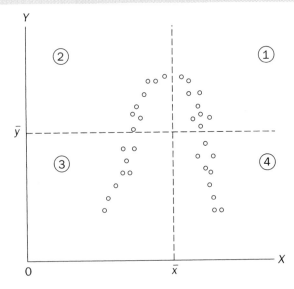

fourth quadrants, giving rise to a negative covariance. This shows that if X and Y are positively related, the covariance and hence the correlation between them will be positive. A negative relation will result in a negative coefficient of correlation. The **sample correlation coefficient** is given by

$$r_{xy} = \frac{s_{xy}}{s_x s_y} = \frac{\Sigma(x_i - \bar{x})(y_i - \bar{y})}{[\Sigma(x_i - \bar{x})^2]^{1/2}[\Sigma(y_i - \bar{y})^2]^{1/2}} \qquad (2.11)$$

where s_x and s_y are the sample standard deviations (square roots of the variances) of X and Y, respectively.

In Section 2.3 we mentioned that the correlation coefficient is a measure of a linear relationship between X and Y. Figure 2.8 is a scatter diagram showing the situation when Y is an approximate quadratic function of X. We note that the points are scattered in all four quadrants, and hence the sum $\Sigma(x_i - \bar{x})(y_i - \bar{y})$ is likely to be small, indicating a low value for r_{xy}. Thus, a low r_{xy} does not mean that X and Y are not closely related, just that they do not have a close *linear* relation.

Exercise 2.24 illustrates the concept of correlation applied to the **Phillips curve.**

For GRETL users, Practice Computer Session 2.3 (see Appendix D, Table D.1) illustrates the calculation of covariance and correlation between college grade point average and high school grade point average for the data in DATA2-2, described in Appendix D. Use your own program with DATA2-2 to verify the results presented here.

Table 2.8   Annotated Partial Computer Output Illustrating Various Summary Statistics

Comments are set in a typeface different from that used for the computer output.

```
x = colgpa = Grade point average in College
y = hsgpa = Grade point average in High School


Correlation between x and y = 0.406662


    Summary Statistics, using the observations 1 - 427


Variable        MEAN        MEDIAN          MIN          MAX
x              2.7855         2.79         0.85         3.97
y             3.55785         3.59         2.29          4.5


Variable        S.D.         C.V.         SKEW      EXCSKURT
x             0.54082     0.194155    -0.203647   -0.0517458
y            0.419577      0.11793    -0.401241    -0.220107
```

Min and Max are the smallest and largest values in the sample. Median is the value of x or y to each side of which there are 50 percent of the observations. C.V. is the coefficient of variation (MEAN/S.D.) discussed in Section 2.2. SKEW is a measure of how far the distribution of the variable deviates from symmetry (this is called skewness). A zero value indicates symmetry around zero. A positive value indicates skewness to the right with a long tail in that direction. A negative value indicates skewness to the left with a long tail in that direction. EXCKURT is excess kurtosis, that is, kurtosis − 3. Kurtosis is a measure of the peakedness of a distribution. The normal distribution has a kurtosis of 3. A flat distribution will have a negative excess kurtosis, and a tall distribution will have a positive excess kurtosis. Skewness and kurtosis have not been discussed in the text because they are not in much use in econometrics. To learn more about those measures see Ramanathan (1993, Section 3.5).

An annotated version of the output is presented in Table 2.8. The table also has additional summary statistics measures not discussed above.

The Method of Least Squares (or Ordinary Least Squares)

In econometrics the most commonly used method of estimating parameters is the **method of least squares** (also known as **ordinary least squares** or **OLS**). Although it is predominantly used to estimate the parameters of a regression model of the type PRICE $= \alpha + \beta$SQFT $+ u$ encountered in Chapter 1, it is also useful in the simpler context of estimating the mean of a single random variable X.

Each of the observations x_i can be thought of as an estimator of the sample mean μ because $E(x_i) = \mu$. The error in this estimator is $e_i = x_i - \mu$ (that is, $x_i = \mu + e_i$). Consider the sum of the square of this error over the entire sample. That is, let ESS$(\mu) = \Sigma e_i^2 = \Sigma(x_i - \mu)^2$. The method of least squares chooses that estimator of μ for which the sample sum of squared errors is a minimum. Squaring the errors accomplishes two things. First, it eliminates the sign of the error. Thus, positive errors and negative errors are treated alike. Second, squaring penalizes large errors because such errors are magnified when squared.

To obtain $\hat{\mu}$, the estimate of μ by minimizing ESS, write ESS as follows:

$$
\begin{aligned}
\text{ESS}(\hat{\mu}) &= \sum (x_i - \hat{\mu})^2 = \sum (x_i - \bar{x} + \bar{x} - \hat{\mu})^2 \\
&= \sum (x_i - \bar{x})^2 + \sum (\bar{x} - \hat{\mu})^2 + 2\sum (\bar{x} - \hat{\mu})(x_i - \bar{x}) \\
&= \sum (x_i - \bar{x})^2 + \sum (\bar{x} - \hat{\mu})^2
\end{aligned}
$$

Because $\bar{x} - \hat{\mu}$ in the third term is a constant, it can be factored out (see Appendix 2.A.1) and, by Property 2.A.4, the third term is zero. Because the first term has no $\hat{\mu}$, we see that ESS is minimized with respect to the choice of $\hat{\mu}$ if and only if we set $\hat{\mu} = \bar{x}$, which would make the second term zero. Therefore, the least squares estimator of μ is the sample mean $\bar{x}$.

In the chapter appendix, another, more advanced estimation procedure is discussed: the maximum likelihood estimator (MLE). Interested readers should read that section.

(To see how the methods described in this section are used in estimating regressions, proceed to Sections 3.1 and 3.2.)

2.6   Properties of Estimators

The two estimation procedures discussed in the previous section chose the sample mean as an estimator of μ. In the heights-of-persons example given in Section 2.5, an alternative estimator is to take the heights of the tallest and shortest persons and average them. Which estimator is better? In order to answer questions of this kind, we need some criteria for choosing among alternative estimators. Numerous criteria have been developed to judge the "goodness" of an estimator, but we discuss in the following sections only those concepts that are most frequently used in econometrics. Some of them refer to small samples and others are appropriate only for large samples.

Small-Sample Properties of Estimators

The standard notation to denote an unknown parameter is θ and an estimator is denoted by $\hat{\theta}$. It should be emphasized that $\hat{\theta}$ is a function of the observations $x_1, x_2, \ldots, x_n$ and does not depend on any unknown parameters. An estimator is thus a sample statistic. However, because the x's are random variables, so is $\hat{\theta}$.

UNBIASEDNESS Because $\hat{\theta}$ is a random variable, it has a probability distribution with a certain mean, which is $E(\hat{\theta})$. If this mean is the same as the unknown parameter θ, we say that the estimator is **unbiased.** Thus, we have the following definition.

DEFINITION 2.7 (Unbiasedness)

An estimator $\hat{\theta}$ is said to be an unbiased estimator of θ if $E(\hat{\theta}) = \theta$. If this equality does not hold, the estimator is said to be biased and the bias is $E(\hat{\theta}) - \theta$.

Although in a given trial $\hat{\theta}$ may not equal θ, if we repeat the trial a large number of times and compute $\hat{\theta}$ each time, the average of these values should be θ if the estimator is to be unbiased. As described in Section 2.4, if we fix the sample size at n, conduct repetitions of the experiment, calculate $\hat{\theta}$ each time, and form a frequency distribution, we obtain the sampling distribution of $\hat{\theta}$. Unbiasedness requires that the mean of this distribution be the true θ.

EFFICIENCY While unbiasedness is clearly a desirable characteristic for any estimator to possess, we need additional criteria because it is possible to construct an infinite number of unbiased estimators. In the example of measuring heights, we know that the sample mean $\bar{x}$ is unbiased because $E(\bar{x}) = \mu$. But the alternative estimator, proposed earlier, that averages the height of the tallest person (call it x_{max}) and that of the shortest person (call it x_{min}) is also unbiased. Let $\hat{\theta} = \frac{1}{2}(x_{max} + x_{min})$. Then $E(\hat{\theta}) = \frac{1}{2}[E(x_{max}) + E(x_{min})] = \mu$, and hence $\hat{\theta}$ is also unbiased. It is easy to verify that any weighted average of the x's is an unbiased estimator of μ, provided the weights are nonrandom and add up to 1. We therefore need more criteria to distinguish between two unbiased estimators.

We have seen that the variance of a random variable is a measure of its dispersion around the mean. A smaller variance means that, on average, the values of the random variable are closer to the mean than those for another random variable with the same mean but a higher variance. This suggests that we could use the variances of two different unbiased estimators as a means of choosing between the two. The one with the smaller variance is clearly more desirable because, on average, it is closer to the true mean θ. This is the concept of **efficiency.**

DEFINITION 2.8 (Efficiency)

a. Let $\hat{\theta}_1$ and $\hat{\theta}_2$ be two unbiased estimators of the parameter θ. If $\mathrm{Var}(\hat{\theta}_1) < \mathrm{Var}(\hat{\theta}_2)$, then we say that $\hat{\theta}_1$ is more efficient than $\hat{\theta}_2$.

b. The ratio $[\mathrm{Var}(\hat{\theta}_1)]/[\mathrm{Var}(\hat{\theta}_2)]$ is called the *relative efficiency*.

c. Among all the unbiased estimators of θ, the one with the smallest variance is called the *minimum variance unbiased estimator*.

Let us apply this to the height example. Let $\hat{\theta}_1$ be the sample mean and $\hat{\theta}_2$ be the mean of the heights of the tallest and shortest persons. From Property 2.10a,

$\mathrm{Var}(\hat{\theta}_1) = \sigma^2/n$ and $\mathrm{Var}(\hat{\theta}_2) = \sigma^2/2$. If the sample size is more than two, $\hat{\theta}_1$ has a smaller variance and hence is clearly preferable. Thus, $\hat{\theta}_1$ is more efficient than $\hat{\theta}_2$.

MEAN SQUARED ERROR   Consider two estimators: One is unbiased and the other, though biased, has a much smaller variance, indicating that, on average, it might be closer to the true mean than the unbiased estimator. In this case, we might be willing to allow some bias in order to gain on the variance side. A measure that permits this trade-off between unbiasedness and variance is the **mean squared error.**

DEFINITION 2.9   (Mean Squared Error)

a.   The mean squared error of an estimator $\hat{\theta}$ is defined as $\mathrm{MSE}(\theta) = E[(\hat{\theta} - \theta)^2]$, which is the expected value of the square of the deviation of $\hat{\theta}$ from θ.

b.   If $\hat{\theta}_1$ and $\hat{\theta}_2$ are two alternative estimators of θ and $\mathrm{MSE}(\hat{\theta}_1) < \mathrm{MSE}(\hat{\theta}_2)$, then $\hat{\theta}_1$ is said to be *mean squared efficient* compared to $\hat{\theta}_2$. If they are both unbiased, $\hat{\theta}_1$ is more efficient, as in Definition 2.8a.

c.   Among all possible estimators of θ, the one with the smallest mean squared error is called the *minimum mean squared error estimator.*

It is easy to show that the mean squared error is equal to the sum of the variance and the square of the bias. Thus, if $b(\theta) = E(\hat{\theta}) - \theta$ is the bias in the estimator $\hat{\theta}$, then $\mathrm{MSE} = \mathrm{Var}(\hat{\theta}) + [b(\theta)]^2$. Note that $b(\theta)$ is independent of the x's and is hence fixed and nonrandom.

$$\mathrm{MSE} = E[(\hat{\theta} - \theta)^2] = E[\hat{\theta} - E(\hat{\theta}) + E(\hat{\theta}) - \theta]^2$$
$$= E[\hat{\theta} - E(\hat{\theta}) + b(\theta)]^2 = E[\hat{\theta} - E(\hat{\theta})]^2 + [b(\theta)]^2 + 2b(\theta)E[\hat{\theta} - E(\hat{\theta})]$$

The first term is the variance of $\hat{\theta}$ and the third term is zero because $E(\hat{\theta})$ is nonrandom and hence $E[\hat{\theta} - E(\hat{\theta})] = E(\hat{\theta}) - E(\hat{\theta}) = 0$. The desired result follows immediately.

The concept of mean squared error is more frequently used to choose among alternative forecasts of a random variable (see Chapter 11). Forecasts are often biased—that is, they systematically overestimate or underestimate the variable of interest—but some of them may have a smaller variance. The mean squared error is therefore a useful measure for taking account of both the bias and the variance of a forecast.

Large-Sample Properties of Estimators

All the properties discussed previously are applicable to samples of finite sizes. Sometimes an estimator may not possess one or more of the desirable properties in a small sample, but when the size of the sample is large, many of the desirable properties might hold. It is therefore of interest to study these large-sample, or *asymptotic,* properties. In the following discussions, we let the sample size n increase indefinitely. Because an estimator will depend on n, we denote it as $\hat{\theta}_n$.

CONSISTENCY The most frequently used large-sample property is that of **consistency.** In intuitive terms, consistency means that as n increases, the estimator $\hat{\theta}_n$ approaches the true value θ. In other words, we draw a random sample of any size from a large population and compute $\hat{\theta}$. Next we draw one more observation and recompute $\hat{\theta}$ with this extra observation. We repeat this process indefinitely, getting a sequence of estimates for θ. If this sequence converges to θ as n increases to infinity, then $\hat{\theta}$ is a consistent estimator of θ. The formal definition of consistency is given in Definition 2.10.

DEFINITION 2.10 (Consistency)

An estimator $\hat{\theta}_n$ is said to be a consistent estimator of θ if $\lim\limits_{n \to \infty} P(\theta - \varepsilon \leq \hat{\theta}_n \leq \theta + \varepsilon) = 1$, for all $\varepsilon > 0$. This property is expressed as $\operatorname{plim}(\hat{\theta}_n) = \theta$.

Let us look at this definition more closely. Consider the fixed (that is, nonrandom) interval $(\theta - \varepsilon, \theta + \varepsilon)$, where ε is any positive number. Because $\hat{\theta}_n$ is an estimator based on a sample of observations, it is a random variable. We can therefore compute the probability that $\hat{\theta}_n$ lies in the interval defined. If this probability increases to 1 as n increases to infinity *for any $\varepsilon > 0$*, we say that $\hat{\theta}_n$ is a *consistent estimator of θ.*

This point is illustrated in Figure 2.9, which graphs the sampling distribution of $\hat{\theta}_n = \bar{x}$ for various values of the sample size n. We note that this distribution becomes more and more "tightly packed" as the sample size increases. In other words, the variance of $\hat{\theta}_n$ approaches zero as the sample size increases. In the limit, the distribution of $\hat{\theta}_n$ collapses to the single point θ.

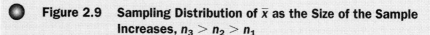

Figure 2.9 Sampling Distribution of $\bar{x}$ as the Size of the Sample Increases, $n_3 > n_2 > n_1$

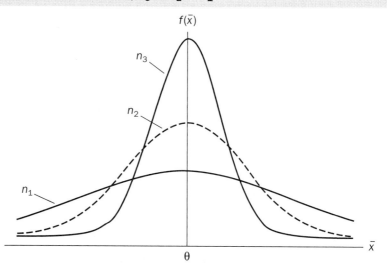

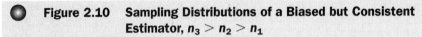

Figure 2.10   Sampling Distributions of a Biased but Consistent Estimator, $n_3 > n_2 > n_1$

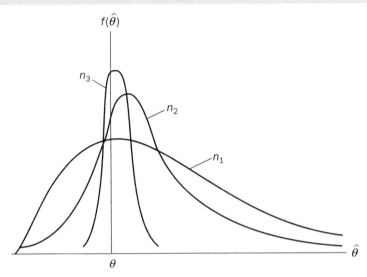

It should be stressed that the concepts of unbiasedness and consistency are conceptually quite different. Unbiasedness can hold for any sample size, but consistency is strictly a large-sample concept. Figure 2.10 illustrates a biased but consistent estimator.

Does unbiasedness imply consistency? Absolutely not, as is seen from the following trivial counterexample. The first observation, x_1, is an unbiased estimator of the mean θ because $E(x_1) = \theta$. But letting $n \to \infty$ is not going to make x_1 approach θ by any means.

(Proceed now to Section 3.3 to see how these concepts are applied in econometrics.)

ASYMPTOTIC UNBIASEDNESS*   The bias in an estimator is the difference between its expected value and the true parameter, θ. This bias might depend on the sample size, n. If the bias goes to zero as n increases to infinity, we say that the estimator is *asymptotically unbiased.*

DEFINITION 2.11   (Asymptotic Unbiasedness)*

An estimator $\hat{\theta}_n$ is said to be asymptotically unbiased if $\lim_{n \to \infty} E(\hat{\theta}_n) = \theta$, or, equivalently, if $\lim_{n \to \infty} b_n(\theta) = 0$, where $b_n(\theta) = E(\hat{\theta}_n) - \theta$.

ASYMPTOTIC EFFICIENCY*   No single estimator can be most efficient (that is, have the smallest variance) for all values of θ. Some are good for certain values of θ and others are more efficient in other ranges of θ. For instance, let $\hat{\theta} = 1.25$, regardless of what the observations are. If the true θ is at or near 1.25, this is a pretty good estimate; but when the true θ is far from 1.25, it is a very poor estimate. When dealing with consistent estimators, however, the range of values of θ for which one estimator is more efficient than another shrinks as the sample size increases. In the limit when $n \to \infty$, the distributions of all consistent estimators collapse to the true parameter θ (recall that the variances go to zero). Preference should therefore be given to those estimators that approach the true θ in the fastest possible way (that is, those whose variances converge to zero the fastest). This is the concept of *asymptotic efficiency* formally defined in Definition 2.12. In intuitive terms, a consistent estimator is asymptotically efficient if, for large samples, its variance is smaller than that of any other consistent estimator.

DEFINITION 2.12   (Asymptotic Efficiency)*

A consistent estimator $\hat{\theta}_1$ is said to be asymptotically efficient if for every other consistent estimator $\hat{\theta}_2$

$$\lim_{n \to \infty} \left[\frac{\text{Var}(\hat{\theta}_1)}{\text{Var}(\hat{\theta}_2)} \right] < 1 \qquad \text{for all } \theta$$

2.7   The Chi-square, t-, and F-distributions

In testing hypotheses on econometric models, four distributions are used predominantly. These are the *normal, chi-square, Student's t-, and Fisher's F-distributions*. The normal distribution and its properties have already been examined. In this section, we discuss the other three distributions.

The Chi-square Distribution

The distribution of the sum of squares of n independent standard normal random variables is called the **chi-square (χ^2) distribution** with n degrees of freedom and is written as χ_n^2. More formally, consider the n random variables $Z_1, Z_2, \ldots, Z_n$, all of which are independently and identically distributed (iid) as the standard normal $N(0, 1)$. Define a new random variable U that is the sum of the squares of the Zs. Thus,

$$U = Z_1^2 + Z_2^2 + \cdots + Z_n^2 = \sum Z_i^2$$

The distribution of the random variable U is χ_n^2. Because U is nonnegative, the chi-square distribution is defined only over $0 \leq u < \infty$. The density function of χ_n^2 depends on only one parameter, called the **degrees of freedom** (frequently abbreviated as **d.f.**). The mean of χ_n^2 can be shown to be n. Figure 2.11 presents the graphs of the chi-square densities for a number of selected values of the degrees of freedom. We note that when $n = 1$, the density function is strictly decreasing. For higher degrees of freedom, it rises quickly to a maximum but tapers off slowly to the

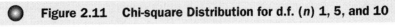

Figure 2.11   Chi-square Distribution for d.f. (*n*) 1, 5, and 10

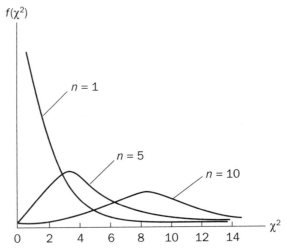

right with a long "tail." A number of properties of the χ^2 distribution are summarized in Property 2.12.

Property 2.12

a. $E(\chi_n^2) = n$; that is, the expected value of a chi-square random variable is its d.f.

b. The chi-square distribution has the additive property; namely, if $U \sim \chi_m^2$ and $V \sim \chi_n^2$ with U and V independent, then their sum $U + V \sim \chi_{m+n}^2$. It follows from this that the sum of several independent chi-square random variables is also chi-square with d.f. equal to the sum of the d.f.

c. If $x_1, x_2, \ldots, x_n$ are independent and normally distributed random variables with mean μ_i and variance σ_i^2, then the sum of squares $U = \Sigma(x_i - \mu_i)^2/\sigma_i^2$ has the chi-square distribution with n d.f. The result follows from the fact that $Z_i = (x_i - \mu_i)/\sigma_i$ has the standard normal distribution and the Zs are independent, thus making their sum of squares χ_n^2. As a special case of this, if $\mu_i = \mu$ and $\sigma_i^2 = \sigma^2$—that is, if the Zs are iid—then $\Sigma(x_i - \mu)^2/\sigma^2 \sim \chi_n^2$.

The table in the inside front cover of the book and Table A.3 of Appendix A present the values of χ^2 for which the areas to the right correspond to specified probabilities. Thus, for example, for 15 d.f. the area to the right of 24.9958 is 0.05. Section 2.8 on testing hypotheses illustrates the use of the chi-square distribution.

The Student's *t*-distribution

The distribution of the ratio of a normal variate to the square root of an independent χ_n^2 is called the **Student's *t*-distribution** with *n* degrees of freedom (and is

written as t_n). Suppose $Z \sim N(0, 1)$ and $U \sim \chi_n^2$, with Z and U independent. Define the random variable $t = Z/\sqrt{U/n} = (Z\sqrt{n})/\sqrt{U}$. The distribution of t is the t-distribution with n degrees of freedom.

The table at the back of the front cover of the book and Table A.2 present the values of t for which the areas in the tails correspond to specified probabilities. Some of the properties of the t-distribution are listed in Property 2.13.

Property 2.13

The t-distribution with n d.f. has the following properties:

a. The t-distribution is symmetric around the origin and has a shape similar to that of the normal distribution.

b. For large n, the t-distribution is approximately distributed as $N(0, 1)$. The approximation is quite good even for $n = 30$.

As an example, for 15 d.f., the area in the right-hand tail for 1.753 is 0.05, that is, $P(t > 1.753) = 0.05$. Because of the symmetry property, $P(t < -1.753$ or $t > 1.753) = 0.10$, that is, the area in both tails is twice the area in a single tail. The t-distribution is the most widely used one in hypothesis testing.

The F-distribution

Another distribution of considerable interest in econometrics is Fisher's **F-distribution**. It is the ratio of two independent chi-squares. Let $U \sim \chi_m^2$ and $V \sim \chi_n^2$ be independent of each other. Then the distribution of $F = (U/m) \div (V/n)$ is called the F-distribution with m and n d.f., and it is written as $F \sim F_{m,n}$. The first number is the degrees of freedom for the numerator and the second number is the degrees of freedom for the denominator. Tables A.4a, A.4b, and A.4c have values of F for several combinations of m, n, and the probabilities 0.01, 0.05, and 0.10. Tables A.4a and A.4b are also reproduced on the inside of the back cover. Some of the properties of the F-distribution are listed in Property 2.14.

Property 2.14

The F-distribution with m and n d.f. has the following properties:

a. The F-distribution has a shape similar to that of a chi-square.

b. If the random variable t has the Student's t-distribution with n d.f., then t^2 has the F-distribution with d.f. 1 and n. Thus, $t_n^2 \sim F_{1,n}$.

For example, from Table A.4b, for 3 d.f. for the numerator (denoted as m) and 15 d.f. for the denominator (denoted as n), $P(F > 3.29) = 0.05$, and from Table A.4a, $P(F > 5.42) = 0.01$.

The Distribution of the Sample Variance

In the case of a random sample from a normal distribution, the distribution of the sample variance s^2 defined in Equation (2.9) is of considerable interest. Note that

$(n - 1)s^2 = \Sigma(x_i - \bar{x})^2$ is the sum of squares of the deviations of a typical observation from the sample mean. We know that $x_i - \bar{x}$ has the normal distribution because it is a linear combination of the xs, which are normal. Earlier we saw that the chi-square was defined as the sum of squares of independent normal random variables. In Property 2.12c, we stated that $\Sigma(x_i - \mu)^2/\sigma^2$ is distributed as χ_n^2. Can we infer from this that $\Sigma(x_i - \bar{x})^2/\sigma^2$ also has the chi-square distribution? The answer is yes, but with a slight modification. Although this sum of squares also has the chi-square distribution, its degrees of freedom is $n - 1$ and not n. By substituting $\bar{x}$ for μ, we "lose a degree of freedom." This is because the deviations $(x_i - \bar{x})$ are not independent, even though the x_is are. The total deviation $\Sigma(x_i - \bar{x})$ is always zero, and hence we can designate only $n - 1$ of them independently. The nth one would be determined by the condition that the n deviations must add up to zero. Hence $(n - 1)s^2/\sigma^2$ has the chi-square distribution with d.f. $n - 1$. This and other related properties are summarized in Property 2.15.

Property 2.15

a. If an independent random sample $x_1, x_2, \ldots, x_n$ is drawn from a normal population with mean μ and variance σ^2, the sample variance $s^2 = \dfrac{1}{n - 1}\Sigma(x_i - \bar{x})^2$ has the property that $(n - 1)s^2/\sigma^2 = \Sigma(x_i - \bar{x})^2/\sigma^2 \sim \chi_{n-1}^2$.

b. Because the mean of a χ^2 is its d.f.—that is, $E(\chi_m^2) = m$—$E\left[\dfrac{(n - 1)s^2}{\sigma^2}\right] = n - 1$. It follows that $E(s^2) = \sigma^2$ and hence s^2 is an unbiased estimator of σ^2. We now see the reason for dividing $\Sigma(x_i - \bar{x})^2$ by $n - 1$. If we had used n instead, the expected value would not have been equal to σ^2, resulting in a bias.

c. We know from Property 2.10b that $Z = \sqrt{n}(\bar{x} - \mu)/\sigma \sim N(0, 1)$. Also from Property 2.15a, $U = (n - 1)s^2/\sigma^2 \sim \chi_{n-1}^2$. It can be shown that Z is independent of U. We note from the definition of the t-distribution that it is derived as the ratio of a standard normal to the square root of a chi-square. Thus, $t = Z/\sqrt{U/(n - 1)}$. Substituting for Z and U from above and simplifying the terms, we get the result that $t = \sqrt{n}(\bar{x} - \mu)/s \sim t_{n-1}$. Comparing this with Property 2.10b, we note that if σ is replaced by s, the resulting distribution is no longer normal but is a t-distribution.

● 2.8 Testing Hypotheses

Aside from estimating unknown parameters, testing hypotheses on those parameters is the most important aspect of an empirical investigation. In Chapter 1, we listed a variety of hypotheses that would be of interest. The procedure for hypothesis testing also requires formal concepts and methodologies. This chapter provides a brief review of those topics. Three steps are basic to any hypothesis-testing procedure: (1) Formulate two opposing hypotheses, (2) derive a test statistic and identify

⬤ **Table 2.9 Null and Alternative Hypotheses**

	(a)	(b)	(c)	(d)
H_0	$\mu = \mu_0$	$\mu = \mu_0$	$\mu \leq \mu_0$	$\mu \geq \mu_0$
H_1	$\mu = \mu_1$	$\mu \neq \mu_0$	$\mu > \mu_0$	$\mu < \mu_0$

its sampling distribution, and (3) derive a decision rule and choose one of the opposing hypotheses.

Null and Alternative Hypotheses

The first step is to formulate two opposing hypotheses: the **null hypothesis** (denoted by H_0) and the **alternative hypothesis** (denoted by H_1). Table 2.9 has examples of null and alternative hypotheses formulated on the mean of a population (μ).

A Statistical Test

A decision rule that selects one of the inferences "reject the null hypothesis" or "do not reject the null hypothesis" for every outcome of an experiment is called a **statistical test.** The procedure usually involves first computing a **test statistic** $T(x_1, x_2, \ldots, x_n)$ calculated from the sample of observations. The next step is to derive the sampling distribution of T under the null hypothesis. The final step is to derive a decision rule based on the observed value of T. The range of values of T for which the test procedure recommends rejecting the null hypothesis is called the **critical region,** and the range for which it recommends not rejecting the null hypothesis is called the **acceptance region** or, more accurately, the **nonrejection region.**

Type I and Type II Errors

For any test procedure three outcomes are possible: (1) a correct decision was made (that is, the procedure accepted a true hypothesis or rejected a false hypothesis), (2) a true hypothesis was rejected, and (3) a false hypothesis was accepted. The error of rejecting H_0 when it is true is called the **type I error.** The error of not rejecting H_0 when it is false is called the **type II error.** Associated with each of these errors is a probability. These are known as the probabilities of type I and type II errors and are denoted by $P(\text{I})$ and $P(\text{II})$. These concepts are better understood with an example from the legal system that was presented by Kohler (1985). Consider a defendant in a criminal trial. The null hypothesis is that the defendant is "not guilty" and the alternative is that the accused is "guilty." The presumption is that the accused is innocent and the burden is on the prosecution to prove that the accused is guilty, that is, to convince the jury to reject the null hypothesis. If the jury declares an innocent person "not guilty" or a guilty person "guilty," a correct decision has been made. If an innocent person is found guilty, a type I error has been made because a true hypothesis has been rejected. A type II error occurs when a guilty person is acquitted.

As a second example, suppose a pharmaceutical company claims to have found a cure for a deadly disease. The null hypothesis would be that the drug is not effective in curing the disease, and the burden of proof that it is effective rests with the pharmaceutical company. A type I error would have occurred if an ineffective drug (that is, one for which H_0 is true) is accepted as effective (that is, H_0 is rejected). A type II error occurs when a truly effective drug is rejected as ineffective.

Ideally, we would like to keep both $P(I)$ and $P(II)$ as low as possible no matter what the value of an unknown parameter is. Unfortunately, an attempt to reduce $P(I)$ automatically increases $P(II)$. For instance, in the criminal trial example, suppose we do not want a single guilty person to be acquitted. The only way this can be achieved is to declare everyone guilty. In this case, $P(II) = 0$, but $P(I) = 1$ because we would have convicted every innocent person also. Similarly, the only way to prevent even a single innocent person from being convicted is to declare everyone not guilty. In this case, we would let all criminals free also with $P(II) = 1$ and $P(I) = 0$.[1] In practice, the trade-off between these errors is not as extreme, but a particular decision rule would be better for some values of the parameter and not for others. *The classical procedure for hypothesis testing is to choose a maximum value for type I error that is acceptable to the investigator and then derive that decision rule for which type II error is a minimum.* In the criminal trial example, this would mean choosing a decision rule that will find an innocent person guilty no more than a certain percent of the time (say, 1 percent) and then minimizing the probability that a guilty person will be set free.

In the pharmaceutical example, we would set the probability of approving an ineffective drug to some maximum and minimize the probability of rejecting an effective drug.

The Level of Significance and the Power of a Test

The largest probability of a type I error when H_0 is true is called the **level of significance** (also known as the **size of a test**). In the criminal trial example, this is the maximum probability of convicting an innocent person. The probability of rejecting a hypothesis when it is false is given by $1 - P(II)$ and is called the **power of a test.** In our example, it is the probability of convicting a guilty person. The standard testing procedure is to find a decision rule for which $P(II)$ is a minimum (or equivalently, the power of the test is a maximum), subject to the restriction that $P(I) \leq a$, where a is a given constant ($0 < a < 1$). Such a test procedure is called a **most powerful test** of size a. The most common levels of significance are 0.01, 0.05, and 0.10.

We now present a few tests of hypotheses frequently used in business and economic decisions. Here we consider only the hypotheses on a normally distributed random variable. The reader should consult one of the references at the end of this chapter for more details on this and other tests.

Testing the Mean of a Normal Distribution

Consider a random variable X that is normally distributed with mean μ and variance σ^2. The most common null hypothesis is of the form $H_0: \mu = \mu_0$. The alternative H_1

---

[1]It should be emphasized that although $P(I) + P(II) = 1$ in these examples, this is generally not the case.

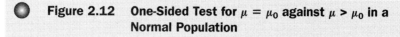

Figure 2.12   One-Sided Test for $\mu = \mu_0$ against $\mu > \mu_0$ in a Normal Population

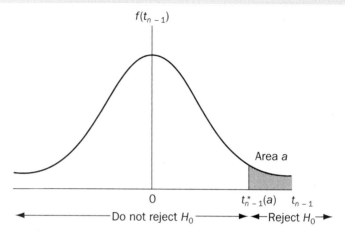

might be **one-sided,** as in $H_1: \mu > \mu_0$, or **two-sided,** as in $H_1: \mu \neq \mu_0$. Each of these cases is now discussed in detail.

A ONE-SIDED TEST   In many situations, the investigator will have prior knowledge of which side of the two-sided alternative the parameter is likely to be on. For instance, we know that the marginal propensity to consume (the extra consumption per unit of extra income) is positive. To test whether the marginal propensity to consume (μ) is zero, the sensible alternative is that $\mu > \mu_0$ (= 0 in our example).

By the method of moments, the sample mean $\bar{x}$ is an unbiased estimate of μ. If the observed $\bar{x}$ is considerably larger than the μ_0 specified in the null hypothesis, we would suspect that the true μ is most probably larger than μ_0. Thus, if $\bar{x} - \mu_0$ is "large" we would reject H_0 that $\mu = \mu_0$. In order to be able to compute probabilities in the distribution of $\bar{x}$ with an unknown σ^2, the actual test statistic used is $t_c = \sqrt{n}(\bar{x} - \mu_0)/s$, where s is the sample standard deviation defined in Equation (2.9). The steps involved in the test are summarized in the following list and are illustrated in Figure 2.12.

Procedure for Testing H_0 against H_1

Step 1 $H_0: \mu = \mu_0$; $H_1: \mu > \mu_0$.

Step 2   The test statistic is $t_c = \sqrt{n}(\bar{x} - \mu_0)/s$. Under the null hypothesis, this has the Student's t-distribution with $n - 1$ d.f.

Step 3   In the t-table (Table A.2), look up the entry corresponding to $n - 1$ d.f. and the given level of significance a, and obtain the point $t^*_{n-1}(a)$ such that $P(t > t^*) = a$, the selected level of significance. t^* is known as the **critical value.**

Step 4   Reject H_0 if the observed $t_c > t^*$. If the alternative is $\mu < \mu_0$, reject H_0 if $t_c < -t^*$. Equivalently, for either alternative, reject if $|t_c| > t^*$.

This is called a **one-sided test** because the alternative is on one side of μ_0 and because the value of t^* is obtained such that the area in one tail of the *t*-distribution is equal to a (see Figure 2.12). It is also referred to as a **one-tailed test.**

● EXAMPLE 2.10

The label on a carton of light bulbs states that it contains "long-life" bulbs with an average life of 935 hours. An unhappy consumer files a complaint with the Department of Commerce alleging that the claim is false and that the life is considerably less than 935 hours. A Commerce Department analyst tested a random sample of 25 light bulbs and found that the average life of the bulbs was 917 hours with a standard deviation of 54 hours. Can the analyst reject the company's claim? Assume that the life of a bulb is distributed normally with mean μ and variance σ^2.

Step 1   The null and alternate hypotheses are H_0: $\mu = 935$ and H_1: $\mu < 935$.
Step 2 $\bar{x} = 917$, $s = 54$, and $n = 25$. The *t*-statistic is $t_c = \sqrt{n}(\bar{x} - \mu_0)/s = \sqrt{25}(917 - 935)/54 = -1.67$. Under the null hypothesis, this has a *t*-distribution with $n - 1 (= 24)$ degrees of freedom.
Step 3   From the *t*-table, $t^*_{24}(.05) = 1.711$.
Step 4   Because $|t_c| < t^*$, we cannot reject the null hypothesis and hence conclude that, *at the 5 percent level of significance, there is no statistical evidence to indicate that the average life is significantly below the company's claim of 935,* even though the observed average is below 935.

A TWO-SIDED TEST   Let H_0 be $\mu = \mu_0$ and H_1 be $\mu \neq \mu_0$. Note that the alternative is a two-sided alternative, that is, that μ can be on either side of μ_0. Many economic and business decisions might require the formulation of two-sided hypotheses. For instance, a tire manufacturer might want to test whether the average life of a tire is 30,000 miles or not. There may be no a priori information about whether the life will be higher or lower than 30,000. In this case, the procedure is first to obtain a random sample of observations $x_1, x_2, \ldots, x_n$. We stated in Property 2.11c that the sample statistic $t = (\bar{x} - \mu)/(s/\sqrt{n})$, where $\bar{x}$ is the sample mean and s is the sample standard deviation defined in Equation (2.9), is distributed as t_{n-1}. If the null hypothesis is true, $\mu = \mu_0$. Under this hypothesis, the value of t calculated from the sample is given by $t_c = (\bar{x} - \mu_0)/(s/\sqrt{n}) \sim t_{n-1}$. If the observed sample mean $\bar{x}$ deviates substantially from the null hypothesis $\mu = \mu_0$, the calculated value t_c will be either too large or too small. When this is the case, we reject H_0. From the *t*-table in Appendix A (Table A.2), obtain $t^*_{n-1}(a/2)$, where t^* is the value in the *t*-distribution with $n - 1$ d.f. such that $P(t > t^*) = a/2$ and a is the level of significance (usually 0.01 or 0.05 or 0.10). Note that because of the symmetry of the *t*-distribution around the origin, $P(t < -t^*)$ is also equal to $a/2$. The procedure for testing H_0 against H_1: $\mu \neq \mu_0$ is to reject H_0 if $t_c > t^*$ or $t_c < -t^*$. The steps involved are summarized in the following list and are illustrated in Figure 2.13.

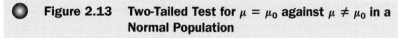

Figure 2.13   Two-Tailed Test for $\mu = \mu_0$ against $\mu \neq \mu_0$ in a Normal Population

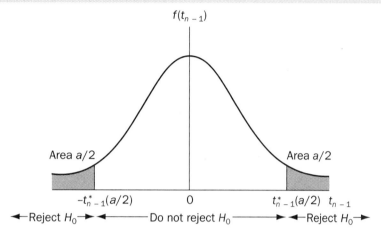

Procedure for Testing H_0 against H_1

Step 1 H_0: $\mu = \mu_0$; H_1: $\mu \neq \mu_0$.

Step 2   The test statistic is $t_c = \sqrt{n}(\bar{x} - \mu_0)/s$. Under the null hypothesis, this has the Student's t-distribution with $n - 1$ d.f.

Step 3   In the t-table (Table A.2), look up the entry corresponding to $n - 1$ d.f. and the given level of significance a, and obtain the point $t^*_{n-1}(a/2)$ such that $P(t > t^*) = a/2$, This gives $P(t < -t^*$ or $t > t^*) = a$, the selected level of significance.

Step 4   Reject H_0 if the observed $t_c > t^*$ or $t_c < -t^*$. Equivalently, reject H_0 if $|t_c| > t^*$.

This test is called a **two-sided** (or more commonly a **two-tailed**) **test** because the alternative is on either side of μ_0 and because the value of t^* is obtained such that the area in either tail of the t-distribution is equal to $a/2$ (see Figure 2.13).

EXAMPLE 2.11

In the light bulb example, suppose the alternative is $\mu \neq 935$. The calculated t-value is still -1.67, and $t^*_{n-1}(a/2) = t^*_{24}(0.025) = 2.064$. Because $|t_c| < t^*$, we do not reject the null hypothesis that $\mu = 935$ and conclude that the average life is not significantly different from 935.

Try Exercise 2.20 and verify your answers with those in Appendix B.

Testing the Coefficient of Correlation between Two Variables

With two variables, the null hypothesis is $H_0: \rho_{xy} = 0$; that is, the population correlation coefficient between X and Y is zero. The alternative hypothesis is $H_1: \rho_{xy} \neq 0$. If the null is not rejected, we conclude that X and Y are uncorrelated. The test statistic is $F_c = [(n - 2)r^2]/(1 - r^2)$, where r^2 is the square of the sample correlation coefficient given in Equation (2.11). Under the null hypothesis, it has an F-distribution with d.f. 1 and $n - 2$. From the F-table, look up $F^*_{1,n-2}(a)$, the point on the F-distribution above to the right of which there is an area of a, the level of significance. Reject H_0 if the computed $F_c > F^*$.

This test could have been done with a t-test also. From Property 2.14b, we note that an F-statistic with 1 d.f. in the numerator is the same as a t^2. The equivalent t-test is to compute $t^*_{n-2}(a/2)$ and reject H_0 if $t_c = \sqrt{F_c} > t^*$.

● EXAMPLE 2.12

Suppose that the correlation coefficient between SAT scores in mathematics and verbal tests, for a sample of 427 students, is $r = 0.42$. Then, $r^2 = 0.1764$, and the F-statistic is

$$F_c = 425 \times 0.1764/(1 - 0.1764) = 91.027 \qquad \sim F(1,425)$$

From Table A.4a we see that for a 1 percent level of significance, the critical F^* is between 6.63 and 6.85. It is readily seen from the F^* value that F_c is extremely significant, implying that we reject the null hypothesis that $\rho_{xy} = 0$. In other words, the two scores are significantly correlated.

Tests for other hypotheses such as difference between means or on variances are excluded here. Refer to Ramanathan (1993, pages 225–227) for details on those.

(For applications of the concepts of hypothesis testing in a regression context, read Section 3.5 now and then continue with Section 2.9.)

● 2.9   Interval Estimation

The estimation procedures discussed in the preceding section result in a single estimated value for the unknown parameters of a distribution. These are known as **point estimates.** The sample mean and the sample variance are examples of point estimates. Although point estimates are useful, they are subject to errors. The variance of an estimator measures this uncertainty and gives the precision with which the estimate has been obtained. **Interval estimation** is a way of directly taking account of this uncertainty. Rather than providing a single estimate, interval estimation would provide a range of possible values. For example, instead of saying that the inflation rate next year is expected to be 3.3 percent, we may wish to say that with a certain probability it will lie between 3 percent and 3.5 percent. This is known as a **confidence interval;** it is illustrated in the following discussion with an example for the mean of the normal distribution.

Confidence Interval for the Mean of a Normal Distribution

Property 2.10a states that if a random variable X is distributed as $N(\mu, \sigma^2)$, then the sample mean $\bar{x}$ is distributed as $N[\mu, (\sigma^2/n)]$. Furthermore, we know from Property 2.15c that the transformed variable $(\bar{x} - \mu)/(s/\sqrt{n})$ has the Student's t-distribution with $n - 1$ d.f. (s is the sample standard deviation). In other words, $t = (\bar{x} - \mu)/(s/\sqrt{n}) \sim t_{n-1}$. Let t^* be the point on this t-distribution such that the area to the right of t^* is 0.025 (that is, $2\frac{1}{2}$ percent). Because the t-distribution is symmetric around zero, it follows that the area to the left of $-t^*$ is also 0.025. Therefore, $P(-t^* \leq t \leq t^*) = 0.95$. Substituting for t in terms of the sample mean and standard deviation, we get the probability statement

$$P\left[-t^* \leq \frac{\bar{x} - \mu}{s/\sqrt{n}} \leq t^* \right] = 0.95$$

Multiplying through by $s/\sqrt{n}$ and rearranging terms, we get

$$P[\bar{x} - (s/\sqrt{n})t^* \leq \mu \leq \bar{x} + (s/\sqrt{n})t^*] = 0.95$$

This means that the true parameter μ lies in the interval $\bar{x} \pm (s/\sqrt{n})t^*$ with probability 0.95. This interval is known as the 95 percent confidence interval for μ. It should be noted that the confidence interval is a random interval because the endpoints $\bar{x} \pm (s/\sqrt{n})t^*$ are themselves random variables. The interpretation of a confidence interval is as follows. If we repeat the experiment of drawing a random sample and computing the confidence interval a large number of times, 95 percent of the intervals will include the true mean μ. The choice of the confidence level is at the discretion of the investigator. If very accurate forecasts are not essential, one may settle for a 90 percent confidence interval. It should be noted that as the sample size n increases, the width of the confidence interval becomes smaller. Similarly, as the estimated standard error (s) decreases, the confidence interval decreases in length. In other words, *for a given level of confidence, the higher the sample size or the lower the standard error, the narrower is the confidence interval and hence the better the precision of the estimate.*

⬤ EXAMPLE 2.13

Suppose that the average life of a light bulb has been estimated as 450 hours and the estimated standard deviation is 25 hours. Here, $\bar{x} = 450$ and $s = 25$. Let the size of the sample (n) be 25. From the t-table in Appendix A (Table A.2), we see that for 24 d.f. (which is $n - 1$) t^* is 2.064 with an area of 2.5 percent to the right of it. The estimated 95 percent confidence interval is therefore $450 \pm (25/\sqrt{25})2.064$, which gives the range (439.68, 460.32).

Relation between Hypothesis Testing and Confidence Intervals

A close relationship exists between two-tailed tests and confidence intervals. In the light bulb example (2.10), we can calculate the confidence interval for the life of a bulb. We note that the confidence interval for μ is $[\bar{x} - (s/\sqrt{n})t^*, \bar{x} + (s/\sqrt{n})t^*]$, which becomes $[917 \pm (54/5)2.064]$ or $(895, 939)$. This is the 95 percent confidence interval for the population mean life of the bulb. We note that this interval includes the value of $\mu_0 = 935$. In this case, we do not reject the null hypothesis. This example shows that the test of hypothesis can be done in another, equivalent way using the confidence interval. The steps are given in the following list:

Step 1   From the test statistic, construct a $1 - a$ confidence interval for the parameter in question (a is the level of significance).

Step 2   Reject the null hypothesis if this confidence interval *does not* include the value of the parameter at the null hypothesis. If the confidence interval includes the value corresponding to H_0, the null hypothesis cannot be rejected.

(See Section 3.8 for the application of confidence intervals to regression parameters.)

Key Terms

Acceptance region
Alternative hypothesis
Binomial distribution
Central limit theorem
Chain rule of differentiation
Chi-square (χ^2) distribution
Coefficient of variation
Conditional expectation of Y given X
Conditional probability
Conditional probability density function
Conditional variance
Confidence interval
Consistency
Correlation
Correlation coefficient
Covariance
Critical region
Critical value
Degrees of freedom (d.f.)
Distribution of the sample mean
Distribution of the sample variance
Efficiency
Estimate
Estimator
Expected value of X
F-distribution
First central moment
Frequency distribution
Histogram
Independent, identically distributed (iid)

Interval estimation
Law of iterated expectations
Law of large numbers
Level of significance
Marginal cost
Marginal density of X
Mean of a distribution
Mean squared error
Method of least squares
Method of moments
Most powerful test
Nonrejection region
Normal distribution
Null hypothesis
One-sided alternative
One-sided test
One-tailed test
Ordinary least squares (OLS)
Parent population
Partial derivative
Perfectly correlated
Phillips curve
Point estimates
Population mean
Population moments
Population parameter
Population variance
Power of a test
Probability density function (PDF)
Probability distribution

Random sampling
Random variable
Regression of Y on X
Sample correlation coefficient
Sample covariance
Sample mean
Sample moments
Sample standard deviation
Sample statistic
Sample variance
Second central moment
Size of a test
Standard deviation (s.d.)
Standard error

Standardized normal
Standard normal distribution
Statistically independent
Statistical test
Student's t-distribution
Test statistic
Two-sided test
Two-tailed test
Type I error
Type II error
Unbiased
Uncorrelated
Variance of the distribution
Z-score

References

Mathematics
The following books give lucid treatments of the mathematical tools needed to understand econometric methodology.

Chiang, A. C. *Fundamental Methods of Mathematical Economics,* 2d ed. New York: McGraw-Hill, 1974.

Dowling, Edward T. *Mathematics for Economists.* New York: McGraw-Hill, 1980.

Taylor, Angus E., and W. Robert Mann. *Advanced Calculus,* 2d ed. Lexington, Mass.: Xerox College Publishing, 1972.

Business Statistics
The following books present probability theory and statistics in less technical detail than those listed in the next section.

Hamburg, Morris. *Statistical Analysis for Decision Making,* 6th ed. Fort Worth, Tex.: The Dryden Press, 1994.

Hey, John D. *Statistics in Economics.* New York: Praeger, 1977.

Kohler, Heinz. *Statistics for Business and Economics.* Glenview, Ill.: Scott, Foresman, 1985.

Lapin, Lawrence L. *Statistics for Modern Business Decisions,* 6th ed. Fort Worth, Tex.: The Dryden Press, 1993.

Newbold, Paul. *Statistics for Business and Economics.* Englewood Cliffs, N.J.: Prentice-Hall, 1984.

Wonnacott, T. H., and R. J. Wonnacott. *Introductory Statistics for Business and Economics.* New York: Wiley, 1990.

Yamane, Taro. *Statistics: An Introductory Analysis.* New York: Harper & Row, 1967.

Mathematical Statistics
The following books should be referred to for mathematical details on probability theory and statistical methods.

Brunk, H. D. *An Introduction to Mathematical Statistics.* Lexington, Mass.: Xerox Corporation, 1975.

DeGroot, Morris H. *Probability and Statistics,* 2nd ed. New York: Addison-Wesley, 1986.

Freund, John E. *Mathematical Statistics,* 5th ed. Englewood Cliffs, N.J.: Prentice-Hall, 1992.

Mood, Alexander M., Franklin A. Graybill, and Duane C. Boes. *Introduction to the Theory of Statistics.* New York: McGraw-Hill, 1974.

Ramanathan, Ramu. *Statistical Methods in Econometrics.* San Diego: Academic Press, 1993.

Economics

Abel, Andrew, B., and Ben S. Bernanke. *Macroeconomics,* 2d ed. New York: Addison-Wesley, 1995.

Phillips, A. W. "The Relation between Unemployment and the Rate of Change of Money Wage Rates in the United Kingdom, 1867–1957." *Economica,* November 1958, pp. 283–299.

Exercises

2.1 If a coin is tossed four times and X denotes the number of heads, derive the probability distribution of X.

2.2 When a pair of dice is thrown, let the total score be denoted by X. Derive the probability for each of the outcomes of scores.

2.3 You need 18 computer memory chips to install in the motherboard of a microcomputer. You order 20 memory chips because you know that 10 percent of all chips are defective. What is the probability that your computer will work?

†2.4 A small commuter airline uses planes with 20 seats. Experience shows that 10 percent of individuals reserving space in a flight do not show up. If the company takes 23 reservations for each flight, what is the probability that it will be able to accommodate everyone appearing without bumping anyone?

2.5 My wife bought a box of 20 gladiola bulbs from the Greenhouse Nursery. The box states that if fewer than 90 percent of the bulbs germinate, the manufacturer will refund the price of the entire box. Suppose the probability of germination is only 0.8. What is the probability that my wife will *not* get a refund on her purchase?

†2.6 Consider the discrete random variable X that can take only the values $x_1, x_2, \ldots, x_n$, with the corresponding probabilities $f(x_i)$, $(i = 1, 2, \ldots, n)$. Prove Property 2.1 for this random variable.

2.7 Let X be a discrete random variable with mean μ_x and variance σ_x^2. Define $Z = a + bX$, where a and b are known constants. Show that $\mu_Z = E(Z) = a + b\mu_x$ and $\sigma_Z^2 = V(Z) = b^2\sigma_x^2$.

2.8 For the distributions in Exercises 2.1 and 2.2, compute the mean, variance, and standard deviation of X.

†2.9 Consider the random variable X, which can take only the values $1, 2, \ldots, n$. Assume that each of these outcomes is equally likely (such a distribution is called the *uniform distribution*) with probability $1/n$. Write down the probability function $f(x)$, and derive the mean and variance of X.

2.10 A company operating a chain of drug stores plans to open a new store in one of two locations. The management of the company figures that at the first location the store will show an annual profit of $20,000 if it is successful and an annual loss of $2,000 if it is not. At the second location, the store will show an annual profit of $25,000 if it is successful and an annual loss of $5,000 if it is not. If the probability of success is one-half for each location, where should the company open the new store so as to maximize expected profit. Show all your work in arriving at your conclusion.

*2.11 An equipment leasing company rents a tractor for $50 per hour, but the machine tends to break down. In a period of t hours, it breaks down X times, which costs a *total* of X^2 dollars to repair. X is a random variable with mean and variance both equal to $2t$. Derive the profit function $\pi(X,t)$ and the expected profit as a function of t. What is the optimum number of hours the company should rent out at a stretch in order to maximize expected profit (this part requires the use of derivatives described in Appendix Section 2.A.2)?

†2.12 Suppose that X denotes the annual incomes, in thousands of dollars, and that, for a particular group of people, X is normally distributed with mean 26 and variance 36.

A random sample of 25 persons is drawn from the group. What is the probability that the average income is between $25,000 and $29,000?

2.13   Prove Properties 2.8a, 2.8c, 2.8e, 2.8f, and 2.9.

†2.14   Let X_1 and X_2 be two random variables, with $\text{Var}(X_i) = \sigma_i^2 (i = 1, 2)$ and $\text{Cov}(X_1, X_2) = \sigma_{12}$ (their means are unknown). Now make the transformations $Y = X_1 + X_2$, and $Z = X_1 - X_2$. Derive $\text{Cov}(Y,Z)$ and the condition under which Y and Z will be uncorrelated.

2.15 X and Y are random variables with means μ_x and μ_y, variances σ_x^2 and σ_y^2, and covariance σ_{xy}. Derive the variance of $Y - bX$, where b is a constant. What value of b will minimize this variance?

2.16   Let $x_1, x_2, \ldots, x_n$ be a random sample drawn from a population with mean μ and variance σ^2. Let $\bar{x} = \dfrac{1}{n}\sum_{i=1}^{n} x_i$ be the sample mean. Show that $E(\bar{x}) = \mu$ and $\text{Var}(\bar{x}) = \sigma^2/n$. Next let $y = \dfrac{1}{n}\sum a_i x_i$, where the a_i's are fixed constants. Derive $E(y)$ and $\text{Var}(y)$. What is the condition for $E(y)$ to be equal to μ? Construct a new random variable Z that depends only on $\bar{x}$, μ, σ, and n, such that it has zero mean and variance 1.

2.17   The random variable X has mean μ and variance σ^2. Two independent observations, x_1 and x_2, are drawn. Consider the estimator of μ given by $\hat{\mu} = 1.1x_1 + bx_2$. What value of b will make $\hat{\mu}$ unbiased? Next compute the variance of $\hat{\mu}$ in terms of σ^2. What value of b will minimize this variance? Do you get the same value of b in both cases?

2.18   Let X be a random variable with mean μ and variance σ^2. Three independent observations are drawn from this distribution: x_1, x_2, and x_3. Consider the three different estimators of μ, $\hat{\mu}_1 = 0.2x_1 + 0.3x_2 + 0.5x_3$, $\hat{\mu}_2 = 0.4x_1 + 0.2x_2 + 0.4x_3$, and $\hat{\mu}_3 = 0.3x_1 + 0.3x_2 + 0.3x_3$. Prove that the first two are unbiased estimators but the last one is biased. Express the variances of the first two estimators (ignore the third) in terms of σ^2. Which one is more efficient and why?

2.19   A market research organization wants to test the claim that 60 percent of all customers in a certain area prefer Brand A cleanser to all competing brands. It is decided to take a random sample of 18 customers and reject the claim if 9 or fewer of them prefer Brand A over all other brands. Carefully derive an expression for the probability that the market research organization will make the error of rejecting the claim even though it is correct, that is, even though 60 percent of customers truly prefer Brand A. Be sure to define all symbols. Use the binomial table in Appendix A (Table A.6), and write down the numerical answer.

‡2.20   A stock market analyst wanted to test whether the rate of return of purchasing stock in a certain company exceeded the average return for the market as a whole. In other words, is the average "excess returns" (company's rate of return minus the market average rate of return) positive or negative? We therefore want to test whether the average returns are zero or not. The excess rate of return was computed for 13 periods, and the average was 3.1 percent with a standard deviation of 1 percent. Test the hypothesis at the 5 percent level of significance, assuming that excess returns are normally distributed. Derive a 95 percent confidence interval for the average excess returns.

2.21   For a period of 26 weeks, it was found that the sample correlation between the percent change in the stock market indices in New York and London was 0.370. Test at the 1 percent level the null hypothesis that the correlation coefficient is zero against the alternative that it is not zero.

2.22   A random sample of 500 owners of single-family homes is drawn from the population of a city. Let the random variable X denote annual household income, in thousands of dollars, and the random variable Y denote the value of the house, also in thousands of dollars. The following information is available:

$$n = 500 \qquad \sum_{i=1}^{n} x_i = 24{,}838 \qquad \sum_{i=1}^{n} y_i = 107{,}226$$

$$\sum (x_i - \bar{x})^2 = 66{,}398 \qquad \sum (y_i - \bar{y})^2 = 1{,}398{,}308$$

$$\sum (x_i - \bar{x})(y_i - \bar{y}) = 194{,}293$$

a. Compute the mean and standard deviation of the value of the houses in this sample. Do the same for household income.
b. Compute the correlation between income and house value.
c. Construct a 95 percent confidence interval for the mean value of houses. What assumptions do you have to make to do this?
d. Using a two-tailed test at the 0.01 level, test the hypothesis that the correlation between income and house value is zero.

2.23 An insurance company needs to estimate the average amount claimed by its policy-holders over one year. A random sample of 81 policyholders reveals that the sample mean claim is $739.98 and the sample standard deviation is $312.70. Compute a 95 percent confidence interval for the average amount claimed. Suppose the insurance company analyst wants to test the hypothesis that the average claim is 800 against the alternative that it is less than 800. Perform this test at the 5 percent level. Be sure to state the assumptions needed to make this a valid test.

2.24 The notion that there might be a trade-off between unemployment and inflation is well known. The perception is that if the government tries to reduce inflation by contractionary monetary and fiscal policy, then unemployment will surely rise. Thus, one would expect a negative correlation between unemployment and inflation. This idea originally came from A. W. Phillips (1958) who examined data (for almost a century) on nominal wage growth and unemployment and found a negative relationship. It is now known as the Phillips curve, although work subsequent to Phillips's focused on the trade-off between unemployment and inflation. For an excellent discussion of the Phillips curve and related research, see Abel and Bernanke (1995). The file DATA2-3 has annual data for the United States for the period 1959–1996 (37 years) for the following variables (the source is the 1996 Economic Report of the President):

unemp = Civilian unemployment rate, Table B-38
cpi   = Consumer price index (1982–1984 = 100), Table B-56
infl = Percent change in cpi (inflation rate) calculated as
          $100 \ast [\text{cpi}(t) - \text{cpi}(t-1)]/\text{cpi}(t-1)$
wggr = Percent change in average weekly earnings, in current dollars, Table B-43

Compute the correlation coefficients between unemployment and inflation separately for the periods 1959–1970, 1971–1980, and 1981–1995. Is there a negative relation? How has it changed over the decades? Redo the analysis using the wage growth rate instead of the inflation rate.

Miscellaneous Derivations

2.A.1 Certain Useful Results on Summations

Because the summation operation is used extensively in probability, statistics, and econometrics, it would be beneficial to summarize a number of properties relating to summations. The sum $X_1 + X_2 + \cdots + X_n$ is denoted by the compact notation $\sum_{t=1}^{t=n} X_t$, where n is the total number of terms in the summation and X_t is a typical term in the summation. The arithmetic mean of the Xs is usually denoted by $\overline{X} = (\sum X_t / n)$. Several simple but useful properties of summations are presented in this section.

Property 2.A.1

If k is a constant, then $\sum_{t=1}^{t=n} k = nk$.
  Because there are n terms, each with a constant k, the result readily follows.

Property 2.A.2

If k is a constant, then $\sum_{t=1}^{t=n} kX_t = k\sum_{t=1}^{t=n} X_t$.
  Because every term has the constant k, it can be factored out of the summation.

Property 2.A.3

$$\sum_{t=1}^{t=n} (X_t + Y_t) = \left(\sum_{t=1}^{t=n} X_t \right) + \left(\sum_{t=1}^{t=n} Y_t \right)$$

Property 2.A.4

If $\overline{X} = (\sum X_t)/n$ is the mean, then $\sum_{t=1}^{t=n}(X_t - \overline{X}) = 0$.
  Thus, the sum of deviations from the mean is zero.

PROOF

$$\sum (X_t - \overline{X}) = \left(\sum X_t \right) - \left(\sum \overline{X} \right) = \left(\sum X_t \right) - n\overline{X}$$

because $\overline{X}$ is the same for each t. But, from the definition of $\overline{X}$, $n\overline{X} = \sum X_t$. Therefore, the last two terms cancel each other and hence $\sum (X_t - \overline{X}) = 0$.

2.A.2 Maximization and Minimization

Estimation of the unknown parameters of a distribution often involves the maximization or minimization of certain objective functions. For example, in estimating relationships an important objective is to find the "best fit" that somehow minimizes errors. In this section we present the methods of maximization or minimization of objective functions; this is especially useful when the investigator has constraints on the problems under study. The basic principles are first studied for the simple case involving only one variable, with no constraints imposed. These are then extended to many variables and to the case when constraints are present.

Functions, Derivatives, Maxima, and Minima

The general relationship between a dependent variable (Y) and an independent variable (X) is expressed in the form of a function denoted by the expression $Y = F(X)$. At the moment, we focus our attention only on functions involving a single variable. We will assume that $F(X)$ is *continuous;* that is, $F(X)$ does not "jump" when X moves only by an infinitesimal amount. A function is said to be *monotonically increasing* if Y increases whenever X increases (see Figure 2.A.1). A supply curve is an example of such a function. If Y decreases as X increases, as in Figure 2.A.2, the function is said to be *monotonically decreasing* (a demand curve for example). In Figure 2.A.1, consider the two points A and B whose coordinates are (X_1, Y_1) and (X_2, Y_2). The ratio $(Y_2 - Y_1)/(X_2 - X_1)$ is the *slope* of the straight line connecting A and B that intersects the graph of the function at A and B. The ratio measures the change in Y per unit change in X. It is also denoted by $\Delta Y/\Delta X$, where $\Delta Y = Y_2 - Y_1$ is the change in Y and $\Delta X = X_2 - X_1$ is the change in X. Suppose we make ΔX smaller and smaller so that ultimately A and B coincide at X. Eventually, the straight line AB just touches the graph of $F(X)$. This is the *tangent* of the curve at the point X; the slope of the tangent is called the derivative of Y with respect to X. This is

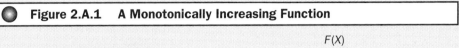

Figure 2.A.1   A Monotonically Increasing Function

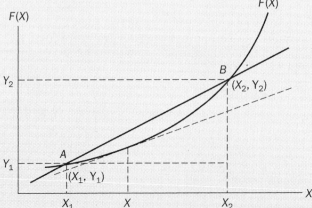

Figure 2.A.2　A Monotonically Decreasing Function

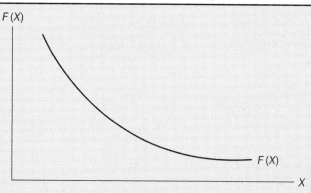

written algebraically as the limit of $\Delta Y/\Delta X$ as ΔX goes to zero, and is denoted either as dY/dX or as $F'(X)$. We thus have the following definition.

DEFINITION 2.A.1

The derivative of Y with respect to X is defined as

$$\frac{dY}{dX} = F'(X) = \lim_{\Delta X \to 0} \frac{\Delta Y}{\Delta X} \quad \text{provided the limit exists}$$

If the limit exists, $F(X)$ is said to be *differentiable* at X. As an example, suppose X is the total quantity of a good produced by a firm and Y is the total cost of producing it. Then $F(X)$ is the total cost function and the derivative, dY/dX, is the added cost of producing one additional unit, which is known as **marginal cost** in microeconomics. It will be noted from Figures 2.A.1 and 2.A.2 that the derivative $F'(X)$ need not be constant but might depend on the value of X at which it is measured. We can therefore differentiate $F'(X)$ again and get $F''(X) = d^2Y/dX^2$, provided this second derivative exists.

In Figure 2.A.1 the derivative is positive for all X for which $F(X)$ is defined. Similarly, it is always negative in Figure 2.A.2. We readily see that for a monotonic function the derivative always has the same sign. In Figure 2.A.3a we note that $F(X)$ is not monotonic but alternatively rises and falls (unemployment rate is an example). Initially, the slope is positive, then it becomes negative, and again becomes positive. The points A and B have the property that the slope of the tangent is zero. Thus, $F'(X) = 0$ at these points. We note that at A, $F(X)$ attains a local maximum and at B it attains a local minimum. A necessary condition for a *local extremum* (that is, maximum or minimum) is that the first derivative $F'(X)$ should be zero. This condition, known as the *first-order condition*, is not sufficient to identify whether $F(X)$ is at a minimum or maximum. Figure 2.A.3b represents $F'(X)$, and we note that it initially decreases and later increases. The slope of $F'(X)$ is the second derivative $F''(X)$,

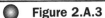

Figure 2.A.3

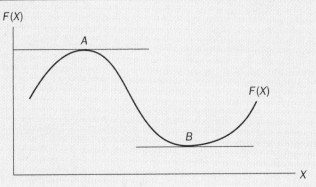

F(*X*)

A

F(*X*)

B

a. A nonmonotonic function

F'(*X*)

F'(*X*)

A

B

X

b. The graph of *F'*(*X*)

which is negative at *A* and positive at *B*. To distinguish between a minimum and a maximum, we need the *second-order condition* that the second derivative *F"*(*X*) should be negative at the point at which the first derivative *F'*(*X*) = 0, in order for *F*(*X*) to attain a maximum. For a minimum, the second-order condition is that *F"*(*X*) be positive at the point at which *F'*(*X*) = 0.

 We state without proof a number of useful results on derivatives.

Property 2.A.5

a. The derivative of a constant is zero.

b. The derivative of *F*(*X*) + *G*(*X*) is the sum of the derivatives *F'*(*X*) + *G'*(*X*).

c. If *a* is a constant, the derivative of *aF*(*X*) equals *aF'*(*X*).

d. The derivative of the power function X^m equals mX^{m-1}. As a special case of this, the derivative of $\sqrt{X}$ (that is, $X^{1/2}$) is $1/(2\sqrt{X})$, or $\frac{1}{2}X^{-1/2}$. Similarly, the derivative of $1/X$ (that is, X^{-1}) is $-1/X^2$ (that is, $-X^{-2}$).

e.   If $Y = F(Z)$ and $Z = G(X)$, then $\dfrac{dY}{dX} = \dfrac{dY}{dZ}\dfrac{dZ}{dX} = F'G' = F'(Z)G'(X) = F'[G(X)]G'(X)$. [This result is known as the **chain rule of differentiation**.]

f.   By the product rule of differentiation, the derivative of $F(X)G(X)$ is $F(X)G'(X) + G(X)F'(X)$.

g.   By the quotient rule of differentiation, the derivative of the ratio $F(X)/G(X)$ is $[G(X)F'(X) - F(X)G'(X)]/[G(X)]^2$.

An Application

Suppose a firm is faced with a cost function $C(q)$ (the relationship between total cost and output), where q is the quantity of output produced. Further assume that the firm is in a competitive industry and can sell the output at the fixed market price p per unit. The firm's decision is to choose the quantity of goods to be produced. Its objective is to maximize profits. The total revenue is pq and profit is total revenue minus total cost. The profit function is therefore given by

$$\pi(q) = pq - C(q)$$

As we noted earlier, a condition for maximizing profits is $\pi'(q) = 0 = p - C'(q)$. C' is the derivative of C with respect to q. It is the additional cost of one more unit produced, which as we saw is the *marginal cost*. The condition, therefore, states that in order to maximize profits, a competitive firm should choose the output at which price equals marginal cost. As a specific example, let $C(q) = 10 - 5q + 2q^2$ and the price per unit be 35. Differentiating $C(q)$ with respect to q, the marginal cost function is $C'(q) = -5 + 4q$. Setting this equal to 35 and solving for q, we get $q = 10$. Thus, the profit-maximizing output is 10. In the general case when the cost function is quadratic (that is, it depends on the square of q), $C(q) = a + bq + cq^2$ and the marginal cost function is $C'(q) = b + 2cq$. The profit-maximizing condition is therefore $p = b + 2cq$. When solved for q, this gives the optimum quantity to produce as $q = (p - b)/2c$. The second-order condition for maximization is $\pi''(q) < 0$. The second derivative of π is $-C''(q) = -2c$. For this to be negative, we need the condition that c must be positive. Also, to give a positive output, p must be greater than b. If b is negative, as in the example above, this condition is automatically satisfied because price will always be positive.

Functions of Several Variables

Here we summarize a number of results for a function that depends on several variables. Applications of the multivariate calculus are presented later in this section.

The general form of a function of several variables is $Y = F(X_1, X_2, \ldots, X_n)$. A simple example of this is a generalization of a straight line: $Y = X_1 + 2X_2 + 3X_3 + \cdots + 8X_8$. As before, Y is the dependent variable and the Xs are the independent variables. The change in Y in response to a change in only one of the Xs is of considerable interest. For the moment, consider $X_2, X_3, \ldots, X_n$ as fixed. Treating Y as a function of only X_1, we can measure the change in Y per unit change in X_1. This analogue of the derivative is called the **partial derivative** of Y with respect to X_1 and is written in a number of ways.

DEFINITION 2.A.2

The partial derivative of Y with respect to X_i is defined as

$$\frac{\partial Y}{\partial X_i} = \frac{\partial F}{\partial X_i} = F_i = \lim_{\Delta X_i \to 0} \frac{\Delta Y}{\Delta X_i}$$

Thus, the partial derivative is the response per unit change in one of the independent variables, *holding the values of all the other independent variables fixed*. In the example we used, $\partial Y/\partial X_8 = 8$.

EXAMPLE 2.A.1

Let $Y = \beta_1 X_1 + \beta_2 X_2 + \cdots + \beta_n X_n$, where each of the βs is a constant. The partial derivative is then $\partial Y/\partial X_i = \beta_i$. As another example, suppose $Y = aK^2 + bKL + cL^2$ (a, b, and c are constants). The partial derivative of Y with respect to K is $\partial Y/\partial K = 2aK + bL$. This is because the derivative of aK^2 is $2aK$, which gives the first term. The partial derivative of bKL with respect to K is bL because L is treated as fixed. The partial derivative of cL^2 with respect to K is zero because it is independent of K.

The chain rule of differentiation is applicable here also. Suppose $Y = F(Z)$ and $Z = G(X_1, X_2, \ldots, X_n)$. Then the partial derivative of Y with respect to X_i can be written as

$$\frac{\partial Y}{\partial X_i} = \frac{\partial Y}{\partial Z}\frac{\partial Z}{\partial X_i} = F'(Z)\frac{\partial G}{\partial X_i}$$

Note that this partial derivative would generally depend on all the Xs.

The concepts of maximum and minimum are extended easily to a multivariate function. In order for $F(X_1, X_2, \ldots, X_n)$ to attain a maximum or a minimum, the following conditions have to be met:

$$\frac{\partial F}{\partial X_i} = 0 \quad \text{for each } i = 1, 2, \ldots, n$$

By setting to zero the partial derivative of F with respect to each X, we get n equations in the n unknowns $X_1, X_2, \ldots, X_n$. Solving these for X_i, we obtain their solutions. When these values are substituted in F, we obtain the maximum or minimum value of Y. Analogous to the second-order condition in a univariate case, there is a similar condition that enables us to distinguish between a maximum point and a minimum point. This condition is very complicated and is not presented here. The reader is referred to the books on mathematics listed at the end of this chapter for more details.

An Application

It is useful to illustrate the preceding concepts with an application. Consider a firm in a competitive industry that faces a fixed commodity price p, a given wage rate w, and a given capital rental rate r. Let $F(K, L)$ be the *production function* that relates the quantity of output produced by the firm to the inputs, capital (K) and labor (L). The firm's objective would be to choose the amounts of labor and capital so as to maximize profits. The profit function $\pi(K, L)$ is given by the value of the output $[pF(K, L)]$ less the cost of capital (Kr) and that of labor (wL).

$$\pi(K, L) = pF(K, L) - rK - wL$$

The two conditions for maximization are $\partial\pi/\partial K = 0$ and $\partial\pi/\partial L = 0$. Taking the partial derivatives of π with respect to K and L and setting them to zero, we get (noting that p, w, and r are fixed)

$$r = p\frac{\partial F}{\partial K} \quad \text{and} \quad w = p\frac{\partial F}{\partial L}$$

$\partial F/\partial K$ is the extra output per unit extra capital input and is called the *marginal product of capital*. Similarly, $\partial F/\partial L$ is the *marginal product of labor*. Also, $p\partial F/\partial L$ and $p\partial F/\partial K$ are the values of the corresponding marginal products. The first-order conditions imply that firms would maximize profits when they choose K and L such that the value of the marginal product of labor equals the wage rate and the value of the marginal product of capital equals the rental rate.

Let us apply this to a specific production function. Let $Y = F(K, L) = K^\alpha L^\beta$, where Y is the quantity of output produced. This is known as the *Cobb–Douglas production function*. The marginal product of capital is

$$\frac{\partial Y}{\partial K} = \alpha K^{\alpha-1}L^\beta = \frac{\alpha K^\alpha L^\beta}{K} = \frac{\alpha Y}{K}$$

Similarly, the marginal product of labor is $\partial F/\partial L = \beta Y/L$. For profit maximization, the first-order conditions are $\alpha Y/K = r/p$ and $\beta Y/L = w/p$. These can be solved for the amounts of labor and capital as $L = \beta Yp/w$ and $K = \alpha Yp/r$.

As a numerical example, let $\alpha = 0.2$, $\beta = 0.6$, $p = 10$, $w = 4$, and $r = 0.1$. From these values, we get $L = \beta Yp/w = 1.5Y$ and $K = \alpha Yp/r = 20Y$. Substituting these in the production function, we obtain

$$Y = (20Y)^{0.2}(1.5Y)^{0.6} = 20^{0.2}1.5^{0.6}Y^{0.8} = 2.321992Y^{0.8}$$

Dividing both sides by $Y^{0.8}$, we get $Y^{0.2} = 2.321992$. Solving this, we get the total output Y as 67.5. The *derived demands* for labor and capital are then obtained as $L = \beta Yp/w = 101.25$ and $K = \alpha Yp/r = 1{,}350$.

Optimization under Constraints

In economics, we frequently encounter the need to maximize or minimize a multi-variate function subject to one or more constraints. For instance, let $U(X_1, X_2)$ be the utility a consumer derives from the consumption of two commodities. X_1 is the consumption of the first commodity and X_2 is the consumption of the second commodity. Let p_1 be the price of the first good, p_2 the price of the second good, and Y the consumer's income, all of which are assumed to be fixed. The objective of the consumer is to maximize the utility function subject to the constraint that the total amounts spent on the two commodities $(p_1X_1 + p_2X_2)$ be exactly equal to the consumer's income (Y). Thus, the problem reduces to choosing the values of X_1 and X_2 such that $U(X_1, X_2)$ is a maximum, subject to the budget condition that $Y = p_1X_1 + p_2X_2$.

As a second example, consider a public utility company that generates electricity and sells it to its customers in a service area. Being a regulated monopoly, it is not permitted to maximize profits. Instead, the public utility commission and the company generate forecasts of the electricity requirements for the next one or two decades and then choose that electricity-generating technology (or combination of technologies) that minimizes the cost of producing the target output. In other words, the firm minimizes the cost of production subject to the constraint that the output must be a fixed quantity.

Both these problems are examples of *constrained optimization*. This topic is usually covered only in third-semester calculus courses. An understanding of this is *not* essential to learning the basics of econometrics. We are discussing it here because some of the theoretical proofs presented, in this and later chapter appendices, depend on this section. Readers not interested in those proofs may skip this section entirely without loss of continuity. However, the discussion here is simple enough to be understood even by those who have not had a course on advanced calculus. Also, the student will find the application presented here useful in other courses.

Lagrange's Method of Constrained Optimization

The general problem is to maximize the function $F(X_1, X_2, \ldots, X_n)$ subject to the constraint $G(X_1, X_2, \ldots, X_n) = 0$. First write the *Lagrangian function*

$$H(X_1, X_2, \ldots, X_n, \lambda) = F(X_1, X_2, \ldots, X_n) + \lambda G(X_1, X_2, \ldots, X_n)$$

where λ is called the *Lagrange multiplier* and is a new unknown. It can be shown that the maximization of F subject to the constraint $G = 0$ is equivalent to maximizing the function H with respect to each of the Xs *without any constraint*. The problem has thus been reduced to the earlier form, with a modified function and an additional unknown (λ). Setting the partial derivatives of H with respect to the unknowns to zero, we get the $n + 1$ first-order conditions, $G(X_1, X_2, \ldots, X_n) = 0$ and $\partial H/\partial X_i = 0$, for $i = 1, 2, \ldots, n$. These conditions can be solved, in general, for the $n + 1$ unknowns $X_1, X_2, \ldots, X_n$ and the Lagrange multiplier λ.

Application to the Cost Minimization Problem

In the electricity generation example, the company minimizes the cost function subject to the constraint that a certain target output must be produced. Let Y_0 be the target output. The constraint is then $Y_0 = F(K, L)$, where $F(\ )$ is the production function encountered earlier. K and L are the amounts of capital and labor the utility will use in order to generate the output Y_0. The cost corresponding to this is $Kr + Lw$, where w is the wage rate and r is the capital rental rate, both assumed fixed. The utility's optimization problem is that of choosing K and L so as to minimize $Kr + Lw$ subject to the constraint $Y_0 = F(K, L)$. The Lagrangian function here is

$$H(K, L, \lambda) = Kr + Lw + \lambda[Y_0 - F(K, L)]$$

The first-order conditions are now given by $\partial H/\partial K = \partial H/\partial L = \partial H/\partial \lambda = 0$. These translate to the following three conditions in the unknowns K, L, and λ, which can be solved, in general, for the optimum levels of capital and labor to use:

$$r = \lambda \frac{\partial F}{\partial K}, \qquad w = \lambda \frac{\partial F}{\partial L}, \qquad Y_0 = F(K, L)$$

Extension to Several Constraints

The Lagrange multiplier principle can be applied even when there is more than one constraint. The modification is to add more Lagrange multiplier terms in the Lagrangian function, one for each constraint. Thus, the problem of maximizing $F(X_1, X_2, \ldots, X_n)$ subject to the two constraints $G(X_1, X_2, \ldots, X_n) = 0$ and $Q(X_1, X_2, \ldots, X_n) = 0$ can be solved with the modified Lagrangian function

$$H(X_1, X_2, \ldots, X_n) = F(X_1, X_2, \ldots, X_n) + \lambda G(X_1, X_2, \ldots, X_n) + \mu Q(X_1, X_2, \ldots, X_n)$$

where λ and μ are the Lagrange multipliers corresponding to the two constraints. The first-order conditions for maximization are the following $n + 2$ conditions:

$$G(X_1, X_2, \ldots, X_n) = 0$$

$$Q(X_1, X_2, \ldots, X_n) = 0$$

$$\frac{\partial F}{\partial X_i} + \lambda \frac{\partial G}{\partial X_i} + \mu \frac{\partial Q}{\partial X_i} = 0 \qquad \text{for } i = 1, 2, \ldots, n$$

2.A.3 More on Estimation

In Section 2.5 we discussed two methods of estimating the unknown parameters of a distribution. In this section we present another, more advanced method.

The Principle of Maximum Likelihood

This method was proposed by the British statistician R. A. Fisher for obtaining estimates of unknown parameters from a sample of observations. It is better explained with an example. Suppose a pharmaceutical company has invented a new drug to combat a disease. The company claims that the cure rate is 90 percent. A chemist from the Food and Drug Administration conducts preliminary tests and disputes that claim, saying that the cure rate is 70 percent. They go to a statistician to resolve the dispute. The statistician's task is to decide whether the cure rate is 70 percent or 90 percent.[1] Because the experiment has only two outcomes (a cure being a "success"), the underlying probability model is the binomial distribution described in Section 2.1. Let p be the probability of a success; that is, that the patient is cured. The statistician's task is to choose between the two alternative estimates for p: 0.9 and 0.7.

To resolve the dispute, the analyst draws a random sample of ten patients (in practice, several thousand observations will be drawn) and finds that eight of them were cured. The question is "Given that eight successes out of ten occurred, is the true probability likely to be 0.7 or 0.9?" The *principle of maximum likelihood* is based on the intuitive notion that "an event occurred because it was most likely to." According to this principle, we compute the probability (which is called *likelihood* in the context of estimation) of the observed outcome under the two alternatives under consideration and choose that alternative for which the probability of observing what we observed is the maximum. The belief is that the observed sample values are more likely to have come from this population than from others. In our example, the probability of observing eight successes out of ten is given by

$$\frac{10!}{8!\ 2!}\ 0.9^8\ 0.1^2 = 0.1937 \qquad \text{if } p = 0.9$$

$$\frac{10!}{8!\ 2!}\ 0.7^8\ 0.3^2 = 0.2335 \qquad \text{if } p = 0.7$$

Because the probability is higher for $p = 0.7$, the *maximum likelihood estimate* of the probability of a cure is 0.7 (when the choice is between 0.9 and 0.7).

The general principle of maximum likelihood uses the following procedure. Let X be the random variable whose probability distribution depends on the unknown parameter θ. The probability density is $f(x|\theta)$. A random sample $x_1, x_2, \ldots, x_n$ of independent observations is drawn. Because the xs are independent, the *joint density* of the sample is the product $f(x_1, \theta) \cdot f(x_2, \theta) \cdots f(x_n, \theta)$. This is called the *likelihood function* and is denoted by $L(\theta|x)$.

$$L(\theta|x) = \prod_{i=1}^{n} f(x_i, \theta) = f(x_1, \theta) \cdot f(x_2, \theta) \cdots f(x_n, \theta)$$

---

[1] In practice, the question will be posed as one of estimating the cure rate without restricting the choice to just two values. To keep the discussion simple, we assume that a choice is to be made only between 0.9 and 0.7.

If the possible values of θ are discrete, the procedure is to evaluate $L(\theta|x)$ for each possible value under consideration and choose the value for which L is the highest. If $L(\theta|x)$ is differentiable, maximize it over the range of permissible values of θ. This gives the first- and second-order conditions

$$\frac{dL}{d\theta} = 0 \quad \text{and} \quad \frac{d^2L}{d\theta^2} < 0$$

If this principle is applied to the drug-testing example used earlier, the maximum likelihood estimate of the probability is 0.8. Taking the logarithm of both sides of the likelihood function, we have

$$\ln L(\theta|x) = \sum \ln[f(x|\theta)]$$

Because logarithm is a *monotonic transformation* (that is, if $x_1 > x_2$, then $\ln x_1 > \ln x_2$), maximizing $L(\theta|x)$ is equivalent to maximizing $\ln L(\theta|x)$. It is often more convenient to maximize this log likelihood function.

Suppose the likelihood function has several unknown parameters θ_i ($i = 1, 2, \ldots, k$) such as, for example, the mean μ (θ_1) and variance $\sigma^2(\theta_2)$ of the distribution. Then the maximization is that of $L(\theta_1, \theta_2, \ldots, \theta_k|x)$. The first-order conditions are then $\partial L/\partial \theta_i = 0$ for $i = 1$ to k. The k resulting equations are jointly solved for the θs. In practice, it is often easier to maximize $\ln L$ and use the conditions $\partial \ln L/\partial \theta_i = 0$ to solve for the θs.

Properties of Maximum Likelihood Estimators

Maximum likelihood estimators have a number of desirable properties. These are listed in Property 2.A.6.

Property 2.A.6

Maximum likelihood estimators are

a.   consistent.

b.   asymptotically efficient; that is, for large n, no other consistent estimator has a smaller variance.

c.   asymptotically normal; that is, for large n, they closely approximate the normal distribution, even if the distribution from which the observations were drawn was not normal.

EXAMPLE 2.A.2

Suppose a random variable X has the normal distribution with mean μ and variance σ^2. A random sample of observations $x_1, x_2, \ldots, x_n$ is drawn. What are the maximum likelihood estimators of μ and σ^2? From Equation (2.4) we know that the density function for x_i is given by

$$f(x_i, \mu, \sigma^2) = \frac{1}{\sigma\sqrt{2\pi}} \, e^{-(x_i-\mu)^2/(2\sigma^2)}$$

The likelihood function is therefore given by

$$L(\mu, \sigma^2|x) = \left[\frac{1}{\sigma\sqrt{2\pi}}\right]^n e^{-[\Sigma(x_i-\mu)^2]/(2\sigma^2)}$$

By taking the logarithm of this we get the log likelihood function as

$$\ln L = -n \ln \sigma - n \ln(\sqrt{2\pi}) - \frac{1}{2\sigma^2} \sum (x_i - \mu)^2$$

We note that $\ln L$ depends on μ only through the last term involving the sum of squares of deviations of x_i from the mean μ. Because there is a minus sign in front of that term, maximizing $\ln L$ is equivalent to minimizing $\Sigma(x_i - \mu)^2$, which is the same as the least squares procedure described earlier. The estimate of μ that minimizes this sum of squares (and hence maximizes the likelihood) is the sample mean $\bar{x}$. Therefore, *the sample mean $\bar{x}$ is the maximum likelihood estimator of μ if X is normally distributed as $N(\mu, \sigma^2)$.*

To get the maximum likelihood estimator of σ^2, partially differentiate $\ln L$ with respect to σ. We get the first-order condition (note that x, n, and μ are treated as constants in this partial differentiation)

$$-\frac{n}{\sigma} - \frac{1}{2} \sum (x_i - \mu)^2 (-2\sigma^{-3}) = 0$$

It is easy to verify that the maximum likelihood estimator of σ^2, denoted by $\hat{\sigma}^2$, is given by $\hat{\sigma}^2 = (1/n)\Sigma(x_i - \bar{x})^2$. In deriving this, we have used the estimate $\bar{x}$ for μ. Comparing this to Equation (2.9), we note that the sample variance s^2 and the maximum likelihood estimator $\hat{\sigma}^2$ are different. Because $E(s^2) = \sigma^2$ by Property 2.15b, $E(\hat{\sigma}^2) \neq \sigma^2$. This establishes the result that *the maximum likelihood estimator of a parameter need not be unbiased.* By Property 2.A.6a, however, it is consistent. It is also asymptotically unbiased.

Basics

This part consists of three chapters that cover the basics of econometrics. Chapter 3 explores in considerable detail the procedures for estimating the simple linear relationship between two variables introduced in Chapter 1. All the basic assumptions and methods of analyses are brought out here. In particular, methods of estimating a model, measures of precision of estimates, and testing hypotheses on them are developed in detail. The techniques presented are illustrated with several examples. Chapter 4 extends the concepts to the case involving several variables. Derivations are kept to the minimum here. Chapter 5 examines the consequences of high correlations among explanatory variables.

Included in these and later chapters are numerous sample computer outputs that walk the reader through the various empirical steps for the estimation and testing procedures. Even if the computer is not used to reproduce the examples, a careful study of the steps described in the outputs would enormously enhance the understanding of the methodologies described here.

CHAPTER 3

The Simple Linear Regression Model

*In Chapter 1 we stated that the first step in any econometric analysis is to formulate a model that describes the underlying structure of the behavior of economic variables. The economic or business analyst then gathers the relevant data and estimates the model for later use in decision making. In this chapter, we start with the simplest of these models and develop in detail the methodology for estimating, hypothesis testing, and forecasting. This model relates a dependent variable (Y) to a single independent variable (X). It is known as the **simple linear regression model**. Although the model is simplistic, and hence unrealistic in most real-world situations, a good understanding of its basic underpinnings will go a long way toward helping you understand more complex models. In fact, a great deal of econometric methodology can be explained with the simple linear regression model. In the body of the chapter, only basic derivations are presented. Tedious derivations, as well as those requiring calculus, have been given in the chapter appendix. Readers with a calculus background may, if interested, read the appendix for a better understanding of the theoretical results.*

3.1 The Basic Model

In Chapter 1 we saw an example of the simple regression model in which the price of a house was related to the number of square feet of living area (see Figure 1.2). We fixed the living area at several levels and enumerated all the houses in the population that had square footage close to the fixed levels. Next we computed the average sale price for each house and plotted it (points denoted by $\times$). A fundamental assumption underlying the simple linear regression model is that these average points lie on a straight line (denoted by $\alpha + \beta$SQFT), which is the **population regression function** and is the *conditional mean* (or expectation) of PRICE for a *given* SQFT. The general formulation of the simple linear regression model is given in Assumption 3.1.

ASSUMPTION 3.1   (Linearity of Model)

$$Y_t = \alpha + \beta X_t + u_t \tag{3.1}$$

where X_t and Y_t are the tth observations ($t = 1$ to n) on the independent and dependent variables, respectively; α and β are unknown parameters to be esti-

---

mated; and u_t is the unobserved error term assumed to be a random variable with certain properties specified later. In particular, the u_ts are drawn independently from a common distribution. α and β are called the **regression coefficients.** (The subscript t can be thought of as referring to "time" in a time series or to a "typical observation" in a cross section.)

The term *simple* in a simple linear regression model is used to denote the fact that only one explanatory variable (X) is used in the model. In the next chapter, we extend this to a *multiple regression model* in which more explanatory variables are added. The term *regression* comes from Francis Galton (1886) who related the heights of sons to those of their fathers and empirically observed that there is a tendency for the average height of sons with a fixed father's height to "regress" (that is, move) toward the average height of the population as a whole. The term $\alpha + \beta X_t$ is the *deterministic part* of the model and is the **conditional mean of Y for a given X,** that is, $E(Y_t|X_t) = \alpha + \beta X_t$, when $E(u_t|X_t) = 0$. The term *linear* refers to the fact that the *population parameters* α and β appear linearly here *and not to the fact that X_t appears linearly.* Thus, the model $Y_t = \alpha + \beta X_t^2 + u_t$ is still called a simple linear regression even though the X term appears as a quadratic. An example of a **nonlinear regression model** is $Y_t = \alpha + X^\beta + u_t$. In this book we do not study such nonlinear regression models, but restrict our attention to models that are linear in the parameters. Such linear models could include nonlinear terms for the explanatory variables (more on that in Chapter 6). For excellent treatments of nonlinear regression models, refer to Greene (2000), Ruud (2000), Davidson and MacKinnon (1993), and Griffiths, Hill, and Judge (1993).

The error (also known as *stochastic* or *disturbance*) term u_t is the unobserved random component and is the difference between Y_t and the deterministic part $\alpha + \beta X_t$. It is actually a combination of the four different effects discussed as follows:

1. *Omitted variables.* Suppose the true model was $Y_t = \alpha + \beta X_t + \gamma Z_t + v_t$, where Z_t is another explanatory variable and v_t is the true error term, but we used the model $Y_t = \alpha + \beta X_t + u_t$. Then $u_t = \gamma Z_t + v_t$. Thus, u_t captures the effect of the omitted variable Z. In the real estate example used earlier, if the true model included the effects of bedrooms and bathrooms but we omitted them and used just the living area, then the u term will include the effects of bedrooms and bathrooms on the sale price of a house.

2. *Nonlinearities.* u_t would also include the effects of nonlinearities in the relationship between Y and X. Thus, if the true model were $Y_t = \alpha + \beta X_t + \gamma X_t^2 + v_t$ and we assumed that it is $Y_t = \alpha + \beta X_t + u_t$, then the effect of X_t^2 would be absorbed into u_t.

3. *Measurement errors.* Errors in measuring X and Y are also captured by u. For example, suppose Y_t is the value of new construction and we want to estimate the function $Y_t = \alpha + \beta r_t + v_t$, where r_t is the interest rate for construction loans and v_t is the true error term (for simplicity of exposition, we are ignoring the effects of income and other variables on investment). In actual estimation, however, we use the model $Y_t = \alpha + \beta X_t + u_t$, where $X_t = r_t + Z_t$ is the prime

rate. Thus, the interest rate is measured with the error Z_t. Substituting for r_t as $X_t - Z_t$ in the original formulation, we get $Y_t = \alpha + \beta(X_t - Z_t) + v_t = \alpha + \beta X_t - \beta Z_t + v_t = \alpha + \beta X_t + u_t$. We readily note that the stochastic term u_t includes the error in measuring the loan interest rate accurately.

4. *Unpredictable effects.* However well-specified an econometric model might be, there will always be inherently unpredictable random effects. These effects will also be absorbed into the error term u_t.

As mentioned earlier, it is unrealistic to conduct a complete census of the population in order to derive the population regression function. In practice, an analyst will draw a sample of houses and measure their attributes in order to derive the **sample regression function.** Table 3.1 has the data for a sample of 14 houses ($n = 14$) sold in an area of San Diego. It is also available on the Internet and the CD as the file DATA3-1. In Figure 3.1, the pairs of data (X_t, Y_t) have been plotted for these values. This diagram is called the **sample scatter diagram** for the data. It is similar to Figure 1.2, but there we plotted (X_t, Y_t) for the population as a whole; Figure 3.1 is based on the sample data only. Suppose, for the moment, that we know the values of α and β. Let us draw the straight line $\alpha + \beta X$ in this diagram. This is the **population regression line.** The vertical deviations of the actual values of the price (Y_t) from the regression line ($\alpha + \beta X$) are the random errors u_t. The slope of the straight line (β) is also $\Delta Y/\Delta X$, which is the *change in Y per unit change in X.* β can therefore be interpreted as the **marginal effect of X on Y.** Thus, if β is 0.14, each 1-square-foot increase in the living area is expected to increase the sale price of the house, on average, by 0.14 thousands of dollars (note that the unit is important), or

Table 3.1   Actual and Estimated Average Price of a House and the Living Area in Square Feet

t	SQFT	Sale Price[1]	Estimated Average Price[2]
1	1,065	199.9	200.386
2	1,254	228	226.657
3	1,300	235	233.051
4	1,577	285	271.554
5	1,600	239	274.751
6	1,750	293	295.601
7	1,800	285	302.551
8	1,870	365	312.281
9	1,935	295	321.316
10	1,948	290	323.123
11	2,254	385	365.657
12	2,600	505	413.751
13	2,800	425	441.551
14	3,000	415	469.351

[1]Prices are in thousands of dollars.
[2]The method of computing the estimated average price is discussed in Section 3.2.

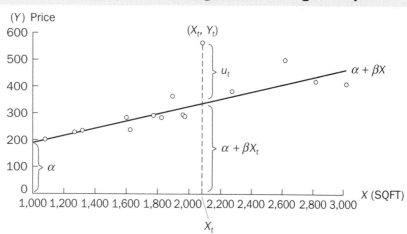

Figure 3.1 Sample Scatter Diagram for PRICE against SQFT

$140. More realistically, a 100-square-foot increase in SQFT is expected to increase the average price by $14,000. Although α is the intercept term and corresponds to the mean of Y when X is zero, it cannot be interpreted as the average price of a vacant lot. This is because α also captures the average effects of omitted variables and hence has no ready interpretation (more on this in Section 4.5).

The first aim of an econometrician is to use the data gathered to estimate the population regression function, that is, to estimate the population parameters α and β. Let $\hat{\alpha}$ (read as "alpha hat") denote the sample estimate of α and $\hat{\beta}$ denote the estimate of β. Then the estimated average relation is $\hat{Y} = \hat{\alpha} + \hat{\beta}X$. This is known as the sample regression function. For a given observation t, we have $\hat{Y}_t = \hat{\alpha} + \hat{\beta}X_t$. This is the predicted value of Y_t for a given X_t. Subtracting this from the observed Y_t, we have an estimate of u_t, called the **estimated residual,** or simply the **residual,** and denoted by $\hat{u}_t$.[1] This is represented in the following equation:

$$\hat{u}_t = Y_t - \hat{Y}_t = Y_t - \hat{\alpha} - \hat{\beta}X_t \tag{3.2}$$

Rearranging the terms, we have

$$Y_t = \hat{\alpha} + \hat{\beta}X_t + \hat{u}_t \tag{3.3}$$

It is important to understand the distinction between the *population regression function* $Y = \alpha + \beta X$ and the *sample regression function* $\hat{Y} = \hat{\alpha} + \hat{\beta}X$. Figure 3.2 represents both these lines and the associated error and residual (study it carefully). Note that "error" refers to u_t and "residual" refers to $\hat{u}_t$.

---

[1]Some authors and instructors prefer to use a for $\hat{\alpha}$, b for $\hat{\beta}$, and e_t for $\hat{u}_t$. We have adopted the $\hat{\ }$ notation conventional in statistical theory because it makes a clear distinction between the true value and an estimated value and also identifies the parameter that is being estimated.

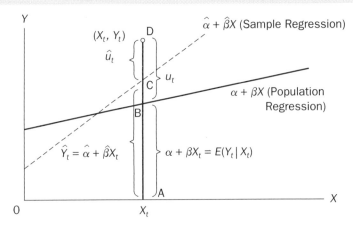

Figure 3.2   Population and Sample Regression Functions

● **PRACTICE PROBLEM 3.1[†]**

Consider the following equations:

a. $Y_t = \alpha + \beta X_t + u_t$

b. $Y_t = \hat{\alpha} + \hat{\beta} X_t + \hat{u}_t$

c. $Y_t = \hat{\alpha} + \hat{\beta} X_t + u_t$

d. $\hat{Y}_t = \alpha + \beta X_t$

e. $\hat{Y}_t = \alpha + \beta X_t + \hat{u}_t$

f. $\hat{Y}_t = \hat{\alpha} + \hat{\beta} X_t + \hat{u}_t$

Carefully explain why equations (a) and (b) are correct but (c), (d), (e), and (f) are incorrect. Figure 3.2 would be useful in answering this question.

● **3.2   Estimation of the Basic Model by the Method of Ordinary Least Squares (OLS)**

In the previous section, we specified the basic linear regression model and distinguished between the population regression and the sample regression. Our next objective is to make use of the data on X and Y and obtain the "best" estimates of the population parameters α and β. In econometrics, the most frequently used estimation procedure is the **method of least squares.** It is more commonly known as **ordinary least squares (OLS),** as opposed to other types of least squares procedures that will be discussed in later chapters. Denoting the estimates of α and β by $\hat{\alpha}$ and $\hat{\beta}$, the estimated residual is equal to $\hat{u}_t = Y_t - \hat{\alpha} - \hat{\beta} X_t$. The optimality criterion used by the least squares procedure is to minimize the objective function

$$\text{ESS}(\hat{\alpha}, \hat{\beta}) = \sum_{t=1}^{t=n} \hat{u}_t^2 = \sum_{t=1}^{t=n} (Y_t - \hat{\alpha} - \hat{\beta} X_t)^2$$

with respect to the unknown parameters $\hat{\alpha}$ and $\hat{\beta}$. ESS is the sum of squared residuals, and the OLS procedure minimizes the sum of squared residuals.[2] It should be noted that ESS is a squared distance measure from the regression line. Using this distance measure, we can say that the OLS procedure finds the straight line that is "closest" to the data.

On a more intuitive level, suppose we choose a particular set of values $\hat{\alpha}$ and $\hat{\beta}$, that is, a particular straight line $\hat{\alpha} + \hat{\beta} X$. The deviation of Y_t from this chosen line is given by the estimated residual $\hat{u}_t = Y_t - \hat{\alpha} - \hat{\beta} X_t$, which can be computed from the data. Next square this and sum it over all the sample observations. The *observed* sum of squares of residuals [referred to as the **error sum of squares (ESS)**] is therefore $\Sigma \hat{u}_t^2$. Associated with each choice of straight line is an error sum of squares. The OLS procedure would select those values $\hat{\alpha}$ and $\hat{\beta}$ for which ESS is a minimum.

Squaring accomplishes two things. First, it removes the sign of the error and hence treats positive errors and negative errors alike. Second, squaring has the property of penalizing large errors substantially. As an example, suppose the sample residuals were $1, 2, -1$, and -2 for a particular choice of the regression coefficients $\hat{\alpha}$ and $\hat{\beta}$. Compare this with another choice that generates the residuals $-1, -1, -1$, and 3. The sum of the absolute values of the errors is the same in both cases. Although the second choice has lowered one of the errors from 2 to 1 in absolute value, it also results in a large error, namely 3, which is undesirable. If we obtain ESS for the two cases, we get the value 10 for the first case ($1^2 + 2^2 + 1^2 + 2^2$) and the value 12 ($1^2 + 1^2 + 1^2 + 3^2$) for the second case. The least squares method imposes a heavy penalty on the large error and hence would have chosen the first straight line. We will see in Section 3.3 that the procedure of minimizing ESS has other desirable properties as well.

The Normal Equations

In Section 3.A.3 of the appendix, the OLS method is formally applied. It is shown there that the conditions for minimizing ESS with respect to $\hat{\alpha}$ and $\hat{\beta}$ are given by the following two equations, known as the **normal equations** (no connection with the normal distribution):

$$\sum \hat{u}_t = 0 = \sum (Y_t - \hat{\alpha} - \hat{\beta} X_t) = \sum Y_t - (n\hat{\alpha}) - \hat{\beta} \sum X_t \tag{3.4}$$

$$\sum (X_t \hat{u}_t) = \sum [X_t(Y_t - \hat{\alpha} - \hat{\beta} X_t)] = 0 \tag{3.5}$$

---

[2]It is somewhat confusing to call the sum of squared residuals ESS, but this notation is used by many well-known computer programs and comes from the analysis of variance literature (see the end of Section 3.5).

In Equation (3.4) we note that $\Sigma\hat{\alpha} = n\hat{\alpha}$ because every term has $\hat{\alpha}$ and there are n terms. Taking the negative terms in Equation (3.4) to the right and dividing every term by n, we get

$$\frac{1}{n}\sum Y_t = \hat{\alpha} + \hat{\beta}\frac{1}{n}\sum X_t \tag{3.6}$$

$(1/n)\Sigma Y_t$ is the sample mean of Y, denoted by $\overline{Y}$, and $(1/n)\Sigma X_t$ is the sample mean of X, denoted by $\overline{X}$. Using these results in Equation (3.6), we get the following equation:

$$\overline{Y} = \hat{\alpha} + \hat{\beta}\overline{X} \tag{3.7}$$

The straight line $\hat{\alpha} + \hat{\beta}X$ is the *estimated* line and is the **sample regression line,** or the **fitted straight line.** We see from Equation (3.7) that the sample regression line passes through the mean point $(\overline{X}, \overline{Y})$. We will see in Exercise 3.12c that this property need not hold unless the constant term α is present in the model.

In Equation (3.5), taking the summation term by term and noting that $\hat{\alpha}$ and $\hat{\beta}$ can be taken out of the summation because they appear for each t, we get

$$\sum(X_tY_t) - \hat{\alpha}\sum X_t - \hat{\beta}\sum X_t^2 = 0$$

or

$$\sum(X_tY_t) = \hat{\alpha}\sum X_t + \hat{\beta}\sum X_t^2 \tag{3.8}$$

Solutions to the Normal Equations

To facilitate the solution of these two equations, the following expressions would be useful. They are proved in Appendix Section 3.A.2.

$$S_{xx} = \sum(X_t - \overline{X})^2 = \sum X_t^2 - n(\overline{X})^2 = \sum X_t^2 - \frac{1}{n}\left(\sum X_t\right)^2 \tag{3.9}$$

$$S_{xy} = \sum(X_t - \overline{X})(Y_t - \overline{Y}) = \left(\sum X_tY_t\right) - n\overline{X}\overline{Y} \tag{3.10}$$

$$= \sum X_tY_t - \left[\left(\sum X_t\right)\left(\sum Y_t\right)/n\right]$$

From Equation (3.7),

$$\hat{\alpha} = \overline{Y} - \hat{\beta}\overline{X} = \frac{1}{n}\sum Y_t - \hat{\beta}\frac{1}{n}\sum X_t \tag{3.11}$$

Substitute for $\hat{\alpha}$ from this into (3.8):

$$\sum X_tY_t = \left[\frac{1}{n}\sum Y_t - \hat{\beta}\frac{1}{n}\sum X_t\right]\left(\sum X_t\right) + \hat{\beta}\sum X_t^2$$

Now group the $\hat{\beta}$ terms together:

$$\sum X_t Y_t = \left[\frac{\left(\sum X_t \right)\left(\sum Y_t \right)}{n} \right] + \hat{\beta}\left[\sum X_t^2 - \frac{\left(\sum X_t \right)^2}{n} \right]$$

Solving this for $\hat{\beta}$ we get

$$\hat{\beta} = \frac{\sum X_t Y_t - \dfrac{\left(\sum X_t \right)\left(\sum Y_t \right)}{n}}{\sum X_t^2 - \dfrac{\left(\sum X_t \right)^2}{n}}$$

Using the simplifying notation introduced in Equations (3.9) and (3.10), this can be expressed as

$$\hat{\beta} = \frac{S_{xy}}{S_{xx}} \tag{3.12}$$

The notation S_{xx} and S_{xy} can be remembered in a more intuitive way. Define $x_t = X_t - \overline{X}$ and $y_t = Y_t - \overline{Y}$, where the bar denotes the sample mean. Thus, the lowercase variable denotes the deviation of the uppercase variable from its mean. The following results are proved in Appendix Sections 2.A.1 and 3.A.2.

$$\sum x_t = 0$$

$$S_{xx} = \sum x_t^2 = \sum (X_t - \overline{X})^2 = \sum X_t^2 - \frac{1}{n}\left(\sum X_t \right)^2 \tag{3.13}$$

$$S_{xy} = \sum x_t y_t = \sum (X_t - \overline{X})(Y_t - \overline{Y}) = \sum X_t Y_t - \frac{1}{n}\left[\left(\sum X_t \right)\left(\sum Y_t \right) \right] \tag{3.14}$$

S_{xy} can thus be remembered as the "sum of x_t times y_t." Similarly, S_{xx} is the sum of x_t times x_t, which is the sum of x_t squared.

Equations (3.11) and (3.12) represent the solution to the normal equations [(3.4) and (3.5)] and give us the **sample estimates** $\hat{\alpha}$ and $\hat{\beta}$ for the **population parameters** α and β.

It should be noted that the estimate of β given in Equation (3.12) cannot be obtained if $S_{xx} = \sum x_t^2 = \Sigma(X_t - \overline{X})^2 = 0$. This term will be zero if and only if each x_t is zero, that is, if and only if all X_t are the same. This leads us to the next assumption.

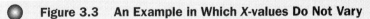

Figure 3.3   An Example in Which *X*-values Do Not Vary

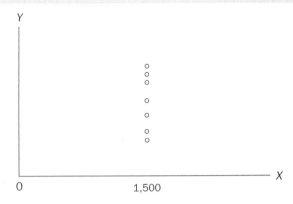

ASSUMPTION 3.2   (Some of the Observed Xs Are Different)

Not all the values of X_t are the same. At least one of the values of X_t is different from the others. In other words, the sample variance $\widehat{\text{Var}(X)} = \frac{1}{n-1}\sum_t(X_t - \overline{X})^2$ is not zero.

This is an important assumption that can never be relaxed (unless $\alpha = 0$) because otherwise the model cannot be estimated. On an intuitive level, if X_t does not vary, we cannot explain why Y_t varies. Figure 3.3 illustrates this assumption graphically. In the house example, suppose information was gathered only about houses with a living area of 1,500 square feet. The sample scatter diagram will be as in Figure 3.3. It is clear from the diagram that this information is inadequate for estimating the population regression line $\alpha + \beta X$.

EXAMPLE 3.1

In the terminology commonly used in econometrics, if we use the data in Table 3.1 and "regress Y (PRICE) against a constant term and X (SQFT)," we obtain the estimated relation (that is, the sample regression function) as $\hat{Y}_t = 52.351 + 0.13875X_t$. $\hat{Y}_t$ is the estimated average price (in thousands of dollars) that corresponds to X_t (see Table 3.1). The regression coefficient for X_t is the estimated *marginal* effect of living area for an average house. Thus, if the living area is increased by one unit, the estimated average price is expected to go up by 0.13875 thousands of dollars (that is, by $138.75). More realistically, for a 100-square-foot increase in the area, the estimated price is expected to go up, on average, by $13,875.

The sample regression function can be used to estimate the average price of a house with a given living area. (Table 3.1 has the average prices in the last column.) Thus, a house with an area of 1,800 square feet would be expected to sell, on average, for $302,551 [52.351 + (0.139 × 1,800)]. But the actual sale price was $285,000. The model has thus overestimated the sale price by $17,551, perhaps because the house in question was not well maintained and hence sold for less. In contrast, for the house with an area of 2,600 square feet, the estimated mean price is $413,751, considerably lower than the actual sale price of $505,000. This difference could be because we have ignored other factors that also affect house prices. For instance, the house might have a large yard and/or a swimming pool, both of which would command a higher price than average. This point underscores the importance of identifying explanatory variables that could affect the values of the dependent variable and including them in the model formulation. Furthermore, it is critical to ask how reliable the estimates of the intercept and slope coefficients of Equation (3.1) are and how good the "fit" of the model is to the actual data.

● PRACTICE PROBLEM 3.2

Copy two columns of numbers in Table 3.1 onto a ruled sheet of paper. In the first column of the worksheet, copy the values for Y_t(PRICE), and in the second column, copy the values for X_t(SQFT). Use a calculator (not a computer) and prepare two more columns of numbers. Square each entry in the second column, and enter it in the third column (X_t^2). Multiply corresponding entries in the first and second columns, and enter the number in the fourth column ($X_t Y_t$). Next, sum each column, and verify the following totals:

$$\sum X_t = 26,753 \qquad \sum X_t^2 = 55,462,515$$

$$\sum Y_t = 4,444.9 \qquad \sum X_t Y_t = 9,095,985.5$$

To avoid overflow and round-off errors, be sure to use as many digits as the calculator will allow. Next, compute S_{xy} from Equation (3.14) and S_{xx} from Equation (3.13). Finally, compute $\hat{\beta}$ from (3.12) and $\hat{\alpha}$ from (3.11), and verify the values presented earlier. (Aren't you glad computers do all the work nowadays?)

● 3.3 Properties of Estimators

Although the least squares procedure gives an estimate of the straight-line relationship that would be the "best fit" for the data, we would like to answer several other questions. For example, what are the statistical properties of $\hat{\alpha}$ and $\hat{\beta}$? What measure of reliability do they have? How can we use them to test hypotheses or generate forecasts? We now take up a discussion of each of these issues. It would be useful at this point to review Section 2.6, which gives a summary of the desirable properties of estimators.

The first property that we examine is that of *unbiasedness*. It was noted in Section 2.4 that an estimator such as $\hat{\alpha}$ and $\hat{\beta}$ is itself a random variable and hence has a statistical distribution. This is because different trials of an experiment with different independent samples will result in different estimates of the parameters. If we repeat the experiment a large number of times, we obtain a large number of estimates. We can then compute the fraction of times these estimates fall in a specified interval. This gives the *sampling distribution of the estimators*. Such a distribution usually has a mean and a variance. If the mean of that distribution is the true parameter (α or β in our case), then we say that the estimator is *unbiased*. *Unbiasedness* is clearly desirable because it means that, on average, the estimated values will be the true values, even though in a particular sample this may not be so.

It is possible to show that the OLS estimators of α and β derived in Section 3.2 possess the unbiasedness property. In order to prove that, however, we need to impose additional assumptions on X_t and u_t. Some of the assumptions are relaxed later and the consequences examined.

ASSUMPTION 3.3   (Conditional Mean of *u*, Given *X*, Is Zero)

Each u_t is a random variable with $E(u_t|X_t) = 0$; that is, the conditional expectation of u_t, given X_t, is 0. By the law of iterated expectations (Property 2.6), this also means that the unconditional expectation $E(u_t) = 0$.

In order to interpret the deterministic part of a regression model, $\alpha + \beta X$, as a "statistical average" relation, we need the assumption that the error terms (u_t) average to zero in the population. Although we only specify that the conditional mean of u_t be zero, because of the law of iterated expectations, the unconditional mean of u_t is also zero. Thus,

$$E(u_t) = E_X[E_{u|X}(u_t|X_t)] = E_X(0) = 0$$

ASSUMPTION 3.4   (Xs Are Given and Hence Can Be Treated as Nonrandom)

Each X_t is treated as a given observation and is hence assumed to be nonrandom (that is, nonstochastic) or, equivalently, it is assumed that X_t is *fixed in repeated samples*. This implies that $\mathrm{Cov}(X_s, u_t) = 0$ for all s and $t = 1, 2, \ldots, n$, that is, that X_s and u_t are uncorrelated.

When we introduced the simple regression model in Chapter 1 (see Figure 1.2), we fixed the values of X and then obtained observations on Y for the given X. This is a common approach with many types of data. For instance, in the real estate example, we fix the characteristics of a house and then ask what the sale price of such a house is. We can specify the characteristics of an employee and ask what his or her salary is, or choose the features of a car and examine its price, and so on. In nonexperimental situations where one cannot select the values of X, Assumption 3.4 is a convenient simplification to derive useful properties of the estimators. We examine later the consequences of a violation of Assumption 3.4—in particular, when we are dealing with a simultaneous equation model (Chapter 13).

It is easy to show that, under Assumption 3.4, $\text{Cov}(X_s, u_t) = 0$ for all s and $t = 1, 2, \ldots, n$. By definition,

$$\text{Cov}(X_s, u_t) = E(X_s u_t) - E(X_s)\, E(u_t)$$

Because X_s is given, it can be treated as fixed and taken out of the expectations. Hence,

$$\text{Cov}(X_s, u_t) = X_s E(u_t) - X_s E(u_t) = 0$$

Property 3.1 states that under Assumptions 3.1 through 3.4, OLS estimators are unbiased.

Property 3.1 (Unbiasedness)	Under Assumptions 3.1 through 3.4, the least squares estimators $\hat{\alpha}$ and $\hat{\beta}$ are unbiased; that is, $E(\hat{\alpha}) = \alpha$ and $E(\hat{\beta}) = \beta$.

PROOF*

(Readers not interested in the proof may skip it without loss of continuity.) In Equation (3.10), substitute for Y_t from Equation (3.1) and also use $n\alpha$ for $\Sigma\alpha$.

$$S_{xy} = \sum X_t(\alpha + \beta X_t + u_t) - \left[\frac{\left(\sum X_t\right)\left(n\alpha + \beta \sum X_t + \sum u_t\right)}{n}\right] \tag{3.15}$$

$$= \alpha \sum X_t + \beta \sum X_t^2 + \sum X_t u_t - \alpha \sum X_t$$

$$- \beta\left[\frac{\left(\sum X_t\right)^2}{n}\right] - \left[\frac{\left(\sum X_t\right)\left(\sum u_t\right)}{n}\right]$$

$$= \beta\left[\sum X_t^2 - \frac{\left(\sum X_t\right)^2}{n}\right] + \left[\sum X_t u_t - \frac{\left(\sum X_t\right)\left(\sum u_t\right)}{n}\right]$$

$$= \beta S_{xx} + S_{xu}$$

where S_{xx} is given by Equation (3.9) and

$$S_{xu} = \sum X_t u_t - \frac{\left(\sum X_t\right)\left(\sum u_t\right)}{n} \tag{3.16}$$

$$= \sum X_t u_t - \bar{X}\sum u_t = \sum (X_t - \bar{X})u_t$$

It follows from Equations (3.12) and (3.15) that

$$\hat{\beta} = S_{xy}/S_{xx} = \beta + (S_{xu}/S_{xx}) \tag{3.17}$$

Taking the conditional expectation of this for a given X, we get

$$E(\hat{\beta}|X) = \beta + E[(S_{xu}/S_{xx})|X]$$

But by Assumption 3.4, X_t is given and hence so is S_{xx}. This means that in taking expectations, terms involving X_t can be brought outside the expectations. Therefore, we have

$$E(\hat{\beta}|X) = \beta + \frac{1}{S_{xx}} E(S_{xu}|X)$$

In Equation (3.16), $\overline{X}$ is the sample mean of X, X_t is given, and the expectation of a sum of terms is equal to the sum of the expectations. Therefore, making use of Assumption 3.3,

$$E(S_{xu}|X) = \Sigma E(X_t u_t|X) - \overline{X}\Sigma E(u_t|X) = \Sigma X_t E(u_t|X) - \overline{X}\Sigma E(u_t|X) = 0$$

It follows from this that $E(\hat{\beta}|X) = \beta$. By the law of iterated expectations, $E(\hat{\beta}) = \beta$, which means that $\hat{\beta}$ is unconditionally unbiased. *In other words, $\hat{\beta}$ is unbiased even if X is random.* The proof is similar for $\hat{\alpha}$. It should be pointed out that Assumptions 3.3 and 3.4—that $E(u_t|X) = 0$ and X_t is given—are crucial in this proof.

● **PRACTICE PROBLEM 3.3**[†]

Using Equation (3.11), show that $\hat{\alpha}$ is unbiased. Clearly state all the assumptions needed for this.

Although unbiasedness is a desirable property, by itself it does not make an estimator "good," and an unbiased estimator is not unique. Consider, for instance, the alternative estimator $\tilde{\beta} = (Y_2 - Y_1)/(X_2 - X_1)$. It will be noted that $\tilde{\beta}$ (read as "beta tilde") is simply the slope of the straight line connecting the first two scatter points (X_1, Y_1) and (X_2, Y_2). It is easy to show that $\tilde{\beta}$ is also unbiased.

$$\tilde{\beta} = \frac{Y_2 - Y_1}{X_2 - X_1} = \frac{(\alpha + \beta X_2 + u_2) - (\alpha + \beta X_1 + u_1)}{X_2 - X_1} = \beta + \frac{u_2 - u_1}{X_2 - X_1}$$

As before, the Xs are nonstochastic and $E(u_2) = E(u_1) = 0$. Therefore, $\tilde{\beta}$ is also unbiased. In fact, it is possible to construct an infinite number of such unbiased estimators. Because $\tilde{\beta}$ throws away observations 3 through n, intuitively it cannot be a "good" estimator. In Exercise 3.6, all the observations are used to construct yet another unbiased estimator, but this too is not as desirable as other possible unbiased estimators. We therefore need additional criteria to judge whether an estimator is "good."

A second criterion to consider is that of *consistency*, which is a large sample property defined in Section 2.6 (Definition 2.10). Suppose we draw a random sample of size n and obtain $\hat{\alpha}$ and $\hat{\beta}$. Now draw one more observation, and reestimate the parameters. Repeat this process a large number of times to obtain a sequence of estimates. Consistency is the property that the estimates converge to the true values as the sample size is increased indefinitely. The estimator $\tilde{\beta}$ presented above is clearly not consistent because increasing the sample size does not affect it. Property 3.2 states the conditions under which an estimator will be consistent.

Property 3.2 (Consistency)

Under Assumptions 3.1 through 3.4, the least squares estimators are consistent.

PROOF*

(This proof also may be skipped without loss of continuity.) From Equation (3.17),

$$\hat{\beta} = \beta + \frac{S_{xu}/n}{S_{xx}/n} \tag{3.18}$$

By the law of large numbers (Property 2.10a), S_{xu}/n converges to its expectation, which is $\text{Cov}(X, u)$. Similarly, S_{xx}/n converges to $\text{Var}(X)$. It follows, therefore, that as n converges to infinity, $\hat{\beta}$ converges to $\beta + [\text{Cov}(X, u)/\text{Var}(X)]$, which would equal β if $\text{Cov}(X, u) = 0$—that is, if X and u are uncorrelated. Thus, $\hat{\beta}$ is a consistent estimator of β.

Although $\hat{\beta}$ is unbiased and consistent, we still need additional criteria because it is possible to construct other unbiased and consistent estimators. Exercise 3.6 has an example of such an estimator. The criterion that we will use next is *efficiency* (defined in Section 2.6). In simple terms, an unbiased estimator is said to be more efficient if it has a smaller variance than another unbiased estimator. In order to establish efficiency, we need more assumptions on u_t.

ASSUMPTION 3.5 (Homoscedasticity)

All the u's are identically distributed with the same conditional variance σ^2, so that $\text{Var}(u_t|X_t) = E(u_t^2|X_t) = \sigma^2$. This is known as **homoscedasticity** (equal scatter).

ASSUMPTION 3.6 (Serial Independence)

The u's are also independently distributed so that $\text{Cov}(u_t, u_s|X_t) = E(u_t u_s|X_t) = 0$ for all $t \neq s$. This is known as **serial independence.**

These assumptions imply that the residuals are independently and identically distributed (iid). We note from Figure 1.2 that for a given X there is a scatter of Y values that determines a *conditional* distribution. The errors u_t are the deviations

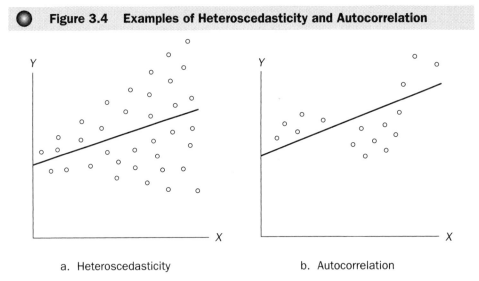

Figure 3.4   Examples of Heteroscedasticity and Autocorrelation

a. Heteroscedasticity

b. Autocorrelation

from the *conditional mean* $\alpha + \beta X_t$. Assumption 3.5 implies that the distribution of u_t has the same variance (σ^2) as that of u_s for a different observation s. Figure 3.4a is an example of **heteroscedasticity** (or unequal scatter) where the variances are not constant across observations but increase with X. Assumption 3.5 is relaxed in Chapter 8. Appendix Section 3.A.1 has a three-dimensional representation of this assumption.

Assumption 3.6 (which is relaxed in Chapter 9) implies that u_t and u_s are independent and hence uncorrelated. In particular, successive errors are uncorrelated and are not clustered together. Figure 3.4b is an example of **autocorrelation** where this assumption is violated. Note that successive observations, being clustered together, are likely to have errors that are correlated.

Property 3.3 (Efficiency, BLUE, and the Gauss–Markov Theorem)	Under Assumptions 3.1 through 3.6, ordinary least squares estimators are most efficient among unbiased linear estimators. The OLS procedure thus yields **best linear unbiased estimates (BLUE).** This result holds even when X is a random variable.

This property (proved in Section 3.A.4) is known as the **Gauss–Markov theorem,** which states that OLS estimators are BLUE; that is, among all linear combinations of the Ys that are unbiased, the OLS estimators of α and β have the smallest variance.

In summary, the ordinary least squares (OLS) procedure of estimating the regression coefficients of a model yields several desirable properties: estimators are (1) unbiased, (2) consistent, and (3) most efficient within the class of linear unbiased estimators.

Using the real estate data, we estimated the parameters as $\hat{\alpha} = 52.351$ and $\hat{\beta} = 0.13875$. The natural question is how good these estimates are and how well the sample regression function $\hat{Y} = 52.351 + 0.13875X$ "fits" the data. In this section, we discuss the procedures for obtaining numerical measures of the precision of the estimates as well as of the **goodness of fit.**

The Precision of the Estimators

We know from the theory of probability that the variance of a random variable is a measure of its dispersion around the mean. The smaller the variance, the closer, on average, individual values are to the mean. Also, when dealing with confidence intervals, we know that the smaller the variance of the random variable, the narrower the confidence interval of a parameter. The variance of an estimator is thus an indicator of the precision of the estimator. It is therefore of considerable interest to compute the variances of $\hat{\alpha}$ and $\hat{\beta}$.

Because $\hat{\alpha}$ and $\hat{\beta}$ depend on the Ys, which in turn depend on the random variables $u_1, u_2, \ldots, u_n$, they are also random variables with associated distributions. The following equations are derived in Section 3.A.6 of the appendix to this chapter (for simplicity of notation, we henceforth omit the condition that X_t is given).

$$\text{Var}(\hat{\beta}) = \sigma_{\hat{\beta}}^2 = E[(\hat{\beta} - \beta)^2] = \frac{\sigma^2}{S_{xx}} \qquad (3.19)$$

$$\text{Var}(\hat{\alpha}) = \sigma_{\hat{\alpha}}^2 = E[(\hat{\alpha} - \alpha)^2] = \frac{\sum X_t^2}{nS_{xx}} \sigma^2 \qquad (3.20)$$

$$\text{Cov}(\hat{\alpha}, \hat{\beta}) = \sigma_{\hat{\alpha}\hat{\beta}} = E[(\hat{\alpha} - \alpha)(\hat{\beta} - \beta)] = -\frac{\overline{X}}{S_{xx}} \sigma^2 \qquad (3.21)$$

where S_{xx} is defined in Equation (3.13) and σ^2 is the variance of the error terms. It should be noted that if S_{xx} increases, these variances and covariance (in absolute value) decrease. This demonstrates that a *higher variation in X and a larger sample size are desirable because they improve the precision with which the parameters are estimated.*

The above expressions are **population variances** and are unknown because σ^2 is unknown. They can, however, be estimated because σ^2 can be estimated from the sample. Note that $\hat{Y}_t = \hat{\alpha} + \hat{\beta}X_t$ is the estimated straight line. Therefore, $\hat{u}_t = Y_t - \hat{\alpha} - \hat{\beta}X_t$ is an estimate of u_t and is the *estimated residual.* An obvious estimator of σ^2 is $\Sigma\hat{u}_t^2/n$ but it happens to be biased. An unbiased estimator of σ^2 is given by (see Section 3.A.7 for proof)

$$s^2 = \hat{\sigma}^2 = \frac{\sum \hat{u}_t^2}{n - 2} \qquad (3.22)$$

The reason for dividing by $n - 2$ is similar to that given for dividing the chi-square by $n - 1$, which was discussed in Section 2.7. There, $n - 1$ was used because of the condition $\Sigma(x_i - \bar{x}) = 0$. Here, there are two conditions given by the normal Equations (3.4) and (3.5), and hence we use $n - 2$. The square root of the estimated variance is called the **standard error of the disturbances** or the **standard error of the regression.** Using this estimate, we can obtain estimates of the variances and covariance of $\hat{\alpha}$ and $\hat{\beta}$. The square roots of the estimated variances are called the **standard errors of the regression coefficients** and are denoted by $s_{\hat{\alpha}}$ and $s_{\hat{\beta}}$. The estimated variances and covariance of the estimated regression coefficients are

$$s_{\hat{\beta}}^2 = \frac{\hat{\sigma}^2}{S_{xx}} \tag{3.23}$$

$$s_{\hat{\alpha}}^2 = \frac{\sum X_t^2}{nS_{xx}} \hat{\sigma}^2 \tag{3.24}$$

$$s_{\hat{\alpha}\hat{\beta}} = -\frac{\bar{X}}{S_{xx}} \hat{\sigma}^2 \tag{3.25}$$

To summarize what we have done so far: First, we obtained the estimated regression coefficients $\hat{\alpha}$ and $\hat{\beta}$ using Equations (3.11) and (3.12). This gave us an estimated relationship between Y and X. We then calculated the predicted value of Y_t as $\hat{Y}_t = \hat{\alpha} + \hat{\beta}X_t$. From this we obtained the residual $\hat{u}_t$ as $Y_t - \hat{Y}_t$. Then we obtained an estimate of the variance of u_t from Equation (3.22). Substituting this in Equations (3.19), (3.20), and (3.21), we obtained the estimates for the variances and covariance of $\hat{\alpha}$ and $\hat{\beta}$.

It should be noted that for the expression of the residual variance s^2 given in Equation 3.22 to be sensible, we need the condition $n > 2$. Without this assumption, the estimated variance could be undefined or negative. A more general version of this condition is stated in Assumption 3.7, which also can never be relaxed.

ASSUMPTION 3.7   (*n* > 2)

The number of observations (n) must be greater than the number of regression coefficients to be estimated (k). In the case of a simple linear regression, this reduces to the condition $n > 2$.

● **EXAMPLE 3.2**

The following standard errors are given for the home price example:

standard error of the residuals $= s = \hat{\sigma} = 39.023$
standard error for $\hat{\alpha} = s_{\hat{\alpha}} = 37.285$
standard error for $\hat{\beta} = s_{\hat{\beta}} = 0.01873$
covariance between $\hat{\alpha}$ and $\hat{\beta} = s_{\hat{\alpha}\hat{\beta}} = -0.671$

Practice Computer Session 3.1 in Appendix D has the commands to reproduce these results as well as those in later sections.

Although we have numerical measures of the precision of the estimates, by themselves they are of no use because they can be made arbitrarily large or small by simply changing the units of measurement (more on this in Section 3.6). The primary use of these measures is in hypothesis testing, a topic discussed in detail in Section 3.5.

The Overall Goodness of Fit

It is clear from Figure 3.1 that no straight line will adequately "fit" the data because many of the values predicted by a straight line will be far away from the actual values. To be able to judge whether a particular relationship describes the observed values better than an alternative relationship, it would be desirable to have a numerical measure of goodness of fit. In this section, we develop such a measure.

In trying to make predictions about the dependent variable Y if the only information we have is that the observed values of Y came from some probability distribution, then perhaps the best we can do is to estimate the mean and variance using $\overline{Y}$ and $\hat{\sigma}_Y^2 = [\Sigma (Y_t - \overline{Y})^2]/(n - 1)$. If we are asked to predict Y, then we simply use the average $\overline{Y}$ because there is no other information to use. The error in predicting observation t is $Y_t - \overline{Y}$. Squaring this and summing over all the observations, we obtain a measure of the **total variation** of Y_t from $\overline{Y}$ as $\Sigma(Y_t - \overline{Y})^2$. This is known as the **total sum of squares (TSS).** The sample standard deviation of Y is a measure of the dispersion of Y_t around its mean $\overline{Y}$ or, equivalently, the dispersion of the error in using $\overline{Y}$ as a predictor. It is given by $\hat{\sigma}_Y = \sqrt{TSS/(n - 1)}$.

Suppose we are now told that Y is related to another variable X according to Equation (3.1). Then we would expect that a prior knowledge of the value that X takes will help us make a better prediction of Y than simply $\overline{Y}$. More specifically, if we have the estimates $\hat{\alpha}$ and $\hat{\beta}$ and also know that X takes the value X_t, then our estimate of Y_t will be $\hat{Y}_t = \hat{\alpha} + \hat{\beta}X_t$. The error in this estimate is $\hat{u}_t = Y_t - \hat{Y}_t$. Squaring this and summing over all the observations, we obtain the error sum of squares (ESS), or the **sum of squares of the residuals,** as ESS $= \Sigma\hat{u}_t^2$. The standard error of the residuals is $\hat{\sigma} = \sqrt{ESS/(n - 2)}$. It measures the dispersion of the error in using $\hat{Y}_t$ as a predictor and is often compared with $\hat{\sigma}_Y$ given above to see how much of a reduction there has been. Because a small ESS is desirable, a large reduction would be ideal. In the example we are using, $\hat{\sigma}_Y = 88.498$ and $\hat{\sigma} = 39.023$, a reduction of more than half the original value.

This method is not satisfactory, however, because the standard errors are very sensitive to the unit in which Y was measured. It would be desirable to have instead a measure of goodness of fit that is not sensitive to the units of measurement. This issue is taken up next.

A measure of the total variation of $\hat{Y}_t$ from $\overline{Y}$ (which is also the mean of $\hat{Y}_t$) for the entire sample is $\Sigma(\hat{Y}_t - \overline{Y})^2$. This is known as the **regression sum of squares (RSS).** In Section 3.A.8 it is shown that

$$\sum (Y_t - \overline{Y})^2 = \sum (\hat{Y}_t - \overline{Y})^2 + \sum \hat{u}_t^2 \qquad (3.26)$$

Thus, TSS = RSS + ESS. We note that $(Y_t - \overline{Y}) = (\hat{Y}_t - \overline{Y}) + \hat{u}_t$. Figure 3.5 illustrates this decomposition. Equation (3.26) states that the same decomposition holds for sum of squares also. If the relationship between X and Y is "close," the scatter points (X_t, Y_t) will lie near the straight line $\hat{\alpha} + \hat{\beta}X$. In other words, ESS will be small and RSS will be large. The ratio

$$\frac{\text{RSS}}{\text{TSS}} = 1 - \frac{\text{ESS}}{\text{TSS}}$$

is called the **coefficient of multiple determination** and is denoted by R^2. The term *multiple* does not apply in the case of simple regression because we use only the one independent variable X. However, because the expression is the same for multiple regression as well, we use the same term here.

$$R^2 = 1 - \frac{\Sigma \hat{u}_t^2}{\Sigma(Y_t - \overline{Y})^2} = 1 - \frac{\text{ESS}}{\text{TSS}} = \frac{\text{RSS}}{\text{TSS}} \qquad 0 \leq R^2 \leq 1 \qquad \textbf{(3.27)}$$

R^2 will clearly lie between 0 and 1. It is unit-free because both the numerator and the denominator have the same units. The closer the observed points are to the estimated straight line, the better the "fit," which means that ESS will be smaller and R^2 will be higher. Thus, R^2 is a measure of the goodness of fit, and a high R^2 is desirable. ESS is also called the **unexplained variation** because $\hat{u}_t$ is the effect of variables other than X_t that are not in the model. RSS is the **explained variation.** Thus, TSS, the total variation in Y, can be broken into two components: (1) RSS, which is that part accounted for by X, and (2) ESS, which is the unaccounted part. A small

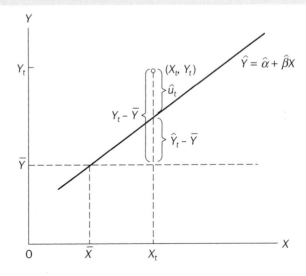

● **Figure 3.5   The Decomposition of Y**

value of R^2 implies that a lot of the variation in Y has not been explained by X. We may have to look for other variables that exert influence over Y.

Besides being the proportion of total variation in Y explained by the model, R^2 has another interpretation. It also measures the correlation between the observed value Y_t and the predicted value $\hat{Y}_t(r_{Y,\hat{Y}_t})$. You should review the discussion of the population and sample correlation coefficients presented in Sections 2.3 and 2.5. It's shown in Section 3.A.9 that

$$r_{Y\hat{Y}}^2 = \frac{\widehat{\mathrm{Cov}^2(Y_t, \hat{Y}_t)}}{\widehat{\mathrm{Var}(Y_t)}\,\widehat{\mathrm{Var}(\hat{Y}_t)}} = \frac{\mathrm{RSS}}{\mathrm{TSS}} = R^2 \qquad (3.27a)$$

Thus, the square of the simple correlation between the observed value Y_t and the value $\hat{Y}_t$ predicted by the regression model is the same as R^2 defined in Equation (3.27). This result holds even if there are more explanatory variables, *provided the regression has a constant term.*

A frequently asked question about the overall goodness of fit is, "How do you decide whether the computed R^2 is high or low?" There is no hard and fast rule about what a high or low value of R^2 is. With time series data, one often finds high R^2 because many time series variables have underlying trends that are highly correlated. It is therefore common to observe R^2 values above 0.9. A value of 0.6 or 0.7 will then be considered low. Cross-section data, however, represent the behavior of varied agents at a single point in time and typically have low R^2. In such cases, 0.6 or 0.7 may not be that bad. The general advice is not to rely too much on the value of R^2. It is simply one measure of the adequacy of a model. It is more important to judge a model by whether the signs of the regression coefficients agree with economic theory, intuition, and the past experience of the investigator.

● **EXAMPLE 3.3**

In the home price example, TSS, ESS, and R^2 have the following values (refer to the output from Practice Computer Session 3.1):

$$\mathrm{TSS} = 101{,}815 \qquad \mathrm{ESS} = 18{,}274 \qquad R^2 = 0.82052$$

Thus, 82.1 percent of the variation in the price of a house in the sample is explained by the corresponding living area. In Chapter 4, we will find that adding other explanatory variables, such as the number of bedrooms and bathrooms, improves the model fit.

● **3.5   Tests of Hypotheses** ✓

As mentioned earlier, testing statistical hypotheses is one of the main tasks of an econometrician. In the regression model (3.1), if β is zero, the predicted value of Y will be independent of X, implying that X has no effect on Y. Thus, the hypothesis $\beta = 0$ is of interest here, and we would strongly hope that it would be rejected. The correlation coefficient (ρ) between the two variables X and Y measures the close-ness of association between the two variables. The sample estimate of ρ is given in Equation (2.11). If $\rho = 0$, the variables are uncorrelated. Another test of interest is therefore $\rho = 0$. In this section, we discuss the procedures for testing hypotheses on α and β only. The test on ρ is undertaken in the next section. We strongly recom-mend that, before proceeding, you review Section 2.8 on hypothesis testing and 2.7 on distributions.

Hypothesis testing consists of three basic steps: (1) formulating two opposing hypotheses (null and alternative hypotheses), (2) deriving a test statistic and its sta-tistical distribution under the null hypothesis, and (3) deriving a decision rule for rejecting or accepting the null hypothesis. In the home price example, the null hy-pothesis is H_0: $\beta = 0$. Because we would expect β to be positive, a natural alternative hypothesis is H_1: $\beta > 0$. Later we also consider the two-sided alternative H_1: $\beta \neq 0$. In order to carry out this test, $\hat{\beta}$ and its estimated standard error $s_{\hat{\beta}}$ are used to de-rive a test statistic. To derive the sampling distributions of $\hat{\alpha}$ and $\hat{\beta}$ that indirectly de-pend on the random error terms $u_1, u_2, \ldots, u_n$ (see Equation 3.15), we need an ad-ditional assumption on the distribution of u_t.

ASSUMPTION 3.8   (Normality of Errors)

For given X_t, each u_t is distributed as $N(0, \sigma^2)$, which implies that the conditional density of Y given X is distributed as $N(\alpha + \beta X, \sigma^2)$.

Thus, the error terms $u_1, u_2, \ldots, u_n$ are assumed to be independently and iden-tically distributed as normal with mean zero and the common variance σ^2. We will see that Assumption 3.8 is fundamental to hypothesis testing. Table 3.2 summarizes all the assumptions made so far. Error terms that satisfy Assumptions 3.3, 3.5, and 3.6 are often referred to as **well-behaved errors** and also as **white-noise errors.**

⬤   **Table 3.2   Assumptions of the Simple Linear Regression Model**

3.1	The regression model is linear in the unknown coefficients α and β; that is, $Y_t = \alpha + \beta X_t + u_t$, for $t = 1, 2, \ldots, n$.
3.2	Not all of the observations on X are the same; at least one of them is different; that is, $\mathrm{Var}(X) > 0$.
3.3	The error term u_t is a random variable with $E(u_t|X_t) = 0$.
3.4	X_t is given and nonrandom, implying that it is uncorrelated with u_s; that is, $\mathrm{Cov}(X_t, u_s) = E(X_t u_s) - E(X_t) E(u_s) = 0$, for all $s, t = 1, 2, \ldots, n$.
3.5	Given X_t, u_t has a constant variance for all t; that is, $\mathrm{Var}(u_t|X_t) = E(u_t^2|X_t) = \sigma^2$.
3.6	Given X_t, u_t and u_s are independently distributed for all $t \neq s$, so that $\mathrm{Cov}(u_t, u_s|X_t) = E(u_t u_s|X_t) = 0$.
3.7	The number of observations (n) must be greater than the number of regression coefficients estimated ($n > 2$ here).
3.8	For a given X_t, u_t is normally distributed so that $u_t|X_t \sim N(0, \sigma^2)$, which implies that $Y_t|X_t \sim N(\alpha + \beta X_t, \sigma^2)$.

Derivation of a Test Statistic

In this section, we show that the test statistic $t_c = (\hat{\beta} - \beta_0)/s_{\hat{\beta}}$, where β_0 is a constant, has the Student's t-distribution, under the null hypothesis, with $n - 2$ degrees of freedom (the d.f. is $n - 2$ here because we are estimating two parameters, α and β). Note that Assumption 3.7 is crucial to ensure that the d.f. are positive.

PROOF*

(Readers not interested in the formal derivation may skip this part.) First, it is possible to show the following property:

Property 3.4

> a. $\hat{\alpha}$ and $\hat{\beta}$ are distributed normally.
> b. $(\Sigma \, \hat{u}_i^2)/\sigma^2 = [(n - 2)\hat{\sigma}^2]/\sigma^2$ has a chi-square distribution with $n - 2$ d.f.
> c. $\hat{\alpha}$ and $\hat{\beta}$ are distributed independently of $\hat{\sigma}^2$.

Property 3.4a follows from the fact that $\hat{\alpha}$ and $\hat{\beta}$ are linear combinations of u_t and that u_t is normally distributed. For the formal proof of parts b and c, refer to Hogg and Craig (1978, pp. 296–298). Utilizing these results we have

$$\hat{\alpha} \sim N(\alpha, \sigma_{\hat{\alpha}}^2), \qquad \hat{\beta} \sim N(\beta, \sigma_{\hat{\beta}}^2), \qquad \frac{\Sigma \, \hat{u}_t^2}{\sigma^2} \sim \chi_{n-2}^2$$

where $\sigma_{\hat{\alpha}}^2$ and $\sigma_{\hat{\beta}}^2$ are the variances of $\hat{\alpha}$ and $\hat{\beta}$ given by Equations (3.19) and (3.20), respectively. By standardizing the distributions of the estimated parameters—that is, subtracting the mean and dividing by the standard deviation—we will get

$$\frac{(\hat{\alpha} - \alpha)}{\sigma_{\hat{\alpha}}} \sim N(0, 1), \qquad \frac{(\hat{\beta} - \beta)}{\sigma_{\hat{\beta}}} \sim N(0, 1), \qquad \frac{(n - 2)\hat{\sigma}^2}{\sigma^2} \sim \chi_{n-2}^2$$

In Section 2.7, the t-distribution was defined as the ratio of a standard normal to the square root of a chi-square independent of it, divided by its number of d.f. Applying this to $\hat{\beta}$ and using Equations (3.19) and (3.23), we obtain

$$t = \frac{(\hat{\beta} - \beta)}{\sigma_{\hat{\beta}}} \div \left[\frac{\hat{\sigma}^2}{\sigma^2} \right]^{1/2} = \frac{\sigma(\hat{\beta} - \beta)}{\hat{\sigma}\sigma_{\hat{\beta}}} = \frac{(\hat{\beta} - \beta)}{s_{\hat{\beta}}} \sim t_{n-2}$$

where

$$s_{\hat{\beta}} = \frac{\hat{\sigma}}{\sqrt{S_{xx}}} = \frac{\hat{\sigma}}{\sigma} \frac{\sigma}{\sqrt{S_{xx}}} = \frac{\hat{\sigma}\sigma_{\hat{\beta}}}{\sigma}$$

$s_{\hat{\beta}}$ is the estimated standard error of $\hat{\beta}$ given in Equation (3.23).

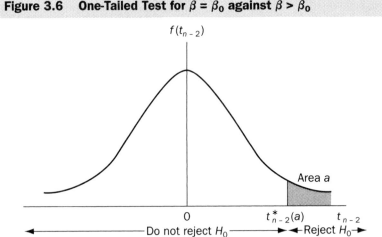

Figure 3.6   One-Tailed Test for $\beta = \beta_0$ against $\beta > \beta_0$

The above t is the test statistic based on which a decision rule is formulated. The test is known as the **t-test.** The steps for testing the desired hypothesis are given next, separately for two-tailed and one-tailed tests.

Decision Rule

ONE-TAILED *t*-TEST

Step 1 H_0: $\beta = \beta_0$, H_1: $\beta > \beta_0$.

Step 2   The test statistic is $t_c = (\hat{\beta} - \beta_0)/s_{\hat{\beta}}$, which can be calculated from the sample. Under the null hypothesis, it has the t-distribution with $n - 2$ d.f. If the calculated t_c is "large," we would suspect that β is probably not equal to β_0. This leads to the next step.

Step 3   In the t-table inside the front cover of the book, look up the entry for $n - 2$ d.f. and the given level of significance (say a) and find the point $t^*_{n-2}(a)$ such that $P(t > t^*) = a$ (t^* is known as the **critical value**).

Step 4   Reject H_0 if $t_c > t^*$. If the alternative had been $\beta < \beta_0$, the test criterion would have been to reject H_0 if $t_c < -t^*$.

This test is illustrated graphically in Figure 3.6 (we are using the symbol a for the level of significance in order to avoid confusion with the intercept term α). If the calculated t-statistic (t_c) falls in the shaded area of the figure (known as the **critical region**), then $t_c > t^*$. In that case, the null hypothesis is rejected and we conclude that β is *significantly greater than β_0*. The test for α is conducted similarly.

● **EXAMPLE 3.4**

In the home price example, $\beta_0 = 0$. Therefore, $t_c = \hat{\beta}/s_{\hat{\beta}}$; that is, the test statistic is simply the ratio of the estimated regression coefficient divided by its standard error.

This ratio is known as the *t*-statistic. The estimate is $\hat{\beta} = 0.13875$, and from Example 3.2, $s_{\hat{\beta}} = 0.01873$. Therefore, the calculated *t*-statistic is $t_c = 0.13875/0.01873 = 7.41$. The degrees of freedom are $n - 2 = 14 - 2 = 12$. Let the level of significance (referred to above as *a*) be 1 percent; that is, $a = 0.01$. From the *t*-table inside the front cover of this book, $t_{12}^{*}(0.01) = 2.681$. Because $t_c > t^{*}$, we reject H_0 and conclude, not surprisingly, that β is **significantly greater than zero** at the 1 percent level of significance. It should be noted that this coefficient is significant even at the 0.05 percent level of significance because $t_{12}^{*}(0.0005) = 4.318$.

To test H_0: $\alpha = 0$, the *t*-statistic for $\hat{\alpha}$ is given by $t_c = 52.351/37.285 = 1.404$ which is smaller than $t_{12}^{*}(0.05) = 1.782$. Hence, we cannot reject H_0 but instead conclude that α is **statistically not greater than zero** at the 5 percent level. The insignificance of $\hat{\alpha}$ points to two things. First, $X = 0$ is well outside the sample range and hence estimating $\hat{Y}$ when $X = 0$ will not be very reliable (more on this in Section 3.9). Second, as can be readily seen from Figure 3.1, the two-variable specification is inadequate for explaining the observed variation in price. It will be seen in Chapter 4 that $\hat{\alpha}$ captures the average effects of omitted variables and nonlinearities, in addition to the effect when X is zero. The net effect could very well make $\hat{\alpha}$ insignificant.

Some Cautions about the Use of the *t*-Test

Although the *t*-test is extremely useful in identifying whether or not a coefficient is statistically significant, it is easy to misunderstand the implications of the test. For instance, in Example 3.4 the *t*-test for α could not reject the null hypothesis that $\alpha = 0$. Does this test therefore "prove" that $\alpha = 0$? The answer is an emphatic no. All we can assert is that *in our data set and in the model specified here,* there is no evidence to refute the contention that $\alpha = 0$. In Chapter 4 we will encounter *t*-tests for several regression coefficients. If one of them is insignificant (that is, we cannot reject the hypothesis that it is zero), it does not mean that the corresponding variable has no effect on the dependent variable or that it is "unimportant." This point is discussed more fully in the next chapter. We will also see in Chapter 5 that when a model specification is changed, the significance of a coefficient might also change. Thus, one should be very careful in carrying out any hypothesis test and not jump to conclusions without subjecting the model and the analysis to further diagnostic tests in order to arrive at a robust conclusion (that is, one that is stable across model specifications).

The *p*-Value Approach to Hypothesis Testing

The *t*-tests can also be carried out in an equivalent way. To motivate this alternative method, known as the ***p*-value approach,** recall that in Example 3.4 the *t*-test for β was first carried out at the 1 percent level of significance and found to be statistically significant (that is, we rejected the null hypothesis that $\beta = 0$). We then showed that it was significantly different from zero even if the level was lowered to 0.05 percent. In contrast, the *t*-test for α was conducted at 5 percent, and we concluded that it was not significantly different from zero (that is, we could not reject the null hypothesis that $\alpha = 0$). If a higher level such as 10 percent had been chosen, we would have rejected the null (verify it). A natural question that arises is, "What is the *smallest level* (known as the *p*-value) at which we would reject H_0: $\alpha = 0$ when the observed *t*-statistic is t_c?" After all, the levels chosen here, namely, 0.01, 0.0005, 0.05, and 0.10, are quite arbitrary. The level of significance is the area to the right of the critical value (referred to earlier as t^*) in the *t*-distribution with $n - 2$ d.f. Recall from Section 2.8 that it is also the probability of a Type I error, that of rejecting a true hypothesis. If t^* is set at any value above the observed t_c, then we would not reject the null hypothesis (see Step 4 of the decision rule given earlier). Therefore, to reject the null, the largest value for t^* must be t_c and the corresponding level is the area to the right of t_c. Thus,

$$p\text{-Value} = P(t > t_c \mid H_0)$$

is also the smallest probability of a Type I error that corresponds to our observed t_c. It is then clear that another way of testing is to compute this *p*-value and ask the question whether this smallest probability of a Type I error is something we would tolerate (say, below the level *a*). If so, we could "safely" reject the null. If not, we would not reject the null.

The modified steps for the *p*-value approach are as follows:

Step 3a   Calculate the probability under H_0 (denoted as *p-value*) that *t* is greater than t_c; that is, compute the area to the right of the *calculated* t_c.

Step 4a   Reject H_0 and conclude that the coefficient is significant if the *p*-value is *less than* the given level of significance (*a*).

To see the equivalence of the two approaches, we note from Figure 3.7 that if $P(t > t_c|H_0)$ is *less than* the level *a*, then the point corresponding to t_c must necessarily be to the *right* of $t^*_{n-2}(a)$. This means that t_c will fall in the rejection region. Similarly, if $P(t > t_c|H_0) > a$, then t_c must be to the left of t^* and hence fall into the nonrejection region.

Figure 3.7   *p*-Value Approach to Hypothesis Testing

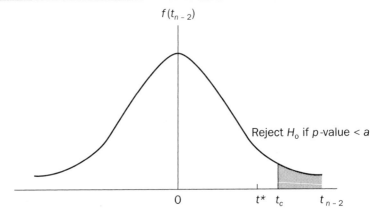

In summary, β is judged to be significantly greater than β_0 if the t-statistic is high or the p-value is low, how high or low being determined by the investigator. The traditional method of hypothesis testing requires one to look up tabulated values for the critical t^*. The p-value approach, however, requires a computer program that calculates the areas in the tail for any given value of t_c. More and more computer programs are providing these p-values and hence this method is not hard to implement. Be careful, however, to check whether the reported p-value measures one tail or both tails.

● EXAMPLE 3.4A

To apply the p-value approach to the home price example, we calculate the probability that t is greater than the observed value of 7.41 for β. Using GRETL, this was calculated as a value less than 0.0001 (refer to the output from Practice Computer Session 3.1). This means that, if we reject the null hypothesis, there is a less than 0.01 percent chance of making a mistake of Type I, and hence it is "safe" to reject H_0 and conclude that β is significantly greater than zero. For the parameter α, the p-value is 0.093; that is, $P(t > 1.404) = 0.093$. Now if $H_0: \alpha = 0$ is rejected, the probability of making a type I error is 9.3 percent, which is higher than 5 percent. Therefore, we cannot reject H_0 at 5 percent, which means that we conclude, as we did before, that (at the 5 percent level of significance) α is statistically not greater than zero. We see from this that the p-value approach has an advantage, namely, we know the precise level at which a coefficient is significant and can judge whether this level is low enough to justify rejecting H_0. After all, there is nothing sacred about values such as 0.01, 0.05, and 0.10.

Two-Tailed t-Test

The procedure for a two-sided alternative is quite similar. The steps are as follows:

Step 1 $H_0: \beta = \beta_0$, $H_1: \beta \neq \beta_0$.

Step 2   The test statistic is $t_c = (\hat{\beta} - \beta_0)/s_{\hat{\beta}}$, which is the same as before. Under the null hypothesis, t_c is distributed as t_{n-2}.

Step 3   In the t-table inside the front cover, look up the entry for $n - 2$ d.f. and the given level of significance (say a), and find the point $t_{n-2}^*(a/2)$ such that $P(t > t^*) = a/2$ (one-half of the level of significance).

Step 3a   To use the p-value approach, calculate

$$p\text{-value} = P(t > t_c \quad \text{or} \quad t < -t_c | H_0) = 2P(t > |t_c| \text{ under } H_0)$$

because of the symmetry of the t-distribution around the origin.

Step 4   Reject H_0 if $|t_c| > t^*$, and conclude that β is **significantly different from β_0 at the level a.**

Step 4a   In the case of the p-value approach, reject H_0 if p-value $< a$, the level of significance.

The two-tailed test is illustrated graphically in Figure 3.8. The degrees of freedom here also are $n - 2$. If the calculated t-statistic (t_c) falls in the shaded area in

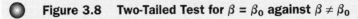

Figure 3.8   Two-Tailed Test for $\beta = \beta_0$ against $\beta \neq \beta_0$

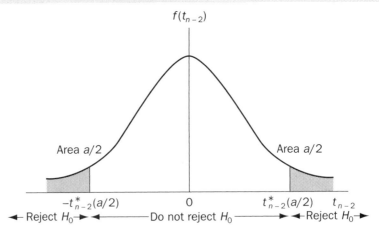

the figure, the null hypothesis is rejected, and we conclude that β is significantly different from β_0. A critical value of $t^* = 2$ is often used as a rule of thumb to judge the significance of a t-statistic at 5 percent (for a two-tailed test). This is because t^* is nearly 2 for degrees of freedom over 25.

EXAMPLE 3.5

The calculated t_c for the home price example is the same as before; that is, it is still 7.41 for $\hat{\beta}$ and 1.404 for $\hat{\alpha}$. From the t-table, $t^*_{12}(0.005) = 3.055$, which means that the area in both tails corresponding to 3.055 is 0.01. Because $t_c > t^*$ for $\hat{\beta}$, we reject H_0 here also and conclude that β is **significantly different from zero** at the 1 percent level of significance. For $\hat{\alpha}$, $t^*_{12}(0.025) = 2.179$, which is greater than t_c. Therefore, we cannot reject the null hypothesis here either (note that we are using a 5 percent test for α). From Step 3a, the p-value for $\hat{\alpha} = 2P(t > 1.404) = 0.186$ (note that the p-value corresponding to t_c for the two-sided case is twice that for the one-sided alternative). Because a Type I error of 18.6 percent is unacceptably high, we cannot reject H_0: $\alpha = 0$. It follows that α is not statistically significant, but β is.

PRACTICE PROBLEM 3.4

For the home price example, test the hypothesis H_0: $\beta = 0.1$ against H_1: $\beta \neq 0.1$ at the levels of significance 0.05 and 0.01.

PRACTICE PROBLEM 3.5[†]

Show that if a coefficient is significant at the 1 percent level, it will also be significant at any level higher than that.

● **PRACTICE PROBLEM 3.6**

Show that if a coefficient is insignificant at the 10 percent level, it will not be significant at any level lower than that.

Testing σ^2

Although a test for the significance of the error variance σ^2 is not common, we present it here for completeness. The steps are as follows:

Step 1 H_0: $\sigma^2 = \sigma_0^2$, H_1: $\sigma^2 > \sigma_0^2$.

Step 2   The test statistic here is $Q_c = (n - 2)\dfrac{\hat{\sigma}^2}{\sigma_0^2}$. From Property 3.4b, the distribution of this, under the null hypothesis, is chi-squared with $n - 2$ d.f. If Q is "large," we would suspect that σ^2 is probably not equal to σ_0^2.

Step 3   From the chi-square table inside the front cover, look up the value $Q_{n-2}^*(a)$ such that the area to the right is a.

Step 4   Reject H_0 at the level a if $Q_c > Q_{n-2}^*(a)$.

The reason that this test is not common is that, in general, an investigator does not have a priori information about which value of σ_0^2 to use in the null hypothesis.

Test of Goodness of Fit

It is possible to conduct a formal test for the goodness of fit. Let ρ be the population correlation coefficient between X and Y defined in Equation (2.7). As seen in Equation (2.11), an estimate of ρ^2 is given by $r_{xy}^2 = S_{xy}^2/(S_{xx}S_{yy})$, where S_{xx} and S_{xy} are defined in Equations (3.9) and (3.10) and

$$S_{yy} = \sum Y_t^2 - \left[\frac{\left(\sum Y_t\right)^2}{n}\right] = \sum(Y_t - \overline{Y})^2 = \text{TSS} \tag{3.28}$$

It is shown in Section 3.A.10 that r_{xy}^2 is identical to R^2 (this holds in the simple regression model only). In Section 2.8 on testing hypotheses, we presented the method of testing for the hypothesis that X and Y are uncorrelated. The test is known as the **F-test.** The steps for the test are as follows:

Step 1 H_0: $\rho_{xy} = 0$, H_1: $\rho_{xy} \neq 0$.

Step 2   The test statistic is $F_c = R^2(n - 2)/(1 - R^2)$. It can also be calculated as $F_c = \text{RSS}\,(n - 2)/\text{ESS}$. Under the null hypothesis, it has an F-distribution with 1 d.f. for the numerator and $n - 2$ d.f. for the denominator.

Step 3   Look up in the F-table the entry corresponding to 1 d.f. for the numerator and $n - 2$ d.f. for the denominator, for the point $F_{1,n-2}^*(a)$, such that the area to the right of F^* is a, the level of significance.

Step 4   Reject the null hypothesis (at the level a) if $F_c > F^*$.

It should be noted that the null hypothesis above is not valid when there are several Xs. It will be seen in Chapter 4 that the test is still F but H_0 will be different.

In the home price example, $R^2 = 0.82052$. $F_c = 0.82052(14 - 2)/(1 - 0.82052) = 54.86$. From Example 3.5, ESS = 18,274, and RSS = TSS − ESS = 83,541. Therefore, F_c could also be calculated using the alternative formula in Step 2: $F_c = 83,541(14 - 2)/18,274 = 54.86$. The degrees of freedom are 1 for the numerator and 12 for the denominator. For a 5 percent level, $a = 0.05$ and hence $F_{1,12}^*(0.05) = 4.75$ from Table A.4b. Because $F_c > F^*$, we reject (at the 5 percent level) the null hypothesis that X and Y are uncorrelated. In fact, because $F_c > F_{1,12}^*(0.01) = 9.33$ from Table A.4a, the null hypothesis is rejected at the 1 percent level also. Thus, even though the value of R^2 is well below 1, it is significantly different from zero.

Presentation of Regression Results

The results of a regression analysis are presented in a variety of ways. A very common way is to write the estimated equation with the t-statistics below each regression coefficient, as in the following:

$$\widehat{PRICE} = 52.351 + 0.13875\ SQFT$$
$$\underset{(1.404)}{} \quad \underset{(7.41)}{}$$

$$R^2 = 0.821 \qquad d.f. = 12 \qquad \hat{\sigma} = 39.023$$

Another form is to have the standard error below a regression coefficient:

$$\widehat{PRICE} = 52.351 + 0.13875\ SQFT$$
$$\underset{(37.29)}{} \quad \underset{(0.019)}{}$$

A preferred form is

$$\widehat{PRICE} = 52.351 + 0.13875\ SQFT$$
$$\underset{(37.29)}{} \quad \underset{(0.019)}{}$$
$$\underset{[0.093]}{} \quad \underset{[<0.0001]}{}$$

If several alternative models have been estimated, it is more convenient to present the results in a tabular form, as in Table 4.2.

The decomposition of the total sum of squares into its components is often summarized in the form known as the **analysis of variance (ANOVA)** table (Table 3.3).

● **Table 3.3   Analysis of Variance Table**

Source	Sum of Squares	d.f.	Mean Square (SS ÷ d.f.)	F
Regression (RSS)	$\sum (\hat{Y}_t - \bar{Y})^2 = 83,541$	1	83,541	$\dfrac{RSS(n-2)}{ESS} = 54.86$
Error (ESS)	$\sum \hat{u}_t^2 = 18,274$	$n - 2 = 12$	1,523	
Total (TSS)	$\sum (Y_t - \bar{Y})^2 = 101,815$	$n - 1 = 13$	7,832	

● 3.6 Scaling and Units of Measurement

Suppose we had measured PRICE in actual dollars rather than in thousands of dollars. In Table 3.1 the column for PRICE would have had entries such as 199,900, 228,000, and so on. How would the estimates of the regression coefficients, their standard errors, R^2, and so on be affected by this change in units? This question is examined here for measuring both PRICE and SQFT in different units. First we reproduce the model here.

$$PRICE = \alpha + \beta SQFT + u$$

Let PRICE* be price in actual dollars. Then PRICE* = 1,000 PRICE. Multiply every term in the equation by 1,000, and substitute PRICE* in the left-hand side. We then obtain

$$PRICE* = 1,000\alpha + 1,000\beta SQFT + 1,000u = \alpha* + \beta*SQFT + u*$$

If we apply the OLS method to this equation and minimize $\Sigma(u_i^*)^2$, we would get estimates of $\alpha*$ and $\beta*$. It is readily seen that the new regression coefficients would be equal to the old values multiplied by 1,000. Thus, *changing the scale of measurement of only the dependent variable in a linear regression model results in the corresponding scaling of each of the regression coefficients.* Because $u* = 1,000u$, the residuals and standard errors will also be multiplied by 1,000. The sum of squares will be multiplied by a million (1,000 squared). It should be noted that the t-statistics, F-statistics, and R^2 will not be affected because they involve ratios in which the scale factor cancels out.

What are the consequences of changing the scale of an *independent variable?* Suppose SQFT was measured in hundreds of square feet rather than in actual square feet, but PRICE was measured in thousands as before. Let SQFT' be square feet in hundreds. Then SQFT = 100SQFT'. Substituting this in the basic model, we get

$$PRICE = \alpha + \beta 100SQFT' + u = \alpha + \beta'SQFT' + u$$

It is evident from this that if we regress PRICE against a constant and SQFT', the only coefficient that will be affected is that of SQFT. If β' is the coefficient of SQFT', then $\hat{\beta}' = 100\hat{\beta}$. Its standard error will also be multiplied by 100. But all other measures—ESS, the t-statistics, R^2, and F-statistics in particular—will be unaffected. In conclusion, *if the scale of measurement of a single independent variable is changed in a linear regression model, its regression coefficient and the corresponding standard errors are affected by the same scale but all other statistics are unchanged.*

There is a particularly good reason to scale values so that the resulting numbers are not large or too small and are similar to those of other variables. This is because large numbers cause overflow errors and small numbers cause round-off errors, especially when sums of squares are computed, which adversely affect the accuracy of results.

To obtain a practical understanding of the consequences of changing units, try Practice Computer Section 3.2 in Appendix D.

● PRACTICE PROBLEM 3.7

Suppose you define a new variable, $X^* = \text{SQFT} - 1,000$ (that is, X^* is the square feet in excess of 1,000), and estimate the model $\text{PRICE} = a + bX^* + v$. Explain how you can derive $\hat{a}$ and $\hat{b}$ from $\hat{\alpha}$ and $\hat{\beta}$, *without really estimating the new model*.

● 3.7 Application: Estimating an Engel Curve Relation between Expenditure on Health Care and Income

In this section, we present a "walk-through" application in which the two-variable regression model is illustrated. The data used are a cross section for the 50 states and the District of Columbia ($n = 51$) and were obtained from the 1995 *Statistical Abstract of the U.S.* The actual data values are in the file DATA3-2. The variables are as follows:

> EXPHLTH = Aggregate expenditures (in billions of dollars) on health care in the state in 1993, Table 153, page 111, range 0.998–9.029.
>
> INCOME = Personal income (in billions of dollars) in the state in 1993, Table 712, page 460, range 9.3–64.1.

The model is the Engel curve derived in Example 1.4 and is applied to the total expenditure on health care in the United States as a function of total personal income. Practice Computer Session 3.3 (see Appendix Table D.1) has the instructions to generate the results. An annotated version of the computer printout is presented in Table 3.4. You are encouraged to study the annotations carefully and to use your own regression program to reproduce the results. The following is the estimated model along with *t*-statistics (in parentheses) and *p*-values (in square brackets):

$$\widehat{\text{EXPHLTH}} = 0.1765 + 0.1417 \ \text{INCOME}$$
$$\underset{[0.707]}{\underset{(0.378)}{}} \quad \underset{[<0.0001]}{\underset{(49.272)}{}}$$

$$R^2 = 0.98 \qquad \text{d.f.} = 49 \qquad F = 2,428 \qquad \hat{\sigma} = 2.547$$

The model fits very well because 98 percent of the variation in health care expenditures is explained by income. As explained in Table 3.4, the constant term is statistically insignificant and is consistent with the theoretical specification derived in Example 1.4, which indicated that $\alpha = 0$. Because EXPHLTH and INCOME are both measured in billions of dollars, the interpretation of $\hat{\beta} = 0.1417$ is that for each additional \$100 billion increase in aggregate personal income, the increase in total expenditures on health care is expected to be, on average, \$14.17 billion. For other details, see the annotations in Table 3.4.

● **Table 3.4   Annotated Computer Output for Section 3.7**

Comments are set in a typeface different than that used for the computer output.

```
exphlth = Aggregate expenditures on health care in a State
income = Personal income in the State

Both variables are measured in billions of dollars.
```

(The graph of expenditures against income shows a close relation)

```
 exphlth
94.178  |                                                        o
        |
        |
78.648  +
        |
        |
        |
        |                                              o
52.7647 +
        |                                    o
        |                               o
        |                          o
        |                     o  o
26.8813 +                o
        |            o      o
        |                o
        |         o
        |     o  ooo
        |   oooo      o
 0.998  +ooo
        |+---------+---------+---------+---------+---------+---------+
         9.3                         income                     683.5
```

```
MODEL 1: OLS estimates using the 51 observations 1-51
Dependent variable: exphlth
```

VARIABLE	COEFFICIENT	STDERROR	T STAT	2Prob(t > |T|)	
0) const	0.1765	0.4675	0.378	0.707414	
2) income	0.1417	0.0029	49.272	0.000000	***

(The estimated income coefficient is $\hat{\beta} = 0.1417$, and the estimated constant term is $\hat{\alpha} = 0.1765$. The t-statistic (coefficient divided by stderror) for income is 49.272, which is extremely significant. 2Prob $(t > |T|)$ is the area on both tails of the t-distribution corresponding to the t-statistic and is the p-value or the probability of Type I error (for a two-tailed test). If the p-value is low by conventional measures (in this case less than 0.0001), we are "safe" in rejecting the null hypothesis that

(continued)

⬤   **Table 3.4   (continued)**

$\beta = 0$ and concluding that the income coefficient is significantly different from zero. The *p*-value of 0.707414 for the constant term suggests that, if we reject the null hypothesis that $\alpha = 0$, we are likely to make a Type I error 70.7 percent of the time. Since this is considerably higher than what one would typically choose as the upper limit, we would not want to reject the null hypothesis. We thus conclude that the constant term is not significantly different from zero. Note that in Example 1.4, the theoretical derivation of the Engel curve suggested that there was no constant term. The insignificance of the estimated constant term is consistent with this theoretical result. The marginal propensity to spend on health care out of income is 0.1417; that is, for each $100 increase in income, individuals are expected to spend, on average, $14.17 on health care.

The value of R-squared shown below indicates that 98 percent of the variation in expenditures is explained by income. The difference between Adjusted and Unadjusted R-squared in the output below is explained in Chapter 4 as are the model selection statistics.

The Durbin–Watson statistic and the first-order serial correlation coefficient are explained in Chapter 9, which deals with the violation of Assumption 3.6 that the error terms of two observations are uncorrelated. The mean of the dependent variable is $\overline{Y}$ and S.D. is the standard deviation s_Y.)

```
Mean of dep. var.            15.069 S.D. of dep. variable          17.927
Error Sum of Sq (ESS)    317.8986 Std Err of Resid. (sgmahat)      2.5471
Unadjusted R-squared          0.980 Adjusted R-squared              0.980
F-statistic (1, 49)         2427.71 p-value for F()              0.000000
Durbin-Watson stat.           2.209 First-order autocorr. coeff   -0.121

MODEL SELECTION STATISTICS

SGMASQ    6.48773      AIC        6.74188      FPE       6.74215
HQ        6.9399       SCHWARZ    7.27247      SHIBATA   6.72219
GCV       6.75253      RICE       6.7638
```

ut = estimated residuals (denoted as $\hat{u}_t$)
yhat = predicted values of dependent variable = observed exphlth − residual (= $\hat{Y}_t$)
    fit = predicted values obtained by the "fit" command in GRETL
    yf = predicted values obtained by the "fcast" command in GRETL

Note that in the following table yhat, autofit, and yf are identical, as they should be:

Obs	exphlth	yhat	autofit	yf	ut
1	0.998	1.49386	1.49386	1.49386	-0.49586172
2	1.499	1.763	1.763	1.763	-0.26400087
3	4.285	2.59875	2.59875	2.59875	1.68625
4	1.573	2.1313	2.1313	2.1313	-0.55829655
5	2.021	1.72051	1.72051	1.72051	0.30049479
6	2.26	2.34377	2.34377	2.34377	-0.083774825
7	1.953	1.98964	1.98964	1.98964	-0.036644364
8	2.103	2.24462	2.24462	2.24462	-0.14161839
9	3.428	3.17952	3.17952	3.17952	0.24847729

Table 3.4 (continued)

Obs	exphlth	yhat	autofit	yf	ut
10	2.277	2.91038	2.91038	2.91038	−0.63338356
11	3.452	3.73197	3.73197	3.73197	−0.27996623
12	3.485	4.05777	4.05777	4.05777	−0.57276626
13	3.433	3.47699	3.47699	3.47699	−0.043992302
14	3.747	4.65271	4.65271	4.65271	−0.90570543
15	4.4	4.66687	4.66687	4.66687	−0.26687065
16	3.878	3.91611	3.91611	3.91611	−0.038114075
17	5.197	4.34107	4.34107	4.34107	0.85592937
18	4.118	4.42606	4.42606	4.42606	−0.30806194
19	6.111	5.6726	5.6726	5.6726	0.43839884
20	6.903	7.3016	7.3016	7.3016	−0.39860129
21	6.187	5.68677	5.68677	5.68677	0.50023362
22	7.341	7.48575	7.48575	7.48575	−0.14474913
23	7.999	8.53398	8.53398	8.53398	−0.53497529
24	8.041	7.96737	7.96737	7.96737	0.073633445
25	12.216	13.251	13.251	13.251	−1.03499
26	10.066	11.0271	11.0271	11.0271	−0.96105374
27	9.029	8.84561	8.84561	8.84561	0.1833899
28	10.384	9.2564	9.2564	9.2564	1.1276
29	10.635	10.2763	10.2763	10.2763	0.35870284
30	12.06	10.3188	10.3188	10.3188	1.74121
31	13.014	10.2763	10.2763	10.2763	2.7377
32	14.194	13.6193	13.6193	13.6193	0.57471128
33	15.154	16.9623	16.9623	16.9623	−1.80828
34	14.502	14.3275	14.3275	14.3275	0.17445035
35	16.203	13.4776	13.4776	13.4776	2.72536
36	15.949	14.6817	14.6817	14.6817	1.26732
37	15.129	16.3957	16.3957	16.3957	−1.26667
38	16.401	15.7016	15.7016	15.7016	0.69942416
39	23.421	20.9852	20.9852	20.9852	2.4358
40	6.682	20.0361	20.0361	20.0361	−13.3541
41	20.104	19.0021	19.0021	19.0021	1.10193
42	18.241	18.5629	18.5629	18.5629	−0.32194997
43	25.741	30.0934	30.0934	30.0934	−4.35244
44	27.136	27.7562	27.7562	27.7562	−0.62017675
45	33.456	31.0425	31.0425	31.0425	2.41349
46	34.747	37.516	37.516	37.516	−2.76901
47	41.521	36.4395	36.4395	36.4395	5.08154
48	44.811	40.3207	40.3207	40.3207	4.49027
49	49.816	49.0465	49.0465	49.0465	0.7694999
50	67.033	64.005	64.005	64.005	3.02803
51	94.178	96.9958	96.9958	96.9958	−2.81776

3.8   Confidence Intervals

It was pointed out in Section 2.9 that one way to take directly into account the fact that α and β are estimated with uncertainty is to compute confidence intervals. Thus, for example, rather than say that $\hat{\beta} = 0.139$ we might want to say that with a certain probability, $\hat{\beta}$ will lie between 0.09 and 0.17. From the derivation of the test statistics in Section 3.5,

$$\frac{\hat{\alpha} - \alpha}{s_{\hat{\alpha}}} \sim t_{n-2} \quad \text{and} \quad \frac{\hat{\beta} - \beta}{s_{\hat{\beta}}} \sim t_{n-2}$$

Let $t_{n-2}^*(0.025)$ be the point on the *t*-distribution with $n - 2$ d.f. such that $P(t > t^*) = 0.025$. This implies that $P(-t^* \leq t \leq t^*) = 0.95$.

$$P\left(-t^* \leq \frac{\hat{\alpha} - \alpha}{s_{\hat{\alpha}}} \leq t^*\right) = 0.95 = P(\hat{\alpha} - t^* s_{\hat{\alpha}} \leq \alpha \leq \hat{\alpha} + t^* s_{\hat{\alpha}})$$

It follows from this that the 95 percent confidence intervals for α and β are, respectively, $\hat{\alpha} \pm t^* s_{\hat{\alpha}}$ and $\hat{\beta} \pm t^* s_{\hat{\beta}}$.

EXAMPLE 3.7

In the home price example, the standard errors for $\hat{\alpha}$ and $\hat{\beta}$ are $s_{\hat{\alpha}} = 37.285$ and $s_{\hat{\beta}} = 0.18373$. Also, from the *t*-table, $t_{12}^*(0.025) = 2.179$. The 95 percent confidence intervals are therefore

$$52.351 \pm (2.179 \times 37.285) = (-28.893, 133.595) \quad \text{for } \alpha$$

$$0.13875 \pm (2.179 \times 0.18373) = (0.099, 0.179) \quad \text{for } \beta$$

Note that these confidence intervals are quite wide. This is an indication of the poor fit of the simple linear regression model specified here. A better specification of the model should make confidence intervals narrower.

PRACTICE PROBLEM 3.8

Derive the confidence intervals for α and β in Application Section 3.7.

3.9   Forecasting

As stated earlier, a common use of the regression model is for forecasting (this topic is discussed more fully in Chapter 11). In the house example, we could ask what the predicted sale price of a home with a living area of 2,000 square feet will be. The estimated regression model is $\hat{Y} = 52.351 + 0.13875X$. Thus, when $X = 2,000$, the forecast of Y is $52.351 + (2,000 \times 0.13875) = 329.851$. Because price is measured in

thousands of dollars, this forecast is also in thousands of dollars. Thus, according to the model, the estimated *average* price of a 2,000-square-foot house is $329,851. It is evident that, in general, if X takes the value X_0, the predicted value of Y_0 is given by $\hat{Y}_0 = \hat{\alpha} + \hat{\beta}X_0$. The conditional mean of the predictor of Y given $X = X_0$ is

$$E(\hat{Y}|X = X_0) = E(\hat{\alpha}) + X_0 E(\hat{\beta}) = \alpha + \beta X_0 = E(Y|X = X_0)$$

Thus, $\hat{Y}_0$ is an unbiased conditional predictor of the average sale price given X_0.

Confidence Interval for the Mean Predictor

Because α and β are estimated with imprecision, the predictor $\hat{Y}_0$ is also subject to error. To take account of this, we compute a standard error and confidence interval for the mean predictor. The following is an estimator of the variance of the predictor (see Section 3.A.11 for proof):

$$s_{\hat{Y}_0}^2 = \hat{\sigma}^2 \left[\frac{1}{n} + \frac{(X_0 - \bar{X})^2}{S_{xx}} \right] \tag{3.29}$$

The confidence interval of the mean forecast is given by

$$[\hat{Y}_0 - t^* s_{\hat{Y}_0}, \ \hat{Y}_0 + t^* s_{\hat{Y}_0}]$$

where t^* is the critical value of the t-distribution obtained earlier. Note that when X_0 is farther away from the mean $\bar{X}$, $s_{\hat{Y}_0}$ is larger and the corresponding confidence interval is wider. This means that if a forecast is made too far outside the sample range, the reliability of the forecast decreases. If $X_0 = \bar{X}$, then the confidence interval has the smallest length. Figure 3.9 gives an idea of the "confidence band" for various values of X_0.

Confidence Interval for the Point Forecast

The sample variance given in the previous section is that for predicting the mean. We would also like the variance of the prediction error for the true value Y_0 that corresponds to X_0. This is derived in Appendix Section 3.A.12 as follows:

$$s_{\hat{u}_0}^2 = \text{Var}(\hat{u}_0) = \hat{\sigma}^2 \left[1 + \frac{1}{n} + \frac{(X_0 - \bar{X})^2}{S_{xx}} \right] > s_{\hat{Y}_0}^2 \tag{3.30}$$

where $\hat{u}_0 = Y_0 - \hat{Y}_0$ is the error in the point forecast. The confidence interval is obtained by using $s_{\hat{u}_0}$ instead of $s_{\hat{Y}_0}$. When the sample size is large, the second and third terms above will be negligible, with $s_{\hat{u}_0}$ nearly equal to $\hat{\sigma}$. Also, t^* will be close to 2 for a 95 percent confidence level. Therefore, a large sample confidence interval is $\hat{Y}_0 \pm 2\hat{\sigma}$.

● EXAMPLE 3.8

In the home price example, we have $s_{\hat{Y}_0}^2 = 111.555$ and $s_{\hat{u}_0}^2 = 1634.353$, and the corresponding confidence intervals for $X_0 = 2,000$ are, respectively, (307, 353) and

⬤ Figure 3.9   Confidence Interval Band for Forecast

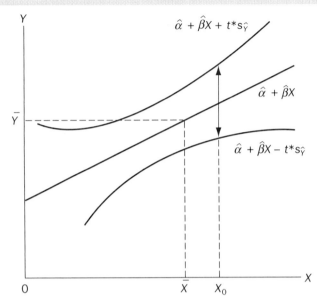

(242, 418). The large sample confidence interval is (252, 408). (See Practice Computer Session 3.4 to reproduce these results.)

Which of these two types of confidence intervals should one choose? Because the main interest is in the forecast error with respect to the true Y_0, Equation (3.30) is to be preferred. Note that this confidence interval is much wider than that based on Equation (3.29).

Comparison of Forecasts

Economic and business analysts often use more than one model to generate forecasts. A common measure used to compare the forecasting performance of different models is the **mean squared error** (or sometimes its square root, called the **root mean squared error**).

Let Y_t^f be the forecast of the dependent variable for the observation t, and Y_t be the actual value. The mean squared error is computed as

$$\text{MSE} = \frac{\sum (Y_t^f - Y_t)^2}{n - 2} \qquad \text{RMSE} = \sqrt{\text{MSE}}$$

If two different models are used to predict Y, the one with a smaller MSE is judged to be superior for forecasting purposes.

Another useful measure is the **mean absolute percent error (MAPE)** given by

$$\text{MAPE} = \frac{1}{n} \sum 100 \, \frac{|Y_t - Y_t^f|}{Y_t}$$

which is meaningful only if all the Ys are positive (see Application Section 3.11). Alternatively, we could compute the **mean squared percentage error (MSPE)** or its square root.

$$\text{MSPE} = \frac{1}{n} \sum \left[100 \frac{Y_t - Y_t^f}{Y_t} \right]^2 \qquad \text{RMSPE} = \sqrt{\text{MSPE}}$$

Yet another method of evaluating a model and its forecasting ability is to carry out a **postsample forecast.** According to this, the analyst would not use the last few observations (for example, the last 10 percent of the observations) in estimating the model, but use the parameter estimates from the first set of observations to predict Y_t for the reserved sample. We can then compute MSE and MAPE for the postsample period. The model that has lower values for these measures would be a better model for forecasting purposes.

3.10 Causality in a Regression Model

In specifying the model as $Y = \alpha + \beta X + u$, we implicitly assumed that X *causes Y*. Although R^2 measures the goodness of fit, it cannot be used to *identify causality*. In other words, the fact that X and Y are highly correlated does not indicate whether changes in X cause changes in Y or vice versa. For example, the correlation coefficient between Australia's kangaroo population and its human population might be quite high. Does that mean that changes in one variable cause changes in the other? Clearly not, because what we have is a case of **spurious correlation.** If we regress one of the variables against the other, we will have a **spurious regression.** As a more realistic example, suppose we regress the number of thefts (Y) in a city against a constant term and the number of police officers (X) and then observe that the estimated slope coefficient is positive, indicating a positive correlation between X and Y. Does this mean that increasing the number of police officers increases theft, therefore implying a policy to reduce the police force? That conclusion is clearly unacceptable. What might be happening is that the causation is reversed; that is, a city employs more police officers because of an increase in thefts, and hence it would make more sense to regress X against Y instead. In reality, however, the two variables would be **jointly determined,** and therefore we should specify two equations, one with Y on X and other variables and the other with X on Y and other variables. This *simultaneous* determination of variables is discussed in detail in Chapter 13. It will be seen there that estimates obtained by ignoring simultaneity will be biased and inconsistent. It is also possible that observed high correlation between X and Y might be due entirely to other variables and neither of them might be directly causing the other. These examples stress the importance of carefully thinking through what the underlying behavioral mechanism is, that is, what the **data-generating process (DGP)** is, and formulating equations appropriately. Economic theory, the investigator's own knowledge of the underlying behavior, past experience, and so on must suggest how a model should be specified. It is, however, possible to test for the apparent direction of causation (more on this in Chapter 10). The reader is referred to the papers by Granger (1969) and Sims (1972) for details.

As an illustration of the importance of correctly specifying causality, suppose we reversed X and Y and estimated the model

$$X_t = \alpha^* + \beta^* Y_t + v_t \tag{3.1'}$$

Would we get the same fitted straight line as before? The answer, in general, is no, because the least squares procedure applied to Equation (3.1) minimizes the sum of squares of vertical deviations from the straight line (see Figure 3.10). In contrast, the reverse straight line minimizes the sum of squares of horizontal deviations v_t. Solving for Y_t in terms of X_t, Equation (3.1') can be rewritten as follows:

$$Y_t = -\left(\frac{\alpha^*}{\beta^*}\right) + \left(\frac{1}{\beta^*}\right)X_t - \left(\frac{v_t}{\beta^*}\right) = \alpha' + \beta' X_t + v_t'$$

Minimizing $\Sigma \hat{u}_t^2$, as was done for Equation (3.1), and minimizing $\Sigma \hat{v}_t^2$ will generally give different answers. More specifically, the estimated value of β' will be different from that of β from Equation (3.1).

● **EXAMPLE 3.9**

The estimated relation when $\Sigma \hat{u}_t^2$ was minimized (see Practice Computer Session 3.5) was

$$\widehat{\text{PRICE}} = 52.351 + 0.13875 \text{ SQFT}$$

● **Figure 3.10 Minimizing Vertical versus Horizontal Sums of Squares**

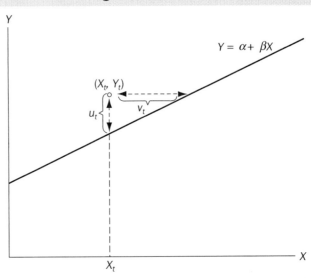

When the causation is reversed and $\Sigma \hat{v}_t^2$ is minimized, we get

$$\widehat{\text{SQFT}} = 33.385 + 5.91366 \text{ PRICE}$$

Inverting the second estimated relation and writing $\widehat{\text{PRICE}}$ as a function of SQFT, we have

$$\widehat{\text{PRICE}} = -\frac{33.385}{5.91366} + \frac{1}{5.91366} \text{ SQFT} = -5.645 + 0.169 \, \text{SQFT}$$

We note that the sign of the constant term is reversed and that the slope term is quite different.

Under what conditions will the two estimated lines be identical? To answer this, first apply OLS to Equation (3.1$'$); that is, minimize $\Sigma \hat{v}_t^2$. Reversing X and Y in Equation (3.12), we have

$$\hat{\beta}* = \frac{S_{xy}}{S_{yy}} = \frac{1}{\hat{\beta}'}$$

and hence $\hat{\beta}' = S_{yy}/S_{xy}$. The least squares estimator that minimizes $\Sigma \hat{u}_t^2$ is $\hat{\beta} = S_{xy}/S_{xx}$. For $\hat{\beta}'$ to be equal to $\hat{\beta}$, the condition is

$$\frac{S_{xy}}{S_{xx}} = \frac{S_{yy}}{S_{xy}} \quad \text{or} \quad \frac{S_{xy}^2}{S_{xx}S_{yy}} = 1$$

But the left-hand side of the second equation is r_{xy}^2, the square of the simple correlation between X and Y (defined in Equation 2.11). Thus, the required condition is that X and Y must be perfectly correlated. Property 2.8d stated that if there is a perfect correlation between two variables, then there must be an exact linear relationship between them. Hence, the fit between X and Y must be perfect in order for us to get the same fitted straight line whether we apply OLS to Equation (3.1) or to (3.1$'$). In general, the correlation between X and Y will not be perfect, and hence we will not get the same straight line. This stresses the importance of specifying the direction of causation appropriately rather than blindly choosing an X and a Y.

As illustrated earlier with the crime example, the causation can also go both ways, a situation known as **feedback.** The price and quantity of a good are also examples of this. Because price and quantity are jointly determined by the interaction of demand and supply, each can influence the other. Similarly, there is feedback between aggregate income and consumption or investment. These situations come under the topic of simultaneous equation models, which are discussed in Chapter 13.

● 3.11 Application: Relation between Patents and the Expenditures on Research and Development (R&D)

This section has another "walk-through" example of regression analysis. The data for this example are in the file DATA3-3, which refers to the following variables:

PATENTS = The number of patent applications filed, in thousands, range 84.5–189.4.

R&D   = Expenditures on research and development, in billions of 1992 dollars, obtained as the ratio of expenditure in current dollars divided by the gross domestic product (GDP) price deflator, range 57.94—166.7.

The data are annual for the United States as a whole, and for the 34 years between 1960 and 1993. The sources are in Appendix D.

If a country spends more on research and development, one would expect that it would result in more innovations that will be protected by patents. Hence, we might expect a positive relationship between the number of patents issued and the R&D expenses. Although the effects of R&D will be felt several years after projects have been started, for the sake of simplicity we ignore that issue here. In later chapters, we deal with the lagged effect of explanatory variables and will revisit this example.

The estimated simple regression model is given below along with *t*-statistics in parentheses (Practice Computer Session 3.6 has the GRETL instructions for reproducing the results of this section and Table 3.5 has the output).

$$\widehat{\text{PATENTS}} = \underset{(5.44)}{34.571} + \underset{(13.97)}{0.792} \text{ R\&D}$$

$$R^2 = 0.859 \qquad \text{d.f.} = 32$$

$$F_c(1, 32) = 195.055 \qquad \hat{\sigma} = 11.172$$

To test the model for overall significance, we use the *F*-statistic, which is 195.055. Under the null hypothesis that patents and R&D expenses are uncorrelated, F_c has the *F*-distribution with 1 d.f. for the numerator and 32 d.f. (34 − 2) for the denominator. From Table A.4a (also inside the back cover), we note that the critical value for $F(1, 32)$ at the 1 percent level is between 7.31 and 7.56. Because F_c is well above these values, we conclude that patents and R&D are significantly correlated. This conclusion is reinforced by the individual *t*-statistics. For a 1 percent two-tailed test, the *t*-table inside the front cover of the book (also in Table A.2) indicates that the critical value for 32 d.f. is between 2.704 and 2.75. Because the observed t_c are well above these values, we conclude that both the intercept and the slope coefficients are significantly different from zero. Since PATENTS is measured as the number of patent applications in thousands and R&D is in billions of dollars, the interpretation of $\hat{\beta} = 0.792$ is that for a $100 billion increase in R&D, on average, 79,200 (= 100 × 0.792 × 1,000) more patent applications would be filed.

The goodness of fit measure R^2 indicates that the model explains 85.9 percent of the variation. Although this appears to be a good fit, we see from Figure 3.11 that

Table 3.5 Annotated Computer Output for Application in Section 3.11

```
Listing 4 variables
  0) const     1) YEAR     2) R&D      3) PATENTS

MODEL 1: OLS estimates using the 34 observations 1960-1993
Dependent variable: PATENTS

    VARIABLE   COEFFICIENT   STDERROR   T STAT   2Prob(t > |T|)

  0)    const     34.5711      6.3579    5.438    0.000006 ***
  3)      R&D      0.7919      0.0567   13.966    0.000000 ***

Mean of dep. var.           119.238   S.D. of dep. variable           29.306
Error Sum of Sq (ESS)     3994.3003   Std Err of Resid. (sgmahat)    11.1724
Unadjusted R-squared          0.859   Adjusted R-squared              0.855
F-statistic (1, 32)         195.055   p-value for F()              0.000000
Durbin-Watson stat.           0.234   First-order autocorr. coeff     0.945

MODEL SELECTION STATISTICS

SGMASQ          124.822   AIC       132.146   FPE       132.164
HQ              136.255   SCHWARZ    144.56   SHIBATA   131.301
GCV             132.623   RICE      133.143
```

(Generate the following variables.)

ut = $\hat{u}_t$ (residuals)
temp = PATENTS - ut   (fitted values)
fitted = int(0.5+(10*temp))/10   (round to one decimal)
error = PATENTS - fitted   (forecast error)
(compute absolute % error to two decimals)
abspcerr = int(0.5+(10000*abs(error)/PATENTS))/100
(print values)

Obs	R&D	PATENTS	fitted	error	abspcerr
1960	57.94	84.5	80.5	4.0	4.73
1961	60.59	88.2	82.6	5.6	6.35
1962	64.44	90.4	85.6	4.8	5.31
1963	70.66	91.1	90.5	0.6	0.66
1964	76.83	93.2	95.4	-2.2	2.36
1965	80.00	100.4	97.9	2.5	2.49
1966	84.82	93.5	101.7	-8.2	8.77
1967	86.84	93.0	103.3	-10.3	11.08
1968	88.81	98.7	104.9	-6.2	6.28
1969	88.28	104.4	104.5	-0.1	0.10
1970	85.29	109.4	102.1	7.3	6.67

(continued)

Table 3.5   (continued)

1971	83.18	111.1	100.4	10.7	9.63
1972	85.07	105.3	101.9	3.4	3.23
1973	86.72	109.6	103.2	6.4	5.84
1974	85.45	107.4	102.2	5.2	4.84
1975	83.41	108.0	100.6	7.4	6.85
1976	87.44	110.0	103.8	6.2	5.64
1977	90.11	109.0	105.9	3.1	2.84
1978	94.50	109.3	109.4	-0.1	0.09
1979	99.28	108.9	113.2	-4.3	3.95
1980	103.64	113.0	116.6	-3.6	3.19
1981	108.77	114.5	120.7	-6.2	5.41
1982	113.96	118.4	124.8	-6.4	5.41
1983	121.72	112.4	131.0	-18.6	16.55
1984	133.33	120.6	140.2	-19.6	16.25
1985	144.78	127.1	149.2	-22.1	17.39
1986	148.39	133.0	152.1	-19.1	14.36
1987	150.90	139.8	154.1	-14.3	10.23
1988	154.36	151.9	156.8	-4.9	3.23
1989	157.19	166.3	159.1	7.2	4.33
1990	161.86	176.7	162.8	13.9	7.87
1991	164.54	178.4	164.9	13.5	7.57
1992	166.70	187.2	166.6	20.6	11.00
1993	165.20	189.4	165.4	24.0	12.67

the model does not quite capture the real variation in patents. The "fitted" straight line is the solid line, and it does not adequately represent the curvilinear nature of the observed scatter. Because of this, the model badly predicts patents in many of the years.

Figure 3.11   U.S. Patents against R&D Expenditures

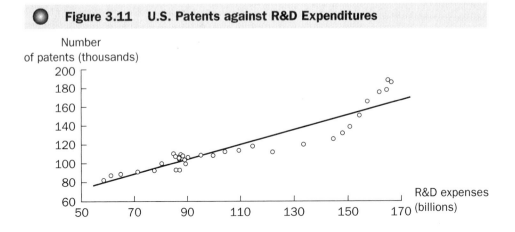

This point is brought out more clearly in Table 3.5, which has other useful statistics. The fourth column has the estimated average values ($\hat{Y}_t$), the fifth column has the residual calculated as the observed minus the estimated mean values ($\hat{u}_t = Y_t - \hat{Y}_t$), and the last column has the absolute percent error (APE), which is given by $100|\hat{u}_t|/Y_t$. The fitted (that is, predicted) values presented in Table 3.5 are rounded to one decimal. Because the original patents data had only one decimal, it does not make sense to have more than one-decimal accuracy for fitted values.

Many of the APEs are above 5 percent, and for several years they are above 10 percent, which is quite high. We also observe that the scatter points are clustered together for the years 1966–1977, indicating that something other than R&D expenses was causing the changes in patents. Thus, a closer look at the results points to model misspecification. In Chapter 6, we use the same data set to estimate a curvilinear model and will examine whether that specification better captures the observed variation in patents.

Summary

Even though a simple two-variable linear regression model has been used in this chapter, almost all the basic aspects of carrying out empirical analyses have been covered here. It will be useful to summarize the results derived so far.

The simple linear regression model is $Y_t = \alpha + \beta X_t + u_t$, ($t = 1, 2, \ldots, n$). X_t and Y_t are the tth observations on the independent variable and the dependent variable, respectively, α and β are unknown population parameters to be estimated from the data on X and Y, u_t is an unobserved error term that is a random variable whose properties are stated below. n is the total number of observations. The slope (β) is interpreted as the marginal effect on Y_t of a unit increase in X_t. $\alpha + \beta X_t$ is the conditional mean of Y given $X = X_t$.

The ordinary least squares (OLS) procedure minimizes the sum of squared errors $\Sigma \hat{u}_t^2$ and obtains estimates (denoted by $\hat{\alpha}$ and $\hat{\beta}$) of the intercept α and the slope β. The only requirement for estimating the parameters by OLS is that n be at least 2 and that at least one of the Xs be different—that is, that not all the Xs be the same. More specifically, $\text{Var}(X) > 0$.

If u_t is a random variable with mean zero and X_t is given and nonrandom, then $E(u_t) = 0$ and $E(X_s u_t) = 0$, for $s, t = 1, 2, \ldots, n$. The normal equations are $\Sigma \hat{u}_t = 0$ and $\Sigma X_t \hat{u}_t = 0$. The solution to these equations yields the OLS estimates of α and β.

Under the assumptions just specified, OLS estimators are unbiased and consistent. Unbiasedness holds even if X_t is random, provided $E(u_t|X_t) = 0$. Consistency holds even if X_t is random, provided $\text{Cov}(X, u) = 0$, that is, provided that X and u are uncorrelated.

If the us are independently and identically distributed (iid) with finite variance, $\hat{\alpha}$ and $\hat{\beta}$ are also best linear unbiased estimators (BLUE); that is, among all the unbiased linear combinations of the Ys, $\hat{\alpha}$ and $\hat{\beta}$ have the lowest variance. This result is known as the Gauss–Markov theorem and means that, besides being unbiased and consistent, OLS estimators are also most efficient.

From $\hat{\alpha}$ and $\hat{\beta}$, the predicted value of Y_t (denoted as $\hat{Y}_t$) is obtained as $\hat{Y}_t = \hat{\alpha} + \hat{\beta} X_t$, and the residual is estimated as $\hat{u}_t = Y_t - \hat{Y}_t$. The standard error of the residuals is an estimator of the standard deviation σ and is given by $\hat{\sigma} = [\Sigma \hat{u}_t^2/(n - 2)]^{1/2}$. From this, the standard errors of $\hat{\alpha}$ and $\hat{\beta}$ ($s_{\hat{\alpha}}$ and $s_{\hat{\beta}}$) can be derived. The smaller the standard errors, the greater the precision of the estimates of the parameters. A higher variation in X is desirable because this tends to improve the precision of individual estimators.

The steps for testing a one-sided alternative on β are as follows:

Step 1 $H_0: \beta = \beta_0$, $H_1: \beta > \beta_0$.

Step 2   The test statistic is $t_c = (\hat{\beta} - \beta_0)/s_{\hat{\beta}}$, where $s_{\hat{\beta}}$ is the estimated standard error for $\hat{\beta}$. Under the null hypothesis, this has the t-distribution with $n - 2$ d.f.

Step 3   Look up in the t-table the entry corresponding to $n - 2$ d.f. and the given level of significance (say, a), and find the point $t^*_{n-2}(a)$ such that $P(t > t^*) = a$.

Step 4   Reject H_0 at the level a if $t_c > t^*$. If the alternative had been $\beta < \beta_0$, H_0 would have been rejected when $t_c < -t^*$.

The test can also be carried out in an equivalent way. The modified Steps 3 and 4 are as follows:

Step 3a   Calculate the probability (denoted as p-value) that $t > |t_c|$, under the null hypothesis.

Step 4a   Reject H_0 and conclude that the coefficient is significant if the p-value is less than the given level of significance (a).

The steps for a two-sided alternative are as follows:

Step 1 $H_0: \beta = \beta_0$, $H_1: \beta \neq \beta_0$.

Step 2   The test statistic is $t_c = (\hat{\beta} - \beta_0)/s_{\hat{\beta}}$. Under the null hypothesis, this has the t-distribution with $n - 2$ d.f.

Step 3   Look up in the t-table the entry corresponding to $n - 2$ d.f. and the level of significance (a), and find the point $t^*_{n-2}(a/2)$ such that $P(t > t^*) = a/2$ (one-half the level of significance).

Step 4   Reject H_0 at the level a if $|t_c| > t^*$.

The modified steps for the p-value approach are as follows:

Step 3a   Calculate p-value $= 2P(t > |t_c|)$ under H_0.

Step 4a   Reject H_0 if the p-value is less than the preselected level of significance.

A statistic that measures the goodness of fit of a model is given by $R^2 = 1 - (\text{ESS}/\text{TSS})$, where $\text{ESS} = \Sigma \, \hat{u}_t^2$ and $\text{TSS} = \Sigma \, (Y_t - \bar{Y})^2 \cdot R^2$ lies between 0 and 1. The higher its value, the better the fit. R^2 has two interpretations: (1) It is the proportion of the total variance in Y that the model explains, and (2) it is the square of the correlation coefficient between the observed value (Y_t) of the dependent variable and the predicted value ($\hat{Y}_t$).

A test for the overall goodness of fit of the model as a whole can be carried out using the value of R^2. The steps are as follows (ρ_{xy} is the population correlation coefficient between X and Y):

Step 1 $H_0: \rho_{xy} = 0$, $H_1: \rho_{xy} \neq 0$.

Step 2   The test statistic is $F_c = R^2(n - 2)/(1 - R^2)$. Under the null hypothesis, it has an F-distribution with d.f. 1 and $n - 2$.

Step 3   Look up in the F-table the entry corresponding to 1 d.f. in the numerator and $n - 2$ d.f. in the denominator and the given level of significance (say, a), and find the point F^* such that $P(F > F^*) = a$.

Step 4   Reject H_0 at the level a if $F_c > F^*$.

The 95 percent confidence interval for β is given by

$$(\hat{\beta} - t^* s_{\hat{\beta}}, \, \hat{\beta} + t^* s_{\hat{\beta}})$$

The conditional predictor of Y, given that X is X_0, is $\hat{Y} = \hat{\alpha} + \hat{\beta}X_0$. Its variance (a measure of the reliability of the prediction) increases with the distance of X_0 from the mean $\overline{X}$. Thus, the farther X_0 is from the mean of X, the less reliable is the forecast.

Changing the scale of measurement of the dependent variable results in the corresponding scaling of each of the regression coefficients. The values of R^2 and the t-statistics are, however, unchanged. If the scale of measurement of an independent variable is changed, its regression coefficient and the corresponding standard errors are affected by the same scale, but all other statistics are unchanged.

It is very important to specify correctly the causality in a regression model. The standard assumption is that X causes Y. If X and Y are reversed, however, and the model estimated is $X_t = \alpha^* + \beta^* Y_t + v_t$, the fitted straight line will generally be different from the one derived from the model $Y_t = \alpha + \beta X_t + u_t$.

Key Terms

Analysis of variance (ANOVA)
Autocorrelation
Best linear unbiased estimator (BLUE)
Coefficient of multiple determination
Conditional mean of Y given X
Critical region
Critical value
Data-generating process (DGP)
Engel curve
Error sum of squares (ESS)
Estimated residual
Explained variation
Feedback
Fitted straight line
F-test
Gauss–Markov theorem
Goodness of fit
Heteroscedasticity
Homoscedasticity
Jointly determined
Marginal effect of X on Y
Mean absolute percent error (MAPE)
Mean squared error (MSE)
Mean squared percentage error (MSPE)
Method of least squares
Nonlinear regression model
Normal equations
Ordinary least squares (OLS)
Population parameters
Population regression function
Population regression line

Population variances
Postsample forecast
p-value approach
Regression coefficients
Regression sum of squares (RSS)
Residual
Root mean squared error (RMSE)
Sample estimates
Sample regression function
Sample regression line
Sample scatter diagram
Serial independence
Significantly different from β_0 at the
    level a
Significantly different from zero
Significantly greater than zero
Simple linear regression model
Spurious correlation
Spurious regression
Standard error of a regression coefficient
Standard error of the disturbances
Standard error of the regression
Statistically not greater than zero
Sum of squares of the residuals (ESS)
Total sum of squares (TSS)
Total variation
t-statistic
t-test
Unexplained variation
Well-behaved errors
White-noise errors

References

Bell, Frederick W., and Neil B. Murphy. "The Impact of Regulation on Inter- and Intra-regional Variation in Commercial Banking Costs." *J. Regional Science* 9 (1969): 225–238.

Davidson, Russell, and James K. MacKinnon. *Estimation and Inference in Econometrics*. Oxford: Oxford University Press, 1993.

Economic Report of the President. Washington, D.C.: U.S. Government Printing Office, 1996.

Galton, Francis. "Family Likeness in Stature." *Proceedings of the Royal Society* 40 (1886): 42–72.

Granger, C. W. J. "Investigating Causal Relations by Econometric Models and Cross-Spectral Models." *Econometrica* 37 (1969): 424–438.

Greene, W. H. *Econometric Analysis*. Upper Saddle River, NJ: Prentice-Hall, 2000.

Griffiths, William E., R. Carter Hill, and George G. Judge. *Learning and Practicing Econometrics*. New York: J. Wiley, 1993.

Hogg, Robert V., and Allen T. Craig. *Introduction to Mathematical Statistics*. New York: Macmillan, 1978.

Ruud, Paul A. *An Introduction to Classical Econometrics*. New York: Oxford University Press, 2000.

Sims, C. A. "Money, Income, and Causality." *American Economic Review* 62 (1972): 540–552.

Statistical Abstract of the United States. Washington, D.C.: U.S. Government Printing Office, 1995.

Exercises

Theoretical Questions

3.1   In the four equations given below, the summations are all for the *sample data*, not the population. Indicate which of the equations are correct as stated and which are not. Carefully justify your answers.

a. $\sum_{t=1}^{n} \hat{u}_t = 0$

b. $\sum_{t=1}^{n} X_t \hat{u}_t = 0$

c. $\sum_{t=1}^{n} u_t = 0$

d. $\sum_{t=1}^{n} X_t u_t = 0$

3.2   What is the distinction between an "error term" and a "residual"? Also explain the difference between u_t and $E(u_t)$. Next show that $E(\hat{u}_t) = 0$. Be sure to explain what the expected value means and state all the assumptions needed to prove it.

†3.3   For the simple linear model $Y_t = \alpha + \beta X_t + u_t$, show that under certain assumptions, OLS estimates give unbiased predictions. That is, show that $E(\hat{Y}_t) = E(Y_t)$. Be sure to state the assumptions essential to the proof.

3.4   Write down the assumptions essential for each of the following statements. Be sure to explain exactly where your assumption is needed.

a.   For estimating α and β by the OLS procedure.

b.   For proving that the OLS estimates of the parameters are unbiased and consistent.

c.   For proving that the OLS estimates are also most efficient.

d.   For carrying out *t*- and *F*-tests.

3.5   Are the following statements correct? If they are only partly correct, identify that part. Justify your answers carefully.

    a.   OLS estimates of the slope are more precisely estimated if the X-values are closer to their sample mean.

    b.   If X_t and u_t are correlated, estimators can still be unbiased.

    c.   Estimators cannot be BLUE unless the u_ts are all normally distributed.

    d.   If the error terms are not normally distributed, then the t- and F-tests cannot be performed.

    e.   If the variance of u_t is large, then confidence intervals for the coefficients will be wider.

    f.   If the X-values have a large variance, confidence intervals will be narrower.

    g.   A high p-value means that the coefficient is significantly different from zero.

    h.   If you choose a higher level of significance, a regression coefficient is more likely to be significant.

    i.   If the errors are serially correlated or heteroscedastic, estimated coefficients will not be unbiased, consistent, or BLUE.

    j.   The p-value is the probability that the null hypothesis is true.

†3.6   Assume that the model is $Y_t = \alpha + \beta X_t + u_t$. Given the n observations (X_1, Y_1), (X_2, Y_2), . . . , (X_n, Y_n), construct an estimate of β as follows: First connect the first and second points of the scatter diagram and compute the slope of that line. Then connect the first and third points and compute its slope. Proceed similarly and finally connect the first and last points and compute the slope of that line. Finally, average all these slopes and call that $\hat{\beta}$, the estimate of β.

    Draw a scatter diagram, give a geometric representation of $\hat{\beta}$, and derive an algebraic expression for it. Next compute the expected value of $\hat{\beta}$. Be sure to state any assumptions you made in computing the expectation. Is the estimate biased or unbiased? Explain. Finally, prove without any derivations why this estimate is inferior to the one we obtained earlier using the OLS procedure. Explain what you mean by "inferior."

3.7   Answer the same questions as in 3.6 when an estimate of β is obtained by the following alternative procedure. Draw a straight line from (X_t, Y_t) to the mean point $(\overline{X}, \overline{Y})$, for each t.

3.8   Assume that the model is $Y_t = \alpha + \beta X_t + u_t$. Given the n observations (X_1, Y_1), (X_2, Y_2), . . . , (X_n, Y_n), construct an estimate of β as follows: First connect the first and second points of the scatter diagram and compute the slope. Then connect the second and third points and compute the slope. Proceed similarly and finally connect the last two points and compute the slope of that line (note: all connections are straight-line segments). Then average all these slopes and call that $\tilde{\beta}$, the estimate of β. Draw a scatter diagram, give a geometric representation of $\tilde{\beta}$, and derive an algebraic expression for it. Next compute the expected value of $\tilde{\beta}$. Be sure to state any assumption you made in computing the expectation. Is the estimate biased or unbiased? Explain.

    Finally, prove without any derivations why this estimate is inferior to the one we obtained in Section 3.1 using the OLS procedure. Explain what you mean by "inferior."

3.9   Assume that the model is $Y_t = \alpha + \beta X_t + u_t$. Given n observations, construct an estimate of β as follows: Draw a straight line from the origin to each point and compute its slope. Then average all these slopes and call that $\tilde{\beta}$, the estimate of β. Draw a scatter diagram, give a geometric representation of $\tilde{\beta}$, and derive an algebraic expression for it. Next compute the expected value of $\tilde{\beta}$. Be sure to state any assumption you made in computing the expectation. Is the estimate biased or unbiased? Explain.

3.10   Suppose the alternative estimator is $\tilde{\beta} = \overline{Y}/\overline{X}$, that is, the ratio of the sample means. Compute the expected value and check whether this is unbiased or not (note: $\alpha \neq 0$).

3.11   In the model $Y_t = \alpha + \beta X_t + u_t$, an estimate of β is obtained as follows:

$$\tilde{\beta} = \frac{1}{n-1} \sum_{t=2}^{t=n} \left[\frac{Y_t - Y_{t-1}}{X_t - X_{t-1}} \right]$$

a.   Give a geometric interpretation of $\tilde{\beta}$.
b.   Show that $\tilde{\beta}$ is unbiased and consistent. Be sure to state the assumptions needed to prove this.
c.   Without actually deriving the variance of $\tilde{\beta}$, argue why this estimator is inefficient relative to the OLS estimator of β.

†3.12   Consider the model $Y_t = \beta X_t + u_t$ in which there is no intercept, that is, $\alpha = 0$. Some of the following questions depend on the appendix to this chapter and can be omitted in an elementary course.

a.   Show that the normal equations $\Sigma \hat{u}_t = 0$ and $\Sigma X_t \hat{u}_t = 0$ yield two different estimates for β. The first one is $\tilde{\beta} = \bar{Y}/\bar{X}$, where $\bar{X}$ and $\bar{Y}$ are the sample means. The second one is $\hat{\beta} = (\Sigma X_t Y_t)/(\Sigma X_t^2)$.
b.   Show that both $\tilde{\beta}$ and $\hat{\beta}$ are unbiased. Be sure to state all the assumptions you make to prove your result.
c.   Show that the fitted line $\hat{Y} = \hat{\beta} X$ will generally *not* go through the average point $(\bar{X}, \bar{Y})$, but that the fitted line $\tilde{Y} = \tilde{\beta} X$ will.
*d.   By proceeding as in Section 3.A.3 show that $\hat{\beta}$ is the OLS estimator of β.
*e.   By proceeding as in Section 3.A.4 show that $\hat{\beta}$ is BLUE.
*f.   Using this result explain why the Gauss–Markov theorem is applicable here, and prove (without any derivations) that $\hat{\beta}$ is superior to $\tilde{\beta}$.

3.13   Suppose the model is as in Exercise 3.12, that is, $Y_t = \beta X_t + u_t$. An estimate of β is derived as follows: In the scatter diagram for X and Y, draw a line from the origin to each of the points (X_1, Y_1), (X_2, Y_2), ..., (X_n, Y_n). Then compute the average (β^*) of the slopes of these lines.

a.   Write an algebraic expression for β^*.
b.   Prove that β^* is an unbiased estimator of β.
c.   Without formal derivations, argue why the OLS estimator given in Exercise 3.12d is superior to β^*.

3.14   Suppose you've specified the regression model as $Y_t = \beta X_t + v_t$ and obtained the OLS estimator as $\hat{\beta} = \Sigma(X_t Y_t)/\Sigma(X_t^2)$. However, the true model has a constant term so that Y_t is actually given by $\alpha + \beta X_t + u_t$, where u_t has zero expectation. Show that $\hat{\beta}$ is biased. Derive the condition under which $\hat{\beta}$ will be unbiased even though the wrong model was used. What is the intuitive interpretation of the condition you derived?

3.15   In the regression model $Y_t = \alpha + \beta X_t + u_t$, let $\hat{\beta}$ be the OLS estimator of β. Then $\hat{u}_t = Y_t - \hat{\alpha} - \hat{\beta} X_t$ is the residual after removing the effect of X_t on Y_t. Show that X_t and $\hat{u}_t$ are uncorrelated; that is, prove that $\text{Cov}(X_t, \hat{u}_t) = 0$.

3.16   Show that the estimated slope coefficient can also be written as

$$\hat{\beta} = \frac{\widehat{\text{Cov}(X, Y)}}{\widehat{\text{Var}(X)}}$$

where $\text{Cov}(X, Y)$ and $\text{Var}(X)$ are the covariance between X and Y and the variance of X, respectively. In other words, $\hat{\beta}$ can also be expressed as the ratio of the estimated covariance between X and Y and the estimated variance of X.

3.17   Show that the OLS estimator $\hat{\beta}$ can also be written as $r(s_y/s_x)$, where r is the sample correlation coefficient between X and Y given in Equation (2.11), s_x^2 is the sample variance of X given in Equation (2.10), and s_y^2 is the sample variance of Y. (*Hint:* Use the relation $\hat{\beta} = \widehat{\text{Cov}(X, Y)}/\widehat{\text{Var}(X)}$ derived in Exercise 3.16.) Also show that the estimated relation can be written as

$$\hat{Y} = \bar{Y} + r(s_y/s_x)(X - \bar{X})$$

†3.18   Consider the regression model $E = \alpha + \beta N + u$, where E is the starting salary (in dollars) of a new employee of a firm and N is the number of years of college attended. There are 50 new employees.

a.   What are the intuitive/economic interpretations of α and β?

b.   The error term u has all the properties you need but you do not know its distribution, although you do know that it is *not* normally distributed.

(1)   List all the properties of the least squares estimators $\hat{\alpha}$ and $\hat{\beta}$ that are still valid. For each property explain briefly why it holds.

(2)   State all the properties of $\hat{\alpha}$ and $\hat{\beta}$ that are no longer valid and any other problems caused by the lack of knowledge. Briefly justify your answer.

c.   Suppose E is measured in hundreds of dollars. Describe the effect of this change in units on the estimated regression coefficients and their standard errors, t- and F-statistics, and the value of R^2.

3.19   You are working for a company that produces a number of health and beauty products. The sales manager gives you the company's total annual sales in millions of dollars for 25 years and you are asked to project the sales for the next 3 years. Formulate a simple regression model that relates sales to a linear time trend, that is, where the independent variable is "time" (t). What would your data table (columns of X_t and Y_t) look like? Write down an expression for the predicted sales in year 28.

3.20   An analyst graphs the observations on a dependent variable (Y_t) against the observations on an independent variable (X_t) and finds it to be as shown in the figure. Is the analyst justified in feeling elated thinking he will get a perfect fit with $R^2 = 1$? Why or why not?

3.21   Consider the model given in Exercise 3.12, that is, $Y_t = \beta X_t + u_t$. Let $\hat{Y}_t = \hat{\beta} X_t$ be the predicted value ($\hat{\beta}$ being the OLS estimator derived in Exercise 3.12d) and $\hat{u}_t = Y_t - \hat{Y}_t$ be the error in prediction. Show that $\Sigma\, Y_t^2 = \Sigma\, \hat{Y}_t^2 + \Sigma\, \hat{u}_t^2$. (Note that $\bar{Y}$ is not subtracted as was done in Equation (3.26).)

Empirical Questions Requiring No Computer Work

3.22   You work for a life insurance company and are preparing for a briefing of the board. Your economics tells you that the best predictor of life insurance (lins) holdings is income. You gather the relevant data (family life insurance and family income, both in thousands of dollars) and want to analyze it, running a regression of life insurance holdings on income. The output, as well as some other statistics, follow.

OLS Estimates Using the 20 Observations 1–20
Dependent Variable—lins

Variable	Coefficient	Standard Error	t-Stat	2 Prob $t > |T|$
Constant	6.854991	7.383473	0.928424	0.365471
Income	3.880186	0.112125	34.606006	< 0.0001***

Mean of dep. var.	236.95	S.D. of dep. variable	114.838319
Error Sum of Sq (ESS)	3710.374715	Std Err of Resid. (sgmahat)	14.357295
Unadjusted R-squared	0.985	Adjusted R-squared	0.984
F-statistic (1, 18)	11197.575635	Prob. F > 1197.576 is < 0.0001	

a.   You need to interpret the regression results, and as the board has not benefited from taking this course, you need to describe in words what is going on. Explain what the following mean (that is, don't just give the numbers, interpret what they mean for the problem):
  (1)   Coefficient on the constant.
  (2)   Coefficient on income.
  (3)   The value $\hat{\alpha} + \hat{\beta}x_0$ for some arbitrary x_0.
  (4)   The value for R^2.

b.   You also need to think about the population regression line.
  (1)   Write down the population regression function.
  (2)   What are the population error terms likely to be (that is, what causes deviations from the population mean)?

c.   Under certain assumptions the coefficient estimates are unbiased.
  (1)   Describe what the property of unbiasedness is in terms of the regression line above, and explain what this means for the chance that your estimates in this particular sample are close to the true values.
  (2)   What assumptions are required on the population model for the estimates to be unbiased?
  (3)   Do you think that they hold here? Make an argument one way or the other.

d.   One of the managers suggests that the industry rule of thumb is that people hold life insurance at five dollars for every dollar of their income. Another suggests that this is unlikely and that the number is too high. You want to examine this difference of opinion.
  (1)   What null and alternative hypotheses would you use here to discriminate between these hypotheses?
  (2)   Test the hypothesis, using a 5 percent Type I error.
  (3)   Compute and interpret (in words) the test statistics for the test.
  (4)   Construct a 95 percent confidence interval for the estimate of the coefficient on income.

e.   You are cross-examined by the board.
  (1)   The manager you disagreed with in question (d) is unhappy. The manager suggests that your whole methodology is flawed and that you should have used the method of maximum likelihood. What is your response?
  (2)   Another manager asks if you think that there are any other economically significant factors that affect life insurance holdings. What is your response?

3.23 The following tax function was estimated using cross-section data for the 50 U.S. states and the District of Columbia. This can be verified using the data file DATA3-4 described in Appendix D.

$$\widehat{\text{Tax}} = -0.221 + \underset{(<0.0001)}{0.142} \text{ Income}$$
$$\underset{(0.087)}{}$$

$$n = 51 \qquad R^2 = 0.997 \qquad \hat{\sigma} = 0.687$$

where Tax is total taxes paid and Income is total income, both measured in billions of dollars, and the numbers in parentheses are the corresponding p-values.

   a. Do the observed signs for the regression coefficients agree with your prior intuition? Explain.
   b. What is the interpretation of the coefficient for income?
   c. State the null and alternative hypotheses that the p-values given above test. Are the coefficients significant at the 5 percent level? Justify your answers.

†3.24 A company produces a sealing compound used in construction. A simple model for the demand for the sealant is given by $Q_t = \alpha + \beta P_t + u_t$, where Q_t is the number of gallons of the sealant shipped in a given month and P_t is the price per gallon in dollars. Using monthly data for 89 periods, the model was estimated; the following table is a partial computer printout (data are in DATA3-5).

Variable	Coefficient	Standard Error
Constant	5962.053755	955.809956
P	−381.092383	104.765725
Error Sum of Sq (ESS) 1.869999e + 08	Std Err of Resid. (sgmahat)	1466.09133
Unadjusted R-squared 0.132	Adjusted R-squared	0.122

   a. What signs would you expect for α and β and why?
   b. Write down the estimated relation and associated statistics in the standard form given in Section 3.5.
   c. Do the observed signs of the regression coefficients agree with your answer in (a)?
   d. What is the interpretation of the coefficient for price? In particular, write down the change in demand when the price per gallon goes up by one dollar.
   e. What can you say about the goodness of fit? Carry out a formal test for overall goodness of fit (choose the level 0.01). Be sure to state the null and alternative hypotheses, the test statistic, its distribution and d.f., and the criterion for rejecting the null. What do you conclude?
   f. Test whether each regression coefficient is significantly different from zero or not (at the 1 percent level). Here also state the null and alternative hypotheses, the test statistics, their distribution and d.f., and the criterion for rejecting the null. What do you conclude?
   g. Suppose price is measured in cents rather than in dollars. How will your answer to (b) change?
   h. Do you think the model is well specified? What other variables do you think should be added to the model?

†3.25 Consider the relation between per-capita savings (income − consumption) and personal income per capita, both in actual dollars, given by $S_t = \alpha + \beta Y_t + u_t$. Using

annual data for the United States for 36 years, the estimated model was the following, with standard errors in parentheses (see DATA3-6):

$$\hat{S}_t = 384.105 + 0.067 \ Y_t$$
$$\quad\quad (151.105) \quad (0.011)$$

$$R^2 = 0.538 \quad\quad \hat{\sigma} = 199.023$$

a. What is the economic interpretation of β?
b. What signs would you expect for α and β and why? Do the actual signs agree with your prior intuition? If there is a conflict, can you give any possible reasons?
c. What can you say about the goodness of fit? Carry out a formal test for overall goodness of fit (choose the level 0.01). Be sure to state the null and alternative hypotheses, the test statistic, its distribution and d.f., and the criterion for rejecting the null. What do you conclude?
d. Test whether or not each regression coefficient is significantly different from zero (at the 1 percent level). Here also state the null and alternative hypotheses, the test statistics, their distribution and d.f., and the criterion for rejecting the null. What do you conclude?
e. Suppose savings and income are both measured in hundreds of dollars rather than in dollars. How will the previous table change?

3.26 Consider the following two models of the expenditures for maintenance of a certain automobile:

$$E_t = \alpha_1 + \beta_1 \ \text{Miles}_t + u_t$$

$$E_t = \alpha_2 + \beta_2 \ \text{Age}_t + u_t$$

where E is the cumulative expenditure on maintenance (excluding gasoline), in dollars, Miles is the cumulative number of miles driven (in thousands), and Age is the age in weeks. Using 57 time series observations, the two models were estimated and the partial computer output is reproduced here (data in DATA3-7).

● **Model A**

Variable	Coefficient	Standard Error	t-Stat	2 Prob $(t > |T|)$
Constant	−625.935025	104.149581	−6.009962	< 0.0001 ***
Age	7.343478	0.32958	22.281356	< 0.0001 ***

Error Sum of Sq (ESS) 7.401653e + 06   Std Err of Resid. (sgmahat)   366.845346
R-squared   0.900

● **Model B**

Variable	Coefficient	Standard Error	t-Stat	2 Prob $(t > |T|)$
Constant	−796.074573	134.74494	−5.908011	< 0.0001 ***
Miles	53.450724	2.926144	18.26661	< 0.0001 ***

Error Sum of Sq (ESS) 1.050175e + 07   Std Err of Resid. (sgmahat)   436.96796
R-squared   0.858

a.   What signs would you expect for β_1 and β_2? Do the observed signs agree with your expectation?

b.   Which of the two models do you think is "better"? Clearly state the criteria you used.

c.   In the better model you chose, use the t-statistics to perform appropriate tests. Be sure to state the null and alternative hypotheses, the distribution of the test statistic including d.f., and your criteria for rejecting or not rejecting the null. What do you conclude?

d.   In Model A suppose Age is measured in days rather than weeks. Rewrite the table.

3.27   U.S. business schools that train MBAs vary a great deal in the tuition they charge. As one would suspect, the gain in salary after the degree compared to the salary before the degree also varies substantially. To examine whether a relationship exists between the two, the following estimated model was obtained using data for 25 business schools highly rated by *Business Week* (see DATA3-8). The values in parentheses are the corresponding standard errors.

$$\widehat{\text{Gain}} = 11.101 + 1.433 \text{ Tuition}$$
$$\quad\quad\quad (12.03)\quad\ (0.562)$$

$$R^2 = 0.186$$

Gain is the gain in salary and Tuition is the annual tuition, both in thousands of dollars.

a.   Would you say from the preceding data that we have a "good fit"? If not, what additional variables would be important to include in the model?

b.   Test each regression coefficient for significance at the 10 percent level. What are the null and alternative hypotheses and the distribution of test statistics, including the d.f.?

c.   Suppose tuition and salary gain were both measured in actual dollars. Write down the new values for the preceding table.

3.28   The Office of the Registrar of a university campus took a random sample of 427 students and obtained their grade point average in college (COLGPA), high school GPA (HSGPA), verbal Scholastic Aptitude Test scores (VSAT), and the mathematics scores in the SAT (MSAT). Three alternative models were estimated and the results were as follows (values in parentheses are standard errors):

$$\widehat{\text{COLGPA}} = 0.92058 + 0.52417 \text{ HSGPA} \quad\quad R^2 = 0.165$$
$$\quad\quad\quad\quad (0.20463)\quad\ (0.05712)$$

$$\widehat{\text{COLGPA}} = 1.99740 + 0.00157 \text{ VSAT} \quad\quad R^2 = 0.070$$
$$\quad\quad\quad\quad (0.14128)\quad\ (0.00028)$$

$$\widehat{\text{COLGPA}} = 1.62845 + 0.00204 \text{ MSAT} \quad\quad R^2 = 0.124$$
$$\quad\quad\quad\quad (0.15135)\quad\ (0.00026)$$

a.   Compute appropriate F-statistics and test each model for overall goodness of fit using a 1 percent level of significance. Are the models significant overall?

b.   Test each regression coefficient (exclude the constant term) for significance at the 1 percent level. Be sure to state the null hypothesis and an appropriate alternative.

c.   What do the low values for R^2 indicate? Which is the "best" model and why?

d.   Explain why the two-variable model is inadequate. What variables do you think would be important in explaining the variation in COLGPA?

†3.29 A staff member for a political campaign estimated the model $V_t = \alpha + \beta P_t + u_t$, for $t = 1, 2, \ldots, 22$, where V_t is voter turnout in precinct t, and P_t is the precinct's population. When the results were being printed out, the printer malfunctioned, smudging some of the results. With the information already provided, fill in the blanks.

Coefficient	Estimate	Standard Error	t-ratio
$\hat{\alpha}$	26.034	____	14.955
$\hat{\beta}$	0.137	0.028	____
ESS = 305.96	$\bar{P} = 54.478$	$s_v^2 = 31.954$	$s_p^2 = 925.91$
$r_{vp} = $ ____	$R^2 = $ ____	$\hat{\sigma}^2 = $ ____	$\bar{V} = $ ____

3.30 Consider the simple regression model $Y_t = \alpha + \beta X_t + u_t$ in which Y_t is total expenditure on travel and X_t is total income for the tth state. Including the District of Columbia, you have data for 51 observations. Both variables are measured in billions of dollars. The following is a partial computer output for the data:

Variable	Coefficient	Standard Error
Constant	0.4981	0.5355
Income	0.0556	0.0033
Error Sum of Squares (ESS)	417.110	
Total Sum of Squares (TSS)	2841.330	

a. What is the economic interpretation of the estimated coefficient for income? Does the numerical value appear reasonable?

b. Test individually whether the coefficients for the constant term and income are significantly different from zero at the 5 percent level. Be sure to state the null and alternative hypotheses, the test statistic and its distribution, the critical value (or range), and the criterion. What is your conclusion?

c. Compute the measure of goodness of fit.

d. Test the model for goodness of fit at the 1 percent level of significance. Show all your derivations. What is your conclusion?

e. Suppose the data on X and Y are converted to thousands and a new model is estimated as $Y_i^* = \alpha^* + \beta^* X_i^* + u_i^*$, where the variables with asterisks are the transformed ones. In the following table, fill in the blanks, indicated by underlined items, that give the values for the transformed model. Show your derivations.

Variable	Estimate	Standard Error
Constant*	____	____
Income*	____	____
Error Sum of Squares (ESS*)	____	____
Total Sum of Squares (TSS*)	____	____
R-squared	____	

3.31   Consider the simple regression model $GAIN_t = \alpha + \beta \, TUITION_t + u_t$, where GAIN is the gain in salary after a student completes an MBA program and TUITION is the tuition. Both are measured in thousands of dollars.

Variable	Coefficient	Standard Error
Constant	11.101	12.000
TUITION	1.433	0.562
	$R^2 = 0.186$	$n = 25$

a.   What is the economic interpretation of the estimated coefficient for tuition? Does the numerical value appear reasonable?

b.   Test individually whether the coefficients for the constant term and income are significantly different from zero at the 5 percent level. Be sure to state the null and alternative hypotheses, the test statistic and its distribution, the critical value (or range), and the criterion. What is your conclusion?

c.   Test the model for goodness of fit at the 1 percent level of significance. Show all your derivations, including the null hypothesis, the test statistic and its distribution with d.f. and the criteria for rejection. What is your conclusion?

d.   Suppose the data on TUITION and GAIN are converted to actual dollars and a new model is estimated as $GAIN_t^* = \alpha + \beta \, TUITION_t^* + u_t^*$ where the variables with asterisks are the transformed ones. In the following table, fill in the blanks, indicated by underlined items, that give the values for the transformed model. Show your derivations.

Variable	Coefficient	Standard Error
Constant*	——	——
TUITION*	——	——
R^2	——	

Empirical Questions Requiring Computer Work

For details on the various data files, see Appendix D.

3.32   Do companies with large assets usually have a high return on invested capital? More specifically, is there a relationship between return on invested capital and the total assets of a company? Address this question using the data for 38 French companies presented in DATA3-9. Return is given in percents and assets in billions of dollars (1995). First estimate a simple linear regression with return as the dependent variable. Test each regression coefficient for statistical significance at 10 percent. Also compute *p*-values and identify the actual levels of significance. Test the model for overall significance. What do you conclude? Do you think the model should include additional variables? Name a few variables that you think ought to be there, justify your choice, and indicate the direction of their effect on returns (that is, positive or negative).

3.33   DATA3-10 has cross-section data on total 1995 sales and profits for 27 German companies.

a.   Estimate the model $PROFITS_t = \alpha + \beta SALES_t + u_t$.

b.   Draw the scatter diagram. Do you expect a good fit? Compute R^2. Is the actual fit good?

c.   Estimate the standard error of the residuals and the standard errors of $\hat{\alpha}$ and $\hat{\beta}$.

d.   Perform t-tests for the hypotheses $\alpha = 0$ and $\beta = 0$, choosing your own level of significance. In each case state the null and alternative hypotheses, the distribution of the test statistic, and the criterion for acceptance or rejection of the null hypothesis.

e.   Suppose profits are measured in dollars instead of millions. Describe the effect of this change in units on regression coefficients, standard errors, t- and F-statistics, and the value of R^2.

f.   What other factors do you think the profits of a company depend on?

3.34   DATA3-11 has data on the salary (in thousands of dollars) and years since a Ph.D. was awarded for a sample of 222 professors at various universities. Estimate the model SALARY $= \alpha + \beta$ YEARS $+ u$. Test the model for overall significance (using your own level of significance). Also test each regression coefficient for significance at the 1 percent level. What does the value of R^2 indicate to you? Graph salary against years, and ask yourself whether the model is adequate for explaining the variations in salary levels. Based on your results, what recommendations would you give to improve the model specification? Examine the implications of measuring salary in actual dollars.

3.35   DATA3-12 has annual data from 1962 through 1994 for the population of the United Kingdom (in millions). Generate a variable called TIME that takes the value 1 for 1962, 2 for 1963, and so on up to 33 for 1994. Graph population against TIME, and state whether a linear time trend is a good approximation. Estimate the linear time trend POP $= \alpha + \beta$TIME $+ u$ using only the data for 1962–1989. As before, test the model for overall significance and for the significance of individual coefficients. Predict population for 1990–1994, and evaluate the model's adequacy in explaining the level of the U.K. population during 1990–1994.

3.36   Carry out a parallel analysis for the United States using the data in DATA3-13. Compare the rates of growth of the two countries, and indicate which country's population has grown faster since World War II.

3.37   A widely used relationship in consumer theory is the **Engel curve,** which relates the expenditure on a particular category to the income of an individual or family (see Example 1.4 and Section 3.7). DATA3-14 presents data on total income and expenditures on domestic travel for each of the 50 states of the United States and for the District of Columbia. Both variables are measured in billions of dollars. Do the same kind of analysis that you have been doing in previous exercises; that is, graph the appropriate relationship, estimate a relevant simple linear regression model, and test it for overall and individual coefficients' significance. What are the interpretations of the intercept and slope coefficients? Should other variables be included in the model? If so, indicate what they are and why you think that they should be included.

3.38   DATA3-15 has annual data for the United States on the population (millions) and the gross domestic product (GDP, in billions of dollars). Estimate the model GDP $= \alpha + \beta POP + u$, and compute the associated standard errors, t-statistics, goodness of fit measure, and so on. Graph GDP against POP and indicate whether you expect a good fit for the simple linear regression model. Next generate a time trend (TIME) as you did in Exercise 3.35 and estimate the alternative model GDP $= \alpha^* + \beta^*$ TIME $+ v$. Which model explains the variations in GDP better? Examine the effects on all statistics of measuring GDP also in millions of dollars.

3.A APPENDIX

Miscellaneous Derivations

3.A.1 Three-Dimensional Representation of the Simple Linear Model

Figure 3.A.1 graphically presents the assumptions listed in Table 3.2 for the case of the simple two-variable regression model. The X and Y axes represent the values of the random variables X and Y. The Z-axis is the probability density function, $f(u)$, of the random error term u. The straight line $\alpha + \beta X$ is the conditional mean of Y given X, assumed to be linear. The statistical distributions drawn around the mean line for the three values X_1, X_2, and X_3 are the corresponding conditional distributions. As mentioned in the text, the assumption that $\mathrm{Var}(u_t|X_t) = \sigma^2$ is called *homoscedasticity*, which means "equal scatter." Figure 3.A.1 depicts this constancy of the error variance for all observations. If these variances are not constant but vary with t [thus, $\mathrm{Var}(u_t|X_t) = \sigma_t^2$], we have *heteroscedasticity* (unequal scatter). Figure 3.A.2 illustrates the case of heteroscedasticity in which the variance increases as X increases. This case is examined in considerable detail in Chapter 8.

3.A.2 More Results on Summations

Equations (3.9) and (3.10) are proved here.

$$S_{xx} = \sum (X_t - \overline{X})^2 = \sum X_t^2 - n(\overline{X})^2 = \sum X_t^2 - \frac{1}{n}\left(\sum X_t\right)^2 \tag{3.9}$$

⬤ **Figure 3.A.1   Graphic Representation of the Simple Linear Regression Model**

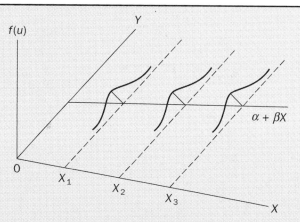

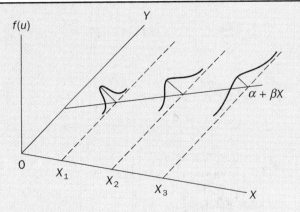

Figure 3.A.2   Illustration of Heteroscedasticity

PROOF

$$\sum (X_t - \overline{X})^2 = \sum [X_t^2 - 2X_t\overline{X} + (\overline{X})^2] = \sum X_t^2 - \sum 2\overline{X}X_t + \sum (\overline{X})^2$$

As before, $\overline{X}$ is the same for each t. Hence, the above $= \Sigma X_t^2 - 2\overline{X}\Sigma X_t + n(\overline{X})^2$. Also, $\Sigma X_t = n\overline{X}$. Therefore, the expression becomes $\Sigma X_t^2 - 2\overline{X}n\overline{X} + n(\overline{X})^2$. Combining the second and third terms, we get the first part of the property. We know that $\overline{X} = (\Sigma X_t)/n$. Substituting for $\overline{X}$ from this, we get the second part of the property.

$$S_{xy} = \sum (X_t - \overline{X})(Y_t - \overline{Y}) = \sum X_tY_t - n\overline{X}\,\overline{Y} = \sum X_tY_t - \left[\left(\sum X_t\right)\left(\sum Y_t\right)/n\right] \quad \textbf{(3.10)}$$

PROOF

$$\begin{aligned}
\sum (X_t - \overline{X})(Y_t - \overline{Y}) &= \sum (X_tY_t - X_t\overline{Y} - Y_t\overline{X} + \overline{X}\,\overline{Y}) \\
&= \sum X_tY_t - \overline{Y}\sum X_t - \overline{X}\sum Y_t + n\overline{X}\,\overline{Y} \\
&= \sum X_tY_t - \overline{Y}n\overline{X} - \overline{X}n\overline{Y} + n\overline{X}\,\overline{Y} \\
&= \sum X_tY_t - n\overline{X}\,\overline{Y}
\end{aligned}$$

Substituting $\overline{X} = (\Sigma X_t)/n$ and $\overline{Y} = (\Sigma Y_t)/n$, we get the second equality.

3.A.3 Derivation of the Normal Equations by Least Squares

In this section, we apply the method of least squares, presented in Section 3.2, and derive the normal Equations (3.4) and (3.5). The least squares criterion is to choose those values of $\hat{\alpha}$ and $\hat{\beta}$ that minimize the sum of squared errors:

$$\text{ESS}(\hat{\alpha}, \hat{\beta}) = \sum_{t=1}^{t=n} \hat{u}_t^2 = \sum_{t=1}^{t=n} (Y_t - \hat{\alpha} - \hat{\beta}X_t)^2$$

To minimize ESS with respect to $\hat{\alpha}$ and $\hat{\beta}$, we set the partial derivatives (see Section 2.A.2 on partial derivatives) $\partial\text{ESS}/\partial\hat{\alpha}$ and $\partial\text{ESS}/\partial\hat{\beta}$ to zero and solve the resulting equations. We have

$$\frac{\partial\text{ESS}}{\partial\hat{\alpha}} = \frac{\sum \partial(\hat{u}_t^2)}{\partial\hat{\alpha}} = \sum 2\hat{u}_t \frac{\partial\hat{u}_t}{\partial\hat{\alpha}} = 2\sum \hat{u}_t(-1) = 2\sum (Y_t - \hat{\alpha} - \hat{\beta}X_t)(-1) = 0$$

$$\frac{\partial\text{ESS}}{\partial\hat{\beta}} = \frac{\sum \partial(\hat{u}_t^2)}{\partial\hat{\beta}} = \sum 2\hat{u}_t \frac{\partial\hat{u}_t}{\partial\hat{\beta}} = 2\sum \hat{u}_t(-X_t) = 2\sum (Y_t - \hat{\alpha} - \hat{\beta}X_t)(-X_t) = 0$$

from which we obtain the following equations:

$$\sum (Y_t - \hat{\alpha} - \hat{\beta}X_t) = 0$$
$$\sum (Y_t - \hat{\alpha} - \hat{\beta}X_t)X_t = 0$$

Taking the summation term by term and noting that $\hat{\alpha}$ and $\hat{\beta}$ can be factored out of summations because they do not depend on t, we get

$$\sum Y_t = n\hat{\alpha} + \hat{\beta}\sum X_t$$

$$\sum Y_t X_t = \hat{\alpha}\sum X_t + \hat{\beta}\sum X_t^2$$

The first equation is equivalent to Equation (3.4) and the second equation is the same as Equation (3.5).

3.A.4 Best Linear Unbiased Estimator (BLUE) and the Gauss–Markov Theorem

From statistical theory we know that one of the desirable properties for an estimator is to be a minimum variance unbiased linear estimator (see Definition 2.8). In other words, among all linear combinations of the dependent variable that are unbiased, we would like to choose the one that has the smallest variance. This is the best linear unbiased estimator (BLUE) property. In this section, we prove the Gauss–Markov theorem, which states that the OLS estimator derived in Section 3.2 also has the BLUE property. For simplicity of notation, the assumption that X_t is given is not explicitly indicated.

First note that the OLS estimator $\hat{\beta}$ can indeed be expressed as a linear combination of Y_t. To see this, we reproduce Equation (3.10) below.

$$S_{xy} = \left[\sum X_t Y_t - \frac{\left(\sum X_t \right)\left(\sum Y_t \right)}{n} \right] \tag{3.10}$$

Noting that $\overline{X} = \Sigma X_t / n$, this can be expressed as

$$\sum X_t Y_t - \overline{X} \sum Y_t = \sum (X_t - \overline{X}) Y_t$$

Because $\hat{\beta} = S_{xy}/S_{xx}$ from Equation (3.12), we have

$$\hat{\beta} = \sum \left[\frac{X_t - \overline{X}}{S_{xx}} \right] Y_t = \sum w_t Y_t$$

which is a linear combination of Y_t with the weight $w_t = \left[\dfrac{X_t - \overline{X}}{S_{xx}} \right]$ that depends on X_t. Now consider a general linear combination of the Ys that takes the form $\tilde{\beta} = \Sigma a_t Y_t$, where a_t is nonrandom. The best linear unbiased estimator (BLUE) has the two properties: (1) $\tilde{\beta}$ is unbiased and (2) $\text{Var}(\tilde{\beta})$ is the smallest.

PROOF

Define $d_t = a_t - w_t$ as the difference between the weights (note that d_t depends only on the Xs and hence can be treated as nonrandom). Then $a_t = w_t + d_t$. It follows that

$$\tilde{\beta} = \sum (w_t + d_t) Y_t = \hat{\beta} + \sum d_t Y_t$$

$$E(\tilde{\beta}) = \beta + \sum E(d_t Y_t) = \beta + \sum d_t E(Y_t) = \beta + \sum d_t (\alpha + \beta X_t)$$

$$= \beta + \alpha \sum d_t + \beta \sum d_t X_t$$

For unbiasedness, we need this to be equal to β, which can happen if and only if

$$\sum d_t = 0 \quad \text{and} \quad \sum d_t X_t = 0$$

The variance of the estimator $\tilde{\beta}$ is given by $\text{Var}[\Sigma(w_t + d_t) Y_t]$. From Property 2.9e, the variance of a sum of independent random variables is the sum of the variances (independence is guaranteed by Assumption 3.6). Also, because of the homoscedasticity Assumption 3.5, u_t and hence Y_t has the constant variance σ^2. It follows from this that

$$\text{Var}(\tilde{\beta}) = \sigma^2 \sum (w_t + d_t)^2 = \sigma^2 \sum w_t^2 + \sigma^2 \sum d_t^2 + 2\sigma^2 \sum w_t d_t$$

The third term is zero because $\sum w_t d_t = \sum \left(\dfrac{X_t - \overline{X}}{S_{xx}} \right) d_t = 0$, since the unbiasedness conditions $\Sigma d_t = 0$ and $\Sigma d_t X_t = 0$ make each of the terms in the summation equal to zero. In the preceding expression for the variance of $\tilde{\beta}$, the first term is independent of the choice variables d_t. Because the second term is a sum of squares, the only way we can minimize that term is to choose each of the ds to be zero. This makes $a_t = w_t$ and therefore $\tilde{\beta} \equiv \hat{\beta}$, thus implying that the OLS estimator is indeed BLUE and hence most efficient. This establishes the Gauss–Markov theorem. It should be noted that the proof of the theorem requires Assumptions 3.5 and 3.6 of homoscedasticity and serial independence. If either of these assumptions is violated, then OLS does not give efficient estimates.

In the preceding proof, we assumed that X is given. Thus, we have proved the Gauss–Markov theorem only for a given X. That is,

$$\mathrm{Var}(\hat{\beta}|X) \leq \mathrm{Var}(\tilde{\beta}|X)$$

for all X values. It is easy to show, however, that the theorem holds even when X is a random variable. Recall from Property 2.7 that

$$\mathrm{Var}(\hat{\beta}) = E_X[\mathrm{Var}(\hat{\beta}|X)] + \mathrm{Var}_X[E(\hat{\beta}|X)]$$

But the second term is zero because $E(\hat{\beta}|X) = \beta$, a constant. A similar expression holds for $\mathrm{Var}(\tilde{\beta})$ also. Since the variance of $\hat{\beta}$ for a given X is no greater than the variance of $\tilde{\beta}$ for a given X, it must be so for the average value too. Therefore,

$$\mathrm{Var}(\hat{\beta}) = E_X[\mathrm{Var}(\hat{\beta}|X)] \leq E_X[\mathrm{Var}(\tilde{\beta}|X)] = \mathrm{Var}(\tilde{\beta})$$

This establishes the theorem for random X also.

3.A.5 Maximum Likelihood Estimation

The motivation for the maximum likelihood estimation method is described in detail in Section 2.A.4. The reader should study that section before starting this one. In that section, the method was applied to the case in which the mean and variance of a normal distribution were estimated. Here we apply the same technique to the regression problem. Because the maximum likelihood principle requires a knowledge of the distribution in question, we need Assumption 3.8. The steps for deriving a maximum likelihood estimator are straightforward. First, set up the likelihood function relating the joint density function of the observations to the unknown parameters. To maximize this, partially differentiate the logarithm of the likelihood function with respect to each unknown parameter and set it to zero. Then solve the resulting first-order conditions for the maximum likelihood estimators. The density function of u is given by [see Equation (2.4)]

$$f(u) = \frac{1}{(\sigma\sqrt{2\pi})} e^{-u^2/(2\sigma^2)}$$

Because the observations were drawn independently, the likelihood function of u_1, $u_2, \ldots, u_n$ is

$$L(\alpha, \beta, \sigma^2) = f(u_1)f(u_2) \cdot \cdots \cdot f(u_n)$$

$$= \frac{1}{(\sigma\sqrt{2\pi})^n} e^{-\Sigma u_t^2/(2\sigma^2)}$$

$$= \frac{1}{(\sigma\sqrt{2\pi})^n} e^{-\Sigma(Y_t-\alpha-\beta X_t)^2/(2\sigma^2)}$$

It is more convenient to maximize the logarithm of the likelihood function, which is equivalent to maximizing L because the logarithm is a monotonic increasing transformation; that is, if $a > b$, then $\ln(a) > \ln(b)$

$$\ln L = -n\ln\sigma - n\ln(\sqrt{2\pi}) - \sum\left[\frac{(Y_t - \alpha - \beta X_t)^2}{2\sigma^2}\right]$$

$$= -n\ln\sigma - n\ln(\sqrt{2\pi}) - \frac{\text{SSE}}{2\sigma^2}$$

where $\text{SSE} = \Sigma(Y_t - \alpha - \beta X_t)^2$. The only place where α and β appear is in SSE. Therefore, maximizing $\ln L$ is equivalent to minimizing SSE (because there is a negative sign before SSE). But minimizing SSE gives the least squares estimators. Therefore, least squares estimators are also MLE provided the us are iid as $N(0, \sigma^2)$. Because maximum likelihood estimators are consistent and asymptotically efficient, so are the OLS estimators.

To obtain the MLE of σ^2, differentiate $\ln L$ partially with respect to σ and set the result to zero. We would then have

$$\frac{\partial(\ln L)}{\partial\sigma} = -\frac{n}{\sigma} + \frac{\text{SSE}}{\sigma^3} = 0$$

Solving this for σ^2, we get $\sigma^2 = \text{SSE}/n$. But SSE depends on α and β. However, we can use their maximum likelihood estimates $\hat{\alpha}$ and $\hat{\beta}$. We therefore get the MLE of the variance of u_t as $\tilde{\sigma}^2 = \Sigma \hat{u}_t^2/n$. As stated earlier, this is not unbiased. An unbiased estimate is obtained by dividing $\Sigma \hat{u}_t^2$ by $n - 2$ and using $\hat{\sigma}^2$ defined in Equation (3.22). This unbiasedness is proved in Appendix Section 3.A.7.

3.A.6 Derivation of the Variances of the Estimators

From Equation (3.12), $\hat{\beta} = S_{xy}/S_{xx}$. Because X is nonrandom by Assumption 3.4, S_{xx} is also nonrandom and hence $\text{Var}(\hat{\beta}) = \text{Var}(S_{xy})/S_{xx}^2$. From Equation (3.15), $S_{xy} = \beta S_{xx} + S_{xu}$, and therefore $\text{Var}(S_{xy}) = \text{Var}(S_{xu})$. We note from Equation (3.16) that $S_{xu} = \Sigma(X_t - \overline{X})u_t$. It is stated in Property 2.A.5c that the variance of a sum of random variables is the sum of the variances provided the covariance terms are zero. By Assumption 3.6, u_t and u_s are uncorrelated for all $t \neq s$ and the covariances are zero. Therefore,

$$\mathrm{Var}(S_{xu}) = \mathrm{Var}\left[\sum (X_t - \overline{X})u_t\right] = \sum \mathrm{Var}[(X_t - \overline{X})u_t] = \sum (X_t - \overline{X})^2 \mathrm{Var}(u_t)$$

By Assumption 3.5, $\mathrm{Var}(u_t) = \sigma^2$. Therefore, $\mathrm{Var}(S_{xu}) = \sigma^2 \sum (X_t - \overline{X})^2 = \sigma^2 S_{xx}$. It follows from this that

$$\mathrm{Var}(\hat{\beta}) = \frac{\mathrm{Var}(S_{xy})}{S_{xx}^2} = \frac{\sigma^2 S_{xx}}{S_{xx}^2} = \frac{\sigma^2}{S_{xx}}$$

We have thus derived Equation (3.19). The procedure for deriving Equations (3.20) and (3.21) is similar and is left as an exercise to the reader.

3.A.7 Unbiased Estimator of the Variance of the Error Term

In Equation (3.22), it was stated that $s^2 = \hat{\sigma}^2 = (\Sigma \hat{u}_t^2)/(n - 2)$ is an unbiased estimator of σ^2. This is proved here.

$$\hat{u}_t = Y_t - \hat{\alpha} - \hat{\beta}X_t = Y_t - (\overline{Y} - \hat{\beta}\overline{X}) - \hat{\beta}X_t$$

using Equation (3.11) for $\hat{\alpha}$. Because Y_t is given by Equation (3.1), $\overline{Y} = \alpha + \beta\overline{X} + \overline{u}$, where $\overline{u}$ is $\Sigma u_t/n$. We therefore have, grouping all the β terms,

$$\hat{u}_t = (\alpha + \beta X_t + u_t) - (\alpha + \beta\overline{X} + \overline{u}) + \hat{\beta}\overline{X} - \hat{\beta}X_t$$

$$= (u_t - \overline{u}) - (\hat{\beta} - \beta)(X_t - \overline{X})$$

The sum of squares of $\hat{u}_t$ is therefore given by

$$\sum \hat{u}_t^2 = \sum (u_t - \overline{u})^2 + (\hat{\beta} - \beta)^2 \sum (X_t - \overline{X})^2 - 2(\hat{\beta} - \beta)\sum (X_t - \overline{X})(u_t - \overline{u})$$

$$= S_{uu} + (\hat{\beta} - \beta)^2 S_{xx} - 2(\hat{\beta} - \beta)S_{xu}$$

using the notation similar to that in Equations (3.9) and (3.10). From Equation (3.15), $S_{xu} = S_{xy} - \beta S_{xx} = S_{xx}(\hat{\beta} - \beta)$. Substituting this in the preceding equation and combining the second and third terms, we have

$$\sum \hat{u}_t^2 = S_{uu} - (\hat{\beta} - \beta)^2 S_{xx}$$

To compute the expected value of the error sum of squares, we need $E(S_{uu})$ and $E[(\hat{\beta} - \beta)^2]$. We note from Property 2.15b that $E(S_{uu}) = (n - 1)\mathrm{Var}(u) = (n - 1)\sigma^2$. Also,

$$E[(\hat{\beta} - \beta)^2] = \mathrm{Var}(\hat{\beta}) = \frac{\sigma^2}{S_{xx}}$$

from Equation (3.19). Putting all this together, we obtain

$$E\left(\sum \hat{u}_t^2\right) = E(S_{uu}) - S_{xx}E[(\hat{\beta} - \beta)^2] = (n-1)\sigma^2 - \sigma^2 = (n-2)\sigma^2$$

Dividing through by $n-2$ we have the desired result that

$$E(\hat{\sigma}^2) = E\left[\frac{\sum \hat{u}_t^2}{n-2}\right] = \sigma^2$$

Hence, $\hat{\sigma}^2$ is an unbiased estimator of σ^2.

3.A.8 Derivation of Equation 3.26

The total sum of squares can be rewritten as follows:

$$\sum (Y_t - \overline{Y})^2 = \sum (Y_t - \hat{Y}_t + \hat{Y}_t - \overline{Y})^2$$

$$= \sum (Y_t - \hat{Y}_t)^2 + \sum (\hat{Y}_t - \overline{Y})^2 + 2\sum (Y_t - \hat{Y}_t)(\hat{Y}_t - \overline{Y})$$

As $\hat{u}_t = Y_t - \hat{Y}_t$, the first two terms are what we had in Equation (3.26). All we need now is to show that $\sum (Y_t - \hat{Y}_t)(\hat{Y}_t - \overline{Y}) = \sum \hat{u}_t(\hat{Y}_t - \overline{Y}) = 0$.

$$\sum \hat{u}_t(\hat{Y}_t - \overline{Y}) = \sum \hat{u}_t(\hat{\alpha} + \hat{\beta}X_t - \overline{Y}) = \hat{\alpha}\sum \hat{u}_t + \hat{\beta}\sum \hat{u}_t X_t - \overline{Y}\sum \hat{u}_t$$

From the first normal Equation (3.4), $\sum \hat{u}_t = \sum (Y_t - \hat{\alpha} - \hat{\beta}X_t) = 0$. From Equation (3.5), $\sum \hat{u}_t X_t = \sum (Y_t - \hat{\alpha} - \hat{\beta}X_t)X_t = 0$, thus proving the result.

3.A.9 Derivation of Equation 3.27a

To derive Equation (3.27a), we first derive the sample covariance (denoted by $\widehat{\text{Cov}}$) between Y_t and $\hat{Y}_t$. From Equation (2.10),

$$\widehat{\text{Cov}}(Y_t, \hat{Y}_t) = \frac{1}{n-1} \sum (Y_t - \overline{Y})(\hat{Y}_t - \overline{Y})$$

Note that the mean of $\hat{Y}_t$ is also $\overline{Y}$ because $\hat{\alpha} + \hat{\beta}\overline{X} = \overline{Y}$. Also,

$$Y_t - \overline{Y} = (Y_t - \hat{Y}_t) + (\hat{Y}_t - \overline{Y}) = \hat{u}_t + (\hat{Y}_t - \overline{Y})$$

Therefore,

$$\widehat{\text{Cov}}(Y_t, \hat{Y}_t) = \frac{\sum \hat{u}_t(\hat{Y}_t - \overline{Y})}{n-1} + \frac{\sum (\hat{Y}_t - \overline{Y})^2}{n-1}$$

It was shown in the previous section that the first term is zero. Hence, the covariance between Y_t and $\hat{Y}_t$ is the same as the second term, which is RSS/$(n-1)$:

$$\widehat{\text{Cov}(Y_t, \hat{Y}_t)} = \frac{\text{RSS}}{n-1}$$

We also have

$$\widehat{\text{Var}(Y_t)} = \frac{\text{TSS}}{n-1} \quad \text{and} \quad \widehat{\text{Var}(\hat{Y}_t)} = \frac{\sum(\hat{Y}_t - \overline{Y})^2}{n-1} = \frac{\text{RSS}}{n-1}$$

It will be recalled from Equation (2.7) that the square of the simple correlation coefficient between Y_t and $\hat{Y}_t$ is given by

$$r_{Y\hat{Y}}^2 = \frac{\widehat{\text{Cov}^2(Y_t, \hat{Y}_t)}}{\widehat{\text{Var}(Y_t)}\,\widehat{\text{Var}(\hat{Y}_t)}}$$

Substituting for the covariance and variances from the expressions just derived and canceling $n-1$, we have

$$r_{Y\hat{Y}}^2 = \frac{\text{RSS}^2}{\text{TSS RSS}} = \frac{\text{RSS}}{\text{TSS}} = R^2$$

Thus, the square of the simple correlation between the observed value Y_t and the value $\hat{Y}_t$ predicted by the regression model is the same as R^2 defined in Equation (3.27).

3.A.10 Proof That $r_{xy}^2 = R^2$ for a Simple Regression Model

Here we show that in the case of a simple regression model, R^2 is also equal to the square of the simple correlation between X and Y. From Equation (2.11), $r_{xy}^2 = S_{xy}^2/(S_{xx}S_{yy})$. S_{yy} is the same as the total sum of squares, TSS. Also, RSS $= \sum(\hat{Y}_t - \overline{Y})^2$. Because $\hat{Y}_t = \hat{\alpha} + \hat{\beta}X_t$ and $\overline{Y} = \hat{\alpha} + \hat{\beta}\overline{X}$, we have $\hat{Y}_t - \overline{Y} = \hat{\beta}(X_t - \overline{X})$. Therefore,

$$\text{RSS} = \sum(\hat{Y}_t - \overline{Y})^2 = \hat{\beta}^2 \sum(X_t - \overline{X})^2 = \hat{\beta}^2 S_{xx}$$

From Equation (3.12), $\hat{\beta} = S_{xy}/S_{xx}$. Substituting this for one of the $\hat{\beta}$s above, we obtain

$$\text{RSS} = \hat{\beta}\left(\frac{S_{xy}}{S_{xx}}\right)(S_{xx}) = \hat{\beta}S_{xy}$$

Substituting for S_{xy} from this and noting that $S_{yy} = \text{TSS}$, we get

$$r_{xy}^2 = \frac{S_{xy}^2}{S_{xx}S_{yy}} = \frac{S_{xy}}{S_{xx}}\frac{S_{xy}}{\text{TSS}} = \frac{\hat{\beta}S_{xy}}{\text{TSS}} = R^2$$

This establishes the result.

3.A.11 Derivation of Equation 3.29

$$\text{Var}(\hat{Y}_0) = E[\,\hat{Y}_0 - E(\hat{Y}|X_0)\,]^2$$

$$= E[\hat{\alpha} + \hat{\beta}X_0 - \alpha - \beta X_0]^2 = E[(\hat{\alpha} - \alpha) + X_0(\hat{\beta} - \beta)]^2$$

$$= \text{Var}(\hat{\alpha}) + X_0^2\text{Var}(\hat{\beta}) + 2X_0\,\text{Cov}(\hat{\alpha}, \hat{\beta})$$

In deriving the above, we have made use of Property 2.8a. Substituting from Equations (3.19), (3.20), and (3.21), we get

$$\text{Var}(\hat{Y}_0) = \sigma^2\left[\frac{\sum X_t^2}{nS_{xx}} + X_0^2\frac{1}{S_{xx}} - 2\frac{X_0\overline{X}}{S_{xx}}\right]$$

where $S_{xx} = \Sigma X_t^2 - n\overline{X}^2$. Noting that $\Sigma X_t^2 = S_{xx} + n\overline{X}^2$ and substituting for that in the expression for the variance, we get

$$\text{Var}(\hat{Y}_0) = \sigma^2\left[\frac{1}{n} + \frac{\overline{X}^2 + X_0^2 - 2X_0\overline{X}}{S_{xx}}\right] = \sigma^2\left[\frac{1}{n} + \frac{(X_0 - \overline{X})^2}{S_{xx}}\right]$$

This establishes Equation (3.29).

3.A.12 Derivation of Equation 3.30

Let $\hat{u}_0 = Y_0 - \hat{Y}_0$ be the error in the point forecast of Y_0, where $\hat{Y}_0 = \hat{\alpha} + \hat{\beta}X_0$ is the predictor of the mean. Therefore we have

$$\mathrm{Var}(\hat{u}_0) = \mathrm{Var}(Y_0) + \mathrm{Var}(\hat{Y}_0) - 2\,\mathrm{Cov}(Y_0, \hat{Y}_0)$$

Because $Y_0 = \alpha + \beta X_0 + u_0$, $\mathrm{Var}(Y_0) = \sigma^2$. Also, $\mathrm{Var}(\hat{Y}_0)$ is given by Equation (3.27). Finally, $\mathrm{Cov}(Y_0, \hat{Y}_0) = 0$, because u_0 is uncorrelated with the other residuals and hence is uncorrelated with $\hat{\alpha}$ and $\hat{\beta}$. We thus have

$$\mathrm{Var}(\hat{u}_0) = \sigma^2 \left[1 + \frac{1}{n} + \frac{(X_0 - \overline{X})^2}{S_{xx}} \right]$$

CHAPTER 4

Multiple Regression Models

In Chapter 3 we confined ourselves to the simple case of a two-variable regression. We now take up **multiple regression,** which relates a given dependent variable Y to several independent variables, $X_1, X_2, \ldots, X_k$. The multiple linear regression model has the following general formulation:

$$Y_t = \beta_1 + \beta_2 X_{t2} + \cdots + \beta_k X_{tk} + u_t \qquad (4.1)$$

X_{t1} is set to 1 to allow for an "intercept." The subscript t refers to the observation number and varies from 1 to n. The assumptions made on the disturbance term, u_t, are identical to those specified in Chapter 3. In the general specification of a multiple regression model, the choice of the dependent and independent variables comes from economic theory, intuition, and past experience. In the real estate example used in Chapter 3, the dependent variable was the price of a single-family home. We mentioned there that the **hedonic price index** depends on the characteristics of a house. Table 4.1 presents additional data for the 14 sample houses sold. Note that the data for X_1 is simply a column of 1s and corresponds to a constant term. Including the constant term, there are k independent variables and hence k unknown regression coefficients to estimate.

The multiple linear model for this example will be as follows:

$$\text{PRICE} = \beta_1 + \beta_2\text{SQFT} + \beta_3\text{BEDRMS} + \beta_4\text{BATHS} + u \qquad (4.2)$$

As before, price is measured in thousands of dollars. Besides the square footage of the living area, price is related to the number of bedrooms as well as the number of bathrooms.

The effect of a change in Y_t when only X_{ti} is changed is given by $\Delta Y_t / \Delta X_{ti} = \beta_i$. Hence, the interpretation of the regression coefficient β_i is that, keeping the values of all the other variables the same, if X_{ti} is changed by one unit, Y_t is expected to change, on average, by β_i units. Thus, β_4 in Equation (4.2) is interpreted as follows: Between two houses with the same SQFT and BEDRMS, the one with an extra bathroom is expected to sell, on average, for β_4 thousand dollars more. Multiple regression analysis thus enables us to control for a subset of explanatory variables and examine the effect of a selected independent variable.

Table 4.1   Data for Single-Family Houses (price in thousands of dollars)

t	Price (Y)	Constant (X_1)	SQFT (X_2)	BEDRMS (X_3)	BATHS (X_4)
1	199.9	1	1,065	3	1.75
2	228	1	1,254	3	2
3	235	1	1,300	3	2
4	285	1	1,577	4	2.5
5	239	1	1,600	3	2
6	293	1	1,750	4	2
7	285	1	1,800	4	2.75
8	365	1	1,870	4	2
9	295	1	1,935	4	2.5
10	290	1	1,948	4	2
11	385	1	2,254	4	3
12	505	1	2,600	3	2.5
13	425	1	2,800	4	3
14	415	1	3,000	4	3

4.1   Normal Equations

In the case of the multiple regression model, Assumption 3.4 is modified as follows: *Each X is given so that* $\text{Cov}(X_{si}, u_t) = E(X_{si} u_t) = 0$ *for each i from* 1 *to k and each s,t from* 1 *to n.* Thus, *each of the independent variables is assumed to be uncorrelated with all the error terms.* In the case of the ordinary least squares (OLS) procedure, we define the sum of squared errors as

$$\text{ESS} = \sum_{t=1}^{n} \hat{u}_t^2 = \sum_{t=1}^{n} (Y_t - \hat{\beta}_1 - \hat{\beta}_2 X_{t2} - \cdots - \hat{\beta}_k X_{tk})^2$$

OLS procedure minimizes ESS with respect to $\hat{\beta}_1, \hat{\beta}_2, \ldots, \hat{\beta}_k$. By proceeding as in Section 3.A.3, we can derive the normal equations, the number of normal equations being equal to the number of coefficients estimated. We thus obtain k equations in the k unknown regression coefficients (the summations are over the index t—that is, over observations):

$$\sum Y_t = n\hat{\beta}_1 + \hat{\beta}_2 \sum X_{t2} + \cdots + \hat{\beta}_k \sum X_{tk}$$
$$\sum Y_t X_{t2} = \hat{\beta}_1 \sum X_{t2} + \hat{\beta}_2 \sum X_{t2}^2 + \cdots + \hat{\beta}_k \sum X_{tk} X_{t2}$$

$$\sum Y_t X_{ti} = \hat{\beta}_1 \sum X_{ti} + \hat{\beta}_2 \sum X_{t2} X_{ti} + \cdots + \hat{\beta}_k \sum X_{tk} X_{ti}$$
$$\sum Y_t X_{tk} = \hat{\beta}_1 \sum X_{tk} + \hat{\beta}_2 \sum X_{t2} X_{tk} + \cdots + \hat{\beta}_k \sum X_{tk}^2$$

The k normal equations can (with a few exceptions noted in Chapter 5) be solved uniquely for the βs. Standard computer programs do all the calculations once the data have been entered and the dependent and independent variables specified. Appendix 4.A.1 describes the steps for a three-variable model in which Y is regressed against a constant term, X_2, and X_3.

Properties 3.1 through 3.3 are valid in the case of multiple linear regression also. Thus, the OLS estimates are BLUE, unbiased, efficient, and consistent. Residuals and predicted values are obtained from the following relations:

$$\hat{u}_t = Y_t - \hat{\beta}_1 - \hat{\beta}_2 X_{t2} - \cdots - \hat{\beta}_k X_{tk}$$

$$\hat{Y}_t = \hat{\beta}_1 + \hat{\beta}_2 X_{t2} + \cdots + \hat{\beta}_k X_{tk} = Y_t - \hat{u}_t$$

● EXAMPLE 4.1

For the model specified in Equation (4.2), the estimated relation is (see Practice Computer Session 4.1)

$$\widehat{\text{PRICE}} = 129.062 + 0.1548\,\text{SQFT} - 21.588\,\text{BEDRMS} - 12.193\,\text{BATHS}$$

We note immediately that the regression coefficients for BEDRMS and BATHS are both negative, which goes against what we would expect. One might intuitively feel that adding a bedroom and/or a bathroom should increase the value of the property. However, the regression coefficient has the proper interpretation only when other things are equal. Thus, if we increase the number of bedrooms by one, *holding* SQFT *and* BATHS *constant,* the average price is expected to go down by $21,588. If the same living area is divided up to provide one more bedroom, each room will be much smaller. The data indicate that, on average, buyers value such a division lower and hence would be willing to pay only a smaller price.

A similar argument also applies to BATHS. Holding SQFT and BEDRMS constant, if we add a bathroom, the average price is expected to decrease by $12,193. Again, adding a bathroom but keeping the total number of square feet the same also means having smaller bedrooms. The results reveal buyers' aversion and hence we observe a reduction in the average price. We note from these arguments that what appeared at first to be unexpected signs (commonly referred to as "wrong signs") had a sensible explanation.

Suppose we add a bedroom and increase the overall number of square feet by 300 (allowing for an additional hallway and other related items). Then BEDRMS will increase by 1 and SQFT will increase by 300. The change in average price (ΔPRICE) as a result of this combined effect will be

$$\Delta\widehat{\text{PRICE}} = \hat{\beta}_2 \Delta\text{SQFT} + \hat{\beta}_3 \Delta\text{BEDRMS} = 300\hat{\beta}_2 + \hat{\beta}_3$$

In the model, this amounts to a net increase of $24,852 in the estimated average price [calculated as $(300 \times 0.1548) - 21.588$, in thousands of dollars], which appears reasonable.

● PRACTICE PROBLEM 4.1

Suppose a bedroom and a bathroom are added, with an increase in the living area of 350 square feet. By how much is the average price expected to go up? Is the numerical value believable?

● PRACTICE PROBLEM 4.2

Forecast the average price of a house with 4 bedrooms, 3 baths, and 2,500 square feet of living area. Does the forecast appear reasonable for the data given in Table 4.1?

An unbiased estimator of the residual variance σ^2 is obtained by $s^2 = \hat{\sigma}^2 = \Sigma \hat{u}_t^2/(n - k)$, where n is the number of observations used in the estimation and k is the number of regression coefficients estimated, including the constant term. The proof of this statement is similar, in principle, to that given in Section 3.A.7, but is much more complicated because there are k normal equations here (see Johnston, 1984, pp. 180–181). In Chapter 3 we divided the error sum of squares by $n - 2$ to get an unbiased estimator of σ^2. Here, the k normal equations impose k constraints, resulting in a "loss" of k degrees of freedom. Hence we divide by $n - k$. Because $\hat{\sigma}^2$ should be nonnegative, n must be larger than k. The procedure for computing standard errors of the $\hat{\beta}$s is similar, but the calculations are now much more tedious. Computer programs provide all the statistics needed to estimate the parameters and test hypotheses on them. It can be shown that $\Sigma \hat{u}_t^2/\sigma^2$ has the chi-square distribution with $n - k$ degrees of freedom (see Johnston, 1984, p. 181). These results are summarized in Property 4.1.

Property 4.1

a. An unbiased estimator of the error variance (σ^2) is given by

$$s^2 = \hat{\sigma}^2 = \frac{\text{ESS}}{n - k} = \frac{\Sigma \hat{u}_t^2}{n - k}$$

where ESS is the sum of squares of the residuals.

b. ESS/σ^2 has the chi-square distribution with $n - k$ d.f. Note that this property critically depends on Assumption 3.8 that the error terms u_t are normally distributed as $N(0, \sigma^2)$.

Forecasts and Their Standard Errors

As in the simple regression model, we would be interested in generating conditional forecasts of the dependent variable for given values of the independent variables. Suppose X_{fi} is the given value of the ith independent variable for $i = 2, \ldots, k$, and $t = f$, for which we wish to forecast Y. Define

$$\beta = \beta_1 + \beta_2 X_{f2} + \cdots + \beta_k X_{fk}$$

Then $\hat{\beta} = \hat{Y}_f$, defined earlier for $t = f$, and hence the required prediction is the estimated value of β, and the corresponding standard error should enable us to construct a confidence interval for the forecast. Solving for β_1 from the preceding equation and substituting in the original model, we obtain

$$Y_t = \beta - \beta_2 X_{f2} - \cdots - \beta_k X_{fk} + \beta_2 X_{t2} + \cdots + \beta_k X_{tk} + u_t$$

Grouping terms appropriately, this can be rewritten as

$$Y_t = \beta + \beta_2(X_{t2} - X_{f2}) + \cdots + \beta_k(X_{tk} - X_{fk}) + u_t$$
$$= \beta + \beta_2 Z_{t2} + \cdots + \beta_k Z_{tk} + u_t$$

where $Z_{ti} = X_{ti} - X_{fi}$, for $i = 2, \ldots, k$. This reformulation suggests the following steps for carrying out the forecast exercise:

Step 1   Given the value X_{fi} for the ith independent variable and $t = f$, generate the new variable $Z_{ti} = X_{ti} - X_{fi}$ for $i = 2, \ldots, k$.

Step 2   Regress Y_t against a constant term and the newly generated variables $Z_{t2}, \ldots, Z_{tk}$.

Step 3   The estimated constant term is the required point forecast. The corresponding confidence interval (see Section 3.8) is given by $(\hat{\beta} - t^* s_f, \hat{\beta} + t^* s_f)$, where t^* is the critical value for the t-distribution with $n - k$ degrees of freedom and the selected level of significance, and s_f is the standard error for the estimated constant term obtained in Step 2.

● EXAMPLE 4.2

In the real estate example, let SQFT = 2,000, BEDRMS = 4, and BATHS = 2.5. The first step is to generate new variables, SQFT2 = SQFT − 2000, BEDRMS2 = BEDRMS − 4, and BATHS2 = BATHS − 2.5. Next regress PRICE against a constant term and SQFT2, BEDRMS2, and BATHS2. From Practice Computer Session 4.1, we note that the predicted average price for this house is $321,830 and the standard error of forecast is $13,865. This gives the 95 percent confidence interval as $321,830 \pm (2.201 \times 13865)$, which gives the interval as (291313, 352347).

● 4.2   Goodness of Fit

When measuring the goodness of fit, the total sum of squares, regression sum of squares, and error sum of squares have the same form as before, and TSS = RSS + ESS here also (provided the model has a constant term). Thus,

$$\text{TSS} = \sum (Y_t - \bar{Y})^2 \qquad \text{RSS} = \sum (\hat{Y}_t - \bar{Y})^2 \qquad \text{ESS} = \sum \hat{u}_t^2$$

The goodness of fit is measured as before by $R^2 = 1 - (\text{ESS}/\text{TSS})$. If the constant term is present in the model, R^2 is also equal to the square of the correlation coefficient between Y_t and $\hat{Y}_t$. This way of defining R^2, however, creates a problem. It can be shown that the addition of any variable (whether or not it makes sense in the context) will never decrease R^2. The algebraic proof of this statement is quite tedious, but we can argue it intuitively. When a new variable is added and ESS minimized, we are minimizing over a larger set of variables and hence the new ESS is likely to be smaller (at least not larger). More specifically, suppose the term $\beta_{k+1} X_{tk+1}$ is added to Equation (4.1) and a new model obtained. If the *minimum* sum of squares for this new model is *higher* than that for the old model, then setting β_{k+1} to zero and using the old estimates for the other βs is better, and hence the new estimates could not have minimized ESS. It follows that when a new variable is added, the corresponding R^2 cannot decrease, but is likely to increase. This being so, one is always tempted to add new variables in order to do just that—increase R^2— regardless of the importance of the variables to the problem at hand.

To penalize this kind of "fishing expedition," a different measure of goodness of fit is used more frequently. This measure is called the **adjusted R^2** or **R^2 adjusted for degrees of freedom** (we encountered this in the computer printouts in Chapter 3). To develop this measure, first recall that R^2 measures the fraction of the variance of Y "explained" by the model; equivalently, it is one minus the fraction "unexplained," which is due to the error variance $\mathrm{Var}(u)$. A natural measure, call it $\overline{R}^2$ (*R*-bar squared), is therefore

$$\overline{R}^2 = 1 - \frac{\widehat{\mathrm{Var}(u)}}{\widehat{\mathrm{Var}(Y)}}$$

We know that an unbiased estimator of $\sigma^2 = \mathrm{Var}(u)$ is given by $\mathrm{ESS}/(n - k)$, and an unbiased estimator of $\mathrm{Var}(Y)$ is given by $\mathrm{TSS}/(n - 1)$. Substituting these in the preceding equation, we obtain

$$\overline{R}^2 = 1 - \frac{\mathrm{ESS}/(n - k)}{\mathrm{TSS}/(n - 1)} = 1 - \frac{\mathrm{ESS}(n - 1)}{\mathrm{TSS}(n - k)}$$

$$= 1 - \frac{n - 1}{n - k}(1 - R^2) = 1 - \frac{\hat{\sigma}^2(n - 1)}{\mathrm{TSS}}$$

The addition of a variable leads to a gain in R^2 but also to a loss of 1 d.f., because we are estimating an extra parameter. The adjusted R^2 is a better measure of goodness of fit because it allows for the trade-off between increased R^2 and decreased d.f. Also note that because $(n - 1)/(n - k)$ is never less than 1, $\overline{R}^2$ will never be higher than R^2. However, although R^2 cannot be negative, $\overline{R}^2$ can be less than zero. For example, when $n = 26$, $k = 6$, and $R^2 = 0.1$, we have $\overline{R}^2 = -0.125$. A negative $\overline{R}^2$ indicates that the model does not describe the data-generating process adequately.

● EXAMPLE 4.3

Table 4.2 presents the estimated regression coefficients and associated statistics for four alternative models (Practice Computer Session 4.1 has instructions for

● **Table 4.2   Estimated Models for the Home Price Data**

Variable	Model A	Model B	Model C	Model D
CONSTANT	52.351 (1.404)	121.179 (1.511)	129.062 (1.462)	317.493 (13.423)
SQFT	0.13875 (7.407)	0.14831 (6.993)	0.1548 (4.847)	
BEDRMS		−23.911 (−0.970)	−21.588 (−0.799)	
BATHS			−12.193 (−0.282)	
ESS	18,274	16,833	16,700	101,815
R^2	0.821	0.835	0.836	0.000
$\bar{R}^2$	0.806	0.805	0.787	0.000
F	54.861	27.767	16.989	180.189
d.f.	12	11	10	13
SGMASQ	1,523*	1,530	1,670	7,832
AIC	1,737*	1,846	2,112	8,389
FPE	1,740*	1,858	2,147	8,391
HQ	1,722*	1,822	2,077	8,354
SCHWARZ	1,903*	2,117	2,535	8,781
SHIBATA	1,678*	1,718	1,874	8,311
GCV	1,777*	1,948	2,338	8,434
RICE	1,827*	2,104	2,783	8,485

Note: Values in parentheses are the corresponding *t*-statistics, that is, coefficient divided by its standard error.
*Denotes the model that is "best" for the criterion, that is, has the smallest value.

reproducing these). Entries below the degrees of freedom (d.f.) are discussed in the next section. Model A is the same as the one presented in Chapter 3. In Model B, BEDRMS has been added, and in Model C both BEDRMS and BATHS have been added. Model D has no explanatory variables, just a constant term. It will be used in Section 4.4. It is clear from Table 4.2 that, as more variables are added, the residual sum of squares steadily decreases and R^2 increases. $\bar{R}^2$, however, decreases as more variables are added. This means that the gain in R^2 is more than offset by the loss in degrees of freedom, resulting in a net loss in the "goodness of fit." Model D has a zero value for R^2 because its ESS and TSS are the same. This is not surprising because there is nothing in the model that explains the variation in PRICE. It is included here because of its usefulness in testing hypotheses (covered in Section 4.4).

In Model A, SQFT explains 80.6 percent of the variation in home prices. When all three variables are included, however, the model explains 78.7 percent of the variation in prices, which is reasonable for a cross-section study. If additional variables had been included, the model's explanatory power would have been higher. For instance, the lot size, the number and type of built-in appliances, and so on are all possible variables to include. As such information was not available in the sample data, however, we could not include more variables. In Chapter 7 we discuss the effect of a swimming pool on the price.

● **PRACTICE PROBLEM 4.3**

Show that $\bar{R}^2$ and $\hat{\sigma}^2$ move inversely to each other; that is, if $\bar{R}^2$ goes up, then $\hat{\sigma}^2$ must necessarily decrease. (Thus, choosing a model that has a higher $\bar{R}^2$ is equivalent to choosing one that has a lower $\hat{\sigma}^2$.)

Computing R^2 and $\bar{R}^2$ When There Is No Constant Term*

The sum of squares decomposition TSS = RSS + ESS is valid only if the model has a constant term. If the model has no constant term, the appropriate decomposition can be shown to be $\Sigma Y_t^2 = \Sigma \hat{Y}_t^2 + \Sigma \hat{u}_t^2$. Note that the mean $\bar{Y}$ is not subtracted here. Some computer programs calculate R^2 as $1 - (\text{ESS}/\Sigma Y_t^2)$ when the intercept term is absent. This formula is recommended by the National Institute of Standards and Technology. It should be pointed out, however, that the value computed this way is not comparable to the value computed with TSS because the denominators are different between the two models. If the goal is to compare the models with and without constant terms, in terms of their goodness of fit, the formula for R^2 should not be model-dependent. It would be better to use $1 - (\text{ESS}/\text{TSS})$ in both cases so that R^2 could be compared. If R^2 is computed using TSS in the denominator, it is possible for it to be negative when the constant term is absent from the model. Such a negative value indicates that the model might be poorly specified. An alternative and perhaps better measure of R^2 is the square of the correlation between Y_t and $\hat{Y}_t$, which is always nonnegative.

We argued earlier that $\bar{R}^2 = 1 - [\widehat{\text{Var}}(u)/\widehat{\text{Var}}(Y)]$ is a better measure of the variation in Y explained by the model. This suggests the formula

$$\bar{R}^2 = 1 - \frac{\text{ESS} \div (n - k)}{\text{TSS} \div (n - 1)}$$

in *all* cases.

Because computer programs differ in the manner in which R^2 and $\bar{R}^2$ values are calculated in the absence of the constant term, it is recommended that the reader test whatever program is being used and identify whether the measures are comparable across models. Investigators often exclude the constant term if it is insignificant in order to improve the statistical significance of the remaining variables. Unless a strong theoretical reason exists for omitting a constant term (for instance, the capital asset pricing model of Example 1.3 did not have a constant term), the practice is discouraged because it may lead to model misspecification (more on this in Section 4.5).

● 4.3   General Criteria for Model Selection

We showed earlier that by increasing the number of variables in a model, the residual sum of squares $\Sigma \hat{u}_t^2$ will decrease and R^2 will increase, but at the cost of a loss in degrees of freedom. $\bar{R}^2$ and the standard error of the residuals, $[\text{ESS}/(n - k)]^{1/2}$, take account of the trade-off between the reduction in ESS and the loss of degrees of freedom. These are the most commonly used criteria for model comparison.

In general, simpler models are recommended for two technical reasons. First, the inclusion of too many variables makes the relative precision of individual coefficients worse. This point will be explored in detail in Chapter 5. Second, the resulting loss of degrees of freedom would reduce the power of tests performed on the coefficients. Thus, the probability of not rejecting a false hypothesis (type II error) increases as the degrees of freedom decrease. Simpler models are also easier to comprehend than complex models. It is therefore desirable to develop criteria that penalize larger models but do not go to the extreme of always choosing a simpler model.

In recent years, several criteria for choosing among models have been proposed. All of these take the form of the residual sum of squares (ESS) multiplied by a penalty factor that depends on the complexity of the model. A more complex model will reduce ESS but raise the penalty. The criteria thus provide other types of trade-offs between goodness of fit and model complexity. A model with a lower value of a criterion statistic is judged to be preferable. In this section, we present a brief summary of penalty factors without going into the technical motivation for each. For a more detailed summary, along with some applications, the reader should refer to the paper by Engle and Brown (1985).

Akaike (1970, 1974) developed two procedures, one known as the **finite prediction error (FPE)** and the other known as the **Akaike information criterion (AIC).** Hannan and Quinn (1979) suggested another procedure (which will be referred to as the **HQ criterion**). Other criteria include those by Schwarz (1978), Shibata (1981), and Rice (1984), and a **generalized cross validation (GCV)** method developed by Craven and Wahba (1979) and used by Engle, Granger, Rice, and Weiss (1986). Each of these statistics is based on some optimality property, details of which will be found in the papers cited (note that the papers require a knowledge of linear algebra). Table 4.3 summarizes the various criteria (n is the number of observations and k is the number of parameters estimated).

There is no need to include $\overline{R}^2$ in the criteria because $\overline{R}^2$ and SGMASQ ($\hat{\sigma}^2$) are inversely related, and hence a lower SGMASQ automatically implies a higher value

Table 4.3 Model Selection Criteria

SGMASQ:	$\left(\dfrac{\text{ESS}}{n}\right)\left[1 - \left(\dfrac{k}{n}\right)\right]^{-1}$	HQ:	$\left(\dfrac{\text{ESS}}{n}\right)(\ln n)^{2k/n}$
AIC:	$\left(\dfrac{\text{ESS}}{n}\right)e^{(2k/n)}$	RICE:	$\left(\dfrac{\text{ESS}}{n}\right)\left[1 - \left(\dfrac{2k}{n}\right)\right]^{-1}$
FPE:	$\left(\dfrac{\text{ESS}}{n}\right)\dfrac{n+k}{n-k}$	SCHWARZ:	$\left(\dfrac{\text{ESS}}{n}\right)n^{k/n}$
GCV:	$\left(\dfrac{\text{ESS}}{n}\right)\left[1 - \left(\dfrac{k}{n}\right)\right]^{-2}$	SHIBATA:	$\left(\dfrac{\text{ESS}}{n}\right)\dfrac{n+2k}{n}$

for $\overline{R}^2$. $\overline{R}^2$ is useful only to determine the fraction of the variation in Y explained by the Xs.

Ideally, we would like a model to have lower values for all these statistics, as compared to an alternative model. Although it is possible to rank some of these criteria for a given ESS, n, and k, this ordering is meaningless because models differ in both ESS and k. Ramanathan (1992) examined certain special cases more closely. In these special cases some of the criteria might become redundant—that is, a model found to be superior under one criterion will also be superior under a different criterion. In general, however, it is possible to find a model superior under one criterion and inferior under another. For example, the Schwarz criterion penalizes model complexity more heavily than do other measures and hence might give a different conclusion. A model that outperforms another in several of these criteria might be preferred. The AIC criterion, however, is a common one used in time series analysis.

⬤ EXAMPLE 4.4

For the home price data, Table 4.2 has the eight model selection statistics for each of the three models. All the criteria prefer the simplest model, in which the only explanatory variable is SQFT. This means that the reduction in ESS due to a more complex model is not enough to offset the penalty factor associated with it. This result should not really surprise us. The living area depends on the number of bedrooms and bathrooms in the house. Model A therefore indirectly accounts for BEDRMS and BATHS. Hence, we should not expect Models B and C to be so much better as to lower ESS sufficiently.

⬤ 4.4 Testing Hypotheses

In this section we discuss three types of hypothesis testing: (1) testing the statistical significance of individual coefficients, (2) testing several regression coefficients jointly, and (3) testing a linear combination of regression coefficients.

Testing Individual Coefficients

As in Chapter 3, the test of hypothesis on a single regression coefficient is carried out with a t-test. The properties that each $\hat{\beta}_i$ has a normal distribution and that $\text{ESS}/\sigma^2 = (n - k)\hat{\sigma}^2/\sigma^2$ has a chi-square distribution extend to the multivariate case also. The only modification is that ESS/σ^2 is distributed as chi-square with $n - k$ d.f. The steps for carrying out tests on an individual coefficient are as follows:

ONE-TAILED t-TEST

Step 1 $H_0: \beta = \beta_0$, $H_1: \beta > \beta_0$.
Step 2   Construct the t-statistic $t_c = (\hat{\beta} - \beta_0)/s_{\hat{\beta}}$, where $\hat{\beta}$ is the estimate and $s_{\hat{\beta}}$ is its estimated standard error. If $\beta_0 = 0$, this t-value reduces to the ratio

of the regression coefficient to its standard error. Under H_0, it has a t-distribution with $n - k$ d.f.

Step 3   Look up in the t-table the entry corresponding to $n - k$ d.f. and find the point $t_{n-k}^*(a)$ such that the area to the right of it is equal to the level of significance (a).

Step 4   Reject the null hypothesis if $t_c > t^*$. If the alternative had been H_1: $\beta < \beta_0$, H_0 would have been rejected if $t_c < -t^*$. Equivalently, for either alternative, reject if $|t_c| > t^*$.

To use the p-value approach, compute p-value $= P(t > |t_c|$, given $H_0)$ and reject H_0 if the p-value is less than the level of significance.

● EXAMPLE 4.5

Let us apply this to Models B and C in Table 4.2. Model B has 11 d.f. $(14 - 3)$ and Model C has 10 d.f. From Table A.2, $t_{11}^*(0.05) = 1.796$ and $t_{10}^*(0.05) = 1.812$ for a 5 percent test. Thus, for a regression coefficient to be significantly positive or negative, the absolute value of the t-statistics given in Table 4.2 must be greater than 1.796 for Model B and greater than 1.812 for Model C. We note that in every model the regression coefficient for SQFT is significant, whereas all the other regression coefficients are insignificant. This means that in those cases we cannot reject the null hypothesis that the corresponding coefficient is zero.

Would a level of significance other than 5 percent have rejected the null hypothesis? After all, there is nothing special about 5 percent. If the actual level of significance were slightly higher, we might still be willing to reject the null hypothesis. We note from Table A.2 that for a 10 percent level, $t_{10}^*(0.1) = 1.372$. The t-statistic for BEDRMS in Model C is 0.799 in absolute value, which is less than 1.372. Therefore, we conclude that BEDRMS is insignificant in Model C, at the 10 percent level of significance. BEDRMS is not significant in Model B even at the 10 percent level.

Using the GRETL program, we computed the p-values for the coefficients of BEDRMS and BATHS (see Practice Computer Session 4.1). They range from 0.175 to 0.39, implying that, if we reject the null hypothesis that these coefficients are zero, there is a 17.5 to 39 percent chance of making a mistake of type I. As these are higher than one would normally tolerate, we do not reject H_0 but instead conclude that the coefficients are not significantly different from zero.

TWO-TAILED t-TEST

Step 1 H_0: $\beta = \beta_0$, H_1: $\beta \neq \beta_0$.

Step 2   Construct the same t-statistic, $t_c = (\hat{\beta} - \beta_0)/s_{\hat{\beta}}$, where $\hat{\beta}$ is the estimate and $s_{\hat{\beta}}$ is its standard error. Under H_0, it has a t-distribution with $n - k$ d.f.

Step 3   Look up in the t-table A.2 the entry corresponding to $n - k$ d.f. and find $t_{n-k}^*(a/2)$ such that the area to the right of it is one-half the level of significance.

Step 4   Reject the null hypothesis if $|t_c| > t^*$.

To use the p-value approach, compute p-value $= 2P(t > |t_c|$, given $H_0)$ and reject H_0 if the p-value is less than the level of significance.

To summarize, a low p-value (which is the same as the probability of a type I error of rejecting a true hypothesis) implies that we are "safe" in rejecting the null hypothesis that the coefficient is zero (for $\beta_0 = 0$) and concluding that it is significantly different from zero. If the p-value is high, then we cannot reject the null but would instead conclude that the coefficient is statistically insignificant.

⬤ EXAMPLE 4.6

Let us apply the two-tailed test to Models B and C. In Model B, the d.f. is 11 and hence $t_{11}^*(0.025)$ is 2.201 for a 5 percent level of significance. In Model C, $t_{10}^*(0.025) = 2.228$. Thus, for a regression coefficient to be significantly different from zero at the 5 percent level, the t-statistics given in Table 4.2 must be greater than 2.201 in absolute value for Model B and greater than 2.228 in absolute value for Model C. We note that in every model the regression coefficient for SQFT is significant, whereas all the other regression coefficients are insignificant. This means that in those cases we cannot reject the null hypothesis that the corresponding coefficient is zero.

Would a level of significance other than 5 percent have rejected the null hypothesis? The p-values are now twice those obtained earlier (that is, 0.35 to 0.78). As these are high, the conclusion is that the observed nonzero values for these regression coefficients could be due to random sampling errors. Thus, given the value of SQFT, the variables BEDRMS and BATHS do not significantly affect the price of a home. This result confirms the earlier one in which Model A was judged superior according to all eight criteria.

⬤ PRACTICE PROBLEM 4.4

Using your regression program, estimate Models B and C, and verify the results in Table 4.2.

It is possible to establish the following property (see Haitovsky, 1969):

Property 4.2

If the absolute value of the t-statistic of a regression coefficient is less than 1, then dropping it from the model will increase the adjusted R^2. Similarly, dropping a variable whose t-statistic is greater than 1 (in absolute value) will reduce $\overline{R}^2$.

This might suggest that, in addition to the critical t-value, we can use a t-value of 1 as a guide in determining whether a variable is a candidate to be dropped. However, since $\overline{R}^2$ is only one of several criteria, it is recommended that individual p-values, model selection statistics, and the theoretical importance of the variables be used to identify candidate variables for elimination (see Sections 4.6 and 4.7 for examples).

Testing Several Coefficients Jointly (The Wald Test)

The *t*-test on individual coefficients is for the significance of particular coefficients. It is also possible to test the **joint significance** of several regression coefficients. For example, consider the following models:

(U) $\text{PRICE} = \beta_1 + \beta_2\text{SQFT} + \beta_3\text{BEDROOMS} + \beta_4\text{BATHS} + u$

(R) $\text{PRICE} = \gamma_1 + \gamma_2\text{SQFT} + v$

Model U (which is Model C in Table 4.2) is called the **unrestricted model,** and Model R (which is Model A in Table 4.2) is called the **restricted model.** This is because β_3 and β_4 are restricted to be zero in Model R. It is possible to test the joint hypothesis $\beta_3 = \beta_4 = 0$ against the alternative that at least one of them is nonzero. The test for this joint hypothesis is known as the **Wald test** (Wald, 1943). The procedure is as follows.

GENERAL WALD TEST   Let the restricted and unrestricted models be (omitting the *t*-subscript):

(U) $Y = \beta_1 + \beta_2 X_2 + \cdots + \beta_m X_m + \beta_{m+1} X_{m+1} + \cdots + \beta_k X_k + u$

(R) $Y = \beta_1 + \beta_2 X_2 + \cdots + \beta_m X_m + v$

Although Model U appears different, it is identical to Equation (4.1). Model R is obtained by omitting several variables from Model U, namely, $X_{m+1}, X_{m+2}, \ldots, X_k$. Thus, the null hypothesis is $\beta_{m+1} = \beta_{m+2} = \cdots = \beta_k = 0$. Note that (U) contains k unknown regression coefficients and (R) contains m unknown regression coefficients. Thus, Model R has $k - m$ fewer parameters. The question we will presently address is whether the $k - m$ excluded variables have a significant *joint* effect on Y.

Suppose these omitted variables have no significant effect on Y. Then we would not expect the error sum of squares of Model R (ESS_R) to be very different from the error sum of squares of Model U (ESS_U). In other words, their difference, $\text{ESS}_R - \text{ESS}_U$, is likely to be small. But how small is small? We know that ESS is sensitive to the units of measurement, and hence it can be made large or small by simply changing the scale. "Small" or "large" is determined by comparing the difference above to ESS_U, the error sum of squares of the full unrestricted model. Thus, $\text{ESS}_R - \text{ESS}_U$ is compared to ESS_U. If the former is "small" relative to the latter, we conclude that omitting $X_{m+1}, X_{m+2}, \ldots, X_k$ has not changed ESS sufficiently to believe that their coefficients are significant.

We know that sums of independent squares have a chi-square distribution (see Section 2.7). Thus, ESS_U/σ^2 is a chi-square with $n - k$ d.f. (*n* observations minus *k* parameters in Model U). It can be shown under the null hypothesis that, because of the additive property of chi-square (Property 2.12b), $(\text{ESS}_R - \text{ESS}_U)/\sigma^2$ is also chi-square with d.f. equal to the number of variables omitted in (R). In Section 2.7, we saw that the ratio of two independent chi-squares has an *F*-distribution that has two parameters: a d.f. for the numerator of the ratio and a d.f. for the denominator. The test statistic is based on this *F*-ratio.

The formal steps for the Wald test (commonly referred to as the **F-test**) are as follows:

Step 1 The null hypothesis is H_0: $\beta_{m+1} = \beta_{m+2} = \cdots = \beta_k = 0$. The alternative hypothesis is H_1: at least one of the βs is nonzero. The null hypothesis has thus $k - m$ restrictions.

Step 2 First regress Y against a constant, $X_2, X_3, \ldots, X_k$, and compute the error sum of squares $\mathrm{ESS_U}$. Next regress Y against a constant, $X_2, X_3, \ldots, X_m$ and compute $\mathrm{ESS_R}$. We know from Property 4.1b that $\mathrm{ESS_U}/\sigma^2$ has the chi-square distribution with d.f. $\mathrm{DF_U} = n - k$ (that is, n observations minus k coefficients estimated). Similarly, under the null, $\mathrm{ESS_R}/\sigma^2$ has the chi-square distribution with d.f. $\mathrm{DF_R} = n - m$. It can be shown that they are independent and, by the additive property of chi-square, their difference $(\mathrm{ESS_R} - \mathrm{ESS_U})/\sigma^2$ is also chi-square, with d.f. equal to the difference in d.f., that is, $\mathrm{DF_R} - \mathrm{DF_U}$. Note that $\mathrm{DF_R} - \mathrm{DF_U}$ is also $k - m$, which is the number of restrictions in the null hypothesis (that is, the number of excluded variables). In Section 2.7, we defined the F-distribution as the ratio of two independent chi-square random variables. This gives the test statistic

$$F_c = \frac{(\mathrm{ESS_R} - \mathrm{ESS_U}) \div (\mathrm{DF_R} - \mathrm{DF_U})}{\mathrm{ESS_U} \div \mathrm{DF_U}} \tag{4.3}$$

$$= \frac{(\mathrm{ESS_R} - \mathrm{ESS_U})/(k - m)}{\mathrm{ESS_U}/(n - k)}$$

$$= \frac{(\text{difference in ESS} \div \text{number of restrictions})}{(\text{error sum of squares of Model U} \div \text{d.f. of Model U})}$$

$$= \frac{(R_U^2 - R_R^2)/(k - m)}{(1 - R_U^2)/(n - k)}$$

where R^2 is the unadjusted goodness-of-fit measure. Division by the degrees of freedom gives the sum of squares per degree of freedom. Under the null hypothesis, F_c has the F-distribution with $k - m$ d.f. for the numerator and $n - k$ d.f. for the denominator.

Step 3 From the entry in the F-table that corresponds to the d.f. $k - m$ for the numerator, $n - k$ for the denominator, and the given level of significance (call it a), obtain $F^*_{k-m, n-k}(a)$ such that the area to the right of F^* is a.

Step 4 The null hypothesis is rejected at the level a if $F_c > F^*$. For the p-value approach, compute p-value $= P(F > F_c|H_0)$ and reject the null hypothesis if p-value is *less than* the level of significance.

⬤ **EXAMPLE 4.7**

In our real estate example, H_0: $\beta_3 = \beta_4 = 0$ and H_1: at least one of the βs is nonzero. Thus, Model U is the same as Model C in Table 4.2, and Model R is Model A. The number of restrictions is therefore 2. Also, $\mathrm{ESS_R} = 18{,}274$ and

ESS_U = 16,700 (see Table 4.2). The degrees of freedom for Model U is 10. Hence, the calculated F-statistic is

$$F_c = \frac{(18{,}274 - 16{,}700)/2}{16{,}700/10} = 0.471$$

From the F-table (Table A.4b), $F^*_{2,\,10}(0.05) = 4.1$. Because F_c is not greater than F^*, we cannot reject the null hypothesis, and hence we conclude that β_3 and β_4 are indeed insignificant at the 5 percent level. Even if the level were 10 percent (see Table A.4c), $F^*_{2,\,10}(0.1) = 2.92 > F_c$. This means that in terms of the significance of the independent variables, the simpler Model A is better. A similar test could have been used to compare Models B and A, but it is unnecessary because the difference between these two models is in only one variable, namely, BEDRMS. In this case, the F-distribution will have only 1 d.f. in the numerator. When this happens, the value of F is simply the square of the t-statistic for BEDRMS (see Property 2.14b). It is easy to verify this. Model B is now unrestricted and hence

$$F_c = \frac{(18{,}274 - 16{,}833)/1}{16{,}833/11} = 0.942$$

whose square root is 0.97, which is the same as the t-statistic in Table 4.2. Thus, the *Wald test need be performed only when there are two or more zero regression coefficients in the null hypothesis.*

The p-value for this example is $P(F > 0.471) = 0.64$. Because a 64 percent chance of rejecting a true H_0 (that the coefficients for BEDRMS and BATHS are zero) is unacceptably high, we do not reject H_0 but instead conclude that the coefficients are statistically insignificantly different from zero.

We see from Table 4.2 that the constant term is not significant in any of the models (except Model D). Nevertheless, it is not wise to drop the constant term from the model. This is because the constant term indirectly captures some of the average effects of omitted variables (this point is discussed more fully in Section 4.5). Hence, dropping the constant term might result in a serious model misspecification.

SPECIAL WALD TEST FOR OVERALL GOODNESS OF FIT   As a special case of the Wald test, consider the following two models:

(U) $Y = \beta_1 + \beta_2 X_2 + \cdots + \beta_k X_k + u$

(SR) $Y = \beta_1 + w$

Model U is the multiple regression model in Equation (4.1), with X_1 being the constant term. In Model SR (super restricted), all but the constant term have been omitted; that is, we have imposed the $k - 1$ restrictions $\beta_2 = \beta_3 = \cdots = \beta_k = 0$. This hypothesis will test the statement "None of the coefficients in the model (excluding the constant term) is statistically significant." A Wald test can be performed for this hypothesis. If the hypothesis is not rejected, we conclude that none of the included variables can jointly explain the variation in Y. This means that we have a poor model and must reformulate it. ESS_U is the error sum of squares for the full model.

To get ESS_{SR}, we first minimize $\Sigma\, w_t^2 = \Sigma\, (Y_t - \beta_1)^2$ with respect to β_1. It is easy to verify that $\hat{\beta}_1 = \overline{Y}$ (see Section 2.5 for proof). Hence, we have $ESS_{SR} = \Sigma(Y_t - \overline{Y})^2$, which is the same as the total sum of squares (TSS_U) of Model U (it is also the total sum of squares for Model SR). The F-statistic now becomes

$$F_c = \frac{(TSS_U - ESS_U)/(k-1)}{ESS_U/(n-k)} = \frac{RSS_U/(k-1)}{ESS_U/(n-k)} = \frac{R^2/(k-1)}{(1-R^2)/(n-k)} \quad \textbf{(4.4)}$$

which can be computed from the unadjusted R^2 of the full model. All regression programs provide this F-statistic as part of the summary statistics for a model. The first task should be to make sure that the null hypothesis of this F-test is rejected, that is, that $F_c > F^*_{k-1,n-k}(a)$. If it is not, we have a model in which none of the independent variables explains the variations in the dependent variable, and hence the model has to be reformulated.

● EXAMPLE 4.8

Table 4.2 provides the Wald F-statistic, given in Equation (4.4), for the home price example. For Model C, $k = 4$, and hence $k - 1 = 3$ and $n - k = 14 - 4 = 10$. The degrees of freedom for the F-statistic are therefore 3 for the numerator and 10 for the denominator. From the F-table, A.4b, the critical value for a 5 percent test is $F^*_{3,10}(0.05) = 3.71$. Because the F-value in Table 4.2 is 16.989 for Model C, we reject the null hypothesis that all the regression coefficients except the constant term are zero. Thus, at least one of the other regression coefficients is significantly different from zero. From the t-test for the coefficient for SQFT, we already know that this is the case. It is easy to verify that $F^*_{2,11}(0.05) = 3.98$ for Model B and $F^*_{1,12}(0.05) = 4.75$ for Model A, and hence all the models reject the null hypothesis that none of the explanatory variables is significant.

We note that the F-statistics for Models B and C are much lower than that for Model A. This is because the differences in R^2 are fairly small, whereas the ratio $(n - 1)/(n - k)$ increases substantially as k increases. We thus see from Equation (4.4) that this can account for the large difference in F. In general, however, the differences in F across models are unimportant. Only the result of the Wald test is of interest.

● PRACTICE PROBLEM 4.5

In Table 4.2, Model D is the super-restricted model that regresses PRICE against only a constant term. Compare this model with Model C as the unrestricted model, and verify the Wald F-value reported in Table 4.2 for Model C. Next do the same for Models A and B. Finally, explain why $R^2 = \overline{R}^2 = 0$ for Model D.

The difference between the two types of *F*-tests should be carefully noted. *The formula given in Equation (4.4) is not applicable when only a few variables have been omitted. It is applicable only when the restricted model has just a constant term.* The *F*-statistic printed by computer programs tests the overall goodness of fit, whereas the *F*-statistic calculated from Equation (4.3) tests whether a subset of the coefficients is significantly different from zero. Also note that the *F*-test is always a one-tailed test.

COMPUTING THE *F*-STATISTIC WHEN THE MODEL HAS NO CONSTANT TERM*   In Section 4.2, we discussed the differences in R^2 measures between two models, one with a constant term and the other without, and argued that the same formula should be used in both cases to compare their relative goodness of fit. When computing the *F*-ratio, however, the formula will be different. To see why this is so, consider the following two models:

(A) $Y = \beta_2 X_2 + \beta_3 X_3 + \cdots + \beta_k X_k + u$

(B) $Y = w$

where the constant term $X_1(=1)$ has been eliminated. Note that the unrestricted Model A has only $k - 1$ parameters now (which means the degrees of freedom is $n - k + 1$) and the restricted Model B has none (with d.f. n). To test for the overall fit of the model, the null hypothesis is again $H_0: \beta_2 = \beta_3 = \cdots = \beta_k = 0$, and the alternative is the same as before. The Wald test is applicable here also and the appropriate formula is Equation (4.3). Let $\text{ESS}_A = \Sigma \hat{u}_i^2$ be the error sum of squares of Model A. In Model B, the error sum of squares will be $\text{ESS}_B = \Sigma Y_t^2$. The value of F is therefore given by

$$F_c = \frac{(\text{ESS}_B - \text{ESS}_A)/(k-1)}{\text{ESS}_A/(n-k+1)} = \frac{\left(\Sigma Y_t^2 - \Sigma \hat{u}_i^2\right)/(k-1)}{\text{ESS}_A/(n-k+1)} \tag{4.4a}$$

$$= \frac{\Sigma \hat{Y}_t^2/(k-1)}{\text{ESS}_A/(n-k+1)}$$

because of the decomposition $\Sigma Y_t^2 = \Sigma \hat{Y}_t^2 + \Sigma \hat{u}_i^2$ in the absence of a constant. Under the null hypothesis, this has an *F*-distribution with $k - 1$ and $n - k + 1$ d.f. The criterion for acceptance/rejection of H_0 is similar. The *F*-statistic presented for Model D tests the hypothesis that the constant term is zero. Because only one coefficient will be omitted here, the *F*-value is the square of the *t*-statistic. Therefore, $F = 180.189$ even though $R^2 = 0$. Note that the formula just given for testing the overall goodness of fit is quite different from that in Equation (4.4).

Testing a Linear Combination of Coefficients

Very often we encounter hypotheses that are stated in terms of linear combinations of regression coefficients. As an illustration, consider the following aggregate consumption function:

$$C_t = \beta_1 + \beta_2 W_t + \beta_3 P_t + u_t$$

where C is the aggregate consumption expenditures in a given region, W is the total wage income, and P is all other income, most of which will be profits and other returns on capital. β_2 is the marginal propensity to consume out of wage income, and β_3 is the marginal propensity to consume out of other income. The hypothesis $\beta_2 = \beta_3$ implies that an *extra* dollar of wage income and an *extra* dollar of other income both contribute the same *extra* amount to average consumption. The t-tests on individual coefficients are no longer applicable because the hypothesis is a linear combination of two regression coefficients. The hypothesis H_0: $\beta_2 = \beta_3$ versus H_1: $\beta_2 \neq \beta_3$ can be tested in three different ways, all of which will lead to the same conclusion.

In later sessions, we will encounter other types of linear combinations, such as $\beta_2 + \beta_3 = 1$ or $\beta_2 + \beta_3 = 0$. We now develop the procedures for testing such linear combinations of regression coefficients. This is done in the context of the following (unrestricted) model with two independent variables (X_2 and X_3):

$$(U) \qquad Y_t = \beta_1 + \beta_2 X_{t2} + \beta_3 X_{t3} + u_t \tag{4.5}$$

METHOD 1 (WALD TEST)

Step 1 Using the restriction, solve for one of the coefficients in terms of the others, and substitute that in the unrestricted model to obtain the restricted model. Thus, to test $\beta_2 = \beta_3$, substitute for β_3 in Equation (4.5) and obtain the following:

$$(R) \qquad Y_t = \beta_1 + \beta_2 X_{t2} + \beta_2 X_{t3} + u_t \tag{4.6}$$

$$= \beta_1 + \beta_2(X_{t2} + X_{t3}) + u_t$$

Rewrite the restricted model by grouping terms appropriately. In our case, we would generate the new variable $Z_t = X_{t2} + X_{t3}$ and write the model as

$$(R) \qquad Y_t = \beta_1 + \beta_2 Z_t + u_t$$

Step 2 Estimate the restricted and unrestricted models, and obtain the error sums of squares, ESS_R and ESS_U.

Step 3 Compute the Wald F-statistic (F_c), using Equation (4.3), and d.f. for the numerator and denominator.

Step 4 From the F-table, obtain the point F^* such that the area to the right is equal to the level of significance. Alternatively, compute p-value $= P(F > F_c)$.

Step 5 Reject H_0 if $F_c > F^*$ or if p-value is less than the level of significance.

● PRACTICE PROBLEM 4.6

Derive the restricted models for the tests $\beta_2 + \beta_3 = 1$ and $\beta_2 + \beta_3 = 0$.

● EXAMPLE 4.9

The file DATA4-2 (see Appendix D) has annual data for the United States for the period 1959–1994 (which gives $n = 36$). The definitions for the variables are as follows:

$CONS(C_t)$ = Real consumption expenditures in billions of 1992 dollars
$GDP(Y_t)$ = Real gross domestic product in billions of 1992 dollars
$WAGES$ = Total compensation of employees (wages, salaries, and supplements) in billions of current dollars
$PRDEFL$ = Implicit price deflator for consumption, 1992 = 100 (this is a price index for consumption goods)

The model we will be estimating is the following consumption function presented earlier:

$$(U) \qquad C_t = \beta_1 + \beta_2 W_t + \beta_3 P_t + u_t \qquad (4.5)$$

where the variables are as defined earlier. Before estimating the model, we have to perform some transformations of the data to get all financial variables in "real" terms (that is, in constant dollars adjusted for inflation).

Consumption is already in real terms. To get the wage income in real terms (W_t), we divide WAGES by PRDEFL and multiply by 100. Total profits and other income from capital are then obtained as GDP minus real wage income.

$$W_t = \frac{100 \, WAGES_t}{PRDEFL_t} \qquad P_t = Y_t - W_t$$

In Equation (4.5), impose the restriction $\beta_2 = \beta_3$. We get

$$(R) \qquad C_t = \beta_1 + \beta_2 W_t + \beta_2 P_t + u_t = \beta_1 + \beta_2 (W_t + P_t) + u_t \qquad (4.6)$$
$$= \beta_1 + \beta_2 Y_t + u_t$$

where $Y_t = W_t + P_t$ is aggregate income. Equation (4.5) is the unrestricted model (with $n - 3$ d.f.) and Equation (4.6) is the restricted model. We can therefore compute the Wald F-statistic given in Equation (4.3) (with $k - m = 1$ because there is only one restriction). Thus,

$$F_c = \frac{(ESS_R - ESS_U)/1}{ESS_U/(n - 3)}$$

will be tested against $F^*_{1, \, n-3}(0.05)$ and the null hypothesis rejected if $F_c > F^*$.

Applying this to the aggregate consumption data, we have the estimated Equations (4.5) and (4.6). (See Practice Computer Session 4.2.)

$$\hat{C}_t = -222.16 + 0.69W_t + 0.74P_t \qquad ESS_U = 38,977$$

$$\hat{C}_t = -221.4 + 0.71Y_t \qquad\qquad ESS_R = 39,305$$

$$F_c = \frac{(39,305 - 38,977)}{38,977/33} = 0.278$$

From Table A.4c, $F^*_{1,33}(0.10)$ is between 2.84 and 2.88. Because $F_c < F^*$, we do not reject the null hypothesis and conclude that the marginal propensities to consume out of wages and profits are not significantly different from each other at the 10 percent level. Thus, although their numerical values are quite different, statistically the difference is due to random chance.

METHOD 2 (INDIRECT t-TEST)   In the second method, the model is transformed in a different way and an indirect t-test carried out. The steps are as follows:

Step 1   Define a new parameter, call it δ, which takes the value zero when the null hypothesis is true. Thus, when H_0 is $\beta_2 = \beta_3$, we would define $\delta = \beta_2 - \beta_3$, and when $\beta_2 + \beta_3 = 1$ is the null hypothesis, $\delta = \beta_2 + \beta_3 - 1$.

Step 2   Express one of the parameters in terms of δ and the remaining parameters, substitute for it in the model, and group terms appropriately.

Step 3   Carry out a t-test using $\hat{\delta}$, the estimate of δ.

● **EXAMPLE 4.10**

In the consumption function case, $\delta = \beta_2 - \beta_3$. The null hypothesis now becomes H_0: $\delta = 0$ versus H_1: $\delta \neq 0$. Also, $\beta_3 = \beta_2 - \delta$. Substituting this in the model we get

$$C_t = \beta_1 + \beta_2 W_t + (\beta_2 - \delta)P_t + u_t$$

$$= \beta_1 + \beta_2(W_t + P_t) - \delta P_t + u_t$$

Because $Y_t = W_t + P_t$, this model becomes

$$C_t = \beta_1 + \beta_2 Y_t - \delta P_t + u_t \qquad\qquad (4.7)$$

which is conceptually equivalent to Equation (4.5). Now regress C against a constant, Y, and P, and use the t-statistic for δ to test the desired hypothesis. In this case, the test reduces to the standard t-test but on a modified model. (As a practice problem, apply the technique to $\beta_2 + \beta_3 = 1$.)

For our data, the estimated Equation (4.7) is (see Practice Computer Session 4.2)

$$\hat{C}_t = \underset{(-11.4)}{-222.16} + \underset{(21.3)}{0.69Y_t} + \underset{(0.5)}{0.04P_t}$$

The values in parentheses are the corresponding *t*-statistics. For $\hat{\delta}$, the *t*-value is 0.5, which is lower than $t_{33}^*(0.05)$, which is between 2.021 and 2.042. Hence, the null hypothesis is not rejected here also.

METHOD 3 (DIRECT *t*-TEST)*   The last method applies a *t*-test directly and does not require the estimation of another regression.

Step 1   As in Method 2, define a new parameter—call it δ—that takes the value zero when the null hypothesis is true. Thus, when H_0 is $\beta_2 = \beta_3$, we would define $\delta = \beta_2 - \beta_3$, and when $\beta_2 + \beta_3 = 1$ is the null hypothesis, $\delta = \beta_2 + \beta_3 - 1$.

Step 2   Derive the statistical distribution of δ directly, and use it to construct a *t*-statistic.

Step 3   Carry out a *t*-test on δ using this directly computed statistic.

The previous test is illustrated here only for the example we have been using, namely, $H_0: \beta_2 = \beta_3$. (As a practice problem, apply this method to the hypothesis $\beta_2 + \beta_3 = 1$.)

Because the OLS estimators are linear combinations of observations on the dependent variable and are hence linear combinations of normally distributed error terms, we know that

$$\hat{\beta}_2 \sim N(\beta_2, \sigma_{\hat{\beta}_2}^2) \qquad \hat{\beta}_3 \sim N(\beta_3, \sigma_{\hat{\beta}_3}^2)$$

where σ^2 refers to the respective variances. Furthermore, a linear combination of normal variates is also normal. Hence,

$$\hat{\beta}_2 - \hat{\beta}_3 \sim N[\beta_2 - \beta_3, \mathrm{Var}(\hat{\beta}_2 - \hat{\beta}_3)]$$

From Property 2.8a, the variance of $\hat{\beta}_2 - \hat{\beta}_3$ is given by $\mathrm{Var}\,(\hat{\beta}_2) + \mathrm{Var}\,(\hat{\beta}_3) - 2\,\mathrm{Cov}(\hat{\beta}_2, \hat{\beta}_3)$. Converting the above to a standard normal distribution (by subtracting the mean and dividing by the standard deviation), we have

$$\frac{\hat{\beta}_2 - \hat{\beta}_3 - (\beta_2 - \beta_3)}{[\mathrm{Var}(\hat{\beta}_2) + \mathrm{Var}(\hat{\beta}_3) - 2\,\mathrm{Cov}(\hat{\beta}_2, \hat{\beta}_3)]^{1/2}} \sim N(0, 1)$$

Under the null hypothesis, $H_0: \beta_2 - \beta_3 = 0$. Also, we do not know the variances and covariance exactly, but they can be estimated (most computer packages provide them as an option). If we substitute estimates of these variances and covariance, the statistic above is not distributed as $N(0, 1)$, but its statistical distribution is $t_{n-k}(n - 3$ in our example). Thus, the same *t*-test can be applied on the *t*-statistic computed from the expression above with appropriate estimates substituted. The calculated *t*-statistic is

$$t_c = \frac{\hat{\beta}_2 - \hat{\beta}_3}{[\widehat{\mathrm{Var}}(\hat{\beta}_2) + \widehat{\mathrm{Var}}(\hat{\beta}_3) - 2\,\widehat{\mathrm{Cov}}(\hat{\beta}_2, \hat{\beta}_3)]^{1/2}}$$

because $\beta_2 = \beta_3$ under the null hypothesis. For a 5 percent level of significance, H_0 is rejected in favor of H_1: $\beta_2 - \beta_3 > 0$ if the computed t_c numerically exceeds $t^*_{n-k}(0.05)$. For a two-sided alternative, H_1: $\beta_2 \neq \beta_3$, obtain $t^*_{n-k}(0.025)$ and reject H_0 if $|t_c| > t^*$. Because this method involves several auxiliary calculations, one of the other methods is recommended over Method 3.

● **EXAMPLE 4.11**

As an illustration, we consider Equation (4.5), which was estimated using the data in DATA4-2 described in Appendix D. The estimated equation with the variances and covariance is the following (see Practice Computer Session 4.2):

$$\hat{C}_t = -222.16 + 0.693W_t + 0.736P_t$$

$$\overline{R}^2 = 0.999 \qquad \text{d.f.} = 33 \qquad \text{ESS} = 38{,}977$$

$$\widehat{\text{Var } \hat{\beta}_2} = (0.032606)^2 \qquad \widehat{\text{Var } \hat{\beta}_3} = (0.048822)^2$$

$$\widehat{\text{Cov } (\hat{\beta}_2, \hat{\beta}_3)} = -0.001552$$

The *t*-statistic is given by

$$t_c = \frac{0.693 - 0.736}{[(0.032606)^2 + (0.048822)^2 - 2(-0.001552)]^{1/2}} = -0.53$$

Because $t^*_{33}(0.05)$, which is between 2.021 and 2.042, is much higher than this numerically, we do not reject the null hypothesis that the marginal propensities to consume out of wages and other income are equal. This result holds whether the alternative is one-sided or two-sided.

We see that all three methods yield the same conclusion. Of the three methods presented, Method 2 is the easiest to implement because it does not require an auxiliary computation but can be used to test the desired hypothesis with a direct *t*-test on a slightly modified model. The Wald test discussed in Method 1 is, however, applicable in more general cases.

● **4.5   Specification Errors**

We mentioned earlier that the choice of independent and dependent variables in an econometric model comes from economic theory, a knowledge of the underlying behavior, and past experience. However, the true relationships among economic variables are never known, and therefore we can expect errors in the specification of econometric models. A **specification error** occurs if we misspecify a model either in terms of the choice of variables, functional forms, or the error structure (that is, the stochastic disturbance term u_t and its properties). In this section we deal with the specification error of the first type. Chapter 6 discusses the choice of functional form, and specification errors in the stochastic disturbance term are discussed in Chapters 8 and 9.

In choosing the independent variables that belong in a model, two types of errors are likely: (1) the omission of a variable that belongs in the model and (2) the inclusion of an irrelevant variable. In a demand function, if we omit the price of the commodity or the income of the household, we are likely to cause misspecification of the first type. In the real estate example used earlier, suppose the type of the roof or the number of built-in appliances or the distance to neighborhood schools do not significantly affect the sale price of a house. If we still include these variables in the model, we would be committing a specification error of the second type, that is, including redundant variables. In the following sections, we examine the theoretical consequences of each of these two types of specification errors and also present empirical evidence.

Omission of an Important Variable

We first consider a case in which a variable that belongs in the model is omitted. Suppose the *true* model is

$$Y_t = \beta_1 + \beta_2 X_{t2} + \beta_3 X_{t3} + u_t$$

but we estimate the model

$$Y_t = \beta_1 + \beta_2 X_{t2} + v_t$$

In other words, the true value of β_3 is nonzero, but we assume that it is zero and hence omit variable X_3 from the specification. The error terms of the true model are assumed to satisfy Assumptions 3.2 through 3.8. The consequences of this type of misspecification are summarized in the following property:

Property 4.3

a.   If an independent variable whose true regression coefficient is nonzero is excluded from a model, the estimated values of all the other regression coefficients will be biased unless the excluded variable is uncorrelated with every included variable.

b.   Even if this condition is met, the estimated constant term is generally biased, and hence forecasts will also be biased.

c.   The estimated variance of the regression coefficient of an included variable will generally be biased, and hence tests of hypotheses are invalid.

We see from Property 4.3 that the consequences of omitting an important variable are very serious. Estimates and forecasts are biased, and tests of hypotheses are no longer valid. The cause of the bias (known as **omitted variable bias**) is fairly easy to see. Comparing the two models, we see that $v_t = \beta_3 X_{t3} + u_t$. The expected value of the error term in the erroneous model is $E(v_t) = \beta_3 X_{t3} \neq 0$. Therefore, v_t violates Assumption 3.3. More seriously, the covariance between X_{t2} and v_t is given by (see Section 2.3 on covariances)

$$\text{Cov}(X_{t2}, v_t) = \text{Cov}(X_{t2}, \beta_3 X_{t3} + u_t) = \beta_3\,\text{Cov}(X_{t2}, X_{t3}) + \text{Cov}(X_{t2}, u_t)$$
$$= \beta_3\,\text{Cov}(X_{t2}, X_{t3})$$

because X_2 and u are uncorrelated. Therefore, unless the covariance between X_2 and X_3 is zero—that is, unless X_2 and X_3 are uncorrelated—the covariance between X_2 and v will not be zero, thus violating Assumption 3.4 also. The properties of unbiasedness and consistency depend on these two assumptions. It follows, therefore, that $\hat{\beta}_2$ will not be unbiased or consistent.

The assertion above can be seen more formally. Let $\hat{\beta}_1$ and $\hat{\beta}_2$ be the estimates of the constant term and the slope coefficient for X_{t2} when we regress Y_t against a constant term and just X_{t2}, that is, excluding X_{t3}. The true expected values of these two estimates are derived in Appendix Section 4.A.2 as follows:

$$E(\hat{\beta}_2) = \beta_2 + \beta_3 \left[\frac{S_{23}}{S_{22}} \right] \quad \text{and} \quad E(\hat{\beta}_1) = \beta_1 + \beta_3 \left[\overline{X}_3 - \overline{X}_2 \frac{S_{23}}{S_{22}} \right]$$

where the variables with the bars are the corresponding means, $S_{23} = \Sigma(X_{t2} - \overline{X}_2)(X_{t3} - \overline{X}_3)$ and $S_{22} = \Sigma(X_{t2} - \overline{X}_2)^2$. We see from this that, unless $S_{23} = 0$, that is, unless X_2 and X_3 are uncorrelated, $E(\hat{\beta}_2) \neq \beta_2$ and therefore $\hat{\beta}_2$ will be biased in general. Also note that $\hat{\beta}_2$ includes a term involving β_3, which is the effect of the omitted variable. Hence we cannot interpret $\hat{\beta}_2$ as the marginal effect of X_2 alone. Part of the effect of the excluded variable is also captured. Thus, the coefficient measures the direct effect of the included variable as well as the indirect effect of the excluded variable. This is true of the estimated constant term also. Note that even if $S_{23} = 0$, $\hat{\beta}_1$ will be biased unless, in addition, the mean of X_3 is zero. Because the conditions derived here are very unlikely to hold, estimates and forecasts based on them will generally be biased.

THE DANGERS OF OMITTING A CONSTANT TERM   We saw above that $\hat{\beta}_1$ and $\hat{\beta}_2$ capture part of the effect of the omitted variable X_3. It was therefore useful to have included the constant term in the model. If the constant term had been omitted, then the regression line would have been forced through the origin, which might be a serious misspecification. We note from the scatter diagram in Figure 3.1 or Figure 3.11 that to constrain the regression line to go through the origin would mean a biased estimate for the slope and larger errors. The conclusion from this discussion is, again, that the constant term should always be retained unless there is a strong theoretical reason not to do so (in Chapter 6 we will encounter a case where theory dictates that the constant term be absent).

● PRACTICE PROBLEM 4.7[†]

In a simple linear model, suppose you had erroneously omitted the constant term; that is, suppose the true model was $Y_t = \alpha + \beta X_t + u_t$, but you estimate it as $Y_t = \beta X_t + v_t$. First verify that the OLS estimate of β, using the wrong model, is $\hat{\beta} = [\Sigma(X_t Y_t)]/[\Sigma(X_t^2)]$. Next substitute for Y_t in this expression from the true model, and then compute $E(\hat{\beta})$. Then show that $\hat{\beta}$ is biased. Finally, derive the condition under which $\hat{\beta}$ would be unbiased even though the wrong model was used. What is the intuitive interpretation of the condition you derived?

[In this and similar exercises at the end of this chapter, proceed as follows: (1) Use the *estimated model* and derive an algebraic expression for the parameter estimate; (2) substitute for Y_t from the *true model* in terms of X_t, u_t, and the parameters of the true model (we use the true model because Y_t is determined by that and not by the wrong model); (3) compute the expected value of the estimator; and (4) compare the expected value with the true value, check for unbiasedness, and, if necessary, derive the conditions for unbiasedness.]

● EXAMPLE 4.12

It is useful to give an empirical illustration of the specification bias due to the omission of important variables. DATA4-3 described in Appendix D has annual data on housing starts in the United States. An estimated relation between housing starts (in thousands), GNP (in billions of 1982 dollars), and the mortgage rate (in percent) is as follows (see Practice Computer Session 4.3 for details):

$$\text{Model A:} \quad \widehat{\text{HOUSING}} = 687.898 + 0.905 \text{ GNP} - 169.658 \text{ INTRATE}$$
$$\phantom{\text{Model A:} \quad \widehat{\text{HOUSING}} = } (1.80) (3.64) \phantom{0.905 \text{ GNP} - } (-3.87)$$

$$\overline{R}^2 = 0.375 \qquad F(2, 20) = 7.609 \qquad \text{d.f.} = 20$$

From basic demand theory, we would expect the demand for housing to rise as income rises. On the other hand, if the mortgage rate increases, the cost of owning a house rises, and hence the demand for housing will decline. We note that the signs of the estimated coefficients agree with our prior intuition. We also see from the t-statistics in parentheses that GNP and INTRATE are very significant. $\overline{R}^2$, however, is not very high for time series data. Suppose we had omitted the important variable INTRATE. The estimated model would be as follows:

$$\text{Model B:} \quad \widehat{\text{HOUSING}} = 1442.209 + 0.058 \text{ GNP}$$
$$\phantom{\text{Model B:} \quad \widehat{\text{HOUSING}} = } (3.39) (0.38)$$

$$\overline{R}^2 = -0.04 \qquad F(1, 21) = 0.144 \qquad \text{d.f.} = 21$$

The change in the results is dramatic. First of all, $\overline{R}^2$ has now become negative, indicating a poor fit. This is reinforced by the F-statistic, which is low and insignificant. The t-statistic for GNP is insignificant, indicating that GNP has a negligible effect on housing starts. Finally, the estimated value of the GNP coefficient is dramatically altered. These results are totally unacceptable and are a consequence of the omission of the mortgage rate, which is an important determinant of housing demand.

Inclusion of an Irrelevant Variable

Suppose that the *true* model is

$$Y_t = \beta_1 + \beta_2 X_{t2} + u_t$$

but we erroneously include the variable X_3 so that we estimate the model

$$Y_t = \beta_1 + \beta_2 X_{t2} + \beta_3 X_{t3} + v_t$$

As before, the true residual u_t is assumed to satisfy Assumptions 3.2 through 3.8 of Chapter 3. What are the consequences of this kind of misspecification? Is the estimator of β_2 biased? Is it still BLUE? Are the tests of hypotheses valid? The answers to these questions are summarized in the following property:

Property 4.4

a.   If an independent variable whose true regression coefficient is zero (that is, the variable is redundant) is included in the model, the estimated values of all the other regression coefficients will still be unbiased and consistent.

b.   Their variance, however, will be higher than that without the irrelevant variable, and hence the coefficients will be inefficient.

c.   Because the estimated variances of the regression coefficients are unbiased, tests of hypotheses are still valid.

The consequences of including an irrelevant variable are thus less serious as compared to omitting an important variable.

PROOF*

It is shown in Section 4.A.3 that

$$E(\hat{\beta}_2) = \beta_2 \quad \text{and} \quad E(\hat{\beta}_3) = 0$$

Therefore, $\hat{\beta}_2$ is unbiased, and the expectation of $\hat{\beta}_3$ is zero. Consistency also holds. These results generalize to a multiple regression model with many explanatory variables. Thus, the inclusion of irrelevant variables does not bias the estimates of the remaining coefficients. Because estimators are unbiased and consistent, so are forecasts based on them.

The next step is to compute the variance of $\hat{\beta}_2$ in order to examine the efficiency property. We have, from Section 4.A.3 (using the notation there),

$$\text{Var}(\hat{\beta}_2) = \frac{\sigma^2}{S_{22}(1 - r^2)}$$

where r^2 is the square of the simple correlation (see Equation 2.11) between X_2 and X_3, defined as $r^2 = S_{23}^2/(S_{22}S_{33})$. Let us compare this with the variance of the OLS estimator (call it β_2^*) that would have been obtained had the true model been used. From Chapter 3 Equations (3.12) and (3.19),

$$\beta_2^* = \frac{S_{y2}}{S_{22}} \quad \text{and} \quad \text{Var}(\beta_2^*) = \frac{\sigma^2}{S_{22}}$$

The relative efficiency (refer to Definition 2.8b) of $\hat{\beta}_2$ with respect to β_2^* is

$$\frac{\text{Var}(\hat{\beta}_2)}{\text{Var}(\beta_2^*)} = \frac{1}{1 - r^2} \geq 1$$

It is therefore clear that the estimator of β_2 using the wrong model is inefficient unless $r^2 = 0$—that is, unless X_2 and X_3 are uncorrelated. Because of this inefficiency, t-statistics tend to be lower, and hence we may erroneously conclude that variables are statistically insignificant when, in fact, they are actually nonzero. It can be shown (see Johnston, 1984, p. 262) that the estimator of the variance of $\hat{\beta}_2$ is unbiased, and hence tests of hypotheses are still valid.

● **EXAMPLE 4.13**

DATA4-3 also has data for population (POP) and the unemployment rate (UNEMP). Population is measured in millions and unemployment is a percentage rate. We can expect that the higher the population, the more the number of housing units started. Unemployment rate is a reasonable measure for the business cycle. When unemployment is high, consumers are likely to postpone the purchase of a house. It therefore seems reasonable to add POP and UNEMP as explanatory variables. The modified model is as follows (with t-values in parentheses):

$$\text{Model C:} \quad \widehat{\text{HOUSING}} = \underset{(0.5)}{5087.434} + \underset{(0.8)}{1.756\,\text{GNP}} - \underset{(-2.9)}{174.692\,\text{INTRATE}}$$

$$\underset{(-0.4)}{- 33.434\,\text{POP}} + \underset{(0.7)}{79.720\,\text{UNEMP}}$$

$$\bar{R}^2 = 0.328 \qquad F(4, 18) = 3.681 \qquad \text{d.f.} = 18$$

Comparing this to Model A we note many significant differences. GNP, which was originally significant, is now insignificant. The t-statistic for INTRATE has also declined, although it still remains significant. This is exactly what the theoretical analysis predicted. Property 4.4b stated that the variances of the coefficients are likely to be larger, which implies that t-statistics are likely to be smaller. The t-statistics for POP and UNEMP are very low, indicating that these variables are probably not important as *additional* determinants of housing, given that GNP and INTRATE measure the size of the economy and the business cycle. In fact, we can perform a Wald test for omitting POP and UNEMP. Treating Model C as the unrestricted model and Model A as the restricted model, the Wald F-statistic (see Equation 4.3) is given by

$$F_c = \frac{(\text{ESS}_A - \text{ESS}_C) \div (\text{d.f.}_A - \text{d.f.}_C)}{\text{ESS}_C \div \text{d.f.}_C}$$

$$= \frac{(1{,}491{,}140 - 1{,}444{,}274)/2}{1{,}444{,}274/18}$$

$$= 0.292$$

The observed F_c is very small and is insignificant even at the 25 percent level (the p-value is 0.75). Thus, the Wald test would not reject the null hypothesis that the regression coefficients for POP and UNEMP are zero. We also note that the signs for POP and UNEMP are opposite to what we expected. However, in view of the insignificance of these coefficients, their signs are irrelevant and can be attributed to chance.

● **PRACTICE PROBLEM 4.8**

Instead of adding both POP and UNEMP, as was done here, add to Model A only the unemployment rate (call this Model D). Compare the results with those of Model A. Are the results very different?

Comparing the theoretical consequences of adding an irrelevant variable with those of omitting an important variable, we observe a trade-off. The former specification error causes estimators to be inefficient, though unbiased. The latter type of error causes bias in estimates and hypothesis tests. Because the true relationships are never known, we face the dilemma of choosing the most appropriate formulation. An investigator who puts more emphasis on unbiasedness, consistency, and reliability of tests would rather keep an irrelevant variable than face the consequences of omitting a crucial variable. On the other hand, if a researcher cannot tolerate inefficient estimators, deleting the offending variable(s) would be preferable. Economic theory and an understanding of the underlying behavior can often help out in the dilemma. The model selection criteria discussed earlier can help as well. In Chapter 6 we will see that tests for specification will also help. All this involves a lot of judgment. Blind adherence to mechanical criteria is to be avoided at all costs.

● **4.6   Application: The Determinants of the Number of Bus Travelers**

The first walk-through application relates the number of people who travel by bus to various factors that affect it. DATA4-4 described in Appendix D has cross-section data for 40 cities across the United States. The variables are as follows:

BUSTRAVL = Measure of urban transportation by bus in thousands of passenger hours
FARE = Bus fare in dollars
GASPRICE = Price of a gallon of gasoline in dollars
INCOME = Average income per capita in dollars
POP = Population of city in thousands
DENSITY = Density of population (persons/sq. mile)
LANDAREA = Land area of the city (sq. miles)

The general specification of the model, often referred to as the "kitchen sink" model, is given below (without the t-subscript):

$$BUSTRAVL = \beta_1 + \beta_2 FARE + \beta_3 GASPRICE + \beta_4 INCOME$$
$$+ \beta_5 POP + \beta_6 DENSITY + \beta_7 LANDAREA + u$$

Before estimating the model, let us examine what signs we would expect, a priori, for the regression coefficients. In this discussion, the supply-side implications are not considered to be that important. Because an increase in the bus fare is likely to decrease the demand for bus travel, we would expect β_2 to be negative. In terms of travel, the automobile is a substitute for a bus, and hence an increase in the price of gasoline might induce some consumers to switch to bus travel. Hence we would expect a positive effect here; that is, β_3 is likely to be positive. When income rises, we would expect the demand for a commodity to rise also, and hence we would ordinarily expect β_4 to be positive. However, if the commodity is an "inferior good," then the income effect (that is, β_4) would be negative. An increase in the size of the population or the density of population is likely to increase the demand for bus travel. Thus, we would expect β_5 and β_6 to be positive. If the land area is high, then the city is spread out and consumers might prefer the automobile as the main mode of transportation. If this is the case, β_7 would be expected to be negative.

Table 4.4 has an annotated partial computer output using the GRETL program (see Practice Computer Session 4.4). The comments are quite detailed and should be studied carefully before proceeding further. All the topics we have studied are brought together in this mini empirical project, and Table 4.4 will help you put the pieces of the puzzle together. Even if you use your own program to verify the results, it is worthwhile to study the remarks in Table 4.4.

● **Table 4.4   Annotated Partial Computer Output for the Number of Travelers by Bus**

MODEL 1: OLS estimates using the 40 observations 1-40
Dependent variable: BUSTRAVL

	VARIABLE	COEFFICIENT	STDERROR	T STAT	2PROB(t > |T|)	
0)	const	2744.6797	2641.6715	1.039	0.306361	
2)	FARE	-238.6544	451.7281	-0.528	0.600816	
3)	GASPRICE	522.1132	2658.2276	0.196	0.845491	
4)	INCOME	-0.1947	0.0649	-3.001	0.005090	***
5)	POP	1.7114	0.2314	7.397	0.000000	***
6)	DENSITY	0.1164	0.0596	1.954	0.059189	*
7)	LANDAREA	-1.1552	1.8026	-0.641	0.526043	

Table 4.4   (continued)

```
Mean of dep. var.            1933.175  S.D. of dep. variable      2431.757
Error Sum of Sq (ESS)     1.8213e+007  Std Err of Resid. (sgmahat) 742.9113
Unadjusted R-squared            0.921  Adjusted R-squared            0.907
F-statistic (6, 33)           64.1434  p-value for F()           0.000000
Durbin-Watson stat.             2.083  First-order autocorr. coeff   -0.156

MODEL SELECTION STATISTICS

SGMASQ          551917    AIC          646146    FPE          648503
HQ              719020    SCHWARZ      868337    SHIBATA      614698
GCV             668991    RICE         700510

Excluding the constant, p-value was highest for variable 3 (GASPRICE)
```

[The adjusted R-squared is 0.907, indicating that 90.7 of the variance of BUSTRAVL is explained collectively by the variables in the model. For a cross-section study, this is quite good. The last column gives the p-value for a two-tailed test for the null hypothesis that the corresponding regression coefficient is zero. Three asterisks (***) indicate that the p-value is less than 1 percent, ** means that it is between 1 and 5 percent, one * implies a p-value between 5 and 10 percent, and no * means that p-value is above 10 percent. Recall that a high p-value means that the probability of a type I error in rejecting the null is high. If this is higher than the chosen level of significance (0.10, for example), then we should not reject the null hypothesis that the coefficient is zero. In other words, holding other variables fixed, this variable has no significant effect on BUSTRAVL. According to this, only INCOME, POP, and DENSITY have significant coefficients at the 10 percent level. The constant term and the coefficients for FARE, GASPRICE, and LANDAREA are statistically insignificant even at levels above 25 percent.

The relevance of the model selection statistics (discussed in Section 4.3) will become apparent later. The Durbin–Watson statistic and the first-order autocorrelation coefficient will be discussed in Chapter 9, but are irrelevant for our purposes.

What should we do next? We have mentioned several times that the constant term has no natural interpretation and captures the mean of the dependent variable as well as the average effects of omitted variables. Therefore, the general rule is to ignore the constant term's significance or lack of it. FARE, GASPRICE, and LANDAREA are, however, "initial candidates" for exclusion from the model because there is no evidence that they have significant effects on BUSTRAVL. We could take a giant step, drop them all, estimate a restricted model, and carry out a Wald F-test as described in Section 4.4. To facilitate this, we have retrieved the error sum of squares and the degrees of freedom for the unrestricted model just estimated. You are cautioned, however, that omitting several variables simultaneously is not a wise thing to do. As you will see next and in later examples, the exclusion of several variables in one sweep might also exclude variables that are on the borderline of being significant or those that have theoretical importance. Therefore, the sensible and cautious thing to do is to omit variables one at a time. There are several sound reasons for omitting variables with insignificant coefficients. First, a simpler model is easier to interpret than a complex model. Second, omission of a variable increases the d.f. and

(continued)

● **Table 4.4   (continued)**

hence improves the precision of the remaining coefficients. Finally, as we will see in the next chapter, having explanatory variables that are highly correlated with each other makes interpretation of individual coefficients difficult. Eliminating variables reduces the chance of this high correlation and hence makes interpretations more meaningful.

The starting point for the process of elimination is to identify the variable with the least significant regression coefficient. This is done by looking at the highest p-value in the model estimates but excluding the constant. On average, the corresponding coefficient is expected to be closest to zero, and hence we trust that any bias caused by its omission is likely to be small. From the results for Model A, we note that the coefficient for GASPRICE has the highest p-value and is hence the least significant. It is therefore sensible to omit this variable from the specification and see what happens. Based on that we could omit more variables. This process is known as **data-based model simplification.**]

```
MODEL 2: OLS estimates using the 40 observations 1-40
Dependent variable: BUSTRAVL
```

	VARIABLE	COEFFICIENT	STDERROR	T STAT	2PROB(t > |T|)
0)	const	3215.8565	1090.4692	2.949	0.005730 ***
2)	FARE	-225.6595	440.4936	-0.512	0.611762
4)	INCOME	-0.1957	0.0638	-3.069	0.004203 ***
5)	POP	1.7168	0.2265	7.581	0.000000 ***
6)	DENSITY	0.1182	0.0580	2.037	0.049453 **
7)	LANDAREA	-1.1953	1.7656	-0.677	0.502980

```
Mean of dep. var.          1933.175  S.D. of dep. variable        2431.757
Error Sum of Sq (ESS) 1.8235e+007  Std Err of Resid. (sqmahat)  732.3323
Unadjusted R-squared         0.921  Adjusted R-squared             0.909
F-statistic (5, 34)         79.204  p-value for F()             0.000000
Durbin-Watson stat.          2.079  First-order autocorr. coeff   -0.155
```

```
MODEL SELECTION STATISTICS
```

SGMASQ	536311	AIC	615352	FPE	616757
HQ	674378	SCHWARZ	792765	SHIBATA	592623
GCV	630954	RICE	651234		

```
Excluding the constant, p-value was highest for variable 2 (FARE)
Of the 8 model selection statistics, 8 have improved.
```

[Note that all eight of the model selection criteria have improved, that is, decreased. Also, the omission of GASPRICE has improved the precision of the remaining coefficients by making some of them more significant—for example, the constant term and DENSITY. The variable with the least significant coefficient, that is, the highest p-value, is now FARE. But bus fare is a price

● **Table 4.4   (continued)**

measure that economic theory says is an important determinant of demand. Therefore, we should not omit it even though the *p*-value suggests that we could. The next step is therefore to omit LANDAREA, which has the next highest *p*-value.]

```
MODEL 3: OLS estimates using the 40 observations 1-40
Dependent variable: BUSTRAVL
```

VARIABLE	COEFFICIENT	STDERROR	T STAT	2Prob(t > |T|)
0) const	3111.1805	1071.0669	2.905	0.006330 ***
2) FARE	-295.7306	424.8354	-0.696	0.490959
4) INCOME	-0.2022	0.0626	-3.232	0.002680 ***
5) POP	1.5883	0.1227	12.950	0.000000 ***
6) DENSITY	0.1490	0.0357	4.173	0.000189 ***

```
Mean of dep. var.          1933.175  S.D. of dep. variable      2431.757
Error Sum of Sq (ESS)    1.848e+007  Std Err of Resid. (sgmahat) 726.6434
Unadjusted R-squared          0.920  Adjusted R-squared            0.911
F-statistic (4, 35)         100.445  p-value for F()           0.000000
Durbin-Watson stat.           1.995  First-order autocorr. coeff  -0.102
```

```
MODEL SELECTION STATISTICS
```

SGMASQ	528011	AIC	593232	FPE	594012
HQ	640287	SCHWARZ	732670	SHIBATA	577512
GCV	603441	RICE	616012		

```
Excluding the constant, p-value was highest for variable 2 (FARE)
Of the 8 model selection statistics, 8 have improved.
```

[The variable DENSITY has increased even further in significance. However, the FARE variable has the *p*-value of 49 percent, which is unacceptably high for any reasonable level of significance. This suggests that, given the presence of the other variables, price may not matter much in affecting the demand for bus travel. In other words, when it comes to bus travel, consumers may not be that price-sensitive. It is therefore worth omitting FARE and seeing what happens.]

```
MODEL 4: OLS estimates using the 40 observations 1-40
Dependent variable: BUSTRAVL
```

VARIABLE	COEFFICIENT	STDERROR	T STAT	2Prob(t > |T|)
0) const	2815.7032	976.3007	2.884	0.006589 ***
4) INCOME	-0.2013	0.0621	-3.241	0.002566 ***
5) POP	1.5766	0.1206	13.071	0.000000 ***
6) DENSITY	0.1534	0.0349	4.396	0.000093 ***

(continued)

⬤   **Table 4.4   (continued)**

```
Mean of dep. var.        1933.175  S.D. of dep. variable       2431.757
Error Sum of Sq (ESS)  1.8736e+007 Std Err of Resid. (sgmahat) 721.4228
Unadjusted R-squared        0.919  Adjusted R-squared             0.912
F-statistic (3, 36)       135.708  p-value for F()             0.000000
Durbin-Watson stat.         1.879  First-order autocorr. coeff   -0.043

MODEL SELECTION STATISTICS

SGMASQ       520451   AIC         572112   FPE        572496
HQ           608137   SCHWARZ     677373   SHIBATA    562087
GCV          578279   RICE        585507

Of the 8 model selection statistics, 8 have improved.
```

[Note that Model 4 has the lowest model selection statistics and all the coefficients are extremely significant. Also, the coefficients for INCOME, POP, and DENSITY are not that different between Models 3 and 4. Thus the bias in omitting FARE might not be serious.

For the sake of completeness, it would be worthwhile to treat Model 1 as the unrestricted model and Model 4 as the restricted model and to carry out an *F*-test to examine whether the coefficients for GASPRICE, LANDAREA, and FARE are jointly different from zero. The result is given below.]

```
F(3, 33): area to the right of 0.315845 = 0.813800
```

[The null hypothesis for the Wald *F*-test is that the coefficients of all the omitted variables are zero, that is, that $\beta_2 = \beta_3 = \beta_7 = 0$. Since the *p*-value for it is 0.8138, which is high by any reasonable standard, we cannot reject the null. Using a calculator and Equation (4.3), verify the *F*-statistic for the omitted variables given above as 0.315845 (note that Model 1 is the unrestricted model and Model 4 is the restricted model for this test). Then use the *F*-table for 10 percent level given in Table A.4c and verify that you cannot reject the null hypothesis at 10 percent. Thus, the coefficients for FARE, GASPRICE, and LANDAREA are jointly insignificant at this level. Based on all the criteria, Model 4 appears to be "best" and is chosen as the final model for interpretation.

The coefficients for income, size of the population, and the density of population are extremely significant. Standard economic theory says that the income effect on the demand for any commodity is usually positive, but the estimated coefficient for INCOME is negative. This suggests, not surprisingly, that bus travel is an "inferior good." As income rises, people are more likely to use automobiles for travel, and hence the amount of bus travel is likely to decrease. If per-capita income goes up by $100, then, on average, bus travel is expected to decrease by $100|\hat{\beta}_4|$, that is, by 20.13 thousands of hours. As expected, the coefficients for POP and DENSITY are positive. In other words, when the size of the population or the population density increases, then more people travel by bus. However, although the numerical value for DENSITY is sensible, that for POP is not because it is greater than 1 (note that both DENSITY and POP are measured in the same units). This suggests a possible model misspecification.

When estimating demand relations, one often asks the question whether demand is "elastic" or "inelastic" with respect to price and income. The answer to that question requires estimating a nonlinear relationship, a topic explored in detail in Chapter 6.]

4.7 Application: Women's Labor Force Participation

The second walk-through application used here is an econometric study of the determinants of women's labor force participation rates—that is, the percent of women over age 16 who are in the labor force either actually employed or seeking employment. DATA4-5 described in Appendix D presents 1990 census data for the 50 states on a variety of variables (the first is the dependent variable):

WLFP = Participation rate (%) of all women over 16 (that is, percent of women in the labor force)
YF = Median earnings (in thousands of dollars) by females
YM = Median earnings (in thousands of dollars) by males
EDUC = Percent of female high school graduates over 24 years of age
UE = Unemployment rate (%)
MR = Marriage rate (%) of women at least 16 years of age
DR = Divorce rate (%)
URB = Percent of urban population in state
WH = Percent of females over 16 years who are white

The econometric model using all the explanatory variables is as follows:

$$\text{WLFP} = \beta_1 + \beta_2\text{YF} + \beta_3\text{YM} + \beta_4\text{EDUC} + \beta_5\text{UE} + \beta_6\text{MR} + \beta_7\text{DR} + \beta_8\,\text{URB} + \beta_9\text{WH} + u$$

Before actually estimating the model it will be useful to discuss the signs of the regression coefficients that one might expect. This discussion is drawn on "economic theory" as opposed to "econometric theory." The reader is referred to the papers by O'Neill (1981), Kelley and Da Silva (1980), and King (1978) for details on some of the theories.

YF: Since this is a measure of money offerings to female workers, we would expect this to have a positive effect on WLFP. In other words, the higher the wage, the more the participation by women. However, we should also bear in mind that labor theory says that the "income effect" on labor is negative; that is, as income rises, workers desire more leisure (less work). At the prevailing wages, the latter effect is likely to be smaller; and hence, on balance, we would expect a positive sign.

YM: As husbands earn more, their wives need not work as much. Hence, we might expect this coefficient to be negative. It is also possible that because many women are well qualified, higher male incomes might induce more females to seek such jobs. However, this would affect the type of job and probably not whether more women would join the labor force.

EDUC: More education implies more (as well as more desirable) job opportunities available to women. Thus, we would expect this coefficient to be positive.

UE: Unemployment rate has both negative and positive effects. The "discouraged worker hypothesis" states that a higher unemployment rate might be an indication to women (and minorities) that searches for employment may be futile. This might induce them to drop out of the labor force, which would give a negative sign.

There is also a positive effect. If a husband loses his job, the wife might enter the labor force to compensate for the loss in earnings. If this effect is not very strong, the negative sign will prevail.

MR: If a woman is married, she tends to have fewer opportunities to work (especially when there are children) and perhaps a reduced desire or need to work. Thus, a higher marriage rate is likely to reduce WLFP.

DR: We would expect a positive sign for this because when the divorce rate is high, more women are likely to enter the labor force to support themselves.

URB: In urban areas employment opportunities are more diverse than in rural areas. One might therefore expect that states having a larger fraction of the population living in urban areas might have a higher women's participation rate. On the other hand, rural women tend to help out by feeding livestock and poultry and doing other farm chores. Thus, they will already be part of the labor force. This means that if a state has a larger rural population (that is, less URB), then women's labor force participation may be higher, resulting in a negative sign. The net effect can be determined only empirically.

WH: There is no clear sign one might expect for this beforehand. If non-White women are relatively unskilled and seek employment as maids and housekeepers, we would expect a negative sign for this coefficient because the higher WH, the fewer the number of non-Whites. Also, if White women are relatively affluent, they may not enter the labor force. This also would yield a negative sign. If these assumptions are false, the result will be a positive sign or zero.

Table 4.5 shows a partial computer output with annotations (see Practice Computer Session 4.5). Use your own regression program and DATA4-5 to reproduce the results. Then carefully study the results before proceeding further.

⬤   **Table 4.5   Annotated Partial Computer Output for Women's Labor Force Participation Rates**

[Model with all variables (often referred to as the "kitchen sink" model)]

```
MODEL 1: OLS estimates using the 50 observations 1-50
Dependent variable: wlfp
```

	VARIABLE	COEFFICIENT	STDERROR	T STAT	2Prob(t > |T|)	
0)	const	44.5096	8.9750	4.959	0.000013	***
2)	yf	0.9880	0.4076	2.424	0.019847	**
3)	ym	-0.1743	0.3062	-0.569	0.572212	
4)	educ	0.2851	0.0932	3.060	0.003888	***
5)	ue	-1.6106	0.3136	-5.136	0.000007	***
6)	mr	-0.0782	0.1731	-0.452	0.653835	
7)	dr	0.4374	0.2583	1.693	0.098035	*
8)	urb	-0.0926	0.0333	-2.779	0.008195	***
9)	wh	-0.0875	0.0398	-2.196	0.033819	**

⬤   **Table 4.5   (continued)**

```
Mean of dep. var.          57.474   S.D. of dep. variable        4.249
Error Sum of Sq (ESS)     193.9742  Std Err of Resid. (sgmahat)  2.1751
Unadjusted R-squared        0.781   Adjusted R-squared           0.738
F-statistic (8, 41)        18.2459  p-value for F()          0.000000
Durbin-Watson stat.         1.637   First-order autocorr. coeff   0.179


MODEL SELECTION STATISTICS


SGMASQ      4.73108      AIC         5.56058     FPE       5.58267
HQ          6.33926      SCHWARZ     7.84492     SHIBATA   5.2761
GCV         5.76961      RICE        6.06169


Excluding the constant, p-value was highest for variable 6 (mr).
```

[Note that ym and mr have high *p*-values and are preliminary candidates for exclusion from the model. We now omit variables one at a time starting with mr, which has the highest *p*-value.)

```
MODEL 2: OLS estimates using the 50 observations 1-50
Dependent variable: wlfp


       VARIABLE    COEFFICIENT    STDERROR    T STAT   2Prob(t > |T|)


   0)    const       41.3460       5.5598      7.437   0.000000 ***
   2)       yf        1.0671       0.3645      2.927   0.005497 ***
   3)       ym       -0.1984       0.2987     -0.664   0.510097
   4)     educ        0.2582       0.0709      3.643   0.000734 ***
   5)       ue       -1.5910       0.3076     -5.171   0.000006 ***
   7)       dr        0.3916       0.2354      1.664   0.103626
   8)      urb       -0.0876       0.0311     -2.814   0.007420 ***
   9)       wh       -0.0851       0.0391     -2.175   0.035271 **


Mean of dep. var.          57.474   S.D. of dep. variable        4.249
Error Sum of Sq (ESS)     194.9397  Std Err of Resid. (sgmahat)  2.1544
Unadjusted R-squared        0.780   Adjusted R-squared           0.743
F-statistic (7, 42)        21.2255  p-value for F()          0.000000
Durbin-Watson stat.         1.649   First-order autocorr. coeff   0.173


MODEL SELECTION STATISTICS


SGMASQ      4.64142      AIC         5.36914     FPE       5.38405
HQ          6.03252      SCHWARZ     7.29064     SHIBATA   5.14641
GCV         5.5255       RICE        5.73352
```

(continued)

● **Table 4.5   (continued)**

```
Excluding the constant, p-value was highest for variable 3 (ym).
Of the 8 model selection statistics, 8 have improved.
```

[Omit ym, which still has a high *p*-value, and note that dr now becomes significant at the 10 percent level.]

```
MODEL 3: OLS estimates using the 50 observations 1-50
Dependent variable: wlfp
```

	VARIABLE	COEFFICIENT	STDERROR	T STAT	2Prob(t > |T|)
0)	const	41.8336	5.4753	7.640	0.000000 ***
2)	yf	0.8493	0.1582	5.370	0.000003 ***
4)	educ	0.2492	0.0691	3.606	0.000804 ***
5)	ue	-1.6776	0.2769	-6.059	0.000000 ***
7)	dr	0.4341	0.2251	1.929	0.060390 *
8)	urb	-0.0942	0.0293	-3.212	0.002500 ***
9)	wh	-0.0961	0.0352	-2.729	0.009156 ***

```
Mean of dep. var.          57.474  S.D. of dep. variable        4.249
Error Sum of Sq (ESS)    196.9882  Std Err of Resid. (sgmahat)  2.1404
Unadjusted R-squared        0.777  Adjusted R-squared           0.746
F-statistic (6, 43)       25.0145  p-value for F()           0.000000
Durbin-Watson stat.         1.668  First-order autocorr. coeff   0.165
```

```
MODEL SELECTION STATISTICS
```

SGMASQ	4.58112	AIC	5.21282	FPE	5.22248
HQ	5.77222	SCHWARZ	6.81281	SHIBATA	5.0429
GCV	5.32688	RICE	5.47189		

```
Of the 8 model selection statistics, 8 have improved
```

[Using Model 3 as the restricted model and Model 1 as the unrestricted model, we can carry out an *F*-test. The result is as follows.]

```
F(2, 41): area to the right of 0.318535 = 0.728997
```

[Using a calculator, verify the Wald test statistic for the omission of ym and dr. The null hypothesis for the test is that $\beta_3 = \beta_7 = 0$. As before, the *p*-value is the probability of a type I error if we reject the null hypothesis. Since 0.729 is too high for any reasonable level of significance, we should not reject the null but instead conclude that ym and dr are jointly insignificant. You should verify this by using the *F*-table in Appendix A.4c for a 10 percent level of significance. All the model selection statistics are lowest for Model 3. Therefore, we choose Model 3 as the final "best" model for further examination. For the interpretation of the results, see the text.]

In Model 3, which is chosen as the "best" final model, the positive sign for YF indicates that the "backward-bending supply curve effect" on labor—namely, that as wages increase workers prefer more leisure and less participation in the labor force—is weak. Other things being equal, a $1,000 increase in a woman's earnings is expected to increase her participation rate, on average, by 0.849 percent.

Men's earnings (YM) was not significant. This may be because it is closely associated with YF and is captured by the coefficient for YF.

As expected, an increase in the education of women induces more women to seek jobs. A 1 percent increase in the percent of women with high school diplomas will increase the participation rate, on average, by 0.249 percent.

The negative sign for UE supports the "discouraged worker hypothesis," which states that when the unemployment rate is high, women seeking employment might get discouraged and drop out of the labor force. The magnitude of this coefficient is quite high. A 1 percent increase in UE means a 1.678 percent decrease in WLFP, on average.

Divorce rate has the expected positive sign. On average, a 1 percent increase in the divorce rate is expected to induce an increase of 0.434 percent in WLFP. Marriage rate (MR), however, was statistically insignificant.

The negative coefficient for URB (-0.094) supports the earlier contention that states with a high rural population (that is, low URB) might also be high in WLFP because rural women perform many of the farm chores and would hence be in the labor force.

The average effect of a 1 percent increase in the White population is to reduce the expected women's participation rate by 0.096 percent.

The value of $\overline{R}^2$ indicates that only about 74 percent of the variation across states in labor force participation is explained by Model C. Thus, we may have omitted some variables that would improve the explanatory power. However, it is quite typical for cross-section data to yield low R^2. Because many time series data generally grow over time, models based on them tend to give relatively good fits. This can be seen from the value of $\overline{R}^2$ (0.999) for the consumption function presented in Example 4.11. With additional data, we might have been able to provide a better explanation of women's labor force participation rates. Possible variables to be included in the regression are as follows:

1. Measure of family size, birth rates, and number of children under a "threshold" age; these would tend to reduce the opportunities for women to work.

2. A variable measuring college-educated women.

3. Age distribution of women.

4. Welfare payments to single women with children; this could dictate whether women work or choose to remain at home (the availability of day care will have the same effect).

5. Measures to capture regional differences; farm states and industrial states may have different behavioral patterns.

Important Remarks on the Interpretation of Regression Coefficients

A great deal of care must be exercised when interpreting the estimated regression coefficients. First, the sign of a regression coefficient might be contrary to what you might expect a priori. If the coefficient is statistically insignificant (that is, you cannot reject the null hypothesis that it is zero), then the wrong sign is irrelevant because, statistically, the numerical value could be equally positive or negative and it is simply random chance that you got the wrong sign. In the annotated remarks in Table 4.4, we stated a number of sensible reasons for omitting a variable with an insignificant coefficient (easier and more meaningful interpretation and better precision). In such a case, you should simply omit the variable and reestimate the model trusting that the omitted variable bias is likely to be negligent. It should be noted that by omitting a variable you are not saying that it has no effect on Y, but that, *other things being equal,* the variable in question does not have a *separate* effect. Its effect might be captured by the presence of another variable that it is correlated with (more on this in the next chapter).

When deciding on the significance or lack of it of a regression parameter, an interesting question is "What level of the p-value should we deem too high for rejecting the null hypothesis of zero effect?" Most analysts use 5 percent (or 0.05) as a benchmark. My personal preference is 10 percent. An advantage of using the higher value is that more variables will be retained in the model (explain why this is the case), thus reducing any omitted variable bias. Unlike medical experiments, where mistakes would be very costly, economic behavior is subject to more uncertainties, and hence a higher tolerance is recommended. If the sample size (n) is very large, however, one should use a stricter p-value. This is because when n is large, standard errors are likely to be small, making almost every coefficient significant.

What should one do if the coefficient with the contrary sign is statistically significant? Then one should look for explanations. For instance, in Example 4.1 on home prices, we found counterintuitive negative signs for BEDRMS and BATHS. However, with the proper meaning of a regression coefficient—namely, that it is the partial effect, *when all other variables are at fixed values*—we saw that the negative coefficients were not so surprising after all. As a second example, in the bus travel model in Section 4.6 (see Table 4.4), we found that the income coefficient was negative, which is contrary to what one would normally expect. By noting that, in this case, the negative sign indicates that bus travel was an "inferior good," we were able to arrive at a sensible explanation. Chapter 5 gives other examples of cases where one encounters counterintuitive signs and suggests remedies. They should be studied carefully.

Another important point to note is that the units in which the variables are measured is critical in interpreting the numerical values of regression coefficients (refresh your memory by reviewing Section 3.6 on changing units). Particular care must be taken when you are dealing with variables expressed as fractions or as percents (for example, unemployment and interest rates). If you carry out your own empirical project, it is good practice in general to avoid fractions or proportions and express such variables as percents. That is because it is easier to interpret the effect of a 1 percent change in a variable rather than a 0.01 change in it. In an empirical article that you read, however, the investigator might have expressed some variables as proportions. In such cases, exercise a great deal of caution in interpreting the numerical values. It is useful at this stage to review the interpretation of the estimated coefficients for the percentage variables in the womens' labor force participation example just discussed.

4.8   Empirical Example: Net Migration Rates and the Quality of Life

Liu (1975) has examined the relationships between the variations in net migration rates among states and a number of explanatory variables, including the "quality of life." The data are cross-sectional over the 50 states, and the basic model used is the following:

$$MIGRATE = f(QOL, Y, E, IS, ES, AP, ED, HW)$$

where

MIGRATE = Net migration rate between 1960 and 1970 (in-migration minus out-migration divided by population)
QOL = Index of the quality of life
Y = Index of state income as a ratio to U.S. income
E = Ratio of state employment to U.S. employment
IS = Index of individual status
ES = Index of economic status
AP = Index of agricultural production
ED = Index of educational development
HW = Index of health and welfare provision

Based on criteria developed by President Eisenhower's Commission of National Goals, Liu constructed each of the indices listed above. QOL is an arithmetic average of the other indices of quality of life. Table 4.6 has the estimated coefficients and related statistics for a number of multiple regression models relating migration rates to the quality-of-life indices. To do justice to the author of this study on migration, students should read the original paper. Although the topics covered in this chapter are adequate to obtain a good understanding of the models and the results, we present here only a brief summary of those results.

The author did not provide information on the residual sums of squares for the models, and hence we cannot compare the models using the general criteria presented earlier. Goodness of fit can be judged only by $\overline{R}^2$. We note that income and employment by themselves do not explain any of the variation in migration. The value of $\overline{R}^2$ is negative for Model 2. QOL by itself explains about 6 percent of the variance in migration. If income and employment are added to QOL (Model 3), $\overline{R}^2$ decreases substantially. This implies that these two variables probably do not belong in the model. In Model 4, the author has excluded Y and E. We note that, with the exception of health and welfare (HW), all the other quality-of-life variables are either significant or almost significant at the 5 percent level of significance. Because HW is insignificant in both models, it would have been better if this had been omitted and the model reestimated in order to get more efficient estimates for the

● **Table 4.6   Estimated Relations between Migration and Quality of Life**

Independent Variable	Model 1	Model 2	Model 3	Model 4	Model 5
CONSTANT	−23.05	104.62	55.94	−16.46	−62.50
QOL	24.06 (2.05)		23.40 (1.93)		
Y		0.36 (0.05)	−0.74 (−0.10)		7.19 (1.11)
E		−103.47 (−0.48)	−77.26 (−0.37)		41.76 (0.23)
IS				28.68 (2.02)	30.21 (2.14)
ES				20.03 (2.24)	20.49 (2.28)
AP				18.73 (2.87)	19.13 (2.89)
ED				−31.56 (−3.46)	−33.48 (−3.59)
HW				−18.45 (−1.41)	−21.69 (−1.57)
$\bar{R}^2$	0.06	−0.03	0.02	0.37	0.36
D.F.	48	47	46	44	42

Note: The values in parentheses are *t*-statistics.

Source: Liu (1975). Reprinted with the permission of the President and Fellows of Harvard College.

remaining coefficients. But the author may have chosen to retain it in order to avoid possible omitted variable bias.

All the quality-of-life variables have the expected positive signs with the exception of the educational development variable (the negative sign for HW can be ignored because it is statistically insignificant). Liu's rationalization for this counterintuitive result is reproduced here (Liu, 1975, p. 333):

> First, while migration is a flow variable the educational variable represents a stock concept. This results in an equilibrium adjustment process in the United States between the stock of educated people and the flow of migration, i.e., states which are known for significant educational development have been exporting highly educated manpower to states where the skilled manpower is relatively scarce and as a result, highly educated migrants have found that in these states greater career opportunities, as well as more rewarding jobs, exist. Second, is that migrants are of heterogeneous educational backgrounds, and their migration decisions are often affected by the friends or relatives at the destination who usually have the same educational training as the migrants. Consequently, states with heterogeneous educational attainments among residents may expect to have a higher net migration rate than states that are relatively homogeneous. However, further research is required to assess the effect of this educational variable on migration.

4.9 Empirical Project

If an empirical project is part of your course on econometrics, you should have followed the directions given in Section 1.3 and obtained some of the data. If you have the information for enough variables, you should enter the data on the computer and make sure that the values are entered accurately (if you are using GRETL, read its manual on setting up your own data file). You could then try a preliminary model, omit variables and carry out a Wald F-test, and then apply the data-based model simplification technique to eliminate variables. All these steps are, however, merely for practice and to reinforce an understanding of the topics covered in this chapter. You should not take the results seriously, because a great deal of theoretical study is essential before undertaking a meaningful model and analysis.

Summary

In the multiple linear regression model, the dependent variable (Y) is regressed against the k independent variables $X_1, X_2, \ldots, X_k$. X_1 is generally set to 1 so that a constant intercept term can be included. As before, the OLS procedure minimizes the error sum of squares $\Sigma \hat{u}_t^2$ and gives k normal equations. These equations can generally be solved uniquely for the coefficients, provided the number of observations is larger than k.

An unbiased estimator of the error variance (σ^2) is given by $s^2 = \hat{\sigma}^2 = (\Sigma \hat{u}_t^2)/(n - k)$. Under the assumption that the error terms u_t are independently and identically distributed as $N(0, \sigma^2)$, the statistic $[(n - k)\hat{\sigma}^2]/\sigma^2$ has a chi-square distribution with $n - k$ d.f.

The goodness of fit is measured in one of two equivalent ways. From the estimated equation, the residual is measured as $\hat{u}_t = Y_t - \hat{\beta}_1 - \hat{\beta}_2 X_{t2} - \cdots - \hat{\beta}_k X_{tk}$. The error sum of squares (ESS) is $\Sigma \hat{u}_t^2$, and the total sum of squares (TSS) is $\Sigma (Y_t - \bar{Y})^2$. The standard error of the regression given by $\hat{\sigma} = [\text{ESS}/(n - k)]^{1/2}$ can be compared with $\hat{\sigma}_Y = [\text{TSS}/(n - 1)]^{1/2}$ to see how much of a reduction there is. A unit-free measure is given by the *adjusted R-squared* (denoted by $\bar{R}^2$), which can be computed as

$$\bar{R}^2 = 1 - \frac{\text{ESS}(n - 1)}{\text{TSS}(n - k)} = 1 - \frac{n - 1}{n - k}(1 - R^2) = 1 - \frac{\hat{\sigma}^2(n - 1)}{\text{TSS}}$$

$\bar{R}^2$ can be interpreted as the variation in Y_t explained by the model. Unlike R^2, which is $1 - (\text{ESS}/\text{TSS})$, $\bar{R}^2$ takes account of the trade-off between a gain in R^2 due to an added variable and a loss in the degrees of freedom.

In this chapter, we also discussed eight different criteria for choosing among competing models. A simpler model is preferable because (1) the inclusion of too many variables makes the relative precision of individual coefficients worse (as will be seen in detail in the next chapter), (2) adding variables means a loss of degrees of freedom, which makes the power of a test worse, and (3) a simpler model is easier to comprehend than a complex one. The model selection criteria take the form of the error sum of squares multiplied by a penalty factor that depends on the complexity of the model. A model is judged to be superior if it has lower values for the criteria statistics in a majority of the specifications. However, in certain special cases one or more of the criteria may become redundant.

To test whether an individual coefficient (β) is significantly different from zero, we first compute the t-statistic (t_c), which is the ratio of the estimated coefficient to its estimated standard error. If $|t_c| > t_{n-k}^*(a/2)$, where t^* is the point on the t-distribution with $n - k$ d.f. such that the probability that $t > t^*$ is equal to one-half of the level of significance a, the null hypothesis $H_0: \beta = 0$ is rejected in favor of the alternative $H_1: \beta \neq 0$. If the alternative is one-sided, we obtain t^* such that the area to the right of it is equal to the level of significance. Then we reject H_0 in favor of $\beta > 0$ if $t_c > t^*$ or in favor of $\beta < 0$ if $t_c < -t^*$.

To apply the *p*-value approach, first calculate twice the area to the right of $|t_c|$ in the *t*-distribution with $n - k$ d.f. Reject H_0 if the *p*-value is less than the level of significance, and conclude that the coefficient is significant.

To test whether a subset of regression coefficients is zero, a joint *F*-test, known as the *Wald test,* is carried out. More specifically, to test $H_0: \beta_{m+1} = \beta_{m+2} = \cdots = \beta_k = 0$ against the alternative that at least one of them is nonzero, we first estimate the unrestricted model (U):

$$(U) \qquad Y = \beta_1 + \beta_2 X_2 + \cdots + \beta_m X_m + \beta_{m+1} X_{m+1} + \cdots + \beta_k X_k + u$$

Next we omit the last $k - m$ variables and estimate the restricted model (R):

$$(R) \qquad Y = \beta_1 + \beta_2 X_2 + \cdots + \beta_m X_m + v$$

Then we compute the Wald *F*-statistic

$$F_c = \frac{(ESS_R - ESS_U)/(k - m)}{ESS_U/(n - k)} = \frac{(R_U^2 - R_R^2)/(k - m)}{(1 - R_U^2)/(n - k)}$$

where R^2 is the unadjusted goodness of fit. The null hypothesis is rejected if $F_c > F^*_{k-m,\ n-k}(a)$, where F^* is that point on the *F*-distribution with $k - m$ and $n - k$ degrees of freedom such that the probability that $F > F^*$ is a (for example, 0.05 or 0.01). The Wald test need not be performed if only one regression coefficient is omitted from the model. This is because a *t*-test on the corresponding coefficient is equivalent.

The Wald test statistic for overall goodness of fit is given by

$$F_c = \frac{R^2/(k - 1)}{(1 - R^2)/(n - k)}$$

which has the *F*-distribution with d.f. $k - 1$ and $n - k$.

Testing a linear combination of regression coefficients may be done in three equivalent ways. A *t*-statistic on the linear combination of estimates has $n - k$ d.f. and can be used in a *t*-test similar to that on an individual regression coefficient. Alternatively, the linear combination may be incorporated into the model and a *t*- or *F*-test performed.

Confidence intervals for individual coefficients are similar to those derived in Chapter 3. A confidence interval of the forecast $\hat{Y} = \hat{\beta}_1 + \hat{\beta}_2 X_2 + \cdots + \hat{\beta}_k X_k$ is easily obtained by estimating a slightly modified model.

Indiscriminate "data mining" to find the "best fit" should be avoided because it often leads to the substantiation of any hypothesis one might think of, however contradictory such substantiations might be. Mechanical criteria should not be applied blindly without regard to theory or some understanding of the underlying behavior.

The consequences of including an irrelevant variable (that is, one for which the true regression coefficient is zero) are as follows:

1. Estimated regression coefficients using the wrong model and forecasts based on these estimates are unbiased and consistent.

2. The estimates are inefficient and are not BLUE because the estimator based on the true model is BLUE.

3.   Tests of hypotheses are still valid because the estimated variances are also unbiased. However, the power of tests is reduced. In other words, the probability of accepting a false hypothesis (type II error) is higher when the wrong model is used.

The consequences of omitting a variable that ought to belong in a model are as follows:

1.   Estimated regression coefficients using the incorrect model and forecasts based on these estimates are biased and inconsistent.

2.   Estimated variances are also biased, and therefore tests of hypotheses are no longer valid.

Comparing the theoretical consequences of adding an irrelevant variable with those of omitting an important variable, we observe a trade-off. The former specification error causes estimators to be inefficient, though unbiased. The latter type of error causes bias in estimates and hypothesis tests. Because the true relationships are never known, we face the dilemma of choosing the most appropriate formulation. An investigator who puts more emphasis on unbiasedness, consistency, and reliability of tests would rather keep an irrelevant variable than face the consequences of omitting a crucial variable. On the other hand, if a researcher cannot tolerate inefficient estimators, deleting the offending variable(s) would be preferable. Economic theory and an understanding of the underlying behavior can often help in the dilemma. The model selection criteria discussed earlier can also help. Tests for specification (Chapter 6) will help as well.

Because the constant term captures the average effects of omitted variables, it is not wise, in general, to omit the constant term from the specification, even if it is very insignificant and/or has an unexpected sign.

Key Terms

Adjusted R^2
Akaike information criterion (AIC)
Data-based model simplification
Finite prediction error (FPE)
F-test
Generalized cross validation (GCV)
Hedonic price index
HQ criterion
Joint significance

Model in deviation form
Multiple regression
Omitted variable bias
Restricted model
R^2 adjusted for degrees of freedom
Specification error
Unrestricted model
Wald test

References

Some of the following references require a knowledge of linear algebra.

Akaike, H. "Statistical Predictor Identification." *Annals Instit. Stat. Math.* 22 (1970): 203–217.
_____. "A New Look at Statistical Model Identification." *IEEE Trans. Auto Control* 19 (1974): 716–723.
Box, G. E. P., and D. R. Cox. "An Analysis of Transformations." *J. Royal Stat. Society,* Series B (1964).
Brealey, Richard, and Stewart Myers. *Principles of Corporate Finance.* New York: McGraw-Hill, 1981.
Craven, P., and G. Wahba. "Smoothing Noisy Data with Spline Functions." *Num. Math.* 13 (1979): 377–403.

Economic Report of the President. Washington, D.C.: U.S. Government Printing Office, 1986, 1987.

Engle, R. F., and Scott Brown. "Model Selection for Forecasting." *J. Computation in Statistics* (1985).

Engle, R. F., C. W. Granger, J. Rice, and A. Weiss. "Semi-parametric Estimates of the Relation Between Weather and Electricity Sales." *J. Amer. Stat. Assoc.* 81 (June 1986).

Friend, Irwin, Marshall Blume, and Jean Crockett. *Mutual Fund and Other Institutional Investors: A New Perspective.* New York: McGraw-Hill, 1970.

Haitovsky, Y. "A Note on the Maximization of $\overline{R}^2$." *American Statistician* (February 1969): 20–21.

Hannan, E. J., and B. Quinn. "The Determination of the Order of an Autoregression." *J. Royal Stat. Society,* Series B 41 (1979): 190–195.

Heien, Dale. "The Cost of the U.S. Dairy Price Support Program: 1949–74." *Review of Economics and Statistics* 59 (February 1977): 1–8.

Johnston, J. *Econometric Methods.* New York: McGraw-Hill, 1984.

Kelley, A. C., and L. M. Da Silva. "The Choice of Family Size and the Compatibility of Female Work Force Participation in the Low-income Setting." *Revue Economique* (November 1980): 1081–1103.

King, A. G. "Industrial Structure, the Flexibility of Working Hours, and Women's Labor Force Participation." *Rev. Econ. Stat.* (August 1978): 399–407.

Klein, L. R., and J. N. Morgan. "Results of Alternative Statistical Treatment of Sample Survey Data." *J. Amer. Stat. Assoc.* 47 (December 1951).

Kmenta, Jan. *Elements of Econometrics.* New York: Macmillan, 1986.

Liu, Ben-chieh. "Differential Net Migration Rates and the Quality of Life." *Review of Economics and Statistics* LVII (August 1975): 329–337.

O'Neil, June. "A Time-Series Analysis of Women's Labor Force Participation." *Amer. Econ. Assoc., Papers and Proceedings* (May 1981): 76–80.

Ramanathan, R. *Introduction to Econometrics with Applications,* 2d ed. Fort Worth: The Dryden Press, 1992.

Rice, J. "Bandwidth Choice for Nonparametric Kernel Regression." *Annals of Stat.* 12 (1984): 1215–1230.

Schwarz, G. "Estimating the Dimension of a Model." *Annals of Stat.* 6 (1978).

Shibata, R. "An Optimal Selection of Regression Variables." *Biometrika* 68 (1981).

Wald, A. "Tests of Statistical Hypotheses Concerning Several Parameters When the Number of Observations Is Large." *Transactions of the Amer. Math. Society* 54 (1943).

Exercises

Theoretical Questions

4.1 In the model $Y_t = \beta_1 + \beta_2 X_{t2} + \beta_3 X_{t3} + u_t$, suppose it is known that $\beta_2 = 1$. Describe how you would obtain the best estimates for β_1 and β_3 when β_2 is known to be 1.

4.2 "In testing hypotheses on several linear combinations of regression coefficients, the difference in the degrees of freedom between the restricted and unrestricted models is the same as the number of restrictions." Do you agree with this statement? If yes, prove it, and, if not, give a counterexample.

4.3 In the model in Exercise 4.1, describe step-by-step how you would test the hypothesis $\beta_2 + \beta_3 = 0$. Be sure to do this using all three methods discussed in Section 4.4.

4.4 In the model in Exercise 4.1, describe step-by-step how you would test the hypothesis $\beta_2 + \beta_3 + 1 = 0$. Be sure to do this using all three methods discussed in Section 4.4.

4.5   In a two-variable regression model, suppose you unnecessarily included a constant term. In other words, the true model is $Y_t = \beta X_t + u_t$, whereas you estimated the model $Y_t = \alpha + \beta X_t + v_t$. Derive the expected value of the OLS estimator of β. Is the estimator biased or not? If yes, state the condition(s) under which it might become unbiased.

†4.6   Suppose you did not have data on an independent variable X_t but used a proxy variable Z_t instead. For instance, you wanted to use the wage rate in the service industry but could only get the wage rate in the manufacturing industry. Examine the consequence of this kind of specification error. More specifically, let the true model be $Y_t = \beta X_t + u_t$, but assume you used the model $Y_t = \beta Z_t + v_t$ instead. Under what conditions will the OLS estimate of β be (a) unbiased and (b) consistent?

4.7   Consider the simple regression model $CATCH_t = \alpha + \beta BOATS_t + u_t$, where CATCH = the total fish catch in thousands of pounds and BOATS = the number of BOATS that went fishing on day t. If BOATS = 0, then CATCH should be zero also, indicating that the true value of α is zero. Thus, the *true model* is $CATCH_t = \beta BOATS_t + v_t$. Suppose, however, you kept the constant term in the model and estimated a constant term and a slope term. What is the nature of the misspecification you are making here; is it adding an irrelevant variable or omitting a relevant variable? Are the estimates (1) biased, (2) consistent, (3) efficient? Are the hypothesis tests valid?

Empirical Questions Requiring No Computer Work

4.8   Using census data for the 50 U.S. states, the following model was estimated (values in parentheses are standard errors).

$$\text{(U)} \quad \widehat{PC} = -0.365 - 0.0009\,D + 0.0094\,NW + 0.0003\,Y$$
$$\underset{(0.978)}{} \quad \underset{(.0006)}{} \quad \underset{(.0104)}{} \quad \underset{(0.0001)}{}$$

$$- 0.099\,U + 1.519\,COP - 0.0068\,AGE1 + 0.0077\,AGE2$$
$$\underset{(0.084)}{} \quad \underset{(0.276)}{} \quad \underset{(0.00034)}{} \quad \underset{(0.0038)}{}$$

$$R^2 = 0.557 \qquad \overline{R}^2 = 0.484 \qquad ESS = 33.41$$

where
   PC = Property crime index
   D = Population density
   NW = Percent of non-White population
   Y = Per-capita income in dollars
   U = Unemployment rate
   COP = Size of police force per thousand population
   AGE1 = Population (in thousands) in the age group 15–24
   AGE2 = Population (in thousands) in the age group 25–34

a.   Does the observed sign of each regression coefficient (ignore the constant) agree with intuition? In other words, what sign would you expect a priori and why? Does any result surprise you?

b.   Test each coefficient (ignore the constant) for statistical significance at the 5 percent level (two tails).

A second model was estimated and the following results are given (with standard errors in parentheses):

$$\text{(R)} \quad \widehat{PC} = -0.037 + 0.0002\,Y + 1.428\,COP - 0.0061\,AGE1 + 0.0068\,AGE2$$
$$\underset{(0.84)}{} \quad \underset{(0.00008)}{} \quad \underset{(0.266)}{} \quad \underset{(0.839)}{} \quad \underset{(0.839)}{}$$

$$R^2 = 0.512 \qquad \overline{R}^2 = 0.468 \qquad ESS = 36.85$$

c. Using both the models U and R, perform an appropriate test at the 5 percent level. Be sure to state (1) the null and alternative hypotheses, (2) the statistical distribution (including degrees of freedom *for your models*), and (3) the test criterion for rejection of the null. What do you conclude from your test?

d. For Model R, the *F*-statistic for overall goodness of fit is 11.8 and the corresponding *p*-value is 0.003. State the null hypothesis for this *F*-test. From the *p*-value would you accept or reject the null? Why?

e. In Model R do the signs of coefficients agree with your intuition? Based on that would you say that the models here are sensible?

4.9 The Office of the Registrar at UCSD took a random sample of 427 students and obtained their grade point averages in college (COLGPA) and high school (HSGPA), verbal Scholastic Aptitude Test scores (VSAT), and mathematics scores in the SAT (MSAT). The following model was estimated (subscript *t* is omitted for simplicity):

$$COLGPA = \beta_1 + \beta_2 HSGPA + \beta_3 VSAT + \beta_4 MSAT + u$$

The estimated coefficients and their standard errors are given as follows:

	Coefficient	Standard Error	Test Statistic	Significance
$\hat{\beta}_1$	0.423	0.220		
$\hat{\beta}_2$	0.398	0.061		
$\hat{\beta}_3$	7.375e-04	2.807e-04		
$\hat{\beta}_4$	0.001015	2.936e-04		

a. The unadjusted R^2 was 0.22. Because this is very low, we might suspect that the model is inadequate. Test the model for overall goodness of fit (using a 1 percent level of significance). Be sure to state the null and alternative hypotheses, the test statistic and its distribution, and the criterion for acceptance or rejection. What is your conclusion?

b. Test each regression coefficient for significance at the 1 percent level against the alternative that the coefficient is positive. Are any of them insignificant? In the table, fill in the test statistic and indicate whether the coefficient is significant or insignificant. State their distribution and d.f.

c. Suppose a student took a special course to improve her SAT scores and increased the verbal and math scores by 100 points each. On average, how much of an increase in college GPA could she expect?

d. Suppose you want to test the hypothesis that the regression coefficients for VSAT and MSAT are equal (but need not be equal to zero). Describe step-by-step how you would do this. State the null and alternative hypotheses, the regression(s) to be run, the test statistic to be computed and its distribution, and the criterion for accepting or rejecting the null hypothesis. Describe these steps for each of the three methods discussed in Section 4.4.

e. List other variables that should have been included in the model. Explain why you think they belong in the model.

4.10 In a study of early retirements, the following equation was estimated using census data for 44 U.S. states:

$$RETRD = \beta_1 + \beta_2 HLTH + \beta_3 MSSEC + \beta_4 MPUBAS$$
$$+ \beta_5 UNEM + \beta_6 DEP + \beta_7 RACE + u$$

where

RETRD = Percent of retired men who are between the ages of 16 and 65
HLTH = Percent of people between 16 and 64 years of age who are prevented from working due to disability
MSSEC = Mean social security income ($)
MPUBAS = Mean public assistance (welfare) income ($)
UNEM = Unemployment rate in percent
DEP = Percent of households that are composed of married couples with children under 18
RACE = Percent of men who are non-White

a.   What signs would you expect for the regression coefficients? Give your reasoning. Using census data, the coefficients were estimated as follows:

	Coefficient	Standard Error	Test Statistic	Omitted/ Retained
$\hat{\beta}_1$	−3.930	9.202		
$\hat{\beta}_2$	1.627379	0.300		
$\hat{\beta}_3$	−5.483e-04	0.0021		
$\hat{\beta}_4$	4.568e-04	0.0017		
$\hat{\beta}_5$	0.549	0.250		
$\hat{\beta}_6$	0.153	0.097		
$\hat{\beta}_7$	0.077	0.034		

The adjusted R^2 for the model was $\overline{R}^2 = 0.654$, and the error sum of squares was 175.08805.

b.   Do all the signs agree with your intuition stated earlier? If not, which are counterintuitive?

c.   For each of the coefficients above (excluding the constant), carry out a test for the null hypothesis $\beta = 0$ against a two-sided alternative. Use a 10 percent level of significance. Based on your test, would you say that the corresponding variable is a candidate to be omitted from the model or retained?

d.   A second model was estimated after omitting MSSEC and MPUBAS and the new error sum of squares is 175.52381. Test the null hypothesis $\beta_3 = \beta_4 = 0$ at the 1 percent level. Be sure to state the alternative hypothesis, the test statistic to compute, its distribution under the null including the d.f., and the criterion for rejection of the null. What is your conclusion about the hypothesis? Is there a conflict between your conclusion here and that in question (c)?

†4.11   The following table presents estimates and related statistics (p-values in parentheses) for four models relating the number of private housing units authorized by building permits and their determinants (if an entry is blank, it means that the variable is absent from the model). The data refer to 40 cities in the United States. The model is as follows:

$$\text{HOUSING} = \beta_1 + \beta_2\text{DENSITY} + \beta_3\text{VALUE} + \beta_4\text{INCOME}$$
$$+ \beta_5\text{POPCHANG} + \beta_6\text{UNEMP}$$
$$+ \beta_7\text{LOCALTAX} + \beta_8\text{STATETAX} + u$$

where

HOUSING = Actual number of building permits issued
DENSITY = Population density per square mile
VALUE = Median value of owner-occupied homes (in hundreds of dollars)
INCOME = Median household income (in thousands of dollars)
POPCHANG = Percent increase in population between 1980 and 1992
UNEMP = Unemployment rate
LOCALTAX = Average local taxes per capita (in dollars)
STATETAX = Average state tax per capita (in dollars)

a.   For each regression coefficient *in Model A*, test whether or not it is zero at the 10 percent level (values in parentheses are *p*-values for a two-sided alternative). Based on your test would you say that the variable should be retained or should be dropped from the model?

b.   In Model A, test the joint hypothesis $H_0: \beta_2 = \beta_6 = \beta_7 = \beta_8 = 0$ at the 10 percent level. Be sure to state the alternative hypothesis, compute the test statistic, state its distribution under the null, and the criterion for acceptance or rejection. State your conclusion.

c.   Which of the models is the "best"? Explain what criteria you used to choose the best model.

d.   For each regression coefficient (ignore the constant term for this) *in your best model*, state whether some of the coefficients are "wrong" in sign. State what sign you would expect and why. Then identify whether it has the right sign.

e.   In Model D, suppose you measure HOUSING in thousands of units *and at the same time* measure income in hundreds of dollars. Write down the estimated coefficients of the new model, the corresponding *p*-values, and the new unadjusted *R*-square.

f.   Interpret the results using those in Sections 4.6 and 4.7 as guides.

Variables	Model A	Model B	Model C	Model D
CONSTANT	813 (0.74)	−392 (0.81)	−1279 (0.34)	−973 (0.44)
DENSITY	0.075 (0.43)	0.062 (0.32)	0.042 (0.47)	
VALUE	−0.855 (0.13)	−0.873 (0.11)	−0.994 (0.06)	−0.778 (0.07)
INCOME	110.411 (0.14)	133.025 (0.04)	125.705 (0.05)	116.597 (0.06)
POPCHANG	26.766 (0.11)	29.185 (0.06)	29.406 (0.001)	24.857 (.08)
UNEMP	−76.546 (0.48)			
LOCALTAX	−0.061 (0.95)			
STATETAX	−1.006 (0.40)	−1.004 (0.37)		
ESS	4.763e+7	4.843e+7	4.962e+7	5.038e+7
Unadj. R^2	0.349	0.338	0.322	0.312
$\hat{\sigma}^2$	1.488e+6	1.424e+6	1.418e+6	1.399e+6
AIC	1.776e+6	1.634e+6	1.593e+6	1.538e+6

Variables	Model A	Model B	Model C	Model D
FPE	1.786e+6	1.638e+6	1.595e+6	1.539e+6
HQ	2.007e+6	1.791e+6	1.719e+6	1.635e+6
SCHWARZ	2.490e+6	2.105e+6	1.967e+6	1.821e+6
SHIBATA	1.887e+6	1.574e+6	1.551e+6	1.511e+6
GCV	1.860e+6	1.676e+6	1.620e+7	1.55e+6
RICE	1.984e+6	1.730e+6	1.654e+6	1.574e+6

4.12   Using quarterly data for 10 years (making the number of observations 40), the following model of demand for new cars was estimated:

$$\text{NUMCARS} = \beta_1 + \beta_2\text{PRICE} + \beta_3\text{INCOME} + \beta_4\text{INTRATE} + \beta_5\text{UNEMP} + u$$

where
NUMCARS = Number of new car sales per thousand population
PRICE = New car price index
INCOME = Per-capita real disposable income (in actual dollars)
INTRATE = Interest rate
UNEMP = Unemployment rate

The following table has the estimates of the coefficients for three alternative models. Values in parentheses are standard errors (if an entry is blank, it means that the variable is absent from the model).

Variables	Model A	Model B	Model C
CONSTANT	−7.453352 (13.5782)	−10.554074 (4.621104)	15.238094 (1.167467)
PRICE	−0.071391 (0.034730)	−0.079392 (0.011022)	−0.024883 (0.007366)
INCOME	0.003159 (0.001763)	0.00356 (0.0006266)	
INTRATE	−0.153699 (0.049190)	−0.146651 (0.039229)	−0.204769 (0.051442)
UNEMP	−0.072547 (0.298195)		
ESS	23.510464	23.550222	44.65914
Adj. R^2	0.758	0.764	0.565
SGMASQ	0.671728	0.654173	1.207004
AIC	0.754701	0.719108	1.29716
FPE	0.755693	0.71959	1.297529
HQ	0.814563	0.764388	1.35795
SCHWARZ	0.932092	0.851414	1.472329
SHIBATA	0.734702	0.706507	1.28395
GCV	0.767689	0.726859	1.304869
RICE	0.783682	0.735944	1.313504

In Model A, test the joint hypothesis $\beta_3 = \beta_5 = 0$ by carrying out the following steps.
a.   Write down the formula for the test statistic and compute it.

b.   State its distribution and d.f.

c.   State the decision rule (for a 1 percent level) and your conclusion.

Next test each of the coefficients *in Model A only,* whether or not it is significantly different from zero, by carrying out the following steps:

d.   Write down the d.f. for the test statistic.

e.   Write down the critical value for a 10 percent level of significance (don't ask whether the test is one-tailed or two-tailed; you decide what it is based on the information given).

f.   Use the information in (e) and test whether or not each coefficient is significant. Clearly show your work and state your conclusion.

g.   Based on your test in (f), would you recommend any of the variables be omitted? If yes, which one? Also state what the advantages of omitting the variable(s) are. What are the disadvantages?

h.   Suppose income is measured in thousands of dollars. Write down the new numerical values of the coefficients and standard errors that changed because of that fact.

i.   For each variable, explain whether the sign of the estimated regression coefficients is as you would expect or is it "the wrong sign"? Justify your answers carefully.

j.   Which of the three models is the "best"? Explain what criteria you used and why you chose the model you did.

k.   Interpret the results using those in Sections 4.6 and 4.7 as guides.

4.13   Using annual data for 31 years, the following model of timber harvest in Oregon was estimated:

$$\text{HARVEST} = \beta_1 + \beta_2\text{EXPORTS} + \beta_3\text{HOUSTART} + \beta_4\text{INDPROD}$$
$$+ \beta_5\text{TIMBPRIC} + \beta_6\text{PRODPRIC} + u$$

where

    HARVEST = Total timber harvested in billion board feet

    EXPORTS = Volume of timber exports to foreign countries in 100 million board feet

    HOUSTART = Total housing starts in the United States in millions

    INDPROD = Index of industrial production for paper and wood products

    TIMBPRIC = Price of timber measured in dollars per 1,000 board feet

    PRODPRIC = Producer price index for all commodities

The following table has the estimates of the βs for three alternative models ($n = 31$ and values in parentheses are standard errors):

	Model A		Model B		Model C	
Variables	**Coeff. (std. err.)**	**Test Stat.**	**Coeff. (std. err.)**	**Test Stat.**	**Coeff. (std. err.)**	**Test Stat.**
CONSTANT	3.913 (0.574)	ignore	4.269 (0.376)	ignore	3.602 (0.533)	ignore
EXPORTS	0.108 (0.082)	——				
HOUSTART	0.524 (0.355)	——			0.618 (0.360)	——

Variables	Model A Coeff. (std. err.)	Test Stat.	Model B Coeff. (std. err.)	Test Stat.	Model C Coeff. (std. err.)	Test Stat.
INDPROD	0.525 (0.127)	———	0.694 (0.080)	———	0.612 (0.091)	———
TIMBPRIC	−0.018 (0.011)	———				
PRODPRIC	−0.456 (0.087)	———	−0.556 (0.079)	———	−0.481 (0.089)	———
d.f.		———		———		———
Critical value		———		———		———
ESS	6.22273		7.90322		7.1265	
Adj. R^2	0.758		0.725		0.743	
SGMASQ	0.248909		0.282258		0.263945	
AIC	0.29562		0.309385		0.297571	
FPE	0.297085		0.309573		0.298002	
HQ	0.323613		0.323702		0.316071	
SCHWARZ	0.390185		0.355441		0.358054	
SHIBATA	0.278437		0.304286		0.289213	
GCV	0.308648		0.3125		0.303047	
RICE	0.327512		0.316129		0.309848	

a.   In the preceding table, enter the appropriate values for the test statistics for testing whether each of the regression coefficients is significantly different from zero (exclude the constant terms).

b.   Also enter the degrees of freedom (d.f.) for each of the models.

c.   Next enter the critical values for a 10 percent level of significance (don't ask whether the test is one-tailed or two-tailed; you decide what it is based on the information given).

d.   Near each of the test statistics you wrote for (a), write down whether the corresponding coefficient is significant or insignificant.

e.   Which of the three models is the "best"? Explain what criteria you used and why you chose the model you did.

f.   Based on your test *for Model A only*, would you say any of the variables should be considered candidates for omission? If yes, which ones? What are the advantages of omitting the variables? What are the disadvantages?

Using Model A as the unrestricted model and Model B as the restricted model, test a relevant joint hypothesis by carrying out the following steps:

g.   Write down the null hypothesis.

h.   Write down the formula for the test statistic and compute it.

i.   State its distribution under the null and d.f.

j.   State the decision rule (for a 10 percent level) and your conclusion. Use numerical values, not symbols.

k.   Suppose EXPORTS is measured in billion board feet. Write down the new numerical values (for Model A only) of the coefficients and standard errors that changed because of that. Be sure to justify how you arrived at the answer. How are the t-statistics, F-statistics, and R^2 affected by the change in units?

l.   Interpret the results using those in Sections 4.6 and 4.7 as guides.

4.14   Using data for 40 top television markets, the following model was estimated:

$$SUB = \beta_1 + \beta_2 HOME + \beta_3 INST + \beta_4 SVC + \beta_5 TV + \beta_6 AGE$$
$$+ \beta_7 AIR + \beta_8 Y + u$$

where
   SUB = Number of subscribers to cable TV (thousands)
   HOME = Number of homes passed by each system (thousands)
   INST = Installation fee ($)
   SVC = Monthly service charge ($)
   TV = Number of signals carried by each cable system
   AGE = Age of the system in years
   AIR = Number of TV signals received with good signals without cable
   Y = Per-capita income in the area

a.   State the null and alternative hypotheses that will enable you to test the model for *overall significance.*
b.   You are given that TSS = 43865.001 and ESS = 4923.914. Derive the numerical value of the test statistic for that hypothesis. (Note: You have all the information needed.)
c.   State the statistical distribution and d.f. for the test statistic.
d.   Obtain the relevant critical value or range (for a 1 percent level of significance), and state whether or not you reject the null hypothesis. Describe your conclusion.
e.   Consider the hypotheses $H_0: \beta_i = 0$ and $H_1: \beta_i \neq 0$ (*separately* for $i = 2, 3, \ldots, 8$). The following table gives the estimated coefficients and the corresponding standard errors. In each case, compute the appropriate test statistic, and write it in the proper column (for the present, ignore the last column).

Coefficient		Standard Error	Test Statistic	Significance
$\hat{\beta}_1$	−6.808	26.7	Ignore	Ignore
$\hat{\beta}_2$	0.406	0.035		
$\hat{\beta}_3$	−0.526	0.476		
$\hat{\beta}_4$	2.039	2.127		
$\hat{\beta}_5$	0.757	0.688		
$\hat{\beta}_6$	1.194	0.502		
$\hat{\beta}_7$	−5.111	1.518		
$\hat{\beta}_8$	0.0017	0.00347		

f.   The test statistic has the _____ distribution with d.f. _____. The critical value or range for a 10 percent level of significance is _____.
g.   In the preceding table, write down for each case whether the coefficient is significant or insignificant.
h.   Based on your results, write down the names of variables that are candidates for omission from the model.
      A second model was also estimated and the results are as follows:

$$\widehat{SUB} = 12.869 + 0.412\, HOME + 1.140\, AGE - 3.462\, AIR$$

$$ESS = 5595.615$$

Use the two models to test a relevant hypothesis.
i.   First state the null and alternative hypotheses.
j.   Derive the numerical value of the test statistic.
k.   State its distribution and d.f.
l.   Derive the critical value or range and the test criterion (use the 10 percent level this time) and state the conclusion.

4.15   The following table presents estimates and related statistics (standard errors in parentheses) for four models relating the list price of an automobile to a number of characteristics using 82 observations. The model is as follows:

$$PRICE = \beta_1 + \beta_2 WBASE + \beta_3 LENGTH + \beta_4 WIDTH + \beta_5 HEIGHT + \beta_6 WEIGHT + \beta_7 CYL + \beta_8 LITERS + \beta_9 GASMPG + u$$

where
    PRICE = List price in thousands of dollars
    WBASE = Wheelbase in inches
    LENGTH = Length of car in inches
    WIDTH = Width of car in inches
    HEIGHT = Height in inches
    WEIGHT = Weight of car in hundreds of pounds
    CYL = Number of cylinders
    LITERS = Engine displacement in liters
    GASMPG = Estimated gas miles per gallon, averaged between city and freeway driving

a.   (For Model A only) I believe that some of the coefficients are "wrong" in sign. For each regression coefficient (ignore the constant term for this), state what sign you would expect and why. Then identify whether it has the right sign.
b.   Test the joint hypothesis that the coefficients for WBASE, WIDTH, CYL, LITERS, and GASMPG are all zero at the 5 percent level. Be sure to state the null and alternative hypotheses, compute the test statistic, state its distribution under the null, and identify the criterion for rejection. State your conclusion.
c.   Which of the models is the "best"? Explain what criteria you used to choose the best model. Interpret the results of this best model.
d.   Test Model A for overall significance at the 1 percent level. Be sure to state the null and alternative hypotheses, compute the test statistic, state its distribution, and specify the decision rule. What do you conclude? (You have all the information you need for this.)

Variables	Model A	Model B	Model C	Model D
CONSTANT	58.866	54.400	65.476	71.554
	(27.33)	(23.19)	(20.1)	(19.93)
WBASE	0.036			
	(0.28)			
LENGTH	−0.394	−0.383	−0.391	−0.403
	(0.14)	(0.117)	(0.117)	(0.118)
WIDTH	−0.104			
	(0.24)			
HEIGHT	−0.748	−0.741	−0.703	−0.839
	(0.46)	(0.43)	(0.43)	(0.42)

(continued)

(continued)

Variables	Model A	Model B	Model C	Model D
WEIGHT	2.184 (0.47)	2.148 (0.43)	1.926 (0.36)	2.227 (0.31)
CYL	0.959 (1.31)	1.046 (0.691)	1.095 (0.69)	
LITERS	0.264 (1.83)			
GASMPG	0.196 (0.22)	0.194 (0.20)		
ESS	2303.751	2309.978	2337.952	2414.724
$\overline{R}^2$ (adjusted)	0.559	0.576	0.576	0.568
$\hat{\sigma}^2$	31.558	30.394	30.363	30.958
AIC	34.991	32.610	32.210	32.466
FPE	35.022	32.618	32.214	32.468
HQ	38.906	34.999	34.164	34.033
SCHWARZ	45.570	38.889	37.301	36.510
SHIBATA	34.262	32.293	31.989	32.321
GCV	35.449	32.794	32.335	32.546
RICE	35.996	33.000	32.472	32.631

Note: Values in parentheses are standard errors.

4.16   Using data for the 58 counties in California, the following model was estimated:

$$\text{MEDINC} = \beta_1 + \beta_2 \text{FAMSIZE} + \beta_3 \text{HIGHSCHL} + \beta_4 \text{COLLEGE} + \beta_5 \text{UNEMP} + \beta_6 \text{URB} + u$$

where
  MEDINC = Median family income in thousands of dollars
  FAMSIZE = Persons per household
  HIGHSCHL = Percent of the population (25 years and over) that had only a high
      school education
  COLLEGE = Percent of the population (25 years and over) that completed four
      years of college or higher
  UNEMP = Percent unemployment rate
  URB = Percent of urban population

a.   What signs would you expect for the regression coefficients and why? (Ignore the
    constant term.)
The estimated model with standard errors in parentheses is given as follows:

$$\widehat{\text{MEDINC}} = -41.464 + 15.382 \text{ FAMSIZE} + 0.335 \text{ HIGHSCHL}$$
$$\begin{array}{ccc} (15.742) & (3.033) & (0.126) \end{array}$$
$$+ 1.021 \text{ COLLEGE} - 0.403 \text{ UNEMP} + 0.029 \text{ URB}$$
$$\begin{array}{ccc} (0.132) & (0.229) & (0.029) \end{array}$$

$$\text{ESS} = 578.7298 \qquad \text{Adjusted } R^2 = \overline{R}^2 = 0.837$$

b.   Carry out a test of the overall significance of the model (you have all the infor-
    mation you need) at the 1 percent level of significance. Be sure to state the null
    and alternative hypotheses, the test statistic to compute and its distribution in-
    cluding the d.f., and the criterion for rejecting the null. What do you conclude?

c.   Do the observed signs of the coefficients agree with what you stated in (a)?

d.   Test whether each of the coefficients, excluding the constant, is significantly different from zero (use a 10 percent level). Here also be sure to state the null and alternative hypotheses, the test statistic to compute and its distribution including the d.f., and the criterion for rejecting the null. Based on your test, are any of the variables candidates for exclusion from the model? If so, which ones?

e.   Suppose MEDINC is measured in hundreds of dollars. Write down the new values for all the statistics presented above.

f.   A second model was estimated and its coefficients and related statistics are given next.

$$\widehat{\text{MEDINC}} = -61.766 + 16.971 \text{ FAMSIZE} + 0.498 \text{ HIGHSCHL}$$
$$\quad\quad (13.584) \quad\quad (2.746) \quad\quad\quad\quad (0.109)$$
$$\quad\quad + 1.213 \text{ COLLEGE}$$
$$\quad\quad\quad (0.079)$$

$$\text{ESS} = 640.229 \quad\quad \text{Adjusted } R^2 = 0.826$$

g.   Use the first model as the unrestricted model and the second as the restricted model, and perform a relevant test at the 10 percent level. Here again be sure to state the null and alternative hypotheses, the test statistic to compute and its distribution including the d.f., and the criterion for rejecting the null. Is there a contradiction between this test and the one you did in (d)? If so, point out where.

[†]4.17   The accompanying table has the estimated results (t-statistics are in parentheses) for a number of models on deaths due to heart disease. The variables are defined for DATA4-7 in Appendix D.

a.   Explain why each of the independent variables might affect the death rate due to coronary heart disease. What signs would you expect a priori for each of the regression coefficients? Do the observed signs agree with your intuition? If not, do you have an alternative explanation for the unexpected sign?

Variables	Model A	Model B	Model C
CONSTANT	226.002	247.004	139.678
	(1.54)	(1.94)	(1.79)
CAL	−69.983	−77.762	
	(−0.89)	(−1.06)	
CIG	10.116	10.640	10.706
	(2.00)	(2.32)	(2.33)
UNEMP	−0.613		
	(−0.39)		
EDFAT	2.810	2.733	3.380
	(1.88)	(2.40)	(3.50)
MEAT	0.112		
	(0.46)		
SPIRITS	21.716	23.650	26.749
	(2.57)	(3.11)	(3.80)
BEER	−3.467	−3.849	−4.132
	(−2.67)	(−4.27)	(−4.79)
WINE	−4.562		
	(−0.28)		
$\bar{R}^2$	0.645	0.674	0.672
F	8.508	14.633	17.932

(continued)

(Continued)

Variables	Model A	Model B	Model C
ESS	1980	2040	2122
SGMASQ	79.212	72.868	73.184
AIC	98.895	85.407	83.766
FPE	100.180	85.727	83.946
HG	113.504	93.624	90.480
SCHWARZ	148.130	111.809	104.846
SHIBATA	89.079	81.188	80.780
GCV	107.728	88.482	85.801
RICE	123.769	92.741	88.430

Note: Values in parentheses are *t*-statistics.

b.   Would you say that the fit is good? What do the values of *F* in the table mean? For-mally test a relevant hypothesis. Be sure to state the null and alternative hypothe-ses, the degrees of freedom for the *F*-statistic, and the criterion for rejecting or accepting the hypothesis. What do you conclude?

c.   Test each of the regression coefficients for statistical significance at the level you choose. Based on your test, would you recommend that any of the variables be dropped?

d.   Perform relevant Wald *F*-tests for excluding variables. State the null and alterna-tive hypotheses and the degrees of freedom. What do you conclude?

e.   Which of the models is the best? Explain your reasons.

f.   Identify any variables that belong in the model but have been omitted.

4.18   The monthly salary (WAGE), age (AGE), number of years of education beyond the eighth grade (EDUC), and the number of years of experience (EXPER) were ob-tained for 49 persons in a certain office. The estimated relation between WAGE and the characteristics of a person is as follows (with *t*-statistics in parentheses):

$$\widehat{\text{WAGE}} = 632.244 + 142.510\ \text{EDUC} + 43.225\ \text{EXPER} - 1.913\ \text{AGE}$$
$$\quad\quad\ (1.493)\quad\quad\quad (4.088)\quad\quad\quad\quad (3.022)\quad\quad\quad\quad (-0.22)$$

a.   The value of $\bar{R}^2$ is 0.277. Using this information, test the model for overall signif-icance. (Note: You have all the information you need to perform the test.)

b.   Test the coefficients for EDUC and EXPER for statistical significance at the 1 per-cent level and AGE for significance at the 10 percent level.

c.   Can you rationalize the negative sign for AGE?

d.   Because the *t*-statistic is low for AGE, someone suggests that AGE be eliminated. If you follow the suggestion, what kind of specification error might you be mak-ing? What are the consequences of that for unbiasedness and consistency of esti-mates and forecasts? Explain.

4.19   Consider the following model relating the gain in salary due to an MBA degree to a number of its determinants (for simplicity, the *t* subscript is omitted):

$$\text{SLRYGAIN} = \beta_1 + \beta_2\ \text{TUITION} + \beta_3\ Z1 + \beta_4\ Z2 + \beta_5\ Z3 + \beta_6\ Z4 + \beta_7\ Z5 + u$$

where SLRYGAIN is post-MBA salary minus pre-MBA salary, in thousands of dollars, TUITION is annual tuition in thousands of dollars, and the other variables are as follows:

$Z1$ = MBA skills, graded by recruiters, in being analysts (1–4, 1 is best)
$Z2$ = MBA skills, graded by recruiters, in being team players (1–4, 1 is best)
$Z3$ = MBA skills, graded by recruiters, in having a global view (1–4, 1 is best)
$Z4$ = Teaching evaluation by MBAs (1–4, 1 is best)
$Z5$ = Curriculum evaluation by MBAs (1–4, 1 is best)

Using data for 25 top business schools gathered by *Business Week*, the coefficients were estimated as follows:

Coefficient		Standard Error	Test Statistic	Retain or Omit
$\hat{\beta}_1$	60.899	2.513	Skip this	Skip this
$\hat{\beta}_2$	0.314	0.750	——	——
$\hat{\beta}_3$	−3.948	2.756	——	——
$\hat{\beta}_4$	−2.016	2.165	——	——
$\hat{\beta}_5$	−2.402	2.948	——	——
$\hat{\beta}_6$	−0.613	3.062	——	——
$\hat{\beta}_7$	−5.325	3.773	——	——

$R^2 = 0.461$ $\bar{R}^2 = 0.282$ ESS = 1288.214

a. To carry out individual tests for the null hypotheses $\hat{\beta}_i = 0$ ($i = 2, 3, \ldots, 7$) against a two-sided alternative, write down in the table the numerical values of the test statistic for each of the coefficients, excluding the constant term.

b. State the statistical distribution of the test statistics, including the degrees of freedom, and the critical value (or range) for a 10 percent test.

c. In each case, write down (in the table) whether the variable is a candidate for omission or retention.

d. Test the model for overall significance at the 10 percent level by carrying out the following steps: (1) State the null and alternative hypotheses. (2) Write down an expression for the test statistic and compute its value. (3) State its distribution under the null including the d.f. (4) State the criterion for rejection of the null (at the 10 percent level) and apply it. What is your conclusion about the overall goodness of fit? Is there a conflict between your conclusion here and that in question (c)? If yes, can you suggest a possible explanation(s)?

e. Another model was estimated after omitting some variables. The estimated model is the following, with *p*-values in parentheses:

$$\widehat{\text{SLRYGAIN}} = 62.438 - 6.398\ Z1 - 5.516\ Z5$$
$$\quad\quad (<0.01) \quad\quad (0.006) \quad\quad (0.052)$$

Error sum of squares = 1494.512 $\bar{R}^2 = 0.318$

Using the first model as the unrestricted model and the second model as the restricted model, test a relevant *joint* hypothesis at the 10 percent level by carrying out the following steps: (1) State the null and alternative hypotheses. (2) Write down an expression for the test statistic and compute its value. (3) State its distribution under the null including the d.f. (4) State the criterion for rejection of the null (at the 10 percent level) and apply it. (5) State whether your test confirms the individual test done in (a) above or contradicts it.

f.   In the two models, do the signs of the regression coefficients agree with your intuition, or do you think that some of the signs are wrong? If the latter, which ones? Considering the goodness of fit, the tests you have done, the conclusions you have drawn from them, and the significance of the regression coefficients, evaluate the adequacy of the model specification.

4.20   The following table presents estimates and related statistics for three models relating the number of private housing units authorized by building permits and its determinants. The data refer to 40 cities in the United States. The model is (omitting the t-subscript)

$$\text{HOUSING} = \beta_1 + \beta_2 \text{ VALUE} + \beta_3 \text{ INCOME} + \beta_4 \text{ LOCALTAX}$$
$$+ \beta_5 \text{ STATETAX} + \beta_6 \text{ POPCHANG} + u$$

where HOUSING is the actual number of building permits issued, VALUE is the median price of owner-occupied homes (in hundreds of dollars), INCOME is median household income (in hundreds of dollars), LOCALTAX is average local taxes per capita (in dollars), STATETAX is average state tax per capita (in dollars), and POPCHANG is the percent increase in population between 1980 and 1982.

Values in parentheses are p-values for a two-sided alternative. Note that you are not given the standard errors or t-statistics and they cannot be calculated from the information given.

Variable	Model A	Model B	Model C
$\hat{\beta}_1$ Constant	−420.323 (0.80)	−1071.982 (0.40)	−973.017 (0.44)
$\hat{\beta}_2$ VALUE	−0.724 (0.15)	−0.864 (0.05)	−0.778 (0.07)
$\hat{\beta}_3$ INCOME	111.898 (0.08)	110.193 (0.08)	116.600 (0.06)
$\hat{\beta}_4$ LOCALTAX	0.503 (0.41)	0.491 (0.41)	
$\hat{\beta}_5$ STATETAX	−0.636 (0.15)		
$\hat{\beta}_6$ POPCHANG	28.257 (0.07)	29.662 (0.05)	24.857 (0.08)
ESS	4.886	4.941	5.038
Unadjusted R^2	0.332	0.325	0.312
SIGMASQ	1.437	1.412	1.399
AIC	1.649	1.586	1.538
FPE	1.653	1.588	1.539
HQ	1.807	1.712	1.635
SCHWARZ	2.124	1.959	1.821
SHIBATA	1.588	1.544	1.511
GCV	1.691	1.613	1.555
RICE	1.745	1.647	1.574

a.   For each regression coefficient *in Model A*, test whether it is significantly different from zero at the 10 percent level (ignore the constant term). Based on your test, which variables are candidates to be dropped from the model and why?

Use Model A as the unrestricted model and Model C as the restricted model, and carry out the following steps for an appropriate test:

b. Write down the null and alternative hypotheses in terms of the βs.

c. Compute the test statistic.

d. State the distribution of your test statistic, under the null, including the degrees of freedom.

e. Write down the critical value (or range) for the test, and state whether or not you would reject the null hypothesis at the 10 percent level.

f. Which of the models is the "best"? Explain what criteria you used to choose the best model.

g. For each regression coefficient (ignore the constant term for this) *in your best model*, state whether some of the coefficients are "wrong" in sign. State what sign you would expect and why. Then identify whether it has the right sign or not.

Empirical Questions Requiring Computer Work

4.21 DATA4-10 (see Appendix D) has the data for a study involving school choice in the United States. It is cross-sectional for all 50 states and Washington, D.C. The variables are described in Appendix D. The dependent variable is the proportion of students enrolled in private schools.

For each explanatory variable, explain why it might have a causal effect on school enrollments, and indicate the direction of effect. Using the data in the disk file DATA4-10, estimate an appropriate model. Perform a test for overall significance. Comment on the goodness of fit. Test each regression coefficient (except the constant term) for significance at the 10 percent level (two-tailed), and identify candidates for omission. First omit them all, reestimate the new model, and perform a Wald test for omission. What do you conclude? Next start with the original model and omit only one at a time (at each stage justify your choice of variable to omit) and reestimate. Do the model selection statistics improve? Proceed until you get a final model (justify your choice of the "best" model), and interpret the results. Is the final model the same as the restricted model when you first omitted all the variables with insignificant coefficients? If not, how would you explain the difference? Do the signs of regression coefficients in the final model agree with your intuition?

4.22 DATA4-12 has cross-section data for the 50 states and Washington, D.C. ($n = 51$) for total mortality rates and their determinants. Details about the variables and sources are in Appendix D. The dependent variable is the total mortality rate per 100,000 population.

For each explanatory variable, explain why it might have a causal effect on total mortality rates, and indicate the direction of effect. Using the data in the disk file DATA4-12, estimate an appropriate model. Perform a test for overall significance. Comment on the goodness of fit. Test each regression coefficient for significance at the 10 percent level (two-tailed), and identify candidates for omission. First omit them all, reestimate the new model, and perform a Wald test for omission. What do you conclude? Next start with the original model and omit only one at a time (at each stage justify your choice of variable to omit) and reestimate. Do the model selection statistics improve? Proceed until you get a final model (justify your choice of the "best" model), and interpret the results. Is the final model the same as the restricted model when you first omitted all the variables with insignificant coefficients? If not, how would you explain the difference? Do the signs of regression coefficients in the final model agree with your intuition?

4.23 DATA4-13 has data on the attendance at baseball games in 78 cities across the United States. Details about the variables and sources are in Appendix D. The dependent variable is the attendance at baseball games (in thousands).

For each explanatory variable, explain why it might have a causal effect on baseball attendance, and indicate the direction of effect. Using the data in the disk file DATA4-13, estimate an appropriate model. Perform a test for overall significance. Comment on the goodness of fit. Test each regression coefficient for significance at the 10 percent level (two-tailed), and identify candidates for omission. First omit them all, reestimate the new model, and perform a Wald test for omission. What do you conclude? Next start with the original model and omit only one at a time (at each stage justify your choice of variable to omit) and reestimate. Do the model selection statistics improve? Proceed until you get a final model (justify your choice of the "best" model), and interpret the results. Is the final model the same as the restricted model when you first omitted all the variables with insignificant coefficients? If not, how would you explain the difference? Do the signs of regression coefficients in the final model agree with your intuition?

4.24   DATA4-14 has additional data on the MBA programs at the top 25 business schools in the United States (see DATA3-8). The variables are defined as follows:

TUITION = Annual tuition in thousands of dollars
SLRYGAIN = Average salary gain (in thousands of dollars) for MBAs (dependent variable); the file also includes additional data on ratings by recruiters and MBAs in various categories; ratings are from 1(A) to 4(D)

$z1$ = MBA skills in being analysts, as graded by recruiters
$z2$ = MBA skills in being team players, as graded by recruiters
$z3$ = MBA skills in having a global view, as graded by recruiters
$z4$ = Teaching evaluation by MBAs
$z5$ = Curriculum evaluation by MBAs

What signs would you expect for the z-variables listed? Estimate the most general model for salary gain. Carry out a test for overall goodness of fit. Carry out a data-based model reduction until you find the "best" model. Explain your procedure step-by-step. Finally, interpret the results of your best model.

4.25   DATA4-9 has the data used in Exercise 4.10. First verify the results in that exercise. Which variables would you recommend be considered for exclusion from the model and why? Omit these one at a time and estimate the new model until you arrive at a "final" model, justifying your action along the way. Use the most general model as the unrestricted model and your final model as the restricted model and carry out a Wald F-test. Be sure to state the null hypothesis for this, the test statistic, its distribution and d.f., and the criterion for rejection of the null. What do you conclude? In the final model do the actual estimates agree with your prior notion? If not, can you rationalize the difference?

4.26   DATA4-11 has the data used in Exercise 4.11. Using this data set, carry out an analysis similar to the one in Exercise 4.25.

4.27   DATA6-5 has the data used in Exercise 4.13. Using this data set, carry out an analysis similar to the one in Exercise 4.25.

4.28   DATA4-8 has the data used in Exercise 4.14. Using this data set, carry out an analysis similar to the one in Exercise 4.25.

4.29   DATA4-6 has the data used in Exercise 4.16. Using this data set, carry out an analysis similar to the one in Exercise 4.25.

4.30   DATA4-7 has the data used in Exercise 4.17. Using this data set, carry out an analysis similar to the one in Exercise 4.25.

4.31   DATA4-16 has data on the same variables as in DATA4-10. Carry out an analysis similar to the one in Exercise 4.21.

4.A APPENDIX

Miscellaneous Derivations

4.A.1 The Three-Variable Regression Model

A three-variable regression model relates the dependent variable Y to a constant term and to the two independent variables X_2 and X_3. The formal model is

$$Y_t = \beta_1 + \beta_2 X_{t2} + \beta_3 X_{t3} + u_t \tag{4.A.1}$$

Taking the mean of each term in the model, we have

$$\overline{Y} = \beta_1 + \beta_2 \overline{X}_2 + \beta_3 \overline{X}_3 + \overline{u} \tag{4.A.2}$$

Subtracting this from (4.A.1), we obtain the **model in deviation form** as

$$y_t = \beta_2 x_{t2} + \beta_3 x_{t3} + e_t \tag{4.A.3}$$

where $y_t = Y_t - \overline{Y}$, $x_{t2} = X_{t2} - \overline{X}_2$, $x_{t3} = X_{t3} - \overline{X}_3$, and $e_t = u_t - \overline{u}$. The lowercase letters indicate that the variables are deviations from the respective means. The advantage in expressing the model in deviation form is that there are only two parameters (β_2 and β_3) to estimate. If $\hat{\beta}_1$, $\hat{\beta}_2$, and $\hat{\beta}_3$ are the estimates of the regression coefficients, $\hat{\beta}_1$ is estimated as

$$\hat{\beta}_1 = \overline{Y} - \hat{\beta}_2 \overline{X}_2 - \hat{\beta}_3 \overline{X}_3$$

An estimate of the residual term is

$$\hat{u}_t = Y_t - \hat{\beta}_1 - \hat{\beta}_2 X_{t2} - \hat{\beta}_3 X_{t3}$$

The OLS procedure minimizes the error sum of squares ESS $= \Sigma \hat{u}_t^2$ with respect to $\hat{\beta}_1$, $\hat{\beta}_2$, and $\hat{\beta}_3$. This is equivalent to (not proven) minimizing $\Sigma \hat{e}_t^2 = \Sigma(y_t - \hat{\beta}_2 x_{t2} - \hat{\beta}_3 x_{t3})^2$. Setting to zero the partial derivatives of this with respect to $\hat{\beta}_2$ and $\hat{\beta}_3$, it is easy to verify that the conditions are

$$\sum x_{t2} \hat{e}_t = 0 = \sum x_{t2}(y_t - \hat{\beta}_2 x_{t2} - \hat{\beta}_3 x_{t3})$$
$$\sum x_{t3} \hat{e}_t = 0 = \sum x_{t3}(y_t - \hat{\beta}_2 x_{t2} - \hat{\beta}_3 x_{t3})$$

This gives the following two normal equations (ignoring the t-subscript):

$$\hat{\beta}_2 \sum x_2^2 + \hat{\beta}_3 \sum x_2 x_3 = \sum y x_2 \tag{4.A.4}$$

$$\hat{\beta}_2 \sum x_2 x_3 + \hat{\beta}_3 \sum x_3^2 = \sum y x_3 \tag{4.A.5}$$

Using a simplifying notation, this can be rewritten as follows:

$$\hat{\beta}_2 S_{22} + \hat{\beta}_3 S_{23} = S_{y2} \tag{4.A.6}$$

$$\hat{\beta}_2 S_{23} + \hat{\beta}_3 S_{33} = S_{y3} \tag{4.A.7}$$

where

$$S_{22} = \sum x_{t2}^2 = \sum (X_{t2} - \overline{X}_2)^2 \tag{4.A.8}$$

$$S_{23} = \sum x_{t2} x_{t3} = \sum (X_{t2} - \overline{X}_2)(X_{t3} - \overline{X}_3) \tag{4.A.9}$$

$$S_{33} = \sum x_{t3}^2 = \sum (X_{t3} - \overline{X}_3)^2 \tag{4.A.10}$$

$$S_{y2} = \sum y_t x_{t2} = \sum (Y_t - \overline{Y})(X_{t2} - \overline{X}_2) \tag{4.A.11}$$

$$S_{y3} = \sum y_t x_{t3} = \sum (Y_t - \overline{Y})(X_{t3} - \overline{X}_3) \tag{4.A.12}$$

The solutions to (4.A.6) and (4.A.7) are

$$\hat{\beta}_2 = (S_{y2} S_{33} - S_{y3} S_{23})/\Delta \tag{4.A.13}$$

$$\hat{\beta}_3 = (S_{y3} S_{22} - S_{y2} S_{23})/\Delta \tag{4.A.14}$$

where

$$\Delta = S_{22} S_{33} - S_{23}^2 \tag{4.A.15}$$

The computation of the variance of the $\hat{\beta}$s is postponed to Appendix 5.A.

4.A.2 Bias Due to the Omission of a Relevant Variable

The true and the estimated models are

True model: $Y_t = \beta_1 + \beta_2 X_{t2} + \beta_3 X_{t3} + u_t$

Estimated model: $Y_t = \beta_1 + \beta_2 X_{t2} + v_t$

OLS estimates of the parameters of the estimated model are given by (see Equations (3.9) and (3.10):

$$\hat{\beta}_2 = S_{y2}/S_{22} \quad \text{and} \quad \hat{\beta}_1 = \overline{Y} - \hat{\beta}_2 \overline{X}_2 \tag{4.A.16}$$

where S_{y2} and S_{22} are defined in Equations (4.A.11) and (4.A.8). The expected value of $\hat{\beta}_2$ is given by $E(S_{y2})/S_{22}$ because S_{22} is nonrandom:

$$S_{y2} = \sum (Y_t - \overline{Y})(X_{t2} - \overline{X}_2) = \sum Y_t (X_{t2} - \overline{X}_2) - \sum \overline{Y}(X_{t2} - \overline{X}_2)$$

$$= \sum Y_t (X_{t2} - \overline{X}_2)$$

because $\overline{Y}$ can be taken out of the summation and $\Sigma\,(X_{t2} - \overline{X}_2) = 0$ by Property 2.A.4. Substitute for Y_t from the true model (because that is the true process by which Y_t is generated):

$$S_{y2} = \sum (X_{t2} - \overline{X}_2)(\beta_1 + \beta_2 X_{t2} + \beta_3 X_{t3} + u_t)$$

$$= 0 + \beta_2 \sum (X_{t2} - \overline{X}_2) X_{t2} + \beta_3 \sum (X_{t2} - \overline{X}_2) X_{t3} + \sum (X_{t2} - \overline{X}_2) u_t$$

The first term is zero because of Property 2.A.4. The second term is

$$\sum (X_{t2} - \overline{X}_2) X_{t2} = \sum (X_{t2} - \overline{X}_2)(X_{t2} - \overline{X}_2 + \overline{X}_2)$$

$$= \sum (X_{t2} - \overline{X}_2)^2 + \overline{X}_2 \sum (X_{t2} - \overline{X}_2) = \sum (X_{t2} - \overline{X}_2)^2$$

because the second term is zero. By proceeding similarly,

$$\sum (X_{t2} - \overline{X}_2) X_{t3} = \sum (X_{t2} - \overline{X}_2)(X_{t3} - \overline{X}_3)$$

Using these results we get

$$S_{y2} = \beta_2 \sum (X_{t2} - \overline{X}_2)^2 + \beta_3 \sum (X_{t2} - \overline{X}_2)(X_{t3} - \overline{X}_3) + \sum (X_{t2} - \overline{X}_2) u_t$$

$$= \beta_2 S_{22} + \beta_3 S_{23} + S_{u2}$$

where the notation for the S-terms is similar to the ones given in Equations (4.A.8) through (4.A.12). Because X_2 and X_3 are nonrandom and uncorrelated with u, and $E(u) = 0$, then

$$E(S_{y2}) = \beta_2 S_{22} + \beta_3 S_{23} + E(S_{u2}) = \beta_2 S_{22} + \beta_3 S_{23}$$

It follows from this that

$$E(\hat{\beta}_2) = \beta_2 + \beta_3 \left[\frac{S_{23}}{S_{22}} \right]$$

Because $\beta_3 \neq 0$, $\hat{\beta}_2$ will be biased unless $S_{23} = 0$—that is, unless X_2 and X_3 are uncorrelated. This proves Property 4.4a for the models used here. The omitted variable bias is given by $\beta_3(S_{23}/S_{22})$. The direction of the bias depends on whether β_3 is positive and whether X_2 and X_3 are positively or negatively correlated. As the sample size increases indefinitely, $\hat{\beta}_2$ will not converge to β_2 (if $S_{23} \neq 0$), and hence the estimator is not consistent.

From Equation (4.A.16), $\hat{\beta}_1 = \overline{Y} - \hat{\beta}_2 \overline{X}_2$, and hence $E(\hat{\beta}_1) = E(\overline{Y}) - \overline{X}_2 E(\hat{\beta}_2)$. Because $\overline{Y} = \beta_1 + \beta_2 \overline{X}_2 + \beta_3 \overline{X}_3 + \overline{u}$, $E(\overline{Y}) = \beta_1 + \beta_2 \overline{X}_2 + \beta_3 \overline{X}_3$. Substituting for this and for the expectation of $\hat{\beta}_2$, we get,

$$E(\hat{\beta}_1) = \beta_1 + \beta_2 \overline{X}_2 + \beta_3 \overline{X}_3 - \overline{X}_2 \left(\beta_2 + \beta_3 \frac{S_{23}}{S_{22}} \right)$$

$$= \beta_1 + \beta_3 \left(\overline{X}_3 - \overline{X}_2 \frac{S_{23}}{S_{22}} \right)$$

We note from this that the necessary and sufficient condition for $\hat{\beta}_1$ to be unbiased is that $[\overline{X}_3 - \overline{X}_2(S_{23}/S_{22})] = 0$. X_2 and X_3 being uncorrelated is not sufficient to guarantee the unbiasedness of the estimate of the intercept term. In addition, the mean of X_3 must be zero. From the expected values of $\hat{\beta}_1$ and $\hat{\beta}_2$, we note that they capture part of the effects of the omitted variable X_3. This point is significant and should be emphasized. Because of this result, one may find that the numerical value of a regression coefficient is quite different from any prior notions we may have about the magnitude. This indicates that the coefficient in question represents not only the direct effect of the corresponding variable but also that of an omitted variable that is correlated with the included variable.

Kmenta (1986, p. 394) has shown that even if $S_{23} = 0$, the estimated variance of $\hat{\beta}_2(s_{\hat{\beta}_2}^2)$ is positively biased; that is, $E(s_{\hat{\beta}_2}^2) = \mathrm{Var}(\hat{\beta}_2) + Q$, where Q is nonnegative. Therefore, the usual tests of hypotheses are no longer valid. The consequences of omitting a relevant variable are therefore quite serious.

4.A.3 Proof of Property 4.4

The estimated model is

$$Y_t = \beta_1 + \beta_2 X_{t2} + \beta_3 X_{t3} + v_t$$

From Equations (4.A.13) and (4.A.14)—repeated here along with (4.A.15)—the OLS estimates for β_2 and β_3 are

$$\hat{\beta}_2 = (S_{y2}S_{33} - S_{y3}S_{23})/\Delta \qquad\qquad \textbf{(4.A.13)}$$

$$\hat{\beta}_3 = (S_{y3}S_{22} - S_{y2}S_{23})/\Delta \qquad\qquad \textbf{(4.A.14)}$$

where

$$\Delta = S_{22}S_{33} - S_{23}^2 \qquad\qquad \textbf{(4.A.15)}$$

To check whether $\hat{\beta}_2$ is unbiased or not, we first need the *true* expectations of S_{y2} and S_{y3}. The true model is (in deviation form)

$$y_t = \beta_2 x_{t2} + u_t - \overline{u}$$

Substituting for y_t from the true model into S_{y2}, we have

$$S_{y2} = \sum y_t x_{t2} = \sum x_{t2}(\beta_2 x_{t2} + u_t - \overline{u}) = \beta_2 S_{22} + S_{u2}$$

$$E(S_{y2}) = \beta_2 S_{22}$$

because x_{t2} is nonrandom or given and $E(S_{u2}) = 0$. The true specification must be used because y_t is generated by it and not by the estimated equation. In a similar manner,

$$S_{y3} = \sum y_t x_{t3} = \sum x_{t3}(\beta_2 x_{t2} + u_t - \overline{u}) = \beta_2 S_{23} + S_{u3}$$

$$E(S_{y3}) = \beta_2 S_{23}$$

Taking the expectations of Equations (4.A.13) and (4.A.14) and substituting for $E(S_{y2})$ and $E(S_{y3})$, we obtain

$$E(\hat{\beta}_2) = [S_{33}\beta_2 S_{22} - S_{23}\beta_2 S_{23}]/\Delta = \beta_2$$

$$E(\hat{\beta}_3) = [S_{22}\beta_2 S_{23} - S_{23}\beta_2 S_{22}]/\Delta = 0$$

Therefore, $\hat{\beta}_2$ is unbiased and the expectation of $\hat{\beta}_3$ is zero, which is the result in Property 4.5a. From the law of large numbers, consistency is easy to establish.

Derivation of the Variance of $\hat{\beta}_2$

The next step is to compute the variance of $\hat{\beta}_2$. We have

$$\text{Var}(S_{y2}) = \text{Var}(\beta_2 S_{22} + S_{u2}) = \text{Var}(S_{u2}) = \sigma^2 S_{22}$$

$$\text{Var}(S_{y3}) = \text{Var}(\beta_2 S_{23} + S_{u3}) = \text{Var}(S_{u3}) = \sigma^2 S_{33}$$

$$\text{Cov}(S_{y2}, S_{y3}) = \text{Cov}(\beta_2 S_{22} + S_{u2}, \beta_2 S_{23} + S_{u3}) = \sigma^2 S_{23}$$

In deriving these, we have made use of the fact that S_{22} and S_{33} can be treated as nonrandom. Using Property 2.4a, we get

$$\text{Var}(\hat{\beta}_2) = [S_{33}^2 \,\text{Var}(S_{y2}) + S_{23}^2 \,\text{Var}(S_{y3}) - 2S_{33}S_{23}\,\text{Cov}(S_{y2}, S_{y3})]/\Delta^2$$

$$= \sigma^2[S_{33}^2 \, S_{22} + S_{23}^2 S_{33} - 2S_{33}S_{23}S_{23}]/\Delta^2$$

$$= \frac{\sigma^2 S_{33}}{S_{22}S_{33} - S_{23}^2} = \frac{\sigma^2}{S_{22} - (S_{23}^2/S_{33})}$$

Using the fact that r^2, the square of the simple correlation between x_2 and x_3, is defined as $r^2 = S_{23}^2/(S_{22}S_{33})$, the preceding equation can be reduced to

$$\text{Var}(\hat{\beta}_2) = \frac{\sigma^2}{S_{22}(1 - r^2)}$$

thus providing an expression for the variance of $\hat{\beta}_2$.

CHAPTER 5

Multicollinearity

*T*he explanatory variables specified in an econometric model usually come from economic theory or a basic understanding of the behavior we are trying to model, as well as from past experience. The data for these variables typically come from uncontrolled experiments and often move together. This is especially true of time series variables that often have common underlying trends. For example, population and gross domestic product are two series that are highly correlated with each other. In the previous chapter, we stated that the regression coefficient for a particular variable is a measure of its own partial effect, that is, its effect when all other variables in the model are at fixed levels *and only its value is changed*. When two explanatory variables move closely together, however, we cannot simply hold one constant and change the other because when the latter is changed, the former is changed. In this situation, it would be difficult to isolate the partial effect of a single variable. Also, changing the model by omitting or adding a variable can drastically alter the results, making the interpretation of the estimates more difficult. This is the problem of **multicollinearity**, which arises when explanatory variables have approximate linear relationships. This chapter examines the consequences of multicollinearity in the context of estimating parameters, studying their statistical properties, and testing hypotheses on them. We first present examples of how multicollinearity might arise in practice and then study the problem in more detail.

5.1 Examples of Multicollinearity

We present two examples in which the addition of apparently sensible variables drastically alters the results. First, we reexamine the housing starts example used in Section 4.5, which relates the number of new housing units started to several aggregate variables; in the second example, we relate the cumulative expenditure for maintaining a car to its age and number of miles driven.

EXAMPLE 5.1

Let $HOUSING_t$ be the number of housing units (in thousands) started in the United States in the year t, POP_t be the U.S. population in millions, GNP_t be the U.S. gross national product in billions of 1982 dollars, and $INTRATE_t$ be the new home mortgage rate in percent. Using the data in DATA4-3 described in Appendix

D, the following three models were estimated: the results are presented in Table 5.1 (see Practice Computer Session 5.1).

$$\text{Model A:} \quad \text{HOUSING}_t = \alpha_1 + \alpha_2 \, \text{INTRATE}_t + \alpha_3 \, \text{POP}_t + u_{1t}$$

$$\text{Model B:} \quad \text{HOUSING}_t = \beta_1 + \beta_2 \, \text{INTRATE}_t + \beta_3 \, \text{GNP}_t + u_{2t}$$

$$\text{Model C:} \quad \text{HOUSING}_t = \gamma_1 + \gamma_2 \, \text{INTRATE}_t + \gamma_3 \, \text{POP}_t + \gamma_4 \, \text{GNP}_t + u_{3t}$$

We would expect the number of housing units to be influenced by both the size of the population and the level of income. Yet in Model C, which has both these variables, the t-statistics are low and insignificant. When POP or GNP is entered alone, however, the corresponding coefficient is very highly significant. A Wald F-test on excluding POP and GNP from Model C yields an F-statistic of 6.42, which is significant even at 1 percent, indicating that they are jointly significant although individually insignificant. There is thus an apparent contradiction in the conclusion. A second result is that the coefficients for POP and GNP in Model C are very different from those in Models A and B. The INTRATE coefficient, however, is less volatile. Although a priori we thought that both population and income belong in the model, the results indicate that when they are present together, drastic changes occur. This is due to the fact that population, gross national product, and interest rate are very highly correlated. The pairwise correlation coefficients for GNP, POP, and INTRATE are

$$r(\text{GNP, POP}) = 0.99 \qquad r(\text{GNP, INTRATE}) = 0.88 \qquad r(\text{POP, INTRATE}) = 0.91$$

Thus, an almost perfect linear relationship exists between GNP and POP, and a near perfect relationship with INTRATE also. As will be shown later, the observed

⬤ **Table 5.1 Estimates of Housing Starts Relations**

Variables	Model A	Model B	Model C
CONSTANT	−3812.93 (−2.40)	687.90 (1.80)	−1315.75 (−0.27)
INTRATE	−198.40 (−3.87)	−169.66 (−3.87)	−184.75 (−3.18)
POP	33.82 (3.61)		14.90 (0.41)
GNP		0.91 (3.64)	0.52 (0.54)
d.f.	20	20	19
$\bar{R}^2$	0.371	0.375	0.348
MSE	75,029	74,557	77,801
MAPE	12.14	12.54	12.23

Note: MSE is mean squared forecast error ($= \hat{\sigma}^2$). MAPE is mean absolute percent error. Values in parentheses are t-statistics.

changes in regression coefficients and *t*-statistics are a direct result of these high correlations. It should be emphasized that a high correlation between the dependent variable and a given independent variable not only does not cause any problem but is in fact highly desirable. It is the close linear relationships among *explanatory variables* that can affect model results.

● EXAMPLE 5.2

Let E_t be the cumulative expenditure at time t on the maintenance (excluding gasoline) for a given automobile, MILES$_t$ be the cumulative mileage in thousands of miles, and AGE$_t$ be its age in weeks since the original purchase. Consider the following three alternative models:

$$\text{Model A:} \quad E_t = \alpha_1 + \alpha_2\,\text{AGE}_t + u_{1t}$$

$$\text{Model B:} \quad E_t = \beta_1 + \beta_2\,\text{MILES}_t + u_{2t}$$

$$\text{Model C:} \quad E_t = \gamma_1 + \gamma_2\,\text{AGE}_t + \gamma_3\,\text{MILES}_t + u_{3t}$$

A car that is driven more will have a greater maintenance expense. Similarly, the older the car, the greater the cost of maintaining it. Also, between two cars of the same age, the one with the higher mileage is likely to have the larger maintenance expenditure. We would therefore expect α_2, β_2, γ_2, and γ_3 to be positive. Table 5.2 presents the estimated coefficients and their *t*-statistics (in parentheses) for the three models, based on actual data for a Toyota station wagon. The data are in DATA3-7 described in Appendix D (see Practice Computer Session 5.2 to verify these results).

It is interesting to note that even though the coefficient for MILES is positive in Model B, it is significantly negative in Model C. Thus, there has been a drastic reversal of the sign. The coefficient for AGE has also changed substantially. Second, the *t*-statistics for AGE and MILES are much lower in Model C. Here also the reason for the significant change in results is the high correlation between two

● Table 5.2   Estimated Models of Auto Expenditure

Variables	Model A	Model B	Model C
CONSTANT	−626.24 (−5.98)	−796.07 (−5.91)	7.29 (0.06)
AGE	7.35 (22.16)		27.58 (9.58)
MILES		53.45 (18.27)	−151.15 (−7.06)
d.f.	55	55	54
$\overline{R}^2$	0.897	0.856	0.946
MSE	135,861	190,941	72,010
MAPE	227.9	278.2	47.3

Note: MSE is mean squared forecast error ($= \hat{\sigma}^2$). MAPE is mean absolute percent error. Values in parentheses are *t*-statistics.

explanatory variables, in this case AGE and MILES, whose correlation coefficient is 0.996.

We see from these examples that high correlation among explanatory variables can make regression coefficients insignificant or reverse their signs. Multicollinearity is not limited to just two independent variables. It can, and often does, occur among many independent variables that have an approximate linear relationship.

5.2   Exact Multicollinearity

If two or more independent variables have a linear relationship between or among them, we have **exact** (or **perfect**) **multicollinearity.** In this case, there is no unique solution to the normal equations derived from the least squares principle. This point is illustrated with a model that has two independent variables, X_2 and X_3, plus the constant. The model is

$$y_t = \beta_2 x_{t2} + \beta_3 x_{t3} + v_t \tag{5.1}$$

in which the constant term is eliminated by expressing each variable as a deviation from its mean (see Section 4.A.1). The corresponding normal equations are as follows (ignoring the t-subscript):

$$\hat{\beta}_2 \sum x_2^2 + \hat{\beta}_3 \sum x_2 x_3 = \sum y x_2 \tag{5.2}$$

$$\hat{\beta}_2 \sum x_2 x_3 + \hat{\beta}_3 \sum x_3^2 = \sum y x_3 \tag{5.3}$$

Let us first consider the simplest case of exact multicollinearity, where $x_3 = 2x_2$. Although one might wonder why an investigator would include x_3 in the model if this is so, as we will see in the next chapter, this situation might arise inadvertently. Substituting for x_3 in Equation (5.3), we get

$$\hat{\beta}_2 \sum x_2(2x_2) + \hat{\beta}_3 \sum x_3(2x_2) = \sum y(2x_2)$$

We readily see that, if we cancel the common factor 2, this equation becomes the same as Equation (5.2). Thus, the two normal equations are not independent of each other, but rather reduce to the same one. A single equation is not enough to obtain a unique solution to the two unknowns $\hat{\beta}_2$ and $\hat{\beta}_3$. Hence, it is not possible to estimate the regression coefficients in the case of exact multicollinearity.

More generally, suppose that x_2 and x_3 were exactly multicollinear with the linear relation $x_3 = ax_2 + b$. Then Equation (5.3) could be rewritten as

$$\hat{\beta}_2 \sum x_2 x_3 + \hat{\beta}_3 \sum x_3 x_3 = \sum y x_3$$

or

$$\hat{\beta}_2 \sum x_2(ax_2 + b) + \hat{\beta}_3 \sum x_3(ax_2 + b) = \sum y(ax_2 + b)$$

or

$$a\hat{\beta}_2 \sum x_2^2 + b\hat{\beta}_2 \sum x_2 + a\hat{\beta}_3 \sum x_2 x_3 + b\hat{\beta}_3 \sum x_3 = a\sum yx_2 + b\sum y$$

Because x_1, x_2, and y are deviations from their means, we have, from Property 2.A.4, $\sum x_2 = \sum x_3 = \sum y = 0$. Therefore, the preceding equation reduces (after canceling a) to

$$\hat{\beta}_2 \sum x_2^2 + \hat{\beta}_3 \sum x_2 x_3 = \sum yx_2$$

This is the same as the first normal Equation (5.2). In a multiple regression model, if some of the independent variables can be expressed as linear combinations of other independent variables, then the corresponding regression coefficients cannot be estimated. It may, however, be possible for linear combinations of parameters to be estimable.

    If an investigator accidentally regresses a model that has exact multicollinearity, most regression programs give an error message of the form "matrix singular" or "exact collinearity encountered." When this happens, one or more of the variables should be dropped from the model. The most frequent case, however, is the situation where a close (but not exact) linear relationship exists. The consequences of this are examined next.

● 5.3   Near Multicollinearity

When explanatory variables are approximately linearly related, the normal equations can usually be solved to yield unique estimates. The questions that arise in that case are (1) what are the consequences of ignoring multicollinearity, (2) how do we go about identifying the presence of it, and (3) what remedies are available to an investigator to circumvent the problem? We now examine these issues one-by-one.

Consequences of Ignoring Multicollinearity

UNBIASEDNESS AND OTHER PROPERTIES   A natural question that arises is whether multicollinearity invalidates the Gauss–Markov theorem, which says that OLS produces best linear unbiased estimators (BLUE). We see from the statement of the Gauss–Markov theorem (see Section 3.3) that Assumptions 3.2 through 3.7 are required to prove the theorem. A high correlation among explanatory variables does not violate any of these assumptions. Therefore, the OLS estimators are still BLUE; that is, they are unbiased, consistent, and efficient. Also, high collinearity has no impact on Assumption 3.8. Therefore, the distribution of the t-statistic is also not affected. By proceeding as we did in Section 3.A.5, we can show that the OLS estimators are still maximum likelihood and are hence consistent. Forecasts are still unbiased and confidence intervals are valid. None of the previous results are therefore affected by multicollinearity. Although the standard errors and t-statistics of regression coefficients are numerically affected, tests based on them are still valid.

EFFECT ON FORECASTS   Although multicollinearity affects individual regression coefficients, its effect on forecasts are often less drastic and may even be beneficial.

For example, in Table 5.1 the sample period mean squared error (MSE) of forecasts as well as the mean absolute percentage error (MAPE) are presented for each model. Note that, while coefficients vary a great deal across models, MSE does not undergo such a drastic change. The MSE and MAPE values are also presented in Table 5.2. It is interesting to note that Model C, in which the coefficient for MILES is the reverse of that of Model B, performs considerably better in terms of MSE and MAPE than either of the other two models. Thus, in this case, the presence of multicollinearity actually helps the forecast performance.

EFFECT ON STANDARD ERRORS It is clear from this discussion that multicollinearity does not cause any severe disruption in terms of theoretical properties or statistical tests. Then why do we care about multicollinearity? It will be seen presently that, although estimates are BLUE, standard errors are usually higher, making t-statistics lower and possibly insignificant. For the model in (5.1), the following equations were derived in Appendix 4.A (r is the correlation between X_2 and X_3, and S_{22} and S_{33} are defined in Appendix 4.A).

$$\text{Var}(\hat{\beta}_2) = \frac{\sigma^2}{S_{22}(1 - r^2)} \tag{5.4}$$

$$\text{Var}(\hat{\beta}_3) = \frac{\sigma^2}{S_{33}(1 - r^2)} \tag{5.5}$$

$$\text{Cov}(\hat{\beta}_2, \hat{\beta}_3) = \frac{-\sigma^2 r}{\sqrt{S_{22} S_{33}}\,(1 - r^2)} \tag{5.6}$$

Suppose r^2 is very close to 1; that is, r is near ± 1 **(near multicollinearity)**. It is evident from Equations (5.4) and (5.5) that the variances, and hence the standard errors, of $\hat{\beta}_2$ and $\hat{\beta}_3$ will be very large when r^2 is close to 1. A large variance means a poor precision and a low t-statistic, which results in insignificance. This explains why, in the first example, we found that when both population and GNP were included, their coefficients became insignificant. Second, we see from Equation (5.6) that the covariance between the regression coefficients will be huge, in absolute value, if r is close to $+1$ or -1. If the estimates are correlated, each coefficient is capturing part of the effect of the other variable, and hence it is difficult to obtain the *separate* effects of X_2 and X_3 on Y. In other words, we cannot hold X_3 constant and increase X_2 alone, because X_3, being correlated with X_2, will also change as a result.

The results of the above discussion are summarized in Property 5.1.

Property 5.1

The consequences of ignoring multicollinearity are as follows:

a. If two or more explanatory variables in a multiple regression model are exactly linearly related, then the model cannot be estimated.

b. If some explanatory variables are nearly linearly related, then OLS estimators (and hence forecasts based on them) are still BLUE and MLE and hence are unbiased, efficient, and consistent.

c. The effect of near multicollinearity among explanatory variables is to increase the standard errors of the regression coefficients and reduce the t-statistics, thus making coefficients less significant (and possibly even insignificant). The tests of hypotheses are, however, valid.

d. The covariance between the regression coefficients of a pair of highly correlated variables will be very high, in absolute value, thus making it difficult to interpret individual coefficients.

e. Multicollinearity may not affect the forecasting performance of a model and may possibly even improve it.

In a model with several variables, the chances of multicollinearity are greater and therefore interpretation of the results could be more difficult. Multicollinearity might result in the insignificance of many of the coefficients, whereas a fit with one of them alone might produce a significant coefficient.

The danger of multicollinearity is a strong argument against the indiscriminate use of explanatory variables. The importance of theory in formulating models should once again be emphasized. There may be strong theoretical reasons for including a variable even if multicollinearity might make its coefficient insignificant. In this case, the variable should be retained in the model even if multicollinearity exists.

ABSENCE OF MULTICOLLINEARITY　For completeness, let us consider the other extreme case, for which $r = 0$ — that is, the case for which X_2 and X_3 are uncorrelated **(absence of multicollinearity)** as opposed to perfectly correlated. In this case, $S_{23} = 0$ and hence the two normal equations become (see Appendix 5.A)

$$S_{22}\hat{\beta}_2 = S_{y2} \quad \text{and} \quad S_{33}\hat{\beta}_3 = S_{y3}$$

Recognize that these are the same as the normal equations when Y is regressed *separately* against X_2 and X_3. It is hence evident that when $S_{23} = 0$, the value of $\hat{\beta}_2$, obtained from having both X_2 and X_3 in the model, is *identical* to the value obtained when Y is regressed against a constant term and just X_2. A similar result holds for $\hat{\beta}_3$. The covariance between the two regression coefficients is zero, indicating that the partial effect is entirely due to the variable included and not due to any indirect effect from another included variable. Ideally, we would like r to be close to zero, but in practice this is often not so.

Identifying Multicollinearity

In a practical situation, multicollinearity often shows up in a number of ways.

HIGH R^2 WITH LOW VALUES FOR t-STATISTICS　As we see in Exercise 5.2, it is possible to find a situation in which every regression coefficient is insignificant (that is, has low t-values) but the Wald F-statistic is very highly significant. Similarly, as was seen in Example 5.1, the Wald F-value for a group of coefficients may be significant even though individual t-values are not.

HIGH VALUES FOR CORRELATION COEFFICIENTS Pairwise correlations among explanatory variables might be high, as was the case in Examples 5.1 and 5.2. It is generally a good practice to obtain the correlations between every pair of variables in a regression model and check for high values among explanatory variables. Note that a high correlation coefficient between the dependent variable and an independent variable is not a sign of multicollinearity. In fact, such a correlation is highly desired.

REGRESSION COEFFICIENTS SENSITIVE TO SPECIFICATION Although a high correlation between pairs of independent variables is a sufficient condition for multicollinearity, the converse need not be true. In other words, multicollinearity may be present even though the correlation between two explanatory variables does not appear to be high. This is because three or more variables may be nearly linear. Yet, pairwise correlations may not be high. Kmenta (1986, p. 434) has presented an example in which three variables are exactly linearly related, but the correlations between any pair of them are no higher than 0.5. In such situations, the real evidence of multicollinearity is the observation that regression coefficients are drastically altered (even possibly reversing signs, as in Example 5.2) when variables are added or dropped.

FORMAL TESTS FOR MULTICOLLINEARITY Although tests have been proposed, these procedures are mentioned only in passing because they are quite controversial. Because multicollinearity is more a problem with the data than with a model itself, many econometricians argue that formal tests are either meaningless or not fruitful (see Maddala, 1977, p. 186).

Farrar and Glauber (1967) proposed a group of tests to identify the severity of multicollinearity. The tests consist of a chi-square test, an F-test, and a t-test. The chi-square test is to identify whether multicollinearity is generally present. This is followed by an F-test, to find which variables are causing the multicollinearity, and finally by the t-test, to discover the nature of the multicollinearity. These tests are formulated in terms of concepts that involve a knowledge of linear algebra. Interested readers with a background in matrix algebra may want to read their paper.

Belsley, Kuh, and Welsch (1980, Ch. 3) suggested a two-step procedure for testing multicollinearity. The first step is to compute a "condition number" for the matrix of data values. Serious collinearity problems are indicated if this number is over 30. In the second step, a "variance decomposition" measure is used. Their method also requires an understanding of linear algebra and is beyond the scope of this book.

Solutions

No single solution exists that will eliminate multicollinearity altogether. A great deal of judgment is required in handling the problem. However, certain general approaches might be useful in treating multicollinearity, and these are discussed next.

BENIGN NEGLECT If an analyst is less interested in interpreting individual coefficients but more interested in forecasting, multicollinearity may not be a serious concern. One can simply ignore it without any dire consequences. Similarly, even with high correlations among independent variables, if the regression coefficients are significant and have meaningful signs and magnitudes, one need not be too concerned about multicollinearity. If a coefficient is significant even in the presence of multicollinearity, then that is clearly a robust result. Finally, if a variable belongs in a model for theoretical reasons, then it might be safer to keep it even if there is multicollinearity.

ELIMINATING VARIABLES   Because multicollinearity is caused by close relationships among explanatory variables, the surest way to eliminate or reduce the effects of multicollinearity is to drop one or more of the variables from a model. As we have noted in numerous examples, this procedure often improves the standard errors of the remaining coefficients and may make formerly insignificant variables significant, since the elimination of a variable reduces any multicollinearity caused by it. Model B of Table 5.1 illustrates this point. Eliminating POP, which had the lowest *t*-statistic (excluding the constant term, which should never be eliminated because it captures the average effects of omitted variables), makes GNP significant and improves the *t*-values of the other two coèfficients. The *data-based model simplification* procedure, introduced in the last chapter, is an effective way of reducing multicollinearity.

Very often, investigators include too many variables in a model for fear of otherwise encountering the omitted-variable bias described in Section 4.5. In such a case, the elimination of variables with low *t*-statistics would generally improve the significance of the remaining variables. What essentially happens in this situation is that the remaining variables are able to capture the effects of the omitted variables with which they are closely associated. It will be recognized that this data-based model simplification is central to the Hendry/LSE general-to-simple modeling approach. There is a danger, however, in dropping too many variables from the model specification, precisely because that would lead to bias in the estimates. It is generally a good practice to consider the theoretical importance of retaining an insignificant variable if its *t*-statistic is at least 1 in absolute value or the *p*-value is less than 0.25. The model selection statistics discussed in Chapter 4 should be useful guides in this task. Remember, however, that when two explanatory variables are strongly correlated and one is left out of the model, the remaining variable captures the effects of both variables and not just the effect of the remaining variable. It is useful at this point to review the discussion of omitted-variable bias in Section 4.5.

REFORMULATING THE MODEL   In many situations, respecifying the model can reduce multicollinearity. For example, we can express variables as per capita rather than include population as an explanatory variable. In Example 5.1 for instance, the dependent variable would be HOUSING/POP and, instead of POP and GNP separately, we would just have GNP/POP. Per-capita GNP is less likely to be correlated with INTRATE than GNP and POP. The estimated model now becomes (see Practice Computer Session 5.3)

$$\left(\frac{\widehat{\text{HOUSING}}}{\text{POP}}\right) = \underset{(0.62)}{2.079} + \underset{(2.55)}{0.936}\frac{\text{GNP}}{\text{POP}} - \underset{(-3.75)}{0.698}\ \text{INTRATE}$$

$$\overline{R}^2 = 0.377 \qquad \text{d.f.} = 20 \qquad r(\text{GNP/POP, INTRATE}) = 0.843$$

Although adjusted R^2 is slightly higher here than in Example 5.1, the two values are not comparable because the dependent variables are different. Also, multicollinearity is not eliminated, only reduced.

Because time series variables typically have underlying trends, one would expect high collinearity among them. A common way to avoid this is to formulate the model in terms of **first differences,** that is, use variables as changes from one time period to another. For instance, rather than formulate a consumption function as

$$C_t = \beta_1 + \beta_2 C_{t-1} + \beta_3 Y_t + \beta_4 Y_{t-1} + u_t$$

in which all the explanatory variables will be highly correlated, we could relate change in consumption to change in income. We would thus have

$$C_t - C_{t-1} = \alpha_1 + \alpha_2 (Y_t - Y_{t-1}) + v_t$$

It should be noted that these two formulations are not equivalent and, in particular, the first explains the level of consumption whereas the second explains changes in consumption. One should use theory to decide a priori which one is appropriate. If the goal is to forecast consumption expenditures, a forecast comparison might be made after using the second model to generate a forecast of the level of consumption for each time period. All of these steps require careful thought and judgment.

Sometimes models are reformulated with linear combinations of correlated variables used instead of each one as a separate variable. A problem with this is to decide on the weights for the linear combination. *Principal component analysis* is a way to address this issue (see Judge et al., 1985).

USING EXTRANEOUS INFORMATION   The method of using extraneous information is often used in studies on the estimation of demand functions. Time series data on income and the price of a commodity often exhibit a high correlation, which makes estimating the income and price elasticities of demand difficult. A solution to this problem is to estimate the income elasticity from cross-section studies and then use that information in the time series model to estimate the price elasticity. The price elasticity cannot be estimated from the cross-section data because, although consumers differ considerably in income levels, they face basically the same price. Hence, there is no variation in price, which is essential for the successful estimation of the price elasticity (refer to the discussion on Assumption 3.2 in Chapter 3). A serious problem with this approach is that the cross-section income elasticity and the time series income elasticity may be measuring entirely different things. This point has been argued by Meyer and Kuh (1957).

INCREASING THE SAMPLE SIZE   The procedure of increasing the sample size is sometimes recommended on the ground that such an increase improves the precision of an estimator and hence reduces the adverse effects of multicollinearity. It will be noted from Equations (5.4) and (5.5) that, if the sample size increases, then S_{22} and S_{33} will also increase. If the value of r^2, including the new sample, goes down or remains approximately the same, then the variances of $\hat{\beta}_2$ and $\hat{\beta}_3$ will indeed decrease and counteract the effects of multicollinearity. If, however, r^2 goes up substantially, then there may be no benefit to adding to the sample size. Furthermore, an investigator typically collects all the data available (subject to budget and time constraints), and hence adding data may not be feasible as a practical matter.

OTHER REMEDIES   A number of methods have been suggested in the literature, most of which are ad hoc, and there is not much agreement among econometricians about their usefulness. Two of these techniques are ridge regression and principal component analysis. They will not be discussed here because they require linear algebra and mathematical statistics beyond the scope of this book. For those with such a background, an excellent treatment of multicollinearity will be found in Judge, Griffiths, Hill, and Lee (1985). Other useful bibliographical readings are listed in the reference section, but some of them require matrix algebra or methods presented in Chapter 11.

5.4 Applications

Automobile Maintenance Expenditure

It was pointed out that one of the effects of multicollinearity is to change the regression coefficients substantially. If, however, the near linear relationship among the independent variables is taken into account, the differences are not likely to be so large. For example, in the Toyota example, if MILES is regressed against a constant and AGE, we get (see Practice Computer Session 5.4)

$$\widehat{\text{MILES}} = 4.191 + 0.134 \text{ AGE}$$
$$\phantom{\widehat{\text{MILES}} = } (8.74) \quad (88.11)$$

The *t*-statistics in parentheses are very highly significant, and the value of $\bar{R}^2$ is 0.993, indicating a near perfect fit. If this relationship is substituted in Model C of Table 5.2, we obtain

$$\hat{E} = 7.29 + 27.58 \text{ AGE} - 151.15(4.191 + 0.134 \text{ AGE})$$

$$= -626.18 + 7.33 \text{ AGE}$$

which is very close to the values in Model A. Thus, even though Model C appears to be quite different from Model A, when the relationship between the two independent variables MILES and AGE is explicitly taken into account, the two models are very close. In practice, however, it is unrealistic to obtain all possible relationships and use them. The solution in such a case is to identify *redundant* variables and delete them from the model.

Poverty Rates and Their Determinants

DATA4-6 has the data on poverty rates and a number of factors that might affect these rates for 58 California counties. The dependent variable is *povrate*, which is the percent of families with income below the poverty level. The independent variables are defined as follows (see Appendix D and Practice Computer Session 5.5 for more details on these):

urb = Percent of urban population
famsize = Persons per household
unemp = Percent unemployment rate
highschl = Percent of the population (25 years and over) that had only high school education
college = Percent of the population (25 years and over) that completed four years of college or higher
medinc = Median family income in thousands of dollars

Table 5.3 has the annotated computer printout, which is worth studying.

● **Table 5.3   Annotated Computer Printout for the Application in Section 5.4**

[The matrix of pairwise correlation coefficients is presented here. The last column stands for the variable numbers. Thus, the correlation between variable #5 (highschl) and variable #4 (unemp) is −0.109. Diagonal elements are all 1.000 because the correlation between a variable and itself is 1. Note that the correlation coefficients show some high values. As expected, college education is positively correlated with median income and negatively correlated with unemployment. We can expect these high correlations to introduce multicollinearity among these variables and affect regression results.]

```
          Correlation Coefficients, using the observations 1 - 58
    2) urb      3) famsize     4) unemp    5) highschl    6) college
    1.000          0.350         0.110         0.211        -0.358   (2
                   1.000         0.485        -0.508        -0.300   (3
                                 1.000        -0.109        -0.757   (4
                                               1.000        -0.358   (5
                                                             1.000   (6


  7) medinc
     -0.084   (2
     -0.035   (3
     -0.714   (4
     -0.280   (5
      0.848   (6
      1.000   (7
```
[Estimate general model with all explanatory variables.]

(continued)

● **Table 5.3   (continued)**

```
MODEL 1: OLS estimates using the 58 observations 1-58
Dependent variable: povrate

      VARIABLE       COEFFICIENT      STDERROR        T STAT    2Prob(t > |T|)

  0)     const         16.8176         8.5026          1.978     0.053350 *
  2)       urb         -0.0187         0.0148         -1.270     0.210010
  3)   famsize          6.0918         1.8811          3.238     0.002116 ***
  4)     unemp         -0.0118         0.1195         -0.099     0.921724
  5) highschl         -0.1186         0.0681         -1.741     0.087742 *
  6)   college          0.1711         0.0982          1.743     0.087355 *
  7)    medinc         -0.5360         0.0704         -7.619     0.000000 ***

Mean of dep. var.            9.903 S.D. of dep. variable          3.955
Error Sum of Sq (ESS)     146.0911 Std Err of Resid. (sgmahat)    1.6925
Unadjusted R-squared         0.836 Adjusted R-squared             0.817
F-statistic (6, 51)        43.3875 p-value for F()             0.000000
Durbin-Watson stat.          1.904 First-order autocorr. coeff     0.040

MODEL SELECTION STATISTICS

SGMASQ      2.86453     AIC         3.20646     FPE         3.21025
HQ          3.53259     SCHWARZ     4.11172     SHIBATA     3.1268
GCV         3.2577      RICE        3.32025

Excluding the constant, p-value was highest for variable 4 (unemp).
```

[We note that urb and unemp have *p*-values well above any reasonably acceptable level and are hence candidates for exclusion from the model, especially since there is no theoretical reason to retain them. More seriously, we note the unexpected positive sign for college. Other things being equal, if a county has a higher percentage of population with a college education, we would expect its poverty rate to be lower. We would thus expect a negative sign for college, which is contrary to the actual estimate. Could multicollinearity be causing this "wrong" sign? Because unemp is extremely insignificant, with a *p*-value of over 90 percent, we can safely omit it without seriously jeopardizing the results.]

```
MODEL 2: OLS estimates using the 58 observations 1-58
Dependent variable: povrate

      VARIABLE       COEFFICIENT      STDERROR        T STAT    2Prob(t > |T|)

  0)     const         16.5654         8.0325          2.062     0.044192 **
  2)       urb         -0.0184         0.0142         -1.296     0.200710
  3)   famsize          6.0496         1.8145          3.334     0.001583 ***
  5) highschl         -0.1166         0.0646         -1.805     0.076822 *
```

Table 5.3 (continued)

VARIABLE	COEFFICIENT	STDERROR	T STAT	2Prob(t > |T|)
6) college	0.1746	0.0905	1.929	0.059138 *
7) medinc	-0.5343	0.0677	-7.894	0.000000 ***

Mean of dep. var.	9.903	S.D. of dep. variable	3.955
Error Sum of Sq (ESS)	146.1190	Std Err of Resid. (sgmahat)	1.6763
Unadjusted R-squared	0.836	Adjusted R-squared	0.820
F-statistic (5, 52)	53.0737	p-value for F()	0.000000
Durbin-Watson stat.	1.901	First-order autocorr. coeff	0.041

MODEL SELECTION STATISTICS

SGMASQ	2.80998	AIC	3.09837	FPE	3.10067
HQ	3.36659	SCHWARZ	3.83444	SHIBATA	3.04053
GCV	3.13421	RICE	3.1765		

Excluding the constant, p-value was highest for variable 2 (urb).
Of the 8 model selection statistics, 8 have improved.

[There is practically no change in the estimated coefficients and standard errors. Urb is still insignificant and is omitted next.]

MODEL 3: OLS estimates using the 58 observations 1-58
Dependent variable: povrate

VARIABLE	COEFFICIENT	STDERROR	T STAT	2Prob(t > |T|)
0) const	19.1721	7.8263	2.450	0.017634 **
3) famsize	5.4140	1.7581	3.079	0.003283 ***
5) highschl	-0.1388	0.0627	-2.214	0.031161 **
6) college	0.1953	0.0897	2.178	0.033882 **
7) medinc	-0.5523	0.0667	-8.284	0.000000 ***

Mean of dep. var.	9.903	S.D. of dep. variable	3.955
Error Sum of Sq (ESS)	150.8385	Std Err of Resid. (sgmahat)	1.6870
Unadjusted R-squared	0.831	Adjusted R-squared	0.818
F-statistic (4, 53)	65.0877	p-value for F()	0.000000
Durbin-Watson stat.	2.025	First-order autocorr. coeff	-0.025

MODEL SELECTION STATISTICS

SGMASQ	2.84601	AIC	3.09003	FPE	3.09135
HQ	3.31139	SCHWARZ	3.69066	SHIBATA	3.04905
GCV	3.1145	RICE	3.14247		

(continued)

● **Table 5.3   (continued)**

```
Of the 8 model selection statistics, 6 have improved.
```

[All the coefficients are now quite significant at levels below 5 percent, but the coefficient for college still has the wrong sign. Other coefficients have changed more substantially. Because median income is determined by the percent of high school and college graduates, it makes sense to exclude that from the model even though it has a strongly significant coefficient. Its effect should be indirectly captured by highschl and college. Refer to the discussion in Section 4.7 on interpreting regression coefficients.]

```
MODEL 4: OLS estimates using the 58 observations 1-58
Dependent variable: povrate
```

VARIABLE	COEFFICIENT	STDERROR	T STAT	2Prob(t > |T|)
0) const	53.2862	9.9879	5.335	0.000002 ***
3) famsize	-3.9594	2.0194	-1.961	0.055081 *
5) highschl	-0.4137	0.0798	-5.182	0.000003 ***
6) college	-0.4744	0.0582	-8.151	0.000000 ***

```
Error Sum of Sq (ESS)     346.1406 Std Err of Resid. (sgmahat)     2.5318
Unadjusted R-squared          0.612 Adjusted R-squared              0.590
F-statistic (3, 54)        28.3753 p-value for F()              0.000000
```

MODEL SELECTION STATISTICS

SGMASQ	6.41001	AIC	6.85058	FPE	6.85208
HQ	7.24045	SCHWARZ	7.8966	SHIBATA	6.79111
GCV	6.88483	RICE	6.92281		

[It is interesting to note that college now has the expected negative sign and is significant. The change might be due to the fact that multicollinearity might exist between medinc and some or all of the other explanatory variables. However, there is a substantial drop in $\bar{R}^2$ from 0.818 to 0.590. Also, all the model selection statistics have worsened. Because a positive sign for college makes no theoretical sense, we should not put medinc back just to increase the adjusted goodness-of-fit measure or to improve the selection criteria. It is clear from this that a good deal of judgment and common sense is required in evaluating the results. Blind reliance on mechanical measures might lead us astray.

To confirm the suspected multicollinearity, we next relate medinc to its determinants.]

```
MODEL 5: OLS estimates using the 58 observations 1-58
Dependent variable: medinc
```

VARIABLE	COEFFICIENT	STDERROR	T STAT	2Prob(t > |T|)
0) const	-44.9132	15.3482	-2.926	0.005042 ***
3) famsize	16.8193	2.6613	6.320	0.000000 ***

Table 5.3   (continued)

VARIABLE	COEFFICIENT	STDERROR	T STAT	2Prob(t > |T|)
4) unemp	-0.4677	0.2193	-2.133	0.037586 **
5) highschl	0.3649	0.1222	2.986	0.004277 ***
6) college	0.9921	0.1287	7.707	0.000000 ***

Mean of dep. var.	35.338	S.D. of dep. variable	8.264
Error Sum of Sq (ESS)	589.6206	Std Err of Resid. (sgmahat)	3.3354
Unadjusted R-squared	0.849	Adjusted R-squared	0.837
F-statistic (4, 53)	74.2331	p-value for F()	0.000000

MODEL SELECTION STATISTICS

SGMASQ	11.1249	AIC	12.0788	FPE	12.084
HQ	12.9441	SCHWARZ	14.4266	SHIBATA	11.9186
GCV	12.1744	RICE	12.2838		

[All the coefficients are very significant and have the expected signs. Also, the adjusted R-squared is quite high, thus confirming that multicollinearity must have been the reason for the unexpected positive sign for college in the poverty rate model.]

Summary

If an exact linear relationship exists between two or more explanatory variables, the variables are said to be *exactly multicollinear*. In such a situation, the regression coefficients corresponding to these independent variables cannot be uniquely estimated.

If several explanatory variables are nearly multicollinear, OLS estimators are still unbiased, consistent, and BLUE. Therefore, forecasts are also unbiased and consistent. Furthermore, all the tests of hypotheses are valid.

The effect of near multicollinearity is to increase the standard errors of the regression coefficients and lower their t-statistics. This tends to make the coefficients less significant than they would be if multicollinearity were absent. One should therefore be cautious in drawing inferences and not jump to the conclusion that every insignificant variable should be omitted.

If two variables are nearly multicollinear, the covariance between that pair of the regression coefficients is high, indicating that each coefficient is capturing part of the effect of another variable. It is possible to have signs reversed when a new variable is added or deleted. This makes interpretation of an individual regression coefficient more difficult. The partial effect of a single variable is, hence, hard to measure.

If a pair of independent variables is uncorrelated, then the regression coefficient of each of them is the same whether or not the other variable is included in the model.

Multicollinearity can be identified by examining the pattern of correlation among explanatory variables. Since time series variables tend to grow together, models based on them are more subject to multicollinearity problems than are cross-section models. If deleting one or more independent variables drastically alters results, multicollinearity is surely the cause.

No single solution exists that will eliminate multicollinearity. If the focus is on forecasting, multicollinearity can frequently be ignored because forecasting ability is often not much affected. If similar variables are present in the model, eliminating redundant ones is recommended. Possible candidates are those with very low *t*-values. Data-based model simplification is a useful approach here. One should, however, bear in mind the omitted-variable bias caused by eliminating important variables. Theory should be used to decide whether a variable should be kept in spite of seeming multicollinearity problems.

Increasing the sample size is also recommended, provided the new data has the same or lesser collinearity than the original one. Other remedies such as ridge regression and principal component analysis may be used, but these are ad hoc procedures and no consensus exists among econometricians about their usefulness.

Key Terms

Absence of multicollinearity

Exact multicollinearity

First differences

Multicollinearity

Near multicollinearity

Perfect multicollinearity

References

Belsley, D. A., E. Kuh, and R. E. Welsch. *Regression Diagnostics, Identifying Influential Data and Sources of Collinearity.* New York: Wiley, 1980.

Burt, Oscar R. "The Fallacy of Differencing to Reduce Multicollinearity." *American Journal of Agricultural Economics* 69 (3) (August 1987): 697–700.

Copeland, Ronald M., and Hassan Espahbodi. "Accommodating Multicollinearity in Financial Forecasting and Business Research." Cheng F. Lee, ed., *Advances in Financial Planning and Forecasting,* vol. 3, A Research Annual. Greenwich, Conn., and London: JAI Press, 1989, 311–322.

Farrar, D. E., and R. R. Glauber. "Multicollinearity in Regression Analysis: The Problem Revisited." *Review of Economics and Statistics* (February 1967).

Hill, Carter R., and George Judge. "Improved Prediction in the Presence of Multicollinearity." *Journal of Econometrics* 35 (1) (May 1987): 83–100.

Judge, George G., William E. Griffiths, R. Carter Hill, and Tsoung-Chao Lee. *The Theory and Practice of Econometrics.* New York: Wiley, 1985.

Kmenta, Jan. *Elements of Econometrics.* New York: McGraw-Hill, 1986.

Maddala, G. S. *Econometrics.* New York: McGraw-Hill, 1977.

Meyer, John, and Edwin Kuh. "How Extraneous Are Extraneous Estimates?" *Review of Economics and Statistics* (November 1957).

Pearce, Douglas K., and Sara A. Reiter. "Regression Strategies When Multicollinearity Is a Problem: A Methodological Note." *Journal of Accounting Research* 23 (1) (Spring 1985): 405–407.

Salinas, Teresita S., and Steven C. Hillmer. "Multicollinearity Problems in Modeling Time Series with Trading-Day Variation." *Journal of Business and Economic Statistics* 5 (3) (July 1987): 431–436.

Trenkler, Gotz. "Some Further Remarks on Multicollinearity and the Minimax Conditions of the Bock Stein-Like Estimator." *Econometrica* 52 (4) (July 1984): 1067–1069.

Wilson, Earl R., and Penny R. Marquette. "Evaluating the Effects of Multicollinearity: A Note on the Use of Ridge Regression." Bill N. Schwartz, ed., *Advances in Accounting,* vol. 6, A Research Annual. Greenwich, Conn., and London: JAI Press, 1988, 143–156.

Exercises

5.1 Suppose that the exact relation between X_2 and X_3 is of the form $x_2 + x_3 = 1$. Show, by proceeding as in Section 5.2, that the second normal equation reduces to the first, thus making it impossible to solve for the regression coefficients.

†5.2 Using 15 years of annual data, planners in San Diego County estimated the following model for water consumption:

$$\widehat{\text{SDWATR}} = -326.9 + 0.305 \text{ SDHOUSE} + 0.363 \text{ SDPOP}$$
$$\quad\quad\quad (-1.7) \quad\quad (0.9) \quad\quad\quad\quad (1.4)$$

$$-0.005 \text{ SDPCY} - 17.87 \text{ PRWATR} - 1.123 \text{ SDRAIN}$$
$$(-0.6) \quad\quad\quad (-1.2) \quad\quad\quad\quad (-0.8)$$

$$n = 15 \quad \overline{R}^2 = 0.93 \quad F = 38.9$$

> SDWATR = Total water consumption (million cubic meters)
> SDHOUSE = Total number of housing units (thousands)
> SDPOP = Total population (thousands)
> SDPCY = Per-capita income (dollars)
> PRWATR = Price of water (dollars/100 cubic meters)
> SDRAIN = Rainfall in inches

The values in parentheses are t-statistics.

a. Based on economic theory and/or intuition, what signs would you expect for the regression coefficients (exclude the constant) and why? Do the observed signs agree with your intuition?

b. Every t-statistic is insignificant, but the F-statistic is significant (verify this statement). What are the reason(s) for this paradoxical result?

c. Would you say the estimates are (1) biased, (2) inefficient, or (3) inconsistent? Carefully justify your answers.

d. You are asked to formulate a model that explains not total water consumption but *consumption per household,* in terms of average family size and other relevant variables. Using the data described, develop a model that would be appropriate.

5.3 Using Example 5.1, estimate the relation between the U.S. gross national product and population as $\text{GNP} = \alpha + \beta \text{ POP} + \text{error}$. Substitute this in Model C of Table 5.1, and compare the results with those in Model A. Would you consider the modified Model C to be close to Model A?

5.4 Indicate whether each of the following statements is justified and explain your reasons:

a. "Because multicollinearity lowers t-statistics, all the insignificant regression coefficients should be dropped from the model because they are redundant."

b. "Multicollinearity raises the standard errors of regression coefficients and hence t- and F-tests are invalid."

5.5 In Exercise 4.9 on grade point, would you expect multicollinearity (MC) among the variables? If so, which variables do you think might cause MC problems? What are the consequences of ignoring MC? In particular, are estimates and forecasts biased, inefficient, inconsistent, not BLUE? Explain.

5.6 In Example 4.9, the correlation between W and P was 0.92. What does this convey about the estimated relationship? Specifically, examine the implications on bias of estimates, confidence intervals, validity of tests of hypotheses, and so on.

5.7 In Exercise 4.17, one might expect multicollinearity to be severe. How can one find out whether this is the case? If it is a problem, discuss the various solutions possible. Which would you recommend most, and why?

5.8   "If there is multicollinearity among independent variables, then a variable that appears significant may not indeed be so." Is this statement valid?

5.9   "High multicollinearity affects standard errors of estimated coefficients and therefore estimates are not efficient." Is this statement valid? If yes, cite what assumptions and properties enable you to agree with this statement. If not, explain why not.

5.10 "Adding an irrelevant variable (that is, one that has a truly zero coefficient) to a model has the same effect as high multicollinearity when it comes to the properties of unbiasedness, consistency, and efficiency of the OLS estimators of parameters." Carefully explain whether this statement is valid. If it is partially valid, indicate which parts are.

Derivation of Equations (5.4) through (5.6)

Using the notation of Section 4.A.1, the normal Equations (5.2) and (5.3) can be solved for the βs as (see Equations 4.A.6 through 4.A.15).

$$\hat{\beta}_2 = \frac{S_{y2}S_{33} - S_{y3}S_{23}}{\Delta} \tag{5.A.1}$$

$$\hat{\beta}_3 = \frac{S_{y3}S_{22} - S_{y2}S_{23}}{\Delta} \tag{5.A.2}$$

where

$$\Delta = S_{22}S_{33} - S_{23}^2 \tag{5.A.3}$$

It is easy to show that

$$E(S_{y2}) = \beta_2 S_{22} + \beta_3 S_{23} \tag{5.A.4}$$

$$E(S_{y3}) = \beta_2 S_{23} + \beta_3 S_{33} \tag{5.A.5}$$

We have

$$S_{y2} = \sum yx_2 = \sum x_2(\beta_2 x_2 + \beta_3 x_3 + v) \tag{5.A.6}$$
$$= \beta_2 S_{22} + \beta_3 S_{23} + S_{v2}$$

using Equation (5.1). Because $E(v) = 0$ and the xs are nonrandom, $E(S_{v2}) = E(\Sigma vx_2) = \Sigma x_2 E(v) = 0$. Therefore, $E(S_{y2}) = \beta_2 S_{22} + \beta_3 S_{23}$, thus proving Equation (5.A.4). The proof for (5.A.5) is similar. We next show that

$$\text{Var}(\hat{\beta}_2) = \frac{\sigma^2 S_{33}}{\Delta} \tag{5.A.7}$$

$$\text{Var}(\hat{\beta}_3) = \frac{\sigma^2 S_{22}}{\Delta} \tag{5.A.8}$$

$$\text{Cov}(\hat{\beta}_2, \hat{\beta}_3) = \frac{-\sigma^2 S_{23}}{\Delta} \tag{5.A.9}$$

From (5.A.6) and Property 2.8c, $\text{Var}(S_{y2}) = \text{Var}(S_{v2})$. From Property 2.9e,

$$\text{Var}(S_{y2}) = \sum x_2^2 \, \text{Var}(v) = \sigma^2 \sum x_2^2 = \sigma^2 S_{22}$$

$$\text{Var}(S_{y3}) = \sum x_3^2 \, \text{Var}(v) = \sigma^2 \sum x_3^2 = \sigma^2 S_{33}$$

$$\text{Cov}(S_{y2}, S_{y3}) = \sum x_2 x_3 \, \text{Var}(v) = \sigma^2 S_{23}$$

Also, from Property 2.4a

$$\text{Var}(\hat{\beta}_2) = \frac{1}{\Delta^2}[S_{33}^2 \, \text{Var}(S_{y2}) + S_{23}^2 \, \text{Var}(S_{y3}) - 2S_{33}S_{23} \, \text{Cov}(S_{y2}, S_{y3})]$$

$$= \frac{\sigma^2}{\Delta^2}[S_{33}^2 S_{22} + S_{23}^2 S_{33} - 2S_{33}S_{23}S_{23}]$$

$$= \frac{\sigma^2}{\Delta^2}[S_{33}^2 S_{22} - S_{23}^2 S_{33}] = \frac{\sigma^2}{\Delta^2} S_{33}[S_{33}S_{22} - S_{23}^2] = \frac{\sigma^2 S_{33}}{\Delta}$$

thus proving (5.A.7). The procedures for (5.A.8) and (5.A.9) are similar.

Let r be the correlation coefficient between X_2 and X_3 (see Equation 2.11). Then by definition, $r^2 = S_{23}^2/(S_{22}S_{33})$. Therefore,

$$\Delta = S_{22}S_{33}(1 - r^2)$$

Using this in Equations (5.A.7), (5.A.8), and (5.A.9), we obtain Equations (5.4), (5.5), and (5.6).

Extensions

Part 3 presents a number of extensions to the basic models studied so far. Chapter 6 deals with the estimation of relationships that are nonlinear. It also includes a discussion of the Hendry/LSE approach of "general to simple" modeling as well as the Lagrange multiplier test for modeling from "simple to general." In addition, the chapter discusses Ramsey's RESET procedure for testing regression specification. Chapter 7 discusses how nonquantitative variables, such as gender, race, season, affiliation to a political party, and so on, can be handled in a regression context by means of binary (or more commonly, dummy) variables. A variety of examples are provided to illustrate the use of dummy variables, especially in testing whether a relationship might have changed over time.

CHAPTER 6

Choosing Functional Forms and Testing for Model Specification

In Chapters 4 and 5 we studied multiple regression in which the dependent variable of interest (Y) is related to many independent variables (Xs). The choice of the independent variables comes from economic theory, intuition, past experience, and other studies. To avoid the omitted-variable bias discussed earlier, an investigator often includes several explanatory variables that are suspected to influence the dependent variable. However, the relationship between Y and the Xs studied so far has been assumed to be linear. This is obviously a severe and often unrealistic constraint on a model. In the application Section 3.11, we noted that the observed scatter diagram between the number of patents issued and the expenditure on R&D (Figure 3.11) indicated a curvilinear relation. We saw that the assumption of linearity gave poor predictions in several of the years. Aside from empirically observed facts of this type, there are often good theoretical reasons for considering general functional forms of relationships between dependent and independent variables. For example, economic theory tells us that average cost curves are U-shaped, and hence the linearity assumption is questionable if we wish to estimate average cost curves.

In this chapter, we explore in considerable detail a variety of ways of formulating and estimating nonlinear relationships. To be able to draw graphs, many of the presentations deal with only one explanatory variable. This is a purely pedagogical device. In examples and applications we relax this constraint.

The chapter also discusses some of the approaches to conducting formal tests of model specification. In particular, the "general to simple" and "simple to general" approaches mentioned in Chapter 1 are discussed, as is Ramsey's RESET procedure (1969).

6.1 Review of Exponential and Logarithmic Functions

The exponential and logarithmic functions are two of the most commonly used functions in model formulations. For this reason, it is useful to review the basic properties of these functions before using them.

The function $Y = a^X (a > 0)$ is an example of an exponential function. In this function, a is the **base** of the function and X is the **exponent.** In mathematics the most common base used in an exponential function is the mathematical constant e, defined by

$$e = \lim_{n \to \infty} \left(1 + \frac{1}{n} \right)^n = 2.71828 \ldots$$

The standard **exponential function** thus has the form $Y = e^X$, also written as exp(X). The inverse of the exponential function is called the **logarithmic function.** The logarithm of a number to a given base a (which must be positive) is defined as the power to which the base must be raised to give the number. We write $X = \log_a Y$. For example, since $32 = 2^5$, the logarithm of 32 to the base 2 is 5. Logarithm to the base e is called the **natural logarithm** and is denoted as $Y = \ln X$, without the base explicitly written. Note that $\ln 1 = 0$ because $e^0 = 1$. A number of properties of the exponential and logarithmic functions are listed below.

Property 6.1

a. The logarithmic and exponential functions are monotonic increasing; that is, if $a > b$, then $f(a) > f(b)$, and vice versa.

b. The logarithm of the product of two numbers is the sum of the logarithms; that is, $\ln(XY) = \ln X + \ln Y$. Also, the logarithm of a ratio is the difference of the logarithms. Thus, $\ln(X/Y) = \ln X - \ln Y$. It follows from this that $\ln(1/X) = -\ln X$.

c. $\ln(a^X) = X \ln a$. It follows from this that $a^X = e^{X \ln a}$.

d. $a^X a^Y = a^{X+Y}$ and $(a^X)^Y = a^{XY}$.

Unlike a straight line, which has a constant slope, general functions $f(X)$, such as the exponential and logarithmic, have varying slopes. The change in Y per unit change in X is the **marginal effect** of X on Y and is usually denoted by $\Delta Y/\Delta X$ (see Figure 2.A.1 and the discussion associated with it). If the change in X is made infinitesimally small, we have the slope of the tangent to the curve $f(X)$ at the point X. This limiting slope is known as the **derivative** of Y with respect to X and is denoted by dY/dX. The derivative is thus the marginal effect of X on Y for a very small change in X. It is an extremely important concept in econometrics, because we are constantly asking what the change in the dependent variable is expected to be when we change the value of an independent variable by a small amount. Important properties of derivatives are summarized in Property 2.A.5 and are worth studying. Property 6.2 lists a few properties of the logarithmic and exponential functions that are extremely useful in econometrics. Figure 6.1 graphs the two functions.

Property 6.2

a. The exponential function with base e has the remarkable property that it equals its own derivative. Thus, if $Y = e^X$, then $dY/dX = e^X$.

b. The derivative of e^{aX} is ae^{aX}.

c. The derivative of $\ln X$ is $1/X$.

d. The derivative of a^X is $a^X \ln a$. This result follows from the fact that $a^X = e^{X \ln a}$ and the property that the derivative of $e^{bX} = be^{bX}$.

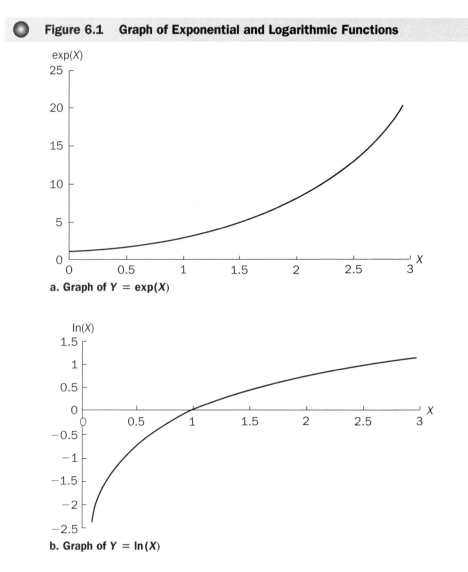

Figure 6.1   Graph of Exponential and Logarithmic Functions

a. Graph of Y = exp(X)

b. Graph of Y = ln(X)

The Concept of Elasticity

The logarithm is closely related to the concept of **elasticity** used in economics. We will see in later sections that this concept is widely used in empirical econometrics as well. In simple terms, the elasticity of Y with respect to X is defined as the *percent change in Y with respect to a percent change in X for a small change in X.* Thus, if ΔY is the change in Y, the percent change is $100\Delta Y/Y$. Similarly, $100\Delta X/X$ is the percent change in X. The ratio of the former to the latter is the elasticity. This gives rise to the following definition.

Table 6.1 **Marginal Effects and Elasticities of Different Functional Forms**

Name	Functional Form	Marginal Effect (dY/dX)	Elasticity $[(X/Y)(dY/dX)]$
Linear	$Y = \beta_1 + \beta_2 X$	β_2	$\beta_2 X/Y$
Linear-log	$Y = \beta_1 + \beta_2 \ln X$	β_2/X	β_2/Y
Reciprocal	$Y = \beta_1 + \beta_2(1/X)$	$-\beta_2/X^2$	$-\beta_2/(XY)$
Quadratic	$Y = \beta_1 + \beta_2 X + \beta_3 X^2$	$\beta_2 + 2\beta_3 X$	$(\beta_2 + 2\beta_3 X)X/Y$
Interaction	$Y = \beta_1 + \beta_2 X + \beta_3 XZ$	$\beta_2 + \beta_3 Z$	$(\beta_2 + \beta_3 Z)X/Y$
Log-linear	$\ln Y = \beta_1 + \beta_2 X$	$\beta_2 Y$	$\beta_2 X$
Log-reciprocal	$\ln Y = \beta_1 + \beta_2(1/X)$	$-\beta_2 Y/X^2$	$-\beta_2/X$
Log-quadratic	$\ln Y = \beta_1 + \beta_2 X + \beta_3 X^2$	$Y(\beta_2 + 2\beta_3 X)$	$X(\beta_2 + 2\beta_3 X)$
Double-log (log-log)	$\ln Y = \beta_1 + \beta_2 \ln X$	$\beta_2 Y/X$	β_2
Logistic	$\ln\left[\dfrac{Y}{1-Y}\right] = \beta_1 + \beta_2 X$	$\beta_2 Y(1 - Y)$	$\beta_2(1 - Y)X$

DEFINITION 6.1

The elasticity of Y with respect to X (denoted by η) is

$$\eta = \frac{\Delta Y}{Y} \div \frac{\Delta X}{X} = \frac{X}{Y}\frac{\Delta Y}{\Delta X} \rightarrow \frac{X}{Y}\frac{dY}{dX} \quad \text{as } \Delta X \text{ tends to zero} \qquad (6.1)$$

Table 6.1 has the marginal effects (dY/dX) and the elasticities $[(X/Y)(dY/dX)]$ for a number of alternative functional forms discussed in this chapter. Note that they sometimes depend on X and/or Y. To calculate them, one often substitutes the mean value $\overline{X}$ and the corresponding predicted $\hat{Y}$.

6.2 Linear-Log Relationship

In a **linear-log model,** the dependent variable is unchanged but the independent variable appears in logarithmic form. Thus,

$$Y = \beta_1 + \beta_2 \ln X + u \qquad (6.2)$$

For positive β_1 and β_2, Figure 6.2 graphs the relation as a nonlinear function. This relation gives $\Delta Y/\Delta X = \beta_2/X$. If $\beta_2 > 0$, the marginal increase in Y with respect to an increase in X is a decreasing function of X. We note that

$$\Delta Y = \beta_2 \frac{\Delta X}{X} = \frac{\beta_2}{100}\left[100 \frac{\Delta X}{X}\right] = \frac{\beta_2}{100} \times \text{percent change in } X$$

It follows from this that a one *percent* change in X will change Y, on average, by $\beta_2/100$ units (*not* percent).

● Figure 6.2   A Linear-Log Functional Form

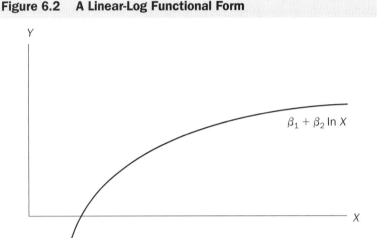

As an example, let Y be the output of wheat and X be the number of acres cultivated. Then $\Delta Y/\Delta X$ is the marginal product of an extra acre cultivated. We hypothesize that the marginal product will decrease as acreage increases. When the acreage is low, we expect that the most fertile land will be cultivated first. As acreage goes up, less fertile areas will be put to use; the additional output from these areas may not be as high as the output from the more fertile lands. This suggests a diminishing marginal product of wheat acreage. A linear-log formulation would enable us to capture this relationship.

As another example, let Y be the price of a house and X be the living area. Consider two houses, one with a living area of 1,300 square feet and another with a living area of 3,200 square feet. We can expect that the *additional price* a consumer will be willing to pay for 100 *additional square feet* of living area will be higher when $X = 1,300$ than when $X = 3,200$. This is because the latter house is already quite large, and a buyer might not be induced to pay much extra to increase it further. This means that the marginal effect of SQFT on PRICE can be expected to decrease as SQFT increases. One way to test this is to fit a linear-log model and test $H_0: \beta_2 = 0$ against $H_1: \beta_2 > 0$. This will be recognized as a one-tailed test. The decision rule is to reject H_0 if $t_c > t^*_{n-2}(0.05)$. We note from Table 6.1 that in this model the elasticity of Y with respect to X is β_2/Y. One can calculate the elasticity at the mean as $\beta_2/\overline{Y}$. If the data are a time series, a more interesting elasticity would be the one corresponding to the most recent observation—for $t = n$. This elasticity is β_2/Y_n.

Although these illustrations were in terms of a simple regression model, the extension to the multivariate case is straightforward. Simply generate logarithms of the relevant explanatory variables, call them Z_1, Z_2, and so on, and regress Y against a constant and the Zs.

● PRACTICE PROBLEM 6.1

Derive an expression for the elasticity of Y with respect to X in the linear and linear-log models and verify the entries in Table 6.1.

● PRACTICE PROBLEM 6.2

Graph Equation (6.2) when $\beta_2 < 0$ (assume for simplicity that $\beta_1 = 0$).

● EXAMPLE 6.1

We estimated the linear-log model using the home price data in Table 4.1 (see Practice Computer Session 6.1 for the instructions to reproduce the results of this example and to verify the assertions made here). The argument of diminishing marginal effect applies equally well to the numbers of bedrooms and bathrooms. We therefore generated logarithms of SQFT, BEDRMS, and BATHS and then regressed PRICE against a constant and these log terms. The logarithms of BATHS and BEDRMS were then omitted one at a time because their coefficients were very insignificant. The "best" model was then chosen in terms of the model selection criteria discussed in Chapter 4. The estimated equations of the best linear model and the best linear-log model are presented next, with the t-statistics in parentheses.

$$\widehat{\text{PRICE}} = 52.351 + 0.139 \text{ SQFT}$$
$$ (1.4) (7.4)$$

$$\overline{R}^2 = 0.806 \qquad \text{d.f.} = 12$$

$$\widehat{\text{PRICE}} = -1{,}749.974 + 299.972 \ln(\text{SQFT}) - 145.094 \ln(\text{BEDRMS})$$
$$ (-6.8) (7.5) (-1.7)$$

$$\overline{R}^2 = 0.826 \qquad \text{d.f.} = 11$$

We note that the value of $\overline{R}^2$ is slightly higher for the linear-log model. This model also had the lowest model selection statistics. However, the coefficient for the logarithm of BEDRMS is significant only at the 11.48 percent level. If this term is omitted, the selection statistics worsen considerably, and therefore we have chosen to retain it. The regression coefficient for ln(SQFT) is highly significant, thus supporting the hypothesis that the marginal effect of the living area decreases as the number of square feet increases. The coefficient for the logarithm of BEDRMS was negative as it was for the linear model, but its effect is statistically weak.

● PRACTICE PROBLEM 6.3

Compute the partial elasticities of PRICE with respect to SQFT for the estimated linear and linear-log models when SQFT is 1,500, 2,000, and 2,500. How do they compare with each other?

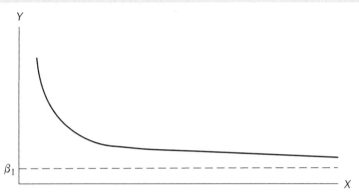

Figure 6.3   A Reciprocal Relationship

6.3   Reciprocal Transformation

A functional form frequently used to estimate demand curves is the reciprocal transformation:

$$Y = \beta_1 + \beta_2\left(\frac{1}{X}\right) + u$$

Because demand curves typically slope downward, we would expect β_2 to be positive. Note that when X becomes large, Y asymptotically approaches β_1 (see Fig. 6.3). The sign and magnitude of β_1 will determine whether the curve intersects the X-axis or not.

● PRACTICE PROBLEM 6.4

Graph the reciprocal function for $\beta_2 < 0, \beta_1 > 0$.

6.4   Polynomial Curve-Fitting

Very often investigators use a polynomial to relate a dependent variable to an independent variable. This model would be

$$Y = \beta_1 + \beta_2 X + \beta_3 X^2 + \beta_4 X^3 + \cdots + \beta_{k+1} X^k + u$$

The estimation procedure consists of creating new variables X^2, X^3, and so on through transformations and then regressing Y against a constant term, X, and against these transformed variables. The degree of the polynomial (k) is constrained by the number of observations. If $k = 3$, we have a cubic relation; and if $k = 2$, we have a quadratic formulation. Quadratic formulations are frequently used to fit U-shaped cost functions and other nonlinear relations. A cubic curve is often fitted to approximate the shape in Figure 6.9 (see the section on the logit model). In general, polynomials of orders greater than 2 should be avoided. One of the reasons for this is the fact that each polynomial term means the loss of an extra degree of freedom. As was mentioned in Chapter 3, a loss of degrees of freedom means a reduction in the precision of the parameter estimates and a reduction in the power of tests. Also, we saw in Chapter 5 that the possible high correlation between X, X^2, and X^3 makes individual coefficients less reliable.

Using properties on derivatives (see Property 2.A.5), we can show that the marginal effect of X on Y is given by

$$dY/dX = \beta_2 + 2\beta_3 X + 3\beta_4 X^2 + \cdots + k\beta_{k+1} X^{k-1}$$

A special case of the polynomial functional form is the quadratic model

$$Y = \beta_1 + \beta_2 X + \beta_3 X^2 + u$$

The marginal effect of X on Y, that is, the slope of the quadratic relation, is given by $dY/dX = \beta_2 + 2\beta_3 X$. Note that the marginal effect of X on Y depends on the value of X at which we calculate the marginal effect. A common value used is the mean, $\overline{X}$. As pointed out in the appendix to Chapter 2, when $dY/dX = 0$, the function attains either a minimum or a maximum. The value of X at which this happens is obtained from solving the condition $\beta_2 + 2\beta_3 X = 0$ as $X_0 = -\beta_2/(2\beta_3)$. To find out whether a minimum or a maximum is attained, we need to compute the second derivative, $d^2Y/dX^2 = 2\beta_3$. If $\beta_3 < 0$, the function attains a maximum at X_0, and if it is positive, the function attains a minimum at X_0. We next present two examples: an average cost function that is a U-shaped relation (Fig. 6.4) and a production function that is a hump-shaped relation (Fig. 6.5).

● EXAMPLE 6.2

DATA6-1 described in Appendix D has data on the per-unit cost (UNITCOST) of a manufacturing firm over a 20-year period, an index of its output (OUTPUT), and an index of its input costs (INPCOST). First we obtained the squares of the two independent variables and then regressed UNITCOST against a constant, OUTPUT, $OUTPUT^2$, INPCOST, and $INPCOST^2$ (see Practice Computer Session 6.2 for details on this). Because $INPCOST^2$ had an extremely insignificant coefficient, it was omitted and the model reestimated. The results are given next, with t-statistics in parentheses.

$$\widehat{\text{UNITCOST}} = 10.522 - 0.175 \text{ OUTPUT} + 0.000895 \text{ OUTPUT}^2$$
$$(14.3) \quad (-9.7) \quad\quad\quad\quad (7.8)$$
$$+ 0.0202 \text{ INPCOST}$$
$$(14.454)$$

$$\overline{R}^2 = 0.978 \quad\quad \text{d.f.} = 16$$

Note that for this model $\hat{\beta}_1$, $\hat{\beta}_3 > 0$ and $\hat{\beta}_2 < 0$, which accounts for the U-shaped relation. The model explains 97.8 percent of the variation in the average cost. It is

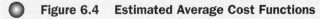

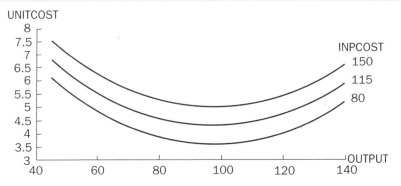

Figure 6.4 Estimated Average Cost Functions

easy to verify that all the regression coefficients are extremely significant. Note that what we have above is a family of average cost curves shifted by the levels of the input cost index. It would be interesting to graph the unit cost function for a typical input cost. Figure 6.4 is the estimated U-shaped average cost function for a range of outputs and three different input cost levels (80, 115, and 150). They take the minimum value at the output index level 98 (verify it).

EXAMPLE 6.3

DATA6-2 described in Appendix D has annual data on the production of white tuna fish (Thunnus Alalunga) in the Basque region of Spain. The output (dependent) variable is total catch in thousands of tonnes and the input (independent) variable is the fishing effort measured in total days of fishing (in thousands). The estimated model is (*t*-statistics in parentheses)

$$\widehat{\text{Catch}} = \underset{(17.1)}{1.642} \text{ Effort} - \underset{(-8.0)}{0.01653} \text{ Effort}^2$$

$$\overline{R}^2 = 0.660 \qquad \text{d.f.} = 32$$

Practice Computer Session 6.3 can be used to verify this. Note that, because the catch cannot be made if there is no effort, β_1 must theoretically be zero for this model. We readily see that $\hat{\beta}_2 > 0$ and $\hat{\beta}_3 < 0$; hence, the production function will graph as in Figure 6.5 with the maximum reached when the effort is 50.

PRACTICE PROBLEM 6.5[†]

Using the home price data, estimate the following quadratic relation between price and square feet:

$$\text{PRICE} = \beta_1 + \beta_2 \text{SQFT} + \beta_3 \text{SQFT}^2 + u$$

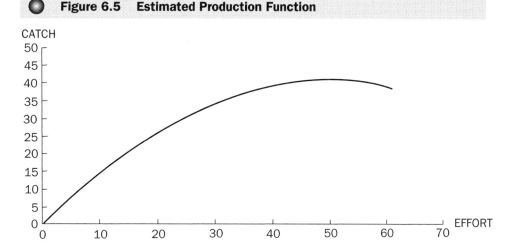

Figure 6.5   Estimated Production Function

What is the economic interpretation of the hypothesis $\beta_3 = 0$? Test this hypothesis against the alternative, $H_1: \beta_3 < 0$. What do you conclude about the marginal effect of SQFT on PRICE? Compare this model, in terms of the selection criteria, with the linear-log model estimated in Example 6.1 (see Practice Computer Session 6.4).

PRACTICE PROBLEM 6.6

Estimate the model PRICE $= \beta_1 + \beta_2 \ln$ SQFT $+ \beta_3$BATHS $+ u$, and compare the results with those in Table 4.2 and those in Practice Problem 6.5.

PRACTICE PROBLEM 6.7

For the relation $Y = \beta_1 + \beta_2 X + \beta_3 X^2$, verify the slope and elasticity given in Table 6.1.

6.5 Interaction Terms

The marginal effect of one explanatory variable may sometimes depend on another variable. To illustrate, Klein and Morgan (1951) proposed a hypothesis regarding the interaction of income and assets in determining consumption patterns. They argued that the marginal propensity to consume will also depend on assets—a wealthier person is likely to have a different marginal propensity to consume out of income. To capture this, let $C = \alpha + \beta Y + u$. The hypothesis is that β, the marginal propensity to consume, depends on assets (A). A simple way to allow for this is to assume that $\beta = \beta_1 + \beta_2 A$. Substituting this in the consumption function, we get $C = \alpha + (\beta_1 + \beta_2 A) Y + u$. This reduces to the model $C = \alpha + \beta_1 Y + \beta_2(AY) + u$. The term AY is known as the **interaction term** because it captures the interaction between the income and asset effects. For estimation purposes, we create a new variable Z, which is equal to the product of Y and A, and then regress C against a constant, Y, and Z. If β_2 is statistically significant, there is evidence of an interaction between income and assets. Note that in this example, $\Delta C / \Delta Y = \beta_1 + \beta_2 A$. To determine the marginal effect of Y on C, we need the value of A.

As a second example, consider the relationship $E_t = \alpha + \beta T_t + u_t$, where E_t is the number of kilowatt-hours of electricity consumption and T_t is the temperature at time t. If this model is estimated for the summer season, we would expect β to be positive because, as the temperature rises in the summer, there will be greater demand for air-conditioning and hence electricity consumption will rise. We may hypothesize, however, that the marginal effect of T on E might depend on the price of electricity (P_t). If electricity is expensive, consumers might postpone turning on the air-conditioner or switch it off sooner. One way to test for this effect is to assume that $\beta = \beta_1 + \beta_2 P_t$. We are thus assuming that the marginal effect of temperature on electricity consumption depends on price. Substituting this in the relation, we get

$$E_t = \alpha + (\beta_1 + \beta_2 P_t) T_t + u_t = \alpha + \beta_1 T_t + \beta_2 (P_t T_t) + u_t$$

To estimate the parameters, we generate $Z_t = P_t T_t$ and regress E against a constant, T, and Z. The significance of β_2 is evidence of an interaction effect between temperature and price. Note that $\Delta E / \Delta P = \beta_2 T$; that is, the marginal effect of P on E depends on temperature. If we let α also depend on P, the model becomes

$$E_t = \alpha_1 + \alpha_2 P_t + \beta_1 T_t + \beta_2 (P_t T_t) + u_t$$

In later chapters, we have several empirical examples of such interaction effects.

Spurious Nonlinearities

In order to identify possible nonlinearities, one might be tempted to graph Y against a particular independent variable (X) and see if any observed nonlinearities exist. This is a dangerous procedure because it might lead to serious model misspecification. Suppose, for instance, Y is linearly related to X, Z, and the interaction term XZ, so that we have

$$Y = \beta_1 + \beta_2 X + \beta_3 Z + \beta_4 (XZ) + u \quad \text{and} \quad \Delta Y / \Delta X = \beta_2 + \beta_4 Z$$

In computing the marginal effect of X on Y, we treat Z as fixed. Note that the marginal effect of X on Y, that is, the slope, depends on Z. The empirically observed scatter diagram between Y and X might look as in Figure 6.6, which appears to suggest a linear-log relation between Y and X. In reality, this is due to two linear relations between Y and X for different values of Z (Z_1 and Z_2). Thus, rather than empirically graph observed Y against each X, you should try to model the DGP using theory and intuition about the underlying behavior and then conduct specification tests. In Sections 6.13, 6.14, and 6.15, we discuss several approaches to testing regression specifications.

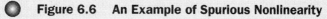

Figure 6.6   An Example of Spurious Nonlinearity

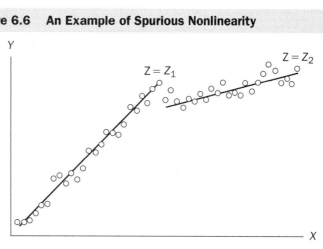

6.6   Lags in Behavior (Dynamic Models)

The effects of economic and other variables are rarely instantaneous; it takes some time for consumers, producers, and other economic agents to respond. Macroeconomic theory tells us that the equilibrium gross national product (Y) is determined by a number of exogenous variables, in particular, by government expenditure (G), taxes (T), money supply (M), exports (X), and so on. Because the equilibrium effect is felt only after the passage of some time, econometric models using time series data are often formulated with **lags in behavior.** An example of such a model is the following:

$$Y_t = \beta_1 + \beta_2 G_t + \beta_3 G_{t-1} + \beta_4 M_t + \beta_5 M_{t-1} + \beta_6 T_t + \beta_7 T_{t-1} + \beta_8 X_t + \beta_9 X_{t-1} + u_t$$

The estimation procedure here is quite straightforward. We simply create the lagged variables G_{t-1}, M_{t-1}, T_{t-1}, and X_{t-1} and regress Y_t against these variables *using observations 2 through n.* Because G_{t-1} and the others are not defined for $t = 1$, we lose the first observation in the estimation. A number of problems arise in this model, however, because the independent variables are correlated with each other and also because degrees of freedom are lost when higher lags are added. These issues are discussed in detail in Chapter 10.

Lags in behavior might also take the form of lags in the dependent variable. The model might thus take the form

$$Y_t = \beta_1 + \beta_2 Y_{t-1} + \beta_3 X_t + \beta_4 X_{t-1} + u_t$$

As an example, let Y_t be the consumption expenditure at time t and X_t be the income. Because consumers tend to maintain the standard of living they are accustomed to, we might expect their consumption to be closely related to their previous consumption. Thus, Y_t can be expected to depend on Y_{t-1} also. More specifically, consider the following formulation:

$$Y_t = \beta_1 + \beta_2 Y_{t-1} + \beta_3 (X_t - X_{t-1}) + u_t$$

Because of "habit patterns," consumers are generally reluctant to alter their style of living, and hence we would expect consumption at time $t(Y_t)$ to depend on previous periods' consumption (Y_{t-1}). However, if the income level (X_t) changes, consumers would adapt their consumption patterns to the amount of increase or decrease in income. We would thus use a dynamic model of the type formulated above and expect all the coefficients to be positive.

● **EXAMPLE 6.4**

DATA6-3 (see Appendix D) has annual data for the United Kingdom for per-capita personal consumption expenditures (C, measured in £) and per-capita disposable income (that is, personal income less taxes, denoted by DI, and also measured in £). To correct for inflation, both variables are expressed in real terms (also known as *constant prices*). The estimated dynamic model is presented here (see Practice Computer Session 6.5), with the *t*-statistics in parentheses.

$$\hat{C}_t = \underset{(-2.07)}{-46.802} + \underset{(123.0)}{1.022\ C_{t-1}} + \underset{(9.93)}{0.706\ (\mathrm{DI}_t - \mathrm{DI}_{t-1})}$$

$$\overline{R}^2 = 0.998 \qquad \text{d.f.} = 38$$

Although the model has an excellent fit and the estimates appear reasonable, it has a number of drawbacks. It will be seen in Chapters 10 and 13 that this model violates the serial independence in Assumption 3.6 as well as Assumption 3.4 that independent variables be uncorrelated with the error terms. This misspecification causes the estimates to be biased. We reexamine this model in Chapters 10 and 13.

● **6.7 Application: Relation between Patents and R&D Expenses Revisited**

In Section 3.11, we estimated a simple linear regression model between patents and R&D expenses and found it to be grossly inadequate because the observed scatter diagram indicated a curvilinear relation (see Fig. 3.11). We also pointed out that there would be a lag between the actual spending on research and development and the fruits of those expenses in terms of patents. Here we estimate a **dynamic** nonlinear **model** and compare the results. However, because there is no economic or other theory about how many years' lags are needed or on what the functional form should be, we arbitrarily use lags up to four years. The four lagged variables generated are R&D($t-1$), R&D($t-2$), R&D($t-3$), and R&D($t-4$). These variables were then squared and a quadratic model with all the variables was estimated.

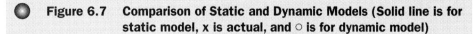

Figure 6.7   Comparison of Static and Dynamic Models (Solid line is for static model, x is actual, and ○ is for dynamic model)

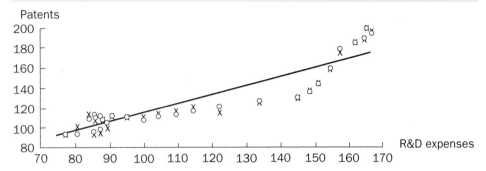

Thus, this is a purely "curve-fitting" exercise rather than one based on economic theory. The annotated computer output in Table 6.2 should be studied carefully (see Practice Computer Session 6.6 for reproducing Table 6.2). Figure 6.7 has plotted actual patents, the fitted values from the static model of Chapter 3 (solid straight line), and those from the final dynamic model. We note that the dynamic model tracks the actual pattern quite well, even during the years when patents and R&D expenses were clustered and during the years 1988–1993 when the linear model was widely off. Thus, a dynamic nonlinear model is a considerably better specification than a simple linear **static model.**

Table 6.2   Annotated Computer Output for the Application in Section 6.7

```
MODEL 1: OLS estimates using the 34 observations 1960-1993
Dependent variable: PATENTS
```

VARIABLE	COEFFICIENT	STDERROR	T STAT	2Prob(t > |T|)
0) const	34.5711	6.3579	5.438	0.000006 ***
3) R&D	0.7919	0.0567	13.966	0.000000 ***

Mean of dep. var.	119.238	S.D. of dep. variable	29.306
Error Sum of Sq (ESS)	3994.3003	Std Err of Resid. (sgmahat)	11.1724
Unadjusted R-squared	0.859	Adjusted R-squared	0.855
F-statistic (1, 32)	195.055	p-value for F()	0.000000
Durbin-Watson stat.	0.234	First-order autocorr. coeff	0.945

(continued)

⬤   **Table 6.2   (continued)**

```
MODEL SELECTION STATISTICS

SGMASQ       124.822    AIC          132.146    FPE        132.164
HQ           136.255    SCHWARZ       144.56    SHIBATA    131.301
GCV          132.623    RICE         133.143
```

[generate lagged variables]   [generate squared variables]

```
R&D1 = R&D(-1)                        sq_R&D = (R&D)²
R&D2 = R&D(-2)                        sq_R&Di = (R&Di)²
R&D3 = R&D(-3)                        for i = 1,2,3, and 4
R&D4 = R&D(-4)
```

[Estimate a general model with all the explanatory variables using only observations 1964–1993, because lagged variables are undefined for the period 1960–1963.]

```
MODEL 2: OLS estimates using the 30 observations 1964-1993
Dependent variable: PATENTS
```

	VARIABLE	COEFFICIENT	STDERROR	T STAT	2Prob(t > |T|)	
0)	const	85.3526	22.1027	3.862	0.001051	***
3)	R&D	-0.0477	1.1251	-0.042	0.966638	
4)	R&D1	0.6033	2.0562	0.293	0.772387	
5)	R&D2	0.0001794	2.1850	0.000	0.999935	
6)	R&D3	-0.5869	2.0522	-0.286	0.777989	
7)	R&D4	-0.1837	1.0994	-0.167	0.869055	
8)	sq_R&D	-0.0007326	0.0049	-0.150	0.882674	
9)	sq_R&D1	-0.0018	0.0089	-0.197	0.845884	
10)	sq_R&D2	0.0017	0.0098	0.177	0.861555	
11)	sq_R&D3	-0.0007564	0.0092	-0.082	0.935597	
12)	sq_R&D4	0.0071	0.0051	1.405	0.176209	

```
Mean of dep. var.           123.330  S.D. of dep. variable          28.795
Error Sum of Sq (ESS)       223.3789 Std Err of Resid. (sgmahat)     3.4288
Unadjusted R-squared          0.991  Adjusted R-squared              0.986
F-statistic (10, 19)        202.626  p-value for F()              0.000000
Durbin-Watson stat.           1.797  First-order autocorr. coeff     0.101

MODEL SELECTION STATISTICS

SGMASQ        11.7568   AIC           15.5026   FPE         16.0676
HQ            18.2719   SCHWARZ       25.9139   SHIBATA     12.9063
GCV           18.5633   RICE          27.9224
```

Table 6.2   (continued)

```
Excluding the constant, p-value was highest for variable 5 (R&D2)
```

[Note that there is a great deal of multicollinearity among the explanatory variables. Current and lagged values of R&D as well as R&D and its square are expected to have high correlations. Thus, it is not surprising that, except for the constant term, nothing is significant. As pointed out in the previous chapter, this does not mean that the variables are "unimportant," just that the multi-collinearity might be hiding variables that ought to be included. According to the data-based model simplification approach used earlier, we should eliminate variables that appear redundant. As a first step, we omit variables with p-values above 0.9. They are R&D, R&D2, and sq_R&D3.]

```
MODEL 3: OLS estimates using the 30 observations 1964-1993
Dependent variable: PATENTS


        VARIABLE      COEFFICIENT      STDERROR      T STAT    2Prob(t > |T|)

    0)     const         84.8409        19.0579       4.452    0.000200 ***
    4)      R&D1          0.6043          0.6351       0.952    0.351669
    6)      R&D3         -0.7352          0.5233      -1.405    0.174012
    7)      R&D4         -0.0745          0.5134      -0.145    0.886004
    8)    sq_R&D      -0.0009491          0.0012      -0.824    0.418554
    9)   sq_R&D1         -0.0017          0.0034      -0.496    0.624855
   10)   sq_R&D2          0.0016          0.0025       0.641    0.527835
   12)   sq_R&D4          0.0066          0.0020       3.364    0.002799 ***


Mean of dep. var.             123.330   S.D. of dep. variable           28.795
Error Sum of Sq (ESS)         223.6243  Std Err of Resid. (sgmahat)      3.1882
Unadjusted R-squared            0.991   Adjusted R-squared               0.988
F-statistic (7, 22)           334.799   p-value for F()               0.000000


MODEL SELECTION STATISTICS


SGMASQ          10.1647   AIC           12.7064   FPE         12.8753
HQ              14.3197   SCHWARZ       18.4628   SHIBATA     11.4297
GCV             13.861    RICE          15.9732


Excluding the constant, p-value was highest for variable 7 (R&D4).
Comparison of Model 2 and Model 3 is given below: Null hypothesis: the
regression parameters are zero for the variables R&D, R&D2, and sq_R&D3.

Test statistic: F(3, 19) = 0.006957, with p-value = 0.999173
Of the 8 model selection statistics, 8 have improved.
```

(continued)

● **Table 6.2   (continued)**

[The high *p*-value for the Wald *F*-test for the excluded variables suggests that we cannot reject the null hypothesis that their coefficients are all zero even at levels as high as 0.9. It therefore makes sense to eliminate them. Also, all eight model selection statistics have decreased, indicating an improvement in the goodness of fit. Although many of the *p*-values have decreased, only one is small enough to be significant—that for variable no. 12. This suggests further elimination. Next, we omit variables R&D4, sq_R&D1, and sq_R&D2, which have *p*-values above 0.5.]

```
MODEL 4: OLS estimates using the 30 observations 1964-1993
Dependent variable: PATENTS

        VARIABLE      COEFFICIENT      STDERROR      T STAT    2Prob(t > |T|)

   0)     const         82.8545        12.0355        6.884     0.000000 ***
   4)     R&D1           0.4771         0.3278         1.455     0.158001
   6)     R&D3          -0.6370         0.2388        -2.667     0.013227 **
   8)    sq_R&D         -0.0011      0.0010000        -1.146     0.262479
  12)    sq_R&D4         0.0065      0.0006784         9.609     0.000000 ***


Mean of dep. var.         123.330   S.D. of dep. variable          28.795
Error Sum of Sq (ESS)    233.5118   Std Err of Resid. (sgmahat)     3.0562
Unadjusted R-squared        0.990   Adjusted R-squared              0.989
F-statistic (4, 25)       637.338   p-value for F()              0.000000
Durbin-Watson stat.         1.844   First-order autocorr. coeff     0.078

MODEL SELECTION STATISTICS

SGMASQ      9.34047    AIC        10.8631    FPE       10.8972
HQ         11.7057     SCHWARZ    13.7206    SHIBATA   10.3783
GCV        11.2086     RICE       11.6756

Excluding the constant, p-value was highest for variable 8 (sq_R&D).
Comparison of Model 3 and Model 4:


Null hypothesis: the regression parameters are zero for the variables
    R&D4, sq_R&D1, and sq_R&D2

Test statistic: F(3, 22) = 0.324242, with p-value = 0.807788
Of the 8 model selection statistics, 8 have improved.
```

[Here also the high *p*-value for the Wald *F*-test for the excluded variables suggests that we cannot reject the null hypothesis that their coefficients are all zero at levels even as high as 0.80. It therefore makes sense to eliminate them too. Also, all eight model selection statistics have decreased, indicating a further improvement in the goodness of fit. There are still two variables (sq_R&D

⬤ **Table 6.2 (continued)**

and R&D1) with *p*-values above 15 percent. We next omit these, but one at a time, yielding the final model in which all of the coefficients are significant at levels below 2 percent.]

```
MODEL 5: OLS estimates using the 30 observations 1964-1993
Dependent variable: PATENTS


          VARIABLE      COEFFICIENT      STDERROR      T STAT    2Prob(t > |T|)

    0)      const          91.3464        6.4046       14.263    0.000000 ***
    6)       R&D3          -0.2951         0.1175       -2.512    0.018286 **
   12)    sq_R&D4           0.0059      0.0005486       10.675    0.000000 ***


Mean of dep. var.            123.330   S.D. of dep. variable          28.795
Error Sum of Sq (ESS)      258.6727   Std Err of Resid. (sgmahat)    3.0952
Unadjusted R-squared          0.989   Adjusted R-squared              0.988
F-statistic (2, 27)         1241.43   p-value for F()              0.000000
Durbin-Watson stat.           1.665   First-order autocorr. coeff     0.166


MODEL SELECTION STATISTICS

SGMASQ        9.58047   AIC           10.5315    FPE          10.5385
HQ           11.0143    SCHWARZ       12.1155    SHIBATA      10.3469
GCV          10.645     RICE          10.778

Of the 8 model selection statistics, 7 have improved.
```

[Compute predicted values and the absolute percent error for each prediction.]

Obs	R&D	PATENTS	Predicted value	Prediction error	Absolute percent error
1964	76.83	93.2	93.1259	0.0740826	0.0794878
1965	80	100.4	93.8292	6.57081	6.54463
1966	84.82	93.5	94.8126	-1.31258	1.40383
1967	86.84	93	97.9126	-4.91264	5.28241
1968	88.81	98.7	102.306	-3.606	3.65349
1969	88.28	104.4	103.795	0.605085	0.579583
1970	85.29	109.4	107.851	1.5492	1.41609
1971	83.18	111.1	109.3	1.80002	1.62018
1972	85.07	105.3	111.483	-6.1826	5.87141
1973	86.72	109.6	111.815	-2.21525	2.02121
1974	85.45	107.4	109.399	-1.99891	1.86118

(continued)

● **Table 6.2   (continued)**

Obs	R&D	PATENTS	Predicted value	Prediction error	Absolute percent error
1975	83.41	108	106.76	1.24028	1.14841
1976	87.44	110	108.135	1.86509	1.69554
1977	90.11	109	110.169	-1.16945	1.07289
1978	94.5	109.3	109.491	-0.191014	0.174761
1979	99.28	108.9	106.285	2.61523	2.4015
1980	103.64	113	109.529	3.4713	3.07194
1981	108.77	114.5	111.009	3.49072	3.04867
1982	113.96	118.4	114.344	4.05551	3.42526
1983	121.72	112.4	118.482	-6.0819	5.41094
1984	133.33	120.6	122.149	-1.54888	1.28431
1985	144.78	127.1	126.998	0.101834	0.0801211
1986	148.39	133	131.477	1.52261	1.14482
1987	150.9	139.8	138.761	1.03908	0.743265
1988	154.36	151.9	152.722	-0.821732	0.540969
1989	157.19	166.3	170.303	-4.00303	2.40711
1990	161.86	176.7	175.76	0.9403	0.532145
1991	164.54	178.4	179.138	-0.737635	0.413472
1992	166.7	187.2	184.487	2.71267	1.44908
1993	165.2	189.4	188.272	1.12779	0.595455

[Except for a few stray years (1965, 1967, 1972, and 1983), all the absolute percent errors are below 5 percent. In fact, most of them are below 2 percent. Also, compared to the linear static model, which has an adjusted R-squared of 0.855, the final model has a value of 0.988.]

● 6.8   Log-Linear Relationship (or Semilog Model)

All the nonlinear relationships discussed so far had the dependent variable Y appear as it was, that is, linearly. Only the independent variables underwent any transformations. It will also be noted that, although we used logs and squares of independent variables, the models were all *linear in the coefficients*. We now examine a number of models in which the dependent variable appears in a transformed way.

Suppose we have a variable P that is growing at a constant rate. More specifically, let $P_t = (1 + g)P_{t-1}$, where g is the fixed growth rate between the time periods $t - 1$ and t. P might be the population and g its rate of growth. By repeated substitution we get $P_t = P_0(1 + g)^t$. Using data on P_t, we wish to estimate the growth rate g. This relationship does not appear in the convenient linear form used in the previous sections. However, it is possible to convert this to the linear form. Taking logarithms of both sides (and using Property 6.1), we obtain $\ln P_t = \ln P_0 + t \ln(1 + g)$. Define $Y_t = \ln P_t$, $X_t = t$, $\beta_1 = \ln P_0$, and $\beta_2 = \ln(1 + g)$. Then the relation may be rewritten as $Y_t = \beta_1 + \beta_2 X_t$. Since Y and X may not satisfy the relationship exactly, we add the error term u_t, making the relationship the familiar simple regression model of Equation (3.1). The transformed model thus becomes

$$\ln P_t = \beta_1 + \beta_2 t + u_t \tag{6.3}$$

Exponentiating this, we get the original model as

$$P_t = e^{\beta_1 + \beta_2 t + u_t} \tag{6.4}$$

Equation (6.4) is an exponential relation and is illustrated in Figure 6.8. It should be noted that the disturbance term in Equation (6.4) is multiplicative. Equation (6.3) is linear when the dependent variable is in a logarithmic form. With $\ln P_t$ on the vertical axis, the formulation becomes a straight line. The first step toward estimating the growth (g) is to transform the observations $P_1, P_2, \ldots, P_n$ using the logarithmic transformation so that we get $Y_t = \ln P_t$. Then we regress Y_t against a constant term and time t. We have

$$\widehat{\ln P_0} = \hat{\beta}_1 \quad \text{and} \quad \widehat{\ln(1 + g)} = \hat{\beta}_2$$

Solving for g and P_0, we have

$$\hat{P}_0 = e^{\hat{\beta}_1} \quad \text{and} \quad \hat{g} = e^{\hat{\beta}_2} - 1 \tag{6.5}$$

Any hypothesis on g can be translated (with trivial exceptions) to an equivalent hypothesis on β_2. Because the transformed dependent variable is in log form, this model is known as the **log-linear model,** or sometimes as the **semilog model.** If the model is written as $\ln P_t = \beta_1 + \beta_2 X_t + u_t$, β_2 is the marginal effect of X on $\ln P_t$ and

Figure 6.8   An Exponential Functional Form

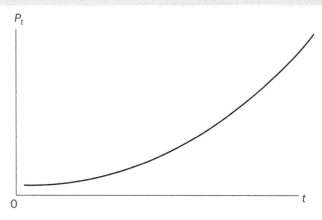

not on P_t. It is known as the **instantaneous rate of growth.** Differentiating both sides with respect to X_t (see Property 6.2 on differentiation), we get

$$\beta_2 = \frac{d(\ln P_t)}{dX_t} = \frac{1}{P_t}\frac{dP_t}{dX_t} \tag{6.6}$$

The term dP_t/P_t can be interpreted as the *change* in P_t divided by P_t. When multiplied by 100, β_2 gives the *percent change in P_t per unit change in X_t*. For a calculation of the elasticity of P with respect to X, see Table 6.1.

Taking the expected values of both sides of Equation (6.4), we get

$$E(P_t) = e^{\beta_1 + \beta_2 t}E(e^{u_t}) \tag{6.7}$$

It can be shown that $E(e^{u_t}) = e^{\sigma^2/2} \neq 1$, and therefore if we predict P_t using the expression $e^{\beta_1 + \beta_2 t}$, the prediction would be biased, inconsistent, and inefficient. The proper expression in this case is

$$\hat{P}_t = \exp[\hat{\beta}_1 + \hat{\beta}_2 t + (\hat{\sigma}^2/2)] \tag{6.8}$$

where $\hat{\sigma}^2$ is the sample variance of the error terms and exp is the exponential function. $\hat{P}_t$ is a consistent estimator of $E(P_t)$.

A similar adjustment is needed in Equation (6.5) because $E(e^{\hat{\beta}_2}) = e^{\beta_2 + [Var(\hat{\beta}_2)/2]}$. Therefore, an unbiased estimator of g is given by

$$\tilde{g} = \exp[\hat{\beta}_2 - 1/2\,\widehat{Var}(\hat{\beta}_2)] - 1$$

It is possible to obtain an adjusted prediction interval for P_t. Earlier, we defined $Y_t = \ln(P_t)$. Let $\hat{Y}_t$ be the prediction for $\ln(P_t)$ in the log-linear model and $s_t = s(\hat{Y}_t)$ be the corresponding estimated standard error. Then the confidence interval for Y_t is $\hat{Y}_t \pm t^*s_t$, where t^* is the point on the t-distribution such that $P(t > t^*)$ = one-half of the level of significance (refer to Section 3.9 on confidence intervals for predictors). Exponentiating this (that is, taking antilog) and adjusting for the bias as shown in Equation (6.8), we obtain the modified confidence interval for predicting P_t as $\exp[\hat{Y}_t \pm t^*s_t + (\hat{\sigma}^2/2)]$, where $\hat{\sigma}^2$ is the sample variance of the error terms. It should be pointed out that this interval will not be symmetric around $\hat{P}_t = \exp[\hat{Y}_t + (\hat{\sigma}^2/2)]$. Refer to Nelson (1973, pp. 161–165) for a discussion of point predictions and their confidence intervals when the dependent variable is log-transformed.

● **EXAMPLE 6.5**

The log-linear model is widely used in human capital literature in which theory suggests that the logarithm of earnings or wages be used as the dependent variable. To motivate this, suppose that the rate of return to an extra year of education is r. Then, for the first period, wages $w_1 = (1 + r)w_0$. For two years of education this becomes $w_2 = (1 + r)^2 w_0$. For s years, we have $w_s = (1 + r)^s w_0$. Taking logarithms, we have (referring to Property 6.1c),

$$\ln(w_s) = s \ln(1 + r) + \ln(w_0) = \beta_1 + \beta_2 s$$

We thus obtain a log-linear relation between wages and years of education. A similar argument applies to the number of years of experience also. The age of an employee is likely to have a different type of effect. We would expect low earnings when a person is young, with rising earnings as he or she grows older, but falling earnings after retirement. This hump-shaped relation may be tested with a quadratic formulation, that is, with AGE and AGE^2. To be really general, we may want to test whether education and experience also exhibit such a quadratic effect. Thus, a general model is of the following form:

$$\ln(\text{WAGE}) = \beta_1 + \beta_2 \text{EDUC} + \beta_3 \text{EXPER} + \beta_4 \text{AGE} + \beta_5 \text{EDUC}^2 \quad \textbf{(6.9)}$$
$$+ \beta_6 \text{EXPER}^2 + \beta_7 \text{AGE}^2 + u$$

DATA6-4 has data on monthly wages, education in number of years after the eighth grade, experience in number of years, and age for a sample of 49 individuals. We first estimated the preceding log-linear model but found several regression coefficients to be insignificant. As before, we carried out a data-based simplification by omitting variables one at a time (see Practice Computer Session 6.7 for reproducing the results), using the p-values for guidance (the highest p-value indicating least significance) until model selection statistics started to worsen. The final model results are presented here, with the t-statistics in parentheses.

$$\widehat{\ln(\text{WAGE})} = 7.023 + 0.005 \, \text{EDUC}^2 + 0.024 \, \text{EXPER} \quad \textbf{(6.10)}$$
$$\underset{(76.0)}{} \quad \underset{(4.3)}{} \quad \underset{(3.9)}{}$$
$$\overline{R}^2 = 0.33 \qquad \text{d.f.} = 46$$

Both education squared and experience are very significant at levels below 0.001. The interpretation of the experience coefficient, 0.024, is that, between two employees with the same education, if one of them had one more year of experience than the other, then he or she can be expected to earn, on average, 2.4 percent more in wages (see Equation 6.6 for this interpretation). It will be noted that EDUC has a quadratic effect, with the marginal effect increasing with the level of education. These results, however, should not be taken too seriously because the goodness-of-fit measure is quite low even for a cross-section data set. More work is clearly needed before we can have some faith in the numbers. We revisit this model in later chapters and obtain more reliable results.

Tansel (1994) has an extensive application of the log-wage model. It is worthwhile studying that carefully.

● PRACTICE PROBLEM 6.8

Using the data in DATA6-4, estimate both the general model in Equation (6.9) and the final model in Equation (6.10). Perform a Wald test using these two models. Be sure to state the null and alternative hypotheses and your conclusion in words.

Suppose wage is measured in hundreds of dollars. How will this affect the regression coefficients? If any of them is changed, write down the new value(s) in Equation (6.10).

● PRACTICE PROBLEM 6.9

Derive the marginal effect (dY/dX) and the elasticity $(X/Y)(dY/dX)$ for the model $\ln Y = \beta_1 + \beta_2 X + \beta_3 X^2 + u$.

● PRACTICE PROBLEM 6.10

Derive the marginal effect and the elasticity for the model $\ln Y = \beta_1 + \beta_2 X + \beta_3(XZ) + u$.

● PRACTICE PROBLEM 6.11

Consider the log-linear model $\ln Y = \beta_1 + \beta_2 X + \beta_3 Z + \beta_4 X^2 + \beta_5 XZ + u$, where X and Z are explanatory variables. Derive an algebraic expression for the elasticity of Y with respect to X. Describe how you would use the Wald test to check whether the nonlinear terms involving X^2 and XZ are statistically significant.

● 6.9 Comparison of R^2 Values between Models

In Example 6.5, if we had used WAGES as the dependent variable instead of its logarithm, the adjusted R^2 would have been 0.338. Since R^2 for the log-linear model was 0.333, does that mean the linear model is slightly better in goodness of fit? The answer is an emphatic no, because it is improper to compare R^2 values when the dependent variables are different. In the linear case, the model explains 33.8 percent of the variation in Y, whereas in the log-linear case, the model explains 33.3 percent of the variation in $\ln(Y)$. For proper comparability, the dependent variables must be the same.

There is, however, a heuristic way of comparing the goodness of fit. The steps for the log-linear case are as follows:

Step 1 Estimate the log-linear model in the usual way and obtain the fitted values of $\ln(Y)$ from it.

Step 2 From these, generate the estimated average for Y by taking antilogs, and be sure to make the bias adjustment as in Equation (6.8). Thus, we would have the following:

$$\hat{Y}_t = \exp[\widehat{\ln(Y_t)} + (\hat{\sigma}^2/2)] \tag{6.11}$$

Step 3 Compute the square of the correlation between Y_t and $\hat{Y}_t$. This is comparable to the unadjusted R^2 of a linear model.

Step 4 Compute the error sum of squares and the variance of the residuals using the relationships

$$\text{ESS} = \sum (Y_t - \hat{Y}_t)^2 \quad \text{and} \quad \hat{\sigma}^2 = \frac{\text{ESS}}{n - k}$$

Step 5   Using ESS, compute the model selection statistics for the new model. This is comparable to similar statistics for the linear model.

● EXAMPLE 6.6

Using the data set in DATA6-4 and the log-linear model estimated in Example 6.5, we carried out these steps and computed the new R^2 measure and the selection criteria statistics (see Practice Computer Session 6.8 for details). It was found that R^2 was 0.37, which is trivially larger than that for the linear model. All the selection statistics were lower for the log-linear model than for the linear model. Thus, in terms of these criteria, the log-linear model has a slight edge.

● 6.10   The Double-Log (or Log-Log) Model

The **double-log** (or **log-log**) model is very popular in estimating production functions as well as demand functions. If Q is the quantity of output of a production process, K is the quantity of the capital input (machine-hours), and L is the quantity of the labor input (worker-hours), then the relation between output and the inputs is the production function written as $Q = F(K, L)$. A common specification of the functional form of this is the **Cobb–Douglas production function,** well known in microeconomic theory. It has the following general form:

$$Q_t = cK_t^\alpha L_t^\beta$$

where c, α, and β are unknown parameters. Taking logarithms of both sides (see Property 6.1) and adding an error term, we get the following econometric formulation ($\beta_1 = \ln c$):

$$\ln Q_t = \beta_1 + \alpha \ln K_t + \beta \ln L_t + u_t$$

If we change only K but keep L constant, then we have (using Property 6.2c)

$$\alpha = \frac{\Delta(\ln Q)}{\Delta(\ln K)} = \frac{(1/Q)\Delta Q}{(1/K)\Delta K} = \frac{K}{Q}\frac{\Delta Q}{\Delta K}$$

$100\Delta(\ln Q) = 100\Delta Q/Q$ is the percent change in Q. Therefore, α is the percent change in Q divided by the percent change in K. This is the **elasticity of output with respect to capital.** In a similar manner, β is the **elasticity of output with respect to labor.** Thus, the regression coefficients in a double-log model are simply the respective elasticities, which are constant. Note that because of this property, the numerical values of the coefficients for different independent variables are directly comparable. Table 6.3 summarizes the interpretation of the regression coefficients in models that have logarithms of variables.

Table 6.3   Interpretation of Marginal Effects in Models Involving Logarithms

Model	Functional Form	Marginal Effect	Interpretation
Linear	$Y = \beta_1 + \beta_2 X$	$\Delta Y = \beta_2 \Delta X$	One *unit* change in X will induce a β_2 *unit* change in Y
Linear-log	$Y = \beta_1 + \beta_2 \ln X$	$\Delta Y = \dfrac{\beta_2}{100}\left[100\,\dfrac{\Delta X}{X}\right]$	One *percent* change in X will induce a $\beta_2/100$ *unit* change in Y
Log-linear	$\ln Y = \beta_1 + \beta_2 X$	$100\,\dfrac{\Delta Y}{Y} = 100\,\beta_2\,\Delta X$	One *unit* change in X will induce a $100\,\beta_2$ *percent* change in Y
Double-log	$\ln Y = \beta_1 + \beta_2 \ln X$	$100\,\dfrac{\Delta Y}{Y} = \beta_2\left[100\,\dfrac{\Delta X}{X}\right]$	One *percent* change in X will induce a β_2 *percent* change in Y

We can derive another interesting result for this model. Suppose the quantities of capital and labor inputs are doubled. Then the output is

$$Q_1 = c(2K)^{\alpha}(2L)^{\beta} = 2^{\alpha+\beta}Q$$

If $\alpha + \beta = 1$, $Q_1 = 2Q$. Thus, the output would also be doubled if $\alpha + \beta = 1$. This is the well-known condition for **constant returns to scale.** If the estimated elasticities are such that $\hat{\alpha} + \hat{\beta} > 1$, they indicate **increasing returns to scale,** and $\hat{\alpha} + \hat{\beta} < 1$ indicates **decreasing returns to scale.** A formal test for constant returns to scale would be of interest. The null hypothesis is $H_0: \alpha + \beta = 1$ and the alternative is $H_1: \alpha + \beta \neq 1$. In Section 4.4, we developed three tests for hypotheses involving linear combinations of regression coefficients. To apply Method 2, define $\beta_2 = \alpha + \beta - 1$. Under the null hypothesis, $\beta_2 = 0$. Solving for β, we get $\beta = \beta_2 + 1 - \alpha$. Substituting this in the model, we get

$$\ln Q_t = \beta_1 + \alpha \ln K_t + (\beta_2 + 1 - \alpha) \ln L_t + u_t$$
$$= \beta_1 + \alpha\,(\ln K_t - \ln L_t) + \ln L_t + \beta_2 \ln L_t + u_t$$

This model cannot be estimated as it stands because the term $\ln L_t$ has no coefficient. For estimation purposes, such variables should be moved to the left-hand side. We thus have

$$\ln Q_t - \ln L_t = \beta_1 + \alpha\,(\ln K_t - \ln L_t) + \beta_2 \ln L_t + u_t$$

Defining $Y_t = \ln Q_t - \ln L_t$, $X_{t1} = \ln K_t - \ln L_t$, and $X_{t2} = \ln L_t$, the model becomes

$$Y_t = \beta_1 + \alpha X_{t1} + \beta_2 X_{t2} + u_t$$

To estimate the model, we transform the original variables to generate the newly de-fined variables and then regress Y_t against a constant term, X_{t1} and X_{t2}. The re-quired test for constant returns to scale is simply a t-test on the coefficient for X_{t2}.

● PRACTICE PROBLEM 6.12[†]

Describe step-by-step how the same test may be performed using Methods 1 and 3 described in Section 4.4.

● PRACTICE PROBLEM 6.13

Assume that constant returns to scale hold; that is, $\alpha + \beta = 1$. Under this assump-tion, describe how the Cobb–Douglas production function can be estimated.

Empirical Example: An Agricultural Production Function

Carrasco-Tauber and Moffitt (1992) have estimated a Cobb–Douglas-type produc-tion function relating the value of agricultural output (in a double-log form) to labor, land, buildings, machinery, other inputs, fertilizer, and pesticide. They have then used the estimated production function to compute the implied marginal products (evaluated at the geometric means) of each of the farm inputs. The data are for 1987 for the states in the United States, excepting Alaska and Hawaii. All the variables are in thousands of dollars per farm, except labor, which is in thousands of days per farm. The estimated model is given here, with t-statistics in parentheses.

$$\widehat{\ln Q} = 4.461 + 0.227 \ln(\text{labor}) + 0.159 \ln(\text{land \& buildings})$$
$$\phantom{\widehat{\ln Q} = } (2.11) \quad (2.12) \quad\quad\quad\quad (2.01)$$

$$+ 0.274 \ln(\text{machinery}) + 0.402 \ln(\text{other inputs})$$
$$(2.42) \quad\quad\quad\quad (8.55)$$

$$+ 0.082 \ln(\text{fertilizer}) + 0.136 \ln(\text{pesticide})$$
$$(0.85) \quad\quad\quad\quad (2.00)$$

Except for the elasticity for fertilizer, the others are statistically significant at the 5 percent level. The estimated marginal products for the inputs were \$44.54 per day for labor, \$0.04 per dollar of land and buildings, \$1.25 per dollar of machinery, \$1.29 per dollar of other inputs, \$4.91 per dollar of fertilizers, and \$5.66 per dollar of pesticides. The authors estimated several alternative models using functional forms not discussed in this chapter and obtained different marginal product mea-sures for some inputs. Interested readers are referred to their paper for full details.

● 6.11   Application: Estimating Elasticities of Bus Travel

Because the double-log model yields regression coefficients that are constant elas-ticities, this formulation is a very common one in estimating demand functions. We illustrate the double-log model by revisiting the determinants of bus travel studied in Section 4.6. The data set is in the file DATA4-4, and Practice Computer Session 6.9 has the instructions for reproducing the results presented here.

The model with all the explanatory variables had insignificant coefficients (at 10 percent) for the logarithm of FARE, GASPRICE, POP, DENSITY, and LAND-AREA, of which the log of population density was least significant (that is, had the highest *p*-value). When it was excluded and the model reestimated, the coefficients for INCOME, POP, and LANDAREA became significant at levels below 0.001. The formal theoretical reasoning for this drastic change is that reduced multicollinearity and the increase in degrees of freedom associated with a smaller model can improve the precision of coefficients. We proceeded to delete variables that had insignificant coefficients until all remaining coefficients were significant. As in the linear case, ln(FARE) was also excluded. The following is the final model, with standard errors in parentheses (not the usual *t*-statistics):

$$\widehat{\ln(\text{BUSTRAVL})} = 45.846 - 4.730 \ln(\text{INCOME}) + 1.820 \ln(\text{POP})$$
$$\underset{(9.614)}{} \quad \underset{(1.021)}{} \quad \underset{(0.236)}{}$$

$$- 0.971 \ln(\text{LANDAREA})$$
$$\underset{(0.207)}{}$$

$$\overline{R}^2 = 0.609 \qquad \text{d.f.} = 36$$

An interesting question that arises is whether bus travel is *elastic* or *inelastic*. If the numerical value (that is, ignoring the sign) of the elasticity is less than 1, then we say that bus usage is inelastic. If it is greater than 1, then it is elastic. The formal null hypothesis is therefore that the coefficient is 1 and the alternative is two-sided. The test statistics for each of the elasticities are

$$\frac{4.73 - 1}{1.021} = 3.65, \qquad \frac{1.82 - 1}{0.236} = 3.47, \qquad \frac{0.971 - 1}{0.207} = -0.14$$

From the *t*-table in the inside front cover, we note that the critical value for 36 d.f. and 0.002 (two-tail) level of significance is between 3.307 and 3.385. Because the calculated *t*-statistics for the coefficients of income and population are higher than this, we conclude that they are significantly elastic. In contrast, however, the coefficient for land area is not significantly different from 1 even at the 0.8 level (critical value lies between 0.255 and 0.256 and is numerically greater than the observed value). In this case, we say that it is **unitary elastic** with respect to land area.

● **PRACTICE PROBLEM 6.14**

Carry out a Wald test similar to the one in Practice Problem 6.8.

● **6.12   Miscellaneous Other Models***

The Logit Model*

In some cases, the dependent variable may take values only between 0 and 1. For instance, we may relate the fraction of people who voted for a particular president to its determinants. Alternatively, we may relate the fraction of people who bought cars in a certain period to its determinants. If an ordinary regression model is used in such cases, there is no assurance that the predicted value will lie between 0 and 1. To make sure that such a situation does not arise, the following functional form (known as the **logistic curve**) is commonly adopted:

$$\ln\left[\frac{P}{1-P}\right] = \alpha + \beta X + u$$

where P is the value of the dependent variable between 0 and 1. This model is more commonly known as the **logit model.** Solving this equation for P (by first exponentiating both sides), we get

$$P = \frac{1}{1 + e^{-(\alpha + \beta X + u)}}$$

It is easy to see that if $\beta > 0$, then P approaches the value 0 when $X \to -\infty$, and 1 when $X \to \infty$. Thus, P can never be outside the range $[0, 1]$. The logistic curve has the shape presented in Figure 6.9. Such a curve is also used to fit growth patterns. For example, the sales of a new product (such as high-definition televisions) might initially grow fast and then taper off. The logit model is estimated by regressing $\ln[P/(1 - P)]$ against a constant and X. Models of this type are explored more fully in Chapter 12.

The Box–Cox Transformation*

Consider the following model, which uses a transformation known as the **Box–Cox transformation** [see Box and Cox (1964)]:

$$\frac{Y^\lambda - 1}{\lambda} = \alpha + \beta \frac{X^\lambda - 1}{\lambda} + u$$

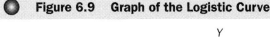

Figure 6.9 Graph of the Logistic Curve

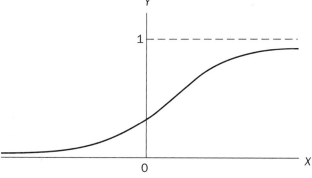

It can be shown that when $\lambda = 0$, this model reduces to the double-log form $\ln Y = \alpha + \beta \ln X + u$. For $\lambda = 1$, we get the linear case $Y - 1 = \alpha + \beta(X - 1) + u$ or $Y = \alpha^* + \beta X + u$, where $\alpha^* = \alpha - \beta + 1$. For other values of λ, we get a nonlinear model that can be estimated by the maximum likelihood procedure using a nonlinear optimization program. The functional form flexibly captures many shapes, and one can test whether $\lambda = 0$ or 1 or neither. If the range of values of λ is known a priori (say -1 to $+1$), we can choose a value of λ and form new variables $Y^* = (Y^\lambda - 1)/\lambda$ and $X^* = (X^\lambda - 1)/\lambda$. Then we regress Y^* against X^* and the constant term and obtain the error sum of squares. We repeat this procedure for different values of λ and choose the one for which the error sum of squares is the smallest. This *search procedure* can be carried out using a linear regression program and does not require a nonlinear regression program. An extension to this approach is to use $X^* = (X^\mu - 1)/\mu$, search over both λ and μ (from -1 to $+1$), and choose that combination for which ESS is a minimum.

For more on the Box–Cox transformation, see Kim and Hill (1993), Showalter (1994), and Wooldridge (1992).

Nonlinearity in Parameters*

We have seen a variety of ways in which nonlinearities in variables can easily be handled in the linear regression context as long as the variables can be suitably transformed so that we obtain a model that is linear in the unknown regression coefficients. There are situations, however, in which this may not be possible. The Box–Cox function is an example of such a situation in which the relationship is **nonlinear in parameters** and cannot be transformed into a linear form except for the special cases discussed. Another example is the *constant elasticity of substitution* (*CES*) production function, which has the following form:

$$Q = \gamma[\delta K^{-\rho} + (1 - \delta)L^{-\rho}]^{-\nu/\rho}e^u \qquad (\gamma > 0, 0 < \delta < 1, \nu > 0, \rho \geq -1)$$

γ, δ, ν, and ρ are the unknown parameters that appear nonlinearly. They can be estimated only by the maximum likelihood procedure or by nonlinear least squares methods. In this case, however, Kmenta (1986, p. 515) has provided the following quadratic approximation:

$$\ln Q = \ln \gamma + \gamma\delta \ln K + \nu(1 - \delta) \ln L - \frac{1}{2}\rho\nu\delta(1 - \delta)[\ln K - \ln L]^2 + u$$

$$= \beta_1 + \beta_2 \ln K + \beta_3 \ln L + \beta_4(\ln K - \ln L)^2 + u$$

The estimates of the original parameters of the CES production function can be obtained from estimates of the βs.

Although it is easy to transform variables and include them in the regression model, indiscriminate use of transformations should be avoided. It is wise to look for some theoretical basis for the transformation and to keep the model as simple as possible.

6.13   The Hendry/LSE Approach of Modeling from "General to Simple"

As stated before, the formulation of a satisfactory econometric model is crucial to any conclusions drawn from it. In the previous sections and chapters, we have discussed a variety of criteria for judging whether a model is "good." The initial formulation of a model is based on economic theory, an investigator's own knowledge of the underlying behavior, other similar studies, and so on. The analyst might also have some general idea of possible nonlinear effects as well as interactions among variables. Because there is no unique way of characterizing the relationship between the dependent variable and the explanatory variables, a researcher often formulates alternative models and then puts them through a number of diagnostic tests.

In judging the acceptability of an econometric model, the signs of the estimated regression coefficients are important, and it is essential that the investigator have some prior notion of what to expect, at least for the key variables. Suppose, for instance, we are estimating a demand relation and find that the estimated price elasticity is positive. This is a clear sign of possible misspecification either in the deterministic part or in the error structure (or both) and/or faulty econometric methodology. Although $\overline{R}^2$ is a useful measure of the goodness of fit, overreliance on this measure is not fruitful. Cross-section studies generally have low $\overline{R}^2$ compared to time series studies, in which most variables exhibit trends and there are high correlations among them. Although low $\overline{R}^2$ signals possible omitted variables, choosing models by maximizing $\overline{R}^2$ is not recommended.

In Chapter 4 we recommended eight model selection criteria as useful measures in judging whether one model is "better" than another. Another criterion often used in judging a model is its ability to predict the dependent variable. If forecasting is an important goal of an econometrician, then it is essential that the model's forecasting ability be carefully evaluated (more on this in Chapter 11).

In the applications and examples on nonlinearities and lagged variables presented in this chapter, we started with a general unrestricted model and then reduced it by eliminating one at a time the variable with the least significant coefficient. This approach, referred to as **"general to simple,"** is strongly advocated by Hendry (1985) and many econometricians at the London School of Economics (see also Hendry and Richards, 1982, 1983; Gilbert, 1986, 1989). Their approach has also been referred to as the **Hendry/LSE approach.** Although Hendry's emphasis was on time series modeling, the principle is equally applicable to cross-section data. The basic idea, in Hendry's terminology, is that there is a **data generation process (DGP)** underlying the values of economic variables and that an investigator's job is to approximate it using economic theory, intuition, and experience and by putting the model through a number of diagnostic tests to see if either model or methodology can be improved. To do this, one would start with a general dynamic model which is **overparametrized,** that is, has more lags and variables (including possible nonlinear terms) than one would normally start with, and then carry out a **data-based simplification** through Wald and t-tests. Example 6.5 and application Section 6.7 on patents and R&D expenditure are concrete examples of this methodology. In Chapters 7, 9, and 10, we will see more examples of the general to simple approach. This data-based model simplification results in a **parsimonious specification,** that is, one with fewer parameters. The advantages of such parsimony are (1) increased precision of estimates because of reduced multicollinearity, (2) more degrees of freedom and hence more reliable estimates, (3) greater power of tests, and (4) a simpler model, which is easier to comprehend than a complex one.

● 6.14 "Simple to General" Modeling Using the Lagrange Multiplier Test

Although the general to specific form is preferable in principle, practical implementation of this in its pure form might be troublesome. For instance, adding new variables that are lags of variables already present in the model causes independent variables to be highly correlated. As was seen in the previous chapter, this high correlation often makes it difficult or impossible to measure *separate* impacts of explanatory variables. Also, an investigator typically has more confidence in a basic specification than in formulating a general model. To avoid these problems, the **"simple to general"** modeling approach would start at the other end with a basic specification about which a researcher has a great deal of confidence and then ask whether more variables should be added. A diagnostic tool frequently used in this approach is the **Lagrange multiplier (LM) test.** Before discussing that, however, it is useful to provide an overview of different approaches to testing for model specification.

A number of formal approaches are used for hypothesis testing, the most common of which are the Lagrange multiplier (LM) test, the **likelihood ratio (LR) test,** and the Wald test. In previous sections, the Wald test has been used extensively. The present section focuses on the LM test as an alternative means of testing for model specification. The LR test is discussed in the appendix. In all these approaches, two models are formulated, a *restricted model* and an *unrestricted model.* The restricted model is obtained by imposing linear or nonlinear constraints on its parameters and corresponds to the null hypothesis. The unrestricted model is the alternative. In earlier sections, we have used the Wald approach to test hypotheses between the unrestricted model and a restricted one in which some of the variables were omitted. This was illustrated in several cross-section and time series applications. The Wald test starts with the alternative (the unrestricted model) and asks whether the null (restricted model) should be preferred. The likelihood ratio test is a direct comparison of the two hypotheses. The Lagrange multiplier principle starts at the null and asks whether a movement toward the alternative is preferred. In other words, the LM procedure specifies a simpler and more parsimonious model and asks whether it pays to add new variables. Thus, we start with a basic formulation and test for the addition of new variables rather than start with the full specification and test whether some of the variables should be omitted. The LM method is quite general and can be applied to other situations, as will be described in later chapters. Both the general to the simple and the simple to the general are useful approaches, and it is recommended that both methods be used to obtain more robust conclusions.

The LM test has been discussed in a number of papers: Aitcheson and Silvey (1958), Silvey (1959), Berndt and Savin (1977), Godfrey (1978), Buse (1982), and Engle (1982, 1984), all of which require a knowledge of linear algebra. In this chapter, we present a simplified summary of the test and illustrate its usefulness with several applications. Some theoretical results are summarized in the chapter appendix, along with an explanation of the terms *Lagrange multiplier* and *likelihood ratio*. A geometrical comparison of the three approaches is also made in the appendix and illustrated with simple examples. In the chapter itself, we specify the steps required to carry out the LM test and apply them to actual data. Although the LM test is a large-sample test, it has been found to be useful even if the number of observations is only 30. The Wald test is applicable to small samples also. The likelihood ratio test sometimes leads to small-sample tests. These points are discussed in more detail in the appendix.

Hypotheses implied by the omission of variables are special cases of **nested hypotheses.** In a nested formulation, the restricted model is a subset of the unrestricted model. **Nonnested hypotheses** compare totally different models in which one cannot be derived as a subset of another. For instance, omitting some variables and adding others will result in nonnested models. In this book, we confine our attention to nested hypotheses only. Readers interested in nonnested hypothesis testing are referred to the papers by Davidson and MacKinnon (1981, 1982) and MacKinnon (1983) but are cautioned that they require a knowledge of linear algebra.

Lagrange Multiplier Test for Adding Variables

The LM test procedure is easily understood in the case in which the economic or business analyst wants to know whether additional variables should be included in the model (for example, whether nonlinear and interaction terms should be included). Consider the following restricted and unrestricted models:

(R) $Y = \beta_1 + \beta_2 X_2 + \beta_3 X_3 + \cdots + \beta_m X_m + u$

(U) $Y = \beta_1 + \beta_2 X_2 + \cdots + \beta_m X_m + \beta_{m+1} X_{m+1} + \cdots + \beta_k X_k + v$

In Model U, the $k - m$ new variables $X_{m+1}, X_{m+2}, \ldots, X_k$ (nonlinear variables, for example) have been added. The null hypothesis of interest is that the regression coefficients for these added variables is zero. The steps for the LM test are as follows:

Step 1 $H_0: \beta_{m+1} = \beta_{m+2} = \cdots = \beta_k = 0.$ H_1: at least one of these βs is nonzero.

Step 2   Estimate the restricted model R.

Step 3   Obtain the estimated residuals from this model as

$$\hat{u}_R = Y - \hat{\beta}_1 - \hat{\beta}_2 X_2 - \hat{\beta}_3 X_3 - \cdots - \hat{\beta}_m X_m$$

Suppose the "true" specification had been Model U; in this case, the variables $X_{m+1}, X_{m+2}, \ldots, X_k$ should have been included. Their effect would be captured by the residual $\hat{u}_R$. Thus, $\hat{u}_R$ should be related to these omitted variables. In other words, if we regress $\hat{u}_R$ against these variables, we should get a good fit, which is an indicator that at least some of the variables $X_{m+1}, X_{m+2}, \ldots, X_k$ should have been included in the model. This argument leads to the next step.

Step 4   Regress $\hat{u}_R$ against a constant and all the Xs, *including the ones in the restricted model*—that is, against all the independent variables in the unrestricted model. We will henceforth refer to this second regression as the **auxiliary**

regression. Engle (1982) has shown that, for large samples, the sample size (n) multiplied by the unadjusted R^2 for this auxiliary regression has the chi-square distribution with degrees of freedom equal to the *number of restrictions in the null hypothesis.* (This is shown in Appendix Section 6.A.3 for the simple regression case.) Thus, in our case, $nR^2 \sim \chi^2_{k-m}$. The reason for including the original variables in the auxiliary regression is to make the test statistic have the convenient form it has. If $nR^2 > \chi^{*2}_{k-m}(a)$, the point on χ^2_{k-m} such that the area to its right is a, the level of significance, we would reject the null hypothesis that the new regression coefficients are all zero. Alternatively, we would compute p-value $= P(\chi^2_{k-m} > nR^2)$ and reject the null if p-value is less than the level of significance. In other words, we would conclude that at least some of the new variables should have been included in the model. The p-values of individual coefficients can give a clue as to which of these omitted variables might be included.

Using the Auxiliary Regression to Select Variables to Be Added to the Basic Model

The auxiliary regression has information as to which of the new variables under consideration might be candidates for adding to the basic model. *In fact, the estimated coefficients and associated statistics for the new variables in the auxiliary regression in an LM test are identical to those one would obtain for the completely unrestricted model that the general to simple approach would start with.* This point is formally proved in Ramanathan (1986) and is illustrated empirically in Example 6.7. Although there is no clear theoretical guidance on how to choose variables from the auxiliary list, a simple rule of thumb might be to include all the variables for which the regression coefficients have p-values less than 0.5. This rule is more conservative than the one that selects only strictly significant variables. As will be seen in Examples 6.7 and 6.8, using strict significance tends to miss variables that might become significant when least-significant variables are omitted. This procedure is equivalent to estimating the full general model and then omitting all variables for which the corresponding p-values are larger than 0.5.

● EXAMPLE 6.7

The LM test approach is illustrated first with the data for estimating the demand for cable television presented in DATA4-8. The data are a cross section for 40 cities for the variables defined here and are described in more detail in Appendix D.

sub = The number of subscribers of each system (in thousands)
home = The number of homes passed by each system
inst = Installation fee in dollars
svc = Monthly service charge of each system in dollars
tv = The number of television signals carried by each cable system
age = The age of each system in years
air = The number of free television signals received
y = Per-capita income in dollars

Table 6.4 has the annotated partial computer output that walks you through the steps just described. To get the complete output, carry out Practice Computer Session 6.10.

Although the LM test statistic in this example was clearly significant, it is sometimes possible for the test to give contradictory signals. This point is illustrated in the next example.

⬤ **Table 6.4   Annotated Partial Computer Output for Example 6.7**

[First, estimate the basic model by regressing sub against a constant, home, inst, svc, tv, age, air, and y. Then, generate the residuals as ut. The auxiliary regression presented here regresses the residual ut against the variables in the basic model plus all the square terms denoted as sq_x (for example, sq_home = $home^2$).]

Dependent variable: ut

	VARIABLE	COEFFICIENT	STDERROR	T STAT	2Prob(t > |T|)	
0)	const	−481.4363	264.2862	−1.822	0.080496	*
2)	home	0.0339	0.0839	0.404	0.689961	
3)	inst	0.9184	2.1242	0.432	0.669195	
4)	svc	10.1055	19.1942	0.526	0.603188	
5)	tv	−1.4180	2.6542	−0.534	0.597895	
6)	age	−2.5507	1.4623	−1.744	0.093391	*
7)	air	23.8229	5.2392	4.547	0.000121	***
8)	y	0.0829	0.0526	1.576	0.127509	
9)	sq_home	0.0002207	0.0002839	0.778	0.444146	
10)	sq_inst	−0.0210	0.0655	−0.321	0.750748	
11)	sq_svc	−0.7790	1.2854	−0.606	0.549977	
12)	sq_tv	0.0484	0.1017	0.476	0.637925	
13)	sq_age	0.1393	0.0734	1.898	0.069252	*
14)	sq_air	−1.5823	0.3732	−4.240	0.000267	***
15)	sq_y	−4.547e−006	2.8346e−006	−1.604	0.121287	

Unadjusted R-squared   0.550 Adjusted R-squared   0.298

[The LM statistic = no. of observations multiplied by the unadjusted R^2 = 21.992652.]

Chi-square (7): area to the right of 21.992652 = 0.002548.

[The null hypothesis for the LM test is that the coefficients for the seven added squared variables are all zero (and, hence, the d.f. is 7). The p-value of 0.002548 suggests that we are "safe" in re-

(continued)

● **Table 6.4   (continued)**

jecting the null hypothesis and concluding that at least some of the added variables belong in the model. (Using a calculator, verify the LM test statistic and carry out the chi-square test using a 1 percent level of significance and the chi-square table.)

The auxiliary regression helps us determine the new variables to be added to the model. However, there is no theoretical guide for the actual selection. We thus use the arbitrary rule of including every new variable that has a *p*-value of less than 0.5, that is, is significant at the 50 percent level. This is much more conservative than the 10 percent cutoff we have used so far and is designed to minimize possible omitted-variable bias caused by not including enough variables. According to the 0.5 rule, the squares of home, age, air, and y are to be added to the basic model. This is done next. Note that the dependent variable is now again sub. A mistake often made at this point is to specify ut again as the dependent variable or include it as another independent variable. This is clearly meaningless and wrong.]

```
Dependent variable: sub


        VARIABLE      COEFFICIENT      STDERROR      T STAT    2Prob(t > |T|)


    0)    const       -407.0791       211.7804       -1.922      0.064813 *
    2)    home           0.4319         0.0792        5.451      0.000008 ***
    3)    inst          -0.1821         0.3957       -0.460      0.648969
    4)    svc            0.2123         1.9666        0.108      0.914822
    5)    tv             0.6962         0.5292        1.315      0.199029
    6)    age           -1.0718         1.2305       -0.871      0.391149
    7)    air           18.1986         4.8824        3.727      0.000868 ***
    8)    y              0.0757         0.0476        1.591      0.122767
    9)  sq_home       0.0002240      0.0002689        0.833      0.411944
   13)   sq_age         0.1174         0.0580        2.025      0.052478 *
   14)   sq_air        -1.5579         0.3383       -4.605      0.000082 ***
   15)    sq_y      -4.049e-006    2.5562e-006       -1.584      0.124383


Mean of dep. var.          24.509   S.D. of dep. variable          33.537
Error Sum of Sq (ESS)   2307.1870   Std Err of Resid. (sgmahat)    9.0774
Unadjusted R-squared        0.947   Adjusted R-squared             0.927
F-statistic (11, 28)      45.8496   p-value for F()             0.000000
Durbin-Watson stat.         1.943   First-order autocorr. coeff     0.001


MODEL SELECTION STATISTICS


SGMASQ        82.3995    AIC          105.099    FPE        107.119
HQ           126.229     SCHWARZ      174.438    SHIBATA     92.2875
GCV          117.714     RICE         144.199


Excluding the constant, p-value was highest for variable 4 (svc)
```

⬤ Table 6.4 (continued)

[The rest of the procedure is to carry out the data-based model reduction that we have adopted before. This is done by successively eliminating the variable with the highest p-value, but one at a time. To avoid cluttering the pages with unnecessary output, only the final model is presented here.)

	VARIABLE	COEFFICIENT	STDERROR	T STAT	2Prob(t > |T|)	
0)	const	-562.6761	158.0817	-3.559	0.001185	***
2)	home	0.4960	0.0283	17.525	0.000000	***
6)	age	-1.5575	0.9037	-1.723	0.094460	*
7)	air	17.3047	4.3410	3.986	0.000364	***
8)	y	0.1108	0.0348	3.186	0.003215	***
13)	sq_age	0.1392	0.0438	3.181	0.003251	***
14)	sq_air	-1.4177	0.2919	-4.856	0.000030	***
15)	sq_y	-5.948e-006	1.8798e-006	-3.164	0.003399	***

Mean of dep. var.	24.509	S.D. of dep. variable	33.537
Error Sum of Sq (ESS)	2521.9340	Std Err of Resid. (sgmahat)	8.8775
Unadjusted R-squared	0.943	Adjusted R-squared	0.930
F-statistic (7, 32)	74.9412	p-value for F()	0.000000
Durbin-Watson stat.	2.069	First-order autocorr. coeff	-0.051

MODEL SELECTION STATISTICS

SGMASQ	78.8104	AIC	94.0571	FPE	94.5725
HQ	106.275	SCHWARZ	131.852	SHIBATA	88.2677
GCV	98.513	RICE	105.081		

[To contrast this simple to general methodology with the Hendry/LSE approach of general to simple modeling, we now estimate the most general model that includes linear and quadratic terms. It is interesting to note that the coefficients and standard errors for the added square terms are *identical* to those in the auxiliary regression above. For a theoretical proof of why this is always the case, see Ramanathan (1986).]

Dependent variable: sub

	VARIABLE	COEFFICIENT	STDERROR	T STAT	2Prob(t > |T|)	
0)	const	-488.2440	264.2862	-1.847	0.076556	*
2)	home	0.4394	0.0839	5.238	0.000020	***
3)	inst	0.3920	2.1242	0.185	0.855089	
4)	svc	12.1443	19.1942	0.633	0.532671	

(continued)

Table 6.4   (continued)

VARIABLE	COEFFICIENT	STDERROR	T STAT	2Prob(t > |T|)	
5) tv	-0.6615	2.6542	-0.249	0.805230	
6) age	-1.3571	1.4623	-0.928	0.362229	
7) air	18.7117	5.2392	3.572	0.001475	***
8) y	0.0845	0.0526	1.608	0.120423	
9) sq_home	0.0002207	0.0002839	0.778	0.444146	
10) sq_inst	-0.0210	0.0655	-0.321	0.750748	
11) sq_svc	-0.7790	1.2854	-0.606	0.549977	
12) sq_tv	0.0484	0.1017	0.476	0.637925	
13) sq_age	0.1393	0.0734	1.898	0.069252	*
14) sq_air	-1.5823	0.3732	-4.240	0.000267	***
15) sq_y	-4.547e-006	2.8346e-006	-1.604	0.121287	

```
Error Sum of Sq (ESS)      2216.6660   Std Err of Resid. (sgmahat)      9.4163
Unadjusted R-squared           0.949   Adjusted R-squared               0.921
```

[Following the data-based model reduction strategy, we eliminate variables with insignificant coefficients one at a time. The final model derived this way is identical to the one derived earlier using the simple to general framework. Thus, in this example, the two approaches are equivalent. Because this need not always be the case, it is recommended that both approaches be applied as a means of cross-checking. If, however, there is a need to choose between the two approaches, the Hendry/LSE approach is preferable because it is surer and does not depend on the arbitrary 0.5 rule of selecting variables from the auxiliary regression. However, we will find in Chapters 8, 9, and 10 that the LM test is an extremely powerful testing procedure in other situations.]

PRACTICE PROBLEM 6.15

In Example 6.7, we omitted variables based strictly on the significance of their regression coefficients. Start with the most general model used in the Hendry/LSE approach and eliminate variables one at a time as before, but retain income, the monthly service charge, and the installation fee until the very end because they are income and price measures in a demand equation and hence have theoretical importance. Compare the final model you get (in terms of the selection criteria and the significance of coefficients) with the final model in Table 6.4. What differences do you perceive? Which model would you recommend as the one to use for the final interpretation? Use that model to interpret the results.

EXAMPLE 6.8

The second illustrative example demonstrates how the LM test can be applied to the problem studied in Example 6.5, that is, in the log-linear model for wages. Table 6.5 has the annotated computer printout for this case (see Computer Practice Ses-

● **Table 6.5   Annotated Partial Computer Output for Example 6.8**

[Estimate the auxiliary regression.]

```
OLS estimates using the 49 observations 1-49
Dependent variable: ut
```

	VARIABLE	COEFFICIENT	STDERROR	T STAT	2Prob(t > |T|)	
0)	const	0.4934	0.8092	0.610	0.545334	
2)	EDUC	-0.1576	0.0864	-1.824	0.075224	*
3)	EXPER	-0.0088	0.0245	-0.361	0.719991	
4)	AGE	-0.0008179	0.0338	-0.024	0.980822	
7)	sq_EDUC	0.0115	0.0063	1.837	0.073294	*
8)	sq_EXPER	0.0004293	0.0011	0.384	0.703130	
9)	sq_AGE	0.0000211	0.0003814	0.055	0.956041	

```
Unadjusted R-squared = 0.079
Value of the LM statistic = 3.861657.
Chi-square(3): area to the right of 3.861657 = 0.276796
```

[Note that the p-value suggests that the null hypothesis cannot be rejected, but the coefficient for EDUC square is significant at the 7.33 percent level.

sion 6.11 for full particulars). The unadjusted R^2 for the auxiliary regression is only 0.079, with a nR^2 statistic of 3.86. Under the null hypothesis that the quadratic terms have coefficients that are zero, this has a chi-square distribution with 3 d.f. The p-value of 0.28 indicates that we cannot safely reject the null hypothesis. This implies that none of the new variables have significant coefficients. We note, however, that the p-value for the coefficient of $EDUC^2$ is significant at the 7.33 percent level, which is acceptable. Thus, the auxiliary regression would suggest that this variable be included in the model (the 0.5 p-value rule would also pick this variable but ignore all others). In contrast, the nR^2 test indicates that none of the variables need be included. Thus, the LM test gives conflicting signals about the importance of adding new variables to the original model. In this example, the general to simple approach is superior because there is no ambiguity. However, if we adopt the 0.5 p-value rule for selecting variables, the two approaches will be identical.

The preceding examples demonstrate that, while the LM test is useful as a diagnostic tool in going from a simple to a general framework, in some cases its usefulness might be limited. We will see in Chapters 8, 9 and 10, however, that the LM test is extremely powerful in other contexts.

● 6.15 Ramsey's RESET Procedure for Regression Specification Error

Ramsey (1969) proposed yet another method for testing a model's specification. It is known as the **RESET (regression specification error test).** The procedure is as straightforward to apply as the LM test described in the previous section. The steps for the RESET procedure are as follows:

Step 1 Estimate the model by the OLS procedure and save the fitted value $\hat{Y}_t$.

Step 2 Add the variables $\hat{Y}_t^2$, $\hat{Y}_t^3$, and $\hat{Y}_t^4$ to the model in Step 1 and estimate the new model.

Step 3 Carry out a Wald F-test for the omission of the three new variables in Step 2. If the null hypothesis that the new variables have no effect is rejected, that is an indication of a specification error.

The rationale for the Ramsey RESET procedure is that the estimated residuals ($\hat{u}_t$) that stand for omitted-variable effects can be approximated by a linear combination of the powers of the fitted values. If those powers had significant effects, then the original model is taken to be misspecified. A major drawback of the RESET method, however, is that the test does not say what kind of misspecification, nor does it throw any light on the appropriate functional form to use. Nevertheless, the test can be useful as a supplement to the Wald and LM tests applied to test for specific nonlinear and dynamic effects. This point is illustrated in the following example.

● EXAMPLE 6.9

In Example 6.2, we used the data in DATA6-1 to estimate an average cost function for a manufacturing firm. We first used the RESET procedure to test whether a linear relationship is adequate (see Practice Computer Session 6.12 for the steps to reproduce the results of this example). Thus, we regressed UNITCOST against a constant, OUTPUT, and INPCOST, and saved the estimated $Y(\hat{Y})$. Next we regressed UNITCOST against the same variables plus the powers of the estimated Y and carried out a Wald F-test on the powers of $\hat{Y}$. The computed F-statistic was 3.7447, which, under the null hypothesis that the added variables have no effect on UNIT-COST, has the F-distribution with 3 d.f. for the numerator and 14 ($= 20 - 6$) d.f. for the denominator. The p-value corresponding to this is 0.036407, which indicates that the coefficients of the added variables are jointly significant at levels below 5 percent. In other words, the RESET procedure points to a model misspecification. In Example 6.2, we added the quadratic term for OUTPUT and found it to have a significant effect (this is not surprising because theory tells us that average cost curves are generally U-shaped). It would be interesting to use the RESET approach to test that model for specification error. This requires first regressing UNITCOST against a constant, OUTPUT, INPCOST, and OUTPUT^2 and saving the estimated Y as before. Then add the powers of the estimated Y as explanatory variables and use the Wald F-test for these added variables. The F-statistic was 0.4826 with a p-value of 0.7. Because this is too high, we cannot reject the null hypothesis that the added variables have zero effect on UNITCOST. Thus, the RESET method suggests that the final model in Example 6.2 may not suffer from misspecification.

● PRACTICE PROBLEM 6.16

Apply the RESET procedure to test for misspecification in the final model in the application in Example 6.7.

● PRACTICE PROBLEM 6.17

Do the same for the final model in Example 6.5.

Summary

The simple linear regression model can be used to handle nonlinear relationships also, *provided the model is linear in the parameters.* Common alternative functional forms used are semilog or log-linear model, linear-log relationship, double-log model, and the reciprocal transformation.

Quadratic and higher powers of independent variables, or lags in variables, are easily accommodated in a regression model provided the *unknown regression coefficients appear linearly.* One simply makes the suitable transformation of the data and incorporates them in the model. The marginal effect of one variable can be made to depend on another explanatory variable through interaction terms. Some models cannot be converted to a form that is linear in parameters. In such cases, the estimation procedure consists of nonlinear least squares or maximum likelihood methods.

It is improper to compare the values of R^2 across models unless they both have the same left-hand-side variables. If the dependent variables are different, one can use the alternative models to predict the value of the same variable and then compute the coefficient of correlation between the predicted and observed values of this variable. These are comparable across models. It should be noted, however, that forecasts of the level of the dependent variable generated from a log-linear or double-log model are biased and inconsistent and need a correction factor.

Three approaches are most commonly used in *nested hypothesis testing*—that is, in hypotheses in which the restricted model is a subset of the more general unrestricted model. They are the *Wald test,* the *likelihood ratio (LR) test,* and the *Lagrange multiplier (LM) test.* The Wald approach (also referred to as the Hendry/LSE "general to simple" approach) formulates a model with many independent variables and their lags and then asks whether some should be eliminated. The LM test involves formulating a basic model and then asking whether other variables should be included. This is the "simple to general" approach. Both use judgment and both are useful, depending on the context. The LR test treats the two models equally.

Although asymptotically (that is, for large samples) the three tests are equivalent, the LM test has been found to be useful in more general contexts. It is also useful in testing for nonlinear effects and for the presence of interaction terms. The LM test requires three basic steps: (1) Regress the dependent variable against a list of basic independent variables, including the constant; (2) obtain the residuals from the OLS procedure carried out in Step (1); and (3) regress the residuals against all the Xs in Step (1), as well as against new variables (*m* in number), which might include nonlinear terms or cross products (squares and interactions) of the independent variables.

If the product of the sample size (n) and the unadjusted R^2 from this auxiliary regression (that is, nR^2) exceeds $\chi^2_m(a)$, the point on the chi-square distribution with m degrees of freedom, to the right of which there is an area a (the level of significance), then the null hypothesis that the m added variables all have zero coefficients is rejected. If the hypothesis is rejected, the t-values in Step (3) will help to identify the variables that could be added to the basic model. Even if the nR^2 test fails to reject the null hypothesis of zero coefficients, the t-statistics of the auxiliary regression might suggest that some variables ought to be included. These variables could then be added to the basic model for a new set of estimates. We will see in later chapters that the principles of the LM test procedure are applicable in more general contexts.

Ramsey's regression specification error test (RESET) can also be used to test for model specification. The model is first estimated and the estimated $Y(\hat{Y})$ is saved. The variables $\hat{Y}^2$, $\hat{Y}^3$, and $\hat{Y}^4$ are then added to the model and a joint F-test carried out on their coefficients. If the coefficients are jointly significant, that is taken as an indication of model misspecification. The procedure, however, does not specify the nature of the misspecification. Nevertheless, the RESET methodology can be a useful supplement to the Wald, LM, and LR tests for model specification.

Key Terms

Auxiliary regression

Base

Box–Cox transformation

Cobb–Douglas production function

Constant returns to scale

Data-based simplification

Data generation process (DGP)

Decreasing returns to scale

Derivative

Double-log model

Dynamic models

Elasticity

Elasticity of output with respect to capital

Elasticity of output with respect to labor

Exponent

Exponential function

General to simple approach

Hendry/LSE approach

Increasing returns to scale

Instantaneous rate of growth

Interaction terms

Lagrange multiplier (LM) test

Lags in behavior

Likelihood ratio (LR) test

Linear-log model

Logarithmic function

Logistic curve

Logit model

Log-linear model

Log-log model

LSE approach

Marginal effect

Natural logarithm

Nested hypotheses

Nonlinearity in parameters

Nonnested hypotheses

Overparametrized

Parsimonious specification

Polynomial curve-fitting

Reciprocal transformation

Regression specification error test (RESET)

Semilog model

Simple to general approach

Spurious nonlinearities

Static models

Trend-fitting

Unitary elastic

References

Several of the following references require a background in linear algebra.

Aitcheson, J., and S. D. Silvey. "Maximum Likelihood Estimation of Parameters Subject to Restraints." *Annals of Math. Stat.* 29 (1958).

Berndt, E. R., and N. E. Savin. "Conflict among Criteria for Testing Hypotheses in the Multivariate Regression Model." *Econometrica* (July 1977): 1263–1278.

Box, G. E. P., and D. R. Cox. "An Analysis of Transformations." *J. Royal Stat. Society,* Series B (1964).

Buse, A. "The Likelihood Ratio, Wald, and Lagrange Multiplier Test: An Expository Note." *The American Statistician* (August 1982): 153–157.

Carrasco-Tauber, C., and L. J. Moffitt. "Damage Control Econometrics: Functional Specification and Pesticide Productivity." *Amer. J. Agric. Econ.* (February 1992): 158–162.

Davidson, R., and J. G. MacKinnon. "Several Tests for Model Specification in the Presence of Alternative Hypotheses." *Econometrica* (1981): 781–793.

———. "Some Non-nested Hypothesis Tests and Relations among Them." *Review of Econ. Stud.* (1982): 551–565.

Engle, R. F. "A General Approach to Lagrangian Multiplier Diagnostics." *Annals of Econometrics* 20 (1982): 83–104.

———. "Wald, Likelihood-Ratio and Lagrangian Multiplier Tests in Econometrics." *Handbook of Econometrics,* ed. Z. Griliches and M. D. Intriligator. New York: North-Holland, 1984.

Gilbert, C. L. "Professor Hendry's Econometric Methodology." *Oxford Bulletin of Economics and Statistics* 48 (1986): 283–307.

———. "LSE and the British Approach to Time Series Econometrics." *Oxford Economic Papers* 41 (1989): 108–128.

Godfrey, L. G. "Testing for Multiplicative Heteroscedasticity." *J. Econometrics* 8 (1978).

Hausman, J. A. "Specifications Tests in Econometrics." *Econometrica* 46 (6) (November 1978): 1251–1271.

Hendry, D. "Econometric Methodology," paper presented to the Econometric Society Fifth World Congress, MIT (1985).

Hendry, D., and J. F. Richards. "On the Formulation of Empirical Models in Dynamic Econometrics." *J. Econometrics* 20 (1982): 3–33.

———. "The Econometric Analysis of Economic Time Series." *International Statistical Review* 51 (1983): 111–163.

Johnston, J. *Econometric Methods.* New York: McGraw-Hill, 1984.

Kim, Minbo, and R. Carter Hill. "The Box–Cox Transformation-of-Variables in Regression." *Empirical Economics* 18 (2) (1993): 307–319.

Klein, L. R., and J. N. Morgan. "Results of Alternatical Statistical Treatment of Sample Survey Data." *J. Amer. Stat. Assoc.* 47 (December 1951).

Kmenta, J. *Elements of Econometrics.* New York: Macmillan, 1986.

Larson, Alexander C., and John S. Watters. "A Convenient Test of Functional Form for Pooled Econometric Models." *Empirical Economics* 18 (2) (1993): 271–280.

MacKinnon, J. G. "Model Specification Tests against Non-nested Alternatives." *Econometric Reviews* (1983): 85–157.

Mood, A. M., F. A. Graybill, and D. C. Boes. *Introduction to the Theory of Statistics.* New York: McGraw-Hill, 1974.

Nelson, Charles R. *Applied Time Series Analysis for Managerial Forecasting.* Holden-Day, 1973.

Ramanathan, Ramu. "A Note on the Lagrange Multiplier Test and Model Selection Criteria." Discussion paper No. 1986–19, UCSD Economics Department.

———. *Statistical Methods in Econometrics.* San Diego: Academic Press, 1993.

Ramsey, J. B. "Tests for Specification Errors in Classical Linear Least Squares Regression Analysis." *J. Royal Stat. Soc.,* Series B, 31 (1969): 350–371.

Showalter, Mark H. "A Monte Carlo Investigation of the Box–Cox Model and a Nonlinear Least Squares Alternative." *Review of Economics and Statistics* 76 (3) (August 1994): 560–570.

Silvey, D. S. "The Lagrange Multiplier Test." *Annals of Math. Stat.* (1959).

Spurr, W. A., and C. P. Bonini. *Statistical Analysis for Business Decisions.* Homewood Ill.: Irwin, 1973.

Tansel, Aysit. "Wage Employment, Earnings and Returns to Schooling for Men and Women in Turkey." *Economics of Education Review* 13 (1994): 305–320.

Wooldridge, Jeffrey M. "Some Alternatives to the Box–Cox Regression Model." *International Economic Review* 33 (4) (November 1992): 935–955.

Exercises

Questions Requiring No Computer Work

6.1   Consider the following functional form (ignoring the error term) of a nonlinear model.

$$Y = \beta_1 + \beta_2 X + \beta_3(1/X)$$

where all the βs are positive.

a.   Derive the expression for the marginal effect of Y with respect to X.

b.   Derive the expression for the elasticity of Y with respect to X and make sure to express it *in terms of X only*.

c.   Graphically indicate the shape of the relationship between Y and X (for $X > 0$).

To test for adding the nonlinear term, you want to start with the basic linear model and then carry out an LM test for adding the term $\beta_3(1/X)$.

d.   First describe the regressions to run and explain how you should compute the test statistic. Explain this as you would to a research assistant.

e.   What is its distribution and d.f.?

f.   Describe how you should decide on whether to reject the null (at the 5 percent level).

g.   Repeat the analysis with ln Y as the dependent variable instead of Y (ignore part c).

†6.2   a.   Derive the marginal effect of Y with respect to X ($\partial Y / \partial X$) for the functional form (ignoring the error term) ln $(Y) = \beta_1 + \beta_2 X + \beta_3 X^2 + \beta_4(XZ)$. [Note: Your answer should not depend on Y.]

b.   Derive the elasticity of Y with respect to X for the same.

To test for adding the terms X^2 and XZ, you want to start with the basic log-linear model and then carry out an LM test for adding the X^2 and XZ terms.

c.   First describe the regressions to run and explain how you should compute the test statistic. Explain this as you would to a research assistant.

d.   What is its distribution and d.f.?

e.   Describe how you should decide on whether to reject the null (at the 5 percent level).

6.3   Consider the relationship (ignoring the error term)

$$Y = \beta_1 + \beta_2 X + \beta_3 \ln X + \beta_4 Z + \beta_5(Z \ln X)$$

where X and Z are explanatory variables.

a.   Derive an algebraic expression for the elasticity of Y with respect to X. [Note: Your answer should not depend on Y.]

To test for adding the terms ln X, Z, and Z ln X, you want to start with the basic linear model and then carry out an LM test for adding the variables.

b.   First describe the regressions to run and explain how you should compute the test statistic. Explain this as you would to a research assistant.

c.   What is its distribution and d.f.?

d.   Describe how you should decide on whether to reject the null (at the 5 percent level).

6.4   Consider the Cobb–Douglas production function $Q_t = e^\alpha K_t^\beta L_t^\gamma e^{u_t}$. You have data on Q, K, and L.

a.   Derive a model (call it Model R) that is estimable using the OLS procedure.

b.   You suspect that the parameters α, β, and γ are not constant but "time-varying," that is, $\alpha = \alpha_1 + \alpha_2 t$ and similarly for β and γ, where t is time, going from 1 to n. Derive another model (call it U) that can be used to obtain the estimates of the new parameters just listed.

c.   What variables would you generate to estimate this model?

d.   State the joint hypothesis on Model U that will result in Model R being the restricted model. What is the alternative hypothesis?

e.   Suppose you have 46 observations ($n = 46$). To use the Wald test, write down an expression for the test statistic. Define all the symbols you use and be sure to put actual numerical values where available.

f.   What is its distribution and d.f.?

g.   Write down the numerical value of the critical value for a 5 percent test.

h.   Describe the decision rule for your test.

6.5   Consider the following model for electricity consumption:

$$\ln E_t = \beta_1 + \beta_2 \ln Y_t + \beta_3 \ln P_t + u_t$$

where E is per-capita electricity consumption in kilowatt-hours, Y is per-capita income, and P is the price of electricity, at time t. Suppose we believe that the price and income elasticity of electricities are not constant but are continuously changing over time. Thus, $\beta_2 = \alpha_1 + \alpha_2 t$ and similarly for β_3.

a.   Formulate an econometric model that will enable you to test this belief.

b.   Describe in detail (including what the null hypothesis is, which regressions to run, test statistics to compute, and so on) how you will test the relevant hypotheses.

†6.6   Let C be total consumption expenditures of a family, Y its income, and N the size of the family. Formulate an econometric model that incorporates the following assumptions: (a) the marginal propensity to consume decreases as income increases, and (b) the marginal effect of family size on consumption decreases as N increases (because of economies of scale in cooking, rents, and so on). Describe how you would test the hypotheses implicit in these statements.

6.7   Consider the household consumption function in double-log form

$$\ln(C) = \alpha + \beta \ln(Y) + u \qquad n = 40$$

where $\ln(C)$ is the logarithm of consumption expenditures and $\ln(Y)$ is the logarithm of household income in a given period. I believe that the parameters α and β are not constant but depend on the number of people (N) in the household, that is, on its size.

a.   Formulate another econometric model that will enable me to allow for the parameters to vary with the family size (clearly define any additional variables I should use).

b.   In the new model, derive an expression for the elasticity of consumption (that is, of C) with respect to family size (that is, N).

c.   State the null and alternative hypotheses in the new model to test the hypothesis that the size of the household does not affect consumption.

d. To use the Lagrange multiplier (LM) test, describe what regression(s) are to be run and how the test statistic is to be computed.

e. Describe the distribution of the test statistic (including the numerical values of the d.f.), and explain how I can apply the *p*-value approach with 10 percent level for acceptance or rejection.

6.8   The sales manager of a company believes that his company's sales (S_t) have been growing according to the model $S_t = S_0(1 + g)^t$. He obtains the following OLS regression results:

$$\widehat{\ln S_t} = 3.6889 + 0.0583t$$

a. What is his estimate of the growth rate (g)?

b. What is his estimate of S_0?

c. Estimate the company's sales five periods into the future.

6.9   Consider the following double-log model of timber harvest in Oregon estimated with annual data for 31 years:

$$\ln(\text{HARVEST}) = \beta_1 + \beta_2 \ln(\text{HOUSESTART}) + \beta_3 \ln(\text{INDPROD})$$
$$+ \beta_4 \ln(\text{PRODPR}) + u$$

The estimated coefficients follow. The last column is the coefficient divided by its standard error.

Indep. Variable	Coeff. ($\hat{\beta}$)	$\hat{\beta}$/std. err.
CONSTANT	0.856	7.228
ln (HOUSESTART)	0.157	2.073
ln (INDPROD)	0.807	7.721
ln (PRODPR)	−0.415	−6.105

HOUSESTART is total housing construction in the United States in millions, INDPROD is an index of industrial production for paper and wood products, and PRODPR is an index of producer prices for all commodities.

a. *For the elasticity of INDPROD only* (call it β), test whether or not it is equal to 1. To do this, be sure to carry out the following steps:

(1) State the null and alternative hypotheses.

(2) Compute the test statistic.

(3) State its distribution and the *numerical value* of the d.f.

(4) State the decision rule for a 5 percent level of significance.

(5) State your conclusion whether the effect is elastic, inelastic, or unitary elastic.

b. Suppose HOUSESTART is measured in thousands instead of millions. How will this affect the coefficients (that is, the βs)? If anything is changed, write down the new value.

6.10   Using quarterly data for the United States for 10 years, which gives 40 observations, the following double-log model was first estimated:

$$\text{Model A:}\quad \widehat{\ln(\text{NUMCARS})} = -39.772 - 2.157 \ln(\text{PRICE})$$
$$+ 4.569 \ln(\text{INCOME})$$
$$+ 3.105 \ln(\text{POP})$$
$$- 0.160 \ln(\text{INTRATE})$$
$$- 0.000784 \ln(\text{UNEMP})$$

where NUMCARS is the number of cars sold, PRICE is a price index, INCOME is per-capita income, POP is total population, INTRATE is the prime interest rate, and UNEMP is the unemployment rate. To test the *joint hypothesis* that the coefficients for ln(UNEMP) and ln(POP) are *both* equal to zero, the following second model was estimated (the values in parentheses are the corresponding standard errors):

$$\text{Model B:} \quad \widehat{\ln(NUMCARS)} = -\underset{(5.544)}{28.069} - \underset{(0.230)}{1.557} \ln(PRICE)$$

$$+ \underset{(0.708)}{4.807} \ln(INCOME) - \underset{(0.058)}{0.208} \ln(INTRATE)$$

The error sum of squares for Model A is 0.309293, and for Model B it is 0.311974.

a.   Compute the numerical value of the test statistic for the preceding joint test (be sure to show your intermediate calculations).

b.   What is its distribution, including the degrees of freedom?

c.   Write down the critical value (or range) for a 10 percent test.

d.   Carry out the test and write down whether you reject the null hypothesis.

e.   Do you conclude from all this that the coefficients for the omitted variables are jointly significant or insignificant? (Explain why.)

f.   In Model B, I want to test the hypothesis that each of the elasticities is numerically equal to 1 or not (that is, ignoring the sign). Compute the numerical values of the test statistics for each of the elasticities (show your calculations).

g.   What is their distribution, including d.f.?

h.   Write down the critical value (or range) for a 5 percent test. (Don't ask whether this is a one-tail or two-tail test; you have the information needed in *f*.)

i.   Carry out the test and write down whether you reject or accept the null hypothesis that each of the elasticities is numerically 1 (show your work).

†6.11   The planning department of a city estimates the following relationship:

$$\widehat{\ln H_t} = \underset{(0.8)}{1.12} + \underset{(10.7)}{1.14} \ln Y_t + \underset{(1.5)}{0.96} \ln P_t$$

$$\overline{R}^2 = 0.98 \qquad T = 27$$

where H_t is the total number, at time t, of single-family dwellings; Y_t is aggregate income in constant dollars (that is, corrected for inflation); and P_t is the city's population. The values in parentheses are *t*-statistics.

a.   Test each of the regression coefficients for significance at the 1, 5, and 10 percent levels. Which are significant and at what levels?

b.   City Councilman A says, "This model is misspecified because per-capita income (Y_t/P_t) should be used *instead of* Y_t." Councilman B says, "Because the model is in double-log form, it doesn't matter whether you use Y_t or (Y_t/P_t) in its place. The models are *essentially identical*." Which of the councilmen is correct and why? If A is correct, what can you say about the bias, hypothesis tests, and so on? If B is correct, show how the regression coefficients of Councilman A's alternative model can be obtained from those given, *without rerunning the regression*.

c.   Councilman C says, "The model is misspecified because other variables that belong are omitted." List at least two important variables that ought to be there. Carefully examine the implications of this misspecification on (1) bias of estimates and forecasts and (2) validity of tests of hypothesis.

6.12 The model in Exercise 4.9 was estimated in double-log form, and the results are as follows (standard errors in parentheses):

$$\widehat{LCOLGPA} = -\underset{(0.378)}{1.753} + \underset{(0.082)}{0.511}\ LHSGPA + \underset{(0.051)}{0.129}\ LVSAT$$

$$+ \underset{(0.062)}{0.207}\ LMSAT$$

$$R^2 = 0.202 \qquad T = 427$$

A staff member at the registrar's office says, "The double-log model is inferior in goodness of fit and hence should be discarded." Is the staff member's claim right? Explain.

Suppose you want to test the hypothesis "The verbal and math SAT score elasticities are equal." Describe how each of the methods in Section 4.4 on testing a linear combination of coefficients would be used to test this hypothesis.

6.13 A labor economist wished to examine the effects of schooling and experience on earnings. Using cross-section data, she obtained the following relationships:

$$\widehat{\ln E} = \underset{(0.113)}{7.71} + \underset{(0.005)}{0.094S} + \underset{(0.009)}{0.023N} - \underset{(0.000187)}{0.000325N^2}$$

$$R^2 = 0.337 \qquad T = 60$$

where $\ln E$ is the natural logarithm of earnings, S is the number of years of schooling, and N is the number of years of experience. R^2 is unadjusted and the values in parentheses are standard errors.

a.   Test the hypothesis (state the null and alternate hypotheses) "Schooling has no effect on earnings." What do you conclude?

b.   Test the hypothesis (state the null and alternate hypotheses) "Neither schooling nor experience has any effect on earnings." (You have all the information needed to perform this test.)

c.   Describe how you would test the hypothesis "Experience has no effect on earnings." More specifically, state the null and alternative hypotheses; describe what additional regression(s), if any, you would run; write an expression for the test statistic; state its distribution, degrees of freedom, and the acceptance/rejection criterion.

d.   Write down or derive the expressions for the elasticity of earnings with respect to (1) schooling and (2) experience. What additional information, if any, do you need to compute these elasticities?

e.   Examine the consequences of measuring E in different units.

6.14 As part of a study on industrial employment in San Diego, the following equation was estimated using annual data for 22 years (value of $\overline{R}^2$ was 0.996):

$$\text{Model A:} \quad \widehat{\ln EMP}_t = -\underset{(-0.56)}{3.89} + \underset{(2.3)}{0.51}\ \ln INCM_t - \underset{(-1.7)}{0.25}\ \ln WAGE_t$$

$$+ \underset{(5.8)}{0.62}\ \ln GOVTEXP_t$$

where EMP is total employment, INCM is total income, WAGE is the average hourly wage rate, and GOVTEXP is the total expenditure of all local governments.

a. Do the signs of the coefficients (excluding the constant term) agree with intuition? Explain. (t-statistics are in parentheses.)
b. Test each of the regression coefficients for significance at the 1, 5, and 10 percent levels.
c. Suppose you had formulated the following alternative model (Model B):

$$\ln EMP = \alpha_0 + \alpha_1 \ln POP + \alpha_2 \ln PERCAPINCM + \alpha_3 \ln WAGE$$
$$+ \alpha_4 \ln GOVTEXP + error$$

and imposed the restriction $\alpha_1 = \alpha_2$ ahead of time. POP is San Diego population and PERCAPINCM = INCM/POP. Show how you would use Model A's estimates and estimate Model B *without rerunning*. In other words, write the estimates for α_1, α_2, α_3, and α_4.

6.15 Suppose you regress Y against a constant, X, and X^2 in a double-log model; that is, you regress $\ln Y$ against a constant, $X_1 = \ln X$, and $X_2 = \ln (X^2)$. Show that the model cannot be estimated because there is exact multicollinearity.

6.16 Using the data in DATA4-3, the following new variables were generated:

LH = ln(HOUSING)   LP = ln(POP)
LG = ln(GNP)   LU = ln(UNEMP)
LR = ln(INTRATE)

The following table has several estimated models. (LH is the dependent variable.)
a. Which of the three models is the "best"? Explain what you mean by "best."
b. In Model A, test the joint hypothesis (at the 5 percent level) that the coefficients for LP, LG, LU, and LR are all zero. State the null and alternative hypotheses, the test statistic, its distribution under the null hypothesis, and the criterion for acceptance/rejection. What do you conclude from the test?
c. Test each regression coefficient in Model A (except the constant term) for significance at the 5 percent level. Based on your results, would you recommend that some of the variables be omitted? If yes, what and why?
d. In Model A, test the joint hypothesis that the coefficients for LP and LU are zero. Based on your result would you recommend that these variables be omitted? Explain why or why not.

Variable	Model A	Model B	Model C
CONSTANT	4.607 (0.21)	−4.968 (−1.51)	−4.759 (−1.45)
LG	2.914 (1.23)	1.904 (3.86)	1.873 (3.79)
LP	−3.349 (−0.44)		
LU	0.319 (0.95)	0.198 (1.08)	
LR	−1.313 (−3.17)	−1.405 (−4.01)	−1.229 (−3.96)

(continued)

Variable	Model A	Model B	Model C
ESS	0.533	0.538	0.571
R^2	0.479	0.474	0.442
$\overline{R}^2$	0.363	0.391	0.386
F	4.140	5.699	7.907
d.f.	18	19	20
SGMASQ	0.0296	0.0283	0.0286
AIC	0.0358	0.0331	0.0322
FPE	0.0360	0.0333	0.0323
GCV	0.0378	0.0343	0.0328
HQ	0.0381	0.0348	0.0335
RICE	0.0410	0.0359	0.0336
SCHWARZ	0.0458	0.0404	0.0374
SHIBATA	0.0332	0.0315	0.0313

Note: Values in parentheses are the corresponding *t*-statistics—that is, the coefficient divided by its standard error.

6.17   You have data on the sale price (PRICE) in thousands of dollars, square feet of living area (SQFT), and square feet of the yard size (YARD) for a sample of 59 single-family homes sold recently. The basic model first estimated was

$$\text{PRICE} = \beta_1 + \beta_2 \, \text{SQFT} + \beta_3 \, \text{YARD} + u$$

You suspect that the terms ln(SQFT) and ln(YARD) should be added to the model. To perform an LM test for the addition of these variables, you obtained the following auxiliary regression:

$$\hat{u}_t = 3265 + 0.255 \, \text{SQFT} - 0.000485 \, \text{YARD} - 507 \, \text{ln(SQFT)} + 6.765 \, \text{ln(YARD)}$$
$$\quad (0.01) \quad (0.012) \qquad\quad (0.917) \qquad\qquad (0.011) \qquad\qquad (0.886)$$

Unadjusted $R^2 = 0.115$, $n = 59$, and the values in parentheses are *p*-values for a two-tailed test.
a.   Carefully describe how you must have obtained $\hat{u}_t$.
b.   Compute the test statistic and state its distribution and d.f.
c.   Use a 5 percent level of significance and actually carry out the test. What do you conclude?
d.   From the information given, write down a model you should estimate. Carefully justify your choice. [Note: This should not be the "kitchen sink" model.]

6.18   Consider the model

$$\text{COLGPA} = \beta_1 + \beta_2 \, \text{HSGPA} + \beta_3 \text{VSAT} + \beta_4 \, \text{MSAT} + u$$

where COLGPA and HSGPA are grade point averages at college and in high school, VSAT is the verbal SAT score, and MSAT is the math SAT score.

You want to test whether you should add the quadratic terms HSGPA^2, VSAT^2, and SAT^2, as well as appropriate variables that capture nonlinearities.
a.   First formulate another model (Model B) that will enable you to test the null hypothesis that the added variables in the previous paragraph have no significant effect. Be sure to define all new variables to be created.

b.   In Model B write down the null and alternative hypotheses to carry out the test specified in part a.

c.   Describe step-by-step how you will use the Wald test (not the LM test) to test the hypothesis specified above. More specifically, (1) describe what regressions to run, (2) how the test statistic is to be computed, (3) its distribution and d.f., (4) and the decision rule. Be sure to provide numerical values wherever available (use a 5% level for this and the next test).

d.   Describe step-by-step how you will use the Lagrange multiplier (LM) test to test the hypothesis specified in part a. More specifically, (1) describe what regressions to run, (2) how the test statistic is to be computed, (3) its distribution and d.f., (4) and the decision rule. Be sure to provide numerical values wherever available.

6.19   Consider the household consumption function (Model A) $C = \alpha + \beta Y + u$, where C and Y are household consumption expenditures and disposable income, respectively. You hypothesize that α is not a constant, but is a simple function of the family size, N, and that β is a function of both N and Y.

a.   Derive another econometric model (Model B) that incorporates all of these beliefs.

b.   State the null hypothesis on the parameters of Model B, which, if true, will make Model A the restricted model.

c.   Describe step-by-step the procedure for using the Lagrange multiplier (LM) test for testing your hypothesis. Wherever numerical values can be provided, you must state them and not use general symbols.

6.20   Consider the double-log model (*t*-subscript is omitted for simplicity)

$$\text{lhouse} = \beta_1 + \beta_2\text{lpcgnp} + \beta_3\text{lunemp} + \beta_4\text{lintrat} + u$$

where lhouse is the natural log of new housing starts in the United States, lpcgnp is the natural log of per-capita GNP, lunemp is ln(unemployment rate), and lintrat is ln(mortgage rate). Housing starts and per-capita GNP are in thousands, and the other two variables are percents. Using data for 23 periods, the following estimates and their standard errors were obtained:

Variable	Coefficient	Stderror
constant	−1.29838	1.27347
lpcgnp	2.31275	0.700321
lunemp	0.245648	0.186777
lintrat	−1.37653	0.331935

All the tests you are asked to conduct next should be at the 5 percent level.

a.   Test whether the elasticity with respect to per-capita GNP (β_2) is equal to 1 or not. Show all your steps and be sure to calculate the test statistic, stating its distribution, including d.f., and the decision rule. What is your conclusion in words? Is housing elastic or inelastic or unitary elastic with respect to GNP?

b.   Test whether the elasticity with respect to unemployment is equal to 0 or not. Show all your steps and be sure to calculate the test statistic, stating its distribution, including d.f., and the decision rule. What is your conclusion in words? Is housing elasticity with respect to unemp significant or not?

c.   Test whether the elasticity with respect to interest rate is equal to −1 or not. Show all your steps and be sure to calculate the test statistic, stating its distribution, including d.f., and the decision rule. What is your conclusion in words? Is housing elastic or inelastic or unitary elastic with respect to interest rate?

d. Suppose housing start data are converted to actual numbers instead of thousands and the new variable (called house*) is used instead of house in a double-log form. How will this unit change affect the estimates in the table? Indicate which coefficients will change and which ones will not. For the ones that change, write the new value.

Questions Requiring Computer Work

For details on data files, see Appendix D.

6.21   Business forecasters often fit time trends to economic data. The method is referred to as **trend-fitting.** Here there is no economic behavioral model, just the belief that past trends are likely to continue. The independent variable is therefore just t, defined as 1 for the first observation, 2 for the second observation, and so on up to n. Forecasters typically estimate a variety of alternative models, choose the one that best describes past data, and then use that to make projections for the future. The topic of forecasting is covered in more detail in Chapter 11, but it is useful to see how the various functional forms we have learned in this chapter can be used for fitting time trends.

The file DATA6-6 has the U.S. farm population as percent of the total population (call it Y_t) for the 44 years 1948–1991. Using your own regression program, generate the time trend variable t ($=$ year $-$ 1947), and estimate each of the following models:

(A)	Linear:	$Y_t = \beta_1 + \beta_2 t + u_t$
(B)	Quadratic:	$Y_t = \beta_1 + \beta_2 t + \beta_3 t^2 + u_t$
(C)	Cubic:	$Y_t = \beta_1 + \beta_2 t + \beta_3 t^2 + \beta_4 t^3 + u_t$
(D)	Linear-log:	$Y_t = \beta_1 + \beta_2 \ln t + u_t$
(E)	Reciprocal:	$Y_t = \beta_1 + \beta_2 (1/t) + u_t$
(F)	Log-linear:	$\ln(Y_t) = \beta_1 + \beta_2 t + u_t$
(G)	Log-reciprocal:	$\ln(Y_t) = \beta_1 + \beta_2 (1/t) + u_t$
(H)	Double-log:	$\ln(Y_t) = \beta_1 + \beta_2 \ln t + u_t$
(I)	Logistic:	$\ln[Y_t/(100 - Y_t)] = \beta_1 + \beta_2 t + u_t$

Use the estimated models to obtain the predicted values $\hat{Y}_t$. Then compute the mean absolute percent error (MAPE) for each model (refer to the discussion of this in Section 3.9). Use those and the model selection statistics to choose the best forecasting model. Note that for the models in which the dependent variable is in logarithmic form, you need the bias correction discussed in Section 6.8 (see Equation 6.8). You can also use each of the models to predict Y_t for the years 1992 onward and compare the predictions with actual values you may be able to obtain from the U.S. *Statistical Abstract* or the *Economic Report of the President.*

6.22   DATA6-5 has annual data on the determinants of the harvest of timber in Oregon during the years 1959–1989. Verify the estimated double-log model presented in Exercise 6.9, and test the model for overall goodness of fit. Omit all the variables with insignificant coefficients at the 10 percent level (ignore the constant term), reestimate the restricted model, and perform a Wald test for omission. Next reestimate the original model, and then omit one variable at a time until all variables have significant coefficients. In the final model, test whether each of the elasticities is equal to 1 (ignore the sign of the coefficient) against a two-sided alternative. Suppose HOUSTART is measured in thousands instead of in millions. Indicate which coefficients will change, and write down the new value(s).

6.23   Redo Exercise 4.11 using a double-log formulation. Carry out a similar exercise as in 6.22.

6.24   Redo Exercise 4.21 using a log-linear specification, and compare the results with those for a linear model.

6.25   Estimate a double-log version of the model you tried in Exercise 4.23, and carry out an analysis similar to 6.22. (Caution: Some of the variables have zero entries for which the logarithm is undefined. Use these variables linearly.)

6.26   Using your multiple regression program, enter the data in DATA4-5 and DATA4-6 and estimate your own alternative models, including any nonlinear terms that might make sense. Do you find any of them to be superior to the ones presented in Chapter 4?

6.27   Chapter 4 has numerous data sets. Take each of the data sets and examine whether any nonlinearities appear to make sense a priori. Use the three approaches to testing model specification described in Sections 6.13, 6.14, and 6.15 to subject your prior notions to diagnostic testing.

6.28   Use DATA3-12, DATA3-13, and DATA3-15 to fit time trends and carry out an analysis similar to that in Exercise 6.21.

More Details on LR, Wald, and LM Tests

This appendix provides theoretical details about the Wald, likelihood ratio, and Lagrange multiplier tests. Before reading this section, however, it is essential that you read Section 2.A.3 on the maximum likelihood principle and Section 3.A.5 on its application to the simple linear regression model. Although these three test procedures are applicable in general situations, we restrict our attention here to the regression context and, in particular, to a model of the following type:

$$y_t = \beta x_t + u_t \tag{6.A.1}$$

The lowercase letters denote the deviations of the variables from the corresponding means. As was seen in Section 4.A.1, the advantage of this approach is that it eliminates the constant term. Under the assumption that the us are normally distributed with mean zero and variance σ^2, the logarithm of the likelihood function for the set of observations $y_1, y_2, \ldots, y_n$ and the unknown parameter β can be written as follows (the procedure is analogous to the one in Section 3.A.5).

$$\ln L = -n \ln \sigma - n \ln(\sqrt{2\pi}) - \frac{\sum (y_t - \beta x_t)^2}{2\sigma^2} \tag{6.A.2}$$

The null hypothesis we examine is of the form $\beta = \beta_0$, and the alternative is $\beta \neq \beta_0$. When $\beta_0 = 0$, this is equivalent to asking whether the variable x belongs in the model. Each of the test procedures is discussed separately, and a geometric comparison of the methods is made. See the papers by Buse (1982) and Engle (1982), as well as Ramanathan (1993), for more details on the three tests.

6.A.1 Likelihood Ratio Test

In statistics, the classical test procedure is based on the *likelihood ratio*, which, in simple terms, is defined as the ratio of the maximum value of the likelihood function under the null hypothesis divided by its maximum value when no restrictions are imposed. More specifically, let $\hat{\beta}$ be the maximum likelihood estimator of the parameter. The likelihood function evaluated at these values is denoted by $L(\hat{\beta})$, ignoring σ^2. Let the likelihood function under the null hypothesis $\beta = \beta_0$ be $L(\beta_0)$. The likelihood ratio is defined as

$$\lambda = \frac{L(\beta_0)}{L(\hat{\beta})}$$

Because the denominator is based on the unrestricted model, its value cannot be smaller than that of the numerator. Therefore, $0 \leq \lambda \leq 1$. If the hypothesis were true, we would intuitively expect λ to be close to 1. If λ is far from 1, the likelihood ratio under the null is very different from that under the unrestricted model, which is the alternative. This suggests that we should reject the null hypothesis if λ is too small. The LR test is formulated as one of rejecting the null if $\lambda \leq K$, where K is determined by the condition that, under the null hypothesis, the probability that $0 \leq \lambda \leq K$ is equal to the level of significance (a); that is, $P(0 \leq \lambda \leq K | \beta = \beta_0) = a$.

In a number of cases, the critical region $\lambda \leq K$ can be translated into another form involving a well-known sample statistic such as the t-statistic or an F. In these situations, the LR test reduces to a t-, F-, or χ^2 test. For examples of these cases, the reader is referred to Mood, Graybill, and Boes (1974) and to Ramanathan (1993), Chapter 9. The various tests presented in Chapter 2 can be derived from this likelihood ratio principle. When λ cannot be conveniently transformed into another statistic whose distribution is known, a large-sample test is often used. It can be shown (see Ramanathan, 1993, p. 228) that, for large sample sizes, the statistic

$$\text{LR} = -2 \ln \lambda = 2 \ln L(\hat{\beta}) - 2 \ln L(\beta_0) \tag{6.A.3}$$

has a chi-square distribution with degrees of freedom equal to the number of restrictions, which is 1 in our example. The idea behind this test can be represented geometrically. In Fig. 6.A.1, the log of the likelihood function is graphed when there is only a single parameter in the model. The graph is below the axis because the log of the likelihood (which is a probability density less than 1) is negative. The point $\hat{\beta}$ corresponds to the case when the likelihood is maximum and β_0

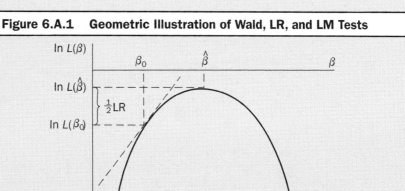

Figure 6.A.1   Geometric Illustration of Wald, LR, and LM Tests

corresponds to the null hypothesis. The LR test is based on the vertical difference, which is the same as one-half LR. If the vertical distance is large, the null hypothesis is rejected.

● EXAMPLE 6.A.1

The likelihood ratio test principle is illustrated for testing the hypothesis $\beta = 0$ in Equation (6.A.1). By proceeding as in Section 3.A.5 and using the notation in Section 3.2, we note that the unrestricted likelihood function L is maximized when $\hat{\beta} = S_{xy}/S_{xx}$ and $\hat{\sigma}^2 = \Sigma \hat{u}_i^2/n = \text{ESS}/n$, where ESS is the error sum of squares. The corresponding maximum value is

$$\hat{L} = \left(\frac{1}{\hat{\sigma}\sqrt{2\pi}}\right)^n \exp\left[-\sum \hat{u}_i^2/(2\hat{\sigma}^2)\right] = \left(\frac{1}{\hat{\sigma}\sqrt{2\pi}}\right)^n e^{-n/2}$$

Under the null hypothesis that $\beta = 0$, the model becomes $y_i = u_i$ and the likelihood function becomes

$$L(\sigma^2) = \left(\frac{1}{\sigma\sqrt{2\pi}}\right)^n \exp\left[-\sum u_i^2/(2\sigma^2)\right] = \left(\frac{1}{\sigma\sqrt{2\pi}}\right)^n \exp\left[-\sum y_i^2/(2\sigma^2)\right]$$

This is maximized when $\tilde{\sigma}^2 = \Sigma y_i^2/n = \text{TSS}/n$, where TSS is the total sum of squares. The maximum under the null is therefore given by

$$\tilde{L} = \left(\frac{1}{\tilde{\sigma}\sqrt{2\pi}}\right)^n e^{-n/2}$$

The likelihood ratio is $\lambda = \tilde{L}/\hat{L} = (\hat{\sigma}/\tilde{\sigma})^n = (\hat{\sigma}^2/\tilde{\sigma}^2)^{n/2}$. The LR test statistic is

$$\text{LR} = -2\ln\lambda = -n\ln(\hat{\sigma}^2/\tilde{\sigma}^2) = -n\ln(\text{ESS/TSS}) = -n\ln(1 - R^2)$$

where R^2 is the unadjusted R^2 of the unrestricted model.

For large samples, LR has a chi-square distribution with 1 d.f. We would reject the null hypothesis that $\beta = 0$ if $\text{LR} > K$, where K is the point on χ_1^2 such that the area to the right of K is the level of significance.

6.A.2 The Wald Test

Unlike the LR test, which used a vertical difference (see Fig. 6.A.1), the Wald test uses a horizontal squared distance measure. Specifically, the squared horizontal distance $(\beta - \beta_0)^2$, weighted by a function of the form $I(\hat{\beta})$, is used:

$$W = (\hat{\beta} - \beta_0)^2 I(\hat{\beta}) \tag{6.A.4}$$

where

$$I(\beta) = -E\left[\frac{\partial^2 \ln L}{\partial \beta^2}\right] \qquad \textbf{(6.A.5)}$$

is the expected value of the second derivative of the log-likelihood function with respect to β. It is a measure of the curvature of the log-likelihood function. The I function is known as the *information matrix*. The computational procedure for this test can be carried out by estimating a restricted model and an unrestricted model, as was done in Chapter 4, and constructing an F-statistic. The formal proof of this requires linear algebra (see Ramanathan, 1993, pp. 273–275).

● EXAMPLE 6.A.2

In the simple regression case, note that $\hat{\beta}$ is distributed as $N(\beta_0, \sigma^2/S_{xx})$. Therefore, $z = (\hat{\beta} - \beta_0)/(\sigma/\sqrt{S_{xx}})$ has the standard normal distribution, and hence z^2 is chi-square with 1 d.f. The Wald test statistic corresponding to the null hypothesis $\beta = 0$ is therefore given by $W = \hat{\beta}^2 S_{xx}/\hat{\sigma}^2$. From Equation (3.12) we have $\hat{\beta} S_{xx} = S_{xy}$. Also, we showed in Section 3.A.10 that $\hat{\beta} S_{xy} = $ RSS, the regression sum of squares. Using these two results, we have

$$W = \frac{\hat{\beta}(\hat{\beta} S_{xx})}{\text{ESS}/n} = \frac{n\,\text{RSS}}{\text{ESS}} = \frac{nR^2}{1 - R^2}$$

As in the LR test case, this has a chi-square distribution for a large sample. The null hypothesis will be rejected if W exceeds the critical value K derived in Example 6.A.1.

6.A.3 The Lagrange Multiplier Test

The LM test is based on the Lagrange multiplier technique for constrained optimization presented in Chapter 2. The restricted model is derived by imposing the condition that β is equal to β_0. This suggests that we maximize the logarithm of the likelihood function with respect to β and σ^2, *subject to the restriction $\beta = \beta_0$*. As we see from Section 2.A.2, this is equivalent to maximizing $\ln L(\beta) - \mu(\beta - \beta_0)$, where μ is the Lagrange multiplier. The first-order condition for maximization is

$$\frac{\partial \ln L}{\partial \beta} = \mu$$

If the null hypothesis $\beta = \beta_0$ is true, the restricted maximum likelihood estimators will be near the unrestricted estimates. We note that if the Lagrange multiplier, μ, is zero, then the equations give the maximum likelihood estimators. Hence, the Lagrange multiplier can be interpreted as being the "shadow price" of the constraint $\beta = \beta_0$. If the price is high, the constraint should be rejected as being inconsistent with the data. That is the motivation behind the LM test. The LM test is based on the partial derivative $(\partial \ln L)/\partial\beta$, which is known as the *score function* and is denoted by $S(\beta)$. Engle (1982) has formally derived the test statistic for a multiple regression model and shown that the test can be performed by running an auxiliary regression on the estimated residuals of the restricted model (also see Ramanathan, 1993, pp. 276–277). The steps for this are in Section 6.14. The LM test statistic is of the form

$$\text{LM} = S^2(\beta_0)\,I(\beta_0)^{-1} \tag{6.A.6}$$

We readily see from Fig. 6.A.1 that the score function, which is the partial derivative of the log likelihood, is the slope of the graph at the point β_0. The alternative hypothesis corresponds to $S(\beta) = 0$; that is, the slope is close to zero. Thus, the Wald test is based on the horizontal distance between $\hat{\beta}$ and β_0 in the graph, the LR test is based on the vertical distance, and the LM test is based on the slope of the curve at β_0. Each is a reasonable measure of the distance between the null and alternative hypotheses. Engle (1982) and Buse (1982) have shown independently that when the log-likelihood function is a quadratic (as is the case in Equation 6.A.2), all three test procedures give the same result. For a general linear model, there is an inequality among the three test criteria. This is given by

$$\text{W} \geq \text{LR} \geq \text{LM}$$

It follows that whenever the LM test rejects the null hypothesis of zero coefficients, so will the others. Similarly, whenever the Wald test fails to reject the null, other tests will too. Computationally, the LR test is the most cumbersome, unless it can be converted to a t-, F-, or χ^2 test. The other two tests are straightforward, as is seen in the text.

● EXAMPLE 6.A.3

In the simple regression case, the score function is given by

$$S = \frac{\partial \ln L}{\partial \beta} = \frac{\sum (y_t - \beta x_t) x_t}{\sigma^2} = \frac{\sum x_t u_t}{\sigma^2}$$

and its variance is $\Sigma x_t^2/\sigma^2 = S_{xx}/\sigma^2$. Therefore,

$$z^2 = \frac{S^2}{\text{Var}(S)} = \frac{\left(\sum x_t u_t\right)^2}{\sigma^2 S_{xx}} \sim \chi_1^2$$

The LM test statistic is therefore given by

$$\text{LM} = \frac{\left(\sum x_t \hat{u}_t\right)^2}{\tilde{\sigma}^2 S_{xx}}$$

Consider the auxiliary regression $\hat{u}_t = \gamma x_t + v_t$. Following steps similar to those in Example 6.A.1, the following equations are easily derived:

$$\hat{\gamma} = \frac{\sum x_t \hat{u}_t}{S_{xx}}, \qquad \mathrm{RSS}_{\mathrm{aux}} = \hat{\gamma} \sum x_t \hat{u}_t, \qquad \tilde{\sigma}^2 = \frac{\sum \hat{u}_t^2}{n}.$$

Substituting these in the LM test statistic, we have

$$\mathrm{LM} = n\left[\mathrm{RSS}_{\mathrm{aux}} \Big/ \left(\sum \hat{u}_t^2 \right) \right] = n[\mathrm{RSS}_{\mathrm{aux}} / \mathrm{TSS}_{\mathrm{aux}}] = nR_{\mathrm{aux}}^2$$

This establishes the result given in the text that the LM test statistic is equal to the number of observations multiplied by the unadjusted R^2 for the auxiliary regression. Although this proof is only for the simple regression case considered here, it is valid in the general multiple regression model also. For details, see Ramanathan (1993), pp. 276–278.

Qualitative (or Dummy) Independent Variables

*A*ll the variables we have encountered so far have been **quantitative** in nature; that is, they have numerically measurable attributes. The behavior of economic variables may, however, also depend on **qualitative** factors such as the gender of a person, educational status, season, public or private, and so on. As a specific example, consider the following simple regression model (for simplicity, the t-subscript has been omitted):

$$Y = \alpha + \beta X + u \tag{7.1}$$

Let Y be the consumption of energy in a given day and X be the average temperature. When temperature rises in the summer, we would expect energy consumption to go up. Hence, the slope coefficient β is likely to be positive. In the winter, however, as temperature rises from, say, 20 degrees to 40 degrees, there is less energy used for heating, and the consumption is likely to decrease as temperature increases. This suggests that β might be negative in the winter. Thus, the nature of the relationship between energy consumption and temperature can be expected to depend on the qualitative variable "season." In this chapter, we study the procedures for taking account of qualitative variables in estimation and hypothesis testing. We confine our attention to qualitative independent variables only. Chapter 12 discusses the case in which the dependent variable is qualitative.

7.1 Qualitative Variables with Two Categories Only

To start with, we consider the simplest case in which a qualitative variable has just two categories. For example, between two houses with the same characteristics, one might have a swimming pool whereas the other might not. Similarly, between two employees of a company with the same age, education, experience, and so on, one might be a male and the other a female. The important question in these examples is how to measure the gender impact on wages or the swimming pool impact on home prices. To motivate the theory, consider the wage example and let Y_t be the monthly wages of the tth employee of a company. For pedagogical simplicity let us ignore, for the time being, the effects of all other variables that affect wages and focus just on gender. Since gender is not a directly quantifiable variable, we define a **dummy variable** (call it D), which is a **binary variable** that takes the value 1 for a male employee and 0 for a female. We will see later that this is fundamentally equivalent to defining D to be 1 for a female and 0 for a male. The choice is therefore arbitrary. The group for which D is equal to 0 is called the **control group.** Table 7.1 has the monthly salary and the value of D for each of the 49 employees in DATA6-4, which we encountered in the previous chapter. Note that there are 26 males and 23 females. The overall average monthly salary is $1,820.20. However, if we separate employees by gender, the average salary is $2,086.93 for males and $1,518.70 for females (verify them). Does this mean that there is "gender discrimination" amounting to an average of $568.23 per month? The answer is clearly no because we have not controlled for other variables, such as experience, education, and so on. It is possible that female employees in this sample had fewer years of education and experience and hence had lower average salaries. We could try to identify male and female employees with identical experience or education and then compute average salaries. This is not only cumbersome but may be infeasible because there may be other characteristics such as ethnicity or type of job that we have to consider. This is where econometric analysis becomes a powerful tool. We would formulate and estimate a model using the dummy variable as one of the explanatory variables. The simplest form of this model is given by

$$Y_t = \alpha + \beta D_t + u_t \tag{7.2}$$

where there is no other explanatory variable (this is known as an **analysis of variance model**). We will gradually extend this to include employee characteristics

●   Table 7.1   Cross-Section Data on Monthly Salary and Gender

Y	D	Y	D	Y	D
1345	0	1566	0	2533	1
2435	1	1187	0	1602	0
1715	1	1345	0	1839	0
1461	1	1345	0	2218	1
1639	1	2167	1	1529	0
1345	0	1402	1	1461	1
1602	0	2115	1	3307	1
1144	0	2218	1	3833	1
1566	1	3575	1	1839	1
1496	1	1972	1	1461	0
1234	0	1234	0	1433	1
1345	0	1926	1	2115	0
1345	0	2165	0	1839	1
3389	1	2365	0	1288	1
1839	1	1345	0	1288	0
981	1	1839	0		
1345	0	2613	1		

other than just gender. We assume that the error term is well behaved and satisfies all the assumptions made in Chapter 3. We can take conditional expectations of Y for given D and obtain the equations

$$\text{Males:} \qquad E(Y_t|D = 1) = \alpha + \beta$$

$$\text{Females:} \qquad E(Y_t|D = 0) = \alpha$$

Thus, α is the average salary for the control group and β is the expected differential in average salary between the two groups, for the population as a whole.

We have seen in Chapter 3 that the normal equations for estimating Equation (7.2) are given as

$$\sum Y_t = n\hat{\alpha} + \hat{\beta}\sum D_t \tag{7.3}$$

$$\sum Y_t D_t = \hat{\alpha}\sum D_t + \hat{\beta}\sum D_t^2 = \hat{\alpha}\sum D_t + \hat{\beta}\sum D_t \tag{7.4}$$

Note that because D is a dummy variable that takes only the values 1 and 0, D^2 is the same as D. In Equation (7.4), ΣD_t on the right-hand side equals the number of male employees (call it n_m) and $\Sigma Y_t D_t$ on the left-hand side equals the sum of their wages. Dividing both sides by n_m, we get

$$\hat{\alpha} + \hat{\beta} = \overline{Y}_m \tag{7.5}$$

where $\overline{Y}_m$ is the average salary of male employees. Thus, the sum of the regression coefficients is an estimate of $E(Y_t|D = 1)$, the population mean of male salaries.

Because $\Sigma D_t = n_m$, Equations (7.3) and (7.4) can be rewritten as

$$\sum Y_t = n\hat{\alpha} + n_m\hat{\beta}$$

$$\sum Y_t D_t = n_m(\hat{\alpha} + \hat{\beta})$$

Subtracting the second equation from the first and canceling the common term on the right-hand side, we get

$$\sum Y_t - \sum Y_t D_t = (n - n_m)\hat{\alpha} = n_f\hat{\alpha}$$

where n_f is the number of female employees. Note that the left-hand side of the equation is simply the sum of the wages of female employees (sum of total salaries minus the sum of male salaries). Therefore, dividing both sides by n_f, we get $\hat{\alpha} = \overline{Y}_f$, the sample average female employee salary, which is an estimate of the population mean $E(Y_t|D = 0)$.

In summary, if we regress Y_t against a constant term and the dummy variable D_t, the intercept $\hat{\alpha}$ estimates the average female salary and the slope coefficient $\hat{\beta}$ estimates the differential between the average male and female salaries. From Practice Computer Session 7.1 (see Appendix Table D.1), we obtain the regression estimates as $\hat{\alpha} = 1,518.70$ and $\hat{\beta} = 568.23$. We thus see that the regression approach is equivalent to dividing the sample into the male and female groups and computing the respective average wages. However, as we will see in later sections, the regression method is more powerful because it can be applied even when employees differ in other characteristics, such as experience and education.

● **PRACTICE PROBLEM 7.1**[†]

Suppose the dummy variable had been defined as $D^* = 1$ for females and 0 for males and the variable D_i^* been used instead of D_i. In other words, consider the new model $Y_t = \alpha^* + \beta^* D_i^* + u_t$. Noting that $D^* = 1 - D$, derive the algebraic relations between the new regression coefficients and the old ones. More specifically, show how we can estimate α^* and β^* *without rerunning the regressions*. Would the standard errors, t-values, R^2, ESS, and the F-statistic be affected? If so, in what way?

Adding Quantitative Explanatory Variables

The next step in the analysis is to add explanatory variables that are quantifiable. To illustrate, let Y be the monthly salary as before but, in addition to the dummy variable D introduced earlier, add experience (call it X) as an explanatory variable. Note that we are now able to control for experience and ask the question "Between two employees with the same experience, is there a gender differential?" A simple way to answer this question is to let the intercept α in Equation (7.1) be different for males and females. This is done by assuming that $\alpha = \alpha_1 + \alpha_2 D$. For females, $D = 0$ and hence $\alpha = \alpha_1$. For males, $D = 1$ and hence $\alpha = \alpha_1 + \alpha_2$. It is readily seen that α_2 measures the differential in the intercept between the two groups. Substituting for α in Equation (7.1) we get the econometric model

$$Y = \alpha_1 + \alpha_2 D + \beta X + u \tag{7.6}$$

Note that α_1, α_2, and β are estimated by regressing Y against a constant, D, and X. The estimated relationships for the two groups are

$$\text{Females:} \qquad \hat{Y} = \hat{\alpha}_1 + \hat{\beta} X \tag{7.7}$$

$$\text{Males:} \qquad \hat{Y} = (\hat{\alpha}_1 + \hat{\alpha}_2) + \hat{\beta} X \tag{7.8}$$

Figure 7.1 graphs these relationships when the αs and β are positive. We notice that the estimated straight lines are parallel to each other. This is because we have assumed that both the groups have the same β. This assumption is relaxed in Section 7.3.

A natural hypothesis to test is that "there is no difference in the relationships between groups." Comparing Equations (7.7) and (7.8), we see that the relationships will be the same if $\alpha_2 = 0$. Thus, we have $H_0: \alpha_2 = 0$ and $H_1: \alpha_2 > 0$ or $\alpha_2 \neq 0$. The appropriate test is the t-test on α_2, which has $n - 3$ d.f.

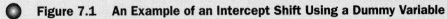

Figure 7.1   An Example of an Intercept Shift Using a Dummy Variable

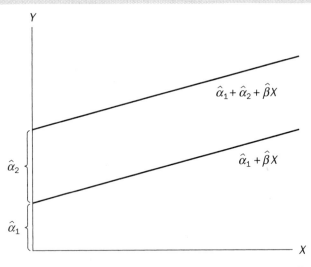

● EXAMPLE 7.1

Using DATA7-2 described in Appendix D, we estimated Equation (7.6) as follows (entries in parentheses are the p-values):

$$\widehat{WAGE} = 1366.27 + 525.63\, D + 19.81\ EXPER$$
$$\hphantom{WAGE = 13}(<0.01)\hphantom{m}(0.003)\hphantom{mmmm}(0.152)$$

$$\overline{R}^2 = 0.197 \qquad n = 49 \qquad F_c(2,\,46) = 6.90$$

To reproduce these results, try Practice Computer Session 7.2. The p-value for the dummy variable is very small, indicating high significance. Thus, controlling for experience, there is a significant gender differential in average salaries. The p-value for experience indicates insignificance at even the 0.15 level. This result should not be taken too seriously, however, because the model does not include other explanatory variables such as education and age and hence the estimates are biased. Also, the dependent variable should have been expressed as a logarithm (refer to Section 6.8). In Section 7.3, we present a more general analysis of the determinants of wage, including the effects of a number of qualitative variables.

● EXAMPLE 7.2

DATA7-3 has additional data on the 14 single-family houses, all of which are dummy variables. POOL takes the value 1 if a house has a swimming pool, 0 otherwise. Similarly, FAMROOM stands for the presence of a family room, and FIREPL represents the presence of a fireplace. One might expect that a house that has these characteristics might command a higher price than a similar house without these amenities. Table 7.2 has the estimated coefficients and related statistics for a number of models, including Model A, which we estimated earlier (the results can be duplicated with the help of Practice Computer Session 7.3).

Comparing Model A with Model E, which has all the new variables, we note that $\overline{R}^2$ has increased from 0.806 to 0.836, but that four of the model selection criteria have worsened. RICE is undefined because it requires that the number of observations be greater than twice the number of coefficients estimated, which is not the case here. The t-statistic for POOL is 2.411, which is significant at levels below 1 percent. The regression coefficients for BEDRMS, BATHS, FAMROOM, and FIREPL are, however, insignificant even at levels well above 25 percent (verify it). In Model F these insignificant variables have been eliminated and the model reestimated. Using Model E as the unrestricted model and Model F as the restricted model, we can perform a Wald F-test to test the null hypothesis that the regression coefficients for BEDRMS, BATHS, FAMROOM, and FIREPL are zero. The computed F-statistic is

$$F_c = \frac{(9,455 - 9,010) \div 4}{9,010 \div 7} = 0.086$$

Table 7.2   Effect of Dummy Variables on Home Price

Variable	Model A	Model E	Model F
CONSTANT	52.351 (1.404)	39.057 (0.436)	22.673 (0.768)
SQFT	0.13875 (7.407)	0.147 (4.869)	0.144 (10.118)
BEDRMS		−7.046 (−0.245)	
BATHS		−0.264 (−0.006)	
POOL		53.196 (2.411)	52.790 (3.203)
FAMROOM		−21.345 (−0.498)	
FIREPL		26.188 (0.486)	
$\overline{R}^2$	0.806	0.836	0.890
ESS	18,274	9,010	9,455
d.f.	12	7	11
SGMASQ	1,523	1,287	860*
AIC	1,737	1,749	1,037*
FPE	1,740	1,931	1,044*
HQ	1,722	1,698	1,024*
SCHWARZ	1,903	2,408	1,189*
SHIBATA	1,678	1,287	965*
GCV	1,777	2,574	1,094*
RICE	1,827	undefined	1,182*

Note: Models B, C, and D are in Table 4.2. Values in parentheses are corresponding t-statistics.
*Denotes the model that is "best" for that criterion.

which has the F-distribution with 4 and 7 d.f. It is readily seen that F_c is not significant even at levels above 0.25. We therefore conclude that the corresponding regression coefficients are not jointly significant.

If these variables are omitted, we see that the t-statistics for SQFT and POOL are much higher. Also, $\overline{R}^2$ rises to 0.89. Thus, elimination of the insignificant variables has improved the overall performance of the model. It should be emphasized that the conclusion is not that the omitted variables are unimportant, only that, *holding* SQFT and POOL *unchanged*, the inclusion of BEDRMS, BATHS, FAMROOM, and FIREPL does not add to the explanatory power of the model. At least some of the effects of the excluded variables are captured by the variables already in the model. In Model F the coefficient for POOL is 52.790, which implies that between two houses with the same square feet of living area, the one with a pool is expected to sell, on average, for $52,790 more than a house without a pool. Considering the cost of installing a pool, this value appears excessively high. A possible explanation is that, along with a swimming pool, these houses might also contain a jacuzzi, a decked patio, or other such features. Thus, the dummy variable POOL might really be a proxy for many other improvements.

● PRACTICE PROBLEM 7.2

In Section 6.2, we argued that the marginal effect of SQFT on PRICE might decrease as SQFT increases. This suggested using ln(SQFT) instead of SQFT. Using your regression program, reestimate Models A, E, and F in Table 7.2 using ln(SQFT) instead of SQFT. Are the results superior? Next try including SQFT also. Do the results improve or worsen? Derive an expression for the *marginal* effect of SQFT on PRICE. (Practice Computer Session 7.4 will be useful in carrying this out.)

Empirical Example: Pay and Performance in Major League Baseball

Sommers and Quinton (1982) carried out a study of the pay and performance in major league baseball in which dummy variables were used to account for qualitative variables such as National League teams, pennant-winning teams, whether a stadium is older or newer, and so on. Before discussing their results, it would be useful to present some background.

The baseball industry is characterized by *monopsony* (or *oligopsony*), in which team owners exercise some degree of control over players' salaries. Until 1975, a baseball player's unsigned contract could be perpetually renewed by the owners. In that year, however, labor arbitrator Peter Seitz ruled that players could seek employment with different owners after playing one year without a signed agreement. Because players could now seek a competitive bidding for their services, we might expect that their wages would be closer to the respective marginal revenue product (the extra revenue per extra hour of labor). More specifically, let R be the total team revenue. Then net profits are $\pi = R - wL - rK$, where L is labor in worker-hours, K represents all other inputs, w is the wage rate, and r is the rental rate. A profit-maximizing team owner would set $\Delta\pi/\Delta L$ to zero, which gives the condition $\Delta R/\Delta L = w$. The left-hand side is the marginal revenue product. Thus, for profits to be maximized, wages should equal the marginal revenue product.

Sommers and Quinton estimated the contribution of a number of individual players toward the marginal revenue and compared this estimate to the players' salaries as free agents. The following two equations were estimated separately using cross-section observations for 50 teams in a number of SMSAs (Standard Metropolitan Statistical Areas) for the years 1976 and 1977:

$$\widehat{PCTWIN} = \underset{(1.97)}{188.45} + \underset{(2.90)}{256.33\ TSA^*} + \underset{(2.85)}{80.87\ TSW^*} - \underset{(-2.62)}{55.33\ XPAN}$$

$$+ \underset{(4.90)}{51.34\ CONT} - \underset{(-6.14)}{72.07\ OUT}$$

$$R^2 = 0.892 \qquad \text{d.f.} = 44$$

$$\widehat{REVENUE} = \underset{(-1.12)}{-2{,}297{,}500} + (\underset{(4.54)}{22{,}736} - \underset{(-1.65)}{2{,}095\ SMSA} + \underset{(3.22)}{415\ SMSA^2})PCTWIN$$

$$\underset{(-0.45)}{-313{,}700\ STD} + \underset{(2.70)}{4{,}298{,}900\ XPAN} - \underset{(-3.74)}{3{,}750{,}200\ TWOTM}$$

$$\underset{(-0.08)}{-2{,}513\ BBPCT}$$

$$R^2 = 0.704 \qquad \text{d.f.} = 42$$

where
  PCTWIN = 100 times the ratio of games won to games played
  REVENUE = Home attendance times average ticket price plus estimated
        concession income plus revenue from broadcasting rights
  TSA* = Team slugging average (total bases divided by total at bats) as a ratio
        to the average for the relevant division of the league
  TSW* = Team strikeout-to-walk ratio (strikeouts divided by walks) to similar
        ratio for league
  XPAN = 1 if the team is an expansion club, 0 otherwise
  CONT = 1 for pennant or divisional winners, 0 for others
  OUT = 1 for teams that were 20 or more games out of first place at the end
        of the season, 0 for others
  SMSA = The population of the SMSA
  STD = 1 if the stadium is older, 0 otherwise
  TWOTM = 1 if the team shares a home SMSA with another team
  BBPCT = Percentage of black players on the team

To allow for an interaction between PCTWIN and the size of the SMSA in the revenue function, the authors assumed that $\Delta REVENUE/\Delta PCTWIN$ is a quadratic function of SMSA. Because the focus in this example is only on the dummy variables, we do not interpret any of the other results. Sommers and Quinton used these estimated equations to calculate the marginal revenue products of 14 players and compared them with the corresponding salaries. Their conclusion was that, contrary to popular opinion, the ballplayers were grossly underpaid.

In the PCTWIN equation all the dummy variables were significant. Expansion clubs finished, on average, 55 points lower. Out-of-first-place teams had 72 fewer points, on average. In the REVENUE equation STD was not significant, indicating that it did not matter whether a stadium was older or newer. The significance of TWOTM and its negative value indicate, not surprisingly, that having a second team in the same city is detrimental to revenue.

● 7.2 Qualitative Variable with Many Categories

The number of possible categories in a qualitative variable might be more than two. For example, let Y be the savings of a household and X be its income. We would expect the relationship between savings and income to be different for different age groups. For a given income, a young household might spend more, on average, than one headed by a middle-aged person. This is because the latter might save more for educating the children and for retirement. A retired family is likely to spend more, on average, because the need to save for the future is reduced. If we have the exact age of the head of a household, this can be entered in a model as a quantitative variable. If, however, only the age group is known (for example, whether the head belongs to the age group under 25, 25 to 55, or over 55), how do we account for the qualitative variable "age group of the head of household"? The procedure here is to choose one of the groups as the control group and define dummy variables for the other two groups. More specifically, we define

$$A_1 = \begin{cases} 1 & \text{if the head of the household is 25 to 55} \\ 0 & \text{otherwise} \end{cases} \tag{7.9}$$

$$A_2 = \begin{cases} 1 & \text{if the head of the household is over 55} \\ 0 & \text{otherwise} \end{cases} \tag{7.10}$$

The control group (that is, the one for which both A_1 and A_2 are zero) is all the households for which the head is under 25 years of age. To allow for α to be different for the different groups, we assume that $\alpha = \alpha_0 + \alpha_1 A_1 + \alpha_2 A_2$. Substituting this into Equation (7.1) we get

$$Y = \alpha_0 + \alpha_1 A_1 + \alpha_2 A_2 + \beta X + u \tag{7.11}$$

For a young household, $A_1 = A_2 = 0$. For the middle-aged group, $A_1 = 1$ and $A_2 = 0$. For the oldest age group, $A_1 = 0$ and $A_2 = 1$. The estimated models for the three groups are as follows:

$$\text{Age} < 25\text{:} \quad \hat{Y} = \hat{\alpha}_0 + \hat{\beta}X \tag{7.12}$$

$$\text{Age } 25\text{--}55\text{:} \quad \hat{Y} = (\hat{\alpha}_0 + \hat{\alpha}_1) + \hat{\beta}X \tag{7.13}$$

$$\text{Age} > 55\text{:} \quad \hat{Y} = (\hat{\alpha}_0 + \hat{\alpha}_2) + \hat{\beta}X \tag{7.14}$$

$\hat{\alpha}_1$ is an estimate of the difference in intercept between a young and a middle-aged household. $\hat{\alpha}_2$ is an estimate of the difference between a young and an old household. Thus, *the intercept shifters are the deviations from the control group.* The estimated lines will be parallel to each other.

Table 7.3   Sample Data Values with Several Qualitative Variables

t	Y	const	X	A_1	A_2	H	E_1	E_2	O_1	O_2	O_3	O_4
1	Y_1	1	X_1	1	0	1	1	0	0	1	0	0
2	Y_2	1	X_2	1	0	0	0	0	0	0	0	1
3	Y_3	1	X_3	0	0	0	0	1	0	0	0	0
4	Y_4	1	X_4	0	1	0	1	0	0	0	1	0
5	Y_5	1	X_5	0	1	0	1	0	0	1	0	0

There is a special reason for not defining a third dummy variable, A_3, that takes the value 1 for a young household and 0 for others. If we had assumed that $\alpha = \alpha_0 + \alpha_1 A_1 + \alpha_2 A_2 + \alpha_3 A_3$, we would have exact multicollinearity because $A_1 + A_2 + A_3$ is always equal to 1, which is the constant term (see Table 7.3). This is known as the **dummy variable trap**. To avoid this problem, *the number of dummy variables is always one less than the number of categories* (see Practice Problem 7.3 for an exception to this). Thus, if we wanted to capture seasonal differences between electricity consumption and temperature, we would define three dummy variables (because there are four seasons). To capture monthly differences, we need 11 dummy variables.

Several hypotheses are of interest here. To test the hypothesis that the senior age group behaves like the young household, we simply carry out a t-test on $\hat{\alpha}_2$. To test the hypothesis that "there is no difference in the savings function due to age," the hypothesis is H_0: $\alpha_1 = \alpha_2 = 0$ and the alternative is H_1: at least one of the coefficients is nonzero. This hypothesis is tested using the Wald test described in Section 4.4. The unrestricted model will be Equation (7.11), and the restricted model is $Y = \alpha_0 + \beta X + u$. The Wald F, derived from the respective sums of squares, will have d.f. 2 and $n - 4$. The hypothesis that "there is no difference in behavior between the middle- and the old-age groups" implies that $\alpha_1 = \alpha_2$. This can be tested using the three methods described in Section 4.4. To apply the Wald test, impose this condition on Equation (7.11). We get the restricted model

$$Y = \alpha_0 + \alpha_1 A_1 + \alpha_1 A_2 + \beta X + u \qquad (7.15)$$

$$= \alpha_0 + \alpha_1(A_1 + A_2) + \beta X + u$$

The procedure for estimating the restricted model is to create a new variable, $Z = A_1 + A_2$, and regress Y against a constant, Z, and X. A Wald test is then carried out between this and Equation (7.11) by comparing the sums of squares of the estimated residuals. The F-statistic will now have d.f. 1 and $n - 4$.

● PRACTICE PROBLEM 7.3

Suppose we had used the third dummy variable A_3 just defined and formulated the model as $Y = \beta_1 A_1 + \beta_2 A_2 + \beta_3 A_3 + \beta X + u$, *without a constant term*. Show that there is no problem here with exact multicollinearity. Describe how estimates of the αs can be obtained from estimates of the βs.

● PRACTICE PROBLEM 7.4[†]

Choose a different age group as the control—say, the middle—and reformulate the model. How are the estimates of the new model related to those in Equation (7.11)? More specifically, derive the estimates of your new model from those for Equation (7.11). Describe how the tests of the hypotheses specified may be conducted in this new formulation.

Several Qualitative Variables

The dummy variable analysis is easily extended to the case in which there are several qualitative variables, some of which may have more than one category. To illustrate, consider the savings function described earlier in which Y is household savings and X is household income. One can hypothesize that besides the age of the head, other factors such as home ownership, education level, occupation status, and so on are also important determinants of household savings. Suppose, for instance, we have information that the household head has a postgraduate degree, a bachelor's degree only, or a high school education. Further, suppose we know that the occupation of the head is one of the following categories: managerial or executive, skilled worker, unskilled worker, clerical, self-employed businessperson or professional. Also, the exact age of head is unknown; we know only which age group he or she belongs to. How do we incorporate these variables into the analysis? The procedure is to define as many dummy variables as needed and enter them all in the model. The unrestricted model would be as follows:

$$Y = \beta_0 + \beta_1 A_1 + \beta_2 A_2 + \beta_3 H + \beta_4 E_1 + \beta_5 E_2 + \beta_6 O_1 \qquad (7.16)$$
$$+ \beta_7 O_2 + \beta_8 O_3 + \beta_9 O_4 + \beta_{10} X + u$$

where

$$A_1 = \begin{cases} 1 & \text{if the age of head is between 25 and 55} \\ 0 & \text{otherwise} \end{cases}$$

$$A_2 = \begin{cases} 1 & \text{if the age of head is over 55} \\ 0 & \text{otherwise} \end{cases}$$

$$H = \begin{cases} 1 & \text{if the household owns the house} \\ 0 & \text{otherwise} \end{cases}$$

$$E_1 = \begin{cases} 1 & \text{if the household head has a postgraduate degree} \\ 0 & \text{otherwise} \end{cases}$$

$$E_2 = \begin{cases} 1 & \text{if the household head has a bachelor's degree only} \\ 0 & \text{otherwise} \end{cases}$$

$$O_1 = \begin{cases} 1 & \text{if the household head is a manager} \\ 0 & \text{otherwise} \end{cases}$$

$$O_2 = \begin{cases} 1 & \text{if the household head is a skilled worker} \\ 0 & \text{otherwise} \end{cases}$$

$$O_3 = \begin{cases} 1 & \text{if the household head is a clerical worker} \\ 0 & \text{otherwise} \end{cases}$$

$$O_4 = \begin{cases} 1 & \text{if the household head is self-employed} \\ 0 & \text{otherwise} \end{cases}$$

It should be noted that the control groups are as follows: age of head under 25, unskilled workers, and households whose head had a high school education only. An example of a data matrix is given in Table 7.3. The estimation of the parameters is done by regressing Y against a constant term, A_1, A_2, H, E_1, E_2, O_1, O_2, O_3, O_4, and X (additional quantitative variables are easily added if the model calls for them). Home-ownership status is tested with a t-test on β_3 (with $n - 11$ d.f.). Educational status is tested with a Wald test under the null hypothesis that $\beta_4 = \beta_5 = 0$. The unrestricted model is Equation (7.16), and the restricted model is the one obtained by omitting E_1 and E_2 from (7.16). The degrees of freedom for the F-statistic would be 2 and $n - 11$. Similarly, to test whether occupational status matters in explaining variations in savings, the Wald test is used for the null hypothesis that $\beta_6 = \beta_7 = \beta_8 = \beta_9 = 0$. Many other tests are possible; these are left as exercises for the reader.

● PRACTICE PROBLEM 7.5

Write the estimated relation for a middle-aged household that owns the home and whose head has a B.A. degree and works as a clerical worker.

● PRACTICE PROBLEM 7.6†

Describe, step-by-step, how each of the following tests of hypotheses is carried out: (a) "The saving behavior of clerical workers is the same as those of skilled workers," and (b) "Occupational status has no significant effect on saving behavior." More specifically, describe the regression(s) to run, the test statistics to compute, the distribution of the statistics under the null hypothesis (including the degrees of freedom), and the criterion for rejection of the null hypothesis.

Analysis of Variance Models*

It is possible for all the independent variables in a model to be binary. Such models are known as **analysis of variance (ANOVA) models.** They are common in agricultural economics, market research, sociology, and psychology. In this section, we introduce ANOVA models only briefly. For more details, refer to a book on statistics or experimental designs.

Consider an agricultural experiment in which the investigator plans to study the average yield per acre due to three types of hybrid seeds treated with four different doses of fertilizer. The designer of the experiment divides a large area of land into a number of plots and applies, at random, various combinations of seeds and doses. The observed yield in each plot is then related to the corresponding type of seed and the dose of fertilizer. An experiment designer would formulate the model as follows:

$$Y_{ijk} = \mu + a_j + b_k + \varepsilon_{ijk}$$

where Y_{ijk} is the observed yield in the ith plot using the jth seed ($j = 1, 2, 3$) and kth dose of fertilizer ($k = 1, 2, 3, 4$), μ is the "grand mean," a_j is the "seed effect," and b_k is the "fertilizer effect." ε_{ijk} is an unobservable random error term. Thus, the average yield is composed of an overall effect common to all plots, which is modified by the type of seed and fertilizer dosage in a particular plot. Because a_j and b_k are deviations from the overall mean, we have the conditions $\Sigma a_j = \Sigma b_k = 0$. Due to these constraints, the eight parameters (μ, three as, and four bs) reduce, in effect, to only six. This model is written as follows for selected combinations:

$$Y_{i12} = \mu + a_1 + b_2 + \varepsilon_{i12}$$

$$Y_{i34} = \mu + a_3 + b_4 + \varepsilon_{i34}$$

The same model can be formulated with only dummy variables. For the seed varieties, define two dummy variables: $S_1 = 1$ if the first seed variety is chosen, 0 otherwise; $S_2 = 1$ if the second seed variety is chosen, 0 otherwise. Similarly, define three dummy variables for the fertilizer doses: $D_1 = 1$ when the first dose is used, $D_2 = 1$ for the second dose, and $D_3 = 1$ for the third dose. Note that the control group is the third variety of seed and the fourth dose. The econometric formulation is

$$Y = \alpha_0 + \alpha_1 S_1 + \alpha_2 S_2 + \beta_1 D_1 + \beta_2 D_2 + \beta_3 D_3 + u$$

Here also there are six unknown parameters to estimate. For the two combinations listed above, the model becomes

$$Y = \alpha_0 + \alpha_1 + \beta_2 + u \qquad (S_1 = D_2 = 1, \ S_2 = D_1 = D_3 = 0)$$

$$Y = \alpha_0 + u \qquad (S_1 = S_2 = D_1 = D_2 = D_3 = 0)$$

In comparing the two approaches, we note that $\alpha_0 + \alpha_1 + \beta_2 = \mu + a_1 + b_2$ and $\alpha_0 = \mu + a_3 + b_4$. It is possible to show a one-to-one correspondence between the econometric model and the experimental design model. The hypothesis that there is no difference among the seeds can be translated as $a_1 = a_2 = a_3 = 0$, or equivalently as $\alpha_1 = \alpha_2 = 0$. Similarly, the hypothesis that there is no difference in yield due to fertilizer dose can be tested by either $b_1 = b_2 = b_3 = b_4 = 0$ or $\beta_1 = \beta_2 = \beta_3 = 0$.

● PRACTICE PROBLEM 7.7

Write all the relations between as, bs, and αs, βs; solve for each a and each b in terms of the αs and βs; and show how the experimental design formulation can be derived from the econometric formulation.

● 7.3 The Effect of Qualitative Variables on the Slope Term (Analysis of Covariance)

Shifts in the Slope Term Only

In this section, we allow for the possibility that β might be different for different qualitative variables. Such models are known as **analysis of covariance models.** For instance, in the wage example, how can we test the hypothesis that β is different between males and females? We first assume that the intercept α is unchanged. (This is relaxed in the next section.) The procedure is analogous to the case in which the intercept shifted between categories. Let $\beta = \beta_1 + \beta_2 D$, where $D = 1$ for males and 0 for females. Equation (7.1) now becomes

$$Y = \alpha + (\beta_1 + \beta_2 D)X + u \tag{7.17}$$

$$= \alpha + \beta_1 X + \beta_2(DX) + u$$

$\beta_2 DX$ represents the interaction term described in Section 6.5. To estimate the model, we multiply the dummy variable by X and create a new variable, $Z = DX$. Then we regress Y against a constant term, X, and Z. The estimated relations are as follows (they are graphed in Fig. 7.2, under the assumption that α and the βs are all positive):

$$\text{Females:} \qquad \hat{Y} = \hat{\alpha} + \hat{\beta}_1 X \tag{7.18}$$

$$\text{Males:} \qquad \hat{Y} = \hat{\alpha} + (\hat{\beta}_1 + \hat{\beta}_2) X \tag{7.19}$$

Because the intercept is assumed to be the same, the straight lines start from the same point but have different slopes. If a female employee gains one more year of experience, she is expected to earn an average of $\hat{\beta}_1$ dollars more in wages. Males with one more year of experience are expected to earn, on average, $\hat{\beta}_1 + \hat{\beta}_2$ more per month. Thus, $\hat{\beta}_2$ measures the difference in the estimated slopes.

The procedure for hypothesis testing is also similar to the previous case, in which only the intercept was shifted. A t-test on β_2 (d.f. $n - 3$) will test that there is no difference in the slopes.

● **Figure 7.2   An Example of a Slope Shift Using a Dummy Variable**

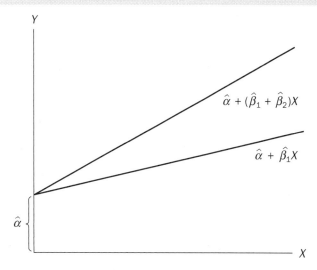

Shifts in Both the Intercept and Slope Terms

Allowing for shifts in both the intercept and the slope is a straightforward procedure. We simply let $\alpha = \alpha_1 + \alpha_2 D$ and $\beta = \beta_1 + \beta_2 D$. Substituting this into Equation (7.1), we get the unrestricted model as

$$Y = \alpha_1 + \alpha_2 D + (\beta_1 + \beta_2 D)X + u \tag{7.20}$$
$$= \alpha_1 + \alpha_2 D + \beta_1 X + \beta_2 (DX) + u$$

Regress Y against a constant, D, X, and the interaction term DX. The estimated relations for the two groups are

$$\text{Males:} \qquad \hat{Y} = (\hat{\alpha}_1 + \hat{\alpha}_2) + (\hat{\beta}_1 + \hat{\beta}_2)X \tag{7.21}$$

$$\text{Females:} \qquad \hat{Y} = \hat{\alpha}_1 + \hat{\beta}_1 X \tag{7.22}$$

Figure 7.3 graphs these relationships when all the αs and βs are positive. In order to test the hypothesis that there is no difference in the entire relationship, we have H_0: $\alpha_2 = \beta_2 = 0$. The test is the Wald F-test, with Equation (7.20) as the unrestricted model and $Y = \alpha_1 + \beta_1 X + u$ as the restricted model. The F-statistic will have 2 and $n - 4$ d.f.

Interpreting Dummy Coefficients in a Log-Linear Model

In Section 6.8 we introduced the log-linear model in which the dependent variable is $\ln(Y)$. 100 multiplied by a regression coefficient was interpreted as the average *percent change* in Y for a *unit change* in the corresponding independent variable. If,

●   **Figure 7.3   An Example of a Shift in the Intercept and Slope**

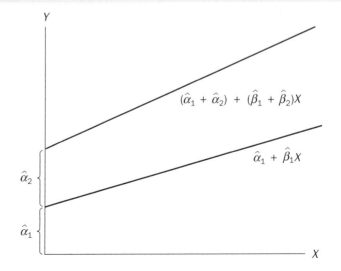

however, the independent variable is a dummy variable, that interpretation is not valid. To see this, consider the model

$$\ln(Y) = \beta_1 + \beta_2 X + \beta_3 D + u$$

where D is a dummy variable. Taking the antilog of this, we get $Y = \exp(\beta_1 + \beta_2 X + \beta_3 D + u)$, where exp is the exponential function. Denote, by Y_1, the dependent variable when $D = 1$, and by Y_0, the value when $D = 0$. Then the percent change between the two categories is $100(Y_1 - Y_0)/Y_0 = 100\,[\exp(\beta_3) - 1]$. The initial impulse is to estimate $\exp^{\beta_3}$ by $\exp^{\hat{\beta}_3}$. However, this is not the appropriate measure, the reason for which was discussed in Section 6.8. The correct measure adjusted for the bias in $\exp^{\hat{\beta}_3}$ is $\exp[\hat{\beta}_3 - \frac{1}{2}\widehat{\mathrm{Var}}(\hat{\beta}_3)]$, where $\widehat{\mathrm{Var}}$ is the estimated variance. We thus have

$$100(\hat{Y}_1/\hat{Y}_0 - 1) = 100\left\{\exp[\hat{\beta}_3 - \tfrac{1}{2}\widehat{\mathrm{Var}}(\hat{\beta}_3)] - 1\right\}$$

If the model has an interactive term so that it becomes

$$\ln(Y) = \beta_1 + \beta_2 X + \beta_3 D + \beta_4 DX + u$$

the corresponding expression is much more complicated. Verify that, in this case, it is

$$100(\hat{Y}_1/\hat{Y}_0 - 1) = 100\left\{\exp[\hat{\beta}_3 + \hat{\beta}_4 X - \tfrac{1}{2}\widehat{\mathrm{Var}}(\hat{\beta}_3 + \hat{\beta}_4 X)] - 1\right\}$$

The variance expression depends on the value of X and also involves a linear combination of random variables. It is readily seen that, when the model has an interactive term between a dummy variable and quantitative variable, the interpretation of the effect of the dummy variable is much more cumbersome.

Although the interpretation of the effect of a dummy variable requires modification in the case of a log-linear model, the marginal effect of a quantitative variable is quite straightforward. We have, $\partial \ln(\hat{Y})/\partial X = \hat{\beta}_2 + \hat{\beta}_4 D$. This gives, using Property 6.2c,

$$100\,\frac{\Delta Y}{Y} = 100(\hat{\beta}_2 + \hat{\beta}_4 D)\,\Delta X$$

It follows that $100\hat{\beta}_2$ is the approximate *percent of change* in Y for a *unit change* in X when $D = 0$ and that $100(\hat{\beta}_2 + \hat{\beta}_4)$ is the approximate percent of change in Y for a unit change in X when $D = 1$.

7.4   Application: Covariance Analysis of the Wage Model

The walk-through application chosen here is the one we used in Example 6.5, namely, the relationship between wages and characteristics of employees. However, there we used only education, experience, age, and their squares. The basic log-linear model was

$$(A) \qquad \ln(\text{WAGE}) = \alpha + \beta\,\text{EDUC} + \gamma\,\text{EXPER} + \delta\,\text{AGE} + u$$

We have seen from earlier analysis that the value of $\overline{R}^2$ for Model A is 0.283, which means that the three explanatory variables explain only 28.3 percent of the variation in ln(WAGE). As pointed out before, this is unimpressive even for a cross-section study, which typically has low $\overline{R}^2$ values. The relationship above is an average over all categories of employees and is likely to be different for different skill levels as well as for different genders and races. DATA7-2, described in Appendix D, has the complete data for a sample of 49 employees at a particular institution. The explanatory variables include the number of years of education (EDUC) beyond the eighth grade when the person was hired, the number of years of experience (EXPER) at the particular institution, and the age of the person (AGE). Also included are dummy variables for gender, race, and job type (e.g., clerical, maintenance, or craft). The categories are male (GENDER = 1), white (RACE = 1), clerical worker (CLERICAL = 1), maintenance worker (MAINT = 1), and craft worker (CRAFTS = 1). The control groups are female, nonwhite, and professional, and we have zero values for these dummy variables.

Suppose we hypothesize that α is not the same for all employees, but differs according to gender, race, and occupational status. To test this, assume that

$$\alpha = \alpha_1 + \alpha_2 \, \text{GENDER} + \alpha_3 \, \text{RACE} + \alpha_4 \, \text{CLERICAL} + \alpha_5 \, \text{MAINT} + \alpha_6 \, \text{CRAFTS}$$

and test the hypothesis that $\alpha_2 = \alpha_3 = \cdots = \alpha_6 = 0$.

Substituting for α in Model A, we obtain Model B, the unrestricted model that relates ln(WAGE) to a number of quantitative as well as dummy variables.

(B) $\ln(\text{WAGE}) = \alpha_1 + \alpha_2 \, \text{GENDER} + \alpha_3 \, \text{RACE} + \alpha_4 \, \text{CLERICAL} + \alpha_5 \, \text{MAINT}$
$\quad + \alpha_6 \, \text{CRAFTS} + \beta \, \text{EDUC} + \gamma \, \text{EXPER} + \delta \, \text{AGE} + u$

A natural question is whether the marginal effects of education, experience, and age also depend on job type, gender, and race. In other words, does an extra year of education or experience contribute more toward the wages of a male employee than toward those of a female or nonwhite employee? Also, are there "diminishing returns" to education and experience? More specifically, do the additional earnings for one additional year of education decrease as education increases? To answer these questions, we should allow the "slope" terms β, γ, and δ to depend on the various employee characteristics. Thus, for example, we could assume

$$\beta = \beta_1 + \beta_2 \, \text{GENDER} + \beta_3 \, \text{RACE} + \beta_4 \, \text{CLERICAL} + \beta_5 \, \text{MAINT}$$
$$+ \beta_6 \, \text{CRAFTS} + \beta_7 \, \text{EDUC}$$

and test whether $\beta_i = 0$ for any i or for $i = 2 - 7$. Similar specifications are possible for γ and δ. If we substitute for α, β, and similar relations for γ and δ into the basic model, we obtain a complete model with numerous quadratic and interaction terms. To save space, we have not written the complete specification. With such a proliferation of variables, the "general to simple" approach will be unwieldy and cumbersome. The LM test approach of starting from the basic Model A is more manageable.

Table 7.4 shows a partial computer printout that illustrates how the Lagrange multiplier test can be used to determine whether some or all of the added terms are significant. Practice Computer Session 7.5 is useful in reproducing those results and in carrying out further analyses.

Comparing the coefficients and related statistics for the added variables in the auxiliary regression (see Table 7.4) to those of the most general Model 3 in Table 7.5,

---

⬤ **Table 7.4   Annotated Partial Output for LM Test Application in Section 7.4**

[The following list includes a number of squared variables and their interactions generated internally through transformations. sq_x refers to the square of x, and x_y refers to the product of x and y.]

```
 0) const      1) WAGE      2) EDUC      3) EXPER     4) AGE
 5) GENDER     6) RACE      7) CLERICAL  8) MAINT     9) CRAFTS
10) sq_EDUC   11) sq_EXPER  12) sq_AGE   13) ED_GEN   14) ED_RACE
15) ED_CLER   16) ED_MAINT  17) ED_CRAFT 18) AGE_GEN  19) AGE_RACE
20) AGE_CLER  21) AGE_MAIN  22) AGE_CRFT 23) EXP_GEN  24) EXP_RACE
25) EXP_CLER  26) EXP_MAIN  27) EXP_CRFT 28) LWAGE
```

[First regress $\ln(\text{WAGE})$ against a constant, EDUC, EXPER, and AGE, and save the residuals $\hat{u}_t$ as ut. The following is the auxiliary regression that regresses the residuals against all the variables in the unrestricted model.]

Dependent variable: ut = $\hat{u}_t$

	VARIABLE	COEFFICIENT	STDERROR	T STAT	2Prob(t > |T|)	
0)	const	-0.8801	1.0029	-0.878	0.389639	
2)	EDUC	0.2627	0.1399	1.878	0.073766	*
3)	EXPER	0.0259	0.0354	0.732	0.471946	
4)	AGE	0.0118	0.0290	0.408	0.686923	
5)	GENDER	0.4091	0.4499	0.909	0.373031	
6)	RACE	-0.3639	0.4476	-0.813	0.424849	
7)	CLERICAL	0.3677	0.7374	0.499	0.622954	
8)	MAINT	-0.2408	0.9154	-0.263	0.794947	
9)	CRAFTS	0.1086	0.7718	0.141	0.889374	
10)	sq_EDUC	-0.0222	0.0109	-2.038	0.053703	*
11)	sq_EXPER	-0.0008053	0.0011	-0.705	0.488381	
12)	sq_AGE	-0.0002380	0.0003148	-0.756	0.457766	
13)	ED_GEN	0.0700	0.0471	1.485	0.151642	
14)	ED_RACE	0.0368	0.0560	0.658	0.517394	
15)	ED_CLER	-0.0761	0.0506	-1.504	0.146848	

(continued)

⬤ Table 7.4   (continued)

VARIABLE	COEFFICIENT	STDERROR	T STAT	2Prob(t > |T|)	
16) ED_MAINT	-0.2094	0.1305	-1.605	0.122645	
17) ED_CRAFT	-0.1245	0.0682	-1.826	0.081493	*
18) AGE_GEN	-0.0151	0.0098	-1.533	0.139646	
19) AGE_RACE	0.0104	0.0100	1.044	0.307974	
20) AGE_CLER	-0.0041	0.0096	-0.426	0.674481	
21) AGE_MAIN	0.0255	0.0121	2.102	0.047225	**
22) AGE_CRFT	0.0114	0.0118	0.968	0.343325	
23) EXP_GEN	-0.0048	0.0178	-0.268	0.791547	
24) EXP_RACE	-0.0229	0.0246	-0.928	0.363564	
25) EXP_CLER	-0.0077	0.0206	-0.375	0.711264	
26) EXP_MAIN	-0.0018	0.0272	-0.068	0.946544	
27) EXP_CRFT	0.0184	0.0188	0.975	0.340112	

```
Unadjusted R-squared        0.818   Adjusted R-squared           0.603
Chi-square(23): area to the right of 40.078742 (LM statistic) = 0.015060
```

[The low *p*-value indicates the rejection of the null hypothesis that the coefficients of the added variables are all zero. The next step is to select variables to be added to the basic model using the simple but arbitrary rule of thumb of including *newly added variables* that have *p*-values less than 0.5. The result is Model 1 in Table 7.5. To obtain the final model, labeled as Model 2 in Table 7.5, we omit variables with insignificant coefficients, a few at a time, until all coefficients are significant at 10 percent. Finally, we estimate the complete model with all square and interaction terms. This is Model 3 in Table 7.5. Note that Model 3 has numerous insignificant terms most likely due to strong multicollinearity.]

we note that they are identical. The value of R^2 for the auxiliary regression is 0.818, the nR^2 statistic is slightly greater than 40, and the corresponding *p*-value is 0.01506. This means that if we *reject* the null hypothesis that all the added variables have insignificant regression coefficients, then the probability of a type I error (of rejecting a true hypothesis) is only 1.5 percent. Because this is very low, we are "safe" in rejecting the null hypothesis and concluding, not surprisingly, that at least some of the included variables do belong in the model.

Here also the question arises, "Which of the new variables in the auxiliary regression should we add to the model specification?" If we go by strict significance (at 10 percent or lower levels), only sq_EDUC (square of EDUC), ED_CRAFT (EDUC*CRAFTS), and AGE_MAIN (AGE*MAINT) will be included. However, we can expect a great deal of multicollinearity among the explanatory variables, which may have caused some of the coefficients to be insignificant. A conservative rule of thumb is to select those variables for which the *p*-values of the coefficients are less than 0.5 (other researchers may prefer some other rule). According to this rule, we would include GENDER, RACE, sq_EDUC, sq_EXPER, sq_AGE, ED_GEN,

Table 7.5 Selected Model Results for the Application

Variable	Model 1	Model 2	Model 3
CONSTANT	6.25809 (11.879)	6.69328 (36.624)	5.95582 (5.939)
EDUC	0.29236 (3.347)	0.22078 (3.618)	0.32721 (2.339)
EXPER	0.04514 (2.095)	0.01794 (4.287)	0.04864 (1.372)
AGE	0.00465 (0.219)		0.01223 (0.422)
GENDER	0.18628 (0.671)		0.40913 (0.909)
RACE	0.00089 (0.004)		−0.36392 (−0.813)
CLERICAL			0.36774 (0.499)
MAINT			−0.24081 (−0.263)
CRAFTS			1.10860 (0.141)
sq_EDUC	−0.01792 (−2.874)	−0.01109 (−2.506)	−0.02219 (−2.038)
sq_EXPER	−0.00085 (−1.098)		−0.00081 (−0.705)
sq_AGE	−0.00015 (−0.633)	−0.00007 (−2.184)	−0.00024 (−0.756)
ED_GEN	0.06650 (2.191)	0.02960 (2.943)	0.06995 (1.485)
ED_RACE			0.03682 (0.658)
ED_CLER	−0.06110 (−5.843)	−0.06169 (−6.525)	−0.07611 (−1.504)
ED_MAINT	−0.22790 (−3.523)	−0.13896 (−3.119)	−0.20945 (−1.605)
ED_CRAFT	−0.11688 (−3.857)	−0.10726 (−5.504)	−0.12452 (−1.826)
AGE_GEN	−0.01081 (−1.492)		−0.01507 (−1.533)
AGE_RACE	0.00721 (1.127)		0.01043 (1.044)
AGE_CLER			−0.00409 (−0.426)
AGE_MAIN	0.02066 (2.554)	0.00758 (1.700)	0.02550 (2.102)
AGE_CRFT	0.01059 (1.945)	0.01152 (3.649)	0.01145 (0.968)
EXP_GEN			−0.00475 (−0.268)
EXP_RACE	−0.02525 (−1.881)		−0.02286 (−0.928)
EXP_CLER			−0.00771 (−0.375)
EXP_MAIN			−0.00185 (−0.068)
EXP_CRFT	0.02402 (2.058)		0.01837 (0.975)

(continued)

● Table 7.5   (continued)

Variable	Model 1	Model 2	Model 3
ESS	0.61473	0.78302	0.574710
$\overline{R}^2$	0.790	0.789	0.733
d.f.	30	38	22
SGMASQ	0.020491*	0.020606	0.026123
AIC	0.027245	0.025036*	0.035307
FPE	0.028437	0.025231*	0.040518
HQ	0.035988	0.029413*	0.052436
SCHWARZ	0.056738	0.038283*	0.100135
SHIBATA	0.022275*	0.023155	0.024655
GCV	0.033469	0.026571*	0.058184
RICE	0.055885	0.029001*	undefined

Note: * Denotes the model that is "best" for that criterion. Values in parentheses are *t*-statistics.

ED_CLER, ED_MAINT, ED_CRAFT, AGE_GEN, AGE_RACE, AGE_MAIN, AGE_CRFT, EXP_RACE, and EXP_CRFT in the model. Such a model was estimated and the results are summarized in Table 7.5 under the label Model 1.

We note that several coefficients have very low *t*-statistics, suggesting insignificance. These were omitted a few at a time until a model was obtained that had all coefficients significant at 10 percent or lower levels (see Practice Computer Session 7.5). The results are shown under Model 2 in the table. Finally, Model 3 is the "kitchen sink" specification, which includes all the quadratic and interaction terms. As one would suspect, Model 3 suffers seriously from multicollinearity problems, which often tend to make coefficients insignificant. In terms of the model selection statistics and the significance of the regression coefficients, Model 2 is clearly superior and is chosen as the final model for interpretation.

INTERPRETATION OF RESULTS   The variables included in the model explain 79 percent of the variation in the logarithm of WAGE. For a cross-section study this is quite good. We now examine the marginal effects of each determinant separately.

Education: The number of years of schooling (beyond the eighth grade) is important in explaining wages. It exhibits significant nonlinearity and it interacts significantly with gender and occupational status. The partial effect is

$$\Delta \widehat{\ln(\text{WAGE})} / \Delta \text{EDUC} = 0.221 - 0.022 \text{ EDUC} + 0.030 \text{ GENDER}$$
$$- 0.062 \text{ CLERICAL} - 0.139 \text{ MAINT} - 0.107 \text{ CRAFTS}$$

It is interesting to note that the marginal effect of schooling decreases with the number of years of education. In other words, the *additional* wages for one *additional* year of education is lower, on average, for a person with an already high level of education as compared to another person with less education. There are thus "diminishing" returns to education. With male and female employees who are similar in other characteristics, a male employee is expected to earn an average of 3 percent more than a female employee for each extra year of education. The type of job interacts significantly with education. As compared to professional employees (the control group), one more year of education means 6.2 percent less in wages for clerical workers, 13.9 percent less for maintenance employees, and 10.7 percent less for craft workers.

Experience: Not surprisingly, the number of years of experience in a given job has a positive effect on wages. There were, however, no significant diminishing returns nor any interaction with the dummy variables. An extra year of experience means an average increase in earnings of only 1.8 percent.

Age: The age of an employee had significant diminishing returns, indicating that, other things being equal, an older employee commands a lower average wage. The marginal effect is

$$\Delta \widehat{\ln(\text{WAGE})} / \Delta \text{AGE} = -0.00014 \text{ AGE} + 0.00758 \text{ MAINT}$$
$$+ 0.01152 \text{ CRAFTS}$$

The age effect is somewhat offset for maintenance and craft employees but not for others.

Gender: We see from Table 7.4 that the partial effect of gender depends on the amount of education. The estimated coefficient is 0.02960 EDUC, and the corresponding estimated variance is $(0.0101 \text{ EDUC})^2$. The positive sign means that a significant gender differential does exist (with comparable male employees earning, on average, a higher salary) and that the gap increases with education. Thus, well-educated women had disproportionately lower average salaries than men with similar characteristics. The estimated marginal effect can be verified to be the following (refer to the derivation in the previous section):

$$100 \left\{ \exp \left[\hat{\beta} \text{ EDUC} - \tfrac{1}{2} \widehat{\text{Var}} (\hat{\beta} \text{ EDUC}) \right] - 1 \right\}$$
$$= 100 \left\{ \exp \left[\hat{\beta} \text{ EDUC} - \tfrac{1}{2} \text{ EDUC}^2 \widehat{\text{Var}} (\hat{\beta}) \right] - 1 \right\}$$

For $\hat{\beta} = 0.02960$ and EDUC = 4 and 8 (that is, high school and college education), these effects are 12.5 percent and 26.3 percent respectively, which are unaccountably high.

Race: None of the race variables was significant, indicating no significant wage differential along racial lines.

Type of Job: The sample employees belonged to four different occupational categories. The control group consisted of professionals, and the others were clerical, maintenance, and craft workers. The estimated partial effects for log wages for each of the noncontrol groups are

Clerical: -0.062 EDUC

Maintenance: $-0.139 \text{ EDUC} + 0.008 \text{ AGE}$

Crafts: $-0.107 \text{ EDUC} + 0.012 \text{ AGE}$

As was pointed out earlier, job type and education interacted very strongly. Age has significant positive effects for maintenance and craft workers but not for the others.

For a real-world application of the log-wage model, refer to the paper by Tansel cited in Chapter 6.

7.5 Estimating Seasonal Effects

Another example of the use of dummy variables occurs in estimating seasonal effects of independent variables. Consider the relationship $E = \alpha + \beta T + u$, presented earlier, between electricity consumption and temperature. In the summer, as the temperature rises, demand for air-conditioning pushes electricity consumption up. Thus, we would expect β to have a positive sign, giving a positive relationship between E and T. In the winter, however, as temperature rises (from, say, 20 degrees to 40 degrees), the demand for heating a house becomes lower, and hence we would expect β to be negative in the winter, giving a negative relation between E and T. How can we capture the effect on E of the qualitative variable "season," which has four classes: fall, winter, spring, and summer? This is accomplished by defining three dummy variables, known as **seasonal dummies.** As explained earlier, we do not define four dummy variables in order to avoid perfect collinearity. The fall season is used here as the control period:

$$D_1 = \begin{cases} 1 & \text{if the season is winter} \\ 0 & \text{otherwise} \end{cases}$$

$$D_2 = \begin{cases} 1 & \text{if the season is spring} \\ 0 & \text{otherwise} \end{cases}$$

$$D_3 = \begin{cases} 1 & \text{if the season is summer} \\ 0 & \text{otherwise} \end{cases}$$

Now let $\alpha = \alpha_0 + \alpha_1 D_1 + \alpha_2 D_2 + \alpha_3 D_3$ and $\beta = \beta_0 + \beta_1 D_1 + \beta_2 D_2 + \beta_3 D_3$. The fully general specification is obtained by substituting these into the relationship between E and T:

$$E = \alpha_0 + \alpha_1 D_1 + \alpha_2 D_2 + \alpha_3 D_3 + \beta_0 T \tag{7.23}$$
$$+ \beta_1 D_1 T + \beta_2 D_2 T + \beta_3 D_3 T + u$$

The estimated models for each of the seasons are as follows (Fig. 7.4 illustrates this):

Fall: $\hat{E} = \hat{\alpha}_0 + \hat{\beta}_0 T$

Winter: $\hat{E} = (\hat{\alpha}_0 + \hat{\alpha}_1) + (\hat{\beta}_0 + \hat{\beta}_1) T$

Spring: $\hat{E} = (\hat{\alpha}_0 + \hat{\alpha}_2) + (\hat{\beta}_0 + \hat{\beta}_2) T$

Summer: $\hat{E} = (\hat{\alpha}_0 + \hat{\alpha}_3) + (\hat{\beta}_0 + \hat{\beta}_3) T$

α_1 is the deviation of the winter intercept term from that of the fall quarter, and β_1 is the deviation of the winter slope term from that of fall. A variety of tests can be

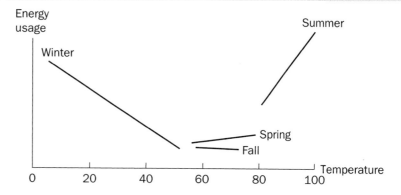

Figure 7.4   Example of Seasonality

performed on these models. For instance, a plausible hypothesis is that there is no difference in the relationships between the fall and spring seasons. Comparing the equations for the fall and the spring, the hypothesis implies that $\alpha_2 = \beta_2 = 0$. This is tested with a Wald test in which Equation (7.23) is the unrestricted model and the restricted model is

$$E = \alpha_0 + \alpha_1 D_1 + \alpha_3 D_3 + \beta_0 T + \beta_1 D_1 T + \beta_3 D_3 T + u \qquad \textbf{(7.24)}$$

Some investigators prefer to retain seasonal dummies in the model even if a few of them are insignificant. It is not clear that this is desirable, however, since redundant dummy variables might unnecessarily reduce the precision of the other parameters. If certain periods are found to be alike (say, the fall and spring), one might consolidate them into one season by defining a dummy $D = 1$ for fall or spring and 0 elsewhere. To test the hypothesis that all the seasons have the same relation, the conditions are $\alpha_1 = \alpha_2 = \alpha_3 = \beta_1 = \beta_2 = \beta_3 = 0$. The unrestricted model will be (7.23), and the restricted model will be $E = \alpha_0 + \beta_0 T + u$. The degrees of freedom for the Wald F-statistics are 6 for the numerator and the number of observations minus 8 for the denominator (explain why). We would expect to reject this hypothesis because we argued earlier that the relationship between E and T will be positive in the summer and negative in the winter.

● PRACTICE PROBLEM 7.8

Redo the previous analysis using the summer quarter instead of the fall as the control.

Instead of defining three dummy variables, suppose we had defined a single variable as follows:

$$D = \begin{cases} 1 & \text{if the season is fall} \\ 2 & \text{if the season is winter} \\ 3 & \text{if the season is spring} \\ 4 & \text{if the season is summer} \end{cases}$$

Next assume that $\alpha = \alpha_0 D$ and $\beta = \beta_0 D$. The model now becomes

$$E = \alpha_0 D + \beta_0 DT + u \qquad (7.25)$$

and the estimated relations now become

Fall:	$\hat{E} = \hat{\alpha}_0 + \hat{\beta}_0 T$
Winter:	$\hat{E} = 2\hat{\alpha}_0 + 2\hat{\beta}_0 T$
Spring:	$\hat{E} = 3\hat{\alpha}_0 + 3\hat{\beta}_0 T$
Summer:	$\hat{E} = 4\hat{\alpha}_0 + 4\hat{\beta}_0 T$

How does this alternative compare with the three-dummy approach we adopted earlier? Note that although the equations for the fall are identical, the others are very different. In particular, comparing fall with winter we see that the difference in intercept between these seasons is α_0. There is no reason why this difference should equal the fall intercept. In fact, the difference in intercept between any two successive seasons is α_0. We are thus assuming that the shift in intercept is the same across all successive seasons. Similarly, the difference in the slopes between any two successive seasons is always β_0. This assumption is too restrictive and is not likely to hold in general. Therefore, the alternative approach will lead to serious model misspecification and should be abandoned in favor of the general approach with three dummy variables presented earlier.

For a real-world application of modeling seasonal effects, see Section 7.8.

7.6   Testing for Structural Change

The relationship between the dependent and independent variables may undergo a **structural change** (also known as **structural instability** or **structural breaks**); that is, the relationship might have changed from one period to another. For example, suppose *C* is the consumption of gasoline in the United States in a given period and the independent variables are price (*P*) and income (*Y*). There have been three periods during 1970–2000 when gasoline prices increased drastically, causing possible changes in the behavioral pattern of gasoline consumption. The first started in 1974 soon after the OPEC (Organization of Petroleum Exporting Countries) cartel started to control world oil prices. The second was in 1979, soon after the revolution in Iran. The last one occurred in 1990 when Iraq invaded Kuwait. It is reasonable to expect the price and income elasticities of gasoline consumption to be different in the four periods divided by these years. The statistical test for structural change is known as the **Chow test** (after Gregory Chow [1960], who first popularized it). This section presents two approaches to testing for structural change. The first one consists of dividing the sample into two or more groups, estimating the model separately for each period and with all the sample pooled, and then constructing an *F*-statistic with which to perform the test. In the second approach, we use dummy variables.

Test Based on Splitting the Sample (Chow Test)

Suppose we want to test whether there has been a structural change at time $t = n_1$. The procedure is to divide the sample of n observations into two groups—group 1 consisting of the first n_1 observations and group 2 consisting of the remaining $n_2 = n - n_1$ observations. Estimate the model (with k regression coefficients) separately for each of the two sample groups and compute the sum of squared residuals ESS_1 and ESS_2. The unrestricted sum of squares is therefore given by $ESS_U = ESS_1 + ESS_2$. When divided by σ^2, this will have a chi-square distribution with d.f. $n_1 - k + n_2 - k = n - 2k$, because estimation of the model separately implies that each equation has k regression coefficients. Next assume that the regression coefficients are the same before and after period n_1 (which gives rise to k restrictions). Estimate the model again but with the pooled sample, and obtain ESS_R. The appropriate test statistic is now

$$F_c = \frac{(ESS_R - ESS_1 - ESS_2) \div k}{(ESS_1 + ESS_2) \div (n - 2k)}$$

The test procedure is to reject the null hypothesis that there is no structural change if F_c exceeds $F^*_{k, \, n-2k}$, the point on the F-distribution with k and $n - 2k$ d.f. such that the area to the right is equal to the level of significance. An important assumption behind this test is that the error variances of the two samples are the same.

Test Based on Dummy Variables

The test can also be conducted using the dummy-variable technique developed in this chapter (see Franklin Fisher, 1970, for more on this approach). This method is illustrated here for the gasoline consumption example just described (for the 1974 and 1979 shifts only).

Let the basic model be

$$\ln C = \alpha + \beta \ln P + \gamma \ln Y + u \tag{7.26}$$

This is a double-log model in which β is the price elasticity and γ is the income elasticity. We define two dummy variables as follows (1974.1 refers to the first quarter of 1974; other quarters are indicated in the same way):

$$D_1 = \begin{cases} 1 & \text{for the period 1974.1 onward} \\ 0 & \text{otherwise} \end{cases}$$

$$D_2 = \begin{cases} 1 & \text{for the period 1979.1 onward} \\ 0 & \text{otherwise} \end{cases}$$

Note that for all the periods from 1979.1, both D_1 and D_2 are 1. To test whether the structures for the three periods (prior to 1974.1, 1974.1 through 1978.4, and 1979.1 onward) are different, the specification must assume the following:

$$\alpha = \alpha_0 + \alpha_1 D_1 + \alpha_2 D_2 \qquad \beta = \beta_0 + \beta_1 D_1 + \beta_2 D_2 \qquad \gamma = \gamma_0 + \gamma_1 D_1 + \gamma_2 D_2$$

Substituting these into Equation (7.26), we get the unrestricted model

$$\ln C = \alpha_0 + \alpha_1 D_1 + \alpha_2 D_2 + (\beta_0 + \beta_1 D_1 + \beta_2 D_2)\ln P$$
$$+ (\gamma_0 + \gamma_1 D_1 + \gamma_2 D_2)\ln Y + u$$
$$= \alpha_0 + \alpha_1 D_1 + \alpha_2 D_2 + \beta_0 \ln P + \beta_1(D_1 \ln P) + \cdots + u$$

To estimate this, we first create the new variables $Z_1 = D_1 \ln P$, $Z_2 = D_2 \ln P$, $Z_3 = D_1 \ln Y$, and $Z_4 = D_2 \ln Y$. Next we regress $\ln C$ against a constant, D_1, D_2, $\ln P$, Z_1, Z_2, $\ln Y$, Z_3, and Z_4. The estimated models are

Prior to 1974.1: $\widehat{\ln C} = \hat{\alpha}_0 + \hat{\beta}_0 \ln P + \hat{\gamma}_0 \ln Y$

1974.1–1978.4: $\widehat{\ln C} = \hat{\alpha}_0 + \hat{\alpha}_1 + (\hat{\beta}_0 + \hat{\beta}_1)\ln P + (\hat{\gamma}_0 + \hat{\gamma}_1)\ln Y$

1979.1 onward: $\widehat{\ln C} = \hat{\alpha}_0 + \hat{\alpha}_1 + \hat{\alpha}_2 + (\hat{\beta}_0 + \hat{\beta}_1 + \hat{\beta}_2)\ln P$
$$+ (\hat{\gamma}_0 + \hat{\gamma}_1 + \hat{\gamma}_2)\ln Y$$

By comparing these relations, we can test a variety of hypotheses. For instance, the hypothesis $\alpha_1 = \alpha_2 = \beta_1 = \beta_2 = \gamma_1 = \gamma_2 = 0$ indicates that there is no structural change whatsoever. A t-test on β_2 will test whether the price elasticity is the same between 1974.1–1978.4 and 1979.1 onward. Many other hypotheses are left as exercises.

The dummy-variable approach has an advantage over splitting the sample; namely, we can test, if we so desire, just a few of the regression coefficients for structural change rather than the entire relation, as the latter method would do.

We see from the unrestricted model for $\ln C$ that if the intercept as well as all the slope coefficients are allowed to be different across periods, the number of interaction terms, and hence the number of regression coefficients to be estimated, could be large. This would result in the loss of several degrees of freedom and a reduction in the power of tests. A researcher is therefore well advised to guard against the proliferation of dummy variables thus leading one to "data mining." A useful approach would be to formulate a basic model without dummy variables and then use the Lagrange multiplier test described in Chapter 6 to test whether additional dummy variables and interaction terms should be included in the model.

● PRACTICE PROBLEM 7.9[†]

Describe how to test the hypothesis that the income elasticity is unchanged in all the three periods.

● PRACTICE PROBLEM 7.10

Describe how to test the hypothesis that the intercept is the same for all the periods.

● **PRACTICE PROBLEM 7.11**

Suppose the dummy variable D_3, defined here, is used instead of D_1:

$$D_3 = \begin{cases} 1 & \text{for the period 1974.1–1978.4} \\ 0 & \text{otherwise} \end{cases}$$

Redo the preceding analysis under this assumption. What is the relation between the coefficients obtained this way and those obtained earlier?

Application: Structural Change in Women's Labor Force Participation Rates

In Section 4.7, we used DATA4-5 and estimated a model for women's labor force participation (WLFP) rates. That data set was for 1990 for the 50 states. In DATA7-4 we have data for both 1990 and 1980. The data for 1990 are "stacked" below those for 1980 with a new column added, namely, D90. This is a dummy variable that takes the value 1 for 1990 and 0 for 1980. It will be interesting to examine whether there has been a structural change in the relationship between WLFP and its determinants. For a complete discussion of the independent variables and their expected effects on WLFP, review Section 4.7 first. Because the entire relation might have shifted between 1980 and 1990, we need to generate all the interaction terms by multiplying D90 with each of the independent variables. Thus, we would generate variables such as D90YF, which is the product of D90 and YF, and do the same for other variables. Table 7.6 has a partial computer output (obtained from Practice Computer Session 7.6). It will be noted that the Chow test for no structural change is rejected even at levels below 0.01 percent. The general model with all the interaction terms has an adjusted R^2 of 0.833, which is much higher than the corresponding measure (0.746) for the 1990 model in Section 4.7. However, as we can suspect, there is likely to be a considerable amount of multicollinearity among variables. We therefore eliminated variables with insignificant coefficients, but one at a time. The final estimated model is given by the following equation, with p-values in parentheses:

$$\widehat{\text{WLFP}} = 47.637 + 0.00478\,\text{YF} - 0.00405\,(\text{D90} \times \text{YF}) + 0.275\,\text{EDUC}$$
$$\scriptstyle (<0.01) \qquad (<0.01) \qquad\qquad (<0.01) \qquad\qquad\qquad (<0.01)$$

$$- 1.061\,\text{UE} - 0.569\,(\text{D90} \times \text{UE}) - 0.207\,\text{MR}$$
$$\scriptstyle (<.01) \qquad\quad (0.085) \qquad\qquad\qquad (0.051)$$

$$+ 0.126\,(\text{D90} \times \text{MR}) + 0.282\,\text{DR} - 0.078\,\text{URB} - 0.111\,\text{WH}$$
$$\scriptstyle (0.015) \qquad\qquad\qquad (0.038) \qquad\quad (<0.01) \qquad\quad (<0.01)$$

$$\bar{R}^2 = 0.842 \qquad \text{d.f.} = 89 \qquad \hat{\sigma} = 2.192$$

To obtain the separate relations for the two periods, we first set D90 to zero, which gives the following equation for 1980:

$$\widehat{\text{WLFP}} = 47.637 + 0.00478\,\text{YF} + 0.275\,\text{EDUC} - 1.061\,\text{UE} - 0.207\,\text{MR}$$

$$+ 0.282\,\text{DR} - 0.078\,\text{URB} - 0.111\,\text{WH}$$

● **Table 7.6   Partial Output for Structural Change Application in Section 7.6**

[First regress WLFP against a constant, YF, YM, EDUC, UE, MR, DR, URB, and WH, and carry out a Chow test for structural change.]

```
Chow test for structural break at observation 50:
  F(9, 82) = 6.903514 with p-value 0.000000   (that is, it is very small)
```

[Note that the null hypothesis of no structural change is soundly rejected. Next, estimate a general model with the original variables plus interaction terms.]

VARIABLE		COEFFICIENT	STDERROR	T STAT	2Prob(t > |T|)	
0)	const	50.8808	11.6760	4.358	0.000038	***
10)	D90	-6.3712	14.9234	-0.427	0.670549	
2)	YF	0.0045	0.0012	3.757	0.000321	***
11)	D90YF	-0.0035	0.0013	-2.770	0.006939	***
3)	YM	-0.0000111	0.0005489	-0.020	0.983935	
12)	D90YM	-0.0001633	0.0006339	-0.258	0.797400	
4)	EDUC	0.2779	0.0674	4.121	0.000090	***
13)	D90EDUC	0.0072	0.1177	0.061	0.951319	
5)	UE	-1.1191	0.2917	-3.836	0.000244	***
14)	D90UE	-0.4915	0.4365	-1.126	0.263485	
15)	D90MR	0.1461	0.2427	0.602	0.548850	
6)	MR	-0.2243	0.1636	-1.371	0.174124	
7)	DR	0.2268	0.1876	1.209	0.230234	
16)	D90DR	0.2106	0.3268	0.645	0.521040	
8)	URB	-0.0691	0.0317	-2.180	0.032124	**
17)	D90URB	-0.0236	0.0469	-0.503	0.616474	
9)	WH	-0.1284	0.0351	-3.654	0.000455	***
18)	D90WH	0.0409	0.0542	0.755	0.452353	

```
Error Sum of Sq (ESS)    416.0265  Std Err of Resid. (sqmahat)    2.2524
Unadjusted R-squared       0.862   Adjusted R-squared             0.833
F-statistic (17, 82)     30.1406   p-value for F()             0.000000
```

MODEL SELECTION STATISTICS

SGMASQ	5.07349	AIC	5.96303	FPE	5.98672
HQ	7.20924	SCHWARZ	9.53062	SHIBATA	5.65796
GCV	6.18719	RICE	6.50041		

[Now omit variables one at a time to yield the final model with coefficients significant at 10%.]

Table 7.6 (continued)

	VARIABLE	COEFFICIENT	STDERROR	T STAT	2Prob(t > |T|)	
0)	const	47.6366	6.5784	7.241	0.000000	***
2)	YF	0.0048	0.0007339	6.512	0.000000	***
11)	D90YF	-0.0041	0.0006821	-5.943	0.000000	***
4)	EDUC	0.2751	0.0455	6.045	0.000000	***
5)	UE	-1.0614	0.2456	-4.322	0.000040	***
14)	D90UE	-0.5694	0.3272	-1.740	0.085324	*
6)	MR	-0.2073	0.1049	-1.976	0.051227	*
15)	D90MR	0.1264	0.0510	2.479	0.015066	**
7)	DR	0.2816	0.1337	2.106	0.037986	**
8)	URB	-0.0785	0.0206	-3.805	0.000260	***
9)	WH	-0.1115	0.0242	-4.599	0.000014	***

Mean of dep. var	53.869	S.D. of dep. variable	5.519
Error Sum of Sq (ESS)	427.5756	Std Err of Resid. (sgmahat)	2.1919
Unadjusted R-squared	0.858	Adjusted R-squared	0.842
F-statistic (10, 89)	53.8705	p-value for F()	0.000000
Durbin-Watson stat.	1.983	First-order autocorr. coeff	0.007

MODEL SELECTION STATISTICS

SGMASQ	4.80422	AIC	5.32792	FPE	5.33268
HQ	5.98311	SCHWARZ	7.09599	SHIBATA	5.21642
GCV	5.398	RICE	5.48174		

The relation for 1990 is obtained by setting D90 to 1 and combining terms for the same variables. For instance, if D90 = 1, the term for YF should be combined with that for D90 × YF. Thus, the estimated relation for 1990 is

$$\text{WLFP} = 47.637 + 0.00073\,\text{YF} + 0.275\,\text{EDUC} - 1.630\,\text{UE} - 0.081\,\text{MR}$$

$$+ 0.282\,\text{DR} - 0.078\,\text{URB} - 0.111\,\text{WH}$$

The final model explains 84.2 percent of the variation in WLFP, which is respectable for cross-section data. The effects of EDUC, DR, URB, and WH had the expected signs and were the same for 1980 and 1990. The marginal effect of the marriage rate (MR) was numerically smaller in 1990 than in 1980. A 1 percent increase in MR decreased WLFP, on average, by 0.207 percent in 1980 but only by 0.081 percent in 1990. This suggests that, compared to 1980, more women stayed in the labor force after marriage. The unemployment rate effect was also significantly different between the two censuses. In 1980, the marginal effect of UE was −1.061, whereas it was −1.630 in 1990. Thus, the discouraged-worker hypothesis was stronger in 1990 than in 1980. The difference in the effect of women's earnings (YF) was also significant—0.00478 in 1980 versus 0.00073 in 1990—a drastic drop in value, the reason for which is not clear. A possible explanation might be the near perfect collinearity between YF and D90 YF, which makes it difficult to obtain separate effects.

7.7   Empirical Example: Motor Carrier Deregulation

Blair, Kaserman, and McClave (1986) studied the effect of deregulation on the price structure of intrastate trucking services in Florida. The deregulation went into effect on July 1, 1980, and the authors' data comprise over 27,000 observations, covering 10 trucking firms and four time periods, one before deregulation. The authors assumed that the supply of trucking services to an individual shipper is infinitely price-elastic at the market rate. The dependent variable was $\ln(\text{PTM})$, where PTM is the price of the shipment per ton-mile in 1980 dollars. The quantitative independent variables were the following: $\ln(\text{WT})$, where WT is the midpoint of the various weight classes; PD is the price of diesel fuel in 1980 cents per gallon; and $\ln(\text{DIST})$, where DIST is the number of miles the shipment traveled. The study also included a number of dummy variables: ORIGJ is 1 when the shipment originated from Jacksonville, ORIGM is 1 if the shipment originated from Miami, CLASSi ($i = 1, 2, 3, 4$) denotes five different shipment classifications, and DEREG is 1 in the postderegulation period. The basic model estimated is as follows, with t-statistics in parentheses:

$$\widehat{\ln(\text{PTM})} = 10.1805 + 0.0305 \text{ ORIGJ} + 0.0254 \text{ ORIGM} - 0.1590 \ln(\text{WT})$$
$$(327.44) \qquad (6.31) \qquad\qquad (5.28) \qquad\qquad (-133.74)$$

$$-0.6398 \ln(\text{DIST}) + 0.2800 \text{ CLASS1} + 0.5871 \text{ CLASS2}$$
$$(-196.00) \qquad\qquad (16.21) \qquad\qquad (97.22)$$

$$+ 0.9086 \text{ CLASS3} + 1.0923 \text{ CLASS4} + 0.0030 \text{ PD} - 0.1581 \text{ DEREG}$$
$$(150.45) \qquad\qquad (175.82) \qquad\qquad (10.42) \qquad (-35.08)$$

$$R^2 = 0.79$$

The regression coefficient of primary interest is that for DEREG. This coefficient is both negative and significant at the 1 percent level, indicating that the hypothesis that deregulation resulted in a significant reduction in trucking rates is supported. Other things being equal, the deregulation of intrastate trucking in Florida resulted in an average rate reduction of nearly 16 percent. The remaining variables are also statistically significant at the 1 percent level and have the correct signs for the coefficients.

The authors also tested for the interaction between the dummy variables and a number of quantitative variables, as well as among the dummy variables themselves, but with mixed results. Details may be found in their paper.

7.8   Application: The Demand for a Sealant Used in Construction

A particular company makes a sealing compound used in concrete work for construction and road building. It believed that a competitor spread a rumor about the quality of the company's product, causing a loss of sales and profits during the period July 1986 through October 1988. The company filed a lawsuit against the competitor and claimed damages. An expert witness on behalf of the company with a sense of humor calls the company Cement Overcoat, Inc. (COI), and himself Rodney Random, so as to protect the confidentiality of the details of the trial.

Figure 7.5 is a graph showing the quantity (in gallons) of the sealant sold by COI in each month from January 1983 through May 1990. Three interesting patterns emerge from the graph. First, there is seasonality in the quantity, and as can be expected, January sales are typically low and sales during August–September are generally high. Second, the sales average appears to have decreased in the "loss" period (July 1986–October 1988) and decreased further in the postloss period. Finally, the height of the summer sales peak has steadily diminished from period to period. Thus, there is some *prima facie* support for the contention that sales were lower during the loss period. In fact, the losses may have continued beyond the litigation period.

Rodney Random obtained data on a number of variables that are likely to affect monthly shipments. DATA 7-5 (see Appendix D) has monthly data for the following variables for the period January 1983 through May 1990:

Q = Shipments of sealing compound used in construction, in gallons/month
P = Price per gallon, in dollars
HS = Housing starts, in thousands
SHC = Index of street and highway construction

Figure 7.5   Shipments of Sealing Compound (gallons/month)

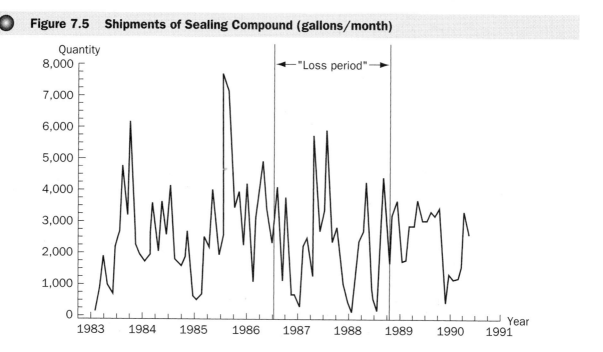

OC = Overall index of public and private construction
L = 1 for July 1986 through October 1988, when company suffered losses
PL = 1 from November 1988 onward, the postloss period

Random did a thorough analysis of the data set, including carrying out many of the testing procedures described in Chapters 8, 9, and 10. Here we present a modified portion of the analysis that illustrates the usefulness of dummy variables. The starting point is the basic model:

(A)　　$Q = \beta_1 + \beta_2 P + \beta_3 HS + \beta_4 SHC + \beta_5 OC + \beta_6 L + \beta_7 PL + u$

It will be noted that the terms L and PL are dummy variables that shift the "intercept." The first period is the control, and β_6, β_7 measure the deviation of the constant term from the base period (note that L is defined as 1 only for the loss period). OLS estimates of the coefficients are given next along with p-values in parentheses (Practice Computer Session 7.7 has all the details for using the GRETL program to reproduce the results of this section).

$$\hat{Q} = -2065 - \underset{(0.003)}{301.670P} + \underset{(0.047)}{14.423HS} + \underset{(0.124)}{0.629\,SHC}$$

$$+\underset{(0.010)}{33.677OC} - \underset{(0.023)}{1{,}075.203L} - \underset{(0.223)}{733.934PL}$$

$$\overline{R}^2 = 0.354 \qquad \text{d.f.} = 82 \qquad \hat{\sigma} = 1{,}258$$

The signs for the regression coefficients for L and PL are negative, indicating that, on average, sales in the latter two periods were below those in the first period, even after correcting for the effects of other explanatory variables such as housing starts, state highway construction, and overall construction. However, the p-value for the coefficient of PL is 0.223, which is unacceptably high. Note that the p-value for the coefficient of L is only 0.023, indicating that average sales were significantly lower in the "loss" period as compared to the first period. However, the model explains only 35.4 percent of the variation in monthly shipments and could use some improvement in specification.

It was noted from Fig. 7.5 that there is a seasonal pattern in the shipment data. This suggests incorporating dummy variables to capture seasonal effects. Accordingly, 11 dummies were defined, one each for February through December (January was omitted in order to avoid the "dummy variable trap"). These were then added to Model A, and a new model (B) was estimated. Because numerous terms exist, the result is not presented here, but it can be obtained using Practice Computer Session 7.7. It was found that the coefficient for L was still significantly negative, but the coefficient for PL, although still negative, was significant only at the 48 percent level. Many of the dummy variables were, however, even more insignificant. We could omit these variables and reestimate the model to see if the significance of the remaining variables would improve. Instead of doing that, we have adopted an approach that directly addresses the loss issue.

The preliminary analysis indicates that there might have been a significant loss in sales during the second period, and perhaps even during the last period. The proper way to obtain a measure of possible sales loss is to exclude the data for the loss and postloss periods. Including them would affect the estimates, thus begging the question we are trying to answer. The procedure adopted estimates the model using the 42 observations for the period 1983.01–1986.06. We can then generate forecasts for the loss and postloss periods and compare them with the actual known values. If the predicted shipments are systematically higher than actual shipments, there is strong evidence of a change in structure and significant losses.

The procedure just described was applied to the first-period data, and a third model (C) was estimated using the explanatory variables constant term, P, HS, SHC, OC, and the 11 monthly dummies, but *excluding* L and PL, which are both zero for the first period. As before, the regression coefficients for many of the dummy variables were insignificant, as was that for housing starts (HS). In order to improve the precision of the remaining coefficients, these variables were omitted and the model reestimated. The estimates for the "final" model (D) are given here, with the *p*-values in parentheses:

$$\hat{Q} = \underset{(0.34)}{-1{,}915} - \underset{(0.096)}{1{,}157} \text{ dummy6} - \underset{(0.002)}{499.986 \text{ P}} + \underset{(0.0004)}{1.896 \text{ SHC}} + \underset{(0.0006)}{51.928 \text{ OC}}$$

$$\overline{R}^2 = 0.513 \qquad \text{d.f.} = 37 \qquad \hat{\sigma} = 1{,}202$$

The coefficient for the June dummy variable was significant at the 9.6 percent level, but all other coefficients (excluding the constant term) were significant at levels below 1 percent. The adjusted R^2 has increased substantially from 0.354, but even the newer model explains only half the variation in shipments. This might be because monthly data are usually volatile (that is, vary a great deal) and are difficult to model.

Model D was next used to forecast shipments for the periods 1986.07–1988.10 and 1988.11–1990.05. Figure 7.6 shows graphs of both the predicted and actual shipments for the entire 89 months. (Practice Computer Session 7.7 computes the numerical values.) Note that during the first period before the alleged rumor about COI, the model tracks the actual values well, except for a few extreme values. This is not very surprising because OLS gives the lowest error sum of squares and has errors that average to zero. In contrast, however, the forecasts for the "loss" period are systematically above those of the actual values. For the postloss period, the difference is more pronounced. This is the strongest evidence that the structure has indeed changed to the detriment of COI's sales and profits. In fact, the losses continued during the postloss period. Measures of the net loss in sales and revenues have been obtained as follows (Σ refers to the net sum of the losses):

$$\text{Sales} = \sum (\hat{Q}_t - Q_t) = 54{,}209 + 38{,}467 = 92{,}676$$

$$\text{Revenues} = \sum P_t(\hat{Q}_t - Q_t) = 481{,}575 + 335{,}597 = 817{,}172$$

Rodney Random submitted his estimates of losses (different from those just given partly because the litigation was in reference to the middle period only) in a detailed report. When the case went to trial, the defendants were so overwhelmed by the strength of Rodney's analysis that all damages to COI were settled out of

Figure 7.6   Actual and Forecast Shipment of Sealing Compound
(Actual is in solid lines and forecast is in broken lines)

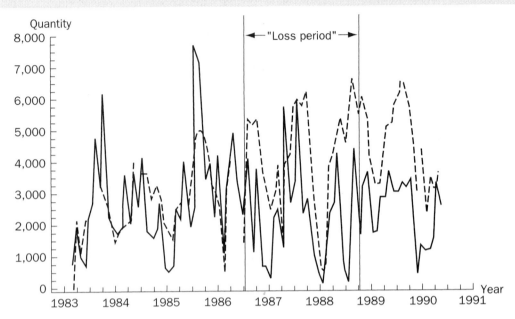

court and he never had a chance to testify. This caused Rodney a great deal of disappointment because he would have been paid $250 an hour for his testimony.

This example demonstrates how useful dummy variables can be in appropriately modeling real behavior.

7.9   Empirical Project

If an empirical project is a required component of your course, you would have followed the directions in Section 4.9, carried out a review of the relevant literature, and collected appropriate data. Now that you have learned how qualitative and nonlinear variables can be handled in a regression context, be sure to define appropriate dummy variables as well as nonlinearities, if needed. Next create a data file and enter all the data on the computer, either by variables or by observations. Then formulate models (see Section 14.3), generate relevant new variables (Section 14.4), and carry out preliminary data analysis (Section 14.5) to ensure that the data have been entered accurately and that explanatory variables do vary across observations (as indicated by the coefficient of variation measure). You might even try estimating an initial model.

The initially estimated results are often disappointing because regression coefficients may be insignificant or their signs may be unexpected (commonly referred to as *wrong signs*). Further diagnostic testing will undoubtedly be needed, but we still have not addressed certain special issues that might call for new types of tests as well as estimation procedures. Empirical analysis will therefore be only partially complete at this stage. You should continue the analysis only after reading more chapters.

Summary

In this chapter we have seen how *qualitative* independent variables such as gender, educational or occupational status, season, public or private, and so on can be handled in an econometric formulation. The method is very straightforward. First we choose one of the categories of the qualitative variable as *control* (the choice is arbitrary). Then we define *dummy variables* (variables that take only the value 1 or 0) for each of the other categories, *the number of dummy variables being one less than the number of categories* (in order to avoid perfect collinearity among the dummy variables). In a model of the form $Y = \alpha + \beta X + u$, if the constant term (α) is to be different for the different categories, then we assume the following:

$$\alpha = \alpha_0 + \alpha_1 D_1 + \alpha_2 D_2 + \cdots + \alpha_{m-1} D_{m-1}$$

where m is the number of categories for the dummy variables, and $D_1, D_2, \ldots, D_{m-1}$ are the dummy variables. D_1 will take the value 1 for observations that belong to category 1 and 0 for all other observations. The other Ds are defined similarly. To shift the slope (β) for the different categories, we assume that

$$\beta = \beta_0 + \beta_1 D_1 + \beta_2 D_2 + \cdots + \beta_{m-1} D_{m-1}$$

To estimate the αs and the βs, we generate the interaction variables $Z_1 = D_1 X$, $Z_2 = D_2 X, \ldots, Z_{m-1} = D_{m-1} X$, where X is a quantitative independent variable. Then we regress Y against a constant term, $D_1, D_2, \ldots, D_{m-1}, X, Z_1, Z_2, \ldots, Z_{m-1}$. The coefficients for the Ds are the $\hat{\alpha}$s and those for the Zs are the $\hat{\beta}$s. Note that the number of coefficients estimated is $2m$ and hence the degrees of freedom are $n - 2m$. This means that unless the number of observations is at least $2m$, the model with the full interaction terms cannot be estimated. If the number of categories is large, the dummy variable and interaction terms can easily proliferate. The problem becomes worse if there are more quantitative variables in the model whose coefficients are to be shifted. A useful approach is to formulate a basic model and then perform LM tests for shifts in intercepts and slopes. Alternatively, we could use the Hendry/LSE data-based reduction from a general model.

Key Terms

Analysis of covariance model

Analysis of variance (ANOVA) model

Binary variables

Chow test

Control group

Dummy variables

Dummy variable trap

Qualitative variables

Quantitative variables

Seasonal dummies

Structural break

Structural change

Structural instability

References

Blair, Roger D., David L. Kaserman, and James T. McClave. "Motor Carrier Deregulation: The Florida Experiment." *Review of Econ. Statistics* (February 1986): 159–164.

Chow, Gregory C. "Tests of Equality between Sets of Coefficients in Two Linear Regressions." *Econometrica* (1960).

Fisher, Franklin M. "Tests on Equality between Sets of Coefficients in Two Linear Regressions: An Expository Note." *Econometrica* (1970).

Grether, D. M., and P. Mieszkowski. "Determinants of Real Estate Values." *J. Urban Economics* 1 (1974).

Kain, J. K. and J. M. Quigley. "Measuring the Value of Housing Quality." *J. Amer. Stat. Assoc.* 65 (June 1970).

Mankiw, N. G., D. Romer, and D. N. Weil. "A Contribution to the Empiries of Economic Growth." *Quarterly J. Economics* (May 1992): 407–437.

Patel, Raman, Andrew Sikula, and John McKenna. "The Mobility of the Business Professor— Why?" *Collegiate News and Views* 37 (Fall 1983).

Ramanathan, Ramu. *Introduction to the Theory of Economic Growth.* Springer-Verlag, Berlin, 1982.

Ridker, R. G., and J. A. Henning. "The Determinants of Residential Property Values with Special Reference to Air Pollution." *Review of Econ. Statistics* (May 1967).

Schmalensee, R., R. Ramanathan, W. Ramm, and D. Smallwood. *Measuring External Effects of Solid Waste Management.* U.S. Environmental Protection Agency, EPA-600/5-7-010 (March 1975).

Sommers, Paul M., and Noel Quinton. "Pay and Performance in Major League Baseball: The Case of the First Family of Free Agents." *J. Human Resources* (1982): 426–436.

Exercises

Questions Requiring No Computer Work

7.1   Consider the following relationship between the amount of money spent by a state on welfare programs (Y) and the state's revenue (X):

$$Y = \alpha_1 + \alpha_2 D1 + \alpha_3 X + \alpha_4(D1{*}X) + u$$

where $D1$ is a dummy variable that takes the value 1 if the state legislature is controlled by Democrats and 0 otherwise, and * means multiplication. Your research assistant decided to define another dummy variable, $D2$, which takes the value 1 if the legislature is controlled by non-Democrats and 0 otherwise, and estimate the following model instead:

$$Y = \beta_1 + \beta_2 D2 + \beta_3 X + \beta_4(D2{*}X) + u$$

Describe step-by-step how you can obtain estimates of the αs from those of the βs, *without running another regression.* That is, you should derive expressions for the αs in terms of the βs.

†7.2   The following table has the estimated coefficients and associated statistics (standard errors in parentheses) for the demand for cigarettes in Turkey. The data are annual for the years 1960–1988 (29 observations). The definitions of the variables are as follows:

LQ = Logarithm of cigarette consumption per adult (dependent variable)
LY = Logarithm of per-capita real GNP in 1968 prices (in Turkish liras)
LP = Logarithm of real price of cigarettes in Turkish liras per kg
$D82$ = 1 for 1982 onward, 0 prior to that
$D86$ = 1 for 1986 onward, 0 prior to that
LYD1 = LY multiplied by $D82$
LYD2 = LY multiplied by $D86$
LPD1 = LP multiplied by $D82$
LPD2 = LP multiplied by $D86$

	Variable	Model A	Model B	Model C	Model D
$\hat{\beta}_1$	CONSTANT	−4.997 (0.511)	−4.800 (0.677)	−4.186 (0.535)	−4.997 (0.509)
$\hat{\beta}_2$	D82	23.364 (5.547)	−0.108 (0.207)	−0.103 (0.026)	21.793 (5.254)
$\hat{\beta}_3$	D86	−36.259 (12.859)	−0.406 (0.236)	−0.103 (0.037)	−28.291 (9.433)
$\hat{\beta}_4$	LY	0.732 (0.069)	0.705 (0.091)	0.621 (0.071)	0.732 (0.068)
$\hat{\beta}_5$	LYD1	−2.798 (0.661)			−2.602 (0.623)
$\hat{\beta}_6$	LYD2	4.251 (1.516)			3.298 (1.098)
$\hat{\beta}_7$	LP	−0.371 (0.097)	−0.337 (0.129)	−0.201 (0.090)	−0.371 (0.097)
$\hat{\beta}_8$	LPD1	0.405 (0.206)	0.016 (0.246)		0.288 (1.787)
$\hat{\beta}_9$	LPD2	−0.236 (0.258)	0.288 (0.250)		
$\overline{R}^2$		0.921	0.859	0.852	0.921
ESS		0.018645	0.036444	0.04195	0.019427

Note: Values in parentheses are the corresponding standard errors.

a. *In Model D,* write down the numerical values of the income and price elasticities of demand for each of the three periods (enter them in the following table).

Period	Income Elasticity	Price Elasticity
1960–1981		
1982–1985		
1986–1988		

Use the information provided to construct a test for the null hypothesis "There has been no structural change in the price and income elasticities over the three periods 1960–1981, 1982–1985, and 1986–1988." To do this, complete the following:

b. Identify the unrestricted and restricted models.
c. Write down the null hypothesis in terms of the βs.
d. Compute the numerical value of the test statistic.
e. State its distribution and d.f.
f. Now actually carry out the test and state whether you would reject the null hypothesis. Use a 1 percent level of significance.
g. Based on your test, would you say there has been a significant structural change in the elasticities? Explain.

Here you are to describe how to carry out a Lagrange multiplier test. Consider the basic model

$$LQ_t = \alpha + \beta LY_t + \gamma LP_t + u_t$$

You want to use the LM test to examine whether *the entire relation* is different across the three time periods for which D82 and D86 are defined.

h. Derive another model that will enable you to carry out the LM test.

i. In your model, write down the null hypothesis for "There has been no structural change in the relation."

j. Carefully describe what regression(s) you will run. (Your answer should say "regress y against $x1$, $x2$, $x3$, . . . " where y, $x1$, $x2$, and so on are actual variable names in your model. Don't use vague terms such as *estimate model* or *compute test statistic.*)

k. Describe the test statistic to compute. (You cannot actually compute it because you do not have enough information.)

l. What is its distribution (including d.f.) under the null hypothesis?

m. Write down the numerical value of the critical value (for a 10 percent level) for your test statistic. (Explain where you got this value.)

n. Describe the decision rule for your test.

7.3   A random sample of 1,629 employees was drawn and the following model was estimated:

$$\widehat{\text{LNWAGE}} = 0.448 + 0.0795 \text{ SCHOOL} + 0.059 \text{ EXP} - 0.00076 \text{ EXP}^2$$
$$+ 0.18725 \text{ URBAN} - 0.04393 \text{ SOUTH}$$
$$- 0.01172 \text{ HEALTH} + 0.03173 \text{ UNION}$$

where LNWAGE is the logarithm of hourly wage rate; SCHOOL is the number of years of schooling; EXP is the number of years of experience; EXP^2 is the square of EXP; URBAN = 1 if the employee lived in a city, 0 otherwise; SOUTH = 1 if the employee lived in a southern state; HEALTH = 1 if the employee had health problems; and UNION = 1 if the employee was a union member.

a. "Experience and experience squared are likely to be highly correlated. Therefore, the estimates are biased and any test of hypotheses based on them is invalid." Is this a correct statement? Explain why or why not.

b. Write down the estimated relation for a union member, with no health problems, living in a southern state (you have all the information needed to answer this question). Note that the model must be expressed in the standard form in which estimated relations are usually written.

c. Derive an expression for the *partial* elasticity of wage with respect to experience, and calculate its numerical value when experience is five years.

†7.4   Using data for 427 University of California at San Diego students, an investigator from the registrar's office estimated the following basic model (call it Model A):

$$\text{UCGPA} = \alpha + \beta \text{ HSGPA} + \gamma \text{ VSAT} + \delta \text{ MSAT} + u$$

where UCGPA and HSGPA are the GPAs at UCSD and in high school and VSAT and MSAT are verbal and math SAT scores. A number of characteristics of each student were also measured: (1) whether the student graduated from a public school or other type of school, (2) whether or not the student lived on campus, and (3) the student's major in five categories—science, social science, humanities, arts, and undeclared. All the following questions relate to this data set. Your answers to questions must therefore be very specific to it and not be general statements.

a. "Because HSGPA, VSAT, and MSAT are likely to be highly correlated, there is multicollinearity, which raises standard errors. Therefore, (1) the t- and F-tests are invalid, and (2) all insignificant variables should be dropped." Carefully explain whether the statements are justified. If not, why not?

b. Formulate another econometric model (call it Model B) that will enable you to test this hypothesis (clearly define any additional variables you might use).

c. State the null and alternative hypotheses *in that model.*

d. Describe what regression(s) should be run and how the test statistic is derived.

e. Describe the criterion for acceptance or rejection of the null hypothesis.

f. Redo the analysis for carrying out a Wald test instead.

7.5 Consider the consumption function (call it Model A) $C = \alpha + \beta Y + u$, where C is the consumption expenditures of a family and Y is its disposable income (income after taxes, measured in thousands of dollars). Consider the hypothesis that (1) α will depend on whether the family owns its residence and on the size of the family (N), and (2) β will depend linearly on the level of Y, whether the family owns its residence, and the family size N. You have data for 40 households.

a. Carefully derive the most general model (Model B) that will enable you to test both hypotheses. Be sure to define any new variables you may have to generate. Do this carefully because your subsequent answers depend very much on your getting this part right.

b. Write down the expression for the estimated relation for a renter. Do the same for a homeowner.

c. In Model B, you want to test the hypothesis that family size has no significant effect on consumption. State the null and alternative hypotheses to test this, and write down the restricted model (Model C).

d. To perform the *Wald test,* describe what regression(s) you will run and what test statistic you would compute (provide numerical values where known).

e. State its distribution and the numerical value(s) of the d.f.

f. Describe how you will use the *p*-value approach to decide whether or not to reject the hypothesis (at the 5 percent level).

g. In your Model B derived in part a, derive *separately* for homeowners and non-homeowners the algebraic expressions for the marginal propensity to consume with respect to income and family size.

h. State the null hypotheses implied by having Model A as the restricted model and Model B as the unrestricted one.

i. Using Model A as the basic model, you want to carry out an LM test for adding the new variables in Model B. Describe what regression(s) you should run and what test statistic you would compute. Clearly explain your steps and provide numerical values where known.

j. State its distribution, the numerical value(s) of the d.f., and the critical value for a 5 percent test.

k. Describe the decision rule for rejecting the null hypothesis.

l. Suppose you reject the null hypothesis. What further steps should you take to obtain a model more general than Model A without using the Wald approach?

m. Suppose Y^* is income measured in hundreds of dollars and Y^* is used instead of Y in Model B derived in part a. Carefully write down the relationships between all the new regression coefficients with the old ones.

7.6 You want to study the determinants of commercial television market shares and have the following basic specification (for simplicity, the *t*-subscript is omitted):

$$\text{SHARE} = \alpha + \beta\,\text{NSTAT} + \gamma\,\text{CABLE} + u \qquad n = 40$$

where SHARE is the market share (as a percent) of a station, NSTAT is the number of competing television stations in the area, and CABLE is the percent of households wired for cable television. You also know whether or not the station is VHF and its network affiliation (ABC, CBS, NBC, or none of these). You believe that the coefficient for NSTAT will depend on the qualitative variables just listed. Carefully describe how you can use the Lagrange multiplier test to verify that belief. More specifically:

a.   Formulate another econometric model that will enable you to test the hypothesis (clearly define any additional variables you should use).

b.   State the null and alternative hypotheses in that model.

c.   Describe the regression(s) to be run and explain how the test statistic is to be computed.

d.   Describe the distribution of the test statistic (including the numerical values of the d.f.) and state the criterion for acceptance or rejection.

e.   Describe how you can select new variables to add to the basic model and explain what you should do thereafter to continue the analysis.

7.7   Using quarterly data for 10 years (40 observations), the following double-log model (Model A) was estimated:

$$\text{LPCCARS} = \alpha + \beta \text{ LPRICE} + \gamma \text{ LPCINCOME} + \delta \text{ LINTRATE} + u$$

where PCCARS is per-capita new car sales, PRICE is new-car price index, PCINCOME is per-capita income, and INTRATE is the prime interest rate. The prefix L for each variable denotes the logarithm. The estimated coefficients and associated statistics are in the following table. (Note: Values in parentheses are t-statistics.) In addition, three seasonal dummies have been defined—SPRING, SUMMER, and FALL—each of which takes the value 1 in the corresponding quarter and 0 otherwise. In Model B these seasonal dummies have been included and in Model C only the SPRING dummy variable is present.

Variable	Model A	Model B	Model C
CONSTANT	−31.852	−33.320	−32.582
	(−5.8)	(−7.6)	(−7.4)
LPRICE	−1.751	−1.774	−1.760
	(−7.6)	(−9.8)	(−9.6)
LPCINCOME	4.732	4.907	4.814
	(6.7)	(8.8)	(8.5)
LINTRATE	−0.193	−0.197	−0.196
	(−3.3)	(−4.3)	(−4.2)
SPRING		0.092	0.125
		(2.8)	(4.6)
SUMMER		−0.051	
		(−1.6)	
FALL		−0.049	
		(−1.5)	
$\overline{R}^2$	0.787	0.867	0.863
ESS	−0.31044	−0.17699	0.19341
SGMASQ	0.8626	0.5363	0.5526
AIC	0.9482	0.6279	0.6209
FPE	0.9488	0.6302	0.6217
HQ	1.0079	0.6987	0.6701
SCHWARZ	1.1226	0.8438	0.7668
SHIBATA	0.9316	0.5973	0.6644
GCV	0.9584	0.6501	0.6316
RICE	0.9704	0.6807	0.6447

a. What is the control season?

b. State the expected signs for each coefficient and your reasons for expecting them.

You want to test the null hypothesis that there is no seasonal difference in the constant term across seasons.

c. Write down another econometric model that will enable you to test this hypothesis.

d. In this model, state the null and alternative hypotheses.

e. Describe how the test statistic for this is calculated.

f. Under the null hypothesis, what is its distribution and the degrees of freedom?

g. Describe the decision rule to reject the hypothesis at the 1 percent level.

h. Based on your analysis, should the null hypothesis be accepted or rejected?

i. Which variables of the model do you think should be dropped from the model and why?

j. Which would you choose as the "best" model and why?

k. You want to test whether the price elasticity (β) is different across seasons. *Starting from Model B,* derive another model that will enable you to test for this.

l. Write down the null hypothesis—in your model it is in part k—to test the hypothesis "There is no seasonal difference in the price elasticity."

m. Describe step-by-step how you would carry out this test. (Note: You cannot actually carry out this test because there is not enough information.) In particular, state what new variables must be created, which regressions should be run, how to compute the test statistic, its distribution and d.f. under the null, and the decision rule.

n. In Model C, test the hypothesis that the demand for new cars is neither price elastic nor inelastic. (Ignore the sign of the coefficient.)

7.8 Consider the model $P_t = \alpha + \beta S_t + u_t$, where P and S are profits and sales of a company at time t. The company's sales manager believes that this relationship is different across the fall, winter, spring, and summer seasons. She gives you data for each season for 20 years ($n = 80$) and wants you to test the null hypothesis that there is no difference in the parameters across the seasons.

a. Derive another model that will enable you to test this hypothesis.

b. Write down the null and alternative hypotheses.

c. Describe how you would test the hypothesis using the Wald approach. In particular, state what regressions you will run, how you will compute the test statistic, its distribution and d.f., and the criterion for acceptance or rejection of the null hypotheses.

d. Do the same using the LM test approach.

7.9 Consider the following model (ignoring the t-subscript) relating the income inequality coefficient, called the *Gini coefficient* (Y), which ranges from 0 to 1, 0 being perfect equality:

$$Y = a + b\,\text{GDP} + c\,\text{POP} + d\,\text{URB} + e\,\text{LIT} + f\,\text{EDU} + g\,\text{AGR} + u$$

where GDP is the growth rate of the gross domestic product, POP is the growth rate of population, URB is the percent of people living in urban areas, LIT is the percent of people in the country who can read and write, EDU is the secondary school enrollment expressed as percent of the total population of secondary school age, and AGR is the share of agriculture in GDP. You suspect that the entire relation will be different for socialist countries versus nonsocialist countries, and we know which country belongs to which category. You have data for 40 countries on these variables.

a. Derive another model that will enable you to use the Lagrange multiplier (LM) test to test whether the structure is different for socialist and other countries. Be sure to define any new variables needed to answer the question.

b. Formally write down the null hypothesis that the structure is the same for all countries.

c. Describe the regressions to be run to carry out the LM test.

d. Describe how to compute the test statistic, its distribution under the null hypothesis, and the numerical value of the d.f.

e. Write down the critical value for a 10 percent test, and describe the decision rule.

f. Repeat the analysis using the Wald test approach.

†7.10 Consider the following model of the demand for airline travel, estimated using annual data for the period 1947–1987. The number of observations is therefore 41.

$$\ln(Q) = \beta_1 + \beta_2 \ln(P) + \beta_3 \ln(Y) + \beta_4 \ln(\text{ACCID}) + \beta_5 \text{FATAL} + u$$

Q = Per-capita passenger miles traveled in a given year
P = Average price per mile
Y = Per-capita income
ACCID = Accident rate per passenger mile
FATAL = Number of fatalities from aircraft accidents

The model is double-log except for the fact that FATAL is not expressed in log form because the observation for some of the years is zero.

In 1979, the airlines were deregulated. Define the dummy variable D that takes the value 0 for 1947–1978 and 1 for 1979–1987. The following table presents the relevant values for three models. Model A is the basic model just given, Model B is the one derived by assuming that there has been a structural change of the entire relation, and Model C is derived after omitting a number of variables from Model B.

	Variable	Model A Coeff (Stderr)	Model B Coeff (Stderr)	Model C Coeff (Stderr)
$\hat{\beta}_1$	CONSTANT	2.938 (1.050)	2.635 (1.326)	2.476 (1.128)
$\hat{\beta}_2$	ln(P)	−1.312 (0.315)	−1.029 (0.377)	−0.991 (0.273)
$\hat{\beta}_3$	ln(Y)	0.716 (0.289)	−0.001 (0.433)	
$\hat{\beta}_4$	ln(ACCID)	−0.541 (0.100)	−0.821 (0.156)	−0.817 (0.035)
$\hat{\beta}_5$	FATAL	0.0004 (0.0003)	0.0009 (0.0003)	0.0009 (0.0003)
$\hat{\beta}_6$	D		−1.688 (0.388)	
$\hat{\beta}_7$	D × ln(P)		0.278 (0.796)	
$\hat{\beta}_8$	D × ln(Y)		0.987 (0.558)	0.883 (0.187)
$\hat{\beta}_9$	D × ln(ACCID)		0.818 (0.252)	0.849 (0.185)
$\hat{\beta}_{10}$	D × FATAL		−0.001 (0.0006)	−0.001 (0.0005)
ESS		1.096191	0.700959	0.711423
$\overline{R}^2$		0.972	0.979	0.981

First carry out a Wald test for the null hypothesis that the structure is the same before and after deregulation. To do this, complete the following steps:

a. Write down the null hypothesis.
b. To use the Wald test, compute the numerical value of the test statistic.
c. State its distribution, including d.f.
d. Write down the numerical value (or range) of the critical value for a 5 percent test.
e. Carry out the test, and indicate your conclusion as to whether or not the structure has significantly changed.
f. Using Model C, write down the complete estimated relation for the dependent variable both before and after deregulation.

In Model C, you want to test the null hypothesis that *during the period 1979–1987* the elasticity for ACCID is equal to 1.

g. First write down Model C in symbolic terms, that is, without any numerical values, just βs.
h. State the null hypothesis for this test. Do this carefully; the rest of the questions depend on a correct answer here.
i. Using Model C as the unrestricted model, derive a restricted model (it must be in terms of parameters and not numerical values) for testing the hypothesis. Show all your derivations; do this carefully also.
j. Write down an expression for the Wald test statistic (define any symbols you use). Be sure to put in numerical values where available.
k. Indicate its distribution under the null and the numerical value(s) of the d.f.
l. Describe how you would use the p-value approach to decide whether or not to accept or reject the null hypothesis.

7.11 Consider the consumption function $C_t = \alpha + \beta Y_t + u_t$, where C is aggregate consumption expenditures in the United States and Y_t is disposable income, both in constant dollars. Suppose you have annual data from 1930 to 1997. Because the World War II years were different, you wish to exclude that data. Furthermore, the postwar consumption function is likely to be different from the prewar function. Describe how you would test for this.

7.12 The relationships between the monthly expenditure on housing (E) and household income (Y) for three age groups are as follows:

$$
\begin{aligned}
\text{Age less than 30:} \quad & E = \alpha_1 + \beta_1 Y + u_1 \\
\text{Age 31 to 55:} \quad & E = \alpha_2 + \beta_2 Y + u_2 \\
\text{Age 56 and over:} \quad & E = \alpha_3 + \beta_3 Y + u_3
\end{aligned}
$$

a. What is the economic interpretation of the hypothesis $\beta_1 = \beta_2 = \beta_3$?
b. Describe step-by-step how the dummy variable approach could be used to test the hypothesis in part a.

7.13 You are studying the determinants of commercial television market shares. The basic specification is

$$
\text{SHARE}_t = \alpha + \beta \, \text{NSTAT}_t + \gamma \, \text{CABLE}_t + \delta \, \text{INCOME}_t + u
$$

where SHARE is the market share (in percent) of the tth station, NSTAT is the number of competing television stations in the same area, CABLE is the percent of households in the area wired for cable television, and INCOME is per-capita income of the locality served by the station.

a.   Explain why we can expect the following signs for the marginal effects:

$$\frac{\partial \text{ SHARE}}{\partial \text{ NSTAT}} < 0, \quad \frac{\partial \text{ SHARE}}{\partial \text{ CABLE}} < 0, \quad \text{and} \quad \frac{\partial \text{ SHARE}}{\partial \text{ INCOME}} = 0$$

b.   Describe step-by-step how you would use the Wald and LM tests to test the hypothesis that

i. α will depend on whether or not the *t*th station is VHF *and* whether or not it is a network affiliate.

ii.   the *entire relation* will depend on the two qualitative variables listed in hypothesis i.

7.14   The following table has four models relating the college grade point average (COL-GPA) of 427 students to their high school grade point average (HSGPA) and to their verbal and math scores in the Scholastic Aptitude Test (VSAT and MSAT). A number of dummy variables are also included: DCAM = 1 if the student lived on campus, DPUB = 1 if the student graduated from a public high school, and several dummy variables for major categories—science (DSCI), social science (DSOC), humanities (DHUM), and arts (DARTS). The control group is the undeclared students. (Note: The entries in parentheses are standard errors.)

Variable	Model A	Model B	Model C	Model D
CONSTANT	0.367 (0.224)	0.368 (0.224)	0.423 (0.220)	0.422 (0.221)
HSGPA	0.406 (0.063)	0.414 (0.062)	0.398 (0.061)	0.389 (0.062)
VSAT	0.00073 (0.00029)	0.00068 (0.00029)	0.00074 (0.00028)	0.00079 (0.00029)
MSAT	0.0011 (0.0003)	0.0011 (0.0003)	0.0010 (0.0003)	0.0010 (0.0003)
DSCI	−0.027 (0.057)	−0.026 (0.057)		
DSOC	0.056 (0.073)	0.054 (0.073)		
DHUM	−0.0041 (0.142)	−0.0068 (0.141)		
DARTS	0.229 (0.189)	0.243 (0.188)		
DCAM	−0.041 (0.052)			−0.040 (0.052)
DPUB	0.029 (0.063)			0.033 (0.063)
ESS	96.204	96.421	97.164	96.932
$\overline{R}^2$	0.211	0.213	0.215	0.213

a.   In the relevant models, test whether there is any difference due to the student's living on campus or off campus. State the null and alternative hypotheses, the test statistic and its distribution, and the test criterion.

b.   In the relevant models, test whether there is any difference due to the student's having graduated from a public or other type of school. State the null and alternative hypotheses, the test statistic and its distribution, and the test criterion.

c.   In Model A, test whether the dummy variables for majors are *jointly significant* at the 10 percent level. Be sure to state the null and alternative hypotheses, the test statistic and its distribution, and the test criterion. Perform the same test with Model B as the unrestricted model. Do you get the same result?

d.   In Model A, test the hypothesis that all of the dummy variables have zero regression coefficients.

7.15   Consider the following model proposed by Patel, Sikula, and McKenna (1983) of the mobility of the business professor:

$$AVGYR = \alpha + \beta\,PAPERS + \gamma AGE + u$$

where AVGYR is the mobility index defined as the average number of years employed in the institution, PAPERS is the number of papers published, and AGE is the age of the professor in years. Information is also available about the rank of the professor (assistant, associate, or full professor), whether opportunity for promotion is good, whether opportunity for jobs for a spouse is good, and whether the professor is happy with the administration.

a.   Develop a model that will enable you to test whether α is the same for professors of all ranks and all the other qualitative characteristics listed. Then describe how you will perform the test "α is the same for all ranks, promotion opportunities, and so on."

b.   Now do the same for the entire relation (that is, α, β, and γ).

7.16   Let E_t be energy consumption at time t and T_t be the temperature at that time. Consider the relation $E_t = a + bT_t + u_t$ examined in Section 7.5. The effect of temperature on energy consumption is likely to depend on the time of day. For instance, a 30° temperature at 2 P.M. will have a different impact than the same temperature at 2 A.M. Thus, this relationship might have a "time-of-day" effect. Describe how you will use the LM test to examine whether the relationship differs according to the time of day.

7.17   Using cross-section data for 59 single-family homes sold in the La Jolla and University City areas of San Diego, data on the following variables were obtained:

   price = Sale price in thousands of dollars (dependent variable)
    sqft = Living area in square feet
   yard = Yard size in square feet
   pool = 1 if the house has a swimming pool, 0 otherwise
   view = 1 if the house has a view, 0 otherwise
lajolla = 1 if the house is located in La Jolla, 0 otherwise

The following table has the coefficients and ESS for two different models. Model B is the basic model and Model A is the most general model that incorporates structural change between the two areas.

Variable	Model A	Model B
constant	33.134	−3.604
sqft	0.056	0.085
yard	0.001	0.001
view	15.888	43.212
pool	12.169	23.126
lajolla	65.553	
lajolla × sqft	0.021	
lajolla × yard	0.001	
lajolla × pool	57.207	
lajolla × view	−4.326	
ESS	2,003,718	3,916,605

    a.   To carry out a Wald test for structural difference in the model between La Jolla and University City, using Model B as the restricted model and Model A as the unrestricted model, write down the null hypothesis.

    b.   Compute the test statistic and write down its distribution under the null and d.f.

    c.   Actually carry out the test at the 1 percent level, and write down your conclusion as to whether there is a significant difference in the structure or not.

    d.   *In Model A,* compute the marginal effect on sale price with respect to each of the independent variables, separately for University City and La Jolla.

    e.   What do the numbers obtained in part d indicate about differences in price patterns between University City and La Jolla? Explain as you would to a senator or congressman.

7.18   Consider the relation $P_t = \alpha + \beta S_t + u_t$, where P is profits and S is sales of a certain firm. You have quarterly time series data for 10 years (40 observations). To allow for seasonal differences, you define three dummy variables, $D_1 = 1$ for fall only, $D_2 = 1$ for spring only, and $D_3 = 1$ for summer only, winter being the control.

    a.   You believe that both the coefficients are different across seasons. Derive the most general model (U) that incorporates that belief.

    b.   Explain why you did not define another dummy variable $D_4 = 1$ for winter, and include that in the model.

    c.   You want to use the Wald test for the null hypothesis "There is no difference in the relation between fall and spring." Carefully write down the null hypothesis for this test.

    d.   Derive the restricted model.

    e.   Describe the regressions to be run for this test.

    f.   Write down the expression for the test statistic and its distribution, including the numerical value(s) of the d.f.

    g.   Describe the decision rule. State numerical values where known.

    h.   You want to use the LM test for the hypothesis "There are no seasonal differences in the basic relationship specified (the one in the first paragraph)." Repeat parts e, f, and g. Provide complete details, including any numerical values.

7.19   Consider the following basic model (ignoring the *t* subscript):

$$\text{LCARS} = \alpha + \beta\,\text{LY} + \gamma\,\text{LP} + \delta\,\text{Lr} + u$$

where LCARS = the logarithm of per-capita new car sales, LY = log of per-capita real income in dollars, LP = log of new car real price index, and Lr = log of interest rate. To capture seasonal differences, three dummy variables were defined: $D_1 = 1$ for spring, 0 otherwise; $D_2 = 1$ for summer; and $D_3 = 1$ for fall. You have quarterly data for 15 years (60 observations).

    What is the control season? You believe that *the entire relation* specified in the basic model is different across seasons.

    a.   Derive the most general econometric model (Model U) that is consistent with that belief. Note that it should be in the standard form in which all models are written.

You want to test the hypothesis "The relationships between fall and spring seasons are identical."

    b.   Carefully derive the null hypothesis for the test.

    c.   Next you want to use the Wald *F*-test to test the hypothesis. Derive the restricted model (Model R) for this. Note that this, too, must be in the standard form.

    d.   Describe step-by-step the procedure for carrying out the test. Provide complete details, including any numerical values.

7.20 In the model formulated in Exercise 6.20, suppose the data were quarterly (with 92 observations) and you want to test whether the elasticity of housing with respect to per-capita GNP is different for different quarters.

    a. Formulate another econometric model that will enable you to test this hypothesis. Be sure to define any new variables needed to perform the test.

    b. State the null hypothesis for testing your belief.

    c. Step-by-step describe the procedure for using the Wald test (not the LM test) appropriate for testing the hypothesis you stated in part b. Give complete details that demonstrate that you really understand the procedure. Wherever numerical values can be provided you must state them and not use general symbols.

Questions Requiring Computer Work

For details on data files see Appendix D.

7.21 DATA7-10 has data on air quality in 30 standard metropolitan statistical areas (SMSAs) in the United States, along with several variables that can contribute to air pollution. The cross-section data refer to the period 1970–1972 for different variables. SMSAs are integrated economic and social units having 5,000 or more inhabitants. Most of them are counties or larger areas.

    a. Carefully explain why each of the possible independent variables might affect air quality. Indicate the sign you would expect for the regression coefficients. If a particular variable is not relevant, state so.

    b. Formulate a basic model with air quality as the dependent variable and a selected list of independent variables (exclude the binary variables at this point). Justify your choice. Using a regression program, estimate this model.

    c. Do your data have any multicollinearity problems? If yes, are your results affected by them?

    d. Describe how the dummy variables might affect the relationship you specified in part b. Formulate a new model and estimate it. Perform appropriate tests to compare the two models. What do you conclude?

    e. After choosing the final model, interpret your results.

7.22 Using cross-section data for the 58 counties in California, data on the following variables were obtained from both the 1980 and the 1990 censuses (this makes the total number of observations 116). The model relates median family income to its determinants listed next.

    MEDINC = Median family income in thousands of dollars (this is the dependent variable)

    FAMSIZE = Persons per household

    HIGHSCHL = Percent of the population (25 years and over) that had only high school education

    COLLEGE = Percent of the population (25 years and over) that completed four years of college or higher

    URB = Percent of urban population

    $D90$ = 1 for the 1990 census and 0 for the 1980 census

The following table has the coefficients, p-values, ESS, and the model selection statistics for four different models. Model B is the basic model and Model A is the most general model that incorporates structural change between the two periods. Note that you are not given the standard errors or t-statistics and they cannot be calculated from the information given.

Variable		Model A Coeff (*p*-value)	Model B Coeff (*p*-value)	Model C Coeff (*p*-value)	Model D Coeff (*p*-value)
β_1	CONSTANT	−16.909 (0.220)	98.434 (<0.01)	−17.040 (0.210)	−40.216 (<0.01)
β_2	FAMSIZE	4.893 (0.117)	−20.215 (<0.01)	4.944 (0.103)	10.029 (<0.01)
β_3	HIGHSCHL	0.224 (0.016)	−0.400 (0.004)	0.223 (0.015)	0.342 (<0.01)
β_4	COLLEGE	0.337 (<0.01)	0.549 (<0.01)	0.339 (<0.01)	0.381 (<0.01)
β_5	URB	0.045 (0.003)	0.017 (0.532)	0.044 (<0.01)	0.041 (<0.01)
β_6	D90	−36.175 (0.046)		−35.767 (0.037)	
β_7	D90 × FAMSIZE	9.881 (0.013)		9.760 (0.007)	2.151 (<0.01)
β_8	D90 × HIGHSCHL	0.201 (0.124)		0.199 (0.118)	
β_9	D90 × COLLEGE	0.872 (<0.01)		0.871 (<0.01)	0.772 (<0.01)
β_{10}	D90 × URB	−0.002 (0.941)			
ESS		763.029	5172.56	763.069	796.560
SGMASQ		7.198	46.600	7.131	7.308
HQ		8.606	51.005	8.378	8.288
GCV		7.877	48.699	7.731	7.777
AIC		7.816	48.606	7.682	7.748
SCHWARZ		9.910	54.731	9.512	9.148
RICE		7.948	48.798	7.786	7.809
FPE		7.819	48.608	7.685	7.749
SHIBATA		7.712	48.435	7.599	7.696

Note: Values in parentheses are *p*-values.

a. To carry out a Wald test for structural change using Model B as the restricted model and Model A as the unrestricted model, state the null hypothesis.

b. Compute the test statistic and state its distribution and d.f.

c. Actually carry out the test at the 1 percent level, and state your conclusion as to whether or not there has been a significant change in the structure.

d. Considering omitted-variable bias, significance of coefficients, and other measures, which model would you choose as the best? Explain why.

e. *In Model C,* compute the marginal effect on median income with respect to famsize, highschl, and college, separately for 1980 and 1990 data, and enter in the following table:

	1980 Data	1990 Data
FAMSIZE		
HIGHSCHL		
COLLEGE		

f. What do the numbers indicate about change in behavior between 1980 and 1990? Explain as you would to a senator or a congressman.

7.23 DATA7-11 has detailed data on 59 single-family houses in the La Jolla and University City communities of San Diego. La Jolla is a coastal community and is well known for its beautiful coves and beaches. It is also a resort city and is considered a prestigious locale to live in. University City is located about 5 to 10 miles inland. Because of their proximity to the ocean and the other reasons mentioned, La Jolla homes tend to be more expensive. Note from DATA7-11 that a number of variables are binary and take only the values 0 and 1.

First use the data to create the new variable LSQFT = ln(SQFT). Then estimate the following basic model:

$$\text{PRICE} = \alpha + \beta \text{SQFT} + \gamma \text{LSQFT} + \delta \text{YARD} + u$$

Do you have a "good" fit? Are the regression coefficients (ignore the constant term) significant? In this model, derive the marginal effect of SQFT on PRICE, and interpret the results. Next estimate a general model that includes other characteristics of the homes as well as ln(YARD). In this unrestricted model, are some variables candidates to be omitted? Why? Exclude these variables, reestimate the model, and perform a Wald F-test to see if the omitted variables are jointly significant. Repeat this process until you have the "best" model. Explain what you mean by "best." Choose your final model and interpret the results. Next repeat the process using the LM test approach of adding variables to the basic specification.

7.24 The data file DATA7-19 contains data (for the 29 years 1960–1988) on the demand for cigarettes in Turkey and its determinants. The definitions of the variables are as follows:

Q = Cigarette consumption per adult (kg)
Y = Per-capita real GNP in 1968 prices (in Turkish liras)
P = Real price of cigarettes in Turkish liras per kg
ED1 = Ratio of enrollments in middle and highs schools to the population 12–17 years old
ED2 = Ratio of enrollments in universities to the population 20–24 years old
D82 = 1 for 1982 onward
D86 = 1 for 1986 onward

In late 1981, health warnings were issued in Turkey regarding the hazards of cigarette smoking. In 1986, one of the national newspapers launched an antismoking campaign. First estimate the basic model relating the logarithm of Q to the logarithms of Y, P, ED1, and ED2. Then use the LM test approach to test whether the dummy variables D82 and D86 should be added to the specification along with interaction terms with the quantitative variables. Based on that, estimate a new model and use data-based reduction to eliminate redundant variables. Next start with a general specification with the entire relation being different across the three time periods and reduce the model by appropriate elimination of variables. Do you get the same final results? Also check whether the model exhibits multicollinearity. In your final model, test whether or not the numerical values of the various elasticities are 1. Is demand price elastic, inelastic, or unitary elastic? Do the same for income.

7.25 DATA7-17 has cross-section data on income inequality for 40 countries. It is measured by the *Gini coefficient,* which ranges from 0 to 1, 0 being perfect equality. For explanatory variables, see Appendix D. As before, use the data to estimate a general model, including slope shifts, and then apply the data-based method to simplify it. Then interpret the results.

7.26   In the theory of economic growth, a well-known model is the Solow–Swan model (see Ramanathan, 1982, for a discussion of the model), which relates the long-run per-capita income of an economy to the saving rate, population growth rate, and the growth rate in technical progress. Mankiw, Romer, and Weil (1992) gathered data for 104 countries and estimated a variety of growth models. The data are in the file DATA7-8 described in Appendix D. The variables are as follows:

$$\text{grth} = \text{Log of change in income 1960–1985 (dependent variable)}$$
$$y60 = \text{Log of income in 1960}$$
$$\text{inv} = \text{Average investment to GNP ratio over 1960–1985}$$
$$\text{pop} = \text{Measure of population growth in logarithms}$$
$$\text{school} = \text{Measure of percent of population in school}$$
$$\text{dn} = \text{Dummy for non–oil-producing countries}$$
$$\text{di} = \text{Dummy for industrialized countries}$$
$$\text{doecd} = \text{Dummy for OECD countries}$$

First estimate a basic model of the form $\text{grth} = \alpha + \beta y60 + \gamma \text{inv} + \delta \text{school} + \epsilon \text{pop} = u$. Next assume that all the regression coefficients are related to the dummy variables dn, di, and doecd and derive the most general model. Then carry out two parallel analyses, one using the data-based model simplification and the other using the LM test approach of going from simple to general modeling. Do you get the same result? Choose a final "best" model (justify your choice) and interpret the results.

7.27   Using the data in the file DATA7-9, verify the estimates presented in Exercise 7.14 for the relationship between college GPA and its determinants. Formulate the most general model that allows for the slope coefficients for high school GPA and verbal and scholastic SAT test scores to vary with the dummy variables. Starting with the basic model specified in Exercise 7.4, use the LM test approach to test whether the new variables in the most general model you specified should be added. From the auxiliary regression, select the independent variables to be added to the basic model, add them, and then carry out a data-based reduction until you find the "best" model (justify your choice). Now start with the most general model and eliminate variables until you reach a final model. Do the two approaches give the same answer? Choose one as the ultimate model and interpret the results.

7.28   The application in Section 5.4 related poverty rates in California counties using 1980 census data. DATA7-6 also contains the data from the 1990 census. A dummy variable, D90, that takes the value 1 for 1990 and 0 for 1980 is also defined. Use this data set to test whether there is structural change between 1980 and 1990, using an approach similar to the one used in the application in Section 7.6. See Section 5.4 for the formulation of the basic model.

7.29   In Exercise 3.34 you related the annual salary of a professor to the number of years since he or she received the Ph.D. degree. DATA7-7 has, in addition, six dummy variables indicating to which one of seven universities the professor belongs. To preserve confidentiality, the specific university for a given professor is not identified. First explain why seven dummy variables are not defined. Next use the basic model in Exercise 3.34 as a starting point and allow the intercept and slope coefficients to be different across universities, thereby deriving the most general model. Test the general and simple models against each other for structural change using both the LM and the Wald tests. Then use both the simple to general and the general to simple approaches to obtain a final model. Interpret the results of the final model. How do the goodness-of-fit and model selection statistics compare between the original basic model and your final model?

7.30   In Exercise 3.35 you fitted a linear time trend for the British population. If you graph population against time, you will note that during the period 1974–1983, population in Britain was pretty much flat. You can see from the graph that the structures are indeed different for the three periods 1962–1973, 1974–1983, and 1984–1994. DATA7-21 has two dummy variables, $D1$ taking the value 1 for 1974–1983 and 0 elsewhere and $D2$ taking the value 1 for 1984–1994 and 0 before 1984. Carry out tests of structural change similar to those done in Exercise 7.28.

7.31   DATA7-12 has data on the list price of 82 new 1995 American-made cars and a variety of characteristics of the car. Appendix D has the detailed definitions of the variables. First state what signs you would expect for each of the explanatory variables. Then estimate the most general model, reduce it using the p-values and other criteria, and interpret the final model. Do the signs of regression coefficients in the final model agree with your prior intuition?

7.32   DATA7-22 described in Appendix D has new data for cable subscriptions and their determinants. Earlier data were used in Example 6.7 to illustrate the LM test. The data in DATA7-22 are for 101 cities, 40 of which were for the original ones (based on 1979 data) used in Example 6.7, and 61 are for new areas (based on 1994 data). The dummy variable D takes the value 1 for the second set of data and 0 for the first set. Carry out a structural change test similar to the one done in Section 7.6 and in Exercises 7.28 and 7.30. Include nonlinear terms as appropriate, and interpret the final results.

7.33   DATA7-14 has cross-section data to estimate the effect of the implementation of capital punishment on homicide rates across the 50 states and Washington, D.C. The variables are described in Appendix D.

Using the data file DATA7-14, estimate the relationship between the homicide rate and all its determinants. Eliminate variables with insignificant coefficients and reduce the model. In the final model, what do you conclude about the legality of capital punishment?

7.34   DATA7-15 has data on voting patterns and their determinants for 38 congressmen/congresswomen. The variables are described in Appendix D. Relate the voting pattern to the other variables, and perform an analysis similar to that in previous exercises.

7.35   DATA7-16 has data on the number of college applications and their determinants for 34 universities and colleges. Using the data in that file, estimate a general model and then use the data-based method to simplify it. Then interpret the results.

7.36   DATA7-18 has cross-section data for 1980 used to explain population differentials for the 58 California counties. As before, use the data to estimate a general model and then apply the data-based method to simplify it. Then interpret the results.

7.37   Data file DATA7-20 has data on NBA (National Basketball Association) players' salaries and their determinants. Estimate a log-linear model of players' salaries using the general to simple method. Interpret the results of the final model.

7.38   The file DATA7-13 has data on families receiving unemployment compensation. For unemployment compensation received, carry out an analysis similar to those used in previous exercises.

7.39   DATA7-24 has data on the sale price and characteristics of homes in two cities within California. Carry out an analysis similar to the one in Exercise 7.17.

7.40   DATA7-25 has data on voting patterns in a number of congressional districts. Carry out an analysis similar to the one in Exercise 7.34.

7.41   DATA7-26 is a combination of DATA4-10 and DATA4-16 with a dummy variable for the second period. Carry out a test for structural change for the model formulated in Exercise 4.21. Use the data-based model simplification to arrive at a final model and interpret the results.

Some Special Issues with Cross-Section and Time Series Data

Part 4 is devoted to a discussion of a variety of issues that arise when an investigator analyzes cross-section and time series data. Chapter 8 deals with heteroscedasticity, a phenomenon that arises when the variance of an error term is not the same across observations. Chapter 9 is concerned with serial correlation (also known as autocorrelation), a phenomenon that occurs when the error term from one observation is correlated with that from another. Serial correlation is a common occurrence in time series data. These chapters begin by exploring the consequences of ignoring heteroscedasticity or autocorrelation and then introduce procedures for testing for the presence of these "problems." They go on to provide alternative approaches for estimating the parameters of a model. Concepts developed in these chapters are explained with the help of several examples and applications.

There are more annotated computer outputs in these chapters than the previous ones. As the new methods are more involved, a careful study of these outputs is strongly encouraged in order to enhance the understanding of the procedures.

CHAPTER 8

Heteroscedasticity

$\boldsymbol{I}$n deriving ordinary least squares (OLS) estimates as well as the maximum likelihood estimates (MLE), we made the assumption that the error terms u_t were identically distributed with mean zero and equal variance σ^2 (refer to Assumption 3.5 of Chapter 3 that stated that $\text{Var}(u_t|x_t) = \sigma^2$ for all t). This assumption of equal variance is known as **homoscedasticity** (which means equal scatter). The variance σ^2 is a measure of dispersion of the error terms u_t around their mean zero. Equivalently, it is a measure of dispersion of the observed value of the dependent variable (Y) around the regression line $\beta_1 + \beta_2 X_2 + \cdots + \beta_k X_k$. Homoscedasticity means that the dispersion is the same across all observations.

In many situations commonly encountered with cross-section data, however, this assumption might be false. Suppose, for example, we survey a random sample of households and obtain information about each household's total consumption expenditure and its income in a given year. Households with a low income do not have much flexibility in spending. Most of the income will go for basic necessities such as food, shelter, clothing, and transportation. Therefore, consumption patterns among such low-income households may not vary very much. On the other hand, rich families have a great deal of flexibility in spending. Some might be large consumers; others might be large savers and investors in real estate, the stock market, and so on. This implies that actual consumption might be quite different from average consumption. In other words, it is very likely that higher-income households have a larger dispersion around mean consumption than lower-income households. In such a case, the scatter diagram between consumption and income would indicate sample points closer to the regression line for low-income households but widely scattered points for high-income households (see Fig. 8.1). Such a situation is called **heteroscedasticity** (which means unequal scatter). Figure 3.A.2 in the Chapter 3 Appendix has a graph of heteroscedasticity in the population.

As a second example, consider a random sample of cities for which we relate the prevalence of crime to the amount of resources available to the city to combat crime. We might expect that the scatter of observed points might be more widely dispersed for large cities as compared to smaller cities. Here again the assumption of constant error variance might be violated.

Heteroscedasticity arises also when one uses grouped data rather than individual data. For instance, we may not have data on individual firms but use industry averages instead. In this case, the model might be $\bar{Y}_t = \alpha + \beta \bar{X}_t + \bar{u}_t$, where the bars indicate averages for the tth industry. The variance of the error term is now $\text{Var}(\bar{u}_t) = \sigma^2/n_t$, where n_t is the number of firms within the tth industry. Because the number of firms is likely to vary, the variance of the error terms will also vary, thus inducing heteroscedasticity.

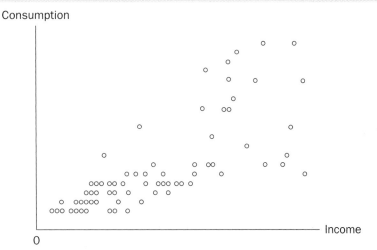

Figure 8.1 An Example of Heteroscedasticity

In this chapter, we relax the assumption that the error variance is constant and assume heteroscedasticity. More formally, we modify Assumption 3.5 as follows:

ASSUMPTION 3.5a

u_t is a random variable with $E(u_t|X_t) = 0$ and $\mathrm{Var}(u_t|X_t) = E(u_t^2|X_t) = \sigma_t^2$, for $t = 1, 2, \ldots, n.$

Thus, each observation has a different error variance. All the other assumptions on the stochastic disturbance terms will be maintained. Figure 3.A.2 provides a three-dimensional representation of heteroscedasticity and Figure 3.A.1 does the same for homoscedasticity.

Heteroscedasticity can occur in time series data also. This issue is discussed in the next chapter.

EXAMPLE 8.1

DATA3-11 has the annual salary and the number of years since earning the Ph.D. for 222 professors from seven universities. We have seen that the log-wage model is the appropriate one to model wages and salaries. The graph in Fig. 8.2 shows the logarithm of the salaries against the corresponding number of years since earning the Ph.D. We note that the spread around an average straight-line relation is not uniform, thus violating the usual assumption of homoscedasticity of the error terms. It is interesting to note that the variance around the conditional mean relation initially increases as the number of years increases but later decreases. This is not surprising, because the salaries of recent Ph.Ds are very competitive in the job market and hence we would not expect salary differentials to be high. Salaries of tenured professors, however, might vary a great deal depending on their productivity

Figure 8.2 Heteroscedasticity in Log Salary

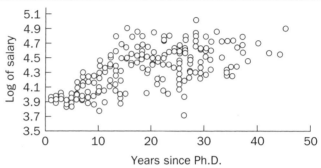

and reputation. After a number of years, salary increases tend to stabilize and hence the variance is likely to be reduced. We explore this example in more detail in Section 8.2 on testing for heteroscedasticity.

Suppose we ignore the heteroscedasticity and use the OLS procedure to estimate the parameters. What are their properties? Are they biased, inefficient, or inconsistent? Are the statistical tests still valid? Is there a procedure that will explicitly take account of heteroscedasticity and give better estimates? These issues are now addressed one by one.

8.1 Consequences of Ignoring Heteroscedasticity

We first study the implications of using the OLS procedure to estimate the regression coefficients in the presence of heteroscedasticity. The model is

$$Y_t = \beta_1 + \beta_2 X_{t2} + \cdots + \beta_k X_{tk} + u_t$$

where $\text{Var}(u_t | x_t) = \sigma_t^2$ for $t = 1, 2, \ldots, n$. The only change is that the error variances are different for different values of t and are unknown.

Effect on the Properties of the Estimators

The proofs of Properties 3.1 and 3.2 (which state that the OLS estimators are unbiased and consistent) depend only on Assumptions 3.3 and 3.4 (that u_t has zero mean and is uncorrelated with X_t) and not on Assumptions 3.5 or 3.5a. Therefore, the properties of unbiasedness and consistency are not violated by ignoring heteroscedasticity and using OLS to estimate the β's. However, while proving the Gauss–Markov theorem (Property 3.3), we used the assumption that $\text{Var}(u_t | x_t) = \sigma^2$ in order to minimize the variance of a linear combination of the Ys. Because that assumption is no longer true, it is not possible to assert that the OLS estimator is also more efficient. This means that the OLS estimator is now inefficient. It is possible to find an alternative unbiased linear estimator that has a lower variance than the OLS estimator. The appendix to this chapter illustrates this for the simple linear regression model.

Effect on the Tests of Hypotheses

It can be shown (see Appendix 8.A) that the estimated variances and covariances of the OLS estimators of the β_is are biased and inconsistent when heteroscedasticity is present but ignored (see Kmenta, 1986, pp. 276–279). Therefore, the tests of hypotheses are no longer valid.

Effect on Forecasting

We just argued that OLS estimators are still unbiased. It follows from this that forecasts based on these estimates will also be unbiased. But because the estimators are inefficient, forecasts will also be inefficient. In other words, the reliability of those forecasts (as measured by their variances) will be inferior to an alternative estimator that is more efficient.

The results obtained in this section are summarized in Property 8.1.

Property 8.1	If heteroscedasticity among the stochastic disturbance terms in a regression model is ignored and the OLS procedure is used to estimate the parameters, then the following properties hold:

a.   The estimators and forecasts based on them will still be unbiased and consistent.

b.   The OLS estimators are no longer BLUE and will be inefficient. Forecasts will also be inefficient.

c.   The estimated variances and covariances of the regression coefficients will be biased and inconsistent, and hence tests of hypotheses (that is, t- and F-tests) are invalid.

● 8.2   Testing for Heteroscedasticity

Because we know that heteroscedasticity invalidates test results, it would be desirable to test formally whether heteroscedasticity is present. In this section, we present the most commonly used tests for heteroscedasticity.

Before actually carrying out any formal tests, however, it is useful to examine the model's residuals visually to get a heuristic feel for whether heteroscedasticity is present. This is achieved by plotting the squares of the residuals obtained by applying OLS to the model under consideration. The squares of the OLS residuals are used because in a regression model the residual $\hat{u}_t$ is an unbiased estimate of the population error term u_t, even in the presence of heteroscedasticity. A sensible, though imperfect, estimate of the error variance $\sigma_t^2 = E(u_t^2 \mid x_t)$ is therefore $\hat{u}_t^2$. In other words, the squared residuals can be used to estimate σ_t^2. We can then graph them against a variable that is suspected to be the cause of heteroscedasticity. If the model has several explanatory variables, one might want to graph $\hat{u}_t^2$ against each of these variables or, better still, graph it against $\hat{Y}_t$, the fitted value of the dependent variable using the OLS estimates. It should be pointed out, however, that this graphing technique is only *suggestive* of heteroscedasticity and is not a substitute for formal testing.

● EXAMPLE 8.2

Using the data set DATA3-11 referred to in Example 8.1, we obtained the following log-quadratic model (see Practice Computer Session 8.1 to verify the results of this section):

$$\widehat{\ln(\text{SALARY})} = 3.809365 + 0.043853\,\text{YEARS} - 6.273475\text{e-04}\,\text{YEARS}^2$$
$$\qquad\qquad\quad (92.15)\qquad\quad (9.08)\qquad\qquad\qquad (-5.19)$$

$$\overline{R}^2 = 0.532 \qquad \text{d.f.} = 219$$

The values in parentheses are *t*-statistics, which indicate very high significance. The quadratic term allows for the possibility that there is diminishing marginal returns to experience. The strongly significant negative coefficient for YEARS^2 supports that hypothesis. For a graphic examination of possible heteroscedasticity, we obtained the squares of the residuals of the equation and plotted them against experience. It is seen from Figure 8.3 that the squared residuals show a tendency to increase with the years and then decrease later, a pattern explained in Example 8.1. Although not shown here (carry out Practice Session 8.1 for this), the graph of squared residuals against the predicted value of ln(SALARY) shows an even more pronounced increase in the variance. There is thus strong suggestive evidence of heteroscedasticity in the model. In the next section, this is put to a formal test.

Lagrange Multiplier (LM) Tests for Heteroscedasticity

There are a number of tests for heteroscedasticity and they vary in the generality and the powers of tests. Among these, the LM test approach has gained popularity in recent years. This is because the test statistic is easy to calculate and a variety of

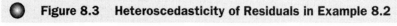

● **Figure 8.3   Heteroscedasticity of Residuals in Example 8.2**

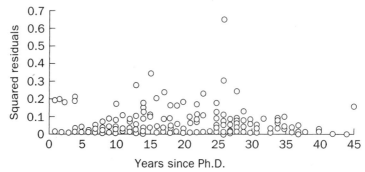

alternatives can be covered. In this section, we discuss the LM test for heteroscedasticity under three alternative assumptions of what causes heteroscedasticity. Let the model be

$$Y_t = \beta_1 + \beta_2 X_{t2} + \beta_3 X_{t3} + \cdots + \beta_k X_{tk} + u_t \tag{8.1}$$

where the error variance is $\sigma_t^2 = E(u_t^2 | x_t)$. If we do not specify the form that σ_t takes, there will be n σs and k regression coefficients to estimate, that is, $n + k$ parameters to estimate. With only n observations this is an impossible task. Therefore, we need to make simplifying assumptions about the error variance. The following three alternatives cover most of the cases discussed in the literature:

$$\sigma_t^2 = \alpha_1 + \alpha_2 Z_{t2} + \alpha_3 Z_{t3} + \cdots + \alpha_p Z_{tp} \tag{8.2a}$$

$$\sigma_t = \alpha_1 + \alpha_2 Z_{t2} + \alpha_3 Z_{t3} + \cdots + \alpha_p Z_{tp} \tag{8.2b}$$

$$\ln(\sigma_t^2) = \alpha_1 + \alpha_2 Z_{t2} + \alpha_3 Z_{t3} + \cdots + \alpha_p Z_{tp} \tag{8.2c}$$

which is equivalent to

$$\sigma_t^2 = \exp(\alpha_1 + \alpha_2 Z_{t2} + \alpha_3 Z_{t3} + \cdots + \alpha_p Z_{tp})$$

where exp stands for the exponential function, p is the number of unknown coefficients, and the Zs are variables with known values (some or all of the Zs might be the Xs in the model). We refer to these equations as the **auxiliary equations** for error variance. The **Breusch–Pagan test** (Breusch and Pagan, 1979) used formulation (8.2a). The **Glesjer test** (Glesjer, 1969) used formulation (8.2b) and the **Harvey–Godfrey test** (Harvey, 1976, and Godfrey, 1978) used Equation (8.2c). The last one is called **multiplicative heteroscedasticity** because the error variance is specified as the product of a number of terms. The **Park test** (Park, 1966) is a special case of the Harvey–Godfrey test and is not covered here separately. It is readily seen that the null hypothesis of homoscedasticity has $p - 1$ restrictions and is given by $\alpha_2 = \alpha_3 = \cdots = \alpha_p = 0$. Under the null the variance will be constant, which means that heteroscedasticity does not exist. Note that in all the formulations we are assuming that known Z variables are responsible for the heteroscedasticity.

Because we do not know σ_t, we use estimates obtained by applying OLS to Equation (8.1). Thus, we would use $\hat{u}_t^2$ for σ_t^2, $|\hat{u}_t|$ (absolute value of u_t) for σ_t, and $\ln(\hat{u}_t^2)$ for $\ln(\sigma_t^2)$. The steps for the LM test are as given next.

Step 1   Regress Y against a constant term, X_2, X_3, . . . , and X_k and obtain the OLS estimates of the βs.

Step 2   Compute the residuals as $\hat{u}_t = Y_t - \hat{\beta}_1 - \hat{\beta}_2 X_{t2} - \hat{\beta}_3 X_{t3} - \cdots - \hat{\beta}_k X_{tk}$.

Step 3a   Square the residuals and regress $\hat{u}_t^2$ against a constant term, Z_{t2}, Z_{t3}, . . . , and Z_{tp}, and obtain the OLS estimates of the αs. This is the **auxiliary regression** corresponding to Equation (8.2a).

Step 3b   Compute the absolute value and regress $|\hat{u}_t|$ against a constant term, Z_{t2}, Z_{t3}, . . . , and Z_{tp} and obtain the OLS estimates of the αs. This is the auxiliary regression corresponding to Equation (8.2b).

Step 3c　Take the logarithm of squared residuals and regress $\ln(\hat{u}_t^2)$ against a constant term, Z_{t2}, Z_{t3}, . . . , and Z_{tp} and obtain the OLS estimates of the αs. This is the auxiliary regression corresponding to Equation (8.2c).

Step 4　Compute the test statistic LM $= nR^2$, where n is the number of observations used in estimating the auxiliary regression and R^2 is the unadjusted R^2 from this regression.

Step 5　Compute p-value $= \text{Prob}(\chi_{p-1}^2 > \text{LM})$, which is the area to the right of LM in the chi-square distribution with $p - 1$ d.f.

Step 6　Reject H_0: $\alpha_i = 0$ for $(i = 2, 3, \ldots, p)$ and conclude that there is significant heteroscedasticity if the p-value is less than the level of significance. Alternatively, look up the chi-square table for $p - 1$ d.f. for the critical value $\chi_{p-1}^2(a)$, where a is the level of significance. Reject H_0 if LM $> \chi_{p-1}^2(a)$. If the test is not rejected, then there is no evidence to support a conjecture of heteroscedasticity. In this case, OLS is the accepted estimation procedure.

The test statistics proposed by the original authors of the tests were not the nR^2 statistic stated here. For instance, the Glesjer test is a Wald test. Harvey proposes a likelihood ratio test (see the Chapter 6 Appendix on the likelihood ratio test). The Breusch–Pagan and Godfrey tests suggest one-half of the regression sum of squares (defined in Chapter 3) of the auxiliary regression as the test statistic, which is distributed as χ_{p-1}^2. As Engle (1984) has pointed out, since all of these tests are large-sample tests, the tests proposed by the various authors are operationally equivalent to the Lagrange multiplier test just given. Because the exact distributions of these statistics are unknown (especially in small samples), they will vary in the powers of the tests. The more accurately one knows exactly what is causing the heteroscedasticity, the better the power of the test. The nR^2 statistic is most convenient to calculate and, since the LM test is asymptotically (that is, for large samples) equivalent to the other tests, it is the recommended test to use. Readers with knowledge of matrix algebra are advised to study the original papers of the authors cited here for more insights into the issues of testing and estimation in the presence of heteroscedasticity. Also refer to Chapter 12 of Greene (2000) for an excellent summary of the issues.

● EXAMPLE 8.3

In Example 8.1 we used the log-quadratic model of professors' salaries with the data from DATA3-11 and graphically demonstrated the presence of heteroscedasticity, with the error variances at first increasing with years since the subjects earned Ph.D.s and then decreasing. This suggests the following quadratic models for the error structure:

(a) Breusch–Pagan:　　$\sigma_t^2 = \alpha_1 + \alpha_2 \, \text{YEARS}_t + \alpha_3 \, \text{YEARS}_t^2$

(b) Glesjer:　　　　　$\sigma_t = \alpha_1 + \alpha_2 \, \text{YEARS}_t + \alpha_3 \, \text{YEARS}_t^2$

(c) Harvey–Godfrey:　$\ln(\sigma_t^2) = \alpha_1 + \alpha_2 \, \text{YEARS}_t + \alpha_3 \, \text{YEARS}_t^2$

The null hypothesis of homoscedasticity is equivalent to H_0: $\alpha_2 = \alpha_3 = 0$. From Practice Computer Session 8.2 and Table 8.1, we see that the LM test statistics are,

Table 8.1   Partial Output for the LM Tests in Example 8.3 Using DATA3-11

[First regress ln(SALARY) against a constant, YEARS, and YEARS^2. Then generate the following variables: usq = $\hat{u}_t^2$, absuhat = $|\hat{u}_t|$, and lnusq = $\ln(\hat{u}_t^2)$. The auxiliary regression for the three LM tests are given below, starting with the Breusch–Pagan test. The null hypothesis is that the coefficients for YEARS and YEARS^2 are both zero.]

```
Dependent variable: usq
```

	VARIABLE	COEFFICIENT	STDERROR	T STAT	2Prob(t > |T|)	
0)	const	-0.0111	0.0135	-0.823	0.411484	
2)	YEARS	0.0061	0.0016	3.866	0.000146	***
4)	YRS2	-0.0001288	0.0000394	-3.271	0.001246	***

```
Unadjusted R-squared        0.075 Adjusted R-squared            0.066
```

```
Chi-square(2): area to the right of (LM =) 16.586551 = 0.000250
```

[The low p-value indicates that because the probability of rejecting a true hypothesis is low, we can safely reject the null hypothesis of homoscedasticity and conclude that there is significant heteroscedasticity. Next is the auxiliary regression for the Glesjer test.]

```
Dependent variable: absuhat
```

	VARIABLE	COEFFICIENT	STDERROR	T STAT	2Prob(t > |T|)	
0)	const	0.0312	0.0241	1.296	0.196278	
2)	YEARS	0.0144	0.0028	5.118	0.000001	***
4)	YRS2	-0.0002975	0.0000704	-4.227	0.000035	***

```
Unadjusted R-squared        0.130 Adjusted R-squared            0.122
```

```
Chi-square(2): area to the right of (LM =) 28.922794 = 0.000001
```

[Such a low p-value indicates the presence of heteroscedasticity. Next is the auxiliary regression for the Harvey–Godfrey test where the p-value is also low, indicating the presence of heteroscedasticity.]

```
Dependent variable: lnusq
```

	VARIABLE	COEFFICIENT	STDERROR	T STAT	2Prob(t > |T|)	
0)	const	-6.5627	0.3592	-18.268	0.000000	***
2)	YEARS	0.2356	0.0420	5.614	0.000000	***
4)	YRS2	-0.0048	0.0011	-4.548	0.000009	***

```
Unadjusted R-squared        0.159  Adjusted R-squared           0.151
```

```
Chi-square(2): area to the right of (LM =) 35.302998 = 0.000000
```

respectively, 16.587, 28.923, and 35.303. From the chi-square table, the critical value with 2 d.f. and the level of significance 0.001 is 13.816. All the LM test statistics are above this, and hence we reject the null hypothesis in all cases and conclude that there is heteroscedasticity. As Table 8.1 shows, the sign of the estimated α_2 is positive and that of the estimated α_3 is negative in all three tests, confirming the graphic pattern of initially increasing and then decreasing variances.

Goldfeld–Quandt Test

An alternative test, proposed by Goldfeld and Quandt (1965), is based on the notion that if the error variances are equal across observations (that is, if they are homoscedastic), then the variance for one part of the sample will be the same as the variance for another part of the sample. One can therefore test for the equality of error variances using an F-test. The test becomes a ratio of two sample variances. The sample of observations is divided into three parts, and the middle observations are discarded. The model is then estimated for each of the other two sets of observations and the residual variances computed. Next an F-test is used to test for the equality of these variances. The formal steps for the **Goldfeld–Quandt test** are as follows:

Step 1   Identify a variable (say Z) to which the error variance σ_t^2 is related. Suppose, for instance, that σ_t^2 is suspected of being positively related to Z_t. Arrange the data set according to increasing values of Z_t (Z_t could be one of the Xs in the regression, such as income or population).

Step 2   Divide the sample of n observations into the first n_1 and the last n_2, thus omitting the middle observations $n_1 + 1$ through $n - n_2$. The number of observations to be omitted is arbitrary and is usually between one-sixth and one-third. Note that n_1 and n_2 must be greater than the number of coefficients to be estimated.

Step 3   Estimate separate regressions for observations 1 through n_1 and $n - n_2 + 1$ through n.

Step 4   Obtain the error sum of squares as follows:

$$\text{ESS}_1 = \sum_{t=1}^{n_1} \hat{u}_t^2 \quad \text{and} \quad \text{ESS}_2 = \sum_{t=n-n_2+1}^{n} \hat{u}_t^2$$

From Property 4.1c we know that ESS/σ^2 has the chi-square distribution. From Section 2.7, we know that the ratio of two independent chi-squares is an F-distribution. This suggests the next step.

Step 5   Compute

$$F_c = \frac{\hat{\sigma}_2^2}{\hat{\sigma}_1^2} = \frac{\text{ESS}_2/(n_2 - k)}{\text{ESS}_1/(n_1 - k)}$$

where k is the number of regression coefficients including the constant term. Under the null hypothesis of homoscedasticity, the computed F_c has an F-distribution with d.f. $n_2 - k$ and $n_1 - k$. If $F_c > F^*$, the point on the F-distribution such that the area to the right is 5 percent, then reject the null hypothesis of homoscedasticity and conclude that heteroscedasticity is present. [Note: If $F_c < 1$, then use $1/F_c$. This is because the alternative hypothesis is usually $\sigma^2_2 > \sigma^2_1$.]

● EXAMPLE 8.4

For the salary data set we have been using here, we first arranged the data in increasing order by YEARS and then estimated the log-quadratic model for the first and last 75 observations, discarding the middle 72 observations. From the output for Practice Computer Session 8.3 we obtain

$$\hat{\sigma}^2_1 = 0.015416 \qquad \hat{\sigma}^2_2 = 0.050608 \qquad F_c = 3.283$$

Under the null hypothesis of homoscedasticity, F_c has the F-distribution with 72 d.f. for the numerator and the same for the denominator. The critical F^* for a 1 percent level is between 1.53 and 1.84 (see Table A.4a). Thus, the test statistic is clearly significant, suggesting that we should reject the null hypothesis and confirming the earlier findings.

White's Test

The Goldfeld–Quandt test is not as useful as the LM tests because it cannot accommodate situations where several variables jointly cause heteroscedasticity, as in Equations (8.2a), (8.2b), and (8.2c). Also, by discarding the middle observations, we are throwing away valuable information. The Breusch–Pagan test has been shown to be sensitive to any violation of the normality assumption. (See Koenker, 1981, for a modification of their test in the presence of nonnormality.) Also, all the previous tests require a prior knowledge of what might be causing the heteroscedasticity. White (1980) has proposed a direct test for heteroscedasticity that is very closely related to the Breusch–Pagan test but does not assume any prior knowledge of the heteroscedasticity. **White's test** is also a large-sample LM test with a particular choice for the Zs, but it does not depend on the normality assumption. For these reasons, this test is recommended over all the previous ones. One might also carry out all the tests and see if the results are robust. The steps for carrying out White's test for heteroscedasticity are described for the following model. The extension for more general models is straightforward.

$$Y_t = \beta_1 + \beta_2 X_{t2} + \beta_3 X_{t3} + u_t \tag{8.3}$$

$$\sigma^2_t = \alpha_1 + \alpha_2 X_{t2} + \alpha_3 X_{t3} + \alpha_4 X^2_{t2} + \alpha_5 X^2_{t3} + \alpha_6 X_{t2} X_{t3} \tag{8.4}$$

Step 1 Estimate (8.3) by the OLS procedure and obtain $\hat{\beta}_1$, $\hat{\beta}_2$, and $\hat{\beta}_3$.

Step 2 Compute the residual $\hat{u}_t = Y_t - \hat{\beta}_1 - \hat{\beta}_2 X_{t2} - \hat{\beta}_3 X_{t3}$, and square it.

Step 3 Regress the squared residual $\hat{u}^2_t$ against a constant, X_{t2}, X_{t3}, X^2_{t2}, X^2_{t3}, and $X_{t2} X_{t3}$. This is the auxiliary regression corresponding to (8.4).

Step 4 Compute the statistic nR^2, where n is the size of the sample and R^2 is the *unadjusted* R-squared from the auxiliary regression of Step 3.

Step 5   Reject the null hypothesis that $\alpha_2 = \alpha_3 = \alpha_4 = \alpha_5 = \alpha_6 = 0$ if $nR^2 > \chi_5^2(a)$, the upper a percent point on the chi-square distribution with 5 d.f.

Although the test is a large-sample test, it has been found useful in samples of 30 or more. If the null hypothesis is not rejected, Equation (8.4) becomes $\sigma_t^2 = \alpha_1$, which implies that the residuals are homoscedastic. White's test is readily generalized for the multiple regression case with several regressors. In this case, for Step 1, we regress Y against a constant (which must be present) and as many regressors, that is, Xs, as needed. Then we obtain the residuals from this model and square them to get $\hat{u}_t^2$. We regress the squared residuals against all the variables in the first step, plus the squares of all the independent variables, plus the cross products of every pair of regressors. Finally, we compute the nR^2 statistic and reject homoscedasticity if $nR^2 > \chi^2(a)$ with level of significance a and degrees of freedom equal to the number of regression coefficients in the *auxiliary regression* with $\hat{u}_t^2$ as the dependent variable, *excluding the constant*. Note that this degrees of freedom is different from that obtained when the LM test is used to test for omitted variables.

Care must be taken in carrying out Step 3, especially if some of the explanatory variables are dummy variables. If X_{t2} is a dummy variable, then X_{t2}^2 is identical to X_{t2} and hence should not be included separately, as otherwise there will be exact multicollinearity and the auxiliary regression cannot be run. Second, if Equation (8.3) has several explanatory variables, Step 3 will involve a large number of variables (because of square and cross-product terms). It is then possible for the number of variables in the auxiliary regression to exceed the number of observations, making it impossible to carry out Step 3. In the general case, with k explanatory variables, *including the constant term*, the auxiliary regression will have $k(k + 1)/2$ terms. The number of observations must be larger than that, and hence $n > k(k + 1)/2$ is a necessary condition. If the degrees of freedom might be a problem, a simple alternative is to regress $\hat{u}_t^2$ against a constant, $\hat{Y}_t$, and $\hat{Y}_t^2$, where $\hat{Y}_t$ is the fitted value of Y_t using OLS estimates. Because $\hat{Y}_t$ depends on all the Xs and $\hat{Y}_t^2$ has all the squares and cross products of the Xs, this procedure is a convenient alternative to circumvent the d.f. problem.

● EXAMPLE 8.5

For the log-quadratic model used earlier, the squared variables will be YEARS^2 and YEARS^4 and the cross-product variable is YEARS^3. Thus, the auxiliary equation for this model is

$$\sigma_t^2 = \alpha_1 + \alpha_2\,\text{YEARS} + \alpha_3\,\text{YEARS}^2 + \alpha_4\,\text{YEARS}^3 + \alpha_5\,\text{YEARS}^4$$

Regressing the squared residuals obtained from applying OLS to the log-quadratic model against a constant and the powers of YEARS, the unadjusted $R^2 = 0.09$ and $n = 222$ (see Practice Computer Session 8.4). Therefore, LM $= nR^2 = 19.98$. The null hypothesis is $\alpha_i = 0$ for $i = 2, \ldots, 5$. Under this, LM has the chi-square distribution with 4 d.f. The critical value for a chi-square with 4 d.f. and level of significance 0.001 is 18.467, which is less than LM. Therefore, we reject homoscedasticity here also.

8.3 Estimation Procedures

If the assumption of homoscedasticity is rejected, we face the problem of trying to find alternative estimation procedures that are superior to ordinary least squares. In this section, we discuss a number of approaches to estimation.

Heteroscedasticity Consistent Covariance Matrix (HCCM) Estimation

In Property 8.1 it was mentioned that the estimated variances of the OLS estimates are biased and inconsistent, and hence statistical inferences will no longer be valid. If, however, consistent estimates can be obtained for the variances of the estimates, then valid inferences are possible *for large samples*. White (1980) has proposed a method of obtaining consistent estimators of the variances and covariances of the OLS estimator, which he called the **heteroscedasticity consistent covariance matrix (HCCM) estimator.** Messer and White (1984) showed how a HCCM estimator may be obtained using conventional regression packages. This has been extended by MacKinnon and White (1985), who studied three different ways of obtaining HCCM estimates. They conclude from sampling experiments that the estimator with the best small-sample properties is based on what statisticians refer to as the **jackknife** (Effron, 1982). In simple terms, a jackknife estimator would first estimate a model n times, each time dropping one observation. This generates a series of estimates whose variability is exploited in constructing the jackknife estimator as an average of individual variances and covariances.

EXAMPLE 8.6

For the salary example we have been using, both OLS and HCCM estimates of the standard errors were obtained using the GRETL and SHAZAM programs (see Practice Computer Session 8.5). The results are given next with the OLS standard errors in parentheses; the HCCM standard errors for GRETL are in square brackets, and the HCCM standard errors for SHAZAM are in braces. HCCM estimates of the variances of the estimators are consistent, whereas the corresponding OLS estimates are not, but the estimates of the regression coefficients and R^2 will be unchanged ($\overline{R}^2 = 0.532$).

$$\widehat{\ln(\text{SALARY})} = 3.809 + 0.044 \text{ YEARS} - 6.274\text{e-}04 \text{ YEARS}^2$$
$$\phantom{\widehat{\ln(\text{SALARY})} = } (0.041) \quad (0.0048) \quad\quad (1.209\text{-}04)$$
$$\phantom{\widehat{\ln(\text{SALARY})} = } [0.027] \quad [0.0046] \quad\quad [1.256\text{e-}04]$$
$$\phantom{\widehat{\ln(\text{SALARY})} = } \{0.026\} \quad \{0.0043\} \quad\quad \{1.171\text{E-}04\}$$

The reason for the very slight difference in the estimates for standard errors between the GRETL and SHAZAM programs is that the former uses the jackknife adjustment discussed earlier, whereas the latter does not. We note that all the coefficients are significant at levels below 0.001.

Generalized (or Weighted) Least Squares

Consider the model in Equation (8.3) and divide every term by σ_t, the standard deviation of u_t. We then obtain the modified model

$$\frac{Y_t}{\sigma_t} = \beta_1 \frac{1}{\sigma_t} + \beta_2 \frac{X_{t2}}{\sigma_t} + \beta_3 \frac{X_{t3}}{\sigma_t} + \frac{u_t}{\sigma_t}$$

or

$$Y_t^* = \beta_1 X_{t1}^* + \beta_2 X_{t2}^* + \beta_3 X_{t3}^* + u_t^* \tag{8.5}$$

where the asterisks denote corresponding variables divided by σ_t. We have

$$\text{Var}(u_t^*) = \text{Var}\left(\frac{u_t}{\sigma_t}\right) = \frac{\text{Var}(u_t)}{\sigma_t^2} = 1$$

Thus, Equation (8.5) satisfies all the conditions required for OLS estimates to possess desirable properties. Hence, estimates obtained by regressing Y_t^* against X_{t1}^*, X_{t2}^*, and X_{t3}^* (with no constant term) will be BLUE. The procedure just described is a special case of a more general method called **generalized least squares (GLS).** Although the GLS procedure appears straightforward, the practical problem is that σ_t is unknown, and hence we cannot estimate Equation (8.5) without additional assumptions.

The GLS procedure applied to the case of heteroscedasticity is also the same as **weighted least squares (WLS).** Define $w_t = 1/\sigma_t$ and note that (8.5) can be rewritten as follows:

$$w_t Y_t = \beta_1 w_t + \beta_2 (w_t X_{t2}) + \beta_3 (w_t X_{t3}) + (w_t u_t) \tag{8.6}$$

Comparing (8.5) and (8.6), we readily see that minimizing the sum of squares of u_t^* is equivalent to minimizing the weighted sum of squares of residuals:

$$\sum (w_t u_t)^2 = \sum (w_t Y_t - \beta_1 w_t - \beta_2 w_t X_{t2} - \beta_3 w_t X_{t3})^2 \tag{8.7}$$

Thus, each observation on each variable (including the constant term) is given the weight w_t, which is inversely proportional to the standard deviation of u_t. This means that observations for which σ_t is large are given less weight in the WLS procedure. It is easy to verify (see Exercise 8.1) that the resulting estimates are identical to those obtained by applying OLS to Equation (8.5). It is possible to show that the weighted least squares estimators are also maximum likelihood (see Exercise 8.2) in the case of normal errors.

It is useful to note that, because the error terms of the transformed Equation (8.5) are "well behaved," by the Gauss–Markov theorem WLS estimators are more efficient than OLS estimators. In fact, they are BLUE, provided the weights are known up to a proportional factor, as is the case in the next section.

Heteroscedasticity with a Known Proportional Factor

First consider the simple case in which the structure of the heteroscedasticity is known to have a particular form. In the model in Equation (8.3), suppose the heteroscedasticity is such that the error standard deviation σ_t is proportional to Z_t, which is known. More specifically, suppose Equation (8.4) is as follows:

$$\text{Var}(u_t) = \sigma_t^2 = \sigma^2 Z_t^2 \quad \text{or equivalently} \quad \sigma_t = \sigma Z_t \tag{8.8}$$

where the values of Z_t are known for all t. In other words, the residual standard deviation is proportional to some known variable Z_t, the constant of proportionality being σ (unknown). In the consumption expenditure example given earlier, Z_t will be household income, and in the crime example, Z_t will be the city's population. Except for this modification, u_t is thought to satisfy all the other assumptions for applying OLS. Dividing every term in Equation (8.3) by Z_t,

$$\frac{Y_t}{Z_t} = \beta_1 \frac{1}{Z_t} + \beta_2 \frac{X_{t2}}{Z_t} + \beta_3 \frac{X_{t3}}{Z_t} + \frac{u_t}{Z_t}$$

or

$$Y_t^* = \beta_1 X_{t1}^* + \beta_2 X_{t2}^* + \beta_3 X_{t3}^* + u_t^* \tag{8.9}$$

where the asterisks denote corresponding variables divided by Z_t. We have

$$\text{Var}(u_t^*) = \text{Var}\left(\frac{u_t}{Z_t}\right) = \frac{\text{Var}(u_t)}{Z_t^2} = \sigma^2$$

Thus, Equation (8.9) satisfies all the conditions required for OLS estimators to have desirable properties. Hence, estimates obtained by regressing Y_t^* against X_{t1}^*, X_{t2}^*, and X_{t3}^* will be BLUE (when $\sigma_t^2 = \sigma^2 Z_t^2$). This is the same as WLS with $w_t = 1/Z_t$. Note that Equation (8.9) does not have a constant term *unless either X_{t2} or X_{t3} is identical to Z_t*. Because the GLS estimators are BLUE, OLS estimators of (8.3) will be inefficient.

● EXAMPLE 8.7

DATA8-2 has cross-section data for the 50 U.S. states and the District of Columbia for the aggregate expenditure on travel (EXPTRAV) and the corresponding personal income (INCOME). Both are measured in billions of dollars. Consider the following Engel curve relation

$$\text{EXPTRAV}_t = \alpha + \beta \, \text{INCOME}_t + u_t$$

We might expect that the error variances are heteroscedastic and increase with population. In other words, states with large populations are likely to have greater variations in the expenditures on travel than small states. A sensible specification is therefore $\sigma_t = \sigma\,POP_t$ or equivalently, $Var(u_t) = \sigma_t^2 = \sigma^2\,POP_t^2$. Assuming that the standard deviation is proportional to the population is equivalent to assuming that the variance is proportional to the square of the population. As the first step, we used the Glesjer test for heteroscedasticity and found it to be significant (see Table 8.2 obtained from Practice Computer Session 8.6). Dividing each term in the model by POP_t, we get

$$\frac{EXPTRAV_t}{POP_t} = \alpha\left(\frac{1}{POP_t}\right) + \beta\left(\frac{INCOME_t}{POP_t}\right) + \frac{u_t}{POP_t} \tag{8.10}$$

It is easy to verify that the error term in Equation (8.10) has a constant variance because of the assumption that $\sigma_t = \sigma POP_t$. We can therefore apply OLS to Equation (8.10). Note that the new dependent variable is simply the per-capita expenditure on travel. Similarly, the new independent variables are per-capita income and the reciprocal of population, *with no constant term*. We thus see that formulating the model in per-capita terms captures any inherent heteroscedasticity caused by the size of the population. If population has a role in a model, it is generally a good practice to express the model in per-capita terms. The estimated model is as follows, with t-statistics in parentheses and adjusted R^2 for the transformed model (see Table 8.2 and Practice Computer Session 8.6):

$$\left(\frac{\widehat{EXPTRAV}}{POP}\right) = \underset{(2.2)}{0.737}\left(\frac{1}{POP}\right) + \underset{(4.8)}{0.059}\left(\frac{INCOME}{POP}\right)$$

$$\overline{R}^2 = 0.174 \qquad F = 42.2$$

It should be pointed out that while OLS is applied to the transformed equation, the interpretation of the coefficients is for the original equation. Thus, the estimated coefficient of $1/POP$ is that of the intercept term, and the estimated coefficient of $INCOME/POP$ is that of the marginal propensity to spend on travel with respect to income.

Although $\overline{R}^2$ appears low, it refers to the transformed model and not to the original specification in levels. The F-statistic, however, is significant at the 1 percent level. Both t-statistics are also significant at levels below 4 percent. As seen in Table 8.2, a Glesjer test was applied to the transformed model and no significant heteroscedasticity was found.

Feasible Generalized Least Squares (FGLS)

The generalized least squares procedure discussed earlier consists of dividing each variable (including the constant term) by σ_t (the standard deviation of the error term) and then applying ordinary least squares to the resulting transformed model. As the structure of the heteroscedasticity is generally unknown (that is, σ_t is unknown), a researcher must first obtain estimates of σ_t by some means and then use the weighted least squares procedure. Harvey (1976) and Greene (2000) refer to this procedure as the **feasible generalized least squares (FGLS).** The actual procedure for

[First regress exptrav against a constant and income and then run the auxiliary regression for the Glesjer test.]

```
Dependent variable: |û_t|

         VARIABLE      COEFFICIENT      STDERROR      T STAT     2Prob(t > |T|)

   0)     const          0.7312          0.4100        1.783      0.080757 *
   3)     pop            0.1774          0.0543        3.264      0.002004 ***

Unadjusted R-squared      0.179                 Adjusted R-squared        0.162
Chi-square(1): area to the right of (LM = ) 9.110000 = 0.002542
```

[The low *p*-value indicates that because the probability of rejecting a true hypothesis is low, we can safely reject the null hypothesis of homoscedasticity and conclude that there is significant heteroscedasticity. The next step is to divide the model by pop and estimate by OLS. First create the following variables.]

pcexp = exptrav/pop
pcincm = income/pop
invpop = 1/pop

```
Dependent variable: pcexp

         VARIABLE      COEFFICIENT      STDERROR      T STAT     2Prob(t > |T|)

   8)     invpop         0.7368          0.3323        2.218      0.031250 **
   7)     pcincm         0.0586          0.0123        4.775      0.000017 ***

R-squared is the square of the correlation between the observed and
fitted values of the dependent variable.

Error Sum of Sq (ESS)    78.6612  Std Err of Resid. (sgmahat)    1.2670
Unadjusted R-squared      0.191   Adjusted R-squared             0.174
```

[Test the transformed model for heteroscedasticity by regressing the absolute value of the residual from the regression above against a constant and population.]

```
         VARIABLE      COEFFICIENT      STDERROR      T STAT     2Prob(t > |T|)

   0)     const          0.8367          0.2018        4.147      0.000133 ***
   3)     pop           -0.0426          0.0267       -1.593      0.117531

Unadjusted R-squared      0.049                 Adjusted R-squared        0.030
Chi-square(1): area to the right of (LM = ) 2.511978 = 0.112984
```

[The high *p*-value suggests that we cannot reject homoscedasticity at 10 percent and hence OLS is acceptable.]

estimating σ_t has, however, varied widely in practice. For details on these and related methods, see Harvey (1976), Judge et al. (1985), Kmenta (1986), and Greene (2000).

In the context of the LM tests discussed in this chapter, the natural method of estimating the error s.d. or variance is to exploit the information contained in the auxiliary regression. Let $\hat{\alpha}_i$ represent the estimates of the parameters of the auxiliary equation. If we substitute these into this equation, we obtain the corresponding predicted variances or s.d. from which the appropriate weights can be constructed. The formal steps for FGLS are as follows.

Step 1   Regress Y against a constant term, $X_2, X_3, \ldots,$ and X_k and obtain the OLS estimates of the βs.

Step 2   Compute the residuals as $\hat{u}_t = Y_t - \hat{\beta}_1 - \hat{\beta}_2 X_{t2} - \hat{\beta}_3 X_{t3} - \cdots - \hat{\beta}_k X_{tk}$.

Step 3a   Regress $\hat{u}_t^2$ against a constant term, $Z_{t2}, Z_{t3}, \ldots,$ and Z_{tp} and obtain the OLS estimates of the αs. This is the auxiliary regression corresponding to Equation (8.2a) for the Breusch–Pagan test and for the White's test in which the Zs are the original Xs, their squares, and the cross products. Next substitute these estimates in Equation (8.2a) and obtain $\hat{\sigma}_t^2$. The weights are the reciprocals of the square roots of the estimated variances; that is, $w_t = 1/\sqrt{\hat{\sigma}_t^2}$.

A problem with this is that there is no guarantee that the predicted variances will be positive for all t. If any of them is exactly zero, then the corresponding weight is undefined. If any of them is negative, we cannot take the square root. If this situation arises for some observations, then we can use the original $\hat{u}_t^2$ and take their positive square roots.

Step 3b   Regress $|\hat{u}_t|$ against a constant term, $Z_{t2}, Z_{t3}, \ldots,$ and Z_{tp} and obtain the OLS estimates of the αs. This is the auxiliary regression corresponding to Equation (8.2b) for the Glesjer test. Next, substitute these estimates in Equation (8.2b) and obtain $\hat{\sigma}_t$. The weights are their reciprocals. Here again we have the nonpositive s.d. problem. If that happens, we could use the corresponding $|\hat{u}_t|$ and its reciprocal, giving $w_t = 1/|\hat{u}_t|$.

Step 3c   Regress $\ln(\hat{u}_t^2)$ against a constant term, $Z_{t2}, Z_{t3}, \ldots,$ and Z_{tp} and obtain the OLS estimates of the αs. This is the auxiliary regression corresponding to Equation (8.2c) for the Harvey–Godfrey test. Next substitute these estimates in Equation (8.2c) and obtain $\ln(\sigma_t^2)$. Take antilog (that is, exponentiate) to get the predicted variances. The weights are the reciprocals of the square roots of the estimated variances. Note that, because exponentiation generates only positive values, there is no negative or zero variance problem in this case. For this reason, the Harvey–Godfrey test and associated variance estimation result is an attractive procedure.

Step 4   Estimate the original model by weighted least squares (WLS) using the weights $w_t = 1/\hat{\sigma}_t$, where $\hat{\sigma}_t$ is the s.d. estimated in Step 3. More specifically, multiply each variable in the model, including the constant, by w_t and regress $(w_t Y_t)$ against $w_t, (w_t X_{t2}), \ldots, (w_t X_{tk})$, *without a constant term*.

The FGLS estimates obtained in this way are consistent, as are OLS estimates. However, unlike OLS, the estimated variances and covariances of the estimates are consistent here. Also, the estimates are asymptotically likely to be more efficient than OLS estimates. Note, however, that by computing weights from the sample, the resulting WLS estimates will not be unbiased.

It should be noted that because the WLS procedure transforms the dependent variable using the weight variable, conventional methods of calculating R^2 are not valid. An intuitively appealing approach is to compute it as the square of the correlation between observed and fitted values of the original dependent variable. Make sure that you know how your program computes the reported R^2.

A word of caution regarding the use of ready-made commands for WLS estimation is also appropriate here because programs differ in the manner of their implementation. For instance, in EVIEWS and GRETL, the weight variable is $w_t = 1/\hat{\sigma}_t$. WLS is done by regressing $(w_t Y_t)$ against w_t and $(w_t X_{ti})$ for each $i = 2, \ldots, k$. In contrast, SHAZAM requires the specified weight to be $1/\hat{\sigma}_t^2$. Before estimation, the positive square root is taken and is multiplied by the dependent and independent variables as indicated here. It is therefore crucial that you clearly understand how your program does the calculations.

● EXAMPLE 8.8

For the professors' salary data, we have seen that the log-quadratic model exhibited heteroscedasticity (see Examples 8.3 and 8.5). We have used the variance formulations proposed by Glesjer, Breusch–Pagan, White, and Harvey–Godfrey to obtain four different estimates of the model. The results are summarized in Table 8.3.

● Table 8.3   FGLS Estimates of Log-Salary Model Using the Auxiliary Regressions from the LM Tests

Variable	Glesjer	Breusch–Pagan	White	Harvey–Godfrey
CONSTANT	3.842 (0.019)	3.869 (0.011)	3.848 (0.013)	3.828 (0.020)
YEARS	0.037 (0.003)	0.031 (0.003)	0.0369 (0.003)	0.038 (0.003)
YRS2	−4.068e-04 (7.949e−05)	−2.392e-04 (6.217e−05)	−4.514e-04 (9.481e−05)	−4.433e-04 (8.272e−05)
Adj Rsq	0.524	0.507	0.528	0.526
SGMASQ	0.043652	0.045382	0.043375*	0.043531
AIC	0.044242	0.045995	0.043961*	0.044119
FPE	0.044242	0.045995	0.043961*	0.044119
HQ	0.045071	0.046857	0.044785*	0.044946
SCHWARZ	0.046324	0.048159	0.046030*	0.046195
SHIBATA	0.044226	0.045978	0.043945*	0.044103
GCV	0.044250	0.046003	0.043969*	0.044127
RICE	0.044259	0.046012	0.043977*	0.044136

Entries in parentheses are the corresponding standard errors. The asterisks denote the model with the lowest selection criteria. It is just a coincidence that the entries for AIC and FPE are identical. They do differ beyond six decimals.

Table 8.4   Computer Steps for Example 8.8 on Estimation by FGLS Using DATA8-1

1. Regress ln(SALARY) against a constant, YEARS, and YEARS^2, and save the residuals ($\hat{u}_t$).
2. Generate absuhat = $|\hat{u}_t|$, usq = $\hat{u}_t^2$, and lnusq = $\ln(\hat{u}_t^2)$.
3. Regress absuhat against a constant, YEARS, and YEARS^2, and save the "fitted" values as absuhat1. This is the estimated σ_t for the Glesjer specification. Luckily, all the values are positive.
4. Compute wt1 = 1/absuhat1 and use it as the weight to obtain the FGLS weighted least squares estimates.
5. For the Breusch–Pagan specification, regress usq against a constant, YEARS, and YEARS^2, and save the "fitted" values as usqhat1. These are the estimated error variances. However, three observations have negative values, which is unacceptable. Replace these negative values with the original usq values, and call the replaced series "usqhat2." An easy way to do this is to first use your regression program to generate a dummy variable, call it d1, that takes the value 1 for all positive values of usqhat1 and 0 otherwise. Then generate usqhat2 = (d1*usqhat1) + ((1 − d1)*usq).
6. Compute wt2 = 1/sqrt(usqhat2), and use it as the weight to obtain the FGLS weighted least squares estimates (sqrt is the square root function).
7. For the White's test specification, regress usq against a constant, YEARS, YEARS^2, YEARS^3, and YEARS^4, and save the "fitted" values as usqhat3. These are the estimated error variances. However, here also three observations have negative values that have to be replaced with the original usq values (see Step 5). Call the replaced series "usqhat4."
8. Compute wt3 = 1/sqrt(usqhat4), and use it as the weight to obtain the FGLS weighted least squares estimates.
9. For the Harvey–Godfrey specification, regress lnusq against a constant, YEARS, and YEARS^2, save the "fitted" values as lnsq1, and take the antilog (that is, exponentiate) to obtain usqhat5, the estimated error variances. Because the exponential function generates only positive values, there is no negative variance problem here.
10. Compute wt4 = 1/sqrt(usqhat5), and use it as the weight to obtain the FGLS weighted least squares estimates.

Table 8.4 describes steps for carrying this out, and they should be studied before proceeding.

We see from Table 8.3 that the estimates are surprisingly robust across the various methodologies used here. All the coefficients are statistically significant at levels below 0.0001. The only deviation is for the Breusch–Pagan estimates for YEARS and YEARS^2. Because the adjusted R^2 and model selection statistics are meaningless for the transformed model obtained by dividing ln(SALARY) by $\hat{\sigma}_t$, they are computed using the error sum of squares for the untransformed log-quadratic model. We see from Table 8.3 that the White approach has the lowest selection statistics. Thus, in terms of these criteria, that is the best formulation. This result is reassuring because we have recommended the White's test over all the others for its generality and its nondependence on the normality assumption. Using these estimates, we have the following estimated model and the corresponding marginal effect of experience on salary (refer to the discussion of the quadratic model in Section 6.4 and the analysis of the log-linear model in Section 6.8):

$$\widehat{\ln(\text{SALARY})} = 3.848 + 0.0369\,\text{YEARS} - 0.0004514\,\text{YEARS}^2 \qquad (8.11)$$

$$\frac{1}{\text{SALARY}} \frac{\Delta \widehat{\text{SALARY}}}{\Delta \text{YEARS}} = 0.0369 - 0.0009028 \, \text{YEARS} \tag{8.12}$$

Setting this to zero and solving for YEARS, we obtain the number of years at which SALARY will attain a maximum (we know that it is a maximum and not a minimum because of the negative coefficient for the quadratic term). The solution is 40.1, which is above most of the sample range. The implication, therefore, is that salaries steadily increase for 40 years but, because of the negative coefficient for YEARS^2, there are diminishing marginal returns. In Equation (8.12), setting YEARS to the values 1, 5, 10, 15, 20, and 25, we obtain the numbers 0.036, 0.032, 0.028, 0.023, 0.019, 0.014. Recall from Section 6.8 that 100 times these values give the approximate percent increase in salaries for one more year of experience. Thus, the marginal salary increase per year varies from a high of 3.6 percent for new Ph.Ds to 1.4 percent for those with 25 years of experience.

Dependent Variable Heteroscedasticity

Sometimes, the standard deviation of $u_t(\sigma_t)$ is specified as being proportional to the expected value of the dependent variable. More formally, suppose $\sigma_t = \sigma E(Y_t)$. Because $\hat{Y}_t$ is an unbiased and consistent estimate of $E(Y_t)$, a suggested procedure is to use the weight $w_t = 1/\hat{Y}_t$, that is, the reciprocal of $\hat{\beta}_1 + \hat{\beta}_2 X_{t2} + \cdots + \hat{\beta}_k X_{tk}$. This procedure is not, however, recommended because here also there is no guarantee that $\hat{Y}_t$ is strictly positive for all t and there is no alternative procedure to substitute for zero or negative $\hat{Y}_t$. Since $E(Y_t)$ is a function of the Xs, this is a special case of the Glesjer formulation specified in Equation (8.2b), with Xs substituted for the Zs used there. Therefore, we recommend that this specification be abandoned in favor of the Glesjer test and the associated method of computing the weights. Better yet, apply all the methods and see if robust results emerge.

8.4 Application: A Model of the Expenditure on Health Care in the United States

In this section, we put together all the topics discussed in this chapter and apply the techniques to a model of health care expenditure in the United States. DATA8-3 has cross-section data on the aggregate personal income and expenditures on health care for the 50 U.S. states and the District of Columbia (see Appendix D for sources). Both are measured in billions of dollars. Also available are data on the U.S. population (in millions) and the percent of seniors 65 or over. We have seen in Example 8.7 that population often induces heteroscedasticity and therefore expressing variables as per-capita, by dividing by population, is a useful way of reducing that effect. The model formulated is, therefore, the following:

$$\frac{\text{EXPHLTH}}{\text{POP}} = \beta_1 + \beta_2 \frac{\text{INCOME}}{\text{POP}} + \beta_3 \, \text{SENIORS} + u$$

We used the tests by Glesjer, Breusch–Pagan, White, and Harvey–Godfrey and found that the null hypothesis of homoscedasticity was rejected at levels below 0.001 by the first three tests. However, the p-value for the LM test statistic for the Harvey–Godfrey test for multiplicative heteroscedasticity was 0.14, which is well above commonly accepted levels. Therefore, we cannot reject the null hypothesis of homoscedasticity, even at the 10 percent level. However, as we note from Table 8.5, which is an annotated partial output, the auxiliary regression for this case shows that per-capita income and its square are quite significant. Therefore, a second test was performed with just those variables, and the p-value was 0.056. Since this is tolerable, we applied the FGLS/WLS procedure using all four approaches.

Table 8.6 summarizes the estimates and related statistics. We note that the Breusch–Pagan and White estimates are very close to each other but the others differ. In terms of the model selection criteria, the Breusch–Pagan estimates are the best. Both the income and seniors coefficients have the expected positive signs and are highly significant at levels below 0.0001. Holding the percent of seniors constant, for a $100 increase in income, an average of $15 is expected to be spent on health care. For a given level of income in the state, a 1 percent increase in the

---

⬤   Table 8.5   **Partial Output for Application in Section 8.4 Using DATA8-3**

(To save space, output has been suppressed except where it is useful.)

[Test using the Harvey–Godfrey approach by first regressing $\ln(\hat{u}_i^2)$ against a constant, x (= income/ pop), seniors, sq_x = x^2, and sq_senio = seniors^2.]

Dependent variable: $\ln(\hat{u}_i^2)$

	VARIABLE	COEFFICIENT	STDERROR	T STAT	2Prob(t > |T|)	
0)	const	18.3709	13.8537	1.326	0.191364	
6)	x	-2.2253	1.1308	-1.968	0.055130	*
4)	seniors	0.1809	0.8672	0.209	0.835647	
10)	sq_x	0.0552	0.0262	2.109	0.040404	**
12)	sq_senio	-0.0149	0.0357	-0.416	0.679121	

Unadjusted R-squared   0.136 Adjusted R-squared   0.061
Chi-square(4): area to the right of (LM) 6.929352 = 0.139669

[Since the p-value is high, we do not reject homoscedasticity. However, because the coefficients for x and x-squared are significant, another LM test is done with just these.]

Chi-square(2): area to the right of (LM) 5.765542 = 0.055979

[Since the p-value is tolerable, we reject homoscedasticity and proceed with FGLS weighted least squares estimation. For a summary discussion of the results, refer to the text.]

Table 8.6   FGLS Estimates of the Health Expenditure Model Using the Auxiliary Regressions from the LM Tests

Variable	Glesjer	Breusch–Pagan	White	Harvey–Godfrey
CONSTANT	−0.402 (0.670)	−1.588 (0.206)	−1.552 (0.195)	0.093 (0.657)
INCOME/POP	0.103 (0.028)	0.150 (0.013)	0.146 (0.013)	0.082 (0.026)
SENIORS	0.092 (0.025)	0.117 (0.015)	0.119 (0.015)	0.086 (0.026)
Adj Rsq	0.416	0.422	0.420	0.403
SGMASQ	0.392697	0.358060*	0.359175	0.422389
AIC	0.415741	0.379071*	0.380251	0.447174
FPE	0.415797	0.379122*	0.380302	0.447235
HQ	0.434192	0.395894*	0.397126	0.467020
SCHWARZ	0.465773	0.424690*	0.426012	0.500990
SHIBATA	0.413080	0.376644*	0.377817	0.444312
GCV	0.417241	0.380439*	0.381623	0.448788
RICE	0.418877	0.381931*	0.383119	0.450548

Entries in parentheses are the corresponding standard errors. The asterisks denote the model with the lowest selection criteria.

number of seniors is expected to increase per-capita health care expenditure, on average, by $116.9 (because it is measured in thousands of dollars). The goodness-of-fit measure indicates that the model explains only about 42 percent of the per-capita expenditure on health care. Perhaps adding nonlinearities would improve the explanatory power. This is left to the reader as an exercise.

8.5   Empirical Project

If you have started an empirical project as part of a course and have carried out the steps described in Sections 4.9 and 7.9, you may be ready to undertake the estimation of models and testing of hypotheses *provided your study involves only cross-section data.* You are cautioned, however, that without reading more chapters in the book, your analysis is likely to be limited. For instance, if your data are time series and your model is dynamic with lags in behavior, you should wait until you have read Chapters 9 and 10, which address special issues involving time series. Also, the nature of the problem you are studying might dictate feedback effects (see Section 3.10) that suggest a simultaneous equations model (discussed in Chapter 13). If you ignore that, your estimates will be biased and inconsistent, and the tests will be invalid. Chapter 12 will be important if you are dealing with a dummy dependent variable or use data that are truncated (for example, only positive values may be observed). Ideally, you should read the first 13 chapters before going on to estimation and hypothesis testing. If, however, your time is limited, seek advice from your instructor regarding any future chapters to read before proceeding with the empirical analysis.

If you go ahead with the analysis of cross-section data, formulate one or more general models and estimate them. If your data includes population as an explanatory variable, express variables in per-capita terms rather than use population as an independent variable. This is to avoid possible heteroscedasticity problems. Be sure to carry out appropriate tests for heteroscedasticity. If it is present, use weighted least squares to obtain more efficient estimates. Then apply the data-based reduction technique to eliminate redundant variables from the model.

Summary

If the variance of the residuals in a linear regression model is the same across all observations, we have *homoscedasticity*. If, on the other hand, the variance is different across the sample, the errors are said to be *heteroscedastic*. If we ignore the presence of heteroscedasticity and apply the OLS procedure, some of the properties of the estimators are altered. OLS estimators are still unbiased and consistent. Forecasts based on them are also unbiased and consistent. Estimates and forecasts, however, are inefficient and hence are no longer BLUE. Because the estimated variances and covariances of the estimates are biased and inconsistent, tests of hypotheses are not valid anymore.

A useful device for identifying heteroscedasticity is to graph the square of OLS residuals ($\hat{u}_t^2$) against variables that are suspected of causing heteroscedasticity or against the fitted values ($\hat{Y}_t^2$). A formal test, however, is preferable.

The presence of heteroscedasticity is determined by a number of tests. The *Goldfeld–Quandt* test consists of (1) identifying a variable that might be causing the heteroscedasticity, (2) arranging the observations in increasing order of that variable, (3) estimating the model for the first n_1 and last n_2 observations (n_1 and n_2 being about a third of n), and (4) using an *F*-test on the ratio of the estimated error variances $\hat{\sigma}_1^2$ and $\hat{\sigma}_2^2$. This test, however, is not recommended, because by discarding nearly a third of the observations we are throwing away valuable information. Also, the test is not applicable if heteroscedasticity is caused jointly by several variables (for example, population and income).

A preferred testing procedure is to use the Lagrange multiplier (LM) test, which is a large-sample test. In this chapter, we have seen four LM tests, each with a different specification of the error variance. The Glesjer test assumes that the s.d. of the tth error (σ_t) depends on a number of variables (denoted by Zs); the Breusch–Pagan test assumes that the variance (σ_t^2) depends on the Zs; the White's test specifies the Zs as the original Xs, their squares, and their cross products; and the Harvey–Godfrey test specifies the logarithm of the variance [$\ln(\sigma_t^2)$] as a function of the Zs, which is equivalent to assuming that heteroscedasticity is multiplicative. In all these cases, the first step is to regress Y against all the Xs, including the constant, and obtain the residuals $\hat{u}_t$. The next step is to regress either $|\hat{u}_t|$ (for the Glesjer test), or $\hat{u}_t^2$ (for the Breusch–Pagan and White tests), or $\ln(\hat{u}_t^2)$ against the Zs, which must include a constant term. This step is the *auxiliary regression*, in which the number of explanatory variables including the constant term is denoted by p. The test statistic is LM $= nR^2$, where n is the number of observations used and R^2 is the unadjusted R^2 in the auxiliary regression. Under the null hypothesis of homoscedasticity, LM has the chi-square distribution with $p - 1$ d.f. Reject the null if LM exceeds the critical $\chi_{p-1}^2(a)$, where a is the level of significance. Alternatively, compute the p-value $= \text{Prob}(\chi_{p-1}^2 > \text{LM}) =$ the area to the right of LM in the chi-square distribution. If the p-value is low (below a), we are "safe" in rejecting the null hypothesis and concluding that there is heteroscedasticity. If the p-value is unacceptably high, we cannot reject homoscedasticity. In this situation, OLS is the acceptable procedure.

If heteroscedasticity is found, one can use *feasible generalized least squares* (FGLS), which are also *weighted least squares* (WLS), to obtain consistent and asymptotically (that is, for large samples) more efficient estimates of the parameters. The procedure is to define a weight, w_t, for each observation equal to the inverse of the standard deviation (that is, $1/\sigma_t$) of the tth error term. Because this standard deviation is unknown, we must either assume that it is proportional to some known variable or use the model to estimate σ_t. In the former case, estimates are BLUE and all tests are valid even for small samples. In the latter case, tests are valid only asymptotically. The general procedure is to use the auxiliary regression to predict the variance or standard deviation. If any of these values is zero or negative, we would substitute the original $|\hat{u}_t|$ for the estimate. An alternative procedure that guarantees that the predicted variances are positive is to regress $\ln(\hat{u}_t^2)$ against the Zs and obtain the predicted values. The antilog (that is, exponentiation) of these will always be positive and can be used as $\hat{\sigma}_t^2$. Next set w_t equal to $1/\hat{\sigma}_t$. Then multiply the dependent variable and each independent variable, *including the constant term* (which must be present in the model), by the corresponding w_t. Finally, regress the transformed dependent variable against all the transformed independent variables. This final regression will not have a constant term. The estimates obtained from this transformed model are known as *feasible generalized least squares* (FGLS) estimates. These are consistent, as are the estimated variances, and hence all tests are valid for large samples. They are, however, biased in small samples.

Key Terms

Auxiliary equation	Heteroscedasticity
Auxiliary regression	Heteroscedasticity consistent covariance
Breusch–Pagan test	matrix (HCCM) estimator
Dependent variable heteroscedasticity	Homoscedasticity
Feasible generalized least squares (FGLS)	Jackknife
Generalized least squares (GLS)	Multiplicative heteroscedasticity
Glesjer test	Park test
Goldfeld–Quandt test	Weighted least squares (WLS)
Harvey–Godfrey test	White's test

References

Amemiya, T. "Regression Analysis When the Variance of the Dependent Variable Is Proportional to the Squares of Its Expectation." *J. American Statistical Association* 68 (December 1973): 928–934.

———. "A Note on a Heteroscedastic Model." *J. Econometrics* 6 (November 1977): 365–370.

Binkley, James K. "Finite Sample Behavior of Tests for Grouped Heteroscedasticity." *Review of Economics and Statistics* 74 (3) (August 1992): 563–568.

Breusch, T. S., and A. R. Pagan. "A Simple Test for Heteroscedasticity and Random Coefficient Variation." *Econometrica* 47 (September 1979): 1287–1294.

Cragg, John G. "Quasi-Aitken Estimation for Heteroscedasticity of Unknown Form." *Journal of Econometrics* 54 (1–3) (October/December 1992): 179–201.

Donald, Stephen G. "Two-Step Estimation of Heteroscedastic Sample Selection Models." *Journal of Econometrics* 65 (2) (February 1995): 347–380.

Effron, B. *The Jackknife, the Bootstrap, and Other Resampling Plans.* Philadelphia: Society for Industrial and Applied Mathematics, 1982.

Engle, R. F. "Autoregressive Conditional Heteroscedasticity with Estimates of Variance of United Kingdom Inflation." *Econometrica* 50 (July 1982): 987–1007.

————. "Wald, Likelihood Ratio, and Lagrange Multiplier Tests in Econometrics." *Handbook of Econometrics,* vol. 2. Ed. Z. Griliches and M. Intriligator. New York: North-Holland, 1984.

Glesjer, H. "A New Test for Heteroscedasticity." *J. Amer. Stat. Assoc.* 64 (1978): 316–323.

Godfrey, L. "Testing for Multiplicative Heteroscedasticity." *J. Econometrics* 8 (1978): 227–236.

Goldfeld, S. M., and R. E. Quandt. "Some Tests for Homoscedasticity." *J. Amer. Stat. Assoc.* 60 (June 1965): 539–547.

————. *Nonlinear Methods in Econometrics.* Amsterdam: North-Holland, 1972.

Greene, W. H. *Econometric Analysis.* Upper Saddle River, NJ: Prentice-Hall, 2000.

Harvey, A. C. "Estimating Regression Models with Multiplicative Heteroscedasticity." *Econometrica* 44 (May 1976): 461–466.

————. *The Econometric Analysis of Time Series.* New York: Wiley, 1981.

Judge, George C., W. E. Griffiths, R. C. Hill, H. Lütkepohl, and T. C. Lee. *The Theory and Practice of Econometrics.* New York: Wiley, 1985.

Kmenta, J. *Elements of Econometrics.* New York: Macmillan, 1986.

Koenker, R. "A Note on Studentizing a Test for Heteroscedasticity." *J. Econometrics* 17 (September 1981): 107–112.

Lee, Byung Joo. "A Heteroscedasticity Test Robust to Conditional Mean Specification." *Econometrica* 60 (1) (January 1992): 159–171.

MacKinnon, J. G., and H. White. "Some Heteroscedasticity-Consistent Covariance Matrix Estimators with Improved Finite Sample Properties." *J. Econometrics* 29 (March 1985): 305–325.

Messer, K., and H. White. "A Note on Computing the Heteroscedasticity Consistent Covariance Matrix Using Instrumental Variable Techniques." *Oxford Bulletin of Economics and Statistics* 46 (May 1984): 181–184.

Park, R. "Estimating with Heteroscedastic Error Terms." *Econometrica* 34 (1966): 888.

Prais, S. J., and H. S. Houthakker. *The Analysis of Family Budgets.* Cambridge: Cambridge University Press, 1955.

Spanos, Aris. "On Modeling Heteroscedasticity: The Student's *t* and Elliptical Linear Regression Models." *Econometric Theory* 10 (2) (June 1994): 286–315.

Statistical Abstract of the United States. Washington, D.C.: U.S. Department of Commerce, 1990.

White, H. "A Heteroscedasticity-Consistent Covariance Matrix and a Direct Test for Heteroscedasticity." *Econometrica* 48 (May 1980): 817–838.

Exercises

Questions Requiring No Computer Work

[†]8.1   Consider the model

$$Y_t = \beta_1 + \beta_2 X_{t2} + \beta_3 X_{t3} + u_t$$

$$\mathrm{Var}(u_t) = \sigma_t^2 = \sigma^2 Z_t^2$$

where data are available on Y, X_1, X_2, and Z. The weighted least squares procedure consists of minimizing

$$\mathrm{ESS} = \sum (w_t u_t)^2 = \sum (w_t Y_t - \beta_1 w_t - \beta_2 w_t X_{t2} - \beta_3 w_t X_{t3})^2$$

with respect to the βs, where w_t is known.

a.   Partially differentiate ESS with respect to β_1, β_2, and β_3, and write down the normal equations (w_t is nonrandom).

b.   Derive the normal equations for Equation (8.9).

c.   Substitute $w_t = 1/Z_t$ in the normal equations obtained in part a and show that they are identical to those derived in part b.

8.2*   In the model given in Exercise 8.1, let the residual u_t be distributed normally as $N(0, \sigma_t^2)$.

a.   Show that the log-likelihood function is given by (refer to Section 3.A.5 of Chapter 3)

$$\ln L = -n \ln \sigma - n \ln(\sqrt{2\pi}) - \sum \left[\frac{(Y_t - \beta_1 - \beta_2 X_{t2} - \beta_3 X_{t3})^2}{2\sigma_t^2} \right]$$

b.   When $\sigma_t^2 = \sigma^2 Z_t^2$, show that the maximum likelihood estimates of the βs are identical to the weighted least squares estimates of Exercise 8.1.

†8.3   Consider the model $Y_t = \beta X_t + u_t$ with $E(u_t) = 0$ and $\sigma_t^2 = \sigma^2 X_t^2$. An estimator of β is constructed as follows. Join each point (X_t, Y_t) to the origin, for $t = 1, 2, \ldots, n$. Next measure the slope of each of those lines and calculate the average of these slopes over the n observations. Call this estimator $\tilde{\beta}$.

a.   Write an algebraic expression for $\tilde{\beta}$ in terms of X_t, Y_t, and the sample size n.

b.   Derive the expected value of $\tilde{\beta}$ and show that it is unbiased.

c.   Derive the weighted least squares estimate of β and show that it is identical to $\tilde{\beta}$. Is it BLUE? Without any explicit derivations, compare the efficiency of $\tilde{\beta}$ relative to the OLS estimate of β.

8.4   Suppose it is known that the error variance is proportional to Z_t. Describe how you would obtain WLS estimates in this case.

8.5   Suppose $Y_t = \beta_1 + \beta_2 X_t + \beta_3 X_t^2 + u_t$ and $\sigma_t^2 = \sigma^2 X_t^2$. Derive the transformed equation and describe how you can obtain WLS estimates of the βs that are BLUE.

8.6   Consider the model $Y_t = \beta_1 + \beta_2 X_{t2} + \beta_3 X_{t3} + u_t$, in which each of the variables has been measured using grouped data so that $\text{Var}(u_t) = \sigma^2/n_t$, where n_t is the known number of observations for the tth group. Describe how you would obtain the best linear unbiased estimators of the parameters of the model.

8.7   Consider the relationship between the expenditure on travel (E_t) and total income (Y_t) given by

$$E_t = \beta_1 + \beta_2 Y_t + u_t$$

I am certain that the error term is heteroscedastic (HSK) with $\text{Var}(u_t) = \alpha P_t^\beta$, where P is the population and α, β are unknown parameters. You have data on E, Y, and P. State the null and alternative hypotheses for no HSK. Describe the regressions to be run for carrying out the test. How would you compute the test statistic? What is its distribution and d.f.? Suppose there is significant HSK and you do not want to ignore it. Describe the steps you would take to get more efficient estimates.

8.8   Consider the simple model $Y_t = \beta X_t + u_t$ for which the variance of the error term is known to be $\sigma_t^2 = \sigma^2 X_t^2$.

a.   Is the OLS estimate of β unbiased, consistent, and efficient (carefully justify the answers)?

b.   Describe step-by-step how you will go about obtaining the weighted least squares estimate of β.

c.   Explicitly derive the WLS estimate of β and give a geometric interpretation of the estimate.

8.9   Consider the following model for real estate values:

$$\text{PRICE}_t = \beta_0 + \beta_1 \text{SQFT}_t + \beta_2 \text{YARD}_t + \beta_3 \text{POOL}_t + u_t$$

where PRICE is price in thousands of dollars, SQFT is the living area in square feet, YARD is the size of the yard in square feet, and POOL is a dummy variable taking the value 1 if the house has a swimming pool.

a. I suspect that the error term u_t might be heteroscedastic and that the *variance* of u_t is proportional to SQFT. Describe step-by-step how I should use the weighted least squares procedure to take care of the problem. Be sure to state the transformations I need and the regression to be run. Write down the assumptions on u_t and the properties of the WLS estimates. Carefully explain why your properties hold.

b. Suppose I did not know the nature of the heteroscedasticity and want to use the White's test for it. Describe carefully all the steps needed to perform the test.

†8.10 Consider the model $S_t = \alpha + \beta Y_t + \gamma A_t + u_t$, where S is the sales of a firm in the tth state, Y is total income in the state, and A is the amount of money spent by the company advertising in that state ($t = 1, 2, \ldots, 50$).

a. You suspect that the random error term u_t is heteroscedastic with a standard deviation σ_t that depends on the size of the population P_t. Describe step-by-step how you will go about testing for this. Be sure to state (1) the null and alternative hypotheses, (2) the regression(s) you will run, (3) the test statistic you will compute and its distribution (including the degrees of freedom), and (4) the criterion for acceptance or rejection of the null hypothesis.

b. Suppose you find that there is heteroscedasticity but ignore it and use OLS to estimate the model. Are your estimates (1) unbiased, (2) consistent, (3) efficient? Carefully justify your answer.

c. Assume that $\sigma_t = \sigma P_t$. Describe step-by-step how you will obtain estimates that are BLUE (define the term). State any theorem that enables you to justify the claim that your estimates are BLUE.

8.11 Consider the following model relating profits to sales of a number of firms:

$$P_t = \beta_1 + \beta_2 S_t + \beta_3 D_t + u_t$$

where P = profits, S = sales, and $D = 1$ if the company is in the manufacturing industry and 0 otherwise.

a. Write down the *most general form* of the auxiliary equation for the variance of u_t so that you can carry out White's test for heteroscedasticity (HSK).

b. State the null hypothesis that there is no HSK.

c. Describe the regressions to be run to conduct the test (be very specific to your model).

d. What is the test statistic, its distribution, and the numerical value of the d.f.?

e. Write down the critical value for a 5 percent test and describe the decision rule.

f. Suppose you reject the null hypothesis and want to apply the weighted least squares (WLS). Describe carefully the steps to be taken to do this (assume that the negative variance problem does not arise here).

8.12 Consider the relationship between the expenditure on travel (E_t) and total income (Y_t) given by

$$E_t = \beta_1 + \beta_2 Y_t + u_t$$

You are certain that the error term is heteroscedastic (HSK) with $\text{Var}(u_t) = \sigma_t^2 = \alpha_1 + \alpha_2 P_t + \alpha_3 P_t^2$, where P is the population. You have data on E, Y, and P.

a. State the null and alternative hypotheses for no HSK.

b. Describe the regressions to be run for carrying out the test.

c. How would you compute the test statistic?

d. What is its distribution and d.f.?

e. Suppose there is significant HSK and you do not want to ignore it. Describe step-by-step how you would use the weighted least squares procedure (that is, FGLS), assuming that you did run into the negative variance problem when using this relation for σ_t^2.

8.13 Consider the model

$$\text{PRICE}_t = \beta_1 + \beta_2 \ln(\text{SQFT}_t) + \beta_3 \ln(\text{YARD}_t) + u_t$$

where PRICE is the sale price of a house in dollars, SQFT is the living area in square feet, and YARD is the size of the yard in square feet.

a. You know from past studies that the variance of u is proportional to the size of the yard. Describe step-by-step how you should apply the weighted least squares procedure (WLS) that makes use of this information. Be sure to state what variables to generate and what regressions to run.

b. In what way are the WLS estimates better than OLS estimates?

In the model, suppose the nature of the heteroscedasticity is unknown.

c. Write down a form of the auxiliary equation for the error variance so that you can apply the Glesjer test.

d. State the null hypothesis that there is no heteroscedasticity.

e. Describe what regression(s) you should run, how you should compute the test statistic, what its distribution is, and the numerical value of the d.f.

Suppose there is heteroscedasticity and you want to apply the WLS procedure using the auxiliary equation you have stated.

f. Describe how you should compute the weights and how you should apply them to obtain WLS estimates (assume that the negative variance problem does not arise).

8.14 Consider the model $S_t = \alpha + \beta A_t + u_t$, in which S_t is the average sales and A_t is the average advertising budget for an industry ($t = 1, 2, \ldots, n$). The average is computed for all the firms in the industry. This makes the variance of u_t not constant but equal to σ^2/N_t, where N_t is the known number of firms in the industry. You have data on S_t, A_t, and N_t.

a. Carefully describe step-by-step how you would obtain weighted least squares (WLS) estimates of α and β. Your instructions should be clear and specific as though to a research assistant. In particular, describe what variables to generate and explain how the OLS method can be used to obtain WLS estimates.

b. Are the WLS estimates biased or unbiased?

c. Are they consistent?

d. Are they BLUE?

e. Are the tests of hypotheses on WLS estimates valid?

8.15 Consider the following model relating profits to sales of a number of firms:

$$\text{LP}_t = \beta_1 + \beta_2 \text{LS}_t + \beta_3 D_t + u_t$$

where LP = $\ln(\text{profits})$, LS = $\ln(\text{sales})$, and $D = 1$ if the company is in the manufacturing industry and 0 otherwise.

a. Write down the most general form of the auxiliary equation for the variance of u_t so that you can carry out White's test for heteroscedasticity (HSK).

b. State the null hypothesis that there is no HSK.

c. Describe the regressions to be run to conduct the test (be very specific to your model).

d. What is the test statistic, its distribution, and d.f.?

e. What is the decision rule?

f. Are the OLS estimates unbiased, consistent, and efficient?

8.16 Consider the model

$$\text{PRICE}_t = \beta_1 + \beta_2 \text{SQFT}_t + \beta_3 \ln(\text{SQFT}_t) + \beta_4 \text{YARD}_t + \beta_5 \ln(\text{YARD}_t) + u_t$$

where PRICE is the price in dollars of a house, SQFT is the living area in square feet, and YARD is the size of the yard in square feet.

a. You suspect that the marginal effect of SQFT on PRICE decreases as SQFT increases and similarly that the marginal effect of YARD on PRICE decreases as YARD increases. If these hypotheses were true, what signs would you expect for β_3 and β_5? Carefully justify your answers.

b. You know from past studies that the variance of u is proportional to the size of the SQFT. Describe step-by-step how you would apply the weighted least squares procedure that makes use of this information. Be sure to state what variables to generate and what regressions to run.

c. In what way is the WLS procedure better than the OLS procedure?

d. In the basic model, suppose the nature of the heteroscedasticity is unknown. Carefully describe the steps to be taken to perform the Harvey–Godfrey test for the model. To do this, first write the auxiliary equation for the error variance and state the null hypothesis of no heteroscedasticity. Then describe the regressions to run, how you will compute the test statistic, and what its distribution and d.f. are.

8.17 The following partial computer printout relates to the model $\text{EXPTRAV}_t = \alpha + \beta \text{INCOME} + u_t$ that was used in Example 8.7. EXPTRAV is the expenditure on travel and INCOME is the total income, both measured in billions of dollars for the 50 U.S. states and the District of Columbia (51 observations).

OLS ESTIMATES USING THE 51 OBSERVATIONS 1–51
Dependent variable – exptrav

VARIABLE	COEFFICIENT	STDERROR	T STAT	PROB t > |T|
0) constant	0.26649	0.32944	0.809	0.4225
2) income	0.06754	0.00350	19.288	0.0000 ***

Error Sum of Sq (ESS)	157.90707	Std Err of Resid. (sgmahat)		1.79516
Unadjusted R-squared	0.884	Adjusted R-squared		0.881

[Generate usq = $\hat{u}_t^2$ and sq_pop = pop^2.]

OLS ESTIMATES USING THE 51 OBSERVATIONS 1–51
Dependent variable – usq

VARIABLE	COEFFICIENT	STDERROR	T STAT	PROB t > |T|
0) constant	-1.37791	2.24070	-0.615	0.5415
1) pop	1.37239	0.67147	2.044	0.0465 **
5) sq_pop	-0.04124	0.03086	-1.337	0.1877

| Error Sum of Sq (ESS) | 3684.47761 | Std Err of Resid. (sgmahat) | 8.76128 |
| Unadjusted R-squared | 0.119 | Adjusted R-squared | 0.082 |

a.   Write down, in symbolic terms, the auxiliary equation for the error variance implicit in the printout.

b.   Next state the null hypothesis that there is no HSK.

c.   Calculate the numerical value of the test statistic.

d.   Write down the distribution and its d.f.

e.   Actually carry out the test (at 5 percent) and state whether HSK is present or not.

f.   Regardless of your answer to part e, suppose you want to use the weighted least squares procedure to estimate the parameters. Your research assistant is a good programmer but does not know any econometrics. Describe step-by-step how your assistant should proceed to estimate the model by weighted least squares. Note that your description must be specific to the model and estimated auxiliary equation (with numerical values from the computer printout wherever available). For simplicity, assume that there is no negative or zero variance problem.

8.18   Consider the model $Y_t = \beta_1 + \beta_2 X_t + \beta_3 S_t + u_t$, where Y = per-capita expenditure on health care, X is per-capita personal income, and S is the percent of seniors (that is, percent of population 65 years or over). Using data for the U.S. states and the District of Columbia (51 observations), the model was estimated by OLS, and the auxiliary regression for testing for heteroscedasticity is given next (it had $R^2 = 0.417$).

$$|\hat{u}_t| = 6.619 - 0.683X_t + 0.017X_t^2 + 0.063S_t - 0.003S_t^2$$

a.   Write down in symbolic terms the auxiliary equation that specifies how heteroscedasticity is determined. In it write down the null hypothesis of homoscedasticity.

b.   Compute the test statistic, state its distribution and d.f., and carry out the test at the 1 percent level, and state your conclusion about homo-/heteroscedasticity in words.

c.   Based on your results, are OLS estimators biased, inconsistent, or inefficient? What can you say about the validity of hypothesis tests based on OLS estimators?

d.   Describe step-by-step how the auxiliary equation can be used to obtain weighted least squares estimates of the βs (you can assume that there is no problem with negative error variance or standard deviation). Note: Your answer should not be in general symbolic terms. It should be quite specific to these models with numerical values indicated wherever they are known.

8.19   Consider the relation $S_t = \alpha + \beta Y_t + u_t$, where S is household savings and Y is household income. You also know the age group the head of the household falls into, but not the actual age. To allow for age-group differences, you define three dummy variables, $D_1 = 1$ for age < 25, $D_2 = 1$ for age 51–65, and $D_3 = 1$ for age > 65. The age group 26–50 is the control. You have data on 50 households.

a.   It is very likely that both coefficients are different across age groups. Derive the most general model (U) that incorporates that belief.

b.   You want to test the null hypothesis, "There is no difference in the relation between age group < 25 and age > 65." Carefully write down the null hypothesis for this test.

c.   Next derive the restricted model.

d.   Describe the steps to carry out this test.

e.   You suspect that the random error term u_t is heteroscedastic (HSK) with a variance σ_t^2 that depends on the size of the family P_t. Write down an appropriate version of the auxiliary equation for the error variance.

    f.   Next state the null hypothesis that there is no HSK.

    g.   Describe the regression(s) to be run using Model U as the basis.

    h.   Write down the test statistic, its distribution, and the numerical value of its d.f.

    i.   Describe the criterion for rejection of the null hypothesis.

    j.   Suppose you find that there is HSK and want to use the weighted least squares procedure to estimate the parameters. Your research assistant is a good programmer, but does not know any econometrics. Describe step-by-step how your R.A. should proceed to estimate Model U by weighted least squares. Note that your description must be specific to the model. For simplicity, assume that there is no negative or zero variance problem.

8.20   Consider the relationship between expenditures on travel (E_t) and total income (Y_t) given by $E_t = \alpha + \beta Y_t + u_t$. Suppose that the error term is heteroscedastic (HSK) with $\text{Var}(u_t) = \sigma_t^2$ that depends on the size of the population P_t. To test this hunch, you use cross-section data for the U.S. states and the District of Columbia (51 observations) and obtain the following estimated auxiliary regression.

```
          OLS ESTIMATES USING THE 51 OBSERVATIONS 1-51
                   Dependent variable - lnusq

   VARIABLE           COEFFICIENT        STDERROR    T STAT    2Prob(t > |T|)

   constant            -1.93858          0.507782   -3.81774  0.000378991 ***
     lnpop              1.21804          0.334229    3.64433  0.000647169 ***

Error Sum of Sq (ESS)   291.971   Std Err of Resid. (sgmahat)        2.44102
Unadjusted R-squared      0.213   Adjusted R-squared                   0.197
F-statistic (1, 49)     13.2811   pvalue = Prob(F > 13.281) is 0.000647169
```

In this table, $\text{lnusq} = \ln(\hat{u}_t^2)$, $\hat{u}_t$ is the residual from the model specified at the top, and $\text{lnpop} = \ln(P_t)$.

    a.   Write down in symbolic terms what the table implies with regard to the error variance. Your answer should be of the form $\sigma_t^2 = f(\ldots)$, where you have to derive explicitly the function $f(\ldots)$ and it should not include any numerical values.

    b.   In the expression derived in part a, state the null hypothesis for no HSK.

    c.   Describe exactly how lnusq was obtained.

    d.   Next carry out the test. That is, compute the test statistic, state its distribution including d.f., the critical value for a 1 percent level, the decision, and the conclusion whether HSK is present or not.

    e.   Regardless of your answer to part d, describe how you can obtain the weighted least squares estimates of the original model. Again be very specific about the steps for the procedure. In particular, it should be relevant to the model at the beginning of the question and include numerical values where available.

    f.   Would you run into the negative variance problem here? Explain why or why not.

8.21   Consider the following model of women's labor force participation rates:

$$\text{WLFP}_t = \beta_1 + \beta_2\,\text{EDUC}_t + \beta_3\,\text{UE}_t + \beta_4\,\text{DR}_t + \beta_5\,\text{URB}_t + \beta_6\,\text{WH}_t + u_t$$

where WLFP = percent in labor force who are female, EDUC = percent of female high school graduates or higher, UE = percent of civilian labor force unemployed, DR = percent of females who are divorced, URB = percent of population living in urban areas, and WH = percent of female population who are white. The model was estimated using data for the 50 states. In order to test for heteroscedasticity, the following auxiliary regression was estimated for the error variance (usq is $\hat{u}_t^2$).

```
OLS ESTIMATES USING THE 50 OBSERVATIONS 1-50
           Dependent variable - usq

   VARIABLE              COEFFICIENT              STDERROR

   constant                105.356               26.4865
   EDUC                     -0.273                0.1412
   UE                       -6.183                4.0648
   DR                       -5.332                3.5786
   URB                      -0.883                0.3877
   WH                       -1.001                0.5165
   UE²                       0.557                0.3020
   DR²                       0.307                0.1732
   URB²                      0.007                0.0029
   WH²                       0.011                0.0044

Error sum of squares (ESS)              888.498
Total sum of squares (TSS)             1725.330
```

a. Write down, using symbols rather than numerical values, the auxiliary equation for error variance implied by these estimates.

b. Write down the null hypothesis for homoscedasticity (that is, no heteroscedasticity).

c. Compute the numerical value of the test statistic (show your derivations).

d. State its distribution under the null including the d.f.

e. Write down the critical value (at the 1 percent level) for the test and state whether the null hypothesis is rejected or not. Does this mean that there is a significant heteroscedasticity? Why or why not?

f. Based on your test, what can you say about the OLS estimators of the model, particularly about unbiasedness, consistency, efficiency, and the reliability of hypothesis tests?

g. Regardless of your answer in part e, assume that there was significant heteroscedasticity. Describe step-by-step how the auxiliary equation can be used to obtain weighted least squares of the βs (assume that you don't face the negative variance problem). Your answer should not be in general symbolic terms but very specific to the numerical values in the table and the variables in the model. Give detailed instructions that demonstrate that you really understand how the procedure works.

8.22 Consider the following model of bus travel:

$$\text{BUSTRAVL}_t = \beta_1 + \beta_2\,\text{FARE}_t + \beta_3\,\text{INCOME}_t + \beta_4\,\text{POP}_t + \beta_5\,\text{DENSITY}_t + u_t$$

where BUSTRAVL = use of urban bus transportation in thousands of passenger hours, FARE = bus fare in dollars, INCOME = average income per capita, POP = population of city in thousands, and DENSITY = density of city in persons/sq. mile. The data are for 40 U.S. cities. In order to test for heteroscedasticity, the following auxiliary regression was estimated for the error variance ($\hat{u}_t^2$ is the dependent variable here). The error and total sums of squares for this auxiliary regression are also given (sq-X refers to X^2).

VARIABLE	COEFFICIENT	STDERROR
Constant	−1.052041e+06	4.295272e+06
FARE	3.601043e+06	2.649295e+06
INCOME	−29.202615	503.752997
POP	804.414977	322.077761
DENSITY	75.042426	100.379415
sq_FARE	−2.147132e+06	1.35584e+06
sq_INCOME	−5.194259e-05	0.014922
sq_POP	−0.05149	0.061621
sq_DENSITY	−0.006809	0.006205
Error sum of squares (ESS)	832.6	
Total sum of squares (TSS)	1672.3	

a. Write down, using symbols rather than numerical values, the auxiliary equation for error variance implied by these estimates.

b. Write down the null hypothesis for homoscedasticity (that is, no heteroscedasticity).

c. Compute the numerical value of the test statistic (show your derivations).

d. State its distribution under the null including the d.f.

e. Write down the critical value (at the 5 percent level) for the test and state whether the null hypothesis is rejected or not. Does this mean that there is a significant heteroscedasticity? Why or why not?

f. Based on your test, what can you say about the OLS estimators of the model, particularly about unbiasedness, consistency, efficiency, and the reliability of hypothesis tests?

g. Regardless of your answer in part e, assume that there was significant heteroscedasticity. Describe step-by-step how the auxiliary equation can be used to obtain weighted least squares estimates of the βs (assume that you don't face the negative variance problem). Your answer should not be in general symbolic terms but very specific to the numerical values in the table and the variables in the model. Give detailed instructions that demonstrate that you really understand how the procedure works.

Questions Requiring Computer Work
Appendix D has details about the data files.

8.23 In the application in Section 8.4, we used DATA8-3 to estimate the relation between expenditure on health care (Y) and its determinants, income (X) and percent of seniors (S) in the state. Suppose we suspect that the marginal effects of these variables are not constant but are themselves dependent on income and seniors. More specifically, consider the following extended model:

$$Y = \beta_1 + \beta_2 X + \beta_3 X^2 + \beta_4 S + \beta_5 S^2 + \beta_6 (X \times S) + u$$

Using the data provided, estimate this model by OLS and save the residuals. Then perform each of the four LM tests discussed in this chapter. Note that when you generate squares and cross products you should avoid exact multicollinearity in the auxiliary equation for the variance. If homoscedasticity is rejected, use the FGLS procedure and obtain estimates of the model. Prepare a summary table similar to Tables 8.3 and 8.5 and interpret the results. How do your results differ from those in Section 8.4?

8.24 Use DATA8-2 and carry out the estimation and hypothesis testing proposed in Exercise 8.7.

8.25 Use DATA8-2 and carry out the estimation and hypothesis testing proposed in Exercise 8.12.

8.26 Using DATA8-2, verify the table in Exercise 8.17. Then use the auxiliary regression to obtain FGLS estimates and compare your results with those in Exercises 8.24 and 8.25.

8.27 DATA7-11 has data on the sale price and corresponding characteristics of a number of homes (see Appendix D for details). Use part of that data to estimate the model in Exercise 8.9 and implement the WLS and FGLS procedure discussed there. Repeat this process after adding more variables to the model.

8.28 DATA7-11 has data on the sale price and corresponding characteristics of a number of homes (see Appendix D for details). Use part of that data to estimate the model in Exercise 8.16 and implement the WLS and FGLS procedures discussed there. Repeat this process after adding more variables to the model.

8.29 In previous chapters, you have used a number of cross-section data and estimated appropriate models. Listed next are a few of them that are particularly interesting. Choosing one item from this data set, start with a general model specification and test for heteroscedasticity using one or more of the LM tests presented in this chapter. If homoscedasticity is rejected, carry out the FGLS procedure and obtain WLS estimates for this general model. Then use the data-based model simplification technique to eliminate redundant variables. Choose a final model and interpret the results.

Data File	Dependent Variable
DATA3-4	Income tax
DATA3-10	Company profits
DATA4-4	Bus travel in cities
DATA4-5	Women's labor force participation
DATA4-6	County poverty rates
DATA4-9	Early retirements
DATA4-11	Housing units authorized
DATA4-14	Salary gain by MBAs
DATA4-15	Gini coefficient of inequality
DATA7-8	Cross-country economic growth
DATA7-10	Air quality in cities
DATA7-12	List price of cars
DATA7-13	Unemployment compensation of individuals
DATA7-17	Inequality among countries
DATA7-18	County population

Properties of OLS Estimators in the Presence of Heteroscedasticity

Here we use the simple linear regression model to demonstrate that OLS estimators are still unbiased and consistent but are inefficient. We also show that the t-statistic used with OLS estimates does not have the Student's t-distribution. Consider the model

$$y_t = \beta x_t + u_t \qquad \text{Var}(u_t) = \sigma_t^2 = \sigma^2 z_t^2 \quad \text{or} \quad \sigma_t = \sigma z_t \qquad \text{(8.A.1)}$$

where z_t is a variable with known values. The constant term is deleted for simplicity of exposition. To simplify the algebra, we have assumed a particular form of heteroscedasticity, namely, that the s.d. of error (σ_t) is proportional to the known variable z_t. The results, however, hold for any general case.

The OLS procedure assumes that $z_t = 1$ and yields the estimates

$$\hat{\beta} = \frac{S_{xy}}{S_{xx}}, \qquad \hat{\sigma}^2 = \frac{\sum \hat{u}_t^2}{n-1}, \qquad \widehat{\text{Var}(\hat{\beta})} = \frac{\hat{\sigma}^2}{S_{xx}} \qquad \text{(8.A.2)}$$

where $S_{xy} = \Sigma x_t y_t$ and $S_{xx} = \Sigma x_t^2$. Substituting for y_t from the model into S_{xy}, we get

$$\hat{\beta} = \frac{\sum x_t(\beta x_t + u_t)}{S_{xx}} = \beta + \frac{\sum x_t u_t}{S_{xx}} \qquad \text{(8.A.3)}$$

Because x_t is given and $E(u_t) = 0$, we have $E(\hat{\beta}) = \beta$, and hence the OLS estimator is still unbiased. Also, $E(x_t u_t) = 0$ and therefore, by the law of large numbers, the probability limit of $\hat{\beta}$ as $n \to \infty$ is equal to its expected value, which is β. Therefore, $\hat{\beta}$ is also consistent. Note that in these proofs we did not make use of the variance of u_t and hence the properties hold even though the errors are heteroscedastic.

From Equation (8.A.3) we obtain the variance of $\hat{\beta}$ as

$$\text{Var}(\hat{\beta}) = \frac{1}{S_{xx}^2} \sum x_t^2 \text{Var}(u_t) = \frac{\sigma^2 \sum z_t^2 x_t^2}{S_{xx}^2} \qquad \text{(8.A.4)}$$

Comparing Equations (8.A.2) and (8.A.4), we see that $E[\widehat{\text{Var}(\hat{\beta})}] = E(\hat{\sigma}^2/S_{xx}) \neq \text{Var}(\hat{\beta})$. The OLS estimate of the variance of $\hat{\beta}$ is thus biased and inconsistent. Since the t-ratio for β is $\hat{\beta}/[\widehat{\text{Var}(\hat{\beta})}]^{1/2}$, which depends on the unbiasedness of the estimated variance, that ratio will no longer have the t-distribution. The tests of hypotheses are therefore invalid.

In the model specified in Equation (8.A.1), divide both sides by z_t. We then have

$$\frac{y_t}{z_t} = \beta\frac{x_t}{z_t} + \frac{u_t}{z_t} \tag{8.A.5}$$

or

$$y_t^* = \beta x_t^* + u_t^* \tag{8.A.6}$$

The variance of u_t^* is given by

$$\mathrm{Var}(u_t^*) = \frac{1}{z_t^2}\mathrm{Var}(u_t) = \sigma^2 \tag{8.A.7}$$

and hence u_t^* is homoscedastic. Therefore, applying OLS to the transformed model in Equation (8.A.6) would yield unbiased, consistent, and efficient estimates (also BLUE) for β. Furthermore, the estimated variance will be unbiased and consistent with the right properties for the new t-ratio. Because the estimate obtained from the transformed model is efficient, the OLS estimator of the original model cannot be efficient.

Although the results have been derived for the simple regression model with a particular form of heteroscedasticity, the results generalize for any multiple regression model with any form of heteroscedasticity.

CHAPTER *9*

Serial Correlation

*T*he method of least squares has been shown to yield parameter estimates that have several desirable properties, provided the error terms (u_t) satisfy a number of assumptions. In particular, the estimates are unbiased, consistent, and most efficient. When an investigator deals with time series data, a number of special problems arise that often result in the violation of some of the assumptions needed to generate the nice properties listed. In this chapter, we explore a particular type of violation of the basic assumptions on the disturbance terms. We first examine the implications of ignoring this violation and using the OLS procedure. One would expect that, as in the case of heteroscedasticity, some properties may no longer hold. Second, we test for the presence of this violation, and finally discuss alternative approaches to the problems.

Assumption 3.6 in Chapter 3 states that the error terms u_t and u_s, for different observations t and s, are independently distributed. This property is called **serial independence.** From Chapter 2, Section 2.3, u_t and u_s being independent implies that they are uncorrelated. When an investigator is analyzing times series data, this assumption is frequently violated. Error terms for time periods not too far apart may be correlated. This property is known as **serial correlation** or **autocorrelation** (these terms will be used interchangeably). In Chapter 3 we listed a number of factors that account for the presence of the error term u_t. These were (1) omitted variables, (2) ignoring nonlinearities, (3) measurement errors, and (4) purely random, unpredictable effects. The first three of these sources can also lead to serially correlated errors. For instance, suppose a dependent variable Y_t is related to the independent variables X_{t1} and X_{t2}, but the investigator does not include X_{t2} in the model. The effect of this variable will be captured by the error term u_t. Because many economic time series exhibit trends over time, X_{t2} is likely to depend on $X_{t-1,2}, X_{t-2,2}, \ldots$. This will translate into apparent correlation between u_t and $u_{t-1}, u_{t-2}, \ldots$, thereby violating the serial independence assumption. Thus, trends in omitted variables could cause autocorrelation in errors.

Serial correlation can also be caused by misspecification of the functional form. Suppose, for example, the relationship between Y and X is quadratic but we assume a straight line. Then the error term u_t will depend on X^2. If X has been growing or falling over time, u_t will also exhibit such a trend, indicating autocorrelation.

Systematic errors in measurement can also cause autocorrelation. For example, suppose a firm is updating its inventory in a given period. If a systematic error occurred in the way it was measured, cumulative inventory stock will reflect accumulated measurement errors. These will show up as serial correlation.

As an example of serial correlation, consider the consumption of electricity during different hours of the day. Because the temperature patterns are similar between successive time periods, we can expect consumption patterns to be correlated between neighboring periods. If the model is not properly specified, this effect may show up as high correlation among errors from nearby periods. Another example of serial correlation is found in stock market data. The price of a particular security or a stock market index at the close of successive days or during successive hours is likely to be serially correlated.

● EXAMPLE 9.1

DATA6-6 has annual data on the farm population as percent of total population in the United States. Figure 9.1 is a graph of the actual farm population and the fitted value obtained from a linear time trend of the form FARMPOP = α + β TIME + u, where TIME is t from 1 to 44. Practice Computer Session 9.1 has the instructions to reproduce this example. We note from the diagram that during the early periods the actual values lie above the least squares line, during the middle periods the scatter points are clustered below the line, and during the last periods they are again consistently above the line. We therefore expect a high correlation between errors of successive and nearby periods, thereby violating the serial independence assumption. In fact, the coefficient of correlation between u_t and u_{t-1} is 0.97. A useful device to identify the presence of serial correlation is the **residual plot.** This is simply a graph of the estimated residuals $\hat{u}_t$ against time t. Figure 9.2 illustrates this residual plot for the farm population case. We observe a clear tendency for successive residuals to cluster on one side of the zero line or the other. This is a graphical indication of the presence of autocorrelation. If u_t were independent, this clustering would not be likely to happen.

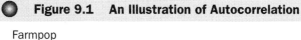

● Figure 9.1   An Illustration of Autocorrelation

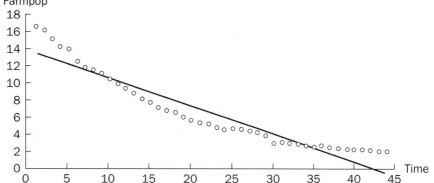

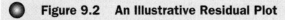

Figure 9.2   An Illustrative Residual Plot

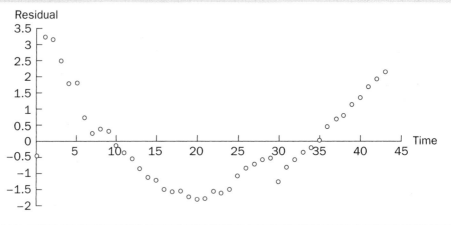

It is evident from this discussion and examples that autocorrelation does indeed violate Assumption 3.6. We now take up a discussion of the consequences of ignoring autocorrelation, present appropriate tests for identifying the presence of serial correlation, and finally discuss alternative estimation methods.

9.1   Serial Correlation of the First Order

Initially, we consider the simplest case of serial correlation called the **first-order serial correlation.** Although we use the simple linear regression model to examine the issues, all the results generalize to the multiple regression case also. If serial correlation is present, then $\text{Cov}(u_t, u_s) \neq 0$ for $t \neq s$; that is, the error for the period t is correlated with the error for the period s. The assumption of first-order autocorrelation is formally stated as follows:

ASSUMPTION 9.1

$$Y_t = \alpha + \beta X_t + u_t \tag{9.1}$$

$$u_t = \rho u_{t-1} + \varepsilon_t \quad -1 < \rho < 1 \tag{9.2}$$

The error u_t is thus related to the previous period's error (u_{t-1}), a new error term (ε_t), and a new parameter ρ. ρ must be less than 1 in absolute value; otherwise, explosive behavior is possible. Because ρ is the coefficient of the error term lagged one period, it is called the **first-order autocorrelation coefficient.** The process described by Equation (9.2) is called the **first-order autoregressive process,** more commonly known as **AR(1).** Later in this chapter (Section 9.5) we consider higher-order autoregressive processes. The new errors ε_t are assumed to satisfy the following conditions:

ASSUMPTION 9.2

The errors ε_t are independently and identically distributed with zero mean and constant variance so that $E(\varepsilon_t) = 0$, $E(\varepsilon_t^2) = \sigma_\varepsilon^2 < \infty$, and $E(\varepsilon_t\varepsilon_{t-s}) = 0$ for $s \neq 0$.

The new error terms are thus assumed to have the same properties that the OLS procedure assumed u_t to have. In the time series literature, a series obeying Assumption 9.2 is known as a **white noise series** with zero mean. Because u_t depends on u_{t-1}, we can expect them to be correlated. Note that u_t does not depend directly on u_{t-2}; however, it does do so indirectly through u_{t-1} because u_{t-1} depends on u_{t-2}. Thus, u_t is correlated with all past errors. If the covariance is positive, there is said to be a *positive autocorrelation,* and when the covariance is negative, we have *negative autocorrelation.* It is shown in Appendix Section 9.A.2 that $\mathrm{Cov}(u_t, u_{t-s}) = \sigma^2\rho^s$, for $s \geq 0$.

● 9.2   Consequences of Ignoring Serial Correlation

In Chapter 3 we proved that under Assumptions 3.3 and 3.4 (that is, that u_t has zero mean and is uncorrelated with X_t), the OLS estimates are unbiased and consistent. Since the proof of these properties did not depend on Assumption 3.6, which is violated by the presence of autocorrelation, *OLS estimates (and forecasts based on them) are unbiased and consistent even if the error terms are serially correlated.* The problem is with the efficiency of the estimates. In the proof of the Gauss–Markov theorem that established efficiency (Section 3.A.4), one of the steps involved minimization of the variance of the linear combination $\sum a_t u_t$:

$$\mathrm{Var}\left(\sum a_t u_t\right) = \sum a_t^2 \sigma^2 + \sum\sum_{t \neq s} a_t a_s \mathrm{Cov}(u_t, u_s) \tag{9.3}$$

where the double summation is over all t and s that are different. If $\mathrm{Cov}(u_t, u_s) \neq 0$, the second term on the right-hand side will not vanish. Therefore, minimizing $\sum a_t^2 \sigma^2$ (which gives OLS normal equations) is not equivalent to minimizing Equation (9.3). For this reason, the best linear unbiased estimator (BLUE) that minimizes (9.3) will not be the same as the OLS estimator. In other words, OLS estimates are not BLUE and are hence *inefficient.* Thus, the consequences of ignoring autocorrelation are the same as those of ignoring heteroscedasticity; namely, the *estimates and forecasts are unbiased and consistent, but are inefficient.* A caveat should be added to this, however. If the X variables include a lagged dependent variable such as Y_{t-1}, then serial correlation will yield inconsistent OLS estimates. This point is proved in the next chapter.

We can also show that if the serial correlation in u_t is positive and the independent variable X_t grows over time (which is often the case), then the estimated

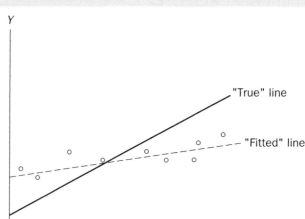

⬤ **Figure 9.3 Underestimation of the Residual Variance**

residual variance ($\hat{\sigma}^2$) will be an underestimate and the value of R^2 will be an over-estimate. In other words, the goodness of fit will be exaggerated and the estimated standard errors will be smaller than the true standard errors. These points are illustrated in Fig. 9.3, a typical scatter diagram, with the help of the simple regression model. The heavy line is the "true" regression line $\alpha + \beta X$. Suppose there is positive autocorrelation; that is, the covariance between two successive stochastic disturbance terms is positive. Further suppose that the first scatter point (X_1, Y_1) is above the true line. This means that u_1 will be positive. Because u_2 and u_1 are positively correlated, u_2 is likely to be positive, putting (X_2, Y_2) also above the line. Hence, the first few scatter points are likely to be above the true regression line. Suppose one of the scatter points happens to be below the true line because of the random nature of the us. Then the next few points are also likely to be below the true line.

Because the least squares procedure minimizes the sum of squared deviations, the "fitted" line will look like the dashed line. The *true* variance of the errors is given by the deviation of (X_t, Y_t) from the true line, which is clearly larger than the *estimated* residual variance, which in turn is calculated from deviations around the fitted line. Hence, *the computed error sum of squares (ESS) will be smaller than the true value, and R^2 will be larger than the true value.*

In the general case, the variances of the regression coefficients will be biased. For a detailed analysis of the nature of the bias, interested readers should refer to Section 8.3 of Kmenta's book (1986).

Effect on Tests of Hypotheses

We just argued that in the common case in which serial correlation is positive and the independent variable is growing over time, estimated standard errors will be smaller than the true ones, and hence the former will be underestimates. This means that the t-statistics will be overestimates, and hence a regression coefficient that appears to be significant may not really be so. The estimated variances of the parameters will be biased and inconsistent. Therefore, the t- and F-tests are no longer valid.

Effect on Forecasting

Although the forecasts will be unbiased (because the estimates are unbiased), they will be inefficient with larger variances. By explicitly taking into account the serial correlation among residuals, it is possible to generate better forecasts than those generated by the OLS procedure. This is demonstrated for the AR(1) error structure specified in Equation (9.2).

Suppose we ignore Equation (9.2) and obtain the OLS estimates $\hat{\alpha}$ and $\hat{\beta}$. We saw in Section 3.9 that the OLS prediction would be $\hat{Y}_t = \hat{\alpha} + \hat{\beta}X_t$. Because u_t is random, it could not be predicted; and hence we set it equal to its mean value, which is zero. In the case of the first-order serial correlation, however, u_t is predictable from Equation (9.2), provided ρ can be estimated (call it $\hat{\rho}$). We have $\hat{u}_t = \hat{\rho}\hat{u}_{t-1}$. At time t, the residual for the previous period ($\hat{u}_{t-1}$) is known. Therefore, the AR(1) prediction will be

$$\tilde{Y}_t = \hat{\alpha} + \hat{\beta}X_t + \hat{\rho}\hat{u}_{t-1} = \hat{\alpha} + \hat{\beta}X_t + \hat{\rho}(Y_{t-1} - \hat{\alpha} - \hat{\beta}X_{t-1}) \qquad (9.4)$$

making use of the fact that $\hat{u}_{t-1} = Y_{t-1} - \hat{\alpha} - \hat{\beta}X_{t-1}$. Equation (9.4) uses the presence of serial correlation to generate the prediction; thus $\tilde{Y}_t$ will be more efficient than that obtained by the OLS procedure. The procedure for estimating ρ is described in Section 9.3.

The results obtained in this section are summarized in Property 9.1.

Property 9.1

If serial correlation among the stochastic disturbance terms in a regression model is ignored and the OLS procedure is used to estimate the parameters, then the following properties hold:

a.   The estimates and forecasts based on them will still be unbiased and consistent. The consistency property does not hold, however, if lagged dependent variables are included as explanatory variables.

b.   The OLS estimates are no longer BLUE and will be inefficient. Forecasts will also be inefficient.

c.   The estimated variances of the regression coefficients will be biased and inconsistent, and hence tests of hypotheses are invalid. If the serial correlation is positive and the independent variable X_t is growing over time, then the standard errors will be underestimates of the true values. This means that the computed R^2 will be an overestimate, indicating a better fit than actually exists. Also, the t-statistics in such a case will tend to appear more significant than they actually are.

9.3   Testing for First-Order Serial Correlation

In this section, we confine ourselves to testing first-order autocorrelation. The procedure is generalized in Section 9.5 to the case of higher orders.

The Durbin–Watson Test

Although the residual plot is a useful graphical device for identifying the presence of serial correlation, formal tests for autocorrelation are essential. In this section, we present the most common test for first-order serial correlation, namely, the **Durbin–Watson (DW) test** (Durbin and Watson, 1950, 1951). A test based on the Lagrange multiplier approach discussed in Chapters 6 and 8 is presented in the next section.

The steps for carrying out the Durbin–Watson test for AR(1) are described for the following multiple regression model:

$$Y_t = \beta_1 + \beta_2 X_{t2} + \beta_3 X_{t3} + \cdots + \beta_k X_{tk} + u_t \qquad (9.5)$$

$$u_t = \rho u_{t-1} + \varepsilon_t \qquad -1 < \rho < 1$$

Step 1   Estimate the model by ordinary least squares and compute the residuals $\hat{u}_t$ as $Y_t - \hat{\beta}_1 - \hat{\beta}_2 X_{t2} - \hat{\beta}_3 X_{t3} - \cdots - \hat{\beta}_k X_{tk}$.

Step 2   Compute the Durbin–Watson statistic:

$$d = \frac{\sum_{t=2}^{t=n} (\hat{u}_t - \hat{u}_{t-1})^2}{\sum_{t=1}^{t=n} \hat{u}_t^2} \qquad (9.6)$$

which is shown later to range from 0 to 4. The exact distribution of d depends on the observations on the Xs. Durbin and Watson showed that the distribution of d is bounded by two distributions. These are used to construct critical regions for the Durbin–Watson test.

Step 3a   To test H_0: $\rho = 0$ against $\rho > 0$ (one-tailed test), look up in Table A.5, Appendix A, the critical values for the Durbin–Watson statistic, and write the numbers d_L and d_U. Note that the table gives k', which is the number of regression coefficients estimated, *excluding the constant*. Reject H_0 if $d \leq d_L$. If $d \geq d_U$, we cannot reject H_0. If $d_L < d < d_U$, the test is inconclusive.

Step 3b   To test for negative serial correlation (that is, for H_1: $\rho < 0$), use $4 - d$. This is done when d is greater than 2. If $4 - d \leq d_L$, we conclude that there is significant negative autocorrelation. If $4 - d \geq d_U$, we conclude that there is no negative autocorrelation. The test is inconclusive if $d_L < 4 - d < d_U$.

The inconclusiveness of the DW test arises from the fact that the small-sample distribution for the DW statistic d depends on the x variables and is difficult to compute. To circumvent this, Durbin and Watson tabulated the critical values for the distributions of the bounds for d, for different values of the sample size n and the number of coefficients k', *not counting the constant term*. Savin and White (1977) extended this to the case of many explanatory variables. When the test is inconclusive, one might try the Lagrange multiplier test described next. Alternatively, other functional forms or estimation procedures could be tried. Some programs such as SHAZAM include the p-value that takes into account the fact that the distribution of d depends on the values of the explanatory variables.

From the estimated residuals we can obtain an estimate of the first-order serial correlation coefficient as

$$\hat{\rho} = \frac{\sum\limits_{t=2}^{t=n} \hat{u}_t \hat{u}_{t-1}}{\sum\limits_{t=1}^{t=n} \hat{u}_t^2} \tag{9.7}$$

This estimate is approximately equal to the one obtained by regressing $\hat{u}_t$ against $\hat{u}_{t-1}$ *without a constant term*. It is shown in Appendix 9.A that the DW statistic d is approximately equal to $2(1 - \hat{\rho})$. Thus,

$$d \approx 2(1 - \hat{\rho}) \tag{9.6a}$$

Because ρ can range from -1 to $+1$, the range for d is 0 to 4. When ρ is 0, d is 2. Thus, a DW statistic of nearly 2 means there is no first-order serial correlation. A strong positive autocorrelation means ρ is close to $+1$. This indicates low values of d. Similarly, values of d close to 4 indicate a strong negative serial correlation; that is, ρ is close to -1. The various possible situations are described in the following diagram. The null hypothesis is H_0: $\rho = 0$.

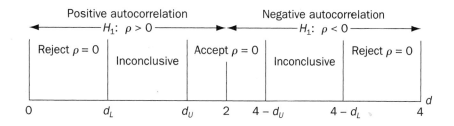

The DW test is invalid if some of the Xs are lags of the dependent variable—that is, if they are of the form $Y_{t-1}, Y_{t-2}, \ldots$. Problems created by such lagged variables are examined in Chapter 10.

● **EXAMPLE 9.2**

For the farm population example for which the residual plot is presented in Fig. 9.2, the DW statistic is $d = 0.056$. (See Practice Computer Session 9.1.) The number of observations is 44 and $k' = 1$. For a one-tailed test, the critical values are obtained (by interpolation) from Table A.5 as $d_L = 1.47$ and $d_U = 1.56$. Since $d < d_L$, this test is rejected at the 5 percent level. We therefore conclude that there is significant serial correlation in the residuals at the 5 percent level.

● EXAMPLE 9.3

As a second example, consider Model C in Exercise 4.17, which relates the death rates due to coronary heart disease to per-capita consumption of cigarettes, per-capita intake of edible fats and oil, per-capita consumption of distilled spirits, and per-capita consumption of beer (see DATA4-7). In this example, we have $n = 34$, $k' = 4$, $d = 1.485$, $d_L = 1.21$, and $d_U = 1.728$. (See Practice Computer Session 9.2.) Because d is between d_L and d_U, we have an inconclusive test. Some computer programs (for example, SHAZAM) calculate the exact p-value based on the user's observations. The p-value is 0.017, which is low, and hence we reject H_0: $\rho = 0$ and conclude that there is significant autocorrelation.

● PRACTICE PROBLEM 9.1

In Example 5.1 of Chapter 5 we related housing starts to variables such as GNP and interest rate and used time series data to estimate several different models. Use the Durbin–Watson test on those models to test for first-order serial correlation. Be sure to state the null and alternative hypotheses and the criterion for acceptance or rejection of the null. Based on your results, what do you conclude about the properties of the OLS estimates obtained in Chapter 5?

The Durbin–Watson test has several drawbacks that make it useless in many contexts. For instance, we have already seen that it can give inconclusive results. Also, the test is invalid if the Xs include lagged dependent variables (more on this in Chapter 10). Third, the test is inapplicable if the autoregressive errors are of higher orders (for example, 4 in the case of quarterly data). Finally, if the number of explanatory variables is large, the bounds d_L and d_U may not be available. If any of these situations arises, an alternative is the LM test discussed next, which does not suffer from any of these criticisms (be sure, however, to have at least 30 d.f., because the LM test is a large-sample test).

The Lagrange Multiplier Test

The LM test described in Chapter 6 is useful in identifying serial correlation not only of the first order but of higher orders as well, but here we confine ourselves to the first-order case. The general case is taken up in Section 9.5.

To motivate this test, note that Equation (9.5) can be rewritten as

$$Y_t = \beta_1 + \beta_2 X_{t2} + \cdots + \beta_k X_{tk} + \rho u_{t-1} + \varepsilon_t$$

The test for $\rho = 0$ can therefore be treated as a Lagrange multiplier (LM) test for the addition of the variable u_{t-1} (which is unknown, and hence one would use $\hat{u}_{t-1}$ instead). The steps for carrying out the LM test are as follows:

Step 1   This step is identical to Step 1 of the DW test; that is, estimate Equation (9.5) by OLS and compute its residuals.

Step 2   Regress $\hat{u}_t$ against a constant, $X_{t2}, \ldots, X_{tk}$, and $\hat{u}_{t-1}$, using the $n-1$ observations 2 through n. This is similar to the auxiliary regression in Step 4 of Section 6.14. Next compute LM $= (n-1)R^2$ from this auxiliary regression. $n-1$ is used because the effective number of observations is $n-1$.

Step 3   Reject the null hypothesis of zero autocorrelation in favor of the alternative that $\rho \neq 0$ if $(n-1)R^2 > \chi^2_1(a)$, the value of χ^2_1 in the chi-square distribution with 1 d.f. such that the area to the right of it is a. Alternatively, compute p-value $= \mathrm{Prob}(\chi^2_1 > \mathrm{LM})$, the area to the right of LM in χ^2_1. If p-value $< a$, it is safe to reject $H_0: \rho = 0$ and conclude that autocorrelation is significant.

If there were serial correlation in the residuals, we would expect $\hat{u}_t$ to be related to $\hat{u}_{t-1}$. This is the motivation behind the auxiliary regression in which $\hat{u}_{t-1}$ is included along with all the independent variables in the model. Note that the LM test does not have the inconclusiveness of the DW test. However, it is a large-sample test and would need at least 30 d.f. to be meaningful.

● EXAMPLE 9.4

In the heart disease example, the auxiliary regression is the following (see Practice Computer Session 9.3):

$$\hat{u}_t = 113.628 - 4.675\ \mathrm{CIG} - 1.579\ \mathrm{EDFAT} + 0.361\mathrm{SPIRITS}$$
$$\quad\ (1.4)\qquad (-1.1)\qquad\quad (-1.6)\qquad\qquad (0.1)$$

$$+\ 0.207\ \mathrm{BEER} + 0.259\ \hat{u}_{t-1}$$
$$\quad (0.3)\qquad\qquad (1.4)$$

$$R^2 = 0.137 \qquad n = 34 \qquad (n-1)R^2 = 4.521$$

The critical chi-square is $\chi^2_1(0.05) = 3.841$, which is less than $(n-1)R^2$. Also, the p-value for 4.521 was 0.033. The LM test thus rejects the null hypothesis of zero autocorrelation, whereas the DW test was inconclusive.

● PRACTICE PROBLEM 9.2

Redo Practice Problem 9.1 using the LM test approach.

● 9.4   Treatment of Serial Correlation

Changing the Functional Form

No estimation procedure can guarantee the elimination of serial correlation because the nature and cause of the autocorrelation are generally unknown. As Hendry and Mizon (1978) have argued forcefully, serial correlation might be more symptomatic of a misspecified model than of misspecified error structure. For instance, suppose that the relation is quadratic and we should have regressed Y

against X and X^2. If X has been systematically rising or falling over time, a regression of Y on X alone will exhibit apparent serial correlation. No sophisticated estimation procedure will be able to correct the problem, which is really due to a misspecification in the deterministic part rather than in the error term. The solution here is to reformulate the model to include the quadratic term so that there is no apparent serial correlation. Another alternative is to use a double-log model. These points are illustrated in Example 9.5. Application Section 9.7 presents another example in which the initial model exhibited autocorrelation, but when the specification was improved, serial correlation was no longer present.

⬤ **EXAMPLE 9.5**

Using the data in DATA6-6, we saw in Figure 9.1 that the percent of the total U.S. population that lives on farms exhibits a nonlinear downward trend from 1947 to 1991. If we fit a linear time trend to this data, we would expect a clustering of successive residuals that appears to indicate serial correlation (see Fig. 9.2). The estimates for such a linear trend are given below (see Practice Computer Session 9.4 for reproducing these results):

$$farmpop_t = \underset{(31.55)}{13.777} - \underset{(-19.2)}{0.325t} \qquad d = 0.056$$

$$\overline{R}^2 = 0.895$$

The values in parentheses are the t-statistics. Note that the Durbin–Watson (DW) statistic is very close to zero, indicating strong serial correlation. Because of this, the t-statistic and the goodness-of-fit measure are exaggerated. It is evident from Figure 9.1 that a nonlinear relation would be more appropriate. A quadratic time trend was next fitted and the results are as follows:

$$farmpop_t = \underset{(113.5)}{17.026} - \underset{(-48.7)}{0.749t} + \underset{(28.4)}{0.00942t^2} \qquad d = 0.601$$

$$\overline{R}^2 = 0.995$$

Although the DW statistic has moved closer to 2, it still indicates significant positive autocorrelation. The first difference in logarithms was tried next. More specifically, we define

$$gfarmpop_t = \ln(farmpop_t) - \ln(farmpop_{t-1})$$

This quantity is known as the **instantaneous rate of growth** and is obtained from an exponential growth path. To see this, suppose Y_t grows exponentially with $Y_t = Y_0 e^{gt}$ (g is the growth rate, which may be negative, indicating an exponential decay of Y). Taking logarithms of both sides, we get

$$\ln(Y_t) = \ln(Y_0) + gt \qquad \text{for time } t$$

$$\ln(Y_{t-1}) = \ln(Y_0) + g(t-1) \qquad \text{for time } t-1$$

Subtracting the second equation from the first we get

$$g = \ln(Y_t) - \ln(Y_{t-1})$$

Thus, the difference in the logarithms is the growth rate. The estimated relation for the farm population was (see Table 9.2)

$$gfarmpop_t = \underset{(-3.9)}{-0.064} + \underset{(0.92)}{0.00058t} \qquad d = 2.266$$

$$\overline{R}^2 = -0.004$$

Note that because the dependent variable is different from the two previous regressions, the values of $\overline{R}^2$ are not comparable. The DW statistic is very close to 2, and it is readily verified that there is no evidence of first-order autocorrelation (since $d > 2$, we would use $4 - d = 1.734$). Thus, an appropriate modification of the functional form has eliminated apparent serial correlation. Does this mean that the third formulation is the "best"? The answer depends on what "best" means. A researcher interested in forecasting farm population will base judgment on the model's ability to forecast it. This issue is addressed more systematically in Chapter 11.

Specifying a More General Dynamic Structure

It is easy to show that a model with an autoregressive error term is a special case of a model with a more general dynamic structure in the deterministic part (see Sargan, 1964, and Hendry and Mizon, 1978). Consider the following model (commonly used in macroeconomics) that relates the dependent variable to its own lagged value, an explanatory variable, and its lag:

$$y_t = \beta_0 + \beta_1 y_{t-1} + \beta_2 x_t + \beta_3 x_{t-1} + \varepsilon_t \qquad |\beta_1| < 1 \tag{9.8}$$

The error term ε_t is assumed to have zero mean, a constant variance, and be serially independent. Equation (9.1) is

$$y_t = \alpha + \beta x_t + u_t \tag{9.1}$$

Solving for u_t in terms of the others and substituting for it in Equation (9.2), we get

$$y_t - \alpha - \beta x_t = \rho(y_{t-1} - \alpha - \beta x_{t-1}) + \varepsilon_t$$

which can be rearranged as follows.

$$y_t = \alpha(1 - \rho) + \rho y_{t-1} + \beta x_t - \beta \rho x_{t-1} + \varepsilon_t \tag{9.1a}$$

Comparing Equations (9.8) and (9.1a), we note that

$$\beta_0 = \alpha(1 - \rho), \qquad \beta_1 = \rho, \qquad \beta_2 = \beta, \qquad \text{and} \qquad \beta_3 = -\rho\beta$$

It is readily seen that the parameters satisfy the nonlinear restriction $\beta_3 + \beta_1\beta_2 = 0$. If this restriction is satisfied in Equation (9.8), then the model reduces to the static model in Equation (9.1) with the autoregressive error structure in Equation (9.2). Equation (9.8) has four parameters to estimate, whereas Equations (9.1) and (9.2) have only three unknown parameters. Thus, serial correlation is a "convenient simplification, not a nuisance" as Hendry and Mizon (1978) have pointed out. They and Sargan (1964) have suggested that one formulate the model generally as in Equation (9.8), test the above nonlinear restriction on it, and if it is accepted, simplify the model along the lines of Equations (9.1) and (9.2). If the nonlinear restriction does not hold, then treating the model as static with an autoregressive error term and a significant Durbin–Watson statistic might yield misleading results.

Model Formulation in First Differences

Granger and Newbold (1974 and 1986) have cautioned against spurious regressions that might arise when a regression is based on levels of trending variables, especially with a significant DW statistic. In empirical econometric work, a common way to get around this problem is to formulate models in terms of a **first difference,** which is the difference between the value at time t and that at time $t - 1$. In this case, we would estimate $\Delta y_t = \beta_0 + \beta\Delta x_t + \varepsilon_t$, where $\Delta y_t = y_t - y_{t-1}$ and $\Delta x_t = x_t - x_{t-1}$. However, the solution of using first differences might not always be appropriate. To see this, note that the first difference model can be rewritten as follows:

$$y_t = y_{t-1} + \beta_0 + \beta x_t - \beta x_{t-1} + \varepsilon_t$$

Comparing this with Equation (9.8), we see that this model is a special case with $\beta_1 = 1$ and $\beta_2 + \beta_3 = 0$. Thus, the preferred approach is to test these two restrictions first and, if both are accepted, then use a first difference specification.

Estimation Procedures

When modified functional forms do not eliminate autocorrelation, several estimation procedures are available that will produce more efficient estimates than those obtained by the OLS procedure. These are discussed next. It should be noted, however, that mechanical "fixes" for autocorrelation may imply restrictions on the time-series properties of the model that are inconsistent with the data. It should also be pointed out that these methods need to be applied only for time series data. With cross-section data one can rearrange the observations in any manner and get a DW statistic that is acceptable. This suggests, however, that the DW test is meaningless for cross-section data. Because time series data cannot be rearranged, an investigator needs to be concerned about possible serial correlation.

Cochrane–Orcutt Iterative Procedure

The **Cochrane–Orcutt (CORC) iterative procedure** (Cochrane and Orcutt, 1949) requires the transformation of the regression model (9.5) to a form in which the OLS procedure is applicable. Rewriting Equation (9.5) for the period $t - 1$ we get

$$Y_{t-1} = \beta_1 + \beta_2 X_{(t-1)2} + \beta_3 X_{(t-1)3} + \cdots + \beta_k X_{(t-1)k} + u_{t-1} \qquad (9.5')$$

Multiplying (9.5') term-by-term by ρ and subtracting from (9.5), we obtain

$$Y_t - \rho Y_{t-1} = \beta_1(1 - \rho) + \beta_2[X_{t2} - \rho X_{(t-1)2}] + \beta_3[X_{t3} - \rho X_{(t-1)3}]$$
$$+ \cdots + \beta_k[X_{tk} - \rho X_{(t-1)k}] + \varepsilon_t$$

where we have used the fact that $u_t = \rho u_{t-1} + \varepsilon_t$. This equation can be rewritten as follows:

$$Y_t^* = \beta_1^* + \beta_2 X_{t2}^* + \beta_3 X_{t3}^* + \cdots + \beta_k X_{tk}^* + \varepsilon_t \qquad (9.9)$$

where

$$Y_t^* = Y_t - \rho Y_{t-1}, \qquad \beta_1^* = \beta_1(1 - \rho), \qquad \text{and} \qquad X_{ti}^* = X_{ti} - \rho X_{(t-1)i},$$
$$\text{for} \quad t = 2, 3, \ldots, n \quad \text{and} \quad i = 2, \ldots, k$$

The transformation that generates the variables Y^* and the X^*s is known as **quasi-differencing,** or **generalized differencing.** β_1^* is just the new constant term. Note that the error term in Equation (9.9) satisfies all the properties needed for applying the least squares procedure. If ρ were known, we could apply OLS to (9.9) and obtain estimates that are BLUE. However, ρ is unknown and has to be estimated from the sample. The steps for carrying out the Cochrane–Orcutt procedure are as follows:

Step 1 Estimate Equation (9.5) by OLS and compute its residual $\hat{u}_t$.

Step 2 Estimate the first-order serial correlation coefficient (call it $\hat{\rho}$) from Equation (9.7).

Step 3 Transform the variables as follows:

$$Y_t^* = Y_t - \hat{\rho} Y_{t-1}, \qquad X_{t2}^* = X_{t2} - \hat{\rho} X_{(t-1)2}, \qquad \text{and so on}$$

Note that the starred variables are defined only for $t = 2$ through n because of the presence of the term involving $t - 1$.

Step 4 Regress Y_t^* against a constant, X_{t2}^*, X_{t3}^*, $\ldots$, X_{tk}^* and get OLS estimates of the transformed Equation (9.9).

Step 5 Use these estimates for the βs in (9.5) and obtain a new set of estimates of u_t. Then go back and repeat Step 2 with these new values until the following stopping rule applies.

Step 6 This iterative procedure can be stopped when the estimates of ρ from two successive iterations differ by no more than some preselected value, such as 0.001. The final $\hat{\rho}$ is then used to get the CORC estimates from Equation (9.9).

Because the constant term is also multiplied by $1 - \hat{\rho}$, $\hat{\beta}_1$ is obtained as $\hat{\beta}_1^*/(1 - \hat{\rho})$, where $\hat{\beta}_1^*$ is the estimated constant term in the *transformed equation* (9.9).

Most standard regression programs carry out all the steps of this procedure with simple commands, thus relieving the user of the drudgery of the iteration process. Most programs report the estimated constant term of the *original model* (that is, $\hat{\beta}_1$), so the user need not (and should not) divide by $(1 - \hat{\rho})$. The user is also cautioned about identifying what the reported R^2, error sum of squares, and so on represent. If they relate to Equation (9.9), the values are not comparable to the corresponding OLS estimates because the left-hand sides of Equations (9.5) and (9.9) are quite different. Similarly, the reported Durbin–Watson statistic often refers to the residuals of (9.9) and not to those of (9.5). A DW test on this would test for a *second-order serial correlation* for $\hat{u}_t$, because the underlying model will be AR(1) on ε_t.

The Cochrane–Orcutt procedure can be shown to converge to the maximum likelihood estimates, which we know are consistent and asymptotically efficient. The iterative procedure generally converges quickly and does not require more than three to six iterations. It should be noted that the number of observations used in estimating (9.9) is only $n - 1$ because we lose the first observation. With k parameters, the degrees of freedom is $n - k - 1$. Hypothesis testing can be done in the usual way. It is possible to preserve the first observation by using the following transformation just for $t = 1$ (the justification for this step is provided in Appendix 9.A):

$$Y_1^* = Y_1(1 - \rho^2)^{1/2} \quad \text{and} \quad X_{1i}^* = X_{1i}(1 - \rho^2)^{1/2} \quad \text{for } i = 1 \text{ to } k$$

● EXAMPLE 9.6

The heart disease example presented in Example 9.4 was found to have significant autocorrelation (according to the LM test), and hence we reestimated the model by CORC. The estimated equation given here was obtained using the GRETL program, which ignores the first observation (see Practice Computer Session 9.5). Because programs differ in the criterion for convergence, answers might differ somewhat from program to program. The difference, however, should not be large.

$$\widehat{\text{CHD}} = 341.023 + 2.903 \text{ CIG} + 0.373 \text{ EDFAT} + 12.045 \text{ SPIRITS} - 2.206 \text{ BEER}$$
$$\quad\quad\quad (4.2) \quad\quad (0.6) \quad\quad\quad (0.4) \quad\quad\quad\quad (1.83) \quad\quad\quad\quad (-2.5)$$

The values in parentheses are *t*-statistics. The number of iterations required is 12 and the final $\hat{\rho}$ is 0.613. We can perform a DW test on the estimated εs from the transformed model (9.9) to check whether the εs exhibit first-order autocorrelation. The DW *d* for the equation was 2.232. From Table A.5 we have (for $n = 33$ and $k' = 4$) $d_L = 1.19$ and $d_U = 1.73$. Because $4 - d = 1.771 > d_U$, we conclude that there is no serial correlation in the εs.

Hildreth–Lu Search Procedure

A frequently used alternative to the Cochrane–Orcutt procedure is the **Hildreth–Lu (HILU) search procedure** (Hildreth and Lu, 1960), which has the following steps:

Step 1   Choose a value of ρ (say ρ_1). Using this value, transform the variables and estimate Equation (9.9) by OLS.

Step 2 From these estimates, derive $\hat{\varepsilon}_t$ from Equation (9.9) and the error sum of squares associated with it. Call it ESS (ρ_1). Next choose a different ρ (ρ_2) and repeat Steps 1 and 2.

Step 3 By varying ρ from -1 to $+1$ in some systematic way (say, at steps of length 0.05 or 0.01), we can get a series of values of ESS(ρ). Choose that ρ for which ESS is a minimum. This is the final ρ that globally minimizes the error sum of squares of the transformed model. Equation (9.9) is then estimated with this final ρ as the optimum solution.

● EXAMPLE 9.7

The original Hildreth–Lu paper presents nearly two dozen examples of estimation by the HILU procedure. We reproduce one of them here. DATA9-1 described in Appendix D has data on the demand for ice cream. The observations refer to four-week periods from March 18, 1951, to July 11, 1953. The variable definitions are as follows:

DEMAND = Per-capita consumption of ice cream in pints
PRICE = Price per pint in dollars
INCOME = Weekly family income in dollars
TEMP = Mean temperature in Fahrenheit

Table 9.1 has the estimated regression coefficients and the error sum of squares of Equation (9.9) for each step of the search procedure. The row corresponding to $\rho = 0$ represents the OLS estimates (using observations 2 through 30). The HILU procedure minimizes ESS(ρ) when $\rho = 0.41$. Note that OLS and HILU estimates differ considerably.

The CORC procedure was also applied to these data. It took only two rounds of iterations for convergence. The final $\hat{\rho}$ was 0.40083, and the CORC estimates and t-statistics are as follows (see Practice Computer Session 9.6 to reproduce this):

$$\widehat{\text{DEMAND}} = 0.157 - 0.892 \, \text{PRICE} + 0.0032 \, \text{INCOME} + 0.00356 \, \text{TEMP}$$
$$\quad\quad\quad (0.5) \quad (-1.1) \quad\quad (2.07) \quad\quad\quad (6.42)$$

These estimates are quite close to the HILU estimates. The DW statistic for Equation (9.9) is 1.55. With $n = 29$ and $k' = 3$, we have $d_L = 1.198$ and $d_U = 1.65$. It is evident that the DW test does not reject the null hypothesis of zero serial correlation of the residuals of Equation (9.9). In particular, the test is inconclusive.

● PRACTICE PROBLEM 9.3

Use the data in DATA9-1 to estimate a double-log model using OLS. The double-log model will give income, price, and temperature elasticities. Perform a DW test on the residuals. Is there evidence of first-order autocorrelation? If there is, use the CORC and HILU procedures and compare the estimates.

⬤ Table 9.1   Hildreth–Lu Estimates of the Demand for Ice Cream

ρ	CONST.	PRICE	INCOME	TEMP	ESS
1.0	.64927	−.9358	−.00197	.00272	.025823
.9	.64166	−.9824	−.00149	.02284	.027317
.8	.53264	−1.0064	−.00044	.00303	.026854
.7	.41572	−1.0001	.00075	.00321	.026470
.6	.30779	−.9728	.00182	.00336	.026022
.5	.22084	−.9342	.00264	.00348	.025622
.42	.16779	−.9004	.00311	.00354	.025459
.41	.16229	−.8967	.00316	.00355	.025452
.4	.15653	−.8916	.00321	.00356	.025453
.39	.15136	−.8876	.00325	.00357	.025454
.3	.11148	−.8502	.00357	.00361	.025674
.2	.08025	−.8101	.00379	.00364	.026395
.1	.05903	−.7733	.00392	.00364	.027666
0	.04406	−.7378	.00398	.00364	.029521
−.1	.03387	−.7058	.00400	.00363	.031964
−.2	.02680	−.6766	.00400	.00362	.034995
−.3	.02210	−.6505	.00398	.00360	.038612
−.4	.01895	−.6270	.00395	.00359	.042810
−.5	.01695	−.6060	.00392	.00357	.047585
−.6	.01580	−.5872	.00388	.00355	.052933
−.7	.01538	−.5707	.00384	.00354	.058846
−.8	.01544	−.5560	.00380	.00352	.065324
−.9	.01587	−.5432	.00376	.00350	.072361
−1.0	.01651	−.5315	.00372	.00349	.079958

Source: Hildreth and Lu (1960), Table 19, 36. Reprinted with the permission of the Michigan State University.

A Comparison of the Two Procedures

The HILU procedure basically searches for the value of ρ between -1 and $+1$ that minimizes the sum of squares of the residuals of Equation (9.9). If the step intervals are small, the procedure involves running a large number of regressions; hence, compared to the CORC procedure, the HILU method is computer-intensive. On the other hand, the CORC procedure iterates to a local minimum of ESS(ρ) and might miss the global minimum if there is more than one local minimum. This observation is illustrated in Fig. 9.4, which has local minima at the points *A* and *B*. The points indicated by circles correspond to the HILU steps. It is quite possible that the CORC technique will iterate to the local minimum at *A*, thus completely missing the global minimum at *B*. Note that the HILU approach would choose the

Figure 9.4   A Comparison of the HILU and CORC Procedures

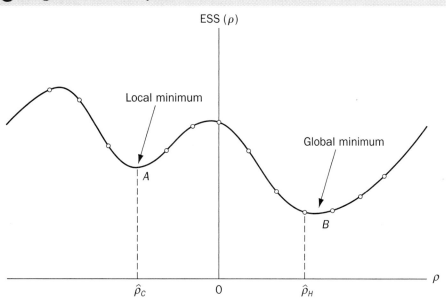

point corresponding to $\hat{\rho}_H$ and miss the true global minimum, but only slightly. Hildreth and Lu experimented with nearly two dozen data sets and found no multiple minima, which might indicate that they are perhaps not common. A hybrid procedure would be to search at broad steps, such as 0.1, which requires 19 regressions (excluding the endpoints -1 and $+1$). Choose the ρ that has the smallest ESS in this first pass as the starting point of a CORC procedure and iterate to a final solution. Thus, in Figure 9.4, HILU will choose $\hat{\rho}_H$ in the first pass, and CORC will then iterate to the global minimum at B.

Most well-known computer programs offer both the iterative procedure and the search procedure; it is wise to use them both to make sure that CORC has not missed the global minimum; better yet, use the hybrid method, because it is more likely to attain the global minimum. It should be noted that the Hildreth–Lu and hybrid procedures are applicable only for AR(1), which is a major limitation. For this reason, the search procedure is no longer common.

EXAMPLE 9.8

We now provide an example in which the CORC and HILU estimates are indeed different (Practice Computer Session 9.7 has the details to reproduce this example). Consider the following model estimated in Chapter 4 using the data in DATA4-2:

$$C_t = \beta_1 + \beta_2 W_t + \beta_3 P_t + u_t$$

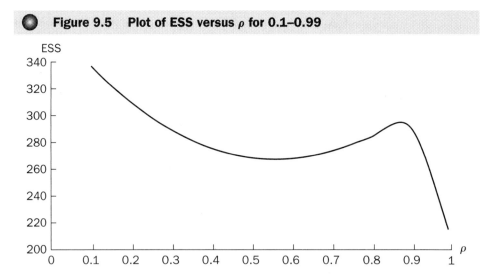

Figure 9.5   Plot of ESS versus ρ for 0.1–0.99

where C_t is aggregate consumption expenditures, W_t is the total employee compensation, and P_t is total profits, all measured in real terms in billions of dollars for the United States for the period 1959–1994.

The Durbin–Watson statistic for first-order autocorrelation is 0.969, which indicates strong serial correlation (verify it). The CORC method starts with the estimated $\rho(0.494)$ obtained from the OLS residuals and performs six iterations to yield the final value of 0.562. The HILU method uses the recommended hybrid procedure and initially searches from -0.9 to $+0.9$ in steps of 0.1 and also at -0.99 and 0.99. In this first pass, ESS is minimum at 0.99. The program then uses this as the starting point and does one CORC iteration to yield the final $\hat{\rho}$ as 0.9903, which is considerably different from the final value of 0.562 obtained by CORC. Figure 9.5 explains why the two procedures give such different $\hat{\rho}$ values. In Fig. 9.5, ESS is plotted against ρ for the range 0.1 to 1.0. It will be noted that CORC starts at 0.494 and converges to the local minimum at 0.562, whereas the hybrid HILU–CORC method has accurately selected 0.99 as the minimum. It is thus evident from this example that the mixed HILU–CORC approach is likely to be superior to using either singly because it exploits the comparative advantage of each method.

9.5   Higher-Order Serial Correlation

As mentioned earlier, the nature of the error structure is generally unknown. The investigator must therefore formulate as general a model as possible for the deterministic part as well as the error structure and let the data discriminate between alternative formulations. The principles explained in the previous sections are applicable to serial correlations of higher order. In this section, we discuss the procedures for testing for higher-order autocorrelation and for estimating model parameters when the disturbance terms follow a general-order serial correlation. The general specification of a model with autoregressive error terms is as follows:

$$Y_t = \beta_1 + \beta_2 X_{t2} + \beta_3 X_{t3} + \cdots + \beta_k X_{tk} + u_t \qquad (9.10)$$

$$u_t = \rho_1 u_{t-1} + \rho_2 u_{t-2} + \rho_3 u_{t-3} + \cdots + \rho_p u_{t-p} + \varepsilon_t \qquad (9.11)$$

Equation (9.11) is known as the **pth-order autoregressive process** of the residuals, or **AR(p).** If we had quarterly data, we might expect that a fourth-order autoregressive model would be appropriate. Similarly, monthly data are likely to exhibit a 12th-order autocorrelation, and hourly data might have a 24th-order serial correlation. We would therefore need measures to identify a general-order autoregressive error structure as well as estimation procedures that take account of such higher orders.

The Breusch–Godfrey LM Test of Higher-Order Autocorrelation

The LM test described in Section 9.3 to test for first-order serial correlation can easily be extended to higher orders, provided the sample size is not small. This test is known as the **Breusch** (1978)–**Godfrey** (1978) **test.** The motivation for the procedure will be apparent if we combine Equations (9.10) and (9.11) as follows:

$$Y_t = \beta_1 + \beta_2 X_{t2} + \cdots + \beta_k X_{tk} + \rho_1 u_{t-1} + \rho_2 u_{t-2} + \cdots + \rho_p u_{t-p} + \varepsilon_t$$

The null hypothesis is that each of the ρs is zero (that is, $\rho_1 = \rho_2 = \cdots = \rho_p = 0$) against the alternative that at least one of them is not zero. The null hypothesis is very similar to the one we carried out in Chapter 6 for testing the addition of new variables. In this case, the new variables are $u_{t-1}, u_{t-2}, \ldots, u_{t-p}$, which can be estimated by $\hat{u}_{t-1}, \hat{u}_{t-2}, \ldots, \hat{u}_{t-p}$. The steps for the test are as follows:

Step 1 Estimate Equation (9.10) by OLS and obtain the residuals $\hat{u}_t$.

Step 2 Regress $\hat{u}_t$ against all the independent variables in Equation (9.10) plus $\hat{u}_{t-1}, \hat{u}_{t-2}, \ldots, \hat{u}_{t-p}$. The effective number of observations used in this auxiliary regression is $n - p$ because $t - p$ is defined only for the period $p + 1$ to n.

Step 3 Compute $(n - p)R^2$ from the auxiliary regression run in Step 2. If it exceeds $\chi_p^2(a)$, the value of the chi-square distribution with p degrees of freedom such that the area to the right is a, then reject H_0: $\rho_1 = \rho_2 = \cdots = \rho_p = 0$ in favor of H_1: *at least one of the ρs is significantly different from zero.*

Although the test procedure itself is straightforward, the investigator has to decide a priori the order p for the autoregressive model given by Equation (9.11). The periodicity of the data (quarterly, monthly, weekly, or whatever) will often suggest the size of p. It was pointed out in Step 2 that the sample size effectively becomes $n - p$. Furthermore, the auxiliary regression has p autoregressive coefficients plus k coefficients for the $k - 1$ explanatory variables and the constant term. Therefore, $n - p$ must be at least $p + k$ (as otherwise we will have negative degrees of freedom), which means that n must be at least $k + 2p$ before the auxiliary regression can even be estimated. If the size of the sample is not adequate, we might drop some of the autoregressive terms. For example, with monthly data, we might formulate lags for $t = 1, 2, 3$, and 12 and set the other autoregressive coefficients to zero. The application in Section 9.7 presents an example of testing for higher-order autocorrelation.

Estimating a Model with General-Order Autoregressive Errors

If the Breusch–Godfrey test rejects the null hypothesis of no serial correlation, we must estimate efficiently the parameters of Equations (9.10) and (9.11). The pth-order generalization of Equation (9.9) is

$$Y_t - \rho_1 Y_{t-1} - \rho_2 Y_{t-2} - \rho_3 Y_{t-3} - \cdots - \rho_p Y_{t-p} \tag{9.12}$$

$$= \beta_1 (1 - \rho_1 - \rho_2 - \cdots - \rho_p)$$

$$+ \beta_2 [X_{t2} - \rho_1 X_{(t-1)2} - \cdots - \rho_p X_{(t-p)2}]$$

$$+ \cdots + \beta_k [X_{tk} - \rho_1 X_{(t-1)k} - \cdots - \rho_p X_{(t-p)k}] + \varepsilon_t$$

The Cochrane–Orcutt algorithm in this general context alternates between Equations (9.11) and (9.12) and is conceptually no more difficult than the case of first-order serial correlation. In fact, standard regression programs are capable of carrying out the necessary steps.

Step 1   Estimate Equation (9.10) by OLS and save the residuals $\hat{u}_t$.

Step 2   Next regress $\hat{u}_t$ against $\hat{u}_{t-1}, \hat{u}_{t-2}, \ldots, \hat{u}_{t-p}$ (with no constant term) to obtain the estimates $\hat{\rho}_1, \hat{\rho}_2$, and so on of the parameters in Equation (9.11). Here also only $n - p$ observations are used.

Step 3   Using these estimates, transform the dependent and independent variables to get the new variables in Equation (9.12).

Step 4   Estimate the transformed model (9.12) and obtain the second-round estimates of the βs.

Step 5   From the new estimates of the βs, compute a revised estimate of the residual u_t using Equation (9.10). Then go back to Step 2 and iterate until some criterion is satisfied. For example, the error sum of squares of Equation (9.12) can be computed and the iteration terminated when its value changes by less than 0.1 percent or some other value. Alternatively, the iteration could continue until the value of the logarithm of the likelihood function for Equation (9.12) does not change by more than some preset percent level.

The final ρs obtained in Step 5 can then be used to make one last transformation of the data to estimate (9.12). At convergence, the estimates of both the βs and the ρs are maximum likelihood. The standard errors and t-statistics obtained from Equation (9.12) are consistent and asymptotically efficient unless some of the Xs contain lagged dependent variables (that is, terms such as Y_{t-1}, Y_{t-2}, and so on). Problems created by such lagged dependent variables are examined in Chapter 10. The preceding method is illustrated in the application in Section 9.7 using the GRETL program, which has an easy command called *ar* for AR(p). Other programs such as B34S, SHAZAM, PcGive, and EViews also provide AR(p) estimation. Because convergence criteria are different between programs, the results may also differ.

Forecasts and Goodness of Fit in AR Models

Equation (9.4) presents an expression for the prediction of Y_t that takes explicit account of the first-order serial correlation in u_t. The corresponding expression for the general AR model is

$$\hat{Y}_t = \hat{\beta}_1 + \hat{\beta}_2 X_{t2} + \cdots + \hat{\beta}_k X_{tk} + \hat{\rho}_1 \hat{u}_{t-1} + \hat{\rho}_2 \hat{u}_{t-2} + \cdots + \hat{\rho}_p \hat{u}_{t-p} \quad (9.13)$$

At time t, all the lagged $\hat{u}$ terms are estimable and hence the forecast of Y_t obtained this way will be more efficient than the OLS prediction that ignores the $\hat{u}$ terms (assuming, of course, that the specified model and error process are correct). Also, it should be noted that the value of R^2 computed for Equation (9.12) measures the variation in the transformed dependent variable and not the variation in Y. It would be more appropriate to compute R^2 as the square of the correlation between the actual Y_t and the predicted $\hat{Y}_t$ obtained from Equation (9.13).

In Section 4.1, we described how one can compute the variance of the forecast $\hat{Y}_t$. In the presence of serial correlation, however, such an analytical expression is impossible to compute because the forecast variance involves numerous terms such as $\text{Var}(\hat{\rho}_1 \hat{u}_{t-1})$ and $\text{Cov}(\hat{\beta}_1, \hat{\rho}_1 \hat{u}_{t-1})$.

9.6   Engle's ARCH Test

The types of serial correlation discussed so far refer only to the error term u_t. Thus, in AR(p) we postulated that u_t depends linearly on the p past errors u_{t-1}, u_{t-2}, . . . , u_{t-p}. Another type of serial correlation is often encountered in time series data, especially when forecasts are generated. Some forecasters have observed that the variance of prediction errors is not a constant but differs from period to period. For instance, when the Federal Reserve Board switched to controlling money growth rather than the interest rate, as was done before, interest rates became quite volatile (that is, they began to vary a great deal around the mean). Forecast errors associated with interest rate predictions were thus heteroscedastic. Although a mere "structural change" in the variance may have been expected, it was found instead that the variance has been changing steadily. A similar heteroscedasticity was observed when exchange rate policy switched from fixed exchange rates to flexible exchange rates. In the latter case, exchange rates fluctuated a great deal, making their forecast variances larger. In monetary theory and the theory of finance, financial asset portfolios are functions of the expected means and variances of the rates of returns. Increased volatility of security prices or rates of return are often indicators that the variances are not constant over time. Engle (1982) introduced a new approach to modeling heteroscedasticity in a time series context. He called it the **ARCH (autoregressive conditional heteroscedasticity) model.** The process by which the variances are generated is assumed to be as follows:

$$\sigma_t^2 = \alpha_0 + \alpha_1 u_{t-1}^2 + \cdots + \alpha_p u_{t-p}^2 \quad (9.14)$$

Equation (9.14) is known as the *p*th-order ARCH process. The term *autoregressive* is applicable because the error variance at time *t* is assumed to depend on previous squared error terms. Also, the variance at time *t* is conditional on those in previous periods and hence the term *conditional heteroscedasticity*. The **ARCH test** is on the null hypothesis $H_0: \alpha_1 = \alpha_2 = \cdots = \alpha_p = 0$. The steps for the test are as follows:

Step 1   Estimate Equation (9.10) by OLS.

Step 2   Compute the residual $\hat{u}_t = Y_t - \hat{\beta}_1 - \hat{\beta}_2 X_{t2} - \hat{\beta}_3 X_{t3} - \cdots - \hat{\beta}_k X_{tk}$, square it, and generate $\hat{u}_{t-1}^2, \hat{u}_{t-2}^2, \ldots, \hat{u}_{t-p}^2$.

Step 3   Regress $\hat{u}_t^2$ against a constant, $\hat{u}_{t-1}^2, \hat{u}_{t-2}^2, \ldots$, and $\hat{u}_{t-p}^2$. This is the auxiliary regression, which uses $n - p$ observations.

Step 4   From the R^2 of the auxiliary regression, compute $(n - p)R^2$. Under the null hypothesis H_0, $(n - p)R^2$ has the chi-square distribution with p d.f. Reject H_0 if $(n - p)R^2 > \chi_p^2(a)$, the point on χ_p^2 with an area a to the right of it.

● EXAMPLE 9.9

When Engle introduced the ARCH model, he applied it to a model of the inflation rate in Britain. The model he used is the following:

$$\dot{p}_t = \beta_1 \dot{p}_{t-1} + \beta_2 \dot{p}_{t-4} + \beta_3 \dot{p}_{t-5} + \beta_4 (p_{t-1} - w_{t-1}) + \beta_5 + u_t$$

where

$\dot{p}_t$ = The first difference of the logarithm of the consumer price index (P_t)—that is, $\ln P_t - \ln P_{t-1}$, the instantaneous rate of change in P_t

$p_t = \ln P_t$

$w_t = \ln W_t$, W_t being the index of wage rates

The data were quarterly for the period 1958.2 through 1977.2. Engle first tested the model for sixth-order serial correlation in the residuals and found no evidence of serial correlation. He next performed an ARCH test for first and fourth orders. The first-order ARCH effect was not significant, but the chi-square statistic for fourth-order ARCH was 15.2. Because $\chi_4^2(0.01) = 13.277$, the fourth-order ARCH model is significant. Since quarterly data were used, finding a fourth-order ARCH effect is not surprising. There was, however, no fourth-order serial correlation effect in the residuals themselves, just their variances.

● EXAMPLE 9.10

The actual testing and estimation for an ARCH model are illustrated with a simplified model of interest rates. DATA9-2 has annual data for the United States for 1960–1995 on the Federal Reserve discount rate (in percent), money supply (M2 in billions of dollars), and Federal deficit (D) in billions of current dollars. The model relating discount rates (r) to the money supply (M) and government budget deficits (D) lagged twice is as follows:

$$r_t = \beta_1 + \beta_2 M_{t-1} + \beta_3 M_{t-2} + \beta_4 D_{t-1} + \beta_5 D_{t-2} + u_t$$

Error variance is assumed to follow ARCH(3) initially:

$$\sigma_t^2 = \alpha_0 + \alpha_1 u_{t-1}^2 + \alpha_2 u_{t-2}^2 + \alpha_3 u_{t-3}^2$$

Practice Computer Session 9.8 has the steps for obtaining the empirical results of this example and Table 9.2 has a partial output. The interest equation was first estimated, its estimated residuals squared, and the auxiliary regression for the variance estimated. R^2 for this regression was 0.126, but $(n - p)R^2 = 3.91$ has p-value 0.27,

---

⬤ Table 9.2 Partial Output for Example 9.10 Using DATA9-2

[Define the following lagged variables.]

```
M1 = M(-1)
M2 = M(-2)
D1 = D(-1)
D2 = D(-2)
```

[Suppress the first two observations, because M2 and D2 are undefined, and estimate the model.]

```
MODEL 1: OLS estimates using the 34 observations 1962-1995
Dependent variable: r
```

	VARIABLE	COEFFICIENT	STDERROR	T STAT	2Prob(t > |T|)	
0)	const	2.8622	0.8085	3.540	0.001371	***
5)	M1	0.0328	0.0064	5.130	0.000018	***
6)	M2	-0.0300	0.0064	-4.662	0.000065	***
7)	D1	-0.0378	0.0131	-2.884	0.007331	***
8)	D2	-0.0076	0.0131	-0.580	0.566637	

[To carry out the Arch(3) test, first generate the following variables:

usq = $\hat{u}_t^2$, where $\hat{u}_t$ is the residual from the model above
usq1 = usq(−1)
usq2 = usq(−2)
usq3 = usq(−3)

Suppress three more observations and estimate the auxiliary regression for ARCH(3) with usq as the dependent variable.]

(continued)

Table 9.2   (continued)

```
MODEL 2: OLS estimates using the 31 observations 1965-1995
Dependent variable: usq
```

	VARIABLE	COEFFICIENT	STDERROR	T STAT	2Prob(t > |T|)
0)	const	2.1770	1.2131	1.795	0.083923 *
10)	usq1	0.3353	0.1915	1.751	0.091306 *
11)	usq2	0.0597	0.2022	0.295	0.770149
12)	usq3	-0.1039	0.1921	-0.541	0.593185

```
Unadjusted R-squared        0.126  Adjusted R-squared          0.029
Chi-square(3): area to the right of (LM) 3.905795 = 0.271818
```

[ARCH(3) is not supported even at the 0.25 level, but ARCH(1) is significant at 9.13 percent. Therefore, it is worth testing for ARCH(1) by regressing usq against a constant and usql. Note that you need to suppress only one observation here.]

```
MODEL 3: OLS estimates using the 33 observations 1963-1995
Dependent variable: usq
```

	VARIABLE	COEFFICIENT	STDERROR	T STAT	2Prob(t > |T|)
0)	const	1.9308	0.9817	1.967	0.058206 *
10)	usq1	0.3454	0.1691	2.043	0.049668 **

```
Unadjusted R-squared        0.119  Adjusted R-squared          0.090
Chi-square(1): area to the right of (LM) 3.914781 = 0.047863
```

[The *p*-value indicates that ARCH(1) is significant at the 5 percent level. Also, although not shown here, all the values of the "fitted" variance (denoted by usqhat) are positive. Next, compute the weight variable as wt=1/sqrt(usqhat) and use this to obtain FGLS estimates by the weighted least squares method.]

```
MODEL 4: WLS estimates using the 33 observations 1963-1995
Dependent variable: r
Variable used as weight: wt
```

	VARIABLE	COEFFICIENT	STDERROR	T STAT	2Prob(t > |T|)
0)	const	3.3075	0.7569	4.370	0.000155 ***
5)	M1	0.0278	0.0058	4.760	0.000053 ***
6)	M2	-0.0255	0.0058	-4.393	0.000145 ***
7)	D1	-0.0323	0.0124	-2.611	0.014355 **
8)	D2	-0.0046	0.0129	-0.358	0.723045

● Table 9.2 (continued)

R-squared is computed as the square of the correlation between observed
and fitted values of the dependent variable.

Unadjusted R-squared   0.520   Adjusted R-squared   0.451

MODEL SELECTION STATISTICS

SGMASQ	3.61497	AIC	4.15292	FPE	4.16269
HQ	4.48215	SCHWARZ	5.20987	SHIBATA	3.99672
GCV	4.2605	RICE	4.40083		

Excluding the constant, p-value was highest for variable 8 (D2)

[Next, omit D2, which has an insignificant coefficient even at the 70 percent level.]

MODEL 5: WLS estimates using the 33 observations 1963-1995
Dependent variable: r
Variable used as weight: wt

	VARIABLE	COEFFICIENT	STDERROR	T STAT	2Prob(t > |T|)	
0)	const	3.3795	0.7186	4.703	0.000058	***
5)	M1	0.0283	0.0056	5.093	0.000020	***
6)	M2	-0.0262	0.0054	-4.898	0.000034	***
7)	D1	-0.0347	0.0103	-3.383	0.002070	***

R-squared is computed as the square of the correlation between observed
and fitted values of the dependent variable.

Unadjusted R-squared   0.515   Adjusted R-squared   0.464

MODEL SELECTION STATISTICS

SGMASQ	3.52526	AIC	3.94783	FPE	3.95256
HQ	4.19629	SCHWARZ	4.73301	SHIBATA	3.84897
GCV	4.0115	RICE	4.0893		

[Comparison of Model 4 and Model 5: Of the 8 model selection statistics, 8 have improved.]

which is not significant. Thus, ARCH(3) is not supported. However, the ARCH(1) term was significant at the level 0.09 (see Table 9.2), so an ARCH(1) specification was tested next. The p-value for this test was 0.048, which indicates significance at the 5 percent level. We then used the estimated auxiliary regression to compute weights and used those to obtain WLS estimates of the model. Because the deficit term $D2$ was insignificant, it was excluded from the model in order to improve the precision of the other variables and to reduce any multicollinearity that might be present. The final model is given next, with p-values in parentheses:

$$\hat{r}_t = \underset{(<0.0001)}{3.380} + \underset{(<0.0001)}{0.0283 \ M_{t-1}} - \underset{(<0.0001)}{0.0262 \ M_{t-2}} - \underset{(0.002)}{0.0347 \ D_{t-1}}$$

$$\overline{R}^2 = 0.464$$

The value of R^2 is calculated as the square of the correlation between observed and fitted values of the interest rate using this equation. We note that the model's goodness-of-fit measure is less than 50 percent. For this reason and because the model is itself simplified and is not for quarterly or monthly data (which would have been more realistic), the results are only illustrative of the technique and are not to be taken seriously.

For a survey of ARCH applications in finance, see Engle and Rothschild (1992). For a generalization of ARCH (called **GARCH**), refer to Bollerslev (1986), Greene (2000, Ch. 18.5), and related citations there.

9.7 Application: Demand for Electricity

The application selected to examine the various issues discussed in this chapter uses quarterly data to model the consumption of electricity by residential customers served by the San Diego Gas and Electric Company. The variable we are interested in explaining is the electricity consumption, as measured in kilowatt-hours (kwh), per residential customer. We are particularly interested in estimating the income and price elasticities of demand for electricity and then studying whether there were any structural changes.

DATA9-3 described in Appendix D presents quarterly data on the following variables from the second quarter of 1972 through the fourth quarter of 1993:

RESKWH = Electricity sales to residential customers
           (millions of kilowatt-hours)
NOCUST = Number of residential customers (thousands)
   PRICE = Average price for the single-family rate tariff (cents/kwh)
      CPI = San Diego consumer price index (1982–1984 = 100)
INCOME = San Diego County total personal income, quarterly rates
           (millions of current dollars)
     CDD = Cooling degree days (explained below)
     HDD = Heating degree days
     POP = San Diego County population (in thousands)

The data have to be transformed suitably before being used in an econometric formulation. Here we use the double-log model, which has the property that all the elasticities are constant (see Section 6.10). The dependent variable (denoted by LKWH) will therefore be the logarithm of the kwh sales per residential customer. We thus have

$$LKWH = \ln(RESKWH/NOCUST)$$

Determinants of the Demand for Electricity

One of the major determinants of the demand for any product is income. Because consumption is measured in per-customer terms, income should be measured as per capita. Furthermore, the measurement must be in "real" terms to adjust for inflation effects. Thus, the relevant income variable is per capita in constant dollars. DATA9-3 has total personal income in current dollars. Per-capita income in current terms is thus INCOME/POP. To convert this to real terms, we need to divide by the price index CPI/100. This will measure per-capita income in constant dollars for the base period (1982–1984 in our case). The relevant variable is therefore

$$LY = \ln\left(\frac{100 * INCOME}{CPI * POP}\right)$$

Another important determinant of demand is the price of the good in question. Thus, the price of electricity is important. There is no single price of electricity, even for residential customers. Price gradually increases depending on actual consumption. One can argue whether the marginal cost or the average cost of electricity should be used as an explanatory variable. We, however, will not discuss those issues here. The reader is referred to an excellent survey by Lester Taylor (1975). Here we use the average price for the single-family rate tariff, which is representative for residential customers. The price is measured in cents per kwh in current terms. As price should also be measured in real terms, it should be divided by CPI/100. The price variable is thus

$$LPRICE = \ln(100 * PRICE/CPI)$$

Perhaps the most important determinant of electricity consumption is the weather. When it is cold in the winter, consumers turn on the heat, and on hot summer days they turn on the air conditioner or a fan. We would therefore expect that the temperature significantly influences the consumption pattern. Because the data are for a three-month period, we need a realistic way of capturing the temperature effect. A common method used by almost all utilities around the country is to compute what are known as *degree days*. In the summer, this will be *cooling degree days* (CDD), and in the winter, it is *heating degree days* (HDD). These variables are defined as follows:

$$CDD = \sum_{d=1}^{d=D} \max\left[\frac{MAXTEMP_d + MINTEMP_d}{2} - 65, 0\right]$$

$$HDD = \sum_{d=1}^{d=D} \max\left[65 - \frac{MAXTEMP_d + MINTEMP_d}{2}, 0\right]$$

where *D* is the number of days in the quarter, MAXTEMP is the maximum temperature, and MINTEMP is the minimum temperature for day *d*.

Although the formula appears complex, it is easy to explain in simple terms. First we compute the average temperature in a day as the mean of the maximum and minimum air temperatures. If this average is exactly 65° Fahrenheit, it is assumed that the customer does not turn on either the heater or the air conditioner. In the summer, if this mean temperature exceeds 65 by a substantial amount, consumers will use the air conditioner. The extent of this excess temperature is measured as the average minus 65. When this is summed over each of the days in the quarter, we get the cooling degree days. If the average is below 65 in the summer, no action is taken, and hence the CDD term for the day is zero. The principle for computing HDD in the winter is similar. If the average temperature is above 65 in the winter, consumers will be happy to turn off the heater, and the contribution to HDD is nil. When the average is below 65, the difference between 65 and the average is the contribution of the day's weather to the HDD term. Adding the heating degree day for each day of the quarter, we get total HDD.

Note from the data that for some quarters HDD and CDD are close to zero. This means that the contribution to these variables was almost zero for every day of the particular quarter. Because of this, we should not take the logarithms of HDD and CDD, and hence they must enter the model linearly.

The Basic Model

The basic model specification is given by the following equation:

$$\text{LKWH} = \beta_1 + \beta_2\text{LY} + \beta_3\text{LPRICE} + \beta_4\text{CDD} + \beta_5\text{HDD} + u \qquad (9.15)$$

The higher the income, the greater the demand for a "normal" good. β_2 can therefore be expected to be positive. When the price of electricity goes up, its demand will go down. Hence, β_3 can be expected to be negative. An increase in CDD implies more days for which average temperature exceeded 65 degrees. We can expect this to increase the demand for air-conditioning, and hence β_4 will be positive. Similarly, if HDD rises, the demand for heating will rise, and hence β_5 will also be positive. The expected signs for the βs (except β_1) are as follows:

$$\beta_2 > 0, \qquad \beta_3 < 0, \qquad \beta_4 > 0, \qquad \beta_5 > 0$$

We have used the 87 observations in DATA9-3 to transform the raw data into the variables specified in Equation (9.15). Applying the OLS procedure, the estimated model is given by (Practice Computer Session 9.9 has the details to reproduce all the empirical results in this application)

$$\widehat{\text{LKWH}} = 0.398 - \underset{(-0.24)}{0.036}\,\text{LY} - \underset{(-3.38)}{0.094}\,\text{LPRICE} + \underset{(7.78)}{0.0002676}\,\text{CDD}$$
$$\underset{(1.87)}{}$$

$$+ \underset{(12.09)}{0.0003607}\,\text{HDD}$$

$$\overline{R}^2 = 0.651 \qquad \text{d.f.} = 82 \qquad \text{DW } d = 1.219$$

The values in parentheses are t-statistics, but if there is serial correlation, these values (and that of $\overline{R}^2$) are meaningless. Also note that LY has a negative sign, which is counterintuitive.

Testing for Serial Correlation

From Table A.5 of Appendix A, we note that for $n = 87$ and $k' = 4$ (the constant term is not counted here), the bounds for the Durbin–Watson statistic (interpolated) are $d_L = 1.556$ and $d_U = 1.749$ for a one-tailed test at the 5 percent level of significance. The computed d is below d_L, and hence there is evidence of significant first-order autocorrelation. However, because the data are quarterly, a fourth-order serial correlation would be more appropriate. The error specification would now be

$$u_t = \rho_1 u_{t-1} + \rho_2 u_{t-2} + \rho_3 u_{t-3} + \rho_4 u_{t-4} + \varepsilon_t$$

The null hypothesis is that $\rho_1 = \rho_2 = \rho_3 = \rho_4 = 0$. Because we are using four lags, the effective number of observations is 83. Also, the unadjusted R^2 for the auxiliary regression was 0.666, which makes the $(n - p)R^2$ statistic 55.3, whose p-value is below 0.0001. There is thus a very strong evidence of fourth-order serial correlation. The model was then estimated by the generalized Cochrane–Orcutt procedure discussed in Section 9.5; the results are presented next, with t-statistics in parentheses.

$$\widehat{\text{LKWH}} = \underset{(1.7)}{0.273} + \underset{(0.9)}{0.102}\, \text{LY} - \underset{(-3.5)}{0.098}\, \text{LPRICE} + \underset{(10.98)}{0.0002756}\, \text{CDD}$$

$$+ \underset{(9.4)}{0.0002288}\, \text{HDD}$$

$$\overline{R}^2 = 0.897 \qquad \text{d.f.} = 78 \qquad \hat{\sigma} = 0.02547$$

Although the coefficients are sensible, the model is seriously misspecified because it is unreasonable to expect that the structure is stable over the 1972–1993 period, especially because of the two "energy crises." We therefore turn our attention to a more complete model formulation and analysis that incorporates possible structural shifts in the parameters.

Modeling Structural Change

During the periods 1973–1974 and 1978–1979, the price of crude oil escalated dramatically and conservation became the watchword for reducing demand. Buildings were better insulated, more energy-efficient appliances and machinery were built, and automobiles became more fuel efficient. One might therefore expect that the relationship between electricity consumption and its determinants has changed. The dramatic increase in price did not continue forever, however. As can be seen from Fig. 9.6, starting from 1983, the real price of electricity has decreased. We may therefore want to test whether further structural change has taken place since 1983.

To allow for a change in the structure, three dummy variables were defined:

D74 = 1 for 1974.1 onward, 0 otherwise
D79 = 1 for 1979.1 onward, 0 otherwise
D83 = 1 for 1983.3 onward, 0 otherwise

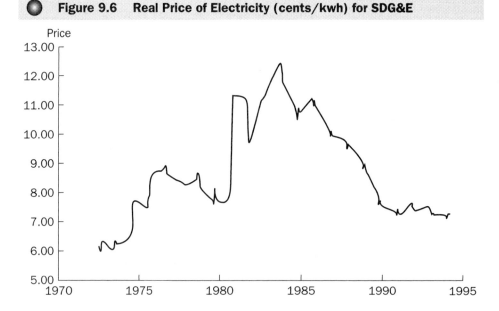

Figure 9.6   Real Price of Electricity (cents/kwh) for SDG&E

Next we let the regression coefficients depend on these dummy variables. For instance, in Equation (9.15) we would have

$$\beta_2 = a_0 + a_1 D74 + a_2 D79 + a_3 D83$$

The income elasticities for the four periods, starting from 1972.2, would be a_0, $a_0 + a_1$, $a_0 + a_1 + a_2$, and $a_0 + a_1 + a_2 + a_3$. Thus, a_1 is the *change* in income elasticity (relative to the period 1972.2–1973.4) attributable to the 1974 structural change, and a_2 is the *additional change* due to the 1979 change in the structure, and similarly for others. In addition to this change, the sensitivity of a weather measure (β_4 and β_5) might also depend on the price of electricity. If, for instance, the price is high, then customers might postpone turning the air conditioner or heater on in order to save money. This possible effect can be captured by letting $\beta_4 = b_0 + b_1 \text{LPRICE} + \cdots$. Because there are numerous terms, we have not written down the complete model, but instead present a list of the variables in Table 9.3.

The formulation of a model with complete interactions with all the dummy variables is in the spirit of the Hendry/LSE approach of going from a general to a simpler model. The Lagrange multiplier test is more cumbersome to apply here because it involves regression of the residuals from the transformed model in Equation (9.12) against similarly transformed variables from the general model. Instead, we estimate the unrestricted model first and then attempt to make it simpler. Table 9.4 has the OLS estimates of a completely general model (see Practice Computer Session 9.9 for commands to duplicate those results). The Durbin–Watson statistic for the unrestricted model was 1.931, which indicates that there is no first-order serial correlation. We can therefore apply OLS and obtain estimates with desirable properties. It is interesting to note that while the basic model specification suffered

● **Table 9.3 Definitions of Transformed Variables**

Name	Definition
LKWH	ln(RESKWH/NOCUST)
LPRICE	ln(100 * PRICE/CPI)
LY	ln[100 * INCOME/(CPI*POP)]
LYD74	LY * D74
LYD79	LY * D79
LYD83	LY * D83
LPRD74	LPRICE * D74
LPRD79	LPRICE * D79
LPRD83	LPRICE * D83
D74CDD	D74 * CDD
D79CDD	D79 * CDD
D83CDD	D83 * CDD
D74HDD	D74 * HDD
D79HDD	D79 * HDD
D83HDD	D83 * HDD
LPRCDD	LPRICE * CDD
LPRHDD	LPRICE * HDD

from the problem of autocorrelation, the more complete model is free of it. However, as can be seen from Table 9.4, most of the regression coefficients have high p-values, indicating insignificance. This is not surprising because, with so many explanatory variables that are cross products, we can expect high multicollinearity among them. To improve the precision of the estimates, insignificant variables with the highest p-values were omitted one or two at a time and the model was reestimated. The "final" model results are given in Table 9.5. It will be noted that this model is also free from first-order serial correlation. Furthermore, all the regression coefficients are significant at levels at or below 5 percent, and the model selection statistics are considerably better than the general model.

Interpretation of the Results

The estimated coefficients for the four time periods are as in Table 9.6 (verify them). It should be pointed out that the control period 1972.2–1973.4 has only seven observations and hence the model results for this period should not be taken too seriously. For instance, income elasticity was statistically insignificant during this period. During the second period of generally rising electricity prices (1974.1–1978.4), income elasticity was almost 1. In the third period it dropped to 0.16, and in the last period, when real electricity prices declined, the income elasticity is negative, indicating that electricity demand was an inferior good during this

Table 9.4 OLS Estimates of the Completely General Model

VARIABLE	COEFFICIENT	StdERROR	T STAT	2Prob(t > |T|)	
CONSTANT	-0.796868	5.714984	-0.139435	0.889538	
D74	-1.004434	5.730953	-0.175265	0.861416	
D79	1.916922	0.706665	2.712631	0.008534	***
D83	0.024624	0.592544	0.041557	0.966979	
LY	-2.636002	6.672636	-0.395047	0.694102	
LYD74	3.586062	6.680982	0.536757	0.593268	
LYD79	-0.7321	0.518463	-1.412058	0.162703	
LYD83	-0.309173	0.444267	-0.695917	0.488962	
LPRICE	2.240851	1.82873	1.225359	0.224862	
LPRD74	-1.884615	1.831642	-1.028921	0.30733	
LPRD79	-0.44734	0.136597	-3.274888	0.001697	***
LPRD83	0.133727	0.064403	2.076425	0.041813	**
CDD	0.001418	4.665718e-04	3.039785	0.003409	***
D74CDD	-2.324821e-04	3.630704e-04	-0.640322	0.524214	
D79CDD	-3.897257e-05	9.707234e-05	-0.40148	0.689384	
D83CDD	7.021266e-05	6.488312e-05	1.082141	0.283188	
LPRCDD	-4.066302e-04	1.677691e-04	-2.42375	0.018153	**
HDD	9.496237e-04	4.176021e-04	2.273992	0.026276	**
D74HDD	-2.830809e-04	3.169507e-04	-0.893139	0.375078	
D79HDD	-4.221766e-05	8.608874e-05	-0.490397	0.625504	
D83HDD	-3.228573e-05	6.658090e-05	-0.48491	0.629371	
LPRHDD	-1.095802e-04	1.558676e-04	-0.703034	0.484545	

```
Mean of dep. var.       0.327332    S.D. of dep. variable        0.080775
Error Sum of Sq (ESS)   0.081511    Std Err of Resid. (sgmahat)  0.035412
Unadjusted R-squared    0.855       Adjusted R-squared           0.808
F-statistic (21, 65)    18.212322   pvalue = Prob (F > 18.212) is < 0.0001
Durbin-Watson Stat.     1.930695    First-order auto corr coeff  0.025
```

MODEL SELECTION STATISTICS

SGMASQ	0.001254	AIC	0.001554	FPE	0.001571
HQ	0.001997	SCHWARZ	0.002898	SHIBATA	0.001411
GCV	0.001678	RICE	0.001896		

Note: Three *s indicate significance (two-tailed) at 1 percent, two *s indicate significance at levels between 1 and 5 percent, and one * indicates significance at levels between 5 and 10 percent.

● Table 9.5   OLS Estimates of the Final Model

VARIABLE	COEFFICIENT	StdERROR	T STAT	2Prob(t > |T|)
Constant	-1.682911	0.395837	-4.251527	< 0.0001 ***
D79	1.949518	0.442915	4.401562	< 0.0001 ***
LYD74	0.980804	0.302486	3.242475	0.001787 ***
LYD79	-0.820708	0.346657	-2.367493	0.020561 **
LYD83	-0.26082	0.097446	-2.676559	0.009179 ***
LPRICE	0.96591	0.21544	4.483422	< 0.0001 ***
LPRD74	-0.684829	0.204703	-3.345484	0.0013 ***
LPRD79	-0.422223	0.120386	-3.507252	0.000779 ***
LPRD83	0.134598	0.052732	2.552504	0.012786 **
CDD	0.001035	2.037711e-04	5.077356	< 0.0001 ***
LPRCDD	-3.316656e-04	8.934507e-05	-3.712187	0.000399 ***
HDD	5.583410e-04	5.809766e-05	9.610388	< 0.0001 ***
D74HDD	-1.217427e-04	5.814511e-05	-2.093773	0.039753 **
D83HDD	-9.335895e-05	2.912222e-05	-3.205764	0.001999 ***

Mean of dep. var.	0.327332	S.D. of dep. variable		0.080775
Error Sum of Sq (ESS)	0.084832	Std Err of Resid. (sgmahat)		0.034089
Unadjusted R-squared	0.849	Adjusted R-squared		0.822
F-statistic (13, 73)	31.527415	pvalue = Prob (F > 31.527) is < 0.0001		
Durbin-Watson Stat.	1.935373	First-order auto corr coeff		0.021

MODEL SELECTION STATISTICS

SGMASQ	0.001162	AIC	0.001345	FPE	0.001349
HQ	0.001578	SCHWARZ	0.002001	SHIBATA	0.001289
GCV	0.001385	RICE	0.001438		

Note: Three *s indicate significance (two-tailed) at 1 percent, two *s indicate significance at levels between 1 and 5 percent, and one * indicates significance at levels between 5 and 10 percent.

period. The price elasticity showed even more dramatic structural change from period to period. The elasticity was as follows:

1972.2–1973.4:	$0.966 - 0.00033167$ CDD
1974.1–1978.4:	$0.281 - 0.00033167$ CDD
1979.1–1983.2:	$-0.141 - 0.00033167$ CDD
1983.3–1990.4:	$-0.007 - 0.00033167$ CDD

There is interaction between cooling degree days and electricity price. Cooling degree days have varied from almost zero to nearly a thousand. During the first

Table 9.6   Estimated Coefficients for the Four Periods

	Variables					
	CONSTANT	**LY**	**LPRICE**	**CDD**	**HDD**	**LPRICE × CDD**
1972.2–1973.4 D74 = D79 = D83 = 0	−1.68291100	0.00000000	0.96591000	0.00103500	0.00055834	−0.00033167
1974.1–1978.4 D74 = 1, D79 = D83 = 0	−1.68291100	0.98080400	0.28108100	0.00103500	0.00043660	−0.00033167
1979.1–1983.2 D74 = D79 = 1, D83 = 0	0.26660700	0.16009600	−0.14114200	0.00103500	0.00043660	−0.00033167
1983.3–1990.4 D74 = D79 = D83 = 1	0.26660700	−0.10072400	−0.00654400	0.00103500	0.00034324	−0.00033167

period, when the electricity price was rising slowly, price elasticity was *positive*, which is contrary to standard economic theory. This might be because electricity consumption grew steadily as a result of growth in income and population, and this dominating trend might have been captured in the regression with a positive sign. It should be noted that when prices started to rise, the positive effect was considerably reduced; and since 1979 consumers have responded with a reduction in the quantity demanded, although this behavior was less pronounced by 1983 when the real price of electricity began to decline.

In an earlier discussion we had argued that the weather effect might depend on the price of electricity, and we see evidence to support that. The marginal effect of cooling degree days is given as follows and is the same in all periods.

$$0.001035 - .00033167 \text{ LPRICE}$$

It is evident that the marginal effect of the weather depends negatively on the price of electricity. In other words, an increase of one cooling degree day results in a smaller increase in electricity usage if the price of electricity is high. Heating degree days also have the expected positive effect, although there is no significant interaction with price. In 1974 and 1983 there were reductions in the marginal HDD effect.

Comparison of Forecasts

It would be interesting to examine how forecasts from different models performed when confronted with actual values. Table 9.7 has the absolute percent errors for three models. Because the dependent variable is in log form, we have applied the bias correction described in Chapter 6 (see Practice Computer Session 9.9 for the steps). Percentage of absolute forecast errors from OLS estimates applied to Equation (9.15) are labeled as Model A, the same model estimated by generalized CORC for AR(4) is labeled as Model B, and Model C refers to the final model in Table 9.6.

It is interesting to note that in terms of forecasting ability, the final model, which incorporated the structural change but did not exhibit serial correlation, is not the best. Both the mean absolute percent error (MAPE) and the mean squared error (MSE) were lowest for Model B. Also, individual percent errors were mostly below 5 percent, with only one exception at 6.08 percent.

● **Table 9.7   Comparison of Absolute Forecast Errors (%)**

Period	Model A	Model B	Model C	Period	Model A	Model B	Model C
1973.2	2.89	3.28	4.08	1983.4	0.33	1.02	1.90
1973.3	0.95	2.93	1.56	1984.1	1.40	2.39	0.26
1973.4	2.45	1.43	2.49	1984.2	2.54	3.58	1.51
1974.1	3.44	6.08	0.49	1984.3	6.99	4.32	4.01
1974.2	5.70	3.48	3.48	1984.4	2.42	3.89	3.91
1974.3	2.48	1.76	1.25	1985.1	3.59	1.54	1.87
1974.4	4.86	3.09	7.39	1985.2	6.14	2.17	5.04
1975.1	1.44	4.07	0.07	1985.3	0.92	4.35	1.56
1975.2	7.73	0.64	5.10	1985.4	0.08	2.20	1.54
1975.3	2.08	0.53	1.11	1986.1	0.12	0.26	2.15
1975.4	4.28	1.03	3.09	1986.2	5.78	1.68	3.97
1976.1	3.03	2.46	2.07	1986.3	0.64	1.21	1.92
1976.2	1.76	5.04	1.77	1986.4	2.63	0.80	4.42
1976.3	2.37	2.33	0.92	1987.1	4.27	0.32	1.28
1976.4	9.41	2.89	5.55	1987.2	5.72	1.12	3.63
1977.1	8.52	4.58	3.34	1987.3	0.12	0.63	1.11
1977.2	2.51	3.49	6.23	1987.4	1.05	1.39	2.92
1977.3	0.49	1.99	3.83	1988.1	3.63	0.73	0.00
1977.4	8.23	0.60	3.78	1988.2	6.17	1.32	3.49
1978.1	11.48	3.04	3.83	1988.3	1.60	1.54	1.95
1978.2	2.34	0.60	5.19	1988.4	0.61	1.90	1.92
1978.3	3.39	2.57	2.49	1989.1	6.62	0.32	1.55
1978.4	7.43	1.88	2.27	1989.2	7.26	3.27	3.90
1979.1	5.83	1.47	3.02	1989.3	0.61	0.56	0.11
1979.2	1.94	0.69	2.86	1989.4	0.05	1.11	2.61
1979.3	1.68	0.95	4.26	1990.1	3.52	2.71	1.91
1979.4	9.44	2.39	4.57	1990.2	6.70	1.00	3.02
1980.1	9.79	0.87	5.19	1990.3	2.21	2.11	0.36
1980.2	0.52	0.39	2.29	1990.4	0.29	0.68	1.75
1980.3	0.47	1.18	3.52	1991.1	4.88	0.48	0.04
1980.4	6.98	0.98	6.39	1991.2	13.51	4.94	9.04
1981.1	6.02	2.14	3.11	1991.3	1.80	2.07	1.43
1981.2	1.74	4.19	2.15	1991.4	1.34	1.73	2.92
1981.3	5.71	6.31	4.09	1992.1	3.01	1.16	1.50
1981.4	4.00	1.17	2.90	1992.2	3.42	3.18	1.61
1982.1	1.57	1.11	2.13	1992.3	3.55	4.26	0.68
1982.2	3.39	0.02	3.43	1992.4	0.16	1.60	1.86
1982.3	3.49	1.33	0.58	1993.1	2.78	2.49	2.07
1982.4	0.83	2.33	0.21	1993.2	5.47	2.78	2.55
1983.1	0.07	1.98	3.38	1993.3	3.35	0.98	1.80
1983.2	0.69	1.71	0.96	1993.4	1.13	0.04	3.72
1983.3	4.39	2.72	0.45				
MAPE	3.57	2.04	2.67				
MSE	21.15	6.12	10.12				

Summary

In this chapter, we explored the impact of *serial correlation* (or *autocorrelation*), that is, correlation among the residual terms of a regression model. We first examined the consequences of ignoring serial correlation and then discussed two tests for the presence of autocorrelation. Assuming serial correlation of the first order, we presented two estimation procedures. Finally, we discussed the case of higher-order serial correlation, both testing and estimation.

In the presence of autocorrelation, OLS estimates and forecasts based on them are still unbiased and consistent, but they are not BLUE and are hence inefficient. The consistency property does not hold, however, if lagged dependent variables are included as explanatory variables. Furthermore, if the exogenous variables have been growing over time, and serial correlation is positive (which is frequently the case), the estimated residual variance will be an underestimate and the value of $\overline{R}^2$ will be an overestimate. This means that the goodness of fit will be exaggerated and the estimated *t*-statistics will be larger than the true values. Most seriously, if serial correlation is ignored and the OLS procedure is applied, the tests of hypotheses will not be valid.

The plot of the estimated residuals is a useful guide that signals the presence of serial correlation. If serial correlation is present, successive residuals will tend to be clustered together.

First-order serial correlation can be tested by the *Durbin–Watson test*. The procedure is to estimate the model by OLS and compute the estimated residuals, $\hat{u}_t$. The Durbin–Watson statistic (d) is next calculated using Equation (9.6). For a one-tailed test for positive serial correlation, two values, denoted by d_L and d_U, are read from Table A.5 in Appendix A. If $d \geq d_U$, we conclude that there is no serial correlation. If $d \leq d_L$, we conclude that there is significant first-order autocorrelation. If d lies between d_L and d_U, the test is inconclusive. For negative autocorrelation, $4 - d$ is compared with d_L and d_U.

The DW test is, however, subject to several drawbacks and is hence not recommended: it often gives inconclusive results, it is invalid if lagged dependent variables are present, and it is not applicable if errors follow a higher-order autoregressive process.

An alternative test that is conclusive in all cases and is applicable more generally is based on the Lagrange multiplier (LM) test described in Chapter 6. This test, called the *Breusch–Godfrey test*, consists of running an auxiliary regression of $\hat{u}_t$ against $\hat{u}_{t-1}$ and all the explanatory variables in the model. Under the null hypothesis of zero autocorrelation, the value of $(n - 1)R^2$ is distributed as chi-square with 1 d.f. If this exceeds the critical value, the conclusion is that there is significant first-order serial correlation.

The Breusch–Godfrey test can be applied to test higher-order serial correlations also. The procedure is to regress $\hat{u}_t$ against $\hat{u}_{t-1}$, $\hat{u}_{t-2}$, . . . , $\hat{u}_{t-p}$ (usually up to the periodicity of the data set), in addition to the variables originally in the model. The value of $(n - p)R^2$ from this auxiliary regression is compared against the critical value in a chi-square distribution with degrees of freedom equal to the number of lagged residuals used in the auxiliary regression (which is p here). The LM test, however, is a large-sample test and requires at least 30 d.f. for it to be meaningful.

Sargan, Hendry, and Mizon have pointed out that observed serial correlation might be symptomatic of a misspecification in the deterministic part of the model and recommend including more dynamics, testing whether a simpler version with static formulation and autoregressive errors is appropriate, and then using appropriate estimating techniques.

If first-order serial correlation is identified, the *Hildreth–Lu (HILU) search procedure* may be used to correct for it. The procedure is to choose a value of ρ, the first-order autocorrelation coefficient, between -1 and $+1$. Then obtain the transformed variables, $Y_t - \rho Y_{t-1}$ and $X_t - \rho X_{t-1}$ for each X in the model. The transformed dependent variable is regressed against the transformed independent variables and the error sum of squares (ESS) of this regression is computed. Next ρ is changed to a new value and the whole procedure repeated. By searching for the value of ρ that gives the lowest ESS, we obtain the Hildreth–Lu estimates, which are consistent and asymptotically more efficient than OLS estimates.

An alternative estimating method is the *Cochrane–Orcutt (CORC) iterative procedure*. In this method, the OLS residuals $\hat{u}_t$ are used to obtain an estimate of ρ using Equation (9.7). This value is used to transform the variables as above and a transformed regression run. The estimates obtained this way are used to recompute $\hat{u}_t$. The procedure is then repeated until two successive ρ-values do not change by more than some prespecified level. This iterative procedure has been found to converge fairly quickly and needs much less computation time than the Hildreth–Lu procedure. However, by searching over the entire range -1 to $+1$, the Hildreth–Lu technique selects the global minimum for ESS. If there are several local minima of ESS, the Cochrane–Orcutt procedure might iterate to a local minimum, which is not a global minimum. Cochrane–Orcutt estimates are also consistent and asymptotically more efficient than OLS estimates. A more desirable procedure is to search in broader steps using the HILU procedure and then fine-tune it using the CORC technique. However, this is applicable only for AR(1).

The Cochrane–Orcutt iterative procedure can be extended to a higher-order serial correlation case also. The procedure is to regress the OLS residuals $\hat{u}_t$ against $\hat{u}_{t-1}$, $\hat{u}_{t-2}$, $\hat{u}_{t-3}$, and so on and obtain $\hat{\rho}_1, \hat{\rho}_2$, and so on. Next transform the dependent variable as $Y_t - \hat{\rho}_1 Y_{t-1} - \hat{\rho}_2 Y_{t-2} - \cdots$, and similarly for each of the Xs. Regress the transformed Y against the transformed Xs. Use the estimates of this transformed regression to recompute $\hat{u}_t$. Repeat the procedure until the error sum of squares of the transformed regression does not change by more than a prespecified percent.

When forecasting in the presence of autocorrelated errors, more efficient forecasts may be obtained by using the error structure.

Key Terms

AR(1)	First-order autoregressive process
AR(p)	First-order serial correlation
ARCH test	GARCH
Autocorrelation	Generalized differencing
Autocorrelation function	Hildreth–Lu (HILU) search procedure
Autoregressive conditional heteroscedasticity (ARCH) model	Instantaneous rate of growth
	pth-order autoregressive process
Breusch–Godfrey (BG) test	Quasi-differencing
Cochrane–Orcutt (CORC) iterative procedure	Residual plot
	Serial correlation
Durbin–Watson (DW) test	Serial independence
First difference	White noise series
First-order autocorrelation coefficient	

References

Bera, Anil K., and Sungsup Ra. "A Test for the Presence of Conditional Heteroscedasticity within ARCH-M Framework." *Econometric Reviews* 14, no. 4 (November 1995): 473–485.

Bollerslev, T. "Generalized Autoregressive Conditional Heteroscedasticity." *J. Econometrics* 31 (1986): 307–327.

Breusch, T. "Testing for Autocorrelation in Dynamic Linear Models." *Australian Econ. Papers* 17 (1978): 334–355.

Cochrane, D., and G. H. Orcutt. "Application of Least Squares Regressions to Relationships Containing Autocorrelated Error Terms." *J. Amer. Stat. Assoc.* 44 (1949): 32–61.

Dezhbakhsh, Hashem, and Jerry G. Thursby. "Testing for Autocorrelation in the Presence of Lagged Dependent Variables: A Specification Error Approach." *Journal of Econometrics* 60, nos. 1–2 (January/February 1994): 251–272.

————"A Monte Carlo Comparison of Tests Based on the Durbin–Watson Statistic with Other Autocorrelation Tests in Dynamic Models." *Econometric Review* 14, no. 3 (1995): 347–365.

Durbin, J., and G. S. Watson. "Testing for Serial Correlation in Least Squares Regression." *Biometrica* 37 (1950): 409–428, and 38 (1951): 159–178.

Engle, R. F. "Autoregressive Conditional Heteroscedasticity with Estimates of the Variance of United Kingdom Inflations." *Econometrica* 50 (1982): 987–1008.

————. "Wald, Likelihood Ratio, and Lagrangian Multiplier Tests in Econometrics." *Handbook of Econometrics.* Eds. Z. Griliches and M. D. Intriligator. New York: North-Holland, 1984.

————. ed. "ARCH: Selected Readings." *Advanced Texts in Econometrics.* Oxford and New York: Oxford University Press, 1995.

Engle, R., and M. Rothschild. "ARCH Model in Finance." *J. Econometrics* 52 (1992).

Fama, Eugene F. "A Pricing Model for the Municipal Bond Market." Manuscript. University of Chicago, 1977.

Godfrey, L. G. "Testing for Higher Order Serial Correlation in Regression Equations When the Regressors Include Lagged Dependent Variables." *Econometrica* 46 (1978): 1303–1310.

Granger, C. W. J. *Forecasting in Business and Economics.* New York: Academic Press, 1989.

Granger, C. W. J., and P. Newbold. "Spurious Regressions in Econometrics." *J. of Econometrics* 2 (1974): 111–120.

————. *Forecasting Economic Time Series.* San Diego: Academic Press, 1986.

Greene, W. H. *Econometric Analysis.* Upper Saddle River N.J.: Prentice-Hall, 2000.

Hamilton, James D., and Raul Susmel. "Autoregressive Conditional Heteroscedasticity and Changes in Regime." *Journal of Econometrics* 64, nos. 1–2 (September/October 1994): 307–333.

Hendry, D. F., and G. E. Mizon. "Serial Correlation as a Convenient Simplification, Not a Nuisance: A Comment on a Study of the Demand for Money by the Bank of England." *The Economic Journal* 88 (September 1978): 549–563.

Hentschel, Ludger. "All in the Family: Nesting Symmetric and Asymmetric GARCH Models." *Journal of Financial Economics* 39, no. 1 (1995): 71–104.

Higgins, Mathew L., and Anil K. Bera. "A Class of Nonlinear ARCH Models." *International Economic Review* 33, no. 1 (February 1992): 137–158.

Hildreth, C., and J. Y. Lu. "Demand Relations with Autocorrelated Disturbances." *Technical Bulletin 276.* Michigan State University (November 1960).

Kim, Kiwhan, and Peter Schmidt. "Unit Root Tests with Conditional Heteroscedasticity." *Journal of Econometrics* 59, no. 3 (October 1993): 287–300.

Kmenta, Jan. *Elements of Econometrics.* New York: Macmillan, 1986.

Lee, John H., and Maxwell L. King. "A Locally Most Mean Powerful Based Score Test for ARCH and GARCH Regression Disturbances." *Journal of Business and Economic Statistics* 11, no. 1 (January 1993): 17–27.

Mizon, Grayham E. "A Simple Message for Autocorrelation Correctors: Don't." *Journal of Econometrics* 69, no. 1 (September 1995): 267–288.

Prais, S. J., and C. B. Winsten. "Trend Estimators and Serial Correlation." *Cowles Commission Discussion Paper 383,* Chicago, 1954.

Sargan, J. D. "Wages and Prices in the United Kingdom: A Study in Econometric Methodology," in *Econometric Analysis for National Income Planning.* Eds. P. E. Hart, G. Mills, and J. K. Whitaker. London: Butterworth, 1964, pp. 25–54.

Savin, N. E., and K. J. White. "The Durbin–Watson Test for Serial Correlation with Extreme Small Samples or Many Regressors." *Econometrica* 45 (November 1977): 1989–1996. See also the correction by R. W. Farebrother. *Econometrica* 48 (September 1980): 1554.

Sullivan, Michael J., and David E. A. Giles. "The Robustness of ARCH/GARCH Tests to First-Order Autocorrelation." *Journal of Quantitative Economics* 11, no. 1 (January 1995): 35–61.

Taylor, Lester. "The Demand for Electricity: A Survey." *The Bell Journal* 6, no. 1 (1975).

Exercises

Questions Requiring No Computer Work

†9.1 Consider the following model estimated by OLS with annual data for the years 1963–1985 for the United States as a whole:

$$\widehat{LH} = -4.759 + 1.873LG - 1.229LR$$
$$\quad\quad\quad (-1.4) \quad\quad (3.8) \quad\quad (-4.0)$$

$$\overline{R}^2 = 0.386 \quad\quad n = 23 \quad\quad DW\ d = 0.794$$

where LH is the logarithm of housing starts, LG is the logarithm of the gross national product, and LR is the logarithm of the mortgage rate. The values in parentheses are *t*-statistics.

a. Test the model for first-order serial correlation under the alternative most common in economics. Be sure to state the null and alternative hypotheses. Based on your conclusions, list the properties of the estimates and associated statistics and the validity of the tests of hypotheses.

b. Describe step-by-step how you would apply the Breusch–Godfrey test for first-order autocorrelation. Your answers must be specific to the model.

c. Describe the procedures for applying the Cochrane–Orcutt and Hildreth–Lu methods of estimating the parameters. Again, your answer should be specific to the model. What are the statistical properties of these estimates?

9.2 Using data for a number of employees of a firm, a labor economist estimated the following model by OLS (*t*-values in parentheses):

$$\widehat{\ln E} = 7.71 + 0.094S + 0.023N - 0.000325N^2$$
$$\quad\quad\quad (6.8) \quad (18.8) \quad\quad (2.6) \quad\quad\quad (-1.7)$$

$$\overline{R}^2 = 0.337 \quad\quad n = 60 \quad\quad DW\ d = 0.53$$

where ln *E* is the natural logarithm of earnings, *S* is the number of years of schooling, and *N* is the number of years of experience. "Because the Durbin–Watson test rejects the null hypothesis of zero first-order serial correlation, the *t*-tests are invalid, and the above R^2 is an overestimate of the true R^2." Do you agree with the quotation? Explain.

9.3 The planning department of a city obtained the following estimated double-log relationship by OLS, with *t*-statistics in parentheses:

$$\widehat{LH}_t = 1.12 + 1.141LY_t + 0.961LP_t$$
$$\quad\quad\quad (0.8) \quad\quad (10.7) \quad\quad\quad (1.5)$$

$$\overline{R}^2 = 0.98 \quad\quad n = 27 \quad\quad DW\ d = 0.65$$

where LH is the logarithm of the number of single-family dwellings, LY is the logarithm of the city's total income in constant dollars, and LP is the logarithm of the city's population. From the DW statistic, what conclusion would you draw about the residuals of the model? What are the implications on (1) bias, if any, of estimates and forecasts; (2) standard errors, goodness of fit, and t-statistics; and (3) validity of tests? If necessary, suggest an alternative procedure of estimating the model. Explain why it might be superior in terms of estimates and their properties (explain what you mean by "superior").

[†]9.4   A study on industrial employment in San Diego estimated the following model by OLS, using annual data for 22 years:

$$\widehat{\text{LEMP}} = \underset{(-0.56)}{-3.89} + \underset{(2.3)}{0.51\text{LINCM}} - \underset{(-1.7)}{0.25\text{LWAGE}} + \underset{(5.8)}{0.62\text{LG}}$$

$$\bar{R}^2 = 0.996 \qquad \text{DW } d = 1.147$$

EMP is total employment, INCM is total income, WAGE is the average hourly wage rate, and G is the total expenditure of the local governments in the area, all in logarithmic terms. Verify that the DW test for first-order autocorrelation is inconclusive. Describe step-by-step how the LM test will be applied in this case. Next describe how the Cochrane–Orcutt procedure can be used to obtain the estimates. Again, your descriptions should be specific to the model.

9.5   Let C_t be real per-capita consumption in the United States at time t, and Y_t be the real per-capita disposable income, both measured in billions of dollars. The following model was estimated by OLS, using annual data for 32 years (LY is the logarithm of Y):

$$\hat{C}_t = \underset{(-39.3)}{-21{,}151} + \underset{(45.0)}{2{,}989.9\text{LY}_t}$$

$$\bar{R}^2 = 0.985 \qquad \text{DW } d = 0.207$$

Test the model for first-order serial correlation. Be sure to state the assumption on the error terms and the null and alternative hypotheses. Based on your result, would you say that we are justified in feeling that the fit is excellent and the regression coefficients extremely significant? Why or why not?

9.6   Consider the following model of the demand for airline travel, estimated using annual data for the period 1947–1987. The number of observations is therefore 41.

$$\ln(Q_t) = \beta_1 + \beta_2 \ln(P_t) + \beta_3 \ln(Y_t) + \beta_4 \ln(\text{ACCID}_t) + \beta_5 \text{FATAL}_t + u_t$$

Q = Per-capita passenger miles traveled in a given year
P = Average price per mile
Y = Per-capita income
ACCID = Accident rate per passenger mile
FATAL = Number of fatalities from aircraft accidents

The model is double-log except for the fact that FATAL is not expressed in log form because the observation for some of the years is zero. The model was estimated by OLS and the Durbin–Watson statistic is 0.97.

a.   To test the model for first-order autocorrelation, write down the auxiliary equation for the error term and the null hypothesis of no serial correlation.

b.   For the Durbin–Watson test, write down the ranges of critical values for a 5 percent level of significance.

c.   Carry out the test and state whether you find significant autocorrelation.

    d.   Based on your conclusion, are the OLS estimates biased or unbiased, consistent or inconsistent, efficient or inefficient, and are the hypothesis tests valid?

    e.   Give three situations in which the DW test is not suitable.

    f.   Suppose you want to estimate the model using the Hildreth–Lu procedure. Describe step-by-step, as you would to your assistant, how to proceed. Provide complete details.

9.7   The planning department of a city obtained estimates for the following double-log model:

$$LH_t = \alpha + \beta\, LY_t + \gamma\, Lr_t + u_t$$

where L is logarithm, H is the number of single-family dwellings per capita, Y is per-capita income, and r is the interest rate. You have quarterly data for 10 years (40 observations). First, you want to test the model for fourth-order autocorrelation.

    a.   Write down the auxiliary equation for the error term.

    b.   State the null and alternative hypotheses for no serial correlation.

    c.   Describe the regressions to be run for carrying out the test.

    d.   How would you compute the test statistic? (Indicate numerical values where known.)

    e.   What is its distribution and d.f.?

    f.   Describe how you would use the p-value approach to decide whether to accept or reject the null hypothesis at 10 percent.

    g.   Suppose significant serial correlation exists, but you ignore it. Are forecasts biased, consistent, efficient?

    h.   Suppose you do not want to ignore autocorrelation. Describe the steps you would take to get more efficient estimates using the generalized Cochrane–Orcutt procedure.

9.8   Consider the double-log model of farm output

$$\ln(Q_t) = \beta_1 + \beta_2 \ln(K_t) + \beta_3 \ln(L_t) + \beta_4 \ln(A_t) + \beta_5 \ln(F_t) + \beta_6 \ln(S_t) + u_t$$

where Q is output, K is capital, L is labor, A is the acreage planted, F is the amount of fertilizers used, and S is the amount of seed planted. Using annual data for the years 1949 through 1988, the model was estimated and the Durbin–Watson statistic was 1.409.

    a.   Write down the auxiliary equation for the error term for using the DW statistic as the test statistic.

    b.   State the null hypothesis you will test and the alternative most common in economics.

    c.   Write down the critical values for the DW test, actually carry out the test, and state what the test result is.

Next you are asked to carry out an LM test for AR(2), that is, second-order autocorrelation.

    d.   Write down the auxiliary equation for the error term and state the null hypothesis of no serial correlation.

The auxiliary equation was estimated, after suppressing the 1949 and 1950 data, and the unadjusted R^2 was 0.687.

    e.   Compute the test LM test statistic and state its distribution and d.f.

    f.   Write down the critical value for the 0.001 level and carry out the test. What do you conclude about serial correlation?

    g.   You want to use the generalized Cochrane–Orcutt procedure for taking account of AR(2) in the errors. Carefully describe the steps you should take to obtain the estimates.

9.9　Consider the following double-log model of the demand for ice cream:

$$LD_t = \beta_1 + \beta_2\, LY_t + \beta_3\, LP_t + \beta_4\, LT_t + u_t$$

where L denotes logs, D is demand, Y is income, P is price, and T is temperature. To test for higher-order serial correlation, the following auxiliary regression was estimated, where $ut1 = \hat{u}(t-1)$, $ut2 = \hat{u}(t-2)$, and $ut3 = \hat{u}(t-3)$.

```
          OLS Estimates Using the 27 Observations 4-30
                 Dependent Variable - ut


VARIABLE       COEFFICIENT      STDERROR      T STAT      2Prob (t > |T|)

constant        -0.51069        1.515891    -0.336891     0.739709
ut1              0.552587       0.246655     2.240318     0.036585  **
ut2             -0.204653       0.297275    -0.688429     0.499091
ut3             -0.064952       0.290782    -0.223372     0.825512
LY               0.140065       0.285781     0.490114     0.629387
LP               0.142403       0.632046     0.225304     0.824029
LT               0.017987       0.081584     0.220473     0.827738


Error Sum of Sq (ESS)   0.17808    Std Err of Resid (sgmahat)      0.094361
Unadjusted R-squared    0.233      Adjusted R-squared              0.003
Durbin-Watson Stat.     1.883646   First-order auto corr coeff    -0.049
```

a.　Write down the auxiliary equation for the error term implied by the equation.
b.　Write down the null hypothesis for no autocorrelation.
c.　Write down the numerical value of the test statistic.
d.　Write down its distribution and d.f.
e.　Write down the critical value for a 10 percent test.
f.　State the decision rule and the conclusion.
g.　Based on your conclusion, are OLS estimates of the parameters of the model unbiased, consistent, and efficient, and are tests valid?

9.10　The following general version of the capital asset pricing model (CAPM) is used in finance literature:

$$(A)\quad SR_t = \beta_1 + \beta_2\, MR_t + \beta_3\, RFR_t + u_t$$

where SR is the rate of return of a company's stock, MR is the rate of return of a market average portfolio (such as the Standard & Poor's stock average), and RFR is the return of a risk-free asset (such as, for example, the three-month Treasury bill). You have data on SR, MR, and RFR for a company for a number of periods.

a.　A more commonly used version of CAPM is the following:

$$(B)\quad SR_t - RFR_t = \alpha(MR_t - RFR_t) + v_t$$

Write down the null hypotheses on the βs (which should not involve α) that will make (B) the restricted model. (Model A would be the unrestricted model.)

b. To use the Wald test on your hypotheses, describe the variables to generate and the regressions to run.

c. Describe how you would compute the test statistic.

d. Write down its distribution and d.f.

e. Suppose the data are time series. You have used appropriate tests and found that there is serial correlation of the first order in the residuals, that is, AR(1). Describe step-by-step how you would go about using the mixed (that is, hybrid) Hildreth–Lu and Cochrane–Orcutt procedure to estimate the parameters of Model A.

9.11 Consider the following double-log model of the demand for a commodity:

$$LQ_t = \beta_1 + \beta_2\, LP_t + \beta_3\, LY_t + u_t$$

where LQ = ln(per-capita quantity demanded), LP = ln(price per unit), and LY = ln(per-capita real income).

a. Write down the general auxiliary equation for AR(4) error specification, and formally state the null hypothesis of no serial correlation.

b. Describe step-by-step how you would use the Breusch–Godfrey test for the fourth-order serial correlation of the errors for this model. Be sure to describe the regressions to run, how you will compute the test statistic, and what its distribution and d.f. are.

c. Suppose you find significant AR(4) in the residuals. Describe the steps for using the generalized Cochrane–Orcutt estimation procedure.

d. Are the estimates unbiased, consistent, and efficient?

Instead of serial correlation, suppose the demand model exhibits a fourth-order ARCH effect.

e. Carefully describe the procedure for using Engle's ARCH test.

f. If there is significant ARCH effect, describe how you would use the weighted least squares procedure (assume that there is no negative variance problem) to obtain estimates better than OLS.

9.12 According to basic macroeconomic theory, the equilibrium gross national product (Y_t) depends on a number of policy variables and other independent variables: money supply (M_t), government expenditure (G_t), taxes (T_t), and exports (X_t). The following computer printout presents the results of an analysis conducted with quarterly U.S. data using the GRETL program.

a. What signs would you expect for each of the regression coefficients (ignore the constant term)? Justify your answers from economic theory.

b. Which of the signs do not agree with your intuition? Do you have any explanation for them?

c. Test (one-tailed) the model for first-order serial correlation at 5 percent. Based on your results, write down the properties of the OLS estimates, their standard errors, R-squared values, validity of tests, and so forth.

d. Use the information provided to test the model for the most general fourth-order serial correlation at the 1 percent level. Be sure to write down the equation for the error term and the null hypotheses.

e. Based on your test in part d, describe the exact procedure (this must be for your model) for using the generalized CORC procedure.

```
List of Variables
    0) const        1) Period     2) Yt       3) Mt       4) Gt
    5) Tt           6) Xt
```

```
        CORRELATION COEFFICIENTS USING THE OBSERVATIONS 1960.1-1984.4

        3) Mt            4) Gt          5) Tt          6) Xt

       1.000            0.998          0.993          0.961        (3
                        1.000          0.992          0.963        (4
                                       1.000          0.981        (5
                                                      1.000        (6
```

```
        OLS ESTIMATES USING THE 104 OBSERVATIONS 1959.1-1984.4
                    Dependent variable - Yt
```

VARIABLE	COEFFICIENT	STDERROR	T STAT	2Prob (t > |T|)	
0) constant	74.31764	8.24521	9.013	< 0.0001	***
3) Mt	0.24260	0.01925	12.601	< 0.0001	***
4) Gt	-0.55270	0.18354	-3.011	0.0033	***
5) Tt	2.20909	0.20321	10.871	< 0.0001	***
6) Xt	2.92166	0.94278	3.099	0.0025	***

```
Error Sum of Sq (ESS) 77577.59973  Std Err of Resid. (sgmahat)    27.99307
Unadjusted R-squared          0.999  Adjusted R-squared               0.999
Durbin-Watson Stat.           0.401  First-order auto corr coeff      0.812
```

[Generate $ut = \hat{u}_t$:
    ut_1 = ut(−1)
    ut_2 = ut(−2)
    ut_3 = ut(−3)
    ut_4 = ut(−4)]

```
        OLS ESTIMATES USING THE 100 OBSERVATIONS 1960.1-1984.4
                    Dependent variable - ut
```

VARIABLE	COEFFICIENT	STDERROR	T STAT	2Prob (t > |T|)	
0) constant	20.10843	5.63716	3.567	0.0006	***
8) ut_1	0.69513	0.10285	6.758	< 0.0001	***
9) ut_2	0.12626	0.12583	1.003	0.3183	
10) ut_3	0.02876	0.12837	0.224	0.8232	
11) ut_4	0.10275	0.10652	0.965	0.3373	
3) Mt	-0.01209	0.01146	-1.054	0.2945	
4) Gt	0.35455	0.12331	2.875	0.0050	***
5) Tt	-0.40493	0.13139	-3.082	0.0027	***
6) Xt	1.24866	0.56477	2.211	0.0295	**

```
Error Sum of Sq (ESS) 24136.15496  Std Err of Resid. (sgmahat)    16.28596
Unadjusted R-squared          0.683  Adjusted R-squared               0.655
```

9.13   Consider the following model of patents and R&D (research and development) expenditures:

$$\text{PATENTS}_t = \alpha + \beta \, \text{R\&D}_t + u_t$$

where PATENTS is the number of patent applications filed in a given year and R&D is the expenditures on research and development in that year. The model was estimated using annual U.S. data for the years 1960 through 1993 ($n = 34$).

You want to use the Durbin–Watson statistic, which had the value $d = 0.234$, to test the model for first-order serial correlation, that is, for AR(1).

a.   Write down the auxiliary equation for the error term implied by the presence of AR(1).

b.   Write down the null hypothesis for no autocorrelation.

c.   Carry out the Durbin–Watson test. Is there significant autocorrelation or not? Show all the details of your procedure.

d.   Describe the auxiliary regression needed to carry out the LM test for AR(1).

e.   Suppose this regression had error sum of squares ESS = 793.09 and total sum of squares TSS = 3,985.38. Compute the numerical value of the test statistic.

f.   Write down its distribution and d.f.

g.   Write down the critical value for a test at the level of 0.001.

h.   State the decision rule and the conclusion.

i.   Based on your conclusion, are OLS estimators of the parameters of the model unbiased, consistent, efficient? Are tests valid?

j.   Write down the assumption(s) that is (are) violated by the presence of serial correlation.

9.14   Consider the double-log model

$$\text{LHARVEST}_t = \beta_1 + \beta_2 \, \text{LHOUSING}_t + \beta_3 \, \text{LINDPRO}_t + \beta_4 \, \text{LTIMBERPR}_t + u_t$$

where L refers to the logarithm, HARVEST is the total softwood timber harvest in Oregon (billion board feet), HOUSING is total U.S. housing starts in millions, INDPRO is the index of industrial production for paper and wood products, and TIMBERPR is the price of timber per 1,000 board feet in dollars. Using annual data for the years 1959 through 1989 (31 observations), the model was estimated by OLS and it was found that the Durbin–Watson statistic was 0.411.

a.   Write down the equation for the error term (u_t) when it follows the AR(1) process, that is, first-order autocorrelation. Define the variables and indicate the null hypothesis of no serial correlation.

b.   Now carry out the test and state whether your test indicates significant autocorrelation or not.

c.   Describe step-by-step how you would use the Cochrane–Orcutt procedure for obtaining the estimates of the βs.

9.15   Using annual data for Turkey for 1960–1988 (29 observations), the following estimated double-log model was obtained (the log terms are elasticities):

$$\ln(Q) = -4.997 + 5.404 \, \text{D86} + 0.732 \ln(Y) - 0.241 \, \text{D82} \times \ln(Y) - 0.371 \ln(P)$$

$$+ 0.500 \, \text{D82} \times \ln(P) - 0.828 \, \text{D86} \times \ln(P) - 1.537 \, \text{D82} \times \ln(\text{ED})$$

$$+ 5.246 \, \text{D86} \times \ln(\text{ED})$$

where
- Q = Cigarette consumption per adult (kg), the dependent variable
- Y = Per-capita real GNP in 1968 prices (in Turkish liras)
- P = Real price of cigarettes in Turkey liras per kg
- ED = Ratio of enrollments in middle and high schools to the population 12–17 years old
- D82 = 1 for 1982 onward, 0 before 1982
- D86 = 1 for 1986 onward, 0 before 1986

a. Write down the numerical values of the elasticities of demand for income (Y), price (P), and education (ED) for each of the three periods (enter them in the following table). Pay close attention to the way the dummy variables are defined.

Variable	1960–1981	1982–1985	1986–1988
Y			
P			
ED			

b. In the table, point out the signs of coefficients that are counterintuitive and explain why you think so. (You need not offer explanations as to why the signs are wrong.)

c. You want to use the Breusch–Godfrey test to check the model for second-order autocorrelation with the error term $u_t = \rho_1 u_{t-1} + \rho_2 u_{t-2} + \varepsilon_t$. What is the null hypothesis that you would use?

d. Describe step-by-step how you will carry out the Breusch–Godfrey LM test at the 5 percent level (give numerical values where known)—specifically, what regressions you will run, how you will compute the test-statistic, its distribution, and the criterion to reject the null hypothesis. Give full details, with your answer being specific to the model at the beginning of the question. Note that this part refers only to testing and not to any estimation.

e. The unadjusted R^2 for the auxiliary regression for the LM test was 0.235. Use this to carry out the test for AR(2) at the 5% level. What do you conclude about serial correlation?

9.16   Consider the model $P_t = \alpha + \beta S_t + u_t$, where P is profits of a company at time t and S is sales. You have quarterly data for 15 years (60 observations). Also, you have found that the model has significant fourth-order autocorrelation with

$$u_t = \rho_1 u_{t-1} + \rho_2 u_{t-2} + \rho_3 u_{t-3} + \rho_4 u_{t-4} + \varepsilon_t$$

Describe step-by-step how you will apply the generalized Cochrane–Orcutt (CORC) iterative procedure. You are not asked how to test for AR(4), just how to estimate the unknown parameters using generalized CORC. Your answer must be specific to the model.

Questions Requiring Computer Work

9.17   Use the data in DATA4-3 (see Appendix D) and generate the variables lph = log(housing/pop), lpcgnp = log(gnp/pop), and lr = log(intrate). Then estimate the following model by OLS:

$$lph = \beta_1 + \beta_2\, lpcgnp + \beta_3\, lr + u$$

Test the model for first-order serial correlation using both the Durbin–Watson and Breusch–Godfrey tests, and indicate your conclusions. Based on your conclusions, what can you say about the properties of the OLS estimates in terms of unbiasedness, consistency, and efficiency?

If significant serial correlation exists, estimate the model by the mixed HILU–CORC procedure. Does serial correlation persist? Next test the model for AR(3) errors. If present, obtain the estimates by the generalized CORC procedure and interpret the results.

9.18   Using the data in DATA9-4 and your regression program, estimate the following model by ordinary least squares:

$$\text{PROFITS} = \alpha + \beta \text{SALES} + u$$

Save the residuals, obtain the residual plot, and examine whether it exhibits signs of serial correlation. Test your model for first-order autocorrelation using both the DW and BG tests. If it is significant, reestimate the model using both CORC and HILU procedures. Retest the model for serial correlation. Are your results meaningful? If not, what modifications do you suggest?

9.19   Use the data in DATA9-1 and estimate the following double-log model by OLS (prefix L denotes logarithms):

$$\text{LDEMAND}_t = \beta_0 + \beta_1 \text{LPRICE}_t + \beta_2 \text{LINCOME}_t + \beta_3 \text{LTEMP}_t + u_t$$

a.   Test the model for first-order serial correlation using both the Durbin–Watson and Breusch–Godfrey tests. Be sure to (1) write down the assumption about the error term u_t, (2) state the null and alternative hypotheses, and (3) state the test criterion and your conclusion.

b.   Based on your conclusion, are your estimates (1) unbiased, (2) consistent, (3) efficient? (Be sure to define each term.) Carefully justify your answer.

c.   Describe step-by-step how you will go about obtaining "better" estimates than OLS. Explain what you mean by "better."

9.20   DATA9-7 contains data on the number of new cars sold in the United States and a number of variables that it might be related to.

a.   Estimate the double-log model (prefix L denotes logs) by OLS.

$$\text{LQNC} = \beta_1 + \beta_2 \text{LPRICE} + \beta_3 \text{LINCOME} + \beta_4 \text{LPRIME}$$
$$+ \beta_5 \text{LUNEMP} + \beta_6 \text{SPRING} + \beta_7 \text{STRIKE} + u$$

(The STOCK variable is ignored in this formulation.)

b.   Compute the correlation coefficients for the independent variables. Is multicollinearity a problem in the data set? If yes, what can you say about the statistical properties of your estimates, t-values, and so on?

c.   Perform the LM test for first-order autocorrelation. Is there evidence of significant serial correlation? In light of your findings, what can you say about the properties of the OLS estimates and associated statistics?

d.   Based on your results, modify the model and reestimate if necessary. Are the model selection statistics better? Check the new model for autocorrelation.

e.   Because the data are quarterly, fourth-order serial correlation is suspected. Test the model for fourth-order serial correlation. What do you conclude? Does your conclusion suggest a "better" method (explain what you mean by "better")? If yes, apply that method and get revised estimates. Are they improved? If not, what other suggested models and/or estimation procedures would you recommend?

9.21   In Exercise 6.22 you estimated a double-log model of timber harvest using the data in DATA6-5. Test that model for first-order serial correlation using both the DW test and the LM test. Next test for AR(3) also. If higher-order autocorrelation is present, use generalized CORC to estimate the model. If AR(1) is present, use the hybrid HILU–CORC method. In the final model you estimate, test the coefficients for unitary elasticity (in numerical terms).

9.22   DATA9-8 has annual data for the following variables:

   POP = Population in millions
   RPM = Revenue air passenger miles (domestic) in billions
   NOP = Number of operators (airlines)
   OPREV = Operating revenue from passengers in millions of dollars
   GNP = Gross national product of the United States in billions of dollars
   ACCID = Number of American planes in an accident
   FATAL = Number of fatalities from aircraft accidents
   REGU = Dummy variable for airline regulation/deregulation: 0 for 1945–1978, and 1 for 1979 onward

First estimate the following model by OLS:

$$\ln(\text{RPM}/\text{POP}) = \beta_1 + \beta_2 \text{REGU} + \beta_3 \ln(\text{OPREV}/\text{RPM})$$
$$+ \beta_4 \ln(\text{GNP}/\text{POP}) + \beta_5 \ln(\text{ACCID}/\text{RPM}) + \beta_6 \text{FATAL} + u$$

RPM/POP is the per-capita revenue passenger miles, GNP/POP is per-capita income, OPREV/RPM measures the average price per mile, and ACCID/RPM measures the accident rate per passenger mile of travel. The model is double-log, except for the fact that REGU and FATAL are not expressed in log form because there are zero entries in the data for these variables. Use both the Durbin–Watson and LM tests for first-order autocorrelation. Given your results, what can you say about the properties of OLS estimates, the goodness of fit, and tests of hypotheses?

Next estimate the model by both CORC and the mixed HILU–CORC procedures and compare the results. Suppose that we want to test whether the intercept and slope coefficients (some of which are elasticities) depend on the variable REGU. In other words, there might have been a structural change when deregulation went into effect. Formulate another model with complete interaction terms and indicate what the null hypothesis of no structural change means. Estimate appropriate models to test for this and carry out such a test. Again, use the mixed HILU–CORC procedure to estimate a general model and then use relevant tests to reduce it to one in which coefficients are significant so that more efficient estimates could be obtained.

Finally, test the model for third-order serial correlation and, if called for, use the generalized Cochrane–Orcutt technique to estimate the model with an appropriate error specification.

9.23   DATA9-5 has annual data for indices of U.S. farm inputs and output with 1982 as the base year. The specific variables are described in Appendix D.

Estimate a double-log model relating the log of output to the log of each of the inputs. Test the model for serial correlation of first and third orders. If significant autocorrelation is present, estimate the models by the CORC, mixed HILU–CORC, and generalized CORC procedures. Eliminate insignificant variables and reestimate the resulting models. Choose your "final" model (justify your choice) and interpret the results.

9.24   The data used in the Application Section 7.8 are a time series. Check the model presented there for serial correlation, both AR(1) and higher orders. If it is significant, redo the analysis using the mixed HILU–CORC procedure and see if your results are the same.

9.25   DATA9-9 has quarterly U.S. data for the following variables for the period 1976.1 through 1985.4:

NUMCARS = Number of new car sales of U.S. dealers in thousands
    PRICE = New car price index
    INCOME = Per-capita disposable personal income in 1982 dollars
    POP = Estimated population obtained by interpolating from annual data (millions)
    INTRATE = Prime interest rate charged by banks
    UNEMP = Unemployment rate for all workers

Estimate the relationship between per-capita new car sales (NUMCARS/POP) and its determinants: price, income, interest rate, and unemployment rate. Formulate the model so that the regression coefficients are all elasticities. Carry out the analysis in three stages. First estimate the model by OLS and test for first-order serial correlation using both the DW and LM tests. If present, estimate the model by CORC and mixed HILU–CORC. Do they give the same results? Eliminate insignificant variables and reestimate the model using appropriate techniques. In the final model, test whether the demand for new car sales is elastic or inelastic with respect to price and income.

In the second stage, test for seasonal effects (omit the unemployment rate variable for the rest of the analysis). In particular, estimate a relevant model assuming that the constant term is different across seasons. Again, test the new model for serial correlation and use appropriate estimation techniques to obtain more efficient estimates.

In the third stage, test the model you started with in the second stage for serial correlation of orders 1 through 4. If present, use generalized CORC to estimate the model. Once again, omit insignificant variables. Choose the model that, in your opinion, best approximates the data-generating process and interpret the results of this model.

9.26   In Exercise 7.24 you estimated a double-log model of Turkish cigarette demand using the data in DATA7-19. Test that model for first-order serial correlation using both the DW test and the LM test. Next test for AR(3) also. If higher-order autocorrelation is present, use generalized CORC to estimate the model. If AR(1) is present, use the hybrid HILU–CORC method. In the final model you estimated, test the coefficients for unitary elasticity (in numerical terms).

9.27   DATA9-10 has data for the weekly sales and related variables for a grocery store in the Del Mar area of southern California. The variable definitions are given in Appendix D.

Formulate a general model (using logs where possible), making sure to use monthly dummies to allow for seasonal differences. Test the model for AR(4) and use appropriate estimation procedures to obtain estimates of the general model. Use data-based simplification to reduce the model. Test the final model for unitary elasticities.

9.28   DATA9-11 has monthly data on the total volume of stocks sold in the United States. The variables are described in Appendix D.

Estimate a model for the sales volume (allow for monthly differences), test it for AR(12), and use appropriate estimation procedures to obtain parameter estimates.

Eliminate redundant variables and reduce the model. Interpret the results of the final model.

9.29   DATA9-12, described in Appendix D, refers to monthly consumption expenditures on new cars.

Estimate an appropriate double-log model with seasonal effects. Test it for AR(12) and use appropriate estimation procedures to obtain parameter estimates. Eliminate redundant variables and reduce the model. Interpret the results of the final model.

9.30   DATA9-13 has monthly data on the returns of stocks for eight banks listed on the New York Stock Exchange as well as a number of possible variables these returns might be related to. Pick a bank and estimate a model relating its returns to variables such as yields, return of T-bill certificates, etc. Carry out tests for serial correlation of order 12. If significant autocorrelation is present, use the generalized Cochrane–Orcutt procedure to reestimate the model. Repeat the process with other banks' data.

Miscellaneous Derivations

9.A.1 Proof That the DW *d* Is Approximately 2(1 − $\hat{\rho}$)

The Durbin–Watson *d* given in Equation (9.6) can be expanded as follows:

$$d = \frac{\displaystyle\sum_{t=2}^{t=n} \hat{u}_t^2 + \sum_{t=2}^{t=n} \hat{u}_{t-1}^2 - 2\sum_{t=2}^{t=n} \hat{u}_t \hat{u}_{t-1}}{\displaystyle\sum_{t=1}^{t=n} \hat{u}_t^2} \tag{9.A.1}$$

Because the residuals, $\hat{u}_t$, are generally small, the summations from 2 to n or from 1 to $n - 1$ are both approximately equal to (denoted by the symbol $\simeq$) the summation from 1 to n. Therefore,

$$\sum_{t=2}^{t=n} \hat{u}_t^2 \simeq \sum_{t=2}^{t=n} \hat{u}_{t-1}^2 \simeq \sum_{t=1}^{t=n} \hat{u}_t^2$$

We note from this that the first two terms of Equation (9.A.1) approximately cancel with the denominator, giving 2. Also, the third term is the same as Equation (9.7), giving $2\hat{\rho}$. It follows from this that *d* is approximately equal to $2(1 - \hat{\rho})$.

9.A.2 Properties of u_t When It Is AR(1)

Substituting repeatedly from Equation (9.2), we get

$$u_t = \rho u_{t-1} + \varepsilon_t = \varepsilon_t + \rho(\varepsilon_{t-1} + \rho u_{t-2}) = \varepsilon_t + \rho\varepsilon_{t-1} + \rho^2(\varepsilon_{t-2} + \rho u_{t-3})$$

$$= \varepsilon_t + \rho\varepsilon_{t-1} + \rho^2\varepsilon_{t-2} + \cdot \cdot \cdot$$

Because $E(\varepsilon_t) = 0$, we have $E(u_t) = 0$. Also, by the independence of the εs,

$$\sigma_u^2 = \text{Var}(u_t) = \text{Var}(\varepsilon_t) + \rho^2\text{Var}(\varepsilon_{t-1}) + \rho^4\text{Var}(\varepsilon_{t-2}) + \cdot \cdot \cdot \tag{9.A.2}$$

$$= \sigma_\varepsilon^2(1 + \rho^2 + \rho^4 + \cdot \cdot \cdot) = \frac{\sigma_\varepsilon^2}{1 - \rho^2}$$

Note that the infinite series will sum to a finite value only if $|\rho| < 1$. Thus, a necessary condition for stationarity is that the first-order autocorrelation be strictly less than 1 in absolute value. If $\rho = 1$, the error process becomes $u_t = u_{t-1} + \varepsilon_t$. The value of u at time t is therefore equal to its value in the previous period plus a purely random effect. This process is known as the *random walk model* and is frequently used in modeling stock price behavior using the "efficient markets" theory, which states that the change in a price from one period to the next is purely random. The covariance between u_t and u_{t-s}, for $s \neq 0$, is given by

$$E(u_t u_{t-s}) = E[(\varepsilon_t + \rho\varepsilon_{t-1} + \rho^2\varepsilon_{t-2} + \cdot \cdot \cdot)(\varepsilon_{t-s} + \rho\varepsilon_{t-s-1} + \rho^2\varepsilon_{t-s-2} + \cdot \cdot \cdot)]$$

All the cross-product terms of the type $\varepsilon_t\varepsilon_{t-s}$, $\varepsilon_{t-1}\varepsilon_{t-s}$, and so on have zero expectations because ε_t and ε_{t-s} are, by assumption, independent. Only the square terms ε_{t-s}^2, ε_{t-s-1}^2 and so on remain. Therefore,

$$\text{Cov}(u_t, u_s) = E(u_t u_{t-s}) = E(\rho^s\varepsilon_{t-s}^2 + \rho^{s+2}\varepsilon_{t-s-1}^2 + \rho^{s+4}\varepsilon_{t-s-2}^2 + \cdot \cdot \cdot) \quad \textbf{(9.A.3)}$$

$$= \rho^s\sigma_\varepsilon^2(1 + \rho^2 + \rho^4 + \cdot \cdot \cdot)$$

$$= \frac{\rho^s\sigma_\varepsilon^2}{1 - \rho^2} = \rho^s\sigma_u^2$$

The coefficient of correlation between u_t and u_s, which is denoted by $r(s)$, is known as the **autocorrelation function** and is given by

$$r(s) = \frac{\text{Cov}(u_t, u_{t-s})}{\text{Var}(u_t)} = \rho^s$$

Since $|\rho| < 1$, as s increases (that is, as you move further into the past), the autocorrelation function decreases in absolute value, the rate of decline being dependent on the numerical value of ρ. At any rate, the error terms are correlated, violating the OLS assumption that they are not.

9.A.3 Treatment of the First Observation under AR(1)

In describing the Cochrane–Orcutt procedure, we transformed the first observation as follows:

$$Y_1^* = Y_1(1 - \rho^2)^{1/2} \quad \text{and} \quad X_{1i}^* = X_{1i}(1 - \rho^2)^{1/2} \quad \textbf{(9.A.4)}$$

To see the justification for this, note that the first observation is

$$Y_1 = \beta_1 + \beta_2 X_{12} + \beta_3 X_{13} + \cdot \cdot \cdot + \beta_k X_{1k} + u_1 \quad \textbf{(9.A.5)}$$

Equation (9.2) is not defined for the first observation because u_0 is undefined. From Equation (9.A.2), the variance of u_t is $\sigma_\varepsilon^2/(1 - \rho^2)$. Suppose we define u_1 to be equal to $\varepsilon_1/(1 - \rho^2)^{1/2}$. Then

$$\text{Var}(u_1) = \frac{1}{1 - \rho^2}\text{Var}(\varepsilon) = \frac{\sigma_\varepsilon^2}{1 - \rho^2}$$

which is in conformity with Equation (9.A.2). Equation (9.A.5) now becomes

$$Y_1 = \beta_1 + \beta_2 X_{12} + \beta_3 X_{13} + \cdot \cdot \cdot + \beta_k X_{1k} + \frac{\varepsilon_1}{(1 - \rho^2)^{1/2}} \tag{9.A.6}$$

Multiplying through by $(1 - \rho^2)^{1/2}$ and using (9.A.4), we get Equation (9.8) for $t = 1$ also. We therefore see that this treatment of the first observation enables us to include it in the estimation, but with a slightly different transformation for the first observation.

Distributed Lag Models

As mentioned in Section 6.6, the impact of policy changes is almost never instantaneous but requires some time to be felt. As an example, suppose the Federal Reserve Board adjusts the discount rate, which is the interest rate that member banks pay when they borrow reserves from the Federal Reserve district banks. Raising the discount rate signals a tighter monetary policy. Its effects on the economy (in particular on investment, inflation, gross domestic product, and so on) will, however, take a while to be noticed. Thus, the gross domestic product, unemployment, and inflation will depend not just on current interest rates but on past interest rates as well. In other words, we need a dynamic model to capture these lagged effects. In Section 6.6 we saw examples of such dynamic models. Dynamic models may also have the lagged dependent variable as an explanatory variable. For example, consumption at time t might depend on consumption at time t − 1, partly because of habit formation and typical consumer resistance to radical changes in lifestyles (see Example 6.4). To capture this lag in behavior, the specification of time series models often includes lagged values of the dependent and independent variables. The inclusion of lagged variables as regressors often creates problems. This chapter examines these problems and suggests solutions to them. The cases of lagged independent variables and lagged dependent variables are treated separately.

10.1 Lagged Independent Variables

Suppose the model under consideration is

$$Y_t = \alpha + \beta_0 X_t + \beta_1 X_{t-1} + \cdots + \beta_p X_{t-p} + u_t \qquad (10.1)$$

In this model, called a **distributed lag model** (because the impacts are distributed over time), only current and lagged values of X—that is, **lagged independent variables**—are used to predict Y_t. As an example, let Y_t be the consumption of electricity at the tth hour of a day and X_t be the temperature at that hour. In the summer, if the temperatures during successive hours are high, the interiors of buildings heat up (this is called the "heat build-up effect"); and hence electricity consumption is likely to depend not only on the current temperature but also on recent past temperatures. The coefficient β_0 is the weight attached to X_t; it is also $\Delta Y_t/\Delta X_t$, the average increase in Y_t when X_t is increased by one unit. β_0 is known as the **impact multiplier**—that is, it is the marginal effect of X on Y in the same time period. β_i is $\Delta Y_t/\Delta X_{t-i}$, the average increase in Y_t for a unit increase in X_{t-i}, that is, for a unit increase in X made i periods prior to t. It is also the average increase in Y an i number of periods from now when X is increased now by one unit. β_i is known as the **interim multiplier of order i.** These points are illustrated in Example 10.1.

Suppose the economy were in a **steady state** (also known as **long-run equilibrium**) in which all the variables were constant over time. Denoting the long-run value with an asterisk, the steady-state relation becomes ($u_t = 0$ in the steady state)

$$Y^* = \alpha + \beta_0 X^* + \beta_1 X^* + \cdots + \beta_p X^* = \alpha + X^*(\beta_0 + \beta_1 + \cdots + \beta_p) \quad \textbf{(10.2)}$$

This gives the cumulative effect over time as $\Delta Y^*/\Delta X^* = \beta_0 + \beta_1 + \cdots + \beta_p$, which is known as the **long-run multiplier.**

● EXAMPLE 10.1

It is known from basic macroeconomic theory that changes in the money supply (M) induce changes in the interest rate (r). Also, if budget deficits (D) are financed by issuing Treasury certificates, they would also affect the interest rate. However, we would expect the changes to take place over time. The following is a dynamic model of the interest rate, and it assumes a fourth-order lag in behavior:

$$r_t = f(M_t, M_{t-1}, M_{t-2}, M_{t-3}, M_{t-4}, D_t, D_{t-1}, D_{t-2}, D_{t-3}, D_{t-4}) + u_t \quad \textbf{(10.3)}$$

DATA10-1 (see Appendix D) has quarterly data for the United States on the three variables for the period 1964.1 through 1991.2. Interest rate (r) is the three-month Treasury bill rate, money supply is in billions of constant 1987 dollars, and deficits are also in billions of dollars but are cyclically adjusted (but it is not clear how this was done). Practice Computer Session 10.1 has the details for reproducing the results of this section. When the model was estimated by OLS, the DW statistic was 0.269, which suggests the presence of autocorrelation. However, because the data are quarterly, we would expect a fourth-order autoregressive error structure. Therefore, an LM test was performed for AR(4). The nR^2 statistic was 82.424 with a p-value less than 0.0001, indicating strong fourth-order serial correlation. We therefore estimated the model by the generalized Cochrane–Orcutt procedure described in Chapter 9. As expected, several of the regression coefficients were insignificant because of severe multicollinearity among the explanatory variables. The model was then reduced by eliminating insignificant variables. The estimates of the "kitchen sink model" (Model A) and those of the final model (Model B) are presented in Table 10.1 along with the p-values in parentheses. The goodness of fit is measured as the square of the correlation coefficient between the observed interest rate and that predicted by the estimated model after taking into account the AR(4) error structure (see Equation 9.13).

It is interesting to note that in Model B all the deficit variables have dropped out and only the current and one-period lagged money supply remain. Thus, *given the presence of these variables,* the other variables have no significant additional effects. The long-run multiplier for money supply is -0.0002 ($= -0.0141 + 0.0139$). Figure 10.1 graphs the observed and predicted interest rates for Model B. We note that the model generally tracks the actual values quite well except for 1980–1982, when interest rates were consistently above 12 percent.

⬤ **Table 10.1   Estimated Models for the Interest Rate**

Variable	Model A	Model B
Constant	5.001 (0.525)	8.2029 (0.167)
$M(t)$	−0.013 (0.005)	−0.0141 (0.0005)
$M(t-1)$	0.014 (0.008)	0.0139 (0.0006)
$M(t-2)$	−0.004 (0.934)	
$M(t-3)$	0.003 (0.596)	
$M(t-4)$	−0.001 (0.727)	
$D(t)$	−0.004 (0.509)	
$D(t-1)$	0.001 (0.940)	
$D(t-2)$	−0.001 (0.869)	
$D(t-3)$	−0.003 (0.693)	
$D(t-4)$	−0.005 (0.411)	
$\hat{u}(t-1)$	1.157 (< 0.0001)	1.135 (< 0.0001)
$\hat{u}(t-2)$	−0.499 (0.0007)	−0.471 (0.0012)
$\hat{u}(t-3)$	0.530 (0.0003)	0.519 (0.0004)
$\hat{u}(t-4)$	−0.264 (0.0078)	−0.259 (0.0089)
Adj. R-squared	0.886	0.893

Note: Entries in parentheses are *p*-values.

⬤ **Figure 10.1   Observed (+) and Predicted (line) Interest Rates (%)**

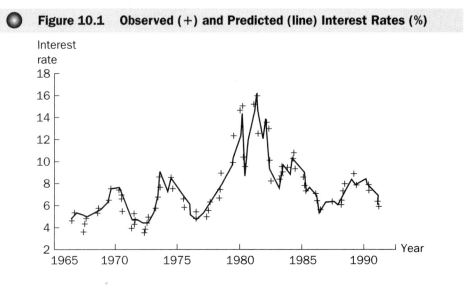

In Equation (10.1), if $X_t, X_{t-1}, \ldots, X_{t-p}$ are all uncorrelated with u_t, which has a zero mean conditional on given Xs, the least squares procedure will give estimates that are BLUE and consistent. Nevertheless, several difficulties are commonly encountered here. The value of p, the largest lag, is often unknown. In this case, we may be tempted to specify a large value for p and select among alternative values for the lag using the AIC or other criterion. But this creates multicollinearity problems because of close relations among $X_t, X_{t-1}, \ldots, X_{t-p}$. In Example 10.1, we encountered severe multicollinearity even when only four lags were used. Second, a large value for p means a considerable loss in degrees of freedom because we can only use the observations in the range $p + 1$ through n. As we know, lower degrees of freedom imply a worsening in the precision of the estimates (that is, their efficiency) and a reduction in the power of tests of hypotheses. It is therefore desirable to devise methods that will alleviate these difficulties. The typical approach is to impose some structure on the βs and reduce from $p + 1$ to a few the number of parameters to be estimated. Only two of the methods are presented here. Details on additional methods are available from the books by Kmenta (1986) and Judge, Griffiths, Hill, and Lee (1985), and Greene (2000).

Koyck Lag (or Geometric Lag)

Koyck (1954) proposed a geometrically declining scheme for the βs, a scheme now known as the **Koyck** (or **geometric**) **lag.** More specifically, he assumed that $\beta_i = \lambda\beta_{i-1}$, with $0 < \lambda < 1$. Thus, the weight for period i is a fraction of the weight for the previous period. By repeated substitution we get $\beta_i = \beta_0\lambda^i$, which gives a geometrically decreasing set of weights. Making the largest lag (p) infinitely large, we have

$$Y_t = \alpha + \beta_0 X_t + \beta_0\lambda X_{t-1} + \beta_0\lambda^2 X_{t-2} + \cdots + u_t$$

Note that the coefficients decline geometrically (see Fig. 10.2) and that there are only three unknown parameters: α, β_0, and λ. The assumption is that the biggest impact of X is felt immediately and that subsequent effects gradually decline to

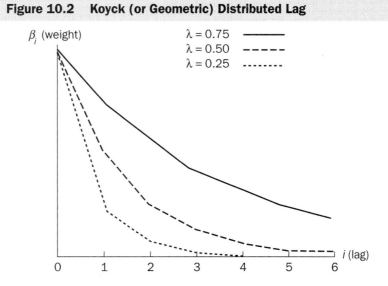

Figure 10.2 Koyck (or Geometric) Distributed Lag

zero. However, because the series is infinite, we cannot use it to estimate β_0 and λ directly. To simplify it, first write down the series for Y_{t-1}:

$$Y_{t-1} = \alpha + \beta_0 X_{t-1} + \beta_0 \lambda X_{t-2} + \beta_0 \lambda^2 X_{t-3} + \cdots + u_{t-1}$$

Next multiply it term-by-term by λ, subtract from the above, and cancel common terms. We then get

$$Y_t - \lambda Y_{t-1} = \alpha(1 - \lambda) + \beta_0 X_t + u_t - \lambda u_{t-1}$$

or

$$Y_t = \alpha^* + \lambda Y_{t-1} + \beta_0 X_t + v_t \tag{10.4}$$

where $\alpha^* = \alpha(1 - \lambda)$. Thus, the Koyck lag procedure is a convenient way to reduce the number of parameters in a distributed lag model, provided the declining geometric approximation is reasonable. In the electricity consumption example this is sensible, because we would expect the largest impact to be due to the temperature at the time period t, with smaller impacts due to temperatures at time periods $t - 1, t - 2$, and so on.

Note that Equation (10.4) now has Y_{t-1}, which is a lagged dependent variable. Furthermore, the error term is not autocorrelated but has a different structure, known as a **moving average,** that will be discussed in detail in the next chapter. The estimation of this model creates a number of problems that are discussed in Section 10.2.

● PRACTICE PROBLEM 10.1

Verify that the long-run multiplier is $\beta_0/(1 - \lambda)$.

● EXAMPLE 10.2

The Koyck lag model is illustrated using data for the electricity usage along with matching temperature data at different hours of the day for an electric company in the northwest region of the United States (see DATA10-2). The data refer to the 744 hours in the month of January 1992. Practice Computer Session 10.2 has the details to reproduce the results. First a static model was estimated relating the electricity load in a given hour (measured in megawatts) to the average temperature in that hour. The estimated model is given next with the p-values in parentheses.

$$\widehat{load}_t = 3{,}132.369 - 11.133 \ temp_t$$
$$(< 0.0001) \quad (0.00053)$$

The adjusted R^2 for this model was only 0.015. However, when the transformed model in Equation (10.4) was estimated, it jumped to 0.848. The estimated coefficients are given next, with p-values in parentheses.

$$\widehat{\text{load}}_t = \underset{(<0.0001)}{405.174} + \underset{(<0.0001)}{0.916 \text{ load}_{t-1}} - \underset{(0.00107)}{4.140 \text{ temp}_t}$$

The long-run multiplier for temp is given by $-4.140/(1 - 0.916) = -49.3$. Because the model refers to time series, we should test for serial correlation. It will be seen in Section 10.2 that, because of the presence of the lagged dependent variable, the Durbin–Watson test for AR(1) is not applicable. The Breusch–Godfrey test, however, is applicable, especially for higher-order autocorrelation. This issue is addressed when we revisit this example in the next section.

● PRACTICE PROBLEM 10.2

Use the data file provided and generate the lagged variables temp_{t-i} for $i = 1, 2, \ldots, 6$; that is, generate 6 lagged *independent* variables. Next estimate a model as in Equation (10.1). Compare the model selection criteria and the long-run multiplier with those of the preceding Koyck transformed model.

Almon Lag (or Polynomial Lag)

An alternative procedure is the **Almon** (or **polynomial**) **lag.** Proposed by Almon (1965), it assumes that the coefficient β_i can be approximated by a polynomial in i, so that

$$\beta_i = f(i) = \alpha_0 + \alpha_1 i + \alpha_2 i^2 + \cdots + \alpha_r i^r$$

Because continuous functions can generally be approximated by a polynomial, this procedure is quite flexible. Figure 10.3 illustrates two commonly assumed shapes that are reasonable in many circumstances. In one of them, endpoint constraints such as $\beta_{-1} = \beta_{p+1} = 0$ are imposed; the other is unconstrained. When there has been a change in government policy (for example, the enactment of a new tax law), we might expect the immediate effect to be negligible. The main effect may be felt in two or three quarters, and thereafter the effect might decline again. A second- or third-degree polynomial is often adequate to capture the shape underlying this behavior. The Almon procedure, however, requires the prior selection of the degree of polynomial (r) and the period of the largest lag used in the model (p). Unlike in the Koyck lag procedure, p in the Almon procedure must be finite. Suppose we choose $r = 3$ and $p = 4$—that is, a cubic polynomial and a lag of four periods. We then have

$$\beta_0 = f(0) = \alpha_0$$

$$\beta_1 = f(1) = \alpha_0 + \alpha_1 + \alpha_2 + \alpha_3$$

$$\beta_2 = f(2) = \alpha_0 + 2\alpha_1 + 4\alpha_2 + 8\alpha_3$$

$$\beta_3 = f(3) = \alpha_0 + 3\alpha_1 + 9\alpha_2 + 27\alpha_3$$

$$\beta_4 = f(4) = \alpha_0 + 4\alpha_1 + 16\alpha_2 + 64\alpha_3$$

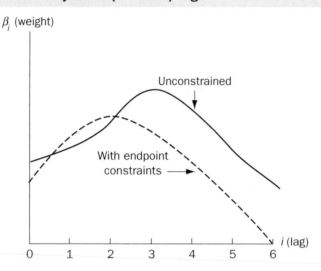

Figure 10.3   Polynomial (or Almon) Lag

Substituting these in the model and grouping terms, we get

$$Y_t = \alpha + \alpha_0 X_t + (\alpha_0 + \alpha_1 + \alpha_2 + \alpha_3) X_{t-1} + (\alpha_0 + 2\alpha_1 + 4\alpha_2 + 8\alpha_3) X_{t-2}$$
$$+ (\alpha_0 + 3\alpha_1 + 9\alpha_2 + 27\alpha_3) X_{t-3} + (\alpha_0 + 4\alpha_1 + 16\alpha_2 + 64\alpha_3) X_{t-4} + u_t$$
$$= \alpha + \alpha_0 (X_t + X_{t-1} + X_{t-2} + X_{t-3} + X_{t-4})$$
$$+ \alpha_1 (X_{t-1} + 2X_{t-2} + 3X_{t-3} + 4X_{t-4})$$
$$+ \alpha_2 (X_{t-1} + 4X_{t-2} + 9X_{t-3} + 16X_{t-4})$$
$$+ \alpha_3 (X_{t-1} + 8X_{t-2} + 27X_{t-3} + 64X_{t-4}) + u_t$$

The unknown αs, and hence the βs, are readily estimated because the variables in parentheses can be obtained through appropriate transformations. If α_3 is insignificant, we may use a second-degree polynomial. If we wish to include additional terms, we may easily do this also. We may change r and p and choose the combination that maximizes $\overline{R}^2$ or, preferably, use model selection statistics such as AIC and SCHWARZ.

EXAMPLE 10.3

The polynomial lag approach was used by Almon to estimate the relation between capital expenditures in manufacturing industries and past appropriations in those industries. Quarterly observations were used for the period 1953–1961. The model was

$$E_t = \alpha_1 S_{t1} + \alpha_2 S_{t2} + \alpha_3 S_{t3} + \alpha_4 S_{t4} + \beta_0 A_t + \beta_1 A_{t-1} + \cdots + \beta_p A_{t-p} + u_t$$

where E_t is capital expenditures at time t (in millions of dollars); A_t, A_{t-1}, and so on are appropriations at time periods t, $t-1$, and so on (also in millions of dollars); and S_{t1}, S_{t2}, S_{t3}, and S_{t4} are seasonal dummies. Almon chose to include all the seasonal dummies without a constant term. The estimated model for all manufacturing industries is (standard errors in parentheses)

$$\hat{E}_t = -283S_{t1} + 13S_{t2} - 50S_{t3} + 320S_{t4} + \underset{(0.023)}{0.048A_t} + \underset{(0.016)}{0.099A_{t-1}} + \underset{(0.013)}{0.141A_{t-2}}$$

$$+ \underset{(0.023)}{0.165A_{t-3}} + \underset{(0.023)}{0.167A_{t-4}} + \underset{(0.013)}{0.146A_{t-5}} + \underset{(0.016)}{0.105A_{t-6}} + \underset{(0.024)}{0.053A_{t-7}}$$

$$\overline{R}^2 = 0.922 \qquad \text{DW } d = 0.890$$

The model was estimated under the endpoint constraints $\beta_{-1} = \beta_8 = 0$. Figure 10.4 graphs the estimated weights. Although the goodness of fit is very good, it may be misleading because the Durbin–Watson statistic indicates the presence of serial correlation. Almon tried a number of variations of the model, the details of which may be found in the paper. The standard errors in parentheses indicate that the weights for the lagged capital appropriations are significant.

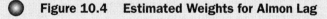

● PRACTICE PROBLEM 10.3

Assume that $r = 2$ and $p = 4$ (that is, a quadratic distributed lag) and derive the estimable econometric model. Describe how you will estimate the relevant parameters.

● **Figure 10.4   Estimated Weights for Almon Lag**

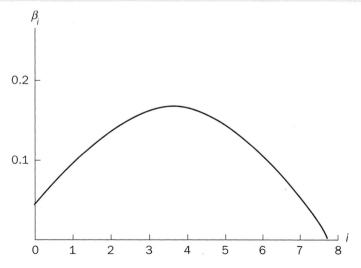

Other Types of Lag Structures

A number of other schemes for reducing the number of parameters in a distributed lag model have also been proposed. We list them here without any discussion. They include *Pascal lag, rational lag, gamma lag, LaGuerre lag,* and *Shiller lag.* Kmenta (1986) gives an excellent treatment of these approaches.

10.2   Lagged Dependent Variables

As mentioned earlier, the presence of the **lagged dependent** (or endogenous) **variable** as a regressor is quite common in economics. In the Koyck lag transformation used previously, Y_{t-1} appears as a regressor. Three other common specifications involving lagged dependent variables are given in the following sections.

Partial Adjustment Model

Suppose Y_t^* is the desired level of inventories of a firm, Y_t is the actual level, and X_t is the sales. Assume that the desired level of inventories depends on sales as

$$Y_t^* = \alpha + \beta X_t \tag{10.5}$$

Because of "frictions" in the market, the gap between the actual and desired levels cannot be closed instantaneously but only with some lag and random shocks. Suppose only a fraction of the gap is closed each period. In this case, the inventory at time t would equal that at time $t-1$, plus an adjustment factor, plus a random error term. More formally,

$$Y_t = Y_{t-1} + \lambda(Y_t^* - Y_{t-1}) + u_t \qquad 0 < \lambda < 1 \tag{10.6}$$

This model is called the **partial adjustment model.** The parameter λ is called the **adjustment coefficient** and $1/\lambda$ is called the **speed of adjustment.** The adjustment coefficient approximates the fraction of the gap closed in one period. The speed of adjustment approximates the number of periods it takes for much of the adjustment to take place. Thus, if $\hat{\lambda} = 0.25$, approximately 25 percent of the gap will be closed in one period. If the desired inventories Y_t^* exceed the actual inventories at the end of the time period $t-1$, we would expect part of that gap to close in the period t, and hence Y_t will go up by $\lambda(Y_t^* - Y_{t-1})$ plus an unpredictable random shock. Combining (10.5) and (10.6), we get the model

$$Y_t = \alpha\lambda + (1-\lambda)Y_{t-1} + \beta\lambda X_t + u_t = \beta_1 + \beta_2 Y_{t-1} + \beta_3 X_t + u_t \tag{10.7}$$

PRACTICE PROBLEM 10.4

Suppose $\hat{\beta}_2 = 0.667$ and $\hat{\beta}_3 = 0.3$. Estimate β and λ from this. What is the marginal effect of sales on (1) desired and (2) actual inventories? What is the average number of periods required for 90 percent of the gap between desired and actual inventories to be closed?

Empirical Example: Cigarette Demand in Turkey

Tansel (1993) has used the partial adjustment framework to examine the characteristics of the demand for cigarettes in Turkey. In particular, she has studied the effects of health warnings as well as education on cigarette consumption. First, desired consumption (Q_t^*) is specified by the following double-log equation:

$$\ln Q_t^* = \alpha + \beta \ln P_t + \gamma \ln Y_t + \delta D_t$$

where P is the cigarette price relative to the consumer price index, Y is per-capita disposable income in constant terms, and D represents two dummy variables, one for the period 1982 onward (when health warnings first appeared on cigarette packages) and another for 1986 onward (when an active antismoking campaign was implemented). Actual consumption (Q_t) is adjusted by the following mechanism:

$$\Delta \ln Q_t = \lambda(\ln Q_t^* - \ln Q_{t-1}) \qquad 0 < \lambda < 1$$

As before, substituting for Q_t^* from the first equation into the second and rearranging terms, we obtain the following estimable equation:

$$\ln Q_t = \beta_1 + \beta_2 \ln P_t + \beta_3 \ln Y_t + \beta_4 \ln Q_{t-1} + \beta_5 D_t + u_t$$

Using annual data from 1960 through 1988, Tansel estimated this model and then subjected it to a number of diagnostic tests. In particular, she tested it for an AR(2) error structure and ARCH effects and also used Ramsey's RESET procedure. The dummy variable for 1986 onward was insignificant and was eliminated. The estimated model is as follows (absolute values of the t-ratios are in parentheses):

$$\widehat{\ln Q_t} = -0.279 + 0.411 \ln Y_t - 0.214 \ln P_t + 0.424 \ln Q_{t-1} - 0.087 \text{ D82}$$
$$\phantom{\widehat{\ln Q_t} =} (3.36) \qquad (3.50) \qquad\quad (2.22) \qquad\quad (3.03) \qquad\quad (3.29)$$

The unadjusted R^2 was 0.878. The long-run income and price elasticities are, respectively, 0.714 and -0.372 (verify them). The significant negative coefficient for the dummy variable indicates that health warnings did have an appreciable impact in reducing cigarette consumption.

Tansel extended the model to include the effects of education. In particular, the ratio of enrollments in middle and high schools to the population 12–17 years old and the ratio of the enrollments in universities to the population 20–24 years old were added as explanatory variables. She found that the school enrollment ratio was not statistically significant, but the university enrollment ratio was negative and significant. The clear policy implication is that education and increasing the price of cigarettes through taxes would significantly reduce cigarette demand. For a fuller discussion of the analysis and policy implications, read Tansel's paper. You should also use the data provided in DATA7-19 and carry out your own analysis (see Exercise 10.14).

Adaptive Expectations Model

Another model that has a lagged dependent variable is the **adaptive expectations model.** Suppose Y_t is consumption, X_t^* is expected income, and X_t is actual income.

Consumption is assumed to be related not to current income, but to expected income. Thus,

$$Y_t = \alpha + \beta X_t^* + u_t \tag{10.8}$$

β is the marginal propensity to consume out of expected income. This equation cannot be estimated in practice because X_t^* is typically unobservable and hence there are no data on it. We therefore need to impose additional structure on the model. Assume that consumers revise their expectations based on how well their earlier expectations were realized. The change in expectation, $X_t^* - X_{t-1}^*$, is assumed to depend on the gap between X_{t-1} and X_{t-1}^*, as follows:

$$X_t^* - X_{t-1}^* = \lambda(X_{t-1} - X_{t-1}^*) \qquad 0 < \lambda < 1 \tag{10.9}$$

If actual income in period $t - 1$ exceeds expectations, we would expect consumers to revise their expectation upward. Equation (10.9) thus becomes

$$X_t^* = \lambda X_{t-1} + (1 - \lambda) X_{t-1}^*$$

We can solve Equation (10.8) for X_t^* in terms of Y_t as $X_t^* = (Y_t - \alpha - u_t)/\beta$. Substituting this in the preceding equation and rearranging terms, we get

$$\frac{Y_t - \alpha - u_t}{\beta} = \lambda X_{t-1} + (1 - \lambda)\left(\frac{Y_{t-1} - \alpha - u_{t-1}}{\beta}\right)$$

Multiplying throughout by β, keeping only Y_t on the left-hand side, and grouping terms, we obtain the following estimable econometric model:

$$Y_t = \alpha\lambda + (1 - \lambda)Y_{t-1} + \lambda\beta X_{t-1} + u_t - (1 - \lambda)u_{t-1} \tag{10.10}$$

$$= \beta_1 + \beta_2 Y_{t-1} + \beta_3 X_{t-1} + v_t$$

where $\beta_1 = \alpha\lambda$, $\beta_2 = 1 - \lambda$, $\beta_3 = \lambda\beta$, and $v_t = u_t - (1 - \lambda)u_{t-1}$. The error term in Equation (10.10) is of the moving average form, encountered in Equation (10.4), which is examined more closely in this chapter in the section on estimation procedures as well as in Chapter 11 on forecasting. Once estimates of the βs have been obtained, α, β, and λ can be estimated as follows:

$$\hat{\lambda} = 1 - \hat{\beta}_2, \qquad \hat{\alpha} = \frac{\hat{\beta}_1}{\hat{\lambda}}, \qquad \hat{\beta} = \frac{\hat{\beta}_3}{\hat{\lambda}}$$

It is interesting to note that we are able to estimate the marginal propensity to consume out of expected income even though there are no data on expected income. This illustrates how one can incorporate unobserved variables in a model and still estimate unknown parameters, provided additional structure is imposed.

The regression coefficient β_3 is $\Delta Y_t / \Delta X_{t-1}$ and is hence the one-period interim multiplier of X on Y. To get the long-run multiplier, set $u_t = 0$, $Y_t = Y^*$, and $X_t = X^*$ for all t. We then have $\hat{Y}^* = \hat{\beta}_1 + \hat{\beta}_2 \hat{Y}^* + \hat{\beta}_3 X^*$. The estimated long-run relation becomes $\hat{Y}^* = (\hat{\beta}_1 + \hat{\beta}_3 X^*)/(1 - \hat{\beta}_2)$. It follows that the estimated long-run multiplier is

$$\frac{\Delta \hat{Y}^*}{\Delta X^*} = \frac{\hat{\beta}_3}{1 - \hat{\beta}_2} = \hat{\beta} \qquad (10.11)$$

● PRACTICE PROBLEM 10.5

Using the same estimates of β_2 and β_3 as in Practice Problem 10.4, estimate the impact multiplier, the long-run multiplier, and the interim multiplier for two, three, and four periods (the interim multiplier for period i is $\Delta Y_t / \Delta X_{t-i}$).

Lagged Dependent Variable as a Generalization of an AR Model

In the previous chapter, we noted the Sargan (1964) and Hendry and Mizon (1978) argument that autoregressive errors might be indicative of model misspecification. We showed there that the model $Y_t = \alpha + \beta X_t + u_t$ with $u_t = \rho u_{t-1} + \varepsilon_t$ can be rewritten as follows:

$$Y_t = \alpha + \beta_1 Y_{t-1} + \beta_2 X_t + \beta_3 X_{t-1} + \varepsilon_t \qquad |\beta_1| < 1 \qquad (10.12)$$

Under serially correlated errors, the parameters of this model satisfy the nonlinear restriction $\beta_3 + \beta_1 \beta_2 = 0$. We readily see that Equation (10.12) has the lagged dependent variable as a regressor.

Consequences of the Presence of Lagged Dependent Variables

Why should we be concerned about the presence of lagged dependent variables as regressors? Why not treat them as any other lagged variable? In other words, why not regress Y_t against a constant, Y_{t-1}, and X_t; then obtain $\hat{\beta}_1$, $\hat{\beta}_2$, and $\hat{\beta}_3$; and finally solve for α, β, and λ in Equation (10.10)? This question is examined with the following simple model. The results generalize to more complicated models.

$$Y_t = \beta Y_{t-1} + u_t \qquad |\beta| < 1 \qquad (10.13)$$

in which u_t is assumed to satisfy all the assumptions made in Chapter 3. In particular, we assume that $E(Y_{t-1} u_t) = 0$—that is, that Y_{t-1} is uncorrelated with u_t.

The least squares estimate of β is (verify)

$$\hat{\beta} = \frac{\sum_{t=2}^{t=n} Y_t Y_{t-1}}{\sum_{t=2}^{t=n} Y_{t-1}^2}$$

Substituting for Y_t from the model and separating the β term, we get

$$\hat{\beta} = \beta + \frac{\displaystyle\sum_{t=2}^{t=n} u_t Y_{t-1}}{\displaystyle\sum_{t=2}^{t=n} Y_{t-1}^2} = \beta + \frac{u_2 Y_1 + u_3 Y_2 + \cdots + u_n Y_{n-1}}{Y_1^2 + Y_2^2 + \cdots + Y_{n-1}^2}$$

Even though Y_{t-1} and u_t may be uncorrelated, Y_{t-1} depends on u_{t-1} (because $Y_{t-1} = \beta Y_{t-2} + u_{t-1}$, from Equation 10.13) and hence many of the terms in the numerator are correlated with terms in the denominator. Thus, the second term in the preceding equation is a ratio of two random variables and is of the form Z_1/Z_2, whose expectation is not easy to compute. In particular, it is not true that $E(Z_1/Z_2) = E(Z_1)/E(Z_2)$. Hurwicz (1950) has shown that $\hat{\beta}$ is biased for any finite sample. In special cases, he has found that the bias might be as much as 25 percent of the true value of the parameter. For samples of about 20 observations, the bias can be about 10 percent.

Because the error term u_t is uncorrelated with all other us and with Y_{t-1}, by Property 3.2 $\hat{\beta}$ is consistent even though biased in small samples. In fact, as Rubin (1950) has shown, for the simple model in Equation (10.13), the consistency property holds even if $|\beta| \geq 1$. If the disturbance term u_t is also normally distributed, then large-sample tests are valid because standard errors can be estimated consistently. We thus have the following property.

Property 10.1

If lags of the dependent variable are present as regressors but the disturbance term u_t satisfies Assumptions 3.2 through 3.8, then

a. OLS estimates of the parameters will be biased in small samples but will be consistent and asymptotically efficient.

b. Estimates of residuals and standard errors are consistent, and hence the tests of hypotheses are valid for large samples. In small samples, however, tests are invalid.

● 10.3 Lagged Dependent Variables and Serial Correlation

Properties 10.1a and 10.1b do not hold if the disturbance term u_t depends on u_{t-1}, either as in Equation (10.4) (that is, the moving average form) or when u_t is serially correlated (that is, the autoregressive form). The combination of lagged dependent variables and serial correlation destroys the consistency property. Furthermore, the Durbin–Watson test for serial correlation is invalid. The DW value tends to be closer to 2 (when $\rho > 0$), and hence we may erroneously conclude that there is no serial correlation.

If $u_t = \rho u_{t-1} + \varepsilon_t$, then Cochrane–Orcutt and Hildreth–Lu procedures will give consistent estimates, but they will be biased in small samples. It can be shown (see Johnston, 1972, Section 10-3) that if the OLS procedure is used, the large-sample limits for the parameters are as follows:

$$\hat{\beta} \to \beta + \frac{\rho(1 - \beta^2)}{1 + \beta\rho}$$

$$\hat{\rho} \to \rho - \frac{\rho(1 - \beta^2)}{1 + \beta\rho}$$

$$d \to 2(1 - \rho) + \frac{2\rho(1 - \beta^2)}{1 + \beta\rho}$$

Therefore, even with a large sample, the OLS estimate $\hat{\beta}$ does not converge to the true value, the estimated autocorrelation coefficient does not converge to the true ρ, and the estimated Durbin–Watson statistic does not converge to $2(1 - \rho)$. We thus have the following property.

Property 10.2

If lags of the dependent variable are present as regressors, but the disturbance term u_t depends on u_{t-1}, u_{t-2}, and so on, then

a. OLS estimates of the parameters, and forecasts based on them, will be biased and inconsistent.

b. Estimates of residuals and standard errors will also be inconsistent, and hence hypotheses tests are no longer valid even for large samples.

c. The Durbin–Watson test for first-order serial correlation is no longer valid.

The Durbin *h*-Test

Durbin (1970) developed a large-sample test, the **Durbin *h*-test,** for first-order serial correlation when lagged dependent variables are present. The steps for the test are as follows:

Step 1 Estimate the model by OLS and obtain the residuals ($\hat{u}_t$).

Step 2 Estimate the first-order autocorrelation coefficient as

$$\hat{\rho} = \frac{\sum \hat{u}_t \hat{u}_{t-1}}{\sum \hat{u}_t^2}$$

or as $(2 - d)/2$, where d is the Durbin–Watson statistic.

Step 3 Construct the following statistic, known as the Durbin *h*-statistic ($n' = n - 1$, the number of observations used):

$$h = \hat{\rho}\left[\frac{n'}{1 - n's_{\hat{\beta}}^2}\right]^{1/2}$$

where $s_{\hat{\beta}}^2$ is the estimated variance of $\hat{\beta}$, the coefficient of Y_{t-1} in the model. In large samples, h has a normal distribution.

Step 4 Reject the null hypothesis of $\rho = 0$ against the alternative $\rho \neq 0$ when $h < -z^*$ or $h > z^*$, where z^* is the point on standard normal $N(0, 1)$

such that the area to the right is 2.5 percent (or 0.5 percent for a 1 percent test).

Breusch–Godfrey Lagrange Multiplier Test

Note that the Durbin h-test will fail if $n's_{\hat{\beta}}^2 > 1$ because then the denominator will be the square root of a negative number. Also, the Durbin h-test is not applicable when terms such as Y_{t-2}, Y_{t-3}, and so on are present, or when autocorrelation is of a higher order. A better alternative is to use the Breusch–Godfrey test LM procedure discussed in Section 9.5. The steps for the LM test are as follows:

Step 1   The model is assumed to be

$$Y_t = \beta_1 + \beta_2 Y_{t-1} + \beta_3 Y_{t-2} + \cdots + \beta_{p+1} Y_{t-p} + \beta_{p+2} X_t + \cdots + u_t$$

with the alternative error structure

$$u_t = \rho_1 u_{t-1} + \rho_2 u_{t-2} + \cdots + \rho_m u_{t-m} + \varepsilon_t$$

where p is the order of the lagged dependent variable and m is the order of the autoregressive error term (it is assumed that $p > m$). The null hypothesis is that $\rho_i = 0$ for $i = 1, 2, \ldots, m$, that is, that there is no autocorrelation among u_t.

Step 2   Estimate the model by OLS and obtain the residuals ($\hat{u}_t$).

Step 3   Regress $\hat{u}_t$ on $\hat{u}_{t-1}, \hat{u}_{t-2}, \ldots, \hat{u}_{t-m}$ and all the explanatory variables in the model, including the lagged dependent variables $Y_{t-1}, Y_{t-2}, \ldots, Y_{t-p}$, and obtain the unadjusted R^2.

Step 4   Compute $(n - p)R^2$ and reject H_0: all $\rho_i = 0$ against H_1: not all the ρs are zero, if it exceeds $\chi_m^2(a)$, the point on χ_m^2 such that the area to the right is a. ($n - p$ is used because the number of observations actually used is $n - p$.)

Although only X_t is used here, the procedure is easily extended to add X_{t-1}, X_{t-2}, . . . as explanatory variables.

The Breusch–Godfrey test can also be used to test whether lagged dependent variables should even be present. Suppose the model formulated is $Y_t = \alpha + \beta X_t + u_t$ and we want to test whether Y_{t-1}, Y_{t-2}, . . . should be included. The LM test for this is exactly the same as the test for adding new variables in the model (discussed in Section 6.14). The first step is to regress Y_t against a constant and X_t, and save the residual $\hat{u}_t$. Next regress $\hat{u}_t$ against a constant, X_t, Y_{t-1}, Y_{t-2}, . . . , and Y_{t-p}. As in Step 4, $(n - p)R^2$ is used as a test statistic.

An alternative to the Breusch–Godfrey test is to regress $\hat{u}_t$ against all the Xs, lagged Ys, and the lagged $\hat{u}$ variables and then carry out an F-test for the exclusion of the lagged $\hat{u}$ variables.

● EXAMPLE 10.4

In Example 10.2 we used DATA10-2 and related the electricity usage at a given time of day to its one-period lag and to the concurrent temperature. With hourly data one can expect serial correlation of order more than one. Here we apply the Breusch–Godfrey test for sixth-order autocorrelation (see Practice Computer Session 10.3 for details on implementing this). The first step is to estimate by OLS the linear regression model

$$\text{load}_t = \beta_1 + \beta_2 \text{load}_{t-1} + \beta_3 \text{temp}_t + u_t$$

The auxiliary regression consists of regressing the residuals from this equation against the variables in it plus the lagged residuals for lags 1 through 6. The LM test statistic for this is 583.299. Under the null hypothesis that there is no serial correlation, this has the chi-square distribution with 6 d.f. The p-value for it is less than 0.0001, indicating strong serial correlation of the sixth order. This means that OLS estimates are biased and inconsistent. In the next section, we address the issue of the appropriate estimation procedure in this situation.

10.4   Estimation of Models with Lagged Dependent Variables

Several procedures are available to estimate models involving lagged dependent variables. The method used depends on the properties of the random disturbance terms.

A Model with "White Noise" Error Terms

As mentioned in Chapter 3, if the disturbance terms (u_t) satisfy Assumptions 3.2 through 3.8, they are often referred to as **well-behaved error** terms (or more commonly as **white noise**). Consider the model

$$Y_t = \beta_1 + \beta_2 Y_{t-1} + \beta_3 X_t + u_t \qquad (10.14)$$

with white noise errors. We have seen that the partial adjustment model leads to an equation of this form. As stated in Property 10.1, the OLS procedure gives consistent and asymptotically efficient estimates of the parameters and their standard errors. Furthermore, tests of hypotheses are valid for large samples. Hence, OLS is applicable, provided the sample size is large enough (usually over 30 d.f.). Small-sample bias will, however, persist, and we cannot get estimates that are BLUE. It should be pointed out that the Durbin–Watson statistic printed by regression packages should not be used to test for serial correlation. Either the Durbin h-test or, preferably, the Breusch–Godfrey test described in the previous section should be applied.

A Model with Autocorrelated Disturbances

If the error terms follow the AR(1) process, the model is of the form

$$Y_t = \beta_1 + \beta_2 Y_{t-1} + \beta_3 X_t + u_t \qquad (10.15)$$

$$u_t = \rho u_{t-1} + \varepsilon_t \qquad (10.16)$$

where the new error term ε_t is assumed to be white noise. We know from Property 10.2 that because u_t depends on u_{t-1}, Y_{t-1} and u_t are directly correlated, and hence applying the OLS procedure to (10.15) will lead to biased and inconsistent estimates. The Cochrane–Orcutt (CORC) procedure is, however, applicable here with a slight modification. The steps are as follows:

Step 1   Estimate the parameters β_1, β_2, and β_3 by OLS and save the residuals $\hat{u}_t = Y_t - \hat{\beta}_1 - \hat{\beta}_2 Y_{t-1} - \hat{\beta}_3 X_t$.

Step 2   Regress $\hat{u}_t$ against $\hat{u}_{t-1}$ (using observations 2 through n) and obtain $\hat{\rho}$.

Step 3   Transform the variables as follows: $Y_t^* = Y_t - \hat{\rho} Y_{t-1}$, $Y_{t-1}^* = Y_{t-1} - \hat{\rho} Y_{t-2}$, and $X_t^* = X_t - \hat{\rho} X_{t-1}$.

Step 4   Regress Y_t^* against a constant, Y_{t-1}^*, and X_{t-1}^*, (using observations 3 through n because Y_t^* is defined only from period 3 onward).

Step 5   Using the estimates of the βs obtained from Step 4, compute a second-round set of residuals $\hat{u}_t$. Next go back to Step 2 and iterate until successive $\hat{\rho}$ estimates do not differ by more than some desired value.

These five steps are identical to those for the CORC method. Although these estimates are consistent even in the presence of lagged dependent variables and autocorrelated errors, the standard errors obtained from that procedure are inconsistent. Consistent standard errors may be obtained by carrying out a final step.

Step 6   Use the final estimates of the βs from Step 4 and compute the residuals of the transformed model; that is, obtain $\hat{\varepsilon}_t$. Next regress $\hat{\varepsilon}_t$ against a constant, Y_{t-1}^*, X_t^*, and $\hat{u}_{t-1}$ (not $\hat{\varepsilon}_{t-1}$). The standard errors of the regression coefficients and that of $\hat{\rho}$ obtained from this step are consistent.

Further details on this technique may be found in Harvey (1990).

A Model with Moving Average Error Terms

In Equations (10.4) and (10.10), the error term was of the form $u_t - \lambda u_{t-1}$, where λ is the adjustment coefficient $(0 < \lambda < 1)$. Such an error term is called a **moving average (MA) error.** It is clear that because Y_{t-1} and u_{t-1} are correlated, OLS estimates will be biased and inconsistent. In this case, we may proceed as follows. First, we reproduce Equation (10.10):

$$Y_t = \alpha\lambda + (1 - \lambda) Y_{t-1} + \lambda\beta X_{t-1} + [u_t - (1 - \lambda) u_{t-1}] \qquad \textbf{(10.17)}$$

Next we define $W_t = Y_t - u_t$. It follows from this that

$$W_t - (1 - \lambda) W_{t-1} = (Y_t - u_t) - (1 - \lambda)(Y_{t-1} - u_{t-1}) \qquad \textbf{(10.18)}$$
$$= Y_t - (1 - \lambda) Y_{t-1} - [u_t - (1 - \lambda) u_{t-1}]$$
$$= \alpha\lambda + \lambda\beta X_{t-1} = \beta_0 + \beta_1 X_{t-1}$$

where $\beta_0 = \alpha\lambda$ and $\beta_1 = \lambda\beta$. We thus have

$$W_t = (1 - \lambda) W_{t-1} + \beta_0 + \beta_1 X_{t-1}$$

By repeated substitution for W_{t-1}, W_{t-2}, and so on, and by setting $\gamma = 1 - \lambda$, we get

$$W_t = \gamma^t W_0 + \beta_0(1 + \gamma + \gamma^2 + \cdots + \gamma^{t-1}) + \beta_1(X_{t-1} + \gamma X_{t-2} + \cdots + \gamma^{t-2} X_1) \tag{10.19}$$

$$= \gamma^t W_0 + \beta_0 \frac{1 - \gamma^t}{1 - \gamma} + \beta_1 Z_t$$

where

$$Z_t = X_{t-1} + \gamma X_{t-2} + \cdots + \gamma^{t-2} X_1$$

Because $W_t = Y_t - u_t$, Equation (10.19) can be rewritten as

$$Y_t = W_t + u_t = \gamma^t W_0 + \beta_0 \frac{1 - \gamma^t}{1 - \gamma} + \beta_1 Z_t + u_t \tag{10.20}$$

$$= \alpha_0 + \alpha_1 \gamma^t + \beta_1 Z_t + u_t$$

where

$$\alpha_0 = \frac{\beta_0}{1 - \gamma} \quad \text{and} \quad \alpha_1 = W_0 - \frac{\beta_0}{1 - \gamma}$$

Because γ lies between 0 and 1 (by assumption), we can use a search procedure similar to that used by Hildreth and Lu. Fix values of γ (at 0.05 or 0.01 intervals from 0 to 1) and for each γ, estimate Equation (10.20) by regressing Y_t against a constant, γ^t, and Z_t. Pick the value of γ for which the error sum of squares of (10.20) is minimum, and obtain the full estimates for that γ.

Several other procedures are available but are not presented here. The reader is referred to Johnston (1984), Kmenta (1986), and Greene (1997).

● PRACTICE PROBLEM 10.6

Show that if u_t is autoregressive, with the special form $u_t = (1 - \lambda) u_{t-1} + \varepsilon_t$, where ε_t is white noise, then the OLS estimates of the parameters in Equation (10.17) will be consistent. Explain why you cannot assert that the estimates are also BLUE. Carefully justify your answers, giving references to assumptions and properties listed in earlier chapters.

Empirical Example: Inflation and the Savings Rate

It has been frequently observed that high rates of inflation and high rates of personal savings are closely related. Davidson and MacKinnon (1983) examined two competing theories on the effect of inflation on the savings rate. The first states that when the rate of inflation increases, interest payments also increase so as to compensate asset holders for the loss in real value of assets. Consumers wishing to maintain the real value of their wealth will refrain from increasing consumption, even though measured income has gone up, because the increase in income is simply an inflation premium. Observed savings will therefore go up. Thus, measured savings and income tend to overestimate real savings and real income. A second theory argues that when inflation is unanticipated, consumers will reduce consumption demand, which thus results in increased involuntary savings.

Davidson and MacKinnon have constructed an econometric model that incorporates both of these theories and have estimated it separately for the United States and Canada. They used quarterly data for 1954.1 and 1979.4. The basic model is as follows (for the theory behind this equation refer to the Davidson–MacKinnon paper):

$$\frac{S_t}{Y_t} = a_0 + (1 - a_0)\alpha\frac{Z_t}{Y_t} + b_1\left[\frac{S_{t-1} - Y_{t-1}}{Y_t}\right] + d_1 \ln\left[\frac{Y_t}{Y_{t-1}}\right] + d_2\pi_t + u_t$$

where S_t is real savings, Y_t is real disposable income, π_t is the inflation rate, and Z_t is the loss in real value of wealth due to inflation. Z_t is measured as $\pi_t I_t / r_t$, where I_t is the real value of interest and dividend payments, and r_t is the nominal rate of interest.

⬤ **Table 10.2   Estimates of the Davidson–MacKinnon Models**

	United States			Canada		
	IIa	**IIb**	**IIab**	**Ia**	**Ib**	**Iab**
a_0 or b_0	0.6476	0.6728	0.6310	0.2485	0.4861	0.2976
	(0.0452)	(0.0650)	(0.0662)	(0.0437)	(0.0785)	(0.0830)
b_1	0.6387	0.6669	0.6209	0.2179	0.4594	0.2690
	(0.0464)	(0.0670)	(0.0686)	(0.0453)	(0.0820)	(0.0859)
α	0.3935	—	0.2708	0.5339	—	0.5909
	(0.1019)		(0.1230)	(0.0722)		(0.1151)
d_2	—	0.7202	0.3223	—	0.8077	−0.1641
		(0.1503)	(0.2296)		(0.2127)	(0.2932)
d_1	—	0.0228	0.0528	—	−0.2603	−0.0683
		(0.0534)	(0.0539)		(0.0882)	(0.0910)
Coefficient on t	−0.1721	−0.1541	−0.1911	−0.3550	−0.3535	−0.3264
($\times$ 1,000)	(0.0412)	(0.0398)	(0.0423)	(0.1716)	(0.1938)	(0.1755)
Coefficient on t^2	—	—	—	0.4036	0.4230	0.3722
($\times$ 100,000)				(0.1368)	(0.1584)	(−0.1438)
Coefficient on	0.1828	0.2178	0.1894	—	—	—
S_{t-2}/Y_t	(0.0617)	(0.0617)	(0.0617)			
log L	380.04	378.95	381.88	343.92	333.65	344.65
Standard error	0.00673	0.00684	0.00669	0.00986	0.01095	0.00991
AR(1)	0.92143	0.4193	0.5968	0.9490	0.0128	0.2727
	(+)	(+)	(−)	(+)	(−)	(−)
AR(4)	0.0382	0.0286	0.0201	0.5923	0.8144	0.4497
	(−)	(−)	(−)	(−)	(−)	(−)
AR(1, 2, 3, 4)	0.2339	0.1982	0.1444	0.7504	0.1495	0.6214
	(− − − −)	(+ − − −)	(− − − −)	(+ + + −)	(− − + −)	(− + + −)

Source: Davidson and MacKinnon, 1983. Reprinted with the permission of Chapman and Hall, Ltd.

If the overmeasurment hypothesis holds, we would expect α to be between zero and 1. If the involuntary savings hypothesis is true, d_1 and d_2 should both be positive. Davidson and MacKinnon estimated the model along with a variety of modifications, including seasonal dummies, time trends, and their powers. Table 10.2 presents estimates of the various models with standard errors in parentheses. The results do not support the theory that unanticipated inflation leads to involuntary savings (for both Canada and the United States). There is, however, tentative support for the first theory, that inflation leads to higher measured savings rates. Davidson and MacKinnon also tested the model for the presence of serial correlation of orders up to 4. Although they found some serial correlation, the models were not reestimated with the more general method presented in Chapter 9.

● 10.5 Application: A Dynamic Model of Consumption Expenditures in the United Kingdom

In this walk-through application, we reexamine the United Kingdom consumption function estimated in Chapter 6 (see Example 6.4) using the techniques learned in this chapter. Three alternative formulations are used, the first being the following static model:

$$\text{(Model A)} \qquad C_t = \alpha + \beta DI_t + u_t$$

Using the data in DATA6-3, the model was estimated by OLS (see Practice Computer Session 10.4 for details on reproducing this application). The DW statistic was 0.25, and it is easy to verify that it is very significant. We therefore used the AR(1) specification for the error term, $u_t = \rho u_{t-1} + \varepsilon_t$. As was seen in Section 9.4, the static model with an AR(1) specification is a special case of the following model:

$$\text{(Model B)} \qquad C_t = \beta_1 + \beta_2 C_{t-1} + \beta_3 DI_t + \beta_4 DI_{t-1} + v_t$$

with the restriction $\beta_4 + \beta_2\beta_3 = 0$. We estimated Model B by OLS and the restricted model by the mixed Hildreth–Lu and Cochrane–Orcutt procedure. A likelihood ratio test (see Section 6.A.1) was then conducted (see Practice Computer Session 10.4 for the steps), the test statistic being

$$\text{LR} = -n \ln(\hat{\sigma}^2/\tilde{\sigma}^2) = n \ln(\text{ESS}_R/\text{ESS}_U)$$

where $\hat{\sigma}^2$ is the estimated error variance for the unrestricted model, $\tilde{\sigma}^2$ is the same for the restricted model, and ESS refers to the error sum of squares of the restricted (R) and unrestricted (U) models. Under the null hypothesis that AR(1) is a special case of Model B, the LR statistic has the chi-square distribution with 1 d.f. Its p-value was 0.006, which indicates that we reject the null hypothesis at less than 1 percent. Thus, Model B is appropriate, and not Model A with AR(1) error terms. Model B was then tested for the presence of first-order autocorrelation. The LM test indicated the absence of AR(1) for Model B.

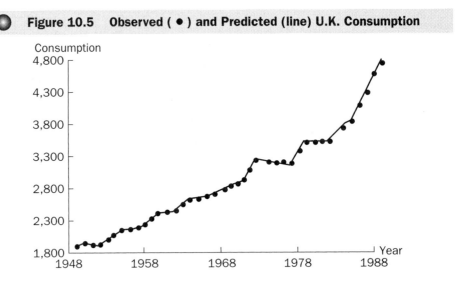

Figure 10.5   Observed (•) and Predicted (line) U.K. Consumption

In Example 6.4, we used the following model for the consumption function:

$$\text{(Model C)} \qquad C_t = \gamma_1 + \gamma_2 C_{t-1} + \gamma_3 (DI_t - DI_{t-1}) + w_t$$

which is another special case of Model B, with the restriction $\beta_4 + \beta_3 = 0$. This restriction can be tested using the Wald F-test described in Chapter 4. The Wald F-statistic was 0.229, with a p-value of 0.635, which is insignificant. Therefore, we cannot reject the restriction. Thus, Model C, which is more parsimonious than Model B, is preferable, provided the model selection statistics confirm that. All eight of the selection statistics were indeed the lowest for Model C. Also, an LM test for AR(1) for Model C did not indicate the presence of serial correlation. Finally, as can be seen in Figure 10.5 in which the observed and predicted consumption expenditures are plotted, Model C tracks consumption patterns extremely well.

10.6   Application: Hourly Electricity Load Model Revisited

In Example 10.4, we used DATA10-2 and estimated an hourly electricity load model using the lagged dependent variable as an explanatory variable and found significant serial correlation of the sixth order. Because we are dealing with hourly data, one might suspect that the error at time t might be correlated with the error 24 hours prior to that. Thus, an AR(24) error structure might be more appropriate. Here we first carried out an LM test for an AR(24) error structure. Practice Computer Session 10.5a has the details for obtaining the relevant computer printout. The first step is to regress load at time t against a constant, load at time $t - 1$, and the temperature at time t, and save the residuals ($\hat{u}_t$). Next regress $\hat{u}_t$ against these variables and the lags $\hat{u}_{t-1}$ through $\hat{u}_{t-24}$. The LM statistic was 657.6, with a p-value less than 0.0001, indicating extreme serial correlation. In the auxiliary regression,

13 of the 24 lags were significant (at the 10 percent level), including those for 21, 23, and 24. It is therefore clear that we should use the generalized Cochrane–Orcutt procedure to estimate the model. This was done in Practice Computer Session 10.5b. Because many of the AR terms were insignificant, they were eliminated so that a parsimonious model with more efficient estimates might be obtained. In the final model, the significant AR coefficients were for the lags 1, 2, 5, 7, 9, 12, 13, 14, 15, 17, 19, 21, 22, 23, and 24. The estimated model is given next.

$$\widehat{\text{load}}_t = 242.858 + 0.941 \, \text{load}_{t-1} - 1.966 \, \text{temp}_t$$

All the p-values were less than 0.0001, and the square of the correlation between the observed load and that predicted, after incorporating the AR terms for the residuals, was 0.987. The mean lag is given by $0.941/(1 - 0.941) = 15.9$, and the long-run multiplier for temperature is $-1.966/(1 - 0.941) = -33.3$. In Fig. 10.6, the actual and predicted hourly loads have been plotted for two of the sample days: January 3 and January 18. For January 3, the model tracks the actual loads quite well except for the evening peak hour. For January 18, the fit is not as good. The overall summary statistics for prediction error indicate that only 24 of the 719 observations $(744 - 25)$ had prediction errors above 5 percent and only one of the observations had a prediction error of about 10 percent. The mean absolute percent error was 1.49. Thus, even the simple model used in this example approximates real behavior quite well. Other improvements to the model would make the approximation even better. For instance, we could introduce dummy variables for weekends because behavior is likely to be different for weekdays. Other enhancements would be to introduce nonlinearities in temperature and to allow for more lags in temperature. For an elaborate analysis of this data set, see the paper by Ramanathan, Engle, Granger, Vahid-Araghi, and Brace (1997).

● 10.7 Unit Roots and the Dickey–Fuller Tests

In a model with a lagged dependent variable (such as the ones in Applications 10.5 and 10.6), we assumed that the coefficient for it was less than 1 in absolute value. This was to avoid explosive behavior. In some situations, the coefficient might be exactly 1. The simplest of this class of models is the **random walk model,** given by $Y_t = Y_{t-1} + u_t$. This means that the value at time t is equal to its value in the previous period plus a random shock. Equivalently, the change in value from one period to the next is a pure white noise random variable. Hourly stock prices have often been shown to follow the random walk model. Note that, in this case, $\text{Var}(Y_t) = \text{Var}(Y_{t-1}) + \text{Var}(u_t)$. By repeated substitutions, we readily see that the variance of Y_t goes to infinity as t goes to infinity. This situation is known as the **unit root** problem. If we ignore the unit root and estimate the model as $Y_t = \rho Y_{t-1} + u_t$, then it can be shown that the distribution of the OLS estimator of ρ is not centered at 1 and the corresponding t-statistic does not have the Student's t-distribution (see Dickey and Fuller, 1979, 1981). Therefore, the usual t-test for $\rho = 1$ does not apply. In this section, we study the tests for unit roots (familiarly known as the **Dickey–Fuller tests**) for a number of different model specifications.

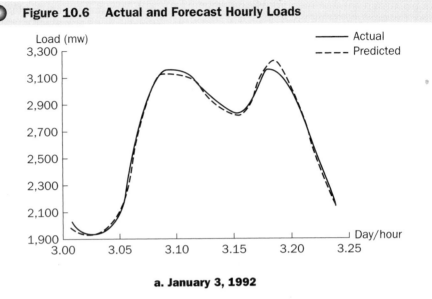

Figure 10.6   Actual and Forecast Hourly Loads

a. January 3, 1992

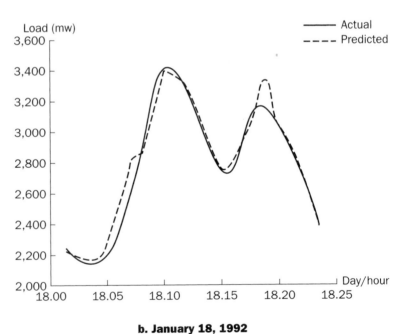

b. January 18, 1992

First consider the basic autoregressive model $Y_t = \alpha + \rho Y_{t-1} + u_t$. The error terms, u_t, are assumed to be white noise, conditional on past Ys, and the first observation, Y_1, is assumed to be fixed. The actual test for a unit root is carried out for a slightly modified model. By subtracting Y_{t-1} from both sides of the equation, we can rewrite the model as follows:

$$\Delta Y_t = \alpha + \lambda Y_{t-1} + u_t$$

where $\lambda = \rho - 1$. We readily see that the unit root test is equivalent to testing $\lambda = 0$, that is, that there exists a unit root. The standard t-statistic for $\hat{\lambda}$ can be used to test $\lambda = 0$, but with the Dickey–Fuller critical values presented in Table 10.3.

We saw in Chapter 9 that if the errors u_t are serially correlated, the model can be transformed to one with a lagged dependent variable (see Equation 9.1a in Section 9.4). This notion can be generalized to any number of terms. Thus, a general form that captures the preceding model as a special case is

$$\Delta Y_t = \alpha + \lambda Y_{t-1} + \sum_{i=1}^{p} \theta_i \Delta Y_{t-i} + u_t \tag{10.21}$$

This formulation is used to allow for serial correlation in ΔY_t. The unit root test for $\lambda = 0$ for this extended model is known as the **augmented Dickey–Fuller test (ADF).** The specific steps for this test are given below.

Step 1 $H_0: \lambda = 0$ (or $\rho = 1$) $H_1: \lambda < 0$ (or $\rho < 1$)
The null hypothesis is that there is a unit root. The alternative $\rho > 1$ is not considered because that will make the model explosive, which is unlikely in one involving economic time series.

⬤ **Table 10.3   Critical Values for the Dickey–Fuller t-Statistics**

	Probability to the Right of Critical Value							
Sample Size	0.99	0.975	0.95	0.90	0.10	0.05	0.025	0.01
	Testing $\lambda = 0$ in the model $\Delta Y_t = \alpha + \lambda Y_{t-1} + \sum_{i=1}^{p} \theta_i \Delta Y_{t-i} + u_t$							
25	−3.75	−3.33	−3.00	−2.62	−0.37	0.00	0.34	0.72
50	−3.58	−3.22	−2.93	−2.60	−0.40	−0.03	0.29	0.66
100	−3.51	−3.17	−2.89	−2.58	−0.42	−0.05	0.26	0.63
250	−3.46	−3.14	−2.88	−2.57	−0.42	−0.06	0.24	0.62
500	−3.44	−3.13	−2.87	−2.57	−0.43	−0.07	0.24	0.61
∞	−3.43	−3.12	−2.86	−2.57	−0.44	−0.07	0.23	0.60
	Testing $\lambda = 0$ in the model $\Delta Y_t = \alpha + \beta t + \lambda Y_{t-1} + \sum_{i=i}^{p} \theta_i \Delta Y_{t-1} + u_t$							
25	−4.38	−3.95	−3.60	−3.24	−1.14	−0.80	−0.50	−0.15
50	−4.15	−3.80	−3.50	−3.18	−1.19	−0.87	−0.58	−0.24
100	−4.04	−3.73	−3.45	−3.15	−1.22	−0.90	−0.62	−0.28
250	−3.99	−3.69	−3.43	−3.13	−1.23	−0.92	−0.64	−0.31
500	−3.98	−3.68	−3.42	−3.13	−1.24	−0.93	−0.65	−0.32
∞	−3.96	−3.66	−3.41	−3.12	−1.25	−0.94	−0.66	−0.33

Source: Fuller (1976), Table 8.5.2. Reproduced with permission from the publishers.

Step 2   Regress ΔY_t against a constant, Y_{t-1}, ΔY_{t-1}, ΔY_{t-2}, . . . , and ΔY_{t-p}. Note that because ΔY_{t-p} ($= Y_{t-p} - Y_{t-p-1}$) is defined only for the observation range $p+2$ to n, we will lose the first $p+1$ observations. Next, compute the t-statistic (t_c) for Y_{t-1} in the usual way, that is, by dividing $\hat{\lambda}$ by the corresponding estimated standard error.

Step 3   Reject the null hypothesis if $t_c < t^*$, where t^* is one of the negative critical values in Table 10.3 that corresponds to the sample size and the chosen probability. For example, for a 10 percent test with $n = 100$, choose 0.90 as the probability to the right of t^* and note that $t^* = -2.58$. The reason for the negative critical value is that we are using the left-tail of the t-distribution because the alternative hypothesis is $\lambda < 0$.

Many economic time series exhibit growth indicating some kind of underlying trend. The modified model for testing a unit root in the presence of a linear trend is

$$\Delta Y_t = \alpha + \beta t + \lambda Y_{t-1} + \sum_{i=1}^{p} \theta_i \Delta Y_{t-1} + u_t \qquad \textbf{(10.21a)}$$

Table 10.3 also has the Dickey–Fuller critical values for testing $\lambda = 0$ in this case. The steps are the same, except that in Step 2, the linear time trend variable t is included as another explanatory variable.

If Y_t grows exponentially (for example, as in the case of population, gross domestic product, money supply, aggregate consumption expenditures, and so on), then it is of the form $\exp(\beta t)$ and hence the linear trend is not appropriate. In this case, we should first take the logarithm and then use a model of the form in (10.21a), substituting $\ln(Y_t)$ wherever Y_t appears.

What should one do if the evidence suggests that there is a unit root creating the infinite variance problem discussed earlier? Note that if $Y_t = \alpha + Y_{t-1} + u_t$, with a white noise u_t, then the first difference of it, namely, ΔY_t, equals $Y_t - Y_{t-1} = \alpha + u_t$, which has a finite variance. Thus, the solution is to difference the series and perhaps test the differenced series for a unit root.

Dickey and Fuller (1981) also proposed a test for the joint hypothesis $\beta = 0$ and $\lambda = 0$ that implies a unit root and no linear trend. The augmented Dickey–Fuller test consists of estimating the unrestricted model in Equation (10.21a) and the restricted model

$$\Delta Y_t = \alpha + \sum_{i=1}^{i=p} \theta_i \Delta Y_{t-i} + u_t$$

and then constructing the usual F-statistic

$$F_c = \frac{(\text{ESSR} - \text{ESSU})/2}{\text{ESSU}/(n-k)}$$

where ESSR and ESSU are the sum of squared residuals for the restricted and unrestricted models, n is the number of observations used in the unrestricted model (Equation 10.21), and k is the number of parameters estimated in the unrestricted

Table 10.4 Critical Values for the Augmented Dickey–Fuller Test

Sample Size (n)	Probability to the Right of Critical Value							
	0.99	0.975	0.95	0.90	0.10	0.05	0.025	0.01
25	0.74	0.90	1.08	1.33	5.91	7.24	8.65	10.61
50	0.76	0.93	1.11	1.37	5.61	6.73	7.81	9.31
100	0.76	0.94	1.12	1.38	5.47	6.49	7.44	8.73
250	0.76	0.94	1.13	1.39	5.39	6.34	7.25	8.43
500	0.76	0.94	1.13	1.39	5.36	6.30	7.20	8.34
∞	0.77	0.94	1.13	1.39	5.34	6.25	7.16	8.27

Source: Dickey and Fuller (1981). Reprinted with the permission of the Econometric Society.

model ($p + 3$ in Equation 10.21a). The usual F-test is, however, not applicable here because, when $\rho = 1$, F_c does not have the well-known F-distribution. Dickey and Fuller have derived the distribution of F_c when $\rho = 1$ and tabulated the critical values (see Table 10.4) for it. It is easily verified that the critical values in Table 10.4 are much higher than those in the standard F table. This implies that a test statistic rejected by the standard F-test may not be rejected by the Dickey–Fuller test. In other words, the standard F-test might lead one to conclude that no unit root exists when in fact there might be a unit root (for example, the model might be a random walk).

● **EXAMPLE 10.5**

DATA9-2 has annual data ($n = 36$) for the United States on the aggregate money supply (M), measured in billions of dollars. As you can see from Figure 10.7, it appears to exhibit an exponential trend that calls for the logarithmic transformation. The steps for carrying out the augmented Dickey–Fuller tests for the unit root in M are as follows (see Practice Computer Session 10.6 for the empirical steps).

Step 1 Generate the variables $Y_t = \ln(M_t)$, $DY_t = \ln(M_t) - \ln(M_{t-1})$, $Y1_t = Y_{t-1}$, and $DY1_t = DY_{t-1} = \ln(M_{t-1}) - \ln(M_{t-2})$.

Step 2 Regress DY_t against a constant, time (t), $Y1_t$, and $DY1_t$, after suppressing the first two observations (explain why). This is the unrestricted model (U).

Step 3 For the Dickey–Fuller t-test for the null hypothesis that the coefficient for $Y_{t-1} = 0$, compute its t-statistic (t_c). We see from Table 10.3 that, for a 10 percent test, the critical t^* is between -3.24 and -3.18. For our data set, $t_c = -0.104 > t^*$, and hence we cannot reject the null hypothesis that a unit root exists. This suggests that we may have to difference the series one more time. (As an exercise, carry out the conventional t-test. Is there a contradiction?)

Figure 10.7　U.S. Money Supply in Billions of Current Dollars

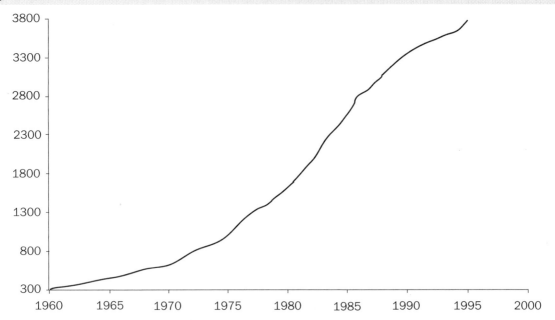

> **Step 4**　For the Dickey–Fuller F-test, the null hypothesis is that the coefficient for both t and Y_{t-1} is zero. To do this, regress DY_t against a constant and $DY1$. This is the restricted model (R). Compute the F-statistic (F_c) shown earlier. From Table 10.4 we see that the critical F^* for a 10 percent test is between 5.61 and 5.91. The actual F_c is 1.372. Since this is not greater than F^*, we cannot reject the joint null hypothesis of a unit root and no linear trend. (Here again, carry out a conventional F-test).

EXAMPLE 10.6

DATA10-3 has monthly data on the exchange rate of deutsche marks per dollar ($n = 157$), which is graphed in Fig. 10.8. To check for a unit root in the exchange rate, we obtained the following estimated model (see Practice Computer Session 10.7):

$$\widehat{\Delta EXCHRATE}_t = 0.074 - 0.0318\, EXCHRATE_{t-1} + 0.3002\, \Delta EXCHRATE_{t-1}$$

The t-statistic for $EXCHRATE_{t-1}$ is -2.042. Note from Table 10.3 that even for a 10 percent test (which corresponds to the column for 0.90 probability), the critical value (t^*) is between -2.58 and -2.57, which is less than $t_c = -2.042$. Therefore, we cannot reject the null hypothesis of the existence of a unit root. It is easy to verify that the conventional t-test would show that the coefficient for $EXCHRATE_{t-1}$ is significant at 5 percent, thus rejecting the null hypothesis of a unit root. In other

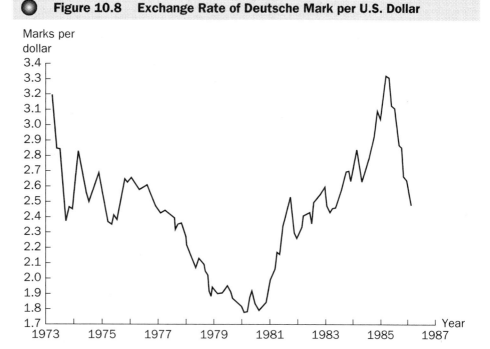

Figure 10.8   Exchange Rate of Deutsche Mark per U.S. Dollar

words, the standard t-test would lead one to conclude that a unit root may not exist when in fact it does.

10.8   Error Correction Models (ECM)

The partial adjustment mechanism is a way of allowing for adjustment costs and/or incomplete information. In recent years, another class of distributed lag models, known as **error correction models,** have gained popularity. The principle behind these models is that there often exists a long-run equilibrium relationship between two economic variables (for example, consumption and income, wages and prices, and so on). In the short run, however, there may be disequilibrium. With the error correction mechanism, a proportion of the disequilibrium in one period is corrected in the next period. For instance, the change in price in one period may depend on the excess demand in the previous period. The error correction process is thus a means to reconcile short-run and long-run behavior. Notable contributions in this area have been made by Sargan (1964), Davidson, Hendry, Srba, and Yeo (1978), Currie (1981), Dawson (1981), Salmon (1982), Hendry (1984), and Engle and Granger (1987), among others. In this section we develop the econometric framework for error correction models and illustrate it with an empirical example.

Suppose that the long-run relation between Y_t and X_t is of the form

$$Y_t = KX_t \qquad (10.22)$$

where K is a fixed constant. As an example, Friedman (1957) formulated the "permanent income hypothesis," which states that consumption (Y_t) is proportional to "permanent income" (X_t). He approximated permanent income by a distributed lag process. Another example is the "life-cycle hypothesis" (see Ando and Modigliani, 1963), which argues that, in the long run, consumption is a constant fraction of wealth. As another example, wages and prices might have nearly equal long-run growth rates, although in the short run their rates of growth might diverge.

Taking logarithms of both sides of Equation (10.22), we obtain

$$\ln Y_t = \ln K + \ln X_t \quad \text{or} \quad y_t = k + x_t \qquad (10.23)$$

where the lowercase letters are used to denote logarithms. Because $y_{t-1} = k + x_{t-1}$, we have

$$\Delta y_t = \Delta x_t \qquad (10.24)$$

where Δ denotes the change in a variable from period $t - 1$ to t. A general short-run model with lagged adjustment is of the following form:

$$y_t = \beta_0 + \beta_1 x_t + \beta_2 x_{t-1} + \alpha_1 y_{t-1} + u_t \qquad (10.25)$$

Under what conditions will the short-run model be consistent with the long-run model? To examine this question, let $y_t = y^*$ and $x_t = x^*$ for all t. Equation (10.25) now becomes (setting $u_t = 0$ in the long run)

$$y^*(1 - \alpha_1) = \beta_0 + (\beta_1 + \beta_2)x^*$$

For this to be compatible with Equation (10.23), we need the condition

$$1 - \alpha_1 = \beta_1 + \beta_2$$

which will give $y^* = k^* + x^*$, where $k^* = \beta_0/(1 - \alpha_1)$. Suppose $1 - \alpha_1 = \gamma = \beta_1 + \beta_2$. Then $\alpha_1 = 1 - \gamma$ and $\beta_2 = \gamma - \beta_1$. Substituting these in (10.25), we get

$$y_t = \beta_0 + \beta_1 x_t + (\gamma - \beta_1)x_{t-1} + (1 - \gamma)y_{t-1} + u_t$$

or

$$y_t - y_{t-1} = \beta_0 + \beta_1(x_t - x_{t-1}) + \gamma(x_{t-1} - y_{t-1}) + u_t$$

That is,

$$\Delta y_t = \beta_0 + \beta_1 \Delta x_t + \gamma(x_{t-1} - y_{t-1}) + u_t \qquad (10.26)$$

Equation (10.26) is the structure of the simplest error correction model. It relates the change in one variable to the change in another variable plus the gap between the two variables in the previous period. It is important to note that the equation captures the short-run adjustment, but at the same time, it is guided by long-run theory. The term $x_{t-1} - y_{t-1}$ provides the short-run disequilibrium adjustment. A test on γ is therefore a test for this disequilibrium component.

The general specification of the error correction model is as follows:

$$\Delta y_t = \beta_0 + \beta_1 \Delta x_t + \gamma_1 x_{t-1} + \gamma_2 y_{t-1} + u_t \tag{10.26a}$$

The steps for estimating this relationship are:

Step 1   Generate the variables $y_t = \ln(Y_t)$, $x_t = \ln(X_t)$, $\Delta y_t = y_t - y_{t-1}$, and $\Delta x_t = x_t - x_{t-1}$.

Step 2   Regress Δy_t against a constant, Δx_t, x_{t-1}, and y_{t-1}.

Note that the general formulation does not assume that $\gamma_2 = -\gamma_1$; in fact, we can test for it. A test on γ_1 and γ_2 is therefore a test for the disequilibrium adjustment term. The most general version of the error correction model has a second equation relating changes in x_t to those in y_t and lagged values. We thus have

$$\Delta x_t = \pi_0 + \pi_1 \Delta y_t + \theta_1 x_{t-1} + \theta_2 y_{t-1} + v_t \tag{10.26b}$$

The error correction framework described in this section is very closely related to the concept of *cointegration* introduced by Granger (1981) and developed in detail by Engle and Granger (1987). This topic is discussed in Section 10.10.

Empirical Example: Wages and Prices in the United Kingdom

Although Phillips (1954) introduced the error correction model, Sargan was the earliest to adopt the approach (1964). In a study of the relationship between wages and prices in the United Kingdom, he formulated a large variety of models, several of which had the error correction formulation. Here we present only a few selected models. You are encouraged to read the original article as well as the other papers previously cited.

Using quarterly data, Sargan estimated the following model (values in parentheses are *t*-statistics):

$$\widehat{w_t - w_{t-1}} = \underset{(-0.058)}{-0.005}(p_{t-1} - p_{t-4}) - \underset{(-2.234)}{0.0143}U_{t-1} - \underset{(-2.904)}{0.395}(w_{t-1} - p_{t-1})$$

$$+ \underset{(1.149)}{0.00085}F_t + \underset{(3.216)}{0.00119}t$$

where w_t is the logarithm of a wage index, p is the logarithm of a price index, U is the logarithm of the unemployment rate, and F is a dummy variable (which took the value 0 up to the fourth quarter of 1951 and 1 thereafter, to incorporate a wage freeze in the earlier period). The model included a time trend to capture the fact that relative wages have been growing over time because of technical progress. The dependent variable is the rate of change of the wage rate (because it is the change in logarithms). Sargan used the rate of change in prices over a whole year rather than over one quarter. The term $w_{t-1} - p_{t-1}$ is the error correction disequilibrium adjustment discussed earlier. The unemployment term captures the business cycle effect. In periods of high unemployment we would not expect wages to rise much.

We note that the rate of price change and the wage freeze factor are insignificant, but the error correction term is significant. When insignificant terms were omitted, the estimated model became the following:

$$\widehat{w_t - w_{t-1}} = \underset{(-2.069)}{-0.0120 U_{t-1}} - \underset{(-3.712)}{0.271\,(w_{t-1} - p_{t-1})} + \underset{(3.694)}{0.00133 t}$$

The significance of the disequilibrium adjustment term is higher. As can be expected, when unemployment rises, wages tend to grow more slowly. Similarly, a rise in real wages reduces the rate of growth of wages. A rise in productivity would cause the wage rate to grow faster. Sargan tried other variations, including longer lags for the explanatory variables, real profits instead of the time trend, and so on. From one of these models, Sargan estimated that the average lag for prices was 4.02 quarters and the mean lag for unemployment was 7.02 quarters.

● 10.9   Application: An Error Correction Model of U.S. Defense Expenditures

Ramanathan and Blackburn (1991) have applied the error correction approach to modeling U.S. defense expenditures. They argued that although the rate of change of military and total government expenditures might diverge in the short run, they have a stable long-run relationship (see Fig. 10.9). This long-run relationship can be derived from a simple static model of utility maximization. Suppose the government has the Cobb–Douglas "objective function"

$$U(M, N) = M^{\alpha} N^{1-\alpha}$$

where M and N are the "quantities" of military and nonmilitary expenditures and α is a fixed parameter. We want to maximize U with respect to M and N, subject to the government budget constraint $G = p_M M + p_N N$. G is the total government expenditure, p_M is the price index of military goods, and p_N is the price index of nonmilitary goods. Using the procedure discussed in Appendix Section 2.A.2, it is easy to show that the "optimum" expenditure on M is $p_M M = \alpha G$, which has the form of Equation (10.22).

The error correction formulation derived from this simple long-run relationship is given by

$$\Delta m_t = \alpha + \beta \Delta g_t + \gamma(g_{t-1} - m_{t-1}) + u_t \tag{10.27}$$

where m_t is the logarithm of military expenditures and g_t is the logarithm of total government expenditures. Thus, the rate of change in military expenditures is de-

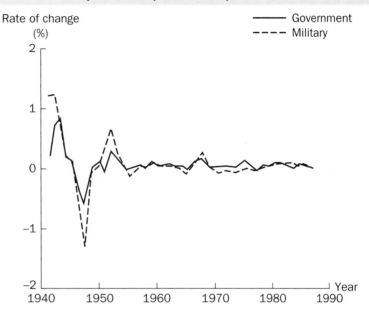

Figure 10.9   Rate of Change of Government and Military Expenditures (1940–1987)

termined by the rate of change in total government expenditure in the same period and the difference between the logarithms of total expenses and the military budget in the previous period. The null hypothesis that $\gamma = 0$ tests for the short-run disequilibrium error correction term. Note that by letting g_{t-1} and m_{t-1} have coefficients that are equal in value but opposite in sign, we have imposed the constraint $\gamma_2 = -\gamma_1$ in Equation (10.26a). This is to simplify the analysis. Interested readers can relax this assumption and test for it using the data provided. As mentioned in Section 10.8, the general structure of the error correction model would also have a second equation relating g_t to m_t and their lagged values, but as such an equation is not meaningful in our context, it has not been specified.

In the empirical analysis, the data used were annual for the period 1940 through 1987, which gives effectively 47 observations. DATA10-4 has data on the following variables:

> UG = Unadjusted annual government outlays expressed in billions of dollars for the years 1940–1987
>
> EM = Total U.S. military outlays expressed in billions of dollars
>
> GNPDEF = Annual implicit GNP deflator for federal government purchases of goods and services, base year 1972
>
> SDEM = Percent of Democrats in the Senate
>
> HDEM = Percent of Democrats in the House of Representatives
>
> PRES = Party of the president in office, Rep = 1, Demo = 0

ELECT = 1 for the year in which the President might have an incentive to increase and decrease military expenditure as a means of stabilizing the government

REAGAN = 1 for the years during which President Reagan was in office

OPP = 1 denotes a year in which the majority party in the Senate is of the opposing party with respect to the President in office, 0 otherwise

WW2 = World War II period, 1941–1945

KWAR = Korean War period, 1951–1953

VWAR = Vietnam War period, 1965–1969

WARSAW = 1 for the years when the Warsaw Pact was in effect, 1955 onward

KRUS = 1 for the years during which Khrushchev may have changed Soviet military policy

GORB = 1 for the years during which Soviet leader Gorbachev may have changed Soviet military policy

SALT = The structural change possibly brought about by the SALT I treaty; 0 = before, 1 = after

Both military and total expenditures are in current dollars and should be converted to real terms. We then need the change in their logarithms. This gives

$$\text{REALMIL} = \text{UM} * 100/\text{GNPDEF}$$

$$\text{REALG} = \text{UG} * 100/\text{DNPDEF}$$

$$\text{MILIT} = \ln(\text{REALMIL}_t) - \ln(\text{REALMIL}_{t-1})$$

$$\text{GOVT} = \ln(\text{REALG}_t) - \ln(\text{REALG}_{t-1})$$

MILIT is the dependent variable representing the difference in the logarithms of total military outlays between the periods t and $t - 1$. In terms of the previous notation, this is Δm_t and measures the instantaneous rate of growth of expenditure on defense. Military expenditures are in billions of constant 1972 dollars. GOVT is Δg_t, the difference between the logarithms of total government expenditure in periods t and $t - 1$. It represents the rate of growth in the total government budget. These data were also in constant 1972 dollars (billions). LONGDEF is $g_{t-1} - m_{t-1}$, the error correction adjustment.

We note from Fig. 10.9 that the rates of change of military and total expenditures deviate substantially from one another during the World War II and Korean War periods, but over the longer run the relationship is more stable.

Ordinary least squares estimates of the coefficients in Equation (10.27) are presented next, with t-statistics in parentheses (use Practice Computer Session 10.8 to reproduce the results of this section):

$$\widehat{\text{MILIT}} = \underset{(-2.8)}{-0.172} + \underset{(12.9)}{1.579\,\text{GOVT}} + \underset{(2.8)}{0.169\,\text{LONGDEF}}$$

$$\text{d.f.} = 44 \qquad \overline{R}^2 = 0.792 \qquad \hat{\sigma} = 0.17241$$

where $\text{MILIT} = \Delta m_t$, $\text{GOVT} = \Delta g_t$, and $\text{LONGDEF} = g_{t-1} - m_{t-1}$.

The Effects of Other Variables

Although all the regression coefficients are statistically significant and the model explains 79.2 percent of the variation in the growth rate of the military budget, tests for first-order serial correlation indicate the presence of autocorrelation in the model. Therefore, the estimates are inefficient and the significance of the regression coefficients is questionable. Although one can use a method such as the Cochrane–Orcutt iterative procedure to correct for serial correlation, this was not done because the basic model relates the military expenditure to only total government expenditure and has to be modified to account for changes due to other variables. We can expect that the short-run adjustment coefficient γ will be related to a number of economic and political variables. To allow for these effects, the authors assume that γ depends on a number of other variables. In particular,

$$\gamma = \gamma_0 + \gamma_1 PRES + \gamma_2 ELECT + \gamma_3 REAGAN + \gamma_4 OPP + \gamma_5 HDEM \quad \textbf{(10.28)}$$
$$+ \gamma_6 SDEM + \gamma_7 WW2 + \gamma_8 KWAR + \gamma_9 VWAR + \gamma_{10} KRUS$$
$$+ \gamma_{11} GORB + \gamma_{12} SALT$$

The variables on the right-hand side are described next. One might want to test whether α and β are also related to these other variables, but because the focus here is on the error correction term, this was not done. Furthermore, that would have added 24 more coefficients to estimate and, as the effective number of observations is only 47, there will be a substantial decrease in the precision of the estimates and the power of tests.

From the above we obtain the following unrestricted model, which includes the interactions between the variables in Equation (10.28) and those in the basic model:

$$MILIT_t = \alpha + \beta GOVT_t + LONGDEF_t(\gamma_0 + \gamma_1 PRES_t \quad \textbf{(10.29)}$$
$$+ \gamma_2 ELECT_t + \gamma_3 REAGAN_t + \gamma_4 OPP_t + \gamma_5 HDEM_t$$
$$+ \gamma_6 SDEM_t + \gamma_7 WW2_t + \gamma_8 KWAR_t + \gamma_9 VWAR_t$$
$$+ \gamma_{10} KRUS_t + \gamma_{11} GORB_t + \gamma_{12} SALT_t) + u_t$$

We now turn our attention to a description of the new variables in the model.

The Political Variables

To test for the presence of a political business cycle, Ramanathan and Blackburn used the binary variable, ELECT, which will have the value of 1 for an election year and the year immediately preceding it, and zero for the other two years following a presidential election. If the political business cycle is present, we would expect this variable to have a positive marginal effect on military expenditures.

To test for the effects of party affiliation, a number of variables were included. The first is PRES, which was given the value of 1 for each year a Republican president was in office. OPP represents a dummy variable assigned the value 1 whenever the President and Senate majority are from opposing parties. Also included are HDEM and SDEM, which represent the percent of seats held by Democrats in the House and Senate, respectively. A dummy variable called REAGAN is also included, with the value 1 from 1981 onward and zero prior to that. This variable is introduced because President Reagan pursued an aggressive policy toward the military budget. To the extent that this was the case, we expect the regression coefficient to be positive.

International Variables

Understandably, several past studies have indicated that a number of exogenous international factors influence levels of defense expenditures. Two factors that have received substantial empirical support are the occurrence of war and changes in peacetime relations between the United States and the Soviet Union (Rattinger, 1975; Ostrom, 1978; Zuk and Woodbury, 1986). Therefore, a number of international variables have been included.

To measure the effects of war, WW2, KWAR, and VWAR were included in the model. All three are binary variables with values of 1 for World War II, the Korean War, and the Vietnam War, respectively. International tension has usually been measured in the form of a tension metric based on events that are concerned with the relations of two nations (Rattinger, 1975). Because this study is not bilateral but takes account of conflicts with other countries as well (Korea, Vietnam, and indirectly China), other variables have been used, which, it was hoped, would capture this broad spectrum of international tension.

Khrushchev conducted a more aggressive policy that culminated in actions such as the building of the Berlin Wall and, more notably, the Cuban Missile crisis, both of which contributed to the cold war between the United States and Soviet Union. Gorbachev was chosen because of his initiation of *perestroika* in an attempt to improve relations. The final variable included is SALT, which was included to test for any structural changes that may have resulted from the signing and ratification of the SALT I arms reduction treaty. This variable was chosen because it represents a culmination of the detente era in U.S.–Soviet relations.

Empirical Results

Equation (10.29) was first estimated by the OLS procedure. The model was then tested for first-order serial correlation coefficient. Because of the presence of the lagged dependent variable, the Durbin–Watson test is not applicable. Therefore, the authors used the Lagrange multiplier test (see Chapters 5 and 9). Basically, the procedure was to regress the estimated residuals $\hat{u}_t$ on $\hat{u}_{t-1}$ and all the variables in Equation (10.29) and compute the test statistic nR^2, where n is the number of observations used in the regression and R^2 is the *unadjusted* R-squared value from the same regression. Under the null hypothesis that the first-order serial correlation coefficient is zero, nR^2 has the χ^2 distribution with one degree of freedom. In our example, $n = 46$ (the first observation is lost because of the $\hat{u}_{t-1}$ term) and $R^2 = 0.138$. Therefore, $nR^2 = 6.348$, which is significant at the 1.2 percent level, thus implying serial correlation. Equation (10.29) was then estimated by a mixed Hildreth–Lu (HILU) and Cochrane–Orcutt (CORC) procedure. This consists of first using the HILU search procedure to obtain an estimate of the first-order serial correlation coefficient and then fine-tuning it using the CORC iterative procedure. We can expect this procedure to converge to the global maximum likelihood estimates. Table 10.5 presents the estimates and associated statistics.

It is unrealistic to expect all the estimated coefficients to be statistically significant. We note that many terms are insignificant. In order to improve the precision of the remaining estimates, these were then omitted one or two at a time, and the resulting model was estimated by the mixed HILU–CORC procedure. Additional diagnostic tests were also performed on this model—the Lagrange multiplier (LM) test for the presence of a lagged dependent variable, the ARCH test for time-varying variances, and the LM test for higher-order serial correlation—but no evidence was found to support any of them (see Chapters 5, 8, and 9 for a discussion of these diagnostic tests). Table 10.6 contains the estimates and associated statistics for the final model. We note that in the final model, most of the regression coefficients are significant at the 1 percent level.

Table 10.5   HILU–CORC Estimates of the General Model In Equation (10.29)

Variable	Coefficient	Std. Error	t-stat	Prob $t > |T|$
CONSTANT	−0.19814	0.03679	−5.386	< 0.0001 ***
GOVT	1.31688	0.07033	18.725	< 0.0001 ***
LONGDEF	0.29021	0.22232	1.305	0.2014
LONGDEF * PRES	0.03553	0.06429	0.553	0.5844
LONGDEF * ELECT	−0.00137	0.02722	−0.050	0.9602
LONGDEF * REAGAN	−0.02705	0.07806	−0.347	0.7313
LONGDEF * OPP	−0.05306	0.06448	−0.823	0.4168
LONGDEF * HDEM	$1.95561e06$	$4.03108e03$	0.000	0.9996
LONGDEF * SDEM	−0.00299	0.00502	−0.595	0.5563
LONGDEF * WW2	0.46665	0.09747	4.788	< 0.0001 ***
LONGDEF * KWAR	0.41699	0.06549	6.367	< 0.0001 ***
LONGDEF * VWAR	0.12367	0.06619	1.868	0.0712 *
LONGDEF * KRUS	0.14522	0.06031	2.408	0.0222 **
LONGDEF * GORB	0.02471	0.04328	0.571	0.5722
LONGDEF * SALT	−0.00534	0.04176	−0.128	0.8991

d.f. = 31 $\overline{R}^2 = 0.943$ $\hat{\sigma} = 0.08178$

Note: Three *s indicate significance at 1 percent, two *s indicate significance between 1 and 5 percent, and one * indicates significance between 5 and 10 percent. $\overline{R}^2$ and $\hat{\sigma}$ are based on the estimated residuals for Equation (10.29) using the mixed estimation procedure described earlier.

● Table 10.6　HILU–CORC Estimates for the Final Model

Variable	Coefficient	Std. Error	t-stat	Prob t > |T|
CONSTANT	−0.20750	0.02992	−6.935	0.0001 ***
GOVT	1.34260	0.06467	20.762	0.0001 ***
LONGDEF	0.35268	0.09435	3.738	0.0006 ***
LONGDEF * SDEM	−0.00413	0.00164	−2.526	0.0158 **
LONGDEF * WW2	0.46914	0.07794	6.019	0.0001 ***
LONGDEF * KWAR	0.42589	0.04811	8.853	0.0001 ***
LONGDEF * VWAR	0.14121	0.04228	3.340	0.0019 ***
LONGDEF * KRUS	0.15773	0.04237	3.722	0.0006 ***

d.f. = 38　　$\bar{R}^2 = 0.951$　　$\hat{\sigma} = 0.07577$

Note: Three *s indicate significance at 1 percent, two *s indicate significance between 1 and 5 percent, and one * indicates significance between 5 and 10 percent. $\bar{R}^2$ and $\hat{\sigma}$ are based on the estimated residuals for Equation (10.29) using the mixed estimation procedure described earlier.

Interpretation of the Results

The variables included in the final model explain 95.1 percent of the variance of the rate of growth of military expenditures, which is considerably higher than that of the basic model. The explanatory variables are classified as follows according to whether they are significant at the 1 or 5 percent levels or are insignificant:

1 percent	GOVT, LONGDEF, LONGDEF * WW2, LONGDEF * KWAR, LONGDEF * VWAR, and LONGDEF * KRUS
5 percent	LONGDEF * SDEM
Insignificant	LONGDEF * PRES, LONGDEF * ELECT, LONGDEF * REAGAN, LONGDEF * OPP, LONGDEF * HDEM, LONGDEF * GORB, and LONGDEF * SALT

As can be seen by the significance of GOVT, military expenditures grew at a significant rate over the sample period, with a marginal effect of 1.343. Thus, a 1 percent increase in government expenditures resulted in a greater increase of 1.343 percent in military expenditures, indicating that military expenditures have become a greater portion of government expenditures. This is confirmed by the significance of the short-run error correction term, LONGDEF.

Most of the variables significant at the 1 percent level are international variables, indicating that, relatively, they have greater influence than the chosen domestic variable. All three of the war variables are significantly positive as expected, although, as can be seen by the differences in their coefficients, World War II and the Korean War had greater marginal effects upon military expenditure than did the Vietnam War.

World War II	0.469 LONGDEF
Korean War	0.426 LONGDEF
Vietnam War	0.141 LONGDEF

This result is plausible since both of the earlier wars involved greater degrees of mobilization in terms of troops and intensity of fighting. KRUS also has a positive marginal effect, 0.158 LONGDEF, which again is as would be expected from the consequences of his aggressive foreign policy.

The only significant domestic variable was SDEM, seeming to indicate that party affiliation in the Senate is indicative of voting patterns on military appropriations. This should not be taken as absolute proof, however, since as can be observed from the magnitude of the effect, -0.00413 LONGDEF, this effect is a small one. In addition, the insignificance of HDEM, PRES, and OPP lead us to the conclusion that party affiliation is not a significant sign of military voting patterns. The significance of SDEM then should be that party affiliation, in the Senate at least, is probably at most an occasional short-run trend that is an insignificant factor in comparison to other events such as war or sensitivity to voting patterns of constituents (Majeski and Jones, 1981).

The insignificance of ELECT seems to indicate that there is no manipulation of defense expenditures in the name of political gain. This does not imply that government expenditures are not used in times of recession for the sake of macroeconomic policy. It is likely in this case that a larger government budget will only in part be supplemented by an augmented military budget, resulting in no significant proportional change. Another possibility is that government spending is used in the same fashion originally suggested for military expenditure.

The insignificance of both GORB and SALT isn't all that surprising either. In the case of GORB it is more likely due to the relatively few years that he was in power with respect to the sample of this study. The fact that SALT is not significant is possibly because it resulted in only a reduction in nuclear arms and it was not part of a general reduction in military expenditures. It could also be so because military funds were redistributed to other portions of the military budget.

Concluding Remarks

The error correction framework used in this study has provided some unique insights into the variation in military expenditure in the United States during World War II and later periods. There is considerable evidence of interaction between the error correction effect and some of the economic and political variables in determining the rates of growth of the military budget. In particular, the short-run adjustment term (LONGDEF) interacts significantly with several policy variables. The scope of this study is limited, however, by the limited degree of freedom. In spite of this, the error correction model has provided a useful benchmark with which to work. Even if the assumption of a stable relationship between two variables is at best a tenuous one, the error correction approach may still provide researchers a powerful instrument with which to carry out studies. This approach is powerful because its unique structure describes a relationship between two related variables and makes short-run and long-run behavior consistent.

10.10 Cointegration

In the previous two sections we introduced the error correction model which related one variable to changes in another variable as well as to the past levels of the two variables. The formulation was based on an underlying long-run relationship between the two variables. This notion is closely related to the concept of **cointegration** introduced by Granger (1981). Before discussing cointegration, we need to define certain new concepts relating to time series data.

Stationarity

In most of the previous discussions we have assumed that a random variable Y_t had finite variance and also that the covariance between Y_t and Y_{t-s} (for $s > 0$) was either zero or depended only on s and not on t. Thus, the correlation between a series and its lagged values was assumed to depend only on the length of the lag and not on when the series started. This property is known as **stationarity**, and any series obeying this is called a **stationary time series.** It is also referred to as a series that is **integrated of order zero** or as **I(0).** The process that generates a stationary series is time-invariant. Under stationarity, $\text{Var}(u_t)$ and $\text{Var}(u_{t-s})$ are the same for $s > 0$. It is readily noted that the residuals of a regression model with an AR(1) structure satisfy the stationarity property, whereas a random walk model or a series that has a time trend has variance increasing with time and is therefore **nonstationary.** Most economic time series are nonstationary because they usually have a linear or exponential time trend. However, it is possible to convert them to a stationary series through the process of differencing, for example, by constructing the first difference $x_t - x_{t-1}$ (see Chapter 11 for more on these concepts). If the differenced series is stationary, then we say that the original series is **integrated of order 1,** that is, **I(1).** A series that follows a random walk is clearly I(1).

Cointegration

Suppose X_t and Y_t are two random walks and hence are not stationary (in particular, their variances increase with t). In general, we would expect that a linear combination of X_t and Y_t would also be a random walk. Yet, the two series may have the property that a particular linear combination of them $(X_t - aY_t)$ is stationary. Thus, X_t and Y_t may each be integrated of order 1 [that is, I(1)], but there may exist an a such that $X_t - aY_t$ is stationary [that is, I(0) with a finite variance]. If such a property holds, then we say that X_t and Y_t are **cointegrated.** Two cointegrated series will thus not drift too far apart over the long run. Examples of possibly cointegrated series are consumption and income, prices of two close substitutes, and prices and wages in two related markets.

Testing for Cointegration

Because the type of model to be estimated might depend on whether a "dependent" variable may be cointegrated with an "independent" variable, it is important to test whether two (or more) variables are cointegrated. Engle and Granger (1987) considered a variety of tests for cointegration, of which we discuss the two recommended by them. To motivate the tests, consider two variables X_t and Y_t that are integrated of order 1.

COINTEGRATING REGRESSION DW TEST   This is the simplest test for cointegration. The procedure is first to estimate the following equation, called the **cointegrating regression:**

$$Y_t = \alpha + \beta X_t + u_t$$

The Durbin–Watson statistic for this is given by

$$DW = \frac{\sum(\hat{u}_t - \hat{u}_{t-1})^2}{\sum \hat{u}_t^2}$$

As mentioned earlier, in general one would expect u to be I(1) if X and Y are I(1). If this were so, the DW statistic will be close to zero and the two series will *not be cointegrated.* Thus, one way of testing for the lack of cointegration is to see if DW is close to zero. If DW is significantly positive, then we would suspect that the two series are cointegrated. The standard tables for the DW test used in Chapter 9 are not applicable here because there the null hypothesis was that $\rho = 0$ for an AR(1) process, rather than that DW = 0. Engle and Granger did a simulation study and obtained the critical values presented in Table 10.7 for a sample of 100 observations.

AUGMENTED DICKEY–FULLER TEST   Here also a cointegration regression is first run. Next obtain the error terms

$$\hat{u}_t = Y_t - \hat{\alpha} - \hat{\beta} X_t$$

Then estimate the following **Dickey–Fuller regression:**

$$\Delta \hat{u}_t = \phi \hat{u}_{t-1} + \sum_{i=1}^{p} b_i \Delta \hat{u}_{t-i} + \varepsilon_t$$

where p is the preselected order of lags for the residuals. The test statistic is the t-statistic for ϕ, but the t-distribution is not appropriate. For this case also Engle and

● **Table 10.7   Critical Values for Testing for Cointegration**

Level of Significance (%)	DW Statistic	Augmented DF t-Statistic
1	0.511	3.77
5	0.386	3.17
10	0.322	2.84

Source: Engle, R. F., and C. W. J. Granger. "Co-integration and Error Correction, Representation, Estimation, and Testing," *Econometrica* 55 (March 1987): 251–276.

Granger have provided critical values using a simulation procedure for 100 observations (see Table 10.7).

EXAMPLE 10.7

DATA10-5 provides annual data on the average hourly wage rates for California and for the United States as a whole for the period 1960–1994, and Fig. 10.10 shows this data graphed. Note that the curves are practically identical except for the fact that the graph for California is consistently above that for the United States. A natural question that arises is whether the two wage rates are cointegrated. Before examining that, however, we should determine whether the two series follow random walks. This was first done with the Dickey–Fuller test described in Section 10.7. The unrestricted model was (W refers to a wage rate)

$$\Delta W_t = \beta_1 + \beta_2 t + \beta_3 W_{t-1} + \beta_4 \Delta W_{t-1} + u_t$$

The null hypothesis that the series is a random walk is $\beta_2 = 0$ and $\beta_3 = 0$. The F statistics for this were 4.283 and 2.754 for the United States and California, respectively (see Practice Computer Session 10.9 to reproduce the results of this example). From the Dickey–Fuller table of critical values presented in Table 10.4 we note that the random walk hypothesis cannot be rejected even at a 10 percent level. To apply the DW test for cointegration, we obtained the following cointegrating regression:

$$CALWAGE_t = 0.309 + 1.0295\ USWAGE_t$$

$$n = 35 \qquad DW = 0.778$$

The DW statistic is well above all the critical values in Table 10.7 and supports the hypothesis that the two wage rates are cointegrated. It should be pointed out,

Figure 10.10   Hourly Wage Rates in the United States and California

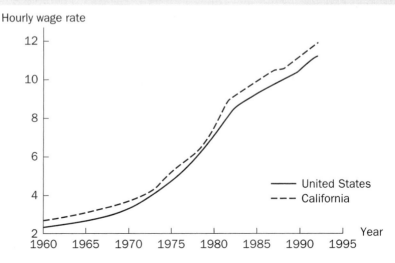

however, that the critical values were based on simulations for 100 observations, whereas we have only 33 observations. The critical values for other sample sizes are not presently available, and the evidence for cointegration is therefore only suggestive.

To apply the augmented Dickey–Fuller test, we saved the residuals from the regression and obtained the following Dickey–Fuller regression, assuming a fourth-order lag process:

$$\Delta \hat{u}_t = -0.396 \hat{u}_{t-1} + 0.193 \, \Delta \hat{u}_{t-1} + 0.011 \, \Delta \hat{u}_{t-2} - 0.201 \, \Delta \hat{u}_{t-3} - 0.010 \, \Delta \hat{u}_{t-4}$$

In view of the lags specified, the effective data period is 1965–1994. The computed t-statistic for the coefficient of $-\hat{u}_{t-1}$ was 1.540, which is considerably below the critical values in Table 10.7. We therefore cannot reject the null hypothesis of no cointegration (the caveat about the smallness of the sample size applies here also).

● **PRACTICE PROBLEM 10.7**

Redo the example above using log wages instead of wages.

Estimation in the Presence of Cointegration

Engle and Granger (1987) have shown that corresponding to a pair of cointegrated variables, there exists an error correction model. This result is known as the **Granger representation theorem.** An ECM can be represented in the form

$$\Delta y_t = \beta_1 \Delta x_t + \beta_2 (y_{t-1} - \beta x_{t-1}) + \varepsilon_t \qquad \textbf{(10.30)}$$

Engle and Granger propose a two-step estimation procedure. First estimate the cointegrating regression $y_t = \beta x_t + u_t$ and save the residuals $\hat{u}_t = y_t - \hat{\beta} x_t$. The second stage consists of estimating Equation (10.30) but using $\hat{u}_{t-1}$ in the second term on the right-hand side. This procedure, however, has some drawbacks. Banerjee et al. (1986) and Stock (1986) have shown that the static model behind the cointegration regression can yield biased estimates. Banerjee et al. suggest using a dynamic form of the cointegrating regression. The reference section of this chapter also has a number of useful citations.

10.11 Causality

When we identify one variable as the "dependent" variable (Y) and another as the "explanatory" variable (X), we have made an implicit assumption that changes in the explanatory variable induce changes in the dependent variable. This is the notion of **causality** in which information about X is expected to affect the conditional distribution of the future values of Y. If X causes Y and Y causes X, then there is a **feedback,** which means that the two variables are **jointly determined** (the price of a commodity and the quantity of goods sold are examples of this feedback effect). In many cases, the apparent direction of causality is not clear. For instance, does the money supply cause changes in the interest rate or is it the other way around? It is therefore of considerable interest to test for causal directions between two variables.

The Granger Test for Causality

The first attempt at testing for the direction of causality was by Granger (1969). The intuition behind the **Granger causality test** is quite straightforward. Suppose X **Granger-causes** Y but Y does not Granger-cause X, then past values of X should be able to help predict future values of Y, but past values of Y should not be helpful in forecasting X. More specifically, consider the following model in which X and Y are expressed as deviations from the respective means:

$$Y_t = \sum_{i=1}^{p} \alpha_i Y_{t-i} + \sum_{j=1}^{q} \beta_j X_{t-j} + u_t \tag{10.31}$$

where u_t is white noise, p is the order of the lag for Y, and q is the order of the lag for X. The null hypothesis that X does not Granger-cause Y is that $\beta_j = 0$ for $j = 1, 2, \ldots, q$. The restricted model is therefore

$$Y_t = \sum_{i=1}^{p} \alpha_i Y_{t-i} + v_t \tag{10.32}$$

The test statistic is the standard Wald F-statistic

$$F_c = \frac{(\text{ESSR} - \text{ESSU})/q}{\text{ESSU}/(n - p - q)}$$

where n is the number of observations used in the unrestricted model in Equation (10.31), ESSU is the error sum of squares for Equation (10.31), and ESSR is the error sum of squares for the restricted model (10.32). Under the null hypothesis of X not Granger-causing Y, F_c has the F-distribution with q d.f. for the numerator and $n - p - q$ d.f. for the denominator. The test is carried out in the usual way. Although Equations (10.31) and (10.32) do not have other explanatory variables, the procedure is the same when such variables are included in the models. The orders of the lags (p and q) are arbitrary and are usually chosen to be large. Alternatively, one could carry out the test for different values of the lags and make sure that conclusions are robust and not model-dependent. The same determination could also have been made with a Lagrange multiplier test.

It should be noted that the procedure tests only for the causal direction from X to Y. Thus, a rejection of the null hypothesis indicates that X Granger-causes Y. To test for causality from Y to X, the variables X and Y will be interchanged in Equations (10.31) and (10.32) and a corresponding test statistic derived. If both tests reject the null hypotheses, then we can conclude that there is a lagged feedback effect.

Since the publication of Granger's paper, a variety of alternatives have been proposed, for example, Sims (1972); Geweke, Meese, and Dent (1983); Pierce (1977); Pierce and Haugh (1977); and Nelson and Schwert (1982).

EXAMPLE 10.8

To illustrate the Granger causality test we examine the direction of causation between money supply and the interest rate. The unrestricted models are the following:

$$r_t = \sum_{i=1}^{6} \alpha_i r_{t-i} + \sum_{j=1}^{6} \beta_j m_{t-j} + u_t$$

$$m_t = \sum_{i=1}^{6} \alpha_i m_{t-i} + \sum_{j=1}^{6} \beta_j r_{t-j} + v_t$$

To carry out the analysis, we have used the quarterly data for the United States provided in DATA10-1 (see Practice Computer Session 10.10 for the commands to reproduce the empirical results presented here). r_t is the interest rate minus its average over the sample period, and similarly m_t is the money supply minus its average.

For the interest rate equation, the Wald F-statistic for the omission of the money supply variables is 0.7007 and the corresponding p-value is 0.650. This implies that the null hypothesis that past money supply values do not influence future interest rates cannot be rejected. For the money supply equation, the Wald F was 8.926 with a p-value less than 0.0001. The hypothesis that past interest rates do not affect future money supply is rejected at levels below 1 percent. There is thus strong evidence of causality in only one direction.

Vector Autoregressive (VAR) Models

The notions of cointegration and causality are closely related to **vector autoregressive models.** They involve specifying several equations relating different independent variables to their own past values as well as those of other independent variables. Such models are extremely popular in empirical macroeconomics literature, especially for forecasting macroeconomic variables. The following is an example of a VAR model with three endogenous (that is, independent) variables and a fourth-order autoregressive specification:

$$X_t = \alpha_0 + \alpha_1 X_{t-1} + \cdots + \alpha_4 X_{t-4} + \alpha_5 Y_{t-1} + \cdots + \alpha_8 Y_{t-4} + \alpha_9 Z_{t-1} + \cdots$$
$$+ \alpha_{12} Z_{t-4} + u_t$$
$$Y_t = \beta_0 + \beta_1 Y_{t-1} + \cdots + \beta_4 Y_{t-4} + \beta_5 X_{t-1} + \cdots + \beta_8 X_{t-4} + \beta_9 Z_{t-1} + \cdots$$
$$+ \beta_{12} Z_{t-4} + v_t$$
$$Z_t = \gamma_0 + \gamma_1 Z_{t-1} + \cdots + \gamma_4 Z_{t-4} + \gamma_5 X_{t-1} + \cdots + \gamma_8 X_{t-4} + \beta_9 Y_{t-1} + \cdots$$
$$+ \beta_{12} Y_{t-4} + w_t$$

It should be noted that in each equation the current values (that is, at time t) of the other two independent variables do not appear, only their past values do. Without this feature, the model will become a regular simultaneous equation model that requires special estimation procedures (more on this in Chapter 13). With the specification made here, the model is estimable by OLS provided the error terms satisfy the standard assumptions made in Chapter 3. If there is serial correlation among the disturbance terms, then the generalized Cochrane–Orcutt procedure is applicable. The order of the autoregressive process is arbitrary and might be dictated by the periodicity of the data series. Alternatively, one can choose to overparametrize the model by specifying several lag terms and then use the data-based model reduction technique and model selection criteria to choose among alternative models. The lag order could also be determined by the model's ability to forecast. In this case, the investigator would withhold a portion of the data set (say, the last 10 percent of data), estimate the model with the remaining data, use it to generate forecasts during the postsample period, compute error statistics such as MSE or MAPE (discussed in Section 3.9), and then choose among the different specifications.

● **EXAMPLE 10.9**

This example uses the quarterly data in DATA10-1 to illustrate the VAR approach for a three-equation model relating money supply (M), interest rate (r), and government deficit (D). The models include constant terms explicitly and have a fourth-order autoregressive process. Practice Computer Session 10.11 has the commands to obtain the results. The complete data set was for the period 1964.1 through 1991.2. Since four quarterly lags are involved, we have to suppress the first four observations when estimating the models. In order to obtain postsample forecasts, only the period 1965.1 through 1988.4 was used. The estimates were then used to forecast r, M, and D, for the 10 quarters 1989.1–1991.2 and to compute the corresponding mean absolute percentage errors (MAPEs). Because the lagged variables were highly correlated, the data-based model reduction procedure was then used to omit variables with insignificant coefficients. The final models' estimates were used to forecast variables for the postsample period. Once again, MAPEs were computed. The following table has the relevant percents:

	Unrestricted Model	Final Model
Interest Rate	6.89	6.39
Money Supply	0.73	0.75
Budget Deficit	15.22	14.39

Note that MAPE is less than 1 percent for the money supply series, whereas for the other two series they are much higher. The final models have a slight edge over the unrestricted models in terms of predictability outside the sample.

● **10.12   Pooling Cross-Sectional and Time Series Data (or Panel Data)**

All the analyses carried out so far have dealt either with time series data or data for a cross section of economic agents at a given point in time. In many cases, however, an investigator might have to collect data over time for a cross section of economic groups. In Chapter 1 we mentioned how a utility might want to select a sample of households, equip them with meters that measure energy consumption at different hours of a day, and follow their consumption patterns for a whole year. Thus, we would have both cross section and time series data that would have to be pooled. Data of this type are referred to as **panel data** or as **pooling cross-section and time series data,** and also as **longitudinal data.** Another example of this type of data is in DATA9-13, which contains monthly rates of return for eight financial stocks listed on the New York Stock Exchange. Panel data of the types listed here need special estimation techniques, and this chapter gives an introduction to a number of alternative approaches. For more details, see the excellent treatment of the issues involved presented in Greene (2000) and Hill, Griffiths and Judge (1997), Judge et al. (1993), Wooldridge (2000), and Kmenta (1986).

To make the presentation easier to understand, we choose the simple linear regression model with just one independent variable. The extension to the general case of many independent variables is straightforward, especially since computer programs such as EViews, SHAZAM, and SAS, can handle panel data easily. The modified general model is

$$Y_{it} = \alpha_{it} + \beta_{it}X_{it} + u_{it} \tag{10.33}$$

where $i = 1, 2, \ldots, G$, represent the G cross-sectional groups (which might be companies, countries, states, cities, individuals, and so on) and $t = 1, 2, \ldots, n$, represent time. Because there are only Gn observations to estimate the $2Gn$ parameters, we need to impose some restrictions to reduce the number of unknown parameters. We now turn to a number of approaches to doing this.

Seemingly Unrelated Regressions (SUR)

One simplification of the model is to assume that α and β vary across the cross-section groups but not over time. Thus, $\alpha_{it} = \alpha_i$ and $\beta_{it} = \beta_i$. If $G = 3$, then Equation (10.33) reduces to the following three equations:

$$Y_{1t} = \alpha_1 + \beta_1 X_{1t} + u_{1t} \tag{10.33a}$$

$$Y_{2t} = \alpha_2 + \beta_2 X_{2t} + u_{2t} \tag{10.33b}$$

$$Y_{3t} = \alpha_3 + \beta_3 X_{3t} + u_{3t} \tag{10.33c}$$

If the error terms (u_{it}) follow the standard assumptions of zero mean, constant but different variances, no autocorrelation, and no *contemporaneous* (that is for a given t) *correlation* between the errors of any two equations, then these equations are essentially unrelated. By applying the OLS procedure to each equation separately, we obtain estimates that are unbiased, consistent, and most efficient. A problem with this approach is that common events that occur in any economy (for example, changes in interest rates, money supply, tax policies, political events, etc.) often affect the different cross-sectional errors in a similar way so that they are **contemporaneously correlated.** We may thus have

$$\text{Cov}(u_{1t}, u_{2t}) = \sigma_{12}, \qquad \text{Cov}(u_{2t}, u_{3t}) = \sigma_{23}, \qquad \text{Cov}(u_{1t}, u_{3t}) = \sigma_{13} \tag{10.34}$$

where the σs are nonzero. By exploiting these covariances, we can obtain better estimates of the parameters than we would get by treating the equations as separate. The steps are as follows:

Step 1   Estimate each equation separately by OLS and obtain the residuals ($\hat{u}_{it}$).
Step 2   Using the residuals, estimate the variances and the covariances (σ_{ij}, for i, $j = 1, 2, \ldots G$—which is 3 here)
Step 3   Use the estimates from Step 2 to obtain feasible generalized least squares (FGLS estimates) estimates of all the parameters.

The well-known computer programs listed earlier perform all the necessary calculations with simple commands. The model above is called **seemingly unrelated regressions (SUR),** a term coined by Zellner (1962), because they appear unrelated except for the correlations among the residuals.

There is one situation in which the joint SUR estimators would be *identical* to the OLS estimators of individual equations, *even if the respective errors are correlated,* and hence there would be no advantage to attempting FGLS estimation. This case arises when $X_{1t} = X_{2t} = X_{3t}$ for $t = 1, 2, \ldots, n$, that is, when the same right-hand side variables are used in all equations. This must be true even if the model contains more X variables. As an example, suppose we specify the demand relations for rice, wheat, and corn, with the quantity consumed of each grain as a function of the three grain prices and income. Thus, each equation will have the same independent variables with the same numerical values of the observations. In this case, OLS estimators have all the desirable properties.

Estimation Using Dummy Variables (Fixed Effects Model)

An alternative approach to estimating models using panel data is using dummy variables for each of the cross-section units (review Section 7.2 on qualitative variables with many categories). To illustrate, define three dummy variables: D_{1t} which takes the value 1 when $i = 1$ and for all the time periods, and 0 otherwise; D_{2t} which takes the value 1 when $i = 2$ and for all the time periods, and 0 otherwise; D_{3t} which takes the value 1 when $i = 3$ and for all the time periods, and 0 otherwise. Shifting just the intercepts in Equation (10.33), the modified model is (for $i = 1, 2, 3$)

$$Y_{it} = \lambda_1 D_{1t} + \lambda_2 D_{2t} + \lambda_3 D_{3t} + \beta_1 X_{it} + u_{it} \tag{10.35}$$

A model of this type is called the **fixed effects model.** It should be noted that we could extend the model to shift the slope terms also by introducing dummy shifts to the slope coefficients. In essence, we are assuming that the error variances in the equations are the same across equations. If this is so, pooling gives more efficient estimates of the parameters because of the considerably increased number of observations.

Random Effects (or Error Components) Model

The fixed effects model treated the dummy variable coefficients as fixed but unknown. In the **random effects model** (commonly known as the **error component**

model), they are treated as random drawings from a common population with a fixed mean (call it θ). The modification is as follows:

$$Y_{it} = \alpha_i + \beta_1 X_{it} + u_{it} \qquad \alpha_i = \theta + \varepsilon_i \qquad (10.36)$$

or

$$Y_{it} = \theta + \beta_1 X_{it} + (u_{it} + \varepsilon_i) = \theta + \beta_1 X_{it} + v_{it} \qquad (10.37)$$

where θ is the fixed mean effect and ε_i is an unobservable time-invariant random effect, specific to the ith cross-section group, assumed to be independent of other εs with a zero mean and constant variance. The combined error term v_{it} has two components (hence the name *error component model*), the group specific error (ε_i) and the overall error u_{it}.

The various error terms are assumed to satisfy the following conditions:

$$E(u_{it}) = E(\varepsilon_i) = 0, \qquad \text{Var}(\varepsilon_i) = \sigma_\varepsilon^2, \qquad \text{Var}(u_{it}) = \sigma_u^2, \qquad \text{Cov}(\varepsilon_i, \varepsilon_j) = 0 \quad \text{for } i \neq j$$

$$\text{Cov}(u_{it}, \varepsilon_j) = 0, \quad \text{for all } i, j, \text{ and } t, \quad \text{and} \quad \text{Cov}(u_{it}, u_{js}) = 0, \quad \text{for } i \neq j \quad \text{and} \quad t \neq s$$

The following results are easy to show (prove it):

$$\text{Var}(v_{it}) = \sigma_u^2 + \sigma_\varepsilon^2 \qquad \text{Cov}(v_{it}, v_{is}) = \sigma_\varepsilon^2 \quad \text{for } t \neq s$$

It is evident that OLS is not the optimal technique but that FGLS produces estimates with desirable properties. The computer programs cited earlier all have the capability of obtaining the appropriate estimates with easy-to-use commands.

10.13 Empirical Project

If you have started an empirical project as part of a course (that is, you have already carried out the steps described in Sections 4.9 and 7.9), and are using time series data, you are ready to undertake the estimation of models and testing of hypotheses. Formulate one or more general models and estimate them. In doing this, be sure to include appropriate dynamics. If your data include population as an explanatory variable, express variables in per-capita terms rather than using population as an independent variable. This is to avoid possible heteroscedasticity and multicollinearity problems. It would also be wise to include financial variables in real terms (that is, corrected for inflation). If you use quarterly or monthly data, you may want to include seasonal dummies also. After estimating the general models by OLS, carry out appropriate LM tests for serial correlation of a general order rather than use just AR(1) and the DW test. If it is present, use the generalized Cochrane–Orcutt procedure to obtain more efficient estimates. Then apply the data-based reduction technique to eliminate redundant variables from the model. Interpret the results of the final model. You may also want to obtain forecasts of the dependent variable and compute error summary statistics. This can be done **in sample** or **out of sample**. In the latter, you should not use the observations for the last 10 percent of the periods in the estimation. Instead, use the first 90 percent of the observations to estimate models and obtain forecasts for the last 10 percent of the periods. Then evaluate the errors and judge how the model performs out of sample.

Summary

This chapter examined the consequences of using lagged variables in a model—both lagged explanatory and lagged dependent (or endogenous) variables. Models involving lags from several periods are known as *distributed lag models.*

A distributed lag model with only lagged explanatory variables is of the form

$$Y_t = \alpha + \beta_0 X_t + \beta_1 X_{t-1} + \cdots + \beta_p X_{t-p} + u_t$$

The partial effect $\Delta Y_t / \Delta X_t$ is known as the *impact multiplier*—that is, it is the marginal effect of X on Y in the same time period. The partial effect $\Delta Y_t / \Delta X_{t-i}$ is known as the *interim multiplier of order i;* that is, it is the marginal effect on Y_t of changes in X made at time $t - i$. *Long-run equilibrium* (or *steady state*) is attained when all the variables are constant over time. We denote the long-run values by Y^* and X^*. The partial effect $\Delta Y^* / \Delta X^*$ is known as the *long-run multiplier,* the effect of X on Y after all the adjustments have taken place and a long-run equilibrium has been attained.

If we apply ordinary least squares to this model, the estimates are still BLUE and consistent, because none of the assumptions is violated. However, because $X_t, X_{t-1}, \ldots$ will generally be highly correlated, multicollinearity problems arise. Furthermore, the larger the value of p, the more the number of parameters to be estimated and the fewer the degrees of freedom. This worsens the precision of the estimates and reduces the powers of tests of hypotheses.

One way to reduce the number of parameters to be estimated is to use the *Koyck lag* (or *geometric lag*) scheme proposed by Koyck. The procedure assumes that the weight for the period i is a fraction of the weight for the previous period. Thus, $\beta_i = \lambda \beta_{i-1}$, where $0 < \lambda < 1$. Such an assumption is reasonable in cases in which most of the impact of X is immediate, with diminished effects as times goes on. The model can now be transformed as

$$Y_t = \alpha(1 - \lambda) + \lambda Y_{t-1} + \beta_0 X_t + u_t$$

which has only three parameters to be estimated.

An alternative procedure to reduce the number of parameters is the *Almon lag* (or *polynomial lag*) proposed by Almon. In this scheme, each coefficient is assumed to be a polynomial in the lags. For instance,

$$\beta_i = \alpha_0 + \alpha_1 i + \alpha_2 i^2 + \cdots + \alpha_r i^r$$

The model can now be transformed to one involving the estimation of the αs. Because the degree of the polynomial is usually no more than 3, the number of parameters to be estimated is limited. The choice of the largest lag (p) and the degree of the polynomial (r) may be made by choosing various combinations and then selecting the one that minimizes most of the model selection statistics.

The Koyck lag transformation converts a distributed lag model to one involving the lagged dependent variable term Y_{t-1}. Other schemes such as a *partial adjustment* or *adaptive expectations* can also result in lag-dependent variables as regressors. If a model has lagged dependent variables and the OLS procedure is used to estimate the parameters, then (1) the estimates and forecasts based on them are biased in small samples but are consistent and asymptotically efficient and (2) estimated standard errors are consistent and tests of hypotheses are valid for large samples, *provided the error terms are well behaved—that is, they satisfy Assumptions 3.2 through 3.8.*

If the error terms are serially correlated or follow a *moving average* in which the errors are linear combinations of other well-behaved random errors, then OLS estimates and forecasts will be biased and inconsistent. Estimated standard errors will also be inconsistent, and hence tests of hypotheses are invalid. Finally, the Durbin–Watson test for serial correlation is not applicable if lagged dependent variables are present in the model. An alternative test is a Durbin *h*-test, but it has limitations. The Breusch–Godfrey Lagrange multiplier test is a better one. The procedure is first to estimate the model by OLS and save the residuals ($\hat{u}_t$). Next regress $\hat{u}_t$ against $\hat{u}_{t-1}$, $\hat{u}_{t-2}$, . . . , $\hat{u}_{t-m}$ and all the explanatory variables in the model, *including the lagged dependent regressors Y_{t-1}, Y_{t-2}, . . . , Y_{t-p},* and compute the unadjusted R^2. The LM test statistic is $(n - p)R^2$, which, under the null hypothesis of zero serial correlation, has a χ_m^2 distribution (m is the order of the serial correlation and $n - p$ is the number of observations actually used in estimating the auxiliary regression). If $(n - p)R^2 > \chi_m^2(0.05)$, the null hypothesis is rejected at the 5 percent level.

Several estimation procedures are available when lagged dependent variables are present. If the errors are white noise, then the OLS procedure gives desirable properties for large samples (usually of size 30 or more). If the errors are serially correlated, the Cochrane–Orcutt procedure will give consistent estimates, but the standard errors will be inconsistent. A slight modification to the CORC procedure will yield consistent standard errors also. If the errors follow a moving average scheme, then the model can be transformed and a search procedure used to get consistent estimates.

If the coefficient for the lag-dependent variable is exactly 1, then we have the *unit root problem,* in which the variance of the dependent variable goes to infinity with the sample size. A *random walk* model is an example of this. It is possible to use the *Dickey–Fuller test* to check whether there is a unit root. The procedure is basically to estimate a restricted and an unrestricted model and compute the F-statistic in the usual way. However, the critical value for the test should not be obtained from the traditional F-table because the distribution is not F. Instead, use the critical values obtained by Dickey and Fuller.

Another way of incorporating short-run adjustments in a model is to use the *error correction mechanism.* The error correction model has the following general structure:

$$\Delta y_t = \beta_0 + \beta_1 \Delta x_t + \beta_2(y_{t-1} - x_{t-1}) + u_t$$

where

$$\Delta y_t = \ln(Y_t) - \ln(Y_{t-1}) \quad \text{and} \quad \Delta x_t = \ln(X_t) - \ln(X_{t-1})$$

are the respective rates of change. The term $y_{t-1} - x_{t-1}$ allows for a short-run disequilibrium adjustment that leads to a long-run situation in which Y_t and X_t grow at the same constant rate.

If a series has time-invariant mean, variance, and serial correlation, then it is called a *stationary series* or *integrated of order zero.* If a nonstationary series becomes stationary after being differenced once, then we say that the series is *integrated of order 1* or I(1).

The concept of *cointegration* is closely related to that of the *error correction model* (ECM). If two series are both I(1), but a particular linear combination of them is stationary, the two series are said to be *cointegrated.* Two cointegrated series will generally not drift too far apart. To test for cointegration, one can use a modified Durbin–Watson test or the *augmented Dickey–Fuller test.*

It is possible to test for the direction of *causality* using the *Granger causality test.* This involves testing whether past values of one variable significantly affect the present and future values of another variable.

Closely related to cointegration and causality are *vector autoregressive* (VAR) models. In these models, involving several dependent variables, each such variable is related to its past values as well as those of the remaining endogenous variables. Estimation of such models can be done separately in a straightforward manner.

There are a variety of techniques available to deal with special data sets that involve the pooling of cross-section and time series data (also known as *panel* data and *longitudinal* data). They typically require feasible generalized least squares estimation that is easily carried out using well-known econometrics programs.

Key Terms

Adaptive expectations model
Adjustment coefficient
Almon lag
Augmented Dickey–Fuller test
Causality
Cointegrated
Cointegration
Cointegrating regression
Contemporaneously correlated
Dickey–Fuller regression
Dickey–Fuller test
Distributed lag model
Durbin *h*-test
Error component model
Error correction model (ECM)
Feedback
Fixed effects model
Geometric lag
Granger causality test
Granger-cause
Granger representation theorem
Impact multiplier
In sample
Integration of order 0 or 1
Interim multiplier of order *i*
Jointly determined

Koyck lag
Lagged dependent variable
Lagged independent variable
Longitudinal data
Long-run equilibrium
Long-run multiplier
Moving average
Moving average (MA) error
Nonstationary
Out of sample
Panel data
Partial adjustment model
Polynomial lag
Pooling cross-section and time series data
Random effects model
Random walk model
Seemingly unrelated regressions (SUR)
Speed of adjustment
Stationarity
Stationary time series
Steady state
Unit root test
Vector autoregressive (VAR) model
Well-behaved errors
White noise errors

References

Almon, S. "The Distributed Lag between Capital Appropriations and Expenditures." *Econometrica* 30 (January 1965): 178–196.

Andersen, L. C., and J. L. Jordan. "Monetary and Fiscal Policy Actions: A Test of Their Relative Importance in Economic Stabilization." *Review of the Federal Reserve Bank of St. Louis* (November 1968): 11–24.

Ando, A., and F. Modigliani. "The 'Life-Cycle' Hypothesis of Saving: Aggregate Implications and Tests." *American Economic Review* 53 (1963): 55–84.

Andrews, Donald W. K., and Ray C. Fair. "Estimation of Polynomial Distributed Lags and Leads with End Point Constraints." *Journal of Econometrics* 53, nos. 1–3 (July/September 1992): 123–139.

Banerjee, A., J. J. Dolado, D. F. Hendry, and G. W. Smith. "Exploring Equilibrium Relationships in Econometrics through Static Models: Some Monte Carlo Evidence." *Oxford Bulletin of Economics and Statistics* 48 (1986): 253–277. See also other papers in the same issue.

Barro, R. J. "Unanticipated Money Growth and Economic Activity in the United States." In *Money, Expectations, and the Business Cycle,* ed. Robert Barro. New York: Academic Press, 1981, 137–169.

Breusch, T. "Testing for Autocorrelation in Dynamic Linear Models." *Australian Econ. Papers* 17 (1978): 334–355.

Campos, Julia, Neil R. Ericsson, and David F. Hendry. "Cointegration Tests in the Presence of Structural Breaks." *Journal of Econometrics* 70, no. 1 (January 1996): 187–220.

Choi, In, and Byung-Chul Ahn. "Testing for Cointegration in a System of Equations." *Econometric Theory* 11, no. 5 (December 1995): 952–983.

Corrigan, E. G. "The Measurement and Importance of Fiscal Policy Changes." *Monthly Review, Federal Reserve Bank of New York* (June 1970): 133–145.

Currie, D. "Some Long-Run Features of Dynamic Time-Series Models." *Economic Journal* 91 (1981): 704–715.

Davidson, J. E. H., D. F. Hendry, F. Srba, and S. Yeo. "Econometric Modeling of the Aggregate Time-Series Relationship between Consumer's Expenditure and Income in the United Kingdom." *Economic Journal* 88 (1978): 661–692.

Davidson, R., and J. G. MacKinnon. "Inflation and the Savings Rate." *Applied Economics* 15 (December 1983): 731–743.

Dawson, A. "Sargan's Wage Equation: A Theoretical and Empirical Reconstruction." *Applied Economics* 13 (1981): 351–363.

Dickey, David A., and Wayne A. Fuller. "Distribution of the Estimators for Autoregressive Time Series with a Unit Root." *J. Am. Stat. Assoc.* 14 (June 1979): 427–431.

———. "Likelihood Ratio Statistics for Autoregressive Time Series with a Unit Root." *Econometrica* 49 (July 1981): 1057–1072.

Durbin, J. "Testing for Serial Correlation in Least Squares Regression When Some of the Regressors Are Lagged Dependent Variables." *Econometrica* 38 (May 1970): 410–421.

Dutkowsky, D. H. "Unanticipated Money Growth, Interest Rate Volatility, and Unemployment in the United States." *Rev. Econ. and Stat.* 69 (February 1987): 144–148.

Economic Report of the President. Washington, D.C.: U.S. Government Printing Office, 1983.

Engle, R. F., and C. W. J. Granger. "Co-integration and Error Correction: Representation, Estimation, and Testing." *Econometrica* 55 (March 1987): 251–276.

Flores, Renato G., Jr., and Ariane Szafarz. "An Enlarged Definition of Cointegration." *Economics Letters* 50, no. 2 (February 1996): 193–195.

Friedman, M. A. *Theory of the Consumption Function.* Princeton, N.J.: Princeton University Press, 1957.

Fuller, W. A. *Introduction to Statistical Time Series.* New York: Wiley, 1976.

Geweke, J., R. Meese, and W. Dent. "Comparing Alternative Tests of Causality in Temporal Systems." *J. Econometrics* 77 (1983): 161–194.

Godfrey, L. G. "Testing for Higher Order Serial Correlation in Regression Equations When the Regressors Include Lagged Dependent Variables." *Econometrica* 46 (1978): 1303–1310.

Granger, C. W. J. "Investigating Causal Relations by Econometric Models and Cross-Spectral Models." *Econometrica* 37 (1969): 424–438.

———. "Some Properties of Time Series Data and Their Use on Econometric Model Specification." *Journal of Econometrics* 16 (1981): 121–130.

Greene, W. H. *Econometric Analysis.* Upper Saddle River, N.J.: Prentice-Hall, 2000.

Gregory, Allan W., and Bruce E. Hansen. "Residual-Based Tests for Cointegration in Models with Regime Shifts." *Journal of Econometrics* 70, no. 1 (January 1996): 99–126.

Gregory, Allan W., James M. Nason, and David G. Watt. "Testing for Structural Breaks in Cointegrated Relationships." *Journal of Econometrics* 71, nos. 1–2 (March 1996): 321–341.

Griffiths W. E., R. C. Hill, and G. Judge. *Learning and Practicing Econometrics.* New York: Wiley, 1993.

Harvey, A. C. *The Econometric Analysis of Time Series.* Cambridge, Mass.: The MIT Press, 1990.

Haug, Alfred A. "Tests for Cointegration: A Monte Carlo Comparison." *Journal of Econometrics* 71, nos. 1–2 (March 1996): 89–115.

Hendry, D. F. "Econometric Modelling of House Prices in the United Kingdom." In *Econometrics and Quantitative Economics,* ed. D. F. Hendry and K. F. Wallis. Oxford: Basil Blackwell, 1984.

Hendry, D. F., and G. E. Mizon. "Serial Correlation as a Convenient Simplification Not a Nuisance: A Comment on a Study of the Demand for Money by the Bank of England." *Economic Journal* 88 (1978): 549–563.

Hill, R. C., W. E. Griffiths, and G. Judge. *Undergraduate Econometrics.* New York: Wiley, 1997.

Horvath, Michael T. K., and Mark W. Watson. "Testing for Cointegration When Some of the Cointegrating Vectors Are Prespecified." *Econometric Theory* 11, no. 5 (December 1995): 984–1014.

Hurwicz, L. "Least-Squares Bias in Time Series." *Statistical Inference in Dynamic Economic Models.* New York: Wiley, 1950.

Johnston, J. *Econometric Methods.* New York: McGraw-Hill, 1972 and 1984.

Judge, G. G., R. C. Hill, W. E. Griffiths, H. Lutkepohl, and T. C. Lee. *Introduction to the Theory and Practice of Econometrics.* New York: Wiley, 1988.

Kmenta, Jan. *Elements of Econometrics.* New York: Macmillan, 1986.

Koyck, L. M. *Distributed Lags and Investment Analysis.* New York: North-Holland, 1954.

Kumar, T. Krishna. "Cointegration and Error Correction Models: A Historical and Methodological Perspective." *Journal of Quantitative Economics* 11, no. 1 (January 1995): 143–154.

Lahiri, Kajal, and Nlandu Mamingi. "Testing for Cointegration: Power versus Frequency of Observation—Another View." *Economics Letters* 49, no. 2 (August 1995): 121–124.

MaeShiro, Asatoshi. "Small Sample Properties of Estimators of Distributed Lag Models." *International Economic Review* 21, no. 3 (October 1980): 721–733.

MaeShiro, Asatoshi. "A Lagged Dependent Variable, Autocorrelated Disturbances, and Unit Root Tests—Peculiar OLS Bias Properties—a Pedagogical Note." *Applied Economics* 31 (1999): 381–396.

Majeski, S. J., and D. L. Jones. "Arms Race Modeling, Causality Analysis and Model Specification." *Journal of Conflict Resolution* 25 (1981): 259–288.

Nelson, C. R., and G. W. Schwert. "Tests for Predictive Relationships between Time Series Variables: A Monte Carlo Investigation." *J. Amer. Stat. Assoc.* 77 (1982): 11–18.

Ostrom, C. "A Reactive Linkage Model of the U.S. Defense Expenditure Policy Making Process." *American Political Science Review* 72 (1978): 941–956.

Phillips, A. W. "Stabilization Policy in a Closed Economy." *Economic Journal* 64 (1954): 290–323.

Phillips, P., and P. Perron. "Testing for a Unit Root in Time Series Regression." *Biometrika* 75 (1988): 335–346.

Pierce, D. A., and L. D. Haugh. "Causality in Temporal System: Characterizations and a Survey." *J. Econometrics* 5 (1977): 265–294.

Ramanathan, Ramu, and Jan Blackburn. "U.S. Defense Expenditures: An Error Correction (Cointegration) Approach," Discussion Paper 91–13, University of California, San Diego, 1991.

Ramanathan, R. R. Engle, C. W. J. Granger, F. Vahid-Araghi, and C. Brace. "Short-Run Forecasts of Electricity Loads and Peaks." *International J. Forecasting* (June 1997): 161–174.

Rattinger, H. "Arms, Detente, and Bureaucracy, the Case of the Arms Race in Europe." *Journal of Conflict Resolution* 19 (1975): 571–595.

Rubin, H. "Consistency of Maximum-Likelihood Estimates in the Explosive Case." *Statistical Inference in Dynamic Economic Models.* New York: Wiley, 1950.

Salmon, M. "Error Correction Mechanisms." *Economic Journal* 92 (1982): 615–629.

Sargan, J. D. "Wages and Prices in the United Kingdom: A Study in Econometric Methodology." In *Econometric Analysis for National Economic Planning*, ed. P. E. Hart, G. Millis, and J. K. Whittaker. London: Butterworth, 1964. Also reprinted in *Econometrics and Quantitative Econometrics*, ed. D. F. Hendry and K. F. Wallis. Oxford: Basil Blackwell, 1984.

Schmidt, P., and R. N. Waud. "Almon Lag Technique and the Monetary Versus Fiscal Debate." *J. Amer. Stat. Assoc.* 68 (March 1973): 11–19.

Sims, C. "Money, Income, and Causality." *Amer. Econ. Rev.* 62 (1972): 540–552.

Stock, J. H. "Asymptotic Properties of Least Squares Estimators of Cointegrating Vectors." *Econometrica* 55 (1986): 1035–1056.

Tansel, A. "Cigarette Demand, Health Scares, and Education in Turkey." *Applied Economics* 25 (1993): 521–529.

Wooldridge, J. *Introductory Econometrics: A Modern Approach.* Cincinnati: South-Western Publishing, 2000.

Young, A. S. "A Comparative Analysis of Prior Families for Distributed Lags." *Empirical Economics* 8, nos. 3–4 (1983): 215–227.

Zellner, A. "An Efficient Method of Estimating Seemingly Unrelated Regressions and Tests of Aggregation Bias." *J. Amer. Stat. Assoc.,* 57 (1962): 348–368.

Zuk, G., and N. R. Woodbury. "U.S. Defense Spending, Electoral Cycles and Soviet–American Relations." *Journal of Conflict Resolution* 30 (1986): 445–468.

Exercises

†10.1 Suppose the demand for money is given by the relation $M_t = \alpha + \beta Y_t^* + \gamma R_t$, where M_t is real cash balances, Y_t^* is "expected" real income, and R_t is the interest rate, at time t. Expectations are revised according to the adaptive rule $Y_t^* = \lambda Y_{t-1} + (1 - \lambda) Y_{t-1}^* + u_t$, $0 < \lambda < 1$. You have data on Y_t, M_t, and R_t but none on Y_t^*.

a. Formulate an econometric model that, in principle, can be used to derive estimates of α, β, γ, and λ. (These estimates won't be unique but you may ignore that problem here.)

b. Suppose $E(u_t) = 0$, $E(u_t^2) = \sigma^2$, $E(u_t u_{t-s}) = 0$ for $s \neq 0$, and Y_{t-1}, R_t, M_{t-1}, and R_{t-1} are all uncorrelated with u_t. Are the OLS estimates (1) unbiased, (2) consistent? Why or why not?

c. Suppose, instead, that $u_t = \rho u_{t-1} + \varepsilon_t$, with ε_t having properties similar to those in part b. Are the OLS estimates (1) unbiased, (2) consistent in this case? Explain.

10.2 Actual business expenditure for new plant and equipment (Y_t) is given by the relation $Y_t = e^\alpha (X_t^*)^\beta e^{u_t}$, where X_t^* is expected sales, α and β are unknown coefficients, and u_t is a random variable. Because X_t^* is not observable, we postulate the adaptive rule $X_t^*/X_{t-1}^* = (X_{t-1}/X_{t-1}^*)^\gamma$, where X_t is actual sales and γ is the adjustment coefficient.

a. Derive a relationship that can be used to estimate α, β, and γ from data on X_t and Y_t.

b. State the assumptions on u_t needed to ensure that the OLS estimates of the model you obtained in part a are consistent. Explain why your assumptions imply consistency.

c. Under the assumptions stated by you, are the OLS estimates also unbiased? Why or why not?

d. Suppose u_t has the normal distribution with mean zero, constant variance, and zero covariance. Are the OLS estimates consistent? Explain why or why not.

10.3 A firm has a desired level of inventories, I_t^*, that is given by $I_t^* = \alpha + \beta S_t$, where S_t is the sales at time t. Because of market frictions and random shocks, actual inventories, I_t, differ from the desired I_t^*, according to the relation

$$I_t = I_{t-1} + \lambda(I_{t-1}^* - I_{t-1}) + u_t$$

where u_t is a random error term whose properties are unspecified at this point. You have data on I_t and S_t but none on I_t^*.

a. State the signs and other restrictions you would expect for the unknown parameters α, β, and λ. Explain your reasoning.

b. Derive a relationship that can be used to estimate α, β, and λ. (Ignore assumptions on u_t here.)

c. State all the assumptions on u_t that will make OLS estimates of the model you got in part b also consistent. Under the assumptions just stated, are the estimates also BLUE? Why or why not?

d. Are α, β, and λ estimable? If not, explain why not. If yes, describe how they can be estimated. That is, express $\hat{\alpha}$, $\hat{\beta}$, and $\hat{\lambda}$ in terms of the estimates of the model you obtained in part b.

†10.4 Let C_t be real per-capita consumption in the United States at time t and Y_t be real per-capita disposable income, both measured in billions of dollars. Using annual data for 32 years, the following model was obtained:

$$\hat{C}_t = -21{,}151 - 2{,}989.9 \ln(Y_t)$$
$$\qquad\quad (-39.3) \qquad\quad (45.0)$$

$$\bar{R}^2 = 0.985 \qquad d = 0.207$$

The values in parentheses are t-statistics and d is the Durbin–Watson statistic.

a. Test the model for first-order serial correlation at the 5 percent level using the alternative most common in economics.

b. Based on your conclusion, what can you say about the properties of the OLS estimates just given, in terms of (1) unbiasedness, (2) BLUE, and (3) the validity of tests of hypotheses?

c. Describe step-by-step an estimation procedure that will give "better" estimates than OLS. Explain why your procedure is superior to OLS.

It is hypothesized that C_t depends on the consumption in the previous period but is adjusted for changes in disposable income. The following model was obtained using OLS (t-values in parentheses):

$$\hat{C}_t = -21.83 + 1.01\, C_{t-1} + 0.769[Y_t - Y_{t-1}]$$
$$\qquad\quad (-0.78) \quad\;\; (107.5) \qquad\quad (7.8)$$

$$\bar{R}^2 = 0.998 \qquad d = 2.11 \qquad \hat{\rho} = -0.07$$

d. Are these estimates unbiased? Explain.

e. Test the model for first-order serial correlation. Write down the null and alternative hypotheses. (Note: You have all the information you need to carry out this test.)

f. Based on your results in part e, are the OLS estimates (1) unbiased, (2) consistent? Explain.

g. If you found significant serial correlation, describe how you can get "better" estimates than those by OLS. Explain what you mean by "better."

10.5 Consider the "desired" savings function $S_t^* = \alpha + \beta Y_t$, where S_t^* is desired saving and Y_t is actual disposable income. Because S_t^* is unknown, consumers use the partial adjustment rule as follows:

$$S_t = S_{t-1} + \lambda(S_{t-1}^* - S_{t-1})$$

You have data on S_t and Y_t for $t = 1, 2, \ldots n$, but none on S_t^*.

a.   State the signs you expect for α, β, and λ, and explain why you think so.

b.   Derive an estimable relation with S_t as the dependent variable. Add the error term u_t at the end.

c.   State all the assumptions on u_t that will make the OLS estimators of the parameters in the model that you obtained in part b consistent. Are the estimators unbiased also? Define the terms "consistent" and "unbiased," and carefully justify your answers. You are cautioned against stating unneeded assumptions.

d.   Suppose the estimates of the model in part b are denoted by $\hat{\beta}_1$, $\hat{\beta}_2$, etc. Carefully explain how you can obtain estimates of α, β, and λ in terms of the $\hat{\beta}$s.

*10.6   Let S_t^* be the desired savings of a household and Y_t^* be its expected income. The relationship between these two variables is of the form $S_t^* = \alpha + \beta Y_t^*$. Consumers revise their desires and expectations according to the partial adjustment and adaptive expectations rules.

$$S_t = S_{t-1} + \lambda(S_{t-1}^* - S_{t-1})$$

$$Y_t^* = Y_{t-1}^* + \mu(Y_{t-1} - Y_{t-1}^*)$$

where S_t is actual saving and Y_t is actual income. You have data on only S_t and Y_t, and none on S_t^* and Y_t^*.

a.   State the signs and other restrictions you would expect for the unknown parameters α, β, λ, and μ. Explain your reasoning.

b.   Derive a relationship that can be used to estimate α, β, λ, and μ (add an error term u_t at the end).

c.   State all the assumptions on u_t that will make OLS estimates of the model you got in part b also consistent. Under the assumptions just stated, are the estimates also BLUE? Why or why not?

d.   Are α, β, λ, and μ estimable? If not, explain why not. If yes, describe how they can be estimated; that is, express $\hat{\alpha}$, $\hat{\beta}$, $\hat{\lambda}$, and $\hat{\mu}$ in terms of the estimates of the model you obtained in part b.

10.7   DATA3-6 has annual data on per-capita consumption (C_t) and personal disposable income (Y_t), both in constant 1992 dollars. Estimate a model similar to Equation (10.1), choosing your own lag period. Test the model for serial correlation and, if it is present, use the mixed HILU–CORC procedure to obtain new estimates. Compute the long-run multiplier for this model and check to see if it is meaningful.

10.8   Suppose consumption is determined not by current income but by "expected income" (Y_t^*). Also assume that consumers revise their expectations according to the adaptive expectations scheme described in Section 10.2. We then have the following two equations (ignoring error terms):

$$C_t = \alpha + \beta Y_t^*$$

$$Y_t^* = \lambda Y_{t-1} + (1 - \lambda) Y_{t-1}^*$$

By proceeding as we did in Section 10.2, derive an estimable econometric formulation. Use the data set in DATA3-6 and estimate the model you obtained. Test it for autocorrelation and correct for it if needed. From your estimates, obtain estimates of the unknown parameters. Compute the long-run multiplier in this example also. Do you get sensible results?

10.9   Use a purely autoregressive framework to relate the logarithm of consumption to its past values only. Estimate the model with the data in DATA3-6 and test for a unit root. Reestimate the model if appropriate. Carry out a similar exercise using the income series.

10.10 Construct an error correction model for the consumption function used in the previous three exercises and estimate it using the same data set. Is the short-run adjustment term significant?

10.11 DATA10-7 has annual data on the population (P_t) of the state of California. Estimate an appropriate log-linear model and test it for a unit root. Carry out a similar exercise with the population data in DATA3-12 and DATA3-13.

10.12 DATA6-6 has annual data on the farm population (Y_t) in the United States. Estimate the following models, which involve only lagged dependent variables and a time trend. Which of the models is "better"? Explain what you mean by "better."

$$Y_t = \beta_0 + \beta_1 Y_{t-1} + \beta_2 Y_{t-2} + \alpha t + u_t$$

$$Y_t = \beta_0 + \beta_1 Y_{t-1} + \alpha t + u_t$$

Use the Durbin *h-* and Breusch–Godfrey tests for first-order serial correlation. Based on your results, what do you conclude about the consistency of the OLS estimates obtained?

10.13 In each of the following questions, a statement has been made in quotation marks. Carefully prove or provide adequate explanations of whether or not the statement is valid. If it is not valid, state the correct version of the assertion. Justify your answers.

    a.   "When it comes to unbiasedness, consistency, and efficiency of the estimates of the parameters of a multiple regression model (with no lagged dependent variable), high multicollinearity, ignoring serial correlation, and adding an irrelevant variable all have similar results."

    b.   Consider two models using time series data:

        (A) $Y_t = \alpha + \beta X_t + u_t$

        (B) $Y_t = \alpha + \beta X_t + \gamma Y_{t-1} + u_t$

    "Model B is likely to have a higher $\bar{R}^2$ than Model A."

    c.   "If a model has a lagged dependent variable as a regressor and the DW statistic d using OLS estimates is less than d_L, then we can reject the null hypothesis that $\rho = 0$, where $u_t = \rho u_{t-1} + \varepsilon_t$."

10.14 DATA7-19 has time series data on cigarette demand in Turkey and a number of its determinants. First convert demand, price, and income to logarithms so that a double-log model can be estimated. Use the partial adjustment mechanism (described in Section 10.2) on the logarithm of demand and estimate a model. Be sure to include the education variables as well as the two dummy variables, but linearly. Test the model for an AR(2) error structure. If it is significant, reestimate the model using the generalized CORC procedure. Eliminate variables with insignificant coefficients, one at a time, and obtain a "final" model. Compute the long-run elasticities for income and price. Do they make sense? Also, are the education and dummy variables significant in the final model? What policy conclusions would you arrive at based on your estimations?

10.15 DATA9-7 contains data on the demand for automobiles and its determinants. Suppose that the desired purchase of new cars in a given period is a function of the cars' average price, consumer income, the prime interest rate (a proxy for auto loan rates), the unemployment rate, a dummy for a General Motors strike, and a dummy for the spring quarter. Actual purchase follows the partial adjustment mechanism described in Section 10.2. Use that to formulate an econometric model (in double-log terms). Next estimate this model and compare the results with those in Exercise 9.20. Also compute the long-run multipliers for each of the exogenous variables. Are the results sensible?

10.16 Redo Exercise 10.15 using the stock variable in DATA9-7 as the dependent variable. In other words, you are modeling the desired stock rather than the desired purchase of new cars.

10.17 According to the theory of economic growth, the long-run rate of inflation equals the rate of growth of the money supply minus the rate of growth of the population. This implies a long-run relationship of the form $P_t = KM_t/N_t$, where P_t is the price index, M_t is money supply, and N_t is the size of the population.

   a.   Show that the result translates to $p_t = k + m_t - n_t$, where the lowercase variables are the logarithms of the corresponding uppercase variables.

   b.   Consider the short-run relation

$$p_t = \beta_0 + \beta_1 p_{t-1} + \beta_2 m_t + \beta_3 m_{t-1} + \beta_4 n_t + \beta_5 n_{t-1} + u_t$$

   Show that if $\beta_1 = 1 - \gamma$, $\beta_3 = \gamma - \beta_2$, and $\beta_5 = -\gamma - \beta_4$, then this short-run relation is consistent with the long-run behavior postulated above.

   c.   Derive an error correction model of the change in log price.

   d.   DATA10-6 has annual data for the United States for the period 1959–1994; N_t is the population in millions; M_t is money supply (in billions of current dollars), defined as M_3 in the *Economic Report of the President;* and P_t is the consumer price, with 1987 as the base year. Using those data, estimate the error correction model you formulated in part c, and interpret the results.

10.18 Application Section 10.9 presented an error correction model of the U.S. military expenditures. Test military and total government expenditures for random walks and cointegration. Do the same for military and nonmilitary expenditures.

10.19 Use the data set in DATA3-6 and carry out tests for both cointegration and causality. Do the same with the U.K. data in DATA6-3.

10.20 Consider the equilibrium relationship for the demand for money given by $\ln(\text{money}) = \alpha + \beta \ln(\text{income}) + \gamma \ln(\text{interest rate}) + u_t$. DATA9-6 has annual data for the United States for these variables. First estimate the static model and test it for third-order autocorrelation. Next use the adaptive expectations variation to this model discussed in Section 10.2 and estimate that model. Check also for serial correlation and, if present, use appropriate estimation techniques. From the final model compute the long-run elasticities for income and interest rate and interpret the results.

10.21 DATA10-8 has data on the Korean exchange rate. Based on that data, formulate an appropriate model of the exchange rate. Include relevant dynamics in the specification, test for serial correlation, and use appropriate estimation procedures to obtain parameter estimates.

10.22 DATA9-13 has monthly data on the returns of stocks for eight banks listed on the New York Stock Exchange as well as a number of possible variables these returns might be related to. Test each series for a unit root. Also use appropriate dynamic models of the stock price of each of the eight banks.

Special Topics

This part covers a number of more advanced topics. Instructors can choose from these topics depending on interest and availability of time. Chapter 11 discusses in detail how forecasts of economic variables can be generated. Both the econometric and time series approaches to forecasting are discussed, as well as the techniques for optimally combining forecasts from different models. The treatment of binary dependent variables and limited dependent variables (e.g., variables that take only positive values or that lie between 0 and 1) is covered in Chapter 12. Chapter 13 examines special problems that arise when a relationship that a researcher is interested in estimating is actually part of a system of several relationships. In other words, the model specification involves several simultaneous equations. In this chapter, a detailed analysis of two-equation models is presented with a brief introduction to extensions for larger models.

CHAPTER 11

Forecasting

*A*n important reason for formulating an econometric model is to generate forecasts of one or more economic variables. In Chapter 1 we presented a number of examples of forecasting, and in Section 3.9 we used the simple regression model to illustrate the basic principles of forecasting.[1] In this chapter, we take up the issue of forecasting in more detail. We describe the various approaches to it, as well as the methods of evaluating forecasts and combining the predictions generated by different models. Because the subject of forecasting is so wide-ranging, however, this chapter only introduces the issues involved. Numerous books have been written on the topic and readers may refer to them for further details.

Although the term **forecasting** (or the equivalent term **prediction**) is generally used in the context of trying to predict the future, the principles apply equally well to predicting cross-section variables. For instance, one could use the real estate example in Chapters 3, 4, 6, and 7 to obtain the predicted average price, given the characteristics of a house.

In categorizing forecasting methodologies, two broad approaches can be distinguished. **Econometric forecasting** is based on a regression model that relates one or more dependent variables to a number of independent variables. This approach has gained enormous popularity because of its ability to explain changes in the dependent variables in terms of changes in economic and other behavioral variables—in particular, changes in policy variables. In contrast to the econometric approach, **time series forecasting** is most commonly based on attempts to predict the values of a variable from past values of the same variable.

These categories are very broad, and the line between them is not clear-cut. For example, while some econometric models are formulated in terms of only past values of the dependent variable, some pure time series (noneconometric) models relate one variable to the values of other variables (for example, vector autoregressive models discussed in Chapter 10). The time series approach has generally been found to be superior to the econometric approach when very short-run predictions are made. Econometric models are better suited to modeling longer-term effects. Models that synthesize these two general approaches offer potentially improved short- and long-run forecasts. Section 11.6 discusses econometric forecasting, and Section 11.7 gives an introduction to time series forecasting.

---

[1]It will be useful to reread Section 3.9 at this point.

11.1   Fitted Values, Ex-post, and Ex-ante Forecasts

In a forecasting environment three time periods are of interest. An investigator first uses the data for the period n_1 through n_2 (for example, 1948 through 1982) to estimate one or more models. From these estimates **fitted values** (sometimes referred to as **in-sample forecasts**) are obtained; that is, forecasts are made for the sample period n_1 through n_2 (1948 through 1982 in our example). As an example, consider the following regression model:

$$Y_t = \beta_1 + \beta_2 X_{t2} + \beta_3 X_{t3} + \cdots + \beta_k X_{tk} + u_t \qquad (11.1)$$

The fitted value for the time period t is

$$\hat{Y}_t = \hat{\beta}_1 + \hat{\beta}_2 X_{t2} + \hat{\beta}_3 X_{t3} + \cdots + \hat{\beta}_k X_{tk} \qquad (11.2)$$

Out-of-sample forecasts are generated next for time periods $n_2 + 1$ onward. This **postsample period** can be divided into two parts: periods $n_2 + 1$ through n_3 (say, 1983 through 1994), for which the actual values of Y and all the Xs are known; and period $n_3 + 1$ onward (say, 1995 onward), for which the values of the Xs and Y are unknown. Forecasts generated for the period $n_2 + 1$ through n_3 are known as **ex-post forecasts,** and those for $n_3 + 1$ onward are known as **ex-ante forecasts.** Figure 11.1 illustrates these three forecasting periods. Since Y_t is known for $n_2 + 1$ through n_3, the forecasts can be compared with these actual values and the out-of-sample performance of the model evaluated (more on that in the next section). Because the data for the ex-post forecast period have not been used to obtain the estimates of the parameters, ex-post forecasts provide a true test of the model's forecasting ability. Ex-ante forecasts are for periods for which neither the dependent nor the independent variables are known and are hence predictions about the unknown future.

Figure 11.1   In-Sample, Ex-ante, and Ex-post Forecast Periods

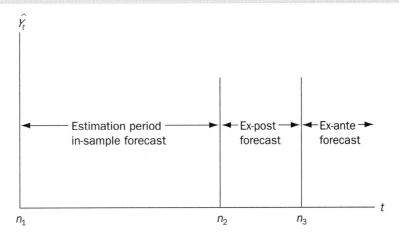

● **EXAMPLE 11.1**

As an example, consider an analyst in the load forecasting department of a utility who is interested in forecasting total residential sales. The analyst has several monthly models that relate residential electricity consumption to weather patterns during the month as well as to other seasonal effects, the price of electricity, the stock of appliances, household income, and so on. Suppose that the forecaster has monthly data for 10 years (120 observations). To compare the forecasting ability of the different models, the investigator might first use observations 1 through 100 to estimate the models (this is the *in-sample* period). She then uses the estimated models to generate *ex-post* forecasts of electricity consumption for the period 101 through 120, *with the known values of the independent variables.* As the values of the dependent variable are also known with certainty in the postsample period, forecasts can be judged against these known values and one of the models selected as the "best." The model finally selected is then reestimated using the entire sample (all 120 observations in our example) and *ex-ante* forecasts (based on this reestimated model) generated for periods beyond 120. These ex-ante forecasts will be the basis on which future electricity-generating capacity is planned and electricity rates are set.

● 11.2 Evaluation of Models

Most forecasters evaluate their models in terms of the models' ability to forecast. Several approaches are used in evaluating forecasting performance. In Section 3.9, the **mean squared error (MSE)** was introduced as a measure for comparing forecasts from different models. For a general model with k regression coefficients, MSE is defined as follows:

$$\text{MSE} = \frac{\sum (Y_t^f - Y_t)^2}{n - k}$$

where n is the number of observations, Y_t is the actual value of the dependent variable, and Y_t^f is the value predicted from a model. In the sample period, MSE is the same as $\hat{\sigma}^2$, the estimate of the variance of the error term u_t.

The model selection criteria discussed in Section 4.3 can also be used to evaluate forecast performance. The procedure is to use each of the competing models to predict the values of Y *during the ex-post period.* Next compute the sum of squared errors (ESS) as $\sum (Y_t^f - Y_t)^2$ and then use the model selection criteria in Table 4.3. A model with lower values of these criterion statistics would be judged superior in terms of forecasting ability.

A third approach used to judge a model is based on the estimation of the following simple linear regression between the forecast and the observed Y:

$$Y_t = a + bY_t^f + e_t$$

If the forecast is perfect for all t, then we would expect $\hat{a}$ to be zero and $\hat{b}$ to be 1. This can be formally tested using an appropriate t-test.

Finally, if all the observations on the dependent variable are positive, one can compute the **absolute percent error,** $\text{APE}_t = 100\,|Y_t - \hat{Y}_t|/Y_t$, and the **mean absolute percent error (MAPE),** defined in Chapter 3 as $(1/n)\Sigma 100|Y_t - \hat{Y}_t|/Y_t$, and choose a model that has a low value for MAPE. We have seen several examples in which the MAPE and MSE have been calculated and model forecastability evaluated.

● 11.3   Conditional and Unconditional Forecasts

In considering ex-post or ex-ante forecasts, it is important to distinguish between *conditional* and *unconditional* forecasts. A **conditional forecast** is obtained when a dependent variable is predicted under the assumption that the independent variables have specific values (which could be known values). As a simple example of a conditional forecast, consider the following model:

$$H_t = \alpha + \beta P_t + u_t \tag{11.3}$$

where H_t is the number of housing units in a certain city and P_t is the city's population. As was noted in Section 3.9, the conditional forecast of H given P, say as P_0, is $\hat{H} = \hat{\alpha} + \hat{\beta}P_0$. Suppose that the population at time $n + 1$ is given as P_{n+1}. Then the conditional forecast for H given that $P = P_{n+1}$ is $\hat{H}_{n+1} = \hat{\alpha} + \hat{\beta}P_{n+1}$. Thus, assuming that next period's population is P_{n+1}, we obtain the conditional prediction for the next period's housing units to be $\hat{\alpha} + \hat{\beta}P_{n+1}$.

Unconditional forecasts are obtained when the values of the exogenous variables are not given a priori but are generated from the model itself or from an auxiliary model. Thus, the independent variables are not measured with certainty but are subject to uncertainty. In the housing unit example, the future population of the city is unknown. An auxiliary model of population migration, births, and deaths may be used to obtain a forecast of the population in the time period $n + 1$ (call it $\hat{P}_{n+1}$). Forecasts of housing units obtained by combining the econometric model with the population model are unconditional. We would thus have $\hat{H}_{n+1} = \hat{\alpha} + \hat{\beta}\hat{P}_{n+1}$, where $\hat{P}_{n+1}$ is the forecast of population obtained from an auxiliary model. VAR models discussed in the previous chapter are excellent devices for generating unconditional forecasts.

Fitted values generated for the in-sample period are conditional (because the values of the Xs are given), but forecasts for the ex-ante period are unconditional because they require that the independent variables be predicted before the dependent variable is predicted. Forecasts for the ex-post period can be either conditional or unconditional depending on how they were obtained.

At this time it is useful to point out some inconsistencies in the literature regarding the use of the terms *conditional* and *unconditional*. Some authors define these terms in exactly the opposite way to the definitions presented here. This is erroneous. The term *conditional* comes from the terminology in probability theory in which we consider the *conditional distribution*, denoted as $P(Y|X)$, of one random variable *given* the value of another random variable. The *conditional mean* of this distribution is $E(Y|X)$. A forecast of Y is an estimate of $E(Y|X)$ and will depend on X. Therefore, the forecast of Y for a given value of X is a *conditional forecast*. The *unconditional mean* of Y, denoted as $E(Y)$, is the expected value of Y over the joint probability density $f(x, y)$ and does not depend on X. An estimate of $E(Y)$ is the *unconditional forecast* in which X is also treated as a random variable.

⬤ EXAMPLE 11.2

The "weather normalization" of sales carried out by electric utilities is a good example of conditional forecasting. In order to set the rates for electricity, utilities are routinely asked by public utilities commissions to obtain "weather-adjusted series" for electricity sales. Such series are obtained by asking the question "What would electricity consumption have been if the weather had been normal?" Normal weather is typically measured by taking the average values for temperature, humidity, wind speed, and so on over a 10-year (or longer) period. The "normal weather" values are then substituted for the weather variables and a forecast is generated. The difference between the forecast of consumption with actual weather and that corresponding to "normal weather" is the weather adjustment. Clearly, there is no such thing as a unique "normal weather." In fact, 10-year averages of weather measures and 20-year averages of weather measures generate two different weather adjustments. The forecasts are thus conditional on the definition of "normal weather." If we also forecast the weather and use it to forecast electricity consumption, we obtain unconditional forecasts.

⬤ 11.4 Forecasting from Time Trends

Most time series of aggregate variables exhibit a steadily increasing or decreasing pattern, known as a **trend.** One can fit a **smooth curve** to an underlying trend. The fitted curve can then be extrapolated to generate forecasts of the dependent variable. This approach to forecasting is called **trend line fitting.** No underlying behavioral econometric model or theory is involved, just the simple assumption that past patterns will continue in the future. In order to decide what type of trend line to fit, an investigator graphs the dependent variable over time and identifies whether the trend is linear, quadratic, or exponential, or has other patterns. We list below a number of commonly used trend lines.

(A)	Straight line:	$Y_t = \beta_1 + \beta_2 t + u_t$
(B)	Quadratic:	$Y_t = \beta_1 + \beta_2 t + \beta_3 t^2 + u_t$
(C)	Cubic:	$Y_t = \beta_1 + \beta_2 t + \beta_3 t^2 + \beta_4 t^3 + u_t$
(D)	Linear-log:	$Y_t = \beta_1 + \beta_2 \ln(t) + u_t$
(E)	Reciprocal:	$Y_t = \beta_1 + \beta_2 (1/t) + u_t$
(F)	Log-linear:	$\ln(Y_t) = \beta_1 + \beta_2 t + u_t;\ Y_t > 0$
(G)	Double-log:	$\ln(Y_t) = \beta_1 + \beta_2 \ln(t) + u_t;\ Y_t > 0$

(H)   Logistic: $\ln\left[\dfrac{Y_t}{1 - Y_t}\right] = \beta_1 + \beta_2 t + u_t; \; 0 < Y_t < 1$

The first five formulations have Y_t as the dependent variable, the next two have $\ln(Y_t)$ as the dependent variable, and the last has a logistic transformation on Y_t. It should be emphasized that the values of $\overline{R}^2$ are comparable only between two models with the same dependent variable. Also, the log transformations require Y_t and $Y_t/(1 - Y_t)$ to be positive. The logistic curve is a useful functional form when Y_t is between 0 and 1 or when Y_t is a percent. As was stated in Section 6.12, the logistic curve ensures that the forecasted value is always between 0 and 1 (or 0 to 100 if the dependent variable is a percent).

We noted in Chapter 6 that if the dependent variable is in logarithmic form, then forecasts are biased. To explore this further, exponentiate the preceding double-log model. We get

$$e^{\ln Y_t} = Y_t = e^{\beta_1 + \beta_2 \ln(t) + u_t} = e^{\beta_1} t^{\beta_2} e^{u_t}$$

Taking the expected value of both sides gives

$$E(Y_t) = e^{\beta_1} t^{\beta_2} E[e^{u_t}] \neq e^{\beta_1} t^{\beta_2}$$

because $E(u_t) = 0$ does not imply that $E[e^{u_t}] = 1$. However, it is possible to estimate $E[e^{u_t}]$ by using the fact that $E[e^{u_t}] = e^{\sigma^2/2}$ (not proved). An estimate of $e^{\sigma^2/2}$ is $e^{\hat{\sigma}^2/2}$. Therefore, a corrected prediction of Y_t is

$$\hat{Y}_t = e^{\hat{\beta}_1} t^{\hat{\beta}_2} e^{\hat{\sigma}^2/2}$$

To generate forecasts from trend lines, the following relations are used (setting the unpredictable error u_t to zero):

Straight line: $\hat{Y}_t = \hat{\beta}_1 + \hat{\beta}_2 t$

Quadratic: $\hat{Y}_t = \hat{\beta}_1 + \hat{\beta}_2 t + \hat{\beta}_3 t^2$

Cubic: $\hat{Y}_t = \hat{\beta}_1 + \hat{\beta}_2 t + \hat{\beta}_3 t^2 + \hat{\beta}_4 t^3$

Linear-log: $\hat{Y}_t = \hat{\beta}_1 + \hat{\beta}_2 \ln(t)$

Reciprocal: $\hat{Y}_t = \hat{\beta}_1 + \hat{\beta}_2 (1/t)$

Log-linear: $\hat{Y}_t = e^{\hat{\beta}_1 + \hat{\beta}_2 t + (\hat{\sigma}^2/2)}$

Double-log: $\hat{Y}_t = e^{\hat{\beta}_1} t^{\hat{\beta}_2} e^{(\hat{\sigma}^2/2)}$

Logistic: $\hat{Y}_t = \dfrac{1}{1 + e^{-[\hat{\beta}_1 + \hat{\beta}_2 t + (\hat{\sigma}^2/2)]}}$

If the trend line exhibits serial correlation in the residuals, improved forecasts can be obtained by exploiting the residual structure, as was described in Chapters 9 and 10.

A common use of trend lines is to remove an underlying trend (known as **detrending**) and then examine the deviation of the observed dependent variable from the fitted trend line. In this case, an analyst first fits one of the curves listed above and then obtains the residuals $\hat{u}_t$. The values of these residuals can then be related to variables that might explain the fluctuations around the trend. This approach is often used by business cycle analysts. They first fit a long-term trend for the dependent variable of interest (stock prices, gross national product, unemployment, or whatever), remove the trend and obtain $\hat{u}_t$, and then relate the residuals to very short-run variables such as the season, government policy announcements, extraordinary international events, and so on.

It should be emphasized that fitting a trend line is generally not an end in itself, but it would be useful as part of a broader modeling strategy in which a dependent variable is related to several independent variables, including, perhaps, trends. Simple curve fitting is not based on any underlying mechanism but on the assumption, often found to be false, that past behavior will continue.

● PRACTICE PROBLEM 11.1

In the preceding log-linear, double-log, and logistic curves, solve for Y_t explicitly as a function of time, and verify the given forecasts. Then graph $\hat{Y}_t$ under various assumptions about the signs of the βs. What different shapes can the curves capture?

Application: Fitting Trend Lines for the Wage Rate in California

DATA10-5 has annual data for 1960–1994 on the average hourly earnings in California. Figure 11.2 graphs this over time, showing that the wage rate was very stable until 1965, when it increased at a substantial rate for two decades and then moder-

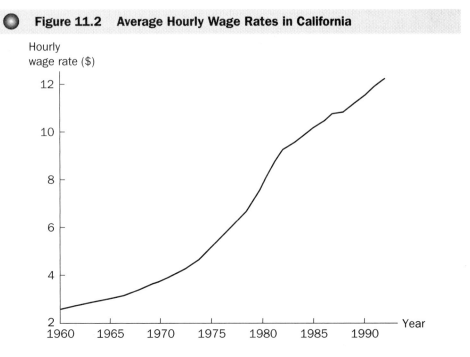

● Figure 11.2   Average Hourly Wage Rates in California

ated. All eight of the trend lines presented earlier were estimated using data for the period 1960–1989. Because there was strong evidence of serial correlation, the parameters were estimated by the Cochrane–Orcutt procedure described in Chapter 9. Out-of-sample forecasts were then generated for 1990–1994, after allowing for the autocorrelation adjustment to the forecast as well as the bias in the forecast for the logarithmic formulations. The regression $Y_t = a + bY_t^f + e_t$, which relates the actual value of the dependent variable to its predicted value, was estimated next. Then the mean absolute percent error (MAPE) and the eight model selection statistics described in Chapter 4 were computed. Table 11.1 presents these summary statistics (Practice Computer Session 11.1 provides the details to reproduce these results). When the forecast is good, we would expect $\hat{a}$ to be close to zero and $\hat{b}$ to be close to 1. In terms of these measures, the quadratic Model B performs the best.

Model B is also the best in terms of MAPE and all the model selection statistics. Table 11.2 has the observed and predicted wage rates as well as the absolute percent errors (APE) for Model B for all the years (see Practice Computer Session 11.2 for details on this). We note that APE exceeded 5 percent only for the years 1961 and 1981, but it was below that for all other years. As mentioned earlier, a true test of a model's prediction capability is how well it forecasts outside the sample period used in the estimation process. It is interesting to note that APE for the postsample period 1990–1994 was no more than 1.68 percent. Thus, Model B, which used a quadratic time trend, performs quite well overall.

● PRACTICE PROBLEM 11.2

Redo the analysis above using the wage data for the United States presented in DATA10-5.

● Table 11.1   Comparison of Forecast Performance of Trend Lines

Models	A	B	C	D	E	F	G
$\hat{a}$	2.879	1.818	−6.296	2.449	2.498	3.854	3.299
$\hat{b}$	0.748	0.849	1.582	0.799	0.795	0.648	0.712
MAPE	1.799	0.610	3.794	0.850	0.876	4.950	2.002
SGMASQ	0.112	0.013	0.385	0.021	0.023	0.673	0.142
AIC	0.149	0.017	0.514	0.029	0.030	0.898	0.190
FPE	0.156	0.018	0.539	0.030	0.032	0.942	0.199
HQ	0.098	0.011	0.338	0.019	0.020	0.590	0.125
SCHWARZ	0.128	0.015	0.440	0.024	0.026	0.768	0.163
SHIBATA	0.121	0.014	0.416	0.023	0.024	0.726	0.154
GCV	0.186	0.022	0.642	0.036	0.038	1.121	0.237
RICE	0.335	0.039	1.156	0.064	0.068	2.018	0.427

Table 11.2   Absolute Percent Errors (APE) for Model B

Year	Wage	Wagehat	APE	Year	Wage	Wagehat	APE
1961	2.72	2.55	6.64	1978	6.43	6.42	0.59
1962	2.79	2.70	3.64	1979	7.03	6.86	2.97
1963	2.88	2.82	2.57	1980	7.70	7.45	3.72
1964	2.96	2.96	0.65	1981	8.56	8.11	5.71
1965	3.05	3.08	1.44	1982	9.24	8.96	3.54
1966	3.16	3.21	2.06	1983	9.52	9.63	1.60
1967	3.29	3.36	2.55	1984	9.77	9.90	1.83
1968	3.44	3.52	2.90	1985	10.12	10.14	0.73
1969	3.62	3.71	2.84	1986	10.36	10.48	1.68
1970	3.80	3.91	3.51	1987	10.75	10.71	0.84
1971	4.02	4.12	3.02	1988	10.80	11.09	3.14
1972	4.25	4.37	3.21	1989	11.16	11.13	0.80
1973	4.44	4.62	4.47	1990	11.48	11.47	0.62
1974	4.76	4.83	1.90	1991	11.87	11.76	1.39
1975	5.22	5.16	1.62	1992	12.19	12.13	1.00
1976	5.59	5.63	1.21	1993	12.38	12.42	0.84
1977	6.00	6.01	0.63	1994	12.44	12.59	1.68

Smoothing an Economic Time Series

When a series is plotted over time, one might notice that there are fluctuations around a smooth trend line. An investigator interested only in the underlying trend might want to try **smoothing** the series by reducing the short-term volatility of the series. This is accomplished in a number of ways. One method is to compute a *moving average* of the form

$$Y_t = \frac{1}{m} \sum (X_t + X_{t-1} + \cdots + X_{t-m+1})$$

where X_t is the original series and Y_t is the new series obtained by averaging m successive terms. For example, where $m = 3$ we would average the first three observations, then average observations 2, 3, and 4, then average 3, 4, and 5, and so on. The extent of smoothness depends on the size of m; the larger m is, the smoother the resulting series. In using Y_t in a regression, however, it should be remembered that Y_t is defined only in the range (m, n), and hence we would lose $m - 1$ observations.

Another approach is **exponential smoothing** in which the new series is obtained as a weighted average of present and past values of series with geometrically declining weights. We would thus have

$$Y_t = \lambda[X_t + (1 - \lambda)X_{t-1} + (1 - \lambda)^2 X_{t-2} + \cdots]$$

with $0 < \lambda < 1$. This can be expressed in a simpler form by noting that for $t - 1$

$$Y_{t-1} = \lambda[X_{t-1} + (1 - \lambda)X_{t-2} + (1 - \lambda)^2 X_{t-3} + \cdots]$$

from which the following equation is easily derived:

$$Y_t = \lambda X_t + (1 - \lambda)Y_{t-1}$$

If λ is close to 1, X_t is given a heavy weight, and hence the resulting series will be as unsmooth as X_t. It follows that the smaller the value of λ, the smoother Y_t will be. Note that exponential smoothing causes only one observation to be lost.

● **EXAMPLE 11.3**

Figure 11.3 shows total nonagricultural employment in the United States, measured in hundred thousands, and two exponentially smoothed series with $\lambda = 0.2$ and 0.7 (Practice Computer Session 11.3 provides the steps to generate the actual numbers). Note that the plot for $\lambda = 0.2$ is smoother than the other two series plots.

Exponential smoothing is also useful when adjusting forecasts to allow for prediction errors made in the recent past. More specifically, let Y_t be the actual value of Y at time t and Y^a_{t+1} be the forecast generated at time $t + 1$ by some model (labeled a).

Figure 11.3   Actual and Exponentially Smoothed Employment Series

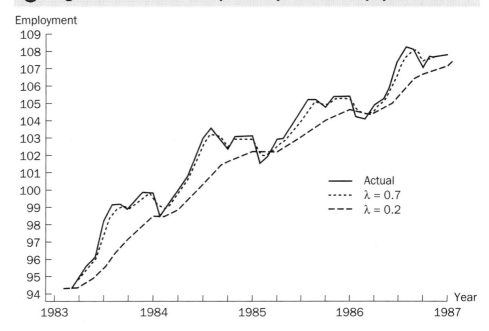

The adjustment made at time $t + 1$ for this initial forecast is a linear combination of previous forecast and adjustment errors. We thus have the **adaptive forecast** Y_{t+1}^b for the time period $t + 1$ as

$$Y_{t+1}^b - Y_{t+1}^a = \lambda(Y_t - Y_t^a) + (1 - \lambda)(Y_t^b - Y_t^a) \qquad 0 < \lambda < 1$$

where Y_t^b is the adaptive forecast made in the previous period. Expanding this and rearranging terms, we obtain the following equation:

$$Y_{t+1}^b - Y_{t+1}^a = (Y_t^b - Y_t^a) + \lambda(Y_t - Y_t^b)$$

where the adjustment factor λ is often chosen to be a small number. To start the process, it is usually assumed that $Y_1^a = Y_1^b$. This method thus has a built-in learning process by which the most recent prediction errors are used to adjust a subsequent period's forecasts.

11.5   Combining Forecasts

In empirical research, the common procedure adopted by analysts is to estimate a number of alternative models, subject them to several tests of hypotheses, and finally choose one as the "best" for whatever purpose the model is intended. If the goal is forecasting, the typical approach (as has been noted before) is to reserve a part of the available data for postsample forecasting exercises, obtain forecasts from different models, and choose that model which has the best forecasting performance in the postsample period. In the previous section, we used several alternative models to forecast wage rates and concluded that the quadratic model was the best from the point of view of forecasting. Models that are judged inferior from a forecasting point of view are usually discarded.

Bates and Granger pointed out in 1969, however, that discarded models do still contain information about the underlying behavior of the dependent variable and argued that **combining forecasts** from several models would outperform those from a single model. As a simple example, suppose f_1 and f_2 are forecasts from two different models or approaches. For simplicity of exposition, assume that they are independent and have the same variance σ^2. Consider an arithmetic average of these two forecasts, $f = \frac{1}{2}(f_1 + f_2)$. The variance of the combined forecast f is $\sigma^2/2$, which is less than the variance of each individual forecast. It is therefore clear that there may be some merit in obtaining combinations of forecasts. In the application of Section 11.2, we found that the quadratic, linear-log, and reciprocal models gave reasonably good forecasts. Combining these forecasts might be useful, but the other models generated very poor forecasts and should be discarded.

In this section, we discuss a number of approaches to combining forecasts and study the properties of such combinations. We consider only linear combinations of forecasts here. The question of interest is how to construct optimum weights for the different forecasts. The steps are as follows:

Step 1   Use the sample period data to estimate the various models.

Step 2   Predict the values of the dependent variable during the sample period.

Step 3   Use the fitted values and actual values of the dependent variable to construct a set of weights for combining the forecasts.

Step 4   Generate out-of-sample forecasts from individual models.

Step 5   Combine these forecasts using the weights obtained in Step 3. If the models are to be evaluated for forecast performance in the postsample period, we need the actual values of the dependent variable.

We present three different methods of combining forecasts and compare their relative merits. The analysis presented here is drawn from a paper by Granger and Ramanathan (1984).

Method A

Let Y_t be the actual value, at time t, of a dependent variable, and $f_{t1}, f_{t2}, \ldots, f_{tk}$ be forecasts generated by k alternative approaches or models. Some of these forecasts may be from econometric models, others from time series models, and yet others from the "expert opinion" of analysts knowledgeable about the behavior of Y. An intuitively obvious approach is to obtain a weighted average of these forecasts, the weights to be determined from some optimality property. Thus, the combined forecast will be $f_t = \beta_1 f_{t1} + \beta_2 f_{t2} + \cdots + \beta_k f_{tk}$.

In the first method, we assume that the weights sum to unity; that is, $\Sigma \beta_i = 1$. The error in the combined forecast is $u_t = Y_t - f_t$. The sum of squared forecast errors is therefore $\Sigma u_t^2 = \Sigma (Y_t - f_t)^2$, where the summation is for the periods 1 through T, for which both forecasts and the actual values of Y are available. The "optimum" method of combining is to choose the weights β_i so that the sum of squared forecast errors is a minimum. It is easily shown that the weights can be estimated using any regression program. To see this, note that

$$Y_t = f_t + u_t = \beta_1 f_{t1} + \beta_2 f_{t2} + \cdots + \beta_k f_{tk} + u_t \qquad (11.4)$$

with $\beta_1 + \beta_2 + \cdots + \beta_k = 1$, or $\beta_k = 1 - \beta_1 - \beta_2 - \cdots - \beta_{k-1}$. Substituting this in Equation (11.4), we get

$$Y_t = \beta_1 f_{t1} + \beta_2 f_{t2} + \cdots + \beta_{k-1} f_{t,k-1} + (1 - \beta_1 - \beta_2 - \cdots - \beta_{k-1}) f_{tk} + u_t$$

Taking f_{tk} to the left side and grouping the β_i terms, we obtain

$$Y_t - f_{tk} = \beta_1 (f_{t1} - f_{tk}) + \beta_2 (f_{t2} - f_{tk}) + \cdots + \beta_{k-1} (f_{t,k-1} - f_{tk}) + u_t \quad (11.5)$$

We readily see that the βs can be estimated by regressing $Y_t - f_{tk}$ against $f_{t1} - f_{tk}$, $f_{t2} - f_{tk}, \ldots, f_{t,k-1} - f_{tk}$, with no constant term in the estimation. β_k is estimated as $1 - \hat{\beta}_1 - \hat{\beta}_2 - \cdots - \hat{\beta}_{k-1}$. Note that the estimated weights could be negative.

Will the mean value of the forecast error ($\hat{u}_t$) due to f be zero? That is, will $(1/n) \Sigma \hat{u}_t = 0$?

$$\sum \hat{u}_t = \sum (Y_t - \hat{f}_t) = \sum (Y_t - \hat{\beta}_1 f_{t1} - \hat{\beta}_2 f_{t2} - \cdots - \hat{\beta}_k f_{tk}) \qquad (11.6)$$

Suppose each of the individual forecasts has zero mean forecast error; that is, suppose that $\Sigma(Y_t - f_{ti}) = 0$, for each i. Then $\Sigma f_{ti} = \Sigma Y_t$. Substituting this in Equation (11.6), we get

$$\sum \hat{u}_t = \sum Y_t - \hat{\beta}_1 \sum Y_t - \hat{\beta}_2 \sum Y_t - \cdots - \hat{\beta}_k \sum Y_t \qquad (11.7)$$

$$= \left(\sum Y_t\right)(1 - \hat{\beta}_1 - \hat{\beta}_2 - \cdots - \hat{\beta}_k) = 0$$

because the sum of the estimated weights is 1. Therefore, a sufficient condition for zero mean combined forecast error is that each forecast have zero mean forecast error. In general, there is no assurance that individual forecasts are unbiased—that is, that they neither overpredict nor underpredict, on average. For this reason, the combined forecast is likely to have nonzero mean forecast error.

Method B

There is nothing inviolable about requiring that the weights for individual forecasts add up to 1. Suppose we do not impose that restriction. Can we get "better" combined forecasts? The answer is yes, provided the criterion for "better" is minimum mean squared forecast error. We see from Equation (11.4) that the procedure now is to regress Y against $f_1, f_2, \ldots, f_k$, again with no constant term, but with no constraints. Because we are minimizing the unconstrained sum of squared forecast errors, the minimum value will be no more than that obtained by Method A. Thus, if ESS_A is the estimated error sum of squares in Equation (11.5) and ESS_B is the same for Method B, then $ESS_B \leq ESS_A$, the gain being $ESS_A - ESS_B$. Will the combined forecast error average to zero in this case? We see that here also

$$\sum \hat{u}_t = \left(\sum Y_t\right)(1 - \hat{\beta}_1 - \hat{\beta}_2 - \cdots - \hat{\beta}_k)$$

if each individual forecast has zero mean error. But, unless the estimated weights happen to sum to unity, the mean forecast error will not be zero. Therefore, although we gain on MSE, we may obtain a combined forecast that has nonzero error mean even though each individual forecast has zero error mean. Note that if any of the individual forecasts is biased, the combined forecast is likely to be biased also.

Is it possible to have the best of both worlds; that is, is it possible to have the lowest mean squared error and zero mean error, even if some of the individual forecasts have nonzero error means? Granger and Ramanathan (1984) have derived such a method of combining forecasts. This is described next.

Method C

If individual forecasts are biased, then their weighted average is also likely to be biased. Suppose we could obtain an estimate of this bias. Then by subtracting this estimated bias we could perhaps get an unbiased forecast of the dependent variable, even though some of the individual forecasts may be biased. This is the motivation behind the Granger–Ramanathan (GR) approach. The trick is to add a constant term to the forecast and let the estimated constant term adjust for the bias.

The modified forecast would therefore be $f_t = \beta_0 + \beta_1 f_{t1} + \beta_2 f_{tk} + \cdots + \beta_k f_{tk}$. No constraints are imposed on any of the βs. The forecast error is $u_t = Y_t - f_t$. The formulation thus becomes the familiar multiple regression model

$$Y_t = \beta_0 + \beta_1 f_{t1} + \beta_2 f_{t2} + \cdots + \beta_k f_{tk} + u_t \qquad (11.8)$$

Note that Method B is a special case of this with the constraint $\beta_0 = 0$, and Method A is a special case of this with $\beta_0 = 0$ and $\beta_1 + \beta_2 + \cdots + \beta_k = 1$. The procedure for estimating the weights is to regress Y_t against a constant, $f_{t1}, f_{t2}, \ldots,$ and f_{tk}, with no constraints. Because an unconstrained minimum is no greater than a constrained minimum, we have $\text{ESS}_C \leq \text{ESS}_B \leq \text{ESS}_A$. Hence Method C is the best in terms of minimum mean squared forecast error. Is the mean combined forecast error zero? To answer this, note that

$$\sum \hat{u}_t = \sum (Y_t - \hat{f}_t) = \sum (Y_t - \hat{\beta}_0 - \hat{\beta}_1 f_{t1} - \hat{\beta}_2 f_{t2} - \cdots - \hat{\beta}_k f_{tk}) \quad (11.9)$$

But the minimization of the mean squared forecast error $\sum \hat{u}_t^2$ with respect to $\hat{\beta}_0$ gives the normal equation

$$\sum (Y_t - \hat{\beta}_0 - \hat{\beta}_1 f_{t1} - \hat{\beta}_2 f_{t2} - \cdots - \hat{\beta}_k f_{tk}) = \sum \hat{u}_t = 0$$

It follows from this that $\sum \hat{u}_t = 0$ and hence the mean combined forecast error is zero. Note that we did not stipulate that any of the individual forecast errors have zero mean. Therefore, Method C is the best because it gives the smallest mean squared forecast error and has an unbiased combined forecast *even if individual forecasts are biased*. For this reason Granger and Ramanathan advocate that the common practice of obtaining a weighted average of alternative forecasts should be abandoned in favor of an unrestricted linear combination *including a constant term*.

Some Extensions to the Standard Forecast Combination

In the regression approach to forecast combination just discussed (Method C), we implicitly assumed that the errors of Equation (11.8) were serially independent with constant variance. This might not be the case, because the errors could be autocorrelated or exhibit ARCH effects. In such situations, we can apply the techniques proposed in Chapter 9 to correct for these problems.

One might also suspect that the weights for combinations (that is, the βs in Equation 11.8) are not constant, but vary over time. Note that this is distinct from errors being correlated over time (serial correlation) or being heteroscedastic (ARCH). It is easy to allow for such **time-varying weights.** A simple approach is to assume that, in Equation (11.8), $\beta_i = \alpha_{i0} + \alpha_{i1} t$, where t represents time from 1 to n, and $i = 0, 1, \ldots, k$. This leads to the modified model,

$$Y_t = \alpha_{00} + \alpha_{01} t + \alpha_{10} f_{t1} + \alpha_{11}(t f_{t1}) + \cdots + \alpha_{k0} f_{tk} + \alpha_{k1}(t f_{tk}) + u_t$$

All we have to do is generate the interaction terms between time and each forecast and then add these new variables to the model in Equation (11.8).

● EXAMPLE 11.4

Bessler and Brandt (1981) combined forecasts for quarterly hog prices from an econometric model, a time series model called ARIMA (described in Section 11.7), and from expert opinions, for the period 1976.1 to 1979.2. Granger and Ramanathan applied each of the three methods to 16 observations from this data set and obtained optimum weights. They then subjected the methods to a postsample forecast exercise for the periods 17 through 24. They also did an in-sample comparison with all 24 observations to estimate the weights. Table 11.3 gives the weights and forecast errors for the 24 in-sample periods, and Table 11.4 shows the out-of-sample forecast errors for the periods 17 through 24. Table 11.3 indicates that the original forecast methods produced somewhat biased forecasts, although these biases did not contribute much to the MSE. The best individual forecast was by the time series ARIMA method. We also note that any kind of combined forecast substantially improved the MSE. As the theory predicts, Method C has zero mean fore-

● Table 11.3   Weights and In-Sample Forecast Errors for Hog Price Data

Forecast	Mean Error	Sum of Squared Errors	Weights for			
			Const.	Econ.	ARIMA	Expert
Original						
Econometric	−1.71	610.4	—	1.00	—	—
ARIMA	−0.03	420.7	—	—	1.00	—
Expert opinion	0.59	522.7	—	—	—	1.00
Combined Method A (no constant, weights sum to 1)						
All three	−0.26	334.7	0.00	0.30	0.27	0.43
Econ. and ARIMA	−0.35	409.8	0.00	0.19	0.81	0.00
ARIMA and expert	0.21	360.8	0.00	0.00	0.45	0.55
Expert and econ.	−0.44	344.6	0.00	0.62	0.00	0.38
Combined Method B (unconstrained, no constant term)						
All three	0.06	331.4	0.00	0.35	0.22	0.43
Econ. and ARIMA	0.11	403.4	0.00	0.26	0.73	0.00
ARIMA and expert	0.14	360.7	0.00	0.00	0.62	0.38
Expert and econ.	0.06	337.4	0.00	0.51	0.00	0.48
Combined Method C (unconstrained with constant)						
All three	0.00	319.6	7.57	0.19	0.26	0.38
Econ. and ARIMA	0.00	372.6	11.80	0.03	0.70	0.00
ARIMA and expert	0.00	325.4	10.65	0.00	0.42	0.34
Expert and econ.	0.00	327.8	6.80	0.36	0.00	0.48

Source: Granger and Ramanathan (1984).

Table 11.4   Weights and Out-of-Sample Forecast Errors for Hog Price Data

Forecast	Mean Error	Sum of Squared Errors	Weights for Const.	Econ.	ARIMA	Expert
Original						
Econometric	−0.95	322.8	—	1.00	—	—
ARIMA	0.78	245.1	—	—	1.00	—
Expert opinion	−2.13	160.2	—	—	—	1.00
Combined Method A (no constant, weights sum to 1)						
All three	−1.14	199.1	0.00	0.47	0.15	0.38
Econ. and ARIMA	0.51	238.6	0.00	0.16	0.84	0.00
ARIMA and expert	0.32	212.2	0.00	0.00	0.84	0.16
Expert and econ.	−1.47	206.6	0.00	0.55	0.00	0.45
Combined Method B (unconstrained, no constant term)						
All three	−0.59	199.8	0.00	0.50	0.16	0.33
Econ. and ARIMA	1.16	246.1	0.00	0.30	0.68	0.00
ARIMA and expert	0.56	217.3	0.00	0.00	0.86	0.14
Expert and econ.	−0.94	205.0	0.00	0.59	0.00	0.40
Combined Method C (unconstrained with constant)						
All three	−0.86	193.4	3.50	0.45	0.13	0.34
Econ. and ARIMA	0.96	233.5	2.89	0.25	0.66	0.00
ARIMA and expert	−0.32	180.2	7.72	0.00	0.63	0.20
Expert and econ.	−1.17	198.8	3.79	0.51	0.00	0.39

Source: Granger and Ramanathan (1984).

cast error and the lowest MSE. Further, as the postsample exercise in Table 11.4 indicates, mean errors are no longer zero if the weights estimated from periods 1 through 16 are used to predict prices for the periods 17 through 24. Although Method C is consistently superior to the other methods, combining three forecasts is not always superior to combining just a pair.

It should be emphasized that the example result may not hold in general for other data sets. It is quite possible that MSE and mean error may be worse in the postsample period than in the in-sample period. Bohara, McNown, and Batts (1987) have shown that, in some cases, individual forecasts for the postsample period might outperform the Granger–Ramanathan method of combining forecasts using Model C, although in the in-sample period the GR method will always be superior. Other studies have found that the GR method outperforms other methods in postsample situations also. As Granger (1989a) has pointed out, the combining of forecasts should be especially fruitful when radically different methods, such as econometric and time series, are used to generate the forecasts. The *Journal of Forecasting* (1989) and the *International Journal of Forecasting* (1989) have each devoted an entire issue to combining forecasts. They contain a number of interesting articles, some using advanced methods.

● 11.6   Forecasting from Econometric Models

The econometric approach to forecasting consists first of formulating an econometric model that relates a dependent variable to a number of independent variables that are expected to affect it. The model is then estimated and used to obtain conditional and/or unconditional forecasts of the dependent variable. The models are generally formulated on both economic and statistical grounds.

Consider, as an example, the problem of forecasting the monthly electricity sales of a utility. Economic theory tells us that consumers choose appliances (including home heating, cooling, and water heating appliances) based on their level of income, the prices of the appliances, and other characteristics such as the demographic composition of the household. The actual usage of these appliances typically varies with the weather as well as with other seasonal effects such as weekdays or weekends, vacations, and holidays. An econometric model of electricity sales would therefore relate monthly electricity sales to weather measures, such as the number of cooling and heating degree days encountered (see the application in Section 9.7), monthly dummy variables that allow for other seasonal effects, income, stock of appliances, and the price of electricity. To evaluate different models and approaches, a forecaster typically obtains conditional forecasts based on the known values of the independent variables for a postsample period. Conditional forecasts are also often obtained under different scenarios of the future: a fast growth in population and income, a medium growth in the economic/demographic variables, or a slow growth. Alternative time paths for the price of electricity can also be selected. To obtain unconditional forecasts of electricity sales, a utility analyst would have to model the behavior of the independent variables themselves. Common approaches used are fitting time trends or using purely time series methods such as those discussed in the next section.

The following are several alternative formulations commonly used in forecasting.

Econometric Forecasting with No Lagged Dependent Variables or Serially Correlated Errors

This is the simplest case of econometric forecasting. The underlying model is of the form in Equation (11.1) in which the errors are well behaved and satisfy Assumptions 3.2 through 3.7. A forecast for the time period $n + h$ (that is, h-steps-ahead forecast) is given by

$$\hat{Y}_{n+h} = \hat{\beta}_1 + \hat{\beta}_2 X_{n+h,\,2} + \hat{\beta}_3 X_{n+h,\,3} + \cdots + \hat{\beta}_k X_{n+h,\,k} \qquad \textbf{(11.10)}$$

As mentioned previously, the forecast will be conditional if the values for $X_{n+h,\,i}$ are assumed to be given from some exogenous mechanism.

Econometric Forecasting with No Lagged Dependent Variables but Serially Correlated Errors

We saw in Chapter 9 that if the errors of a regression model are serially correlated, we can obtain improved predictions by using that information. In Equation (11.1), suppose that u_t follows the first-order autoregressive process (ε_t are assumed to be well behaved):

$$u_t = \rho u_{t-1} + \varepsilon_t \tag{11.11}$$

If $\hat{\rho}$ is an estimate of the serial correlation coefficient, we have

$$\hat{u}_{n+1} = \hat{\rho}\,\hat{u}_n, \qquad \hat{u}_{n+2} = \hat{\rho}\,\hat{u}_{n+1} = \hat{\rho}^2 \hat{u}_n, \qquad \hat{u}_{n+h} = \hat{\rho}^h \hat{u}_n$$

Because $\hat{u}_n$ is obtainable from the sample, we can obtain a better prediction of the forecast error h steps ahead and hence obtain the following revised forecast of Y_{n+h}:

$$\hat{Y}_{n+h} = \hat{\beta}_1 + \hat{\beta}_2 X_{n+h,\,2} + \hat{\beta}_3 X_{n+h,\,3} + \cdots + \hat{\beta}_k X_{n+h,\,k} + \hat{\rho}^h \hat{u}_n \tag{11.12}$$

In the general case of a qth-order autoregressive error structure,

$$u_t = \rho_1 u_{t-1} + \rho_2 u_{t-2} + \cdots + \rho_q u_{t-q} + \varepsilon_t \tag{11.13}$$

a one-step-ahead forecast error is estimated as

$$\hat{u}_{n+1} = \hat{\rho}_1 \hat{u}_n + \hat{\rho}_2 \hat{u}_{n-1} + \cdots + \hat{\rho}_q \hat{u}_{n+1-q} \tag{11.14}$$

The one-step-ahead forecast of Y_{n+1} is therefore

$$\hat{Y}_{n+1} = \hat{\beta}_1 + \hat{\beta}_2 X_{n+1,\,2} + \hat{\beta}_3 X_{n+1,\,3} + \cdots + \hat{\beta}_k X_{n+1,\,k} + \hat{u}_{n+1} \tag{11.15}$$

Subsequent forecasts would be generated in a similar way.

Econometric Forecasting with Lagged Dependent Variables and Serially Correlated Errors

The most general econometric formulation of a single dependent variable is the one with both lagged dependent variables and autocorrelated errors:

$$Y_t = \alpha_0 + \alpha_1 Y_{t-1} + \cdots + \alpha_p Y_{t-p} + \beta_1 X_{t1} + \cdots + \beta_k X_{tk} + u_t \tag{11.16}$$

$$u_t = \rho_1 u_{t-1} + \rho_2 u_{t-2} + \cdots + \rho_q u_{t-q} + \varepsilon_t \tag{11.17}$$

The procedure for estimating a simpler version of this model was described in Section 10.2. For given values $X_{n+1,\,1}, X_{n+1,\,2}, \ldots, X_{n+1,\,k}$, a one-step-ahead forecast is given by

$$\hat{Y}_{n+1} = \hat{\alpha}_0 + \hat{\alpha}_1 Y_n + \hat{\alpha}_2 Y_{n-1} + \cdots + \hat{\alpha}_p Y_{n+1-p} \tag{11.18}$$
$$+ \hat{\beta}_1 X_{n+1,\,1} + \hat{\beta}_2 X_{n+1,\,2} + \cdots + \hat{\beta}_k X_{n+1,\,k} + \hat{u}_{n+1}$$

where

$$\hat{u}_{n+1} = \hat{\rho}_1 \hat{u}_n + \hat{\rho}_2 \hat{u}_{n-1} + \cdots + \hat{\rho}_q \hat{u}_{n+1-q} \qquad (11.19)$$

For higher steps, this procedure will be repeated with $\hat{Y}_{n+1}$ instead of Y_{n+1}.

Empirical Example: Short-Term Forecasts of Electricity Sales

Engle and Granger (1986) carried out a comparative analysis of several alternative models and methodologies for forecasting monthly electricity sales. A portion of their study is presented here. For details, refer to their paper. The data refer to monthly series for 1964 through 1981 for California. The estimation was done for 168 periods (approximately 1964–1977), and ex-post forecasts were obtained for 36 periods during 1978–1980. Table 11.5 presents the estimates for one of the models

● **Table 11.5   Diagnostic Tests for California Model Auto-A**

Test Stat.	d.f.	% of Dist.	Test	Test Dist.
2.749	1	90.269	AUTO1	CHI-SQ
1.998	1	84.254	AUTON	CHI-SQ
18.600	10	95.436	AUTO1-N	CHI-SQ
0.898	1	65.668	AUTO MAX	CHI-SQ
4.019	1	95.501	YLAGD1	CHI-SQ
2.669	1	89.769	YLAGDN	CHI-SQ
9.320	12	32.468	YLAG1-N	CHI-SQ
0.627	1	57.186	Y-MAX	CHI-SQ
13.765	1	99.979	ARCH1	CHI-SQ
0.308	1	42.153	ARCHN	CHI-SQ
19.761	12	92.826	ARCH1-N	CHI-SQ
26.913	24	69.147	ARCH1-2N	CHI-SQ
1.212	1	72.918	TIME TND	CHI-SQ
12.175	2	99.773	CDDMA * TIME, HDDMA * TIME	
9.597	6	85.733	CDD^2, HDD^2, $CDD(-1)^2$, $HDD(-1)^2$, $CDD(-2)^2$, $HDD(-2)^2$	
6.368	2	95.859	RELCP250, RELCP500	
4.432	3	78.158	TIME, D70, T70	
7.466	3	94.156	TIME, D72, T72	
20.915	3	99.989	TIME, D74, T74	
2.7491	1	90.269	AUTO-2	
3.8405	3	72.079	AUTO-3, AUTO-4, AUTO-6	

Source: Engle and Granger, 1986. Reprinted with the permission of the Electric Power Research Institute.

used, and Table 11.6 presents LM test statistics for a number of types of model specifications. The dependent variable is residential electricity consumption per customer. CDD and HDD are the cooling and heating degree days defined in the application of Section 9.7. In Table 11.6, RPINC/C is real per-capita income and RELCP750 is the real average price of electricity. The model also includes monthly dummy variables (MAY is omitted to avoid exact multicollinearity). AUTO refers to serial correlation terms (lags 1, 12, and 13 were used). The values labeled "% of

Table 11.6   California Estimates of Model Auto-A

DEPENDENT VARIABLE = DELC/C
SUM OF SQUARED RESIDUALS = 11,245
MEAN OF DEPENDENT VARIABLE = 394.63
STANDARD DEVIATION = 64.732
STANDARD ERROR OF THE REGRESSION = 8.806
R-SQUARED = 0.983
ADJUSTED R-SQUARED = 0.981
F-STATISTIC (22,145) = 403.55
NUMBER OF OBSERVATIONS = 168

Variable	Lag	Beta/Rho	Std. Error	t-stat
CDD	0	0.123	0.028	4.406
CDD	1	0.171	0.028	6.047
CDD	2	0.102	0.027	3.672
HDD	0	0.063	0.012	4.952
HDD	1	0.010	0.013	7.418
HDD	2	0.032	0.013	2.522
RPINC/C	0	13.492	36.630	0.368
RELCP750	0	−8.780	4.716	−1.861
JAN	0	77.899	11.159	6.980
FEB	0	38.327	10.277	3.729
MAR	0	23.834	8.599	2.771
APR	0	3.743	6.043	0.619
JUN	0	17.025	6.559	2.595
JUL	0	32.158	10.978	2.929
AUG	0	29.562	14.513	2.036
SEP	0	35.415	15.522	2.281
OCT	0	26.262	13.761	1.908
NOV	0	33.551	11.741	2.857
DEC	0	53.550	11.100	4.824
CONST	0	516.190	247.140	2.088
AUTO	1	0.709	0.061	11.603
AUTO	12	0.580	0.072	7.962
AUTO	13	−0.315	0.083	−3.789

Source: Engle and Granger, 1986. Reprinted with the permission of the Electric Power Research Institute.

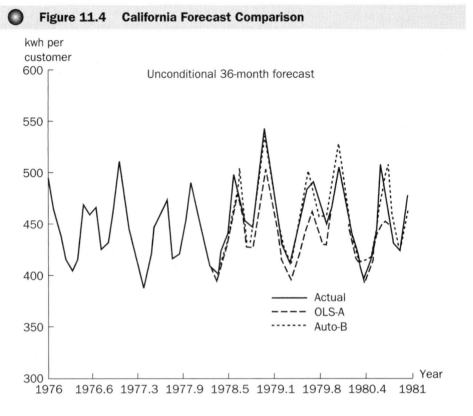

Figure 11.4   California Forecast Comparison

Dist" (Table 11.5) are probabilities in the chi-square distribution to the *left* of the observed chi-square (100 minus the level of significance). Entries over 95 percent indicate significance at 5 percent. The interactions between CDD and time as well as HDD and time were the only significant ones. Engle and Granger reestimated the model including these interaction terms.

Unconditional forecasts obtained from this model (labeled AUTO-B) and a simple model with no serial correlation (labeled OLS-A) are graphed in Figure 11.4. The root mean squared error (RMSE) for a one-step-ahead forecast was 15.4 for OLS-A and 13.6 for AUTO-B. Both the figure and the RMSE values show that the model with autoregressive error terms performed better. Engle and Granger also estimated a variety of other models for ten different states. These are discussed in their paper.

11.7   Forecasting from Time Series Models

As mentioned earlier, econometric models are generally based on some underlying behavior of the agents involved in an economic system. A widely used alternative class of models, however, especially for short-run forecasting, is known as *time series models.* These typically relate a dependent variable to its past values and to random errors that may be serially correlated. Time series models are generally not based on any underlying economic behavior. Until about 30 years ago, time series models were most common in engineering and the physical sciences. In the last two decades, however, the time series approach has gained enormous popularity in economics, especially for short-run forecasting for which time series models have proven to be better suited than econometric models. In this section, we present a brief introduction to the issues involved in the time series approach. For an excellent treatment of time series models and forecasting at the undergraduate level, refer to the books by Granger (1989b) and Diebold (2001). For an advanced treatment of the subject, see Harvey (1990) and Granger and Newbold (1986).

A time series is often modeled as the sum (or product) of three components: (1) a **trend term,** (2) a **seasonal term,** and (3) a **random** (or **stochastic**) term. We thus have

$$Y_t = T_t + S_t + u_t \quad \text{or} \quad Y_t = T_t S_t u_t$$

where Y is the dependent variable, T is the trend component, S is the seasonal component, and u is the random error term. An example of a simple linear time trend is $T_t = \alpha + \beta t$. In Section 11.4, several other forms of trends were fitted. If Y_t has been growing exponentially, it should be converted first to logarithms. As the name indicates, a seasonal component is one that is due to a regularly occurring seasonal phenomenon such as the month or a quarter, week, day, hour, public holidays, and so on. We have seen many examples in which seasonal dummies can be used to estimate seasonal patterns. Very sophisticated techniques were developed to estimate these components, but by the 1930s investigators were disenchanted with the methods, and a different structure was formulated for time series variables. This structure is discussed next.

The Structure of Time Series Models

AUTOREGRESSIVE (AR) MODELS   A purely autoregressive time series model (which is a special case of Equation 11.16) has the following structure:

$$Y_t = \alpha_1 Y_{t-1} + \alpha_2 Y_{t-2} + \cdots + \alpha_p Y_{t-p} + u_t \qquad \textbf{(11.20)}$$

where Y_t is the tth observation on the dependent variable *after subtracting its mean,* and u_t is a well-behaved error term with zero mean and constant variance that is uncorrelated with u_s for $t \neq s$ (such a term is known as **white noise**). The constant term is omitted because Y_t is expressed as a deviation from the mean. Readers should readily recognize that this is a special case of the distributed lag model discussed in Chapter 10 and a special case of Equation (11.16) with all the βs set to zero. In other words, Y_t is modeled only with its own past and not with other independent variables. These are **autoregressive,** or **AR, models,** and the one in Equation (11.20) is referred to as an AR(p) model, p being the order of the autoregressive structure.

MOVING AVERAGE (MA) MODELS   The following model is referred to as a **moving average,** or **MA, model** of order q, denoted by $MA(q)$:

$$Y_t = v_t - \beta_1 v_{t-1} - \beta_2 v_{t-2} - \cdots - \beta_q v_{t-q} \tag{11.21}$$

where v_t is a white noise error series. Y_t is thus a linear combination of white noise random variables. We encountered such an error term in Section 10.2.

ARMA MODELS   A mixture of the autoregressive and moving average formulations is known as an **ARMA model.** Thus, an ARMA (p, q) model is of the general form

$$Y_t = \alpha_1 Y_{t-1} + \alpha_2 Y_{t-2} + \cdots + \alpha_p Y_{t-p} \tag{11.22}$$
$$+ \ v_t - \beta_1 v_{t-1} - \beta_2 v_{t-2} - \cdots - \beta_q v_{t-q}$$

The Autocorrelation Function and the Correlogram

Consider the correlation coefficient $r(s)$ between u_t and u_{t-s} for values of s from 0 to $t - 1$. This function is called the **autocorrelation function.** The autocorrelation function is thus defined as

$$r(s) = \mathrm{Cor}(u_t, u_{t-s}) = \frac{\mathrm{Cov}(u_t, u_{t-s})}{\mathrm{Var}(u_t)} = \frac{E(u_t u_{t-s})}{E(u_t^2)}$$

which can be estimated by the sample correlation coefficient between u_t and u_{t-s}.

The **correlogram** is the graph of $r(s)$ against s, for $s = 0, 1, 2, \ldots, t - 1$. It is a useful guide for determining how correlated the error term (u_t) is to the past errors $u_{t-1}, u_{t-2}, \ldots$.

It is shown in Appendix 9.A that in the case of the first-order autoregressive process [AR(1)] given by Equation (9.2), the autocorrelation function takes the form $r(s) = \rho^s$. The correlogram for AR(1) is presented in Fig. 11.5 for $\rho = 0.3, 0.6$, and 0.9 for $s = 1$ through 10. Figure 11.6 presents the same for negative values of ρ. Note that $r(s)$ is independent of t. Also, if $|\rho| < 1$, the variance of u_t will be finite (proved in Appendix 9.A). Hence, the AR(1) process is stationary provided the autoregressive coefficient ρ does not exceed 1 in absolute value. If ρ is negative, $r(s)$ will alternate in sign. If ρ is high, then the correlogram for AR(1) declines slowly over time, whereas for a low ρ, the function quickly decreases to zero. The usefulness of the autocorrelation function and the correlogram is discussed in more detail later in this chapter.

Stationarity

In this chapter, we restrict ourselves only to the case in which the autocorrelation function $r(s)$ is independent of t, the time period from which current and past residual correlations are measured, and depends only on the distance (s) between the time period t and the period $(t - s)$ for which the correlation is calculated. Furthermore, u_t is assumed to have a finite variance. As noted in Section 10.10, this property is known as **stationarity,** and any time series obeying this is called a

Figure 11.5 Correlogram for AR(1) Model ($\rho > 0$)

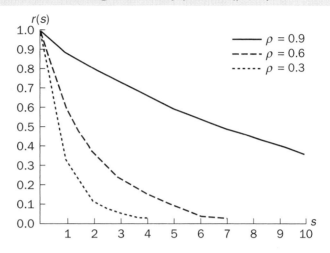

Figure 11.6 Correlogram for AR(1) Model ($\rho < 0$)

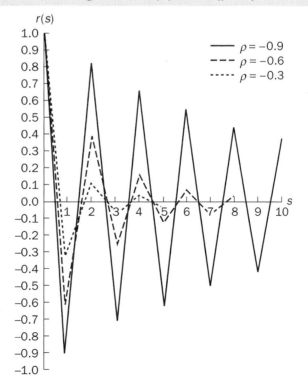

stationary time series. Thus, the process that generates the stochastic disturbances is time-invariant. Under stationarity, $\text{Var}(u_{t-s})$ and $\text{Var}(u_t)$ are the same. Granger (1989a) and Diebold (2001) have more details on the correlogram, stationarity, and autoregressive formulations.

NONSTATIONARITY, DIFFERENCING, AND ARIMA MODELS We just saw that stationarity has the property that the correlation between a variable at time t (Y_t) and its value at time s (Y_s) depends only on the distance $t - s$ between the two time periods. A stationary series has a constant (not necessarily zero) mean and a variance that does not change through time. The process that generates the series is thus time-invariant. Most economic series, however, have **nonstationarity** because they steadily grow over time. For instance, if Y_t has a linear or exponential time trend, it will not be stationary. Estimation of the ARMA process requires that Y_t be a stationary time series. What can one do in such a case? It is possible to convert most nonstationary time series to stationary form through the process of **differencing.** Consider a linear trend of the form $Y_t = \alpha + \beta t$. The **first difference** of Y_t is defined as $\Delta Y_t = Y_t - Y_{t-1}$. We see that

$$\Delta Y_t = \alpha + \beta t - \alpha - \beta(t - 1) = \beta$$

which is constant and hence stationary. Thus, a linear trend can be removed by differencing once. If a series is growing exponentially at a constant rate, the logarithm $\ln(Y_t)$ has a linear trend that can be differenced. It is easily shown that a quadratic trend can be removed by differencing twice. The **second difference** (denoted as $\Delta^2 Y$) is defined as the first difference of the first difference. Thus,

$$\Delta^2 Y_t = (Y_t - Y_{t-1}) - (Y_{t-1} - Y_{t-2}) = Y_t - 2Y_{t-1} + Y_{t-2} \qquad \textbf{(11.23)}$$

Another form in which nonstationarity often arises is seasonality. Nonstationarity in monthly and quarterly series can often be removed by taking appropriate differencing: $\Delta_4 = Y_t - Y_{t-4}$ for quarterly data and $\Delta_{12} = Y_t - Y_{t-12}$ for monthly series.

● PRACTICE PROBLEM 11.3

a. Show that the quadratic trend $Y_t = \alpha + \beta t + \gamma t^2$ can be removed with a second difference.

b. Show that the quarterly differencing $\Delta_4 = Y_t - Y_{t-4}$ also removes a linear trend, and similarly for Δ_{12}.

Suppose a nonstationary time series can be converted to a stationary one by differencing d times. Then the series is said to be **integrated of order d** and is written as **I(d).** The differenced stationary series can then be modeled as an ARMA(p, q). In this case the process that generates the series Y_t is called an **autoregressive integrated moving average,** and the models are **ARIMA models,** denoted as ARIMA(p, d, q).

Estimation and Forecasting with an ARIMA Model

Box and Jenkins (1970) proposed a specific approach to time series modeling, which consists of three stages:

1. **Identification,** which is the specification of p, d, and q.
2. **Estimation,** which consists of estimating the parameters in Equation (11.22) in which the left-hand side is the series differenced d times.
3. **Diagnostic checking,** which consists of applying a variety of tests to see whether the estimated model fits the data adequately. If the model is found to be inadequate, the process is repeated.

IDENTIFICATION   Because most economic time series vary over time in a systematic way, the first step in identification is to choose d, the number of times to difference a series to make it approximately stationary. A plot of the series over time often gives a clue as to the nature of the series. If the series appears to grow exponentially, first take the logarithm and plot it against time. If a linear trend is apparent, difference the series (or its logarithm) once and plot the differenced series. If this also exhibits a trend, a second differencing might be required. Economic time series rarely require differencing more than twice.

A second way to identify whether differencing is required is to calculate the autocorrelation function (ACF) defined earlier and plot the correlogram. The correlogram is a plot of the coefficients of correlation between a series and its past values. If this plot declines slowly (as for $\rho = 0.9$ in Fig. 11.4), then differencing is indicated. Next plot the correlogram of the first differences. If this plot also declines slowly, a second difference is indicated.

Nonstationarity due to seasonal effects is handled by **deseasonalizing** the series. A simple way to take out the seasonal component in a monthly data series is to obtain the difference $Y_t - Y_{t-12}$. Alternatively, we could regress Y_t against seasonal dummy variables and then obtain the residuals of the fitted equation, which would be free of seasonal effects. Other, more sophisticated methods are discussed in Granger (1989a), Granger and Newbold (1986), and Diebold (2001). If seasonal effects are present, the ACF will have "spikes" at regular intervals (see Fig. 11.7 for an illustration with monthly data). The difference $Y_t - Y_{t-12}$ often removes the seasonal and linear trend effects (see Fig. 11.8 for an illustration with the same monthly data).

The initial choices of the order of the autoregressive and moving average terms (p and q) are usually made simultaneously. For large values of the lag (denoted by k), the theoretical ACF of the AR(p) model is approximately of the form $A\rho^k$ (with $-1 < \rho < 1$). If ρ is positive, the ACF will steadily decline (see Fig. 11.5). If ρ is negative, the function will be bounded by a pair of curves, as in Figure 11.9. For the MA(q) model, the theoretical correlogram is zero for all lags greater than q but has no particular shape before q (see Fig. 11.10). The estimated correlogram can be used as a guide to choosing a value of q. If the correlogram remains near zero after a particular lag, then that lag will be a good choice for q.

To choose the initial value of p, another function, called the **partial autocorrelation function (PACF),** and the associated graph, called the **partial correlogram,** are used. Suppose we fit a first-order autoregressive model of the form

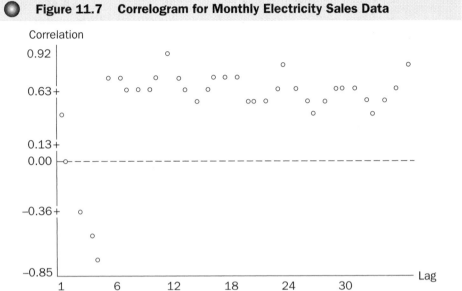

Figure 11.7   Correlogram for Monthly Electricity Sales Data

$Y_t = a_{11}Y_{t-1} + u_t$ and estimate a_{11} by OLS (the constant term is omitted by letting Y_t be the deviation from the mean of the series). Next we estimate an AR(2) model of the form $Y_t = a_{21}Y_{t-1} + a_{22}Y_{t-2} + u_t$ and obtain $\hat{a}_{22}$. By proceeding in this way, we can obtain $\hat{a}_{kk}$, the estimated regression coefficient of Y_{t-k} when a kth-order autoregressive model is estimated. The plot of $\hat{a}_{kk}$ is the partial correlogram. It is the correlation between Y_t and Y_{t-k}, after the effects of the other Ys have been removed. The theoretical partial correlogram has the property that, if the order of autore-

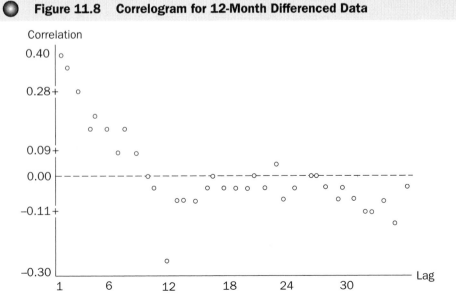

Figure 11.8   Correlogram for 12-Month Differenced Data

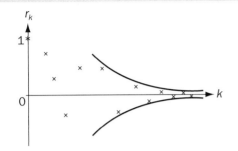

Figure 11.9   Correlogram for AR(p)

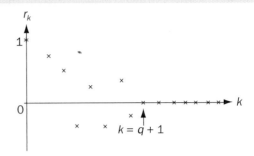

Figure 11.10   Correlogram for MA(q)

gression is p, then $a_{kk} = 0$ for all $k > p$. The estimated partial correlogram can therefore be used as a guide in choosing a value of p. If the partial correlogram remains near zero after a particular lag, then that lag will be a good choice for p. The guidelines for identifying an initial time series model can be summarized as follows:

1.   If the correlogram remains near zero after a certain lag, say q, then the appropriate choice for the order of MA is q.

2.   If the partial correlogram remains near zero after a certain lag, say p, then the appropriate choice for the order of AR is p.

3.   If neither of these happens but both plots eventually decline to zero, we could start with a simple ARMA(1, 1) model.

ESTIMATION   The procedure for estimating the parameters of a time series model is quite complicated and involves solving a set of nonlinear equations. Many computer programs that compute correlograms and partial correlograms used in identifying a model, and then automatically carry out the estimation process, are available (EViews, FORECAST MASTER, FORECAST PRO, TSP, Micro TSP, to name a few).

DIAGNOSTIC CHECKING   The diagnostic-checking stage consists of subjecting the estimated model to a variety of tests to make sure that it fits the data adequately. The best way to examine whether a model is adequate is to conduct a postsample exercise—that is, reserve a part of the sample (which will not be used in the estimation) for ex-post forecasting and then compare the forecasted values with the known values of Y. Commonly used summary statistics are the mean squared error and the Akaike information criterion (see Section 4.3). Another simple approach is to *overfit* the model—that is, fit a slightly higher-order model and then test whether the extra parameters are significantly different from zero.

In any case, if the model fits the data well, the residuals from the model ($\hat{v}_t$ in Equation 11.22) should be white noise. The usual procedure is to compute the residuals and their autocorrelation function and then examine whether the residuals approximate a white noise series. Box and Pierce (1970) have proposed a formal test for this. The procedure is to compute the **Box–Pierce statistic:**

$$Q = n \sum_{k=1}^{k=K} r_k^2 \qquad\qquad (11.24)$$

where r_k is the kth-order autocorrelation of the residuals $(\hat{v}_t)$, n is the number of observations, and K is a preselected number of autocorrelations (say, 20 or more). If the residual series is white noise, then Q will have a chi-square distribution with $K - p - q$ degrees of freedom. If Q is larger than a critical value of chi-square, we conclude that the residual series is not white noise. A more recent test now in common use is by Ljung and Box (1978). The **Ljung–Box test statistic** is given by

$$\text{LJB} = n'(n' + 2) \sum_{k=1}^{k=K} \left[\frac{r_k^2}{n' - k} \right] \tag{11.25}$$

where $n' = n - d$, the number of observations used after the series has been differenced d times. Under the null hypothesis that the residuals are indeed white noise, LJB has a chi-square distribution with $K - p - q$ degrees of freedom. The criterion for acceptance or rejection of the test is similar to that of the Box–Pierce test.

FORECASTING   The final step is to obtain the actual forecasts. We see from Equation (11.22) that a one-step-ahead forecast is given by (setting v_{n+1} to 0):

$$\hat{Y}_{n+1} = \hat{\alpha}_1 Y_n + \hat{\alpha}_2 Y_{n-1} + \cdots + \hat{\alpha}_p Y_{n+1-p} \tag{11.26}$$

$$- \hat{\beta}_1 \hat{v}_n - \hat{\beta}_2 \hat{v}_{n-1} - \cdots - \hat{\beta}_q \hat{v}_{n+1-q}$$

If the series had to be differenced in order to make it stationary, then this forecast would have been for $\widehat{\Delta Y}_{n+1} = \hat{Y}_{n+1} - \hat{Y}_n$, from which $\hat{Y}_{n+1}$ is obtained as

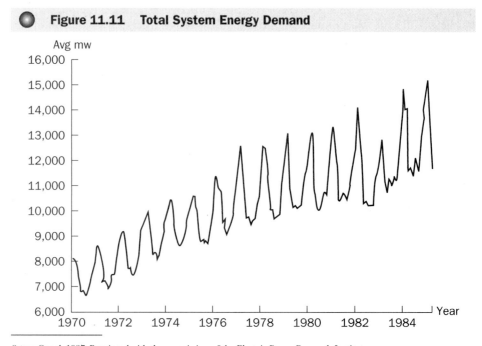

⬤ Figure 11.11   Total System Energy Demand

Source: Gunel, 1987. Reprinted with the permission of the Electric Power Research Institute.

$\hat{Y}_n + \widehat{\Delta Y}_{n+1}$. If the series had been differenced twice, we would have had, from Equation (11.23),

$$\hat{Y}_{n+1} = 2Y_n - Y_{n-1} + \widehat{\Delta^2 Y_{n+1}}$$

Empirical Example: Forecasting Monthly Electricity Sales

Gunel (1987) has carried out a comparative study of a number of different approaches to forecasting Ontario Hydro Electric Company's monthly system energy demand; one of these approaches was the Box–Jenkins method described here. Figure 11.11 is a graph of the total system energy demand for the period January 1970 to April 1984. The graph indicates both strong seasonality and an upward trend. The AIC criterion and the root mean squared error (RMSE) are presented here for four different ARMA models:

ARMA Order	AIC	RMSE
(1, 1)	1,930	320
(4, 1)	1,927	312
(1, 4)	1,926	311
(0, 4)	1,924	311

Figure 11.12 Box–Jenkins Forecast of System Energy

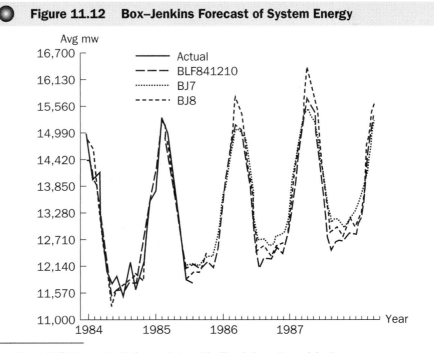

Source: Gunel, 1987. Reprinted with the permission of the Electric Power Research Institute.

ARMA(0, 4) is the best, but Gunel found strong seasonality indicated by the ACF. To remove the nonstationarity due to seasonal effects, Gunel regressed the energy series against a constant and 11 monthly dummy variables and computed the residuals. The residuals were then modeled using the Box–Jenkins methodology. ARIMA(0, 1, 4) appeared to be superior to a number of alternatives the author tried. Postsample forecasts were made through June 1985. Figure 11.12 is a comparison of a number of different models. Although the graph does not show it very clearly, the model (labeled BJ7 in the graph) does well in forecast performance. The statistical measures also indicated that the model has no serial correlation and the lowest forecast error.

Summary

One of the major applications of an econometric model is that of *forecasting* or *prediction*. There are two broad approaches to forecasting: *econometric* and *time series*. *Econometric forecasting* is based on a regression model that relates one or more dependent variables to several independent variables. *Time series forecasting* relates a dependent variable to its past values and attempts to use the relationship to predict the dependent variable.

A forecasting environment consists of three time periods. An investigator uses a sample of observations and estimates the model. The predicted values of the dependent variable during this *in-sample* period are also known as *fitted values*. *Out-of-sample* forecasts can be either ex-post or ex-ante. *Ex-post* forecasts are for the period during which actual values of the dependent and independent variables are known. Such forecasts are often compared with the actual values to evaluate the forecasting performance of a model. *Ex-ante* forecasts are predictions of the future with values of the independent variables predicted from other models.

Forecasts can be conditional or unconditional. When the values of the independent variables are given (or known), we obtain *conditional forecasts*. *Unconditional forecasts* are generated when the values of the exogenous variables are not given a priori but are generated from the model itself or from an auxiliary model.

The evaluation of the forecasting ability of a model is done in a number of ways. First we withhold a portion of the sample and do not use it for estimation purposes. Next we generate forecasts for the withheld sample (this is the ex-post forecast) and compute prediction errors and the sum of squared prediction errors (ESS). This can be used to calculate the model selection statistics presented in Table 4.3. A model that has lower values for most of the criterion statistics is judged to be superior. In addition, we regress the predicted value against a constant and the actual value. If the forecast is perfect we would expect the estimated constant term to be near zero and the estimated slope term to be near 1.

Trend line fitting is a commonly used forecasting technique that expresses the dependent variable as a function of just time. The assumed functional form could be linear, quadratic, linear-log, reciprocal, log-linear, double-log, or logistic.

An investigator interested only in the underlying trend of a time series rather than in fluctuations around the trend might *smooth* the data using either an average of several successive terms (called the *moving average*) or an exponential smoothing, which obtains a weighted average of current and past values of the series, the weights declining exponentially as we move back in time. The technique can be used on forecast errors in order to obtain *adaptive forecasts*.

When several alternative models appear to generate reasonably good forecasts, it is better to combine the forecasts rather than select one model as the "best" and discard the others. The optimum method of combining forecasts is to regress (using sample period data or ex-post data) the actual values against a constant and the forecasts generated by the alternative models. The estimated coefficients are then used as weights to combine forecasts. In the sample period, the combined forecast has the lowest sum of squared errors with zero mean forecast error, *even if individual forecasts are biased.*

In econometric models, forecasts are generated by substituting predicted or assumed values for the independent variables. If there is serial correlation in the residuals, the errors can be modeled with an autoregressive process and the information used in obtaining more efficient forecasts.

As mentioned earlier, time series models relate a dependent variable to its own past values. A purely autoregressive time series (AR *model*) would relate the dependent to its past values with white noise errors. A moving average model (MA *model*) relates a dependent variable to a linear combination of white noise error terms. An ARMA *model* combines the AR and MA features into a single model.

The *correlogram* is a useful diagram for identifying patterns in correlation among series. It plots the *autocorrelation function,* which gives the coefficient of correlation between the values of a series at time t and those at time $t - s$, for different values of s.

The property of *stationarity* has the feature that the series has a time-invariant mean and variance, and the correlation between a variable at time t and that at time s ($t \neq s$) depends only on the distance $t - s$ between the two periods. A nonstationary series can often be differenced (by obtaining the change from one period to the next) to make it stationary. Sometimes it may have to be differenced many times or converted to logarithms before differencing. A linear trend can be removed by differencing once, a quadratic trend can be removed by differencing twice, and so on. Quarterly and monthly data often exhibit seasonal effects that can be removed by differences of order 4 or 12—that is, by $Y_t - Y_{t-4}$ or $Y_t - Y_{t-12}$. ARIMA *models* are models that are first differenced many times to produce stationarity and then have an ARMA model fitted to them.

The estimation of a time series model consists of three steps: (1) identification, (2) estimation, and (3) diagnostic checking. Identification is the process of specifying the orders of differencing, autoregressive modeling, and moving average modeling. Correlograms and partial correlograms are used in identifying models. Diagnostic checking is the process of subjecting the model to tests to see whether it fits adequately. Two tests frequently used here are the *Box–Pierce test* and the *Ljung–Box test.* Once the model has been judged adequate, forecasts are generated from the estimated model.

Key Terms

Absolute percent error (APE)
Adaptive forecast
ARIMA models
ARMA models
Autocorrelation function
Autoregressive integrated moving average
Autoregressive (AR) models
Box–Pierce statistic
Combining forecasts
Conditional forecast
Correlogram
Deseasonalization
Detrending
Diagnostic checking
Differencing
Econometric forecasting

Estimation
Ex-ante forecast
Exponential smoothing
Ex-post forecast
First difference
Fitted value
Forecasting
Identification
In-sample forecast
Integrated of order d, I(d)
Ljung–Box test statistic
Mean absolute percent error (MAPE)
Mean squared error (MSE)
Moving average (MA) model
Nonstationarity
Out-of-sample forecast

Partial autocorrelation function (PACF)
Partial correlogram
Postsample period
Prediction
Random term
Seasonal term
Second difference
Smooth curve
Smoothing
Stationarity

Stationary time series
Stochastic term
Time series forecasting
Time-varying weights
Trend
Trend line fitting
Trend term
Unconditional forecast
White noise

References

Bates, J. M., and C. W. J. Granger. "The Combination of Forecasts." *Operations Research Quarterly* 20 (1969): 451–469.

Bessler, D. A., and J. A. Brandt. "Forecasting Livestock Prices with Individual and Composite Methods." *Applied Economics* 13 (1981): 513–522.

Bohara, A., R. McNown, and J. T. Batts. "A Re-evaluation of the Combination and Adjustment of Forecasts." *Applied Economics* 19 (1987): 437–455.

Box, G. E. P., and G. M. Jenkins. *Time Series Analysis, Forecasting, and Control.* San Francisco: Holden Day, 1970.

Box, G. E. P., and D. A. Pierce. "Distribution of Residual Autocorrelations in Autoregressive Integrated Moving Average Time Series Models." *J. Amer. Stat. Assoc.* 65 (1970): 1509–1526.

Brailsford, Timothy J., and Robert W. Faff. "An Evaluation of Volatility Forecasting Techniques." *Journal of Banking and Finance* 20, no. 3 (April 1996): 419–438.

Clements, Michael P., and David F. Hendry. "Macro-economic Forecasting and Modelling." *Economic Journal* 105, no. 431 (July 1995): 1001–1013.

Diebold, F. X. *Elements of Forecasting.* Cincinnati: South Western, 2001.

Economic Report of the President. Washington, D.C.: U.S. Government Printing Office, 1987.

Engle, R. F., and C. W. J. Granger. *Forecasting Electricity Sales over the Short Term: A Comparison of New Methodologies,* Section 2. Electric Power Research Institute, EM-4772, September 1986.

Granger, C. W. J. "Combining Forecasts—Twenty Years Later." *Journal of Forecasting,* 1989a.

———. *Forecasting in Business and Economics.* New York: Academic Press, 1989b.

Granger, C. W. J., and P. Newbold. *Forecasting Economic Time Series.* Orlando: Academic Press, 1986.

Granger, C. W. J., and Ramu Ramanathan. "Improved Methods of Combining Forecasts." *Journal of Forecasting* 3 (1984): 197–204.

Gunel, I. "Forecasting System Energy Demand." *Forecast Master Program Case Studies.* Electric Power Research Institute, EM-5114, April 1987.

Hamilton, J. D. *Time Series Analysis.* Princeton, N.J.: Princeton University Press, 1994.

Harvey, A. C. *The Econometric Analysis of Time Series.* Cambridge, Mass.: The MIT Press, 1990.

Howrey, E. Philip. "An Analysis of RSQE Forecasts: 1971–1992." *Atlantic Economic Journal* 23, no. 3 (September 1995): 203–219.

International Journal of Forecasting. Special section on combining forecasts (November 1989).

Jansen, Dennis W., and Ruby Pandey Kishan. "An Evaluation of Federal Reserve Forecasting." *Journal of Macroeconomics* 18, no. 1 (Winter 1996): 89–109.

Journal of Forecasting. Special issue on combining forecasts (July 1989).

Ljung, G. M., and G. E. P. Box. "On a Measure of Lack of Fit in Time Series Models." *Biometrika* 65 (1978): 297–303.

McNees, Stephen K. "An Assessment of the 'Official' Economic Forecasts." *New England Economic Review* (July/August 1995): 13–23.

Ramanathan, R., R. F. Engle, C. W. J. Granger, F. Vahid-Araghi, and C. Brace. "Short-Run Forecasts of Electricity Loads and Peaks." *International J. Forecasting,* June 1997.

Townsend, Henry. "A Comparison of Several Consensus Forecasts." *Business Economics* 31, no. 1 (January 1996): 53–55.

Yokum, J. Thomas, and J. Scott Armstrong. "Beyond Accuracy: Comparison of Criteria Used to Select Forecasting Methods." *International Journal of Forecasting* 11, no. 4 (December 1995): 591–597.

Exercises

11.1 Define each of the following terms and provide examples to illustrate them: *fitted values, conditional, unconditional, ex-post forecast, ex-ante forecast.*

11.2 Describe step-by-step how you would go about evaluating the forecasts from a model.

11.3 Suppose you have forecasts from three different approaches: the econometric approach, the time series approach, and expert opinion. Y_t is the dependent variable and the forecasts are f_{t1}, f_{t2}, and f_{t3}. Describe the exact steps for combining the forecasts using the Granger–Ramanathan method, Method C.

11.4 You have quarterly sales for a company for several years. Describe how the dummy variable approach can be used to "deseasonalize" the series (define the term in quotes).

11.5 Describe how you would "detrend" a series Y_t (define *detrending*).

†11.6 Consider the model $Y_t = \alpha + \beta X_t + u_t$, with $u_t = \rho u_{t-1} + \varepsilon_t$. Describe how you would use the estimated models to generate forecasts, taking account of the serial correlation. Suppose the error structure was $u_t = \rho_1 u_{t-1} + \rho_3 u_{t-3} + \varepsilon_t$. What is the forecasting procedure in this case?

11.7 Suppose the error term of a regression model is MA(1), so that $u_t = \varepsilon_t - \lambda \varepsilon_{t-1}$, where ε_t is white noise. Derive an expression for the autocorrelation function $r(s) = \text{Cor}(u_t, u_{t-s})$, $t \neq s$.

†11.8 You have monthly data for electricity sales for a utility for a number of years. It exhibits both seasonal variation and exponential growth over the years. Describe how you would formulate econometric and time series models to capture these effects.

11.9 Suppose $Y_t = Y_0 e^{\lambda t}$; that is, Y is growing exponentially. Show that the first difference in log of Y becomes stationary (define the term *stationary*).

†11.10 Consider an adaptive expectations model derived in Section 10.2. Explain whether the model is AR, MA, ARMA, or ARIMA.

11.11 You have quarterly data for several years for a company. Describe how you would use the time series approach to model the series.

11.12 In many of the previous chapters, time series data were used to relate a dependent variable to its determinants. For each case, withhold the last 10 or 15 observations and estimate a linear and a double-log model with the rest of the data. Next use the models to generate forecasts for the last 10 or 15 periods, using the known values of the independent variables. Compare the forecasts for the observed values (derive appropriate criterion statistics for this) and evaluate the forecasting ability of the models. Also use the Granger–Ramanathan method, Method C, to combine the forecasts and then evaluate them. If serial correlation or ARCH effects are detected, apply appropriate corrections.

CHAPTER *12*

Qualitative and Limited Dependent Variables

In all the topics discussed so far, we have treated the values of a dependent variable as if they varied continuously. Many situations arise, however, in which this is not the case. Suppose, for instance, we wish to model the purchasing decision of a household, in particular, the decision whether to buy a car. In a given survey period, a typical family either bought a car or it did not. In this situation, we have a **qualitative dependent variable**—that is, one that takes the value 1 if the household purchased a car and the value 0 if it did not. Other household decisions such as whether to buy a house, furniture, appliances, or other durable goods are examples in which the dependent variable might be a dummy variable. In the labor market, whether to enter the labor force, strike an employer, or join a union are examples of binary dependent variables. In these cases, the interpretation of the dependent variable is that it is a probability measure for which the realized value is 0 or 1, although the theoretical value could be any intermediate value.

In Chapter 7, we introduced dummy (or binary) variables and demonstrated their usefulness in capturing the effects of qualitative independent variables on the dependent variable. Special problems arise when the dependent variable is binary. Models involving dependent variables of this type are referred to as **discrete choice models** or as **qualitative response models.**

The dependent variable might also take other forms in which it is not continuous. For instance, in the car purchase example, suppose we related the expenditure on a car, in a given period, to a number of determinants such as household income and family size. In such a case, the dependent variable will be continuous, but with a big jump from 0—expenditure will be zero if a family did not buy a car. Thus, the sample might contain a number of observations with zero values along with observations with values in the thousands. This situation also calls for a special type of analysis. Dependent variables of this type are known as **limited dependent variables.** This chapter examines the special problems created by qualitative and limited dependent variables and the techniques needed to address those problems. Because the methodology uses the maximum likelihood principle (described in the appendices to Chapters 2 and 3), which is beyond the scope of this book, only an introduction to these topics is presented here. Empirical examples are, however, presented to illustrate the techniques. For more details on the approaches, see Greene (2000), Maddala (1983), and Amemiya (1981). GRETL, SHAZAM, and EViews have the necessary commands for these techniques.

12.1   Linear Probability (or Binary Choice) Models

In the car purchase example, let Y_t be the probability that a particular household (tth in the sample) will purchase a car in a given year. Let X_t be the household income. Consider the simple regression model $Y_t = \alpha + \beta X_t + u_t$. Although the interpretation of Y_t is as a probability, the *observed* value for a given household will either be 1 or 0 because, in the survey period, the household either bought the car or it did not. Hence, the dependent variable takes a binary form here. Such models are known as **linear probability** or **binary choice models.** Why should that cause any problems? Why not estimate α and β by regressing the dummy variable Y against a constant and income? The answer is that, as will be shown presently, in the case of a dummy dependent variable, the residuals will be heteroscedastic, and hence the application of OLS will yield inefficient estimates.

Let p_t be the probability that $Y_t = 1$, or equivalently, that $u_t = 1 - \alpha - \beta X_t$ (see Table 12.1). Then $1 - p_t$ is the probability that $Y_t = 0$, or that $u_t = -\alpha - \beta X_t$. The random variable u_t is therefore not normally distributed, as is usually assumed, but has the binomial distribution (refer to Section 2.1) with only two outcomes. The expected value of u_t must be zero, and hence we have

$$0 = E(u_t) = p_t(1 - \alpha - \beta X_t) + (1 - p_t)(-\alpha - \beta X_t)$$

Solving this equation for p_t, we have $p_t = \alpha + \beta X_t$. The variance of u_t (σ_t^2) is $E(u_t^2)$ because $E(u_t) = 0$. By definition,

$$\sigma_t^2 = p_t(1 - \alpha - \beta X_t)^2 + (1 - p_t)(-\alpha - \beta X_t)^2$$
$$= p_t(1 - p_t)^2 + (1 - p_t)p_t^2 = p_t(1 - p_t)$$

which makes use of the fact that $\alpha + \beta X_t = p_t$. Hence $\sigma_t^2 = (1 - \alpha - \beta X_t)$ $(\alpha + \beta X_t)$, which varies with t, thus establishing the heteroscedasticity of the errors u_t.

Even though the normality assumption of u_t is violated, OLS estimates of α and β are unbiased and consistent but inefficient because of the heteroscedasticity. The tests of hypotheses critically depend on normality. However, we can invoke the central limit theorem (Property 2.7b), which states that if several random variables are identically distributed, their mean will be asymptotically normal even if the

Table 12.1   Probability Distribution of u_t

u_t	Probability
$1 - \alpha - \beta X_t$	p_t
$-\alpha - \beta X_t$	$1 - p_t$

random variables were originally not normal. Because OLS estimates are linear combinations of such random variables, the normality holds for large samples. However, because heteroscedasticity invalidates tests, they are no longer valid. We saw in Chapter 8 that we can get asymptotically efficient estimates by applying the weighted least squares (WLS) procedure here, provided we can obtain suitable estimates of σ_t^2. Using the OLS estimates $\hat{\alpha}$ and $\hat{\beta}$, we can estimate the residual variance as

$$\hat{\sigma}_t^2 = (\hat{\alpha} + \hat{\beta}X_t)(1 - \hat{\alpha} - \hat{\beta}X_t) = \hat{Y}_t(1 - \hat{Y}_t)$$

We can now set $w_t = 1/\hat{\sigma}_t$ and apply weighted least squares in the manner described in Chapter 8. However, a potential problem arises when the predicted value $\hat{Y}_t$ is 0 or 1, or is outside the interval 0 to 1. In this case, $\hat{\sigma}_t^2$ will not be positive. There is no assurance that OLS will not make such unacceptable predictions. When it does happen, however, we can modify the procedure slightly. If the predicted σ_t^2 is not positive, set w_t to zero. This is basically equivalent to omitting such observations. The steps for estimating a linear probability model are as follows:

Step 1   Estimate the model by the ordinary least squares (OLS) procedure and obtain the predicted values of the dependent variable ($\hat{Y}_t$).
Step 2   Estimate the residual variance as $\hat{\sigma}_t^2 = \hat{Y}_t(1 - \hat{Y}_t)$.
Step 3   Construct the weight for the tth observation as $w_t = 1/\hat{\sigma}_t$, provided $\hat{\sigma}_t^2$ is positive. If $\hat{\sigma}_t^2$ is 0 or negative, set w_t to zero.
Step 4   Obtain weighted least squares (WLS) estimates (see Section 8.3) using w_t as the weight for the tth observation.

As mentioned, because the predicted values are not guaranteed to be between 0 and 1 (even after applying WLS), this model is not used much today.

12.2   The Probit Model

An alternative to the linear probability model described in the previous section is the **probit model.** To illustrate that it does not have the drawbacks of the former model, consider the example of an employee of a company who has to decide whether or not to join a union. The assumption underlying probit analysis is that there is a response function of the form $Y_t^* = \alpha + \beta X_t + u_t$, where X_t is observable but Y_t^* is an unobservable variable. $\dfrac{u_t}{\sigma}$ has the standard normal distribution. What we observe in practice is Y_t, which takes the value 1 if $Y_t^* > 0$ and 0 otherwise. We thus have

$$Y_t = 1 \qquad \text{if } \alpha + \beta X_t + u_t > 0$$
$$Y_t = 0 \qquad \text{if } \alpha + \beta X_t + u_t \leq 0$$

If we denote by $F(z)$ the cumulative distribution function of the standard normal distribution, that is, $F(z) = P(Z \leq z)$, then

$$P(Y_t = 1) = P(u_t > -\alpha - \beta X_t) = 1 - F\left(\frac{-\alpha - \beta X_t}{\sigma}\right)$$

$$P(Y_t = 0) = P(u_t \leq -\alpha - \beta X_t) = F\left(\frac{-\alpha - \beta X_t}{\sigma}\right)$$

The joint probability density of the sample of observations (called the *likelihood function* in the Chapter 2 appendix) is therefore given by

$$L = \prod_{Y_t=0} F\left(\frac{-\alpha - \beta X_t}{\sigma}\right) \prod_{Y_t=1} \left[1 - F\left(\frac{-\alpha - \beta X_t}{\sigma}\right)\right]$$

where Π denotes the product of terms. The parameters α and β are estimated by maximizing this expression, which is highly nonlinear in the parameters and cannot be estimated by conventional regression programs. Programs such as LIMDEP, EViews, GRETL, SHAZAM, PROBIT, MIDAS, and SAS can perform the specialized nonlinear optimization needed here.

An Empirical Example: A Probit Model of Television Station Behavior

Foster and Hull (1986) used probit analysis to model the decision as to whether a television station should subscribe to the Television Code of the National Association of Broadcasters (NAB). The sample data were for 89 U.S. commercial television stations sold between January 1976 and March 1982, when the NAB suspended the code's advertising provisions.

Let C_t^* be the index of incentive for station t to abide by the code, which depends on a number of characteristics. The model used by Foster and Hull is as follows (omitting the t subscript):

$$C^* = \beta_1 + \beta_2 A + \beta_3 Ca + \beta_4 Nc + \beta_5 Y + \beta_6 V + \beta_7 N$$
$$+ \beta_8 CPo + \beta_9 \% \Delta CP + \beta_{10} T + u_t$$

with $C = 1$ if $C^* > 0$ and 0 otherwise. The explanatory variables are as follows (refer to the original paper for details about these variables as well as for a variety of other models estimated by the authors):

A = Station audience size
Ca = Percent of designated market area (DMA) households wired for cable
Nc = Number of large commercial stations viewable
Y = Per-capita income of the area
V = 1 if station has VHF channel, 0 otherwise
N = 1 if station was network affiliate, 0 otherwise
CPo = Index of potential cartel effectiveness
CP = Another index of potential cartel effectiveness
T = Number of months between sale date and March 1982

The estimated model was (with absolute values of t-ratios in parentheses)

$$\hat{C}* = -3.281 + 0.015A + 0.008\ Ca - 0.113\ Nc + 0.380Y - 0.551V$$
$$\quad\ \ (1.22)\quad\ \ (3.02)\quad\ \ (0.55)\quad\quad\ (1.29)\quad\quad\ (1.90)\quad\quad\ (1.42)$$

$$+\ 1.081N - 0.002\ CPo + 0.0003\ \%\Delta CP + 0.004T$$
$$\quad\ (2.12)\quad\quad (0.11)\quad\quad\quad\ (0.02)\quad\quad\quad\quad (0.42)$$

If cartel effects are important, we would expect *CPo*, $\%\Delta CP$, and *T* to have significant positive effects on the probability of subscribing to the Television Code; that is, β_8, β_9, and β_{10} would be positive. However, when the authors tested the null hypothesis that $\beta_8 = \beta_9 = \beta_{10} = 0$, it could not be rejected at the 10 percent level. If all the insignificant variables are dropped from the specification, the estimated model is the following:

$$\hat{C}* = -3.450 + 0.013A + 0.347Y + 0.982N$$
$$\quad\quad (2.45)\quad\ (2.93)\quad\ (1.92)\quad\ (2.57)$$

The numerical values of this regression have no particular interpretation. However, we can conclude that the higher the size of the station's audience or the per-capita income of the area, the greater the likelihood of the station subscribing to the NAB Television Code. Also, network affiliation has a positive impact on the likelihood. Other variables included in the original model have no significant impact on the chances of the station subscribing to the code.

12.3   The Logit Model

In Section 6.12, we introduced the **logit model** (also known as the *logistic model*) and pointed out its usefulness when the dependent variable takes values only between 0 and 1 (or between 0 and 100, if it is in percent form). The logistic model has the following functional form:

$$\ln\left[\frac{P}{1-P}\right] = \alpha + \beta X + u \tag{12.1}$$

where *P* is the value of the dependent variable between 0 and 1. The rationale for this form can be seen by solving the equation for *P* (by first exponentiating both sides). We then obtain the value *P* as follows:

$$P = \frac{1}{1 + e^{-(\alpha + \beta X + u)}} \tag{12.2}$$

It is easy to see that if $\beta X \to +\infty$, $P \to 1$, and when $\beta X \to -\infty$, *P* approaches 0. Thus, *P* can never be outside the range [0, 1].

The estimation procedure depends on whether the observed *P* is between 0 and 1, or whether it is binary and takes the value 0 or the value 1. Models in which the dependent variable is binary are called **binomial logit models.** For an excellent example of such a model, see Wunnava and Ewing (2000). In the case in which *P* is strictly between 0 and 1 (for example, *P* is the fraction of households purchasing a car), the method is simply to transform P and obtain $Y = \ln[P/(1 - P)]$. Then regress Y against a constant and X (more explanatory variables are easily added). If, however, P is binary, then the logarithm of $P/(1 - P)$ is undefined when P is either 0 or 1. The procedure used in such a case is the maximum likelihood method discussed in Sections 2.A.3 and 3.A.5.

The marginal effect of X on P is calculated by taking the partial derivative of P with respect to X. The estimated marginal effect is given as follows:

$$\frac{\Delta \hat{P}}{\Delta X} = \frac{\hat{\beta} e^{-(\hat{\alpha} + \hat{\beta} X)}}{[1 + e^{-(\hat{\alpha} + \hat{\beta} X)}]^2} = \hat{\beta} \hat{P}(1 - \hat{P})$$

A number of computer programs estimate the logit model in more general contexts. They include GRETL, EViews, SAS, SHAZAM, MLOGIT, and QUAIL. Refer to Amemiya's 1981 survey for more details.

⬤ EXAMPLE 12.1

In this example we use the logistic model to estimate the relation between women's labor force participation rates and their determinants. The estimated model using the data in DATA4-5 (see Practice Computer Session 12.1) is

$$\ln \left[\frac{\widehat{WLFP}}{100 - WLFP} \right] = \underset{(-1.53)}{-0.355} + \underset{(5.03)}{0.03316 YF} + \underset{(4.17)}{0.01175 EDUC}$$

$$\underset{(-5.53)}{-0.0587\, UE} - \underset{(-2.71)}{0.00315 URB} - \underset{(-2.75)}{0.00414 WH}$$

Because the dependent variable here is not WLFP, the regression coefficients are not comparable, nor are the adjusted R^2 values. One way of comparing the goodness of fit of a linear model with that of a logit is to use the latter to forecast WLFP and then compute the error sum of squares and the model selection statistics. When this was done, we found that the logit model is better. See Practice Computer Session 12.1 for details.

Empirical Example: Career Interruptions Following Childbirth

Even (1987) has used the logit model to examine the effect of childbirth on the probability that a woman will return to work.[1] The basic assumption behind the model he uses is that "a woman will resume employment in the first time period following childbirth in which her full wage (W) exceeds the value of her time in the home or her reservation wage (R)." The data used were from the 1973 National Survey of Family Growth, for 866 white married women who had at least one child

---

[1]More specifically, what is modeled is the hazard rate, the conditional probability of returning to work at time t, given that the woman has not returned prior to t.

and who worked sometime during their most recent pregnancy. The explanatory variables are the following:

s = Number of time periods after childbirth
KIDS = Number of children in the family
DKIDS = The variable KIDS multiplied by the number of quarters of career interruptions since childbirth
AGE = Mother's age at the most recent birth
HINC = Father's income reported at the time of interview
MQPRIOR = Number of months that the mother ceased employment prior to her most recent childbirth
EXP = Number of years of labor market experience
DEXP = The variable EXP multiplied by the number of quarters of nonemployment since childbirth
OCC = 1 if the mother's occupation is professional or technical, 0 otherwise
EDUC = Number of years of education
DEDUC = The variable EDUC multiplied by the number of quarters of nonemployment since childbirth

Table 12.2 presents the estimated coefficients (with *t*-statistics in parentheses) for a number of alternative model specifications, the dependent variable being the probability of returning to work. We note that EDUC is not statistically significant in any of the models, whereas a priori we would have expected a positive effect on wages. As an explanation, Even suggests that a high wage might also induce a woman to demand a high child quality and, consequently, she might quit her job to improve child quality. The insignificance of the interaction term DEDUC indicates that the marginal effect of EDUC does not depend on the number of quarters of nonemployment since childbirth.

The coefficient for KIDS is insignificant, but that for the interaction DKIDS is significantly positive (at the 5 percent level of significance). This means that additional children have a negligible effect on the probability immediately after childbirth, but the marginal effect increases as time passes. This might be due to older children requiring less attention and to the fact that their presence might increase the demand for market goods.

AGE has the expected negative sign and is significant. Similarly, the higher the husband's income, the lower the probability of returning to work. Experience has the expected positive effect on the probability, as does the dummy variable for professional women.

The variable MQPRIOR, which is the number of months that the mother ceased employment prior to childbirth, has a very strong negative effect. Thus, quitting earlier during pregnancy increases the probability that the woman will not (or will not be able to) return to work.

● 12.4 Limited Dependent Variables

As mentioned in the introduction to this chapter, the observed values of an independent variable sometimes have a discrete jump at zero. For instance, if we take a

⬤ Table 12.2   Estimated Logit Models

	(1)	(2)	(3)	(4)	(5)	(6)
Constant	−0.286 (0.69)	−0.45 (1.08)	0.095 (0.18)	0.34 (0.66)	0.75 (1.44)	0.97 (1.80)
s	*	*	−0.12 (1.62)	−0.28 (4.01)	−0.58 (6.31)	−0.79 (5.45)
s^2	*	*	*	0.0097 (7.02)	0.050 (6.13)	0.096 (3.67)
$s^3/100$	*	*	*	*	−0.13 (4.90)	−0.47 (2.54)
$s^4/1000$	*	*	*	*	*	0.077 (1.88)
DKIDS	*	0.018 (2.29)	0.023 (2.78)	0.015 (2.03)	0.013 (1.82)	0.013 (1.82)
DEXP	*	−0.0080 (2.77)	−0.0074 (2.49)	−0.0053 (2.03)	−0.0055 (2.23)	−0.0055 (2.23)
DEDUC	*	−0.010 (5.21)	−0.0019 (0.34)	−0.0031 (0.65)	−0.0026 (0.54)	−0.0025 (0.53)
KIDS	0.082 (1.70)	0.026 (0.41)	0.0010 (0.02)	0.047 (0.76)	0.051 (0.81)	0.051 (0.81)
AGE	−0.046 (2.87)	−0.046 (2.78)	−0.045 (2.73)	−0.044 (2.67)	−0.044 (2.66)	−0.045 (2.69)
HINC	−0.027 (3.83)	−0.016 (2.27)	−0.016 (2.28)	−0.015 (2.12)	−0.015 (2.13)	−0.015 (2.12)
MQPRIOR	−0.148 (8.06)	−0.12 (6.63)	−0.12 (6.55)	−0.12 (6.30)	−0.12 (6.16)	−0.12 (6.11)
EXP	0.033 (2.26)	0.076 (3.84)	0.073 (3.66)	0.063 (3.30)	0.063 (3.29)	0.064 (3.30)
OCC	0.311 (2.45)	0.28 (2.12)	0.29 (2.20)	0.27 (2.02)	0.25 (1.90)	0.25 (1.97)
EDUC	−0.025 (0.92)	0.025 (0.89)	−0.014 (0.38)	−0.0090 (0.26)	−0.0091 (0.26)	−0.0089 (0.25)
Log-likelihood	−1806.8	−1698.1	−1696.8	−1674.8	−1661.6	−1659.9
Goodness-of-fit statistics	459.65 (0)	98.84 (2.2E−11)	97.14 (4.4E−11)	61.34 (2.0E−5)	37.82 (0.027)	33.91 (0.066)

Source: Adapted from Even, 1987, Table 2, p. 266. Reprinted with the permission of the University of Chicago Press.

random sample of women and record their wages, we may observe many zero values because recorded wages are available only for working women. Thus, in the simple regression model $Y_t = \alpha + \beta X_t + u_t$, we observe the dependent variable only when $Y_t > 0$. As another example, if we obtain a random sample of households and record their expenditure on durable goods, some of the entries may be zero while others are positive. We therefore never observe negative values. What are the consequences of disregarding this fact and regressing Y against a constant and X? We note that, in this situation, the errors will not satisfy the condition $E(u_t) = 0$, which is required for the unbiasedness of estimates. A dependent variable with the property that it has a discrete jump at zero (or any other threshold value) is known as a *limited dependent variable*. One of the first applications (in economics) of the limited dependent variable model was given by Tobin (1958). He applied it to model household expenditure on automobiles. Such models are referred to as **tobit models** or as **censored regressions**.

The Tobit Model (or Censored Regressions)

In the Tobit model, there is an asymmetry between observations with positive values of Y and those with negative values. In this case, the model becomes

$$Y_t = \begin{cases} \alpha + \beta X_t + u_t & \text{if } Y_t > 0 \quad \text{or} \quad u_t > -\alpha - \beta X_t \\ 0 & \text{if } Y_t \leq 0 \quad \text{or} \quad u_t \leq -\alpha - \beta X_t \end{cases}$$

The basic assumption behind this model is that there exists an index function $I_t = \alpha + \beta X_t + u_t$ for each economic agent being studied. If $I_t \leq 0$, the value of the dependent variable is set to zero. If $I_t > 0$, the value of the dependent variable is set to I_t. Suppose u has the normal distribution with mean zero and variance σ^2. We note that $Z = u/\sigma$ is a standard normal random variable. Denote by $f(z)$ the probability density of the standard normal variable Z, and by $F(z)$ its cumulative density—that is, $P[Z \leq z]$. Then the joint probability density for those observations for which Y_t is positive is given by (see Section 3.A.5) the following expression:

$$P_1 = \prod_{i=1}^{i=m} \frac{1}{\sigma} f\left[\frac{Y_i - \alpha - \beta X_i}{\sigma} \right]$$

where Π denotes the product and m is the number of observations in the subsample for which Y is positive. For the second subsample (of size n) for which the observed Y is zero, the random variable $u \leq -\alpha - \beta X$. The probability for this event is

$$P_2 = \prod_{j=1}^{j=n} P[u_j \leq -\alpha - \beta X_j]$$

$$= \prod_{j=1}^{j=n} F\left[\frac{-\alpha - \beta X_j}{\sigma} \right]$$

The joint probability for the entire sample is therefore given by $L = P_1 P_2$. Because this is nonlinear in α and β, the OLS procedure is not appropriate here. The procedure for obtaining estimates of α and β is to maximize L with respect to the parameters. This is the maximum likelihood procedure described in Section 3.A.5.

Among others, the computer programs EViews, LIMDEP, SAS, SHAZAM, and TSP have procedures for estimating the Tobit model.

Empirical Example: A Tobit Model of Charitable Contributions

Reece (1979) has carried out a study of charitable contributions using a Tobit model. Although he examined a number of components of charitable contributions, here we focus on just three: total of all contributions, contributions to charities, and a category called "CONTRIB," which excludes from the total gifts support to nonhousehold members and certain miscellaneous contributions. Most of the data were obtained (for a large number of households) from the Consumer Expenditure Survey of the Bureau of Labor Statistics for 1972 and 1973. Households were from a number of Standard Metropolitan Statistical Areas (SMSAs). Other sources of data were the U.S. Bureau of the Census and the Department of Health, Education, and Welfare. Table 12.3 presents the estimated elasticities implied by

Table 12.3 Estimated Tobit Models

	Equations		
	(1) Charity + Deducted	(2) All	(3) Contrib.
PRICE	−0.976	−1.401	−1.192
	−114.60 (−2.67)	−787.88 (−4.63)	−396.71 (−4.15)
INCOME	1.423	0.550	0.877
	0.0095 (9.99)	0.0176 (4.87)	0.0166 (8.01)
AGE	0.309	0.484	0.380
	0.8808 (1.44)	6.60 (2.79)	3.06 (2.30)
ASSISTANCE	−0.097	−0.186	0.102
	−0.0108 (−0.29)	−0.0996 (−0.67)	0.0322 (0.39)
RECIPIENT	−0.138	0.327	0.351
	−0.0017 (−0.37)	0.0190 (1.06)	0.0121 (1.20)
COL	−1.511	0.518	−0.542
	−0.1420 (−1.21)	0.2329 (0.51)	−0.1443 (−0.57)
SECOND	−0.016	0.005	−0.012
	−3.42 (−0.27)	5.32 (0.11)	−7.30 (−0.26)
CONSTANT	124.70 (0.95)	113.33 (0.22)	183.61 (0.64)
$1 - e'e/s^2$	0.342	0.175	0.282
$1 - e'e/y'y$	0.466	0.405	0.529

Note: The elasticity, coefficient, and *t*-statistic (in parentheses) are given for each variable.
Source: Adapted from Reece, 1979, Table 1, p. 147. Reprinted with the permission of the American Economic Association.

the coefficients of the index function, the coefficients themselves, and the corresponding *t*-statistics. The independent variables are as follows:

PRICE = Price of contributions
INCOME = Average of current and previous years' family income (before taxes) plus net return from home ownership
ASSISTANCE = Average public assistance
RECIPIENT = Lower quintile family income for the SMSA
COL = An index of family budget for the SMSA
AGE = Age of the head of the household
SECOND = 1 for the sample from 1973, 0 for the sample from 1972

Reece defines the price of a dollar of contribution to be the amount of consumption forgone by the household in making the contribution. Because of the tax deductibility of the contributions, the price will generally be less than 1. For more details on the exact measure used, those interested should refer to the original paper. In order to take account of differences in the price of consumption goods across households, a cost-of-living index variable (COL) is used. The variable RECIPIENT is used to approximate the effect of the social environment. The assumption is that, aside from themselves, households are concerned mostly about other families living in the same geographical area (this is the "utility interdependence" hypothesis). If the other families' average income is low, the household might be more generous with its contributions. The income below which 20 percent of the families reside in the area (the lower quintile) is used as RECIPIENT.

The last two rows of Table 12.3 show two goodness-of-fit measures. Although they are not very high, they are reasonable, considering the fact that it is difficult to get high goodness-of-fit measures in cross-section data (especially one for a large number of households). The dependent variable CHARITY + DEDUCTED includes all charitable contributions, whether they were deducted from pay or not. The PRICE and INCOME variables are statistically significant and have the expected signs. The social environment variables ASSISTANCE and RECIPIENT have insignificant negative coefficients. This suggests a lack of support for the "utility interdependence" hypothesis. The coefficient for SECOND is negative and significant. This indicates that contributions decreased, on average, in 1973 as compared to 1972. This result is to be expected because 1972 was an election year. The results also indicate that (1) the tax deductibility of contributions to charity is an important element in determining the amount of contributions made and (2) religious organizations gain even more when contributions are tax deductible.

Summary

This chapter concerned the special treatment needed when the dependent variable (Y) either takes a binary form or has a discrete jump at zero. Whenever an economic agent's decision takes the form of whether or not to pursue a particular course of action (for example, buy a car or house, strike against an employer, return to work after childbirth, vote for a particular candidate, and so on), the observed value of Y is 1 or 0. Models that address this type of dependent variable are known as *discrete choice models*. *Linear probability models*, *probit models*, and *logit models* are examples of discrete choice models. OLS is not applicable to a model with a binary dependent variable because the error terms are heteroscedastic. Using a binomial framework, it is possible to estimate the heteroscedasticity and apply weighted least squares. However, there is no guarantee that the predicted value of the dependent variable (which is interpreted as a probability measure) will be between 0 and 1. To avoid this difficulty, logit models are often used. The dependent variable now takes the form $\ln[P/(1 - P)]$, where P is the observed fraction of times a particular decision is favored and ln is the natural logarithm. The logit model has the property that the predicted value of P is always between 0 and 1. If Y is not the observed fraction but is binary (taking the values 0 and 1 only), then a probit model is appropriate.

In many situations, Y may be bounded by zero (or some other threshold value). Thus, the observed value of Y might always be positive or zero, but never negative. Endogenous variables of this type are known as *limited dependent variables*. The *Tobit model* is frequently used to address limited dependent variables. OLS is not applicable here either because the condition $E(u) = 0$ (u is the error term), needed for unbiasedness of estimates, is not satisfied. The appropriate procedure here is the maximum likelihood method.

Key Terms

Binary choice models

Binomial logit model

Censored regressions

Discrete choice models

Limited dependent variable

Linear probability models

Logit models

Probit models

Qualitative dependent variable

Qualitative response models

Tobit models

References

The references given here include a number of excellent surveys on the topics.

Amemiya, T. "Qualitative Response Models: A Survey." *Journal of Economic Literature* 19 (December 1981): 1488–1536.

———. "Tobit Models: A Survey." *Journal of Econometrics* 24 (January/February 1984): 3–61.

Even, William. "Career Interruptions Following Childbirth." *Journal of Labor Economics* 5 (April 1987): 255–277.

Foster, Carroll B., and Brooks Hull. "An OPEC in Fantasyland: The NAB Television Code as Cartel." University of Michigan–Dearborn, Working Paper No. 41, 1986.

Greene, W. H. *Econometric Analysis.* Upper Saddle River, N.J.: Prentice-Hall, 2000.

Ham, John C., and Samuel A. Rea, Jr. "Unemployment Insurance and Male Unemployment Duration in Canada." *Journal of Labor Economics* 5 (July 1987): 325–353.

Maddala, G. S. *Limited Dependent and Qualitative Variables in Econometrics.* Cambridge: Cambridge University Press, 1983.

Reece, William S. "Charitable Contributions: New Evidence on Household Behavior." *American Economic Review* 69 (March 1979): 142–151.

Tobin, James. "Estimation of Relationships for Limited Dependent Variables." *Econometrica* 26 (1958): 24–36.

Tracy, Joseph. "An Empirical Test of an Asymmetric Information Model of Strikes." *Journal of Labor Economics* 5 (April 1987): 149.

Wunnava, P. V., and B. T. Ewing, "Union–Nonunion Gender Wage and Differential across Establishment Sizes." *Small Business Economics* 15 (2000): 47–57.

Exercises

†12.1 A company did a survey of employees between 55 and 65 years of age who had either retired recently or were eligible for retirement but had not yet retired. Let P be probability of retirement, A be the age of the employee or retiree, N be the number of years employed, and S be the salary at the present time or at retirement. The observed values of P are either 0 or 1. Describe how you would formulate a linear probability model for the probability of retirement. Next describe the estimation procedure. What signs would you expect for each of the explanatory variables? Justify your answers carefully.

12.2 DATA12-1 has the data on the acceptance or rejection to medical school for a sample of 60 applicants, along with a number of their characteristics. The variables are the following:

ACCEPT = 1 if granted an acceptance, 0 if otherwise
GPA = Cumulative undergraduate grade point average
BIO = Score in biology portion of the Medical College Admissions Test (MCAT)
CHEM = Score in chemistry portion of MCAT
PHY = Score in physics portion of MCAT
RED = Score in reading portion of MCAT
PRB = Score in problem portion of MCAT
QNT = Score in quantitative portion of MCAT
AGE = Age of applicant
GENDER = 1 if male, 0 if female

First estimate a relation between ACCEPT and the other variables using OLS. Use the estimates to obtain the predicted acceptance rates and then reestimate the model by WLS, as described in Section 12.1. Use the revised estimates to predict the probability of acceptance for each of the applicants. Check whether they lie between 0 and 1. Based on your analysis, what do you conclude about the usefulness of the linear probability model?

If you have access to one of the programs that estimate the probit model described in Section 12.1, use it to estimate the relation between ACCEPT and the other variables.

†12.3 Suppose you have a sample of companies for which you have data on the following variables:

P = The fraction of employees between 55 and 65 years of age who have recently retired
A = The median age of employees or recent retirees
N = The median number of years employed
S = The median salary

Formulate a logit model of the probability of retirement and explain how you would estimate it.

12.4 Let H be the fraction of households in a given SMSA that purchased a house in a certain period, Y be the median income of the SMSA, P be the median price of a single-family house in the area, and R be the average mortgage rate prevailing in the city. To model the probability of purchasing a house, is a linear probability model or a logit model more appropriate? Formulate a model and describe how you would estimate it.

12.5 A union wants to model the relationship between the probability that an employee will join the union and a number of characteristics of the employee. It hires you to conduct a survey and construct appropriate models. What kind of survey would be appropriate here: a survey of individual employees in a company or a survey of employees in several companies? Describe the kind of data you would obtain and the model you would formulate. For the model you construct, describe the estimation procedure.

12.6 An analyst for the Justice Department obtains a random sample of the names of persons arrested for a crime and gathers the following information: whether the person was convicted, the annual income, number of years of schooling, race, male or female, and the number of previous arrests. Formulate an appropriate model for the probability of conviction and describe how you would estimate it. Do you have any prior notion of what sign to expect for each of the independent variables? Explain.

12.7   A labor economist draws a random sample of women, both employed and unemployed but in the labor force, and gathers the following data: monthly wages (which will be zero if the woman is unemployed), age of the woman, number of years of education, skill status (unskilled, clerical or equivalent, and professional), race (white or nonwhite), and the number of years or prior experience. What is the appropriate framework for modeling the wages? Describe how you would estimate the model you formulate.

CHAPTER 13

Simultaneous Equation Models

*A*ll *the econometric models discussed so far have dealt with a single dependent variable. In many economic models, however, several endogenous (that is, dependent) variables are determined simultaneously. Estimating demand and supply equations is an example of this type of formulation; here the price and quantity are jointly determined. Macroeconomic models are also examples of simultaneous equation specification. In this chapter, we study the special problems that arise when simultaneous equation models are estimated. Only the basics of simultaneous equation models are presented, however. The reader is referred to the bibliography at the end of this chapter for more details and generalizations.*

13.1 Structure and Reduced Forms of Simultaneous Equation Models

Structural Equations

Consider the following equations representing the demand and supply of wheat (for simplicity, the t-subscript is omitted):

$$q_d = \alpha_0 + \alpha_1 p + \alpha_2 y + u \tag{13.1}$$

$$q_s = \beta_0 + \beta_1 p + \beta_2 r + v \tag{13.2}$$

$$q_d = q_s \tag{13.3}$$

where q_d is the quantity of wheat demanded, q_s is the supply of wheat, p is the price, y is income, r is the amount of rainfall, and u and v are stochastic disturbance terms. The first equation is the demand relation, in which the quantity demanded is related to price and income. Equation (13.2) specifies the quantity supplied as a function of price and the amount of rainfall. Although other variables such as the amount of fertilizer, machines used, and so on, are important determinants of supply, they have been excluded in order to simplify the exposition. Equations (13.1) and (13.2) are known as **behavioral equations** (because they are determined by the behavior of economic agents). Basic economic theory tells us that the equilibrium price and quantity sold are determined by the equality of supply and demand. Equation (13.3) is thus the equilibrium condition that determines price and quantity sold. The simultaneous equation system therefore consists of two behavioral equations and one equilibrium condition.

Equations (13.1), (13.2), and (13.3) are known as the **structural equations** of the simultaneous equation model, and the regression coefficients—the αs and βs—are known as the **structural parameters.** Because price and quantity are jointly determined, they are both **endogenous variables.** We note that price influences quantity and vice versa. This is known as **feedback,** a feature common among simultaneous equation models. Income and rainfall are not determined by the specified model but are given exogenously, and hence they are the **exogenous variables.** In single-equation models we used the terms *exogenous variable* and *explanatory variables* interchangeably. In simultaneous equation modeling this is no longer possible. In Equation (13.1), price is an explanatory variable but is not an exogenous variable.

Although the model just specified has three equations, by setting $q_d = q_s = q$, we can reduce the model to a two-equation specification. The simultaneous equation model therefore consists of two equations in two endogenous variables (p and q) and three exogenous variables (a constant term, income, and rainfall). The number of equations in a system (which is the same as the number of endogenous variables) is denoted by G, and the number of exogenous variables by K.

A simultaneous equation model might also have other types of equations and variables. These are best understood with an example. Consider the following simple macro model:

$$C_t = \alpha_0 + \alpha_1 DY_t + \alpha_2 DY_{t-1} + u_t \tag{13.4}$$

$$I_t = \beta_0 + \beta_1 Y_t + \beta_2 Y_{t-1} + v_t \tag{13.5}$$

$$DY_t = Y_t - T_t \tag{13.6}$$

$$Y_t = C_t + I_t + G_t \tag{13.7}$$

where C is consumption expenditure, I is investment, Y is the gross national product (GNP), G is government expenditure, T is total taxes, and DY is disposable income. Equation (13.6) defines disposable income as GNP less taxes. This equation is thus an *identity.* Equations (13.4) and (13.5) are the behavioral equations, and Equation (13.7) is the equilibrium condition, well known in macro models. The model thus consists of four structural equations in the four endogenous variables Y_t, C_t, I_t, and DY_t (that is, $G = 4$). The variable DY_{t-1} is disposable income in the previous period. At time t, this lagged endogenous variable is known and is hence predetermined, as is Y_{t-1}. We therefore see that a simultaneous equation model consists of endogenous variables whose behavior we are trying to explain, exogenous variables whose values are given outside the system, and **predetermined variables** that consist of lagged endogenous variables. To avoid confusion, we henceforth include all exogenous variables under the category *predetermined.* A model will thus consist of endogenous variables (G in number) and predetermined variables (K in number). In the macro example, G is 4 and K is 5 (G_t, T_t, Y_{t-1}, DY_{t-1}, and a constant).

Another type of equation, not specified in the examples given previously, is a **technical equation.** For example, we could have added a production function to the macro model, relating the aggregate supply (Q) to inputs such as the capital stock (K) and labor (L). The types of equations encountered in simultaneous equation models are thus behavioral, technical, equilibrium conditions, and identities.

Reduced Form Equations

Equating (13.1) and (13.2) and solving for p, we obtain the following relation:

$$p = \frac{\beta_0 - \alpha_0}{\alpha_1 - \beta_1} - \frac{\alpha_2}{\alpha_1 - \beta_1} y + \frac{\beta_2}{\alpha_1 - \beta_1} r + \frac{v - u}{\alpha_1 - \beta_1} \tag{13.8}$$

which can be written in the form

$$p = \lambda_0 + \lambda_1 y + \lambda_2 r + \varepsilon_1 \tag{13.9}$$

Substituting this in Equation (13.1), we get (q is the equilibrium quantity sold):

$$q = (\alpha_0 + \alpha_1 \lambda_0) + (\alpha_1 \lambda_1 + \alpha_2)y + \alpha_1 \lambda_2 r + \varepsilon_2 = \mu_0 + \mu_1 y + \mu_2 r + \varepsilon_2 \tag{13.10}$$

ε_1 and ε_2 are new error terms that depend on u and v. Equations (13.9) and (13.10) specify each of the endogenous variables in terms of only the predetermined variables, the parameters of the model, and the stochastic disturbance terms. Note that the right-hand sides of (13.9) and (13.10) do not contain any endogenous variables. These two equations are known as the **reduced form equations,** and the λs and μs are known as the **reduced form parameters.** Reduced form equations are obtained by solving for each of the endogenous variables in terms of the predetermined variables, the unknown parameters, and the disturbance terms. We readily see that a *reduced form equation will generally contain the error terms from all the equations.* Thus, the reduced form equation for GNP in the macro model will depend on a constant, G_t, T_t, Y_{t-1}, DY_{t-1}, all the structural parameters, and the error terms u_t and v_t.

● PRACTICE PROBLEM 13.1

Derive the reduced form for the macro model in Equations (13.4)–(13.7).

● 13.2   Consequences of Ignoring Simultaneity

Suppose we treat each of the equations in a simultaneous equation model as a separate single-equation model and estimate the parameters, if any, by OLS. What are the properties of the estimators? In particular, are they unbiased, consistent, efficient, BLUE, and so on? For example, to estimate Equation (13.4), suppose we regress C_t against a constant, DY_t, and DY_{t-1}. It is useful to know the properties of these estimators. This issue is examined next with a simple macroeconomic model. The conclusions, however, generalize to models with many equations.

Consider the following well-known income determination model presented in introductory courses on macroeconomics:

$$C_t = \alpha + \beta Y_t + u_t \qquad 0 < \beta < 1 \tag{13.11}$$

$$Y_t = C_t + I_t \tag{13.12}$$

where C_t is consumption expenditure, Y_t is net national product, and I_t is net investment. The only modification made here is the addition of u_t, a stochastic disturbance term. Equation (13.11) is the familiar consumption function, and Equation (13.12) is the equilibrium condition. In this model, investment is treated as exogenous (and hence I_t and u_t are uncorrelated by assumption). The endogenous variables are C_t and Y_t, and the predetermined variables are the constant term and I_t.

Substituting for Y_t from Equation (13.12) into Equation (13.11) and solving for C_t, we obtain the reduced form for C_t:

$$C_t = \frac{\alpha}{1 - \beta} + \frac{\beta I_t}{1 - \beta} + \frac{u_t}{1 - \beta} \tag{13.13}$$

Similarly, substituting for C_t from Equation (13.13) into Equation (13.12) and solving for Y_t, we obtain the reduced form for Y_t:

$$Y_t = \frac{\alpha}{1 - \beta} + \frac{I_t}{1 - \beta} + \frac{u_t}{1 - \beta} \tag{13.14}$$

Let us now examine the consequences of estimating Equation (13.11), ignoring the fact that it is part of a simultaneous equation system. First of all, we can readily see that the estimators will be biased. Property 3.1 states that the least squares procedure yields unbiased estimates provided u_t has zero mean and is uncorrelated with the independent variables. This means that u_t should be uncorrelated with Y_t. But, as is seen from the reduced form equation for Y_t, this assumption is false. It is evident that Y_t depends on u_t, and hence applying ordinary least squares will give biased estimates. This is true for models with more equations. The simultaneity implies that endogenous variables appearing on the right-hand side of a given equation will be correlated with the corresponding residual, thus making OLS estimates biased.

Will the estimates be at least consistent; that is, will the bias be small in large samples and the estimates converge to the true values when the sample size is increased indefinitely? To answer this we need some formal analysis. The limit of the OLS estimate $\hat{\beta}$ as the number of observations n increases indefinitely is derived in the chapter appendix as follows:

$$\lim_{n \to \infty} \hat{\beta} = \frac{\beta \sigma_I^2 + \sigma_u^2}{\sigma_I^2 + \sigma_u^2} = \beta + \frac{(1 - \beta)\sigma_u^2}{\sigma_I^2 + \sigma_u^2} \tag{13.15}$$

where σ_I^2 and σ_u^2 are, respectively, the variances of I and u. Because $\beta \neq 1$ and $\sigma_u^2 \neq 0$, we see that $\hat{\beta}$ does not converge to the true β. Therefore, $\hat{\beta}$ is not only biased but is also inconsistent. The bias in $\hat{\beta}$ is known as the **least squares bias** or as the **simultaneous equation bias.** Even with a large sample, the bias does not become small but is positive, giving an overestimate of β. It is interesting to note that even though there are no unknown coefficients or stochastic error terms in Equation (13.12), the very fact that it implies a feedback effect causes bias and inconsistency. Standard errors of the estimates are also biased, and hence tests of hypotheses are invalid. The consequences of ignoring simultaneity are summarized in Property 13.1.

Property 13.1

If simultaneity among variables is ignored and the OLS procedure is applied to estimate the parameters of a system of simultaneous equations, the estimates will be biased and inconsistent. Forecasts based on them will also be biased and inconsistent. Furthermore, tests of hypotheses on parameters will be invalid.

In Section 4.5 we estimated a relationship between housing starts and GNP. Although changes in GNP affect housing starts, there is also a feedback effect because housing starts affect the equilibrium level of GNP. They are thus jointly determined by other factors. The estimates presented in Section 4.5 therefore suffer from least squares bias.

13.3 The Identification Problem

The reduced form Equation (13.9) expresses price as a function of the predetermined variables: constant, income, and rainfall. Because the predetermined variables are not endogenous, and hence are uncorrelated with the error terms, OLS can be applied to the reduced form to yield unbiased, consistent, and efficient estimates of the reduced form parameters (λs and μs in the example used here), provided the reduced form errors are "well behaved." A natural question is whether we can obtain consistent estimates of the original parameters of the structural equations (αs and βs in our example). When an investigator obtains the estimates of the reduced form equations and then attempts to go back and solve for the structural parameters, he or she finds one of three situations: (1) it is not possible to go from the reduced form back to the structure, (2) it is possible to go back in a unique way, or (3) there is more than one way to go back. This problem of being able to go back and reconstruct estimates of the structural parameters from estimates of the reduced form coefficients is known as the **identification problem.** The first type, in which it is not possible to go from the reduced form to the structure, is known as the **unidentified equation** or **underidentification.** The second case, the unique situation, is called **exact identification.** The final case, in which more than one structural estimate is obtainable, is called **overidentification.** We examine each of these cases with a number of models of demand and supply equations.

Model 1

Consider the following supply and demand model (say, for wheat) presented in elementary textbooks without random error terms (for simplicity the *t*-subscript is omitted):

Structure:

$$q_d = \alpha_0 + \alpha_1 p + u \qquad \text{(demand equation)}$$

$$q_s = \beta_0 + \beta_1 p + v \qquad \text{(supply equation)}$$

$$q_d = q_s = q \qquad \text{(equilibrium condition)}$$

Reduced form (obtained by solving separately for p and q):

$$p = \frac{\beta_0 - \alpha_0}{\alpha_1 - \beta_1} + \frac{v - u}{\alpha_1 - \beta_1} = \lambda_0 + \varepsilon_1$$

$$q = \frac{\alpha_1 \beta_0 - \alpha_0 \beta_1}{\alpha_1 - \beta_1} + \frac{\alpha_1 v - \beta_1 u}{\alpha_1 - \beta_1} = \mu_0 + \varepsilon_2$$

where u and v are random error terms and $q = q_d = q_s$. Applying OLS to the reduced forms gives the following two equations:

$$\hat{\lambda}_0 = \bar{p} \quad \text{or} \quad \frac{\beta_0 - \alpha_0}{\alpha_1 - \beta_1} = \bar{p}$$

$$\hat{\mu}_0 = \bar{q} \quad \text{or} \quad \frac{\alpha_1 \beta_0 - \alpha_0 \beta_1}{\alpha_1 - \beta_1} = \bar{q}$$

where $\bar{p}$ and $\bar{q}$ are the sample means of price and quantity. As there are only two equations in the four unknowns α_0, α_1, β_0, and β_1, we cannot obtain their estimates. We are thus faced with the problem of not being able to go back to the structure from the reduced form estimates. This is the case of underidentification.

Why the simple demand and supply curves are not estimable can be explained intuitively. Note that the observations (p_t, q_t) are equilibrium points and hence are the intersections of the demand and supply curves at various points. Suppose for argument that the supply curve is fixed over time but the demand curve is shifting. The intersection points (which are also the observations) would be as in Figure 13.1.

● **Figure 13.1   Demand Curve Shifting but Supply Curve Fixed**

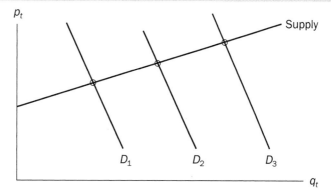

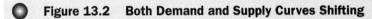

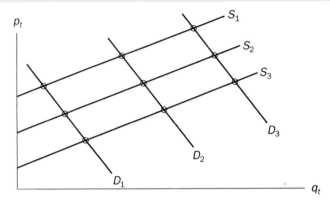

Figure 13.2   Both Demand and Supply Curves Shifting

The observed values of p and q would then trace the supply curve, but we may erroneously conclude that it is the demand curve with a wrong slope. Similarly, if we are interested in the supply curve, which in actuality has shifted while the demand curve has remained fixed, we would estimate not the supply curve but the demand curve. In practice, however, both the demand and supply curves shift with the intersection points, as in Figure 13.2. The observation points (denoted by circles) trace neither the demand curve nor the supply curve. Thus, without additional information as to how these curves are shifting, these relations are not identifiable.

Model 2

Let us modify Model 1 to take shifts explicitly into account as follows:

$$\text{Demand:} \qquad q = \alpha_0 + \alpha_1 p + \alpha_2 y + u$$

$$\text{Supply:} \qquad q = \beta_0 + \beta_1 p + v$$

where y is income and is exogenous. We have thus assumed that the supply curve is fixed whereas the demand curve shifts with income. As we saw in Figure 13.1, in this situation the supply curve can be estimated, but the demand curve cannot. Let us verify this formally. The reduced form is

$$p = \frac{\beta_0 - \alpha_0}{\alpha_1 - \beta_1} - \frac{\alpha_2}{\alpha_1 - \beta_1} y + \frac{v - u}{\alpha_1 - \beta_1}$$

$$= \lambda_0 + \lambda_1 y + \varepsilon_1$$

$$q = (\beta_0 + \beta_1 \lambda_0) + \beta_1 \lambda_1 y + \varepsilon_2$$

$$= \mu_0 + \mu_1 y + \varepsilon_2$$

Since y is exogenous and hence is independent of ε_1 and ε_2, we can apply OLS to the reduced form and obtain $\hat{\lambda}_0$, $\hat{\lambda}_1$ by regressing p against y and the constant term, and $\hat{\mu}_0$, $\hat{\mu}_1$ by regressing q against y and the constant. Note that $\hat{\beta}_1 = \hat{\mu}_1 / \hat{\lambda}_1$ and

$\hat{\beta}_0 = \hat{\mu}_0 - \hat{\lambda}_0\hat{\beta}_1$, and hence the supply curve is identified. But the demand curve is not identified because

$$\hat{\lambda}_0 = \frac{\hat{\beta}_0 - \alpha_0}{\alpha_1 - \hat{\beta}_1} \qquad \hat{\lambda}_1 = \frac{-\alpha_2}{\alpha_1 - \hat{\beta}_1}$$

are only two equations in the three unknowns α_0, α_1, and α_2. We are therefore unable to go back to the structure of the demand equation from the reduced form, but can uniquely go back to the supply equation.

In a two-equation model, if one of the equations has an omitted variable, then it is identified. In Model 2, for example, the income variable is absent from the supply equation and hence is identified. This result is not proved. A similar condition must be satisfied in multiequation models. How can the demand equation be identified? By the rule that one of the variables present in the supply equation must be absent from the demand equation. This is so in the next model.

Model 3

Let r be the rainfall and consider the following model, used earlier:

$$\text{Demand:} \quad q = \alpha_0 + \alpha_1 p + \alpha_2 y + u$$

$$\text{Supply:} \quad q = \beta_0 + \beta_1 p + \beta_2 r + v$$

The exogenous variables are y, r, and the constant, and the endogenous variables are p and q. The reduced form is

$$p = \frac{\beta_0 - \alpha_0}{\alpha_1 - \beta_1} - \frac{\alpha_2}{\alpha_1 - \beta_1}y + \frac{\beta_2}{\alpha_1 - \beta_1}r + \varepsilon_1$$

$$= \lambda_0 + \lambda_1 y + \lambda_2 r + \varepsilon_1$$

$$q = (\alpha_0 + \alpha_1\lambda_0) + (\alpha_1\lambda_1 + \alpha_2)y + \alpha_1\lambda_2 r + \varepsilon_2$$

$$= \mu_0 + \mu_1 y + \mu_2 r + \varepsilon_2$$

Note that the reduced form consists of exogenous variables from all the equations. We can run a regression of p on the constant, y, and r to get $\hat{\lambda}_0$, $\hat{\lambda}_1$, and $\hat{\lambda}_2$ and run a regression of q on the constant, y, and r to get $\hat{\mu}_0$, $\hat{u}_1$, and $\hat{\mu}_2$. From these, the structural parameters are obtained as follows:

$$\hat{\alpha}_1 = \frac{\hat{\mu}_2}{\hat{\lambda}_2} \qquad\qquad \hat{\alpha}_2 = \hat{\mu}_1 - \hat{\alpha}_1\hat{\lambda}_1$$

$$\hat{\alpha}_0 = \hat{\mu}_0 - \hat{\alpha}_1\hat{\lambda}_0 \qquad\qquad \hat{\beta}_1 = \hat{\alpha}_1 + \left(\frac{\hat{\alpha}_2}{\hat{\lambda}_1}\right)$$

$$\hat{\beta}_2 = \hat{\lambda}_2(\hat{\alpha}_1 - \hat{\beta}_1) \qquad\qquad \hat{\beta}_0 = \hat{\alpha}_0 + \hat{\lambda}_0(\hat{\alpha}_1 - \hat{\beta}_1)$$

Thus, all the structural parameters can be estimated unambiguously.

Model 4

We now present a model that is overidentified:

$$\text{Demand:} \qquad q = \alpha_0 + \alpha_1 p + \alpha_2 y + u$$

$$\text{Supply:} \qquad q = \beta_0 + \beta_1 p + \beta_2 r + \beta_3 f + v$$

where f is the amount of fertilizer used and is another exogenous variable. The difference between this and Model 3 is that two of the exogenous variables (r, f) are absent from the demand equation. The reduced form is

$$p = \frac{\beta_0 - \alpha_0}{\alpha_1 - \beta_1} - \frac{\alpha_2 y}{\alpha_1 - \beta_1} + \frac{\beta_2 r}{\alpha_1 - \beta_1} + \frac{\beta_3 f}{\alpha_1 - \beta_1} + \varepsilon_1$$

$$= \lambda_0 + \lambda_1 y + \lambda_2 r + \lambda_3 f + \varepsilon_1$$

$$q = (\alpha_0 + \alpha_1 \lambda_0) + (\alpha_1 \lambda_1 + \alpha_2)y + \alpha_1 \lambda_2 r + \alpha_1 \lambda_3 f + \varepsilon_2$$

$$= \mu_0 + \mu_1 y + \mu_2 r + \mu_3 f + \varepsilon_3$$

First regress p and q on all the exogenous variables—y, r, f—and the constant to obtain the λs and μs. As $\alpha_1 \lambda_2 = \mu_2$, we can estimate α_1 as $\hat{\mu}_2 / \hat{\lambda}_2$. However, we also have $\alpha_1 \lambda_3 = \mu_3$. Therefore, $\hat{\alpha}_1 = \hat{\mu}_3 / \hat{\lambda}_3$ is another estimate of $\hat{\alpha}_1$. Only by a rare coincidence will we find the two estimates to be the same. Depending on which of these we choose, we will get different estimates of the parameters. Thus, there is more than one way to get back to the structure, and we have overidentification.

To summarize, we can assign any given structural equation to one of three identification categories:

1. *Unidentified:* There is no way to go back to the structure from the reduced form. Both equations of Model 1 and the demand equation of Model 2 are unidentified.
2. *Exactly identified:* There is a unique way to go back, as in Model 3.
3. *Overidentified:* There is more than one way to go back to the structure from the reduced form, as in Model 4. Note from Model 4 that there is an implicit nonlinear restriction among the parameters, namely, $\mu_2 / \lambda_2 = \mu_3 / \lambda_3$. These are known as the **overidentifying restrictions.**

To determine the identifiability of a system of equations, two sets of conditions are checked: the *order condition* and the *rank condition*. The order condition is only a necessary condition and is not sufficient; that is, if the order condition is not satisfied, the model is not identified. However, the fact that the order condition is satisfied does not guarantee the model's identifiability. The rank condition is also needed. The order condition can be stated in three different forms.

Property 13.2

For the order condition of identifiability, the number of variables excluded (that is, absent) from an equation must be greater than or equal to $G - 1$, where G is the number of structural equations. Alternatively, the number of predetermined variables (which consist of exogenous variables and all lagged variables, including lagged endogenous variables) excluded from an equation must be greater than or equal to the number of included endogenous variables minus 1. In general, the number of prior restrictions on the parameters should not be less than the number of equations in the model minus 1 $(G - 1)$.

● **EXAMPLE 13.1**

Consider the following three-equation model, in which the Ys are the endogenous variables and the Xs and the constant term are the predetermined variables:

$$Y_1 = \alpha_0 + \alpha_1 Y_2 + \alpha_2 Y_3 + \alpha_4 X_1 + \alpha_5 X_2 + u_1$$

$$Y_2 = \beta_0 + \beta_1 Y_3 + \beta_2 X_1 + u_2$$

$$Y_3 = \gamma_0 + \gamma_1 Y_2 + u_3$$

Because G equals 3 here, for the order condition to be satisfied, at least two variables should be absent from each equation. In the first equation all the variables are present; that is, none are absent. This equation is therefore not identified. In the second equation Y_1 and X_2 are absent, and hence the order condition is satisfied. In the third equation Y_1, X_1, and X_2 are absent, and therefore this equation also satisfies the order condition.

The statement of the rank condition requires a knowledge of matrix algebra and is beyond the scope of this book. Readers familiar with linear algebra are referred to the books listed at the end of this chapter.

● **PRACTICE PROBLEM 13.2**

Derive the reduced form equations for the system in Example 13.1 and indicate whether you can go back and reconstruct structural parameters from those of the reduced form.

● **13.4   Estimation Procedures**

Indirect Least Squares

We have seen that if a model is exactly identified, then there is a unique way to obtain the structural estimates from the reduced form estimates. This procedure is called the **indirect least squares (ILS) procedure** and is illustrated with the simple macro model presented in Section 13.2.

The reduced form for C_t can be rewritten as

$$C_t = \lambda_0 + \lambda_1 I_t + \varepsilon_t \tag{13.16}$$

where $\lambda_0 = \alpha/(1 - \beta)$, $\lambda_1 = \beta/(1 - \beta)$, and $\varepsilon_t = u_t/(1 - \beta)$. The exogenous variable I_t is uncorrelated with u_t, and hence OLS is applicable to the reduced form. This property generalizes to a multiequation model. Thus, the error terms in the reduced form of a simultaneous equation model always satisfy the assumptions for applying OLS to the reduced form. *OLS estimates of the reduced form parameters (λ_0 and λ_1 in our example) are therefore BLUE.* Applying OLS to Equation (13.16) and using the notation in Equations (13.A.2) and (13.A.3) in the chapter appendix, we can obtain estimates of α and β (denoted by $\sim$).

$$\frac{\widetilde{\beta}}{1 - \widetilde{\beta}} = \widetilde{\lambda}_1 = \frac{S_{CI}}{S_{II}} \quad \text{or} \quad \widetilde{\beta} = \frac{S_{CI}}{S_{CI} + S_{II}}$$

$$\widetilde{\alpha} = (1 - \widetilde{\beta})\widetilde{\lambda}_0$$

Because transformations of consistent estimates are also consistent, $\widetilde{\alpha}$ and $\widetilde{\beta}$ are consistent. They are, however, not unbiased because the transformations are nonlinear. The procedure, then, consists of first applying OLS to the reduced form equations and then using them to solve indirectly for the structural parameters.

The ILS method is not commonly used because (1) most simultaneous equation models tend to be overidentified and (2) if the system has several equations, solving for the reduced form and back to the structure would be tedious. A number of alternatives are therefore used. Here we present only two of those methods. For other methods, refer to any of the excellent books mentioned in the bibliography.

Instrumental Variable Procedure

We have seen that the reason why OLS estimates of a structural equation are not consistent is that the right-hand side endogenous variable (call it Y_2) is correlated with the error term. Suppose we find a variable (call it Z) that has the following properties: (1) Z is uncorrelated with the error term, and (2) Z is highly correlated with the right-hand side endogenous variable Y_2. Z will then serve as a good substitute variable for Y_2. Estimates obtained using Z will be consistent because it is uncorrelated with the error term. Such a variable is called an **instrumental variable,** and the method just described, in which the instrumental variable is used as a substitute for the endogenous variable causing least squares bias, is called the **instrumental variable technique (IV).**

To illustrate this procedure, consider the following two-equation model in which the constant terms have been eliminated by expressing the variables as deviations from their means (for simplicity, we have also omitted the *t*-subscript).

$$y_1 = \alpha_1 y_2 + \alpha_2 x_1 + u$$
$$y_2 = \beta_1 y_1 + \beta_2 x_2 + v$$

If we had applied OLS to the first equation, we would have used the sample analogs of the conditions $\text{Cov}(y_2, u) = 0$ and $\text{Cov}(x_1, u) = 0$, which are the following:

$$\sum y_2 \hat{u} = 0 \quad \text{and} \quad \sum x_1 \hat{u} = 0$$

However, the first of the two covariances is not zero because of simultaneity, and therefore we cannot use the first condition. To obtain another equation, the instrumental variable technique would use the fact that $\text{Cov}(x_2, u) = 0$, because x_2 is exogenous. Thus, x_2 is used as the instrument for y_2, and the second condition will be $\Sigma x_2 u = 0$. Using the fact that $u = y_1 - \alpha_1 y_2 - \alpha_2 x_1$, it is readily verified that the normal equations, using the IV approach, would be as follows:

$$\sum x_1 y_1 = \alpha_1 \sum x_1 y_2 + \alpha_2 \sum x_1^2$$

$$\sum x_2 y_1 = \alpha_1 \sum x_2 y_2 + \alpha_2 \sum x_1 x_2$$

In this example, the structural parameters are exactly identified, and hence the number of normal equations is the same as the number of parameters. If one of the equations is overidentified, however, the number of possible instruments for y_2 would be more than 1, and we would get too many normal equations. For instance, suppose the second equation had also the exogenous variable x_3. Then a third normal equation, $\Sigma x_3 u = 0$, would result in three equations for the two unknowns, α_1 and α_2. To avoid this overidentification, the standard procedure is to use a linear combination of the xs in all the equations as the instrument for y_2. It can be shown that this procedure yields consistent and asymptotically (that is, for large samples) efficient estimates. If the equations are all linear in the parameters, then the IV method is equivalent to the **two-stage least squares (TSLS) procedure,** which is computationally easier than the instrumental variable approach. The TSLS procedure is described next.

Two-Stage Least Squares Procedure

The TSLS procedure can be applied to obtain unique estimates that are consistent and asymptotically efficient. This technique is useful in the case of exact identification also, and it will give the same estimates as those given by the ILS procedure. Therefore, it can be applied whether a model is exactly identified or overidentified. TSLS is easy to apply and is illustrated here for Model 4 of Section 13.3. An empirical example and a "walk-through" application are presented later.

Stage 1 First estimate the reduced form for all the endogenous variables that appear on the right-hand side. In Model 4, p is the only endogenous variable appearing on the right-hand side. So regress p on y, r, f, and the constant. Then save $\hat{p}$, the predicted values of p as obtained from the reduced form estimates. Thus, $\hat{p} = \hat{\lambda}_0 + \hat{\lambda}_1 y + \hat{\lambda}_2 r + \hat{\lambda}_3 f$.

Stage 2 Estimate the structural equation but use as instruments the predicted endogenous variables obtained in the first stage. In Model 4 this means that we regress q on the constant, $\hat{p}$, and y for the demand equation. Regress q on the constant, $\hat{p}$, r, and f for the supply equation. Thus, we are estimating the structural equations but are replacing p by $\hat{p}$. $\hat{p}$ is the instrumental variable here. In computing standard errors, however, the original p will be used. Also, when computing R^2, it is better to obtain it as the square of the correlation between the observed and predicted values of the dependent (that is, endogenous) variable. It can be shown that this procedure leads to consistent estimates.

Another procedure, known as the **three-stage least squares method,** takes into account the covariances between the error terms of different equations. This procedure and other procedures such as *limited information maximum likelihood* and *full information maximum likelihood* are beyond the scope of this book. Interested readers with a background in matrix algebra are referred to the bibliography at the end of this chapter.

Lagrange Multiplier Test for Omitted Variables

In Chapter 6, we discussed the procedure to use the LM test for adding variables to a single-equation model. The test is also applicable in the context of a simultaneous equation but requires some modification. Wooldridge (1990) has shown that the test procedure used for a single-equation model is not applicable because the distribution of the nR^2 statistic calculated in the usual way is unknown even for a large sample. He proposed, instead, the following procedure:

Step 1   Let the general model be $Y_t = \beta_1 X_{t1} + \beta_2 X_{t2} + u_t$, in which the goal is to test the null hypothesis $\beta_2 = 0$. X_{t1} and X_{t2} are used generically to represent a basic set of variables and an added set of variables, respectively (X_{t1} will include a constant term also). Denote by Z_t the variables in the reduced form that will be used as instruments.

Step 2   Estimate the restricted model $Y_t = \beta_1 X_{t1} + u_t$ by TSLS and save the corresponding residuals as $\tilde{u}_t$.

Step 3   Regress X_{t1} against Z_t and obtain the "fitted" values $\tilde{X}_{t1}$.

Step 4   Do the same with X_{t2} and denote the fitted values by $\hat{X}_{t2}$.

Step 5   Regress $\tilde{u}_t$ against $\tilde{X}_{t1}$ and $\hat{X}_{t2}$ and compute the test statistic nR^2. Under the null hypothesis that $\beta_2 = 0$, and for large samples, this will have an approximate $\chi^2_{k_2}$ distribution with d.f. k_2 equal to the number of restrictions in $\beta_2 = 0$. This can be used in the usual way to test the null hypothesis.

Wooldridge also presents an *F*-statistic analog to the Wald test statistic in single-equation models.

Serial Correlation in a Simultaneous Equation Model*

If time series data are used to estimate a simultaneous equation model, it is very likely that the disturbance terms are serially correlated. The LM test can be used to test for serial correlation, but it, too, requires modification similar to the one made earlier (see Wooldridge, 1991). The steps are as follows:

Step 1   Estimate the model $Y_t = \beta X_t + u_t$ by TSLS and save the residuals $\hat{u}_t$.

Step 2   Regress X_t by Z_t, the variables in the reduced form that serve as instruments, and obtain the fitted values $\hat{X}_t$.

Step 3   Regress $\hat{u}_t$ against $\hat{X}_t$ and $\hat{u}_{t-1}, \hat{u}_{t-2}, \ldots, \hat{u}_{t-p}$ and compute $(n - p)R^2$. Serial correlation of order p can be tested with this using the χ^2 distribution with p degrees of freedom.

If serial correlation is present, using the standard TSLS procedure is inappropriate, and one can use a modified model or methodology.

REFORMULATING THE MODEL   We saw in Chapters 9 and 10, in particular in Equation (10.12), that serial correlation is a special case of more general dynamics. An easy way to handle that is to include lagged dependent and independent variable terms in the model. Thus, for example, we would include the terms C_{t-1} and DY_{t-2} in Equation (13.4) and the terms I_{t-1} and Y_{t-2} in Equation (13.5). The modified model will then be estimated by TSLS.

MODIFIED ESTIMATION PROCEDURES   The Hildreth–Lu and Cochrane–Orcutt methods can be modified to deal with serial correlation. This modified method is described with the following two-equation model, but the principle is the same for models with more equations:

$$Y_{t1} = \alpha_{12}Y_{t2} + \beta_{11}X_{t1} + \beta_{12}X_{t2} + u_t \qquad (13.17)$$

$$Y_{t2} = \alpha_{21}Y_{t1} + \beta_{21}X_{t1} + \beta_{23}X_{t3} + v_t \qquad (13.18)$$

$$u_t = \rho_1 u_{t-1} + \varepsilon_{t1} \qquad (13.19)$$

$$v_t = \rho_2 v_{t-1} + \varepsilon_{t2} \qquad (13.20)$$

where Y_1 and Y_2 are the endogenous variables and X_1, X_2, and X_3 are the predetermined variables. The structural disturbances are assumed to follow an AR(1) process, with the εs being white noise. The quasidifferenced version of Equation (13.17) is given by

$$Y_{t1} - \rho_1 Y_{t-1,1} = \alpha_{12}(Y_{t2} - \rho_1 Y_{t-1,2}) + \beta_{11}(X_{t1} - \rho_1 X_{t-1,1}) \qquad (13.21)$$
$$+ \beta_{12}(X_{t2} - \rho_1 X_{t-1,2}) + \varepsilon_{t1}$$

The Hildreth–Lu search procedure and the Cochrane–Orcutt iterative procedure are applicable here, but note that because the modified reduced form for Y_{t2} will contain lags of X_1, X_2, and X_3, the first stage must include these as regressors. The steps for estimating Equation (13.17) are therefore the following:

Step 1   Regress Y_{t2} against X_{t1}, X_{t2}, X_{t3}, $X_{t-1,1}$, $X_{t-1,2}$, and $X_{t-1,3}$ and save the predicted value $\hat{Y}_{t2}$.

Step 2   Choose a value for ρ_1 and estimate Equation (13.21) by OLS using $\hat{Y}_{t2}$ as an instrument for Y_{t2}.

Step 3   Repeat Step 2 for various values of ρ_1 between -1 and $+1$ and choose that ρ_1 for which the error sum of squares of Equation (13.21) is minimum. This is the modified Hildreth–Lu search procedure. The Cochrane–Orcutt technique is also similar to the one in Chapter 9. The only difference is that $\hat{Y}_{t2}$ is used instead of Y_{t2}.

If the model has lagged dependent variables as predetermined variables, then the first-stage regression for Y_{t2} should include $Y_{t-1,1}$ and $Y_{t-2,1}$ (as well as, possibly,

$Y_{t-1,2}$ and $Y_{t-2,2}$) as regressors. To see this, suppose that X_{t1} was really $Y_{t-1,1}$. Then we see that Equation (13.23) will have $Y_{t-1,1}$ and $Y_{t-2,1}$ on the right-hand side, and hence these must be included as regressors in the first-stage regression. Fair (1970) has shown that this procedure gives consistent estimates of the structural equations.

13.5 Empirical Example: Regulation in the Contact Lens Industry

In a study, Haas-Wilson (1987) has examined the effects of state restrictions prohibiting the fitting of contact lenses by independent opticians on the price and quality of contact lenses. A two-equation model is used to relate the price and quality of contact lenses, and the parameters are estimated by two-stage least squares. Before looking at the empirical formulation let us examine the background.

The purchase of contact lenses involves three steps: (1) a visit to an ophthalmologist or optometrist for examination and prescription, (2) a fitting examination to measure the radius of curvature of the cornea, and (3) purchase and evaluation of the lenses. The contact lens industry is characterized by oligopoly, in which many sellers have some degree of market power. A number of states have tying requirements (that is, requirements that the purchase of one product, such as contact lenses, must be accompanied by the purchase of another product, such as the services of an optometrist or ophthalmologist) that prohibit the fitting of contact lenses by independent opticians. The question for examination is whether the tying requirements result in an increase in the price of contact lenses and, if so, by how much.

Haas-Wilson formulates an oligopoly model in which sellers maximize profits with respect to price. Without going through the intermediate steps for the econometric specification (details are in the paper), we simply give here the two equations formulated (P and QUALW are the endogenous variables and the others are exogenous):

$$P = f(\text{QUALW, SOFT, FITOPH, FITOPTOM, EXOPH, Y, INPUT, R-FIT,}$$
$$\text{LIC, R-AD, REG})$$
$$\text{QUALW} = g(\text{P, FITOPH, FITOPTOM, SEX, AGE, FAIL, WEARTIME, HOURS,}$$
$$\text{DIRT, DAMAGE, WARP, SOFT, R-FIT, R-AD, LIC, REG})$$

where

$$
\begin{aligned}
\text{P} &= \text{Price of contact lenses} \\
\text{QUALW} &= \text{A weighted index of eye health} \\
\text{SOFT} &= \text{1 for soft contact lenses, 0 otherwise} \\
\text{FITOPH} &= \text{1 if fitting was done by an ophthalmologist} \\
\text{FITOPTOM} &= \text{1 if fitting was done by an optometrist} \\
\text{EXOPH} &= \text{1 if examined by an ophthalmologist} \\
\text{Y} &= \text{Income} \\
\text{INPUT} &= \text{Price of inputs} \\
\text{R-FIT} &= \text{1 if the consumer's state has restrictions on fitting by opticians} \\
\text{R-AD} &= \text{1 if the consumer's state restricts advertising}
\end{aligned}
$$

LIC = 1 if the state requires licenses for opticians
REG = Index of other commercial practice restrictions
SEX = 1 for male
AGE = Age of consumer
FAIL = 1 if consumer was unsuccessful in wearing contact lenses before
WEARTIME = Wear time prior to the exam
HOURS = Average hours worn per day
DIRT = 1 if lenses were dirty
DAMAGE = 1 if lenses were damaged
WARP = 1 if lenses were warped

This model was estimated with 354 observations obtained by the Federal Trade Commission during the period 1976–1979 from consumers in 18 urban areas. Two-stage least squares estimates of the parameters are as follows (standard errors are in parentheses):

$$\hat{P} = 167.30 - 0.64\text{QUALW} + 53.92\text{SOFT} + 17.87\text{FITOPH} + 2.72\text{FITOPTOM}$$
$$\phantom{\hat{P} = }(43.3) \quad (0.9) \quad\quad (6.5) \quad\quad (10.8) \quad\quad (13.9)$$

$$+ 28.48\text{EXOPH} - 0.01\text{Y} - 18.52\text{INPUT} + 17.29\text{R-FIT} - 4.45\text{LIC}$$
$$(13.8) \quad\quad (0.0) \quad (39.0) \quad\quad (7.9) \quad\quad (7.3)$$

$$R^2 = 0.29 \quad\quad T = 354 \quad\quad F = 12.73$$

$$\widehat{\text{QUALW}} = 8.02 - 0.08\text{P} + 3.39\text{FITOPH} - 0.06\text{FITOPTOM} + 3.61\text{SEX}$$
$$\phantom{\widehat{\text{QUALW}} = }(9.1) \quad (0.1) \quad (2.7) \quad\quad (2.0) \quad\quad (1.6)$$

$$- 0.07\text{AGE} - 283\text{FAIL} - 0.83\text{WEARTIME} - 0.83\text{HOURS}$$
$$(0.1) \quad\quad (1.9) \quad\quad (0.3) \quad\quad\quad (0.5)$$

$$- 1.65\text{DIRT} + 1.03\text{DAMAGE} + 0.07\text{WARP} + 7.85\text{SOFT}$$
$$(1.0) \quad\quad (0.9) \quad\quad (1.1) \quad\quad (4.1)$$

$$- 0.10\text{R-FIT} + 0.06\text{R-AD} - 0.53\text{LIC} + 0.53\text{REG}$$
$$(1.5) \quad\quad (2.3) \quad\quad (1.3) \quad\quad (0.7)$$

$$R^2 = 0.14 \quad\quad T = 354 \quad\quad F = 3.51$$

The null hypothesis of main interest is that the coefficient for R-FIT is zero in the price equation. This hypothesis is rejected at the 5 percent level, indicating that the tying requirements do significantly affect the price of contact lenses. In states that restrict contact lens prescriptions by opticians, prices are expected to be higher, on average, by $17.29. The author also used a double-log model for the price and estimated that contact lens prices were 8 percent higher in states with restrictions. The results suggest, too, that quality, measured as eye health, does not significantly affect price. Other types of restrictions, such as those on the use of trade names and the number of branch offices an optometrist may operate, are also associated with higher contact lens prices. The quality equation estimates suggest that tying requirements do not significantly affect quality. Finally, the quality provided by opticians is not significantly different from that provided by optometrists or ophthalmologists. Advertising and other restrictions do not appear to affect quality significantly.

See Wunnava and Mehdi (1994) for another example of the application of the two-stage least squares procedure.

13.6   Application: A Simple Keynesian Model

We use a simple Keynesian model to illustrate the principles discussed in this chapter. The discussion here is, however, not exhaustive. Extensions to the analysis are suggested in the exercises. You are encouraged to use the data provided to formulate other variations and estimate them. The structural equations of the model are the following:

$$C_t = \alpha_0 + \alpha_1 C_{t-1} + \alpha_2 DY_t + \alpha_3 DY_{t-1} + u_{t1}$$

$$I_t = \beta_0 + \beta_1 I_{t-1} + \beta_2 Y_t + \beta_3 Y_{t-1} + \beta_4 r_t + \beta_5 r_{t-1} + u_{t2}$$

$$r_t = \gamma_0 + \gamma_1 r_{t-1} + \gamma_2 Y_t + \gamma_3 Y_{t-1} + \gamma_4 M_t + \gamma_5 M_{t-1} + u_{t3}$$

$$T_t = t_0 + t_1 Y_t + u_{t4}$$

$$IMP_t = m_0 + m_1 Y_t + u_{t5}$$

$$DY_t = Y_t - T_t$$

$$Y_t = C_t + I_t + G_t + X_t - IMP_t$$

where C is aggregate consumption expenditure, I is investment, Y is gross domestic product (GDP), DY is disposable income, G is total government expenditure, M is the money supply, X is exports, IMP is imports, T is total tax receipts (federal, state, and local), r is the interest rate, and the us are stochastic error terms. To correct for inflation and population effects, all financial variables are measured in real per-capita terms. To allow for the kind of dynamics discussed in Section 10.2 (see Equation 10.12), we have included lag terms in the behavioral equations. The jointly determined endogenous variables are C, I, r, DY, Y, T, and IMP. The predetermined variables are the constant term, G, X, M, and the lagged variables.

The first equation is the consumption function, and the second equation is the investment function. The third equation determines the interest rate and is derived from equilibrium in the money market. To see this, let the money demand function (also known as the *liquidity preference function*) be $M_d = L(Y, r)$. In equilibrium, this will equal the money supply, M. Solving the equation $M = L(Y, r)$ for r in terms of Y and M and adding the dynamic adjustment terms, we get the third equation. The fourth and fifth equations define the tax and import functions. The sixth equation is an identity defining disposable income. The last equation is the condition for equilibrium in the goods market.

Note that the model is purely Keynesian because it has no price determination. DATA13-1 has annual data for the United States for the 35 years 1959–1993. The definitions of the variables are given as follows:

GDP = Gross domestic product in billions of 1987 dollars
CONS = Personal consumption expenditures in billions of 1987 dollars

> INV = Gross private domestic investment in billions of 1987 dollars
> GOVEXP = Government purchases of goods and services in billions of 1987 dollars
> EXPORTS = Exports of goods and services in billions of 1987 dollars
> IMPORTS = Imports of goods and services in billions of 1987 dollars
> GOVREC = Federal, state, and local government receipts in billions of dollars
> MONYSUP = Money supply measure M2; currency, demand deposits, savings deposits, Eurodollar, overnight repurchase agreements, in billions of current dollars
> Pt = Implicit price deflators for gross domestic product, base year 1987
> rt = Corporate Aaa bond yields as percent
> POP = U.S. population in millions

Because the model's variables are in per-capita real terms, the data have to be transformed appropriately. The relations between the variables in the model and those in DATA13-1 are given as follows:

$$Y_t = \text{GDP/POP}$$
$$C_t = \text{CONS/POP}$$
$$I_t = \text{INV/POP}$$
$$G_t = \text{GOVEXP/POP}$$
$$X_t = \text{EXPORTS/POP}$$
$$IMP_t = \text{IMPORTS/POP}$$
$$TAX_t = 100 \text{ GOVREC/Pt}$$
$$DY_t = (\text{GDP} - \text{TAXt})/\text{POP}$$
$$M_t = 100 \text{ MONYSUP}/(\text{Pt} \times \text{POP})$$
$$T_t = \text{TAXt/POP}$$

The two-stage least squares estimates of the structural parameters are presented next along with the absolute values of t-statistics in parentheses (see Practice Computer Session 13.1 for reproducing these results). Goodness of fit is measured as the square of the correlation between the observed and predicted dependent variable and then adjusted for degrees of freedom.

$$\hat{C}_t = \underset{(1.35)}{-0.4045} + \underset{(9.81)}{0.8521 C_{t-1}} + \underset{(7.59)}{0.7414 DY_t} - \underset{(5.12)}{0.5621 DY_{t-1}} \qquad \overline{R}^2 = 0.998$$

$$\hat{I}_t = \underset{(2.16)}{-0.2156} + \underset{(5.67)}{0.4861 I_{t-1}} + \underset{(10.41)}{0.6353 Y_t} - \underset{(8.78)}{0.5561 Y_{t-1}}$$

$$+ \underset{(2.82)}{0.0698 r_t} - \underset{(2.25)}{0.0532 r_{t-1}} \qquad \overline{R}^2 = 0.970$$

$$\hat{r}_t = \underset{(3.74)}{3.4645} + \underset{(15.53)}{1.1159 r_{t-1}} - \underset{(2.46)}{0.7935 Y_t} + \underset{(5.1)}{2.5464 M_t}$$

$$+ \underset{(4.67)}{3.421 M_{t-1}} \qquad \overline{R}^2 = 0.933$$

$$\hat{T}_t = \underset{(9.24)}{-0.9653} + \underset{(54.78)}{0.3591 Y_t} \qquad \overline{R}^2 = 0.989$$

$$\widehat{IMP}_t = -2.1553 + 0.2217Y_t \qquad\qquad \overline{R}^2 = 0.938$$
$$\phantom{\widehat{IMP}_t = -}(13.61)\quad\;\;(22.32)$$

In the interest rate equation, Y_{t-1} was omitted because it was insignificant even at the 75 percent level. All the regression coefficients are highly significant and the goodness-of-fit measures indicate good fits. Because of the simultaneity and because all the variables are highly multicollinear, the regression coefficients are not useful to measure the impact of the exogenous variables or to calculate short-run multipliers. For example, in the interest rate equation, the impact of M_t is not just -2.5464 because Y_t also depends on money supply through the equilibrium condition. Furthermore, since M_t is highly correlated with M_{t-1}, its separate effect is hard to measure. For meaningful implications, we need to obtain the **implied reduced form estimates,** namely, the reduced form after solving for the endogenous variables. In particular, the long-run relationships would be of interest. To obtain these, set each variable to be at the steady state denoted by an asterisk. For the consumption function, we would have

$$C^* = -0.4045 + 0.8521C^* + 0.1793(Y^* - T^*)$$

which can be solved for C^* as

$$C^* = -2.735 + 1.2123Y^* - 1.2123T^*$$

Similarly, for the other equations we have (verify it)

$$r^* = -29.8921 + 6.8464Y^* - 7.5462M^*$$
$$I^* = -1.385 + 0.3753Y^* - 0.2438M^*$$
$$T^* = -0.9653 + 0.3591Y^*$$
$$IMP^* = -2.1553 + 0.2217Y^*$$
$$Y^* = C^* + I^* + G^* + X^* - M^*$$

After substituting for the individual terms and solving for Y^*, we get the following long-run relation for GDP.

$$Y^* = -11.4317 - 3.5065M^* + 14.3885(G^* + X^*)$$

We note that the negative sign for money supply is counterintuitive because we would expect money supply to be expansionary in the long run and not contractionary. This suggests possible model misspecification. For instance, money supply might actually not be exogenous as we have assumed here but might actually be determined by recent past values of GDP, interest rate, and so on. Also, there may be serial correlation in the error terms. This can be treated by adding additional lagged variables in the model. Interested readers are strongly recommended to use the data provided to estimate modified models and see how the results differ.

Summary

This chapter discussed the special problems that arise when a regression equation of interest is part of a system of simultaneous equations. A simultaneous equation system consists of a number of *structural equations* involving several *endogenous variables* whose values are determined within the specified system. Their values also depend on several *exogenous variables* whose values are specified outside the system and also on lagged values of variables, known as *predetermined variables.* To avoid confusion, exogenous variables are also considered predetermined. Structural equations can be behavioral, technical, identities, or equilibrium conditions. If each of the endogenous variables is solved in terms of the exogenous and predetermined variables, we obtain a system of *reduced form equations.* These equations will not contain any endogenous variables, but will depend on the stochastic terms of all the equations.

If the simultaneity is ignored and ordinary least squares applied, the estimates will be biased and inconsistent. Consequently, forecasts will be biased and inconsistent. In addition, tests of hypotheses will no longer be valid.

Because the exogenous and predetermined variables are independent of all the error terms, OLS can be applied to the reduced form to obtain estimates that are BLUE and consistent. The natural question that arises at this point is "Why not apply OLS to the reduced form and then solve backward for the structural coefficients?" Unfortunately, this is not always possible. This is the *identification problem.* If it is not possible to solve for the coefficients of a structural equation from estimates of the coefficients of the reduced form equation, we have a model that is *unidentified* or *underidentified.* If a unique set of structural estimates can be estimated, we have an *exactly identified* equation. If more than one structural estimate is possible, we have an *overidentified* specification.

If an equation is exactly identified, we can apply *indirect least squares* by first estimating the reduced form and solving backward for the structural coefficients. This procedure, however, is cumbersome, especially if several equations exist. A better method that gives consistent estimates is the *instrumental variable technique,* in which one finds a substitute variable (say *Z*) for an endogenous variable with the following properties: (1) *Z* is uncorrelated with the error term, and (2) *Z* is highly correlated with the endogenous variable. The variable *Z* (known as an *instrumental variable*) is used in place of the endogenous variable, and the structural equation is estimated. A frequently used instrumental variable technique is the *two-stage least squares procedure,* which is especially appropriate when an equation is overidentified. In the first stage, each of the reduced form equations is estimated and the predicted values of the endogenous values saved. These are then used in place of the endogenous variables, and the structural equation is estimated. In calculating residuals and standard errors, however, the actual values of the endogenous values are used instead of the predicted values.

Once the structural estimates have been obtained, we can use them to get the *implied reduced form estimates* by solving each of the endogenous variables in terms of the exogenous and predetermined variables. Because TSLS estimates take account of overidentifying restrictions, the implied reduced form estimates obtained from them are more efficient than direct reduced form estimates.

From the implied (or direct) reduced form estimates we can obtain the multipliers of the endogenous variables with respect to the exogenous variables, many of which will be policy variables.

Key Terms

Behavioral equations

Endogenous variable

Exact identification

Exogenous variable

Feedback

Identification problem

Implied reduced form estimates
Indirect least squares (ILS) procedure
Instrumental variable
Instrumental variable (IV) technique
Least squares bias
Overidentification
Overidentifying restrictions
Predetermined variables
Reduced form equation

Reduced form parameter
Simultaneous equation bias
Structural equations
Structural parameters
Technical equation
Three-stage least squares method
Two-stage least squares (TSLS) procedure
Underidentification
Unidentified equation

References

Economic Report of the President. Washington, D.C.: U.S. Government Printing Office, 1991.

Fair, Ray C. "The Estimation of Simultaneous Equation Models with Lagged Endogenous Variables and First Order Serially Correlated Errors." *Econometrica* 38 (May 1970): 507–516.

Greene, W. H. *Econometric Analysis.* Upper Saddle River, N.J.: Prentice Hall, 2000.

Haas-Wilson, Deborah. "Tying Requirements in Markets with Many Sellers: The Contact Lens Industry." *Review of Economics and Statistics* 69 (February 1987): 170–175.

Haugh, L. D. "Checking the Independence of Two Covariance-Stationary Time Series: A Univariate Residual Cross-correlation Approach." *J. Amer. Stat. Assoc.* 71 (1976): 378–385.

Johnston, J. *Econometric Methods.* New York: McGraw-Hill, 1984.

Judge, G. G., W. E. Griffiths, R. C. Hill, and T. Lee. *The Theory and Practice of Econometrics.* New York: John Wiley & Sons, 1985.

Kmenta, Jan. *Elements of Econometrics.* New York: Macmillan, 1986.

Peirce, D. A. "Relationships—and the Lack Thereof—between Economic Time Series, with Special Reference to Money and Interest Rates." *J. Amer. Stat. Assoc.* 72 (1977): 11–22.

Pindyck, R. S., and D. L. Rubenfeld. *Econometric Models and Economic Forecasts.* New York: McGraw-Hill, 1976.

Wooldridge, J. "A Note on the Lagrange Multiplier and F-Statistics for Two-Stage Least Squares Regression." *Economics Letters* 34 (1990): 151–155.

———. "On the Application of Robust Regression-rooted Diagnostics to Models of Conditional Means and Conditional Variables." *J. Econometrics* 47 (1991): 5–46.

Wunnava, P. V., and S. A. Mehdi. "The Effect of Unemployment Insurance on Unemployment Rate and Average Duration: Evidence from Pooled Cross-Sectional Time-Series Data." *Applied Economics Letters* 1 (1994):114–118.

Exercises

†13.1   Thirty years ago, it was possible to write papers estimating the simple consumption function $C_t = \alpha + \beta Y_t + u_t$ using the OLS assumptions on u_t.

    a.   Based on what you have learned so far, give alternative reasons as to why this model may be misspecified, either in the deterministic part (that is, in the $\alpha + \beta Y_t$ part) or in the error structure (that is, in assumptions on u_t). State clearly the nature of the misspecification in each case.

    b.   Choose two of the reasons, one for the deterministic part and one for the error structure, and in each case examine the OLS estimates of this consumption function from the point of view of (1) unbiasedness, (2) BLUE, and (3) consistency. State, with adequate reasons, whether these properties hold.

13.2   This question refers to the macro model presented in Section 13.2 and the ILS procedure discussed in Section 13.4. Using the relation $Y = C + I$, first show that

$S_{YI} = S_{CI} + S_{II}$. Then write the reduced form for GNP as $Y_t = \mu_0 + \mu_1 I_t + v_t$ and show that the OLS estimates $\hat{\mu}_0$ and $\hat{\mu}_1$ are given by

$$\hat{\mu}_0 = \overline{Y} - \hat{\mu}_1 \overline{I} \quad \text{and} \quad \hat{\mu}_1 = \frac{S_{YI}}{S_{II}}$$

Finally, estimate α and β indirectly from these and show that they are identical to those obtained earlier. Thus, in this example, it does not matter which reduced form is used to obtain indirect least squares estimates of the structural parameters.

†13.3   The structural form of a two-equation model is as follows (the t-subscript is omitted):

$$P = \alpha_1 + \alpha_2 N + \alpha_3 S + \alpha_4 A + u$$

$$N = \beta_1 + \beta_2 P + \beta_3 M + v$$

where P and N are endogenous and S, A, and M are exogenous.
a.   For each equation, examine whether it is under-, over-, or exactly identified.
b.   What explanatory variables, if any, are correlated with u? What explanatory variables, if any, are correlated with v?
c.   What happens if OLS is used to estimate the αs and the βs?
d.   Can the αs be estimated by ILS? If yes, derive the estimates. Answer the same equation about the βs.
e.   Explain step-by-step how the TSLS method can be applied on the second equation.

13.4   Consider the following simple three-equation model:

$$A = X - M \qquad\qquad \text{Endogenous: } A, M, X$$

$$M = \alpha_1 + \alpha_2 Y + \alpha_3 P + \alpha_4 U + u \qquad \text{Exogenous: } Y, P, U$$

$$X = \beta_1 + \beta_2 P + \beta_3 A + v \qquad\qquad \text{Error terms: } u, v$$

a.   Check whether the order condition is satisfied for the second and third equations. What is your conclusion?
b.   Derive the reduced form equations.
c.   How would you use the TSLS estimation procedure on the third equation?
d.   Explain why we can use the OLS method on the second equation. What properties do the estimates have?
e.   Suppose we had used OLS to estimate the third equation. What properties will those estimates have?

13.5   Consider the following three-equation model relating crime in a city to a number of determinants:

$$\text{PROPCRIME} = \alpha_1 + \alpha_2 \text{ MEDHOME} + \alpha_3 \text{ POPDEN} + \alpha_4 \text{ UNEMP}$$
$$+ \alpha_5 \text{ POLICE} + u$$

$$\text{VIOLNTCRIME} = \beta_1 + \beta_2 \text{ POLICE} + \beta_3 \text{ DEATH} + \beta_4 \text{ MEDAGE} + v$$

$$\text{POLICE} = \gamma_1 + \gamma_2 \text{ PROPCRIME} + \gamma_3 \text{ VIOLNTCRIME} + w$$

where PROPCRIME is property crime, VIOLNTCRIME is violent crime, POLICE is the expenditure on police, DEATH is a dummy variable that takes the value 1 if the city is in a state that allows the death penalty, MEDHOME is median value of homes,

POPDEN is the density of population (number of people per square mile), UNEMP is the unemployment rate, and MEDAGE is the median age of the city's population.

a.   What signs would you expect a priori for each of the coefficients?

b.   Check the order conditions on each equation.

c.   Describe step-by-step how you would use TSLS to estimate each of the equations.

13.6   Consider the following two-equation model in which the ys are endogenous and the xs are exogenous:

$$y_1 = \alpha_1 y_2 + \alpha_2 x_1 + u$$

$$y_2 = \beta_1 y_1 + \beta_2 x_2 + \beta_3 x_3 + v$$

Explicitly derive the reduced form equations for y_1 and y_2. Use these to check whether each of the parameters is (1) unidentified, (2) exactly identified, or (3) overidentified. Then describe the appropriate estimation procedure for each of the parameters.

13.7   Consider the following two-equation model in which the ys are endogenous and the xs are exogenous:

$$y_1 = \alpha_1 y_2 + \alpha_2 x_1 + u$$

$$y_2 = \beta_1 x_1 + \beta_2 x_2 + v$$

Suppose that u and v are uncorrelated with both x_1 and x_2. Show that, in this example, there is no simultaneous equation bias. Is OLS appropriate in this case?

13.8   Consider the following two-equation model in which x and y are both endogenous:

$$y_t = \alpha_1 y_{t-1} + \alpha_2 x_t + u_t$$

$$x_t = \beta_1 x_{t-1} + \beta_2 y_{t-1} + v_t$$

Both u_t and v_t are uncorrelated with the lagged variables x_{t-1} and y_{t-1}. Explain why this model also exhibits no simultaneous equation bias.

13.9   Redo the analysis in Section 13.6 using aggregate levels of financial variables rather than per-capita values. Are the qualitative results the same or different?

13.10   In the equations in Section 13.6, add one more lag for both the endogenous and predetermined variables and reestimate the equations by two-stage squares. This approach allows for serial correlation in the original models.

Derivation of the Limits for OLS Estimates

In this appendix, we compute the limit of the OLS estimate of β ($\hat{\beta}$) for Equation (13.11) and show that it is not equal to the true value, thus proving that the estimate is inconsistent. Applying the OLS procedure to Equation (13.11), we obtain the following expression for $\hat{\beta}$ (see Equation 3.12):

$$\hat{\beta} = \frac{S_{CY}}{S_{YY}} \tag{13.A.1}$$

where

$$S_{CY} = \sum (C_t - \overline{C})(Y_t - \overline{Y}) \tag{13.A.2}$$

$$S_{YY} = \sum (Y_t - \overline{Y})^2 \tag{13.A.3}$$

From the reduced forms of the model (Equations 13.13 and 13.14), we have

$$C_t - \overline{C} = \frac{\beta}{1 - \beta}(I_t - \overline{I}) + \frac{u_t - \overline{u}}{1 - \beta} \tag{13.A.4}$$

$$Y_t - \overline{Y} = \frac{I_t - \overline{I}}{1 - \beta} + \frac{u_t - \overline{u}}{1 - \beta} \tag{13.A.5}$$

where the bar above a variable represents the sample mean. Multiplying the left-hand sides of Equations (13.A.4) and (13.A.5) and summing, we have

$$S_{CY} = \frac{\beta}{(1 - \beta)^2} S_{II} + \frac{1}{(1 - \beta)^2} S_{uu} + \frac{1 + \beta}{(1 - \beta)^2} S_{Iu}$$

where S_{II}, S_{uu}, and S_{Iu} are defined similarly to S_{CY} and S_{YY}. As $n \to \infty$, S_{uu}/n converges to the variance σ_u^2 (by the law of large numbers), S_{Iu}/n converges to 0 because I_t and u_t are uncorrelated, and S_{II}/n converges to the variance σ_I^2. Therefore, S_{CY}/n converges to $(\beta \sigma_I^2 + \sigma_u^2)/(1 - \beta)^2$. Similarly,

$$S_{YY} = \frac{S_{II}}{(1 - \beta)^2} + \frac{S_{uu}}{(1 - \beta)^2} + \frac{2S_{Iu}}{(1 - \beta)^2}$$

and hence S_{YY}/n converges to $(\sigma_I^2 + \sigma_u^2)/(1 - \beta)^2$. Thus, the asymptotic limit of $\hat{\beta}$ is as follows:

$$\lim_{n \to \infty} \hat{\beta} = \frac{\beta \sigma_I^2 + \sigma_u^2}{\sigma_I^2 + \sigma_u^2} = \beta + \frac{(1 - \beta)\sigma_u^2}{\sigma_I^2 + \sigma_u^2}$$

This establishes Equation (13.15).

Practice

This part, which contains only one chapter, takes the reader through the various steps involved in carrying out an empirical project and in preparing a report. It also provides details that will help in choosing a topic, obtaining sources for review of existing literature, and looking for data. Students who are expected to conduct an empirical study may be assigned this chapter early in the course.

CHAPTER 14

Carrying Out an Empirical Project

In Chapter 1, we gave a brief description of the various stages of an empirical study, from formulating the problem to be studied to interpreting the results. Although most of the chapters have presented illustrative applications in the form of mini projects, a student will learn more about econometrics from a complete empirical project than from dozens of lectures. This chapter further elaborates each of the steps presented in Chapter 1. If an instructor is requiring an empirical project, students should study this chapter earlier, especially the parts about formulating a research question, specifying an initial model in general form, and gathering the data.

As one might easily infer, there is no unique way to conduct an empirical study and no magic formula one can apply. Practice is the only way to learn the steps involved in applied research and to develop the intuition needed to judge results and draw conclusions. This chapter, therefore, can offer only general guidelines and suggestions for approaches.

14.1 Selecting a Topic

If you are a professional researcher, the problem for study is usually dictated by the requirements of the job and/or assigned by your superiors. For instance, one of the major tasks of an analyst in the load forecasting department of an electric utility is to estimate the relationship between the demand for electricity and its various determinants, such as weather and seasonal patterns, the price of electricity, income, stock of appliances, industrial and demographic mix of the utility service area, and so on. The estimated relation is then used to generate load forecasts. These forecasts are evaluated by the state's public utilities commission to determine what the new rate structure should be and whether any new power plants are required to service the area's demand. In this example, the research question is easily posed as that of relating the demand for electricity to its determinants and that of generating forecasts.

If you are a student in a course on econometrics, however, the instructor might require that you carry out an empirical project and may not assign any specific problem to be examined. The first task, then, is to select a topic for study, which naturally raises the question, "What do I do and how do I get started?" To answer this, consider the following. Before taking a course in econometrics you undoubtedly took other economics courses, some of which might have been at the upper-division level. You would have studied many theories about the behavior of economic agents and the relationships among economic variables. So ask yourself now which of the theoretical relationships you studied would be worth empirically estimating and which bodies of theories can be put to empirical tests. In the courses you took, there might have been a discussion of an equation or of someone's study that interested you. This would be worth following up. Your former professors might be willing to help you focus on one of the problems of interest, but don't impose on them or take advantage of their generosity. Some possible topic areas are the following[1]:

1. *Macroeconomics:* Estimate a consumption or investment or money demand function. These usually require time series analysis and two-stage least squares. You might try to estimate a Phillips curve, either with international data for many countries or with time series data for a given country. Macro topics have the advantage that the data are relatively easy to come by.

2. *Microeconomics:* Estimating production, cost, supply, and demand functions are obvious choices, but data are generally hard to obtain.

3. *Urban and regional economics:* Estimate the demand for housing, transportation, schools and other public facilities, and so on for a city, county, or state. Measure the sensitivity of industrial location to differences across regions in tax rates, energy prices, zoning laws, degree of unionization, availability of skilled labor, and so on.

4. *International economics:* Estimate import and export functions for a given country over time or across many countries. Relate exchange rates to their determinants.

5. *Development economics:* Measure the determinants of per-capita income (GNP) across countries.

6. *Labor economics:* Test theories on unionization, early retirement, labor force participation rates, wage differentials among women, minorities, and young workers, and so on.

7. *Industrial organization:* Measure the effects of advertising on sales and profits or on the concentration (that is, market share) in industries. Estimate the relationship between expenditures on research and development (R&D) and employee productivity. Study the relationship between industry concentration and profitability due to merger activity. You are cautioned, however, that because of confidentiality, data on research and development expenditures and advertising budgets of individual companies would be practically impossible to obtain.

8. *Public finance:* Estimate the relationship between local government tax revenue and its characteristics, such as population, demographic and industrial

---

[1] This list is drawn from a similar list provided to me by Carrol Foster. For other excellent examples of possible empirical projects, see Wooldridge (2000, pp. 635–640), Lott and Ray (1992), Berndt (1991), and Intriligator, Bodkin, and Hsiao (1996).

mix, wages, income, and so on. Also relate the expenditures on health, roads, education, and so on to their determinants.

9. *Socioeconomics:* Explain variations across cities, counties, and states in crime, poverty, divorce rates, family size, and so on.

10. *Politics:* Relate voter turnout to a number of characteristics of precincts, candidates, and so on. Explain the vote obtained by a politician in different districts.

A very convenient way to look for topics and to find published papers on the topics is to use an Internet service such as EconLit, which is likely to be available through your college or university. EconLit would enable you to search on-line by subject, author, or key words from a large collection of journal articles. Another useful reference source available on the Internet is the *Social Science Citation Index.* This periodical provides a list (typically by authors' names) of journals, books, and so on that have cited a particular research work.

Yet another systematic way to approach the problem of choosing a specific topic is to make effective use of a classification system adopted by the *Journal of Economic Literature (JEL)*, which is a quarterly publication that presents a classified list of books and journal articles published in the preceding quarter (see Table 14.1 for a copy of this list). A compact disc version is available for purchase from the American Economic Association. As an example, if you are interested in studying labor mobility, first look up the entry in Table 14.1 under "Labor and Demographic Economics" and note that the relevant classification number is J6. Next turn to the "Subject Index of Articles in Current Periodicals," which contains a detailed list of recent articles published under the various classifications, and make a list of those that interest you. The journal also lists the contents of current periodicals and has abstracts on selected books and articles. The abstracts will help you learn more about particular topics and help you decide whether a paper is too theoretical for your tastes.

Journals such as *Applied Economics, Applied Econometrics, Review of Economics and Statistics, International Monetary Fund Staff Papers,* and the *Brookings Paper on Economic Activity* are predominantly application-oriented and would be useful starting points. Some journals specialize in certain fields (for example, *Journal of Human Resources, Journal of Urban Economics, Journal of Regional Science*). These can be identified from a list of journals that the *JEL* uses for abstracts (Table 14.2 has a partial listing). If you have a general field in mind, these specialized journals might be helpful in narrowing down a specific research question. Be sure to write down the names and other references for books and journals that relate to the topic of your choice. Take a quick look at the papers to see if you wish to pursue the topic further. Bibliographical citations in these papers are also worth looking into because they contain additional references on the same topic. The list you compile at this stage will be indispensable in future stages. After selecting a topic, prepare a statement of the problem you intend to study.

The Web site *www.rfe.org* (Resources for Economists) is a good starting point for searching for a variety of economics material on the Web.

Table 14.1 Journal of Economic Literature Classification System

MAJOR FIELDS Code List

A General Economics and Teaching
A0 General
A1 General Economics
A2 Teaching of Economics

B Methodology and History of Economic Thought
B0 General
B1 History of Economic Thought through 1925
B2 History of Economic Thought since 1925
B3 History of Thought: Individuals
B4 Economic Methodology

C Mathematical and Quantitative Methods
C0 General
C1 Econometric and Statistical Methods: General
C2 Econometric Methods: Single-Equation Models
C3 Econometric Methods: Multiple/Simultaneous Equation Models
C4 Econometric and Statistical Methods: Special Topics
C5 Econometric Modeling
C6 Mathematical Methods and Programming
C7 Game Theory and Bargaining Theory
C8 Data Collection and Estimation Methodology; Computer Programs
C9 Design of Experiments

D Microeconomics
D0 General
D1 Household Behavior and Family Economics
D2 Productions and Organizations
D3 Distribution
D4 Market Structure and Pricing
D5 General Equilibrium and Disequilibrium
D6 Economic Welfare
D7 Analysis of Collective Decision Making
D8 Information and Uncertainty
D9 Intertemporal Choice and Growth

E Macroeconomics and Monetary Economics
E0 General
E1 General Aggregative Models
E2 Consumption, Saving, Production, Employment, and Investment
E3 Prices, Business Fluctuations, and Cycles
E4 Money and Interest Rates
E5 Monetary Policy, Central Banking, and the Supply of Money and Credit
E6 Macroeconomic Aspects of Public Finance, Macroeconomic Policy, and General Outlook

F International Economics
F0 General
F1 Trade
F2 International Factor Movements
F3 International Finance
F4 Macroeconomic Aspects of International Trade and Finance

G Financial Economics
G0 General
G1 General Financial Markets
G2 Financial Institutions and Services
G3 Corporate Finance and Governance

H Public Economics
H0 General
H1 Structure and Scope of Government
H2 Taxation and Subsidies
H3 Fiscal Policies and Behavior of Economic Agents
H4 Publicly Provided Goods
H5 National Government Expenditures and Related Policies
H6 National Budget, Deficit, and Debt
H7 State and Local Government; Intergovernmental Relations
H8 Miscellaneous Issues

I Health, Education, and Welfare
I0 General
I1 Health
I2 Education
I3 Welfare and Policy

J Labor and Demographic Economics
J0 General
J1 Demographic Economics
J2 Time Allocation, Work Behavior, and Employment Determination
J3 Wages, Compensation, and Labor Costs
J4 Particular Labor Markets
J5 Labor–Management Relations, Trade Unions, and Collective Bargaining
J6 Mobility, Unemployment, Vacancies
J7 Discrimination

K Law and Economics
K0 General
K1 Basic Areas of Law
K2 Regulation and Business Law
K3 Other Substantive Areas of Law
K4 Legal Procedures, the Legal System, and Illegal Behavior

L Industrial Organization
L0 General
L1 Market Structure, Firm Strategy, and Market Performance
L2 Firm Objectives, Organization, and Behavior
L3 Nonprofit Organizations and Public Enterprise
L4 Antitrust Policy
L5 Regulation and Industrial Policy
L6 Industry Studies: Manufacturing
L7 Industry Studies: Primary Products and Construction
L8 Industry Studies: Services
L9 Industry Studies: Utilities and Transportation

(continued)

Table 14.1   (continued)

MAJOR FIELDS Code List (continued)

M Business Administration and Business Economics: Marketing; Accounting
M0   General
M1   Business Administration
M2   Business Economics
M3   Marketing and Advertising
M4   Accounting

N Economic History
N0   General
N1   Macroeconomics; Growth and Fluctuations
N2   Financial Markets and Institutions
N3   Labor; Demography; Education; Income and Wealth
N4   Law and Regulation
N5   Agriculture, Natural Resources, and Extractive Industries
N6   Manufacturing and Construction
N7   Transport, Trade, and Other Services

O Economic Development, Technological Change, and Growth
O0   General
O1   Economic Development
O2   Development Planning and Policy
O3   Technological Change
O4   Economic Growth and Aggregate Productivity
O5   Economywide Country Studies

P Economic Systems
P0   General
P1   Capitalist Systems
P2   Socialist Systems
P3   Socialist Institutions
P4   Other Economic Systems
P5   Comparative Economic Systems

Q Agricultural and Natural Resource Economics
Q0   General
Q1   Agriculture
Q2   Renewable Resources and Conservation; Environmental Management
Q3   Nonrenewal Resources and Conservation
Q4   Energy

R Urban, Rural, and Regional Economics
R0   General
R1   General Spatial Economics
R2   Household Analysis
R3   Production Analysis and Firm Location
R4   Transportation Services
R5   Regional Government Analysis

Z Other Special Topics
Z0   General
Z1   Cultural Economics

Source: Journal of Economic Literature. Reprinted with permission of the American Economic Association.

Table 14.2   A Selected List of Periodicals

American Economic Review	*Economic Studies Quarterly*
American Journal of Agricultural Economics	*Economics of Education Review*
American Journal of Economics and Sociology	*Economics Letters*
Annals of Regional Science	*Empirical Economics*
Antitrust Bulletin	*Energy Economics*
Applied Economics	*Energy Journal*
Australian Economic Review	*Environment and Planning*
Brookings Papers on Economic Activity	*European Economic Review*
Cambridge Journal of Economics	*Federal Reserve Bank Reviews*
Canadian Journal of Agricultural Economics	*Federal Reserve Bulletin*
Canadian Journal of Economics	*Finance and Development*
Contemporary Economic Policy	*Financial Review*
Eastern Economic Journal	*Indian Economic Journal*
Econometrica	*Indian Economic Review*
Economica	*Industrial Relations*
Economic Analysis and Worker's Management	*International Journal of Industrial Organization*
Economic Development and Cultural Change	*International Journal of Transport Economics*
Economic Inquiry	*International Labor Review*
Economic Journal	*International Monetary Fund Staff Papers*
Economic Modeling	*Journal of Agricultural Economics*
Economic Record	*Journal of Applied Econometrics*

⬤   Table 14.2   (continued)

Journal of Banking and Finance	Journal of Regional Science
Journal of Business	Journal of Urban Economics
Journal of Business and Economic Statistics	Land Economics
Journal of Consumer Research	Managerial and Decision Economics
Journal of Development Economics	Manchester School of Economics and Social Studies
Journal of Econometrics	Marine Resource Economics
Journal of Economic Education	Monthly Labor Review
Journal of Economic Issues	National Tax Journal
Journal of Economics and Business	Natural Resources Journal
Journal of Environmental Economics and Management	Oxford Bulletin of Economics and Statistics
Journal of Finance	Oxford Economic Papers
Journal of Financial and Quantitative Analysis	Oxford Review of Economic Policy
Journal of Financial Economics	Pakistan Development Review
Journal of Financial Research	Public Choice
Journal of Health Economics	Quarterly Journal of Business and Economics
Journal of Human Resources	Quarterly Journal of Economics
Journal of Industrial Economics	Quarterly Review of Economics and Business
Journal of International Economics	Quarterly Review of Economics and Finance
Journal of Labor Economics	Rand Journal of Economics
Journal of Law, Economics, and Organization	Regional Science and Urban Economics
Journal of Macroeconomics	Review of Financial Studies
Journal of Monetary Economics	Review of Income and Wealth
Journal of Money, Credit, and Banking	Review of Social Economy
Journal of Political Economy	Social Science Quarterly
Journal of Public Economics	Southern Economic Journal
Journal of Quantitative Economics	Survey of Current Business

⬤   14.2   Review of Literature

The next step after choosing a topic and formulating a research question is to find out what other researchers have done on that topic. This bibliographic search is crucial because you will not only learn how models have been formulated and estimated but also what the data sources are. The starting point for the literature review is, again, the *Journal of Economic Literature*. In the process of selecting a topic, you will have compiled a list of relevant papers or books on the subject. First read each of these quickly to see if it is worth devoting more time to. In particular, note the bibliography items for other papers on the same topic. Another useful reference source is the *Social Science Citation Index* mentioned earlier. If a selected reference item looks interesting, read it carefully and take notes. In particular, identify the dependent and independent variables, the types of models formulated, whether cross-section or time series data were used, the techniques of estimation and tests of hypotheses used, and the data sources and measures. Next prepare a three- to five-page summary of each article or book chapter that relates to your research question. It is recommended that you prepare at least four such summaries.

14.3 Formulating a General Model

Based on the literature review, you should construct a general formulation of your own model. This might require an optimizing framework such as utility maximization, profit maximization, or cost minimization. State the initial model in broad terms and identify the dependent and independent variables for which you would like to get data. You should also decide at this stage whether a simultaneous equation model is called for. If your variables have feedback effects (that is, X affects Y and Y affects X), your model should be a simultaneous equation model, unless you are interested only in the reduced form described in Chapter 13. At this stage you should also decide whether cross-section or time series data are appropriate for your stated objectives. If your goal is to explain what makes the values of the dependent variable change over time, then the relevant data will be time series. If, on the other hand, you wish to investigate why different groups (such as different countries, states, counties, firms, industries, employment groups) behave differently at a given point in time, then cross-section data are called for. The relationships estimated with cross-section data might not be stable over time. To examine this issue you need pooled data. Prepare a write-up explaining why you believe the independent variables you have chosen are likely to affect the dependent variable(s). Describe the hypotheses you plan to test and the expected nature of the effect of independent variables. In particular, discuss the expected signs of regression coefficients, whether nonlinearity might be present, what kinds of interactions among independent variables you should look for, and so on. It is important that you think through carefully whether variables should be in logarithmic form or in squares or in other forms.

14.4 Collecting the Data

Now come the long, and often tedious, tasks of gathering the data, organizing them in a form that computers can process, and finally entering them on a computer for future analysis. How much data should one obtain, and what are the sources from which data can be gathered? We have seen that the higher the degrees of freedom, the better the precision of an estimate and the greater the power of tests of hypotheses. Increasing the degrees of freedom means having more observations relative to the number of independent variables. In the wage determination application of Section 7.3, the number of independent variables was quite large (see Table 7.5) because of the numerous interaction terms. We saw in Chapters 9 and 10 that if a time series model has many lag terms or higher-order serial correlation, we lose several initial observations. To compensate for this we need more observations. Finally, the Lagrange multiplier test and tests for heteroscedasticity are large-sample tests that suggest the need for more observations. A rule of thumb is to have at least 30 degrees of freedom.

Data Sources

The amount of published data is so voluminous that it is impossible to list all the sources here. Therefore, only certain broad types, especially the most frequently used ones, are described here.

MACHINE-READABLE DATA   In this computer age, many data series are already available in machine-readable form. For example, the library at the University of California, San Diego, has a *Social Science Data Base* that has on-line access to a variety of economics data: *Citibase, International Financial Statistics,* and the *Census of Population and Housing,* to name a few. Other campuses may have similar databases. The Center for Research on Security Prices (CRSP) has volumes of data on the security prices of numerous companies, readily accessible by computers. Many companies are now marketing personal computer diskettes that contain data on a variety of fields. Some of them are available in CD-ROM formats. COMPUSERVE is a well-known source of databases. Contact your library personnel to see whether they have the data you require in machine-readable form.

The increasingly popular **World Wide Web** has numerous **on-line databases** available. This book's Web site at *http://econ.ucsd.edu/~rramanat/embook5.htm* has a list of several of these and a direct link to the corresponding Web site.

The advantage of having data in a form accessible directly by a computer is that they are very convenient to get and are usually error-free. However, they often require some text editing for input into a regression program. For instance, the population data might be available for over 50 years, but interest rate data might be available for only 30 years. Before you can use the data for regression analysis, you should select a common period of analysis and prepare a data file with complete data for this period.

Although it is preferable to obtain data from an on-line source, you should not neglect the multitude of data sources from published tables. Some of these are discussed next.

DATA AT THE INTERNATIONAL LEVEL   As mentioned earlier, *International Financial Statistics* is an excellent data source at the international level. Other publications of use are *United Nations Statistical Yearbook, World Development Report, Demographic Yearbook,* and World Health Organization and International Monetary Fund publications.

DATA AT THE NATIONAL LEVEL   Almost all countries have statistical abstracts that usually contain aggregated data for the country as a whole. Some countries may have specialized periodicals with data (for instance, *Economic Trends* in the United Kingdom and the *Economic Report of the President* of the United States). *Survey of Current Business, Federal Reserve Bulletin, Agricultural Statistics, Monthly Labor Review, Census of Population and Housing, Census of Manufacturing, Annual Housing Survey, State and Metropolitan Data Book,* and Bureau of Labor Statistics publications are examples of other sources.

DATA AT THE REGIONAL LEVEL   In the United States, one can get, for most states, the *Economic Report of the Governor* that has statistical appendices. These will have data for the state as a whole and for subregions such as counties, districts, cities, or SMSAs (Standard Metropolitan Statistical Areas). *County and City Data Book* is also a useful source, as is the *State and Metropolitan Data Book* supplement of the *Statistical Abstract of the United States.*

Specialized Data

Monthly or quarterly data on a variety of economic and business indicators can be obtained from the *Survey of Current Business* or from publications from Dun and Bradstreet. A number of the data series are available by industries classified by **SIC codes** *(Standard Industrial Classification codes)*. The *Federal Reserve Bulletin* is a valuable source for financial statistics, as are the Standard & Poors and Moody's ratings of securities and other financial information. Information relating to agriculture is available from *Agricultural Statistics*. For statistics on education, a variety of sources are available: *Digest of Education Statistics, Financial Statistics of Institutions of Higher Education, Admissions Testing Program Summary Reports,* publications by the National Center for Education Statistics, and so on.

Although these data sources can provide a researcher with a starting point, the amount of published data is so voluminous that it is impossible to list them all here. Fortunately, however, compendia are available that, like the *Journal of Economic Literature,* provide a classified listing of data sources. The most valuable of these is the *Statistical Reference Index* compiled by the Congressional Information Service. As its cover page indicates, it is a "selective guide to American statistical publications from private organizations and state government sources." This index has three parts: (1) an index volume that lists the publications, with minimal detail about the exact data series; (2) an abstracts volume, which provides considerable information about each of the data series; and (3) microfiche containing selected recent data.

Index Numbers

It was mentioned in Chapter 1 that **index numbers** play an important role in economic data. The most well known of these is the **consumer price index,** compiled by the U.S. Bureau of Labor Statistics. It measures the average cost of living, at different points in time, of a fixed "market basket" of commodities and services purchased by wage earners and salaried clerks in urban areas. A **base year** of reference is first chosen along with a fixed bundle of goods (known as **weights**) that a typical consumer (often defined as a family of two adults and two children) is likely to purchase. The average prices are compiled for each point in time. These are then rescaled, with the base period's value set to 100 and the others expressed relative to it. As an example, consider the commonly used price index known as the **Laspeyres index.** Let b refer to the base period, t a typical period, i a typical commodity ($i = 1, \ldots, n$), P_{bi} the price of the ith commodity in the base period, Q_{bi} the quantity (which will remain fixed) of the ith commodity in the base period, Q_{ti} the quantity of the ith commodity at time t, and P_{ti} the price of the ith commodity at time t. The steps for computing the Laspeyres index are as follows:

1. Multiply the price of each item in each period (P_{ti}) by the base period quantity of that item (Q_{bi}). This gives $P_{bi} Q_{bi}$ as the value of the ith good in the base period and $P_{ti} Q_{bi}$ as the value of the ith good in period t, *using the base period quantity.*

2. Obtain the sum of these products over the n commodities, which gives us the total value of the basket of goods in the base period as $\sum_{i=1}^{n} P_{bi}Q_{bi}$ and the value of the *same basket of goods* at time t as $\sum_{i=1}^{n} P_{ti}Q_{bi}$.

3. Divide the total value of the bundle of goods at time t by its value in the base period and multiply by 100 to give the following Laspeyres price index for the time period t with b as the base period:

$$P_b^t = 100 \frac{\Sigma P_{ti} Q_{bi}}{\Sigma P_{bi} Q_{bi}}$$

The actual computation of the Laspeyres price index is somewhat different from this procedure. This is to accommodate the fact that consumers periodically use substitute goods (an inexpensive store brand for a well-known national brand, for example). The weights are then modified to allow the freedom to substitute. Weight revisions are also made when the base period is changed. When obtaining index number data, an investigator must be acutely aware of any changes in the base period. If such a change has taken place, appropriate conversions must be made to the data that used a previous period for base. This topic is taken up next.

Changing the Base Period

When a researcher obtains index number data, many of the series would have different base years. Also, the government periodically revises the base period to a more recent one. To make interpretation of results more meaningful, it is important to be able to convert all the data to a common base year. The process, however, is quite straightforward and is easily understood with the hypothetical numbers provided in the following table:

Year	Index with 1995 as Base	Index with 2000 as Base
1995	100	78.13
1996	110	85.94
1997	116	90.63
1998	124	96.88
1999	132	103.13
2000	128	100.00
2001	126	98.44
2002	140	109.38
2003	145	113.28

We readily see that the procedure is to divide each of the values in the old series (the second column here) by the corresponding value for the *new base year* (128 here) and multiply the result by 100. The conversion formula is thus

$$\text{Newindex}_t = 100 \; \text{Oldindex}_t / \text{Oldindex}_{\text{newbase}}$$

Data in Constant (or "Real") Dollars

The total value of a group of commodities is the sum of the products of prices and the corresponding quantities. This value will change from period to period because of changes in both prices and quantities. In economics, however, we are often interested in the value in **real dollars** (also known as **constant dollars**), that is, when prices are held constant. To obtain the value in constant dollars, we take the value in **current (or nominal) dollars,** divide it by the corresponding period's price index, and multiply by 100. For instance, real wages are obtained by dividing nominal wages by the consumer price index and multiplying by 100. This principle obviously applies to currencies other than dollars. The price index used here is often referred to as the **deflator.** The government generally uses different deflators for different series. For instance, to obtain the gross domestic product (GDP) in constant dollars, one would use the GDP deflator, which is a price index of the commodities and services that the GDP measures. Similarly, we have the *personal consumption expenditures* (PCE) *deflator,* which is different from the consumer price index.

A variation of the Laspeyres index is the **Paasche Index,** which uses as weights the quantities of the time period t. For an excellent treatment of index numbers, refer to the book by Chu (1989).

Work Sheets

If the data you seek are available in printed form rather than in machine-readable form, you have the task of copying them down and then making them machine-readable. You accomplish this through the use of **work sheets.** The work sheet might be prepared so that the data are arranged by observations as in a spreadsheet or by variables, that is, series by series. The choice is largely a matter of convenience and the way the published data are arranged. For each series be sure to note the exact data source (with page and table numbers, name and year of publication, the agency that publishes the data, and so on). This is important because you may wish to go back later to verify entries or look for additional data. It is also crucial that the units of measurement be noted. As we have seen, interpreting the numerical values of regression coefficients depends critically on the units in which the variables are measured. Finally, check whether there have been any changes in the definitions of variables or in the base periods for price and other indices. If there were changes, you have to adjust the data accordingly. In the case of time series data, note whether they are already adjusted seasonally.

Because computers can do all the arithmetic calculations, you do not need to convert data manually to suit your model. For instance, if your model calls for per-capita real income, gather information about nominal income, a price index, and population. Then let the computer perform the appropriate transformation to obtain per-capita real income.

Entering the Data on a Computer

Next comes the task of entering the data into a computer for access by a regression program. How they are entered depends very much on the regression package you plan to use to analyze them. In order to do this, you need a **text editor,** which is basically a word processing program. You may also use a **spreadsheet** program (such as EXCEL or Lotus 1-2-3) to enter the data. Most regression programs accept the data in **ASCII** form. ASCII stands for the *American Standard Code for Information Interchange* and is a widely used standard for entering data and text. If your word processing program does not store the data in ASCII form, it is likely to give you the option of preparing an ASCII version of the data. Be sure to choose this option if your regression program will not accept non-ASCII files. Many regression programs have their own built-in editors. Before you actually attempt to enter the data on the computer, study the data input requirements of the regression program you plan to use. *It is also important to remember that your final data set used in regressions must not have any missing entries.*

Generating New Variables

In carrying out empirical analyses, an analyst often works with transformed variables rather than with the original variables for which the data were assembled. We have seen many examples of this. Double-log models require that all the variables be transformed into logarithms. Quadratic and interaction terms require the multiplication of variables. If population has a role in your model, express relevant variables in per-capita terms. To convert variables to real terms, the nominal variables need to be divided by a price index. To calculate percentage change, the transformation $100(X_t - X_{t-1})/X_{t-1}$ is required. To calculate the "instantaneous rate of change," use the transformation $\ln(X_t) - \ln(X_{t-1})$—that is, the difference in the logarithm between two successive observations. Regression packages have the capability of transforming data internally. Take advantage of this capability.

Computers vary in the precision with which numerical calculations are made. Some programs and machines are more subject to round-off and overflow errors than others. It is generally a good practice to avoid using very small or very large values in the actual analysis. The sum of squares associated with such large values may be astronomically large, causing bad overflow and truncation errors. For instance, rather than enter population as 2,157,899, convert it to ten-thousandths and enter it as 215.7899. It is also generally a good practice to scale variables so that the entered values are in the range 1 to 1,000. For example, rather than enter the unemployment rate as 0.043, enter it as 4.3. This applies to other fractions as well.

● 14.5   Empirical Analysis

Analysis is obviously the most important stage of an empirical study. It consists of first putting the data through some preliminary checking, then estimating the models formulated initially, performing appropriate tests, and, if necessary, reformulating them and reestimating them.

Preliminary Data Analysis

Before actually using the data to estimate models, it is important that the data be subjected to some preliminary analysis in order to catch typing errors, **outliers** (which are extreme values), and lack of variation in the data. Some common typing mistakes are using an "el" instead of a "1" (possibly an old habit from using typewriters that did not have a separate key for unity) and using an "oh" for a "0." A raw listing of the data is very useful in spotting obvious mistakes.

The next step is to plot each series against the observation number. In other words, plot X_t against t for each series. Outliers are easier to identify with this plot.

If *t* stands for time, the graph will be a time series plot and will give you an idea of the time path of the variable and the underlying growth rate. A common temptation is to graph the values of the dependent variable against values of each independent variable in order to see whether some nonlinearity can be identified. Although such graphs might be useful in some cases, they are often misleading. The graph between observed *Y* and observed *X does not hold other variables constant.* Thus, what appears to be a nonlinear relation between *Y* and *X* might really be a series of linear relationships that are being shifted by the movement of a third variable *Z* (refer to the discussion on spurious nonlinearities in Section 6.5). Such "data mining" to identify relationships should be avoided. Instead, use theory about behavior to formulate models and perform appropriate tests for model specification, including nonlinearity.

In addition to a plot of the data to identify outliers, it is useful to obtain summary statistics such as the minimum, maximum, mean, standard deviation, and the coefficient of variation, which is the ratio of the standard deviation to the mean. Although there is no hard-and-fast rule about the coefficient of variation, a low value such as 0.05 indicates that the standard deviation is only about 5 percent of the mean. This means that the variable in question does not vary much and might not exhibit any significance if used as an independent variable in a regression (refer to the discussion in Chapter 3 on Assumption 3.2).

Finally, obtain the matrix of correlation coefficients—that is, the correlation coefficients for every pair of variables used in the analysis. A high correlation between the dependent variable and a given independent variable is clearly desirable. A high correlation between two independent variables might cause multicollinearity problems and is worth noting ahead of time. Be cautioned, however, that a low correlation between two independent variables does not mean that multicollinearity need not arise. This point was discussed in detail in Chapter 5.

Model Estimation and Hypothesis Testing

We are now ready to estimate the general model formulated in Section 14.3. Estimate the model and examine the *F*-statistic and $\overline{R}^2$. What percent of the variation in the dependent variable does the model capture? The first model estimated often has disappointing results. Signs of some of the regression coefficients might be contrary to prior expectations, *t*-statistics might indicate insignificance of variables, adjusted R^2 might be low, serial correlation might be present if time series data are used, and so on. Here again there is no general formula as to how to proceed. A considerable amount of judgment is required at each stage, and researchers differ a great deal on the approaches.

Certain general guidelines are nevertheless useful. A fundamental lesson is to avoid hasty conclusions without subjecting the model to more analysis. The approach that is recommended is to formulate models based on some theoretical framework and an understanding of the underlying behavior and then perform a battery of diagnostic tests to assure yourself that the conclusions are robust—that is, that they are not too sensitive to model specification. We have seen throughout that the Wald and Lagrange multiplier tests are extremely useful in testing for the inclusion of omitted variables, nonlinearities, interactions, the presence of lagged dependent variables, serial correlation of higher orders, and whether new variables should be added to the specification. When several similar models are formulated, the model selection criteria can be used to judge the superiority of one model over another. If a certain variable is insignificant under alternative formulations, you can safely conclude that perhaps it is redundant, and its omission might not result in serious misspecification.

Check the correlations among explanatory variables and see if high values can explain unexpected signs and/or insignificant coefficients. If you find serial correlation to be present with time series data, reformulate the model to see if serial correlation can be eliminated. If necessary, apply the Cochrane–Orcutt and/or Hildreth–Lu methods. Similarly, if heteroscedasticity is found, the weighted least squares procedure described in Chapter 8 would be appropriate. For simultaneous equation models, adopt the two-stage least squares procedure to avoid least squares bias and the inconsistency of estimates. The estimation and diagnostic testing of models often involves several stages of reestimation and retesting. *Be sure, however, to report all your steps, including intermediate failures.* Your project should be reproducible by another investigator.

Writing a Report

The final stage of the study is to write a report describing the various steps and interpreting the results. First, prepare a brief title for the study that describes the nature of the question examined. In writing the report, keep the style simple and straightforward. Sedulously eschew all polysyllabic profundities (in other words, don't use big words). A suggested outline for the final report is as follows:

1. Statement of the Problem
2. Review of Literature
3. Formulation of a General Model
4. Data Sources and Description
5. Model Estimation and Hypothesis Testing
6. Interpretation of the Results and Conclusions
7. Limitations of the Study and Possible Extensions
8. Acknowledgements
9. References

Statement of the Problem: In a paragraph to a page, describe the problem you have studied, the questions you have asked, and the broad hypotheses you have tested. You can also give a brief indication of your conclusions.

Review of Literature: Assemble the literature review you conducted earlier and attach it here. As mentioned in Section 14.2, this section will contain a summary of each paper and book you read that relates to your study, with the models and methods used, the data sources, and the conclusions arrived at by the author(s).

Formulation of a General Model: Describe here the initial model you formulated in Section 14.3. Point out the differences between your approach and those of others who have studied similar problems.

Data Sources and Description: Present a table of variable names and their definitions. Be sure to specify the units of measurement. List the data sources and attach a copy of the raw data. Include in the table the transformations that generated the variables actually used in estimation (see Table 9.3 for an example).

Model Estimation and Hypothesis Testing: Present the regression results in one or more tables similar to Table 4.2. Although many authors present standard errors in parentheses below regression coefficients, it is recommended that the *t*-statistics or *p*-values be presented instead, with possible asterisks to identify significant coefficients. Also present useful summary statistics such as adjusted R^2, the Durbin–Watson statistic, model selection criteria, the *F*-statistic, degrees of freedom, and so on. In the text, describe the models you estimated, the various tests you carried out, and the results. The extent to which the actual econometric analysis should be described depends very much on the audience. If you are submitting a term paper to an instructor, it might be important to be informative about every stage of the analysis. Recall the earlier comment that another investigator should be able to reproduce your results. If the audience is not likely to be very technically oriented, move such technical details to appendices.

Interpretation of the Results and Conclusions: State what you observe in terms of the original hypotheses and expectations. If you found unexpected results, present some rationalization for them. The interpretation of results sections in the applications and Sections 4.7, 7.4, and 9.7 are useful guides here. Provide some concluding remarks regarding your study and put it in perspective with other studies.

Limitations of the Study and Possible Extensions: It is important to recognize your study's limitations. Such limitations might be due to a lack of available data or of computer programs for a specific method you deem appropriate, or to other reasons. Suggest where one can go from here and what possible extensions would be interesting.

Acknowledgements: During the course of conducting the empirical study, you might have received the help of a number of persons: professors, teaching assistants, personnel in the library who helped you with the bibliography, people who helped you obtain the data, and so on. It is common courtesy to acknowledge their help.

References: Attach an alphabetical list of the references you compiled earlier in preparing for the analysis. The list should include the bibliography for the literature review as well as the references for your data sources. Avoid numbering the bibliography items and using corresponding numerical references in the text because if you add a bibliographical citation later, you will have to renumber the references and make numerous text changes. If you list the bibliography alphabetically and make text references to it by authors' names and year of publication, you will need to make only minor, if any, alterations to handle subsequent changes. The format used in this book is a useful one.

Key Terms

ASCII	Consumer price index
Base year	Current dollars
Constant dollars	Deflator

Index numbers
Laspeyres index
Nominal dollars
On-line database
Outliers
Paasche index
Real dollars

SIC code
Spreadsheet
Text editor
Weights
Work sheet
World Wide Web

References

Berndt, E.R. *The Practice of Econometrics.* Reading, Mass.: Addison-Wesley, 1991.

Chu, Y. *Statistical Analysis for Business and Economics.* New York: Elsevier, 1989.

Intriligator, M., R. G. Bodkin, and C. Hsiao. *Economic Models, Techniques and Applications.* 2d ed. Upper Saddle River, N.J.: Prentice Hall, 1996.

Lott, W., and S. C. Ray. *Applied Econometrics: Problems and Data Sets.* Fort Worth, Tex.: The Dryden Press, 1992.

Wooldridge, J. *Introductory Econometrics: A Modern Approach.* South-Western College Publishing, 2000.

APPENDIX A

Statistical Tables

A.1   Areas under the Standard Normal Curve from 0 to z

A.2   Percentage Points of the t-Distribution

A.3   Upper Percentage Points of the Chi-Square Distribution

A.4a   Upper 1% Points of the F-Distribution

A.4b   Upper 5% Points of the F-Distribution

A.4c   Upper 10% Points of the F-Distribution

A.5   Durbin–Watson Test: 5% Significance Points of d_L and d_U in One-Tailed Tests

A.6   Cumulative Terms for the Binomial Distribution $\sum_{x=x'}^{x=n} \binom{n}{x} p^x (1-p)^{n-x}$

Table A.1 Areas under the Standard Normal Curve from 0 to z

z	0.00	0.01	0.02	0.03	0.04	0.05	0.06	0.07	0.08	0.09
0.0	0.0000	0.0040	0.0080	0.0120	0.0160	0.0199	0.0239	0.0279	0.0319	0.0359
0.1	0.0398	0.0438	0.0478	0.0517	0.0557	0.0596	0.0636	0.0675	0.0714	0.0753
0.2	0.0793	0.0832	0.0871	0.0910	0.0948	0.0987	0.1026	0.1064	0.1103	0.1141
0.3	0.1179	0.1217	0.1255	0.1293	0.1331	0.1368	0.1406	0.1443	0.1480	0.1517
0.4	0.1554	0.1591	0.1628	0.1664	0.1700	0.1736	0.1772	0.1808	0.1844	0.1879
0.5	0.1915	0.1950	0.1985	0.2019	0.2054	0.2088	0.2123	0.2157	0.2190	0.2224
0.6	0.2257	0.2291	0.2324	0.2357	0.2389	0.2422	0.2454	0.2486	0.2518	0.2549
0.7	0.2580	0.2612	0.2642	0.2673	0.2704	0.2734	0.2764	0.2794	0.2823	0.2852
0.8	0.2881	0.2910	0.2939	0.2967	0.2995	0.3023	0.3051	0.3078	0.3106	0.3133
0.9	0.3159	0.3186	0.3212	0.3238	0.3264	0.3289	0.3315	0.3340	0.3365	0.3389
1.0	0.3413	0.3438	0.3461	0.3485	0.3508	0.3531	0.3554	0.3577	0.3599	0.3621
1.1	0.3643	0.3665	0.3686	0.3708	0.3729	0.3749	0.3770	0.3790	0.3810	0.3830
1.2	0.3849	0.3869	0.3888	0.3907	0.3925	0.3944	0.3962	0.3980	0.3997	0.4015
1.3	0.4032	0.4049	0.4066	0.4082	0.4099	0.4115	0.4131	0.4147	0.4162	0.4177
1.4	0.4192	0.4207	0.4222	0.4236	0.4251	0.4265	0.4279	0.4292	0.4306	0.4319
1.5	0.4332	0.4345	0.4357	0.4370	0.4382	0.4394	0.4406	0.4418	0.4429	0.4441
1.6	0.4452	0.4463	0.4474	0.4484	0.4495	0.4505	0.4515	0.4525	0.4535	0.4545
1.7	0.4554	0.4564	0.4573	0.4582	0.4591	0.4599	0.4608	0.4616	0.4625	0.4633
1.8	0.4641	0.4649	0.4656	0.4664	0.4671	0.4678	0.4686	0.4693	0.4699	0.4706
1.9	0.4713	0.4719	0.4726	0.4732	0.4738	0.4744	0.4750	0.4756	0.4761	0.4767
2.0	0.4772	0.4778	0.4783	0.4788	0.4793	0.4798	0.4803	0.4808	0.4812	0.4817
2.1	0.4821	0.4826	0.4830	0.4834	0.4838	0.4842	0.4846	0.4850	0.4854	0.4857
2.2	0.4861	0.4864	0.4868	0.4871	0.4875	0.4878	0.4881	0.4884	0.4887	0.4890
2.3	0.4893	0.4896	0.4898	0.4901	0.4904	0.4906	0.4909	0.4911	0.4913	0.4916
2.4	0.4918	0.4920	0.4922	0.4925	0.4927	0.4929	0.4931	0.4932	0.4934	0.4936
2.5	0.4938	0.4940	0.4941	0.4943	0.4945	0.4946	0.4948	0.4949	0.4951	0.4952
2.6	0.4953	0.4955	0.4956	0.4957	0.4959	0.4960	0.4961	0.4962	0.4963	0.4964
2.7	0.4965	0.4966	0.4967	0.4968	0.4969	0.4970	0.4971	0.4972	0.4973	0.4974
2.8	0.4974	0.4975	0.4976	0.4977	0.4977	0.4978	0.4979	0.4979	0.4980	0.4981
2.9	0.4981	0.4982	0.4982	0.4983	0.4984	0.4984	0.4985	0.4985	0.4986	0.4986
3.0	0.49865	0.4987	0.4987	0.4988	0.4988	0.4989	0.4989	0.4989	0.4990	0.4990
4.0	0.49997									

Note: If $z = 0.93$, $p(0 \leq Z \leq z) = 0.3238$.

Source: Morris Hamburg, *Statistical Analysis for Decision Making*, 4th ed., 1987. Reprinted with the permission of Harcourt Brace College Publishers.

Table A.2   Percentage Points of the *t*-Distribution

d.f.	1T=0.4 2T=0.8	0.25 0.5	0.1 0.2	0.05 0.1	0.025 0.05	0.01 0.02	0.005 0.01	0.0025 0.005	0.001 0.002	0.0005 0.001
1	0.325	1.000	3.078	6.314	12.706	31.821	63.657	127.32	318.31	636.62
2	.289	0.816	1.886	2.920	4.303	6.965	9.925	14.089	22.327	31.598
3	.277	.765	1.638	2.353	3.182	4.541	5.841	7.453	10.214	12.924
4	.271	.741	1.533	2.132	2.776	3.747	4.604	5.598	7.173	8.610
5	0.267	0.727	1.476	2.015	2.571	3.365	4.032	4.773	5.893	6.869
6	.265	.718	1.440	1.943	2.447	3.143	3.707	4.317	5.208	5.959
7	.263	.711	1.415	1.895	2.365	2.998	3.499	4.029	4.785	5.408
8	.262	.706	1.397	1.860	2.306	2.896	3.355	3.833	4.501	5.041
9	.261	.703	1.383	1.833	2.262	2.821	3.250	3.690	4.297	4.781
10	0.260	0.700	1.372	1.812	2.228	2.764	3.169	3.581	4.144	4.587
11	.260	.697	1.363	1.796	2.201	2.718	3.106	3.497	4.025	4.437
12	.259	.695	1.356	1.782	2.179	2.681	3.055	3.428	3.930	4.318
13	.259	.694	1.350	1.771	2.160	2.650	3.012	3.372	3.852	4.221
14	.258	.692	1.345	1.761	2.145	2.624	2.977	3.326	3.787	4.140
15	0.258	0.691	1.341	1.753	2.131	2.602	2.947	3.286	3.733	4.073
16	.258	.690	1.337	1.746	2.120	2.583	2.921	3.252	3.686	4.015
17	.257	.689	1.333	1.740	2.110	2.567	2.898	3.222	3.646	3.965
18	.257	.688	1.330	1.734	2.101	2.552	2.878	3.197	3.610	3.922
19	.257	.688	1.328	1.729	2.093	2.539	2.861	3.174	3.579	3.883
20	0.257	0.687	1.325	1.725	2.086	2.528	2.845	3.153	3.552	3.850
21	.257	.686	1.323	1.721	2.080	2.518	2.831	3.135	3.527	3.819
22	.256	.686	1.321	1.717	2.074	2.508	2.819	3.119	3.505	3.792
23	.256	.685	1.319	1.714	2.069	2.500	2.807	3.104	3.485	3.767
24	.256	.685	1.318	1.711	2.064	2.492	2.797	3.091	3.467	3.745
25	0.256	0.684	1.316	1.708	2.060	2.485	2.787	3.078	3.450	3.725
26	.256	.684	1.315	1.706	2.056	2.479	2.779	3.067	3.435	3.707
27	.256	.684	1.314	1.703	2.052	2.473	2.771	3.057	3.421	3.690
28	.256	.683	1.313	1.701	2.048	2.467	2.763	3.047	3.408	3.674
29	.256	.683	1.311	1.699	2.045	2.462	2.756	3.038	3.396	3.659
30	0.256	0.683	1.310	1.697	2.042	2.457	2.750	3.030	3.385	3.646
40	.255	.681	1.303	1.684	2.021	2.423	2.704	2.971	3.307	3.551
60	.254	.679	1.296	1.671	2.000	2.390	2.660	2.915	3.232	3.460
120	.254	.677	1.289	1.658	1.980	2.358	2.617	2.860	3.160	3.373
∞	.253	.674	1.282	1.645	1.960	2.326	2.576	2.807	3.090	3.291

Note: 1T = area under one tail; 2T = area under both tails.

For 25 degrees of freedom (d.f.), $P(t > 2.060) = 0.025$ and $P(t < -2.060$ or $t > 2.060) = 0.05$.

Source: Biometrika Tables for Statisticians, Vol. I, 3rd ed., edited by E. S. Pearson and H. O. Hartley, 1966. Reprinted with the permission of the Biometrika Trustees.

Table A.3   Upper Percentage Points of the Chi-Square Distribution (ν Is the Degrees of Freedom and Q Is the Area in the Right Tail)

ν \ Q	0.250	0.100	0.050	0.025	0.010	0.005	0.001
1	1.32330	2.70554	3.84146	5.02389	6.63490	7.87944	10.828
2	2.77259	4.60517	5.99146	7.37776	9.21034	10.5966	13.816
3	4.10834	6.25139	7.81473	9.34840	11.3449	12.8382	16.266
4	5.38527	7.77944	9.48773	11.1433	13.2767	14.8603	18.467
5	6.62568	9.23636	11.0705	12.8325	15.0863	16.7496	20.515
6	7.84080	10.6446	12.5916	14.4494	16.8119	18.5476	22.458
7	9.03715	12.0170	14.0671	16.0128	18.4753	20.2777	24.322
8	10.2189	13.3616	15.5073	17.5345	20.0902	21.9550	26.125
9	11.3888	14.6837	16.9190	19.0228	21.6660	23.5894	27.877
10	12.5489	15.9872	18.3070	20.4832	23.2093	25.1882	29.588
11	13.7007	17.2750	19.6751	21.9200	24.7250	26.7568	31.264
12	14.8454	18.5493	21.0261	23.3367	26.2170	28.2995	32.909
13	15.9839	19.8119	22.3620	24.7356	27.6882	29.8195	34.528
14	17.1169	21.0641	23.6848	26.1189	29.1412	31.3194	36.123
15	18.2451	22.3071	24.9958	27.4884	30.5779	32.8013	37.697
16	19.3689	23.5418	26.2962	28.8454	31.9999	34.2672	39.252
17	20.4887	24.7690	28.5871	30.1910	33.4087	35.7185	40.790
18	21.6049	25.9894	28.8693	31.5264	34.8053	37.1565	42.312
19	22.7178	27.2036	30.1435	32.8523	36.1909	38.5823	43.820
20	23.8277	28.4120	31.4104	34.1696	37.5662	39.9968	45.315
21	24.9348	29.6151	32.6706	35.4789	38.9322	41.4011	46.797
22	26.0393	30.8133	33.9244	36.7807	40.2894	42.7957	48.268
23	27.1413	32.0069	35.1725	38.0756	41.6384	44.1813	49.728
24	28.2412	33.1962	36.4150	39.3641	42.9798	45.5585	51.179
25	29.3389	34.3816	37.6525	40.6465	44.3141	46.9279	52.618
26	30.4346	35.5632	38.8851	41.9232	45.6417	48.2899	54.052
27	31.5284	36.7412	40.1133	43.1945	46.9629	46.6449	55.476
28	32.6205	37.9159	41.3371	44.4608	48.2782	50.9934	56.892
29	33.7109	39.0875	42.5570	45.7223	49.5879	52.3356	58.301
30	34.7997	40.2560	43.7730	46.9792	50.8922	53.6720	59.703
40	45.6160	51.8051	55.7585	59.3417	63.6907	66.7660	73.402
50	56.3336	63.1671	67.5048	71.4202	76.1539	79.4900	86.661
60	66.9815	74.3970	79.0819	83.2977	88.3794	91.9517	99.607
70	77.5767	85.5270	90.5312	95.0232	100.425	104.215	112.317
80	88.1303	96.5782	101.879	106.629	112.329	116.321	124.839
90	98.6499	107.565	113.145	118.136	124.116	128.299	137.208
100	109.141	118.498	124.342	129.561	135.807	140.169	149.449
X	+0.6745	+1.2816	+1.6449	+1.9600	+2.3263	+2.5758	+3.0902

Note: For 25 d.f., $P(\chi^2 > 37.6525) = 0.05$.

For $\nu > 100$ take

$$\chi^2 = \nu\left\{1 - \frac{2}{9\nu} + X\sqrt{\frac{2}{9\nu}}\right\}^3 \quad \text{or} \quad \chi^2 = \tfrac{1}{2}\left\{X + \sqrt{(2\nu - 1)}\right\}^2,$$

according to the degree of accuracy required. X is the standardized normal deviate corresponding to $P = 1 - Q$ and is shown in the bottom line of the table.

Source: Biometrika Tables for Statisticians, Vol. I, 3rd ed., edited by E. S. Pearson and H. O. Hartley, 1966. Reprinted with the permission of the Biometrika Trustees.

Table A.4a Upper 1% Points of the F-Distribution

n \ m	1	2	3	4	5	6	7	8	9	10	12	15	20	24	30	40	60	120	∞
1	4052	4999.5	5403	5625	5764	5859	5928	5981	6022	6056	6106	6157	6209	6235	6261	6287	6313	6339	6366
2	98.50	99.00	99.17	99.25	99.30	99.33	99.36	99.37	99.39	99.40	99.42	99.43	99.45	99.46	99.47	99.47	99.48	99.49	99.50
3	34.12	30.82	29.46	28.71	28.24	27.91	27.67	27.49	27.35	27.23	27.05	26.87	26.69	26.60	26.50	26.41	26.32	26.22	26.13
4	21.20	18.00	16.69	15.98	15.52	15.21	14.98	15.80	14.66	14.55	14.37	14.20	14.02	13.93	13.84	13.75	13.65	13.56	13.46
5	16.26	13.27	12.06	11.39	10.97	10.67	10.46	10.29	10.16	10.05	9.89	9.72	9.55	9.47	9.38	9.29	9.20	9.11	9.02
6	13.75	10.92	9.78	9.15	8.75	8.47	8.26	8.10	7.98	7.87	7.72	7.56	7.40	7.31	7.23	7.14	7.06	6.97	6.88
7	12.25	9.55	8.45	7.85	7.46	7.19	6.99	6.84	6.72	6.62	6.47	6.31	6.16	6.07	5.99	5.91	5.82	5.74	5.65
8	11.26	8.65	7.59	7.01	6.63	6.37	6.18	6.03	5.91	5.81	5.67	5.52	5.36	5.28	5.20	5.12	5.03	4.95	4.86
9	10.56	8.02	6.99	6.42	6.06	5.80	5.61	5.47	5.35	5.26	5.11	4.96	4.81	4.73	4.65	4.57	4.48	4.40	4.31
10	10.04	7.56	6.55	5.99	5.64	5.39	5.20	5.06	4.94	4.85	4.71	4.56	4.41	4.33	4.25	4.17	4.08	4.00	3.91
11	9.65	7.21	6.22	5.67	5.32	5.07	4.89	4.74	4.63	4.54	4.40	4.25	4.10	4.02	3.94	3.86	3.78	3.69	3.60
12	9.33	6.93	5.95	5.41	5.06	4.82	4.64	4.50	4.39	4.30	4.16	4.01	3.86	3.78	3.70	3.62	3.54	3.45	3.36
13	9.07	6.70	5.74	5.21	4.86	4.62	4.44	4.30	4.19	4.10	3.96	3.82	3.66	3.59	3.51	3.43	3.34	3.25	3.17
14	8.86	6.51	5.56	5.04	4.69	4.46	4.28	4.14	4.03	3.94	3.80	3.66	3.51	3.43	3.35	3.27	3.18	3.09	3.00
15	8.68	6.36	5.42	4.89	4.56	4.32	4.14	4.00	3.89	3.80	3.67	3.52	3.37	3.29	3.21	3.13	3.05	2.96	2.87
16	8.53	6.23	5.29	4.77	4.44	4.20	4.03	3.89	3.78	3.69	3.55	3.41	3.26	3.18	3.10	3.02	2.93	2.84	2.75
17	8.40	6.11	5.18	4.67	4.34	4.10	3.93	3.79	3.68	3.59	3.46	3.31	3.16	3.08	3.00	2.92	2.83	2.75	2.65
18	8.29	6.01	5.09	4.58	4.25	4.01	3.84	3.71	3.60	3.51	3.37	3.23	3.08	3.00	2.92	2.84	2.75	2.66	2.57
19	8.18	5.93	5.01	4.50	4.17	3.94	3.77	3.63	3.52	3.43	3.30	3.15	3.00	2.92	2.84	2.76	2.67	2.58	2.49
20	8.10	5.85	4.94	4.43	4.10	3.87	3.70	3.56	3.46	3.37	3.23	3.09	2.94	2.86	2.78	2.69	2.61	2.52	2.42
21	8.02	5.78	4.87	4.37	4.04	3.81	3.64	3.51	3.40	3.31	3.17	3.03	2.88	2.80	2.72	2.64	2.55	2.46	2.36
22	7.95	5.72	4.82	4.31	3.99	3.76	3.59	3.45	3.35	3.26	3.12	2.98	2.83	2.75	2.67	2.58	2.50	2.40	2.31
23	7.88	5.66	4.76	4.26	3.94	3.71	3.54	3.41	3.30	3.21	3.07	2.93	2.78	2.70	2.62	2.54	2.45	2.35	2.26
24	7.82	5.61	4.72	4.22	3.90	3.67	3.50	3.36	3.26	3.17	3.03	2.89	2.74	2.66	2.58	2.49	2.40	2.31	2.21
25	7.77	5.57	4.68	4.18	3.85	3.63	3.46	3.32	3.22	3.13	2.99	2.85	2.70	2.62	2.54	2.45	2.36	2.27	2.17
26	7.72	5.53	4.64	4.14	3.82	3.59	3.42	3.29	3.18	3.09	2.96	2.81	2.66	2.58	2.50	2.42	2.33	2.23	2.13
27	7.68	5.49	4.60	4.11	3.78	3.56	3.39	3.26	3.15	3.06	2.93	2.78	2.63	2.55	2.47	2.38	2.29	2.20	2.10
28	7.64	5.45	4.57	4.07	3.75	3.53	3.36	3.23	3.12	3.03	2.90	2.75	2.60	2.52	2.44	2.35	2.26	2.17	2.06
29	7.60	5.42	4.54	4.04	3.73	3.50	3.33	3.20	3.09	3.00	2.87	2.73	2.57	2.49	2.41	2.33	2.23	2.14	2.03
30	7.56	5.39	4.51	4.02	3.70	3.47	3.30	3.17	3.07	2.98	2.84	2.70	2.55	2.47	2.39	2.30	2.21	2.11	2.01
40	7.31	5.18	4.31	3.83	3.51	3.29	3.12	2.99	2.89	2.80	2.66	2.52	2.37	2.29	2.20	2.11	2.02	1.92	1.80
60	7.08	4.98	4.13	3.65	3.34	3.12	2.95	2.82	2.72	2.63	2.50	2.35	2.20	2.12	2.03	1.94	1.84	1.73	1.60
120	6.85	4.79	3.95	3.48	3.17	2.96	2.79	2.66	2.56	2.47	2.34	2.19	2.03	1.95	1.86	1.76	1.66	1.53	1.38
∞	6.63	4.61	3.78	3.32	3.02	2.80	2.64	2.51	2.41	2.32	2.18	2.04	1.88	1.79	1.70	1.59	1.47	1.32	1.00

Note: m = degrees of freedom for the numerator
n = degrees of freedom for the denominator

Source: Handbook of Tables for Mathematics, edited by Robert C. West and Samuel M. Selby, 1970. Reprinted with the permission of the CRC Press, Inc.

APPENDIX A

Table A.4b   Upper 5% Points of the F-Distribution

n \ m	1	2	3	4	5	6	7	8	9	10	12	15	20	24	30	40	60	120	∞
1	161.4	199.5	215.7	224.6	230.2	234.0	236.8	238.9	240.5	241.9	243.9	245.9	248.0	249.1	250.1	251.1	252.2	253.3	254.3
2	18.51	19.00	19.16	19.25	19.30	19.33	19.35	19.37	19.38	19.40	19.41	19.43	19.45	19.45	19.46	19.47	19.48	19.49	19.50
3	10.13	9.55	9.28	9.12	9.01	8.94	8.89	8.85	8.81	8.79	8.74	8.70	8.66	8.64	8.62	8.59	8.57	8.55	8.53
4	7.71	6.94	6.59	6.39	6.26	6.16	6.09	6.04	6.00	5.96	5.91	5.86	5.80	5.77	5.75	5.72	5.69	5.66	5.63
5	6.61	5.79	5.41	5.19	5.05	4.95	4.88	4.82	4.77	4.74	4.68	4.62	4.56	4.53	4.50	4.46	4.43	4.40	4.36
6	5.99	5.14	4.76	4.53	4.39	4.28	4.21	4.15	4.10	4.06	4.00	3.94	3.87	3.84	3.81	3.77	3.74	3.70	3.67
7	5.59	4.74	4.35	4.12	3.97	3.87	3.79	3.73	3.68	3.64	3.57	3.51	3.44	3.41	3.38	3.34	3.30	3.27	3.23
8	5.32	4.46	4.07	3.84	3.69	3.58	3.50	3.44	3.39	3.35	3.28	3.22	3.15	3.12	3.08	3.04	3.01	2.97	2.93
9	5.12	4.26	3.86	3.63	3.48	3.37	3.29	3.23	3.18	3.14	3.07	3.01	2.94	2.90	2.86	2.83	2.79	2.75	2.71
10	4.96	4.10	3.71	3.48	3.33	3.22	3.14	3.07	3.02	2.98	2.91	2.85	2.77	2.74	2.70	2.66	2.62	2.58	2.54
11	4.84	3.98	3.59	3.36	3.20	3.09	3.01	2.95	2.90	2.85	2.79	2.72	2.65	2.61	2.57	2.53	2.49	2.45	2.40
12	4.75	3.89	3.49	3.26	3.11	3.00	2.91	2.85	2.80	2.75	2.69	2.62	2.54	2.51	2.47	2.43	2.38	2.34	2.30
13	4.67	3.81	3.41	3.18	3.03	2.92	2.83	2.77	2.71	2.67	2.60	2.53	2.46	2.42	2.38	2.34	2.30	2.25	2.21
14	4.60	3.74	3.34	3.11	2.96	2.85	2.76	2.70	2.65	2.60	2.53	2.46	2.39	2.35	2.31	2.27	2.22	2.18	2.13
15	4.54	3.68	3.29	3.06	2.90	2.79	2.71	2.64	2.59	2.54	2.48	2.40	2.33	2.29	2.25	2.20	2.16	2.11	2.07
16	4.49	3.63	3.24	3.01	2.85	2.74	2.66	2.59	2.54	2.49	2.42	2.35	2.28	2.24	2.19	2.15	2.11	2.06	2.01
17	4.45	3.59	3.20	2.96	2.81	2.70	2.61	2.55	2.49	2.45	2.38	2.31	2.23	2.19	2.15	2.10	2.06	2.01	1.96
18	4.41	3.55	3.16	2.93	2.77	2.66	2.58	2.51	2.46	2.41	2.34	2.27	2.19	2.15	2.11	2.06	2.02	1.97	1.92
19	4.38	3.52	3.13	2.90	2.74	2.63	2.54	2.48	2.42	2.38	2.31	2.23	2.16	2.11	2.07	2.03	1.98	1.93	1.88
20	4.35	3.49	3.10	2.87	2.71	2.60	2.51	2.45	2.39	2.35	2.28	2.20	2.12	2.08	2.04	1.99	1.95	1.90	1.84
21	4.32	3.47	3.07	2.84	2.68	2.57	2.49	2.42	2.37	2.32	2.25	2.18	2.10	2.05	2.01	1.96	1.92	1.87	1.81
22	4.30	3.44	3.05	2.82	2.66	2.55	2.46	2.40	2.34	2.30	2.23	2.15	2.07	2.03	1.98	1.94	1.89	1.84	1.78
23	4.28	3.42	3.03	2.80	2.64	2.53	2.44	2.37	2.32	2.27	2.20	2.13	2.05	2.01	1.96	1.91	1.86	1.81	1.76
24	4.26	3.40	3.01	2.78	2.62	2.51	2.42	2.36	2.30	2.25	2.18	2.11	2.03	1.98	1.94	1.89	1.84	1.79	1.73
25	4.24	3.39	2.99	2.76	2.60	2.49	2.40	2.34	2.28	2.24	2.16	2.09	2.01	1.96	1.92	1.87	1.82	1.77	1.71
26	4.23	3.37	2.98	2.74	2.59	2.47	2.39	2.32	2.27	2.22	2.15	2.07	1.99	1.95	1.90	1.85	1.80	1.75	1.69
27	4.21	3.35	2.96	2.73	2.57	2.46	2.37	2.31	2.25	2.20	2.13	2.06	1.97	1.93	1.88	1.84	1.79	1.73	1.67
28	4.20	3.34	2.95	2.71	2.56	2.45	2.36	2.29	2.24	2.19	2.12	2.04	1.96	1.91	1.87	1.82	1.77	1.71	1.65
29	4.18	3.33	2.93	2.70	2.55	2.43	2.35	2.28	2.22	2.18	2.10	2.03	1.94	1.90	1.85	1.81	1.75	1.70	1.64
30	4.17	3.32	2.92	2.69	2.53	2.42	2.33	2.27	2.21	2.16	2.09	2.01	1.93	1.89	1.84	1.79	1.74	1.68	1.62
40	4.08	3.23	2.84	2.61	2.45	2.34	2.25	2.18	2.12	2.08	2.00	1.92	1.84	1.79	1.74	1.69	1.64	1.58	1.51
60	4.00	3.15	2.76	2.53	2.37	2.25	2.17	2.10	2.04	1.99	1.92	1.84	1.75	1.70	1.65	1.59	1.53	1.47	1.39
120	3.92	3.07	2.68	2.45	2.29	2.17	2.09	2.02	1.96	1.91	1.83	1.75	1.66	1.61	1.55	1.50	1.43	1.35	1.25
∞	3.84	3.00	2.60	2.37	2.21	2.10	2.01	1.94	1.88	1.83	1.75	1.67	1.57	1.52	1.46	1.39	1.32	1.22	1.00

Note: m = degrees of freedom for the numerator

n = degrees of freedom for the denominator

Source: Handbook of Tables for Mathematics, edited by Robert C. West and Samuel M. Selby, 1970. Reprinted with the permission of the CRC Press, Inc.

Table A.4c Upper 10% Points of the F-Distribution

n \ m	1	2	3	4	5	6	7	8	9	10	12	15	20	24	30	40	60	120	∞
1	39.86	49.50	53.59	55.83	57.24	58.20	58.91	59.44	59.86	60.19	60.71	61.22	61.74	62.00	62.26	62.53	62.79	63.06	63.33
2	8.53	9.00	9.16	9.24	9.29	9.33	9.35	9.37	9.38	9.39	9.41	9.42	9.44	9.45	9.46	9.47	9.47	9.48	9.49
3	5.54	5.46	5.39	5.34	5.31	5.28	5.27	5.25	5.24	5.23	5.22	5.20	5.18	5.18	5.17	5.16	5.15	5.14	5.13
4	4.54	4.32	4.19	4.11	4.05	4.01	3.98	3.95	3.94	3.92	3.90	3.87	3.84	3.83	3.82	3.80	3.79	3.78	3.76
5	4.06	3.78	3.62	3.52	3.45	3.40	3.37	3.34	3.32	3.30	3.27	3.24	3.21	3.19	3.17	3.16	3.14	3.12	3.10
6	3.78	3.46	3.29	3.18	3.11	3.05	3.01	2.98	2.96	2.94	2.90	2.87	2.84	2.82	2.80	2.78	2.76	2.74	2.72
7	3.59	3.26	3.07	2.96	2.88	2.83	2.78	2.75	2.72	2.70	2.67	2.63	2.59	2.58	2.56	2.54	2.51	2.49	2.47
8	3.46	3.11	2.92	2.81	2.73	2.67	2.62	2.59	2.56	2.54	2.50	2.46	2.42	2.40	2.38	2.36	2.34	2.32	2.29
9	3.36	3.01	2.81	2.69	2.61	2.55	2.51	2.47	2.44	2.42	2.38	2.34	2.30	2.28	2.25	2.23	2.21	2.18	2.16
10	3.29	2.92	2.73	2.61	2.52	2.46	2.41	2.38	2.35	2.32	2.28	2.24	2.20	2.18	2.16	2.13	2.11	2.08	2.06
11	3.23	2.86	2.66	2.54	2.45	2.39	2.34	2.30	2.27	2.25	2.21	2.17	2.12	2.10	2.08	2.05	2.03	2.00	1.97
12	3.18	2.81	2.61	2.48	2.39	2.33	2.28	2.24	2.21	2.19	2.15	2.10	2.06	2.04	2.01	1.99	1.96	1.93	1.90
13	3.14	2.76	2.56	2.43	2.35	2.28	2.23	2.20	2.16	2.14	2.10	2.05	2.01	1.98	1.96	1.93	1.90	1.88	1.85
14	3.10	2.73	2.52	2.39	2.31	2.24	2.19	2.15	2.12	2.10	2.05	2.01	1.96	1.94	1.91	1.89	1.86	1.83	1.80
15	3.07	2.70	2.49	2.36	2.27	2.21	2.16	2.12	2.09	2.06	2.02	1.97	1.92	1.90	1.87	1.85	1.82	1.79	1.76
16	3.05	2.67	2.46	2.33	2.24	2.18	2.13	2.09	2.06	2.03	1.99	1.94	1.89	1.87	1.84	1.81	1.78	1.75	1.72
17	3.03	2.64	2.44	2.31	2.22	2.15	2.10	2.06	2.03	2.00	1.96	1.91	1.86	1.84	1.81	1.78	1.75	1.72	1.69
18	3.01	2.62	2.42	2.29	2.20	2.13	2.08	2.04	2.00	1.98	1.93	1.89	1.84	1.81	1.78	1.75	1.72	1.69	1.66
19	2.99	2.61	2.40	2.27	2.18	2.11	2.06	2.02	1.98	1.96	1.91	1.86	1.81	1.79	1.76	1.73	1.70	1.67	1.63
20	2.97	2.59	2.38	2.25	2.16	2.09	2.04	2.00	1.96	1.94	1.89	1.84	1.79	1.77	1.74	1.71	1.68	1.64	1.61
21	2.96	2.57	2.36	2.23	2.14	2.08	2.02	1.98	1.95	1.92	1.87	1.83	1.78	1.75	1.72	1.69	1.66	1.62	1.59
22	2.95	2.56	2.35	2.22	2.13	2.06	2.01	1.97	1.93	1.90	1.86	1.81	1.76	1.73	1.70	1.67	1.64	1.60	1.57
23	2.94	2.55	2.34	2.21	2.11	2.05	1.99	1.95	1.92	1.89	1.84	1.80	1.74	1.72	1.69	1.66	1.62	1.59	1.55
24	2.93	2.54	2.33	2.19	2.10	2.04	1.98	1.94	1.91	1.88	1.83	1.78	1.73	1.70	1.67	1.64	1.61	1.57	1.53
25	2.92	2.53	2.32	2.18	2.09	2.02	1.97	1.93	1.89	1.87	1.82	1.77	1.72	1.69	1.66	1.63	1.59	1.56	1.52
26	2.91	2.52	2.31	2.17	2.08	2.01	1.96	1.92	1.88	1.86	1.81	1.76	1.71	1.68	1.65	1.61	1.58	1.54	1.50
27	2.90	2.51	2.30	2.17	2.07	2.00	1.95	1.91	1.87	1.85	1.80	1.75	1.70	1.67	1.64	1.60	1.57	1.53	1.49
28	2.89	2.50	2.29	2.16	2.06	2.00	1.94	1.90	1.87	1.84	1.79	1.74	1.69	1.66	1.63	1.59	1.56	1.52	1.48
29	2.89	2.50	2.28	2.15	2.06	1.99	1.93	1.89	1.86	1.83	1.78	1.73	1.68	1.65	1.62	1.58	1.55	1.51	1.47
30	2.88	2.49	2.28	2.14	2.05	1.98	1.93	1.88	1.85	1.82	1.77	1.72	1.67	1.64	1.61	1.57	1.54	1.50	1.46
40	2.84	2.44	2.23	2.09	2.00	1.93	1.87	1.83	1.79	1.76	1.71	1.66	1.61	1.57	1.54	1.51	1.47	1.42	1.38
60	2.79	2.39	2.18	2.04	1.95	1.87	1.82	1.77	1.74	1.71	1.66	1.60	1.54	1.51	1.48	1.44	1.40	1.35	1.29
120	2.75	2.35	2.13	1.99	1.90	1.82	1.77	1.72	1.68	1.65	1.60	1.55	1.48	1.45	1.41	1.37	1.32	1.26	1.19
∞	2.71	2.30	2.08	1.94	1.85	1.77	1.72	1.67	1.63	1.60	1.55	1.49	1.42	1.38	1.34	1.30	1.24	1.17	1.00

Note: m = degrees of freedom for the numerator
n = degrees of freedom for the denominator

Source: Handbook of Tables for Mathematics, edited by Robert C. West and Samuel M. Selby, 1970. Reprinted with the permission of the CRC Press, Inc.

⬤ Table A.5   Durbin–Watson Test: 5% Significance Points of d_L and d_U in One-Tailed Tests

		$k' = 1$		$k' = 2$		$k' = 3$		$k' = 4$		$k' = 5$	
	n	d_L	d_U	d_L	d_U	d_L	d_U	d_L	d_U	d_L	d_U
	6	0.610	1.400	—	—	—	—	—	—	—	—
	7	0.700	1.356	0.467	1.896	—	—	—	—	—	—
	8	0.763	1.332	0.559	1.777	0.368	2.287	—	—	—	—
	9	0.824	1.320	0.629	1.699	0.455	2.128	0.296	2.588	—	—
	10	0.879	1.320	0.697	1.641	0.525	2.016	0.376	2.414	0.243	2.822
	11	0.927	1.324	0.758	1.604	0.595	1.928	0.444	2.283	0.316	2.645
	12	0.971	1.331	0.812	1.579	0.658	1.864	0.512	2.177	0.379	2.506
	13	1.010	1.340	0.861	1.562	0.715	1.816	0.574	2.094	0.445	2.390
	14	1.045	1.350	0.905	1.551	0.767	1.779	0.632	2.030	0.505	2.296
	15	1.077	1.361	0.946	1.543	0.814	1.750	0.685	1.977	0.562	2.220
	16	1.106	1.371	0.982	1.539	0.857	1.728	0.734	1.935	0.615	2.157
	17	1.133	1.381	1.015	1.536	0.897	1.710	0.779	1.900	0.664	2.104
	18	1.158	1.391	1.046	1.535	0.933	1.696	0.820	1.872	0.710	2.060
	19	1.180	1.401	1.074	1.536	0.967	1.685	0.859	1.848	0.752	2.023
	20	1.201	1.411	1.100	1.537	0.998	1.676	0.894	1.828	0.792	1.991
	21	1.221	1.420	1.125	1.538	1.026	1.669	0.927	1.812	0.829	1.964
	22	1.239	1.429	1.147	1.541	1.053	1.664	0.958	1.797	0.863	1.940
	23	1.257	1.437	1.168	1.543	1.078	1.660	0.986	1.785	0.895	1.920
	24	1.273	1.446	1.188	1.546	1.101	1.656	1.013	1.775	0.925	1.902
	25	1.288	1.454	1.206	1.550	1.123	1.654	1.038	1.767	0.953	1.886
	26	1.302	1.461	1.224	1.553	1.143	1.652	1.062	1.759	0.979	1.873
	27	1.316	1.469	1.240	1.556	1.162	1.651	1.084	1.753	1.004	1.861
	28	1.328	1.476	1.255	1.560	1.181	1.650	1.104	1.747	1.028	1.850
	29	1.341	1.483	1.270	1.563	1.198	1.650	1.124	1.743	1.050	1.841
	30	1.352	1.489	1.284	1.567	1.214	1.650	1.143	1.739	1.071	1.833
	31	1.363	1.496	1.297	1.570	1.229	1.650	1.160	1.735	1.090	1.825
	32	1.373	1.502	1.309	1.574	1.244	1.650	1.177	1.732	1.109	1.819
	33	1.383	1.508	1.321	1.577	1.258	1.651	1.193	1.730	1.127	1.813
	34	1.393	1.514	1.333	1.580	1.271	1.652	1.208	1.728	1.144	1.808
	35	1.402	1.519	1.343	1.584	1.283	1.653	1.222	1.726	1.160	1.803
	36	1.411	1.525	1.354	1.587	1.295	1.654	1.236	1.724	1.175	1.799
	37	1.419	1.530	1.364	1.590	1.307	1.655	1.249	1.723	1.190	1.795
	38	1.427	1.535	1.373	1.594	1.318	1.656	1.261	1.722	1.204	1.792
	39	1.435	1.540	1.382	1.597	1.328	1.658	1.273	1.722	1.218	1.789
	40	1.442	1.544	1.391	1.600	1.338	1.659	1.285	1.721	1.230	1.786
	45	1.475	1.566	1.430	1.615	1.383	1.666	1.336	1.720	1.287	1.776
	50	1.503	1.585	1.462	1.628	1.421	1.674	1.378	1.721	1.335	1.771
	55	1.528	1.601	1.490	1.641	1.452	1.681	1.414	1.724	1.374	1.768
	60	1.549	1.616	1.514	1.652	1.480	1.689	1.444	1.727	1.408	1.767
	65	1.567	1.629	1.536	1.662	1.503	1.696	1.471	1.731	1.438	1.767
	70	1.583	1.641	1.554	1.672	1.525	1.703	1.494	1.735	1.464	1.768
	75	1.598	1.652	1.571	1.680	1.543	1.709	1.515	1.739	1.487	1.770
	80	1.611	1.662	1.586	1.688	1.560	1.715	1.534	1.743	1.507	1.772
	85	1.624	1.671	1.600	1.696	1.575	1.721	1.550	1.747	1.525	1.774
	90	1.635	1.679	1.612	1.703	1.589	1.726	1.566	1.751	1.542	1.776
	95	1.645	1.687	1.623	1.709	1.602	1.732	1.579	1.755	1.557	1.778
	100	1.654	1.694	1.634	1.715	1.613	1.736	1.592	1.758	1.571	1.780
	150	1.720	1.746	1.706	1.760	1.693	1.774	1.679	1.788	1.665	1.802
	200	1.758	1.778	1.748	1.789	1.738	1.799	1.728	1.810	1.718	1.820

Note: n = number of observations
k' = number of explanatory
variables excluding the
constant term

k′ = 6		k′ = 7		k′ = 8		k′ = 9		k′ = 10	
d_L	d_U	d_L	d_U	d_L	d_U	d_L	d_U	d_L	d_U
—	—	—	—	—	—	—	—	—	—
—	—	—	—	—	—	—	—	—	—
—	—	—	—	—	—	—	—	—	—
—	—	—	—	—	—	—	—	—	—
—	—	—	—	—	—	—	—	—	—
0.203	3.005	—	—	—	—	—	—	—	—
0.268	2.832	0.171	3.149	—	—	—	—	—	—
0.328	2.692	0.230	2.985	0.147	3.266	—	—	—	—
0.389	2.572	0.286	2.848	0.200	3.111	0.127	3.360	—	—
0.447	2.472	0.343	2.727	0.251	2.979	0.175	3.216	0.111	3.438
0.502	2.388	0.398	2.624	0.304	2.860	0.222	3.090	0.155	3.304
0.554	2.318	0.451	2.537	0.356	2.757	0.272	2.975	0.198	3.184
0.603	2.257	0.502	2.461	0.407	2.667	0.321	2.873	0.244	3.073
0.649	2.206	0.549	2.396	0.456	2.589	0.369	2.783	0.290	2.974
0.692	2.162	0.595	2.339	0.502	2.521	0.416	2.704	0.336	2.885
0.732	2.124	0.637	2.290	0.547	2.460	0.461	2.633	0.380	2.806
0.769	2.090	0.677	2.246	0.588	2.407	0.504	2.571	0.424	2.734
0.804	2.061	0.715	2.208	0.628	2.360	0.545	2.514	0.465	2.670
0.837	2.035	0.751	2.174	0.666	2.318	0.584	2.464	0.506	2.613
0.868	2.012	0.784	2.144	0.702	2.280	0.621	2.419	0.544	2.560
0.897	1.992	0.816	2.117	0.735	2.246	0.657	2.379	0.581	2.513
0.925	1.974	0.845	2.093	0.767	2.216	0.691	2.342	0.616	2.470
0.951	1.958	0.874	2.071	0.798	2.188	0.723	2.309	0.650	2.431
0.975	1.944	0.900	2.052	0.826	2.164	0.753	2.278	0.682	2.396
0.998	1.931	0.926	2.034	0.854	2.141	0.782	2.251	0.712	2.363
1.020	1.920	0.950	2.018	0.879	2.120	0.810	2.226	0.741	2.333
1.041	1.909	0.972	2.004	0.904	2.102	0.836	2.203	0.769	2.306
1.061	1.900	0.994	1.991	0.927	2.085	0.861	2.181	0.795	2.281
1.080	1.891	1.015	1.979	0.950	2.069	0.885	2.162	0.821	2.257
1.097	1.884	1.034	1.967	0.971	2.054	0.908	2.144	0.845	2.236
1.114	1.877	1.053	1.957	0.991	2.041	0.930	2.127	0.868	2.216
1.131	1.870	1.071	1.948	1.011	2.029	0.951	2.112	0.891	2.198
1.146	1.864	1.088	1.939	1.029	2.017	0.970	2.098	0.912	2.180
1.161	1.859	1.104	1.932	1.047	2.007	0.990	2.085	0.932	2.164
1.175	1.854	1.120	1.924	1.064	1.997	1.008	2.072	0.952	2.149
1.238	1.835	1.189	1.895	1.139	1.958	1.089	2.022	1.038	2.088
1.291	1.822	1.246	1.875	1.201	1.930	1.156	1.986	1.110	2.044
1.334	1.814	1.294	1.861	1.253	1.909	1.212	1.959	1.170	2.010
1.372	1.808	1.335	1.850	1.298	1.894	1.260	1.939	1.222	1.984
1.404	1.805	1.370	1.843	1.336	1.882	1.301	1.923	1.266	1.964
1.433	1.802	1.401	1.837	1.369	1.873	1.337	1.910	1.305	1.948
1.458	1.801	1.428	1.834	1.399	1.867	1.369	1.901	1.339	1.935
1.480	1.801	1.453	1.831	1.425	1.861	1.397	1.893	1.369	1.925
1.500	1.801	1.474	1.829	1.448	1.857	1.422	1.886	1.396	1.916
1.518	1.801	1.494	1.827	1.469	1.854	1.445	1.881	1.420	1.909
1.535	1.802	1.512	1.827	1.489	1.852	1.465	1.877	1.442	1.903
1.550	1.803	1.528	1.826	1.506	1.850	1.484	1.874	1.462	1.898
1.651	1.817	1.637	1.832	1.622	1.847	1.608	1.862	1.594	1.877
1.707	1.831	1.697	1.841	1.686	1.852	1.675	1.863	1.665	1.874

(continued)

Table A.5   (continued)

n	k' = 11 d_L	k' = 11 d_U	k' = 12 d_L	k' = 12 d_U	k' = 13 d_L	k' = 13 d_U	k' = 14 d_L	k' = 14 d_U	k' = 15 d_L	k' = 15 d_U
16	0.098	3.503	—	—	—	—	—	—	—	—
17	0.138	3.378	0.087	3.557	—	—	—	—	—	—
18	0.177	3.265	0.123	3.441	0.078	3.603	—	—	—	—
19	0.220	3.159	0.160	3.335	0.111	3.496	0.070	3.642	—	—
20	0.263	3.063	0.200	3.234	0.145	3.395	0.100	3.542	0.063	3.676
21	0.307	2.976	0.240	3.141	0.182	3.300	0.132	3.448	0.091	3.583
22	0.349	2.897	0.281	3.057	0.220	3.211	0.166	3.358	0.120	3.495
23	0.391	2.826	0.322	2.979	0.259	3.128	0.202	3.272	0.153	3.409
24	0.431	2.761	0.362	2.908	0.297	3.053	0.239	3.193	0.186	3.327
25	0.470	2.702	0.400	2.844	0.335	2.983	0.275	3.119	0.221	3.251
26	0.508	2.649	0.438	2.784	0.373	2.919	0.312	3.051	0.256	3.179
27	0.544	2.600	0.475	2.730	0.409	2.859	0.348	2.987	0.291	3.112
28	0.578	2.555	0.510	2.680	0.445	2.805	0.383	2.928	0.325	3.050
29	0.612	2.515	0.544	2.634	0.479	2.755	0.418	2.874	0.359	2.992
30	0.643	2.477	0.577	2.592	0.512	2.708	0.451	2.823	0.392	2.937
31	0.674	2.443	0.608	2.553	0.545	2.665	0.484	2.776	0.425	2.887
32	0.703	2.411	0.638	2.517	0.576	2.625	0.515	2.733	0.457	2.840
33	0.731	2.382	0.668	2.484	0.606	2.588	0.546	2.692	0.488	2.796
34	0.758	2.355	0.695	2.454	0.634	2.554	0.575	2.654	0.518	2.754
35	0.783	2.330	0.722	2.425	0.662	2.521	0.604	2.619	0.547	2.716
36	0.808	2.306	0.748	2.398	0.689	2.492	0.631	2.586	0.575	2.680
37	0.831	2.285	0.772	2.374	0.714	2.464	0.657	2.555	0.602	2.646
38	0.854	2.265	0.796	2.351	0.739	2.438	0.683	2.526	0.628	2.614
39	0.875	2.246	0.819	2.329	0.763	2.413	0.707	2.499	0.653	2.585
40	0.896	2.228	0.840	2.309	0.785	2.391	0.731	2.473	0.678	2.557
45	0.988	2.156	0.938	2.225	0.887	2.296	0.838	2.367	0.788	2.439
50	1.064	2.103	1.019	2.163	0.973	2.225	0.927	2.287	0.882	2.350
55	1.129	2.062	1.087	2.116	1.045	2.170	1.003	2.225	0.961	2.281
60	1.184	2.031	1.145	2.079	1.106	2.127	1.068	2.177	1.029	2.227
65	1.231	2.006	1.195	2.049	1.160	2.093	1.124	2.138	1.088	2.183
70	1.272	1.986	1.239	2.026	1.206	2.066	1.172	2.106	1.139	2.148
75	1.308	1.970	1.277	2.006	1.247	2.043	1.215	2.080	1.184	2.118
80	1.340	1.957	1.311	1.991	1.283	2.024	1.253	2.059	1.224	2.093
85	1.369	1.946	1.342	1.977	1.315	2.009	1.287	2.040	1.260	2.073
90	1.395	1.937	1.369	1.966	1.344	1.995	1.318	2.025	1.292	2.055
95	1.418	1.929	1.394	1.956	1.370	1.984	1.345	2.012	1.321	2.040
100	1.439	1.923	1.416	1.948	1.393	1.974	1.371	2.000	1.347	2.026
150	1.579	1.892	1.564	1.908	1.550	1.924	1.535	1.940	1.519	1.956
200	1.654	1.885	1.643	1.896	1.632	1.908	1.621	1.919	1.610	1.931

$k' = 16$		$k' = 17$		$k' = 18$		$k' = 19$		$k' = 20$	
d_L	d_U	d_L	d_U	d_L	d_U	d_L	d_U	d_L	d_U
—	—	—	—	—	—	—	—	—	—
—	—	—	—	—	—	—	—	—	—
—	—	—	—	—	—	—	—	—	—
—	—	—	—	—	—	—	—	—	—
—	—	—	—	—	—	—	—	—	—
0.058	3.705	—	—	—	—	—	—	—	—
0.083	3.619	0.052	3.731	—	—	—	—	—	—
0.110	3.535	0.076	3.650	0.048	3.753	—	—	—	—
0.141	3.454	0.101	3.572	0.070	3.678	0.044	3.773	—	—
0.172	3.376	0.130	3.494	0.094	3.604	0.065	3.702	0.041	3.790
0.205	3.303	0.160	3.420	0.120	3.531	0.087	3.632	0.060	3.724
0.238	3.233	0.191	3.349	0.149	3.460	0.112	3.563	0.081	3.658
0.271	3.168	0.222	3.283	0.178	3.392	0.138	3.495	0.104	3.592
0.305	3.107	0.254	3.219	0.208	3.327	0.166	3.431	0.129	3.528
0.337	3.050	0.286	3.160	0.238	3.266	0.195	3.368	0.156	3.465
0.370	2.996	0.317	3.103	0.269	3.208	0.224	3.309	0.183	3.406
0.401	2.946	0.349	3.050	0.299	3.153	0.253	3.252	0.211	3.348
0.432	2.899	0.379	3.000	0.329	3.100	0.283	3.198	0.239	3.293
0.462	2.854	0.409	2.954	0.359	3.051	0.312	3.147	0.267	3.240
0.492	2.813	0.439	2.910	0.388	3.005	0.340	3.099	0.295	3.190
0.520	2.774	0.467	2.868	0.417	2.961	0.369	3.053	0.323	3.142
0.548	2.738	0.495	2.829	0.445	2.920	0.397	3.009	0.351	3.097
0.575	2.703	0.522	2.792	0.472	2.880	0.424	2.968	0.378	3.054
0.600	2.671	0.549	2.757	0.499	2.843	0.451	2.929	0.404	3.013
0.626	2.641	0.575	2.724	0.525	2.808	0.477	2.892	0.430	2.974
0.740	2.512	0.692	2.586	0.644	2.659	0.598	2.733	0.553	2.807
0.836	2.414	0.792	2.479	0.747	2.544	0.703	2.610	0.660	2.675
0.919	2.338	0.877	2.396	0.836	2.454	0.795	2.512	0.754	2.571
0.990	2.278	0.951	2.330	0.913	2.382	0.874	2.434	0.836	2.487
1.052	2.229	1.016	2.276	0.980	2.323	0.944	2.371	0.908	2.419
1.105	2.189	1.072	2.232	1.038	2.275	1.005	2.318	0.971	2.362
1.153	2.156	1.121	2.195	1.090	2.235	1.058	2.275	1.027	2.315
1.195	2.129	1.165	2.165	1.136	2.201	1.106	2.238	1.076	2.275
1.232	2.105	1.205	2.139	1.177	2.172	1.149	2.206	1.121	2.241
1.266	2.085	1.240	2.116	1.213	2.148	1.187	2.179	1.160	2.211
1.296	2.068	1.271	2.097	1.247	2.126	1.222	2.156	1.197	2.186
1.324	2.053	1.301	2.080	1.277	2.108	1.253	2.135	1.229	2.164
1.504	1.972	1.489	1.989	1.474	2.006	1.458	2.023	1.443	2.040
1.599	1.943	1.588	1.955	1.576	1.967	1.565	1.979	1.554	1.991

Source: N. E. Savin and K. J. White, "The Durbin–Watson Test for Serial Correlation with Extreme Small Samples or Many Regressors," *Econometrica* 45 (November 1977): 1989–1996 and corrected by R. W. Farebrother, *Econometrica* 48 (September 1980): 1554. Reprinted by permission of the Econometric Society.

Table A.6   Cumulative Terms for the Binomial Distribution $\sum_{x=x'}^{x=n} \binom{n}{x} p^x (1-p)^{n-x}$

							p				
n	x'	0.05	.10	.15	.20	.25	.30	.35	.40	.45	.50
2	1	.0975	.1900	.2775	.3600	.4375	.5100	.5775	.6400	.6975	.7500
	2	.0025	.0100	.0225	.0400	.0625	.0900	.1225	.1600	.2025	.2500
3	1	.1426	.2710	.3859	.4880	.5781	.6570	.7254	.7840	.8336	.8750
	2	.0072	.0280	.0608	.1040	.1562	.2160	.2818	.3520	.4252	.5000
	3	.0001	.0010	.0034	.0080	.0156	.0270	.0429	.0640	.0911	.1250
4	1	.1855	.3439	.4780	.5904	.6836	.7599	.8215	.8704	.9085	.9375
	2	.0140	.0523	.1095	.1808	.2617	.3483	.4370	.5248	.6090	.6875
	3	.0005	.0037	.0120	.0272	.0508	.0837	.1265	.1792	.2415	.3125
	4	.0000	.0001	.0005	.0016	.0039	.0081	.0150	.0256	.0410	.0625
5	1	.2262	.4095	.5563	.6723	.7627	.8319	.8840	.9222	.9497	.9688
	2	.0226	.0815	.1648	.2627	.3672	.4718	.5716	.6630	.7438	.8125
	3	.0012	.0086	.0266	.0579	.1035	.1631	.2352	.3174	.4069	.5000
	4	.0000	.0005	.0022	.0067	.0156	.0308	.0540	.0870	.1312	.1875
	5	.0000	.0000	.0001	.0003	.0010	.0024	.0053	.0102	.0185	.0312
6	1	.2649	.4686	.6229	.7379	.8220	.8824	.9246	.9533	.9723	.9844
	2	.0328	.1143	.2235	.3447	.4661	.5798	.6809	.7667	.8364	.8906
	3	.0022	.0158	.0473	.0989	.1694	.2557	.3529	.4557	.5585	.6562
	4	.0001	.0013	.0059	.0170	.0376	.0705	.1174	.1792	.2553	.3438
	5	.0000	.0001	.0004	.0016	.0046	.0109	.0223	.0410	.0692	.1094
	6	.0000	.0000	.0000	.0001	.0002	.0007	.0018	.0041	.0083	.0156
7	1	.3017	.5217	.6794	.7903	.8665	.9176	.9510	.9720	.9848	.9922
	2	.0444	.1497	.2834	.4233	.5551	.6706	.7662	.8414	.8976	.9375
	3	.0038	.0257	.0738	.1480	.2436	.3529	.4677	.5801	.6836	.7734
	4	.0002	.0027	.0121	.0333	.0706	.1260	.1998	.2898	.3917	.5000
	5	.0000	.0002	.0012	.0047	.0129	.0288	.0556	.0963	.1529	.2266
	6	.0000	.0000	.0001	.0004	.0013	.0038	.0090	.0188	.0357	.0625
	7	.0000	.0000	.0000	.0000	.0001	.0002	.0006	.0016	.0037	.0078
8	1	.3366	.5695	.7275	.8322	.8999	.9424	.9681	.9832	.9916	.9961
	2	.0572	.1869	.3428	.4967	.6329	.7447	.8309	.8936	.9368	.9648
	3	.0058	.0381	.1052	.2031	.3215	.4482	.5722	.6846	.7799	.8555
	4	.0004	.0050	.0214	.0563	.1138	.1941	.2936	.4059	.5230	.6367
	5	.0000	.0004	.0029	.0104	.0273	.0580	.1061	.1737	.2604	.3633
	6	.0000	.0000	.0002	.0012	.0042	.0113	.0253	.0498	.0885	.1445
	7	.0000	.0000	.0000	.0001	.0004	.0013	.0036	.0085	.0181	.0352
	8	.0000	.0000	.0000	.0000	.0000	.0001	.0002	.0007	.0017	.0039
9	1	.3698	.6126	.7684	.8658	.9249	.9596	.9793	.9899	.9954	.9980
	2	.0712	.2252	.4005	.5638	.6997	.8040	.8789	.9295	.9615	.9805
	3	.0084	.0530	.1409	.2618	.3993	.5372	.6627	.7682	.8505	.9102
	4	.0006	.0083	.0339	.0856	.1657	.2703	.3911	.5174	.6386	.7461
	5	.0000	.0009	.0056	.0196	.0489	.0988	.1717	.2666	.3786	.5000
	6	.0000	.0001	.0006	.0031	.0100	.0253	.0536	.0994	.1658	.2539
	7	.0000	.0000	.0000	.0003	.0013	.0043	.0112	.0250	.0498	.0898
	8	.0000	.0000	.0000	.0000	.0001	.0004	.0014	.0038	.0091	.0195
	9	.0000	.0000	.0000	.0000	.0000	.0000	.0001	.0003	.0008	.0020
10	1	.4013	.6513	.8031	.8926	.9437	.9718	.9865	.9940	.9975	.9990

		p									
n	x'	0.05	.10	.15	.20	.25	.30	.35	.40	.45	.50
10	2	.0861	.2639	.4557	.6242	.7560	.8507	.9140	.9536	.9767	.9893
	3	.0115	.0702	.1798	.3222	.4744	.6172	.7384	.8327	.9004	.9453
	4	.0010	.0128	.0500	.1209	.2241	.3504	.4862	.6177	.7340	.8281
	5	.0001	.0016	.0099	.0328	.0781	.1503	.2485	.3669	.4956	.6230
	6	.0000	.0001	.0014	.0064	.0197	.0473	.0949	.1662	.2616	.3770
	7	.0000	.0000	.0001	.0009	.0035	.0106	.0260	.0548	.1020	.1719
	8	.0000	.0000	.0000	.0001	.0004	.0016	.0048	.0123	.0274	.0547
	9	.0000	.0000	.0000	.0000	.0000	.0001	.0005	.0017	.0045	.0107
	10	.0000	.0000	.0000	.0000	.0000	.0000	.0000	.0001	.0003	.0010
11	1	.4312	.6862	.8327	.9141	.9578	.9802	.9912	.9964	.9986	.9995
	2	.1019	.3026	.5078	.6779	.8029	.8870	.9394	.9698	.9861	.9941
	3	.0152	.0896	.2212	.3826	.5448	.6873	.7999	.8811	.9348	.9673
	4	.0016	.0185	.0694	.1611	.2867	.4304	.5744	.7037	.8089	.8867
	5	.0001	.0028	.0159	.0504	.1146	.2103	.3317	.4672	.6029	.7256
	6	.0000	.0003	.0027	.0117	.0343	.0782	.1487	.2465	.3669	.5000
	7	.0000	.0000	.0003	.0020	.0076	.0216	.0501	.0994	.1738	.2744
	8	.0000	.0000	.0000	.0002	.0012	.0043	.0122	.0293	.0610	.1133
	9	.0000	.0000	.0000	.0000	.0001	.0006	.0020	.0059	.0148	.0327
	10	.0000	.0000	.0000	.0000	.0000	.0000	.0002	.0007	.0022	.0059
	11	.0000	.0000	.0000	.0000	.0000	.0000	.0000	.0000	.0002	.0005
12	1	.4596	.7176	.8578	.9313	.9683	.9862	.9943	.9978	.9992	.9998
	2	.1184	.3410	.5565	.7251	.8416	.9150	.9576	.9804	.9917	.9968
	3	.0196	.1109	.2642	.4417	.6093	.7472	.8487	.9166	.9579	.9807
	4	.0022	.0256	.0922	.2054	.3512	.5075	.6533	.7747	.8655	.9270
	5	.0002	.0043	.0239	.0726	.1576	.2763	.4167	.5618	.6956	.8062
	6	.0000	.0005	.0046	.0194	.0544	.1178	.2127	.3348	.4731	.6128
	7	.0000	.0001	.0007	.0039	.0143	.0386	.0846	.1582	.2607	.3872
	8	.0000	.0000	.0001	.0006	.0028	.0095	.0255	.0573	.1117	.1938
	9	.0000	.0000	.0000	.0001	.0004	.0017	.0056	.0153	.0356	.0730
	10	.0000	.0000	.0000	.0000	.0000	.0002	.0008	.0028	.0079	.0193
	11	.0000	.0000	.0000	.0000	.0000	.0000	.0001	.0003	.0011	.0032
	12	.0000	.0000	.0000	.0000	.0000	.0000	.0000	.0000	.0001	.0002
13	1	.4867	.7458	.8791	.9450	.9762	.9903	.9963	.9987	.9996	.9999
	2	.1354	.3787	.6017	.7664	.8733	.9363	.9704	.9874	.9951	.9983
	3	.0245	.1339	.2704	.4983	.6674	.7975	.8868	.9421	.9731	.9888
	4	.0031	.0342	.0967	.2527	.4157	.5794	.7217	.8314	.9071	.9539
	5	.0003	.0065	.0260	.0991	.2060	.3457	.4995	.6470	.7721	.8666
	6	.0000	.0009	.0053	.0300	.0802	.1654	.2841	.4256	.5732	.7095
	7	.0000	.0001	.0013	.0070	.0243	.0624	.1295	.2288	.3563	.5000
	8	.0000	.0000	.0002	.0012	.0056	.0182	.0462	.0977	.1788	.2905
	9	.0000	.0000	.0000	.0002	.0010	.0040	.0126	.0321	.0698	.1334
	10	.0000	.0000	.0000	.0000	.0001	.0007	.0025	.0078	.0203	.0461
	11	.0000	.0000	.0000	.0000	.0000	.0001	.0003	.0013	.0041	.0112
	12	.0000	.0000	.0000	.0000	.0000	.0000	.0000	.0001	.0005	.0017
	13	.0000	.0000	.0000	.0000	.0000	.0000	.0000	.0000	.0000	.0001

(continued)

Table A.6   (continued)

						p					
n	*x'*	0.05	.10	.15	.20	.25	.30	.35	.40	.45	.50
14	1	.5123	.7712	.8972	.9560	.9822	.9932	.9976	.9992	.9998	.9999
	2	.1530	.4154	.6433	.8021	.8990	.9525	.9795	.9919	.9971	.9991
	3	.0301	.1584	.3521	.5519	.7189	.8392	.9161	.9602	.9830	.9935
	4	.0042	.0441	.1465	.3018	.4787	.6448	.7795	.8757	.9368	.9713
	5	.0004	.0092	.0467	.1298	.2585	.4158	.5773	.7207	.8328	.9102
	6	.0000	.0015	.0115	.0439	.1117	.2195	.3595	.5141	.6627	.7880
	7	.0000	.0002	.0022	.0116	.0383	.0933	.1836	.3075	.4539	.6047
	8	.0000	.0000	.0003	.0024	.0103	.0315	.0753	.1501	.2586	.3953
	9	.0000	.0000	.0000	.0004	.0022	.0083	.0243	.0583	.1189	.2120
	10	.0000	.0000	.0000	.0000	.0003	.0017	.0060	.0175	.0426	.0898
	11	.0000	.0000	.0000	.0000	.0000	.0002	.0011	.0039	.0114	.0287
	12	.0000	.0000	.0000	.0000	.0000	.0000	.0001	.0006	.0022	.0065
	13	.0000	.0000	.0000	.0000	.0000	.0000	.0000	.0001	.0003	.0009
	14	.0000	.0000	.0000	.0000	.0000	.0000	.0000	.0000	.0000	.0001
15	1	.5367	.7941	.9126	.9648	.9866	.9953	.9984	.9995	.9999	1.0000
	2	.1710	.4510	.6814	.8329	.9198	.9647	.9858	.9948	.9983	.9995
	3	.0362	.1841	.3958	.6020	.7639	.8732	.9383	.9729	.9893	.9963
	4	.0055	.0556	.1773	.3518	.5387	.7031	.8273	.9095	.9576	.9824
	5	.0006	.0127	.0617	.1642	.3135	.4845	.6481	.7827	.8796	.9408
	6	.0001	.0022	.0168	.0611	.1484	.2784	.4357	.5968	.7392	.8491
	7	.0000	.0003	.0036	.0181	.0566	.1311	.2452	.3902	.5478	.6964
	8	.0000	.0000	.0006	.0042	.0173	.0500	.1132	.2131	.3465	.5000
	9	.0000	.0000	.0001	.0008	.0042	.0152	.0422	.0950	.1818	.3036
	10	.0000	.0000	.0000	.0001	.0008	.0037	.0124	.0338	.0769	.1509
	11	.0000	.0000	.0000	.0000	.0001	.0007	.0028	.0093	.0255	.0592
	12	.0000	.0000	.0000	.0000	.0000	.0001	.0005	.0019	.0063	.0176
	13	.0000	.0000	.0000	.0000	.0000	.0000	.0001	.0003	.0011	.0037
	14	.0000	.0000	.0000	.0000	.0000	.0000	.0000	.0000	.0001	.0005
	15	.0000	.0000	.0000	.0000	.0000	.0000	.0000	.0000	.0000	.0000
16	1	.5599	.8147	.9257	.9719	.9900	.9967	.9990	.9997	.9999	1.0000
	2	.1892	.4853	.7161	.8593	.9365	.9739	.9902	.9967	.9990	.9997
	3	.0429	.2108	.4386	.6482	.8029	.9006	.9549	.9817	.9934	.9979
	4	.0070	.0684	.2101	.4019	.5950	.7541	.8661	.9349	.9719	.9894
	5	.0009	.0170	.0791	.2018	.3698	.5501	.7108	.8334	.9147	.9616
	6	.0001	.0033	.0235	.0817	.1897	.3402	.5100	.6712	.8024	.8949
	7	.0000	.0005	.0056	.0267	.0796	.1753	.3119	.4728	.6340	.7228
	8	.0000	.0001	.0011	.0070	.0271	.0744	.1594	.2839	.4371	.5982
	9	.0000	.0000	.0002	.0015	.0075	.0257	.0671	.1423	.2559	.4018
	10	.0000	.0000	.0000	.0002	.0016	.0071	.0229	.0583	.1241	.2272
	11	.0000	.0000	.0000	.0000	.0003	.0016	.0062	.0191	.0486	.1051
	12	.0000	.0000	.0000	.0000	.0000	.0003	.0013	.0049	.0149	.0384
	13	.0000	.0000	.0000	.0000	.0000	.0000	.0002	.0009	.0035	.0106
	14	.0000	.0000	.0000	.0000	.0000	.0000	.0000	.0001	.0006	.0021
	15	.0000	.0000	.0000	.0000	.0000	.0000	.0000	.0000	.0001	.0003
	16	.0000	.0000	.0000	.0000	.0000	.0000	.0000	.0000	.0000	.0000

							p				
n	*x′*	0.05	.10	.15	.20	.25	.30	.35	.40	.45	.50
17	1	.5819	.8332	.9369	.9775	.9925	.9977	.9993	.9998	1.0000	1.0000
	2	.2078	.5182	.7475	.8818	.9499	.9807	.9933	.9979	.9994	.9999
	3	.0503	.2382	.4802	.6904	.8363	.9226	.9673	.9877	.9959	.9988
	4	.0088	.0826	.2444	.4511	.6470	.7981	.8972	.9536	.9816	.9936
	5	.0012	.0221	.0987	.2418	.4261	.6113	.7652	.8740	.9404	.9755
	6	.0001	.0047	.0319	.1057	.2347	.4032	.5803	.7361	.8529	.9283
	7	.0000	.0008	.0083	.0377	.1071	.2248	.3812	.5522	.7098	.8338
	8	.0000	.0001	.0017	.0109	.0402	.1046	.2128	.3595	.5257	.6855
	9	.0000	.0000	.0003	.0026	.0124	.0403	.0994	.1989	.3374	.5000
	10	.0000	.0000	.0000	.0005	.0031	.0127	.0383	.0919	.1834	.3145
	11	.0000	.0000	.0000	.0001	.0006	.0032	.0120	.0348	.0826	.1662
	12	.0000	.0000	.0000	.0000	.0001	.0007	.0030	.0106	.0301	.0717
	13	.0000	.0000	.0000	.0000	.0000	.0001	.0006	.0025	.0086	.0245
	14	.0000	.0000	.0000	.0000	.0000	.0000	.0000	.0005	.0019	.0064
	15	.0000	.0000	.0000	.0000	.0000	.0000	.0000	.0001	.0003	.0012
	16	.0000	.0000	.0000	.0000	.0000	.0000	.0000	.0000	.0000	.0001
	17	.0000	.0000	.0000	.0000	.0000	.0000	.0000	.0000	.0000	.0000
18	1	.6028	.8499	.9464	.9820	.9944	.9984	.9996	.9999	1.0000	1.0000
	2	.2265	.5497	.7759	.9009	.9605	.9858	.9954	.9987	.9997	.9999
	3	.0581	.2662	.5203	.7287	.8647	.9400	.9764	.9918	.9975	.9993
	4	.0109	.0982	.2798	.4990	.6943	.8354	.9217	.9672	.9880	.9962
	5	.0015	.0282	.1206	.2836	.4813	.6673	.8114	.9058	.9589	.9846
	6	.0002	.0064	.0419	.1329	.2825	.4656	.6450	.7912	.8923	.9519
	7	.0000	.0012	.0118	.0513	.1390	.2783	.4509	.6257	.7742	.8811
	8	.0000	.0002	.0027	.0163	.0569	.1407	.2717	.4366	.6085	.7597
	9	.0000	.0000	.0005	.0043	.0193	.0596	.1391	.2632	.4222	.5927
	10	.0000	.0000	.0001	.0009	.0054	.0210	.0597	.1347	.2527	.4073
	11	.0000	.0000	.0000	.0002	.0012	.0061	.0212	.0576	.1280	.2403
	12	.0000	.0000	.0000	.0000	.0002	.0014	.0062	.0203	.0537	.1189
	13	.0000	.0000	.0000	.0000	.0000	.0003	.0014	.0058	.0183	.0481
	14	.0000	.0000	.0000	.0000	.0000	.0000	.0003	.0013	.0049	.0154
	15	.0000	.0000	.0000	.0000	.0000	.0000	.0000	.0002	.0010	.0038
	16	.0000	.0000	.0000	.0000	.0000	.0000	.0000	.0000	.0001	.0007
	17	.0000	.0000	.0000	.0000	.0000	.0000	.0000	.0000	.0000	.0001
	18	.0000	.0000	.0000	.0000	.0000	.0000	.0000	.0000	.0000	.0000
19	1	.6226	.8649	.9544	.9856	.9958	.9989	.9997	.9999	1.0000	1.0000
	2	.2453	.5797	.8015	.9171	.9690	.9896	.9969	.9992	.9998	1.0000
	3	.0665	.2946	.5587	.7631	.8887	.9538	.9830	.9945	.9985	.9996
	4	.0132	.1150	.3159	.5449	.7369	.8668	.9409	.9770	.9923	.9978
	5	.0020	.0352	.1444	.3267	.5346	.7178	.8500	.9304	.9720	.9904
	6	.0002	.0086	.0537	.1631	.3322	.5261	.7032	.8371	.9223	.9682
	7	.0000	.0017	.0163	.0676	.1749	.3345	.5188	.6919	.8273	.9165
	8	.0000	.0003	.0041	.0233	.0775	.1820	.3344	.5122	.6831	.8204
	9	.0000	.0000	.0008	.0067	.0287	.0839	.1855	.3325	.5060	.6762
	10	.0000	.0000	.0001	.0016	.0089	.0326	.0875	.1861	.3290	.5000

(continued)

Table A.6   (continued)

						p					
n	*x'*	0.05	.10	.15	.20	.25	.30	.35	.40	.45	.50
19	11	.0000	.0000	.0000	.0003	.0023	.0105	.0347	.0885	.1841	.3238
	12	.0000	.0000	.0000	.0000	.0005	.0028	.0114	.0352	.0871	.1796
	13	.0000	.0000	.0000	.0000	.0001	.0006	.0031	.0116	.0342	.0835
	14	.0000	.0000	.0000	.0000	.0000	.0001	.0007	.0031	.0109	.0318
	15	.0000	.0000	.0000	.0000	.0000	.0000	.0001	.0006	.0028	.0096
	16	.0000	.0000	.0000	.0000	.0000	.0000	.0000	.0001	.0005	.0022
	17	.0000	.0000	.0000	.0000	.0000	.0000	.0000	.0000	.0001	.0004
	18	.0000	.0000	.0000	.0000	.0000	.0000	.0000	.0000	.0000	.0000
	19	.0000	.0000	.0000	.0000	.0000	.0000	.0000	.0000	.0000	.0000
20	1	.6415	.8784	.9612	.9885	.9968	.9992	.9998	1.0000	1.0000	1.0000
	2	.2642	.6083	.8244	.9308	.9757	.9924	.9979	.9995	.9999	1.0000
	3	.0755	.3231	.5951	.7939	.9087	.9645	.9879	.9964	.9991	.9998
	4	.0159	.1330	.3523	.5886	.7748	.8929	.9556	.9840	.9951	.9987
	5	.0026	.0432	.1702	.3704	.5852	.7625	.8818	.9490	.9811	.9941
	6	.0003	.0113	.0673	.1958	.3828	.5836	.7546	.8744	.9447	.9793
	7	.0000	.0024	.0219	.0867	.2142	.3920	.5834	.7500	.8701	.9423
	8	.0000	.0004	.0059	.0321	.1018	.2277	.3990	.5841	.7480	.8684
	9	.0000	.0001	.0013	.0100	.0409	.1133	.2376	.4044	.5857	.7483
	10	.0000	.0000	.0002	.0026	.0139	.0480	.1218	.2447	.4086	.5881
	11	.0000	.0000	.0000	.0006	.0039	.0171	.0532	.1275	.2493	.4119
	12	.0000	.0000	.0000	.0001	.0009	.0051	.0196	.0565	.1308	.2517
	13	.0000	.0000	.0000	.0000	.0002	.0013	.0060	.0210	.0580	.1316
	14	.0000	.0000	.0000	.0000	.0000	.0003	.0015	.0065	.0214	.0577
	15	.0000	.0000	.0000	.0000	.0000	.0000	.0003	.0016	.0064	.0207
	16	.0000	.0000	.0000	.0000	.0000	.0000	.0000	.0003	.0015	.0059
	17	.0000	.0000	.0000	.0000	.0000	.0000	.0000	.0000	.0003	.0013
	18	.0000	.0000	.0000	.0000	.0000	.0000	.0000	.0000	.0000	.0002
	19	.0000	.0000	.0000	.0000	.0000	.0000	.0000	.0000	.0000	.0000
	20	.0000	.0000	.0000	.0000	.0000	.0000	.0000	.0000	.0000	.0000
21	1	.6594	.8906	.9671	.9908	.9976	.9994	.9999	1.0000	1.0000	1.0000
	2	.2830	.6353	.8450	.9424	.9810	.9944	.9996	.9997	.9999	1.0000
	3	.0849	.3516	.6295	.8213	.9255	.9729	.9914	.9976	.9994	.9999
	4	.0189	.1520	.3887	.6296	.8083	.9144	.9669	.9890	.9969	.9993
	5	.0032	.0522	.1975	.4140	.6326	.8016	.9076	.9630	.9874	.9967
	6	.0004	.0144	.0827	.2307	.4334	.6373	.7991	.9043	.9611	.9867
	7	.0000	.0033	.0287	.1085	.2564	.4495	.6433	.7998	.9036	.9608
	8	.0000	.0006	.0083	.0431	.1299	.2770	.4635	.6505	.8029	.9054
	9	.0000	.0001	.0020	.0144	.0561	.1477	.2941	.4763	.6587	.8083
	10	.0000	.0000	.0004	.0041	.0206	.0676	.1632	.3086	.4883	.6682
	11	.0000	.0000	.0001	.0010	.0064	.0264	.0772	.1744	.3210	.5000
	12	.0000	.0000	.0000	.0002	.0017	.0087	.0313	.0849	.1841	.3318
	13	.0000	.0000	.0000	.0000	.0004	.0024	.0108	.0352	.0908	.1917
	14	.0000	.0000	.0000	.0000	.0001	.0006	.0031	.0123	.0379	.0946
	15	.0000	.0000	.0000	.0000	.0000	.0001	.0007	.0036	.0132	.0392
	16	.0000	.0000	.0000	.0000	.0000	.0000	.0001	.0008	.0037	.0133
	17	.0000	.0000	.0000	.0000	.0000	.0000	.0000	.0002	.0008	.0036
	18	.0000	.0000	.0000	.0000	.0000	.0000	.0000	.0000	.0001	.0007
	19	.0000	.0000	.0000	.0000	.0000	.0000	.0000	.0000	.0000	.0001

						p					
n	x'	0.05	.10	.15	.20	.25	.30	.35	.40	.45	.50
21	20	.0000	.0000	.0000	.0000	.0000	.0000	.0000	.0000	.0000	.0000
	21	.0000	.0000	.0000	.0000	.0000	.0000	.0000	.0000	.0000	.0000
22	1	.6765	.9015	.9720	.9926	.9982	.9996	.9999	1.0000	1.0000	1.0000
	2	.3018	.6608	.8633	.9520	.9851	.9959	.9990	.9998	1.0000	1.0000
	3	.0948	.3800	.6618	.8455	.9394	.9793	.9899	.9984	.9997	.9999
	4	.0222	.1719	.4248	.6680	.8376	.9319	.9755	.9924	.9980	.9996
	5	.0040	.0621	.2262	.4571	.6765	.8355	.9284	.9734	.9917	.9978
	6	.0006	.0182	.0999	.2674	.4832	.6866	.8371	.9278	.9729	.9915
	7	.0001	.0044	.0368	.1330	.3006	.5058	.6978	.8416	.9295	.9738
	8	.0000	.0009	.0114	.0561	.1615	.3287	.5264	.7102	.8482	.9331
	9	.0000	.0001	.0030	.0201	.0746	.1865	.3534	.5460	.7236	.8569
	10	.0000	.0000	.0007	.0061	.0295	.0916	.2084	.3756	.5650	.7383
	11	.0000	.0000	.0001	.0016	.0100	.0387	.1070	.2281	.3963	.5841
	12	.0000	.0000	.0000	.0003	.0029	.0140	.0474	.1207	.2457	.4159
	13	.0000	.0000	.0000	.0001	.0007	.0043	.0180	.0551	.1328	.2617
	14	.0000	.0000	.0000	.0000	.0001	.0011	.0058	.0215	.0617	.1431
	15	.0000	.0000	.0000	.0000	.0000	.0002	.0015	.0070	.0243	.0669
	16	.0000	.0000	.0000	.0000	.0000	.0000	.0003	.0019	.0080	.0262
	17	.0000	.0000	.0000	.0000	.0000	.0000	.0001	.0004	.0021	.0085
	18	.0000	.0000	.0000	.0000	.0000	.0000	.0000	.0001	.0005	.0022
	19	.0000	.0000	.0000	.0000	.0000	.0000	.0000	.0000	.0001	.0004
	20	.0000	.0000	.0000	.0000	.0000	.0000	.0000	.0000	.0000	.0001
	21	.0000	.0000	.0000	.0000	.0000	.0000	.0000	.0000	.0000	.0000
	22	.0000	.0000	.0000	.0000	.0000	.0000	.0000	.0000	.0000	.0000
23	1	.6926	.9114	.9762	.9941	.9987	.9997	1.0000	1.0000	1.0000	1.0000
	2	.3206	.6849	.8796	.9602	.9884	.9970	.9993	.9999	1.0000	1.0000
	3	.1052	.4080	.6920	.8668	.9508	.9843	.9957	.9990	1.0000	1.0000
	4	.0258	.1927	.4604	.7035	.8630	.9462	.9819	.9948	.9988	.9998
	5	.0049	.0731	.2560	.4993	.7168	.8644	.9449	.9810	.9945	.9987
	6	.0008	.0226	.1189	.3053	.5315	.7312	.8691	.9460	.9814	.9947
	7	.0001	.0058	.0463	.1598	.3463	.5601	.7466	.8760	.9490	.9827
	8	.0000	.0012	.0152	.0715	.1963	.3819	.5864	.7627	.8848	.9534
	9	.0000	.0002	.0042	.0273	.0963	.2291	.4140	.6116	.7797	.8950
	10	.0000	.0000	.0010	.0089	.0408	.1201	.2592	.4438	.6364	.7976
	11	.0000	.0000	.0002	.0025	.0149	.0546	.1425	.2871	.4722	.6612
	12	.0000	.0000	.0000	.0006	.0046	.0214	.0682	.1636	.3135	.5000
	13	.0000	.0000	.0000	.0001	.0012	.0072	.0283	.0813	.1836	.3388
	14	.0000	.0000	.0000	.0000	.0003	.0021	.0100	.0349	.0937	.2024
	15	.0000	.0000	.0000	.0000	.0001	.0005	.0030	.0128	.0411	.1050
	16	.0000	.0000	.0000	.0000	.0000	.0001	.0008	.0040	.0153	.0466
	17	.0000	.0000	.0000	.0000	.0000	.0000	.0002	.0010	.0048	.0173
	18	.0000	.0000	.0000	.0000	.0000	.0000	.0000	.0002	.0012	.0053
	19	.0000	.0000	.0000	.0000	.0000	.0000	.0000	.0000	.0002	.0013
	20	.0000	.0000	.0000	.0000	.0000	.0000	.0000	.0000	.0000	.0002
	21	.0000	.0000	.0000	.0000	.0000	.0000	.0000	.0000	.0000	.0000
	22	.0000	.0000	.0000	.0000	.0000	.0000	.0000	.0000	.0000	.0000
	23	.0000	.0000	.0000	.0000	.0000	.0000	.0000	.0000	.0000	.0000

APPENDIX A

(continued)

Table A.6   (continued)

							p					
n	x'	0.05	.10	.15	.20	.25	.30	.35	.40	.45	.50
24	1	.7080	.9202	.9798	.9953	.9990	.9998	1.0000	1.0000	1.0000	1.0000
	2	.3391	.7075	.8941	.9669	.9910	.9978	.9995	.9999	1.0000	1.0000
	3	.1159	.4357	.7202	.8855	.9602	.9881	.9970	.9993	.9999	1.0000
	4	.0298	.2143	.4951	.7361	.8850	.9576	.9867	.9965	.9992	.9999
	5	.0060	.0851	.2866	.5401	.7534	.8889	.9578	.9866	.9964	.9992
	6	.0010	.0277	.1394	.3441	.5778	.7712	.8956	.9600	.9873	.9967
	7	.0001	.0075	.0572	.1889	.3926	.6114	.7894	.9040	.9636	.9887
	8	.0000	.0017	.0199	.0892	.2338	.4353	.6425	.8081	.9137	.9680
	9	.0000	.0003	.0059	.0362	.1213	.2750	.4743	.6721	.8270	.9242
	10	.0000	.0001	.0015	.0126	.0547	.1528	.3134	.5109	.7009	.8463
	11	.0000	.0000	.0003	.0038	.0213	.0742	.1833	.3498	.5461	.7294
	12	.0000	.0000	.0001	.0010	.0072	.0314	.0942	.2130	.3849	.5806
	13	.0000	.0000	.0000	.0002	.0021	.0115	.0423	.1143	.2420	.4194
	14	.0000	.0000	.0000	.0000	.0005	.0036	.0164	.0535	.1341	.2706
	15	.0000	.0000	.0000	.0000	.0001	.0010	.0055	.0217	.0648	.1537
	16	.0000	.0000	.0000	.0000	.0000	.0002	.0016	.0075	.0269	.0758
	17	.0000	.0000	.0000	.0000	.0000	.0000	.0004	.0022	.0095	.0320
	18	.0000	.0000	.0000	.0000	.0000	.0000	.0001	.0005	.0028	.0113
	19	.0000	.0000	.0000	.0000	.0000	.0000	.0000	.0001	.0007	.0033
	20	.0000	.0000	.0000	.0000	.0000	.0000	.0000	.0000	.0001	.0008
	21	.0000	.0000	.0000	.0000	.0000	.0000	.0000	.0000	.0000	.0001
	22	.0000	.0000	.0000	.0000	.0000	.0000	.0000	.0000	.0000	.0000
	23	.0000	.0000	.0000	.0000	.0000	.0000	.0000	.0000	.0000	.0000
	24	.0000	.0000	.0000	.0000	.0000	.0000	.0000	.0000	.0000	.0000
25	1	.7226	.9282	.9828	.9962	.9992	.9999	1.0000	1.0000	1.0000	1.0000
	2	.3576	.7288	.9069	.9726	.9930	.9984	.9997	.9999	1.0000	1.0000
	3	.1271	.4629	.7463	.9018	.9679	.9910	.9979	.9996	.9999	1.0000
	4	.0341	.2364	.5289	.7660	.9038	.9668	.9903	.9976	.9995	.9999
	5	.0072	.0980	.3179	.5793	.7863	.9095	.9680	.9905	.9977	.9995
	6	.0012	.0334	.1615	.3833	.6217	.8065	.9174	.9706	.9914	.9980
	7	.0002	.0095	.0695	.2200	.4389	.6593	.8266	.9264	.9742	.9927
	8	.0000	.0023	.0255	.1091	.2735	.4882	.6939	.8464	.9361	.9784
	9	.0000	.0005	.0080	.0468	.1494	.3231	.5332	.7265	.8660	.9461
	10	.0000	.0001	.0021	.0173	.0713	.1894	.3697	.5754	.7576	.8852
	11	.0000	.0000	.0005	.0056	.0297	.0978	.2288	.4142	.6157	.7878
	12	.0000	.0000	.0001	.0015	.0107	.0442	.1254	.2677	.4574	.6550
	13	.0000	.0000	.0000	.0004	.0034	.0175	.0604	.1538	.3063	.5000
	14	.0000	.0000	.0000	.0001	.0009	.0060	.0255	.0778	.1827	.3450
	15	.0000	.0000	.0000	.0000	.0002	.0018	.0093	.0344	.0960	.2122
	16	.0000	.0000	.0000	.0000	.0000	.0005	.0029	.0132	.0440	.1148
	17	.0000	.0000	.0000	.0000	.0000	.0001	.0008	.0043	.0174	.0539
	18	.0000	.0000	.0000	.0000	.0000	.0000	.0002	.0012	.0058	.0216
	19	.0000	.0000	.0000	.0000	.0000	.0000	.0000	.0003	.0016	.0073
	20	.0000	.0000	.0000	.0000	.0000	.0000	.0000	.0001	.0004	.0020
	21	.0000	.0000	.0000	.0000	.0000	.0000	.0000	.0000	.0001	.0005
	22	.0000	.0000	.0000	.0000	.0000	.0000	.0000	.0000	.0000	.0001
	23	.0000	.0000	.0000	.0000	.0000	.0000	.0000	.0000	.0000	.0000
	24	.0000	.0000	.0000	.0000	.0000	.0000	.0000	.0000	.0000	.0000
	25	.0000	.0000	.0000	.0000	.0000	.0000	.0000	.0000	.0000	.0000

n	x'						p				
		0.05	.10	.15	.20	.25	.30	.35	.40	.45	.50
30	1	.7854	.9576	.9924	.9988	.9998	1.0000	1.0000	1.0000	1.0000	1.0000
	2	.4465	.8163	.9520	.9895	.9980	.9997	1.0000	1.0000	1.0000	1.0000
	3	.1878	.5886	.8486	.9558	.9894	.9979	.9997	1.0000	1.0000	1.0000
	4	.0608	.3526	.6783	.8773	.9626	.9907	.9981	.9997	1.0000	1.0000
	5	.0156	.1755	.4755	.7448	.9021	.9698	.9925	.9985	.9998	1.0000
	6	.0033	.0732	.2894	.5725	.7974	.9234	.9767	.9943	.9989	.9998
	7	.0006	.0258	.1526	.3930	.6519	.8405	.9414	.9828	.9960	.9993
	8	.0001	.0078	.0698	.2392	.4857	.7186	.8762	.9565	.9879	.9974
	9	.0000	.0020	.0278	.1287	.3264	.5685	.7753	.9060	.9688	.9919
	10	.0000	.0005	.0097	.0611	.1966	.4112	.6425	.8237	.9306	.9786
	11	.0000	.0001	.0029	.0256	.1057	.2696	.4922	.7085	.8650	.9506
	12	.0000	.0000	.0008	.0095	.0507	.1593	.3452	.5689	.7673	.8998
	13	.0000	.0000	.0002	.0031	.0216	.0845	.2198	.4215	.6408	.8192
	14	.0000	.0000	.0000	.0009	.0082	.0401	.1263	.2855	.4975	.7077
	15	.0000	.0000	.0000	.0002	.0027	.0169	.0652	.1754	.3552	.5722
	16	.0000	.0000	.0000	.0001	.0008	.0064	.0301	.0971	.2309	.4278
	17	.0000	.0000	.0000	.0000	.0002	.0021	0124	.0481	.1356	.2923
	18	.0000	.0000	.0000	.0000	.0001	.0006	.0045	.0212	.0714	.1808
	19	.0000	.0000	.0000	.0000	.0000	.0002	.0014	.0083	.0334	.1002
	20	.0000	.0000	.0000	.0000	.0000	.0000	.0004	.0029	.0138	.0494
	21	.0000	.0000	.0000	.0000	.0000	.0000	.0001	.0009	.0050	.0214
	22	.0000	.0000	.0000	.0000	.0000	.0000	.0000	.0002	.0016	.0081
	23	.0000	.0000	.0000	.0000	.0000	.0000	.0000	.0000	.0004	.0026
	24	.0000	.0000	.0000	.0000	.0000	.0000	.0000	.0000	.0001	.0007
	25	.0000	.0000	.0000	.0000	.0000	.0000	.0000	.0000	.0000	.0002
	26	.0000	.0000	.0000	.0000	.0000	.0000	.0000	.0000	.0000	.0000
	27	.0000	.0000	.0000	.0000	.0000	.0000	.0000	.0000	.0000	.0000
	28	.0000	.0000	.0000	.0000	.0000	.0000	.0000	.0000	.0000	.0000
	29	.0000	.0000	.0000	.0000	.0000	.0000	.0000	.0000	.0000	.0000
	30	.0000	.0000	.0000	.0000	.0000	.0000	.0000	.0000	.0000	.0000
35	1	.8339	.9750	.9966	.9996	1.0000	1.0000	1.0000	1.0000	1.0000	1.0000
	2	.5280	.8776	.9757	.9960	.9995	.9999	1.0000	1.0000	1.0000	1.0000
	3	.2542	.6937	.9130	.9810	.9967	.9995	.9999	1.0000	1.0000	1.0000
	4	.0958	.4690	.7912	.9395	.9864	.9976	.9997	1.0000	1.0000	1.0000
	5	.0290	.2693	.6193	.8565	.9590	.9909	.9984	.9998	1.0000	1.0000
	6	.0073	.1316	.4311	.7279	.9024	.9731	.9942	.9990	.9999	1.0000
	7	.0015	.0552	.2652	.5672	.8080	.9350	.9830	.9966	.9995	.9999
	8	.0003	.0200	.1438	.4007	.6777	.8674	.9581	.9898	.9981	.9997
	9	.0000	.0063	.0689	.2550	.5257	.7659	.9110	.9740	.9943	.9991
	10	.0000	.0017	.0292	.1457	.3737	.6354	.8349	.9425	.9848	.9970
	11	.0000	.0004	.0110	.0747	.2419	.4900	.7284	.8877	.9646	.9917
	12	.0000	.0001	.0037	.0344	.1421	.3484	.5981	.8048	.9271	.9795
	13	.0000	.0000	.0011	.0142	.0756	.2271	.4577	.6943	.8656	.9552
	14	.0000	.0000	.0003	.0053	.0363	.1350	.3240	.5639	.7767	.9123
	15	.0000	.0000	.0001	.0018	.0158	.0731	.2109	.4272	.6624	.8447
	16	.0000	.0000	.0000	.0005	.0062	.0359	.1256	.2997	.5315	.7502
	17	.0000	.0000	.0000	.0001	.0022	.0160	.0682	.1935	.3976	.6321
	18	.0000	.0000	.0000	.0000	.0007	.0064	.0336	.1143	.2751	.5000
	19	.0000	.0000	.0000	.0000	.0002	.0023	.0150	.0615	.1749	.3679

APPENDIX A

(continued)

n	x'	p									
		0.05	.10	.15	.20	.25	.30	.35	.40	.45	.50
35	20	.0000	.0000	.0000	.0000	.0001	.0008	.0061	.0300	.1016	.2498
	21	.0000	.0000	.0000	.0000	.0000	.0002	.0022	.0133	.0536	.1553
	22	.0000	.0000	.0000	.0000	.0000	.0001	.0007	.0053	.0255	.0877
	23	.0000	.0000	.0000	.0000	.0000	.0000	.0002	.0019	.0109	.0448
	24	.0000	.0000	.0000	.0000	.0000	.0000	.0001	.0006	.0042	.0205
	25	.0000	.0000	.0000	.0000	.0000	.0000	.0000	.0002	.0014	.0083
	26	.0000	.0000	.0000	.0000	.0000	.0000	.0000	.0000	.0004	.0030
	27	.0000	.0000	.0000	.0000	.0000	.0000	.0000	0000	.0001	.0009
	28	.0000	.0000	.0000	.0000	.0000	.0000	.0000	.0000	.0000	.0003
	29	.0000	.0000	.0000	.0000	.0000	.0000	.0000	.0000	.0000	.0001
	30	.0000	.0000	.0000	.0000	.0000	.0000	.0000	.0000	.0000	.0000
	31	.0000	.0000	.0000	.0000	.0000	.0000	.0000	.0000	.0000	.0000
	32	.0000	.0000	.0000	.0000	.0000	.0000	.0000	.0000	.0000	.0000
	33	.0000	.0000	.0000	.0000	.0000	.0000	.0000	.0000	.0000	.0000
	34	.0000	.0000	.0000	.0000	.0000	.0000	.0000	.0000	.0000	.0000
	35	.0000	.0000	.0000	.0000	.0000	.0000	.0000	.0000	.0000	.0000
40	1	.8715	.9852	.9985	.9999	1.0000	1.0000	1.0000	1.0000	1.0000	1.0000
	2	.6009	.9195	.9879	.9985	.9999	1.0000	1.0000	1.0000	1.0000	1.0000
	3	.3233	.7772	.9514	.9921	.9990	.9999	1.0000	1.0000	1.0000	1.0000
	4	.1381	.5769	.8698	.9715	.9953	.9994	.9999	1.0000	1.0000	1.0000
	5	.0480	.3710	.7367	.9241	.9840	.9974	.9997	1.0000	1.0000	1.0000
	6	.0139	.2063	.5675	.8387	.9567	.9914	.9987	.9999	1.0000	1.0000
	7	.0034	.0995	.3933	.7141	.9038	.9762	.9956	.9994	.9999	1.0000
	8	.0007	.0419	.2441	.5629	.8180	.9447	.9876	.9979	.9998	1.0000
	9	.0001	.0155	.1354	.4069	.7002	.8890	.9697	.9939	.9991	.9999
	10	.0000	.0051	.0672	.2682	.5605	.8041	.9356	.9844	9973	.9997
	11	.0000	.0015	.0299	.1608	.4161	.6913	.8785	.9648	.9926	.9989
	12	.0000	.0004	.0120	.0875	.2849	.5594	.7947	.9291	.9821	.9968
	13	.0000	.0001	.0043	.0432	.1791	.4228	.6857	.8715	.9614	.9917
	14	.0000	.0000	.0014	.0194	.1032	.2968	.5592	.7888	.9249	.9808
	15	.0000	.0000	.0004	.0079	.0544	.1926	.4279	.6826	.8674	.9597
	16	.0000	.0000	.0001	.0029	.0262	.1151	.3054	.5598	.7858	.9231
	17	.0000	.0000	.0000	.0010	.0116	.0633	.2022	.4319	.6815	.8659
	18	.0000	.0000	.0000	.0003	.0047	.0320	.1239	.3115	.5609	.7852
	19	.0000	.0000	.0000	.0001	.0017	.0148	.0699	.2089	.4349	.6821
	20	.0000	.0000	.0000	.0000	.0006	.0063	.0363	.1298	.3156	.5627
	21	.0000	.0000	.0000	.0000	.0002	.0024	.0173	.0744	.2130	.4373
	22	.0000	.0000	.0000	.0000	.0000	.0009	.0075	.0392	.1331	.3179
	23	.0000	.0000	.0000	.0000	.0000	.0003	.0030	.0189	.0767	.2148
	24	.0000	.0000	.0000	.0000	.0000	.0001	.0011	.0083	.0405	.1341
	25	.0000	.0000	.0000	.0000	.0000	.0000	.0004	.0034	.0196	.0769
	26	.0000	.0000	.0000	.0000	.0000	.0000	.0001	.0012	.0086	.0403
	27	.0000	.0000	.0000	.0000	.0000	.0000	.0000	.0004	.0034	.0192
	28	.0000	.0000	.0000	.0000	.0000	.0000	.0000	.0001	.0012	.0083
	29	.0000	.0000	.0000	.0000	.0000	.0000	.0000	.0000	.0004	.0032
	30	.0000	.0000	.0000	.0000	.0000	.0000	.0000	.0000	.0001	.0011
	31	.0000	.0000	.0000	.0000	.0000	.0000	.0000	.0000	.0000	.0003
	32	.0000	.0000	.0000	.0000	.0000	.0000	.0000	.0000	.0000	.0001
	33	.0000	.0000	.0000	.0000	.0000	.0000	.0000	.0000	.0000	.0000
	34	.0000	.0000	.0000	.0000	.0000	.0000	.0000	.0000	.0000	.0000
	35	.0000	.0000	.0000	.0000	.0000	.0000	.0000	.0000	.0000	.0000

n	x'	0.05	.10	.15	.20	.25	.30	.35	.40	.45	.50
						p					
40	36	.0000	.0000	.0000	.0000	.0000	.0000	.0000	.0000	.0000	.0000
	37	.0000	.0000	.0000	.0000	.0000	.0000	.0000	.0000	.0000	.0000
	38	.0000	.0000	.0000	.0000	.0000	.0000	.0000	.0000	.0000	.0000
	39	.0000	.0000	.0000	.0000	.0000	.0000	.0000	.0000	.0000	.0000
	40	.0000	.0000	.0000	.0000	.0000	.0000	.0000	.0000	.0000	.0000
45	1	.9006	.9913	.9993	1.0000	1.0000	1.0000	1.0000	1.0000	1.0000	1.0000
	2	.6650	.9476	.9940	.9995	1.0000	1.0000	1.0000	1.0000	1.0000	1.0000
	3	.3923	.8410	.9735	.9968	.9997	1.0000	1.0000	1.0000	1.0000	1.0000
	4	.1866	.6711	.9215	.9871	.9984	.9999	1.0000	1.0000	1.0000	1.0000
	5	.0729	.4729	.8252	.9618	.9941	.9993	.9999	1.0000	1.0000	1.0000
	6	.0239	.2923	.6858	.9098	.9821	.9974	.9997	1.0000	1.0000	1.0000
	7	.0066	.1585	.5218	.8232	.9554	.9920	.9990	.9999	1.0000	1.0000
	8	.0016	.0757	.3606	.7025	.9059	.9791	.9967	.9996	1.0000	1.0000
	9	.0003	.0320	.2255	.5593	.8275	.9529	.9909	.9988	.9999	1.0000
	10	.0001	.0120	.1274	.4120	.7200	.9066	.9780	.9964	.9996	1.0000
	11	.0000	.0040	.0651	.2795	.5911	8353	.9531	.9906	.9987	.9999
	12	.0000	.0012	.0302	.1741	.4543	.7380	.9104	.9784	.9964	.9996
	13	.0000	.0003	.0127	.0995	.3252	.6198	.8453	.9554	.9910	.9988
	14	.0000	.0001	.0048	.0521	.2159	.4912	.7563	.9164	.9799	.9967
	15	.0000	.0000	.0017	.0250	.1327	.3653	.6467	.8570	.9591	.9920
	16	.0000	.0000	.0005	.0110	.0753	.2538	.5248	.7751	.9238	.9822
	17	.0000	.0000	.0002	.0044	.0395	.1642	.4017	.6728	.8698	.9638
	18	.0000	.0000	.0000	.0017	.0191	.0986	.2887	.5564	.7944	.9324
	19	.0000	.0000	.0000	.0006	.0085	.0549	.1940	.4357	.6985	.8837
	20	.0000	.0000	.0000	.0002	.0035	.0283	.1215	.3214	.5869	.8144
	21	.0000	.0000	.0000	.0001	.0013	.0135	.0708	.2223	.4682	.7243
	22	.0000	.0000	.0000	.0000	.0005	.0060	.0382	.1436	.3526	.6170
	23	.0000	.0000	.0000	.0000	.0001	.0024	.0191	.0865	.2494	.5000
	24	.0000	.0000	.0000	.0000	.0000	.0009	.0089	.0483	.1650	.3830
	25	.0000	.0000	.0000	.0000	.0000	.0003	.0038	.0250	.1017	.2757
	26	.0000	.0000	.0000	.0000	.0000	.0001	.0015	.0120	.0582	.1856
	27	.0000	.0000	.0000	.0000	.0000	.0000	.0005	.0053	.0308	.1163
	28	.0000	.0000	.0000	.0000	.0000	.0000	.0002	.0021	.0150	.0676
	29	.0000	.0000	.0000	.0000	.0000	.0000	.0001	.0008	.0068	.0362
	30	.0000	.0000	.0000	.0000	.0000	.0000	.0000	.0003	.0028	.0178
	31	.0000	.0000	.0000	.0000	.0000	.0000	.0000	.0001	.0010	.0080
	32	.0000	.0000	.0000	.0000	.0000	.0000	.0000	.0000	.0004	.0033
	33	.0000	.0000	.0000	.0000	.0000	.0000	.0000	.0000	.0001	.0012
	34	.0000	.0000	.0000	.0000	.0000	.0000	.0000	.0000	.0000	.0004
	35	.0000	.0000	.0000	.0000	.0000	.0000	.0000	.0000	.0000	.0001
	36	.0000	.0000	.0000	.0000	.0000	.0000	.0000	.0000	.0000	.0000
	37	.0000	.0000	.0000	.0000	.0000	.0000	.0000	.0000	.0000	.0000
	38	.0000	.0000	.0000	.0000	.0000	.0000	.0000	.0000	.0000	.0000
	39	.0000	.0000	.0000	.0000	.0000	.0000	.0000	.0000	.0000	.0000
	40	.0000	.0000	.0000	.0000	.0000	.0000	.0000	.0000	.0000	.0000
	41	.0000	.0000	.0000	.0000	.0000	.0000	.0000	.0000	.0000	.0000
	42	.0000	.0000	.0000	.0000	.0000	.0000	.0000	.0000	.0000	.0000
	43	.0000	.0000	.0000	.0000	.0000	.0000	.0000	.0000	.0000	.0000
	44	.0000	.0000	.0000	.0000	.0000	.0000	.0000	.0000	.0000	.0000
	45	.0000	.0000	.0000	.0000	.0000	.0000	.0000	.0000	.0000	.0000

Note: Linear interpolation will be accurate at most to two decimal places.
Source: Handbook of Tables for Mathematics, 4th ed., The Chemical Rubber Co., 1970.

APPENDIX B

Answers to Selected Problems

T his appendix sketches the answers to selected practice problems and end-of-chapter exercises. Because Chapters 2, 3, and 4 are fundamental to a good understanding of econometric methodology, answers are provided for more of the problems in these chapters. In later chapters, many of the questions involve empirical analysis and have no single answer.

Chapter 1

Exercises

1.2   The output of corn will depend on a number of inputs to the production process. One possible formulation of the model is as follows.

$$\text{OUTPUT} = \beta_1 + \beta_2 \text{ ACRES} + \beta_3 \text{ LABOR} + \beta_4 \text{ CAPITAL}$$
$$+ \beta_5 \text{ FERT} + \beta_6 \text{ INSECT} + u$$

where ACRES is the number of acres of corn cultivated, LABOR is the number of worker-hours, CAPITAL is the number of machine-hours used, FERT is the number of pounds of fertilizers used, INSECT is the number of pounds of insecticides used, and u is the unobserved error term. If a larger area of land is devoted to growing corn, we would expect total corn output to go up. Similarly, if more workers and machinery are used in the production process, then more output is likely to be produced. The same argument applies to fertilizers also. However, for insecticide we have to be guarded. If too many pesticides are used, the produce might become toxic. Therefore, in safe doses, increased pesticide usage would increase production. We would therefore expect all the effects to be positive.

1.5   The proper formulation of a linear regression model is like the one in the answer to Exercise 1.2 in which each of the explanatory variables is multiplied by a coefficient to be estimated. In the given model, all the coefficients are assumed to be exactly 1, which is clearly wrong. Furthermore, it may not make sense to add two variables directly. For example, in Exercise 1.2, ACRES is measured in acres, LABOR is in hours, and FERT is in pounds. It is totally nonsensical to add these and formulate the model with all the βs set to 1.

Chapter 2

Practice Problems

2.7   Given that $X = 1, 2, \ldots, 5$ with probability 0.2, we want the correlation coefficient between X and X^2. First we need the following:

$$\text{Cov}(X, X^2) = E(X^3) - E(X)E(X^2)$$

$$V(X) = E(X^2) - [E(X)]^2 \quad \cdot \quad V(X^2) = E(X^4) - [E(X^2)]^2$$

These can be calculated as follows:

$$E(X) = 0.2(1 + 2 + \cdot \cdot \cdot + 5) = 3$$

$$E(X^2) = 0.2(1^2 + 2^2 + \cdot \cdot \cdot + 5^2) = 11$$

$$E(X^3) = 0.2(1^3 + 2^3 + \cdot \cdot \cdot + 5^3) = 45$$

$$E(X^4) = 0.2(1^4 + 2^4 + \cdot \cdot \cdot + 5^4) = 195.8$$

$$\text{Cov}(X, X^2) = 45 - (3 \times 11) = 12$$

$$V(X) = 11 - 9 = 2$$

$$V(X^2) = 195.8 - 121 = 74.8$$

The correlation coefficient between X and X^2 is therefore given by $\dfrac{12}{\sqrt{(2 \times 74.8)}} = 0.9811$, which is slightly below 1.

Exercises

2.4   Let X be the number of persons who do not show up, out of 23 reservations. The probability of a "no show" is $p = 0.1$. The company can accommodate everyone if no more than 20 people wish to board the plane, that is, if at least 3 people do not arrive. Thus, we need $P(X \geq 3)$, when $n = 23$ and $p = 0.1$. From Table A.6 this is given as 0.4080.

2.6   a. $E(X - \mu) = \Sigma f(x_i)(x_i - \mu) = \Sigma x_i f(x_i) - \mu \Sigma f(x_i)$. Because $\Sigma f(x_i) = 1$ and the first term is $E(X) = \mu$, the above expression becomes $E(X) - \mu = 0$.

   b. $E(c) = c \Sigma f(x_i) = c$.

   c. $E[cg(X)] = \Sigma cg(x_i)f(x_i) = c \Sigma g(x_i)f(x_i) = cE[g(X)]$.

   d. $E[u(X) + v(X)] = \Sigma [u(x_i) + v(x_i)]f(x_i) = \Sigma u(x_i)f(x_i) + \Sigma v(x_i)f(x_i) = E[u(X)] + E[v(X)]$.

2.9   Because each of the elementary outcomes is equally likely, the density function is

$$f(x) = 1/n, \quad \text{for } x = 1, 2, \ldots, n$$

$$E(X) = \frac{1}{n}(1 + 2 + \cdot \cdot \cdot + n) = (n + 1)/2$$

$$E(X^2) = \frac{1}{n}(1^2 + 2^2 + \cdot \cdot \cdot + n^2)$$

$$= (n + 1)(2n + 1)/6$$

Therefore,

$$V(X) = E(X^2) - [E(X)]^2 = \frac{(n+1)(2n+1)}{6} - \frac{(n+1)^2}{4}$$

$$= (n^2 - 1)/12$$

2.12 Let $\overline{X}$ be the average income. Then, by Property 2.10a, $\overline{X} \sim N(\mu, \sigma^2/n) = N(26, 1.44)$. We need $P(25 \le \overline{X} \le 29)$. If we subtract the mean and divide by the standard deviation, the resulting random variable has the standard normal distribution (Z). Therefore, the probability is equal to

$$P\left(\frac{25 - 26}{1.2} \le Z \le \frac{29 - 26}{1.2}\right) = P(-0.83 \le Z \le 2.5)$$

Using the symmetry of the distribution, we have

$$P(-0.83 \le Z \le 2.5) = P(0 \le Z \le 0.83) + P(0 \le Z \le 2.5)$$

$$= 0.2967 + 0.4938 = 0.7905$$

2.14 Given that $V(X_i) = \sigma_i^2 (i = 1, 2)$ and $\text{Cov}(X_1, X_2) = \sigma_{12}$, using Property 2.8g we have

$$\text{Cov}(X_1 + X_2, X_1 - X_2) = \text{Cov}(X_1, X_1) - \text{Cov}(X_1, X_2)$$

$$+ \text{Cov}(X_2, X_1) - \text{Cov}(X_2, X_2)$$

$$= V(X_1) - V(X_2) = \sigma_1^2 - \sigma_2^2$$

Y and Z will be uncorrelated if and only if $\sigma_1 = \sigma_2$.

2.20 Given $n = 13$, $\overline{x} = .031$, and $s = 0.01$. The null hypothesis is $H_0: \mu = \mu_0 = 0$ and the alternative is $H_1: \mu \neq 0$. The test statistic is $t_c = \sqrt{n}(\overline{x} - \mu_0)/s = \sqrt{13}(0.031/0.01) = 11.1772$. We see from the t-table that for 12 d.f. all the critical values (t^*) in the table are below t_c. Therefore, H_0 is rejected at all the tabulated values, implying that the excess rate of return is significantly different from zero. The 95 percent confidence interval is $\overline{x} \pm (t^*s/\sqrt{n}) = 0.031 \pm (2.179 \times 0.01/\sqrt{13}) = (0.025, 0.037)$.

Chapter 3

Practice Problems

3.1 From Figure 3.2 we note the following.

$$Y_t = AD; \quad \hat{Y}_t = \hat{\alpha} + \hat{\beta}X_t = AC; \quad \alpha + \beta X_t = AB; \quad u_t = BD; \quad \hat{u}_t = CD$$

Since the only correct decompositions of the line segment AD are $AB + BD$ and $AC + CD$, only equations (a) and (b) are correctly specified. It is easy to verify that the other equations are incorrect.

3.3 From Equation (3.9), $\hat{\alpha} = \overline{Y} - \hat{\beta}\overline{X}$. $E(\hat{\alpha}) = E(\overline{Y}) - E(\hat{\beta}\overline{X}) = E(\overline{Y}) - \overline{X}E(\hat{\beta})$ because, X_t being given (Assumption 3.4), $\overline{X}$ can be taken out of the expectation. Because $\hat{\beta}$ is unbiased (Property 3.1), $E(\hat{\beta}) = \beta$. The expected value of $\bar{Y}$ is given by (summation is over t)

$$E(\bar{Y}) = E\left(\frac{\sum Y_t}{n}\right) = \frac{\sum E(Y_t)}{n} = \left(\frac{1}{n}\right)\sum E(\alpha + \beta X_t + u_t)$$

Because X_t is nonrandom, $E(X_t) = X_t$. Also, $\Sigma \alpha$ is equal to $n\alpha$ because there are n terms and each is α. Therefore,

$$E(\bar{Y}) = \left(\frac{1}{n}\right)(n\alpha) + \left(\frac{1}{n}\right)\beta\sum X_t + \left(\frac{1}{n}\right)\sum E(u_t)$$

$$= \alpha + \beta\bar{X} + \left(\frac{1}{n}\right)\sum E(u_t)$$

By Assumption 3.3, $E(u_t) = 0$. Therefore, $E(\bar{Y}) = \alpha + \beta\bar{X}$. It follows that $E(\hat{\alpha}) = E(\bar{Y}) - \beta\bar{X} = \alpha$, which implies that α is also unbiased.

3.5   We sketch the proof for a one-tailed test only. If a coefficient is significant at the 1 percent level, then $t_c > t^*_{n-2}(0.01)$, where t^* is the point on the t-distribution with $n - 2$ d.f. such that the area to the right is 0.01. Note that the critical t^* for a higher level (say, 0.05) must be such that $t^*_{n-2}(0.01) > t^*_{n-2}(0.05)$. It follows that $t_c > t^*_{n-2}(0.05)$, which implies that the coefficient is significant at the 5 percent level also.

Exercises

3.3   Since X_t is given (Assumption 3.4), $E(Y_t) = \alpha + \beta X_t + E(u_t) = \alpha + \beta X_t$, under Assumption 3.3 that $E(u_t) = 0$. $E(\hat{Y}_t) = E(\hat{\alpha}) + E(\hat{\beta}X_t)$. We showed in Property 3.1 that $\hat{\alpha}$ and $\hat{\beta}$ are unbiased, that is, $E(\hat{\alpha}) = \alpha$ and $E(\hat{\beta}) = \beta$. Substituting this above and noting that X_t is nonrandom, we have $E(\hat{Y}_t) = \alpha + \beta X_t = E(Y_t)$.

3.6   In the scatter diagram drawn here, we first compute the slope of each of the straight lines and then obtain the average slope. The slope of the straight line connecting (X_1, Y_1) and (X_t, Y_t) is given by $(Y_t - Y_1)/(X_t - X_1)$. Noting that there are $n - 1$ such straight lines, we have

$$\hat{\beta} = \frac{1}{n-1}\sum_{t=2}^{t=n}\left[\frac{Y_t - Y_1}{X_t - X_1}\right]$$

$$E\left[\frac{Y_t - Y_1}{X_t - X_1}\right] = E\left[\frac{(\alpha + \beta X_t + u_t) - (\alpha + \beta X_1 + u_1)}{X_t - X_1}\right]$$

$$= \beta + E\left[\frac{u_t - u_1}{X_t - X_1}\right] = \beta$$

because the Xs are nonrandom and $E(u_t) = 0$. This means that each of the terms in the summation has expectation β and hence the average will also have the same expectation, thus implying unbiasedness. By the Gauss–Markov theorem, $\hat{\beta}$ is inferior because it is less efficient than the OLS estimator of β.

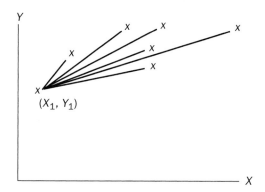

3.12 a. The OLS method in Section 3.2 yields two conditions, $\Sigma \hat{u}_t = 0$ and $\Sigma X_t \hat{u}_t = 0$. For the model given here, the first equation gives $\Sigma(Y_t - \tilde{\beta} X_t) = 0$, or $\Sigma Y_t = \tilde{\beta} \Sigma X_t$. Solving this, we have $\tilde{\beta} = \bar{Y}/\bar{X}$. (Note that this requires that $\bar{X}$ not be zero.) The second equation is $\Sigma X_t(Y_t - \hat{\beta} X_t) = 0$, or $\Sigma X_t Y_t = \hat{\beta} \Sigma X_t^2$, which gives $\hat{\beta} = (\Sigma X_t Y_t)/(\Sigma X_t^2)$.

   b. $E(\hat{\beta}) = E(\Sigma X_t Y_t / \Sigma X_t^2)$. Because X_t is nonrandom (Assumption 3.4), ΣX_t^2 is also nonrandom and hence can be taken out of the expectation. Also, the expectation of a sum is the sum of expectations. Therefore,

$$E(\hat{\beta}) = \left(\frac{1}{\sum X_t^2}\right) \sum E(X_t Y_t) = \left(\frac{1}{\sum X_t^2}\right) \sum E[X_t(\beta X_t + u_t)]$$

$$= \left(\frac{1}{\sum X_t^2}\right)\beta \sum (X_t^2) + \left(\frac{1}{\sum X_t^2}\right) \sum X_t E(u_t) = \beta$$

   because $E(u_t) = 0$ by Assumption 3.3. Hence $\hat{\beta}$ is unbiased. The proof for $\tilde{\beta}$ is similar.

   c. For the fitted line $\hat{Y} = \hat{\beta} X$ to go through the point $(\bar{X}, \bar{Y})$, $\hat{\beta}\bar{X}$ must be equal to $\bar{Y}$. However,

$$\hat{\beta}\bar{X} = \frac{\sum X_t Y_t}{\sum X_t^2} \bar{X}$$

   which will generally not be equal to $\bar{Y}$. This means that the point $(\bar{X}, \bar{Y})$ is not likely to lie on the straight line $\hat{Y} = \hat{\beta} X$. In contrast, however, $\tilde{\beta}\bar{X} = \bar{Y}$ and hence the straight line $\hat{Y} = \tilde{\beta} X$ passes through the point $(\bar{X}, \bar{Y})$.

   d. The OLS procedure minimizes the error sum of squares

$$\text{ESS} = \sum \hat{u}_t^2 = \sum(Y_t - \hat{\beta} X_t)^2$$

   with respect to $\hat{\beta}$. Taking the partial derivative with respect to $\hat{\beta}$ (see the chapter appendix, Section 3.A.1), we get

APPENDIX B

$$\frac{\partial \text{ESS}}{\partial \hat{\beta}} = \sum \left[2\hat{u}_t \left(\frac{\partial \hat{u}_t}{\partial \hat{\beta}} \right) \right] = 2 \sum (Y_t - \hat{\beta} X_t)(- X_t) = 0$$

Solving this for $\hat{\beta}$, we obtain the same expression as in part a.

e.   To establish this, proceed exactly as in Section 3.A.4, except set α to zero throughout.

f.   The Gauss–Markov theorem states that the OLS estimator $(\hat{\beta})$ is BLUE; that is, it is most efficient, with the lowest variance among all linear unbiased estimators. Thus, any other linear unbiased estimator, in particular $\tilde{\beta}$, is less efficient. Therefore, $\hat{\beta}$ is superior to $\tilde{\beta}$.

3.18   The model is $E = \alpha + \beta N + u$, where E is the starting salary and N is the number of years of college attended.

a. $\alpha + \beta N$ is the population average starting salary for a person with N years of college education. If N is zero, then the average salary is α. Thus, α is the average starting salary for a person with no college education. β is the change in E per unit charge in N—that is, dE/dN. Thus, β is the extra starting salary for each extra year of college education.

b.   We require that the error terms be normally distributed only when the statistical distributions of $\hat{\alpha}$ and $\hat{\beta}$ are derived for hypothesis testing. Therefore, the properties of unbiasedness, consistency, and efficiency (BLUE) are valid, provided Assumptions 3.2 through 3.7 hold. If the distribution of u_t is unknown, then all tests of hypotheses are invalid.

c.   Let E^* be the salary measured in hundreds of dollars. Then $E = 100E^* = \alpha + \beta N + u$. It follows that $E^* = (\alpha/100) + (\beta/100)N + (u/100)$ is the new model, with E^* as the dependent variable. If α^* and β^* are the parameters of the new model, we have $\alpha^* = \alpha/100$ and $\beta^* = \beta/100$. Therefore, the new regression coefficients will be one-hundredths of the regression coefficients of the original model. Similarly, the new standard errors will be one-hundredths of the old standard errors. Because R^2, t- , and F-statistics are ratios, they are independent of the scale of units and hence will be unchanged.

3.24 a.   As price increases, the demand for the sealing compound would decrease and hence we would expect β to be negative. The intercept α will be positive because there will be a high demand for the compound when price is low or near zero.

b.
$$\hat{Q} = 5962.053755 - 381.092383P$$
$$\quad\quad\quad (955.809956) \quad\quad (104.765725)$$

$$R^2 = 0.132 \quad\quad \text{d.f.} = 87 \quad\quad \hat{\sigma} = 1466.09133$$

c.   The signs agree with our prior intuition.

d.   The coefficient for price is the expected decrease, on average, in the number of gallons of sealant shipped in a month for a \$1 increase in the price. This average is 381 gallons.

e.   Since only 13.2 percent of the variation in the demand for sealant is explained by the model, the fit is not very good. The null hypothesis for goodness of fit is that the coefficient of correlation (ρ) between Q and P is zero and the alternative is that it is not zero. The test statistic is given by $F_c = R^2(n-2)/(1-R^2) = 0.132 \times 87/(1-0.132) = 13.23$. Under the null hypothesis this has the F-distribution with 1 d.f. for the numerator and 87 d.f. for the denominator. From the F-table for the 1 percent level, the critical value F^* lies between 6.85 and 7.08. Because $F_c > F^*$, we reject the null hypothesis and conclude that the correlation coefficient is significantly different from zero, even though its numerical value is low.

f. The null hypothesis is that the regression coefficient is zero and the alternative is that it is not zero. The test statistic (t_c) is the coefficient divided by the corresponding standard error. Under the null hypothesis, it has a t-distribution with d.f. $n-2 = 87$. From the t-table, for a 1 percent level and 87 d.f., the critical t^* for a two-tailed test is between 2.617 and 2.66. If the calculated t_c is numerically greater than these values, we would reject the null hypothesis and conclude that the corresponding coefficient is significantly different from zero. For the constant term, $t_c = 5962.053755/955.809956 = 6.24$. For the slope coefficient, $|t_c| = 381.092383/104.765725 = 3.64$. Because these are greater than the critical t, we reject the null hypothesis and conclude that both α and β are significantly different from zero.

g. Let P^* be price in cents. Then $P^* = 100P$ and hence $P = P^*/100$. The model now becomes $Q = \alpha + \beta P^*/100 + u = \alpha + \beta^* P^* + u$. Thus, the slope coefficient and the corresponding standard error will be affected but not the others. The new slope coefficient is the old one divided by 100. The new estimated model is therefore

$$\hat{Q} = 5962.053755 - 3.81092383 P^*$$
$$\phantom{\hat{Q} = }(955.809956) \quad\quad (1.04765725)$$

$$R^2 = 0.132 \quad\quad \text{d.f.} = 87 \quad\quad \hat{\sigma} = 1466.09133$$

h. The model is not well specified because it is missing other explanatory variables such as housing starts and some measure of highway, street, and other construction that might require the sealant.

3.25 a. β is the marginal propensity to save out of extra income. In other words, it is the expected average change in per-capita saving when per-capita income is increased by one dollar.

b. When income is zero, households will still have expenses and hence we would expect average saving to be negative. Thus, we would expect α to be negative. If an individual earns an extra \$1 income, we would expect that some of that would be saved. Hence, the expected sign for β is positive. The observed marginal propensity to save (the slope coefficient) has the expected positive sign but the intercept is not negative as suggested above. This might be due to model misspecification. For instance, we would expect the size of a family to affect the amount of saving of a household. This omitted variable might have influenced the estimated intercept term. Another possibility is that the linear specification may not be right.

c.   The model explains 53.8 percent of the variation in saving. For time series data one would expect R^2 to be higher. The null hypothesis for a goodness-of-fit test is that the correlation between saving and income is zero and the alternative is that it is not zero. The test statistic is $F_c = R^2(n-2)/(1-R^2) = 0.538 \times 34/0.462 = 39.59$. Under the null hypothesis, this has the F-distribution with 1 d.f. for the numerator and 34 d.f. for the denominator. From the F-table, the critical F^* for a 1 percent level is between 7.31 and 7.56. Because $F_c > F^*$, we reject the null hypothesis and conclude that the correlation coefficient is not zero.

d.   To test individual coefficients, the null hypothesis is that the coefficient is zero and the alternative is that it is not zero. The test statistic (t_c) is the ratio of the coefficient divided by the corresponding standard error. Under the null hypothesis this has the t-distribution with $n-2 = 34$ d.f. From the t-table, the critical t^* for a two-tailed 1 percent test is between 2.704 and 2.75. If the calculated t_c is numerically higher than this, we would reject the null hypothesis. For the intercept coefficient, $t_c = 384.105/151.105 = 2.54$. Because this is less than the critical t^*, we cannot reject the null hypothesis that $\alpha = 0$ and conclude that it is statistically insignificant. For the slope coefficient $t_c = 0.067/0.011 = 6.09$, which is greater than t^*. Therefore, we reject the null hypothesis and conclude that the slope coefficient is significantly different from zero.

e.   Let S^* be savings in hundreds of dollars and Y^* be income in hundreds of dollars. Then, $S^* = S/100$ and $Y^* = Y/100$. Substituting for S and Y into the model, we get $100\,S^* = \alpha + \beta(100\,Y^*) + u$. Dividing both sides by 100, we get $S^* = (\alpha/100) + \beta Y^* + (u/100) = \alpha^* + \beta Y^* + u^*$. The intercept and the error terms are affected but not the slope term. The new estimated model will be as follows:

$$\hat{S} = 3.84105 + 0.067\,Y$$
$$\quad\quad (1.51105) \quad (0.011)$$

$$R^2 = 0.538 \quad\quad \hat{\sigma} = 1.99023$$

3.29   The t-ratio is the coefficient divided by its standard error. Use the values given for two of them and solve for the third, $\hat{\sigma}^2 = \text{ESS}/(n-2) = 305.96/(22-2) = 15.298$. $R^2 = 1 - (\text{ESS}/\text{TSS})$. We therefore need TSS. But, from Equation (2.9),

$$S_v^2 = \frac{1}{(n-1)}\sum(V_t - \bar{V})^2 = \frac{1}{(n-1)}\text{TSS}$$

We can therefore solve for TSS as $(n-1)s_v^2$. R^2 is now readily obtained. From Equation (3.7), $\bar{V} = \hat{\alpha} + \hat{\beta}\bar{P}$. From Section 3.A.10, $r_{vp}^2 = R^2$. The square root of this is r_{vp}. The confidence interval for β is derived in Section 3.10 as $\hat{\beta} \pm t^*s_{\hat{\beta}}$, where $s_{\hat{\beta}}$ is the standard error of $\hat{\beta}$ and t^* is the point on the t-distribution with 20 d.f. $(= n-2)$ such that the area to the right is 0.025.

Chapter 4

Practice Problems

4.7   The estimated coefficient is $\hat{\beta} = [\Sigma(X_tY_t)/\Sigma\ X_t^2]$ (see Exercise 3.12, part d, for proof). Substitute for Y_t from the true model to obtain

$$\hat{\beta} = \frac{\sum[X_t(\alpha + \beta X_t + u_t)]}{\sum X_t^2} = \alpha\frac{\sum X_t}{\sum X_t^2} + \beta + \frac{\sum X_t u_t}{\sum X_t^2}$$

The expected value of the third term is zero because $E(u_t) = 0$. But, for $\hat{\beta}$ to be unbiased, the first term must also be zero. Thus, unless $\Sigma\ X_t = 0$, which means that unless the sample mean of X is zero, the estimate will be biased.

Exercises

4.6   The true model is $Y_t = \beta X_t + u_t$ and the estimated model is $Y_t = \beta Z_t + v_t$. The estimated regression coefficient is (see the answer to Exercise 3.12, part d) $\hat{\beta} = (\Sigma\ Y_tZ_t)/(\Sigma\ Z_t^2)$. The expected value of this is

$$E(\hat{\beta}) = E\left[\frac{\sum Y_t Z_t}{\sum Z_t^2}\right] = \frac{1}{\sum Z_t^2}\ E\left(\sum Y_t Z_t\right) = \frac{1}{\sum Z_t^2}\sum E(Y_t Z_t)$$

making use of the facts that Z_t is nonrandom and the expectation of a summation is the sum of the expectations. Because the true process that generates Y_t is given by $\beta X_t + u_t$, and because $E(u_t) = 0$, we have

$$E(Y_t Z_t) = E[Z_t(\beta X_t + u_t)] = \beta Z_t X_t$$

Therefore, $E(\hat{\beta}) = \beta(\Sigma\ Z_tX_t/\Sigma\ Z_t^2)$, which will be equal to β only if the expression in parentheses is equal to 1. The same condition is needed for consistency also.

4.11   a.   The table gives the p-values directly. Therefore, there is no need to compute t-statistics or look up the t-table. $H_0: \beta = 0$; $H_1: \beta \neq 0$ for each β, level of significance = 0.10.
         Decision rule: If p-value < 0.10, then the probability of making a mistake if we reject H_0 is small and hence we are "safe" in rejecting H_0. Therefore, we should reject H_0 whenever p-value < 0.10. Rejection means $\beta \neq 0$, that is, *β is significantly different from zero.* Since all the coefficients have p-values above 10 percent, none of the coefficients is significant. We thus have the strange result that all the variables are candidates for omission from the model. As mentioned in the text, however, a prudent step is to be selective in excluding variables. For instance, VALUE, INCOME, and POPCHANG have p-values only slightly above 0.1. In Model C, which excluded UNEMP, LOCALTAX, and STATETAX, these variables have significant coefficients.

         b. H_1: at least one of β_2, β_6, β_7, and β_8 is nonzero.
         Test statistic: The unrestricted model is A and the restricted model is D.

Compute

$$F_c = \frac{(\mathrm{ESS}_D - \mathrm{ESS}_A)/4}{\mathrm{ESS}_A/(40 - 8)} = \frac{(5.038 - 4.763)/4}{4.763/32} = 0.462$$

Distribution: Under H_0, $F_c \sim F_{4,32}$.
Decision rule: Look up $F^*_{4,32}$ such that the area to the right is 0.10. F^* is between 2.09 and 2.14. Since $F_c < F^*$, we cannot reject H_0. We therefore conclude that β_2, β_6, β_7, and β_8 are all jointly insignificant.

c. All eight model selection criteria are lowest for Model D and hence we would choose this model as the best. In this model, VALUE, INCOME, and POPCHANG have coefficients significant at levels below 10 percent. The constant term is not significant but is retained to capture the mean effects of the dependent and omitted variables.

d. As INCOME increases, we would expect demand for housing to increase. Hence, we would expect $\hat{\beta}_4 > 0$, and it is. As population increases, housing would increase also. So, we would expect $\hat{\beta}_5 > 0$, and it is. As the price of a house as measured by the median value increases, we would expect fewer people to demand housing; that is, the expected sign for $\hat{\beta}_3$ is negative. The actual sign agrees with this intuition. What is surprising and counterintuitive are the insignificance of local and state taxes. Because an increase in taxes would reduce disposable incomes, we would expect the demand for housing to decrease. Although this is the case in Model A, their effects are quite weak.

e. The estimated relation using Model D is

$$\widehat{\mathrm{HOUSING}} = -973 - 0.778\,\mathrm{VALUE} + 116.597\,\mathrm{INCOME}$$
$$+ 24.857\,\mathrm{POPCHANG}$$

HOUSING is in actual units and INCOME is in thousands.
Let

HOUSING* = HOUSING in thousands = HOUSING/1,000
INCOME* = income in hundreds = 10 INCOME
HOUSING = 1,000 HOUSING* and INCOME = INCOME*/10

Substitute in the model:

$$1{,}000\,\widehat{\mathrm{HOUSING}}{}^* = -973 - 0.778\,\mathrm{VALUE} + 116.597$$
$$(\mathrm{INCOME}^*/10) + 24.857\,\mathrm{POPCHANG}$$

Divide by 1,000:

$$\widehat{\mathrm{HOUSING}}{}^* = -0.973 - 0.000778\,\mathrm{VALUE} + 0.0116597\,\mathrm{INCOME}^*$$
$$+ 0.024857\,\mathrm{POPCHANG}$$

R^2 is unaffected by the change in units. *p*-values are also unaffected.

f. Model D was chosen earlier as the "best" model for final interpretation. In that model, only VALUE, INCOME, and POPCHANG are statistically significant. DENSITY, UNEMP, LOCALTAX, and STATETAX had no significant effects. Other things being equal, a $1,000 increase in median household income is expected to increase the total number of private housing authorized in the city, on average, by 117 units. If population increased by 1 percentage point when income and house value are held constant, then housing units are expected to increase, on average, by 25 units. If the median value of owner-occupied homes increased by $100, with no change in other variables, then average housing demand is expected to decrease by 1 unit.

4.17 a. Calcium is supposed to improve the bone structure, and it is not clear whether it has any effect on CHD. The sign could be either positive or negative. Cigarette smokers have been shown to have a higher incidence of coronary problems. Thus, we would expect the coefficient for CIG to be positive. This is the case in all the models. Unemployment puts stress on a worker and, in turn, can lead to heart problems. Hence, we expect a positive sign for this variable. Higher consumption of fats has been shown to affect the arteries and hence increase the risk of death due to heart disease. Thus, this coefficient would be expected to be positive, and it is so in all the models. Meat contains animal fat and hence the same argument applies. Alcoholic drinks have a mixed effect. Doctors say that moderate drinkers have a lower incidence of heart problems but that both nondrinkers and heavy drinkers have problems. Because heavy drinkers have a much higher incidence of heart disease, we would expect positive signs for SPIRITS, BEER, and WINE. The observed signs differ from this expectation. The unexpected signs can be rationalized by *multicollinearity*, a topic discussed in Chapter 5.

b. The values of $\overline{R}^2$ range from 0.645 to 0.672. Considering that the data are time series, we would expect higher R^2. The F-statistics reported in the table test the null hypothesis that every regression coefficient except the constant term is zero. The alternative hypothesis is that at least one of them is nonzero. Under the null hypothesis, the calculated F has an F-distribution with degrees of freedom for the numerator equal to the number of restrictions in the null hypothesis (eight for Model A) and the degrees of freedom for the denominator equal to the number of observations minus the number of regression coefficients *including the constant* ($34 - 9 = 25$ here). From Table A.4b, $F^*_{8,25}(0.05)$ is 2.34. Because the observed $F(8.508) > F^*$, we reject the null hypothesis (at the 5 percent level) and conclude that at least one of the regression coefficients is nonzero. This result is not surprising because we note that many of the t-values appear significant (using the rule-of-thumb value of 2). The tests for Models B and C are similar.

c. Here also the tests are conducted for Model A only and for two-sided alternatives. To test a single regression coefficient for significance, we use the t-test. The d.f. is 25 ($34 - 9$). For a 5 percent level of significance, $t^*_{25}(0.025) = 2.06$. For statistical significance, the calculated t must be greater than t^* in absolute value. According to this criterion, the regression coefficients for SPIRITS and BEER are significant (at the 5 percent level), but those for the other variables are not. The other variables are thus candidates to be dropped. However, we must not be hasty and drop them simultaneously (recall the omitted-variable bias discussed in Section 4.5). It is quite possible that if we eliminate the most insignificant one (which is WINE, because it has the lowest t-value), some of the other coefficients will become significant.

d. Suppose we eliminate all the variables with t-values below 0.5 in absolute value. We would then exclude UNEMP, MEAT, and WINE from the model. This results in Model B. We could then perform a joint F-test (the Wald test) for these coefficients. Treating Model A as the unrestricted model and Model B as the restricted one, we get the following calculated F:

$$F_c = \frac{(\text{ESS}_B - \text{ESS}_A)/3}{\text{ESS}_A/25} = 0.2525$$

From Table A.4c, $F_{3,25}^*(0.1) = 2.32$. Therefore, these three regression coefficients are not jointly significant even at the 10 percent level. This suggests that all three of them can be dropped.

e. One should use a variety of criteria to determine whether one model is better than another. The model selection criteria given in Section 4.3 will certainly help. According to the values in the table, Model C is the "best" (has the smallest value for most of the criteria). The significance of the coefficients is another factor to consider. In Model A many coefficients are insignificant. In Model B calcium is insignificant, but in Model C all the regression coefficients, except the constant term, are significant. Because the constant term captures the average effect of omitted variables, it should always be retained.

f. It would have been desirable to obtain data on exercise, diet patterns, weight patterns, and so on. A cross-section study with data on individuals would have been even better.

Chapter 5

Exercises

5.2 a. Other things being equal, the higher the San Diego population or the higher the number of houses, the greater will be the demand for water. We would therefore expect positive signs for SDHOUSE and SDPOP. Higher-income persons may be expected to use more water, but we don't expect this to be strong. The expected sign for SDPCY is positive. If water is more expensive, users are likely to conserve its use and hence we expect the coefficient for PRWATER to be negative. If it rains heavily in San Diego, lawn and other garden or crop field requirements for water will be less. Hence, the coefficient for SDRAIN is likely to be negative. All the signs agree with intuition except SDPCY, which has an unexpected sign.

b. The *t*-statistic being insignificant means that the variable, by itself, does not appear to be significant. The *F*-statistic tests whether the variables are jointly significant. The degrees of freedom for a *t*-test is 9 $(15 - 6)$. The critical t^* for a 10 percent level is 1.833. Note that all the *t*-values are below this in absolute value and are hence insignificant, even at a 10 percent level. The degrees of freedom for the numerator of the *F*-statistic is 5 and for the denominator is 9. For a 1 percent test, the critical F^* is 6.06. The observed *F* is larger than this, indicating joint significance of the regression coefficients. The conflicting result is due to multicollinearity. SDHOUSE, SDPOP, and SDPCY would all be highly correlated. This would lower their *t*s and could make them insignificant. PRWATER and SDRAIN could be insignificant for a different reason. If the values of a variable have not changed much over the sample period, then its effect cannot be measured well. These two variables may not have changed much over the years and hence their effects may be difficult to measure.

c. Multicollinearity is a problem with the observations of the independent variables and has no effect on the assumptions made in Chapter 3. Therefore, the properties of unbiasedness, consistency, efficiency, and BLUE still hold. However, the variances of the estimates will be larger than another case in which there is no multicollinearity.

d. The new dependent variable is consumption per household (= SDWATER/SDHOUSE). The water consumption by a household should be related to household characteristics. These are AVGFAMSIZE, FAMILY INCOME, PRWATER, and AVGRAIN. AVGFAMSIZE may be obtained by dividing SDPOP by SDHOUSE. Also, FAMILY INCOME = SDPCY * AVGFAMSIZE and AVGRAIN = SDRAIN/SDHOUSE. A model that would be appropriate (others are also possible) is

$$\frac{\text{SDWATER}}{\text{SDHOUSE}} = \alpha_0 + \alpha_1 \frac{\text{SDPOP}}{\text{SDHOUSE}} + \alpha_2 \text{SDPCY} * \text{AVGFAMSIZE} + u$$

Chapter 6

Practice Problems

6.5 Differentiating PRICE partially with respect to SQFT, we get

$$\frac{\partial \text{PRICE}}{\partial \text{SQFT}} = \beta_2 + 2\beta_3 \text{SQFT}$$

This means that if β_3 is zero, the marginal effect of SQFT on PRICE is a constant for all SQFT. If β_3 is negative, then the marginal effect decreases as SQFT increases. In other words, as SQFT increases, the extra price for each extra square foot of living area decreases. Thus, the slope of the relation between price and square feet decreases as square feet increase.

6.12 *Method 1:* First, regress ln Q_t against a constant, ln K_t, and ln L_t, and compute the unrestricted error sum of squares, ESS_U. Next, impose the restriction $\alpha +$ $\beta = 1$; that is, let $\beta = 1 - \alpha$. The restricted model is ln $Q_t = \beta_1 + \alpha$

$\ln K_t + (1 - \alpha) \ln L_t + u_t = \beta_1 + \alpha(\ln K_t - \ln L_t) + \ln L_t + u_t$. Bringing the term $\ln L_t$, which has no unknown coefficient, to the left, we have

$$\ln Q_t - \ln L_t = \beta_1 + \alpha(\ln K_t - \ln L_t) + u_t$$

Regress the left-hand side against a constant and $(\ln K_t - \ln L_t)$, and obtain ESS_R, the restricted error sum of squares. The test is the standard Wald F-test with 1 d.f. for the numerator and $n - 3$ d.f. for the denominator (see Equation 4.3).

Method 3: This method depends on a t-statistic for $\hat{\alpha} + \hat{\beta} - 1$. The t-statistic to compute is

$$t_c = \frac{\hat{\alpha} + \hat{\beta} - 1}{[\widehat{\mathrm{Var}(\hat{\alpha})} + \widehat{\mathrm{Var}(\hat{\beta})} + 2\widehat{\mathrm{Cov}(\hat{\alpha}, \hat{\beta})}]^{1/2}}$$

Under the null hypothesis that $\alpha + \beta = 1$, this has a t-distribution with d.f. $n - 3$. Reject the null hypothesis (at the 5 percent level) if $|t_c| > t^*_{n-3}(0.025)$, where t^* is the point in the t-distribution with an area of 0.025 on each tail.

Exercises

6.2 a.   The derivative of $\ln(Y)$ with respect to X is $(1/Y)(\partial Y/\partial X)$. Therefore, differentiating the model partially with respect to X, we get $(1/Y)(\partial Y/\partial X) = \beta_2 + 2\beta_3 X + \beta_4 Z$. This gives the marginal effect as $\partial Y/\partial X = Y(\beta_2 + 2\beta_3 X + \beta_4 Z)$. But the question wants the expression to be independent of Y. First solve for Y by exponentiating the log model. This gives $Y = \exp(\beta_1 + \beta_2 X + \beta_3 X^2 + \beta_4 XZ)$ from which we have

$$\partial Y/\partial X = (\beta_2 + 2\beta_3 X + \beta_4 Z) \exp(\beta_1 + \beta_2 X + \beta_3 X^2 + \beta_4 XZ)$$

b.   The elasticity of Y with respect to X is $(X/Y)(\partial Y/\partial X) = X(\beta_2 + 2\beta_3 X + \beta_4 Z)$.

c.   First estimate the basic log-linear model by regressing $\ln(Y)$ against a constant and X, and save the residual as $\hat{u} = \ln(Y) - \hat{\beta}_1 - \hat{\beta}_2 X$. Next estimate the auxiliary regression by regressing $\hat{u}$ against a constant, X, X^2, and XZ. Then compute the test statistic $\mathrm{LM} = nR^2$, where n is the number of observations used and R^2 is the unadjusted R^2 in the auxiliary regression.

d.   Under the null hypothesis that $\beta_3 = \beta_4 = 0$, LM has the chi-square distribution with 2 d.f.

e.   From the chi-square table, find the critical value for 2 d.f. and the level of significance. Reject the null if LM is greater than the critical value. Alternatively, compute p-value = area to the right of LM in chi-square with 2 d.f. Reject the null if p-value is less than the level of significance.

6.6   Let $C = \alpha + \beta Y + \gamma N + u$ be the basic consumption function. The marginal propensity to consume with respect to Y is β. A simple way to allow for this to depend on income is to assume that $\beta = \beta_0 + \beta_1 Y$. For this to decrease as income increases, we need $\beta_1 < 0$. The effect for family size is similar. Thus, we would have $\gamma = \gamma_0 + \gamma_1 N$. Combining these, we get the following model:

$$C = \alpha + (\beta_0 + \beta_1 Y) Y + (\gamma_0 + \gamma_1 N) N + u$$
$$= \alpha + \beta_0 Y + \beta_1 Y^2 + \gamma_0 N + \gamma_1 N^2 + u$$

The required tests are $\beta_1 = 0$ against $\beta_1 < 0$, and $\gamma_1 = 0$ against $\gamma_1 < 0$. Using the argument for a linear-log model (see Section 6.2), we could also use the logarithmic function to test the hypotheses. An alternative version is

$$C = \alpha_0 + \alpha_1 Y + \alpha_2 \ln Y + \alpha_3 N + \alpha_4 \ln N + v$$

The relevant tests are $\alpha_2 = 0$ against $\alpha_2 > 0$, and $\alpha_4 = 0$ against $\alpha_4 > 0$.

6.11 a. We use a t-test for each regression coefficient. The degrees of freedom are $27 - 3 = 24$. The critical values for the 1, 5, and 10 percent levels are (for two-tailed tests) 2.797, 2.064, and 1.711, respectively. At these three levels of significance, only the t-statistic for $\ln Y_t$ is significant.

  b. Let the original model be written as

$$\widehat{\ln H_t} = \hat{\beta}_0 + \hat{\beta}_1 \ln Y_t + \hat{\beta}_2 \ln P_t$$

Suppose we had used $Y_t^* = Y_t / P_t$ instead of Y_t. The new model would be

$$\widehat{\ln H_t} = \hat{\alpha}_0 + \hat{\alpha}_1 \ln Y_t^* + \hat{\alpha}_2 \ln P_t$$
$$= \hat{\alpha}_0 + \hat{\alpha}_1 \ln (Y_t / P_t) + \hat{\alpha}_2 \ln P_t$$
$$= \hat{\alpha}_0 + \hat{\alpha}_1 \ln Y_t - \hat{\alpha}_1 \ln P_t + \hat{\alpha}_2 \ln P_t$$
$$= \hat{\alpha}_0 + \hat{\alpha}_1 \ln Y_t + (\hat{\alpha}_2 - \hat{\alpha}_1) \ln P_t$$

We note that each version can be readily derived from the other and hence they are essentially the same. The estimates of the constant term and the coefficient for $\ln Y_t$ are the same as before. $\hat{\alpha}_2$ is obtained from $\hat{\beta}_2 = \hat{\alpha}_2 - \hat{\alpha}_1$ as $\hat{\alpha}_2 = \hat{\beta}_2 + \hat{\beta}_1$.

  c. The demand for a product would depend on its price and hence the price of a single-family dwelling is an important variable. Similarly, the mortgage rate is important. If the price of condominiums is low, the demand for single-family houses will decrease. Therefore, the price of condominiums might be relevant as well. Property 4.3 summarizes the consequences of omitting an important variable.

Chapter 7

Practice Problems

7.1   In the new model, $Y_t = \alpha^* + \beta^* D_t^* + u_t$, substitute $D^* = 1 - D$. We have

$$Y_t = \alpha^* + \beta^*(1 - D_t) + u_t = \alpha^* + \beta^* - \beta^* D_t + u_t = \alpha + \beta D_t + u_t$$

We therefore see that $\beta^* = -\beta$, and $\alpha^* = \alpha - \beta^* = \alpha + \beta$. Thus, the new parameters are readily obtained from the original model estimates. R^2 and F are invariant under this linear transformation and hence will be unchanged.

Since u_t is the same, ESS will also not be affected. The standard error for β^* will be the same as that for β, its t-value will have the same value but the opposite sign, and the variance of $\hat{\alpha}^*$ is given by $\mathrm{Var}(\hat{\alpha}^*) = \mathrm{Var}(\hat{\alpha}) + \mathrm{Var}(\hat{\beta}) + 2\,\mathrm{Cov}(\hat{\alpha}, \hat{\beta})$. Its standard error is therefore the square root of this. The new t-statistic will be the sum of the regression coefficients divided by the new standard error just computed.

7.4   Let $A_3 = 1$ for young households (under 25 years of age) and 0 for others. If the middle group is the control, then, omitting A_2, the relevant dummy variables are A_3 and A_1 and the new model is

$$Y = a_0 + a_1 A_1 + a_2 A_3 + bX + u$$

Because $A_1 + A_2 + A_3 = 1$, $A_3 = 1 - A_1 - A_2$. Substituting this into the model we obtain

$$Y = a_0 + a_1 A_1 + a_2(1 - A_1 - A_2) + bX + u$$

$$= (a_0 + a_2) + (a_1 - a_2)A_1 - a_2 A_2 + bX + u$$

It follows from this that $\alpha_0 = a_0 + a_2$, $\alpha_1 = a_1 - a_2$, $-a_2 = \alpha_2$, and $b = \beta$. The coefficients of the new model can be derived from those of the previous model as follows:

$$\hat{b} = \hat{\beta}, \qquad \hat{a}_2 = -\hat{\alpha}_2, \qquad \hat{a}_1 = \hat{\alpha}_1 - \hat{\alpha}_2, \quad \text{and} \quad \hat{a}_0 = \hat{\alpha}_0 + \hat{\alpha}_2$$

The hypothesis that the senior age group behaves as a young household does is now tested with a t-test on a_2. The joint hypothesis $\alpha_1 = \alpha_2 = 0$ translates to $a_1 = a_2 = 0$ and can be tested with a Wald F-test. The hypothesis $\alpha_1 = \alpha_2$ now becomes $a_1 = 0$ and can be tested with a t-test on $\hat{a}_1$. We readily see that the two versions are basically equivalent, and hence it is immaterial which way the model is formulated.

7.6   Only part a is answered here; part b is left as an exercise. First write the saving relation for clerical workers and the same for skilled workers. The models are (ignoring the error term):

Clerical: $Y = (\beta_0 + \beta_8) + \beta_1 A_1 + \beta_2 A_2 + \beta_3 H + \beta_4 E_1 + \beta_5 E_2 + \beta_{10} X$

Skilled: $Y = (\beta_0 + \beta_7) + \beta_1 A_1 + \beta_2 A_2 + \beta_3 H + \beta_4 E_1 + \beta_5 E_2 + \beta_{10} X$

If the two groups behave identically, then β_7 must be equal to β_8. Therefore, the null hypothesis to test is $\beta_7 = \beta_8$. The unrestricted model is Equation (7.16), and the restricted model is obtained by imposing the condition $\beta_7 = \beta_8$.

$$Y = \beta_0 + \beta_1 A_1 + \beta_2 A_2 + \beta_3 H + \beta_4 E_1 + \beta_5 E_2$$
$$+ \beta_6 O_1 + \beta_7 O_2 + \beta_7 O_3 + \beta_9 O_4 + \beta_{10} X + u$$

Combining the β_7 terms, we get

$$Y = \beta_0 + \beta_1 A_1 + \beta_2 A_2 + \beta_3 H + \beta_4 E_1 + \beta_5 E_2$$
$$+ \beta_6 O_1 + \beta_7 (O_2 + O_3) + \beta_9 O_4 + \beta_{10} X + u$$

Before estimating this restricted model, create a new variable $Z = O_2 + O_3$. The actual test procedure is the Wald F-test, described in Section 4.4.

7.9   The income elasticities in the three periods are $\gamma_0, \gamma_0 + \gamma_1$, and $\gamma_0 + \gamma_1 + \gamma_2$. These elasticities will be the same only if $\gamma_1 = \gamma_2 = 0$. The test for this is the familiar Wald test. First estimate the unrestricted model given in Section 7.6. Next set γ_1 and γ_2 to 0 and estimate the restricted model. The relevant test statistic is F with 2 d.f. for the numerator and $n - 9$ d.f. for the denominator.

Exercises

7.2   a.   For the 1960–1981 period, D82 and D86 are both zero. The income elasticity is the coefficient of LY, which is 0.732, and the price elasticity is the coefficient of LP, which is -0.371. For the period 1982–1985, D82 = 1 and D86 = 0. Therefore, LYD1 becomes just LY. Hence, to get the income elasticity we should add the coefficients for LY and that for LYD1, which gives $0.732 - 2.602 = -1.870$. Similarly, price elasticity is $-0.371 + 0.288 = -0.083$. For the 1986–1988 period, D82 and D86 are both 1. Thus, the corresponding elasticities will be for income $0.732 - 2.602 + 3.298 = 1.428$, and for price $-0.371 + 0.288 = -0.083$.

b.   The unrestricted model is A. If there has been no structural change in the three periods, then the coefficients involving the dummy variable terms must be zero. The restricted model is therefore C.

c.   The null hypothesis is $\beta_5 = \beta_6 = \beta_8 = \beta_9 = 0$.

d.   The test statistic is the F-statistic given in Equation (4.3).

$$F_c = \frac{(\text{ESS}_C - \text{ESS}_A)/4}{\text{ESS}_A/(29 - 9)} = \frac{(0.04195 - 0.018645)/4}{0.018645/20} = 6.2497$$

e.   Under the null hypothesis, F_c has the F-distribution with 4 d.f. for the numerator and 20 d.f. for the denominator.

f.   From the F-table, $F^*_{4,20}(0.01) = 4.43$. Since $F_c > F^*$, we reject the null hypothesis.

g.   Rejecting the null implies that at least some of the βs in the null are not zero. This means that there has been significant structural change in the relationship.

7.4   a.   Multicollinearity does raise the standard errors, but none of the Assumptions 3.2 through 3.8 made in Chapter 3 are violated and hence OLS estimates are BLUE and t- and F-tests are valid. The statement is therefore invalid.

It is dangerous to jump to the conclusion that all insignificant variables should be dropped. Because of multicollinearity, it is possible that when just one variable is dropped, other previously insignificant variables become significant. By blindly omitting all insignificant variables we would have dropped variables that belong in the model, thus causing the omitted-variable bias problem. Estimates will then be biased and inconsistent, and all tests of hypotheses are invalid if variables that belong are omitted.

b.   The first step is to define a number of dummy variables as follows:

$D1$ = 1 if the student graduated from a public school, 0 otherwise
$D2$ = 1 if the student lived on campus, 0 otherwise
$D3$ = 1 if the student is a science major, 0 otherwise
$D4$ = 1 if the student is a social science major, 0 otherwise
$D5$ = 1 if the student is a humanities major, 0 otherwise
$D6$ = 1 if the student is an arts major, 0 otherwise

To avoid exact multicollinearity, we do not define a dummy for the undeclared major. It thus becomes the control group.

The hypothesis is that α is different across categories. Let $\alpha = a0 + a1\ D1 + a2\ D2 + a3\ D3 + a4\ D4 + a5\ D5 + a6\ D6$. Substituting this into Model A, we get Model B as

$$\text{UCGPA} = a0 + a1\ D1 + a2\ D2 + a3\ D3 + a4\ D4 + a5\ D5$$
$$+ a6\ D6 + \beta\ \text{HSGPA} + \gamma\ \text{VSAT} + \delta\ \text{MSAT} + u$$

c.   The null hypothesis is that α is *not* different for the different groups. Thus, H_0 is $a1 = a2 = a3 = a4 = a5 = a6 = 0$. The alternative is H_1: at least one of these is nonzero.

d.   To perform the LM test, first estimate the basic Model A and save its residuals as, say, UA. Next regress UA against all the variables in Model B, that is, a constant, HSGPA, VSAT, MSAT, and the six dummies. Compute the unadjusted R^2 from this auxiliary regression. The test statistic is $\text{LM} = 427\ R^2$. Under the null hypothesis, this has a chi-square distribution with 6 d.f. (the number of restrictions).

e.   From the chi-square table look up Chisq*(.05) for 6 d.f. and reject the null hypothesis (at the 5 percent level) if LM is greater than this. Alternatively, compute p-value = area to the right of LM in chi-square 6. Reject the null if the p-value is less than 0.05.

f.   Estimate Models A and B and save their error sum of squares as ESSA and ESSB. The Wald F-statistic is

$$F_c = \frac{(\text{ESSA} - \text{ESSB})/(\text{DFA} - \text{DFB})}{\text{ESSB}/\text{DFB}}$$

where DFA is the d.f. in Model A (= 427 − 4) and DFB is the d.f. in Model B (= 427 − 10). Under the null hypothesis, this has an F-distribution with 6 d.f. in the numerator and 417 d.f. in the denominator. From the

F-table look up *F**(.05) for the above d.f. and reject the null hypothesis if F_c is greater than *F**.

7.10 a.   Model B is the unrestricted model and Model A is the restricted model. Thus, the null hypothesis is $\beta_6 = \beta_7 = \beta_8 = \beta_9 = \beta_{10} = 0$.

b.   The Wald statistic is the *F*-statistic given in Equation (4.3).

$$F_c = \frac{(\text{ESS}_A - \text{ESS}_B)/5}{\text{ESS}_B/(41 - 10)} = \frac{(1.096191 - 0.7000959)/5}{0.700959/31} = 3.496$$

c.   Under the null hypothesis, F_c has the *F*-distribution with 5 d.f. for the numerator and 31 d.f. for the denominator.

d.   From the *F*-table, $F_{5,31}^*(0.05)$ is between 2.45 and 2.53.

e.   Since $F_c > F^*$, we reject the null hypothesis and conclude that at least some of the βs in the null are not zero. This means that there has been significant structural change in the relationship.

f.   For 1947–1978, $D = 0$ and hence

$$\ln(Q) = 2.476 - 0.991 \ln(P) - 0.817 \ln(\text{ACCID}) + 0.0009 \text{ FATAL}$$

For 1979–1987, $D = 1$ and hence

$$\ln(Q) = 2.476 - 0.991 \ln(P) - 0.817 \ln(\text{ACCID}) + 0.0009 \text{ FATAL}$$
$$+ 0.883 \ln(Y) + 0.849 \ln(\text{ACCID}) - 0.001 \text{ FATAL}$$
$$= 2.476 - 0.991 \ln(P) + 0.032 \ln(\text{ACCID})$$
$$+ 0.883 \ln(Y) - 0.0001 \text{ FATAL}$$

g.   We have

$$\ln(Q) = \beta_1 + \beta_2 \ln(P) + \beta_4 \ln(\text{ACCID}) + \beta_5 \text{ FATAL} + \beta_8 D$$
$$\times \ln(Y) + \beta_9 D \times \ln(\text{ACCID}) + \beta_{10} D \times \text{FATAL} + u$$

h.   The elasticity of ACCID in 1979–1987 when $D = 1$ is $\beta_4 + \beta_9 = 1$. Therefore, the null hypothesis is $\beta_4 + \beta_9 = 1$.

i.   Solve for β_9 as $1 - \beta_4$ and substitute in part g.

$$\ln(Q) = \beta_1 + \beta_2 \ln(P) + \beta_4 \ln(\text{ACCID}) + \beta_5 \text{ FATAL} + \beta_8 D \times \ln(Y)$$
$$+ (1 - \beta_4) D \times \ln(\text{ACCID}) + \beta_{10} D \times \text{FATAL} + v$$

Grouping terms and bringing $D \times \ln(\text{ACCID})$, which has no coefficient, to the left, we get

$$\ln(Q) - D \times \ln(\text{ACCID}) = \beta_1 + \beta_2 \ln(P) + \beta_4(1 - D) \ln(\text{ACCID})$$
$$+ \beta_5 \text{ FATAL} + \beta_8 D \times \ln(Y) + \beta_{10} D \times \text{FATAL} + u$$

This is the restricted Model R.

j.   The Wald statistic is the F-statistic given in Equation (4.3).

$$F_c = \frac{(\text{ESS}_R - \text{ESS}_U)/1}{\text{ESS}_U/(41 - 7)}$$

where ESS is the error sum of squares.

k.   Under the null hypothesis, F_c has the F-distribution with 1 d.f. for the numerator and 34 d.f. for the denominator.

l.   Compute p-value = area to the right of F_c in $F_{1,34}$. Reject the null if the p-value is less than the level of significance.

Chapter 8

Exercises

8.1

$$Y_t = \beta_1 + \beta_2 X_{t2} + \beta_3 X_{t3} + u_t$$

$$\sigma_t^2 = \sigma^2 Z_t^2$$

$$\text{ESS} = \sum (w_t Y_t - \beta_1 w_t - \beta_2 w_t X_{t2} - \beta_3 w_t X_{t3})^2$$

a. $\partial \text{ESS}/\partial \beta_1 = 0$ gives $\sum (w_t Y_t - \beta_1 w_t - \beta_2 w_t X_{t2} - \beta_3 w_t X_{t3}) w_t = 0$.
     $\partial \text{ESS}/\partial \beta_2 = 0$ gives $\sum (w_t Y_t - \beta_1 w_t - \beta_2 w_t X_{t2} - \beta_3 w_t X_{t3}) w_t X_{t2} = 0$.
     $\partial \text{ESS}/\partial \beta_3 = 0$ gives $\sum (w_t Y_t - \beta_1 w_t - \beta_2 w_t X_{t2} - \beta_3 w_t X_{t3}) w_t X_{t3} = 0$.

b.   Equation (8.9) is reproduced here:

$$\frac{Y_t}{Z_t} = \beta_1 \frac{1}{Z_t} + \beta_2 \frac{X_{t2}}{Z_t} + \beta_3 \frac{X_{t3}}{Z_t} + \frac{u_t}{Z_t}$$

The corresponding normal equations are the following:

$$\sum \left[\frac{Y_t}{Z_t} - \beta_1 \frac{1}{Z_t} - \beta_2 \frac{X_{t2}}{Z_t} - \beta_3 \frac{X_{t3}}{Z_t} \right] \frac{1}{Z_t} = 0$$

$$\sum \left[\frac{Y_t}{Z_t} - \beta_1 \frac{1}{Z_t} - \beta_2 \frac{X_{t2}}{Z_t} - \beta_3 \frac{X_{t3}}{Z_t} \right] \frac{X_{t2}}{Z_t} = 0$$

$$\sum \left[\frac{Y_t}{Z_t} - \beta_1 \frac{1}{Z_t} - \beta_2 \frac{X_{t2}}{Z_t} - \beta_3 \frac{X_{t3}}{Z_t} \right] \frac{X_{t3}}{Z_t} = 0$$

c.   It is readily seen that if w_t is replaced by $1/Z_t$, both sets of normal equations become identical.

8.3

$$Y_t = \beta X_t + u_t \qquad E(u_t) = 0 \qquad \sigma_t^2 = \sigma^2 X_t^2$$

a.   The slope of the straight line joining (X_t, Y_t) to the origin is Y_t/X_t. The average of this is

$$\tilde{\beta} = \frac{1}{n} \sum_{t=1}^{n} \left(\frac{Y_t}{X_t} \right)$$

b. Since $Y_t/X_t = \beta + (u_t/X_t)$, then $\tilde{\beta} = \beta + (1/n)\Sigma(u_t/X_t)$. Because X_t is nonrandom, $E(u_t/X_t) = [E(u_t)]/X_t = 0$. Hence $\tilde{\beta}$ is unbiased.

c. $Y_t = \beta X_t + u_t$ and $\mathrm{Var}(u_t) = \sigma^2 X_t^2$. Divide both sides of the model by X_t. We get $Y_t/X_t = \beta + u_t/X_t = \beta + v_t$. $E(v_t) = 0$ and $\mathrm{Var}(v_t) = \mathrm{Var}(u_t/X_t) = \sigma^2$. Therefore, v_t has all the properties for the application of OLS, including homoscedasticity. OLS can thus be applied to the transformed model to get an estimate of β that is BLUE. The OLS estimate for β in this model is given by

$$\min_{\beta} \Sigma v_t^2 = \min_{\beta} \Sigma\left(\frac{Y_t}{X_t} - \beta\right)^2$$

This gives

$$\Sigma\left(\frac{Y_t}{X_t} - \tilde{\beta}\right) = 0 \quad \text{or} \quad \tilde{\beta} = \frac{1}{n}\Sigma\left(\frac{Y_t}{X_t}\right)$$

which is the same as that derived in part a. It follows that $\tilde{\beta}$ is BLUE for β, which means that any other unbiased estimate, such as the OLS estimate using the original model $Y_t = \beta X_t + u_t$, will have a variance at least as large as that of $\tilde{\beta}$. $\tilde{\beta}$ is therefore most efficient.

8.10 $$S_t = \alpha + \beta Y_t + \gamma A_t + u_t$$

a. If σ_t depends on the size of the population P_t, then the variance σ_t^2 will depend on P_t^2. Assume that $\sigma_t^2 = \alpha_0 + \alpha_1 P_t^2 + \varepsilon_t$. The null hypothesis to test is $\alpha_1 = 0$. The steps are as follows:

Step 1 Estimate the model by OLS, save the residual $\hat{u}_t$, and square it to obtain $\hat{u}_t^2$.

Step 2 Regress $\hat{u}_t^2$ against a constant and P_t^2. (If the structure of the heteroscedasticity is unknown, the auxiliary regression is $\hat{u}_t^2$ against a constant, Y_t, A_t, Y_t^2, A_t^2, and $Y_t A_t$.)

Step 3 Compute nR^2, where n is the number of observations and R^2 is the unadjusted R^2 from the auxiliary regression of Step 2. Under the null hypothesis, this has a chi-square distribution with 1 d.f. (5 d.f. in the case of the unknown heteroscedasticity structure).

Step 4 Reject the null hypothesis of homoscedasticity (at the 5 percent level) if $nR^2 > \chi_1^2(0.05)$, the point on the distribution such that the area to the right is 0.05.

b. If heteroscedasticity is ignored, OLS estimates are still unbiased and consistent, but are not efficient (that is, not BLUE). This is because the proofs of unbiasedness and consistency depend only on the assumptions $E(u_t) = 0$ and $E(X_t u_t) = 0$, which are unaffected by heteroscedasticity. BLUE, on the other hand, requires that the error terms have constant variance.

c.　It is now given that $\sigma_t = \sigma P_t$. Divide the model by P_t:

$$\frac{S_t}{P_t} = \alpha\frac{1}{P_t} + \beta\frac{Y_t}{P_t} + \gamma\frac{A_t}{P_t} + \frac{u_t}{P_t}$$

Because $\mathrm{Var}(u_t/P_t)$ is σ^2, the OLS procedure can be applied to this transformed model, giving estimates that are BLUE. The procedure is to regress S_t/P_t against $1/P_t$, Y_t/P_t, and A_t/P_t, without a constant term.

Chapter 9

Exercises

9.1　a.　The assumption on the error term is that $u_t = \rho u_{t-1} + \varepsilon_t$, where ε_t is well behaved. The null hypothesis is that $\rho = 0$, and the alternative most common in economics is that $\rho > 0$. The number of observations is 23 and k' $(= k - 1)$ is 2. From Table A.5, the critical values are $d_L = 1.168$ and $d_U = 1.543$. Because the observed d is less than d_L, we reject the null hypothesis of no autocorrelation and conclude that there is significant first-order serial correlation. The OLS estimates are still unbiased and consistent, but are no longer efficient. Furthermore, all tests of hypotheses are invalid.

　　b.　First regress LH against a constant, LG, and LR, and save the residual as $\hat{u}_t$. Next regress $\hat{u}_t$ against a constant, LG, LR, and $\hat{u}_{t-1}$, and compute the unadjusted R^2 of this auxiliary regression. Reject the null hypothesis if $22R^2 > \chi_1^2(0.05)$, where $\chi_1^2(0.05)$ is the point on the chi-square distribution with 1 d.f. such that the area to the right is 0.05.

　　c.　For the Hildreth–Lu procedure, choose a ρ (call it ρ_1) and obtain $\mathrm{LH}_t^* = \mathrm{LH}_t - \rho_1\mathrm{LH}_{t-1}$, $\mathrm{LG}_t^* = \mathrm{LG}_t - \rho_1\mathrm{LG}_{t-1}$, and $\mathrm{LR}_t^* = \mathrm{LR}_t - \rho_1\mathrm{LR}_{t-1}$. Then regress LH_t^* against a constant, LG_t^*, and LR_t^*, and save the error sum of squares (ESS) of this regression. Next choose a different ρ_1 and repeat the process. By systematically searching from -1 to $+1$, we get a series of ESS values. The final estimate of ρ is the one that minimizes this ESS. This ρ is then used to transform the variables and a final regression run.

　　　　In the Cochrane–Orcutt procedure, the first step is to regress LH against a constant, LG, and LR, and save the residual as $\hat{u}_t$. Next compute $\hat{\rho} = (\Sigma \, \hat{u}_t\hat{u}_{t-1})/(\Sigma \, \hat{u}_t^2)$. Use this to obtain LH*, LG*, and LR* as in the Hildreth–Lu case. Then regress LH* against a constant, LG*, and LR*, and obtain new estimates of the regression coefficients. Use these then to obtain a second round of residuals, $\hat{u}_t$. The process is repeated until two successive estimates of ρ do not differ by more than some specified value.

　　　　Estimates obtained by the Hildreth–Lu and Cochrane–Orcutt procedures are more efficient than OLS estimates.

9.4　For $n = 22$, $k' = k - 1 = 3$, $d_L = 1.053$, $d_U = 1.664$. Because d $(= 1.147)$ is between these two values, the Durbin–Watson test is inconclusive. To apply the LM test, the first step is to regress LEMP against a constant, LINCM, LWAGE, and LG, and save the residual $\hat{u}_t$. Next regress $\hat{u}_t$ against a constant,

LINCM, LWAGE, LG, and $\hat{u}_{t-1}$, and compute R^2. The test statistic is $21R^2$ which, under the null hypothesis of zero first-order serial correlation, has a chi-square distribution with 1 d.f. Reject the null hypothesis at the 5 percent level if $21R^2 > \chi_1^2(0.05)$, the point such that the area to the right of it is 0.05. The steps for the Cochrane–Orcutt procedure are as follows:

Step 1　First estimate the model by OLS and obtain the residuals $\hat{u}_t =$ LEMP$_t$ + 3.89 − 0.51LINCM$_t$ + 0.25LWAGE$_t$ − 0.62LG$_t$.

Step 2　Estimate $\hat{\rho} = (\Sigma \hat{u}_t \hat{u}_{t-1})/(\Sigma \hat{u}_t^2)$.

Step 3　Transform the data as follows:

$$Y^* = \text{LEMP}_t - \hat{\rho}\text{LEMP}_{t-1}$$

$$X_1^* = \text{LINCM}_t - \hat{\rho}\text{LINCM}_{t-1}$$

and similarly for LWAGE and LG as X_2^* and X_3^*.

Step 4　Regress Y^* on a constant, X_1^*, X_2^*, and X_3^*, using

$$Y^* = \alpha_0 + \alpha_1 X_1^* + \alpha_2 X_2^* + \alpha_3 X_3^* + \text{error}$$

Step 5　From these estimates, obtain $\hat{u}_t$ of the *original* model again. Next go back to Step 2. The iteration ends when two successive estimates of ρ do not differ by more than some prespecified value.

This procedure gives consistent estimates that are more efficient than OLS estimates, but they are not unbiased or BLUE.

Chapter 10

Exercises

10.1

$$M_t = \alpha + \beta Y_t^* + \gamma R_t$$

$$Y_t^* = \lambda Y_{t-1} + (1 - \lambda) Y_{t-1}^* + u_t$$

a.　Multiplying the second equation by β, we have

$$\beta Y_t^* = \lambda \beta Y_{t-1} + (1 - \lambda)\beta Y_{t-1}^* + \beta u_t$$

Substituting this into the first equation, we get

$$M_t - \alpha - \gamma R_t = \lambda \beta Y_{t-1} + (1 - \lambda)(M_{t-1} - \alpha - \gamma R_{t-1}) + \beta u_t$$

$$M_t = \alpha - \alpha(1 - \lambda) + \lambda \beta Y_{t-1} + \gamma R_t$$
$$+ (1 - \lambda)M_{t-1} - (1 - \lambda)\gamma R_{t-1} + \beta u_t$$
$$= \alpha \lambda + \lambda \beta Y_{t-1} + \gamma R_t + (1 - \lambda)M_{t-1}$$
$$- (1 - \lambda)\gamma R_{t-1} + \beta u_t$$

which is estimable as

$$M_t = \beta_0 + \beta_1 Y_{t-1} + \beta_2 R_t + \beta_3 M_{t-1} + \beta_4 R_{t-1} + v_t$$

There is a problem here in that the estimates are not unique. For instance, $1 - \lambda = \beta_3$. Hence $\hat{\lambda} = 1 - \hat{\beta}_3$. Also, $\beta_2 = \gamma$ and $\beta_4 = -(1-\lambda)\gamma$. Therefore, $1 - \lambda = -\beta_4/\beta_2$ and, thus, $\tilde{\lambda} = 1 + (\hat{\beta}_4/\hat{\beta}_2)$. There is no reason to believe that $\hat{\lambda}$ and $\tilde{\lambda}$ will be the same. What is essentially happening is that there is a nonlinear restriction among the βs, namely, $\beta_2\beta_3 + \beta_4 = 0$. Any estimation procedure must take this into account.

b. Under the assumptions given, $E(u_t) = 0$ and u_t is not correlated with any of the independent variables. Therefore, OLS estimates are consistent. However, because M_{t-1} is on the right-hand side, we have a lagged dependent variable. This gives biased estimates in small samples.

c. If $u_t = \rho u_{t-1} + \varepsilon_t$, then M_{t-1} and u_t are correlated. Hence $E(M_{t-1}u_t) \neq 0$. To get unbiased and consistent estimates we need u_t to be uncorrelated with M_{t-1}, R_{t-1}, R_t, and Y_t. As this is not the case here, we get biased and inconsistent estimates.

10.4 a. H_0: $\rho = 0$, H_1: $\rho > 0$, where ρ is the first-order serial correlation; $n = 32$, $k' = 1$, $d_L = 1.373$, and $d_U = 1.502$. Because $d = 0.207 < d_L$, we reject H_0. We thus conclude that there is significant serial correlation.

b. The proof of unbiasedness does not require ρ to be equal to 0. Hence, OLS estimates are still unbiased. BLUE requires serial independence of errors and hence the estimates are no longer BLUE. Tests of hypotheses are invalid if there is serial correlation.

c. If $u_t = \rho u_{t-1} + \varepsilon_t$ is a good approximation to the error process, then the following procedure will "improve" the estimates:

Step 1   Use OLS on the model and get $\hat{u}_t$, the residuals.
Step 2   Compute $\hat{\rho} = (\Sigma \hat{u}_t \hat{u}_{t-1})/\Sigma(\hat{u}_t^2)$, an estimate of ρ.
Step 3   Transform the variables and obtain

$$C_t^* = C_t - \hat{\rho} C_{t-1} \quad \text{and} \quad Y_t^* = \ln Y_t - \hat{\rho} \ln Y_{t-1}$$

Step 4   Regress C^* against Y^* and a constant. From these obtain new estimates $\hat{u}_t$.
Step 5   Go back to Step 2 and iterate until two successive values of $\hat{\rho}$ differ by no more than a prespecified number (for example, 0.01).

By transforming the models, we get consistent and efficient estimates, and the tests of hypotheses are valid.

d. The new model has C_{t-1}, the lagged dependent variable. The presence of such a variable destroys the unbiasedness property. Therefore, the estimates are biased.

e. H_0: $\rho = 0$, H_1: $\rho > 0$. Because there is a lagged dependent variable, the Durbin *h*-test is the appropriate one:

$$h = \hat{\rho}\left[\frac{n'}{1 - n'\, s_{\hat{\beta}}^2}\right]^{1/2} = -0.39$$

where $n' = n - 1 = 31$. To get $s_{\hat{\beta}}^2$, divide the regression coefficient of C_{t-1} by its t-value and then square it. Because $|h| < 1.645$, the 10 percent critical value of the standard normal distribution, we fail to reject the null hypothesis (even at a 10 percent level), and conclude that there is no serial correlation.

f. Even though there is no serial correlation, because of the presence of a lagged independent variable, OLS estimates are biased. However, $\rho = 0$ implies that they are consistent.

Chapter 11

Exercises

11.6 The case of the first-order serial correlation is presented in Equation (9.4). If $u_t = \rho_1 u_{t-1} + \rho_3 u_{t-3} + \varepsilon_t$, then the forecast at time t is $\hat{Y}_t = \hat{\alpha} + \hat{\beta}X_t + \hat{\rho}_1\hat{u}_{t-1} + \hat{\rho}_3\hat{u}_{t-3}$. This forecast is defined only for $t = 4$ onward. Setting $\hat{u}_1 = \hat{u}_2 = \hat{u}_3 = 0$, we have the following:

$$\hat{Y}_4 = \hat{\alpha} + \hat{\beta}X_4 \qquad\qquad \hat{u}_4 = Y_4 - \hat{Y}_4$$
$$\hat{Y}_5 = \hat{\alpha} + \hat{\beta}X_5 + \hat{\rho}_1\hat{u}_4 \qquad\qquad \hat{u}_5 = Y_5 - \hat{Y}_5$$
$$\hat{Y}_6 = \hat{\alpha} + \hat{\beta}X_6 + \hat{\rho}_1\hat{u}_5 \qquad\qquad \hat{u}_6 = Y_6 - \hat{Y}_6$$
$$\hat{Y}_7 = \hat{\alpha} + \hat{\beta}X_7 + \hat{\rho}_1\hat{u}_6 + \hat{\rho}_3\hat{u}_4 \qquad\qquad \hat{u}_7 = Y_7 - \hat{Y}_7$$

The remaining periods are similar to $t = 7$.

11.8 Seasonal variations can be captured by 11 monthly dummies. Growth can be modeled by first converting the dependent variable to logarithms. Thus, a possible model is the following:

$$\ln(\text{SALES}_t) = \beta_0 + \beta_1 D_{t1} + \beta_2 D_{t2} + \cdots + \beta_{11} D_{t11} + \lambda t + u_t$$

$$u_t = \rho_1 u_{t-1} + \rho_2 u_{t-2} + \cdots + \rho_{12} u_{t-12} + \varepsilon_t$$

where λ is the exponential growth rate and D_{ti} is the tth observation on the dummy variable for the ith month. The second equation could also be modeled as a moving average—that is, as $\alpha_1\varepsilon_{t-1} + \alpha_2\varepsilon_{t-2} + \cdots + \alpha_{12}\varepsilon_{t-12}$.

11.10 Equation (10.10) has both a lagged dependent variable and a moving average error term, and hence the model is ARMA.

Chapter 12

Exercises

12.1 The linear probability model is $P_t = \beta_0 + \beta_1 A_t + \beta_2 N_t + \beta_3 S_t + u_t$, where t refers to the tth employee. The older an employee is, the greater is the probability of retirement. The longer the employee has been with the company, the greater is the probability of retirement. The higher the salary of the employee, the higher the pension and hence the smaller the opportunity cost of not working and hence the higher the probability of retirement. We would therefore expect β_1, β_2, and β_3 to be positive. The estimation procedure is to first regress the dummy variable P_t against a constant, A_t, N_t, and S_t. Next obtain the predicted probability of retirement as $\hat{P}_t = \hat{\beta}_0 + \hat{\beta}_1 A_t + \hat{\beta}_2 N_t + \hat{\beta}_3 S_t$. If $\hat{\sigma}_t^2 = \hat{P}_t(1 - \hat{P}_t)$ is positive, set the weight for the tth observation to $w_t = 1/\hat{\sigma}_t$; otherwise, set w_t to zero. Obtain weighted least squares estimates by regressing $(w_t P_t)$ against w_t, $(w_t A_t)$, $(w_t N_t)$, and $(w_t S_t)$.

12.3 If P_t is the fraction of employees who have recently retired, then the logit model is to regress $\ln[P_t/(1 - P_t)]$ against a constant, A_t, N_t, and S_t.

Chapter 13

Exercises

13.1 The model is $C_t = \alpha + \beta Y_t + u_t$.

a. *Functional form:* The model assumes that the marginal propensity to consume (MPC) is a constant β at all income levels. This is erroneous. Evidence indicates the MPC decreases with income. Thus,

$$C_t = \alpha + \beta Y_t + \gamma Y_t^2 + u_t \quad \text{or} \quad C_t = \alpha + \beta \ln Y_t + u_t$$

would be more appropriate.

Omitted variables: The model assumes that income is the only determinant of consumption. This is also wrong. Other variables such as wealth, past consumption, family size, or population are also important. Thus, such crucial variables are omitted. Similarly, with time series data, lagged variables should be included.

Heteroscedasticity: In cross-section studies it has been found that consumption patterns are much more varied for high-income groups than for low-income groups. Thus, the assumption that $E(u_t^2) = \sigma^2$ is unrealistic. It is more likely that σ_t^2 increases with income.

Serial correlation: In time series data, successive error terms are often correlated; that is, the assumption that $E(u_t u_s) = 0$ for $t \neq s$ is invalid in this case. Here also the error structure is misspecified. The assumption $u_t = \rho u_{t-1} + \varepsilon_t$ is better.

Simultaneous equation bias: At the aggregate level, $C_t = \alpha + \beta Y_t + u_t$ may be a part of a simultaneous equation model. For instance, $Y_t = C_t + I_t$ may be a second equation. Thus, there is a feedback effect from C to Y.

b. *Functional form:* Wrong functional form of the type specified is a misspecification in the deterministic part. $E(u_t) \neq 0$ here and hence estimates are biased. They can therefore not be BLUE. Estimates need not be consistent. F- and t-tests are therefore invalid.

Omitted variables: Same as above.

Heteroscedasticity: If heteroscedasticity is ignored, we still have $E(u_t) = 0$, and hence OLS estimates are unbiased. However, they are not BLUE because $E(u_t^2)$ is not a constant. As long as Y and u are uncorrelated, they will be consistent also.

Serial correlation: $E(u_t) = 0$ still holds, and hence OLS estimates are unbiased here also. But because $E(u_t u_s) \neq 0$ for $t \neq s$, they will not be BLUE. If Y_t and u_t are uncorrelated, estimates will be consistent.

Simultaneous equations bias: Now Y_t and u_t are correlated. Therefore, the estimates are biased and not consistent. They cannot be BLUE.

13.3
$$P = \alpha_1 + \alpha_2 N + \alpha_3 S + \alpha_4 A + u$$
$$N = \beta_1 + \beta_2 P + \beta_3 M + v$$

Endogenous: P and N, Exogenous: S, A, and M

a. This model corresponds to Model 4 of Section 13.3. We noted that the model is overidentified.
b. Because S, A, and M are exogenous, they are uncorrelated with both u and v. P and N are endogenous and are correlated with both u and v.
c. OLS estimates are biased and inconsistent.
d. Because the model is overidentified, indirect least squares is not applicable here.
e. In the first stage, regress P against a constant, S, A, and M, and save the predicted value $\hat{P}$. Similarly, regress N against a constant, S, A, and M, and save the predicted value $\hat{N}$. In the second stage, regress P against a constant, $\hat{N}$, S, and A to obtain TSLS estimates of the first equation. Regress N against a constant, $\hat{P}$, and M to obtain TSLS estimates of the second equation.

Practice Computer Sessions

As mentioned in the text, you are strongly encouraged to use your own regression program to reproduce the results of various examples and applications discussed in this book. All the data sets for the book are available (both on the CD accompanying the book and on the Internet at *http://econ.ucsd.edu/~rramanat/embook5.htm*) for access by almost every econometrics software package. The files are identified by the name DATAX-Y.suf, where *X* is the chapter number, *Y* is the file number within the chapter, and *suf* is the suffix for the file. For instance, DATA4-3.XLS refers to the data number 3 in Chapter 4, formatted as an Excel file. The suffix WK1 refers to an EViews workfile, the suffix LBL refers to the labels that the GRETL program uses, and the suffix HDR refers to a text file that contains the variable names, data sources, and units of measurement (described in detail in Appendix D). ASCII text files containing just the numerical data are denoted without any suffix (for example, DATA4-3).

The CD contains data in ASCII, EViews, and Excel formats, in "zipped" (that is, compressed) files. These can be unzipped using either WinZip *(http://www. winzip.com)* or PKUnzip *(http://www.pkware.com)*. Also available on the CD and the Internet is the *free* open source econometrics program GRETL developed by Professor Allin Cottrell. Details about this as well as other well-known econometrics software programs are provided next.

B34S

The B34S Data Analysis System is a full-featured econometrics package developed by Houston H. Stokes at the University of Illinois, Chicago *(hhstokes@uic.edu)*, with the help of others. The program is documented in *Specifying and Diagnostically Testing Econometric Models*, 2d ed. (Quorum, 1997) by Houston H. Stokes. Professor Stokes has implemented all the data sets in the present book in a file that can be read by his econometrics program at the address *http://www.uic.edu/~hhstokes/hhstokes/b34s.htm*. There is a free student version of B34S that can be downloaded from the Web. B34S is documented in his book (see his Web page). On the B34S page there are quick-start help documents. There is also an executable file that will install the program and our data set *ram.mac* on your machine. Once B34S is up, under FILE, select "run Macro." Then select *c:\b34slm\ram.mac* and you will have a menu of the data set.

EViews

This well-rounded econometrics package, developed by Quantitative Micro Software *(http://www.eviews.com)*, provides state-of-the-art time-series modeling techniques and a variety of single and simultaneous equation regression models, including limited dependent variable models and a number of other new estimators. A student version of EViews is available at an affordable price. As mentioned, all the data sets in the book are available in the EViews format. If you have the CD, unzip the file *eviews.zip* to get all the data files in the form DATAX-Y.WK1 and move them to the appropriate directory for loading with EViews. Otherwise, you can download *eviews.zip* from the file transfer address *ftp://ricardo.ecn.wfu.edu/pub/gretl_cdrom/data.*

Excel

Users who prefer the Microsoft Windows Excel program should use the data files set up as .XLS files. If you have the CD, unzip the file *excel.zip* to get all the data files in the form DATAX-Y.XLS and move them to the appropriate directory for loading with Excel. Otherwise, you can download *excel.zip* from the file transfer address *ftp://ricardo.ecn.wfu.edu/pub/gretl_cdrom/data.*

PcGive

PcGive is a statistical package, written by Jurge Doornik and David Hendry of Nuffield College, University of Oxford, U.K., that is particularly well suited for time series modeling involving the general-to-specific model building approach described in Chapter 6. The data sets and command files to reproduce the examples in this book using PcGive are available from *http://econ.ucsd.edu/~rramanat/pcgive.htm.* For details about free as well as professional versions of PcGive, visit *http://www.timberlake.co.uk/software/pcgive/pcgive.htm.*

SHAZAM

SHAZAM, authored by David Bates, Diana Whistler, Kenneth White, and Donna Wong of the University of British Columbia, Vancouver, Canada, is also an internationally popular program. It contains the techniques for estimating most econometric models. From the links to this book's site at *http://econ.ucsd.edu/~rramanat/shazam.htm* you can obtain sample documentation and data and run SHAZAM programs remotely. SHAZAM is also available on a CD that contains the data sets and commands for a number of econometrics texts, including this one.

Other Econometrics Programs

There are numerous other regression packages not directly linked to this book. Interested readers are referred to the Web site *http://www.oswego.edu* for details about them. If you plan to use the book's data sets with one of these programs, unzip the file *ascii.zip* in the CD to get the data files that contain just the numerical values of the data as the ASCII text file DATAX-Y, without a suffix. There is a corresponding header file, DATAX-Y.HDR, that contains the variable names, data sources, and units of measurement (also described in Appendix D). Move these files to the appropriate directory for loading with your regression program. If you don't have the

CD, visit *ftp://ricardo.ecn.wfu.edu/pub/gretl_cdrom/data* to download the file *ascii.zip,* and unzip it.

GRETL

The GRETL program (Gnu Regression, Econometrics, and Time-series Library) is mentioned last because this relatively new program is used extensively in this book to illustrate the examples. GRETL is included in the accompanying CD. As mentioned in the Preface, GRETL is the successor to ESLWIN, which was distributed with the previous edition of this book. The program is also available in other platforms such as Unix and Linux. GRETL is built around a freely shared library that may be accessed using a command-line interface program (GRETLCLI) or a graphical user interface (GRETL). If you have the CD, simply run the self-extracting executable program *setup.exe*. If you don't have the CD, download *gretl_install.exe* from *http://ricardo.ecn.wfu.edu/gretl/win32* and run it. You will be prompted for a location to install the package (the default is *c:\userdata\gretl,* but you can change it to suit your situation). The complete manual is also available on the CD as the PDF file *manual.pdf* and from the Web site *http://ricardo.ecn.wfu.edu/gretl/#man.* It is readable by Adobe Acrobat Reader, which is available free at the address *http://www.adobe.com/products/acrobat/readstep2.html.* If you plan to use GRETL, be sure to print out the complete manual and keep it handy. Since the GRETL program is updated often, it is wise to check periodically for updates. You can get on the GRETL mailing list and be notified of changes by signing up with *gretl-announce@ricardo.ecn.wfu.edu.* To reproduce all the examples in the book, there are 73 command files labeled "scripts" (denoted by the label PSX-Y.INP, where *X* is the chapter number) that can be readily run from GRETLCLI and GRETL.

Practice Computer Session

Interactive Mode
First click the GRETL icon to load the program. Next click "File," "Open data," "sample file," and "Ramanathan." You will see a list of the data files and a brief description of each one with *data2-1* highlighted. Appendix D has details about the units of measurement, sources, and so on. Click "open" and notice a list of variable names and descriptions with *vsat* highlighted. Next select (that is, click) "data" and "read info" to obtain more information about the variables in this data set. Then close this window and select "variable" and "frequency distribution." You will see a frequency distribution for *vsat.* Close this window and repeat the process for *msat.* Close all the windows and exit the program (for the present, say "no" to saving commands).

Batch Mode
Executing a file that contains a sequence (or batch) of ready-made commands is batch mode. To see this, run the program and select "File," "Open command file," "practice file," and "Ramanathan." The ready-made file *ps2-1.inp* will be highlighted. Selecting "open" will present a list of the GRETL commands in this file. Next choose "File" and "Run." All the commands will be executed and the results

printed on the screen. You can then choose "Save" from the "File" menu, and re-place the asterisk with a name (say *out2-1*). The resulting output file is *out2-1.txt* and can be viewed and printed using *Notepad* or *Winword*. You can also copy and paste parts or all of the results to another file for reporting purposes. After you have read all of Chapter 3 and later chapters, you should rerun GRETL and browse to learn more of its features. Address questions on GRETL to *cottrell@wfu.edu*.

Reproducing the Book's Examples Using GRETLCLI

The book's examples can also be reproduced using the command-line interface pro-gram GRETLCLI. This is run as the DOS command *gretlcli -b scriptfile > outfile.txt*. As an example, first exit temporarily to DOS, change the directory to the GRETL direc-tory (*cd c:\userdata\gretl*, for instance) and then type *gretlcli -b ps2-1.inp > out2-1.txt*. The ready-made command file *ps2-1.inp* will be run and the output stored as the ASCII text file *out2-1.txt*, which can be read by *Notepad* or *Winword*. Repeat this for *ps2-2.inp* and choose the name *out2-2.txt* for the output file.

APPENDIX D

Descriptions of the Data
and Practice Computer Sessions

This appendix describes in detail the data sets included on the accompanying disk and also posted on the Internet. All data values are arranged by observations, that is, in tabular form as in a spreadsheet. Table D.1 specifies where these data are used.

DATA2-1

Verbal and SAT scores of 427 first-year undergraduate students at UCSD.

vsat = Verbal SAT score (range 200–700)
msat = Math SAT score (range 330–770)

DATA2-2

High school and college GPA of 427 undergraduate students. Data reflect the first-year achievement.

colgpa = Grade point average in college (range 0.85–3.97)
 hsgpa = High school GPA (range 2.29–4.5)

DATA2-3

Annual data for the United States on unemployment and inflation rates and wage growth. Source: *1996 Economic Report of the President.*

　year = 1959–1995, 37 observations
unemp = Civilian unemployment rate (percent), Table B-38, range 3.5–9.7
　　cpi = Consumer price index (1982–1984 = 100), Table B-56, range
　　　　　29.1–152.4
　　infl = Percent change in cpi (inflation rate) calculated as
　　　　　$100*[\text{cpi}(t) - \text{cpi}(t-1)]/\text{cpi}(t-1)$ (range 0.69–13.5)
　wggr = Percent change in average weekly earnings, in current dollars,
　　　　　Table B-43 (range 1.9–8.5)

DATA3-1

Selling price and living area of 14 single-family homes in the University City community of San Diego in 1990.

price = Sale price in thousands of dollars (range 199.9–505)
sqft = Square feet of living area (range 1,065–3,000)

DATA3-2

Aggregate personal income and expenditures on health care, both measured in billions of dollars, for the U.S. states and Washington, D.C., in 1993. Source: *1995 Statistical Abstract of the U.S.*

exphlth = Personal health care expenditures, Table 153, page 111 (range 0.998–9.029)
income = Personal income, Table 712, page 460 (range 9.3–64.1)

Number of observations = 51

DATA3-3

Annual data on U.S. patents and R&D expenditures. Source for R&D expenditures: *1995 Statistical Abstract of the U.S.,* Table 979, page 611, and earlier issues. Source for GDP deflator: *1996 Economic Report of the President,* Table B-3, page 284. Source for patents: *Statistical Abstract of the U.S.,* various years.

YEAR = 1960–1993 (34 observations)
PATENTS = Patents in the number of applications filed in thousands (range 84.5–189.4)
R&D = R&D expenditures, billions of 1992 dollars obtained as the ratio of expenditure in current dollars divided by the GDP price deflator (range 57.94–166.7)

DATA3-4

Data on adjusted gross income and taxes by states (1992), including the District of Columbia (51 observations). Source: *1995 Statistical Abstract of the U.S.,* Table 537, page 347.

tax = Total income tax in billions of current dollars (range 0.895–62.48)
income = Adjusted gross income in billions of current dollars (range 6.198–453.941)

DATA3-5

Sealing compound shipment data, compiled by "Rodney Random." Monthly data for the period January 1983 through May 1990 (89 observations).

Q = Shipments of sealing compound used in construction in gallons/month (range 90–7,723)
P = Price per gallon in dollars (range 5.48–14.21)

DATA3-6

Per-capita consumption and disposable income in the United States. Source: *1996 Economic Report of the President.* Table B-27, page 311. (Range for Ct is 7,876–17,152 and for Yt is 8,641–18,320.)

year = 1959–1994 (36 observations)
   Ct = Personal consumption expenditures in constant 1992 dollars
   Yt = Per-capita disposable personal income in constant 1992 dollars

DATA3-7

Data for a Toyota station wagon (57 observations).

  cost = Cumulative repair cost in actual dollars (range 11–3,425)
  age = Age of car in weeks of ownership (range 5–538)
miles = Miles driven in thousands (range 0.8–74.4)

DATA3-8

Annual tuition and average salary gain for MBAs at the 25 top business schools in the country. Both measures are in thousands of dollars. Source: *Business Week,* October 21, 1996.

slrygain = Salary gain (range 27–60)
  tuition = Tuition (range 11.854–24.655)

DATA3-9

Data on return on equity and assets for 38 French companies (1995). Return is in percent (range 2.2–24.3) and assets are in billions of dollars (range 0.714–308.621). Source: *Business Week,* July 8, 1996, page 54.

DATA3-10

Data on total profits and sales of 27 German companies (1995). Profits are in millions of dollars (range 26–1,618) and sales are in billions of dollars (range 1.199–58.112). Source: *Business Week,* July 8, 1996, pages 54–55.

DATA3-11

Data on annual (1995) salary for 222 professors at the seven universities: UC Berkeley, UCLA, UC San Diego, Illinois, Michigan, Stanford, and Virginia.

salary = Annual salary in thousands of dollars (range 41.3–153)
  years = Number of years since Ph.D. (range 1–45)

DATA3-12

Population, in millions, of the United Kingdom for 1962–1994 (33 observations) (range 53.292–58.395). Source: *Annual Abstract of Statistics,* Central Statistical Office, 1996, Table 2.1, page 16.

DATA3-13

Annual data on U.S. population in millions for 1948–1995 (48 observations) (range 146.631–263.034). Source: *Economic Report of the President,* 1996, Table B-30, page 315.

DATA3-14

Aggregate expenditures on domestic travel and personal income, both measured in billions of dollars (1993), for the U.S. states and Washington, D.C. (51 observations). Source: *1995 Statistical Abstract of the U.S.* Travel expenditures, Table 428, page 266 (range 0.708–42.48); personal income, Table 712, page 460 (range 9.3–683.5).

DATA3-15

Annual data on U.S. population and GDP. Source: *Economic Report of the President,* 1996.

year = 1959–1994 (36 observations)
gdp = Real gross domestic product in billions of 1992 dollars, seasonally adjusted annual rates, Table B-2 (range 2,212.3–6,604.2)
pop = Population in millions, Table B-30, page 315 (range 177.82–260.66)

DATA4-1

Data on single-family homes in University City community of San Diego in 1990 (14 observations).

price = Sale price in thousands of dollars (range 199.9–505)
sqft = Square feet of living area (range 1,065–3,000)
bedrms = Number of bedrooms (range 3–4)
baths = Number of bathrooms (range 1.75–3)

DATA4-2

Annual data for the United States. Source: *1996 Economic Report of the President.*

YEAR = 1959–1994 (36 observations)
Ct = Real consumption expenditure in billions of 1992 dollars, Table B-2, page 282 (range 1,393.6–4,471.1)
Yt = Gross domestic product in billions of 1992 dollars, Table B-2, page 282 (range 2,212.3–6,604.2)

WAGES = Total compensation of employees in billions of current dollars, Table
　　　　　B-24, page 306 (range 281.2–4,008.3)
PRDEFL = Implicit price deflator for consumption expenditures, 1992 = 100,
　　　　　Table B-3, page 284 (range 22.8–105.1)

DATA4-3

Annual data on new housing units and their determinants. Source: *1987 Economic
Report of the President*. Because the housing series has been discontinued, this data
set could not be updated.

　　year = 1963–1985 (23 observations)
　housing = Total new housing units started in thousands, Table B-50 (range
　　　　　　1,072.1–2,378.5)
　　　pop = U.S. population in millions, Table B-30 (range 189.242–239.283)
　　　gnp = Gross national product in constant 1982 dollars in billions, Table B-2
　　　　　　(range 1,873.3–3,585.2)
　　unemp = Unemployment rate, in percents, among all workers, Table B-35 (range
　　　　　　3.4–9.5)
　intrate = New home mortgage yields, FHLBB, in percents, Table B-68 (range
　　　　　　5.81–15.14)

DATA4-4

Demand for bus travel and its determinants. All data are for 1988 for 40 cities across
the United States. Data compiled by Sean Naughton, sources unknown.

　BUSTRAVL = Demand for urban transportation by bus in thousands of
　　　　　　　passenger hours (range 18.1–1,310.3)
　　　　FARE = Bus fare in dollars (range 0.5–1.5)
　GASPRICE = Price of a gallon of gasoline in dollars (range 0.79–1.03)
　　INCOME = Average income per capita (range 12,349–21,886)
　　　　POP = Population of city in thousands (range 167–7,323.3)
　DENSITY = Density of city in persons per square mile (range 1,551–24,288)
LANDAREA = Land area of the city in square miles (range 18.9–556.4)

DATA4-5

The following are 1990 census data for the 50 U.S. states. The dependent variable is
the participation rate (in percents) of all women over 16. Data compiled by Louis
Cruz.

　wlfp = Persons 16 years and over—percent in labor force who are female (range
　　　　　42.6–66.4)
　　yf = Median earnings (in thousands of dollars) by females 15 years and over
　　　　　with income in 1989 (range 14.271–25.62)
　　ym = Median earnings (in thousands of dollars) by males 15 years and over with
　　　　　income in 1989 (range 21.425–35.622)

educ = Females 25 years and over—percent high school graduate or higher (range 64.5–86.1)

ue = Civilian labor force—percent unemployed (range 3.5–9.6)

mr = Female population 15 and over—percent now married (excluding separated) (range 46.88–60.92)

dr = Female population 15 and over—percent who are divorced (range 6.42–15.06)

urb = Percent of population living in urban areas (range 32.2–92.6)

wh = Female population—percent 16 years and over who are white (range 24.69–77.73)

DATA4-6

Data on poverty rates and determinants across California counties. The following was extracted from the *County and City Data Book* (1994) for California counties by Kalena Cortes ($n = 58$).

povrate = Percent of families with income below poverty level (range 3–20.8)

urb = Percent of population in urban area (range 2.7–94.3)

famsize = Persons per household (range 2.29–3.26)

unemp = Percent unemployment rate (range 4–21.3)

highschl = Percent of the population (25 years and over) that had only high school education (range 43–68.5)

college = Percent of the population (25 years and over) that completed four years of college or higher (range 9–44)

medinc = Median family income in thousands of dollars (range 24.364–59.147)

DATA4-7

Death rates in the United States due to coronary heart disease and their determinants. Data compiled by Jennifer Whisenand for 1947–1980 (34 observations).

chd = Death rate per 100,000 population (range 321.2–375.4)

cal = Per-capita consumption of calcium per day in grams (range 0.9–1.06)

unemp = Percent of civilian labor force unemployed in persons 16 years and older (range 2.9–8.5)

cig = Per-capita consumption of cigarettes in pounds of tobacco by persons 18 years and older—approximately 339 cigarettes per pound of tobacco (range 6.75–10.46)

edfat = Per-capita intake of edible fats and oil in pounds–includes lard, margarine, and butter (range 42–56.5)

meat = Per-capita intake of meat in pounds—includes beef, veal, pork, lamb, and mutton (range 138–194.8)

spirits = Per-capita consumption of distilled spirits in taxed gallons for individual 18 and older (range 1–2.9)

beer = Per-capita consumption of malted liquor in taxed gallons for individuals 18 and older (range 15.04–34.9) wine = Per-capita consumption of wine measured in taxed gallons for individuals 18 and older (range 0.77–2.65)

DATA4-8

Data on cable systems in the top 40 television markets in 1979 (DATA7-22 has the 1994 data also). Source: *Broadcasting Yearbook 80.* Data compiled by David Andersen.

sub = Number of subscribers of each system in thousands (range 1–170)

home = Number of homes (in thousands) passed by each system (range 1.7–350)

inst = Installation fee in dollars (range 5.95–25)

svc = Monthly service charge of each system (range 5.6–10)

tv = Number of television signals carried by each cable system (range 6–22)

age = Age of each system in years (range 0.17–26)

air = Number of television signals received (range 4–13)

y = Per-capita income for each television market with cable in dollars (range 7,683–11,741)

DATA4-9

Data on early retirement and its determinants for 1979–1980, compiled by David Andersen for 44 U.S. states. Source unknown.

rtrd = Percent of retired men who are between the ages of 16 and 65 (range 5.4–18.7)

hlth = Percent of people between 16 and 64 years who are prevented from working due to a disability (range 1.6–7.6)

mssec = Mean Social Security income in dollars (range 3,449–4,399)

mpubas = Mean public assistance income in dollars (range 1,854–3,079)

unemp = Unemployment rate in percent (range 3.6–9.5)

dep = Percent of households that are made up of married couples with children under 18 years of age (range 12.6–42.6)

race = Percent of men who are nonwhite (range 0.8–72.8)

DATA4-10

The following data were compiled by Jeffrey Wong for a study involving parental school choice in the United States. All data are for 1986, unless otherwise noted, and are for all 51 states (including Washington, D.C.).

ENROLL = Proportion of students that enroll in private schools. (The data for private school enrollment for each state was found by indexing public school enrollment values of 1980 and 1986. This index was then used to calculate the private school enrollment for 1986. Thus, the private school enrollment values are indexed numbers. This should not cause any problem in the model because the enrollment trends in public and private education do not alter drastically from year to year.) Source: *Digest of Education Statistics,* 1990. (range 0.16–0.255)

CATHOL = Proportion of population, in each state, that is Catholic. Source: *The Official Catholic Directory,* 1986 (range 0.02105–0.65234)

PUPIL = Pupil-to-teacher ratio for public schools in each state. Source: *Digest of Education Statistics,* 1990 (range 13.7–23.4)

WHITE = Proportion of population, in each state, that is white. Source: *United States Statistical Abstract,* 1988 (range 0.3–0.987)

ADMEXP = Proportion of educational expenditures devoted to administrative expenses. Source: *Condition of Education,* 1990 (range 0.268–0.518)

REV = Per-pupil education revenue (in thousands of dollars) for each state. Source: *Condition of Education,* 1990 (range 1.933–5.982)

MEMNEA = Proportion of all public teachers who are members of the National Education Association. Source: *National Education Association Handbook* (range 0.0573–0.999)

INCOME = Per-capita income (in thousands of dollars) of household families. Source: *United States Statistical Abstract,* 1988 (range 9.665–19.548)

COLLEGE = Proportion of the population that has completed at least four years of college. Source: *United States Statistical Abstract Supplement, State and Metropolitan Data Book,* 1986 (range 0.104–0.275).

DATA4-11

Data on private housing units authorized, compiled by Susan Huberman. The data are cross-sectional for 40 cities in the United States.

HOUSING = New private housing units authorized by building permits for 1992 in number of houses (range 39–5,222)

DENSITY = Population density per square mile for 1992 in number of persons (range 746–23,671)

VALUE = Median value for owner-occupied home during 1990 in hundreds of dollars (range 256–2,989)

INCOME = Median household income for 1989 in thousands of dollars (range 16.925–46.206)

POPCHANG = Percent change in population from 1980 to 1992 (range 15.9–59.1)

UNEMP = Unemployment rate for civilian labor force during 1990 in percents (range 4.7–19.7)

(Data for variables above taken from *County and City Data Book, 1994,* cities tables, pages 650–853.)

LOCALTAX = Average local taxes per capita for 1992 in dollars (range 239–2,341)

STATETAX = Average state tax per capita for 1993 in dollars (range 1,005–1,725)

(Data for variables above taken from 1995 *Statistical Abstract of the U.S.,* Tables 502 and 492.)

DATA4-12

This data set was compiled by Marc Selznick. It relates the mortality rate in a state to a number of socioeconomic variables. Data are for the U.S. states and Washington, D.C. ($n = 51$). All variables are in per-capita amounts or represent proportions of state populations.

MORT = Total mortality rate per 100,000 population. Source: National Center for Health Statistics, "Advance Report of Final Mortality Statistics, 1985," August 28, 1987, Table 17, pages 42–43 (range 396.2–1,120.5)

INCC = Per-capita income by state in dollars. Source: *Pennsylvania Department of Labor and Industry Annual, 1986,* Table 20 (range 9,187–18,187)

POV = Proportion of families living below the poverty line. Source: *Statistical Abstract of the United States,* 1990, Table 742 (range 0.079–0.239)

EDU1 = Proportion of population completing four years of high school. Source: U.S. Department of Education, *Digest of Education Statistics,* 1987, Table 10 (range 0.531–0.825)

EDU2 = Proportion of population completing four or more years of college. Source: U.S. Department of Education, *Digest of Education Statistics,* 1987, Table 10 (range 0.104–0.275)

ALCC = Per-capita consumption of alcohol in gallons. Source: Metropolitan Life Insurance Company, "Alcohol Use in the U.S.," January–March 1987, page 22 (range 1.53–5.34)

TOBC = Per-capita consumption of cigarettes in packs. Source: *Tobacco Institute Annual,* 1987, "Tax Burden on Tobacco," Table 11 (range 66.5–201.1)

HEXC = Per-capita health care expenditures in dollars (personal, state, and federal spending). Source: *Almanac of the 50 States,* 1987, various tables (by state), pages 9–357 (range 1,203–3,872)

PHYS = Physicians per 100,000 population. Source: Health Insurance Association of America, *Source Book of Health Insurance Data, 1986–7,* Table 7.1 (range 117–552)

URB = Proportion of population over the age of 65. Source: *Statistical Abstract of the United States,* 1990, page xii, state rankings section (range 0.2–1)

AGED = Proportion of population over the age of 65. Source: U.S. Department of Commerce, *Current Population Reports,* 1987, Table 8, page 86 (range 0.034–0.177)

DATA4-13

Data on the factors affecting baseball attendance in 78 metropolitan areas, compiled by Scott Daniel.

ATTEND = Attendance in thousands for 1984–1986. Source: *The Sporting News Official Baseball Guide,* 1985, 1986, and 1987, pages 267, 286, and 287 (range 655.181–3,264.593)

POP = Population of the metropolitan area where the team is located in thousands. Source: *Statistical Abstract of the United States: 1981,*

Table 23, pages 18–20. For the Canadian cities, the source is the *Canada Year Book*, 1980–1981, Table 4.9, page 133 (range 1,327–9,120)

CAPACITY = Capacity of the stadium where the team plays its home games in thousands. Source: *The Sporting News Official Baseball Guide*, 1984, 1985, and 1986, pages 280–320 (range 33.583–74.208)

PRIORWIN = Number of wins the team had in the year prior to the year under examination. Source: *The Sporting News Official Baseball Guide*, 1984, 1985, and 1986, pages 86 and 160 for the 1984 edition, pages 86 and 160 for the 1985 edition, and pages 86 and 160 for the 1986 edition (range 57–104)

CURNTWIN = Number of wins the team had in the year under study. Source: editions of *The Sporting News Baseball Guide*, 1985, 1986, and 1987, pages 86 and 160 for 1985 and 1986 editions, pages 78 and 162 for the 1987 edition (range 57–108)

G1 = Number of games behind the division leader the team is in the standings on April 30. These are calculated using the individual team reports found in *The Sporting News Official Baseball Guide*, 1985, 1986, 1987, located from pages 30–160 in each edition (range 0–10.5)

G2 = Number of games behind the division leader the team is on May 31; see above for source (range 0–19.5)

G3 = Number of games behind the division leader the team is on June 30; see above for source (range 0–22.5)

G4 = Number of games behind the division leader the team is on July 31; see above for source (range 0–31)

G5 = Number of games behind the division leader the team is on August 31; see above for source (range 0–37)

GF = Number of games behind the division leader the team is after the season was over; see above for source (range 0–44)

OTHER = Number of other baseball teams in the metropolitan area (range 0–1)

TEAMS = Number of football, basketball, or hockey teams found in the metropolitan area. The leagues included are the NFL, the CFL, the NBA, and the NHL. This was independently researched by going through old *Sporting News Guides* for each of these individual leagues. The years covered were the guides for 1984, 1985, and 1986 for the NFL and the CFL, and the 1984–1985, 1985–1986, 1986–1987 guides for the NHL and the NBA (range 1–7)

DATA4-14

Annual tuition and salary gain for MBAs at the 25 top business schools in the country. This data set is an expanded version of DATA3-8.

slrygain = Average salary gain in thousands of dollars
tuition = Annual tuition in thousands of dollars

Range for tuition is 11.854–24.655 and range for salary gain is 27–60. The file also includes additional data on ratings by recruiters and MBAs in various categories. Ratings are from 1 (A) to 4 (D). Source: *Business Week,* October 21, 1996.

$z1$ = MBA skills graded by recruiters in being analysts
$z2$ = MBA skills graded by recruiters in being team players
$z3$ = MBA skills graded by recruiters in having a global view
$z4$ = Teaching evaluation by MBAs
$z5$ = Curriculum evaluation by MBAs

DATA4-15

Cross-country data ($n = 41$) on inequality coefficients for 1989 base, compiled by Elmer Gamoning.

Y = Gini coefficient range $0 < Yt < 1$; 0 is perfect equality. Source: Deininger, Klaus, and Lyn Squire, "Measuring Income Inequality: A New Database" (range 0.183–0.596)
Gnp = Per-capita gross national product (base 1989). Source: World Bank: World Data CD-Rom 1995 (range 200–25,450)
Gdp = Growth rate (percent) of gross domestic product. Source: World Bank: World Data CD-Rom 1995 (range 8.9–12.7)
pop = Growth rate of population (percent). Source: World Bank: World Data CD-Rom 1995 (range 0.1–3.3)
urb = Measure of people living in urban areas (percent) (range 10.9–100)
lit = Percent of people in country who can read and write. Sources: Charity A. Dorgan, editor. *Gale Country and World Rankings Reporter,* Gale Research, MI. 1995; *Social Indicators of Development,* The Johns Hopkins University Press, MD, 1996; *Statistical Yearbook,* 40th issue, United Nations Publications, 1995 (range 29.2–99)
edu = Secondary school enrollment expressed as percent of the total population of secondary school age. Source: *World Tables 1995,* The Johns Hopkins University Press, MD, 1995 (range 12–99).
agr = Share of agriculture of GDP (percent). Source: *Statistical Abstract of the World* (range 0.7–56.3)

DATA4-16

Data on private school enrollment and its determinants for the 50 U.S. States and the District of Columbia, compiled by Colleen Dempsey.

enroll = Percent of students that enrolled in private schools. Data year: 1993. Sources: *Digest of Education Statistics,* 1996, *Projections of Education Statistics to 2007.*
cathol = Percent of the population in each state that is Catholic. Data year: 1990. Source: *Churches and Church Membership in the United States,* 1990.
pupil = Pupil-to-teacher ratio for public schools in each state. Data year: 1990. Source: *Digest of Education Statistics,* 1996.

white = Percent of population in each state that is white. Data year: 1990. Source: *1993 Statistical Abstract of the U.S.*

admexp = Percent of educational expenditures devoted to administration. Data year: 1993. Source: *Digest of Education Statistics,* 1996.

revenue = Per-pupil education revenue in thousands of dollars. Data year: 1991. Sources: *Digest of Education Statistics,* 1996. *1997 Statistical Abstract of the U.S.* Projections of Education Statistics to 2007.

memnea = Percent of all public school teachers who are members of the National Education Association. Data year: 1986. Source: *National Education Association Handbook.*

income = Per-capita income in thousands of dollars. Data year: 1990. Source: *1997 Statistical Abstract of the U.S.*

college = Percent of the population who has completed at least four years of college. Data year: 1990. Source: *1997 Statistical Abstract of the U.S.*

DATA4-17

Data on AFDC (Aid to Families with Dependent Children) payments and their determinants, compiled by Simon Park for the 58 counties of California, June 1999.

afdc = Percent of population on AFDC

unemp = Unemployment rate

welfexp = Percent of local government finances for public welfare

income = Median household income

hseduc = Percent of population with high school education (for population 25 yrs. and older)

colgeduc = Percent of population with college education (for population 25 yrs. and older)

white = Percent of population who are white

hispanic = Percent of population who are Hispanic

women = Percent of population who are women

femhh = Percent of female family householder (no spouse present)

poverty = Percent of population below poverty level

mother20 = Percent of mothers who are under age 20

unwed = Percent of mothers who are unmarried

mothredc = Percent of mothers who have under 12 years of education

medical = Percent of births funded by MEDI-CAL

DATA6-1

Data on cost function for a company for 20 years. Source: W. A. Spurr and C. P. Bonini, *Statistical Analysis for Business Decisions,* Irwin, 1973, page 535.

UNITCOST = Cost per unit in dollars (range 3.65–6.62)

OUTPUT = Index of output (range 50–104)

INPCOST = Index of input costs (range 80–150)

DATA6-2

Data on the white tuna (Thunnus Alalunga) fishery production in the Basque region of Spain. Data compiled by Felix Telleria.

year = 1961–1994 (34 observations)
catch = Total catch in thousands of tonnes (range 16.608–51.8)
effort = Total days of fishing in thousands (range 10.31185–61.24754)

DATA6-3

United Kingdom annual data. Source: *Economic Trends*, Annual Supplement, 1991 edition, a publication of the Government Statistical Service, London, UK.

Year = 1948–1989 (42 observations)
Cons = Per-capita consumption expenditure in British pounds (range
         1,858–4,744)
  DI = Per-capita personal disposable income in British pounds (range
         1,875–5,084)

DATA6-4

Data on salaries and employment characteristics of 49 employees in a certain company. Data compiled by Susan Wong.

WAGE = Wage rate per month (range 981–3,833)
EDUC = Years of education beyond eighth grade when hired (range 1–11)
EXPER = Number of years at the company (range 1–23)
  AGE = Age of employee (range 25–64)

DATA6-5

This is time series data from 1959 to 1989 ($n = 31$) measuring Oregon's total softwood harvest. All data are entered on a yearly basis. Compiled by Anthony Hazen.

HARVEST = Total softwood timber harvested from Oregon in a given year. Data
             are in billion board feet (range 5.1212–8.743)
EXPORTS = Volume of timber exports to foreign destinations measured in 100
             million board feet (range 1.469–13.874)
HOUSTART = Total housing starts in the United States in millions (range
             1.072–2.379)
INDPROD = Index of industrial production for paper and wood products
             (range 4.75–15.57)
TIMBPRIC = Stumpage prices for the Pacific Northwest. Prices are measured in
             dollars per 1,000 board feet (range 2.48–43.22)
PRODPRIC = Producer price index for all commodities (range 3.16–10.87)

DATA6-6

Annual data on U.S. farm population. Source: *1996 Economic Report of the President,* Table B-96.

　　year = 1948–1991 (44 observations)
farmpop = Farm population as percent of total population (range 1.9–16.6)

DATA7-1

Data on salaries and gender of 49 employees in a certain company. Data compiled by Susan Wong.

WAGE = Wage rate per month (range 981–3,833)
　　D = 1 for male, 0 for female

DATA7-2

Data on salaries and employment characteristics of 49 employees in a certain company. Data compiled by Susan Wong.

　　　WAGE = Wage rate per month (range 981–3,833)
　　　EDUC = Years of education beyond eighth grade when hired (range 1–11)
　　 EXPER = Number of years at the company (range 1–23)
　　　 AGE = Age of employee (range 25–64)
　GENDER = 1 for male, 0 for female
　　 RACE = 1 for white, 0 for nonwhite
CLERICAL = 1 for clerical workers, 0 for others
　 MAINT = 1 for workers in maintenance, 0 for others
　 CRAFTS = 1 if employee was in crafts, 0 otherwise

Control group is composed of professionals.

DATA7-3

Determinants of the sale price of single-family homes ($n = 14$) in the University City community of San Diego in 1990.

　　　price = Sale price in thousands of dollars (range 199.9–505)
　　　 sqft = Living area in square feet (range 1,065–3,000)
　 bedrms = Number of bedrooms (range 3–4)
　　 baths = Number of bathrooms (range 1.75–3)
　　　 pool = 1 if the house has a swimming pool, 0 otherwise
famroom = 1 if the house has a family room, 0 otherwise
　　 firepl = 1 if the house has a fireplace, 0 otherwise

DATA7-4

The following are from 1980 and 1990 census data by state ($n = 100$). The data for 1980 were compiled by Katherine McGregor and the data for 1990 were compiled by Louis Cruz.

WLFP = Persons 16 years and over—percent in labor force who are female (range 36.5–66.4)

YF = Median earnings in dollars by females 15 years and over with income in 1979 (observations 1–50) and 1989 (observations 51–100) (range 2,366–25,620)

YM = Median earnings in dollars by males 15 years and over with income in 1979 (observations 1–50) and 1989 (observations 51–100) (range 5,842–35,622)

EDUC = Females 25 years and over—percent who are high school graduates or have obtained higher education (range 49.8–86.1)

UE = Civilian labor force—percent unemployed (range 2.8–9.6)

MR = Female population 15 and over—percent now married (excluding separated) (range 46.88–65.2)

DR = Female population 15 and over—percent who are divorced (range 3–16.8)

URB = Percent of population living in urban areas (range 32.2–92.6)

WH = Female population—percent 16 years and over who are white (range 24.69–99.2)

D90 = 1 for 1990 census, 0 for 1980 census

DATA7-5

Sealing compound shipment data, compiled by "Rodney Random," for January 1983 through May 1990 ($n = 89$).

Q = Shipments of sealing compound used in construction in gallons per month (range 90–7,723)

P = Price per gallon in dollars (range 5.48–14.21)

HS = Housing starts in thousands (range 75–188.2)

SHC = Index of street and highway construction (range 403.1–1,978.8)

OC = Overall index of public and private construction (range 107–186)

L = 1 for July 1986 through October 1988, when company suffered losses due to rumors spread by a rival company

PL = 1 from November 1988 onward, the postloss period

DATA7-6

Data on poverty rates and determinants across 58 California counties. 1980 census data were compiled by Susan Wong. 1990 census data were extracted from the *County and City Data Book* (1994) for California counties by Kalena Cortes.

povrate = Percent of families with income below poverty level (range 4.5–18.1)

urb = Percent of urban population (range 0–100)

famsize = Persons per household (range 2.76–3.73)

unemp = Percent unemployment rate (range 3.5–17.6)

highschl = Percent of the population (25 years and over) that had only a high school education (range 41.3–65.5)

college = Percent of the population (25 years and over) that completed four years of college or higher (range 9–38.3)

medinc = Median family income in thousands of dollars (range 13.522–29.721)
D90 = 1 for the 1990 census, 0 for the 1980 census

DATA7-7

Data on annual (1995) salary for 222 professors at the seven universities: UC Berkeley, UCLA, UC San Diego, Illinois, Michigan, Stanford, and Virginia. This is an expanded version of DATA3-11.

salary = Annual salary in thousands of dollars (range 41.3–153)
years = Number of years since Ph.D. (range 1–45)

In addition, $d1$ through $d6$ are dummy variables for six universities, but they are not specifically identified so as to maintain the confidentiality.

DATA7-8

Cross-country data for economic growth and its determinants. Data are from Mankiw, Romer, and Weil, *Q JE*, 1992.

grth = Log of change in income 1960–1985 (dependent variable)
y60 = Log of income in 1960
inv = Average investment to GNP ratio over 60–85
pop = Measure of population growth expressed in logarithms
school = Measure of percent of population in school
dn = Dummy for nonoil
di = Dummy for industrialized
doecd = Dummy for OECD

DATA7-9

Data reflects first-year achievement of 427 students who entered college in Fall 1985. Compiled by Susan Wong.

colgpa = Grade point average at college, Fall 1986 (range 0.85–3.97)
hsgpa = High school GPA (range 2.29–4.5)
vsat = Verbal SAT score (range 200–700)
msat = Math SAT score (range 330–770)
dsci = 1 for a science major, 0 otherwise
dsoc = 1 for a social science major, 0 otherwise
dhum = 1 for a humanities major, 0 otherwise
darts = 1 for an arts major, 0 otherwise
dcam = 1 if student lives on campus, 0 otherwise
dpub = 1 if student attended public high school, 0 otherwise

DATA7-10

Data on air quality and its determinants for 30 SMSAs (Standard Metropolitan Statistical Areas) in California. Data compiled by Susan Wong are for 1970–1972.

airqual = Weight of suspended particle matter (range 59–165)

popln = Population in thousands (range 372–11,529)

valadd = Value added by industrial manufactures in 1972 in thousands of dollars (range 992.9–19,733.8)

rain = Rainfall in inches (range 12.63–68.13)

coast = 1 for SMSAs on the coast, 0 otherwise

density = Population per square mile of area (range 271.59–12,957.5)

medincm = Median per-capita income (range 853–59,460)

poverty = 100 times the percent of families with income less than poverty levels (range 117–1,939)

electr = Electricity consumed by industrial manufacturers in megawatt hours (range 1.7–169.8)

fueloil = Thousands of barrels of fuel oil consumed in industrial manufacturing (range 18.4–1,912.9)

indestab = Number of industrial establishments with 20 or more employees (range 221–9,466)

DATA7-11

Data on 59 single-family houses sold in 1984 in the La Jolla and University City areas of San Diego. Obtained from multiple listing service.

price = Sale price in thousands of dollars (range 110–590)

age = Age of house in years (range 1–60)

aircon = 1 if house has central air-conditioning, 0 otherwise

baths = Number of bathrooms (range 1–5)

bedrms = Number of bedrooms (range 2–5)

cond = Condition of house from poor (1) to excellent (6)

corner = 1 if the house is a corner lot, 0 otherwise

culd = 1 if the house is in a cul-de-sac, 0 otherwise

dish = 1 if the house has a built-in dishwasher, 0 otherwise

fence = 1 if the house has a fence, 0 otherwise

firepl = Number of fireplaces (range 0–2)

floors = Number of floors (range 1–2)

garage = Number of car spaces in garage (range 0–3)

irreg = 1 if lot is irregular in shape, 0 otherwise

lajolla = 1 if the house is located in La Jolla, 0 otherwise

lndry = 1 if the house has a laundry area, 0 otherwise

patio = Number of patios (range 0–2)

pool = 1 if the house has a swimming pool, 0 otherwise

rooms = Number of rooms excluding bedrooms and baths (range 1–5)

sprink = 1 if there is a sprinkler system, 0 otherwise

sqft = living area in square feet (range 950–3,775)

view = 1 if the house has a view, 0 otherwise

yard = yard size in square feet (range 1,530–36,304)

DATA7-12

Data on list price and characteristics of 1995 model, American-made, two-door sedans and hatchbacks only. Source: *1995 Wards Automotive Yearbook,* pages 239–244.

price = List price in thousands of dollars (range 8.395–68.603)
hatch = 1 for a hatchback, 0 for sedan
wbase = Wheel base in inches (range 93.1–113.8)
length = Length of car in inches (range 149.4–207.3)
width = Width of car in inches (range 53.9–75.5)
height = Height in inches (range 46.3–55.2)
weight = Weight of car in hundreds of pounds (range 18.08–38.18)
cyl = Number of cylinders (range 3–8)
liters = Engine displacement in liters (range 1–2.3)
gasmpg = Estimated gas mile per gallon, averaged between city and freeway driving (range 20.5–51.5)
trans = 1 for automatic transmission, 0 otherwise

DATA7-13

Data on 252 families receiving unemployment compensation in 1982. All data are from the Panel Study of Income Dynamics, 1983 interviewing year, Wave XVI. Data compiled by David Arroyo.

UCOMP = Amount of unemployment compensation received in dollars (range 95–9,672)
UHOURS = Head of household's hours of unemployment in 1982 (range 40–2,080)
HEADY = Head of household's labor income in 1982 in dollars (range 0–32,000)
SPOUSEY = Spouse's labor income in 1982 in dollars (range 0–18,000)
EDUC = Number of grades of school completed by the head of household (range 7–17)
MALE = Gender of head of household, 1 if male, 0 if female
MARRIED = Marital status of head of household, 1 if married, 0 otherwise
FAMSIZE = Size of family unit (range 1–9)
WHITE = Race of head of household, 1 if white, 0 otherwise

DATA7-14

Data on homicide and related rates for 50 U.S. states and Washington, D.C. Source: *1995 Statistical Abstract of the U.S.* All data are for 1993.

mr = Murder per 100,000 population, Table 310, page 200 (range 1.6–78.5)
exec = Number under sentence of death and executed, Table 357, page 220 (range 0–17)
south = 1 for a southern state, 0 otherwise
ue = Percent unemployed, Table 664, page 423 (range 2.6–10.8)

capital = 1 if capital punishment allowed, Table 357, page 220

pcy = Per-capita personal income in thousands of 1987 dollars, Table 713, page 461 (range 11.647–23.302)

DATA7-15

Data compiled by Scott Murch for 38 congressmen/women.

pvote = Proportion of vote for 1988 election of congressmen/women elected before 1986 and that is the dependent variable. Data are cross sectional by individuals. Source: *Politics in America* (range 0.5–0.99)

pvote86 = Proportion vote for 1986 election (range 0.55–0.88)

pvote84 = Proportion vote for 1984 election (range 0.52–1.0)

vbush = Proportion of voters voting for Bush in 1988 presidential election in each district (range 0.19–0.71)

terms = Number of previous terms in office (range 3–13)

amtinc = Amount spent by the incumbent in the 1988 election in thousands (range 65–1,755)

amtchall = Amount spent by the challenger in the 1988 election in thousands (range 0–1,633)

resources = Amount raised by the incumbent for the 1988 election in thousands (range 86–1,731)

lcvrate = Environmental rating of the incumbent for 1988 as determined by the League of Conservation Voters with 0 = worst and 100 = best. Source: *Almanac of American Politics,* 1990 (range 6–94)

demo = Dummy variable reflecting party affiliation: Democrat = 1, Republican = 0

DATA7-16

Data on the number of college applications and its determinants for 34 schools. Compiled by Ho Lee.

applied = Number of applications for Fall 1987 (range 1,589–23,670)

founded = Year the school was founded (range 1636–1965)

applfee = Application fee in dollars (range 10–50)

tuition = Tuition fee in dollars (range 858–12,960)

room = Room and board in dollars (range 2,046–5,416)

R&D = Federal obligations for research and development in the sciences in thousands of dollars in 1986 (Range 21,418–188,120)

pp = Private (1) or public (0)

satv = Percent of freshmen with an SAT verbal score higher than 600 (range 5–81)

satm = Percent of freshmen with an SAT math score higher than 600 (range 19–100)

DATA7-17

Data (compiled by Denise Lerner) are a cross section for 40 countries, including Chad, India, Niger, Tanzania, Madagascar, Thailand, Honduras, Philippines, Zambia, El Salvador, Colombia, Ecuador, Peru, Tunisia, Costa Rica, Chile, Jamaica, Lebanon, Mexico, Brazil, Panama, Iraq, Uruguay, Argentina, Yugoslavia, Venezuela, Greece, Spain, Israel, Sudan, United Kingdom, New Zealand, Japan, Norway, Canada, United States, Sweden, Hungary, Poland, and Czechoslovakia.

   Y = Gini coefficient range $0 < Yt < 1$; 0 is perfect equality. Todaro, *Development Economics in the Third World* (range 0.18–0.66)
Gnp = Per-capita gross national product (base 1976). Source: Same (range 63–3,603)
Gdp = Growth rate (percent) of gross domestic product. Source: *World Development Report,* 1978 (range 0.3–10.5)
 pop = Growth rate of population (range 0.3–3.5)
 urb = Measure of people living in urban areas (percent) (range 5–78)
  lit = Percent of people in country who can read and write (range 5–99)
 edu = Secondary school enrollment expressed as a percent of the total population of secondary school age (range 0–74)
 agr = Share of agriculture in GDP (percent) (range 4–66)
 soc = 1 if country is socialist, 0 if not

All sources not mentioned are from the *World Development Report,* 1978.

DATA7-18

Cross-sectional data on the 58 California counties for the year 1990 to explain population differentials. Compiled by Alvin Chan. Sources: *California Statistical Abstract. California Cities, Towns & Counties.*

     pop = County population in thousands (range 1.192–9,149.81)
 educexp = Local government expenditures on education per student in dollars (range 3,869–9,438)
 recrexp = Expenditures per capita on recreation and cultural services in dollars (range 0–3,138)
 policexp = Local government expenditures per capita on police protection in dollars (range 79–674)
  vcrime = Number of violent crimes per 100,000 population (range 230–1,587)
 othrcrim = Number of other crimes per 100,000 population (range 2,130–16,946)
 unemprt = Unemployment rate (percent) (range 4.8–24.9)
    city = Dummy variable that equals 1 if there is a city in the county with a population of more than 100,000 inhabitants
  inland = Dummy variable that takes the value 1 when the county does not border the Pacific Ocean
 central = Dummy variable that takes the value 1 when the county is located in the central portion of the state and 0 when it is in either the northern or southern portion of the state

south = Dummy variable that takes the value 1 when the county is located in the southern portion of the state and 0 if it is in the central or northern portion of the state

DATA7-19

Data on demand for cigarette consumption in Turkey. Source: "Cigarette Demand, Health Scares, and Education in Turkey," by Aysit Tansel, *Applied Economics,* 1993, pages 521–529.

year = 1960–1988 ($n = 29$)
- Q = Cigarette consumption per adult (kg) (range 1.86–2.723)
- Y = Per-capita real GNP in 1968 prices in Turkish liras (range 2,560–5,723)
- P = Real price of cigarettes in Turkish liras per kg (range 1.361–3.968)
- ED1 = Ratio of enrollments in middle and high schools to the population 12–17 years old (range 0.112–0.451)
- ED2 = Ratio of enrollments in universities to the population 20–24 years old (range 0.026–0.095)
- D82 = 1 for 1982 onward
- D86 = 1 for 1986 onward

DATA7-20

Data on 56 NBA players' salaries and their determinants. Compiled by Michael Pepek.

SALARY = Salary earned by players in the 1989–1990 NBA season in thousands of dollars. Source: *San Diego Union,* December 10, 1989, page H10 (range 1,000–3,750)

YRS = Number of years that player has been in the NBA (range 1–13)

HT = Height of the players in inches. Source: *The Sporting News Pro-Basketball Handbook,* 1989–1990 (range 73–88)

WT = Weight of each player in pounds. Source: *Pro-Basketball Handbook* (range 175–290)

AGE = Age of each player determined by his age in 1989. For example, if his birth date is 4-5-63, then his age is determined by 1989 − 1963 = 26 years old. Source: *Pro-Basketball Handbook* (range 23–36)

GAMES = Number of games that each player played in the 1988–1989 season. Source: *HOOPS*–basketball stats book 1989–1990 (range 6–82)

GAMESTRT = Number of games out of the total games played in which the player started. Source: *HOOPS* (range 0–82)

FORWARD = Dummy variable for whether the player is primarily a forward. 1 if forward, 0 if not. Source: *San Diego Union.*

GUARD = Dummy variable if player is primarily a guard. 1 = guard, 0 not. Source: *San Diego Union.*

MIN = Number of minutes that each player played during season. Source: *HOOPS* (range 189–3,255)

FGA = Field goal attempts. All shots taken by the player. This does not include free throws. Source: *Sporting News,* May 1989 (range 104–1,881)

FGPRCNT = Fraction of shots that each player made. 1.000 is perfect shooting. Source: *Sporting News* (range 0.431–0.579)

FTA = Free throw attempts. The total number of free throws attempted by each player after being fouled. Source: *Sporting News* (range 19–918)

FTPRCNT = Fraction of the shot free throws that were made. Source: *Sporting News* (range 0.553–0.911)

REBOUNDS = The number of total rebounds by each player. BRDS is short for boards. Source: *Sporting News* (range 37–1,105)

ASSISTS = Number of assists by player. An assist is when one player makes a pass to another player who scores because of that pass. Source: *Sporting News* (range 29–1,118)

STEALS = Number of times that player stole ball away from other team. Source: *Sporting News* (range 6–564)

BLOCKS = Number of blocked shots. Source: *Sporting News* (range 5–315)

POINTS = Number of points that the player scored in the full season. Source: *Sporting News* (range 116–2,633)

AVGPNTS = Average points per games played. Source: *Sporting News* (range 4.7–32.5)

RACE = Dummy variable to tell whether the player is white or nonwhite. 0 = white, 1 = nonwhite. Source: *Sporting News NBA Guide,* 1987–1988.

EW = Dummy variable to tell whether each player is in the eastern or the western division. 1 = east, 0 = west. Source: *Boston Celtics 1988–1989 Media Guide.*

TRD = Dummy variable telling whether player has been traded in the last two years. 1 = has been traded, 0 = has not. Source: *Sporting News.*

WINTM = Dummy variable telling whether the team that the player is on had more than 45 wins out of the 82-game schedule. Source: *Sporting News.*

ALLSTAT = Dummy variable telling whether the player was on the All-Star team in the 1990–1991 season. The reason for using this year's AS team is based on the theory that players make it onto the AS team the year after they deserved it. 1 = on the AS team, 0 = not. Source: *San Diego Union.*

XPAN = Dummy variable denoting whether the team was an expansion team in the last two seasons. 1 = expansion team. Source: *Boston Celtics Media Guide.*

DATA7-21

Population of the United Kingdom. Source: *Annual Abstract of Statistics,* Central Statistical Office, 1996, Table 2.1, page 16.

year = 1962–1994 ($n = 33$)
pop = Population in millions (range 53.292–58.395)

d1 = 1 for the period 1974–1983, 0 otherwise
d2 = 1 for the period 1984–1994, 0 otherwise

DATA7-22

Data on cable systems in 1979 and 1994. This is updated from DATA4-8. Sources: *Broadcasting Yearbook,* 1980, for 1980 data, and the following for 1994 data: *Broadcasting and Cable Year Book, 1996, Television and Cable Fact Book,* 1996, and *Editor & Publisher Market Guide,* 1995. The 1979 data were compiled by David Andersen and the 1994 data were compiled by Cecilia Steen.

$$sub = \text{Number of subscribers of each system in thousands (range 1–462)}$$
$$homes = \text{Number of homes (in thousands) passed by each system (range 1.7–1,201.09)}$$
$$inst = \text{Installation fee in dollars (range 5.95–75)}$$
$$svc = \text{Monthly service charge of each system (range 5.08–24.93)}$$
$$cblchanl = \text{Number of television signals carried by each cable system (range 6–120)}$$
$$tvchanl = \text{Number of television signals received (range 3–15)}$$
$$pcincome = \text{Per-capita income for each television market with cable in dollars (range 7.683–28.597)}$$
$$D = 1 \text{ for 1994, 0 for 1979}$$

DATA7-23

Data are cross section for 76 countries. 1976 data were compiled by Denise Lerner and 1989 data were compiled by Elmer Gamoning. See DATA4-15 and DATA7-17 for data sources.

$$Y = \text{Gini coefficient range } 0 < Yt < 1; 0 \text{ is perfect equality}$$
$$Gnp = \text{Per-capita gross national product (base 1976)}$$
$$Gdp = \text{Growth rate (percent) of gross domestic product}$$
$$pop = \text{Growth rate of population}$$
$$urb = \text{Measure of people living in urban areas (percent)}$$
$$lit = \text{Percent of people in country who can read and write}$$
$$edu = \text{Secondary school enrollment expressed as percent of the total population of secondary school age}$$
$$agr = \text{Share of agriculture in GDP (percent)}$$
$$d = 1 \text{ for 1989 base, 0 for 1976 base}$$

DATA7-24

Data on the sale price and characteristics of 224 homes in the Dove Canyon and Coto de Caza areas of Orange County, California, compiled by Jody Schimmel. Dove Canyon is a neighborhood built around a golf course with single-family tract homes with relatively small lots. Coto de Caza is a more upscale area. It is more rural, with large custom homes, some with horse corrals.

Salepric = Sale price in thousands of dollars
    sqft = Living area in square feet
bedrms = Number of bedrooms
  baths = Number of baths
 garage = Number of car spaces
    age = Age of house in years
    city = 1 for Coto de Caza, and 0 for Dove Canyon

DATA7-25

Data on congressional elections in 47 districts, compiled by Kameron Kordestani.

        CD = Congressional district
WINVOTE = Number of votes of winning candidate in November, 1996, general
            election
LOSVOTE = Number of votes of losing candidate in November, 1996, general
            election
    WIN$ = Total campaign expenditures, in dollars, of winning candidate in the
            1996 general election cycle
    LOS$ = Total campaign expenditures, in dollars, of losing candidate in the
            1996 general election cycle
 CLINT96 = Total district vote for Democratic candidate for President, Bill
            Clinton, in 1996 general election
  DOLE96 = Total district vote for Republican candidate for President, Bob Dole,
            in 1996 general election
 CLINT92 = Total district vote for Democratic candidate for President, Bill
            Clinton, in 1992 general election
    CCUS = Chamber of Commerce of the United States (CCUS), a probusiness
            interest group, rating of congressperson's voting record, with 100
            being the highest possible score, 0 being lowest score
   PARTY = Political party of winning candidate for House of Representatives
            seat (Democrat = 0, Republican = 1)

Source: Philip D. Duncan, and Christine C. Lawrence, *Congressional Quarterly's Politics in America: 1998*, Washington, D.C.: Congressional Quarterly Press, 1997.

DATA7-26

This data set is the combination of DATA4-10 and DATA4-16 with a dummy variable indicating possible structural change. D = 0 for DATA4-10 and D = 1 for DATA4-16.

DATA8-1

Data on annual (1995) salary for professors at the seven universities: UC Berkeley, UCLA, UC San Diego, Illinois, Michigan, Stanford, and Virginia. This data set is the same as DATA3-11 but arranged in increasing order of years for the Goldfeld–Quandt test of heteroscedasticity.

salary = Annual salary in thousands of dollars (range 41.3–153)
years = Number of years since Ph.D. (range 1–45)

DATA8-2

Aggregate personal income and expenditures on domestic travel (1993) for the U.S. states and Washington, D.C. This is an expanded version of DATA3-14. Source: *1995 Statistical Abstract of the U.S.*

exptrav = Travel expenditures in billions of dollars, Table 428, page 266 (range 0.708–42.48)
income = Personal income in billions in dollars, Table 712, page 460 (range 9.3–683.5)
pop = Population in millions, Table 27, page 28 (range 0.47–31.217)

DATA8-3

Aggregate personal income and expenditures on health care for the U.S. states and Washington, D.C., for 1993. This is an expanded version of DATA3-2.

exphlth = Aggregate expenditures on health care in billions of dollars
income = Aggregate personal income in billions of dollars
pop = U.S. population in millions. Source: *1995 Statistical Abstract of the U.S.* Population, Table 27, page 28 (range 0.47–31.217) Personal Income, Table 712, page 460 (range 9.3–683.5) Personal Health Care Expenditures, Table 153, page 111 (range 0.998–94.178)
Seniors = Percent 65 or over in 1993. Source: *1994 Statistical Abstract of the U.S.*, page 32 (range 4.4–18.6)

DATA9-1

Data for the demand for ice cream. Source: Hildreth–Lu paper, Table D16, page 73. Four-week periods from March 18, 1951, to July 11, 1953 ($n = 30$).

demand = Per-capita consumption of ice cream in pints (range 0.256–0.548)
income = Weekly family income in dollars (range 76–96)
price = Price of ice cream in dollars per pint (range 0.26–0.292)
temp = Mean temperature in Fahrenheit (range 24–72)

DATA9-2

Annual data for the United States on discount rate, money supply, and government deficits. Source: *1996 Economic Report of the President.*

year = 1960–1995 ($n = 36$)
r = Discount rate (percent), Table B-69, page 360 (range 3–13.42)
M = M2 in billions of current dollars, Table B-65, page 355 (range 312.3–3,780.7)
D = Federal deficit in billions of current dollars, Table B-74, page 367 (range −3.2–290.4)

APPENDIX D

DATA9-3

Quarterly data for San Diego Gas and Electric Company.

period = 1972.2 through 1993.4 ($n = 87$)
reskwh = Kilowatt-hour sales to residential customers (millions) at quarterly rates
(range 586.608–1,512.306)
nocust = Average number of residential customers (thousands) (range
459.903–1,007.706)
price = Average price in cents per kwh for the single-family rate tariff (range
2.207–12.42)
cpi = San Diego consumer price index (1982–1984 = 100) (range
36.54–150.9)
incm = Total personal income in millions of current dollars in San Diego
County, at quarterly rates (range 1,815.148–13,870.889)
cdd = Cooling degree days—summation over the quarter of max [(daily max
+ min/2) − 65, 0] (range 0.374–973.493)
hdd = Heating degree days—summation over the quarter of max [65 − (daily
max + min/2), 0] (range 0.042–950.17)
pop = San Diego County population in thousands (range 1,422.64–2,678.544)

DATA9-4

Annual data for the manufacturing sector in the United States. Source: *Economic Report of the President, 1996*, Table B-89. Range for profits is 23.2–85.8 and that for sales is 1,060.6–2,220.9.

year = 1974–1994 ($n = 21$)
profits = Corporate profits (after taxes) in billions of dollars
sales = Sales in billions of dollars

DATA9-5

Indices of farm inputs and output for 1948–1993 with 1982 = 100. Source: *Economic Report of the President, 1996*, Tables B-95 and B-96.

year = 1948–1993 ($n = 46$)
output = Farm output (range 51–116)
labor = Farm labor (range 81–278)
land = Farm real estate (range 89–102)
machines = Durable equipment (range 38–102)
energy = Energy used (range 65–125)
fert = Agricultural chemicals used (range 35–133)
seedfeed = Seed, feed, and livestock purchases (range 55–102)
others = Other purchased inputs (range 73–127)

DATA9-6

Data on log(money), log(income), and interest rate for the United States. Source: Stock and Watson (1993) *Econometrica*—unsmoothed data. Period is 1900–1989 (annual data). Data compiled by Graham Elliott for the 90 years 1900–1989.

DATA9-7

Quarterly data compiled by Ophir Gottlieb. All real-dollar data are in 1982–1984 dollars.

YEAR = 1975.1–1990.4 (64 observations)

QNC = Number of new cars sold in thousands. Source: *Wards Automotive Yearbook* (range 1,754–3,337)

PRICE = Average real price index of a new car. Source: *Economic Report of the President* (range 60.2–121.4)

INCOME = Per-capita disposable personal income in thousands of 1982 dollars. Source: *Citibase Data Series* (range 8.985–11.93)

PRIME = Prime interest rate (percent). Source: *Economic Report of the President* (range 4.89–15.08)

UNEMP = Unemployment rate (percent). Source: *Employment and Earnings* (range 4.4–8.7)

STOCK = Number of cars on road in thousands. Source: *Statistical Abstract of the U.S.* (range 79.231–107.585)

POP = Population in millions. Source: Interpolated from annual values from the *Economic Report of the President* (range 215.973–251.966)

WINTER = 1 for the winter quarter, 0 otherwise. The other seasonal dummies are defined similarly.

DATA9-8

Annual data for estimating domestic revenue passenger miles. Source: *Statistical Abstract of the United States,* 1947–1989. Data compiled by Graham Rushall.

year = 1947–1987 ($n = 41$)

pop = Population in millions (range 144.83–243.915)

rpm = Domestic revenue passenger miles in billions (range 6–324.5)

nop = Number of operators (airlines) (range 31–106)

oprev = Operating revenue from passengers in millions of dollars (range 256–37,309)

gnp = Gross national product of United States in billions of dollars (range 232.2–4,526.7)

accid = Number of American planes in an accident (range 12–69)

fatal = Number of fatalities from aircraft accidents (range 0–460)

regu = Dummy variable for airline regulation/deregulation, 1 for 1979–1987, 0 for 1947–1978

DATA9-9

Quarterly data on the number of new car sales in the United States. Compiled by Brian Robertson.

period = 1976.1–1990.4 (60 observations)

nocars = Number of new car sales in thousands. Source: *Wards Automotive Yearbook,* various years (range 1,280.413–2,775.774)

pop = Population in millions. Source: *Economic Report of the President,* various years (range 218.035–251.966)

Y = Disposable personal income per capita in thousands of 1982 dollars. Source: *Citibase Data Series* (range 9.376–11.930)

price = New car price index, 1982 base year. Source: *Economic Report of the President,* various years (range 68.3–122.0)

primert = Prime interest rate charged by banks (percent). Source: *Economic Report of the President,* various years (range 6.3–20.3)

unemp = Unemployment rate (percent). Source: *Economic Report of the President,* various years (range 5.0–10.6)

DATA9-10

Weekly store sales of a Del Mar supermarket ($n = 69$). Data compiled by James McMillen.

Y = Weekly sales from weekend 1-6-91 to 4-26-92 in thousands (range 257.803–336.274)

X2 = Labor dollars for store weekend in thousands (range 22.064–32.499)

X3 = Weekly sales of same week last year lag_52 in thousands (range 287.755–407.501)

X4 = 1 if holiday week, 0 if not

X5 = 1 if summertime, 0 if not

X6 = 1 if race season at Del Mar race track

X7 = 1 if top 5 holiday week

X8 = 1 if Del Mar fair is at the fairgrounds

X9 = 1 if adjacent stores close

X10 = 1 if construction or closure of area streets

X11 = Percent of reduction in the price of items in the ad (range 28.28–57.27)

X12 = 1 if there was a special promo for the week at half-price sales

X13 = Average weekly water temperature at Del Mar (range 56.57–67.86)

X14 = Average weekly high air temperature at Del Mar (range 63.43–79.43)

X15 = Average weekly low air temperature at Del Mar (range 38–67)

X16 = Total rainfall in Del Mar for the week (range 0–2.935)

DATA9-11

Monthly data on the volume of stock market shares sold. Compiled by Brian Wampler. Sources: *United States Statistical Abstract,* Standard & Poor's quarterly reports. *Citibase Data Series,* and the University of Alabama Web page at *http://bos.business.uab.edu.*

> period = 1980.1–1995.09 (189 observations)
> volume = NYSE reported share volume, measured in millions of shares (range 674–8,835)
> sp500 = S&P's common stock price index, measured in dollars (range 102.97–578.77)
> tbill = U.S. Treasury bills (3-month), measured as a percent (range 2.84–16.295)
> long = U.S. Treasury bonds (10+ years), measured as a percent (range 5.9–14.14)
> gdp = Gross domestic product (gdpmon = GDP quarterly/3), measured in billions of dollars (range 906.467–2,432.833)
> cconf = Consumer confidence index, measured as 1985 = 100 (range 47.3–120.7)
> cexpect = Consumer expectations index, measured as 1985 = 100 (range 50–124.3)
> csent = University of Michigan's index of consumer sentiment, measured as February 1966 = 100 (range 51.7–101)

DATA9-12

Monthly data on personal consumption expenditures on new cars. Data compiled by Johnfar Kerlee (SA is seasonally adjusted). Source: *Citibase Data Series.*

> period = 1975.01–1991.10 (202 observations)
> pcecars = Personal consumption expenditures on new cars in billions of 1982 dollars (range 76.402–174.364)
> pop = U.S. population in millions (range 215.973–254.727)
> pcdpy = Per-capita disposable personal income in thousands of 1982 dollars (range 8.7–11.61)
> cpinew = Consumer price index for new cars (1982–1984 = 100, SA) (range 60.2–126)
> cpiall = Consumer price index for all items (1982–1984 = 100, SA) (range 52.3–137.3)
> cpiused = Consumer price index for used cars (1982–1984 = 100, SA) (range 42.4–121.8)
> cpigas = Consumer price index for gasoline (1982–1984 = 100, SA) (range 42.8–117)
> cpiinsur = Consumer price index for auto insurance (1982–1984 = 100, SA) (range 45.7–197)
> repair = Consumer price index for maintenance and repair (1982–1984 = 100, SA) (range 51.7–138.4)
> credit = Installment credit outstanding in millions of current dollars (range 160.034–742.066)

primert = Prime commercial paper, 30 days (range 4.51–18.95)

pubtrans = Consumer price index for public transportation (1982–1984 = 100, SA) (range 41.7–156.2)

unemprt = Unemployment rate for all workers 16 years and over (range 5–10.8)

DATA9-13

Monthly data from 1990.01 through 1998.12 for eight stocks listed on the NYSE, compiled by Sebastian Badali.

bkret = Monthly returns on Bank of New York stock

btret = Monthly returns on Bankers Trust stock

cmbret = Monthly returns on Chase Manhattan Bank stock

cret = Monthly returns on Citigroup stock

fturet = Monthly returns on First Union stock

melret = Monthly returns on Mellon Bank stock

oneret = Monthly returns on Bank One stock

wfcret = Monthly returns on Wells Fargo stock

30yr = Monthly yield on the 30-year treasury bond

3mtbill = Monthly yield on the 3-month T-bill

3mret = Monthly returns on the 3-month T-bill

bkdiv = Monthly dividend yield on Bank of New York stock

btdiv = Monthly dividend yield on Bankers Trust stock

cmbdiv = Monthly dividend yield on Chase Manhattan Bank stock

cdiv = Monthly dividend yield on Citigroup stock

ftudiv = Monthly dividend yield on First Union stock

meldiv = Monthly dividend yield on Mellon Bank stock

onediv = Monthly dividend yield on Bank One stock

wfcdiv = Monthly dividend yield on Wells Fargo Bank stock

emi = Monthly change of the ifc emerging market index

usd = Monthly change of the index tracking the U.S. dollar vs. international currencies

sp500 = Monthly returns of the S&P 500 equity index

discrate = Monthly Federal Reserve discount rate

inf = Monthly data on the annualized rate of inflation

def = Difference between index of baa rated bonds and index of caa rated bonds

DATA10-1

Quarterly data for the United States. Source: *Citibase Data Series;* interest rate and money supply are averaged from monthly data.

period = 1964.1 to 1991.2 (110 observations)

r = Interest rate: U.S. Treasury bills, auction average, 3-month (percent) (range 3.514–15.904)

M = Money supply M2 in billions of 1987 dollars (range 1,461.733–2,915.233)

D = Federal cyclically adjusted budget: deficit $(+)$ or surplus $(-)$ in billions
of dollars (range 0.6–213)

DATA10-2

Hourly load and temperature data for an electric company in the northwest region
of the United States for the period January 1, 1992, through January 31, 1992. Data
compiled by Casey Brace. ($n = 744$)

day_hour = Day and hour (range 1.01–31.24)
   load = Electricity usage in megawatts (range 1,646–3,833)
   temp = Temperature in Fahrenheit (range 27–59)

DATA10-3

Monthly data on German foreign exchange rate.

  period = 1973.01–1986.01 (157 observations)
exchrate = Deutsche marks per U.S. dollar. Source: *International Financial Statistics*
       (range 1.725–3.303)

DATA10-4

Annual data on U.S. military expenditures and their determinants. Data compiled
by Jan Blackburn from the *History of American Statistics from Colonial Times* and *Historical Tables: Budget of the U.S. Government.*

   year = 1940–1987 (48 years)
     ug = Unadjusted annual government outlays expressed in billions of dollars
       (range 9.589–1,004.586)
     um = Total U.S. military outlays expressed in billions of dollars for 1940–1987
       (range 1.504–273.966)
 gnpdef = Annual implicit GNP deflator for federal government purchases of
       goods and services, base year 1972 (range 22.7–270.5)
  hdem = Percent of Democrats in the House of Representatives (range
       43.318–67.810)
  sdem = Percent of Democrats in the Senate (range 46–71.875)
   pres = Party of the President in office, Republican = 1, Democrat = 0
  elect = 1 for the year in which the President might have to increase or
       decrease military expenditure as a means of stabilizing the government,
       0 otherwise
 reagan = 1 for the years during which President Reagan was in office, 0 otherwise
   opp = 1 denotes a year in which the majority party in the Senate is of the
       opposing party with respect to the President in office, 0 otherwise
   ww2 = 1 during the World War II period, 1941–1945, 0 elsewhere
  kwar = 1 during the Korean War period, 1951–1953, 0 elsewhere
  vwar = 1 during the Vietnam War period, 1965–1969, 0 elsewhere
  krus = 1 for the years during which Kruschev may have changed Soviet military
       policy, 0 otherwise

gorb = 1 for the years during which Soviet leader Gorbachev may have changed Soviet military policy, 0 otherwise

salt = The structural change possibly brought about by the SALT I treaty: 0 = before, 1 = after

DATA10-5

Average hourly earnings in dollars for the United States and California. Source: *1995 Economic Report of the Governor,* State of California, Table 9, page A-8.

year = 1960–1994 (35 years)
calwge = Wage rate in California (range 2.62–12.44)
uswage = Wage rate in the United States (range 2.26–12.06)

DATA10-6

Annual data for the United States.

YEAR = 1959–1994 (36 years)
  N = Population in millions. Source: *Economic Report of the President,* 1996, Table B-30 (range 177.83–260.66)
  M = Money supply in billions, M3. Source: *Economic Report,* 1996, Table B-65 (range 299.8–4,303.9)
  P = GDP deflator, 1992 = 100. Source: *Economic Report,* 1996, Table B-3 (range 23–105)

DATA10-7

Annual data on the population of the state of California. Source: *Economic Report of the Governor,* 1995, Table 1, page A-1.

year = 1960–1994 (35 years)
pop = Population in millions (range 15.863–32.14)

DATA10-8

Exchange rate and determinants for Korea. All data sets were obtained from the *International Financial Statistics.* Data compiled by Patrick Wise.

period = 1982.1–1995.3 (55 observations)
 exrate = Exchange rate of Korean won/U.S. dollars (quarterly average) (range 571.01–891.37)
curracc = Current account balance for Korea (range 3,623–4,829)
  trade = Trade balance for Korea (range 3,419–4,070)
  m1_k = Money (M1) supply for Korea (range 2,960.2–30,643.9)
  m1_u = Money (M1) supply for United States (range 384.73–1,094.57)
irate_k = Yield on Korean government bonds (range 11.1–27.9)
irate_u = Yield on U.S. government bonds (range 5.62–14.85)
 pricek = Wholesale price index for Korea (1985 = 100) (range 64.8–108.97)

priceu = Wholesale price index for the United States (1985 = 100) (range 74.4–103.1)

DATA11-1

Monthly data on total number of full-time nonagricultural wage and salary workers in the United States. Source: *Employment & Earnings*. Compiled by William C. Ryburn.

PERIOD = 1983.01–1986.12 (48 observations)
TOTEMP = Total employment in the hundred thousands (range 94,341–108,176)

DATA12-1

Data represent a random selection of 60 individuals applying to the University of California, San Diego, School of Medicine for the year 1988. Compiled by Steven Bramson.

Accept = 1 if granted an acceptance, 0 otherwise
GPA = Cumulative undergraduate grade point average (range 1.88–2.9)
Bio = Score in biology portion of the Medical College Admissions Test (MCAT) (range 2–9)
Chem = Score in chemistry portion of MCAT (range 2–9)
Phy = Score in physics portion of MCAT (range 3–9)
Red = Score in reading portion of MCAT (range 3–7)
Prb = Score in problem portion of MCAT (range 2–7)
Qnt = Score in quantitative portion of MCAT (range 2–7)
Age = Age of applicant (range 21–23)
Gender = 1 if male, 0 if female

DATA13-1

U.S. annual data from the 1994 *Economic Report of the President* for 1959–1993 (35 observations). Compiled by Sigalit Orr.

GDP = Gross domestic product in billions of 1987 dollars, Table B-2 (range 1928.8–5,132.7)
CONS = Personal consumption expenditures in billions of 1987 dollars, Table B-2 (range 1,178.9–3,452.5)
INV = Gross private domestic investment in billions of 1987 dollars, Table B-2 (range 289.4–820.9)
EXPORTS = Exports of goods and services in billions of 1987 dollars, Table B-2 (range 73.8–596.4)
IMPORTS = Imports of goods and services in billions of 1987 dollars, Table B-2 (range 95.3–675.7)
GOVEXP = Government purchases of goods and services in billions of 1987 dollars, Table B-2 (range 475.3–946.3)
GOVREC = Federal, state, and local government receipts in billions of dollars, Table B-81 (range 128.8–1,969.1)

MONYSUP = Money supply measure M2, currency, demand deposits, savings deposits, Eurodollar, overnight repurchase agreements in billions of current dollars, Table B-68 (range 297.8–3,551.7)

Pt = Implicit price deflators for gross domestic product, base year 1987, Table B-3 (range 25.6–124.2)

rt = Corporate Aaa bond yields as a percent, Table B-72 (range 4.26–14.17)

POP = U.S. population in millions, Table B-32 (range 177.83–258.233)

● **Table D1   Data and GRETL Command Files for Practice Computer Sessions**

Section	Reference	Data File	Input File
2.1	Frequency distribution	DATA2-1	PS2-1.INP
2.2	Mean, s.d., coefficient of variation	DATA2-2	PS2-2.INP
2.5	Covariance and correlation	DATA2-2	PS2-3.INP
3.2	Example 3.1	DATA3-1	PS3-1.INP
3.4	Example 3.2	DATA3-1	PS3-1.INP
3.4	Example 3.3	DATA3-1	PS3-1.INP
3.5	Example 3.4	DATA3-1	PS3-1.INP
3.5	Example 3.4a	DATA3-1	PS3-1.INP
3.5	Example 3.5	DATA3-1	PS3-1.INP
3.5	Example 3.6	DATA3-1	PS3-1.INP
3.6	Scaling and units of measurement	DATA3-1	PS3-2.INP
3.7	Engel curve application (Table 3.3)	DATA3-2	PS3-3.INP
3.8	Example 3.7	DATA3-1	PS3-1.INP
3.9	Example 3.8	DATA3-1	PS3-4.INP
3.10	Example 3.9	DATA3-1	PS3-5.INP
3.11	Application of patents (Table 3.4)	DATA3-3	PS3-6.INP
4.1	Examples 4.1 and 4.2	DATA4-1	PS4-1.INP
4.2	Example 4.3	DATA4-1	PS4-1.INP
4.3	Example 4.4	DATA4-1	PS4-1.INP
4.4	Examples 4.5 through 4.8	DATA4-1	PS4-1.INP
4.4	Examples 4.9, 4.10, and 4.11	DATA4-2	PS4-2.INP
4.5	Examples 4.12 and 4.13	DATA4-3	PS4-3.INP
4.6	Bus travel application in Table 4.4	DATA4-4	PS4-4.INP
4.7	Women's participation rates (Table 4.5)	DATA4-5	PS4-5.INP
5.1	Example 5.1, Table 5.1	DATA4-3	PS5-1.INP
5.1	Example 5.2, Table 5.2	DATA3-7	PS5-2.INP
5.3	Model reformulation	DATA4-3	PS5-3.INP
5.4	Auto expenditure application	DATA3-7	PS5-4.INP
5.4	Poverty rate application	DATA4-6	PS5-5.INP
6.2	Example 6.1	DATA4-1	PS6-1.INP
6.4	Example 6.2	DATA6-1	PS6-2.INP
6.4	Example 6.3	DATA6-2	PS6-3.INP
6.4	Practice Problems 6.5 and 6.6	DATA4-1	PS6-4.INP
6.6	Example 6.4	DATA6-3	PS6-5.INP
6.7	R&D and patents revisited (Table 6.2)	DATA3-3	PS6-6.INP

Section	Reference	Data File	Input File
6.8	Example 6.5	DATA6-4	PS6-7.INP
6.9	Example 6.6	DATA6-4	PS6-8.INP
6.11	Estimating demand elasticities	DATA4-4	PS6-9.INP
6.14	Example 6.7 (Table 6.3)	DATA4-8	PS6-10.INP
6.14	Example 6.8 (Table 6.4)	DATA6-4	PS6-11.INP
6.15	Example 6.9	DATA6-1	PS6-12.INP
7.1	Male–female wage differential	DATA7-1	PS7-1.INP
7.1	Example 7.1	DATA7-2	PS7-2.INP
7.1	Example 7.2 and Table 7.2	DATA7-3	PS7-3.INP
7.1	Practice Problem 7.2	DATA7-3	PS7-4.INP
7.4	Covariance analysis application	DATA7-2	PS7-5.INP
7.6	Structural change application	DATA7-4	PS7-6.INP
7.8	Sealing compound application	DATA7-5	PS7-7.INP
8.2	Examples 8.1 and 8.2	DATA3-11	PS8-1.INP
8.2	Example 8.3	DATA3-11	PS8-2.INP
8.2	Example 8.4	DATA8-1	PS8-3.INP
8.2	Example 8.5	DATA8-1	PS8-4.INP
8.3	Example 8.6	DATA8-1	PS8-5.INP
8.3	Example 8.7	DATA8-2	PS8-6.INP
8.3	Example 8.8	DATA8-1	PS8-7.INP
8.4	Application in Section 8.4	DATA8-3	PS8-8.INP
9.1 and 9.3	Examples 9.1 and 9.2	DATA6-6	PS9-1.INP
9.3	Example 9.3	DATA4-7	PS9-2.INP
9.3	Example 9.4 and Table 9.1	DATA4-7	PS9-3.INP
9.4	Example 9.5 and Table 9.2	DATA6-6	PS9-4.INP
9.4	Example 9.6	DATA4-7	PS9-5.INP
9.4	Example 9.7	DATA9-1	PS9-6.INP
9.4	Example 9.8	DATA4-2	PS9-7.INP
9.6	Example 9.10 and Table 9.4	DATA9-2	PS9-8.INP
9.7	Application Section 9.7	DATA9-3	PS9-9.INP
10.1	Example 10.1	DATA10-1	PS10-1.INP
10.1	Example 10.2	DATA10-2	PS10-2.INP
10.4	Example 10.4	DATA10-2	PS10-3.INP
10.5	U.K. consumption expenditures	DATA6-3	PS10-4.INP
10.6	Hourly electricity load model	DATA10-2	PS10-5a.INP
10.6	Hourly electricity load model	DATA10-2	PS10-5b.INP
10.7	Example 10.5	DATA9-2	PS10-6.INP
10.7	Example 10.6	DATA10-3	PS10-7.INP
10.9	Error correction model	DATA10-4	PS10-8.INP
10.10	Example 10.7	DATA10-5	PS10-9.INP
10.11	Example 10.8	DATA10-1	PS10-10.INP
10.11	Example 10.9	DATA10-1	PS10-11.INP
11.4	Fitting time trends	DATA10-5	PS11-1.INP
11.4	Evaluating model forecasts	DATA10-5	PS11-2.INP
11.4	Example 11.3 on exponential smoothing	DATA11-1	PS11-3.INP
12.3	Example 12.1	DATA4-5	PS12-1.INP
13.6	A simple Keynesian model	DATA13-1	PS13-1.INP

Copyrights and Acknowledgments

TABLE 4.6 "Estimated Relations between Migration and Quality of Life," adapted from "Differential Net Migration and the Quality of Life" by Ben-Chieh Liu from *Review of Economics and Statistics,* August 1975. Reprinted with permission of the President and Fellows of Harvard College.

EXAMPLE 9.7 From "Demand Relations and Autocorrelated Disturbances," *Technical Bulletin* 276, by Clifford Hildreth and John Y. Lu. Reprinted by permission of Michigan State University, Agricultural Experiment Station.

TABLE 10.2 "Estimates of the Davidson–MacKinnon Models," adapted from "Inflation and the Savings Rate" by Russell Davidson and James G. MacKinnon from *Applied Economics,* 1983. Reprinted by permission of Chapman & Hall, Ltd.

TABLE 10.3 "Critical Values for the Dickey–Fuller t-Statistics," adapted from *Introduction to Statistical Time Series,* by W. A. Fuller. Copyright © 1976 by Wiley. Reprinted with permission.

TABLE 10.4 "Critical Values for the Augmented Dickey–Fuller Test" by D. A. Dickey and W. A. Fuller. Copyright: The Econometric Society.

TABLE 10.7 "Critical Values for Testing for Cointegration." Copyright: The Econometric Society.

FIGURE 11.4 "California Forecast Comparison." Copyright © 1986 Electric Power Research Institute. EPRI EM-4772. *Forecasting Electricity Sales Over the Short Term: A Comparison of New Methodologies.* Reprinted with permission.

FIGURE 11.11 "Total System Energy Demand." Copyright © 1987 Electric Power Research Institute. EPRI RM-5114. *FORECAST MASTER Program Case Studies.* Reprinted with permission.

FIGURE 11.12 "Box–Jenkins Forecast of System Energy." Copyright © 1987 Electric Power Research Institute. EPRI RM-5114. *FORECAST MASTER Program Case Studies.* Reprinted with permission.

TABLE 11.5 "Diagnostic Tests for California Model Auto-A." Copyright © 1986 Electric Power Research Institute. EPRI EM-4772. *Forecasting Electricity Sales Over the Short Term: A Comparison of New Methodologies.* Reprinted with permission.

Name Index

A

Aitcheson, J., 262
Almon, S., 439, 440, 441
Andersen, David, 645
Arroyo, David, 656

B

Badali, Sebastian, 668
Banerjee, A., 475
Bates, J. M., 504
Batts, J. T., 509
Belsley, D. A., 217
Berndt, E. R., 262
Bessler, D. A., 508
Blackburn, Jan, 464, 669
Blair, Roger D., 320
Boes, D. C., 285
Bohara, A., 509
Bollerslev, T., 406
Box, G. E. P., 519
Brace, Casey, 455, 669
Brandt, J. A., 508
Breusch, T. S., 349, 361
Brown, Scott, 152
Buse, A., 262, 284, 288

C

Carrasco-Tauber, C., 257
Chan, Alvin, 658
Chou, Y., 578
Chow, Gregory, 314
Cochrane, D., 392
Cortes, Kalena, 644, 653
Craig, Allen T., 97
Craven, P., 152
Cruz, Louis, 643, 652
Currie, D., 461

D

Da Silva, L. M., 177
Davidson, J. E. H., 461
Davidson, Russell, 77, 263, 451, 452, 453
Dawson, A., 461
Dempsey, Colleen, 649
Dent, W., 476
Dickey, David A., 455, 458

Diebold, F. X., 515
Durbin, J., 386, 447

E

Effron, B., 355
Elliot, Graham, 665
Engle, R. F., 152, 262, 264, 284, 288, 350, 401, 406, 455, 461, 463, 472, 475, 512
Even, William, 533
Ewing, B. T., 532

F

Fair, Ray C., 556
Farrar, D. E., 217
Fisher, Franklin, 315
Fisher, R. A., 72
Foster, Carroll B., 531
Freund, John E., 20
Friedman, M. A., 462
Fuller, Wayne A., 455, 458

G

Galton, Francis, 77
Gamoning, Elmer, 649
Geweke, J., 476
Gilbert, C. L., 261
Glauber, R. R., 217
Glesjer, H., 349, 361
Godfrey, L. G., 262, 349, 350, 361
Goldfeld, S. M., 352
Gottlieb, Ophir, 665
Granger, C. W. J., 113, 152, 392, 455, 461, 463, 472, 475, 476, 504, 505, 506, 509, 512, 515
Graybill, F. A., 285
Greene, W. H., 77, 350, 358, 360, 406, 437, 451, 479, 528
Griffiths, William E., 77, 220, 437, 479
Gunel, I., 523

H

Haas-Wilson, Deborah, 562
Haitovsky, Y., 155
Hannan, E. J., 152

Harvey, A. C., 349, 350, 358, 360, 361, 450, 515
Haugh, L. D., 476
Hazen, Anthony, 651
Hendry, D. F., 261, 389, 391, 392, 445, 461
Hildreth, C., 394
Hill, R. Carter, 77, 220, 437, 479
Hogg, Robert V., 97
Hull, Brooks, 531

J

Jenkins, G. M., 519
Johnston, J., 147, 170, 451
Jones, D. L., 471
Judge, George G., 77, 219, 220, 360, 437, 479

K

Kaserman, David L., 320
Kelley, A. C., 177
Kerlee, Johnfar, 667
Kim, Minbo, 260
King, A. G., 177
Klein, L. R., 241
Kmenta, Jan, 208, 217, 347, 360, 384, 437, 442, 451, 479
Koenker, R., 353
Kordestani, Kameron, 662
Kuh, Edwin, 217, 219

L

Lee, Ho, 657
Lee, Tsoung-Chao, 220, 437
Lerner, Denise, 658
Liu, Ben-chieh, 184
Lu, J. Y., 394

M

MacKinnon, J. G., 263, 355, 451, 452, 453
MacKinnon, James K., 77
Maddala, G. S., 217, 528
Majeski, S. J., 471
McClave, James T., 320

677

McGregor, Katherine, 652
McMillen, James, 666
McNown, R., 509
Meese, R., 476
Mehdi, S. A., 558
Messer, K., 355
Meyer, John, 219
Mizon, G. E., 389, 391, 392, 445
Moffitt, L. J., 257
Mood, A. M., 285
Morgan, J. N., 241
Murch, Scott, 657

N

Nelson, Charles R., 252, 476
Newbold, P., 392, 515

O

Orcutt, G. H., 392
Ostrom, C., 468

P

Pagan, A. R., 349, 361
Park, R., 349
Park, Simon, 650
Pepek, Michael, 659
Phillips, A. W., 463
Pierce, D. A., 476

Q

Quandt, R. E., 352
Quinn, B., 152
Quinton, Noel, 296, 297

R

Ramanathan, Ramu, 30, 56, 264, 267, 284, 285, 287, 288, 455, 464, 505, 506
Ramsey, J. B., 270
Random, Rodney, 653
Rattinger, H., 468
Reece, William S., 536
Rice, J., 152
Richards, J. F., 261
Robertson, Brian, 666
Rothschild, M., 406
Rushall, Graham, 665
Ruud, Paul A., 77

S

Salmon, M., 461
Sargan, J. D., 391, 445, 461, 463
Savin, N. E., 262
Schwarz, G., 152
Schwert, G. W., 476
Seitz, Peter, 296
Selznick, Marc, 647
Shibata, R., 152
Showalter, Mark H., 260
Silvey, S. D., 262
Sims, C. A., 113, 476
Sommers, Paul M., 296, 297
Srba, F., 461
Stock, J. H., 475

T

Tansel, Aysit, 253, 443, 659
Taylor, Lester, 407

Telleria, Felix, 651
Tobin, James, 535

V

Vahid-Araghi, F., 455

W

Wahba, G., 152
Wald, A., 156
Watson, G. S., 386
Weiss, A., 152
Welsch, R. E., 217
Whisenand, Jennifer, 644
White, H., 353, 355, 361
Wise, Patrick, 670
Wong, Jeffrey, 645
Wong, Susan, 651, 652, 653, 654
Woodbury, N. R., 468
Wooldridge, Jeffrey M., 260, 479, 554
Wunnava, P. V., 532, 558

Y

Yeo, S., 461

Z

Zellner, A., 480
Zuk, G., 468

Subject Index

A

Absence of multicollinearity, 216
Absolute percent error, 497
Acceptance region, 51
Adaptive expectations model, 443
Adaptive forecast, 504
Adjusted R^2, defined, 149
Adjustment coefficient, 442
AFDC payments data sets, 650
Aggregation, defined, 11–12
Agricultural production function
    (example), 257
Air quality data sets, 654–655
Akaike information criterion (AIC),
    152
Almon lag procedure, 439–441
Alternative hypothesis, 51
Analysis of covariance models, 302–305
Analysis of variance (ANOVA)
    model, 291, 301–302
    table, 104
Annual salary data sets, 641, 654,
    662–663
AR(1). *See* First-order autoregressive
    process
AR(p). *See* pth-order autoregressive
    process
ARCH test, 401–406
ARIMA model
    estimating and forecasting with,
    519–522
    example, 508–510
ARMA models, 516
ASCII standard, 578
Assets
    data sets, 641
    risk-return relationship of, 8–9
Asymptotic efficiency, 46–47
Asymptotic unbiasedness, 46
Augmented Dickey-Fuller test
    cointegration regression and,
    473–474
    steps for, 457–461
Autocorrelation
    defined, 90, 380
    function, 432, 516, 518, 519
    higher-order, 399–400
    illustration of, 381
    positive, 383
Automobile maintenance expenditure
    (application), 220
Autoregressive (AR) models, 515–517
Autoregressive conditional
    heteroscedasticity (ARCH) model
    defined, 401
    example, 402–406
Autoregressive errors, 400–401
Autoregressive integrated moving
    average, 518
Auxiliary equations, 349
Auxiliary regression
    defined, 263
    example, 389
    heteroscedasticity and, 349
    LM test approach and, 268–269
    selecting variables with, 264
    unrestricted model and, 307–308

B

B34S software, 635
Bar diagram. *See* Histogram
Base
    defined, 232
    period, 12
    year, 576
Behavioral equations, 542
Best linear unbiased estimates (BLUE)
    Gauss-Markov theorem and, 90,
    135–137
    multicollinearity and, 214–216
    serial correlation and, 383
Binary choice models
    defined, 529
    estimating, 529–530
Binary variable, 291
Binomial distribution
    cumulative terms for, 596–605
    defined, 20
Binomial logit models, 532
Bivariate distributions, 26
Box-Cox transformation, 259
Box-Pierce statistic, 521
Breusch-Godfrey test
    of higher-order autocorrelation,
    399–400
    for lagged dependent variables,
    448–449
Breusch-Pagan test, 349, 350
Bus travel(ers)
    data set for demand for, 643
    determinants of (application),
    171–177
    estimating elasticities of, 257–258

C

Cable television/system
    data sets, 645, 661
    demand for, 264–268
Capital asset pricing model (CAPM),
    7–8
Causality
    defined, 475–476
    in linear regression model, 113–115
    testing for, 476–477
Censored regressions, 535–536
Census data sets, 643–644, 652–653
Central limit theorem, 37–38
Chain rule of differentiation, 67–68
Charitable contributions, Tobit model
    of, 536–538
Chi-square (χ^2) distribution
    hypothesis testing and, 47–48
    practice problems, 607–608
Chi-square distribution, 156, 588
Chow test
    based on dummy variables, 315–317
    based on splitting the sample, 315
    defined, 314
Cigarette consumption data sets, 659
Cobb-Douglas production function, 69
    double-log model and, 255
    example, 257
Cochrane-Orcutt (CORC) iterative
    procedure
    vs. Hildreth-Lu (HILU) search
    procedure, 396–398
    serial correlation and, 392–394,
    468–469, 555
Coefficient(s). *See also* Regression
    coefficients
    added variables and, 308–312
    adjustment, 442

correlation, 32, 217
dummy, 304–305
first-order autocorrelation, 382
linear combination of, 160–165
of multiple determination, 94
perfectly correlated, 32
sample correlation, 40
testing, 153–160
of variation, 26
Cointegration
defined, 463, 472
testing for, 472–475
College applications data sets, 657
Combining forecasts
extensions to, 507–510
methods of, 504–507
Conditional distribution, 29, 89
Conditional expectation of Y given X, 30
Conditional forecast, 497–498
Conditional mean, 86
Conditional mean of Y for a given X, 77
Conditional probability, 27–28
Conditional variance, 30
Confidence interval(s)
defined, 56
example, 110
hypotheses testing and, 57–58
for the mean of normal distribution, 57
for the mean predictor, 111
for the point forecast, 111–112
Congressional elections data sets, 662
Consistency
defined, 45
estimators and, 88–89
Constant dollars, defined, 578
Constant elasticity of substitution, 260
Constant returns to scale, defined, 256
Constant term
dangers of omitting, 167–168
F-statistic and, 160
Constrained optimization
Lagrange's method of, 70–71
overview of, 70
Consumer price index
defined, 12
purpose of, 576
Consumption expenditures
(application), 453–454
Consumption income relationship, 8
Contemporaneous correlation, 479
Continuous random variable, 16

Control group, defined, 291
Correlation
coefficients, 32, 217
contemporaneous, 479
defined, 31
first-order serial, 382, 386–389, 467–471
positive, 39
spurious, 113
Correlogram
for AR model, 517
autocorrelation function and, 516
for electricity sales data, 520
partial, 519
Cost functions, 239–240, 270–271
Covariance, 26–27
analysis of wage model, 305–312
sample, 39
between X and Y, 31
Critical region, 51, 98
Critical value, defined, 53, 98
Cross-section data
defined, 11
heteroscedasticity and, 344
Cubic curve, 239
Current (or nominal) dollars, defined, 578
Curve(s)
cubic, 239
demand, 238
Engel, 9, 106–109
logistic, 259–260
normal, 586
Phillips, 40
smooth, 498

D

Data
aggregation, 11–12
base period and, 577
in constant dollars, 577–578
cross-section, 11, 344
entering, 578–579
estimating economic relationships from, 2
experimental, 10
files, 14
gathering, 10–12, 574–579
index numbers and, 576–577
nonexperimental, 11
observational, 10–11
panel, 11
sample survey, 10
sources, 574–575
specialized, 576

time series, 11, 392, 472, 478–481
work sheets and, 578
Data-based model simplification
defined, 174
Hendry/LSE approach and, 218
Data generating process (DGP)
defined, 13
general to simple modeling and, 261–262
regression model and, 113
Data sets
AFDC payments, 650
air quality, 654–655
annual data for UK, 651
annual data for US, 642–643, 671–672
annual salary for professors, 641, 654, 662–663
annual tuition and salary gain, 641, 648–649
cable system, 645, 661
California counties, 658–659
census data, 643–644, 652–653
cigarette consumption, 659
college applications, 657
congressional elections, 662
congressmen/women, 657
cost function for a company, 650
cross-sectional data for countries, 658, 661
death rates, 644–645
demand for bus travel, 643
demand for ice cream, 663
discount rate and money supply, 663
domestic revenue passenger miles, 665
early retirement, 645
economic growth, 654
exchange rate, 669–671
expenditures on domestic travel, 642
factors affecting baseball attendance, 647–648
farm input and output, 664
gas and electric company, 664
grade point average, 17–18, 639
gross income and taxes, 640
homicide rates, 656–657
hourly earnings in dollars, 670
hourly load and temperature data, 669
housing units, 643, 646
on inequality coefficients, 649
inflation rates, 639
manufacturing sector, 664
military expenditures, 669–670
mortality rate, 647

NBA players' salaries, 659–660
new car sales, 666
parental school choice, 645–646
per-capita consumption and disposable income, 641
personal consumption expenditures, 640, 663, 667–668
population, 642, 652, 660–661, 670
poverty rates, 644, 653–654
private school enrollment, 649–650
return on equity and assets, 641
salary and employment characteristics of employees, 651, 652
sale prices and characteristics of homes, 661–662
SAT scores, 639
sealing compound shipment, 640, 653
sedans and hatchbacks, 656
single-family homes, 639–640, 642, 652, 655
softwood harvest, 651
stock market shares, 666–668
supermarket weekly sales, 666
unemployment compensation, 656
wage growth rate, 639
white tuna fishery production, 651
Death rates data sets, 644–645
Decision rule, 98
Decreasing returns to scale, defined, 256
Defense expenditures
    application, 464–471
    data sets, 669–670
Deflator, defined, 578
Degrees of freedom (d.f.), defined, 47
Demand
    for bus travel, 643
    for cable television (example), 264–268
    for cigarettes, 443
    curves, 238
    derived, 69
    for electricity, 406–415
    for ice cream, 663
    for sealing compound (application), 320–324
    supply equations, 5
    theory, 168
Dependent variable, 4, 238
    LM test and, 307–308
    log-linear models and, 250–254
Derivation
    of normal equations, 135, 140–143
    of variance, 138–139, 209

Derivatives, 64–71, 233
Deseasonalizing, 519
Detrending, defined, 499
Diagnostic checking, 521–522
Dickey-Fuller tests, 455–461
Differencing process, 518
Direct t-test, 164
Discrete choice models, 528
Discrete random variable
    defined, 16
    example, 23–24
    mean of a distribution and, 21
    probability function and, 26–27
Distributed lag model, 434
Distribution(s)
    binomial, 20, 596–605
    bivariate, 26
    chi-square, 47–48, 156, 588, 607–608
    conditional, 29, 89
    F-distribution, 49, 589–591
    frequency, 17
    joint probability, 26, 27
    large-sample, 37–38
    marginal, 28
    mean of, 21
    multivariate, 34–35
    normal, 19, 24–25, 52–55, 57
    probability, 17, 18, 21–22
    of the sample mean, 36
    of sample variance, 36, 49–50
    sampling, 36–37, 46
    standard normal, 19
    student's t-distribution, 48–49
    variance of, 23
Disturbance term, defined, 6
Double-log (log-log) model, 255–257
    applications, 257–258
    dummy-variable approach and, 315–317
Dummy coefficients, 304–305
Dummy variable(s)
    Chow test based on, 315–317
    defined, 291
    effect of, 294–296
    estimation using, 480
    independent variables and, 312–314
    intercept shift example using, 294
    pay and performance study with, 296–298
    regression coefficients and, 320–324
    several qualitative variables and, 300–301
    slope shift using, 303
    structural change testing based on, 315–316
    trap, 299

Durbin h-test, 447–448
Durbin-Watson test
    for first-order serial correlation, 386–388
    tables, 592–595
Dynamic models, 243–244
    application, 244–250
    of consumption expenditures, 453–454
    of interest rate, 435–437
    vs. static model, 245

E

Early retirement data sets, 645
Econometric(s)
    conditional expectations in, 30
    defined, 2
    exercises, 15, 607
    forecasting, 494, 510–514
    model, 6
    software programs, 635–637
Economic behavior, testing hypotheses about, 3
Economic growth data sets, 654
Economic relationships, estimating, 2
Economic time series, smoothing an, 502–504
Efficiency
    asymptotic, 46–47
    concept of, 43
    defined, 43–44
    estimators and, 89–90
Elasticity
    of bus travel, estimating, 257–258
    concept of, 234
    of functional forms, 235
    of output with respect to capital, 255
    of output with respect to labor, 255
Electricity
    demand for, 406–415
    load model, 454–455
    sales forecast, 512–514, 523–524
Empirical example/project
    career interruptions following childbirth, 533–534
    collecting data for, 10–12, 574–579
    data analysis for, 579–580
    dummy variables and, 324–325
    estimating models for, 12, 481–482, 580–581
    flowchart for steps of, 5
    forecasting electricity sales, 512–514, 523–524
    formulating model for, 4–10, 574
    heteroscedasticity and, 365–366

how to carry out, 13–14
hypothesis testing for, 12–13,
    580–581
inflation and savings rate, 451–453
interpreting results for, 13
literature review for, 573
practicing computer session for, 14
probit model of TV station behavior,
    531–532
regulation in contact lens industry,
    556–558
selecting topic for, 568–570
Tobit model of charitable
    contributions, 536–538
wages and prices in UK, 463–464
writing report for, 581–582
Endogenous variables, 543
Engel curve
    defined, 9
    relation, estimating, 106–109
Equation(s). *See also* Normal equations
    auxiliary, 349
    behavioral, 542
    demand and supply, 5
    reduced form, 544
    solution to normal, 82–84
    structural, 542–544
    technical, 543, 544
    unidentified, 546
Equity data sets, 641
Error(s)
    absolute percent, 497
    autoregressive, 400–401
    component model, 480–481
    correction model, 461–471
    finite prediction, 152
    forecasts and, 147–148
    general-order autoregressive,
        400–401
    mean squared, 44, 112, 496–497
    measurement, 77–78
    multicollinearity and, 215–216
    normality of, 96
    root mean squared, 112
    serially correlated, 510–512
    specification, 165–171
    standard, 36, 92, 147–148
    systematic, 380
    term, 6
    type I, 51–52
    type II, 51–52
    variances, 348–350, 352
    well-behaved, 96, 449
    white-noise, 96, 449
Estimated relationships
    defined, 38

forecasting and, 3–4
Estimated residual, 79
Estimation
    with ARIMA model, 519–522
    of demand curve, 238
    HCCM, 355
    interval, 56–57
    with lagged dependent variables,
        449–453
    of linear-log model, 235–236
    maximum likelihood, 137–138
    of parameters, 38–42
    of polynomial curve-fitting, 238–241
    procedures, 355–363, 392–395
    of simultaneous equation models,
        551–553
    using dummy variables, 480
Estimator(s)
    best linear unbiased, 90, 135–137,
        214–216, 383
    consistency and, 88–89
    defined, 38
    derivation of variances of, 138–139
    efficiency and, 89–90
    HCCM, 355
    heteroscedasticity and, 346–347
    maximum likelihood, 73–74
    precision of, 91–95
    properties of, 42–47, 85–90
    unbiasedness and, 85–88, 147
EViews software, 635–636
Exact identification, defined, 546
Exact multicollinearity, 213–214
Ex-ante forecasts, 495
Excel program, 636
Exchange rates data sets, 670–671
Exercises/practice problems
    chapter 1, 15, 607
    chapter 2, 33–35, 607–609
    chapter 3, 80, 88–89, 102, 122–125,
        127–128, 130, 609–614
    chapter 4, 167–168, 189, 191–193,
        199–200, 615–618
    chapter 5, 227, 618–619
    chapter 6, 240–241, 257, 274–275,
        277, 619–621
    chapter 7, 293, 300–301, 316, 326,
        328–329, 332–333, 621–626
    chapter 8, 368–370, 626–628
    chapter 9, 419–420, 628–629
    chapter 10, 487–488, 629–631
    chapter 11, 527, 631
    chapter 12, 539–540, 631–632
    chapter 13, 562–563, 632–633
Exogenous variables, 4, 543
Expected value of X, 21, 29

Experimental data, 10
Explained variation, defined, 94
Explanatory variables, 4, 210, 212–213
Exponent
    defined, 232
    functions, 232–234
Exponential smoothing, 502–503
Ex-post forecasts, 495

F

Farm population data sets, 652
F-distribution, 49, 589–591
Feasible generalized least squares
    (FGLS)
    for health care expenditure
        application, 363–365
    heteroscedasticity and, 358–363
Feedback, 115, 475, 543
Finite prediction error (FPE), 152
First central moment, defined, 21
First differences, 219, 392, 518
First moment around the origin, 21
First-order autocorrelation coefficient,
    382
First-order autoregressive process
    defined, 382
    miscellaneous derivations with,
        431–433
First-order serial correlation
    autocorrelation and, 467–471
    defined, 382
    testing for, 386–389
Fitted straight line, defined, 82
Fitted values, 495
Fixed effects model, 480
Forecast(ing)
    adaptive, 504
    with ARIMA model, 519–523
    combining, 504–510
    comparison of, 414–415
    conditional, 497–498
    defined, 3
    econometric, 494, 510–514
    errors and, 147–148
    estimated relationships and, 3–4
    fitted values, ex-post, and ex-ante,
        495–496
    goodness of fit and, 401
    heteroscedasticity and, 348
    in-sample, 495, 508
    linear regression model and,
        110–113
    model evaluation and, 496–497
    multicollinearity and, 214–216
    out-of-sample, 495, 501, 509

point, 111–112
postsample, 113
sales, 523–524
serial correlation and, 385
short-term, 512–514
time series, 494, 514–515
from time trends, 498–504
unconditional, 497–498
Frequency distribution, 17, 639
F-statistic, computing, 160
F-test
defined, 103, 157–158
for error variances, 352
Function(s)
agricultural production, 257
autocorrelation, 432, 516, 518, 519
Cobb-Douglas production, 69, 255
cost, 239–240, 270–271
exponent, 232–234
likelihood, 72
logarithmic, 233, 234
monotonically
decreasing/increasing, 64–65
probability, 26–27
production, 69, 240–241
sample regression, 78, 79–80,
84–85
of several variables, 67–68
Functional forms
exponential, 232–233, 251
linear-log, 236
logarithmic, 233
marginal effects and elasticities of,
235
reciprocal transformation, 238
serial correlation and, 389–391

G

Gaussian distribution. *See* Normal
distribution
Gauss-Markov theorem
best linear unbiased estimates and,
90, 135–137
heteroscedasticity and, 346–347
multicollinearity and, 214–216
Generalized differencing, defined,
393
Generalized least squares (GLS), 356
General normal distribution, 24–26
General-order autoregressive errors,
400–401
General to simple modeling, 10,
261–262
Geometric lag model, 437–439
Glesjer test, 349, 350

Goldfeld-Quandt test, 352–353
Goodness of fit
defined, 91
forecasts and, 401
measurement of, 148–151
precision of estimators and, 91–95
test of, 103–104
Wald test for, 158–160
Granger causality test, 476–477
Granger representation theorem, 475
GRETL program, 14, 19, 637

H

Harvey-Godfrey test, 349, 350
Health care expenditures (application)
Engel curve relation between income
and, 106–109
FGLS procedure for, 363–365
Hedonic price index, 6, 144
Hendry/LSE approach
data-based model simplification and,
218
defined, 10
of modeling from general to simple,
261–262
Heteroscedasticity
consequences of ignoring, 346–347
defined, 133, 344
dependent variable, 363
error variances and, 348–350
example, 345
FGLS procedure and, 358–363
GLS procedure and, 356
Goldfeld-Quandt test for, 352–353
illustration of, 134
with a known proportional factor,
357–358
Lagrange multiplier (LM) test for,
348–352
in log-wage model, 345–346
testing for, 347–348
White's test for, 353–354
WLS procedure and, 356
Heteroscedasticity consistent covariance
matrix (HCCM) estimator, 355
Hildreth-Lu (HILU) search procedure
vs. CORC procedure, 396–398
serial correlation and, 394–395,
468–469, 555
Histogram
defined, 17
graphic representation of, 18
Homicide rates data sets, 656–657
Homoscedasticity
defined, 89, 133, 344

example, 90
log-quadratic model and, 354
null hypothesis of, 350–351, 353
Housing units data sets, 643, 646
HQ criterion, defined, 152
Hypotheses testing
confidence intervals and, 57–58
defined, 3
for empirical project, 12–13, 580–581
heteroscedasticity and, 348
likelihood ratio (LR) test and, 262
linear regression model and, 95–104
model estimation and, 580–581
nested, 263
nonnested, 263
p-value approach to, 100
serial correlation and, 384–385
steps to, 50–52
types of, 153–160

I

Identification problem
defined, 546
model 1, 546–548
model 2, 548–549
model 3, 549
model 4, 550–551
Identification process, 519–521
Impact multiplier, defined, 434
Implied reduced form estimates, 560
Increasing returns to scale, defined,
256
Independent, identically distributed
(iid) random variables, 36
Independent variables, 4, 238
estimating seasonal effects of,
312–314
vector autoregressive (VAR) models
and, 477–478
Index numbers
defined, 12
role in economic data, 576–577
Indirect least squares (ILS) procedure,
551–552
Indirect t-test, 163
Inflation rate data sets, 639
In-sample forecasts, 495, 508
Instantaneous rate of growth, 252, 390
Instrumental variable technique (IV),
552–553
Integrated of order 1, defined, 472
Integrated of order d, 518
Integrated of order zero, defined, 472
Interaction terms, 241–243
Intercept shift/term

example, 294
slope terms and, 304
Interim multiplier of order *i*, defined, 435
Interval estimation, 56–57

J

Jackknife, defined, 355
Jointly determined variables, 113, 475
Joint probabilities, 26–27
Joint significance, defined, 156
Journal of Economic Literature (JEL), 570–572

K

Keynesian model, 558–560
Koyck lag model, 437–439

L

Labor force participation rates, 177–183, 317–320
Lagged dependent variables
adaptive expectations model and, 443–445
defined, 442
econometric forecasting and, 510–512
as generalization of an AR model, 445–446
model estimation with, 449–453
partial adjustment model and, 442
serial correlation and, 446–449
Lagged independent variables
defined, 434
distributed lag model and, 434–442
Lagged variables, 243–245
Lagrange multiplier, defined, 70
Lagrange multiplier (LM) test
for adding variables, 263–264
example, 264–269, 287–289
for first-order serial correlation, 388–389
for heteroscedasticity, 348–352
for omitted variables, 554
for simple to general modeling, 262–263
for wages, 307–312
Lags in behavior (dynamic models), 243–244
Laspeyres index, 576
Law of large numbers, 37, 89
Least squares bias, 545

Least squares method
defined, 41–42
derivation of normal equations by, 135
model estimation with, 80–81
normal equations and, 145–146
Left-hand side variable, 4
Level of significance, defined, 52
Likelihood function, 72
Likelihood ratio (LR) test
example, 284–286
hypothesis testing and, 262
Limited dependent variables
application of, 534–536
defined, 528
Linear-log model, 235–237
Linear probability models
defined, 529
estimation of, 529–530
Linear regression model
applications, 106–109, 116–119
assumptions of, 96
causality in, 113–115
defined, 6, 75, 76
estimation of, 80–85
estimators precision and, 91–95
estimators properties and, 85–90
example, 9
forecasting and, 110–113
formulation of, 76–80
graphic representation of, 133
hypothesis testing and, 95–104
scaling and units of measurement and, 105–106
Ljung-Box test statistic, 522
Logarithmic functions
graphic representation of, 234
properties of, 233
Logistic curve
defined, 259
graphic representation of, 259–260
Logit model, 258–260
estimated, 535
estimation procedure, 532–533
Log-linear model (semilog model)
interpreting dummy coefficients in, 304–305
transformed dependent variable and, 250–254
Log-log model, 255–257
Log-quadratic model
FGLS estimates of, 361
heteroscedasticity in, 345–346
homoscedasticity and, 354
Long-run behavior, error correction model and, 461–464

Long-run equilibrium, 435
Long-run multiplier, 435

M

Machine-readable data, 575
Marginal cost, defined, 65
Marginal density of *X*, defined, 28
Marginal distributions, 28
Marginal effect
defined, 233
of functional forms, 235
interpretation of, 256
Marginal effect of *X* on *Y*, defined, 78
Marginal product of capital, 69
Marginal propensity, 9
Mathematical expectation
mean, variance and, 20–26
in two-variable case, 29
of *X*, 21
Maximization and minimization
functions, derivatives, maxima and minima and, 64–67
functions of several variables and, 67–69
Maximum likelihood estimation, 137–138
Maximum likelihood estimators, 73–74
Maximum likelihood principle, 72
Mean
conditional, 86
of the distribution, 21
mathematical expectation and, 20–26
population, 38
predictor, 111
sample, 36
Mean absolute percent error (MAPE)
defined, 112
model evaluation and, 497
multicollinearity and, 214–216
Mean squared error, 44
defined, 112
evaluation of models and, 496–497
Mean squared percentage error (MSPE), 113
Measurement, units of, 105–106
Method of moments, 38–40
Microsoft Excel program, 636
Minimization, maximization and, 64–71
Model(s). *See also specific types*
adaptive expectations, 443
ANOVA, 291, 301–302
ARCH, 401–406
ARIMA, 508–510, 519–522
ARMA, 516

autoregressive, 515–517
binary choice, 529–530
binomial logit, 532
CAPM, 7–8
defined, 4
discrete choice, 528
distributed lag, 434
double-log, 255–257
dynamic, 243–250, 435–437, 453–454
econometric, 6, 510–514
error component, 480–481
estimation, 12, 400–401, 580–581
evaluation, 496–497
fixed effects, 480
formulation, 4–10, 232–233, 607
hedonic price index, 6
Hendry/LSE approach to, 10
interpretation of marginal effects in, 256
Keynesian, 558–560
Koyck lag, 437
with lagged dependent variables, 449–453
linearity of, 76–77
linear-log, 235–237
linear regression, 113–115
load, 454–455
logit, 258–260, 532–533, 535
log-linear, 250–254, 304–305
log-log, 255–257
moving average, 516
multicollinearity and, 218–219
overparametrized, 261
partial adjustment, 442
probit, 530–532
R^2 values between, 254–255
random effects, 480–481
random walk, 455
regression, 205–206
restricted, 156, 262, 263
semilog, 250–254
simultaneous-equation, 5–8
single-equation, 4–5
static, 245
Tobit, 536–538
unrestricted, 156, 262, 307–308
VAR, 477–478
wage, 305–312
Modeling
general to simple, 10
Hendry/LSE approach of, 261–262
simple to general, 10
Moments
method of, 38–40
population, 38
sample, 38

Monotonically decreasing function, 64–65
Monotonically increasing function, 64
Mortality rate data sets, 647
Most powerful test procedure, 52
Motor carrier deregulation (empirical example), 320
Moving average
autoregressive integrated, 518
defined, 438
error terms, 450–451
models, 516
smoothing and, 502–503
Multicollinearity
absence of, 216
applications, 220–225
consequences of ignoring, 214–216
defined, 210
exact, 213–214
examples, 210–213
identifying, 216–217
solutions for, 217–220
tests for, 217
Multiple regression model
applications, 171–183
defined, 7
empirical example, 183–185
goodness of fit measurement and, 148–151
hypothesis testing and, 153–165
normal equations and, 145–148
selection criteria, 151–153
specification errors and, 165–171
Multiplicative heteroscedasticity, 349
Multivariate distributions, 34–35

N

Natural logarithm, 233
Nested hypotheses testing, 263
Newly added variables, 308
Nonexperimental data, 11
Nonlinearities
in parameters, 260
spurious, 242–243
Nonlinear regression model, 77
Nonnested hypotheses testing, 263
Nonrejection region, 51
Nonstationarity, stationary series and, 518
Nonstationary, defined, 472
Normal distribution
confidence interval for mean of, 57
defined, 19
properties of, 24–25

testing mean of a, 52–55
Normal equations
defined, 81
derivation of, 135
multiple regression model and, 145–148
solutions to, 82–84
Null hypothesis, 51

O

Observational data, 10–11
OLS. See Ordinary least squares (OLS)
Omitted variable(s)
bias, 166
LM test for, 554
Wald test and, 156
One-sided test, 53–54
One-tailed test, 53–54, 98, 592–595
One-tailed t-test, 98, 153–154
Optimization
under constraints, 70
Lagrange's method of, 70–71
Ordinary least squares (OLS)
defined, 41–42
estimates, 565–566
estimating model with, 80–81
FGLS procedure and, 360–361
GLS procedure and, 356–357
heteroscedasticity and, 344, 346–348
normal equations and, 145–146
serial correlation and, 383–385
Outliers, defined, 579
Out-of-sample forecasts, 495, 501, 509
Overidentification, defined, 546
Overidentifying restrictions, defined, 550
Overparametrized model, 261

P

Paasche Index, 578
Panel data, 11
Parameters
estimation of, 38–42
nonlinearities in, 260
population, 7, 36, 83
reduced form, 544
structural, 543
true, 7
Parental school choice data sets, 645–646
Parent population, defined, 35
Park test, 349
Parsimonious specification, 262
Partial adjustment model, 442

Partial autocorrelation function
    (PACF), 519
Partial correlogram, 519
Partial derivative, 68
Patents and expenditures, relation
    between, 116–119, 244–245
PcGive software, 636
Perfectly correlated coefficient, 32
Perfect multicollinearity, 213–214
Periodicals, list of economic,
    572–573
Periodicity, defined, 11
Phillips curve, 40
Point forecast, 111–112
Polynomial curve-fitting, 238–241
Polynomial lag procedure, 439–441
Pooling cross-sectional and time series
    data, 11, 478–481
Population
    data sets, 642, 652, 660–661, 670
    mean, 38
    moments, 38
    parameters, 7, 36, 83
    parent, 35
    regression, 7
    regression line, 78
    regression model, 76
    sampling from normal, 37
    variances, 38, 91
Positive autocorrelation, 383
Postsample forecast, 113
Postsample period, 495
Poverty rates
    application, 220–221
    data sets, 644
Power of a test, 52
Practice problems. See
    Exercises/practice problems
Predetermined variables, 543
Prediction. See Forecast(ing)
Principal component analysis, 219
Private school enrollment data sets,
    649–650
Probabilities, joint, 26–27
Probability density function (PDF), 19
Probability distribution
    defined, 17
    example, 17, 21–22
    graphic representation of, 18
Probit model
    defined, 530–531
    of television station behavior,
        531–532
Production function, 69, 240–241
pth-order autoregressive process, 399
p-value approach

to hypothesis testing, 99–101
    steps to, 120

Q
Qualitative dependent variable, 528
Qualitative response models, 528
Qualitative variables
    defined, 290
    dummy variables and, 300–301
    with many categories, 298–302
    slope term and, 302–305
    with two categories, 290–293
Quantitative variables, 290, 293–296
Quasi-differencing, defined, 393

R
R^2 adjusted for degrees of freedom,
    defined, 149
R^2 values between models, 254–255
Random effects model, 480–481
Random sampling, 35–36
Random term, 515
Random variables
    covariance between two, 31
    defined, 16–17
    example, 25–26
    properties involving two, 34
    variance and standard deviation of,
        23–24
Random walk model, 455
Real dollars, defined, 578
Reciprocal transformation, 238
Reduced form equations, 544
Reduced form parameters, 544
Redundant variables, 220
Regressand, 4
Regression. See also Auxiliary regression
    censored, 535–536
    cointegrating, 473
    Dickey-Fuller, 473–474
    model, 205–206
    population, 7
    ridge, 220
    sample, 7
    seemingly unrelated, 479–480
    spurious, 113
    sum of squares, 93
    of Y on X, 30
Regression coefficients
    defined, 77
    in double-log model, 255–257
    dummy variables and, 320–324
    interpretation of, 182–183
    multicollinearity and, 217–218

standard error of, 92
    testing individual coefficients and,
        155
    testing several coefficients and, 156
    variables and, 467
Regression specification error test
    (RESET), 270–271
Regressor, 4
Relationship(s)
    economic, 2
    estimated, 3–4, 38
    linear-log, 235–237
    log-linear, 250–254
    reciprocal, 238
Research and development (R&D),
    patents and expenses on, 116–119,
        244–245
RESET procedure, 270–271
Residual
    defined, 79
    heteroscedasticity of, 348–349
    variance, 384
Residual plot
    defined, 381
    illustration of, 382
Restricted model
    defined, 156
    LR test and, 262
    nested hypotheses and, 263
Right-hand side variable, 4
Root mean squared error, 112

S
Sample correlation coefficient, 40
Sample covariance, 39
Sample estimates, 83
Sample mean, 36
Sample moments, 38
Sample regression, 7
Sample regression function
    defined, 78
    population regression function and,
        79–80
    use of, 84–85
Sample regression line, 82
Sample scatter diagram, 78
Sample size, multicollinearity and,
    219–220
Sample standard deviation, 36
Sample statistic, 36
Sample survey data, 10
Sample variance, 36
Sampling
    defined, 35
    distributions, 36–37, 46

from a normal population, 37
random, 35–36
SAT scores data sets, 639
Scaling, units of measurement and, 105–106
Sealing compound shipment data sets, 640, 653
Seasonal dummies, 312
Seasonality, example, 313–314
Seasonal term, 515
Second central moment, 23
Second difference, 518
Second moment of the distribution, 21
Seemingly unrelated regression (SUR), 479–480
Semilog model, 250–254
Serial correlation
ARCH test and, 401–406
causes of, 380
consequences of ignoring, 383–385
defined, 380
demand for electricity and, 406–415
of the first order, 382–383
higher-order, 398–401
lagged dependent variables and, 446–449
residual plot and, 381–382
in simultaneous-equation models, 554–556
treatment of, 389–398
Serial independence, 89, 380
SHAZAM software, 636
Short-run behavior, error correction model and, 461–464
SIC codes, 576
Significantly different from zero, defined, 102
Significantly greater than zero, defined, 99
Simple linear regression model. *See* Linear regression model
Simple to general modeling, 10, 262–263
Simultaneous-equation models
consequences of ignoring simultaneity and, 544–546
defined, 5
estimation of, 551–554
examples, 5–8
identification problem and, 546–551
serial correlation in, 554–556
structure and reduced forms of, 542–544
Single-equation models, 4–5
Single-family homes data sets, 639–640, 642, 652, 655

Size of a test, defined, 52
Slope term(s)
intercept terms and, 304
qualitative variables and, 302–305
Smooth curve, 498
Smoothing
defined, 502
exponential, 502–503
Social Science Citation Index, 570, 573
Software
B34S, 635
EViews, 635–636
Excel, 636
GRETL, 637
PcGive, 636
SHAZAM, 636
Specialized data, 576
Specification error(s)
defined, 165
types of, 166–171
Speed of adjustment, defined, 442
Spreadsheet program, 578
Spurious correlation, 113
Spurious nonlinearities, 242–243
Spurious regression, 113
Squared variables, 307
Standard deviation (s.d.), 23
Standard error(s)
defined, 36
forecasts and, 147–148
Standard error of the disturbances, 92
Standard error of the regression coefficients, 92
Standard normal distribution, 19
Static model vs. dynamic model, 245
Stationarity
autocorrelation function and, 516, 518
defined, 472
Stationarity time series, 472
Stationary time series, 518
Statistically independent variables, 27
Statistically not greater than zero, 99
Statistical software, 636
Statistical tables
areas under standard normal curve, 586
percentage points of *t*-distribution, 587
upper percentage points of chi-square distribution, 588
Statistical test, 51
Steady state, defined, 435
Stochastic disturbance terms, 385
Stochastic term, 6, 515
Stochastic variables, 16–17

Structural change
defined, 314
testing for, 314–317
in women's labor force, 317–320
Structural equations, 542–544
Structural instability. *See* Structural change
Structural parameters, 543
Student's *t*-distribution, 48–49
Summations, properties of, 63
Sum of squares
minimizing vertical vs. horizontal, 114–115
regression, 93
of the residuals, 93
total, 93

T
t-distribution, percentage points of, 587
Technical equation, 543, 544
Test(ing)
for causality, 476–477
coefficient of correlation between two variables, 56
for cointegration, 472–475
of goodness of fit, 103–104
for heteroscedasticity, 347–348
individual coefficients, 153–155
linear combination of coefficients, 160–165
mean of a normal distribution, 52–55
most powerful, 52
several coefficients, 156–160
statistical, 51
statistics, 97, 110
for structural change, 314–317
Text editor program, 578
Three-stage least squares method, 554
Time series, smoothing an economic, 502–504
Time series data
concepts related to, 472
defined, 11
pooling cross-sectional and, 478–481
serial correlation and, 392
Time series forecasting, 494
Time series model
forecasting from, 514–515
structure of, 515–516
Time-varying weights, 507
Tobit models
application of, 536
defined, 535
Total sum of squares (TSS), 93
Total variation, 93

Trend
    defined, 498
    term, 515
Trend-fitting, defined, 282
Trend line(s)
    commonly used, 498–499
    fitting, 498
    uses of, 499–500
    wage rates application and, 500–502
True parameters, 7
t-statistic
    defined, 99
    multicollinearity and, 220
t-test
    cautions about using, 99
    defined, 98
Two-sided test, 54–55
Two-stage least squares (TSLS)
        procedure
    application, 553–554
    defined, 553
    empirical example, 556–558
Two-tailed test, 54–55, 101–102
Two-tailed t-test, 154–155
Two-variable regression model, 106
Type I error, 51–52
Type II error, 51–52

U

Unbiased, defined, 43
Unbiasedness, estimators and, 85–88,
    147
Unconditional forecasts, 497–498
Uncorrelated, defined, 32
Underidentification, defined, 546
Unemployment compensation data sets,
    656
Unexplained variation, defined, 94
Unidentified equation, 546
Unitary elastic, defined, 258
Unit roots, Dickey-Fuller tests and,
    455–461
Unrestricted model
    auxiliary regression and, 307–308
    defined, 156
    LR test and, 262
US military expenditures data sets,
    669–670

V

Variable(s). See also specific types
    in auxiliary regression, 264, 308–312

binary, 291
continuous random, 16
dependent, 4, 238, 250–254, 307–308
discrete random, 16, 21, 23–24,
    26–27
dummy, 291, 480
endogenous, 543
exercises, 15, 607
exogenous, 4, 543
explanatory, 4, 210, 212–213
functions of several, 67–68
generating new, 579
independent, 4, 238, 312–314,
    477–478
instrumental, 552
international, 468
irrelevant, 168–171
jointly determined, 113, 475
lagged, 243–245
lagged independent, 434
left-hand side, 4
limited dependent, 528, 534–536
LM test for adding, 263–264
multicollinearity and, 218
newly added, 308
omitted, 77, 156, 166–168, 206–208,
    554
political, 467–468
predetermined, 543
qualitative, 290, 298–305
qualitative dependent, 528
quantitative, 290, 293–296
random, 16–17, 23–26, 31, 34
redundant, 220
regression coefficients and, 467
right-hand side, 4
squared, 307
statistically independent, 27
testing coefficient of correlation
    between two, 56
time series, 219
transformed, 411
Variance
    conditional, 30
    derivation of, 138–139, 209
    of distribution, 23
    mathematical expectation and,
        20–26
    population, 38, 91
    residual, 384
    sample, 36, 49–50
    unbiased estimator of, 139–140, 147
Variation
    coefficient of, 26

explained, 94
total, 93
unexplained, 94
Vector autoregressive (VAR) models
    defined, 477
    independent variables and, 477–478

W

Wage growth rate data sets, 639
Wage rates
    covariance analysis of, 305–307
    example, 474–475
    fitting trend lines for, 500–502
    LM test approach for, 268–269,
        307–312
    log-linear relationship between
        education and, 252–254
    relationship between prices and,
        463–464
Wald test
    defined, 156
    example, 286–287
    general, 156–158
    special, 158–160
    testing linear combination of
        coefficients with, 161–163
    unrestricted model and, 262–263
Web site(s)
    book, 575
    for econometric software, 636–637
    for economics material, 570
Weighted least squares (WLS), 356
Weights, defined, 576
Well-behaved errors
    defined, 96
    model with, 449
White noise, 515
    errors, 96, 449
    series, 383
White's test, 353–354
Women in labor force, 177–183,
    317–320
Work sheets, defined, 578

Z

Z-score, defined, 24

Upper 10% Points of the *F*-Distribution

n \ m	1	2	3	4	5	6	7	8	9	10	12	15	20	24	30	40	60	120	∞
1	39.86	49.50	53.59	55.83	57.24	58.20	58.91	59.44	59.86	60.19	60.71	61.22	61.74	62.00	62.26	62.53	62.79	63.06	63.33
2	8.53	9.00	9.16	9.24	9.29	9.33	9.35	9.37	9.38	9.39	9.41	9.42	9.44	9.45	9.46	9.47	9.47	9.48	9.49
3	5.54	5.46	5.39	5.34	5.31	5.28	5.27	5.25	5.24	5.23	5.22	5.20	5.18	5.18	5.17	5.16	5.15	5.14	5.13
4	4.54	4.32	4.19	4.11	4.05	4.01	3.98	3.95	3.94	3.92	3.90	3.87	3.84	3.83	3.82	3.80	3.79	3.78	3.76
5	4.06	3.78	3.62	3.52	3.45	3.40	3.37	3.34	3.32	3.30	3.27	3.24	3.21	3.19	3.17	3.16	3.14	3.12	3.10
6	3.78	3.46	3.29	3.18	3.11	3.05	3.01	2.98	2.96	2.94	2.90	2.87	2.84	2.82	2.80	2.78	2.76	2.74	2.72
7	3.59	3.26	3.07	2.96	2.88	2.83	2.78	2.75	2.72	2.70	2.67	2.63	2.59	2.58	2.56	2.54	2.51	2.49	2.47
8	3.46	3.11	2.92	2.81	2.73	2.67	2.62	2.59	2.56	2.54	2.50	2.46	2.42	2.40	2.38	2.36	2.34	2.32	2.29
9	3.36	3.01	2.81	2.69	2.61	2.55	2.51	2.47	2.44	2.42	2.38	2.34	2.30	2.28	2.25	2.23	2.21	2.18	2.16
10	3.29	2.92	2.73	2.61	2.52	2.46	2.41	2.38	2.35	2.32	2.28	2.24	2.20	2.18	2.16	2.13	2.11	2.08	2.06
11	3.23	2.86	2.66	2.54	2.45	2.39	2.34	2.30	2.27	2.25	2.21	2.17	2.12	2.10	2.08	2.05	2.03	2.00	1.97
12	3.18	2.81	2.61	2.48	2.39	2.33	2.28	2.24	2.21	2.19	2.15	2.10	2.06	2.04	2.01	1.99	1.96	1.93	1.90
13	3.14	2.76	2.56	2.43	2.35	2.28	2.23	2.20	2.16	2.14	2.10	2.05	2.01	1.98	1.96	1.93	1.90	1.88	1.85
14	3.10	2.73	2.52	2.39	2.31	2.24	2.19	2.15	2.12	2.10	2.05	2.01	1.96	1.94	1.91	1.89	1.86	1.83	1.80
15	3.07	2.70	2.49	2.36	2.27	2.21	2.16	2.12	2.09	2.06	2.02	1.97	1.92	1.90	1.87	1.85	1.82	1.79	1.76
16	3.05	2.67	2.46	2.33	2.24	2.18	2.13	2.09	2.06	2.03	1.99	1.94	1.89	1.87	1.84	1.81	1.78	1.75	1.72
17	3.03	2.64	2.44	2.31	2.22	2.15	2.10	2.06	2.03	2.00	1.96	1.91	1.86	1.84	1.81	1.78	1.75	1.72	1.69
18	3.01	2.62	2.42	2.29	2.20	2.13	2.08	2.04	2.00	1.98	1.93	1.89	1.84	1.81	1.78	1.75	1.72	1.69	1.66
19	2.99	2.61	2.40	2.27	2.18	2.11	2.06	2.02	1.98	1.96	1.91	1.86	1.81	1.79	1.76	1.73	1.70	1.67	1.63
20	2.97	2.59	2.38	2.25	2.16	2.09	2.04	2.00	1.96	1.94	1.89	1.84	1.79	1.77	1.74	1.71	1.68	1.64	1.61
21	2.96	2.57	2.36	2.23	2.14	2.08	2.02	1.98	1.95	1.92	1.87	1.83	1.78	1.75	1.72	1.69	1.66	1.62	1.59
22	2.95	2.56	2.35	2.22	2.13	2.06	2.01	1.97	1.93	1.90	1.86	1.81	1.76	1.73	1.70	1.67	1.64	1.60	1.57
23	2.94	2.55	2.34	2.21	2.11	2.05	1.99	1.95	1.92	1.89	1.84	1.80	1.74	1.72	1.69	1.66	1.62	1.59	1.55
24	2.93	2.54	2.33	2.19	2.10	2.04	1.98	1.94	1.91	1.88	1.83	1.78	1.73	1.70	1.67	1.64	1.61	1.57	1.53
25	2.92	2.53	2.32	2.18	2.09	2.02	1.97	1.93	1.89	1.87	1.82	1.77	1.72	1.69	1.66	1.63	1.59	1.56	1.52
26	2.91	2.52	2.31	2.17	2.08	2.01	1.96	1.92	1.88	1.86	1.81	1.76	1.71	1.68	1.65	1.61	1.58	1.54	1.50
27	2.90	2.51	2.30	2.17	2.07	2.00	1.95	1.91	1.87	1.85	1.80	1.75	1.70	1.67	1.64	1.60	1.57	1.53	1.49
28	2.89	2.50	2.29	2.16	2.06	2.00	1.94	1.90	1.87	1.84	1.79	1.74	1.69	1.66	1.63	1.59	1.56	1.52	1.48
29	2.89	2.50	2.28	2.15	2.06	1.99	1.93	1.89	1.86	1.83	1.78	1.73	1.68	1.65	1.62	1.58	1.55	1.51	1.47
30	2.88	2.49	2.28	2.14	2.05	1.98	1.93	1.88	1.85	1.82	1.77	1.72	1.67	1.64	1.61	1.57	1.54	1.50	1.46
40	2.84	2.44	2.23	2.09	2.00	1.93	1.87	1.83	1.79	1.76	1.71	1.66	1.61	1.57	1.54	1.51	1.47	1.42	1.38
60	2.79	2.39	2.18	2.04	1.95	1.87	1.82	1.77	1.74	1.71	1.66	1.60	1.54	1.51	1.48	1.44	1.40	1.35	1.29
120	2.75	2.35	2.13	1.99	1.90	1.82	1.77	1.72	1.68	1.65	1.60	1.55	1.48	1.45	1.41	1.37	1.32	1.26	1.19
∞	2.71	2.30	2.08	1.94	1.85	1.77	1.72	1.67	1.63	1.60	1.55	1.49	1.42	1.38	1.34	1.30	1.24	1.17	1.00

Note: m = degrees of freedom for the numerator
n = degrees of freedom for the denominator

Source: Handbook of Tables for Mathematics, edited by Robert C. West and Samuel M. Selby. 1970. Reprinted with the permission of the CRC Press, Inc.

Upper 5% Points of the F-Distribution

n \ m	1	2	3	4	5	6	7	8	9	10	12	15	20	24	30	40	60	120	∞
1	161.4	199.5	215.7	224.6	230.2	234.0	236.8	238.9	240.5	241.9	243.9	245.9	248.0	249.1	250.1	251.1	252.2	253.3	254.3
2	18.51	19.00	19.16	19.25	19.30	19.33	19.35	19.37	19.38	19.40	19.41	19.43	19.45	19.45	19.46	19.47	19.48	19.49	19.50
3	10.13	9.55	9.28	9.12	9.01	8.94	8.89	8.85	8.81	8.79	8.74	8.70	8.66	8.64	8.62	8.59	8.57	8.55	8.53
4	7.71	6.94	6.59	6.39	6.26	6.16	6.09	6.04	6.00	5.96	5.91	5.86	5.80	5.77	5.75	5.72	5.69	5.66	5.63
5	6.61	5.79	5.41	5.19	5.05	4.95	4.88	4.82	4.77	4.74	4.68	4.62	4.56	4.53	4.50	4.46	4.43	4.40	4.36
6	5.99	5.14	4.76	4.53	4.39	4.28	4.21	4.15	4.10	4.06	4.00	3.94	3.87	3.84	3.81	3.77	3.74	3.70	3.67
7	5.59	4.74	4.35	4.12	3.97	3.87	3.79	3.73	3.68	3.64	3.57	3.51	3.44	3.41	3.38	3.34	3.30	3.27	3.23
8	5.32	4.46	4.07	3.84	3.69	3.58	3.50	3.44	3.39	3.35	3.28	3.22	3.15	3.12	3.08	3.04	3.01	2.97	2.93
9	5.12	4.26	3.86	3.63	3.48	3.37	3.29	3.23	3.18	3.14	3.07	3.01	2.94	2.90	2.86	2.83	2.79	2.75	2.71
10	4.96	4.10	3.71	3.48	3.33	3.22	3.14	3.07	3.02	2.98	2.91	2.85	2.77	2.74	2.70	2.66	2.62	2.58	2.54
11	4.84	3.98	3.59	3.36	3.20	3.09	3.01	2.95	2.90	2.85	2.79	2.72	2.65	2.61	2.57	2.53	2.49	2.45	2.40
12	4.75	3.89	3.49	3.26	3.11	3.00	2.91	2.85	2.80	2.75	2.69	2.62	2.54	2.51	2.47	2.43	2.38	2.34	2.30
13	4.67	3.81	3.41	3.18	3.03	2.92	2.83	2.77	2.71	2.67	2.60	2.53	2.46	2.42	2.38	2.34	2.30	2.25	2.21
14	4.60	3.74	3.34	3.11	2.96	2.85	2.76	2.70	2.65	2.60	2.53	2.46	2.39	2.35	2.31	2.27	2.22	2.18	2.13
15	4.54	3.68	3.29	3.06	2.90	2.79	2.71	2.64	2.59	2.54	2.48	2.40	2.33	2.29	2.25	2.20	2.16	2.11	2.07
16	4.49	3.63	3.24	3.01	2.85	2.74	2.66	2.59	2.54	2.49	2.42	2.35	2.28	2.24	2.19	2.15	2.11	2.06	2.01
17	4.45	3.59	3.20	2.96	2.81	2.70	2.61	2.55	2.49	2.45	2.38	2.31	2.23	2.19	2.15	2.10	2.06	2.01	1.96
18	4.41	3.55	3.16	2.93	2.77	2.66	2.58	2.51	2.46	2.41	2.34	2.27	2.19	2.15	2.11	2.06	2.02	1.97	1.92
19	4.38	3.52	3.13	2.90	2.74	2.63	2.54	2.48	2.42	2.38	2.31	2.23	2.16	2.11	2.07	2.03	1.98	1.93	1.88
20	4.35	3.49	3.10	2.87	2.71	2.60	2.51	2.45	2.39	2.35	2.28	2.20	2.12	2.08	2.04	1.99	1.95	1.90	1.84
21	4.32	3.47	3.07	2.84	2.68	2.57	2.49	2.42	2.37	2.32	2.25	2.18	2.10	2.05	2.01	1.96	1.92	1.87	1.81
22	4.30	3.44	3.05	2.82	2.66	2.55	2.46	2.40	2.34	2.30	2.23	2.15	2.07	2.03	1.98	1.94	1.89	1.84	1.78
23	4.28	3.42	3.03	2.80	2.64	2.53	2.44	2.37	2.32	2.27	2.20	2.13	2.05	2.01	1.96	1.91	1.86	1.81	1.76
24	4.26	3.40	3.01	2.78	2.62	2.51	2.42	2.36	2.30	2.25	2.18	2.11	2.03	1.98	1.94	1.89	1.84	1.79	1.73
25	4.24	3.39	2.99	2.76	2.60	2.49	2.40	2.34	2.28	2.24	2.16	2.09	2.01	1.96	1.92	1.87	1.82	1.77	1.71
26	4.23	3.37	2.98	2.74	2.59	2.47	2.39	2.32	2.27	2.22	2.15	2.07	1.99	1.95	1.90	1.85	1.80	1.75	1.69
27	4.21	3.35	2.96	2.73	2.57	2.46	2.37	2.31	2.25	2.20	2.13	2.06	1.97	1.93	1.88	1.84	1.79	1.73	1.67
28	4.20	3.34	2.95	2.71	2.56	2.45	2.36	2.29	2.24	2.19	2.12	2.04	1.96	1.91	1.87	1.82	1.77	1.71	1.65
29	4.18	3.33	2.93	2.70	2.55	2.43	2.35	2.28	2.22	2.18	2.10	2.03	1.94	1.90	1.85	1.81	1.75	1.70	1.64
30	4.17	3.32	2.92	2.69	2.53	2.42	2.33	2.27	2.21	2.16	2.09	2.01	1.93	1.89	1.84	1.79	1.74	1.68	1.62
40	4.08	3.23	2.84	2.61	2.45	2.34	2.25	2.18	2.12	2.08	2.00	1.92	1.84	1.79	1.74	1.69	1.64	1.58	1.51
60	4.00	3.15	2.76	2.53	2.37	2.25	2.17	2.10	2.04	1.99	1.92	1.84	1.75	1.70	1.65	1.59	1.53	1.47	1.39
120	3.92	3.07	2.68	2.45	2.29	2.17	2.09	2.02	1.96	1.91	1.83	1.75	1.66	1.61	1.55	1.50	1.43	1.35	1.25
∞	3.84	3.00	2.60	2.37	2.21	2.10	2.01	1.94	1.88	1.83	1.75	1.67	1.57	1.52	1.46	1.39	1.32	1.22	1.00

Note: m = degrees of freedom for the numerator
n = degrees of freedom for the denominator

Source: Handbook of Tables for Mathematics, edited by Robert C. West and Samuel M. Selby, 1970. Reprinted with the permission of the CRC Press, Inc.